# Using CourseCompass

CourseCompass

## How do I get started with CourseCompass?

### Turn the page to learn how to:

- Register, enroll in your course, and log in to CourseCompass (see page I-ii)
- Get around in CourseCompass (see page I-iv)
- Use the tools on the My CourseCompass page (see page I-v)
- Explore the content in your course (see page I-vii)
- Take a test online (see page I-xi)

For more information, you can always look in the online Help.

Look for this symbol to learn about cool stuff you can do with CourseCompass!

# Registering and logging in

To open your CourseCompass course, you need a *student access code* and a *course ID*. You can find your student access code on the back side of the first page. Your instructor will give you the **Course ID**.

Once you have both your access code and the course ID, you can register in CourseCompass and enroll in your course. To do so, follow these general steps:

1. Go to **http://students.pearsoned.com**.
2. Click Register .
3. Enter your six-word student access code when prompted. Type one word in each of the boxes provided. Do not type the hyphens.

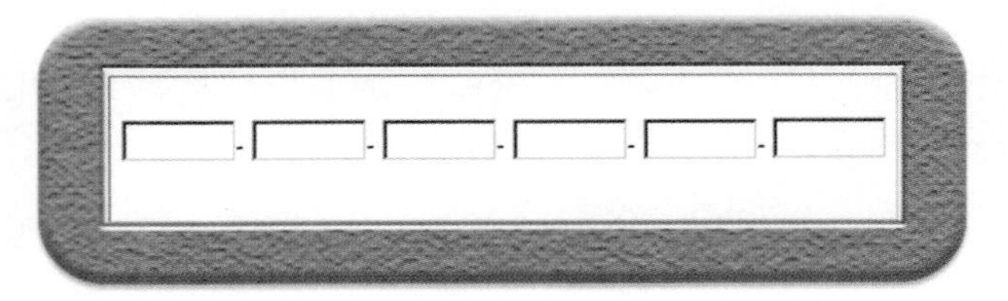

4. If you already have a login name and password for another Pearson Education product, type them in. If you don't have a CourseCompass login and password, just skip this step—you'll create them in step 8.
5. When asked, enter the course ID your instructor gave you.

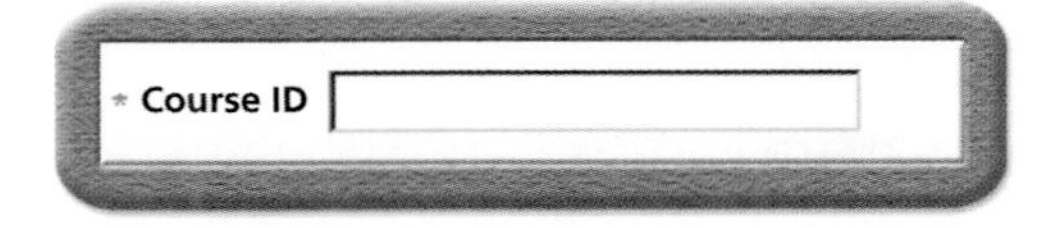


6. Enter the contact information requested, including your first and last name, your school's zip code, and your email address.

   Make sure you provide an email address that you check regularly because this is where CourseCompass sends registration information.
7. Click the down arrow beside Institution Name and select your school from the list. If the name of your school doesn't appear in the list, click Other and enter its city and country.

8 Enter the login name (user ID) and password you want to use for CourseCompass. You'll also be able to use this login name and password for other Pearson Education products.

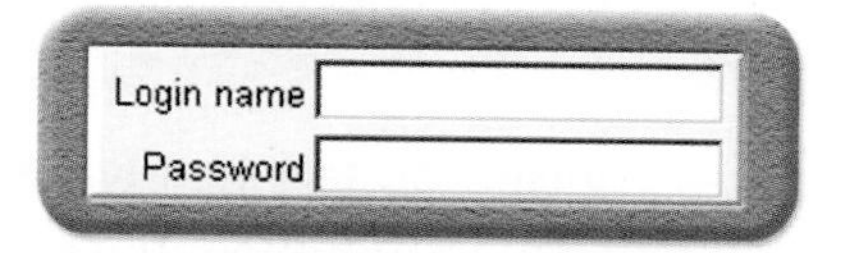


**Tip** To see examples of login names and passwords, click the **Need Help?** link. Because login names must be unique, you may need to add one or more numbers to the end of your first choice.

9 Just in case you ever forget your login name or password, select and answer the question you want CourseCompass Customer Support to use to verify your identity.

10 Click the **License Agreement** link to display the agreement in a separate window. To confirm your agreement with the terms and conditions in the license, return to the registration page and click the **I agree** box.

11 Review the information in the summary area on the left. If you need to change it, click the Back button.

12 CourseCompass confirms your registration. Print a copy of this page, which includes your *summary information, login name,* and *password*.

13 Click the http://students.pearsoned.com link, and click the **Log In** button.

14 Type your **login name** and **password** in the appropriate boxes, and then click the **Log in** button to see your customized My CourseCompass page.

Congratulations! You've registered in CourseCompass and enrolled in this course. To enter this course from now on, just go to http://students.pearsoned.com and log in to CourseCompass.

# Getting started in CourseCompass

Now that you've enrolled in your online course and logged in, you can begin exploring CourseCompass.

When you enter your course, you see the **My CourseCompass** page. This page contains lots of information that's already customized for you–such as your name and the title of this course. You can make other customizations yourself, such as changing the color scheme of the page.

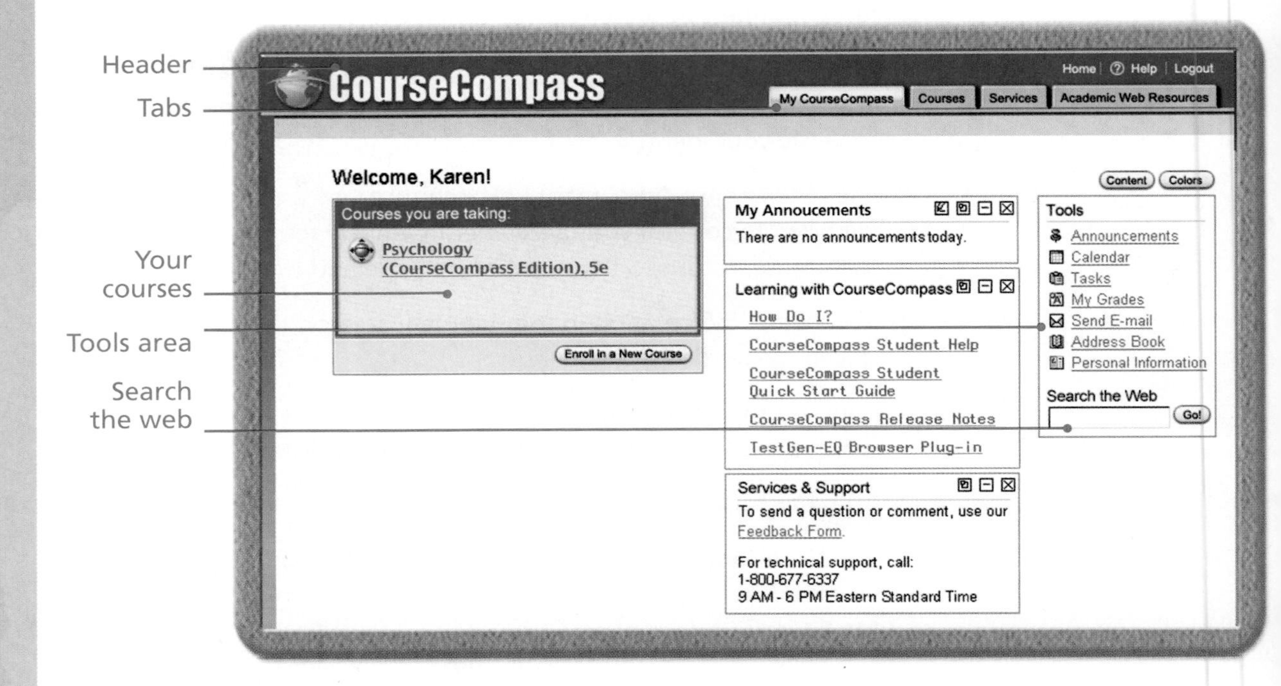


## Header

In the header area, which is always visible in CourseCompass, you can click:

- **Home** to return to your starting point within CourseCompass
- ⓘ **Help** to open CourseCompass online student Help
- **Logout** to exit from CourseCompass

## Tabs

In addition to the My CourseCompass page, there are other main pages in CourseCompass. To access one of these pages, click its tab.

- The **Courses** page lists all the online courses you are taking. You click the title of a course to go directly to it.

- The **Services** page tells you how to contact CourseCompass Customer Support and explains the requirements to run CourseCompass.
- The **Academic Web Resources** page provides access to the Blackboard Resource center, where you can find links related to your class subject.

## Tools area

The **My CourseCompass** page also has a Tools area with links to announcements for all your online courses, a personal "To Do" list, your grades on homework and tests, and an Address Book. You can even send email and search the web right from CourseCompass!

## Modules

The main part of the My CourseCompass page contains boxes, called *modules*, that give you access to CourseCompass courses, features, and information. These modules might include:

- **Courses**, which lists and lets you link to all the courses you are taking
- **Announcements**, which displays system-wide announcements and announcements for all your courses
- **News from Pearson Education**, which shows you updates about Pearson Education products and services
- **Learning with CourseCompass**, which links to resources to help you work in CourseCompass
- **Services and Support**, which tells you how to contact CourseCompass Customer Support

### Picking your own colors for the My CourseCompass page

You can change the color of the text and the background of the module title bars on the My CourseCompass page:

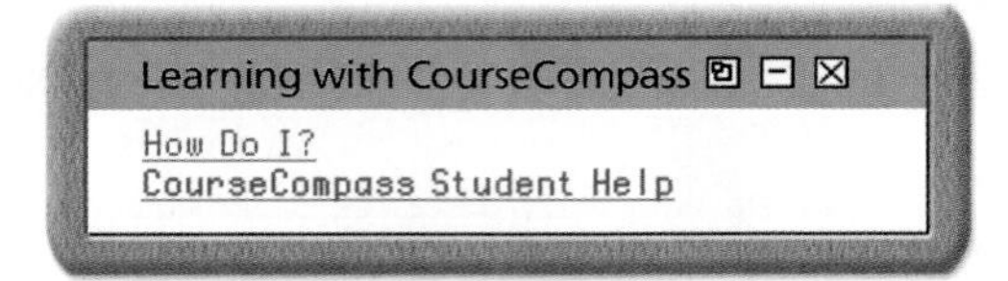


### To customize the colors:

1. Click (Colors) in the upper-right corner of the My CourseCompass page.
2. To change the color of the module title bars on the My CourseCompass page, click (Pick) next to Select Module Banner Color. Click a color in the ColorPicker.
3. To change the color of the text in the module headers, click (Pick) next to Select Banner Text Color. Click a color in the ColorPicker.
4. Click (Submit).

CourseCompass displays the My CourseCompass page with the new color scheme:

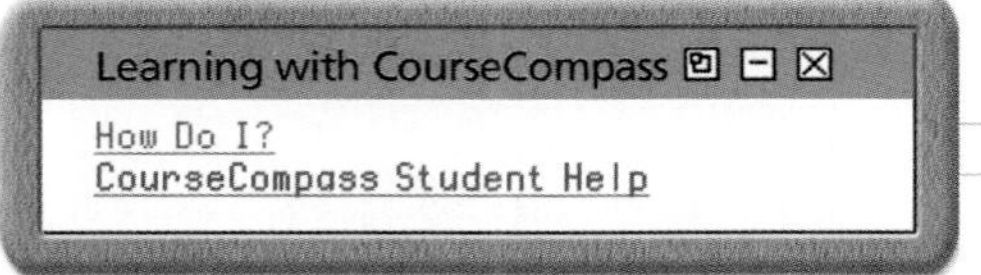

# Exploring your course

Now you're ready to check out your course! You can open your course in two ways:

- Click the course title on the My CourseCompass page:

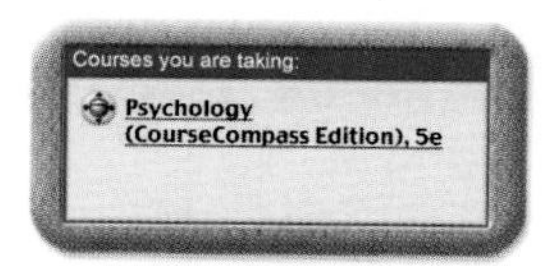


or

- Click the **Courses** tab and then click the course's title on the Course List page.

The Course Home page appears, with an outline of the course. You can explore the contents of your instructor's course by clicking on the links in this outline view and by clicking the buttons on the left. To return to this view, click the Course Home button.

## Viewing course announcements

From the Course Home page, click the Announcements button. You can view all the announcements related to this course, or you can view course announcements for a limited period of time by clicking one of the tabs in the announcements area.

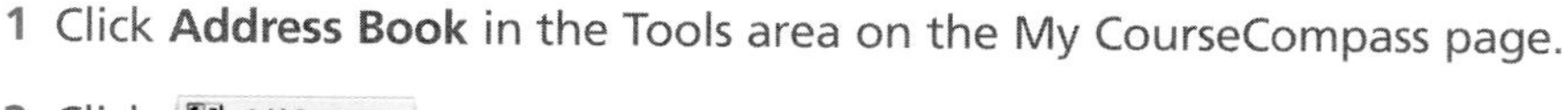

## Adding your friends to your **Address Book**

### To add a contact to your Address Book:

1 Click **Address Book** in the Tools area on the My CourseCompass page.

2 Click  .


3 Under Personal Information, enter the person's first name (required), last name (required), and email address. Add any other information that you want to track for this person, such as phone numbers.

4 Click Submit, and then click OK.

## Viewing course information

You access different areas in your course by clicking the buttons on the left side of the page. Your instructor can store course materials in any of the CourseCompass content areas represented by these navigation buttons.

These are some of the buttons you might see:

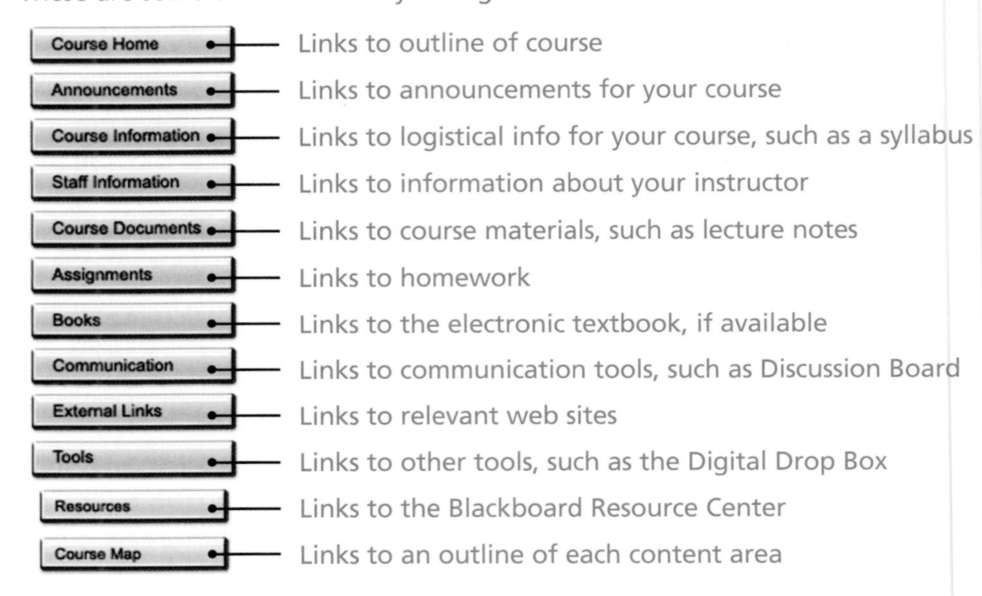


Your instructor might have changed the names of some of these buttons or added new ones. In any case, clicking navigation buttons is one way to get to content in your course.

### Adding events to your personal calendar

CourseCompass automatically creates a calendar for each course, which you can view within your course. Alternatively, you can click Calendar in the Tools area on the My CourseCompass page to see scheduled events for all your courses. You can also add your own personal appointments to this calendar.

To do so:

1 Click **Calendar** in the Tools area on the My CourseCompass page.

2 Click Add Event.

3 Fill in the event information, time, and date. Click Submit, and then click OK.

Your calendar appears, with the event you just added. Depending on the date of your event, and how you are viewing your calendar—by day, week, or month—you may have to click another calendar tab to see your event.

## Viewing and printing your course syllabus

One of your first tasks in CourseCompass will be to find and print your course syllabus. If your instructor has not told you where to locate the syllabus, look in Course Information. To do so:

1 Click your course's title on the My CourseCompass page.

2 Click Course Information .

3 Click the syllabus link, if one appears, as shown here:

Depending on how your instructor created the course syllabus, clicking the syllabus link either displays the syllabus in CourseCompass or opens another application to display a linked syllabus file.

4 If your computer is connected to a printer, you can print the syllabus. To do so, click **File** and then **Print** on your browser's menu.

If you didn't find a syllabus in the Course Information area, click the Course Documents button or open the course map to see whether you can find a link to the syllabus. If all else fails, you can email your instructor!

## Delivering an assignment using the Digital Drop Box

You can deliver completed online assignments using the Digital Drop Box. You can upload and send the file all at once, or you can post the file and send it later. To do so:

1 Click your course's title on the My CourseCompass page.

2 Click Tools .

3 Click the Digital Drop Box link.

4 Click Add File to upload the file but not send it to your instructor right away.

or

Click Send File to upload the file and send it now.

5 Type the assignment title.

6 Click Browse... and find the directory on your computer where you saved your assignment. Click the file name and click Open.

7 Optionally, type additional information or instructions in the Comments box.

8 Click Submit, and then click OK.

Your file appears in the Digital Drop Box:

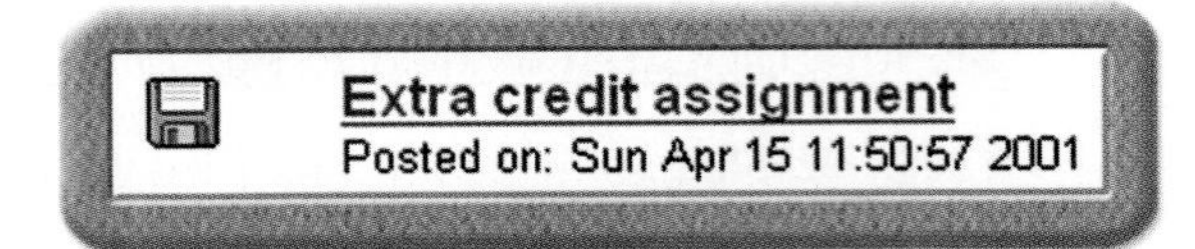


**Note** To send a file at a later date, go to the Digital Drop Box, click Send File, click the arrow at the edge of the Select file box, and click the name of the file you want to deliver to your instructor.

## Participating in a Discussion Board

Your instructor can set up Discussion Board forums to let you hold course-related discussions with other students outside of class time. A Discussion Board forum is like a string of email messages. Unlike a chat session, you can participate in a Discussion Board forum at any time.

Within a forum, CourseCompass groups related messages into threads. Depending on how your instructor set up your course, you can create a message to start a new thread or reply to existing messages.

To participate in a Discussion Board forum:

1 Click your course's title on the My CourseCompass page.

2 Click Communication.

3 Click the Discussion Board link.

4 Click the title of the Discussion Board forum you want to enter:

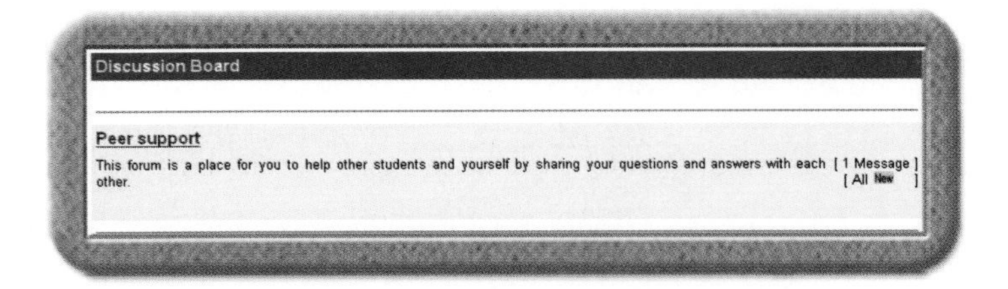

5 Click Add New Thread to begin a new conversation thread.

or

Click the title of a message to which you want to reply, and click Reply.

6 Type a subject for the message. If you are replying to an existing message, the subject box already contains text that you can replace if you want.

7 Type the message or reply.

8 If the forum allows anonymous postings and you want to hide your identity, click the box next to Post Message as Anonymous.

9 Click Browse... to attach a file, if that option is available.

10 Click Preview if you want to see how your message will look.

11 Click Submit.

The Discussion Board page appears, with your message or response.

## Taking tests online

Your instructor may assign assessments for you to complete online. These assessments can range in length and complexity from pre-class exercises, to short quizzes, to full-length exams. To complete any type of online assessment:

1 Click your course's title on the My CourseCompass page.

2 Click Assignments or Course Documents and find the assessment.

**Note** Your instructor can place assessments in any content area of CourseCompass. If you don't find your course assessments in the Assignments or Course Documents area, use the Course Home page to quickly locate them.

3 Click the **Take quiz** link below the assessment you want to take, and then click OK.

4 Click or type an answer to each question.

5 Click Submit at the bottom of the page, and then click OK.

## Checking your grades

You can see how you're doing in your course by checking your grades online in CourseCompass. CourseCompass lists your scores and also shows you your current standing in the course compared to your classmates.

To check your grades:

1. Click your course title on the My CourseCompass or Course List page.
2. Click Tools.
3. Click the Check Grade link.

4. Examine the user statistics, your scores, and, for comparison, the class average on each assessment.

### Creating your own "to do" list

You can use the Tasks list in CourseCompass to keep track of all the stuff you need to do. You can even prioritize each task so you can stay focused on what's most important.

#### To create your Tasks list:

1. Click Tasks in the Tool area on the My CourseCompass page.
2. Click Add Task.
3. Under Task Information, type a title and description for the task.
4. Next to Due Date, click the arrows to select the month, day, and year by which the task must be completed.
5. Next to Priority, click the arrow and select Low, Normal, or High. CourseCompass displays a different symbol, depending on your choice.
6. Next to Status, click the arrow and select Not Started, In Progress, or Completed. CourseCompass displays a different symbol, depending on your choice.
7. Click Submit, and then click OK.

CourseCompass adds your task to the list:

# Examining your CourseCompass Edition media resources

In your textbook, you will see icons in the margin alerting you to audio files, video files, or weblinks that will help you further master core concepts discussed in the chapter.

Weblink:
*Psychology, Fifth Edition*

**Audio and Video Clips:** The audio clips and video clips offer a dynamic presentation of the main topics in each chapter. The audio clips include Robert Baron's reviews of topics featured in the textbook, and discussions of what the author's research and that conducted by other psychologists and scientists have revealed about human behavior. Video clips include selections from actual research studies and help to illustrate how ideas discussed in the textbook have been applied to real-life situations.

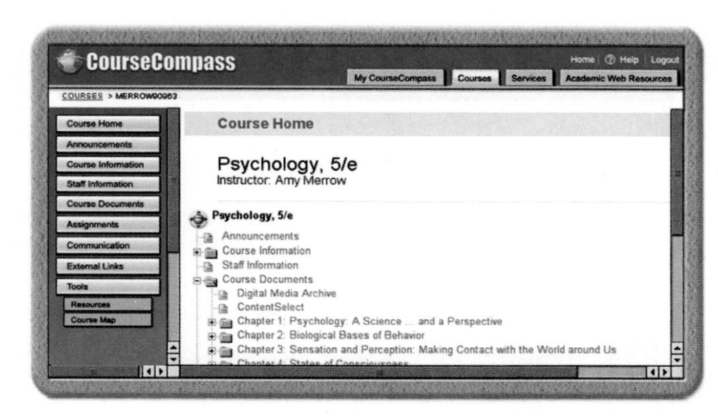


**To locate these media resources:**

1. Click your course's title on the My CourseCompass page.
2. Click on **Course Documents**.
3. Scroll down to find the chapter you are currently studying and click on the link.
4. For each chapter you will see:

   **Objectives**
   **PowerPoint Presentation**
   **Mastering the Web**
   **Chapter Audio/Video**

5. Click the Chapter Audio/Video link to access these media resources.

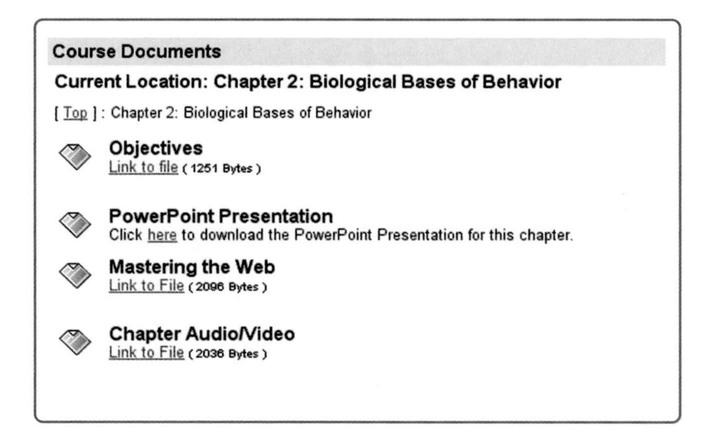

**Weblinks:** Weblinks, also found in Course Documents, provide access to numerous sites in which the content covered in *Psychology, 5th Edition* is presented in greater detail. From links to articles and documents on specific topics to interactive exhibits and enrichment activities, these sites will help reinforce the material presented in both your textbook and your class.

**ContentSelect:** The ContentSelect research database consists of customized collections of articles from top-tier psychology publications and journals. A significant amount of the content in ContentSelect is not available anywhere on the "open" Web. The collections contain high quality, peer-reviewed material that can only be found in premium research services.

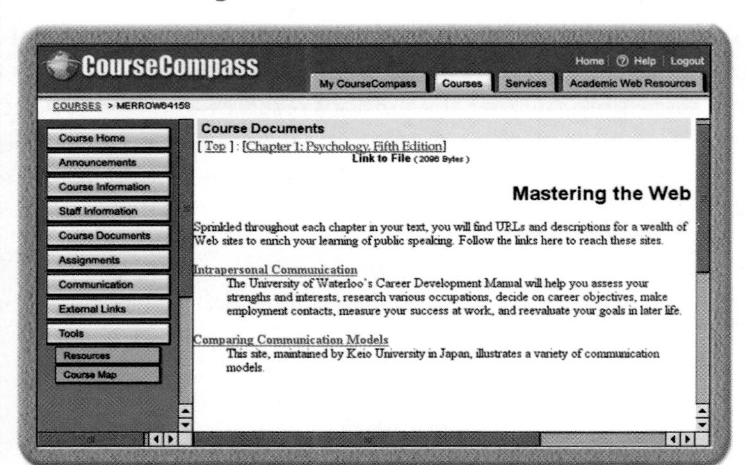


To access the ContentSelect Research Database, click on the ContentSelect link within Course Documents.

## Taking notes with the Electric Blackboard

The Electric Blackboard is like an online memo pad. You can use it to take and store notes in CourseCompass.

1 Click your course's title on the My CourseCompass page.

2 Click Tools.

3 Click the Electric Blackboard link.

4 Type your notes in the large box.

5 Click Submit, and then click OK.

6 Close the Electric Blackboard by clicking the X in the upper-right corner of the window.

When you come back to the Electric Blackboard, your notes will still be there.

## Sending email from **CourseCompass**

You can send email to your classmates right from CourseCompass.

### To send email:

1 Click **Send email** in the Tools area on the My CourseCompass page and click the appropriate course title.

or

Click your course title on the My CourseCompass, page click [Communication], and then click **Send email**.

2 Click Select Users.

3 Click [☑] next to the name of each person you want to email.

4 Enter the subject and message of the email.

5 Select Send Copy of Message to Self to receive a copy of the email.

6 If you want to attach a file to the message, click (Add). Click [Browse...], find the directory on your computer where you saved the file, click the file's name, click Open, and then click (Submit).

7 Click (Submit), and then click OK.

**Tip** For information about sending email to all students or small groups in your course, see online student Help.

## Customer support

The CourseCompass Customer Support Center is open weekdays from 9 AM to 6 PM Eastern Standard Time. You can contact Customer Support by:

1 Calling **1-800-677-6337** during the above service hours

2 Sending email to **support@coursecompass.com** with a detailed description of your computer system and the technical problem. Our Customer Service Support Center will get back to you promptly.

3 Clicking the link to **Feedback Form** on the Services page

# Getting help

To find out more about what you can do in CourseCompass, click on the How Do I? link from the Learning with CourseCompass module or you can explore the online student Help provided.

1 Click ⓘ **Help** in the CourseCompass header area.

2 CourseCompass student Help opens in a separate window so you can read Help as you work with CourseCompass.

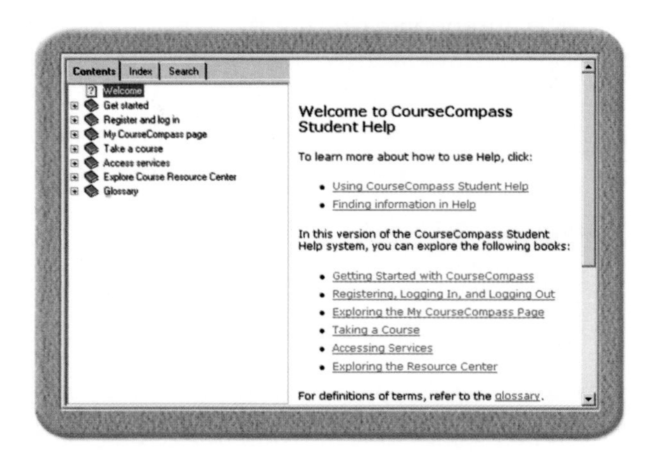


**Tip** Because Help contains a lot of information, it can take a little while to open. You might want to open the Help window when you start CourseCompass, and leave it open so you can quickly access Help topics as you need them.

The Help window has three tabs:

- **Contents** displays Help books and their pages. To open a book and show its pages, click the plus sign (+) to the left of the book icon. To close a book, click the minus sign (-). Click a page to view the corresponding topic.
- **Index** provides a list of keywords. Double-click a keyword to view the corresponding topic. If several topics reference the same keyword, click the title of the topic you want to view.
- **Search** lets you type a word or phrase you want to locate and then click Find. A list of all relevant topics appears. Double-click a topic to display it.

A topic might include additional links, which appear underlined in blue. You can click links to display more detail.

You can also click **Related Topics** at the end of a topic to display a list of other relevant topics.

# Psychology

CourseCompass Edition

# Psychology

FIFTH EDITION

**Robert A. Baron**
*Rensselaer Polytechnic Institute*

With the special assistance of
**Michael J. Kalsher**

ALLYN AND BACON
*Boston / London / Toronto / Sydney / Tokyo / Singapore*

Executive Editor: Carolyn Merrill
Developmental Editor: Jodi Devine
Editorial Assistant: Lara Zeises
Senior Marketing Manager: Caroline Croley
Editorial-Production Administrator: Annette Joseph
Editorial-Production Service: Colophon
Text Designer: Carol Somberg, Omegatype Typography, Inc.
Photo Researcher: Katharine Cook
Electronic Composition: Omegatype Typography, Inc.
Composition Buyer: Linda Cox
Manufacturing Buyer: Megan Cochran
Cover Administrator: Linda Knowles
Cover Designer: Studio Nine

A Pearson Education Company
160 Gould Street
Needham Heights, MA 02494

Internet: *www.abacon.com*



**Library of Congress Cataloging-in-Publication Data**
Baron, Robert A.
Psychology / Robert A. Baron; with the special assistance of Michael J. Kalsher.-- 5th ed.
p. cm.
Includes bibliographical references and indexes.
ISBN 0-205-31402-3 (alk. paper)
1. Psychology. I. Kalsher, Michael J. II. Title.

BF121 .B32 2000
150--dc21 00-027284

CourseCompass Edition Copyright © 2002 ISBN 0-205-34969-2

Printed in the United States of America

10 9 8 7 6 5 4 3 2 1 VHP 05 04 03 02 01

**Photo and Figure Credits** continue on page I-28, which constitutes a continuation of the copyright page.

**Photo Credits:** All Chapter-Opener Art by Heidi Younger
**Chapter 1:** p. 6(l): National Library of Medicine; p. 6(r): Corbis; p. 7(l): Archives of the History of American Psychology—The University of Akron; p. 7(r): National Library of Medicine; p. 14: Michael Newman/PhotoEdit; p. 18: Ulrike Welsch Photography; p. 23: Patti McConville/Image Bank; p. 24: Robert Harbison; p. 26: Courtesy of Robert A. Baron; p. 28(l): Greg Johnson/International Stock; p. 28(r): Jerry Mesmer/Folio, Inc.; p. 33: Courtesy of Robert A. Baron; p. 34: Bios/Peter Arnold, Inc.; p. 36: Courtesy of Robert A. Baron; **Chapter 2:** p. 73: Science Photo Library/Photo Researchers, Inc.; p. 75: T. K. Wanstal/The Image Works; p. 77(l): Courtesy of Wallace Nutting; p. 77(r): Courtesy of Lincoln Faurer; **Chapter 3:** p. 86(l): Dallas & John Heaton/The Stock Shop, Inc.; p. 86(r): Courtesy of Michael J. Kalsher; p. 91: Peter Menzel/Stock, Boston; p. 92: J. & L. Weber/Peter Arnold, Inc.; p. 95: Courtesy of David A. Johnson M. D. at http://www.lasikdoc.com; p. 111: Geoff Tompkinson/Science Photo Library/Photo Researchers, Inc.; p. 115(l): Stone/Bill Ross; p. 115(m): Stone/Robert E. Daemmrich; p. 115(r): Stone/John Ibbotson; p. 116 (top): Steve McCalidter/Image Bank; p. 116(l,bottom): Tommy L. Thompson/Black Star; p. 116(r,bottom): Stone/Steve Marts; p. 117: Ron Pretzer/Luxe; p. 119: AnimalsAnimals/©Robert Maier; p. 120: Courtesy of *Games Magazine*, August 1993 issue; **Chapter 4:** p. 130: Courtesy of Robert A. Baron; p. 131: Roland Seitre/Peter Arnold, Inc.; p. 134(top): Jeff Greenberg/Photo Researchers, Inc.; p. 134(bottom): Charles Gupton/Stock, Boston; p. 141: ChromoSohm/Sohm/Photo Researchers, Inc.; p. 147: Felicia Martinez/PhotoEdit; p. 151: The Kobal Collection; p. 155: Courtesy of Robert A. Baron; p. 158: David Young-Wolff/PhotoEdit; p. 159: Florian Franke/Image Bank; p. 160: The Everett Collection; **Chapter 5:** p. 169: AP/Wide World Photos; p. 170: The Image Works Archives; p. 171: National Library of Medicine; p. 174: Courtesy of Michael J. Kalsher; p. 180: David

## Dedication

To Jessica and Ted; may they have a long, happy, and fulfilling life together.

And

To Stuart, whose intellect and curiosity would be outstanding even in academe, and are truly exceptional outside it!

R.A.B.

To Joe and LaVera, the true believers.

And

To Ryan, the light of my life.

M.J.K.

# Brief Contents


1 **Psychology:** A Science . . . and a Perspective 2

2 **Biological Bases of Behavior** 40

3 **Sensation and Perception:** Making Contact with the World Around Us 82

4 **States of Consciousness** 128

5 **Learning:** How We're Changed by Experience 167

6 **Memory:** Of Things Remembered . . . and Forgotten 208

7 **Cognition:** Thinking, Deciding, Communicating 246

8 **Human Development I:** The Childhood Years 284

9 **Human Development II:** Adolescence, Adulthood, and Aging 328

10 **Motivation and Emotion** 368

11 **Intelligence:** Cognitive, Practical, Emotional 410

12 **Personality:** Uniqueness and Consistency in the Behavior of Individuals 448

13 **Health, Stress, and Coping** 488

14 **Mental Disorders:** Their Nature and Causes 530

15 **Therapies:** Techniques for Alleviating Mental Disorders 576

16 **Social Thought and Social Behavior** 617

# Contents


*Preface* xix

*Acknowledgments* xxix

*About the Authors* xxxii

1

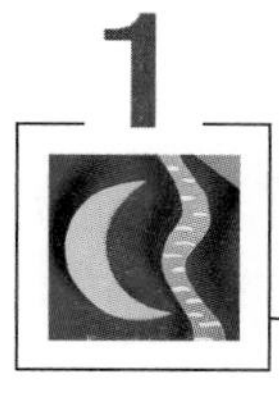

## Psychology: A Science . . . and a Perspective 2

**Modern Psychology: What It Is and How It Originated 5**

Psychology's Parents: Philosophy and Physiology 5

Early Battles over What Psychology Should Study: Structuralism, Functionalism, Behaviorism 7

Challenges to Behaviorism—and the Emergence of Modern Psychology 8

**Psychology: Its Grand Issues and Key Perspectives 10**

Key Perspectives in Psychology: The Many Facets of Behavior 11

**Psychology 2000: Trends for the New Millennium 12**

Psychology and Diversity: The Multicultural Perspective 13

Evolutionary Psychology: A New Perspective on "Human Nature" 15

The Exportation of Psychology: From Science to Practice 17

*From Science to Practice:*

- Preventing Deaths under Anesthesia: Human Factors (Engineering Psychology) to the Rescue 18

**Psychology and the Scientific Method 19**

The Scientific Method: Its Basic Nature 19

The Role of Theory in the Scientific Method 20

Advantages of the Scientific Method: Why Common Sense Often Leads Us Astray 21

**Research Methods in Psychology: How Psychologists Answer Questions about Behavior 24**

Observation: Describing the World around Us 24

Correlation: The Search for Relationships 26

The Experimental Method: Knowledge through Systematic Intervention 28

Ethical Issues in Psychological Research 31

**Using This Book: An Overview of Its Special Features 35**

*Making Psychology Part of Your Life:*

- How to Study Psychology—or Any Other Subject—Effectively 36

2

## Biological Bases of Behavior 40

**Neurons: Building Blocks of the Nervous System 44**

Neurons: Their Basic Structure 44

Neurons: Their Basic Function 45

Neurotransmitters: Chemical Keys to the Nervous System 48

**The Nervous System: Its Basic Structure and Functions 50**

The Nervous System: Its Major Divisions 50

The Endocrine System: Chemical Regulators of Bodily Processes 52

**The Brain: Where Consciousness . . . Is 55**

The Brain Stem: Survival Basics 55

The Hypothalamus, Thalamus, and Limbic System: Motivation and Emotion 56

*Beyond the Headlines:*

■ As Psychologists See It—Is Violence the Result of Faulty Neural Brakes? 57

The Cerebral Cortex: The Core of Complex Thought 58

Two Minds in One Body? Our Divided Brains 61

*Research Methods:*

■ How Psychologists Study the Nervous System and the Brain 64

**The Brain and Human Behavior: Where Biology and Consciousness Meet 66**

How the Brain Functions: An Example from Visual Perception 67

The Brain and Human Speech 69

The Brain and Higher Mental Processes 70

**Heredity and Behavior: Genetics and Evolutionary Psychology 72**

Genetics: Some Basic Principles 73

Disentangling Genetic and Environmental Effects: Research Strategies 74

*From Science to Practice:*

■ Identifying Genetic Factors in Human Disorders: Decoding Iceland 75

Evolutionary Psychology: Genes in Action 76

*Making Psychology Part of Your Life:*

■ The Nature–Nurture Controversy in the New Millennium: Adopting a Balanced View of the Role of Genetic Factors in Human Behavior 78

**3 Sensation and Perception: Making Contact with the World around Us 82**

**Sensation: The Raw Materials of Understanding 85**

Sensory Thresholds: How Much Stimulation Is Enough? 86

*Research Methods:*

■ How Psychologists Measure Sensory Thresholds—The Role of Psychophysical Procedures 87

Sensory Adaptation: "It Feels Great Once You Get Used to It" 90

**Vision 91**

The Eye: Its Basic Structure 91

Light: The Physical Stimulus for Vision 93

Basic Functions of the Visual System: Acuity, Dark Adaptation, and Eye Movements 94

Color Vision 96

Vision and the Brain: Processing Visual Information 97

**Hearing 98**

The Ear: Its Basic Structure 98

Sound: The Physical Stimulus for Hearing 99

Pitch Perception 100

Sound Localization 101

*Beyond the Headlines:*

■ As Psychologists See It—Premature Hearing Loss: The High Cost of Modern Living 102

**Touch and Other Skin Senses 104**

Pain: Its Nature and Control 104

**Smell and Taste: The Chemical Senses 106**

Smell and Taste: How They Operate 106

Smell and Taste: Some Interesting Facts 108

**Kinesthesia and Vestibular Sense 109**

*From Science to Practice:*

■ How a Basic Understanding of Sensory Processes Can Improve the Usefulness of Virtual Technologies 111

**Perception: Putting It All Together 112**

Perception: The Focus of Our Attention 112

Perception: Some Organizing Principles 113

Constancies and Illusions: When Perception Succeeds—and Fails 114

Some Key Perceptual Processes: Pattern and Distance 118

**The Plasticity of Perception: To What Extent Is It Innate or Learned? 121**

Perception: Evidence That It's Innate 121

Perception: Evidence That It's Learned 122

Must We Resolve the Nature–Nurture Controversy? 122

**Extrasensory Perception: Perception without Sensation? 123**

Psi: What Is It? 123

Psi: Does It Really Exist? 123

*Making Psychology Part Of Your Life:*

■ Managing Your Pain: Some Useful Tips 124

4

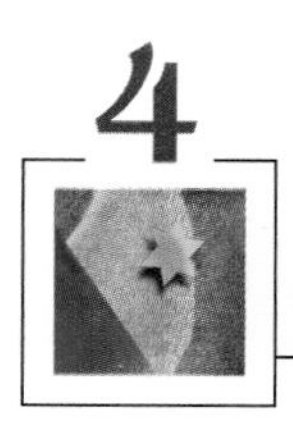

## States of Consciousness 128

**Biological Rhythms: Tides of Life—and Conscious Experience 131**

Circadian Rhythms: Their Basic Nature 131

Longer-Term Biological Rhythms: Mechanisms That Govern Mating and Hibernation 132

Individual Differences in Circadian Rhythms: Are You a Morning Person or a Night Person? 132

Disturbances in Circadian Rhythms: Jet Lag and Shift Work 133

*From Science to Practice:*

- Counteracting the "Drowsy Driver" Syndrome: When Sounds—and Scents—Save Lives 135

**Waking States of Consciousness 136**

Controlled and Automatic Processing: Two Modes of Thought 136

Self-Awareness: Some Effects of Thinking about Ourselves 139

**Sleep: The Pause That Refreshes? 142**

*Research Methods:*

- How Psychologists Study Sleep 142

Sleep: What Functions Does It Serve? 144

Effects of Sleep Deprivation 145

Sleep Disorders: No Rest for Some of the Weary 146

Dreams: "Now Playing in Your Private, Inner Theater . . ." 148

**Hypnosis: Altered State of Consciousness . . . or Social Role Playing? 150**

Hypnosis: How It's Done and Who Is Susceptible to It 150

Hypnosis: Contrasting Views about Its Nature 151

**Consciousness-Altering Drugs: What They Are and What They Do 154**

Consciousness-Altering Drugs: Some Basic Concepts 155

Psychological Mechanisms Underlying Drug Abuse: Contrasting Views 156

Consciousness-Altering Drugs: An Overview 157

*Beyond The Headlines:*

- As Psychologists See It—Can You Buy the Fountain of Youth on the Internet? "Buyer Beware" Strikes Again 161

*Making Psychology Part of Your Life:*

- Are You High or Low in Private Self-Consciousness? A Self-Assessment 162

5

## Learning: How We're Changed by Experience 166

**Classical Conditioning: Learning That Some Stimuli Signal Others 169**

Pavlov's Early Work on Classical Conditioning: Does This Ring a Bell? 171

Classical Conditioning: Some Basic Principles 171

Classical Conditioning: The Neural Basis of Learning 175

Classical Conditioning: Exceptions to the Rules 175

Classical Conditioning: A Cognitive Perspective 178

Classical Conditioning: Turning Principles into Action 179

*Beyond The Headlines:*

- As Psychologists See It—A New Approach to Teen Crime 181

**Operant Conditioning: Learning Based on Consequences 182**

The Nature of Operant Conditioning: Consequential Operations 183

*From Science To Practice:*

- "Horse Whispering": Applying Operant Conditioning to Treat Troubled Horses 185

Operant Conditioning: Some Basic Principles 186

Operant Conditioning: A Cognitive Perspective 194

*Research Methods:*

- How Psychologists Study Applications of Operant Conditioning 197

Applying Operant Conditioning: Solving Problems of Everyday Life 199

**Observational Learning: Learning from the Behavior and Outcomes of Others 200**

Observational Learning: Some Basic Principles 200

Observational Learning and Aggression 201

Observational Learning and Culture 202

Observational Learning: Some Practical Applications 203

*Making Psychology Part of Your Life:*

- Getting in Shape: Using Principles of Learning to Get Fit and Stay Fit 204

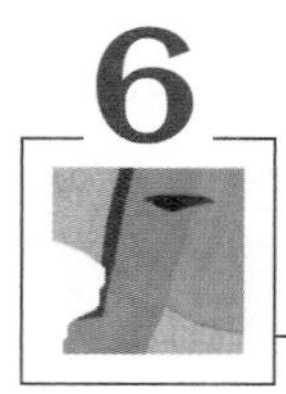

## 6 Memory: Of Things Remembered . . . and Forgotten 208

**Human Memory: Two Influential Views 210**

The Atkinson and Shiffrin Model 211

Neural Networks Models: Parallel Processing of Information 212

**Kinds of Information Stored in Memory 214**

Working Memory: The Workbench of Consciousness 215

*Research Methods:*

- How Psychologists Study Memory 218

Memory for Factual Information: Episodic and Semantic Memory 219

Memory for Skills: Procedural Memory 223

**Forgetting: Some Contrasting Views 225**

Forgetting as a Result of Interference 225

Forgetting and Retrieval Inhibition 226

**Memory Distortion and Memory Construction 226**

Distortion and the Influence of Schemas 227

Memory Construction: Remembering What Didn't Happen 228

**Memory in Everyday Life 230**

Repression: "What's Too Painful to Remember, We Simply Choose to Forget" 230

Autobiographical Memory: Remembering the Events of Our Own Lives 232

Memory for Emotionally Laden Events: Flashbulb Memories and the Effects of Mood on Memory 234

*From Science to Practice:*

- Mental Contamination and the Legal System: Can Jurors Really "Strike It from the Record"? 236

**Memory and the Brain: Evidence from Memory Impairments and Other Sources 237**

Amnesia and Other Memory Disorders: Keys for Unlocking Brain–Memory Links 237

Memory and the Brain: A Modern View 239

*Beyond the Headlines:*

- As Psychologists See It—Can Chewing Gum Improve Your Memory? 241

*Making Psychology Part of Your Life:*

- Improving Your Memory: Some Useful Steps 242

## 7 Cognition: Thinking, Deciding, Communicating 246

**Thinking: Forming Concepts and Reasoning to Conclusions 249**

Basic Elements of Thought: Concepts, Propositions, Images 250

*Research Methods:*

- How Psychologists Study Cognitive Processes 253

Reasoning: Transforming Information to Reach Conclusions 254

**Making Decisions: Choosing among Alternatives 258**

Heuristics: Using Quick—but Fallible—Rules of Thumb to Make Decisions 259

Framing and Decision Strategy 260

Escalation of Commitment: Getting Trapped in Bad Decisions 262

Emotions and Decision Making: The Magnifying Effects of Unexpected Loss and Gain 263

*Beyond the Headlines:*

- As Psychologists See It—Was It the Weather, or Did Faulty Reasoning Kill JFK Jr.? 264

Naturalistic Decision Making: Making Choices in the Real World 266

**Problem Solving: Finding Paths to Desired Goals 267**

Problem Solving: An Overview 267

Methods for Solving Problems: From Trial and Error to Heuristics 268

Facilitating Effective Problem Solving: The Role of Metacognitive Processing 269

Factors That Interfere with Effective Problem Solving 270

Artificial Intelligence: Can Machines Really Think? 272

*From Science to Practice:*

- Intelligent Agents: Just How Smart Are They? 273

**Language: The Communication of Information 275**

Language: Its Basic Nature 275

The Development of Language 275

Language and Thought: Do We Think What We Say or Say What We Think? 278

Language in Other Species 279

*Making Psychology Part of Your Life:*

- Making Better Decisions 281

**8**

**Human Development I: The Childhood Years 284**

**Physical Growth and Development 287**

The Prenatal Period 287

Prenatal Influences on Development 288

*Beyond the Headlines:*

- As Psychologists See It—Playpen Peril? The Potentially Harmful Effects of Plastic Toys 290

Physical Development during Our Early Years 291

**Perceptual Development 294**

*Research Methods:*

- How Psychologists Study Development 296

**Cognitive Development: Changes in Our Ability to Understand the World around Us 298**

Piaget's Theory: An Overview 298

Piaget's Theory: A Modern Assessment 302

Beyond Piaget: Children's Theory of Mind and Research on the Information-Processing Perspective 304

**Moral Development: Reasoning about "Right" and "Wrong" 307**

Kohlberg's Stages of Moral Understanding 308

Evidence Concerning Kohlberg's Theory 309

**Social and Emotional Development: Forming Relationships with Others 311**

Emotional Development and Temperament 311

Attachment: The Beginnings of Love 313

School and Friendships: Key Factors in Social Development 317

*From Science to Practice:*

- Making Playgrounds Safer: Some Concrete Steps 318

Do Parents Really Matter? A Recent—and Continuing—Controversy 319

**From Gender Identity to Sex-Category Constancy: How Children Come to Understand That They Are Female or Male 321**

Children's Growing Sophistication with Respect to Gender 322

Gender Development: Contrasting Explanations of How It Occurs 322

*Making Psychology Part of Your Life:*

- Combating Childhood Obesity 324

**9**

**Human Development II: Adolescence, Adulthood, and Aging 328**

**Adolescence: Between Child and Adult 330**

Physical Development during Adolescence 330

Cognitive Development during Adolescence 332

Social and Emotional Development during Adolescence 333

Adolescence in the New Millennium: A Generation at Risk? 338

*Beyond The Headlines:*

- As Psychologists See It—Preventing Teen Pregnancies: Should Adolescents Decide? 340

**Development during Our Adult Years 343**

Contrasting Views of Adult Development: Stage Theories versus the Contextual Approach 343

Physical Change during Our Adult Years 347

Cognitive Change during Adulthood 351

Social and Emotional Development during Adulthood 355

**Aging, Death, and Bereavement 359**

Theories of Aging: Contrasting Views about Why We Grow Old 359

*From Science to Practice:*

- Living Longer—and Healthier—Lives: Some Concrete Steps 360

Meeting Death: Facing the End of Life 361
Bereavement: Coming to Terms with the Death of Loved Ones 363

*Making Psychology Part of Your Life:*

- Helping Others Cope with Bereavement: Effective Condolence Behavior 365

# 10

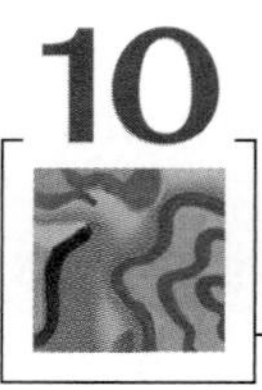

## Motivation and Emotion 368

**Motivation: The Activation and Persistence of Behavior 371**

Theories of Motivation: Some Major Perspectives 372

*From Science to Practice:*

- Using Goal Setting to Increase Occupational Safety—and Save Lives 375

Hunger: Regulating Our Caloric Intake 378
Sexual Motivation: The Most Intimate Motive 381
Aggressive Motivation: The Most Dangerous Motive 386

*Research Methods:*

- How Psychologists Study Aggression 389

Achievement Motivation: The Desire to Excel 390

*Beyond the Headlines:*

- As Psychologists See It—The Need for Stimulation . . . and How It Can Get Out of Hand 393

Intrinsic Motivation: How, Sometimes, to Turn Play into Work 394

**Emotions: Their Nature, Expression, and Impact 395**

The Nature of Emotions: Some Contrasting Views 396
The Biological Basis of Emotions 399
The External Expression of Emotion: Outward Signs of Inner Feelings 401
Emotion and Cognition: How Feelings Shape Thought and Thought Shapes Feelings 402
Subjective Well-Being: Some Thoughts on Personal Happiness 404

*Making Psychology Part of Your Life:*

- Some Tips on Winning the Battle of the Bulge 406

# 11

## Intelligence: Cognitive, Practical, Emotional 410

**Intelligence: Contrasting Views of Its Nature 413**

Intelligence: Unitary or Multifaceted? 413
Gardner's Theory of Multiple Intelligences 414
Sternberg's Triarchic Theory: The Value of Practical Intelligence 415
Cattell's Theory of Fluid and Crystallized Intelligence 416

**Measuring Intelligence 416**

IQ: Its Meaning Then and Now 417
The Wechsler Scales 417
Individual Tests of Intelligence: Measuring the Extremes 419

*Beyond the Headlines:*

- As Psychologists See It—Williams Syndrome: Mentally Challenged Persons with Music in Their Souls 420

Group Tests of Intelligence 421

*Research Methods:*

- How Psychologists Evaluate Their Own Assessment Tools: Basic Requirements of Psychological Tests 422

The Cognitive Basis of Intelligence: Processing Speed 424
The Neural Basis of Intelligence: Intelligence and Neural Efficiency 425

*From Science to Practice:*

- Predicting Career Success: Competency Assessment 426

**Human Intelligence: The Role of Heredity and the Role of Environment 428**

Evidence for the Influence of Heredity 428
Evidence for the Influence of Environmental Factors 431
Environment, Heredity, and Intelligence: Summing Up 433

**Group Differences in Intelligence Test Scores: Why They Occur 434**

Group Differences in IQ Scores: Evidence for the Role of Environmental Factors 434
Group Differences in IQ Scores: Is There Any Evidence for the Role of Genetic Factors? 435
Gender Differences in Intelligence 437

**Emotional Intelligence: The Feeling Side of Intelligence 439**

Major Components of Emotional Intelligence 439

Emotional Intelligence: Evidence on Its Existence and Effects 441

**Creativity: Generating the Extraordinary 442**

Contrasting Views of Creativity 443

Research on Creativity: Evidence for the Confluence Approach 444

*Making Psychology Part Of Your Life:*

- Managing Your Own Anger: A Very Useful Skill 445

## 12 **Personality:** Uniqueness and Consistency in the Behavior of Individuals 448

**Personality: Is It Real? 450**

**The Psychoanalytic Approach: Messages from the Unconscious 452**

Freud the Person 452

Freud's Theory of Personality 453

Research Related to Freud's Theory: Probing the Unconscious 458

Freud's Theory: An Overall Evaluation 461

Other Psychoanalytic Views: Freud's Disciples . . . and Defectors 461

**Humanistic Theories: Emphasis on Growth 463**

Rogers's Self Theory: Becoming a Fully Functioning Person 464

Maslow and the Study of Self-Actualizing People 465

Research Related to Humanistic Theories: Studying the Self-Concept 466

*Beyond the Headlines:*

- As Psychologists See It—What's In a Name? Ask the People Who Have Unusual Ones 467

Humanistic Theories: An Evaluation 468

**Trait Theories: Seeking the Key Dimensions of Personality 468**

The Search for Basic Traits: Initial Efforts by Allport and Cattell 469

The "Big Five" Factors: The Basic Dimensions of Personality? 470

Trait Theories: An Evaluation 471

**Learning Approaches to Personality 472**

Social Cognitive Theory: A Modern View of Personality 473

Research on the Learning Perspective 474

*From Science to Practice:*

- The Potential Benefits of Boosting Self-Efficacy: Helping Unemployed Persons to Help Themselves 474

Evaluation of the Learning Approach 475

**Measuring Personality 476**

Self-Report Tests of Personality: Questionnaires and Inventories 476

Projective Measures of Personality 478

Other Measures: Behavioral Observations, Interviews, and Biological Measures 479

**Modern Research on Personality: Applications to Personal Health and Behavior in Work Settings 479**

Personality and Health: The Type A Behavior Pattern, Sensation Seeking, and Longevity 480

Personality and Behavior in Work Settings: Job Performance and Workplace Aggression 482

*Making Psychology Part of Your Life:*

- Are You a Type A? 484

## 13 

**Health, Stress, and Coping** 488

**Health Psychology: An Overview 490**

*Research Methods:*

- How Psychologists Study Health Behavior 493

**Stress: Its Causes, Effects, and Control 494**

Stress: Its Basic Nature 494

Stress: Some Major Causes 497

Stress: Some Major Effects 500

**Understanding and Communicating Our Health Needs 504**

Health Beliefs: When Do We Seek Medical Advice? 504

Doctor–Patient Interactions: Why Can't We Talk to Our Doctors? 505

*From Science to Practice:*

- Surfing for Solutions to Medical Problems on the Internet: Using Information Technologies to Diagnose Our Illnesses 507

**Behavioral and Psychological Correlates of Illness: The Effects of Thoughts and Actions on Health 509**

Smoking: Risky for You and Everyone around You 510

*Beyond the Headlines:*

- As Psychologists See It—A New Weapon in the Antismoking Arsenal 512

Diet and Nutrition: What You Eat May Save Your Life 513

Alcohol Consumption: Here's to Your Health? 515

Emotions and Health 517

AIDS: A Tragic Assault on Public Health 518

**Promoting Wellness: Developing a Healthier Lifestyle 521**

Primary Prevention: Decreasing the Risks of Illness 521

Secondary Prevention: The Role of Early Detection in Disease and Illness 524

*Making Psychology Part of Your Life:*

- Managing Stress: Some Useful Tactics 525

## 14

## Mental Disorders: Their Nature and Causes 530

**Models of Abnormality: Changing Conceptions of Mental Disorders 533**

From the Ancient World to the Age of Enlightenment 533

Modern Perspectives: Biological, Psychological, Sociocultural, and Diathesis–Stress Models 535

**Assessment and Diagnosis: The DSM-IV and Other Tools 537**

*Research Methods:*

- How Psychologists Assess Mental Disorders 540

**Disorders of Infancy, Childhood, and Adolescence 541**

Disruptive Behavior 542

*From Science to Practice:*

- Preventing Conduct Disorder—or Worse! 543

Attention-Deficit/Hyperactivity Disorder (ADHD) 544

Feeding and Eating Disorders 544

Autism: A Pervasive Developmental Disorder 546

**Mood Disorders: The Downs and Ups of Life 549**

Depressive Disorders: Probing the Depths of Despair 549

Bipolar Disorders: Riding the Emotional Roller Coaster 550

The Causes of Depression: Its Biological and Psychological Roots 550

Suicide: When Life Becomes Unbearable 551

**Anxiety Disorders: When Dread Debilitates 553**

Phobias: Excessive Fear of Specific Objects or Situations 553

Panic Disorder and Agoraphobia 554

Obsessive–Compulsive Disorder: Behaviors and Thoughts outside One's Control 555

Posttraumatic Stress Disorder 556

**Dissociative and Somatoform Disorders 558**

Dissociative Disorders 558

Somatoform Disorders: Physical Symptoms without Physical Causes 560

**Sexual and Gender Identity Disorders 561**

Sexual Dysfunctions: Disturbances in Desire and Arousal 561

Paraphilias: Disturbances in Sexual Object or Behavior 561

Gender Identity Disorders 563

**Personality Disorders: Traits That Harm 563**

*Beyond The Headlines:*

- As Psychologists See It—Life without a Conscience: The Antisocial Personality Disorder in Action 566

**Schizophrenia: Losing Touch with Reality 567**

The Nature of Schizophrenia 567

The Onset and Course of Schizophrenia 568

Causes of Schizophrenia 569

**Substance-Related Disorders 571**

*Making Psychology Part of Your Life:*

- Preventing Suicide: How You Can Help 572

# 15 Therapies: Techniques for Alleviating Mental Disorders 576


**Psychotherapies: Psychological Approaches to Mental Disorders 579**

Psychodynamic Therapies: From Repression to Insight 580

Phenomenological/Experiential Therapies: Emphasizing the Positive 582

Behavior Therapies: Mental Disorders and Faulty Learning 584

Cognitive Therapies: Changing Disordered Thought 587

**Alternatives to Individual Psychotherapy: Group Therapy, Marital Therapy, Family Therapy, and Psychosocial Rehabilitation 589**

Group Therapies: Working Together to Solve Personal Problems 590

Marital and Family Therapies: Therapies Focused on Interpersonal Relations 591

*Beyond the Headlines:*

- As Psychologists See It—Is Better Sex the Key to a Happier Marriage? Don't Bet on It! 593

Self-Help Groups: When Misery Derives Comfort from Company 595

Psychosocial Rehabilitation 596

**Biological Therapies 597**

Drug Therapy: The Pharmacological Revolution 597

Electroconvulsive Therapy 601

Psychosurgery 602

**Psychotherapy: Is It Effective? 603**

*Research Methods:*

- How Psychologists Study the Effectiveness of Psychotherapy 603

The Effectiveness of Psychotherapy: An Overview of Key Findings 604

Are Some Forms of Therapy More Successful Than Others? 605

Culturally Sensitive Psychotherapy 607

**The Prevention of Mental Disorders: Community Psychology and Its Legacy 608**

**Legal and Ethical Issues Relating to Mental Disorders 610**

The Rights of Individuals and the Rights of Society 610

Ethical Issues in the Practice of Psychotherapy 611

*Making Psychology Part of Your Life:*

- How to Choose a Therapist: A Consumer's Guide 612


# 16 Social Thought and Social Behavior 616


**Social Thought: Thinking about Other People 619**

Attribution: Understanding the Causes of Others' Behavior 619

*From Science to Practice:*

- Attributional Augmenting and Perceptions of Female Entrepreneurs 623

Social Cognition: How We Process Social Information 624

Attitudes: Evaluating the Social World 628

*Research Methods:*

- How Psychologists Measure Attitudes—from Attitude Scales to the "Bogus Pipeline" 631

**Social Behavior: Interacting with Others 636**

Prejudice: Distorted Views of the Social World . . . and Their Effects 636

Social Influence: Changing Others' Behavior 641

*Beyond the Headlines:*

- As Psychologists See It—What Happens When Social Norms Encourage a "Lifestyle to Die For"? 643

Attraction and Love 647

Leadership: One Important Group Process 653

*Making Psychology Part of Your Life:*

- Some Guidelines for Having a Happy Romantic Relationship 656


# Appendix: Statistics: Uses—and Potential Abuses 659


**Descriptive Statistics: Summarizing Data 659**

Measures of Central Tendency: Finding the Center 661

Measures of Dispersion: Assessing the Spread 661
The Normal Curve: Putting Descriptive Statistics to Work 662

**Inferential Statistics: Determining Whether Differences Are or Are Not Real 663**

**Correlation and Prediction 665**

**The Misuse of Statistics: Numbers Don't Lie . . . or Do They? 666**

Random Events Don't Always Seem Random 666
Large Samples Provide a Better Basis for Reaching Conclusions Than Small Ones 667
Unbiased Samples Provide a Better Basis for Reaching Conclusions Than Biased Ones 667
Unexpressed Comparisons Are Often Meaningless 667
Some Differences Aren't Really There 668

**Glossary G–1**

**References R–1**

**Name Index I–1**

**Subject Index I–13**

# Preface

## "Taking Psychology with You" Revisited: Some Thoughts on the Value of Psychology—and on Psychologists' Tendency to Be Too Modest

In the previous edition of this book, I commented that I have always viewed psychology as a field that everyone can—and *should*—use throughout life. Not only does it offer a fascinating body of findings and knowledge about human behavior, it also provides a way of looking at the world—and ourselves—that everyone should gain from their first course in psychology. That's the basis for the theme noted above: "taking psychology with you."

Although change is indeed a constant, and I am as subject to changes of heart and mind as anyone else, I find that now, as I write these words, I believe more intensely than ever in the accuracy of this view. Why is this so? Partly because in recent years my own research has focused on topics that have brought me into contact with people from many different fields and walks of life. My studies of workplace aggression and of the social and cognitive factors that influence entrepreneurs' success have been of interest to researchers in many fields outside psychology (e.g., political science, economics, management, finance) as well as to individuals in government and business. As a result, I have often been invited to speak to audiences very different from ones I addressed in the past, and I have had numerous opportunities to interact with scholars and practitioners from a very wide range of backgrounds. These experiences have led me to three important conclusions about psychology and the way it is perceived in society as a whole: (1) The importance of psychology is recognized by virtually everyone; (2) persons in many different fields turn to it to answer important questions relating to their own work; and (3) psychology is generally viewed as the single most valuable and reliable source of knowledge about human behavior—indeed, in my experience, nothing else is even close.

These conclusions, in turn, have led me to realize that psychologists—including me!—have often been too modest about the intrinsic value of their field. They have tended to overlook the important ways in which the findings and principles of psychology are used to solve a wide range of practical problems, not just by psychologists but by persons in other fields as well. I think this is a point worth emphasizing. After all, if psychology is, as I contend, extremely valuable to society, why not accentuate this point? Why not call attention to the *value and usefulness of psychology to society?* Actually, I see doing so as an expansion of the basic theme of "taking psychology with you"; because to the extent that students recognize the many ways in which the findings of psychology are being used for beneficial purposes outside psychology itself, they will be encouraged to apply these findings to their own lives, too. How have I sought to emphasize the value and usefulness of psychology? Primarily, through the steps and features outlined below.

## Emphasizing the Practical Value of Psychology: From Science to Practice Sections

To illustrate the great practical value of psychology in concrete terms, I have included special **From Science to Practice** sections throughout the book. These sections illustrate how the findings and principles of psychology are being used to address important problems in many different fields—medicine, education, law, and business, to mention just a few. Here are some examples of these new sections:

- Preventing Deaths under Anesthesia: Human Factors (Engineering Psychology) to the Rescue (Chapter 1)
- Identifying Genetic Factors in Human Disorders: Decoding Iceland (Chapter 2)
- Counteracting the "Drowsy Driver" Syndrome: When Sounds—and Scents—Save Lives (Chapter 4)
- "Horse Whispering": Applying Operant Conditioning to Treat Troubled Horses (Chapter 5)
- Mental Contamination and the Legal System: Can Jurors Really "Strike It from the Record"? (Chapter 6)
- Intelligent Agents: Just How Smart Are They? (Chapter 7)
- Making Playgrounds Safer: Some Concrete Steps (Chapter 8)
- Using Goal Setting to Increase Occupational Safety—and Save Lives (Chapter 10)
- Predicting Career Success: Competency Assessment (Chapter 11)
- Surfing for Solutions to Medical Problems on the Internet: Using Information Technologies to Diagnose Our Illnesses (Chapter 13)

# Other Features Relating to the Theme of "Taking Psychology with You"

To further encourage readers to recognize the intrinsic usefulness and value of psychology, and so to take it with them throughout life, I've also improved several features present in the previous edition:

## Beyond the Headlines: As Psychologists See It

All of these special sections, which describe what psychological research has to say about the topics covered in recent news stories, are new. Some examples of **Beyond the Headlines** sections:

Is Violence the Result of Faulty Neural Brakes? (Chapter 2)

Premature Hearing Loss: The High Cost of Modern Living (Chapter 3)

Can You Buy the Fountain of Youth on the Internet? "Buyer Beware" Strikes Again (Chapter 4)

BEYOND the HEADLINES: As Psychologists See It

A New Approach to Teen Crime

Counteracting Teen Violence: Therapeutic Breakthrough?—Or New Application of Established Principles of Learning?

CRITICAL THINKING QUESTIONS

Can Chewing Gum Improve Your Memory? (Chapter 6)

Was It the Weather, or Did Faulty Reasoning Kill JFK Jr.? (Chapter 7)

Preventing Teen Pregnancies: Should Adolescents Decide? (Chapter 9)

The Need for Stimulation . . . and How It Can Get Out of Hand (Chapter 10)

Williams Syndrome: Mentally Challenged Persons with Music in Their Souls (Chapter 11)

Life without a Conscience: The Antisocial Personality Disorder in Action (Chapter 14)

Is Better Sex the Key to a Happier Marriage? Don't Bet on It! (Chapter 15)

What Happens When Social Norms Encourage a "Lifestyle to Die For"? (Chapter 16)

## Research Methods: How Psychologists Study . . .

These sections, which describe the methods used by psychologists to study important topics, have been improved and refined to better illustrate the methods used by psychologists to study important aspects of behavior. I continue to believe that describing **Research Methods** in close proximity to discussions of the areas of investigation in which they are used is a more effective strategy than describing them all in a separate chapter at the beginning of the book.

Thinking: Forming Concepts and Reasoning to Conclusions **253**

seems to help people avoid the *planning fallacy*—our tendency to underestimate the resources (such as time or money) necessary to achieve a goal, and to overestimate how easily the goal can be achieved (Buehler, Griffin, & Ross, 1994). (See the discussion of the "optimistic bias" in Chapter 16 for additional information on the planning fallacy.)

For more information on how psychologists study various aspects of thinking, please see the **Research Methods** section below.

**Reaction Time:** Time that elapses between the presentation of a stimulus and a person's reaction to it.

*Research Methods:*
**How Psychologists Study Cognitive Processes**

People think—that's obvious. But how do psychologists measure aspects of cognition since it is difficult to measure these processes directly? One of the earliest techniques used by psychologists to study cognitive processes is **reaction time:** the time that elapses between the presentation of a stimulus and a person's reaction to it. Why measure reaction time? If thinking involves distinct processes, then each process must take some time to complete. As I noted in Chapter 1, the development of computers has made it possible to measure the speed of people's reactions to specific stimuli with great precision. Researchers have used the information derived from reaction-time experiments as the basis for drawing inferences about underlying cognitive processes.

In a typical reaction-time experiment, participants are asked to respond verbally or press a button as quickly as possible following the presentation of a cue; say, a light, a tone, or the appearance of a particular stimulus on a computer screen. What can reaction time tell us about cognitive processes? Actually, plenty. Reaction time can be used to indicate how long it takes for a person to complete various types of perceptual tasks; for example, to react to the presentation of a visual stimulus, identify letters presented on a computer screen, or decide whether a letter is a vowel or a consonant. Researchers can then use the pattern of reaction times obtained on various tasks to determine the speed of the component mental processes involved; for example, the time required to detect a visual stimulus, reach a decision, or make a manual response to the stimulus.

Through the use of reaction-time measures, psychologists have gained tremendous insight into the timing of mental events. Still, an overreliance on reaction-time measures—or on any measure—can be limiting and, in certain respects, misleading. Why? One reason is that reaction time is an aggregate measure that represents only the final output of what is often a complicated series of cognitive events. As a result, important aspects of cognitive processing may not be revealed through reaction time.

To illustrate this point, let's consider the cognitive changes associated with old age. Among the most commonly observed of these are declines in memory, in attention, and in mental processing speed. These changes—usually gauged by measures of accuracy and reaction time—have led researchers to conclude that age-related changes in cognitive ability stem from an overall decline in mental processing, a decline that is magnified as the complexity of the task increases (Cerella, Poon, & Williams, 1980). But is this true? Recent findings using *event-related brain potentials*, or *ERPs*, cast doubt on this possibility (see Figure 7.4).

As we discussed in Chapter 2, ERPs reflect the momentary changes in brain electrical activity that occur as a person performs a cognitive task (Ashcraft, 1998). To measure ERPs, researchers place electrodes at standard locations on the scalp, and a computer analyzes the underlying neural patterns. The series of changes in brain electrical activity reflect different aspects of cognitive activity.

**Figure 7.4**
**Event-Related Brain Potentials: A Tool for Measuring Cognitive Processes**

Event-related brain potentials, or ERPs, are one of several high-tech tools psychologists use to measure aspects of cognitive processing.

## Making Psychology Part of Your Life

These sections, which appear at the end of each chapter, describe ways in which readers can apply the findings and principles of that chapter to their own lives. Many **Making Psychology Part of Your Life** sections are new to this edition. A few examples:

The Nature–Nurture Controversy in the New Millennium: Adopting a Balanced View of the Role of Genetic Factors in Human Behavior (Chapter 2)

Managing Your Pain: Some Useful Tips (Chapter 3)

Are You High or Low in Private Self-Consciousness? A Self-Assessment (Chapter 4)

Combating Childhood Obesity (Chapter 8)

Helping Others Cope with Bereavement: Effective Condolence Behavior (Chapter 9)

Some Guidelines for Having a Happy Romantic Relationship (Chapter 16)

78 CHAPTER 2 Biological Bases of Behavior

*Making* **Psychology** *Part of Your Life*

**The Nature–Nurture Controversy in the New Millennium: Adopting a Balanced View of the Role of Genetic Factors in Human Behavior**

When I was a graduate student, the idea that complex aspects of human behavior (e.g., intelligence or mating preferences) could be influenced by genetic factors was deeply out of favor. A pure "environmentalism" ruled in psychology; almost everything, most psychologists believed, was shaped by the world around us and our experiences in it. Now, however, the pendulum of scientific opinion has swung far back the other way. As I noted in this chapter, growing evidence suggests that everything from mental disorders to gender differences in dominance—and even (as we'll see in later chapters) job satisfaction—can be influenced by genetic factors, at least to a degree. As is often the case, this shift in scientific opinion has been magnified by the media. Magazines, newspapers, and television programs have jumped on the bandwagon, suggesting that genetic factors are all-powerful and are, in fact, *the* controlling influence in our lives.

Where should *you* stand on this important issue? I strongly recommend a balanced view that recognizes the potential role of genetic factors and evolution in human behavior, but which also takes note of the limitations of this theory and of the evidence for it. Here are a few points I think you should try to keep in mind in the years ahead:

- **Even if a form of behavior is influenced by genetic factors, this doesn't mean that it can't be modified.** It's an error I've seen many, many times: People assume that because some illness or some difference between groups of people is inherited, it is etched in stone and can't be changed. This is completely false. Hundreds of millions of people around the world (including me) have faulty vision, but this in no way dooms them to being unable to see clearly. On the contrary, eyeglasses, contact lenses, and now simple laser operations permit the huge majority of these persons to attain something close to normal vision. So remember: The fact that an aspect of behavior is influenced by genetic factors—even strongly influenced—in no way implies that it can't be changed.
- **Environmental factors almost always play a role, too.** Another common error you should avoid is the view that because an aspect of behavior is strongly influenced by genetic factors, environmental ones are relatively unimportant. Wrong! Genes don't determine behavior; they merely produce *predispositions* toward certain traits (physical or otherwise), and predispositions may or may not be translated into reality. Whether they are usually depends to an important degree on environmental factors. For example, consider a strong genetically determined tendency to gain weight. Does this mean that persons having this tendency will always be overweight? Absolutely not. If they live at a time and in a place where there is an overabundance of food, this genetic tendency may show up in their actual weight. But if they live at a time and in a place where food is scarce or where there are very strong norms against being overweight, they may never have the chance to become obese—or may fight this tendency successfully. Again, biology is definitely *not* destiny.
- **We are not simply servants of our genes.** Another common error involves a basic misinterpretation of the evolutionary perspective. Because much emphasis is placed on inherited adaptive mechanisms and how these contribute to reproductive success, some people jump to the conclusion that we exist merely to reproduce—to get our genes into the next generation. This is a highly questionable point of view. Yes, certain physical traits or forms of behavior increase the likelihood that individuals will reproduce, and as a result these traits or forms of behavior tend to become more common in a population. But this in no way implies that all our energy or motivation is directed toward reproducing. This principle merely describes what *tends* to happen, over long periods of time, in large populations; it has little or nothing to do with individuals or with the causes of complex forms of human behavior.
- **Evolution is the scientific view of how species change over time and is supported by a huge amount of data; but it is not the only view and, to date, has not been "proved" in the same manner as many other scientific theories.** The fossil record provides powerful evidence for the view that species change over time (sometimes tremendously) and that many forms of life once existed on earth but have now disappeared (e.g., dinosaurs). However, because we can't travel backward in time to observe evolution directly, and because evolution usually requires extremely long periods of time, it can't be proved through direct experimentation as many

## Expanded Practice in Critical Thinking

As in the previous edition, Critical Thinking Questions are included in each **Beyond the Headlines** section throughout the text, and at the end of each chapter. In addition, I have added Food for Thought questions to several sets of Review Questions in each chapter. These questions are designed to encourage readers to think critically about the information presented in the previous section.

## Increased Coverage of the Biological/Genetic Perspective

Interest among psychologists in the biological and genetic bases of behavior has increased sharply in recent years. This growing interest is reflected in the text by many discussions of these topics and of the field of evolutionary psychology. To call these discussions to readers' attention, each is highlighted with this special symbol.

## Integrated Coverage of Gender and Diversity Issues

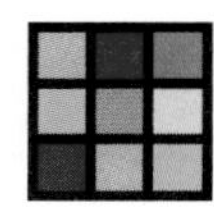

Interest in gender and diversity issues, too, remains an important theme in modern psychology. These topics are treated throughout the text in an integrated fashion and are highlighted by this special symbol.

## What Remains the Same

This books retains several features of the previous edition to which students and colleagues reacted favorably:

- *Incidents and experiences from my own life:* As in the fourth edition, I use these (occasionally) to help illustrate both the practical value of psychology and the unique perspective it provides on human behavior.
- *Marginal glossary:* This feature will be retained, but to avoid giving the margins a cluttered look, I avoid listing several definitions in a row.
- *Special labeling of all graphs and figures:* These labels help students read and interpret these illustrations. Such labels are a hallmark of all my texts, and I've received many favorable comments on them over the years.

## Additional Features Worthy of Note

- *Up-to-date content:* I have always believed that a textbook should reflect a field as it is *now,* not as it was in the past. As a result, I've included the most up-to-date information I could obtain on each topic. *In fact, many new references from 1998, 1999, and even 2000 appear in every chapter.* Truly, I don't know how to do any better than this!
- *Displaced Preface:* Many students don't bother to read prefaces, so I've included a description of the special features of the text and its major themes right in Chapter 1. That way, I feel, readers won't miss this important framework-generating information.
- *Clear references to all illustrations in the text:* Nothing confuses students as much as coming upon a figure, table, or photo that seems totally disconnected from the text. To avoid this problem, all illustrations are numbered and mentioned in the text so that students will know when to look at them and can quickly find them.

## Changes in Content

Psychology is an ever changing field, so woe to any textbook that doesn't reflect this fact! With this point in mind, I've made many important changes in content. Here are just a few of the most important ones:

## Chapter 2: Biological Bases of Behavior

Often, students wonder why they are asked to read a chapter on biology and the nervous system in a course on psychology. The answer, of course, is that the biological structures and processes described are intimately linked to important aspects of behavior. However, these links often get lost in a virtual blizzard of detail. In revising Chapter 2, I have made vigorous efforts to put behavior back on center stage. For example, I have included a new section entitled *The Brain and Human Behavior: Where Biology and Consciousness Meet,* which emphasizes the role of the brain in such functions as analysis of visual information, speech, and higher mental processes (e.g., reasoning). This and other sections remind students that the focus of this chapter is, ultimately, *behavior*—not biology. I believe that this approach will be very helpful for students, and it is also in keeping with modern psychology's increased interest in biological and genetic factors.

## Chapter 8: Human Development I: The Childhood Years

Chapter 8 has been greatly revised to reflect major new advances with respect to such topics as *symbolic play,* children's *theory of mind,* and children's social and emotional development (e.g., new discussions of the development of empathy, the role of fathers, and adjustment of immigrant children).

## New Topics within Chapters

In addition to these changes, literally dozens of new topics have been included—so many that I could not possibly list all of them here. Here is a *small* sample of these new topics:

A new section on current trends (Psychology 2000) that includes a detailed discussion of evolutionary psychology (Chapter 1)

A new, expanded section on the history of psychology (Chapter 1)

A new discussion of brain mechanisms in speech (Chapter 2)

New information on subliminal perception (Chapter 3)

New discussions of pain perception and aromatherapy (Chapter 3)

New information on the ironic monitoring process (Chapter 4)

New findings on the role of genetic factors in alcohol abuse (Chapter 4)

Recent findings on factors that affect ability to delay gratification (Chapter 5)

Role of a genetic predisposition (hypohedonia) in learned helplessness (Chapter 5)

Neutral network models of memory (Chapter 6)

Organization of autobiographical memory (Chapter 6)

New section on physical reasoning (Chapter 7)

Recent findings on the linguistic relativity hypothesis (Chapter 7)

New section on perceptual development (Chapter 8)

Discussion of Harris's contention that parents don't matter (Chapter 8)

Development of children's theory of mind (Chapter 8)

Parenting styles and their effects on adolescents (Chapter 9)

Contextual theory of adult development (Chapter 9)

Friendship and the convoy model in adulthood (Chapter 9)

Recent findings on the role of genetic factors in intelligence (e.g., studies of qualitative trait loci) (Chapter 11)

New evidence on the Flynn effect (Chapter 11)

Cognitive approaches to understanding creativity (Chapter 11)

New findings on the "big five" dimensions of personality (Chapter 12)

New findings about self-efficacy (Chapter 12)

New findings concerning the causes and effects of smoking (Chapter 13)

Why people prefer to eat high-fat foods (Chapter 13)

Developmental psychopathology (Chapter 14)

New section on childhood disorders (e.g., oppositional defiant disorder, conduct disorder, attention-deficit/hyperactivity disorder, autistic disorder) (Chapter 14)

Prodromal pruning theory of schizophrenia (Chapter 14)

Psychosocial rehabilitation (Chapter 15)

Ethnic and gender differences in responses to psychoactive drugs (Chapter 15)

Legal and ethical issues relating to mental disorders and psychotherapy (Chapter 15)

Cultural factors in the correspondence bias (Chapter 16)

Self-affirmation as a technique for reducing dissonance (Chapter 16)

New section on leadership (Chapter 16)

# Ancillaries: Helping Students Learn

*Psychology*, Fifth Edition, is accompanied by a complete teaching and learning package. The key parts of this package are described below.

## Electronic Supplements

Allyn and Bacon offers you two exciting ancillaries from which to choose when you purchase new copies of Baron's *Psychology*, Fifth Edition. Choose between the SuperSite, which includes Psychology Place and a whole host of activities, weblinks, audio clips, video clips, and practice tests. Or select Mind Matters, an interactive CD–ROM designed to supplement Introductory Psychology courses. Your choice of either interactive, technologically based supplement is available to you and your students free with new textbook purchases.

The **SuperSite for Baron's *Psychology* (PIN required)** contains The Psychology Place, a subscription-based Web resource for psychology students and educators, and is customized for Baron, *Psychology*, Fifth Edition. Developed by Peregrine Publishers in conjunction with The Psychology Place Faculty and Allyn and Bacon, this custom site is offered free to you and your students with purchases of new copies of *Psychology*, Fifth Edition.

For Students: To directly support daily coursework, all components of this unparalleled resource are indexed according to the chapters of the textbook. This site currently contains extensive learning activities, news updates, research reports, weblinks, practice tests, and other helpful study aids to reinforce and extend your learning.

For Instructors: The customized version of The Psychology Place offers diverse opportunities for student investigation and collaboration all in an easy-to-use format that reflects your syllabus! An extensive selection of teaching resources is also available for each chapter of the text. The customized version of The Psychology Place will help you:

- Stay abreast of recent Research News and launch your students' own Web investigations;
- Quickly find scientifically accurate and appropriate Web resources using Best of the Web;
- Readily integrate on-line investigative and collaborative Learning Activities into your course;
- Communicate with other educators and share your teaching ideas and challenges by participating in the Op Ed Forum;
- Keep up with Teaching News and Resources each month to learn about the latest books, journals, and conferences; and
- Easily optimize your computer to make the most of the Web's capabilities with the Toolkit.

Additional on-line materials are arranged by major chapter headings for each chapter and present students with hundreds of links to audio clips, video clips, activities, flashcards, and practice tests. These links are annotated with brief descriptions that help students understand the value and purpose of each element in the context of the chapter. The 25-question multiple-choice practice test for each chapter is a terrific study aid for students as it supplies answer justifications for incorrect answers.

Your other option is the **Allyn and Bacon Mind Matters CD–ROM,** developed by James Hilton of the University of Michigan and Charles Perdue of West Virginia State College. A unique learning tool, the Mind Matters CD–ROM helps students explore psychology by combining interactivity with clear explanation, fostering active learning and reinforcing core concepts in introductory psychology. This CD–ROM contains a wide range of learning opportunities including activities with immediate scoring and feedback, video clips of historical experiments and current research, animations, simulations, and an interactive glossary. Introductions and conclusions are provided to place all activities in context. Learning is reinforced through two forms of student assessment, Rapid Reviews after each topic, and more extensive Quick Quizzes after each unit. Easy navigation allows students to work through each unit in a linear or nonlinear format. The Mind Matters CD–ROM is accompanied by an extensive Faculty Guide with descriptions of all activities, outlines, text correlation guides, and test questions for each unit. For more information and a demonstration of this CD, please go to www.abacon.com/mindmatters.

Features of Mind Matters CD-ROM:

- Topical coverage reflects those areas most difficult for students and most applicable for reinforcement through use of technology (biopsychology, sensation and perception, for example).
- Rapid Review concept checks and more extensive Quick Quizzes provide extensive assessment. Students are provided with feedback for questions answered incorrectly.
- Wide range of activities, simulations, and animations provide a rich and exciting learning environment to reinforce coverage in standard introductory psychology textbooks.
- Accessible introductions and conclusions place all activities in context to reinforce learning.

- Easy navigation allows students to move within and between units to explore a wide range of concepts without worry of getting lost.
- An extensive Faculty Guide provides descriptions of all activities, outlines, text correlations, and test questions for each unit. Allyn and Bacon text correlation guides can also be accessed from the Main Screen of the Mind Matters CD–ROM and at www.abacon.com/mindmatters.

## Supplements for Instructors

**Test Bank:** Created by Thomas Jackson of Fort Hays State University, the Test Bank contains more than 2,800 questions—mainly multiple choice but also including true/false, fill-in-the-blank, and short-answer items. Each chapter begins with learning objectives. Each question is designated as applied, conceptual, or factual, depending on the type of question; and as easy, medium, or challenging, depending on the difficulty of the question. More than 40 percent of the questions are new in this edition.

**Computerized Test Bank:** A computerized version of the Test Bank, on Mac, DOS, or Windows, is also available.

**Instructor's Resource Manual:** The Instructor's Resource Manual is created by Debra Hollister of Valencia Community College. Each chapter contains learning objectives, a chapter overview, a Chapter-at-a-Glance table, an Annotated Lecture Outline, video listings, and a list of what is new in this edition. The Chapter-at-a-Glance table correlates all of the available instructional ideas and supplemental items in one easy-to-read table. The Annotated Lecture Outline for each chapter is arranged according to the major headings of the text and contains key terms, classroom demonstrations, lecture examples, critical thinking opportunities, journal entries, and diversity topics. Also included in the Instructor's Resource Manual are Handout Masters, which can be turned into transparencies or individual student handouts.

**Website:** The Allyn and Bacon Companion Website, which can be accessed at www.abacon.com/baron, offers a wide range of resources to both instructors and students. Instructors will find the table of contents, learning objectives, and links to stable URLs with brief descriptions of what will be found at each site, who the author is, and how the site is relevant to the chapter material.

**Allyn and Bacon Digital Media Archive CD–ROM for Psychology, 2.0 Version:** Allyn and Bacon offers an array of media products to help enliven your classroom presentations. The Digital Media Archive provides charts, graphs, tables, and figures electronically on one cross-platform CD–ROM. The Digital Media Archive goes one step further by including video and audio clips and hot weblinks along with the electronic images.

**PowerPoint Presentation:** Fred Whitford of Montana State University prepared a PowerPoint Presentation specifically for Baron's *Psychology*, Fifth Edition, which is available on CD–ROM.

**Transparencies:** 200 color transparencies accompany Baron's *Psychology*, Fifth Edition.

**Allyn and Bacon Interactive Video and Video User's Guide:** Video clips illustrate topics in each chapter and are tied to the text by a narrator who introduces the clips for each chapter and also provides a conclusion after the clips have been viewed. Critical Thinking Questions appear on the screen following related clips. A Video User's Guide accompanies each video and provides additional resources for instructors, such as page references to the text and additional lecture ideas. Contact your local Allyn and Bacon sales representative for information on other available videos.

**Course Management System:** Course Management enables you to easily create password-protected on-line courses and empowers you to manage them in ways never before possible. For more information on Course Management, please go to www.abacon.com/techsolutions and select Course Management Systems Partnerships.

## Supplements for Students

**Study Guide Plus:** The Study Guide Plus, created by Catherine Seta of Wake Forest University and John Seta of the University of North Carolina at Greensboro, is designed to help students review the text material by providing exercises that will check their comprehension and their ability to think critically about the material in the text. This study guide includes a very active approach to learning and carries over the themes of the text so that students apply the material to their lives. Outlines and learning objectives are provided to help students organize the material, and practice tests include multiple-choice questions as well as essay and short-answer questions.

**Practice Tests:** The Practice Tests, created by Thomas Jackson of Fort Hays State University, provide students with multiple-choice questions complete with answer justifications for the incorrect choices. Students will be able to test their knowledge before taking the classroom test; they will be able to use the page references to easily turn to the text and review a section on which they are unclear.

**Allyn and Bacon Website:** The Allyn and Bacon Companion Website, which can be accessed at www.abacon.com/baron, offers a wide range of resources to both the instructors and students. Students will find learning objectives, practice tests, and links to stable URLs with brief descriptions of what will be found at each site, who the author is, and how the site is relevant to the chapter material.

**Allyn and Bacon Quick Guide to the Internet for Psychology, 2001 Edition:** Updated to reflect the most current URLs related to the study of psychology, this easy-to-read guide helps point students in the right direction as they explore the tremendous array of psychology-related information on the Internet.

***Cross-Cultural Explorations: Activities in Culture and Psychology:*** This book by Susan Goldstein focuses on comparing specific behaviors across cultures. *Cross-Cultural Explorations* is composed of activities that revolve around case studies, self-administered scales, mini-experiments, and the collection of analytic, observational, and interview data. The majority of the activities are derived from cross-cultural psychology, although research findings from indigenous psychology, cultural psychology, ethnic psychology, and psychological anthropology are used as well. This activity book provides students with a cross-cultural perspective by encouraging them to explore their own cultural background, interview others with specific cross-cultural experiences, make cross-cultural comparisons using a broad interpretation of culture, and read about cultures different from their own.

Additional supplements for students include:

- *Evaluating Psychological Information: Sharpening Your Critical Thinking Skills,* Second Edition, by James Bell
- *Studying Psychology: A Manual for Success,* by Robert T. Brown
- *Writing for Psychology,* by Christopher Thaiss and James F. Sanford

# Some Final Comments . . . and a Request for Help

I have said it before, but it bears repeating: I personally *hate* a complacent, standpat attitude. I will close, then, by asking for your help once again. I have truly worked hard to make this new edition the best yet. I realize, however, that only you, the readers of this book, can tell me whether and to what extent I've succeeded. So please do write, call, e-mail, or fax your comments and suggestions. I'll listen carefully, and the chances are good that you'll see your ideas reflected in the next edition. My sincere thanks, in advance, for your help.

Robert A. Baron
2114 Pittsburgh Building
Rensselaer Polytechnic Institute
Troy, New York 12180–3590

(518) 276–2864
(518) 276–8661 (FAX)
baronr@rpi.edu

# Acknowledgments

## Words of Thanks

This is the forty-third book with my name somewhere on the cover, so people often ask me, "How do you do it?" My answer always includes two parts: (1) I spend lots of time alone, during which I enter an altered state of consciousness I sometimes describe as my "writing frenzy" (as in sharks' "feeding frenzy"); and (2) I have lots of help from talented friends and colleagues. In preparing this text, as in all my writing projects, I've once again been the recipient of lots of good help. I wish to acknowledge that assistance here.

First and foremost, my sincere thanks to my good friend and colleague Michael J. Kalsher. He played a primary role in preparing several chapters, in working with me to enhance the website for the book, and in many other ways. It was certainly a lucky day for me when he first came to interview at Rensselaer, and an even happier one when he agreed to join our faculty.

Second, I wish to express my thanks to the many colleagues who, through their excellent feedback and suggestions, helped to shape the content and form of this book. These individuals are listed below.

## User Survey Responders and Expert Reviewers for the Fourth Edition

Susan Borsky, Northern Arizona University
Charisse Chappell, Salisbury State University
Stephen L. Chew, Samford University
Joan Cook, County College of Morris
Randy Cornelius, Vassar College
Donald Evans, Drake University
Mark Faust, University of South Alabama
Lee Fernandez, Modesto Junior College
Diane Finley, Towson University
Edwin E. Gantt, Brigham Young University
E. Scott Geller, Virginia Polytechnic Institute and State University
Vernon Hall, Syracuse University
Susan Harris, Northern Arizona University
Judith Horowitz, Medaille College
Bobby Hutchison, Modesto Junior College
Jerdan Johnson, Middle Tennessee State University
Paul E. Jose, Loyola University of Chicago
Charles Kutscher, Syracuse University
Joshua D. Landau, York College of Pennsylvania
Tim Lehmann, Valencia Community College
Gary Levy, University of Wyoming
Christopher M. Lowry, Brigham Young University

Linda M. Montgomery, University of Texas of the Permian Basin
Kristi S. Multhaup, Davidson College
John Nield, Utah Valley State College
Antonio Nunez, Michigan State University
Lynne Schmecter-Davis, Brookdale Community College
Joseph R. Scotti, West Virginia University
Eric Shiraev, Northern Virginia Community College
Karin Sieger, Valencia Community College
Linda Skinner, Middle Tennessee State University
Stephen M. Smith, North Georgia College and State University
Ric Wynn, County College of Morris

## Reviewers for the Fifth Edition

Joel Alexander, Western Oregon University
Bem P. Allen, Western Illinois University
Eric Anderson, Indiana State University
Robert F. Bornstein, Gettysburg College
Rhonda Douglas Brown, Texas Tech University
David M. Buss, University of Texas
Bernardo J. Carducci, Indiana University Southeast
Paul Finn, Saint Anselm College
Joseph M. Fitzgerald, Wayne State University
William F. Flack, Jr., Indiana University of Pennsylvania
Howard Friedman, University of California–Riverside
Debra L. Hollister, Valencia Community College
Brian Kaufman, University of Maine at Farmington
Mark D. Kelland, Lansing Community College
Richard A. Lambe, Providence College
James M. Lampinen, University of Arkansas
Douglas W. Matheson, University of the Pacific
Joel Morgovsky, Brookdale Community College
Elaine H. Olaoye, Brookdale Community College
Lillian M. Range, University of Southern Mississippi
Brad Redburn, Johnson County Community College
Linda C. Reinhardt, University of Wisconsin–Rock County

I also want to extend my personal thanks to Executive Editor Carolyn Merrill of Allyn and Bacon. Her support, advice, encouragement, and friendship have certainly played an important role in the form and features of the new edition, and I look forward to working with her for many years to come. (Please, Carolyn, don't leave Allyn and Bacon!)

It's also a pleasure to express my appreciation to Jodi Devine, my developmental editor. Jodi's comments and suggestions were helpful in many ways—and moreover, she always communicated these to me in a kind and considerate manner. Thanks, Jodi!

Next, I'd like to thank Annette Joseph, my production editor, for her outstanding help in keeping the project on track and pulling all the loose (and often maddening!) ends together.

I also wish to thank Jay Howland for a careful, intelligent, professional, and constructive job of copy-editing. She helped me to clarify important points and to avoid errors and inconsistencies that might otherwise have escaped my notice.

And speaking of slipping through the cracks, I want to take this opportunity to thank Peg Latham of Colophon for her outstanding work in coordinating many elements of production. This is a complex process, and it works only if everything comes together at the right time and in the right place. Peg handled this task with her usual degree of aplomb, with the result that we experienced the minimum number of problems and emergencies possible.

Finally, my thanks to several friends and colleagues for their outstanding work on various ancillaries. These aids are essential to helping students learn, so I'm truly indebted to these colleagues for their help. Debra Hollister of Valencia Community College has produced an exceptionally complete and useful set of instructor materials. Thomas Jackson of Fort Hays State University has prepared superior test items to accompany the text. Catherine Seta of Wake Forest University and John Seta of the University of North Carolina at Greensboro have prepared an excellent study guide that gets students involved in the material in many different ways.

To all these exceptional people, and to many others, too, I offer my warmest personal regards.

# About the Authors

**ROBERT A. BARON** *(right)* is Professor of Psychology and Professor of Management at Rensselaer Polytechnic Institute. He received his Ph.D. from the University of Iowa in 1968. Professor Baron has held faculty appointments at Purdue University, the University of Minnesota, University of Texas, University of South Carolina, University of Washington, and Princeton University. In 1982 he was a Visiting Fellow at Oxford University. From 1979 to 1981 he served as a Program Director at the National Science Foundation. He is a Fellow of both the American Psychological Association and American Psychological Society.

Professor Baron has published more than one hundred articles in professional journals and twenty-eight chapters in edited volumes. He is the author or co-author of forty-one books, including *Social Psychology,* (9th ed.), *Behavior in Organizations* (7th ed.), *Human Aggression* (2nd ed.), and *Understanding Human Relations* (4th ed.).

He holds three U.S. patents, and is President of Innovative Environmental Products, Inc., a company that applies the findings and principles of psychology to the development of new products designed to enhance the quality of everyday life. The company's newest project is a device to help drivers remain alert on long road trips.

Professor Baron's current research interests focus mainly on (1) workplace aggression and violence, (2) cognitive and social factors that contribute to entrepreneurs' success (e.g., their social skills), and (3) effects of the physical environment (e.g., temperature, air quality, lighting) on social behavior.

His hobbies include (1) music (he plays the piano and wrote and copyrighted a song released in the 1960s), (2) fine woodworking (he makes everything from small wooden boxes to furniture), and (3) coin collecting. Professor Baron has been a runner for more than twenty years and has had a lifelong interest in good food and wine.

**MICHAEL J. KALSHER** *(left)* is Associate Professor of Psychology and Chair of the Department of Philosophy, Psychology, and Cognitive Science at Rensselaer Polytechnic Institute. He received his Ph.D. from Virginia Tech in 1988. Professor Kalsher is a member of both the American Psychological Society and the American Psychological Association. He is also a member of the Human Factors and Ergonomics Society where he serves as the Chairman of the Safety Technical Group.

Professor Kalsher has published more than fifty articles in professional journals, a number of chapters in edited books, and he has given more than one hundred presentations at professional meetings.

He consults regularly for business and industry on issues ranging from safety to psychometrics and testing. He is currently President of Behavioral Ergonomics and a founding partner of U.S. Ergonomics and Safety, consulting firms that specialize in applying the principles of psychology to enhance workplace safety.

Professor Kalsher's current research interests focus mainly on (1) workplace safety, (2) development and evaluation of warnings and instructions, and (3) the effects of the physical environment (e.g., sound, fragrance) on human performance.

Professor Kalsher has a longstanding interest in sports, especially running. A native of Montana, he enjoys horseback riding and spending time in the outdoors.

Chapter 1

# Psychology: A Science . . . and a Perspective

## CHAPTER OUTLINE


**MODERN PSYCHOLOGY: WHAT IT IS AND HOW IT ORIGINATED 5**

Psychology's Parents: Philosophy and Physiology

Early Battles over What Psychology Should Study: Structuralism, Functionalism, Behaviorism

Challenges to Behaviorism—and the Emergence of Modern Psychology

**PSYCHOLOGY: ITS GRAND ISSUES AND KEY PERSPECTIVES 10**

Key Perspectives in Psychology: The Many Facets of Behavior

**PSYCHOLOGY 2000: TRENDS FOR THE NEW MILLENNIUM 12**

Psychology and Diversity: The Multicultural Perspective

Evolutionary Psychology: A New Perspective on "Human Nature"

The Exportation of Psychology: From Science to Practice

■ FROM SCIENCE TO PRACTICE *Preventing Deaths under Anesthesia: Human Factors (Engineering Psychology) to the Rescue*

**PSYCHOLOGY AND THE SCIENTIFIC METHOD 19**

The Scientific Method: Its Basic Nature

The Role of Theory in the Scientific Method

Advantages of the Scientific Method: Why Common Sense Often Leads Us Astray

**RESEARCH METHODS IN PSYCHOLOGY: HOW PSYCHOLOGISTS ANSWER QUESTIONS ABOUT BEHAVIOR 24**

Observation: Describing the World around Us

Correlation: The Search for Relationships

The Experimental Method: Knowledge through Systematic Intervention

Ethical Issues in Psychological Research

**USING THIS BOOK: AN OVERVIEW OF ITS SPECIAL FEATURES 35**

■ MAKING PSYCHOLOGY PART OF YOUR LIFE *How to Study Psychology—or Any Other Subject—Effectively*

It never fails. I'm at a party, talking to someone I've just met, and they ask: "What's your field?" When I answer, "I'm a psychologist," they usually react in one of three ways. Some people—I think of them as "fans"—express great enthusiasm about psychology. Usually, I get into a spirited discussion with such persons about one or more aspects of human behavior—anything from weight loss to eyewitness testimony or workplace violence. A second group, whom I describe as "volunteer patients," react quite differently. They view meeting me as an opportunity for free counseling. They tell me about their personal problems (often revealing intimate details I'd rather not know), ask me to interpret their dreams, and sometimes request the name of a good hypnotist!

I describe the third group as "skeptics," and such persons let me know right away that they are *not* impressed. They tend to do this in two contrasting ways. Some tell me that in their opinion psychology is just "common sense," so it's really nothing new and is definitely *not* in the same league as chemistry, physics, or other fields of science. Others grudgingly admit that psychology might be scientific in nature, but express the strong belief that it is not really useful: In their view, it is just so much fun and games—mainly for psychologists themselves.

What do these experiences tell me? Primarily, two things. First, the fact that the first group ("fans") is by far the largest suggests that most people are deeply interested in psychology. They view it as a source of fascinating information about themselves and other persons, and as a source of valuable help with their personal problems. Second, these experiences remind me that not everyone shares these views. On the contrary, the group I label "skeptics" have serious doubts about the value, scientific nature, and usefulness of psychology.

In a sense, this book is dedicated to all three groups. For those who already believe that psychology is interesting and valuable, it will offer a vast array of intriguing and potentially useful information about human behavior. For the skeptics, it will provide a solid basis for changing their minds—for coming to see psychology as the fascinating and eminently *useful* field that it is.

But this book is designed to do more than this. It also seeks to provide you with a *new perspective on human behavior.* I have long believed that psychology offers far more than a collection of interesting facts; it also provides a new way of thinking about your own feelings, thoughts, and actions, and those of other persons. After reading this book, I believe, *you will never think about yourself, other people, and your relations with them in quite the same way as before.* And I also predict that this new perspective will enrich your life in many different ways.

"Come on, Professor Baron, get real!" I can almost hear you saying. "Psychology is OK and might be fun, but it can't be *that* good." I realize that words alone can't convince you on this score, so I ask only that you reserve judgment until you have read several chapters. After you have, I believe, you will understand the basis for my own enthusiasm about my field, and may well come to share it.

Before turning to the specific content of psychology—what it has discovered about human behavior—it is important that you have a framework for interpreting this information and, ultimately, using it. A basic finding of cognitive psychology (one important branch of the field) is that new information is understood best when a mental framework for holding it already exists. Given this fact, I'll use the remainder of this introductory chapter for providing you with such a framework. This will involve several tasks.

First, I'll define psychology, provide a brief overview of its origins, and describe some of the major issues with which it grapples. An example: To what extent is our behavior shaped by experience versus built-in, inherited tendencies? Second, I'll comment on the scientific nature of psychology, describing the *scientific method,* how it is used by psychologists, and how you too can put it to good use. Included here will be a discussion of *critical thinking*—the careful, cautious, and open-minded approach that is one of the key building blocks of all branches of science. Third, I'll describe basic *research methods* used by psychologists in their efforts to increase our knowledge of human behavior. Since the vast majority of the information and findings reported in this book were acquired through research, it is important for you to understand these methods before proceeding. Conducting research raises complex and important ethical issues, so I'll also touch on these as well.

After completing these tasks, I'll summarize the special features of this book—features designed to enhance the value of this, your first college-level course in psychology. Finally, I'll provide you with some concrete suggestions on how to study psychology—or any other subject—effectively. Now, to begin at the beginning, let's consider what psychology is and how it developed.

## Modern Psychology: What It Is and How It Originated

Web Link: *Today in the History of Psychology*

Suppose that you stopped fifty people on the street and asked them to define the field of psychology; what would they say? Probably, many different things, such as "The field that studies the unconscious," "The study of rats in mazes," or perhaps "Hypnotism, ESP, and stuff like that." If you posed this question to fifty psychologists, however, you'd obtain much greater agreement: They would largely agree that **psychology** is best defined as *the science of behavior and cognitive processes.* Two parts of this definition deserve further comment. First, note that psychologists view their field as basically *scientific* in nature. Second, this definition suggests that psychologists view their field as being very broad in scope; indeed, they perceive it as being concerned with virtually everything we do, feel, think, or experience.

By the term *behavior,* in other words, psychologists mean any observable action or reaction of a living organism—everything from overt actions (anything we say or do) through subtle changes in the electrical activity occurring deep inside our brains. If it can be observed and measured, then it fits within the boundaries of psychology. Similarly, by *cognitive processes,* psychologists mean every aspect of our mental life—our thoughts, memories, mental images, reasoning, decision making, and so on—in short, all aspects of the human *mind.*

Psychology was not always defined in this way, however. During the field's formative years, in fact, there were stormy intellectual battles over what psychologists should study and how this endeavor should proceed. Since these debates shaped psychology as we know it today, it is worth taking a brief look at them here. Before turning to these competing early views, though, we'll consider an even more basic question: How did the idea of a scientific field of psychology originate in the first place?

### Psychology's Parents: Philosophy and Physiology

**Psychology:** The science of behavior and cognitive processes.

Let's begin with a basic fact: Scientific progress never occurs in a vacuum. Rather, new advances or breakthroughs emerge when existing streams of research and thought meet and mesh, thus creating insights that did not exist before. The idea of a scientific field of psychology definitely emerged in this way. It occurred when certain ideas in *philosophy* combined with findings and methods in the field of *physiology*—a branch of biology that studies the functioning of living organisms.

By the late nineteenth century, many philosophers had turned their attention to questions about the human mind: How do we perceive the world around us? Do people have free will, or are their actions determined by events outside and inside their bodies? What is the link between mind and body—between the physical world (in which our bodies clearly exist) and our thoughts, feelings, and consciousness?

Philosophers had long attempted to answer these questions through careful reasoning (rationalism). For instance, René Descartes, a French philosopher (1596–1650), suggested that mind and body are distinct entities and that they interact through the *pineal gland,* found deep within the brain; this view is known as *dualism.* Other philosophers, in contrast, suggested that mind can influence body and body can influence mind—a view known as *interactionism.* Perhaps even more important, by the end of the nineteenth century, many philosophers had reached the conclusion that questions about the human mind could not be answered solely by means of reasoning but required careful observation—an empirical approach. This, in turn, raised a thorny question: How could such observations be made?

This is where *physiology* entered the picture. Physiologists had been using the scientific method to answer questions about the nervous system and our senses for decades. During the period from 1860 to 1880, Johannes Müller described how electrical signals were conducted by nerves within the body; Hermann von Helmholtz showed how receptors in the eyes and ears receive and interpret sensations from the outside world; and Gustav Fechner demonstrated that our perceptions of physical stimuli—for instance, the loudness of a sound or brightness of a light—are related in lawful, predictable ways to the physical energies of these stimuli. When these findings were combined with the growing conviction among philosophers that the human mind could be studied through empirical means, a new idea emerged: the possibility of a *scientific field of psychology.* And once this idea took shape, the new field of psychology itself quickly developed.

By 1879, in fact, Wilhelm Wundt had founded the first formal laboratory for research in psychology at the University of Leipzig. Because of this and other contributions, Wundt is often described as the "founder of experimental psychology." (Actually, though, Alexander Bain, a philosopher, founded the influential journal *Mind* in 1876, wrote several books about psychology, and trained a large number of graduate students who went on to do significant work in psychology. So, in a sense, he, too, is a candidate for this title—although perhaps less directly than Wundt.) One of Wundt's students, G. Stanley Hall (1844–1924), was influential in bringing psychology to the United States. He founded the first laboratory of psychology at Johns Hopkins in 1883, helped start the American Psychological Association in 1892, and then became its first president. Psychology was a big hit in the United States—perhaps because universities there were relatively young and so were more receptive to change than older universities elsewhere. By 1893, twenty-four U.S. universities had established psychology laboratories (see Figure 1.1). All was not smooth sailing

**Figure 1.1**
**Wilhelm Wundt and the Early Growth of Psychology**

Wilhelm Wundt *(left)* founded the first laboratory of psychology in Germany in 1879. One of his students, G. Stanley Hall *(right),* was instrumental in bringing the new field to the United States, where it grew rapidly: By 1893, twenty-four U.S. universities had established their own laboratories of psychology.

for the new field, however. In fact, it was soon rocked to its foundations by heated controversies concerning its focus—what, exactly, it should study.

**Structuralism:** An early view of psychology suggesting that the field should focus on identifying the basic structures of the human mind.

**Functionalism:** An early view of psychology suggesting that it should focus on the functions of consciousness.

**Behaviorism:** The view that only observable, overt activities that can be measured scientifically should be studied by psychology.

## Early Battles over What Psychology Should Study: Structuralism, Functionalism, Behaviorism

Wilhelm Wundt was a powerful personality, so he didn't simply found the first laboratory in psychology; he also argued forcefully for his view of what the new field should study. Briefly, he proposed that psychology should focus on analyzing the contents of consciousness in order to determine its basic elements and the relationships between them—a view known as **structuralism.** This task, he argued, could be carried out by *introspection*—a method in which trained individuals report in detail on their conscious experiences in response to specific stimuli (e.g., sounds, optical illusions, other visual stimuli) that are presented to them under carefully controlled conditions. If you have trouble relating such work to the definition of psychology offered above, don't be alarmed. Neither the topics studied by structuralists nor the methods they employed have survived the test of time. However, the strict insistence by Wundt and his followers that psychology adopt rigorous research methods did survive and helped place psychology on a firm scientific footing.

Structuralism's focus on identifying the elements (structure) of consciousness was soon challenged by William James and other psychologists who felt that their new field should focus not on the structure of consciousness, but on its *functions.* **Functionalism** was strongly influenced by Darwin's theory of natural selection; its proponents argued that since consciousness is a uniquely human characteristic, it must serve important functions for us—otherwise it would never have evolved. With this thought in mind, James and other functionalists focused on understanding the functions of consciousness—how it helps human beings cope with the challenging and changing world around them. This gave a practical slant to the research conducted by functionalists, who began to focus on such topics as child development and the relative benefits of various educational practices. Although functionalism itself gradually faded away as an identifiable "ism" or "school," its practical orientation left a lasting impact on the field. Moreover, the idea that aspects of consciousness or behavior have evolved to serve important functions has recently received new attention in the field of *evolutionary psychology,* which we'll soon consider.

It has sometimes been suggested that given enough time, functionalism would have moved toward an approach quite similar to modern psychology: Functionalists appeared to be largely on the right track. They never got the chance, however, because both structuralism and functionalism were soon consigned to the dustbin of history by another approach—**behaviorism.** Behaviorism burst upon the field in 1913, in a provocative article by a brilliant—but brash—young psychologist, John B. Watson (see Figure 1.2). Watson argued passionately for the view that psychology should focus not on consciousness or experience but on *behavior*—actions that can be observed and measured. As Watson (1924, p. 6) put it: "The behaviorist asks: Why don't we make what we can observe the real field of psychology? Let us limit ourselves to things that can be observed and formulate laws concerning only those things. What can we

**Figure 1.2**
**Watson and Skinner: Influential Behaviorists**

John B. Watson *(left)* and B. F. Skinner *(right)* were strong and influential supporters of *behaviorism*—the view that psychology should study only observable forms of behavior, while ignoring cognition and other internal states.

observe? We can observe *behavior*—what the organism does or says. . . ." Many psychologists had already begun to lose interest in studying consciousness and in using introspection as a research method, so Watson's views quickly won general acceptance. Indeed, the idea that psychology should focus only on observable behavior dominated the field for several decades. Moreover, it was emphasized still further by B. F. Skinner, perhaps the most famous behaviorist of all (see Figure 1.2). He argued that because internal mental states cannot be studied scientifically, they should not be part of psychology. Rather, the field should focus only on overt responses to various stimuli. So, for example, we should not make any assumptions about internal states such as motivation. For instance, we can watch an animal who hasn't eaten for several hours press a lever to obtain food, but we cannot directly observe its hunger motivation. Therefore, Skinner contended, we should focus only on the observable behavior and ignore internal states. In short, by the 1930s psychology's early battles seemed to be over: Behaviorism, in one form or another, had won the day.

## Challenges to Behaviorism—and the Emergence of Modern Psychology

Although behaviorism dominated psychology for decades, it never had things all its own way. Even as Watson was issuing his call for focusing on overt behavior, psychologists were listening with growing interest to the theories of a Viennese psychiatrist named Sigmund Freud, who argued strongly for the role of the unconscious and other internal processes in human behavior and mental disorders. Another challenge to behaviorism occurred in the 1950s, when *humanistic psychologists* argued that contrary to what behaviorists proposed, people really *do* have free will—they do not simply repeat behaviors that yield positive outcomes while avoiding behaviors that produce negative ones (a basic principle of behaviorism that we'll examine in detail in Chapter 5). Moreover, people are strongly motivated by future plans and goals, and by the desire for personal growth. (Humanists also rejected Freud's view that much of our behavior stems from innate aggressive and sexual urges; see Chapter 12.)

The ultimate challenge to behaviorism and the narrow definition of psychology it proposed, however, came from what psychologists often describe as the *cognitive revolution*—a renewal of interest in all aspects of cognition. This "revolution" had been brewing for some time, as psychologists quietly went about studying memory, reasoning, problem solving, and other cognitive processes. By the 1960s, the development of computers provided such researchers with important new tools for conducting their research. For instance, computers made it possible to expose individuals to specific stimuli in a very precise manner, and to measure the speed of their reactions with great precision. Researchers could then use such information as the basis for drawing inferences about underlying mental processes. For instance, suppose that research participants are first exposed to some stimuli (e.g., a list of words, such as *hotel, river, stadium*). Then they are shown parts of these words (e.g., *hot, riv, stad*) along with parts of other words they have *not* seen and are asked to complete all the words. Generally, words participants have seen previously have an advantage—they are identified more quickly or accurately than the new words. Yet if asked, participants are often unaware of this and believe they have simply guessed. Findings like these provide evidence that our memory holds information we can't readily put into words.

These advances in research methods were soon followed by techniques for observing activity within the brains of fully awake people as they performed various cognitive tasks—trying to remember words they had previously heard or seen, or working on various kinds of problems (see Chapter 2). The result? Processes that

**Figure 1.3**
**Some Milestones in the History of Psychology**

Many events played important roles in the development of modern psychology. A few of the ones generally regarded as most important are shown here.

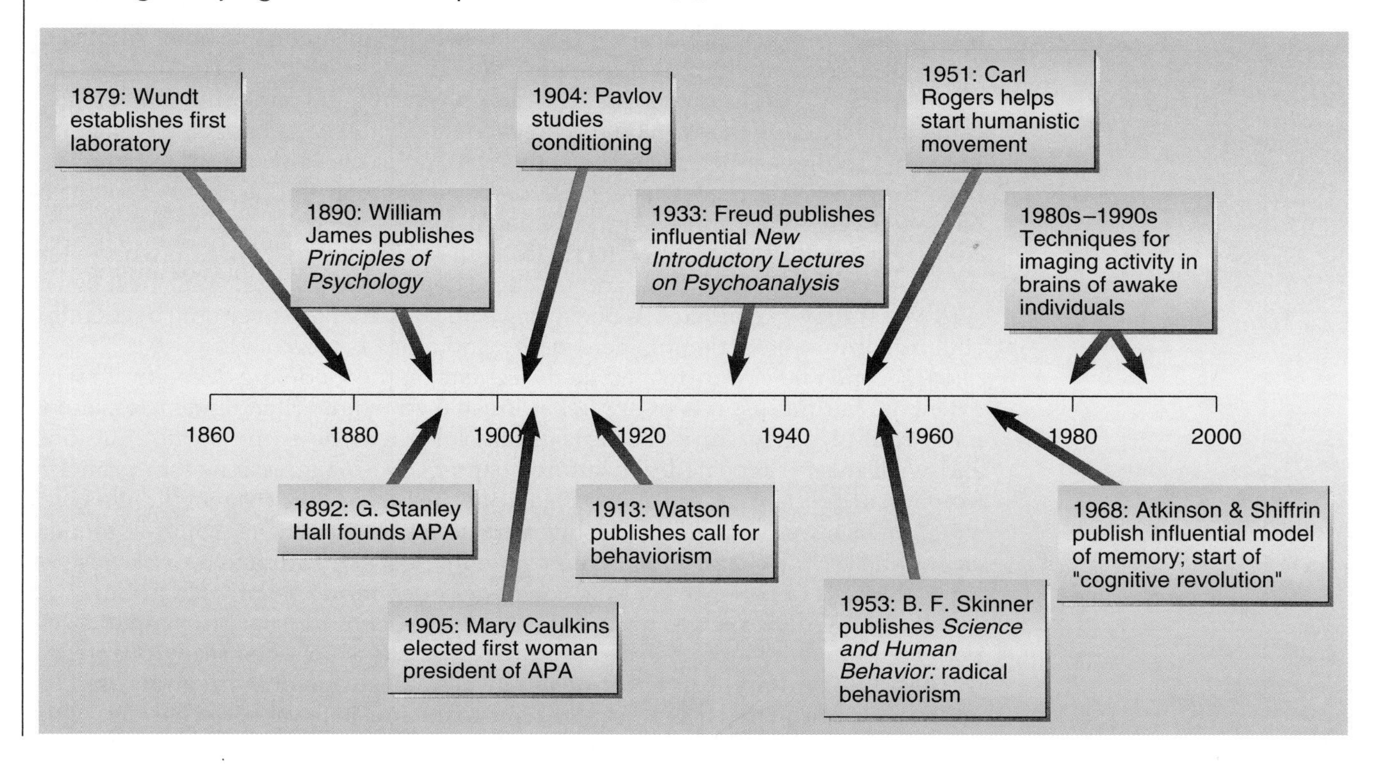


early behaviorists once thought to be unobservable became observable, and the behaviorists' objection to studying them faded away. The study of cognitive processes is now one of the most vigorous areas of research in psychology.

In short, modern psychology truly *is* the science of behavior and cognitive processes. It studies all aspects of human behavior—everything we think, feel, experience, or do—and is no longer restrained by the boundaries imposed on it by the various schools or "isms" I have described. If this statement leads you to expect a lot from the chapters that follow, that's perfectly correct: Modern psychology is truly a "movable feast" with something of interest in it for everyone. But it's interesting to contemplate, as I've done in this section, how we got *here*—to modern, eclectic psychology—from *there*—a new field, struggling to establish a clear identity and a useful agenda for its work. (For an overview of some key events in the history of psychology, please see Figure 1.3.)

**REVIEW QUESTIONS**

- What is the definition of psychology as it exists today?
- What ideas in philosophy and findings in natural science contributed to the establishment of psychology as an independent field?
- According to structuralism, functionalism, and behaviorism, what should psychology study?

## Psychology: Its Grand Issues and Key Perspectives

Several years ago, I went to the thirtieth reunion of my high school class. I hadn't been to any previous reunions, so I knew I was in for an interesting time. Would I be able to recognize my former classmates? Would they be able to recognize me? The results were mixed. Everyone had changed physically, of course; but, amazingly, I could still recognize many people. And even those who had changed so much that I couldn't recognize their faces still showed many of the same traits I remembered from thirty years earlier. This experience calls attention to one of what might be termed psychology's three "grand issues"—large-scale questions or themes that crosscut the field. This question has to do with *stability versus change:* To what extent do we remain stable over time, and to what extent do we change? We'll meet this issue over and over again in this book, as we address changes over time in cognitive abilities, physical functioning, personality, and other aspects of behavior.

A second and closely related theme centers on the following question: To what extent are various aspects of our behavior shaped by inherited tendencies, and to what extent are they learned? This is usually known as the *nature–nurture* question, and we'll meet it repeatedly in future chapters. Does aggression stem primarily from innate tendencies, or is it the result of experiences that "trigger" it in a given situation? Do we find certain persons attractive because we have built-in tendencies to find certain characteristics (e.g., smooth, clear skin) attractive, or because we learn through experience what is considered beautiful in our own culture? As you'll soon see, the answer to such questions is *not* one suggesting that either experience or heredity dominates; rather, many aspects of behavior seem to represent the result of complex interactions between these factors. In any case, the nature–nurture question has recently come to the fore in psychology because of the development of a field that focuses on the potential role of evolution in our behavior—*evolutionary psychology.* This field is so intriguing and controversial, and has stirred so much interest among psychologists, that I'll discuss it in more detail in a later section of this chapter.

Now for the third major theme. Answer quickly: Would you eat a chocolate shaped exactly like a cockroach—hairy legs, long antennae, and all? If you feel some reluctance, you are like many people. But now ask yourself, *Why* would you be reluctant do so? The chocolate has no relationship to a real insect, so why should the fact that it is shaped like one stop you from eating it? The answer, in most general terms, is this: In many cases, we are not completely rational. We know very well what the logical response or reaction would be in a given situation, but our reason is overridden by other factors—our emotions, our gut-level feelings, and so on. This is one illustration of a third major theme you'll find throughout this book: *rationality versus irrationality.* Need more examples? Then consider these: Have you ever underestimated the amount of time it would take you to complete a task? Have you ever lashed out at another person not because of something he or she did or said, but simply because you were in a rotten mood? Have you ever stuck with a bad decision even though increasing evidence indicated that it was wrong (e.g., continuing to invest more and more money in an old car that was forever needing new parts)? If so, then you already have direct experience with the less than completely rational side of human nature (see Figure 1.4). Psychologists are fascinated by these and other illustrations of the fact that we are not always perfectly logical, because such behaviors often offer insights into how the mind works. We'll return to this theme again and again as we examine such issues as decision making, eyewitness testimony, and how we form first impressions of other persons.

Be on the lookout for these three grand issues—they are central questions that have captured the attention of psychologists for decades and have played an important role in shaping the questions asked by psychologists in their research.

**Figure 1.4**
**Human Behavior: Not Always Rational**

As suggested by this cartoon, human behavior and human thought often depart from 100 percent rationality to a surprising—and somewhat disturbing—degree.

(*Source:* DILBERT reprinted with permission of United Feature Syndicate, Inc.)

## Key Perspectives in Psychology: The Many Facets of Behavior

Here's a scene from my own life that happens over and over again: I look for something—a tie, a shirt, a book—and after a few minutes, I give up and ask my wife to help. Usually, her first response is to tell me where to search. When I do, however, I usually still don't find the object. At that point she stops whatever she is doing and joins the search; within a few seconds, she usually finds the object I want. "I don't understand," I often hear myself saying. "I looked there, but I didn't see it." Her reply: "I guess you didn't look very hard, did you?" with just a touch of sarcasm in her voice.

How would a psychologist interpret such events? The answer is: from any of several different perspectives. In other words, it is possible to focus on these events from different viewpoints. One, known as the *behavioral* perspective, would emphasize the overt behavior occurring—my attempts to find the object, my wife's advice, and her attempt to locate it. Here, attention might be focused on what she does differently than I do—differences in our search strategies. Another perspective would be *cognitive* and would focus on my thoughts: how I decide when it's time to give up and call my wife, and how she, as compared to me, thinks about solving this kind of everyday problem. A third perspective would emphasize the *biological factors* that play a role. Is my visual system operating properly? Does my wife's work better than mine? What emotions do I experience as I search for the object and then give up? What emotions does my wife experience when I interrupt her work, and when she hands me the object I couldn't find? Related to this biological approach is the possibility that my failure and her success can be traced to the effects of evolution, which has operated to produce superior object-finding skills among females. I'll comment further on this possibility in the discussion of evolutionary psychology that follows. A fourth perspective is *developmental* and would focus on the question of whether these gender differences in the ability to find "lost" objects are present throughout life, or appear only in adulthood.

Yet another perspective that could be adopted by a psychologist studying this "lost object" puzzle would focus on factors relating to hidden forces within my personality and that of my wife. Perhaps I really don't want to find the lost object, because I want my wife to do it as a sign of her affection for me; and perhaps she wants to find lost objects for me, because it gives her a chance to remind me of her female superiority! The *psychodynamic* perspective focuses on such internal, and often unconscious, motives.

Finally, a psychologist interested in this topic could seek to understand it in terms of *social or cultural* factors. Is my wife better at finding objects because gender stereotypes in our culture say that she should be, with the result that she tries harder than I do to find lost objects? Or is this one aspect of our long-term relationship? In other words, have we divided tasks so that she finds lost objects while I take out the trash and mow the lawn?

**TABLE 1.1**

**Major Perspectives of Modern Psychology**

As shown here, psychology studies behavior from many different perspectives

| Perspective | Description |
|---|---|
| Behavioral | Focuses on overt behavior |
| Cognitive | Focuses on cognitive processes such as memory, thought, reasoning |
| Biological | Focuses on the biological events and processes that underlie behavior |
| Evolutionary | Focuses on the possible role of evolved psychological mechanisms (inherited tendencies shaped by evolution) in human behavior |
| Developmental | Focuses on changes in behavior and cognitive processes over the life span |
| Psychodynamic | Focuses on the role of hidden, often unconscious, internal processes (e.g., unconscious motives) |
| Social and cultural | Focuses on social and cultural factors that can influence behavior |

The key point to remember is this: Human behavior is extraordinarily complex and is influenced by many different factors. Thus, any aspect of behavior can be examined from many different perspectives. All these add to our understanding of behavior, so all will be represented throughout this book. (Table 1.1 summarizes these contrasting points of view or approaches.)

**REVIEW QUESTIONS**

- What are the three "grand issues" about behavior addressed by psychology?
- What are the major perspectives adopted by psychologists, and how do they differ?

## Psychology 2000: Trends for the New Millennium

Web Link: *American Psychological Society Homepage*

Psychology is a tremendously diverse field—and quite a large one; in fact, there are currently more than 200,000 psychologists in North America alone, and more than 500,000 worldwide (American Psychological Association, 1999). And, as shown in Table 1.2, psychologists specialize in many different aspects of behavior. As a result, there is always a lot going on, and the field develops and changes in many ways at once. Among recent trends, however, two seem so important that they are worthy of special note: psychology's growing attention to *diversity* and its focus on the possible role of *evolution* in human behavior. In addition, there is another important trend occurring—one that many psychologists themselves have not yet recognized: increasing use of the findings of psychology in other fields. Since this change, too, has important implications for psychology, I'll comment briefly on it as well.

TABLE 1.2

**Major Subfields of Psychology**

Psychologists specialize in studying many different aspects of behavior. The approximate percentage of all psychologists in each specialty is shown in this table; other subfields not listed separately make up the missing few percent.

| Subfield | Description | Percentage |
|---|---|---|
| Clinical psychology | Studies diagnosis, causes, and treatment of mental disorders | 43 |
| Counseling psychology | Assists individuals in dealing with many personal problems that do not involve psychological disorders | 10 |
| Developmental psychology | Studies how people change physically, cognitively, and socially over the entire life span | 5 |
| Educational psychology | Studies all aspects of the educational process | 6 |
| Experimental psychology | Studies all basic psychological processes, including perception, learning, and motivation | 14* |
| Cognitive psychology | Investigates all aspects of cognition—memory, thinking, reasoning, language, decision making, and so on | (Included under experimental) |
| Industrial/ organizational psychology | Studies all aspects of behavior in work settings | 4 |
| Psychobiology and evolutionary psychology | Investigates biological bases of behavior and the role of evolution in human behavior | 1 |
| Social psychology | Studies all aspects of social behavior and social thought—how we think about and interact with others | 6 |

*Figure includes cognitive psychology.

## Psychology and Diversity: The Multicultural Perspective

Web Link: *U.S. Census Data*

When I entered graduate school in 1964, psychology was largely an American field: A large majority of psychologists lived and worked in North America. Moreover, most research in the field was conducted in North America with North Americans as participants. The result? There was little recognition or appreciation of the importance of *diversity*—differences in the behavior or characteristics of individuals from different cultures or ethnic groups. Indeed, there was even little recognition of or interest in possible differences between males and females! The prevailing point of view was that if such cultural or gender differences exist, they are relatively unimportant. After all, psychology is a science, many people reasoned; so the principles and laws it establishes should apply to *all* human beings, regardless of where they live, their personal background, or their cultural identity.

As you can readily guess, this point of view no longer prevails. Although psychologists have not abandoned the goal of developing a body of knowledge that

**Figure 1.5**
**Domestic Violence: Strongly Affected by Cultural Values**

Views about domestic violence vary greatly across cultures. In order to fully understand this serious problem, therefore, psychologists must take account of such diversity-related factors.

applies to all human beings, they have become far more aware of the importance of the tremendous cultural and ethnic diversity that is so much a part of our human heritage; and they now recognize that such differences must be included as a key part of our efforts to understand human behavior. As a result, psychology now adopts a **multicultural perspective** that pays careful attention to the role of such differences.

This perspective is demonstrated not only in the research conducted by psychologists but also in the guidelines they follow in providing psychological services (such as counseling) to ethnically and culturally diverse populations (American Psychological Association, 1993b). These guidelines require that psychologists recognize cultural diversity and take full account of it in all their activities. For example, psychologists must provide information to clients in forms and languages that people from different cultural groups can understand; they must be certain that psychological tests are valid for use with various ethnic groups; and in understanding psychological processes, including psychological disorders, they must recognize ethnic background and culture as important factors. In short, the guidelines insist that practicing psychologists be sensitive to cultural, ethnic, and linguistic differences and that they build awareness of these differences into all their professional activities.

A concrete example of this multicultural perspective in operation is provided by recent efforts by psychologists to understand the causes of domestic violence—acts of violence by one family member against one or more others (e.g., Walker, 1999). Many of the factors that contribute to this tragic behavior appear to be constant across different cultures—high levels of emotional distress, poverty, and consumption of alcohol and other drugs play a role in the occurrence of such behavior all around the world. And across many cultures, most domestic violence appears to be male assaults on females and children (see Figure 1.5). Yet it is also clear that cultural factors, too, play a role. For example, in Russia, where more than 16,000 women are murdered by their spouses each year (Horne, 1999), violence by husbands against their wives is endorsed by certain cultural values. One widely quoted proverb, for instance, states: "Beat the wife for better cabbage soup." Similarly, in Japan, cultural values view violence as appropriate forms of discipline and punishment; thus, physical punishment of children by parents or even by teachers is considered to be nothing out of the ordinary. And within the family, wives refer to their husbands as *shujin,* which translates as "master"; this, in turn, opens the door for cultural endorsements, or at least an absence of cultural censure, of spouse abuse (Kozu, 1999). Similar attitudes prevail in many Latin countries, such as Nicaragua and Chile (Elisberg et al., 1999; McWhirter, 1999), and contribute to high rates of spouse abuse in these countries. Together, such findings indicate that a full understanding of the nature and causes of domestic violence must include careful attention to cultural factors, because such violence always occurs against a backdrop of cultural values and beliefs that influence its incidence, specific forms, and targets. We will discuss diversity throughout this book, and specific spots where these issues are considered are marked with the special symbol shown at left.

**Multicultural Perspective:** In psychology, an approach that pays careful attention to the effects of ethnic and cultural forces on behavior.

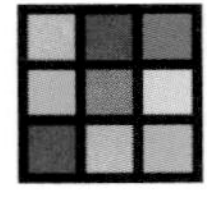

*Separated at birth, the Mallifert twins meet accidentally.*

**Figure 1.6**
**Genetic Factors and Human Behavior**

During the past decade there has been growing recognition among psychologists of the potential role of genetic factors in many aspects of human behavior—including complex processes such as creativity.

(*Source:* © The New Yorker Collection. 1981 Charles Addams from cartoonbank.com All rights reserved.)

## Evolutionary Psychology: A New Perspective on "Human Nature"

Is there such a thing as "human nature"—a set of qualities or behaviors that define us as a unique species? Until about ten years ago, most psychologists would have expressed skepticism on this point. While they would certainly have agreed that our biological nature is partly inherited, many would have pointed to learning and the effects of experience rather than genes or evolution as the main sources of our behavior. In recent years, however, the pendulum of scientific opinion in psychology has swung strongly in the opposite direction. Today, most psychologists believe that genetic factors do indeed play some role in many aspects of our behavior—everything from mate selection and mating strategies (e.g., why males seem to prefer having many different sexual partners more than females do), to creativity (see Figure 1.6), to our desire for status and prestige and our pleasure in the downfall of "tall poppies"—people who are exceptionally high in these dimensions (e.g., Pinker, 1997).

One major reason for this shift in opinion has been the development and rapid growth of **evolutionary psychology** (Buss, 1999). This branch of psychology suggests that our species, like all others on the planet, has been subject to the process of biological evolution throughout its history, and that as a result of this process, we now possess a large number of *evolved psychological mechanisms* that help (or once helped) us to deal with important problems relating to survival. Before turning to these, let's first take a quick look at the process of evolution itself.

**Evolutionary Psychology:** A branch of psychology suggesting that as a result of evolution, human beings possess many evolved psychological mechanisms that help (or once helped) us to deal with important problems relating to survival.

Evolution—which was first hypothesized by Charles Darwin almost 150 years ago—involves three basic components: variation, inheritance, and selection. *Variation* refers to the fact that organisms belonging to a given species vary in many different ways; indeed, such variation is a basic part of life on our planet. Human beings, as you already know, come in a wide variety of shapes and sizes, and vary

**Figure 1.7**
**Evolution: An Overview**

As shown here, evolution involves three major components: variation, inheritance, and selection.

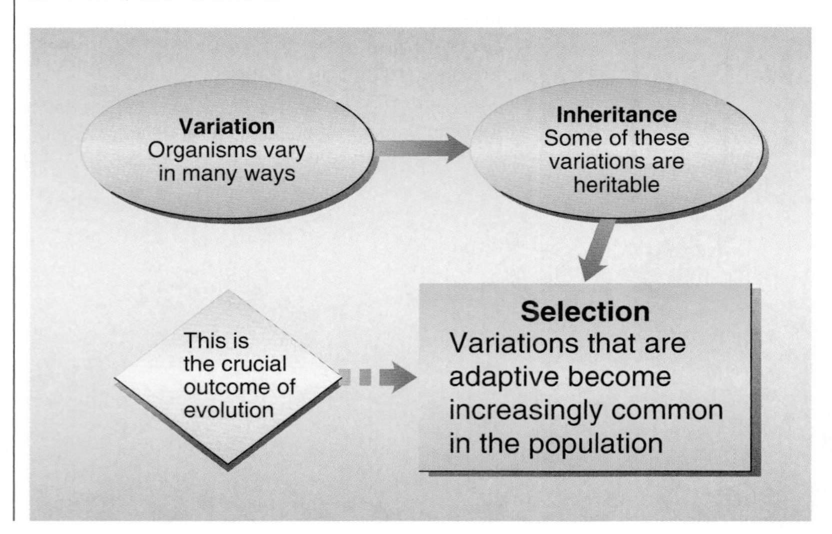


on what sometimes seems to be an almost countless number of dimensions. (We'll examine some of these in detail in Chapters 11 and 12.)

*Inheritance* refers to the fact that some of these variations can be passed from one generation to the next. Darwin didn't understand the mechanism through which this occurs, but today we know that inheritance involves complex genetic mechanisms, which we'll describe in detail in Chapter 2.

*Selection* refers to the fact that some variations give the individuals who possess them an edge in terms of reproduction: These individuals are more likely to survive, find mates, and pass these variations on to succeeding generations. The result is that over time, more and more members of the species possess these variations. This change in the characteristics of a species over time—often, over immensely long periods of time—is the concrete outcome of evolution. (See Figure 1.7 for a summary of this process.)

Now, back to human nature and human behavior. Evolutionary psychology suggests that human beings, like all other species on the planet, have always faced basic problems relating to survival: obtaining food, finding shelter, avoiding predators and other dangers, resisting disease. Over time, natural selection assured that variations that helped our ancestors to survive and to reproduce became increasingly common in the species. Together, these inherited tendencies constitute our human nature—and often play an important role in shaping our behavior. Does this mean that our behavior is genetically determined and cannot be changed? Absolutely not! Rather, it suggests that as human beings we come equipped with a set of mechanisms that interact with the environment; it is this interaction that determines whether, to what extent, and in what form these mechanisms are actually expressed. For instance, one evolved mechanism we possess is the ability to form calluses (hard patches of skin) on our feet. Do we develop them? Only if we walk on hard surfaces. If we spend our days walking on soft carpets or clover, calluses never appear. Similarly, evolved psychological mechanisms provide only the *potential* for certain behaviors or tendencies to occur; whether they do or do not depends on external factors or experience. As for our ability to change, consider this: Once we know what leads to the development of calluses, we can take steps to prevent them—for instance, wearing shoes with soft rubber soles or avoiding hard surfaces. I have been a runner for twenty-two years, but I don't have calluses on my feet, because I always run on soft surfaces such as grass. So yes, evolutionary psychology suggests that our behavior is influenced by inherited mechanisms or tendencies; but *no,* emphatically, it does not imply that behavior is totally determined solely by these mechanisms—far from it!

We'll return to evolutionary psychology and some of its intriguing findings in Chapter 2 and at many other points throughout this book; such places will be marked by a special symbol (at left) (for evolutionary psychology) in the margin. For the moment, though, let's return to the finding-lost-objects example I mentioned earlier. Can the evolutionary perspective shed any light on why I can't seem to find various items but my wife can locate them with ease? In fact, it can. Several psychologists (e.g., Silverman & Phillips, 1998) suggest that before the development of civilization, when human beings lived by hunting and gathering, these crucial tasks were divided between the males and females: Males hunted game, while females searched for nuts, berries, roots, and other edible plants. One result of this division of labor was that selection favored different variations in the two genders. Males who were able to find their way back to camp from long distances away, and who could track moving game, were more successful in obtaining food and so became more desirable mates; thus, they were more likely to pass their genes on to the next generation. In contrast, females who could locate objects, such as plants that provided food, had an edge. So my wife's greater ability to find "lost" objects may reflect the fact that she has a more finely evolved psychological mechanism for doing so than I do. Evidence for this reasoning is provided by several studies (e.g., Silverman & Eals, 1992) that used these procedures: Male and female participants worked on several tasks in a small room. In one condition, they were told to try to remember the locations of various objects in the room; in another, no mention was made of this additional task. Later, when asked to name the objects in the room and indicate their locations, women outperformed men in both conditions. However, their advantage was much larger in the condition in which participants were *not* told to focus on locating the objects. These findings also illustrate the point I made above about our ability to modify our evolved psychological mechanisms: Men could partially compensate for their inferior skills in locating objects by concentrating on this task. But when they were not told to do so, gender differences in this mechanism were larger.

In closing this discussion, I want to emphasize two points. First, evolutionary psychology is a relatively new field and is still quite controversial. Many psychologists have strong reservations about explaining complex forms of behavior as the end product of evolution. Moreover, although evolution itself is widely accepted by biologists and other scientists, many persons perceive it as contrary to their religious beliefs. I fully appreciate these facts and have presented evolutionary psychology here merely as one thought-provoking perspective on human behavior—not as established fact. Second, I want to note, again, that the existence of evolved psychological mechanisms does not in any way imply that our genes force us to act in certain ways, that we can't resist these impulses, or that our sole motivation in life is to reproduce. Rather, evolutionary psychology merely suggests that as human beings, we come equipped with many mechanisms designed to help us survive in a complex and often challenging world. These mechanisms are real, but they interact with the external environment and our experience, and leave tremendous room for individuality and change.

## The Exportation of Psychology: From Science to Practice

Most people realize that several branches of psychology are *applied*—not only do they seek to acquire basic knowledge about human behavior, they also attempt to put it to practical use. For instance, *clinical psychologists* help individuals deal with emotional and psychological problems, while *industrial/organizational psychologists* focus on solving practical problems relating to work (e.g., increasing motivation, evaluating employees' performance fairly and accurately). So, as I noted in the discussion of functionalism (one early school of psychology), psychology has always had a practical as well as a scientific side.

In recent years, however, application of psychology's knowledge about human behavior has expanded beyond psychology itself. Many other fields have found answers to some of their most important questions in the findings and principles of psychology, and have begun to draw upon this knowledge to an increasing degree. In other words, as psychology has matured and become an ever richer source of knowledge about human behavior, persons in other fields have recognized this resource and put it to good use. How have they used the findings of psychology?

In many ways: to improve procedures for the selection and training of employees, to enhance the performance of athletes, to improve classroom instruction, and to train police for better community relations, to mention just a few instances.

Please don't misunderstand: I'm not referring here to people who are not trained psychologists but who try to practice psychology anyway—for example, to conduct therapy, design psychological tests, or advise businesses about how to handle their employees. Rather, I'm referring to a much more legitimate use of psychological knowledge, often with the help and guidance of trained psychologists who serve as "exporters" of the knowledge of their field. Perhaps the best way of illustrating what I mean is through a concrete example, and it is provided in the following **From Science to Practice** section.

from SCIENCE to PRACTICE

## Preventing Deaths under Anesthesia: Human Factors (Engineering Psychology) to the Rescue

Consider this fact: Until about fifteen years ago, about one person in ten thousand who underwent general anesthesia in the United States died because the anesthesiologist inserted the breathing tube into the patient's throat (esophagus) instead of into the trachea, or windpipe, which leads to the lungs. This amounted to more than *3,500 deaths each year in the United States alone* (Gawande, 1999). Could anything be done to reduce this alarming waste of life? In 1982 Dr. Ellison Pierce was elected vice president of the American Society of Anesthesiologists, and he set out to try. He had long been concerned about this state of affairs, because some years earlier good friends of his had taken their eighteen-year-old daughter to the hospital to have her wisdom teeth pulled under general anesthesia. The anesthesiologist inserted the breathing tube into her esophagus, and, deprived of oxygen, she died within minutes.

This tragedy galvanized Dr. Pierce and set him on a quest for help for his field. Where did he turn? To a branch of psychology known as *human factors*—a branch concerned, in part, with designing equipment so that it is most convenient and useful for human beings. When he discussed the problems of anesthesiology with human factors psychologists, they quickly noted that better equipment could readily prevent errors of the type described above. For example, instead of relying on their own judgment, the anesthesiologists could work with special monitoring devices that would tell them with absolute certainty whether they had placed the breathing tube correctly. One type of monitor, for example, could detect carbon dioxide being exhaled from the lungs; if carbon dioxide were not present at certain levels, then the doctor would know at once that the tube was not where it belonged. Another type of monitor could track patients' blood oxygen; if this dropped below certain limits, then the doctor would know immediately that the tube was not correctly placed (see Figure 1.8).

Dr. Pierce was so impressed with these recommendations from human factors psychologists that he worked hard to have them adopted as required procedure in all operations

**Figure 1.8**
**Psychology: Beneficial Effects for Medical Practice**

Psychologists (especially those in the field of *human factors*) have helped to save many thousands of lives by providing physicians with equipment designed to prevent human error.

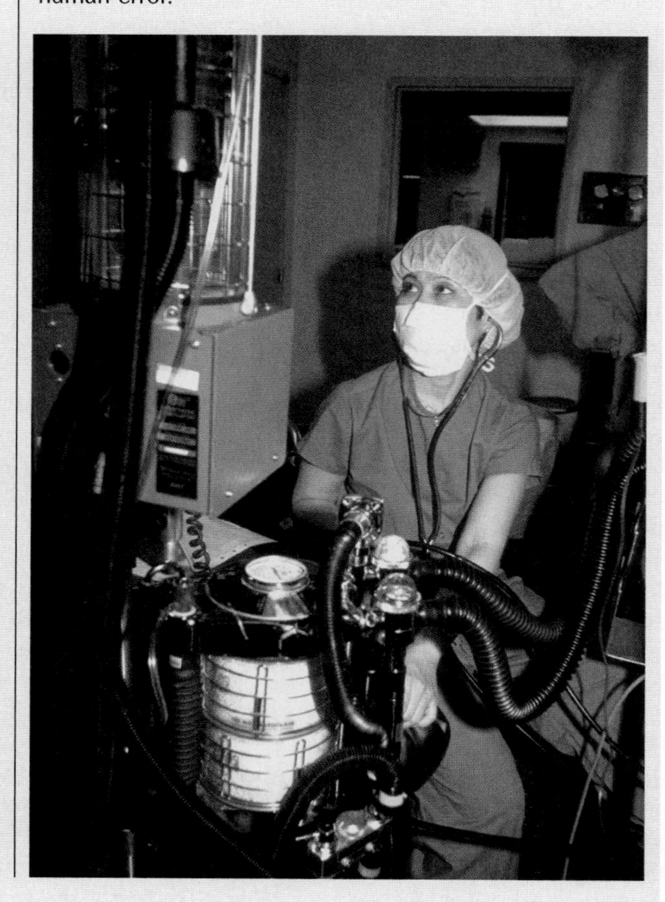

involving general anesthesia. He succeeded, and the results were gratifying: The death rate among patients dropped to just one in more than two hundred thousand cases—less than one twentieth of what they had been, thus saving more than three thousand lives each year in the United States alone.

I believe that the growing use of psychological knowledge in other fields is extremely important—so much so that I will provide examples of it in every chapter in special sections titled (like this one) **From Science to Practice.** I think you will find them interesting. And since I myself have often played the role of "exporter" where psychology is concerned (e.g., my recent research has focused on topics such as workplace violence and the cognitive and social factors that contribute to entrepreneurs' success), I can't help but believe that psychology has *much* to offer to many other fields.

**REVIEW QUESTIONS**

- What is the multicultural perspective, and how do psychologists take account of it in their research and practice?
- What is evolutionary psychology, and how does it contribute to our understanding of human behavior?
- What is meant by the "exportation of psychology"?

**Food for Thought**

Suppose some aspect of behavior made individuals highly attractive to the opposite sex—but also shortened their lives so that they died before they were fifty. According to evolutionary psychology, would this behavior become increasingly common, or would it die out?

# Psychology and the Scientific Method

In a sense, we are all psychologists; we often think about our own feelings, actions, and motives, or those of other persons. In addition, we have at our disposal the thoughts of countless poets, philosophers, and writers—many of whom have offered brilliant insights into the nature of human behavior. Given these facts, an interesting question arises: Is the knowledge provided by psychology different in any important way from this accumulated wisdom of the ages or from our own informal observations? My answer is simple: Absolutely! The knowledge acquired by psychologists *is* different, because in obtaining it psychologists rely heavily on the *scientific method.* To back up this confident reply, I'll now explain the scientific method and how it helps psychologists reach conclusions about human behavior that are far more accurate and useful than those provided by intuition or common sense.

## The Scientific Method: Its Basic Nature

To many people, the term *science* conjures up images of white-coated persons working around complex equipment in impressive laboratories. On the basis of such images, people then conclude that the word *science* applies only to fields such as chemistry, physics, or biology. Actually, though, this term refers simply to a special approach for acquiring knowledge—an approach involving the use of several key values or standards. Viewed in this light, the phrase *scientific method* refers simply to using these methods and adopting these values in efforts to study virtually any topic—any aspect of the world around us. We as human beings are part of the natural world, and thus the scientific method can certainly be applied to the study of our behavior and cognition. It is this adoption of the scientific method that makes psychology a science—and that makes the information it acquires so valuable.

The actual procedures used by psychologists in applying the scientific method are described in detail in a later section; here, I'll focus on the values and standards that are essential components of the scientific method. Among the most important are these:

- *Accuracy:* A commitment to gathering and evaluating information about the world in as careful, precise, and error-free a manner as possible.
- *Objectivity:* A commitment to obtaining and evaluating such information in a manner as free from bias as humanly possible.
- *Skepticism:* A commitment to accepting findings as accurate only after they have been verified over and over again, preferably by many different scientists.
- *Open-mindedness:* A commitment to changing one's views—even views that are strongly held—in the face of evidence that these views are inaccurate.

Psychology, as a field, is deeply committed to these values. It is primarily for this reason that it can be described as a branch of science. In other words, because psychology plays by the rules—accepts and follows the guidelines of the scientific method—it qualifies for membership in the broad family of sciences that, together, have greatly enhanced human life.

Web Link: *Scientific Reasoning*

## The Role of Theory in the Scientific Method

There is one more aspect of the scientific method we should consider. In their research, scientists seek to do more than simply describe the world; they want to be able to *explain* it as well. For example, a chemist is not content merely to describe what happens when two chemicals are brought together in a test tube—the chemist also wants to be able to explain *why* this reaction happens. Similarly, a psychologist studying memory is not content merely to describe the extent to which individuals forget various kinds of information; as a scientist, the psychologist also wants to be able to explain *why* such forgetting occurs (see Chapter 6 for information on this question). To accomplish this task, scientists in all fields engage in the construction of **theories**—frameworks for explaining various events or processes. The procedure involved goes something like this:

1. On the basis of existing evidence, a theory is formulated.
2. This theory, which consists of some basic concepts and statements about how these concepts are related, helps to organize existing information and also makes predictions about observable events.
3. These predictions, known as **hypotheses,** are then tested by actual observations—by research.
4. If results of new observations are consistent with the theory, confidence in it is increased. If they are not, the theory is modified and further tests of its predictions are performed.
5. Ultimately, the theory is either accepted as accurate or rejected as inaccurate. Even if it is accepted as accurate, however, it remains open to further refinement as additional research is conducted.

All this is a bit abstract, so a concrete example may help. Imagine that a psychologist has formulated a theory to explain why, often, people seem to become trapped by their own bad decisions: Once they have made a decision, they stick with it, even if growing evidence indicates that it was wrong. (This is known as *escalation of commitment* and is discussed in detail in Chapter 7.) For instance, sometimes a person who has purchased a stock will continue to hold it even as more and more bad news about the company appears in the newspapers and the stock price continues to drop. Similarly, people often remain in a bad marriage or bad relationship even though it is increasingly clear that their partner will never change or treat them better. A theory designed to explain escalation of commitment might be as follows: People get trapped in bad decisions because once they have made them,

**Theories:** In science, frameworks for explaining various events or processes.

**Hypotheses:** Testable predictions derived from theories.

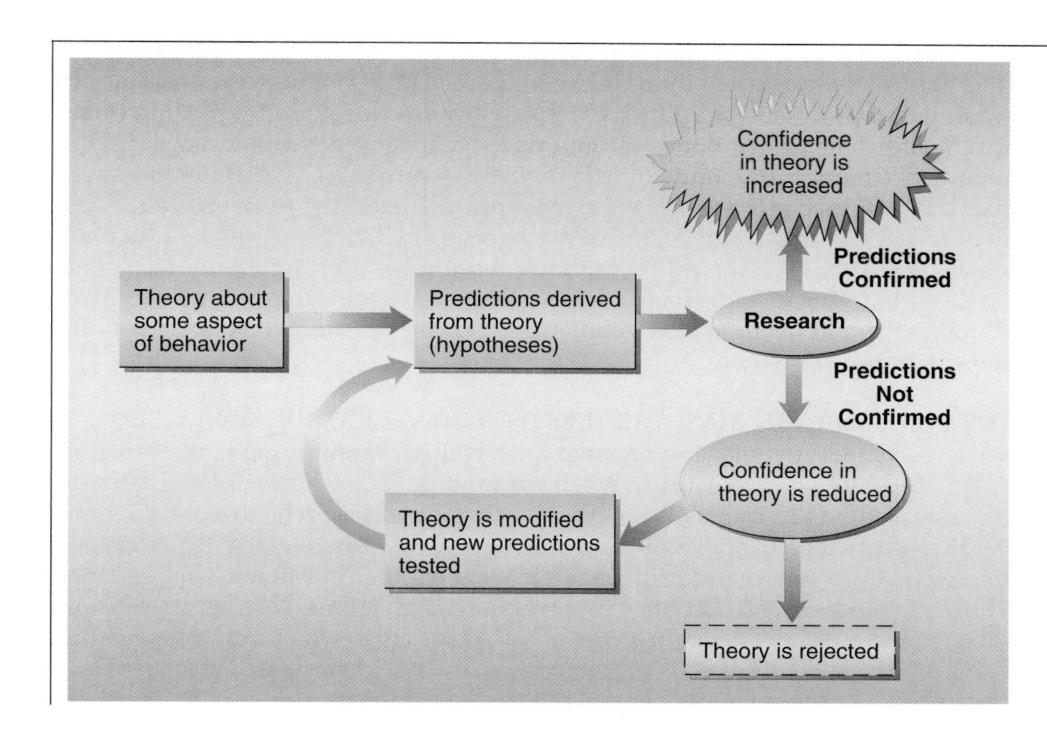


**Figure 1.9**
**The Role of Theory in Psychological Research**

Theories both organize existing knowledge and make predictions about how various events or processes will occur. Predictions derived from a theory (hypotheses) are tested through research. If results agree with the predictions, confidence in the theory is increased. If results do not agree with the predictions, confidence in the accuracy of the theory is reduced, and the theory is either altered or rejected.

they feel a strong need to justify these decisions to others. Admitting they made a mistake would run counter to this need, so they find it very hard to escape from what is an increasingly negative situation. The psychologist would now derive predictions from this theory, and proceed to test them. One such prediction might be: If reversing an initial bad decision involves actions that other people can observe (e.g., divorce), it may be especially hard for persons to escape from the trap of escalating commitment. If, in contrast, reversal of the initial decision doesn't involve actions others can observe (e.g., selling a stock in private), it may be easier to escape.

The psychologist would then conduct research to test this hypothesis. If findings are consistent with the prediction, confidence in the theory is strengthened; if they are not, confidence in it is reduced, and the theory may be modified or ultimately rejected. This process, which lies at the core of the scientific method, is summarized in Figure 1.9. Many different theories relating to human behavior will be discussed in later chapters, so you will soon learn about many examples of this process as it actually operates in psychology.

## Advantages of the Scientific Method: Why Common Sense Often Leads Us Astray

Earlier, I noted that conclusions based on the scientific method are superior, in several ways, to conclusions based on common sense or "folk wisdom." Here, I'll explain why. Two factors are most important in this respect. First, conclusions about behavior based on common sense are often inconsistent and contradictory. Consider the following statement: "Absence makes the heart grow fonder." Do you agree? Is it true that when people are separated they miss each other and so experience even stronger feelings of attraction? Perhaps, but what about *this* statement: "Out of sight, out of mind." It suggests exactly the opposite. Or how about this pair of statements: "Birds of a feather flock together" (people who are similar like each other) and "Opposites attract." I could continue, but by now I'm sure you see the point: Common sense is often a faulty guide to human behavior.

This is not the only reason why we must be wary of common sense, however; another relates to the fact that, unlike Mr. Spock of *Star Trek*, we are *not* perfect information-processing machines. On the contrary, echoing the "rationality versus irrationality" theme mentioned earlier, and as we'll note over and over again in this book (see Chapters 6, 7, and 16), our thinking is subject to several forms of error that can lead us badly astray. While these errors often save us mental effort and may in fact reflect evolved cognitive mechanisms that are generally helpful to us, they suggest that we should be cautious about relying on intuition or common sense when trying to understand human behavior. What are these errors like? We'll examine them in detail in later chapters, but let's take a brief look at some of the most important ones here.

**THE CONFIRMATION BIAS: THE TENDENCY TO VERIFY OUR OWN VIEWS** If you are like most people, you prefer to have your views confirmed rather than refuted. Consider what this means when we attempt to use informal observation as a source of knowledge about human behavior. Because we prefer to have our views confirmed, we tend to notice and remember mainly information that lends support to these views—information that confirms what we already believe. This tendency, known as the **confirmation bias,** is very strong (e.g., Johnson & Eagly, 1989); and when it operates, it places us in a kind of closed system in which only evidence that confirms our existing beliefs is processed. Clearly, this is one tendency that can lead to errors in our efforts to understand others and ourselves.

**THE AVAILABILITY HEURISTIC: EMPHASIZING WHAT COMES TO MIND FIRST OR MOST READILY** Quick: Are there more words in English that start with the letter *k* (e.g., *king*) or more words in which *k* is the third letter (e.g., *awkward*)? If you answered, "More words that begin with *k*" you are like most people. Actually, though, this answer is wrong—more words have the letter *k* in the third position. What's responsible for this type of error? A mental shortcut known as the **availability heuristic.** Because of this shortcut, which is designed to save us mental effort, the easier it is to bring something to mind, or the more information we can think of about it, the more importance we attribute to it—and the greater its impact on subsequent decisions or judgments. In general, this tendency makes sense: When we can bring information about something to mind easily, it often *is* important. But the availability heuristic can also lead us into error. Why? Because sometimes what we can bring to mind most readily isn't especially important; it's just highly memorable because it is dramatic or unusual (e.g., Rothman & Hardin, 1997). For instance, because airplane crashes are more dramatic and easier to remember than automobile accidents, many people believe that the chances of being killed in a plane are higher than those of being killed while driving—a conclusion that is totally false. Judgments based on common sense or intuition are often strongly influenced by the availability heuristic, so they are often untrustworthy for this reason.

Audio 1.1: *Effect of Mood on Judgment*

**Confirmation Bias:** The tendency to notice and remember primarily information that lends support to our views.

**Availability Heuristic:** A mental shortcut suggesting that the easier it is to bring something to mind, the more frequent or important it is.

**RATIONAL VERSUS INTUITIVE THOUGHT: THE DANGER OF "GUT-LEVEL" THINKING** During the 1990s, laws requiring automobiles to have air bags were passed in the United States and many other countries. Further, many insurance companies began to offer discounts for vehicles equipped with antilock brakes. Did these safety devices provide the benefits many people believed they would provide? So far, results are not encouraging. As you probably know, air bags have been found to injure some passengers—especially women and small children (see Figure 1.10). And many drivers don't use antilock brakes correctly, pumping them instead of putting steady pressure on the pedal. This is puzzling: Weren't these devices tested carefully before being put into millions of vehicles? To some extent they were; but in fact they were adopted largely because many persons simply felt, at a gut level, that they would work! This is a prime illustration of yet another reason why we cannot always trust common sense: our tendency to engage in *intuitive* rather than careful, rational thought (e.g., Epstein, 1994).

I could continue, because there are many other aspects of our thinking that can lead us astray. The main point, though, is clear: Because our thinking is subject to such potential sources of bias, we really can't rely on informal observation or common sense as a basis for valid conclusions about human behavior. We are on much firmer ground if we employ the scientific method, which is specifically designed to reduce such potential sources of error, and if we are careful to engage in **critical thinking.** Such thinking closely examines all claims and assumptions, carefully evaluates existing evidence, and cautiously assesses all conclusions. In actual practice, critical thinking involves the following guidelines:

- Never jump to conclusions; gather as much information as you can before making up your mind about any issue.
- Keep an open mind; don't let your existing views blind you to new information or conclusions.
- Always ask "How?" as in "How was the evidence obtained?"
- Be skeptical; always wonder about *why* someone is making an argument, offering a conclusion, or trying to persuade you.
- Never be stampeded into accepting some view because others accept it.
- Be aware of the fact that your own emotions can strongly influence your thinking, and try to hold such effects to a minimum.

By adopting the scientific method and using critical thinking, psychologists vastly increase the probability that their efforts to attain valid information about human behavior will succeed. It is these commitments to the scientific method and careful thought that set psychology apart from other efforts to understand human behavior and make its findings so valuable from the perspective of enhancing human welfare. While you yourself may never become a psychologist or conduct research on human behavior, you can benefit greatly from using critical thinking. For this reason, I'll provide you with many opportunities to practice it throughout this text. Enhancing your skills in this respect will definitely be one of the important benefits you will gain from your first course in psychology.

**Figure 1.10**
**Intuitive Thought: Sometimes It Poses Real Dangers**

Public and government support for some safety devices—such as air bags and antilock brakes—was based at least in part on "gut-level" intuitive thinking: It just seemed reasonable that these devices would work. In fact, however, accident data indicate that these devices are less effective than many people believed. These findings illustrate the potential dangers of intuitive thought.

## REVIEW QUESTIONS

- Why can psychology be viewed as a branch of science?
- What values are central to the scientific method?
- What are theories, and what is their role in the scientific method?
- Why are common sense or "folk wisdom" such uncertain guides to human behavior?
- What are the confirmation bias, the availability heuristic, and intuitive thinking, and what role do they play in our efforts to understand human behavior?
- What is critical thinking, and what role does it play in psychology?

**Critical Thinking:** Thinking that avoids blind acceptance of conclusions or arguments but instead closely examines all assumptions, evidence, and conclusions.

**Systematic Observation:** A basic method of science in which the natural world, or various events or processes in it, are observed and measured in a very careful manner.

**Naturalistic Observation:** A research method in which behavior is studied in the settings were it usually occurs.

CourseCompass
Web Link: *American Psychological Society—Psychological Research on the Net*

# Research Methods in Psychology: How Psychologists Answer Questions about Behavior

Now that I've explained what modern psychology is and described the scientific method and its relation to critical thinking, it's time to turn to another key issue: How do psychologists actually go about the task of adding to our knowledge about human behavior? Primarily, you'll soon see, through the use of three basic procedures: *observation, correlation,* and *experimentation.*

## Observation: Describing the World around Us

One basic technique for studying behavior—or any other aspect of the world—involves carefully observing it as it occurs. Such observation is not the kind of informal inquiry that all of us practice from childhood on; rather, in science, it is observation accompanied by careful, accurate measurement. For example, scientists studying the formation of tornadoes often drive hundreds of miles in order to be present at spots where tornadoes are likely to form. They do this because they wish to make careful observations of the physical events that occur as tornadoes actually take shape. The use of such **systematic observation** takes several different forms in the study of behavior.

CourseCompass
Video 1.1: *Scientists Use Naturalistic Observation*

**NATURALISTIC OBSERVATION: OBSERVING BEHAVIOR WHERE IT NORMALLY OCCURS** Bonobo chimpanzees are a fascinating species. These small primates live in the tropical forests of Zaire and a few other countries, and they have recently been the subject of scientific interest. Why? Primarily because, in contrast to other primate species, including our own, they seem to live together in almost total harmony. Fights, bullying, and all other forms of aggression are almost unknown. What accounts for their calm and peaceful existence? One possibility involves their sexual behavior. Bonobos win the prize among all primates for high interest in sex. They often have sexual relations twenty or more times a day, and females are just as enthusiastic about these activities as males; indeed, females have twenty different gestures for signaling to males that they are interested! Bonobos seem to use sexual relations as a means of reducing tension or anxiety: Whenever they are frightened or upset, they quickly pair up and begin mating. Is there a lesson here for our own species—evidence that the 1970s slogan "Make love, not war" may well have some validity? No one knows for sure, but research on bonobos carried out through **naturalistic observation**—systematic study of their behavior in natural settings (Linden, 1992)—has certainly provided us with much food for thought.

**Figure 1.11**
**Naturalistic Observation of Human Behavior**

Psychologists sometimes observe human behavior in the locations where it normally occurs. For example, recent studies have used such methods to study how and when people touch each other in public places.

While naturalistic observation is often used in the study of animal behavior, it is sometimes applied to human beings as well—especially to behavior in public places such as airports, shopping malls, and hotel lobbies (e.g., Hall & Veccia, 1991) (see Figure 1.11). Who touches whom in such locations? How do people use gestures? Information on these and many other forms of behavior can often be obtained from naturalistic observation, and we'll examine such research in several later chapters.

**CASE STUDIES: GENERALIZING FROM THE UNIQUE** Every human being is unique; each of us possesses a distinctive combination of traits, abilities, and characteristics. Given this fact, is it possible to learn anything about human behavior from detailed study of one individual or perhaps a few persons? Several famous psychologists have suggested that it is. They have adopted the **case method,** in which detailed information is gathered on specific individuals. The researchers then use this information to formulate principles or reach conclusions that, presumably, apply to large numbers of persons—perhaps to all human beings. By far the most famous practitioner of the case method was Sigmund Freud, who used a small number of cases as the basis for his famous theories of personality and mental illness. (We'll discuss these in Chapter 12.)

Is the case method really useful? In the hands of talented researchers such as Freud, it does seem capable of providing insights into various aspects of behavior. Moreover, when the behavior involved is very unusual, the case method can be quite revealing. In Chapter 6, we'll see how several unique cases have added to our understanding of the biological bases of memory. These cases involve individuals who experienced specific kinds of damage to the brain and, as a result, showed certain kinds of memory loss. By studying the pattern of such losses, psychologists have been able to piece together a more complete picture of how memories are stored in the brain (e.g., Squire, 1991). So, much can sometimes be learned from the case method. However, this method suffers from several important drawbacks. First, if the persons studied *are* unique, it can be misleading to generalize from them to other human beings. Second, because researchers using the case method often have repeated contact with the individuals they study, there is the real risk that they will become emotionally involved with these persons and so lose their scientific objectivity, at least to a degree. Because of such drawbacks, the case method is not widely used by psychologists today.

**SURVEYS: THE SCIENCE OF SELF-REPORT** At the opposite end of the scale where systematic observation is concerned is the **survey method.** Here, instead of focusing in detail on a small number of persons, researchers obtain a very limited sample of behavior from large numbers of individuals, usually through their responses to questionnaires. Surveys are used for many purposes—to measure attitudes toward specific issues, voting preferences, and consumer reactions to new products, to mention just a few. Surveys can also be repeated over long periods of time in order to track changes in public opinion or other aspects of behavior. For instance, surveys of job satisfaction—individuals' attitudes toward their jobs—have continued for more than forty years. And changing patterns of sexual behavior have been followed by the Kinsey Institute since the 1940s.

Web Link: *Survey Method*

The survey method offers several advantages. Information can be gathered quickly and efficiently from many thousands of persons. I used it myself recently to obtain information on the kinds of workplace aggression people encounter in their jobs, and results were clear: Most of the workplace aggression respondents witnessed or experienced was subtle and covert—not the kind of violence often emphasized by the mass media (Baron, Neuman, & Geddes, 1999; see Figure 1.12 on page 26). Further, since surveys can be constructed quickly, public opinion on new issues can be obtained almost as soon as the issues arise. To be useful as a research tool, however, a survey must meet certain requirements. First, if the goal is to predict some event (for example, the outcome of an election), great care must be devoted to the issue of **sampling**—how the persons who will participate in the survey are selected. Unless these persons are representative of the larger population about which predictions will be made, serious errors can result.

Another issue deserving careful attention is the way in which surveys are worded. Even changing a single word in a question can sometimes shift the meaning—and strongly influence the results. Recently, for example, the governor of the state where I live reduced the number of state employees in the capital by 450. How did people react to these reductions? In one poll they were asked to indicate how they felt about the governor's "slashing" of the workforce; in another, they were

**Case Method:** A research method in which detailed information about individuals is used to develop general principles about behavior.

**Survey Method:** A research method in which large numbers of people answer questions about aspects of their views or their behavior.

**Sampling:** In the survey method, the methods used to select persons who respond to the survey.

**Figure 1.12**
**Workplace Aggression: Not What the Media Suggest**

Recent research using the survey method indicates that contrary to what many news reports suggest, overt physical assaults are very rare in work settings. In contrast, covert and subtle forms of aggression (e.g., failing to return messages, spreading false rumors about another person, using up supplies another person needs) are far more common.

asked to indicate how they felt about the governor's "pruning" of the workforce. You can guess what happened: Results of the "slashing" poll suggested that the public was strongly against this action, while the responses to "pruning" indicated public support for the governor's action!

In sum, the survey method can be a useful approach for studying some aspects of human behavior, but the results obtained are accurate only to the extent that issues relating to sampling and wording are carefully addressed.

## Correlation: The Search for Relationships

At various times, you have probably noticed that some events appear to be related to each other: As one changes, the other appears to change too. For instance, you have probably observed that as people grow older, they often seem to gain weight; that when interest rates drop, the stock market rises; and that the richer people are, the more conservative they tend to be. When such relationships between events exist, we say that the events are *correlated* with each other (or that a *correlation* between them exists). This means that as one changes, the other tends to change too. Psychologists and other scientists refer to aspects of the natural world that can take different values as *variables,* so from now on that's the term I'll use here.

From the point of view of science, the existence of a correlation between two variables can be very useful. This is so because when a correlation exists, it is possible to predict one variable from information about one or more other variables. The ability to make such *predictions* is one important goal of science, and psychologists often attempt to make predictions about human behavior. To the extent predictions can be made accurately, important benefits follow. For instance, consider how useful it would be if we could predict from current information such future outcomes as a person's success in school or in various occupations, effectiveness as a parent, length of life, or likelihood of developing a serious mental disorder.

The discovery of correlations between variables allows us to make such predictions. In fact, the stronger such correlations are, the more accurate the predictions that can be made. These facts constitute the basis for an important method of research—the **correlational method.** In this approach, psychologists or other scientists attempt to determine whether, and to what extent, variables are related to each other. This involves making careful observations of each variable and then performing statistical analyses to determine whether and to what extent the variables are correlated—to what extent changes in one are related to changes in the other. Correlations range from –1.00 to +1.00, and the more they depart from zero, the stronger the correlation. For instance, a correlation of –.82 is stronger than one of +.23. Positive correlations indicate that as one variable increases, the other increases too. For instance, the greater the number of hours students study for their psychology tests, the higher their grades tend to be. Negative correlations indicate that as one variable increases, the other decreases. For example, the less satisfied people are with their jobs, the more likely they are to search for another one and to leave. As job satisfaction decreases, in other words, quitting increases. (The Appendix at the end of this book provides more information about correlations and how they are computed.) Now let's examine a concrete example of how psychologists actually use the correlational method.

**THE CORRELATIONAL METHOD OF RESEARCH: AN EXAMPLE** Suppose that a psychologist wanted to test the following hypothesis: *Use of small magnets strapped to various parts of one's body reduces joint and muscle pain.* How could research on this topic be conducted by the correlational method? Many possibilities exist, but one approach would be to measure both variables: the extent to which people used magnets and the amount of muscle or joint pain they experienced. The psychologist could measure magnet use by asking individuals to report the number of hours they wore magnets each day, or perhaps the number of magnets they used. Pain could be assessed by means of a rating scale on which the research participants would rate the intensity of the pain they experienced (e.g., from 1 for little or no pain, to 5 for intense pain). The researcher would then analyze these two sets of numbers through statistical procedures (statistics are a form of mathematics) to determine if they were correlated. If a positive correlation were obtained, this would offer support for the hypothesis, and would suggest that magnet use may indeed be linked to pain reduction.

Audio 1.2: *Using the Correlational Method on Research*

So far, so good. But watch out, for we are approaching a real danger zone—one in which many people seem to get confused. On the basis of findings indicating that as the use of magnets increased, pain decreased, many people would then jump to the following conclusion: Wearing magnets *causes* reductions in pain. This seems to make sense; after all, the greater people's use of magnets, the less pain they reported experiencing. But, in fact, such conclusions would not be justified, because correlational research does not, by itself, provide strong or direct evidence about cause-and-effect relationships. Indeed, this is one of the major drawbacks of such research. In this case, we may find that as magnet use increases, pain decreases—but *we do not know whether these effects result from magnet use or from some other variable that is related to both magnet use and pain reduction.*

For instance, it is quite possible that wearing magnets restricts people's movement. As a result, the more they wear them, the less they move around. This, in turn, might allow their injured muscles or joints to heal. If this were true, then it would not be the magnets themselves that cause pain reductions, but rather physical rest. Similarly, it could be the case that the more people use magnets, the stronger their beliefs that magnets work. These beliefs, not magnets themselves, may be responsible for reported reductions in pain. (Please see Figure 1.13 on page 28 for another illustration of why even strong correlations between variables do not necessarily mean that changes in one cause changes in the other.) In short, although the correlational method of research can be very valuable—and is, for reasons we'll soon describe, sometimes the only method psychologists can use to study a specific topic or question—it cannot answer the question "Why?" (as in "Why is magnet use related to pain reduction?") in a very definitive way. For this reason, psychologists often use another research method, to which we'll now turn.

**Correlational Method:** A research method in which researchers attempt to determine whether, and to what extent, different variables are related to each other.

**Figure 1.13**
**Correlation Does Not Equal Causation**

As shown by this example, the fact that two variables are strongly correlated does *not* guarantee that they are causally linked—that changes in one cause changes in the other. Instead, changes in both variables may stem from the influence of another factor—in this case, age.

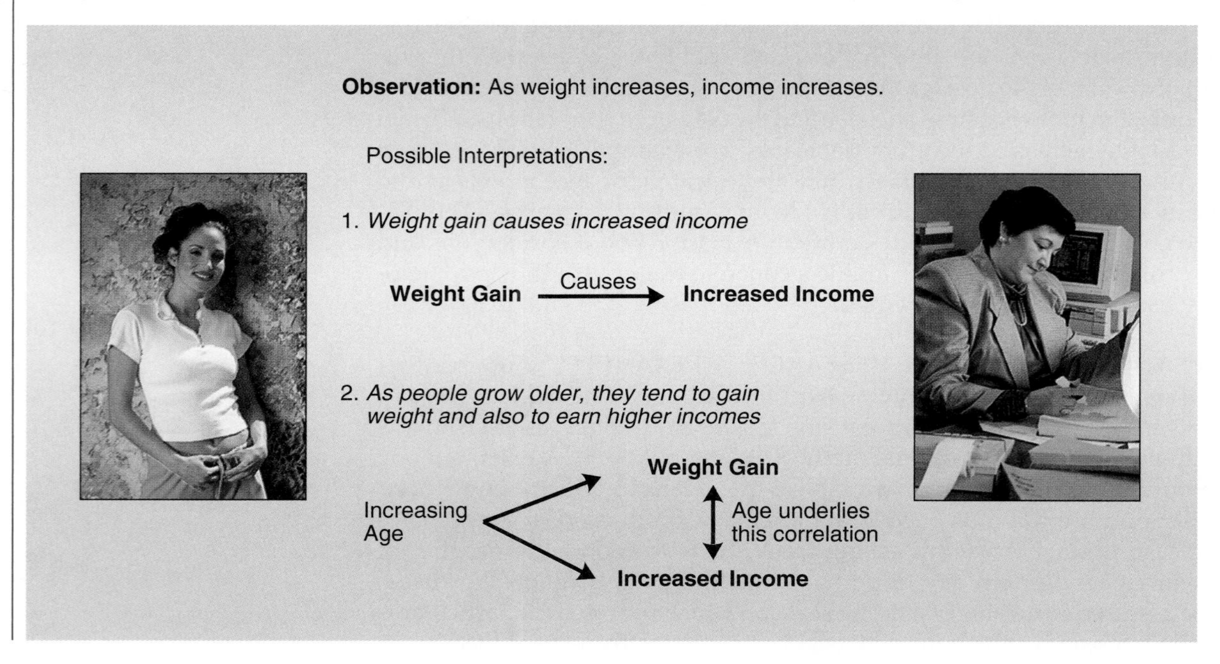


**REVIEW QUESTIONS**

- What is naturalistic observation?
- What is the correlational method of research, and how do psychologists use it?
- Why are even strong correlations between variables *not* evidence that changes in one cause changes in the other?

## The Experimental Method: Knowledge through Systematic Intervention

**Experimentation (the Experimental Method):** A research method in which researchers systematically alter one or more variables in order to determine whether such changes influence some aspect of behavior.

The method I mentioned above is known as **experimentation** or the **experimental method.** As the heading of this section suggests, experimentation involves a strategy built on intervention—making changes in the natural world to see what effects, if any, these changes produce. Specifically, one variable is changed systematically by the scientist, and the effects of these changes on one or more other variables are carefully measured. If changes in one variable produce changes in one or more other variables (and if additional conditions we'll shortly consider are also met), it is then possible to conclude with reasonable certainty that there is indeed a causal relationship between these variables—in other words, that changes in one variable do indeed *cause* changes in the other. Because the experimental method is so valuable in answering this kind of question, it is frequently the method of choice in psychology, just as it is in many other branches of science. But bear in mind that there is no single "best" method of research; rather, psychologists choose the method that is most appropriate for studying a given topic, and one that is consistent with practical and ethical constraints that we'll soon consider.

**EXPERIMENTATION: ITS BASIC NATURE** In its most basic form, the experimental method in psychology involves two key steps: (1) The presence or strength of some variable believed to affect behavior is systematically altered, and (2) the effects of such alterations (if any) are carefully measured. The logic behind these steps is this: If the variable that is systematically changed does indeed influence some aspect of behavior, then individuals exposed to different levels or amounts of that factor should differ in their behavior. For instance, exposure to a low amount of the variable should result in one level of behavior, while exposure to a higher amount should result in a different level, and so on.

The factor systematically varied by the researcher is termed the **independent variable,** while the aspect of behavior studied is termed the **dependent variable.** In a simple experiment, then, different groups of participants are exposed to contrasting levels of the independent variable (such as low, moderate, and high). The researcher then carefully measures the research participant's behavior to determine whether it does in fact differ depending on the level of the independent variable to which they are exposed.

To illustrate the basic nature of experimentation in psychological research, let's return to the possible effects of magnets on muscle or joint pain. One way in which a psychologist could study this topic through the experimental method is as follows. First, the psychologist would recruit persons who had considerable muscle or joint pain as participants in the research; this could be accomplished through ads in local newspapers, by referrals from physicians, or in other ways. These persons would make appointments to come to the psychologist's office or laboratory; there, the psychologist would give them metal disks and ask them to wear these for some specific amount of time (e.g., for one hour). One group would receive real magnets, while another group (known as a *control* condition) would receive disks that looked exactly the same but were not magnets. This is the *independent variable*—whether people wear magnets or nonmagnetized metal disks. At the end of the hour, participants would be asked to rate the amount of muscle or joint pain they felt as they performed a series of simple movements (e.g., raising their arms, moving their legs). They would rate their pain on a simple rating scale (e.g., 0 = no pain, 1 = mild pain, 2 = moderate pain, and so on); pain level would be the *dependent variable.* The psychologist would then compare the pain reported by the two groups. If the group that received the real magnets reported less pain, this would provide evidence that magnets are effective; if the two groups reported identical levels of pain, this would suggest that perhaps magnets are ineffective.

This, of course, is the simplest form of experiment the psychologist could perform. The researcher could make the study more informative by varying the number of magnets (or metal disks) participants wear (e.g., one disk, two, four, and so on) or by varying the number of hours they wear the disks (0.5, 1.0, 2.0, 4.0 hours). In addition, other variables—such as the strength of the magnets or their specific placement on the body—could also be introduced and varied systematically. The data from such expanded studies would provide more evidence concerning whether, and under what conditions, magnets reduce pain. But the basic logic would remain the same: The experimenter would vary each factor systematically in order to determine whether it had any effect on participants' pain.

**Independent Variable:** The variable that is systematically changed in an experiment.

**Dependent Variable:** The variable that is measured in an experiment.

**EXPERIMENTATION: TWO REQUIREMENTS FOR ITS SUCCESS** In order to provide clear information on cause-and-effect relationships, experiments must

**Random Assignments of Participants to Experimental Conditions:** Ensuring that all research participants have an equal chance of being exposed to each level of the independent variable (that is, of being assigned to each experimental condition).

**Confounding** (of variables): Confusion that occurs when factors other than the independent variable are permitted to vary across experimental conditions; can invalidate the apparent results of an experiment.

meet two key requirements. The first involves what is termed **random assignment of participants to conditions.** This means that all participants in an experiment must have an equal chance of being assigned to each group in the study—an equal chance of being exposed to each level of the independent variable. The reason for this rule is simple: If participants are *not* randomly assigned to each condition, it may later be impossible to tell whether differences in their behavior stem from differences they brought with them to the study, from the impact of the independent variable, or both. Imagine that in the study on magnets just described, all of the persons who receive the real magnets are strong believers in the benefits of these devices, while all those who receive the nonmagnetic metal disks are skeptical of such effects. Now assume that those receiving the magnets report less pain. Is this difference due to the effects of the magnets, the participants' belief in the benefits of magnets, or both factors? We can't tell. If, in contrast, the believers and the skeptics are randomly assigned to each condition, a difference between the conditions will be revealing: It will suggest that the magnets really may have some real, measurable effects.

The second requirement essential for successful experimentation is this: To as great a degree as possible, all factors *other* than the independent variable that might also affect participants' behavior must be held constant. To see why this is, consider what may happen in the study on magnets if those who get the real magnets are treated in a kind and soothing manner by the experimenter, while those who get the nonmagnetic disks are treated in a rude and harsh fashion. Again, those who get the real magnets report less pain. Why? We can't tell, because of **confounding** of variables: The independent variable (exposure to real magnets or blank metal disks) is confounded with another variable (the way in which the experimenter treats the participants). Kind, soothing treatment may help reduce pain, while rude, harsh treatment may increase stress and so intensify pain (see Chapters 4 and 13 for more discussion of this topic). The moral is clear: To the extent that variables other than the independent variable are permitted to change in an experiment, the value of the study may be greatly reduced or even totally eliminated (see Figure 1.14).

**Figure 1.14**
**Confounding of Variables: A Fatal Flaw in Experimentation**

In the experiment illustrated here, the independent variable—wearing magnets—is confounded with another variable—different treatment by the experimenter. This person is kind and soothing to those who wear real magnets, but rude and harsh to those who wear nonmagnetic metal disks. As a result of this confounding, it is impossible to tell whether any differences between the pain levels of participants in the two conditions stem from the independent variable, the confounding variable, or both.

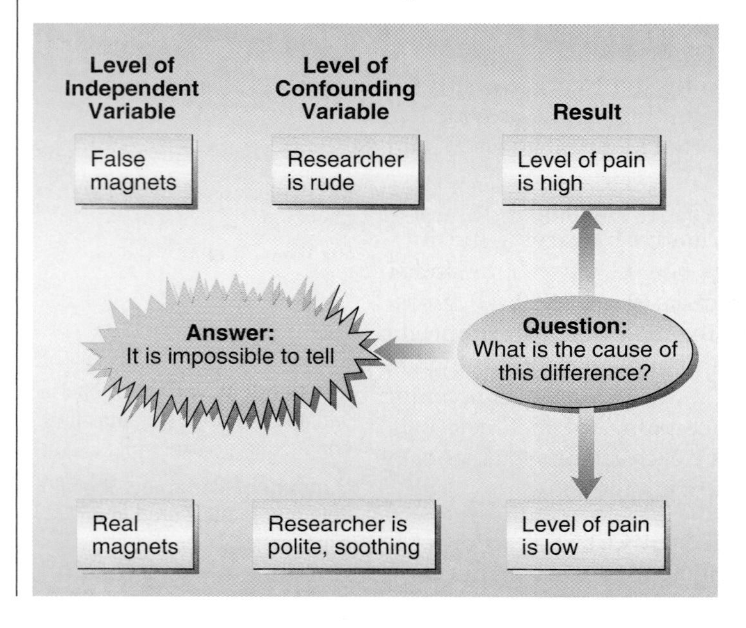


But why, you may be wondering, would a psychologist (or any other type of scientist) make such a mess of her or his own study? The answer, of course, is that no researcher would do so on purpose. But sometimes confounding of variables occurs because researchers aren't aware of the "other" variable and don't realize that it may be influencing the behavior they are studying. For example, suppose magnets can reduce pain, but only for people below the age of forty. Not realizing this, a researcher assigns more people over age forty to the magnet condition, and fewer people over age forty to the no-magnet group. Now, no difference between the conditions is found. Does this mean that magnets don't reduce pain? The researcher may accept this conclusion but will be on shaky ground, because of the potential influence of the confounding variable of which she or he is unaware.

One important source of confounding is subtle differences in experimenters' behavior that can influence research participants. For instance, a researcher who believes that magnets do have beneficial effects may act in a *slightly* friendlier or more reassuring manner toward participants who receive real magnets than toward ones who do not. These subtle differences may be unintentional and unconscious, but they can still affect participants' behavior. Such unintended effects produced by researchers are known as **experimenter effects,** and they can be deadly to the scientific value of a research project. This is one reason why many studies in psychology employ a **double-blind procedure,** in which researchers who have contact with participants do not know the hypothesis under investigation or the condition to which participants have been assigned. In our magnet example, use of the double-blind procedure would mean that the researcher who interacted with participants would not know the hypothesis being studied and would also be unaware of whether each participant received real or bogus magnets.

In sum, experimentation is, in several respects, the crown jewel among psychology's research methods. Why, then, isn't it the only method used by psychologists? One reason is that the other methods do indeed offer advantages (e.g., the vast amount of information that can be collected quickly through the survey method, or the high generalizability provided by naturalistic observation). Another reason is that in many cases, practical and ethical constraints prevent psychologists from using experimentation. For instance, suppose a psychologist believed that painting school buses a color different from the one widely used now (yellow) would make them more visible and so reduce accidents. Could this psychologist persuade school districts to paint their buses a different color? Perhaps, but perhaps not. In this case and in many others, psychologists can imagine useful experiments but can't conduct them because of practical constraints.

Turning to ethical constraints, suppose that a psychologist suspected that certain kinds of experiences cause individuals to think seriously about committing suicide. Could the psychologist conduct an experiment in which some people were exposed to these conditions while others were not, and then see how many committed suicide? Obviously not; this would be totally unethical, and no psychologist would seriously contemplate such research. In short, although experimentation is a powerful tool and one often preferred by psychologists, it cannot be used to investigate all questions about behavior. Please see Table 1.3 on page 32 for an overview of the advantages and disadvantages of all the research methods described in this section.

Web Link: *APA Ethics Information*

Web Link: *Ethical Issues in Psychology*

## Ethical Issues in Psychological Research

Strange as it may seem, the phrase *psychological research* has an ominous ring for some people. When they hear these words, they visualize scenes in which all-knowing psychologists somehow induce unwary research participants to reveal their deepest secrets and wildest fantasies. Do such concerns have any basis in fact? Is psychological research ever harmful to the people and animals being studied, and therefore unethical?

While I certainly don't wish to gloss over a complex and serious issue, my answer is "virtually never." All research conducted by trained psychologists is currently performed in accordance with strict ethical standards designed to protect the safety, privacy, and well-being of all research participants. These standards, which were developed both by government agencies and by the American Psychological Association, are carefully enforced in all settings where research occurs. Thus, many safeguards are built into the system, and together these assure that the disturbing image of psychological research mentioned above has little connection to reality.

Having said this, I should note that two ethical issues deserving of careful attention do remain. One has to do with the use of **deception**—the temporary

**Experimenter Effects:** Unintended effects, caused by researchers, on participants' behavior.

**Double-Blind Procedure:** Procedure in which the researchers who have contact with participants do not know the hypothesis under investigation.

**Deception:** The temporary withholding of information about a study from participants.

TABLE 1.3

**Various Research Methods: Advantages and Disadvantages**

As shown here, psychologists use several different research methods. Each offers a mixture of advantages and disadvantages, so the guiding rule generally is: Use whichever method is best for studying a particular research question.

| Method | Description | Advantages | Disadvantages |
|---|---|---|---|
| Systematic observation | Systematic study of behavior in natural settings | Behavior is observed in the settings where it normally occurs | Cannot be used to establish cause-and-effect relationships; often costly and difficult to perform |
| Case method | Detailed study of a small number of persons | Detailed information is gathered; individuals can be studied for long periods of time | Generalizability of results is uncertain; objectivity of researcher may be compromised |
| Surveys | Large numbers of persons are asked questions about their attitudes or views | Large amount of information can be acquired quickly; accurate predictions of large-scale trends can sometimes be made | Generalizability may be questionable unless persons surveyed are a representative sample of a larger population |
| Correlational research | Researchers measure two or more variables to determine if they are related in any way | Large amount of information can be gathered quickly; can be used in field as well as laboratory settings | Difficult to establish cause-and-effect relationships |
| Experimentation | The presence or strength of one or more variables is varied | Cause-and-effect relationships can be established; precise control can be exerted over other, potentially confounding variables | Results can be subject to several sources of bias (e.g., experimenter effects); generalizability can be doubtful if behavior is observed under highly artificial conditions |

withholding of information about a study from the persons who participate in it. The other issue has to do with the use of animals in psychological research.

Audio 1.3: *Using Deception in Research*

**DECEPTION: THE ETHICS OF MISLEADING RESEARCH PARTICIPANTS** Suppose you are a participant in a study designed to test the following hypothesis: The more attractive people are, the better first impressions they make on others. To test the hypothesis, the experimenter arranges for you to meet several people—one who is unattractive, another who is average in appearance, and a third who is a real knockout—and then asks you to rate your liking for each. Suppose that before the study begins, the psychologist explains the hypothesis to you. Do you think this knowledge could influence your behavior? Perhaps. One possibility is that, knowing what the psychologist hopes to find, you decide to "help"; this means that you express even greater liking for the attractive person than you might normally do. Another possibility is that you decide to show the researcher that you are not so easy to predict, so you actually report liking the *unattractive* person most.

It is in order to avoid such effects that psychologists sometimes choose to withhold information about the hypothesis they are investigating and other details of the research. They believe that such information may change participants' behavior and so render the results of the research useless. While this reasoning is

**Figure 1.15**
**Careful Debriefing: A Requirement after Experiments That Use Deception**

After an experiment is completed, participants should be provided with *debriefing*—full information about the experiment's goals and the reasons why temporary deception was used.

sound, the use of deception also raises important ethical issues. Is it appropriate for psychologists to withhold information from research participants, or even to mislead them? Although this issue remains somewhat controversial, most psychologists believe that deception is permissible, provided that two basic principles are followed.

The first involves obtaining **informed consent**—providing research participants with as much information as possible about events and procedures a study will involve *before* they agree to participate in it. This must be coupled with a clear statement that they are completely free to leave at any time during the study.

The second principle, known as **debriefing,** requires that research participants be given full information about all aspects of a study, including deception, after they have participated in it (see Figure 1.15). The goal is for participants to leave a study possessing a clear understanding of its major purposes and feeling *at least* as good as when they entered.

Existing evidence suggests that informed consent and thorough debriefing go a long way toward eliminating any adverse effects of temporary deception (Mann, 1994; Sharpe, Adair, & Roese, 1992). However, despite such findings, there is still the possibility—confirmed by recent research (e.g., Epley & Huff, 1998)—that exposure to deception can leave participants with increased feelings of suspicion about what researchers tell them. Thus, it is definitely unwise to take the safety or appropriateness of deception for granted. On the contrary, psychologists must always be vigilant to protect the rights and well-being of persons who, by offering their time, effort, and cooperation, help to advance our understanding of human behavior.

**Informed Consent:** A principle requiring that research participants be provided with information about all events and procedures a study will involve before they agree to participate in it.

**Debriefing:** Providing research participants with full information about all aspects of a study after they have participated in it.

**RESEARCH WITH ANIMALS** While most research conducted by psychologists involves human participants, some studies (about 8 percent) are performed with animals (Beckstead, 1991). Why do psychologists conduct such research? For several reasons. First, they may want to study the behavior of endangered species so that they can assist in protecting them from extinction. Research on the mating habits of the giant panda of China has helped to increase the world population of these beautiful animals, which do not readily reproduce in zoos (see Figure 1.16 on page 34). Second, psychologists conduct research on animals in order to examine the generality of basic principles of behavior—for example, certain forms of learning. Does learning occur in much the same manner across many different species,

**Figure 1.16**
**Helping to Save Endangered Species: One Reason for Research with Animals**

Psychologists sometimes conduct research with animals in order to obtain information that will help save endangered species from extinction. This was true in the case of the giant panda, because these animals do not breed readily in captivity.

or does the unique evolutionary history of each species alter this process in important ways? Research conducted with several species can help answer such questions.

The most important reason for conducting research with animals, however, is also the one that raises important ethical issues: Some research exposes animal subjects to conditions or treatments that could not be used with human beings. For obvious ethical and legal reasons, researchers cannot operate on the brains of healthy people in order to study the roles of various parts of their brains in memory, learning, or other aspects of behavior. Similarly, researchers cannot place human beings on diets lacking in important nutrients in order to determine how deficiencies affect their development. In these and many other cases, there appears to be no choice: If the research is to be conducted, it must be conducted with animals.

But is it appropriate to expose rats, pigeons, monkeys, or other animals to such treatment? This is a complex issue on which different persons hold sharply contrasting views. Supporters of animal rights contend that the procedures employed in research with animals expose them to harsh or dangerous treatment; this, they contend, makes such research unethical. Psychologists respond in two ways. First, they note that harsh procedures are virtually *never* used in their research; such conditions are much more frequent in medical studies, in which researchers do indeed inject animals with dangerous microbes or drugs in order to develop improved medical treatments. Second, psychologists note that research with animals has contributed to human welfare in many important ways. For example, it has led to improved means for treating emotional problems, controlling high blood pressure, and reducing chronic pain. In addition, psychological research with animals has increased our understanding of the neural mechanisms underlying memory loss, senility, and various addictions (Miller, 1985). Many persons would contend that these benefits far outweigh the risks to animals studied in psychological research.

This issue is a complex one, so there are no easy answers. Whether the benefits of research with animals—medical or psychological—justify such studies is a value judgment, largely outside the realm of science. Only you, as an individual who thinks critically, can make up your own mind.

## REVIEW QUESTIONS

- What is the basic nature of experimentation?
- Why is random assignment of participants to conditions required in experiments?
- What is confounding of variables in an experiment?
- What are experimenter effects and the double-blind procedure?

*Continued*

- What is deception? Informed consent? Debriefing?
- What ethical issues are raised by research with animals?

Food for Thought

Human behavior is influenced by a very large number of factors. Given this fact, can confounding of variables ever be completely prevented in psychological research? If not, does this necessarily reduce the value of the results?

# Using This Book: An Overview of Its Special Features

Although it's many years ago, I can still remember my own first course in psychology very well. I also remember struggling long and hard to understand many sections of the textbook we used. Because I don't want *you* to have the same kind of memories, I've worked hard to make this book as easy to understand, interesting, and useful as I could. Here are some of the steps I've taken to reach these goals.

Each chapter beings with an outline and ends with a summary. Within the text itself, key terms are printed in **dark type like this** and are defined. These terms are also defined in a running marginal glossary, and in a glossary at the end of the book. In addition, throughout each chapter, I call your attention to important points in special **Review Questions** sections. If you can answer these questions, that's a good sign that you understand the central points in each section. (The questions are answered for you at the end of the chapter.) As you'll soon notice, all figures are clear and simple, and most contain special labels and notes designed to help you understand them.

Second, in keeping with my goal of providing you with a new perspective on human behavior, I've included several types of special sections. One of these, designed to give you practice in critical (scientific) thinking, is labeled **Beyond the Headlines: As Psychologists See It.** These sections take an actual newspaper headline relating to human behavior and examine it from the perspective of psychology, thus illustrating how psychologists think critically about human behavior—and encouraging you to do the same. Additional practice in critical thinking is provided by special **Food for Thought** questions included in selected Review Questions sections, and in **Critical Thinking Questions** at the end of each chapter.

You've already seen another type of special section earlier in this chapter—**From Science to Practice.** These sections indicate how the knowledge acquired by psychologists is currently being used in many different fields—medicine, law, business, and education, to mention just a few. Thus, they provide concrete illustrations of the practical value of psychology as we move into a new millennium.

A third type of special section is labeled **Research Methods: How Psychologists Study. . . .** These sections describe the research methods developed by psychologists working in different branches of the field. Because these different branches address different aspects of behavior, the research methods, too, differ; but all are consistent with the basic methods described in this chapter.

Discussions relating to biological bases of behavior (and evolutionary psychology) and to diversity are highlighted by distinct symbols: and

Watch for these, because they are your signal that information linked to these important current themes in psychology is being presented. Finally, each chapter concludes with a special section entitled **Making Psychology Part of Your Life.** These sections are designed to illustrate how you personally can apply the information in each chapter to enhance your own life.

I hope that together, these features will help to make reading this book a stimulating and enjoyable experience. I also hope that combined with the contents of each chapter, they will provide you with that new perspective on human behavior I mentioned at the very start. In any case, I'm confident that in the pages that follow, you will discover something I first learned almost forty years ago: Psychology is indeed fascinating, useful, and . . . fun!

## Making Psychology Part of Your Life

### How to Study Psychology—or Any Other Subject—Effectively

Among the topics that psychologists know most about are learning, memory, and motivation. (We'll examine these in Chapters 5, 6, and 10.) Fortunately, all of these topics are directly relevant to one activity you must perform as a student: studying. You must be motivated to study, must learn new materials, and must remember them accurately after they have been mastered. Knowledge gained by psychologists can be very useful to you in accomplishing these tasks. Drawing on what psychology knows about these topics, here are some useful tips to help you get the most out of the time you spend studying.

- **Begin with an overview.** Research on memory indicates that it is easier to retain information if it can be placed within a cognitive framework. So when you begin to study, try to see "the big picture." Examine the outline at the start of each chapter and thumb through the pages once or twice. That way, you'll know what to expect and will form an initial framework for organizing the information that follows.
- **Eliminate (or at least minimize) distractions.** In order to enter information into your memory accurately, you must devote careful attention to it. This means that you should reduce all distractions; try to study in a quiet place, turn off the television or radio, put those magazines out of sight, and unhook your phone. The result? You will learn more in less time.
- **Don't do all your studying at once.** All-nighters are very inefficient. Research findings indicate that it is easier to learn and remember new information when learning is spaced out over time than when it is crammed into a single long session. So try to spread your study sessions out; in the final analysis, this will give you a much greater return for your effort (see Figure 1.17).
- **Set specific, challenging goals—but make sure these are attainable.** One of the key findings of industrial/organizational psychology is that setting certain kinds of goals can increase both motivation and performance on many different tasks. This principle can be of great help to you in studying, and it's relatively easy to apply. First, set a concrete goal for each session—for example, "I'll read twenty pages and review my class notes." Merely telling yourself

**Figure 1.17**
**All-Nighters: Not the Best Strategy**
Findings of psychological research indicate that we learn more efficiently when we spread our work sessions out over time. For this reason, all-nighters are usually not the best or most efficient way to study.

"I'll work until I'm tired" is less effective, because it fails to give you something concrete to shoot for. Second, try to set challenging goals, but ones you can attain. Challenging goals will encourage you to "stretch"—to do a little bit more. But impossible ones are simply discouraging. You are the world's greatest expert on your own limits and your own work habits, so you are the best judge of what would be a challenging but attainable goal for *you*. Set such goals when you begin, and the results may surprise you.

- **Reward yourself for progress.** As you'll see in Chapter 5, people often perform various activities to attain external rewards, ones delivered to them by others. But in many cases we can provide our own rewards; we can pat ourselves on the back for reaching goals we've set or for other accomplishments. This "pat on the back" can take many different forms: eating a favorite dessert, watching a favorite TV program, visiting friends. Again, you are the world's greatest expert on your own rewards, so you can readily choose ones that are appropriate. Whatever you choose, however, be sure to provide yourself with rewards for reaching your goals; you deserve it, and these intervals of pleasure will add to your efficiency.
- **Engage in active, not passive, studying.** As you probably know, it is possible to sit in front of a book or a set of notes for hours without accomplishing much—except daydreaming! In order to learn new information and retain it, you must do mental work—that's an inescapable fact of life. You must think about the material you are reading, ask yourself questions about it, relate this new information to things you already know, and so on. The Review Questions sections in each chapter are designed to help you do this, but in the final analysis, it's up to you. To the extent that you really try to answer the questions and engage in other forms of active learning, you will absorb more information, more efficiently.

I know, following these guidelines sounds like a lot of . . . work! But once you master these techniques, and learn to use them, the whole process will tend to get easier. You will learn and remember more, get better grades, improve the value of your own education—and do it more efficiently than ever before. Truly, this is one of those cases where a little extra effort can yield impressive returns.

# Summary and Review

## Modern Psychology: What It Is and How It Originated

- **What is the definition of psychology as it exists today?** Psychology is the science of behavior and cognitive processes.
- **What ideas in philosophy and findings in natural science contributed to the establishment of psychology as an independent field?** Philosophy supplied the ideas that knowledge can be gathered through careful reasoning (rationalism) and through careful observation (empiricism). Natural science provided new information suggesting that human behavior could be studied through scientific means.
- **According to structuralism, functionalism, and behaviorism, what should psychology study?** These three early schools suggested, respectively, that psychology should study the structure of consciousness, the functions of consciousness, or observable behavior.

### Key Terms

psychology, p. 5 • structuralism, p. 7 • functionalism, p. 7 • behaviorism, p. 7

## Psychology: Its Grand Issues and Key Perspectives

- **What are the three "grand issues" about behavior addressed by psychology?** The three issues are stability versus change, nature versus nurture, and rationality versus irrationality.
- **What are the major perspectives adopted by psychologists, and how do they differ?** Major perspectives in psychology include the behavioral, cognitive, biological, evolutionary, developmental, psychodynamic, and social approaches. These perspectives focus on different aspects of behavior but are complementary rather than competing in nature.

## Psychology 2000: Trends for the New Millennium

- **What is the multicultural perspective, and how do psychologists take account of it in their research and practice?** In psychology, the multicultural perspective is recognition of the important influence on behavior of cultural and ethnic diversity. This perspective is now a major focus of many lines of research and is reflected in widely accepted guidelines for the practice of psychology.

- **What is evolutionary psychology, and how does it contribute to our understanding of human behavior?** This new branch of psychology suggests that human beings have been subject to the process of biological evolution and, as a result, possess many evolved psychological mechanisms that influence our behavior.
- **What is meant by the "exportation of psychology"?** The use of psychological knowledge to solve practical problems in other fields.

### Key Terms

multicultural perspective, p. 14 • evolutionary psychology, p. 15

## Psychology and the Scientific Method

- **Why can psychology be viewed as a branch of science?** Psychology can be viewed as a branch of science because psychologists adopt the scientific method in their efforts to study human behavior.
- **What values are central to the scientific method?** Values central to the scientific method include accuracy, objectivity, skepticism, and open-mindedness.
- **What are theories, and what is their role in the scientific method?** Theories organize existing knowledge and make predictions that can be tested in research. They help scientists attain explanations of natural phenomena—understanding of why certain events or processes occur as they do.
- **Why are common sense and "folk wisdom" such uncertain guides to human behavior?** Common sense often suggests inconsistent and contradictory conclusions about behavior, and it is influenced by several important forms of bias.
- **What are the confirmation bias, the availability heuristic, and intuitive thinking, and what role do they play in our efforts to understand human behavior?** These are cognitive errors we make in thinking about the world around us. They often lead us to false conclusions about human behavior.
- **What is critical thinking, and what role does it play in psychology?** Critical thinking closely examines all claims and assumptions, carefully evaluates existing evidence, and cautiously assesses all conclusions. Such thinking is a basic aspect of the scientific method and is an integral part of efforts by psychologists to understand behavior.

### Key Terms

theories, p. 20 • hypotheses, p. 20 • confirmation bias, p. 22 • availability heuristic, p. 22 • critical thinking, p. 23

## Research Methods in Psychology: How Psychologists Answer Questions about Behavior

- **What is naturalistic observation?** Naturalistic observation involves carefully observing behavior in the settings where it normally occurs.
- **What is the correlational method of research, and how do psychologists use it?** This is a basic method in which researchers carefully observe two or more variables to see if changes in one are related to changes in the other. Psychologists use it to make predictions about one variable from observations of another variable.
- **Why are even strong correlations between variables *not* evidence that changes in one cause changes in the other?** Even strong correlations don't necessarily indicate causality because changes in both variables may stem from the influence of some other variable.
- **What is the basic nature of experimentation?** In experimentation, researchers produce systematic changes in one variable (the independent variable) in order to observe whether these changes affect another variable (the dependent variable).
- **Why is random assignment of participants to conditions required in experiments?** Because if participants are *not* randomly assigned to each condition, it may later be impossible to tell whether differences in their behavior stem from differences they brought with them to the study, from the impact of the independent variable, or both.
- **What is confounding of variables in an experiment?** Confounding occurs when one or more variables other than the independent variable are permitted to vary during an experiment.
- **What are experimenter effects and the double-blind procedure?** Experimenter effects are unintentional effects on research participants' behavior produced by researchers. Such effects can be prevented by double-blind procedures, in which experimenters who have contact with research participants do not know the hypothesis or the condition to which participants have been randomly assigned.
- **What is deception? Informed consent? Debriefing?** Deception is the temporary withholding of information about a study from research participants. Obtaining informed consent involves informing participants about all procedures to be used in a study before they agree to participate in it. Debriefing involves providing participants with full explanation of all aspects of a study after they participate in it.
- **What ethical issues are raised by research with animals?** Critics of such research suggest that it is unethical to expose animals to treatments or conditions that can potentially harm them.

### Key Terms

systematic observation, p. 24 • naturalistic observation, p. 24 • case method, p. 25 • survey method, p. 25 • sampling, p. 25 • correlational method, p. 27

• experimentation, p. 28 • independent variable, p. 29 • dependent variable, p. 29 • random assignment of participants to conditions, p. 30 • confounding, p. 30 • experimenter effects, p. 31 • double-blind procedure, p. 31 • deception, p. 31 • informed consent, p. 33 • debriefing, p. 33

# Critical Thinking Questions

## Appraisal

Most psychologists view their field as being scientific in nature. Do you agree? Explain why you accept this view.

## Controversy

Do you think that there is such a thing as "human nature"—a set of tendencies or preferences all human beings possess because they are the result of the evolutionary history of our species?

## Making Psychology Part of Your Life

Suppose that one day you read a news story reporting that results of a survey indicate that 40 percent of women and 30 percent of men have little or no interest in sex. How could you use critical thinking to interpret this report? What kinds of questions would you ask about the source of the data, the way the study was conducted, and the background (e.g., age) of the participants?

Chapter 2

# Biological Bases of Behavior

## CHAPTER OUTLINE

**NEURONS: BUILDING BLOCKS OF THE NERVOUS SYSTEM 44**

Neurons: Their Basic Structure
Neurons: Their Basic Function
Neurotransmitters: Chemical Keys to the Nervous System

**THE NERVOUS SYSTEM: ITS BASIC STRUCTURE AND FUNCTIONS 50**

The Nervous System: Its Major Divisions
The Endocrine System: Chemical Regulators of Bodily Processes

**THE BRAIN: WHERE CONSCIOUSNESS . . . IS 55**

The Brain Stem: Survival Basics
The Hypothalamus, Thalamus, and Limbic System: Motivation and Emotion

- BEYOND THE HEADLINES—As Psychologists See It: *Is Violence the Result of Faulty Neural Brakes?*

The Cerebral Cortex: The Core of Complex Thought
Two Minds in One Body? Our Divided Brains

- RESEARCH METHODS *How Psychologists Study the Nervous System and the Brain*

**THE BRAIN AND HUMAN BEHAVIOR: WHERE BIOLOGY AND CONSCIOUSNESS MEET 66**

How the Brain Functions: An Example from Visual Perception
The Brain and Human Speech
The Brain and Higher Mental Processes

**HEREDITY AND BEHAVIOR: GENETICS AND EVOLUTIONARY PSYCHOLOGY 72**

Genetics: Some Basic Principles
Disentangling Genetic and Environmental Effects: Research Strategies

- FROM SCIENCE TO PRACTICE *Identifying Genetic Factors in Human Disorders: Decoding Iceland*

Evolutionary Psychology: Genes in Action

- MAKING PSYCHOLOGY PART OF YOUR LIFE *The Nature-Nurture Controversy in the New Millennium: Adopting a Balanced View of the Role of Genetic Factors in Human Behavior*

I've been a runner for more than twenty years, but I never had an injury until two years ago. I was visiting friends and ran an especially long route, much of which was on pavement. Then, since it was a hot day, I jumped into my friends' pool; it was icy cold. That night I had some stiffness in my left side, so I did a few extra exercises to "work it out." The next day it was worse; we drove home that day, so I spent many hours in the car. On the third day I awoke with intense pain. The pain got worse as the day progressed, until I was in total agony. It felt as though someone were running a burning needle down my back, into my leg. I didn't sleep a wink, and in the morning I phoned the doctor for an appointment. "Severe muscle strain," he pronounced when I saw him. He explained that I had torn the muscle and that it had swelled, thus pressing on my sciatic nerve. He gave me some medicine and recommended hot baths. The first prescription, a muscle relaxant, made me feel groggy but didn't reduce my pain. In fact, I suffered so much that night that I remember thinking, "If I had this pain all the time, I'd rather be dead." My doctor prescribed another pill, a powerful pain-killer; this made me so groggy that although I could still feel the pain, it didn't bother me much. In fact, I was so dazed that I literally passed out briefly while shaving. After that I gave up on pills and concentrated on hot baths—I took five or six every day. After about a week, the pain subsided and I could sleep. But I still have twinges from that injury even today.

Why do I start with this painful (!) episode from my life? Because it illustrates the basic theme of this chapter: *Everything we think, feel, or do has a basis in biological processes and events*—and primarily in activities occurring in our brains and other portions of the nervous system. Do you understand these words? It is the result of activity in your brain. Do you feel hungry? It is the result of activity in your brain and other biological events. Can you remember what your psychology professor looks like? Again, it's the result of activity in several areas of your brain. I could go on, but by now I'm sure you get the point: *Everything psychological is, ultimately, biological,* in the sense that it is ultimately associated or linked with biological processes or events.

It is only fitting, therefore, to begin our study of psychology by considering the biological processes that underlie all aspects of our behavior. The goal is certainly not to make you an expert on these processes: This is a course in psychology, not biology, and I promise not to forget it. But as you'll soon see, we really can't obtain full answers to many questions about behavior without attention to biological factors—especially activity in our brains. How did an injury to my lower back produce blinding pain in my leg? Clearly, the answer involves the way in which our nervous system is "wired" and the ways in which our brain interprets information from injuries as pain (we'll discuss pain in detail in Chapter 3). How did the second drug my doctor gave me reduce my pain—or at least my emotional reaction to it? Answers to these and countless other questions about behavior involve biological processes, so including them as part of the total picture is essential.

This is not the only reason why psychologists are interested in the biological events that are the foundations of behavior, however. In addition, they realize that an understanding of these roots may often suggest effective treatments for behavioral problems. As we'll see in Chapter 14, science has made much progress in understanding the biological causes of mental disorders—depression, schizophrenia, and anxiety disorders, to name just a few. Such knowledge, in turn, has led to the development of effective drugs for treating these disorders (we'll examine these in detail in Chapter 15). Similarly, growing understanding of the biological mechanisms that play a role in drug addiction is now pointing the way toward more effective treatment of this serious problem. As a third example, consider human aggression. As we'll see in Chapter 10, such behavior stems from a wide range of causes, including other persons' actions (e.g., they insult or provoke us), environmental conditions (it is stiflingly hot and this makes us irritable), and social norms (aggression is approved or disapproved by society). But aggression involves biological processes as well. For instance, some evidence suggests that people with high levels of *testosterone,* an important male sex hormone, are more likely to engage in assaults against others than persons with lower levels (Archer, 1994). And in some cases, especially among individuals who show ruthless, cold-blooded aggression against innocent victims, aggression may involve disorders in brain functioning that make it difficult for these persons to experience negative emotions such as fear (e.g., they are unconcerned about the possibility that others might retaliate or about any pain they themselves may experience) (Patrick, Bradley, & Lang, 1993). Understanding the biological basis of such behavior can help us develop effective ways of reducing it. In sum, there are indeed strong reasons for psychologists—and for you!—to be interested in the biological foundations of behavior. No, the answers will never be as simple as those shown in Figure 2.1, but there *are* indeed answers!

**Figure 2.1**
**Brain and Behavior: There Are Important Links!**

Although their procedures are much more sophisticated than this one, psychologists recognize that everything psychological is ultimately biological. Thus, they often conduct research to investigate the biological bases of behavior. (*Source:* © The New Yorker Collection. 1988. Gahan Wilson from cartoonbank.com. All rights reserved.)

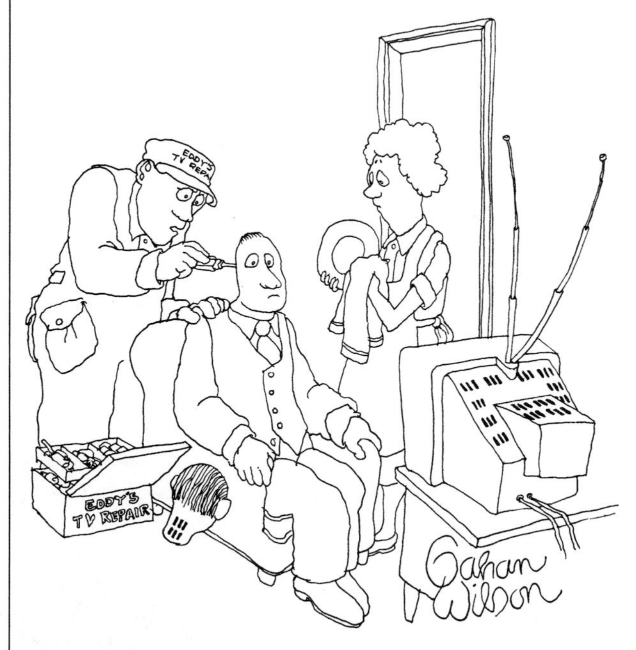


*"Here's your problem."*

There's still one more reason for beginning with this chapter, and it has to do with scientific progress. When I took my first course in psychology in 1962, psychologists wondered about what goes on in the brain when we think, experience emotions, understand speech or produce it, or bring memories to mind; but they had few tools for answering such questions. This situation has changed dramatically in recent decades, as modern technology has provided impressive new tools for studying the living brain—for seeing where activity is centered as people solve problems, listen to music, reason, or memorize new information (e.g., Besson et al., 1998; Waltz et al., 1999). These new tools, which are described in the **Research Methods** section on page 64, have done for psychologists what the microscope did for biology and medicine and what the telescope did for astronomy: They have provided researchers with new ways of examining events and processes that were previously totally hidden from view. The results have been nothing short of a revolution in our understanding of how the brain works and the role it plays in the complex behaviors, feelings, and experiences that make us human. So get ready for some amazing surprises; we are truly on the verge of obtaining a much fuller understanding of the mysteries of the human mind than we ever had before.

To provide you with an overview of these exciting new discoveries, I'll proceed as follows. First, I'll examine the structure and function of *neurons,* the building blocks of the nervous system. As you'll soon see, understanding how neurons function—and especially how they communicate with one another—provides important insights into such diverse topics as how drugs exert their effects and how, perhaps, serious forms of mental illness develop. Next, I'll turn to the structure and function of the *nervous system,* devoting special attention to the *brain,* the marvelous organ that is ultimately responsible for consciousness—and for the fact that you are now reading and understanding these words. After this, I'll put psychology rather than biology at center-stage by examining important links between the brain and behavior. In this section, I'll describe a sampling of recent findings concerning the roles of various portions of the brain in how we perceive the world around us, and in what are often described as our *higher mental processes*—human speech (how we understand and produce it), reasoning, and problem solving. As we'll soon see, the modern research tools I mentioned have provided new insights into all these topics. Finally, I'll conclude by examining the role of *genetic factors* in human behavior, and the possible role of evolution in our behavior—a topic investigated by the field of *evolutionary psychology.* In one respect, it might make sense to start with genetic factors rather than to end with them. However, I think you'll be in a better position to understand these factors—and to appreciate their importance—after acquiring some basic information about the nervous system and, especially, the brain. So let's turn now to neurons—the building blocks of which, ultimately, our consciousness is composed.

# Neurons: Building Blocks of the Nervous System

You are driving down the road when suddenly your friend, who is sitting in the seat next to you, shouts: "Watch out for that truck!" Immediately, you experience strong anxiety, step on the brake, and look around in every direction. The process seems automatic, but think about it for a moment: How did information from your ears get "inside" and trigger your emotions and behavior? The answer involves the activity of **neurons:** cells within our bodies that are specialized for the tasks of receiving, moving, and processing information.

CourseCompass

Video 2.1: *Scientists Study Squid to Understand How the Human Axon Works*

## Neurons: Their Basic Structure

Neurons are tremendously varied in appearance. Yet most consist of three basic parts: (1) a *cell body,* (2) an *axon,* and (3) one or more *dendrites.* **Dendrites** carry information toward the cell body, whereas **axons** carry information away from it. Thus, in a sense, neurons are one-way channels of communication. Information usually moves from dendrites or the cell body toward the axon and then outward along this structure. A simplified diagram of a neuron and actual neurons are shown, magnified, in Figure 2.2. Scientists estimate that the human brain may contain more than 100 billion neurons.

In many neurons the axon is covered by a sheath of fatty material known as *myelin.* The myelin sheath (fatty wrapping) is interrupted by small gaps (places where it is absent). Both the sheath and the gaps in it play an important role in the neuron's ability to transmit information, a process we'll consider in detail shortly. Damage to the myelin sheath surrounding axons can seriously affect synaptic transmission. In diseases such as *multiple sclerosis* (MS), progressive deterioration of the myelin sheath leads to jerky, uncoordinated movement in the affected person. Richard Pryor, a noted comedian, suffers from MS.

The myelin sheath is actually produced by another basic set of building blocks within the nervous system, **glial cells.** Glial cells, which outnumber neurons by

**Neurons:** Cells specialized for communicating information, the basic building blocks of the nervous system.

**Dendrites:** The parts of neurons that conduct action potentials toward the cell body.

**Axon:** The part of the neuron that conducts the action potential away from the cell body.

**Glial Cells:** Cells in the nervous system that surround, support, and protect neurons.

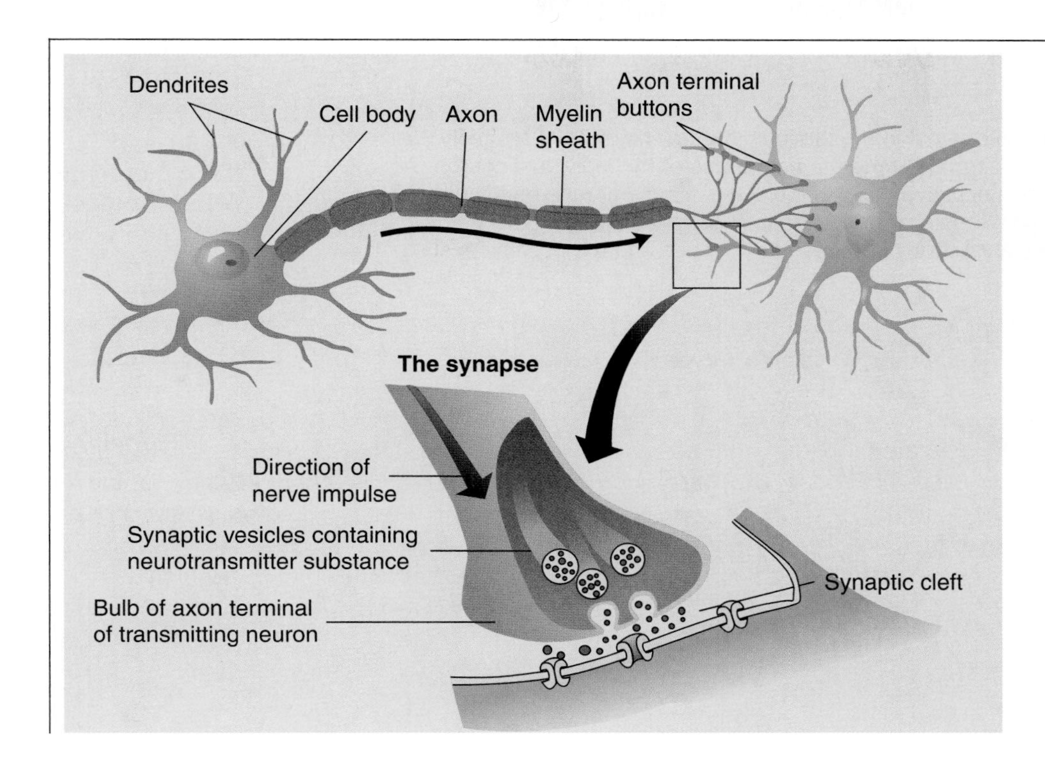


**Figure 2.2**
**Neurons: Their Basic Structure**

Neurons vary in form, but all possess the basic structures shown here: a cell body, an axon (with axon terminals), and one or more dendrites.

about ten to one, serve several functions in our nervous system; they form the myelin sheath around axons and perform basic housekeeping chores, such as cleaning up cellular debris. They also help form the *blood–brain barrier*—a barrier that prevents certain substances in the bloodstream from reaching the brain.

Near its end, the axon divides into several small branches. These, in turn, end in round structures known as **axon terminals** that closely approach, but do not actually touch, other cells (other neurons, muscle cells, or gland cells). The region at which the axon terminals of a neuron closely approach other cells is known as the **synapse.** The manner in which neurons communicate with other cells across this tiny space is described next.

## Neurons: Their Basic Function

As we consider how neurons function, two questions arise: (1) How does information travel from point to point within a single neuron? And (2) how is information transmitted from one neuron to another or from neurons to other cells of the body?

### COMMUNICATION WITHIN NEURONS: GRADED AND ACTION POTENTIALS

The answer to the first question is complex but can be summarized as follows. When a neuron is at rest, there is a tiny electrical charge (–70 millivolts) across the cell membrane. That is, the inside of the cell has a slight negative charge relative to the outside. This electrical charge is due to the fact that several types of ions (positively and negatively charged particles) exist in different concentrations outside and inside the cell. As a result, the interior of the cell membrane acquires a tiny negative charge relative to the outside. This resting potential does not occur by accident; the neuron works to maintain it by actively pumping positively charged ions back outside if they enter, while retaining negatively charged ions in greater concentrations than are present outside the cell.

Stimulation, either directly (by light, heat, or pressure) or by chemical messages from other neurons, produces **graded potentials**—a basic type of signal

**Axon Terminals:** Structures at the end of axons that contain transmitter substances.

**Synapse:** A region where the axon of one neuron closely approaches other neurons or the cell membrane of other types of cells such as muscle cells.

**Graded Potential:** A basic type of signal within neurons that results from external physical stimulation of the dendrite or cell body. In contrast to the all-or-nothing nature of action potentials, graded potentials vary in proportion to the size of the stimulus that produced them.

**Figure 2.3**
**The Action Potential**

The action potential—the most basic signal in the nervous system—consists of a rapidly moving wave of depolarization that travels along the membrane of the individual neuron. As the action potential moves, the negative charge across the cell membrane briefly disappears—largely as a result of positively charged particles moving inside. After the action potential passes, these particles are actively pumped back outside and the negative resting potential is restored.

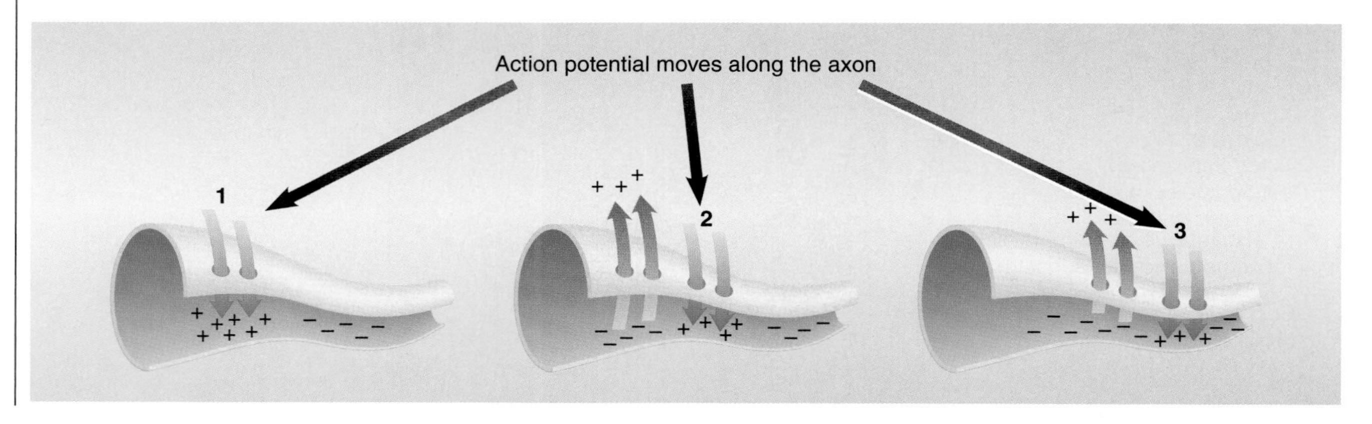


*within* neurons. An important feature of graded potentials is that their magnitude varies in proportion to the size of the stimulus that produced it. Thus, a loud sound or bright light produces graded potentials of greater magnitude than a softer sound or dim light. Because graded potentials tend to weaken quickly, they typically convey incoming information over short distances, usually along the dendrite toward the neuron's cell body. Please note that neurons receive information from many other cells—often from thousands of them.

If the overall pattern of graded potentials reaching the cell body is of sufficient magnitude—if it exceeds the *threshold* of the neuron in question—complex biochemical changes occur in the cell membrane, and an *action potential* is generated (please refer to Figure 2.3). During an action potential, some types of positively charged ions are briefly allowed to enter the cell membrane more readily than before. This influx of positive ions reduces, then totally eliminates the resting potential. Indeed, for a brief period of time, the interior of the cell actually attains a net positive charge relative to the outside. This change in electrical potential across the cell membrane moves rapidly along the neuron, and it is this moving disturbance, known as the **action potential,** is the basic signal within our nervous system—the signal that is ultimately the basis of everything we sense, think, or do.

After a very brief period (1 or 2 milliseconds), the neuron actively pumps the positive ions back outside and allows other ions, which flowed outside via their own ion channels, to reenter. As a result, the resting potential is gradually restored, and the cell becomes ready to "fire" once again. Unlike graded potentials, the action potential is an *all-or-none response.* Either it occurs at full strength or it does not occur at all; there is nothing in between. Also, the speed of conduction of an action potential is very rapid in neurons possessing a myelin sheath. In a sense, the action potential jumps from one small gap in the sheath to another—openings known as **nodes of Ranvier.** Speeds along myelinated axons can reach 270 miles per hour.

**Action Potential:** A rapidly moving wave of depolarization (shift in electrical potential) that travels along the cell membrane of a neuron. This disturbance along the membrane communicates information within the neuron.

**Nodes of Ranvier:** Small gaps in the myelin sheath surrounding the axons of many neurons.

**COMMUNICATION BETWEEN NEURONS: SYNAPTIC TRANSMISSION** I noted earlier that neurons closely approach, but do not actually touch, other neurons (or other cells of the body). How, then, does the action potential cross the gap between them? Existing evidence points to the following answer.

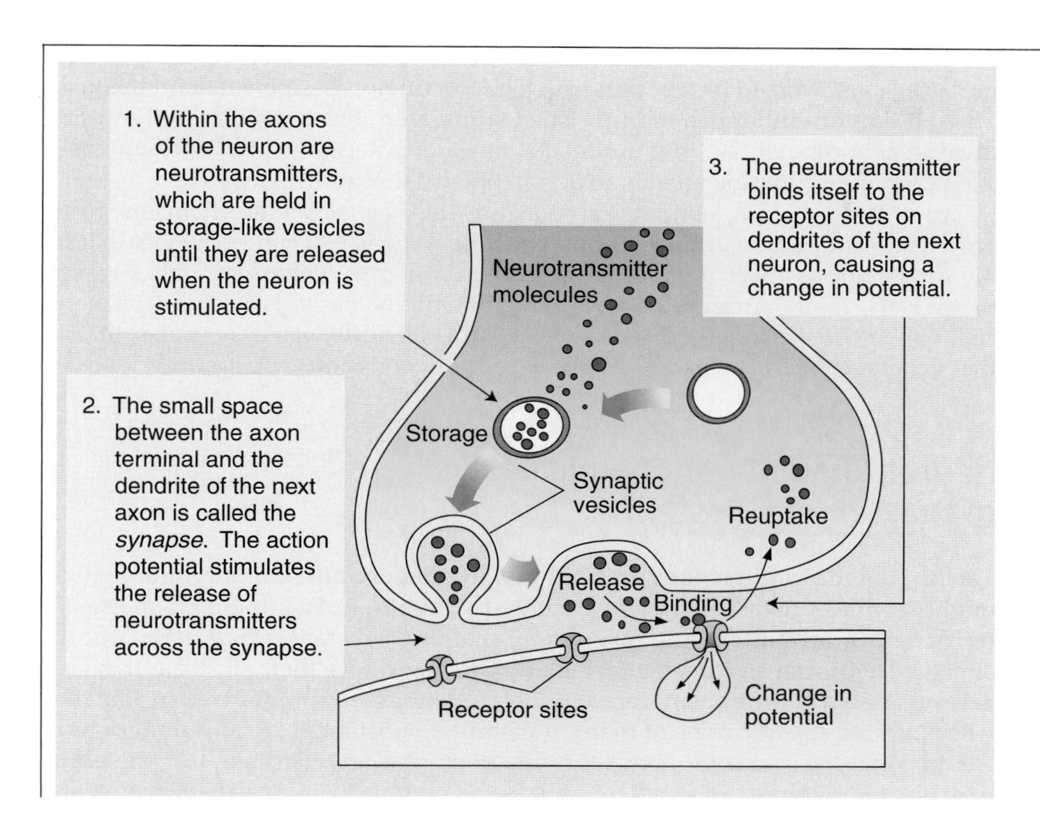


**Figure 2.4**
**Synaptic Transmission**

The axon terminals found on the ends of axons contain many *synaptic vesicles.* When an action potential reaches the axon terminal, these vesicles move toward the cell membrane. Once there, the vesicles fuse with the membrane and release their contents *(neurotransmitters)* into the synapse.

When a neuron "fires," the action potential that is produced travels along the membrane of the axon to the axon terminals. Within the axon terminals are many structures known as **synaptic vesicles.** Arrival of the action potential causes these vesicles to approach the cell membrane, where they fuse with the membrane and then empty their contents into the synapse (see Figure 2.4). The chemicals thus released—known as **neurotransmitters**—travel across the tiny synaptic gap until they reach specialized receptor sites in the membrane of the other cell.

These receptors are complex protein molecules into whose structure neurotransmitter substances fit like chemical keys into a lock. Specific neurotransmitters can deliver signals only at certain locations on cell membranes, thereby introducing precision into the nervous system's complex communication system. Upon binding to their receptors, neurotransmitters either produce their effects directly, or function indirectly through the interaction of the neurotransmitter and its receptor with other substances.

Neurotransmitters produce one of two effects. If their effects are *excitatory* in nature, they make it more likely for the neuron they reach to fire. If, instead, their effects are *inhibitory,* they make it less it less likely that the neuron will fire. What happens to neurotransmitters *after* they cross the synapse from one neuron to another? Either they are taken back for reuse in the axon terminals of the neuron that released them, a process known as *reuptake,* or they are broken down by various enzymes present at the synapse—in a sense, chemically deactivated.

It is important to note that in my comments so far, I have greatly simplified reality by describing a situation in which one neuron contacts another across a single synapse. In fact, this is rarely, if ever, the case. Most neurons actually form synapses with many others—ten thousand or more in some cases. Thus, at any given moment, most neurons are receiving a complex pattern of excitatory and inhibitory influences from many neighbors.

Whether a neuron conducts an action potential or not, then, depends on the total pattern of this input; for example, whether excitatory or inhibitory input

**Synaptic Vesicles:** Structures in the axon terminals that contain various neurotransmitters.

**Neurotransmitters:** Chemicals, released by neurons, that carry information across synapses.

predominates. Further, the effects of excitatory and inhibitory input can be cumulative over time, in part because such effects do not dissipate instantaneously. Thus, if a neuron that has recently been stimulated, but not sufficiently to produce an action potential, is stimulated again soon afterwards, the two sources of excitation may combine so that an action potential is generated.

In one sense, then, neurons serve as tiny *decision-making* mechanisms, firing only when the pattern of information reaching them is just right. The fact that individual neurons affect and are, in turn, affected by many others strongly suggests that it is the total pattern or network of activity in the nervous system that is crucial. As we will see in later discussions, it is this intricate web of neural excitation that generates the richness and complexity of our conscious experience.

## Neurotransmitters: Chemical Keys to the Nervous System

The fact that transmitter substances produce either excitatory or inhibitory effects might seem to suggest that there are only two types. In fact, there are many different neurotransmitters, and many more chemical substances that can mimic the effects of neurotransmitters; in fact, many drugs produce their effects in this way. Several known neurotransmitters and their functions are summarized in Table 2.1. Although the specific roles of many transmitter substances are still under study, we are now fairly certain about the functions of a few. Perhaps the one about which we know most is *acetylcholine.* It is the neurotransmitter at every junction between motor neurons (neurons concerned with muscular movements) and mus-

**TABLE 2.1**

**Neurotransmitters: An Overview**

Neurons communicate with one another across the synapse through neurotransmitters. Several of these are listed and described here.

| Neurotransmitter | Location | Effects |
|---|---|---|
| Acetylcholine | Found throughout the central nervous system, in the autonomic nervous system, and at all neuromuscular junctions. | Involved in muscle action, learning, and memory. |
| Norepinephrine | Found in neurons in the autonomic nervous system. | Primarily involved in control or alertness and wakefullness. |
| Dopamine | Produced by neurons located in a region of the brain called the substantia nigra. | Involved in movement, attention, and learning. Degeneration of dopamine-producing neurons has been linked to Parkinson's disease. Too much dopamine has been linked to schizophrenia. |
| Serotonin | Found in neurons in the brain and spinal cord. | Plays a role in the regulation of mood and in the control of eating, sleep, and arousal. Has also been implicated in the regulation of pain and in dreaming. |
| GABA (gamma-amino-butyric acid) | Found throughout the brain and spinal cord. | GABA is the major inhibitory neurotransmitter in the brain. Abnormal levels of GABA have been implicated in sleep and eating disorders. |

cle cells. Anything that interferes with the action of acetylcholine can produce paralysis. South American hunters have long used this fact to their advantage by dipping their arrow tips in *curare*—a poisonous substance that occupies acetylcholine receptors. As a result, paralysis is produced, and the unlucky animal dies quickly through suffocation. Some evidence suggests that the severe memory loss characteristic of persons suffering from *Alzheimer's disease* results from a degeneration of cells that produce acetylcholine. Examinations of the brains of persons who have died from this disease show unusually low levels of this substance (Coyle, Price, & DeLong, 1983).

**THE ENDORPHINS** During the 1970s, researchers studying the effects of morphine and other opiates made a surprising discovery: There appeared to be special receptor sites for such drugs within the brain (Hughes et al., 1975). Why should such receptors exist? It was soon discovered that naturally occurring substances that closely resemble morphine in chemical structure are produced by the brain. These substances, known as *endorphins,* seemed to act as neurotransmitters, stimulating specialized receptor sites. Why should the brain produce such substances? Research suggests that endorphins are released by the body in response to pain or vigorous exercise and so help reduce sensations that might otherwise interfere with ongoing behavior (Fields & Basbaum, 1984). Additional evidence indicates that endorphins also serve to intensify positive sensations—for example, the "runner's high" many people experience after vigorous exercise. In short, it appears that the brain possesses an internal mechanism for moderating unpleasant sensations and magnifying positive ones, and that the effects of morphine and other opiates stem, at least in part, from the fact that these drugs act on this naturally existing system.

CourseCompass
Web Link: *Understanding Addiction: Basic Science Information*

**DRUGS AND NEUROTRANSMITTERS** Remember the powerful painkiller I took for my back injury? Now that we have considered the nature and function of neurotransmitters, we are in a better position to understand how that drug produced its effects. In many cases, drugs affect our feelings or behavior by altering the process of synaptic transmission. They do this because they are similar enough in chemical structure to neurotransmitters to occupy the receptor sites normally occupied by the neurotransmitters themselves (e.g., Kalivas & Samson, 1992). In this respect, drugs can produce two basic effects: They can mimic the effects of the neurotransmitter, in which case they are described as being **agonists,** or they can inhibit the effects normally produced by the neurotransmitter, in which case they are described as being **antagonists.** Many painkillers (analgesics) occupy receptor sites normally stimulated by endorphins; thus, they block pain and produce a temporary high. Addicting drugs such as opium, heroin, and crack cocaine also occupy these sites, and produce more intensely pleasurable sensations than endorphins. This seems to play a key role in their addicting properties. The influence of both agonists and antagonists is illustrated in Figure 2.5 on page 50.

CourseCompass
Audio 2.1: *Drugs and Neurotransmitters*

Web Link: *National Institute on Drug Abuse*

**REVIEW QUESTIONS**

- What do neurons do, and what are their basic parts?
- What are action potentials and graded potentials? How do neurons communicate with one another?
- What are the effects of neurotransmitters?
- How do drugs produce their effects? What are agonists? Antagonists?

**Agonist:** A chemical substance that mimics the action of a neurotransmitter at a receptor site.

**Antagonist:** A chemical substance that inhibits the effect normally produced by a neurotransmitter at a receptor site.

**Figure 2.5**
**How Drugs Affect the Nervous System: Agonists and Antagonists**

Naturally occurring neurotransmitters fit receptor sites on neurons like a key fitting into a lock. Some drugs are close enough in structure to these neurotransmitters to fit into the same receptor sites. Drugs that then mimic the effects of the neurotransmitter are said to act as *agonists*. Drugs that block the effects normally produced by the neurotransmitter are termed *antagonists*.

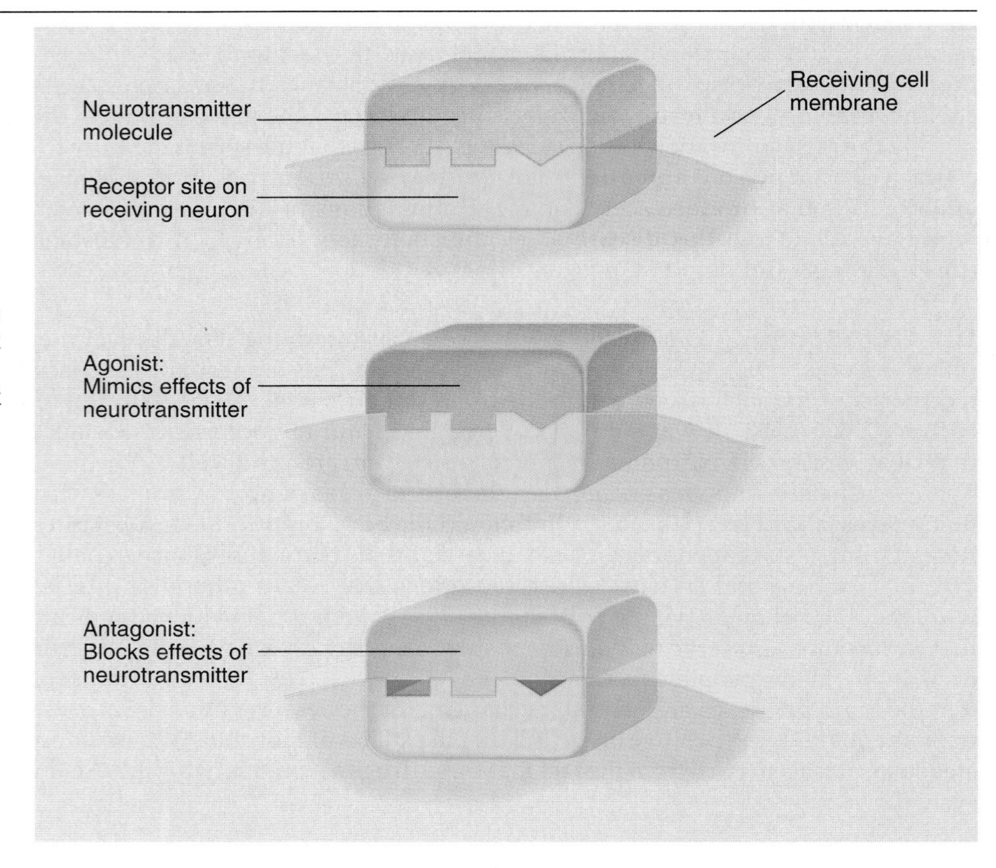

CourseCompass
Web Link: *Organization of the Nervous System*

**Nervous System:** The complex network of neurons that regulates bodily processes and is ultimately responsible for all aspects of conscious experience.

**Central Nervous System:** The brain and the spinal cord.

**Peripheral Nervous System:** The portion of the nervous system that connects internal organs, glands, and voluntary and involuntary muscles to the central nervous system.

**Afferent Nerve Fibers:** Nerve fibers in the spinal cord that carry information from receptors throughout the body toward the brain.

**Efferent Nerve Fibers:** Nerve fibers in the spinal cord that carry information from the brain to muscles and glands throughout the body.

# The Nervous System: Its Basic Structure and Functions

If neurons are building blocks, then the **nervous system** is the structure that they, along with other types of cells, combine to erect. The nervous system is actually a complex network of neurons that regulates our bodily functions and permits us to react to the external world in countless ways, so it deserves very careful attention. But remember: This is *not* a course in biology, so the main reason for focusing on the nervous system is to provide a foundation for understanding its role in all aspects of our behavior.

## The Nervous System: Its Major Divisions

Although the nervous system functions as an integrated whole, it is often viewed as having two major portions—the **central nervous system** and the **peripheral nervous system.** These and other divisions of the nervous system are presented in Figure 2.6.

**THE CENTRAL NERVOUS SYSTEM** The central nervous system (CNS) consists of the brain and the spinal cord. I'll soon describe the structure of the brain in detail, so we won't examine it here. The spinal cord runs through the middle of a bony column of hollow bones known as vertebrae. You can feel them by moving your hand up and down the middle of your back.

The spinal cord has two major functions. First, it carries sensory information via **afferent** (sensory) **nerve fibers** from receptors throughout the body to the brain and conducts information via **efferent** (motor) **nerve fibers** from the brain to mus-

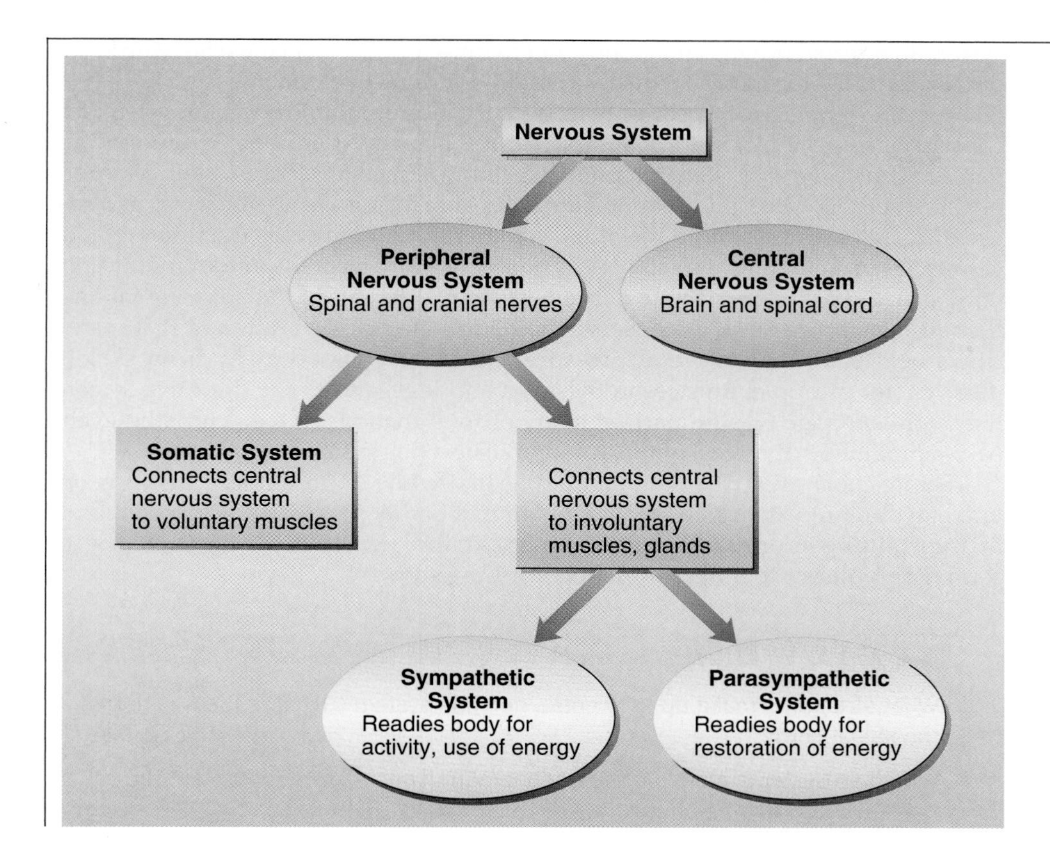


**Figure 2.6**
**Major Divisions of the Nervous System**

As shown here, the nervous system consists of several major parts.

cles and glands. Second, it plays a key role in various reflexes. These are seemingly automatic actions evoked rapidly by particular stimuli. Withdrawing your hand from a hot object or blinking your eye in response to a rapidly approaching object are common examples of reflex actions. In their simplest form, reflexes involve neural circuits in which information from various receptors is carried to the spinal cord, where it stimulates other neurons known as interneurons. These then transmit information to muscle cells, thus producing reflex actions. In fact, reflexes are usually much more complex than this. Hundreds or even thousands of neurons may influence a reflex, and input from certain areas of the brain may be involved as well. Whatever their precise nature, though, spinal reflexes offer an obvious advantage: They permit us to react to potential dangers much more rapidly than we could if the information first had to travel all the way to the brain.

**THE PERIPHERAL NERVOUS SYSTEM** The peripheral nervous system consists primarily of nerves, bundles of axons from many neurons, which connect the central nervous system with sense organs and with muscles and glands throughout the body. Most of these nerves are attached to the spinal cord; these spinal nerves serve all of the body below the neck. Other nerves known as cranial nerves extend from the brain. They carry sensory information from receptors in the eyes and ears and other sense organs; they also carry information from the central nervous system to muscles in the head and neck.

As you can see in Figure 2.6, the peripheral nervous system has two subdivisions: the **somatic** and **autonomic nervous systems.** The somatic nervous system connects the central nervous system to voluntary muscles throughout the body. Thus, when you engage in almost any voluntary action, such as ordering a pizza or reading the rest of this chapter, portions of your somatic nervous system are involved. In contrast, the autonomic nervous system connects the central nervous

**Somatic Nervous System:** The portion of the peripheral nervous system that connects the brain and spinal cord to voluntary muscles.

**Autonomic Nervous System:** The part of the peripheral nervous system that connects internal organs, glands, and involuntary muscles to the central nervous system.

system to internal organs and glands and to muscles over which we have little voluntary control—for instance, the muscles in our digestive system.

We can't stop dividing things here, because the autonomic nervous system, too, consists of two distinct parts. The first is known as the **sympathetic nervous system.** In general, this system prepares the body for using energy, as in vigorous physical actions. Thus, stimulation of this division increases heartbeat, raises blood pressure, releases sugar into the blood for energy, and increases the flow of blood to muscles used in physical activities. The second portion of the autonomic system, known as the **parasympathetic nervous system,** operates in the opposite manner. It stimulates processes that conserve the body's energy. Activation of this system slows heartbeat, lowers blood pressure, and diverts blood away from skeletal muscles (for example, muscles in the arms and legs) and to the digestive system. Figure 2.7 on page 53 summarizes many of the functions of the sympathetic and parasympathetic divisions of the autonomic nervous system.

Before concluding, I should emphasize that while the autonomic nervous system plays an important role in the regulation of bodily processes, it does so mainly by transmitting information to and from the central nervous system. Thus, it is the central nervous system that ultimately runs the show.

### REVIEW QUESTIONS

- What structures make up the central nervous system? What is the function of the spinal cord?
- What two systems make up the peripheral nervous system? What are the roles of these two systems?
- What are the functions of the sympathetic and parasympathetic nervous systems?

CourseCompass

Web Link: *Endocrine Disorders and Surgery*

CourseCompass

Audio 2.2: *New Research on the Endocrine System*

**Sympathetic Nervous System:** The portion of the autonomic nervous system that readies the body for expenditure of energy.

**Parasympathetic Nervous System:** The portion of the autonomic nervous system that readies the body for restoration of energy.

**Endocrine System:** A system for communication within our bodies; it consists of several glands that secrete hormones directly into the bloodstream.

**Hormones:** Substances secreted by endocrine glands that regulate a wide range of bodily processes.

**Pituitary Gland:** An endocrine gland that releases hormones to regulate other glands and several basic biological processes.

## The Endocrine System: Chemical Regulators of Bodily Processes

The nervous system is our primary system for moving and processing information—for responding to the world around us and to our own internal states. Another system exists as well, however: the **endocrine system,** which consists of a variety of *glands*. Endocrine glands release chemicals called **hormones** directly into the bloodstream. These hormones exert profound effects on a wide range of processes related to basic bodily functions (see Figure 2.8 on page 54). Of special interest to psychologists are *neurohormones*—hormones that interact with and affect the nervous system. Neurohormones, like neurotransmitters, influence neural activity. Because they are released into the circulatory system rather than into synapses, however, they exert their effects more slowly, at a greater distance, and often for longer periods of time than neurotransmitters.

One major part of the endocrine system is the **pituitary gland** (refer to Figure 2.8). It is sometimes described as the master gland of the body, for the hormones it releases control and regulate the actions of other endocrine glands. This gland is also closely connected to important regions of the brain that play a role in emotion—areas we'll discuss in the next section.

The pituitary is really two glands in one, the *posterior pituitary* and the *anterior pituitary.* The posterior pituitary releases hormones that regulate reabsorption of water by the kidneys and, in females, the production and release of milk. It is the

**Figure 2.7**
**The Autonomic Nervous System: An Overview**

The autonomic nervous system consists of two major parts, the sympathetic and parasympathetic nervous systems. Some of the functions of each are shown here. (*Source:* Carlson, 1999.)

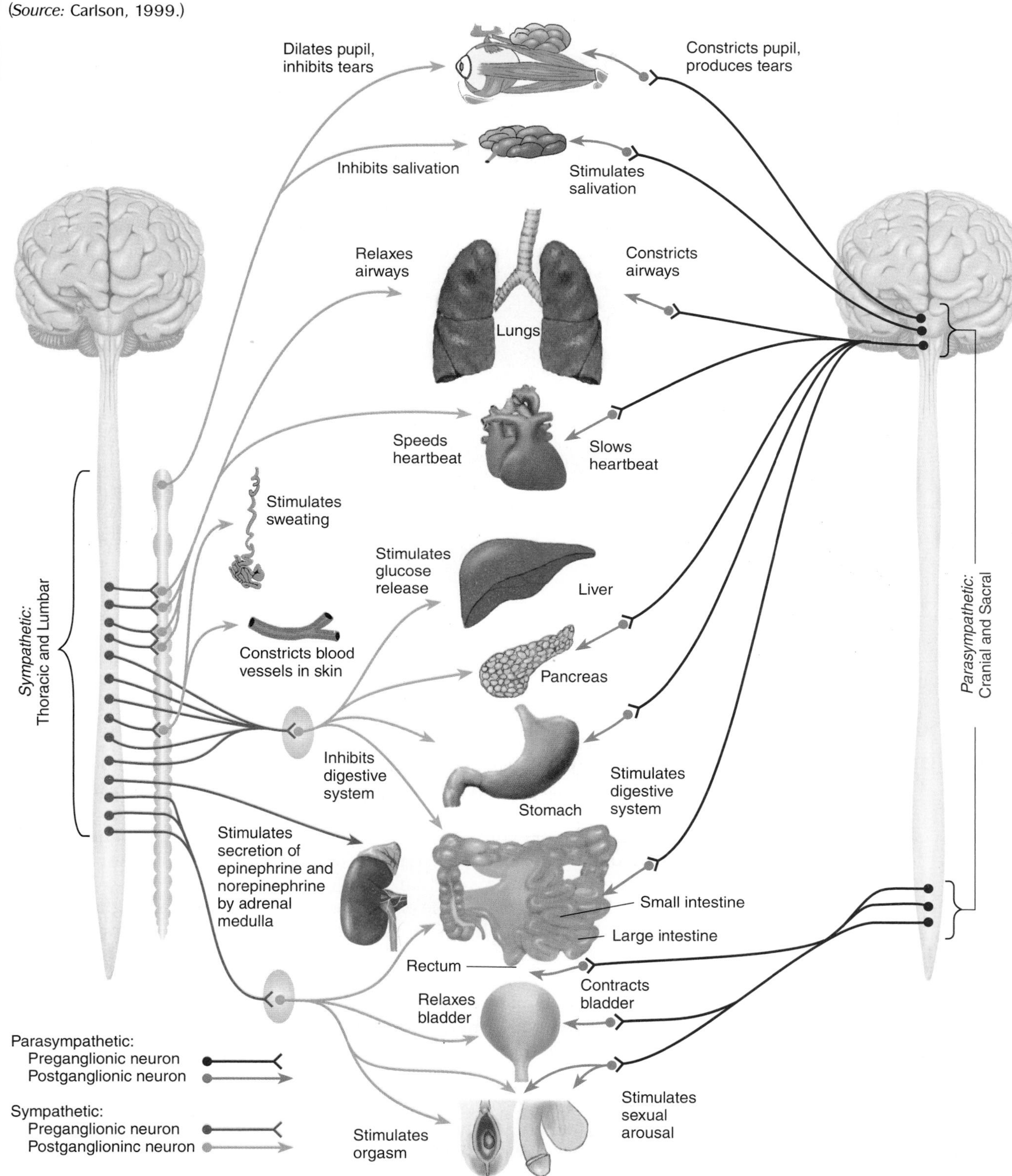

**Figure 2.8**
**The Endocrine System**

The endocrine system consists of several glands. The location of key glands are shown here.

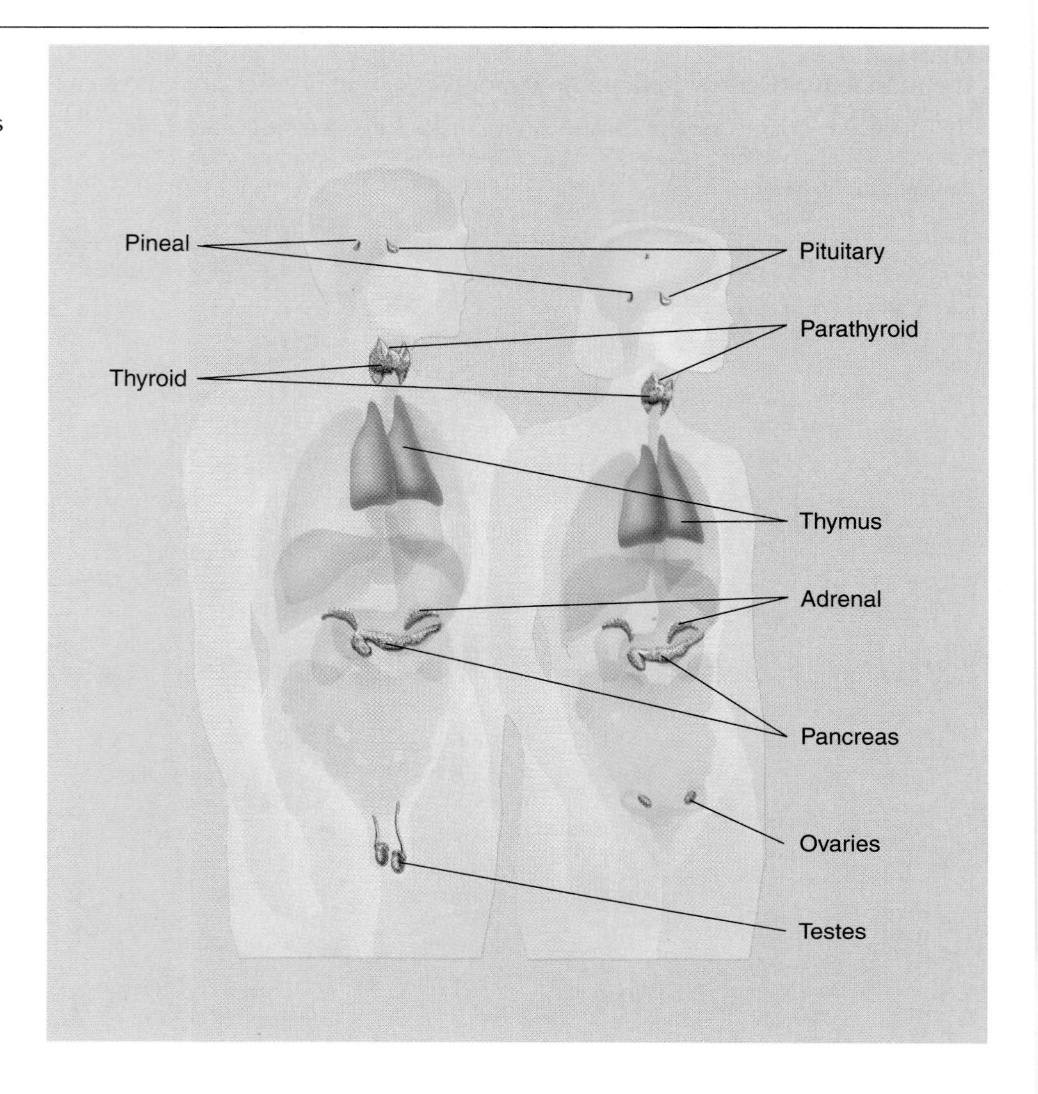


anterior pituitary that releases the hormones that regulate the activity of other endocrine glands. One such hormone, ACTH, stimulates the outer layer of the adrenal gland, the *adrenal cortex,* causing it to secrete cortisone. Cortisone, in turn, affects cells in many parts of the body. The pituitary also secretes hormones that influence sexual development, govern the functioning of the sexual glands (regulating the amount of hormones they release), and help control basic bodily functions relating to metabolism and excretion.

Another important part of the endocrine system is the **adrenal glands,** which sit on top of the kidneys. In response to messages from the autonomic nervous system, the adrenal glands release *epinephrine* and *norepinephrine* (also known as *adrenaline* and *noradrenaline*). These hormones help the body handle emergencies—increasing heart rate, blood pressure, and sugar in the blood. The location and function of these and other parts of the endocrine system (e.g., the thyroid gland, which plays a role in the regulation of metabolism) are shown in Figure 2.8.

**Adrenal Glands:** Glands that release hormones to help the body handle emergencies by, for example, increasing heart rate, blood pressure, and blood sugar levels.

**REVIEW QUESTIONS**

- What is the endocrine system?
- What are some of its major parts?

# The Brain: Where Consciousness . . . Is

Have you ever read *The Hitchhiker's Guide to the Galaxy* or seen it on television? It is a humorous science fiction story filled with interesting characters. One of them, however, always caught my attention. It was a huge, mile-high computer known as Deep Thought. And it was brilliant; in fact, it was designed to answer the following question: "What is the nature of the universe?" The computer's reply: "Tricky, very tricky . . . you'll have to wait." And then it took several million years to come up with the answer. (I won't tell you what it was—read the book!) The main point is that this computer was, supposedly, a fully conscious being. But while such computers exist in science fiction, they are a long way off on this planet. Modern computers are impressive, but none can match the amazing abilities packed within the three pounds of the human brain. And even if we could build a computer as brilliant as Deep Thought, it could not, as far as we can tell, have the emotional experiences, imagery, insights, desires, motives, and creativity of the human brain (see Figure 2.9). Our brain is a marvelous organ indeed!

Not surprisingly, this impressive performance requires a complex organ, and the brain certainly meets that description. For our purposes, though, it can be divided into three major components: portions concerned with basic bodily functions and survival; portions concerned with motivation and emotion; and portions concerned with our higher mental processes, including language, planning, problem solving, and reasoning.

**Medulla:** A structure in the brain concerned with the regulation of vital bodily functions such as breathing and heartbeat.

**Pons:** A portion of the brain through which sensory and motor information passes and which contains structures relating to sleep, arousal, and the regulation of muscle tone and cardiac reflexes.

**Reticular Activating System:** A structure within the brain concerned with sleep, arousal, and the regulation of muscle tone and cardiac reflexes.

Web Link: *Virtual Hospital—The Human Brain*

## The Brain Stem: Survival Basics

Let's begin with the basics: the structures in the brain that regulate the bodily processes we share with many other life forms on earth. These structures are located in the *brain stem,* the portion of the brain that begins just above the spinal cord and continues into the center of this complex organ (refer to Figure 2.10 on page 56).

Two of these structures, the **medulla** and the **pons,** are located just above the point where the spinal cord enters the brain. Major sensory and motor pathways pass through both of these structures on their way to higher brain centers or down to effectors (muscles or glands) in other parts of the body. In addition, both the medulla and the pons contain a central core consisting of a dense network of interconnected neurons. This is the **reticular activating system,** and it has long been viewed as a part of the brain that plays a key role in sleep and arousal—a topic I'll discuss in greater detail in Chapter 4. Recent evidence, however, indicates that the reticular activating system is also concerned with many other functions, such as muscle tone, cardiac and circulatory reflexes, and attention (Pinel, 1993). Thus, referring to it as a single "system" is somewhat misleading. The medulla contains several *nuclei*—collections of neuron cell bodies—that control vital functions such as breathing, heart rate, and blood pressure, as well as coughing and sneezing.

**Figure 2.9**
**The Thinking, Feeling Computer?**

Impressive as they are, modern computers do not even come close to matching the impressive abilities of the human brain. And, in contrast to what this cartoon suggests, they do not, as far as we can tell, possess the emotions, desires, or consciousness that make us human. (*Source:* © The New Yorker Collection. 1983. Warren Miller from cartoonbank.com. All rights reserved.)

**Figure 2.10**
**Basic Structure of the Human Brain**

In this simplified drawing, the brain has been split down the middle to reveal its inner structure, the way you would cut an apple in half through its core.

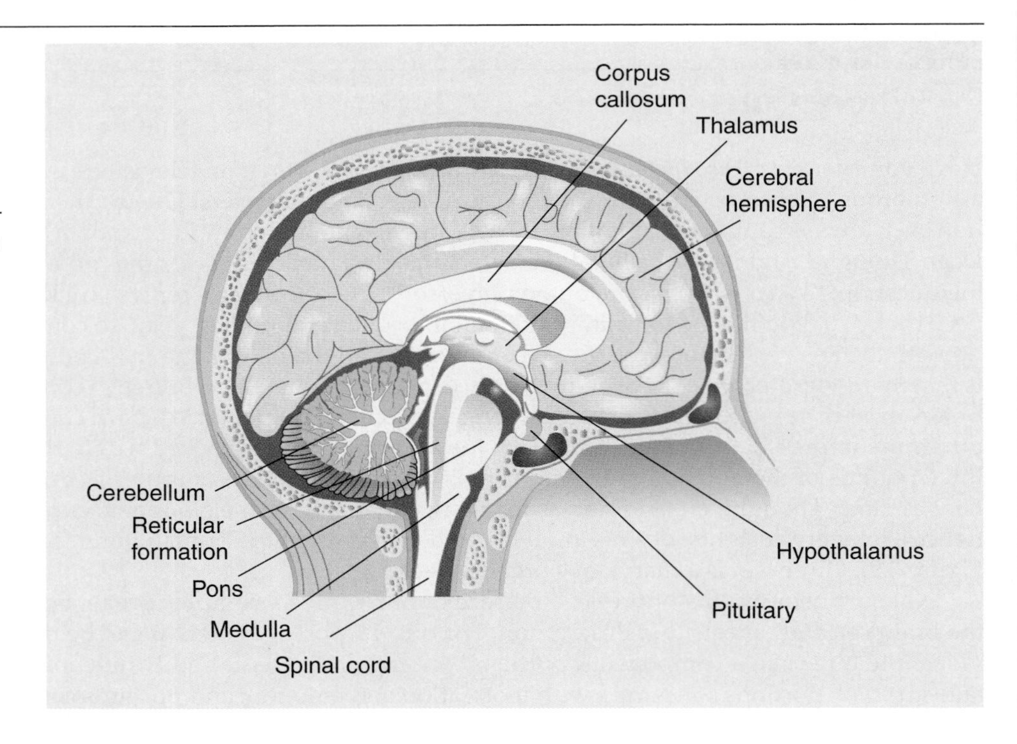


Behind the medulla and pons is the **cerebellum** (refer again to Figure 2.10). It is primarily concerned with the regulation of motor activities, serving to orchestrate muscular activities so that they occur in a synchronized fashion. Damage to the cerebellum results in jerky, poorly coordinated muscle functioning. If such damage is severe, it may be impossible for a person to stand, let alone to walk or run. In addition, the cerebellum may also play a role in certain cognitive processes, such as learning (e.g., Daum et al., 1993).

Above the medulla and pons, near the end of the brain stem, is a structure known as the **midbrain.** It contains an extension of the reticular activating system as well as primitive centers concerned with vision and hearing: the *superior colliculi* (vision) and the *inferior colliculi* (hearing). The midbrain also contains structures that play a role in such varied functions as the pain-relieving effects of opiates and the guidance and control of motor movements by sensory input.

**Cerebellum:** A part of the brain concerned with the regulation of basic motor activities.

**Midbrain:** A part of the brain containing primitive centers for vision and hearing. It also plays a role in the regulation of visual reflexes.

**Hypothalamus:** A small structure deep within the brain that plays a key role in the regulation of the autonomic nervous system and of several forms of motivated behavior such as eating and aggression.

## The Hypothalamus, Thalamus, and Limbic System: Motivation and Emotion

Ancient philosophers identified the heart as the center of our emotions. While this poetic belief is still reflected on many valentine cards, modern science indicates that it is wrong. If there is indeed a center for our appetites, emotions, and motives, it actually lies deep within the brain in several interrelated structures, including the *hypothalamus, thalamus,* and the *limbic system.*

Although the **hypothalamus** is less than one cubic centimeter in size, this tiny structure exerts profound effects on our behavior. First, it regulates the autonomic nervous system, thus influencing reactions ranging from sweating and salivating to the shedding of tears and changes in blood pressure. Second, it plays a key role in *homeostasis*—the maintenance of the body's internal environment at optimal levels. Third, the hypothalamus seems to play a role in the regulation of eating and drinking. Initial studies seemed to indicate that damage to the *ventromedial* portion of the hypothalamus caused laboratory animals (usually rats) to overeat—to the point of obesity, in fact. In contrast, damage to the *lateral hypothalamus* resulted in reduced food intake and a generally reduced responsiveness to all sensory input. In short, the role of the hypothalamus seemed clear. However, these results were called into question when it was discovered that the procedures used to damage structures within the hypothalamus also destroyed fibers passing through the hypothalamus en route to other structures.

The results of additional studies reveal a more sharply defined role for the lateral hypothalamus: It coordinates communication between the parts of the brain that monitor and regulate aspects of the body's internal state (including thirst and hunger) and the frontal cortex—the structure responsible for planning and executing behavior (Winn, 1995). Thus, when damage is confined strictly to cells of the lateral hypothalamus, the brain continues its monitoring function, thereby detecting the need to eat or drink. However, this information does not reach the frontal cortex. As a result, this information is not converted into action—eating. (Please see Chapter 10 for further discussion of the regulation of eating and of several eating disorders.)

The hypothalamus also plays a role in other forms of motivated behavior, such as mating and aggression. It exerts this influence, at least in part, by regulating the release of hormones from the *pituitary gland.*

Above the hypothalamus, quite close to the center of the brain, is another important structure, the **thalamus.** This structure consists of two football-shaped parts, one in each hemisphere. This has sometimes been called the great relay station of the brain, and with good reason. The thalamus receives input from all of our senses except olfaction (smell), performs some preliminary analyses, and then transmits the information to other parts of the brain.

Finally, we should consider a set of structures that together are known as the **limbic system.** The structures that make up the limbic system play an important role in emotion and in motivated behavior, such as feeding, fleeing from danger, fighting, and sex. The largest of these structures, the **hippocampus,** plays a key role in the formation of memories (e.g., Eichenbaum & Bunsey, 1995; Gluck & Myers, 1995), a topic we'll consider in Chapter 6. The **amygdala,** also part of the limbic system, is involved in aspects of emotional control and in the formation of emotional memories. In animals, damage to this structure can produce striking differences in behavior; for example, a typically docile cat may become uncontrollably violent. Much more disturbing, recent findings indicate that dysfunctions in the limbic system—or in other parts of the brain that influence it—may play a role in human violence. For a discussion of this issue, please see the **Beyond the Headlines** section below.

**Thalamus:** A structure deep within the brain that receives sensory input from other portions of the nervous system and then transmits this information to the cerebral hemispheres and other parts of the brain.

**Limbic System:** Several structures deep within the brain that play a role in emotional reactions and behavior.

**Hippocampus:** A structure of the limbic system that plays a role in the formation of certain types of memories.

**Amygdala:** A limbic system structure involved in aspects of emotional control and formation of emotional memories.

## the HEADLINES: *As Psychologists See It*

## Is Violence the Result of Faulty Neural Brakes?

### Researchers Link Violence to Dysfunction in Brain

WASHINGTON POST (APRIL 14, 1998)—An engineer described as friendly and outgoing flies into a rage during a family argument and beats his wife and 13-month-old daughter to death with a champagne bottle. . . . A young man who has a "quick temper" goes back to the auto parts store from which he'd been fired and kills three of his former coworkers. . . . Sociologists, psychiatrists, criminologists and others have long struggled to understand what makes some people turn violent. Childhood abuse clearly can be a factor, but researchers have wondered whether some people are born with the tendency—and a new report suggests some are.

In the first study of its kind, neuroscientists used high-tech imaging technology to peer inside the minds of killers to try to determine whether their brains differ in some fundamental way. The researchers found evidence that some people are born with brains that may make them prone to violence . . . specifically, the part of their brains involved in creating a sense of "conscience" may be dysfunctional. . . . The researchers found that 26 murderers from comparatively benign backgrounds, who had not suffered child abuse, showed 14.2% less activity in a part of the medial prefrontal cortex known as the orbitofrontal cortex on the right hemisphere. The medial prefrontal cortex, located just behind the forehead, has been shown in animal research to be involved in inhibiting the limbic system, a region . . . that produces aggressive behavior. Animal research also has shown that the right orbitofrontal cortex is involved in fear conditioning—the association between antisocial behavior and punishment that in humans is thought to be key to developing a conscience. "When you train a dog, you punish it every time it does something wrong. A conscience is really just a set of conditioned responses," Andrian Raine, leader of the research team, noted. "There are a lot of factors involved in crime," Raine added, "and brain function is just one of those. But by understanding the brain function, we will be in a much better position to understand the complete causes of violent behavior."

A neural basis for conscience and for violent behavior? Wow! And the results do sound convincing: Among a group of murderers, a region of the brain that acts as a neural brake on another region (the limbic system) known to be involved in aggression showed reduced activity.

But there are some potential problems in this interpretation. First, we can't tell whether this reduced activity is the cause of the violent behavior shown by these people or the result of it. Other research indicates that after committing aggressive crimes, or perhaps simply after repeated exposure to films or television shows containing violence, many persons demonstrate reduced arousal in response to the pain and suffering of others (e.g., Baron, 1993a). Thus, it is possible that the murderers studied in this research showed reduced activity in their neural "braking" systems as a result of having engaged in violence rather than the reverse. Second, murderers—especially ones who commit the kind of unpremeditated violent actions shown by these persons—are a special group; they may differ from other people in many ways, and it may be *these* differences, not reductions in neural activity in a specific part of their brains, that are responsible for their behavior. Third, the size of this sample is very small—only twenty-six persons; moreover, we don't know if they are representative of all persons who commit such violent crimes. And finally, it is always risky to jump from studies with animals to humans; the fact that the right orbitofrontal cortex plays a role in fear conditioning for animals in no way guarantees that it plays the same function for humans. For all these reasons, it is probably best to view these findings as suggestive rather than conclusive.

Still, this study provides a clear example of current efforts to understand the role of various portions of the brain in key aspects of human behavior, so I don't want to sound too critical of it. On the contrary, such research has already added greatly to our understanding of important brain-to-behavior links, and will certainly continue to do so in the future. But this doesn't mean we should jump to hasty conclusions, either; that would be a violation of the basic rules of science that are the foundation of all psychological research.

### CRITICAL THINKING QUESTIONS

1. Suppose that other research confirms the findings described in the report; what would be the practical implications?
2. If some people are born with brain dysfunctions that predispose them toward violence, does this mean that they will necessarily engage in such behavior?
3. Do you think the lack of a conscience plays a key role in the kind of violent unpremeditated explosions shown by the persons studied in this research? Why or why not?

Web Link: *The Phineas Gage Information Page*

**Cerebral Cortex:** The outer covering of the cerebral hemispheres.

## The Cerebral Cortex: The Core of Complex Thought

Now, at last, we come to the part of the brain that seems to be responsible for our ability to reason, plan, remember, and imagine—the **cerebral cortex.** This outer surface of the brain is only about one eighth of an inch thick, but it contains billions of neurons, each one connected to thousands of others. The predominance of cell bod-

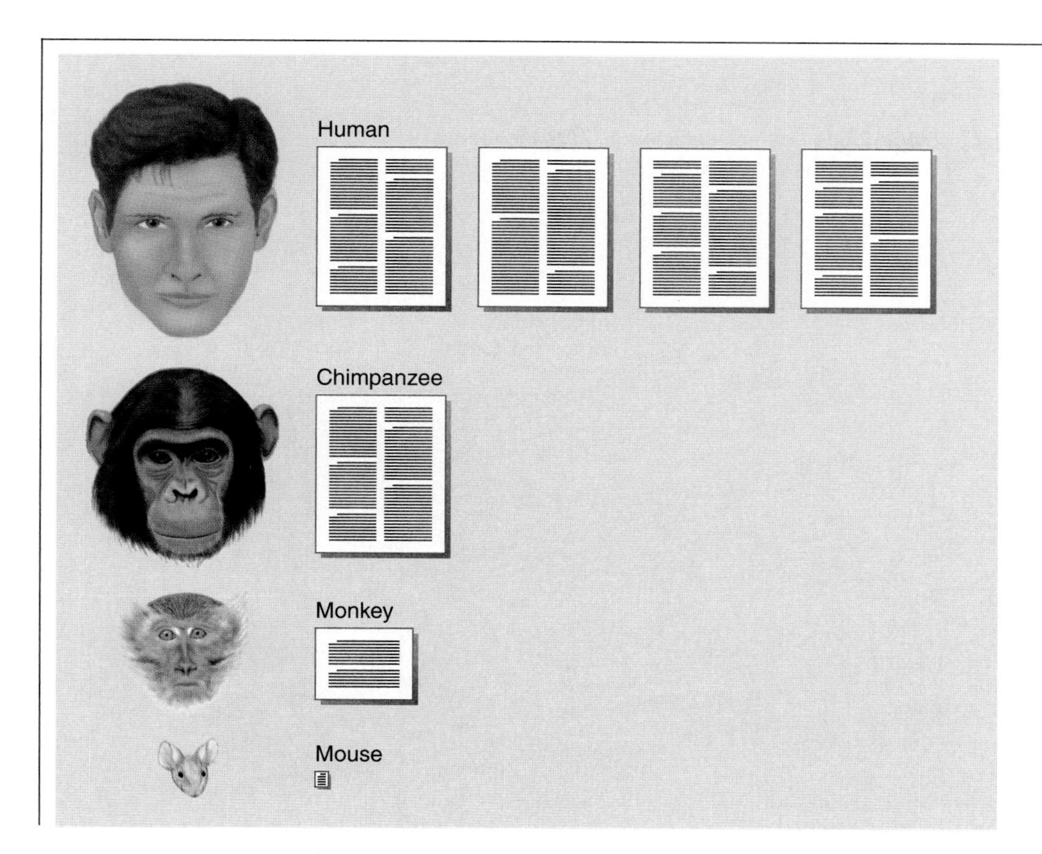


**Figure 2.11**
**Our Cerebral Cortex: Truly "Giant Size" Compared to That of Other Species**

As shown here, the human cerebral cortex is much larger in area than that of other species. If it were not folded, we would need much larger skulls to hold it.

Web Link: *Neuropsychology Central*

ies gives the cortex a brownish-gray color. Because of its appearance, the cortex is often referred to as gray matter. Beneath the cortex are myelin-sheathed axons connecting the neurons of the cortex with those of other parts of the brain. The large concentrations of myelin gives this tissue an opaque appearance, and hence it is often referred to as white matter. It is important to note that the cortex is divided into two nearly symmetrical halves, the *cerebral hemispheres.* Thus, many of the structures described in the following sections appear in both the left and right cerebral hemispheres. As we'll soon see, however, this similarity in structure is not entirely matched by similarity in function. The two hemispheres appear to be somewhat specialized in the functions they perform.

In humans, the cerebral hemispheres are folded into many ridges and grooves. In other organisms, there are fewer folds or no folds at all. The result is that the human cortex covers much more area than is true in other species (see Figure 2.11). Each hemisphere is usually described, on the basis of the largest of these grooves or fissures, as being divided into four distinct regions or lobes: the frontal, parietal, occipital, and temporal lobes. We'll discuss each in detail next.

**THE FRONTAL LOBE** Occupying the area of the brain nearest the face, the **frontal lobe** is bounded by the deep *central fissure.* Lying along this fissure, just within the frontal lobe, is the *motor cortex,* an area concerned with the control of body movements (see Figure 2.12 on page 60). Damage to this area does not produce total paralysis. Instead, it often results in a loss of control over fine movements, especially of the fingers. This illustrates an important fact about the human brain: While a specific area may normally perform a given function, other regions can often take up the slack if that area is damaged and may gradually come to perform the same functions. Such *plasticity,* as it is often termed, is greater at a young age than after maturity, but it seems to operate to some extent throughout life.

**Frontal Lobe:** The portion of the cerebral cortex that lies in front of the central fissure.

**Figure 2.12**
**Major Regions of the Cerebral Cortex**

The cerebral cortex is divided into four major lobes *(left).* Specific areas in these lobes are concerned with sensory and motor functions, as well as with our higher mental processes *(right).*

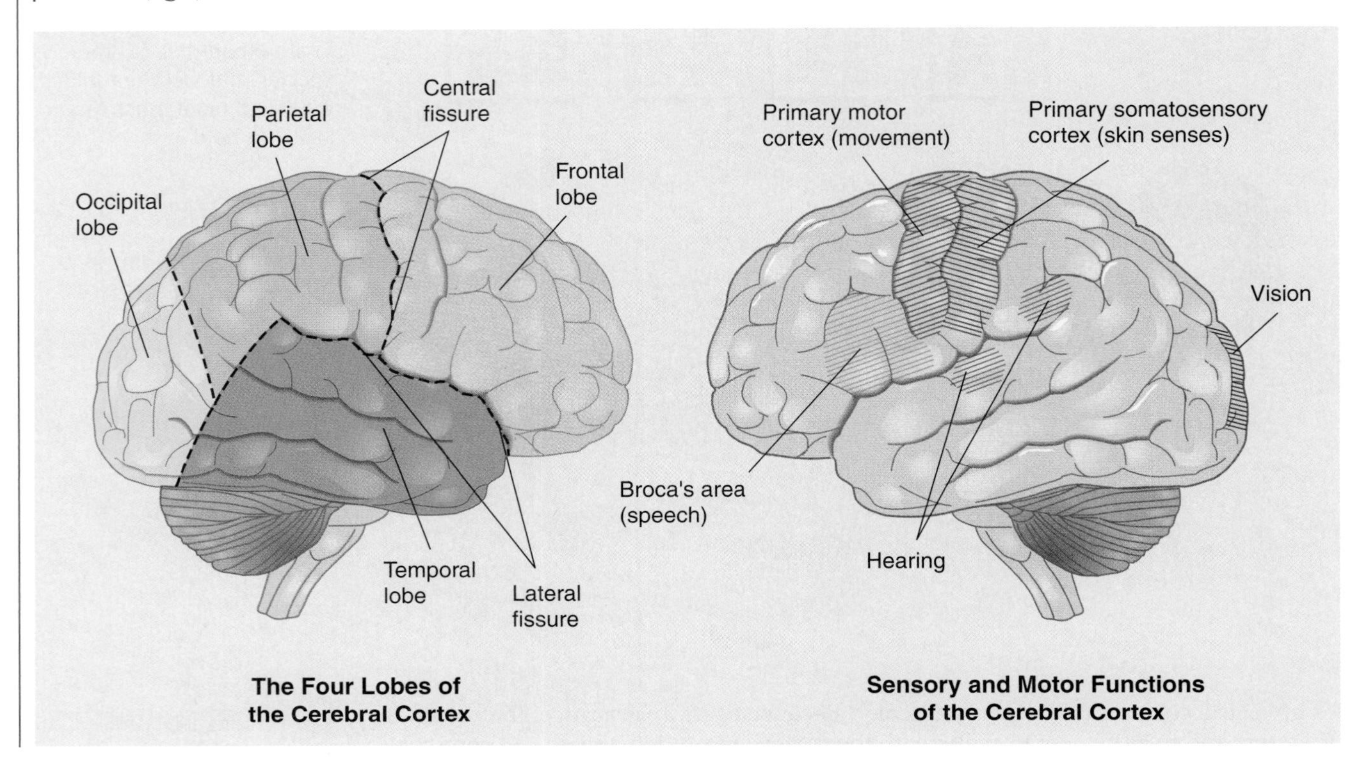


**THE PARIETAL LOBE** Across the central fissure from the frontal lobe is the **parietal lobe.** This area contains the *somatosensory cortex,* to which information from the skin senses—touch, temperature, pressure, and so on—is carried (refer to Figure 2.12). Discrete damage to this area produces a variety of effects, depending in part on whether injury occurs to the left or right cerebral hemisphere. If damage involves the left hemisphere, individuals may lose the ability to read or write, or they may have difficulty knowing where parts of their own body are located. In contrast, if damage occurs in the right hemisphere, individuals may seem unaware of the left side of their body. For example, a man may forget to shave the left side of his face.

**Parietal Lobe:** A portion of the cerebral cortex, lying behind the central fissure, that plays a major role in the skin senses: touch, temperature, pressure.

**Occipital Lobe:** The portion of the cerebral cortex involved in vision.

**Temporal Lobe:** The lobe of the cerebral cortex that is involved in hearing.

**THE OCCIPITAL LOBE** The **occipital lobe** is located near the back of the head. Its primary functions are visual, and it contains a sensory area that receives input from the eyes. Damage to this area often produces a "hole" in the person's field of vision: Objects in a particular location can't be seen, but the rest of the visual field may remain unaffected. As with other brain structures, injury to the occipital lobe may produce contrasting effects depending on which cerebral hemisphere is affected. Damage to the occipital lobe in the right hemisphere produces loss of vision in the left visual field, whereas damage to the occipital lobe in the left hemisphere produces loss of vision in the right visual field.

**THE TEMPORAL LOBE** Finally, the **temporal lobe** is located along the side of each hemisphere (see Figure 2.12). The location makes sense, for this lobe plays a key role in hearing and contains a sensory area that receives input from the ears. Damage to the temporal lobe, too, can result in intriguing symptoms. When such injuries occur in the left hemisphere, people may lose the ability to understand spoken words. When damage is restricted to the right hemisphere, they may be able to recognize speech but may lose the ability to recognize other organizations of sound—for example, melodies, tones, or rhythms. We'll examine the neural mechanisms that play a role in human speech in more detail in a later section.

It is interesting to note that when added together, areas of the cortex that either control motor movements (*motor cortex*) or receive sensory input (*sensory cortex*) account for only 20 to 25 percent of the total area. The remainder is known as the *association cortex* and, as its name suggests, is assumed to play a critical role in integrating the activities in the various sensory systems and in translating sensory input into programs for motor output. In addition, the association cortex seems to be involved in complex cognitive activities such as thinking, reasoning, remembering, language, recognizing faces, and a host of other complex cognitive functions. I'll return to several of these in the next major section.

**REVIEW QUESTIONS**

- What structures make up the brain stem? What are their functions?
- What are the functions of the hypothalamus and thalamus?
- What evidence suggests that brain dysfunctions may play a role in violence?
- What is the role of the cerebral cortex?

**Food for Thought**

Suppose that research clearly identified certain parts of the brain that, when they malfunction, cause persons to engage in violence. Would it be ethical to perform operations on these persons to repair these malfunctioning areas?

## Two Minds in One Body? Our Divided Brains

Web Link: *Splitting the Human Brain*

At first glance, the two hemispheres of the brain appear to be mirror images of one another. Yet a large body of evidence suggests that the cerebral hemispheres do differ, if not in appearance, then in terms of function. In fact, the right and left hemispheres show a considerable degree of **lateralization of function:** Each specializes, to an extent, in the performance of somewhat different tasks. In general terms the left hemisphere is the verbal hemisphere—it is specialized for speech and other verbal tasks. In contrast, the right specializes in the control of certain motor movements, in synthesis (putting isolated elements together), and in the comprehension and communication of emotion. Evidence from two kinds of research points to these conclusions: (1) studies of persons whose cerebral hemispheres have been isolated from each other through either accident or (more typically) surgery performed for medical reasons, and (2) studies of the rest of us—persons in whom the two cerebral hemispheres are connected in the normal way.

**RESEARCH WITH SPLIT-BRAIN PERSONS** Under normal conditions, the two hemispheres of the brain communicate with each other through the **corpus callosum,** a wide band of nerve fibers that passes between them (Hoptman & Davidson, 1994). Sometimes, though, it is necessary to cut this link for medical reasons—for example, to prevent the spread of epileptic seizures from one hemisphere to the other. Such operations largely eliminate communication between the two hemispheres, so they provide a unique opportunity to study the effects that result. Careful study of individuals who have undergone such operations provides intriguing

**Lateralization of Function:** Specialization of the two hemispheres of the brain for the performance of different functions.

**Corpus Callosum:** A band of nerve fibers connecting the two hemispheres of the brain.

**Figure 2.13**
**Some Intriguing Effects of Severing the Corpus Callosum**

A man whose corpus callosum has been cut stares at a central point on a screen. The word *tenant* is flashed across the screen so that the letters *ten* appear to the left of the central point and the letters *ant* appear to the right. Because of the way our visual system is constructed, stimuli presented to the *left* visual field of each eye stimulate only the *right* hemisphere of the brain; items on the *right* side of the visual field of each eye stimulate only the *left* hemisphere. Therefore, when asked "What do you see?" the man answers: "Ant." But when asked to *point* to the word he saw with his left hand he points to the "ten" in the word "tenant." Findings such as these provide evidence for lateralization of function in the two cerebral hemispheres.

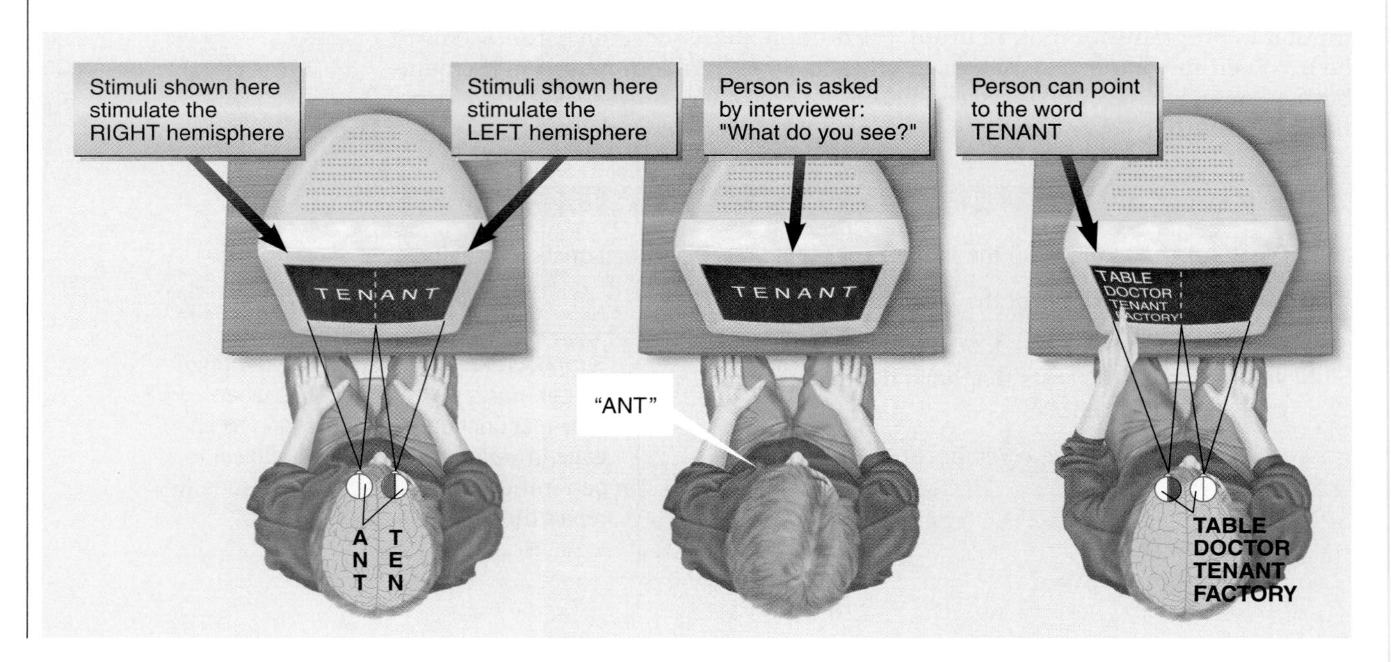


evidence for the view that the two hemispheres of the brain are indeed specialized for performing different tasks (Gazzaniga, 1984, 1985; Sperry, 1968).

Consider, for instance, the following demonstration. A man whose corpus callosum has been cut is seated before a screen and told to stare, with his eyes as motionless as possible, at a central point on the screen. Then simple words such as *tenant* are flashed across the screen so that the letters *ten* appear to the left of the central point and the letters *ant* appear to the right. What does the man report seeing? Before you guess, consider the following fact: Because of the way our visual system is constructed, stimuli presented to the *left* visual field of each eye stimulate only the *right* hemisphere of the brain; items on the *right* side of the visual field of each eye stimulate only the *left* hemisphere.

Now, what do you think our split-brain person reports? If you said "ant," you are correct; see Figure 2.13. This would be expected, because only the left hemisphere, which controls speech, can answer verbally. However, when asked to *point* to the word he saw with his left hand (which is controlled by the right hemisphere), the man reacts differently: He points with his left hand to the word *ten* (part of the word *tenant*). So the right hemisphere has indeed seen and recognized this stimulus; it can't describe it in words, but it can point to it. Thus, the fact that the right hemisphere is less verbal than the left does not mean that it is inferior in other respects. In fact, it is *superior* to the left hemisphere in copying drawings, recognizing faces, and expressing emotion. For instance, look at the photos in Figure 2.14.

Which one shows the emotion of disgust most clearly? Most people choose the photo on the right (photo number 3). Now consider the nature of these photos. The one in the middle is a photo of an actual person. Photo number 1 is based only on the right side of his face—it was constructed by taking the right side and a mirror image of the right side and pasting these together. Photo number 3, in contrast, is based on the left side only—the side controlled by the right hemisphere of the brain. So what does the fact that photo 3 shows more intense emotion suggest? That the right hemisphere, which controls expressions on the left side of the face, is better at expressing emotion (e.g., Sackheim & Gur, 1978).

**Figure 2.14**
**Evidence for Superiority of the Right Hemisphere in the Expression of Emotions**

Which face shows most clearly the emotion of disgust? Most people choose photo 3, which is constructed from mirror images of the *left* side of the face—the side controlled by the right cerebral hemisphere. In contrast, photo 1 is constructed from mirror images of the *right* side of the face—the side controlled by the left hemisphere. It seems to show much less intense emotion. (Photo 2 shows the person as he really appears.)
(*Source:* Sachkheim & Gur, 1978.)

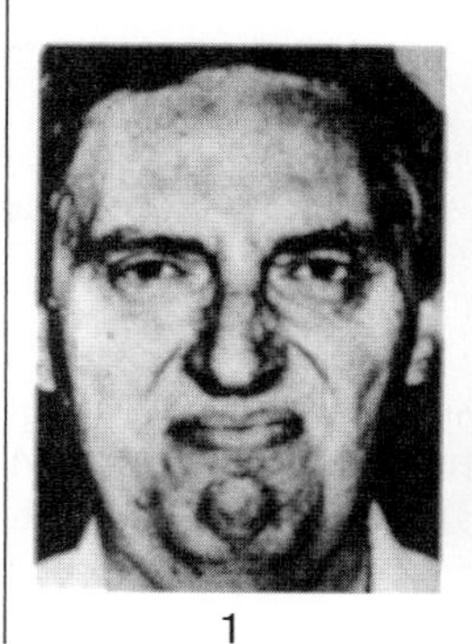
1

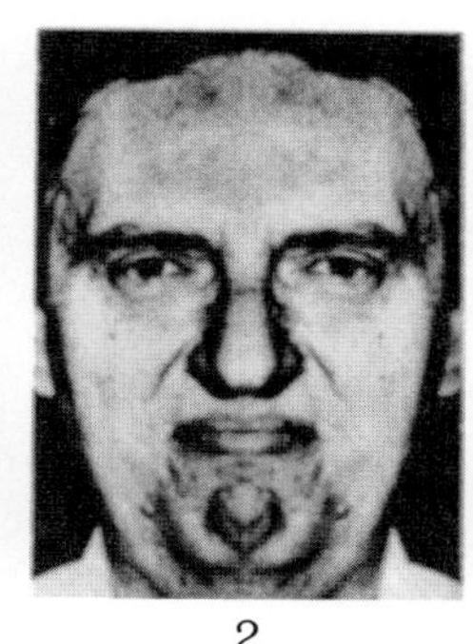
2

3

**RESEARCH WITH PERSONS WHOSE HEMISPHERES ARE CONNECTED** Additional evidence for specialization of function in the two hemispheres is provided by research on persons whose corpus callosum is intact—as in the great majority of us. For instance, consider the following kind of research, conducted with persons who are about to undergo brain surgery. First, participants are asked to describe traumatic emotional events (e.g., a near fatal traffic accident). Not surprisingly, they do so in vivid terms. Then, as preparation for surgery, they receive a drug injected into an artery that leads to the right hemisphere; as a result, this hemisphere is anesthetized. When asked to describe the same events again, they do so in much less intense terms. This provides evidence for the view that the right hemisphere plays a key role in the experience and expression of emotions (e.g., Ross, Homan, & Buck, 1994).

Studies using a procedure we'll consider in the following **Research Methods** section, known as PET scanning, provide further support for the view that the two hemispheres are specialized for different functions. PET scans can reveal which parts of the brain are active when people perform specific tasks. Studies using this technique indicate that when individuals speak or work with numbers, activity in the left hemisphere increases. In contrast, when they work on perceptual tasks—for instance, tasks in which they compare various shapes—activity increases in the right hemisphere (e.g., Springer & Deutsch, 1985). Interestingly, additional research suggests that while individuals are making up their minds about some issue, activity is higher in the left than in the right hemisphere (Cacioppo, Petty, & Quintanar, 1982). Once logical thought is over and a decision has been made, however, heightened activity occurs in the right hemisphere, which seems to play a larger role in global, nonanalytic thought—for instance, overall reactions of the "I like it" or "I don't like it" type.

In sum, a large body of evidence suggests that in a sense, we *do* seem to possess two minds in one brain: The two cerebral hemispheres are specialized for performing somewhat different asks. We are unaware of this fact in everyday life, because the hemispheres generally work together in a unified manner. Why does such specialization exist? From an evolutionary perspective, the answer might be "Because it is beneficial and increases our chances of survival." For example, it appears that emotional expressions appear sooner on the left side of the face than the right (e.g., Hauser, 1993). This suggests that the right hemisphere, because it is nonverbal, responds to emotion-provoking events more quickly than the left,

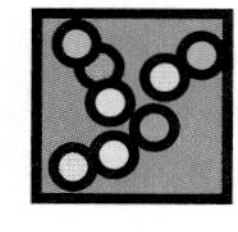

**Figure 2.15**
**The Benefits of Lateralization of Function in the Brain**

As suggested by this cartoon, the fact that our two cerebral hemispheres are specialized for performing somewhat different tasks is beneficial; in fact, it is one more case in which "the whole is greater than the sum of its parts."
(*Source:* © The New Yorker Collection. 1994. George Booth from cartoonbank.com. All rights reserved.)

*"Mama and I fixed a lovely dinner. I used the right side of my brain, and she used the left side of her brain."*

**Electroencephalography (EEG):** A technique for measuring the electrical activity of the brain via electrodes placed at specified locations on the skull.

**Computerized Tomography (CT):** A method of brain scanning in which a series of X-ray images are synthesized and analyzed by computer.

**Magnetic Resonance Imaging (MRI):** A method for studying the intact brain in which technicians obtain images by exposing the brain to a strong magnetic field.

verbal hemisphere. This, in turn, can increase our speed of recognizing potential dangers or threats and so responding to them: Because of specialization of the two hemispheres, we don't have to think in words to recognize a threat—we can respond in a quicker gut-level manner. So, as the cartoon in Figure 2.15 suggests, specialization in our two hemispheres may produce synergy—a case in which the whole is indeed more than the sum of its parts.

Now that we've examined the structure of the brain and the functions of its major parts, we are just about ready to explore its complex and fascinating role in many forms of behavior. Before discussing this topic, however, we'll pause to survey briefly the ingenious methods used by psychologists to find out what happens in our brains, and where this activity occurs, when we speak, reason, and perform many other kinds of behavior. These methods are described in the following **Research Methods** section.

## Research Methods: How Psychologists Study the Nervous System and the Brain

Throughout this chapter, I've stressed the fact that modern technology has provided psychologists and other scientists with an impressive array of new tools for studying the brain—especially for studying the brain in living organisms, including human beings. These new tools are impressive, and worthy of our careful attention. They are not, however, the only techniques available to *physiological psychologists* and other *neuroscientists* (scientists who study the structure and functions of the nervous system). In this section, then, we'll examine not only the newly developed tools but more traditional ones as well. While many procedures for studying the nervous system exist, most fit under these major headings: *observing the effects of damage*—(e.g., damage caused by accidents, disease, medical operations, or experimental procedures); *recording and stimulating neural activity;* and *studying the intact living brain* through new high-tech methods.

### Observing the Effects of Naturally Produced Damage

The world, unfortunately, can be a dangerous place. Many people sustain damage to their brains in automobile or industrial accidents; many others develop illnesses that damage their brains directly, or that lead to medical procedures (e.g., surgery) that cause damage. While these events are tragic for the persons who experience them, they provide psychologists with invaluable research opportunities. By observing the symptoms or deficits shown by such persons, psychologists can sometimes determine what portions of their brains are involved in various forms of behavior. For instance, consider a woman who shows the following baffling set of symptoms. If one object is held in front of her, she can name it. If two objects are held in front of her, however, she will name one of them *but not the other.* In addition, she can recognize that one wooden block is larger than another; but when asked to pick one block up, she fails to adjust the distance between her fingers and thumb according to the size of the object. What is responsible for these strange symptoms? By studying a number of persons who show them, psychologists have determined that the symptoms stem from damage to an area of the brain on the border between the parietal and occipital lobes (e.g., Broussaud, di Pellegrino, & Wise, 1996; Goodale et al., 1994). In many instances, then, studying persons who have experienced damage to areas of their brains can provide valuable information.

### Experimental Ablation: Observing the Effects of Damage

Where human beings are concerned, psychologists must wait for naturally occurring damage to see what effects this produces. But with laboratory animals, it is possible to damage the brain in order to study the effects produced. While this may sound cruel, it is, of course, done under highly humane conditions, and it causes no pain in subjects (the brain has no pain receptors). Usually, researchers damage specific areas of the brain (create brain lesions) by inserting tiny electrodes that emit very high-frequency alternating current. The current produces heat that destroys cells in the chosen area. Because electrodes can be placed with high accuracy (often by means of equipment such as that shown in Figure 2.16), this experimental *ablation* can be a valuable tool for determining the functions of specific regions of the brain.

**Figure 2.16**
**Apparatus for Studying the Brain**

This device (known as *stereotaxic apparatus*) enables psychologists to place tiny electrodes within the brains of animals with great precision.
(*Source:* Carlson, 1999.)

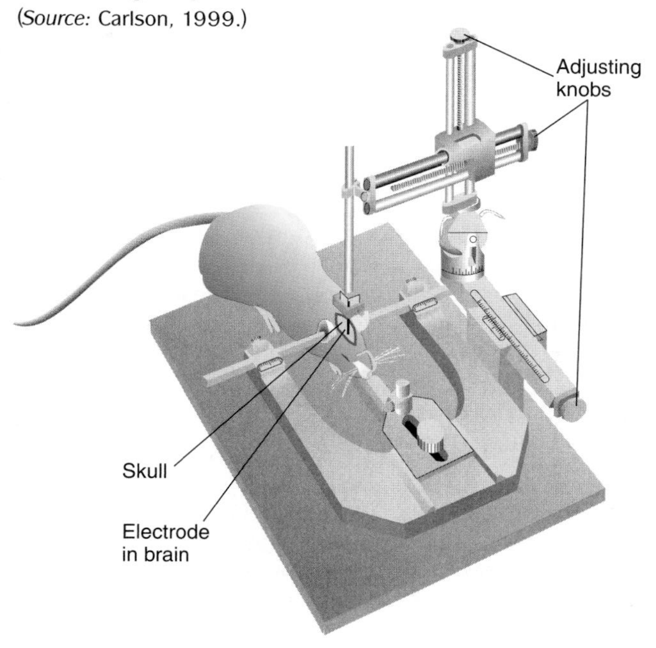


### Recording and Stimulating Neural Activity

A third method for studying the brain involves recording the electrical activity that occurs within it. This can involve recording the activity of individual neurons (with tiny *microelectrodes* implanted into the brain) or of brain regions (with larger *macroelectrodes*). In both cases, changes in patterns of activity that occur in response to specific stimuli, or during various activities, are recorded. (Changes in response to specific stimuli or events are referred to as *event-related brain potentials,* or ERPs for short.) The results can often help researchers identify the specific functions of different regions of the brain. With humans, electrodes cannot generally be implanted in the brain; so recordings are made from the outside of the scalp, a procedure known as **electroencephalography (EEG).**

### Images of the Living, Intact Brain

And now for the newer methods provided by advances in technology. One of these is **computerized tomography (CT).** This procedure uses X rays to scan the patient's head from many different angles. A computer then produces two-dimensional pictures; each picture is like a slice through a loaf of bread or an apple, and these are compared to determine where, for instance, damage to the brain exists. A second and even more valuable procedure for studying the functions of the brain is **magnetic resonance imaging,** or **MRI.** Here, images of the brain are obtained by means of a strong magnetic field. Hydrogen atoms, found in all living tissue, emit measurable waves of energy when exposed to such a field. In MRI, these waves are measured and combined to form images of the brain. These MRI images are impressively clear and therefore extremely useful in the diagnosis of many brain disorders. A recent development is *functional MRI,* in which images can be scanned much more quickly than in the past.

A third recently developed imaging device is called **SQUID**—short for **superconducting quantum interference device.** SQUID produces images based on its ability to detect tiny changes in magnetic fields in the brain. When neurons fire, they create an electric current. Electric currents, in turn, give rise to magnetic fields that the SQUID interprets as neural activity. Researchers have used SQUIDs to map various brain functions, including constructing a representation of the hearing part of the brain.

Finally, scientists use **positron emission tomography,** or **PET,** scans to see what's happening in the brain as it performs various functions. PET scans accomplish this by measuring blood flow in various neural areas, or by gauging the rate at which glucose, the brain's fuel, is metabolized. Individuals undergoing PET scans are injected with small amounts of harmless radioactive isotopes attached to either water or glucose molecules. Blood flow (containing the radioactive water molecules) is greatest in the most active areas of the brain. Similarly, glucose is absorbed by brain cells in proportion to their level of activity, with the most active cells taking in the greatest amount of glucose. As a result, PET scans allow scientists to map activity in various parts of a person's brain as she or he reads, listens to music, or engages in a mental activity such as solving math problems. For instance, look at the PET scans in Figure 2.17. The top row shows activity while a person is in a relaxed state; the lower scans show the same person's brain while he is clenching and unclenching his fist. Scans can be made while people perform almost any activity you can imagine, or in order to compare persons with various mental disorders with persons who do not show such disorders. As you can guess, PET scans provide psychologists with an extremely valuable tool.

Now that I've described the basic methods used by psychologists to study the brain, let's see what recent research using such methods has revealed. These methods have definitely lived up to their promise; they have added tremendously to our knowledge of the intricate—and intimate—links between the brain and behavior.

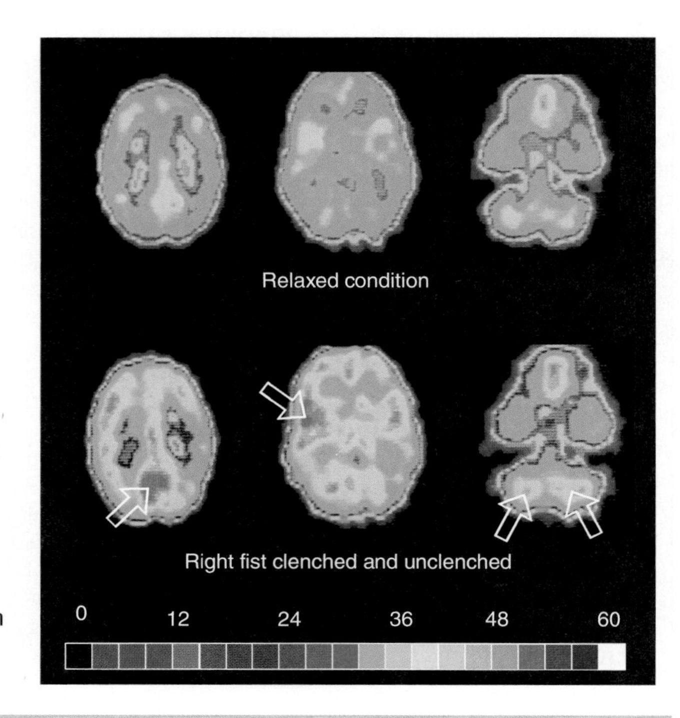


**Figure 2.17**
**PET Scans: An Example**

PET scans reveal the amount of activity occurring in different parts of the brain as individuals perform various tasks. The scans in the top row were made while the individual was at rest. The ones in the bottom row were made as he clenched his right fist and then unclenched it. Clearly, this motor action was associated with increased activity in many parts of the brain. (The brighter the color, the more activity, as shown in the color chart below the photos.)
(*Source:* SUNY/Brookhaven National Laboratory.)

**REVIEW QUESTIONS**

- Who are "split-brain" persons? What evidence do they provide for specialization of functions in the two cerebral hemispheres?
- What evidence from persons with intact brains supports such specialization?
- What methods are used by psychologists to study the brain and its role in behavior?

Web Link: *Gender and the Brain*

**SQUID (Superconducting Quantum Interference Device):** An imaging technique that captures images of the brain through its ability to detect tiny changes in magnetic fields in the brain.

**Positron Emission Tomography (PET):** An imaging technique that detects the activity of the brain by measuring glucose utilization or blood flow.

## The Brain and Human Behavior: Where Biology and Consciousness Meet

Armed with the new techniques and procedures described in the Research Methods section on page 64, psychologists and other scientists have begun to understand how the brain functions to produce human consciousness—our perceptions of the world around us, our thoughts and memories, our emotions. As you can probably guess, the findings of this research are complex; but they also tell a fascinating story. So read on for a look at one of the true cutting edges of modern science.

## How the Brain Functions: An Example from Visual Perception

So far, we've taken the brain apart, examining its major parts and considering evidence that the two hemispheres are specialized for somewhat different tasks. Let's now try to put it back together by looking at how, according to modern research, the brain actually functions. I could illustrate this perspective in many ways; but our knowledge of visual perception—how we perceive the color, shape, and location of physical objects—is perhaps the most advanced, so it is a good place to begin.

Let's start with this question: Do modern computers provide a good model of how the brain works? As we'll see in Chapter 6, such a model has been useful in the study of memory, because our brains and computers do seem similar in certain respects. Both can receive information, enter it into storage (memory), and retrieve it at a later time. But, in fact, computers and the human brain are different in a fundamental way. Modern computers are *serial* devices: They work on information one step at a time. In contrast, our brains appear to process information in a *parallel* fashion; this means that many *modules*—collections of interconnected neurons—process information in different ways simultaneously. These modules may be scattered at widely different locations in the brain. Moreover, each may work on a different aspect of a task. The more complex the task, the greater the number of modules that are called into operation. The result is that even very complex tasks can be handled very quickly, because different aspects of them are performed at the same time. In contrast, a computer proceeds in a serial manner, working on one step at a time, and this can result in slower performance, especially for complex tasks.

As a concrete illustration of this difference, let's consider visual perception. We could readily program modern computers to differentiate between simple shapes such as triangles and squares. How would the computer do this? If we started with a drawing of, for instance, a triangle, this could be scanned by an input device (e.g., a scanner). The computer (really, its program) would then use this information to calculate the location of each line in the drawing, the angles between lines, and so on. It would then compare this information to definitions of "triangle" and "square" previously entered into its memory (or the program) and would classify each figure as a "triangle" or "square" depending on how closely it matched these definitions. So far so good. But what if we wanted the computer to recognize human faces? The program for *this* task would be truly immense, and step-by-step serial processing might take a long time indeed. In contrast, because our brains employ parallel processing by large numbers of modules, we can handle this task with ease. In fact, while computers take much longer to recognize complex patterns, human beings do not. So the fact that our brains act as parallel processors is a big advantage. (Figure 2.18 illustrates the difference between these two kinds of processing.)

**Figure 2.18**
**Serial versus Parallel Processing**

In serial processing, tasks are performed one step at a time, in sequence. In parallel processing, in contrast, tasks are divided into subtasks, and all of these are performed simultaneously. Growing evidence suggests that our brains function through parallel processing, in which separate *modules* (collections of interconnected neurons) work on various parts of a task simultaneously.

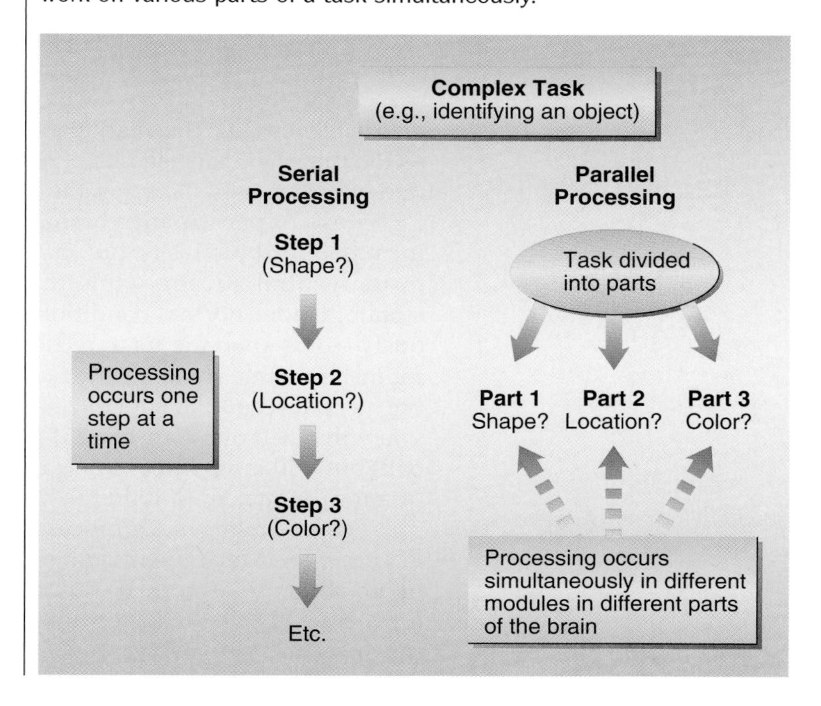

**Figure 2.19**
**Parallel Processing in the Visual System**

Information from our eyes arrives at the *extrastriate cortex*, where it divides into two separate streams. One stream (ventral) carries information downward to part of the temporal lobe; such information is concerned with *where* an object is or how we can react to it physically. The other stream (dorsal) moves upward to areas in the parietal lobe; such information is concerned primarily with *what* the object is—identifying it. Because both types of processing occur at once (in parallel) we can analyze visual information and respond to it very quickly.
(*Source:* Carlson, 1999.)

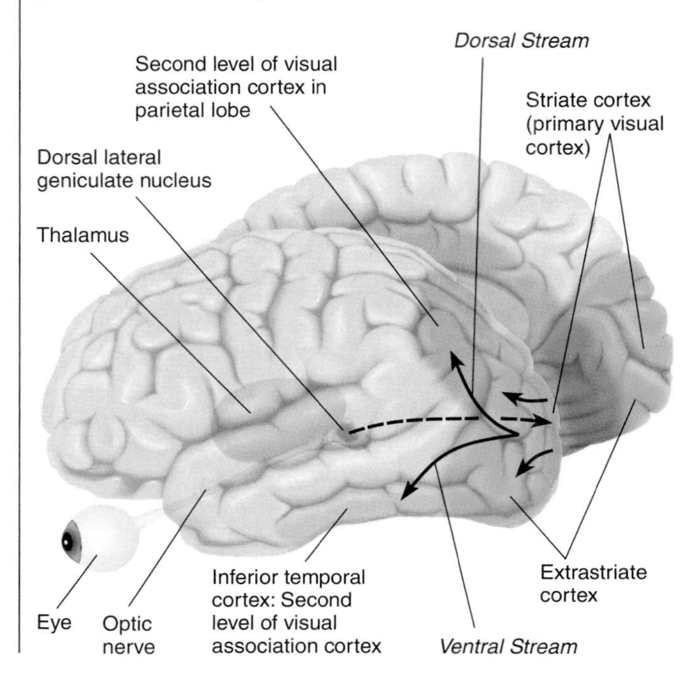


More direct evidence for this view of how the brain functions is provided by research on visual perception. As humans we are largely visual creatures, and this means that when we look around us, we can readily recognize vast numbers of objects, tell where they are in space, and use this information to react to them (e.g., pick them up or get out of their way!). How do we do this so quickly and effortlessly? Parallel processing provides part of the answer. In fact, it appears that from the level of our eyes up, we possess cells specialized for performing different functions—for analyzing different aspects of the visual world. For instance, various cells (or modules) respond to new objects we have not previously seen rather than to ones with which we are very familiar (e.g., Logothetis, Pauls, & Poggio, 1995); to different views (e.g., from different angles) of the same stimulus (Wange, Tanaka, & Tanifjui, 1996); and even specifically to faces (e.g., Desimone et al., 1984). Perhaps even more surprising, we seem to possess different systems for responding to *what* an object is and for determining *where* it is and how we can deal with it (reach for or touch it) (Goodale et al., 1994; Ungerleider & Mishkin, 1982). Research findings indicate that information from our eyes arrives at the *extrastriate cortex* and from there divides into two separate streams. One stream (ventral) carries information downward to part of the temporal lobe; such information is concerned with where an object is or how we can react to it physically. The other stream (dorsal) moves upward to areas in the parietal lobe; such information is concerned primarily with identifying what the object is (see Figure 2.19).

A study by Haxby and his colleagues (1994) provides clear evidence for this difference. Participants were shown either a human face or a random pattern, and then a second face or pattern. In a *form discrimination* task, they had to indicate whether the second stimulus was the same as the first they had seen. In a *location* task, they had to indicate whether the second stimulus was shown in the same place as the first (the location could vary). PET scans of participants' brains indicated that activity in the extrastriate cortex increased for both tasks, but that the form discrimination task increased activity in the ventral stream, while the location task increased activity in the dorsal stream. Under normal conditions, processing occurs in both streams simultaneously—thus enabling us to recognize and react to objects very quickly. Suppose, for instance, that someone throws something to you and shouts "Catch!" You have only a split second to recognize the object and react; yet the chances are good that you will reach out your hand if it is something safe and acceptable (e.g., a tennis ball) but will jump out of the way if it is something less desirable—a sharp object or a messy one. Your ability to do this is a good illustration of the advantages of parallel processing; such processing allows us to recognize objects, their location in space, their movement, and other features with amazing speed. This example of our ability to respond so quickly to the word "Catch!" also neatly sets the stage for the next brain–behavior link we will consider: our ability to understand and use speech.

## The Brain and Human Speech

I have been a professor for more than thirty-two years, and from time to time I've taken a step back to marvel at the wonders of human speech. How, I've often asked myself, can I stand up there for an hour or more, emitting a continuous stream of (I hope!) meaningful words? And how, when students in my classes ask me questions that are often totally unexpected, can I understand what they are saying and then quickly reply? Truly, our capacities to produce and understand speech are amazing. But these remarkable abilities aren't nearly as mysterious as they once were. In recent decades, psychologists and other scientists have gained a much clearer picture of the regions of our brains that play key roles in speech. I say "regions" because, in fact, several areas are important. It is the integrated functioning of all of them that allows us to produce and understand speech.

Let's start with speech production. Here, a region in the frontal lobe near the primary motor cortex, known as **Broca's area,** is crucial. Damage to this area disrupts the ability to speak, producing a condition known as *Broca's aphasia.* People with Broca's aphasia produce slow, laborious speech that is agrammatical in nature—it does not follow normal rules of grammar. For instance, on being asked to describe a picture of a girl giving flowers to her teacher, one patient said: "Girl . . . wants to . . . flowers . . . flowers and wants to. . . . The woman wants to. . . . The girls wants to . . . the flowers and the women" (Saffran, Schwartz, & Marin, 1980). In addition, persons with Broca's aphasia can't seem to find the word they want; and even if they do, they have difficulty pronouncing these words. What do all these symptoms mean? One interpretation is that this portion of the brain, and the regions immediately around it, contain memories of the sequences of muscular movements in the mouth and tongue that produce words. When Broca's area is damaged, therefore, the ability to produce coherent speech is impaired.

The task of speech comprehension—understanding what others say—seems to be focused largely in another region of the brain located in the temporal lobe. Damage to this region—known as **Wernicke's area**—produces three major symptoms: inability to recognize spoken words (i.e., to tell one word from another), inability to understand the meaning of these words, and inability to convert thoughts into words. Together, these symptoms are known as *Wernicke's aphasia.* Careful study of these symptoms has revealed that in fact they stem from somewhat different kinds of damage to the brain. If Wernicke's area alone is damaged, *pure word deafness* occurs—individuals can't understand what is said to them and can't repeat words they hear; that's the first major symptom listed above. They aren't deaf, however; they can recognize the emotion expressed by the tone of another person's speech (e.g., that the person is angry or sad) and can hear other sounds, such as doorbells or the barking of a dog. Further, they can understand what other people say by reading their lips.

If an area behind Wernicke's area (sometimes known as the posterior language area) is damaged but Wernicke's area itself is spared, persons can repeat words they hear but have no understanding of their meaning—that's the second major symptom listed above. The fact that such persons can repeat words they hear suggests that there is a direct link between Wernicke's area and Broca's area; and, in fact, such a connection has been found to exist. If injury to the posterior language area completely isolates it from Wernicke's area, the third symptom listed above occurs: Affected persons can no longer produce meaningful speech on their own—something that patients with damage to Wernicke's area alone can do. Finally, if both Wernicke's area and the posterior language area are damaged, then all three symptoms of Wernicke's aphasia result: Persons with such injuries can't recognize spoken words, understand their meaning, or convert their ideas and thoughts into words.

**Broca's Area:** A region in the prefrontal cortex that plays a role in the production of speech.

**Wernicke's Area:** An area in the temporal lobe that, through its connection with other brain areas, plays a role in the comprehension of speech.

**Figure 2.20**
**The Neural Basis of Human Speech: One Model**

Existing research suggests that *comprehension* of speech involves the flow of information from Wernicke's area to the posterior language area and then to sensory association areas and back again. (The meanings of words may be stored in sensory association areas.) Speech *production* involves the flow of information from sensory association areas to the posterior language area and then to Broca's area.
(*Source:* Carlson, 1999.)

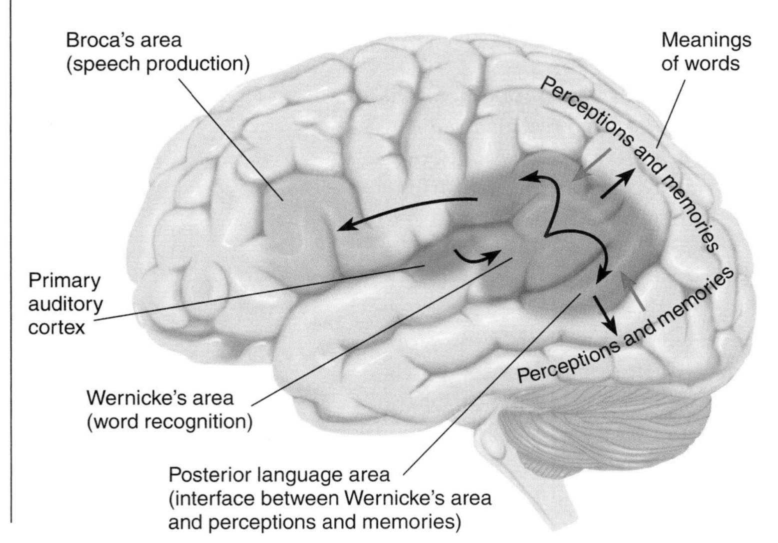


Putting all of these findings together, psychologists have developed the following model of human speech. The meanings of words involve our memories for them—what the words represent (objects, actions)—and such memories are stored in sensory association areas outside Broca's and Wernicke's areas. *Comprehension* of speech involves a flow of information from Wernicke's area to the posterior language area and then to sensory association areas and back again. Speech *production* involves the flow of information from sensory association areas to the posterior language area and then to Broca's area. This is probably an oversimplification of a highly complex process, but it is consistent with current knowledge about the role of the brain in speech. Figure 2.20 summarizes this emerging model.

## The Brain and Higher Mental Processes

Try this simple problem: Sandra has longer hair than Shalana. Shalana has longer hair than Marielena. Does Sandra have longer hair than Marielena? The answer is obvious, but how do you obtain it so effortlessly? How, in short, do you know that if Sandra's hair is longer than Shalana's, and Shalana's is longer than Marielena's, then Sandra's hair must also be longer than Marielena's? Remember our basic theme: Everything psychological is ultimately biological. So reasoning, problem solving, planning, and all of our *higher mental processes* must involve events occurring in our brains. But what parts of our brains? And what kind of events? These are among the questions currently being investigated by psychologists in their efforts to understand the role of the brain in all aspects of human behavior (e.g., Robin & Holyoak, 1995). We can get only a glimpse of this work here, but I'm confident that even that will start you thinking about the complexities—and rewards—of investigating brain–behavior links.

**RELATIONAL REASONING** Let's begin with reasoning, and specifically the kind of *relational reasoning* illustrated by the hair-length example above. In essence, reasoning depends on the ability to manipulate mental representations of relations between objects and events in our minds: You don't have to see Sandra, Shalana, and Marielena to know that Sandra's hair is longer—you can tell just from reasoning about them. But here's the crucial point: While you can tell that Sandra's hair is longer than Shalana's directly from the sentence "Sandra's hair is longer than Shalana's," there is no statement comparing Sandra and Marielena; so here you must mentally integrate multiple relations to attain the correct solution. This ability, many experts believe, may underlie several of our higher mental processes. For instance, take planning. To formulate effective plans, we must be able to arrange many goals and subgoals according to their importance. This, again, involves being able to integrate multiple relations so that we can see, for instance, that Goal C is more important than Goal D, which in turn is more important to us than Goal F (e.g., Delis et al., 1992).

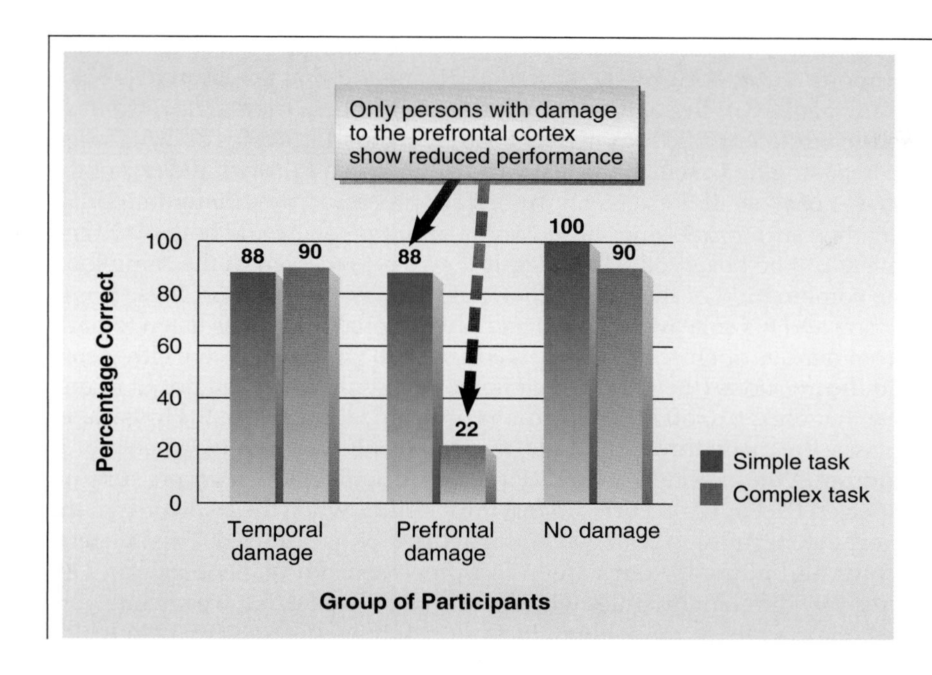


**Figure 2.21**
**Evidence for the Role of the Prefrontal Cortex in Relational Reasoning**

Research participants with damage to their prefrontal cortex performed about as well as persons with damage to other areas of the brain or no brain damage when tasks did not require relational reasoning. However, they did much more poorly on these tasks when they were more complex and *did* require relational reasoning. (Only results for one task, which involved inferences about the heights of imaginary persons, are shown here.)

Now for the key question: Does any part of the brain play a special role in such reasoning? A growing body of evidence suggests that the *prefrontal cortex*—part of the association areas of the brain—is a likely candidate (e.g., Graham & Hodges, 1997). For example, in one recent investigation, Waltz and his colleagues (1999) studied three groups of persons: individuals who had experienced damage to the prefrontal cortex, individuals with damage to the temporal lobes, and a group of persons who had no brain injury. All three groups performed two different tasks—a deductive reasoning task involving the height of several persons (e.g., Sam is taller than Nate; Nate is taller than Roy), and an inductive reasoning task in which participants were asked to choose the geometric pattern that would complete a series of patterns. For each task, there were different levels of complexity—one level that did not involve relational reasoning, and another that did. The researchers predicted that all groups would perform equally well when the tasks were simple, but that when the tasks were complex, participants with injuries to the prefrontal cortex would show a sharp drop in performance, because this part of the brain—crucial in relational reasoning—would not be functioning normally. As you can see in Figure 2.21, results confirmed these predictions. These findings, and those of many other studies (e.g., Bechara et al., 1997), suggest that the prefrontal cortex plays a key role in reasoning and many other higher mental functions. So much for the old and now discredited view that the association areas of the brain are mere backups for more crucial regions!

**MUSIC TO OUR EARS—OR BRAINS?** Remember the modular model of brain function I described earlier? This model suggests that our brains act like parallel processors: Incoming information is often processed simultaneously at several points within the brain. Thus, for instance, a complex task is broken down into parts, and different parts are processed by different modules. This makes for greatly increased efficiency and speed. A great deal of evidence points to this conclusion, but recent studies of how we process music—especially vocal music—are especially revealing (e.g., Patel et al., in press). Findings from previous research indicate that when a word in a sentence is incongruous—its meaning doesn't fit with the rest of the sentence—distinctive patterns of electrical activity occur in our brains. (As noted earlier, these are known as ERPs—*event-related potentials*.) In particular, semantic (meaning) incongruities produce ERPs that can be recorded at several locations on the cortex (e.g., frontal, parietal) and that are known as N400 (N stands for negative). In contrast, musical incongruities—notes played out of tune—produce different ERPs known as P300 (P stands for positive). What happens if we hear singing in which the last word sung doesn't fit with the rest of the sentence *and* is off key? If these incongruities are processed by different modules in the brain, then such processing should occur simultaneously and both N400 and P300 ERPs should be observed. However, if they are processed at the same locations, some combination of the two ERPs would be observed. To test these possibilities, Besson and his colleagues (1998) had professional musicians listen to parts of songs from famous operas. The excerpts ended with words that were either congruous and incongruous (they fit the meaning of the sentence or did not fit it) and were sung either on key or off key. Recordings of electrical activity in the musicians' brains (EEGs) were made throughout the session. Results were clear: When words were incongruous, the expected N400 ERPs occurred, and when they were sung off key, the expected P300 ERPs occurred. Most importantly, when the last words in the excerpts were incongruous in both ways, *both* of these ERPs occurred. This suggests that the words and music in songs are in fact processed simultaneously—and independently—by different modules within the brain. The fact that we are unaware of this division provides a compelling illustration of the remarkable way in which the brain combines information from many different modules in a smooth and seemingly effortless way to provide us with the continuing stream of experience we know as consciousness.

## REVIEW QUESTIONS

- What is the modern view of how the brain functions?
- What evidence suggests that processing of visual information occurs in a parallel fashion?
- What is the modern view of speech production and speech comprehension?
- What portions of the brain are involved in relational reasoning?
- What evidence suggests that the words and music in songs are processed by different modules within the brain?

### Food for Thought

Do you think it will ever be possible to build computers that use true parallel rather than serial processing? If so, will such computers truly have a "mind"?

Web Link: *DNA and Behavior—Is our Fate in Our Genes?*

**Heredity:** Biologically determined characteristics passed from parents to their offspring.

**Chromosomes:** Threadlike structures containing genetic material, found in nearly every cell of the body.

## Heredity and Behavior: Genetics and Evolutionary Psychology

By now, I hope, the basic theme of this chapter is clear: All aspects of behavior, including our consciousness, result from complex biological processes within our bodies. Given this basic fact, it makes a great deal of sense to consider the relationship of **heredity**—biologically determined characteristics—to behavior. After all, many aspects of our biological nature are inherited; so in an indirect manner, and always through the filter of our experience and environmental factors, heredity can indeed influence behavior (Rushton, 1989a, 1989b). In this final section we'll examine several aspects of heredity that appear to be relevant to an understanding of the biological bases of behavior.

## Genetics: Some Basic Principles

Every cell of your body contains a set of biological blueprints that enable it to perform its essential functions. This information is contained in **chromosomes,** threadlike structures found in the nuclei of nearly all cells (see Figure 2.22). Chromosomes are composed of a substance known as DNA, short for deoxyribonucleic acid. DNA, in turn, is made up of several simpler components arranged in the form of a double helix—something like the twisting water slides found by the sides of large swimming pools. Chromosomes contain thousands of **genes**—segments of DNA that serve as basic units of heredity. Our genes, working in complex combinations and together with forces in the environment, ultimately determine many aspects of our biological makeup.

Most cells in the human body contain forty-six chromosomes, existing in pairs (refer to Figure 2.22). When such cells divide, the chromosome pairs split; then, after the cells have separated, each chromosome replicates itself so that the full number is restored. This kind of cell division is known as **mitosis.** In contrast, sperm and ova—the male and female sex cells, or gametes—contain only twenty-three chromosomes. Thus, when they join to form a fertilized ovum from which a new human being will develop, the full number (forty-six) is attained. For each of us, then, half of our genetic material comes from our mother and half from our father.

These basic mechanisms explain why persons who are related resemble one another more than persons who are totally unrelated, and also why the closer the familial tie between individuals, the more similar they tend to be physically. The closer such links, the greater the proportion of chromosomes and genes family members share. And because genes determine many aspects of physical appearance, similarity increases with closeness of relationship. Thus, siblings (children of the same parents) tend to be more alike than cousins (the children of siblings). In the case of identical twins, or *monozygotic* twins, a single fertilized egg splits in two and forms two embryos; in contrast, nonidentical or *fraternal* twins grow from two eggs fertilized by two different sperm. Identical twins, sharing all of their genes, are usually remarkably similar in appearance. They are surprisingly similar in other respects as well, including—amazingly—their religious beliefs, their television-viewing preferences, and even their grief responses (e.g., Segal & Bouchard, 1993).

Impressive progress has been made toward determining the role of genetic factors in a wide range of physical and mental disorders. For example, researchers have discovered the gene that causes **Huntington's disease,** a rare, progressive neuromuscular disorder. Persons afflicted with Huntington's disease experience a gradual onset of uncontrollable, jerky movements in their limbs. Unfortunately, there is at present no cure for this disease (Pinel, 1993). Children of an affected person have a 50 percent chance of inheriting the gene that causes the disorder. Ironically, the onset of symptoms usually appears after age forty—long after many parents have their children, and therefore too late for them to reconsider their decision to start a family. Although scientists are not yet sure how the gene actually causes the disease, it is now possible to detect its presence before the onset of symptoms (e.g., Rothland et al., 1993; Giordani et al., 1995) and, more importantly, in time to let parents avoid passing the lethal gene to their children.

Merely possessing a particular gene, however, does not always mean that a specific effect will follow. Genes do not control behavior or other aspects of life directly. Rather, they exert their influence indirectly, through their impact on chemical reactions in the brain or other organs. These reactions, in turn, may depend on, or be strongly influenced by, environmental conditions. One example is **phenylketonuria (PKU),** a genetically based disorder in which persons lack the enzyme necessary to break down *phenylalanine*—a substance present in many foods. Affected

**Figure 2.22**
**Human Chromosomes**

Chromosomes are composed of DNA (deoxyribonucleic acid). Each human cell contains twenty-three pairs of chromosomes. The twenty-third pair determines sex. In males the twenty-third pair contains one X and one Y chromosome. In females the twenty-third pair contains two X chromosomes. As you can see, the person whose chromosomes are shown here is a male.

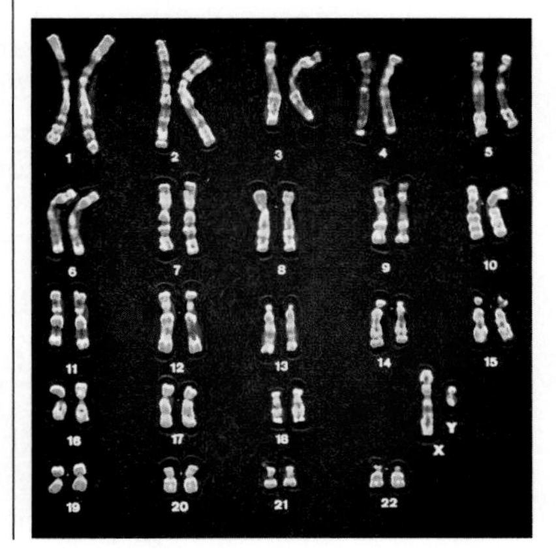

**Genes:** Segments of DNA that serve as biological blueprints, shaping development and all basic bodily processes.

**Mitosis:** Cell division in which chromosome pairs split and then replicate themselves so that the full number is restored in each of the cells produced by division.

**Huntington's Disease:** A genetically based fatal neuromuscular disorder characterized by the gradual onset of jerky, uncontrollable movements.

**Phenylketonuria (PKU):** A genetically based disorder in which persons lack the enzyme to break down phenylalanine, a substance present in many foods. The gradual buildup of body phenylalanine levels contributes to subsequent outcomes that include retardation.

persons on a normal diet tend to accumulate phenylalanine in their bodies. This, in turn, interferes with normal development of the brain and leads to mental retardation, seizures, and hyperactivity (Nyhan, 1987). Altering environmental conditions, however, can prevent this chain of events. Hospitals now routinely screen infants' blood for high levels of phenylalanine. If PKU is detected during the first few weeks of life, babies placed on a diet low in phenylalanine do not develop the PKU symptoms. Dietary restrictions can then be relaxed in late childhood after the majority of brain development is complete. So, as I'll note repeatedly in the rest of this book, biology is *not* necessarily destiny where human beings are concerned. Our genes do predispose us toward showing certain patterns of behavior or developing certain physical conditions or characteristics, but the environments in which we live play a major role in determining whether, and to what extent, such tendencies become reality. Moreover, most human traits are determined by more than one gene. In fact, hundreds of genes, acting in concert with environmental forces, may be involved in shaping complex physical or cognitive abilities (Lerner, 1993; McClearn et al., 1991). So, while there is increasing evidence for the role of genetic factors in many aspects of human behavior, heredity is only part of the total story.

## Disentangling Genetic and Environmental Effects: Research Strategies

If both heredity and environment influence human behavior, the next question is obvious: "How do we separate these factors in order to determine the relative contribution of each to any particular aspect of behavior?" This question relates, of course, to the *nature–nurture controversy* described in Chapter 1, and psychologists use many different methods to address it. Two of these, however, have been most useful: *twin studies* and *adoption studies.*

Twin studies are helpful in disentangling the relative roles of genetic and environmental factors in a given form of behavior because of the fact mentioned above: Identical twins share all the same genes, while fraternal twins do not. Under normal conditions, however, both kinds of twins are raised in environments that, if not identical, are at least very similar. After all, twins generally are raised in the same home, attend the same schools, and so on. Thus, if a given aspect of behavior is strongly influenced by genetic factors, we'd expect identical twins to resemble each other more closely in this respect than fraternal twins. If an aspect of behavior is *not* influenced by genetic factors, however, we would not anticipate such differences. As we'll see in Chapter 14, psychologists have used this approach to investigate the role of genetic factors in many forms of mental disorder and have found that indeed, genetic factors *do* play a role in several of these (e.g., phobias, autistic disorders, depression, and schizophrenia) (e.g., Merkelbach et al., 1996).

A major problem with such twin studies, however, is obvious: The environments in which twins are raised are often *not* precisely identical. This is especially true for fraternal twins, who may differ in gender, and so experience quite different treatment by parents and other persons. For this reason, twin studies, while suggestive, cannot provide conclusive evidence on the relative role of genetic and environmental factors. Actually, no single type of study can provide such evidence; but a second research approach—*adoption studies*—does seem to come closer to this goal. Such research focuses on identical twins who, because they are adopted into different homes, are separated very soon after birth. Because the twins have identical genes, differences between them with respect to various aspects of behavior can reasonably be attributed to environmental factors. I'll describe research using this approach at several points in this book; and, as we'll see in those discussions, adoption studies involving identical twins provide compelling evidence for the

**Heritability:** The extent to which variations among individuals with respect to a given aspect of behavior or a given trait are due to genetic factors.

role of genetic factors in many aspects of human behavior. Even when they are raised in sharply contrasting environments, identical twins show remarkable degrees of similarity in everything from various aspects of their personality to attitudes and values, hobbies, career choices, and even job satisfaction (see Figure 2.23) (Hershberger, Lichtenstein, & Knox, 1994; Lykken et al., 1992).

Using such methods, psychologists have been able to arrive at estimates of what is known as **heritability** for various traits. This term refers to the extent to which variations among individuals with respect to a given aspect of behavior or a given trait are due to genetic factors. For example, if heritability for a given trait is .50, this means that 50 percent of the variability in this trait appears to be shown by individuals due to genetic factors. Suppose it were found that the heritability of intelligence is .50. This means that 50 percent of the variation in intelligence among individuals in the population for which heritability was estimated is due to genetic factors. It does *not* mean that half of each person's intelligence is determined by genetic factors and half by environmental factors. So heritability estimates should be treated with caution. Still, they do provide a rough index of the extent to which genetic factors influence any aspect of behavior, and so are of considerable interest.

**Figure 2.23**
**Identical Twins: More than Mere Look-Alikes**

Growing evidence suggests that identical twins are highly similar with respect to many aspects of behavior—not just in the way they look. Moreover, this is so even if they are separated very early in life and raised in different environments. These findings suggest that genetic factors play a role in a much wider range of human behavior than was once believed.

Can information on the role of genetic factors in human behavior be put to practical use? Major projects now under way assume that it can. For information on one of these, see the following **From Science to Practice** section.

from SCIENCE to PRACTICE

## Identifying Genetic Factors in Human Disorders: Decoding Iceland

Suppose that we identify ten people around the world, all of whom suffer from deep depression. We examine the DNA of all of them to try to find out whether they share some genetic factor that plays a role in their mental disorder. Will we succeed? Probably not; because these persons come from diverse populations, their DNA will differ in so many ways that we will not be able to determine which of these differences contribute to their mental disorders. But now suppose that we repeat this study with a very homogeneous population—one in which nearly everyone is related to everyone else; further, imagine that instead of 10 participants, our study includes almost 300,000. Finally, suppose that we have computer programs that can analyze the DNA of all these people to look for genetic similarities in persons who develop certain diseases. Will we succeed now?

The people of Iceland are betting on it. They recently voted to allow a private company named Decode to obtain DNA samples from all residents of Iceland, plus access to all medical records (Specter, 1999). Because Iceland experienced little or no immigration for almost a thousand years—not until recent decades—the population is exceptionally homogeneous. Further, medical records are unusually complete and accurate, and have been kept for more than one hundred years. Finally, Decode possess highly sophisticated computer programs for comparing the DNA of all participants in the study, and thus identifying common patterns among those who have developed various illnesses—mental and otherwise. Given these factors, the scientists who operate Decode are confident that they will soon crack the genetic code of Icelanders and will be able to identify the genetic factors that play a role in many important diseases.

What if they succeed? The next step will be for major drug companies with whom Decode is working to use this information to develop drugs for treating these disorders—everything from depression to various forms of cancer. Of course, it is a big step from identifying genetic factors to developing effective drugs. But knowing which genes, or genetic anomalies (deviations from the norm), are linked to various diseases is an important first step.

This huge project has a potential downside, however. Many scientists and citizens in Iceland and elsewhere are concerned about the ethical issues it raises. For instance, suppose the study succeeds in identifying genes that confer longevity—people with these genes live longer than those without them. Insurance companies might then want to test all applicants for life insurance policies so they could reject the people who do not have these long-life genes. Similarly, persons possessing genes that predispose them toward cancer or mental disorders might find themselves eliminated from certain jobs or occupations. As is always the case, scientific progress involves complex ethical and social issues that must be carefully considered. Still, given the potential benefits of the Iceland project, it is not surprising that Icelanders voted for it, and that scientists all around the world are awaiting the results with eager anticipation.

## Evolutionary Psychology: Genes in Action

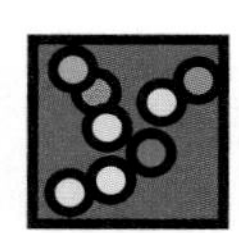

Do you recall our discussion of the new field of *evolutionary psychology* in Chapter 1? To refresh your memory, this field suggests that our species, like all others on the planet, has been subject to the process of biological evolution throughout its history. As a result, we now possess a large number of *evolved psychological mechanisms* that help (or once helped) us to deal with important problems relating to survival. These mechanisms have evolved because organisms vary greatly in many different ways, and some of these variations can be passed from one generation to the next through genes. Some of these heritable variations give individuals who possess them an advantage in terms of reproduction, so natural selection ensures that over time these variations become more common in the species.

Clearly, this process is relevant to our discussion of the role of heredity in human behavior; in fact, it describes one mechanism through which genes, acting over immense periods of time, can shape our behavior. More precisely, an evolutionary perspective suggests that we definitely do *not* inherit specific patterns of behavior; rather, we inherit tendencies or predispositions that may or may not be translated into reality, depending on the environments in which we live. For instance, consider an individual who is born with the potential to become a world-class swimmer: Her genes determine that her body shape and muscles are such that they suit her for this activity. Yet although she is descended from people who once lived on the shore, she now lives far from the ocean, and in a culture that does not view swimming as a worthwhile activity. The result: She never develops this potential and may, in fact, be unable even to stay afloat.

In Chapter 1 I provided some examples of what evolutionary psychology can contribute to our understanding of human behavior, but this new perspective has generated so much interest among psychologists that providing one more seems worthwhile. Let's consider the finding, repeated in many studies, that men and women differ in terms of *dominance motivation*—the desire to attain power and high status in one's society (e.g., Buss, 1999). Specifically, men are higher in dominance motivation. This difference has been observed all around the world in many different countries (e.g., Pratto, 1996), so it seems to be quite universal in our species. Why should such a difference exist? Evolutionary psychologists reason as follows. In many species, ranging from insects to primates, dominant males have much greater access to females, and therefore produce more offspring, than nondominant males (e.g., Ellis, 1995). They attain this greater access in two ways: Females tend to find them more attractive, and high-dominance males prevent other males from mating with the most desirable (i.e., youngest, most attractive) females. At the present time, monogamy is common in most human societies, so even dominant human males tend to have only one wife. However, they still tend to have more affairs and mate with more women than less dominant males (Buss, 1999). In the past, of course, such restrictions did not exist, and historical records going back more than four thousand years indicate that dominant males in many societies had huge numbers of wives and concubines. So, for men, dominance did translate into more offspring; and according to evolutionary principles, this would produce strong natural selection favoring strong motivation to attain dominance.

The situation is different for females. No matter how many mates they have, they can have only a limited number of offspring. Thus, for them, access to more males carries no obvious reproductive advantage. The result: Natural selection would *not* operate to produce high dominance motivation among females. But such pressures *would* operate to produce a tendency for females to find dominant males attractive; after all, such males would be more likely to provide the resources needed by females for raising their offspring, and females who attained high-dominance mates would be more likely to see their children survive.

**Figure 2.24**
**Facial Dominance: A Plus for Success in Some Careers**

West Point cadets who had dominant-looking faces *(left)* rose to higher military rank than cadets who had non-dominant-looking faces *(right).* Findings such as these suggest that dominance—or even the mere appearance of dominance—is linked to positive life outcomes, at least for males. These findings are consistent with predictions from the field of evolutionary psychology.

This reasoning offers one explanation for the fact that males score higher than females in dominance motivation, but it is largely speculative in nature. We can't go back in time and determine if dominant males did in fact produce more offspring over countless generations, or if the desire to seek dominance is in fact genetically determined. What we *can* do is to try to determine what personal characteristics are related to dominance and see if these are linked to positive outcomes—which, in turn, might be linked to reproductive success. In fact, several traits related to being perceived by others as dominant have been identified. These include height, nonverbal posture cues (standing tall), and even facial characteristics. Further, the greater the extent to which men possess these traits, the greater their success in their careers and the more sexual relations they tend to have (e.g., Mazur, Helpern, & Udry, 1994). In one intriguing study, for example, Mueller and Mazur (1996) rated the facial dominance cues of 434 West Point cadets and then followed the cadets through their military careers. Results indicated that those with dominant-looking faces reached higher military rank (see Figure 2.24).

In sum, evolutionary psychology provides a unique and intriguing perspective on the question of how our genes can, over time, shape our behavior. Whether the explanations it offers will turn out to be valid, however, can only be determined by further careful research.

**REVIEW QUESTIONS**

- How do psychologists seek to separate the roles of genetic and environmental factors in many forms of behavior?
- What is heritability?
- Why is the DNA of everyone living in Iceland being measured?
- How does evolutionary psychology explain the greater dominance motivation in males than in females?

**Food for Thought**

In view of the fact that we can't do experiments on many hypotheses offered by evolutionary psychology, is the evolutionary perspective really a valuable one for psychology?

## Making Psychology Part of Your Life

### The Nature–Nurture Controversy in the New Millennium: Adopting a Balanced View of the Role of Genetic Factors in Human Behavior

When I was a graduate student, the idea that complex aspects of human behavior (e.g., intelligence or mating preferences) could be influenced by genetic factors was deeply out of favor. A pure "environmentalism" ruled in psychology; almost everything, most psychologists believed, was shaped by the world around us and our experiences in it. Now, however, the pendulum of scientific opinion has swung far back the other way. As I noted in this chapter, growing evidence suggests that everything from mental disorders to gender differences in dominance—and even (as we'll see in later chapters) job satisfaction—can be influenced by genetic factors, at least to a degree. As is often the case, this shift in scientific opinion has been magnified by the media. Magazines, newspapers, and television programs have jumped on the bandwagon, suggesting that genetic factors are all-powerful and are, in fact, *the* controlling influence in our lives.

Where should *you* stand on this important issue? I strongly recommend a balanced view that recognizes the potential role of genetic factors and evolution in human behavior, but which also takes note of the limitations of this theory and of the evidence for it. Here are a few points I think you should try to keep in mind in the years ahead:

- **Even if a form of behavior is influenced by genetic factors, this doesn't mean that it can't be modified.** It's an error I've seen many, many times: People assume that because some illness or some difference between groups of people is inherited, it is etched in stone and can't be changed. This is completely false. Hundreds of millions of people around the world (including me) have faulty vision, but this in no way dooms them to being unable to see clearly. On the contrary, eyeglasses, contact lenses, and now simple laser operations permit the huge majority of these persons to attain something close to normal vision. So remember: The fact that an aspect of behavior is influenced by genetic factors—even strongly influenced—in no way implies that it can't be changed.
- **Environmental factors almost always play a role, too.** Another common error you should avoid is the view that because an aspect of behavior is strongly influenced by genetic factors, environmental ones are relatively unimportant. Wrong! Genes don't determine behavior; they merely produce *predispositions* toward certain traits (physical or otherwise), and predispositions may or may not be translated into reality. Whether they are usually depends to an important degree on environmental factors. For example, consider a strong genetically determined tendency to gain weight. Does this mean that persons having this tendency will always be overweight? Absolutely not. If they live at a time and in a place where there is an overabundance of food, this genetic tendency may show up in their actual weight. But if they live at a time and in a place where food is scarce or where there are very strong norms against being overweight, they may never have the chance to become obese—or may fight this tendency successfully. Again, biology is definitely *not* destiny.
- **We are not simply servants of our genes.** Another common error involves a basic misinterpretation of the evolutionary perspective. Because much emphasis is placed on inherited adaptive mechanisms and how these contribute to reproductive success, some people jump to the conclusion that we exist merely to reproduce—to get our genes into the next generation. This is a highly questionable point of view. Yes, certain physical traits or forms of behavior increase the likelihood that individuals will reproduce, and as a result these traits or forms of behavior tend to become more common in a population. But this in no way implies that all our energy or motivation is directed toward reproducing. This principle merely describes what *tends* to happen, over long periods of time, in large populations; it has little or nothing to do with individuals or with the causes of complex forms of human behavior.
- **Evolution is the scientific view of how species change over time and is supported by a huge amount of data; but it is not the only view and, to date, has not been "proved" in the same manner as many other scientific theories.** The fossil record provides powerful evidence for the view that species change over time (sometimes tremendously) and that many forms of life once existed on earth but have now disappeared (e.g., dinosaurs). However, because we can't travel backward in time to observe evolution directly, and because evolution usually requires extremely long periods of time, it can't be proved through direct experimentation as many ▶

other scientific theories have been. Thus, although evolution is the accepted scientific view, other interpretations also exist, including ones based on deeply held religious beliefs.

- **Beware of politically driven interpretations of scientific data.** Despite many changes in recent decades, bigotry is, alas, far from dead. And one way in which bias continues to rear its ugly head is through politically driven interpretations of scientific data. For instance, as we'll see in Chapter 11, growing evidence suggests that intelligence is strongly affected by genetic factors. Some individuals use this finding as a basis for suggesting that group differences on IQ tests must also stem from genetic factors. As I'll note in Chapter 11, the logic behind such assertions is seriously flawed. So please beware of efforts by extremist groups to bend evidence for the role of genetic factors in human behavior to their own purposes. Recognize such efforts for what they are: attempts to use science as camouflage for questionable political agendas, or even for outright bigotry.

# Summary and Review

## Neurons: Building Blocks of the Nervous System

- **What do neurons do, and what are their basic parts?** Neurons are cells specialized for receiving, processing, and moving information. They are made up of a cell body, an axon, and one or more dendrites.
- **What are action potentials and graded potentials? How do neurons communicate with one another?** Action potentials are rapid changes in the electrical properties of the cell membranes of neurons. They constitute a mechanism by which information travels through the nervous system. Graded potentials occur within a neuron in response to a physical stimulus or stimulation by another neuron; they weaken quickly, and their strength is directly proportional to the intensity of the physical stimulus that produced them. Neurons communicate that by means of neurotransmitters across the tiny gaps (synapses) that separate them.
- **What are the effects of neurotransmitters?** Neurotransmitters produce one of two effects: Excitatory effects make it more likely that a nerve cell will fire; inhibitory effects make it less likely that the cell will fire.
- **How do drugs produce their effects? What are agonists? Antagonists?** Many drugs produce their effects by influencing synaptic transmission. Agonists are drugs that mimic the impact of neurotransmitters at specific receptors; drugs that inhibit their impact are termed antagonists.

### Key Terms

neurons, p. 44 • dendrites, p. 44 • axon, p. 44 • glial cells, p. 44 • axon terminals, p. 45 • synapse, p. 45 • graded potential, p. 45 • action potential, p. 46 • nodes of Ranvier, p. 46 • synaptic vesicles, p. 47 • neurotransmitters, p. 47 • agonist, p. 49 • antagonist, p. 49

## The Nervous System: Its Basic Structure and Functions

- **What structures make up the central nervous system? What is the function of the spinal cord?** The central nervous system (CNS) includes the brain and the spinal cord. The spinal cord carries sensory information from receptors of the body to the brain via afferent nerve fibers and carries information from the brain to muscles and glands via efferent nerve fibers. It also plays an important role in reflexes.
- **What two systems make up the peripheral nervous system? What are the roles of these two systems?** The peripheral nervous system consists of the somatic and autonomic nervous systems. The somatic nervous system connects the brain and spinal cord to voluntary muscles throughout the body; the autonomic nervous system connects the central nervous system to internal organs and glands and to muscles over which we have little voluntary control.
- **What are the functions of the sympathetic and parasympathetic nervous systems?** The sympathetic nervous system prepares the body for using energy, whereas the parasympathetic nervous system activates processes that conserve the body's energy.
- **What is the endocrine system?** The endocrine system is an internal communication system consisting of glands that release hormones into the bloodstream.
- **What are some of its major parts?** The endocrine system includes the pituitary and adrenal glands, plus several others.

### Key Terms

nervous system, p. 50 • central nervous system, p. 50 • peripheral nervous system, p. 50 • afferent nerve fibers, p. 50 • efferent nerve fibers, p. 50 • somatic nervous system, p. 51 • autonomic nervous system, p. 51 • sympathetic nervous system, p. 52 • parasympathetic nervous system, p. 52 • endocrine system, p. 52 • hormones, p. 52 • pituitary gland, p. 52 • adrenal glands, p. 54

## The Brain: Where Consciousness . . . Is

- **What structures make up the brain stem? What are their functions?** The brain stem includes the medulla, pons, and cerebellum and is concerned primarily with the regulation of basic bodily functions. The cerebellum, however, may also be involved in higher cognitive processes, such as learning.
- **What are the functions of the hypothalamus and thalamus?** The hypothalamus is a brain structure involved in the regulation of motivated behavior and emotion. The thalamus serves as a relay station, directing afferent messages to appropriate brain regions.
- **What evidence suggests that brain dysfunctions may play a role in violence?** Recent studies indicate that some murderers may show reduced activity in portions of the brain that act as a brake on the limbic system and that play a role in fear conditioning.
- **What is the role of the cerebral cortex?** The cerebral cortex is the hub for higher mental processes such as thinking, planning, reasoning, and memory.
- **Who are "split-brain" persons? What evidence do they provide for specialization of functions in the two cerebral hemispheres?** Split-brain persons are individuals whose cerebral hemispheres have been isolated from each other through surgery. Evidence these persons provide suggests that the left hemisphere is specialized for verbal tasks, whereas the right hemisphere is specialized for perceptual tasks and the expression and recognition of emotions.
- **What evidence from persons with intact brains supports such specialization?** PET scans of normal persons reveal that when they speak or work with numbers, activity in the left hemisphere increases. When they work on perceptual tasks, activity increases in the right hemisphere.
- **What methods are used by psychologists to study the brain and its role in behavior?** These methods involve examining the effects of damage to various portions of the brain or nervous system, recording and stimulating neural activity, and obtaining images of the intact living brain.

### Key Terms

medulla, p. 55 • pons, p. 55 • reticular activating system, p. 55 • cerebellum, p. 56 • midbrain, p. 56 • hypothalamus, p. 56 • thalamus, p. 57 • limbic system, p. 57 • hippocampus, p. 57 • amygdala, p. 57 • cerebral cortex, p. 58 • frontal lobe, p. 59 • parietal lobe, p. 60 • occipital lobe, p. 60 • temporal lobe, p. 60 • lateralization of function, p. 61 • corpus callosum, p. 61 • electroencephalography (EEG), p. 64 • computerized tomography (CT), p. 64 • magnetic resonance imaging (MRI), p. 64 • SQUID (superconducting quantum interference device), p. 66 • positron emission tomography (PET), p. 66

## The Brain and Human Behavior: Where Biology and Consciousness Meet

- **What is the modern view of how the brain functions?** The brain processes information in parallel, in many modules.
- **What evidence suggests that processing of visual information occurs in a parallel fashion?** Evidence indicates that visual information about object identification is processed separately than information about where an object is or how we can react to it.
- **What is the modern view of speech production and speech comprehension?** Speech *production* involves the flow of information from sensory association areas to the posterior language area and then to Broca's area. *Comprehension* of speech involves a flow of information from Wernicke's area to the posterior language area and then to sensory association areas and back again.
- **What portions of the brain are involved in relational reasoning?** Such reasoning seems to occur primarily in the prefrontal cortex.
- **What evidence suggests that the words and music in songs are processed by different modules within the brain?** Words that are sung off key and words that have incongruous meanings produce two distinctly different event-related potentials (ERPs) simultaneously.

### Key Terms

Broca's area, p. 69 • Wernicke's area, p. 69

## Heredity and Behavior: Genetics and Evolutionary Psychology

- **How do psychologists seek to separate the roles of genetic and environmental factors in many forms of behavior?** They do this primarily through twin studies and adoption studies.
- **What is heritability?** Heritability is defined as the extent to which variations among individuals with respect to a given aspect of behavior or a given trait are due to genetic factors.
- **Why is the DNA of everyone living in Iceland being measured?** The Decode scientists are attempting to relate genetic anomalies to medical records, in order to identify genetic causes of major illnesses.
- **How does evolutionary psychology explain the greater dominance motivation in males than in females?** Dominance provides males with access to more females, and so increases the number of offspring they father. For females, access to more males does not necessarily lead to more offspring, so there is less reason for females to seek dominance.

### Key Terms

heredity, p. 72 • chromosomes, p. 72 • genes, p. 73 • mitosis, p. 73 • Huntington's disease, p. 73 • phenylketonuria (PKU), p. 73 • heritability, p. 74

# Critical Thinking Questions

## Appraisal

A primary theme of this chapter is that our thoughts, feelings, and actions stem from basic biological processes. Do you think that all of our conscious experience can be reduced to events within our nervous system, especially our brains? If so, why? If not, what *is* the basis for our thoughts and feelings?

## Controversy

If scientists succeed in decoding human DNA (and it seems likely that they will), this may open the door to genetic tinkering with our species—efforts to improve human health or performance through artificial alteration of the DNA of unborn fetuses, or even of human egg cells. Do you think such efforts should be encouraged? Totally banned? Carefully regulated? Why do you hold this view?

## Making Psychology Part of Your Life

Legal systems throughout the world are based on the premise that unless individuals are suffering from serious mental illness, they know what they are doing and should be held responsible for their actions. But now, research findings suggest that some people may behave aggressive because of malfunctions in portions of their brains—an absence of appropriate "neural brakes." Suppose you were asked, as a juror, to judge the guilt or innocence of a person who was charged with committing a violent crime. Would this knowledge about the role of the brain in violence influence your decision? *Should* it have such influence?

# Chapter 3

# Sensation and Perception:

## Making Contact with the World around Us

# CHAPTER OUTLINE


**SENSATION: THE RAW MATERIALS OF UNDERSTANDING 85**

Sensory Thresholds: How Much Stimulation Is Enough?

■ RESEARCH METHODS *How Psychologists Measure Sensory Thresholds—The Role of Psychophysical Procedures*

Sensory Adaptation: "It Feels Great Once You Get Used to It"

**VISION 91**

The Eye: Its Basic Structure
Light: The Physical Stimulus for Vision
Basic Functions of the Visual System: Acuity, Dark Adaptation, and Eye Movements
Color Vision
Vision and the Brain: Processing Visual Information

**HEARING 98**

The Ear: Its Basic Structure
Sound: The Physical Stimulus for Hearing
Pitch Perception
Sound Localization

■ BEYOND THE HEADLINES—As Psychologists See It: *Premature Hearing Loss: The High Cost of Modern Living*

**TOUCH AND OTHER SKIN SENSES 104**

Pain: Its Nature and Control

**SMELL AND TASTE: THE CHEMICAL SENSES 106**

Smell and Taste: How They Operate
Smell and Taste: Some Interesting Facts

**KINESTHESIA AND VESTIBULAR SENSE 109**

■ FROM SCIENCE TO PRACTICE *How a Basic Understanding of Sensory Processes Can Improve the Usefulness of Virtual Technologies*

**PERCEPTION: PUTTING IT ALL TOGETHER 112**

Perception: The Focus of Our Attention
Perception: Some Organizing Principles
Constancies and Illusions: When Perception Succeeds—and Fails
Some Key Perceptual Processes: Pattern and Distance

**THE PLASTICITY OF PERCEPTION: TO WHAT EXTENT IS IT INNATE OR LEARNED? 121**

Perception: Evidence That It's Innate
Perception: Evidence That It's Learned
Must We Resolve the Nature–Nurture Controversy?

**EXTRASENSORY PERCEPTION: PERCEPTION WITHOUT SENSATION? 123**

Psi: What Is It?
Psi: Does It Really Exist?

■ MAKING PSYCHOLOGY PART OF YOUR LIFE *Managing Your Pain: Some Useful Tips*

During a recent visit to my parents' home, I happened to answer their telephone. To my delight, I heard the unmistakable voice of a former girlfriend from my high school days. After briefly catching up on what each one of us had been up to, Rhonda abruptly changed the focus of the conversation, revealing the true purpose of the call. As it turns out, during a chance encounter with my parents at the local mall, she had learned from my mother that I was a psychologist and that I would be visiting soon. She had called to get an "expert's" opinion of psychics and the predictions they make, apparently believing that my training qualified me to offer such advice! Rhonda confessed that she had phoned a psychic hotline—"purely out of curiosity," she assured me. As Rhonda continued with her story, I could tell from her voice that the psychic's accuracy in knowing intimate facts about her and the detailed predictions he offered concerning her future had left her shaken. Although I was eventually able to convince my friend that the psychic's abilities were probably more practiced than mystical, this anecdote does raise questions that relate to topics we will discuss in this chapter. For example, if psychics really *could* know the future, how could they do this? In other words, what is the physical mechanism by which they could detect information about events yet to come? Currently, no objective evidence exists to support the claims of people who purport to have psychic abilities. The same is true for several other hypothesized processes that we'll consider later in this chapter, including subliminal perception and extrasensory perception (ESP).

As illustrated by my conversation with Rhonda, the world around us is complicated. Moreover, the processes that help us make sense out of the sights, sounds, smells, tastes, and other sensations that constantly bombard us are not as simple or direct as common sense might suggest. Careful psychological research conducted over the past one hundred years has shown that we do not understand the external world in a simple, automatic way. Rather, we actively construct our interpretation of sensory information through several complex processes, as illustrated by the interesting visual interpretation in Figure 3.1.

**Sensation:** Input about the physical world provided by our sensory receptors.

To clarify how we make sense of the world around us, psychologists distinguish between two key concepts: *sensation* and *perception*. The study of **sensation** is concerned with the initial contact between organisms and their physical environment. It focuses on describing the relationship between various forms of sensory stimulation (including electromagnetic, sound waves, pressure) and how these inputs are registered by our sense organs (the eyes, ears, nose, tongue, and skin). In contrast, the study of **perception** is concerned with identifying the processes through which we interpret and organize this information to produce our conscious experience of objects and relationships among objects. It is important to remember that perception is not simply a passive process of decoding incoming sensory information. If this were the case, we would lose the richness of our everyday stream of conscious experiences.

The dual processes of sensation and perception play a role in virtually every topic we will consider in later chapters. For these reasons, we will devote careful attention to them here. We'll begin by exploring in detail how the receptors for each sensory system transduce (convert) raw physical energy into an electrochemical code. As we'll soon note, our sensory receptors are exquisitely designed to detect various aspects of the world around us. As part of our discussion of sensation, we'll consider a unique set of procedures psychologists have developed to measure the sensitivity of our sensory organs. We'll also consider the possibility of subliminal perception—perception without any underlying sensation. Next, we'll turn our attention to the active process of perception. Here, we'll focus on how the brain integrates and interprets the constant flow of information it receives from our senses. In our discussion of perception, we'll also consider the contributions of heredity and experience to our perception of the world around us. Finally, we'll conclude by examining evidence concerning the possibility of extrasensory perception, or *psi.*

**Figure 3.1**
**Constructing the World around Us: The "Active" Role of Perception**

As illustrated by the *mis*perception depicted in this cartoon, the way we see ourselves and the world around us is the result of complex processes occurring within the nervous system.

(*Source:* IN THE BLEACHERS. © Steve Moore. Reprinted with permission of UNIVERSAL PRESS SYNDICATE. All rights reserved.)

## Sensation: The Raw Materials of Understanding

CourseCompass
Web Link: *Seeing, Hearing, and Smelling the World*

The sight of a breathtaking sunset, the pleasant fragrance of a summer rose, the smooth texture of a baby's skin, the sharp "crack" of a starter's pistol at the beginning of a race: Exactly how are we able to experience these events (please refer to Figure 3.2 on page 86)? As you may recall from Chapter 2, all of these sensory experiences are based on complex processes occurring within the nervous system. This highlights an intriguing paradox: Although we are continually bombarded by various forms of physical energy, including light, heat, sound, and smells, our brain cannot directly detect the presence of these forces. Instead, it can respond only to intricate patterns of action potentials conducted by *neurons,* special cells within our bodies that receive, move, and process sensory information. Thus, a critical question is how the many forms of physical energy impacting our sensory systems are converted into signals our nervous system can understand.

Highly specialized cells known as **sensory receptors,** located in our eyes, ears, nose, tongue, and elsewhere, are responsible for accomplishing this task. Thus, sights, sounds, and smells that we experience are actually the product of **transduction,** a process in which the physical properties of stimuli are converted into neural signals that are then transmitted to our brain via specialized sensory nerves. To illustrate how our nervous system makes sense out of the physical energies in our environment, we'll begin by focusing on two critical concepts: *thresholds* and *sensory adaptation.*

**Perception:** The process through which we select, organize, and interpret input from our sensory receptors.

**Sensory Receptors:** Cells of the body specialized for the task of transduction—converting physical energy (light, sound) into neural impulses.

**Transduction:** The translation of a physical energy into electrical signals by specialized receptor cells.

**Figure 3.2**
**Experiencing the World around Us: The Role of Sensory Processes**

Our ability to experience events such as the ones pictured here is the result of complex processes occurring within the nervous system.

Web Link: *Sensation/Perception Jeopardy*

Web Link: *The Museum of Science, Art, and Human Perception*

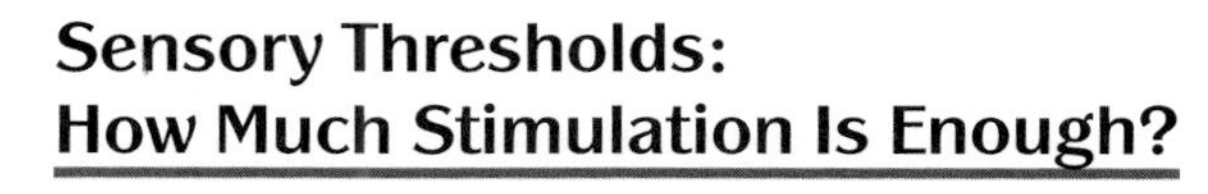

## Sensory Thresholds: How Much Stimulation Is Enough?

Try to focus on all of the sensory information impacting you at this moment—sights, sounds, smells, tastes, the feel of clothing against your skin. Although we are immersed in sensory information, we thrive rather than drown. Our bodies seem well prepared to deal with this abundance of information; so well prepared that when deprived of all sensory input—in a condition termed *sensory deprivation*—our brains may produce hallucinations to fill the void. But what is the slightest amount of stimulation that our sensory systems can detect? In other words, how much physical stimulation is necessary in order for us to experience a sensation? Actually, it turns out to be impressively low for most aspects of sensation. We can hear a watch tick twenty feet away in a quiet room; we can detect the taste of a single teaspoon of sugar in two gallons of water; we can smell a single drop of perfume in an empty three-room apartment; and on a clear dark night, we can see a dim candle thirty miles away (Galanter, 1962).

Although our receptors are remarkably efficient, they do not register all the information available in the environment at any given moment. We are able to smell and taste certain chemicals but not others; we hear sound waves only at certain frequencies; and our ability to detect light energy is restricted to a relatively narrow band of wavelengths. The range of physical stimuli that we and other species can detect, however, is uniquely designed to maximize survival potential. Given that human survival is tied to our unique capacity for spoken language, it is not surprising that our auditory system is best at detecting sound frequencies that closely match the frequencies of human speech (Coren, Ward, & Enns, 1999).

For more than a century, psychologists have investigated the sensory capabilities of the various sense organs. An important goal of this work has been to establish the relationship between physical properties of stimuli, such as brightness and loudness, and people's psychological experience of them. A casual observer might assume such a relationship to be a direct one. In other words, given a stimulus of sufficient intensity, we should always be able to detect its presence. This suggests that at levels above a certain intensity, a person would always report detecting the stimulus. In practice, this pattern of results almost never occurs. Why? One reason is that our sensitivity to stimuli changes from moment to moment. Bodily functions change constantly in order to maintain the body's internal environment at optimal levels, a state termed *homeostasis.* It is not surprising that as a result of these changes, the sensitivity of our sensory organs to external stimuli also varies. For this reason, psychologists have coined the term *absolute threshold* to denote our sensory threshold; they define **absolute threshold** as the smallest magnitude of a stimulus that can be reliably discriminated from no stimulus at all 50 percent of the time. Let's now turn to a discussion in the following **Research Methods** section of procedures psychologists have developed to measure the sensitivity of our sensory organs.

**Absolute Threshold:** The smallest amount of a stimulus that we can detect 50 percent of the time.

**Psychophysical Methods:** A set of procedures psychologists have developed to investigate sensory thresholds.

## Research Methods: How Psychologists Measure Sensory Thresholds—The Role of Psychophysical Procedures

Suppose that the U.S. Navy has developed a device for SEALs—an elite fighting force that is frequently deployed behind enemy lines—to use to detect the presence of hidden explosives during their missions. The tiny sensing device emits a beeping sound that gets higher in pitch as a person approaches an explosive object. Although the warning device has great potential for saving lives, it has one serious drawback. If the tone is too loud, it could alert enemy troops nearby to the SEALs' presence. The navy would like to start using the device; but they realize that before doing so, they need to determine the minimum level of sound necessary to alert the SEALs without disclosing their location to the enemy. How will the navy solve its problem? A good starting point may involve the use of **psychophysical methods,** a set of procedures psychologists have developed to investigate sensory thresholds. There are actually three such methods, and we'll consider all three in this section.

### The Method of Limits

The first of these psychophysical methods is known as the *method of limits,* and it works like this. After a test participant (e.g., one of the SEALs) is seated comfortably and fitted with headphones, a series of ascending and descending trials begins. *Ascending trials* start with the presentation of a tone that is inaudible (no one can hear it), followed by tones that gradually increase in intensity until the person reports, "I hear it." *Descending trials* proceed in just the opposite way; they begin with the presentation of a tone that is loud enough for anyone to hear, followed by tones that gradually decrease in intensity until the person says, "I don't hear it." Our sensitivity to various stimuli tends to shift due to fluctuations in our nervous system. Therefore, both types of trials are repeated several times to provide a more reliable estimate of the threshold. A basic assumption of this method is that people change their response each time the sensory threshold is crossed. For this reason, the threshold for each trial is presumed to lie somewhere between the intensities of the last two stimuli presented. Experimenters obtain an overall estimate of the threshold by computing the average threshold across all individual ascending and descending trials.

The use of both ascending and descending series also helps researchers take account of two common tendencies. The first, referred to as *errors of habituation,* is participants' tendency to continue to say no in an ascending series and yes in a descending series—independent of whether the participant actually hears the sound. The second, termed *errors of anticipation,* is people's tendency to jump the gun; in other words, to change their response to a stimulus before such a change is warranted.

### The Staircase Method

In the *staircase method,* the experimenter may begin with a descending series, initially presenting an audible tone. Each time the participant says, "Yes, I hear it," the intensity of the sound is decreased, in small steps, until the person reports, "No, I do not hear it." But at this point the series does not end, as in the method of limits. Instead, the experimenter switches to an ascending series and increases the intensity of each tone until the person says, "Yes, I hear it." This process is repeated until the threshold is located. The staircase method offers several practical advantages over the method of limits. First, it is more efficient, allowing the experimenter quickly to zero in on the sensory threshold. This, in turn, eliminates testing sound intensities well above or below the threshold value. Second, it allows the experimenter to track changes in sensitivity that may occur during the test session. Finally, participants can be trained to adjust the intensity of the stimulus themselves and thus save time for the experimenter.

### The Method of Constant Stimuli

In the *method of constant stimuli,* the range of sound intensities to be tested are selected in advance, and each tone is presented many times in an irregular order. Stimuli are chosen so that some sounds are below the threshold (participants cannot hear them) and others are at or above the threshold. As with the other procedures, participants are asked to respond "Yes" when they hear the sound and "No" when they do not. An important advantage of this method is that it eliminates some of the biases associated with the method of limits. This makes it the preferred method when accuracy is important; for example, when it is used to help solve problems such as the navy SEALs example described earlier in this section. As you might expect, however, the method of constant stimuli is time-consuming and requires that experimenters pretest the range of stimuli in advance. To summarize, all of these methods work, and work well, so choosing between them is largely a matter of efficiency.

Audio 3.1: *Example of Signal Detection Theory*

**SENSORY THRESHOLDS: SOME COMPLICATIONS** Our discussion so far seems to indicate that sensory thresholds are not really fixed but instead change in response to a variety of factors, including fatigue, lapses in attention, and moment-to-moment fluctuations that occur within our nervous system. Additional research suggests that *motivational factors,* or the rewards or costs associated with detecting various stimuli, may also play an important role.

According to **signal detection theory,** complex decision mechanisms are involved whenever we try to determine if we have or have not detected a specific stimulus (Erev, 1998; Swets, 1992). For instance, imagine that you are a radiologist. While scanning a patient's X-ray, you think you detect a faint spot on the film, but you're not quite sure. What should you do? If you conclude that the spot is an abnormality, you must order more scans or tests—an expensive and time-consuming alternative. If further testing reveals an abnormality, such as cancer, you may have saved the patient's life. If no abnormality is detected, though, you'll be blamed for wasting resources and unnecessarily upsetting the patient. Alternatively, if you decide the spot is *not* an abnormality, then there's no reason to order more tests. If the patient remains healthy, then you've done the right thing. However, if the spot is really cancerous tissue, the results could be fatal. Clearly, your decision is likely to be influenced by the rewards and costs associated with each choice alternative.

**Figure 3.3**
**Difference Thresholds: How Much Change Is Enough?**

In the example depicted here, the students' threshold of ability to notice the change in the intensity of sound present in the room has clearly been exceeded.

(*Source:* CLOSE TO HOME. © John McPherson. Reprinted with permission of UNIVERSAL PRESS SYNDICATE. All rights reserved.)

**Equipped with a series of tiny microphones under her fingernails and a 200-watt amplifier, Mrs. Raffner relished the moment she spotted a student dozing off.**

Interestingly, an incident very similar to this scenario was recently reported in the media. Two Boston area pathologists misread the tissue biopsies of twenty patients (Noonan, 1999); the doctors informed the men they did not have cancer, when in fact they had the disease. The mistakes were revealed during a review of 279 tests performed between 1995 and 1997. Please note that it is not clear whether motivational factors (e.g., cost considerations) contributed to the apparent misdiagnosis. The doctors' error does illustrate, however, that deciding whether we have detected a given stimulus is not always easy. Indeed, these decisions involve much more than a simple determination of the relationship between the amount of physical energy present in a stimulus and the resulting psychological sensations.

**DIFFERENCE THRESHOLDS: ARE TWO STIMULI THE SAME OR DIFFERENT?** A good cook tastes a dish, then adds salt to it, then tastes it again to measure the change. This illustrates another basic question relating to our sensory capacities: How much change in a stimulus is required before a shift can be noticed? Psychologists refer to the amount of change in a stimulus required for a person to detect it as the **difference threshold.** Obviously, the smaller the change we can detect, the greater our sensitivity. In other words, the difference threshold is the amount of change in a physical stimulus necessary to produce a **just noticeable difference (jnd)** in sensation (Figure 3.3). As it turns out, our ability to detect differences in stimulus intensity depends on the magnitude of the initial stimulus; we easily detect even small changes in weak stimuli, but we require much larger changes before we notice differences in strong stimuli. If you are listening to your favorite tunes at a low sound intensity, even small adjustments to the volume are noticeable. But if you are listening to very loud music, much larger changes are required before a difference is apparent. As you might guess, we are also more sensitive to changes in some types of stimuli than to changes in others. For example, we are able to notice very small shifts in temperature (less than one degree Fahrenheit) and in the pitch of sounds (a useful ability for people who tune musical instruments), but we are somewhat less sensitive to changes in loudness or in smells.

**STIMULI BELOW THRESHOLD: CAN THEY HAVE AN EFFECT?** For decades, **subliminal perception** has been a source of controversy. Subliminal perception first captured the public's attention in the 1950s when a marketing executive announced he had embedded subliminal messages like "Eat popcorn" and "Drink Coke" into a then popular movie. Supposedly, the embedded messages were flashed on the screen in front of movie audiences so briefly (a fraction of a second) that audience members were not aware of them (Brean, 1958). Although the executive later confessed to the hoax (no messages were actually presented), many people remained convinced that subliminal messages can be powerful sources of persuasion.

Web Link: *Subliminal Perception*

During the 1980s, public attention was again drawn to the issue of subliminal perception, this time in response to concerns over *backward masking,* a procedure in which "evil" messages are recorded backward and embedded into songs on rock albums. In a highly publicized trial, subliminally embedded messages were alleged to be instrumental in the suicides of two young men. The judge in the case eventually dismissed the charges, citing a lack of evidence that the messages actually *caused* the shootings (*Vance et al. v. Judas Priest et al.*, 1990).

An important question raised by these incidents is whether we can in fact sense or be affected by stimuli that remain outside our conscious awareness (Greenwald, 1992; Merikle, 1992). The most direct answer to this question seems to come from studies that have used a technique called *visual priming.* In a typical experiment, participants are "primed" with brief exposures (less than one-tenth of a second) to words or simple pictures. The duration of the exposure is long enough to be detected by the nervous system, but too brief for people to be consciously aware of its presence. Participants are usually unable to name the visual "primes," but their reactions to stimuli presented subsequently (e.g., words or pictures) do seem to be affected (Merikle & Daneman, 1998). Indeed, systematic research has demonstrated that subliminally presented visual stimuli can have measurable effects on many aspects of our cognition and emotion, including liking for ambiguous stimuli (Murphy & Zajonc, 1993), attraction to members of the opposite sex (Bargh et al., 1995), and even liking for words (Greenwald, Draine, & Abrams, 1996). People primed with the word *happy,* for example, tend to rate the target word *bomb* as more pleasant than persons primed with the word *kill.* The results of these studies suggest that the priming stimuli, despite their brief duration, are registered at some level within the nervous system. (Psychologists also use priming to study certain aspects of memory; see Chapter 6.)

New research is beginning to reveal how subliminal stimuli—stimuli sufficiently intense to be registered by the nervous system, but outside our conscious awareness—are processed by the brain. In one recent study, Bar and Biederman (1998) primed participants with brief exposures (one-twentieth of a second) to pictures of common objects and asked them to name each object as it was presented. As expected, the participants performed poorly on this task, correctly naming only a small percentage of the objects shown (refer to Figure 3.4 on page 90). The pictures

**Signal Detection Theory:** A theory suggesting that there are no absolute thresholds for sensations. Rather, detection of stimuli depends on their physical energy and on internal factors such as the relative costs and benefits associated with detecting their presence.

**Difference Threshold:** The amount by which two stimuli must differ in order to be just noticeably different.

**Just Noticeable Difference (jnd):** The smallest amount of change in a physical stimulus necessary for an individual to notice a difference in the intensity of the stimulus.

**Subliminal Perception:** The presumed ability to perceive a stimulus that is below the threshold for conscious experience.

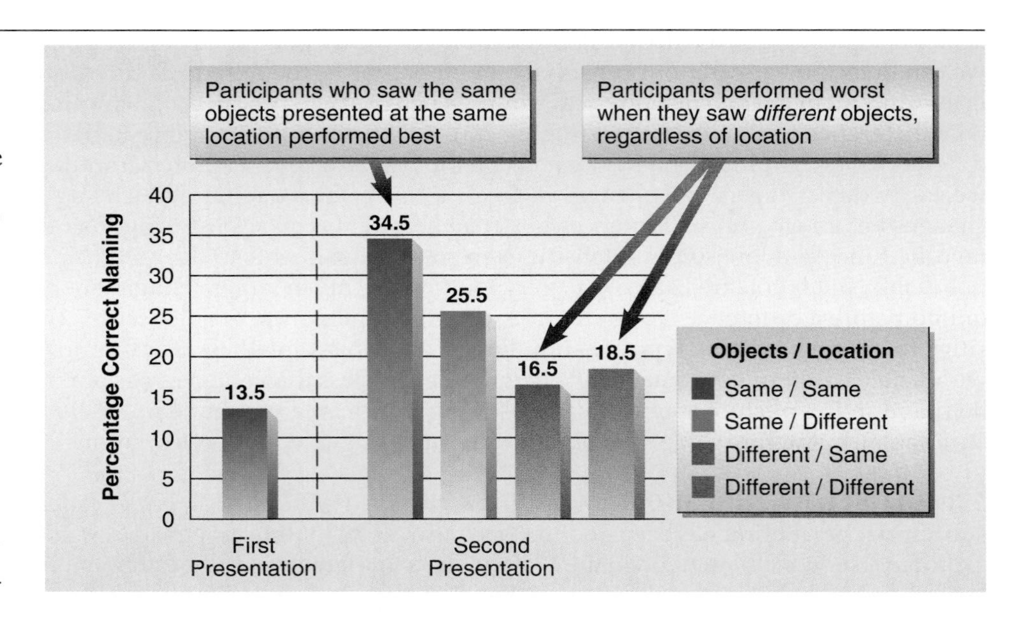


**Figure 3.4**
**Subliminal Perception and Visual Priming**

Participants were able to name only a small percentage of images presented briefly (for less than one-twentieth of a second). Naming accuracy increased significantly when the same image was repeated at the same screen location. The increase in naming accuracy was somewhat diminished when the same images were presented at a different screen location. Naming accuracy did not increase significantly for different images, regardless of their location. These results indicate that subliminal visual priming may be sufficient to activate brain processes involved in object identification. (*Source:* Based on data from Bar & Biederman, 1998.)

were presented again several minutes later, but they were changed in the following ways: (1) Participants viewed either the same objects or similar objects bearing the same name (e.g., a kitchen chair on the first presentation but an office chair the second time); and (2) objects appeared either at the same screen location or at a slightly different location. As shown in Figure 3.4, the performance of participants who viewed the same objects in their original location increased dramatically. A somewhat smaller increase was evident for people who viewed the same object presented at a slightly different location. In contrast, naming performance did not increase among those exposed to different objects, regardless of their location. These results seem to indicate that subliminal visual priming may be sufficient to activate brain processes necessary for object identification, but not sufficient to activate processes necessary to make more subtle distinctions about objects (Wagner et al., 1997).

What are the practical implications of the results of visual priming studies? They are less dramatic than you might expect, for the following reasons. First, the effects of visual priming are generally small and are obtained only under controlled laboratory conditions. Second, most studies show that the effects of priming are short-lived. In most instances, the target stimuli must be presented within a few minutes following the prime for the effect to be obtained (Bar & Biederman, 1998).

So, rest easy! No evidence currently supports the idea that subliminal messages are a powerful means of persuasion. Predictably, this fact has not slowed the current explosion of self-help materials that offer to assist people to lose weight, stop smoking, get smarter, or improve their sex life. Their manufacturers continue to insist that the effectiveness of these products is due to the presence of subliminal messages. Are these claims true? As we've seen throughout this section, systematic evidence casts doubt on this possibility (Greenwald et al., 1991; Urban, 1992). Instead, the improvements people experience appear to stem from other factors, such as motivation and expectations.

## Sensory Adaptation: "It Feels Great Once You Get Used to It"

I have vivid memories of summer camping trips I took as a young boy with my friends. On particularly hot afternoons we would cool off with a dip into an icy mountain lake or stream. Although the initial shock of the icy water was overpowering, as illustrated in Figure 3.5, it eventually felt refreshing. This experience illustrates the process of **sensory adaptation:** the fact that our sensitivity to an unchanging stimulus tends to decrease over time. When we first encounter a stimulus, such as icy water, our temperature receptors fire vigorously. Soon, however, they fire less vigorously; and through the process of sensory adaptation, the water then feels just right.

Sensory adaptation has some practical advantages. If it did not occur, we would constantly be distracted by the stream of sensations we experience each day. We would not adapt to our clothing rubbing our skin, to the feel of our tongue in our mouth, or to bodily processes such as eye blinks and swallowing. However, sensory adaptation is not always beneficial and can even be dangerous. After about a minute, for example, our sensitivity to most odors drops by nearly 70 percent. Thus, in situations where smoke or harmful chemicals are present, sensory adaptation may actually reduce our sensitivity to existing dangers. In general, though, the process of sensory adaptation allows us to focus on important changes in the world around us, and that ability to focus on and respond to stimulus change is usually what is most important for survival.

Now that we've considered some basic aspects of sensation, let's examine in detail each of the major senses: vision, audition, touch, smell, taste, and the kinesthetic and vestibular senses.

**Figure 3.5**
**Sensory Adaptation**

At first icy water feels freezing; but later, because of sensory adaptation, it feels refreshing.

**REVIEW QUESTIONS**

- What is the primary function of our sensory receptors?
- What does the term *absolute threshold* refer to, and what are psychophysical methods?
- Why is signal detection theory important?
- What is a difference threshold?
- Can subliminal messages affect our behavior?
- What is the role of sensory adaptation in sensation?

## Vision

Web Link: *Retina Reference*

Light, in the form of energy from the sun, is part of the fuel that drives the engine of life on earth. Thus, it is not surprising that we possess remarkably adapted organs for detecting this stimulus: our eyes. Indeed, for most of us, sight is the most important way of gathering information about the world. Figure 3.6 on page 92 shows a simplified diagram of the human eye.

### The Eye: Its Basic Structure

How is light energy converted into signals our brain can understand? The answer lies in the basic structure of the eye. It is in the eye that light energy is converted into

**Sensory Adaptation:** Reduced sensitivity to unchanging stimuli over time.

**Figure 3.6**
**The Human Eye**

Light filters through layers of retinal cells before striking receptors (rods and cones) located at the back of the eye and pointed away from the incoming light. The rods and cones then stimulate bipolar cells, which, in turn, stimulate the ganglion cells. The axons of these cells form the fibers of the optic nerve.

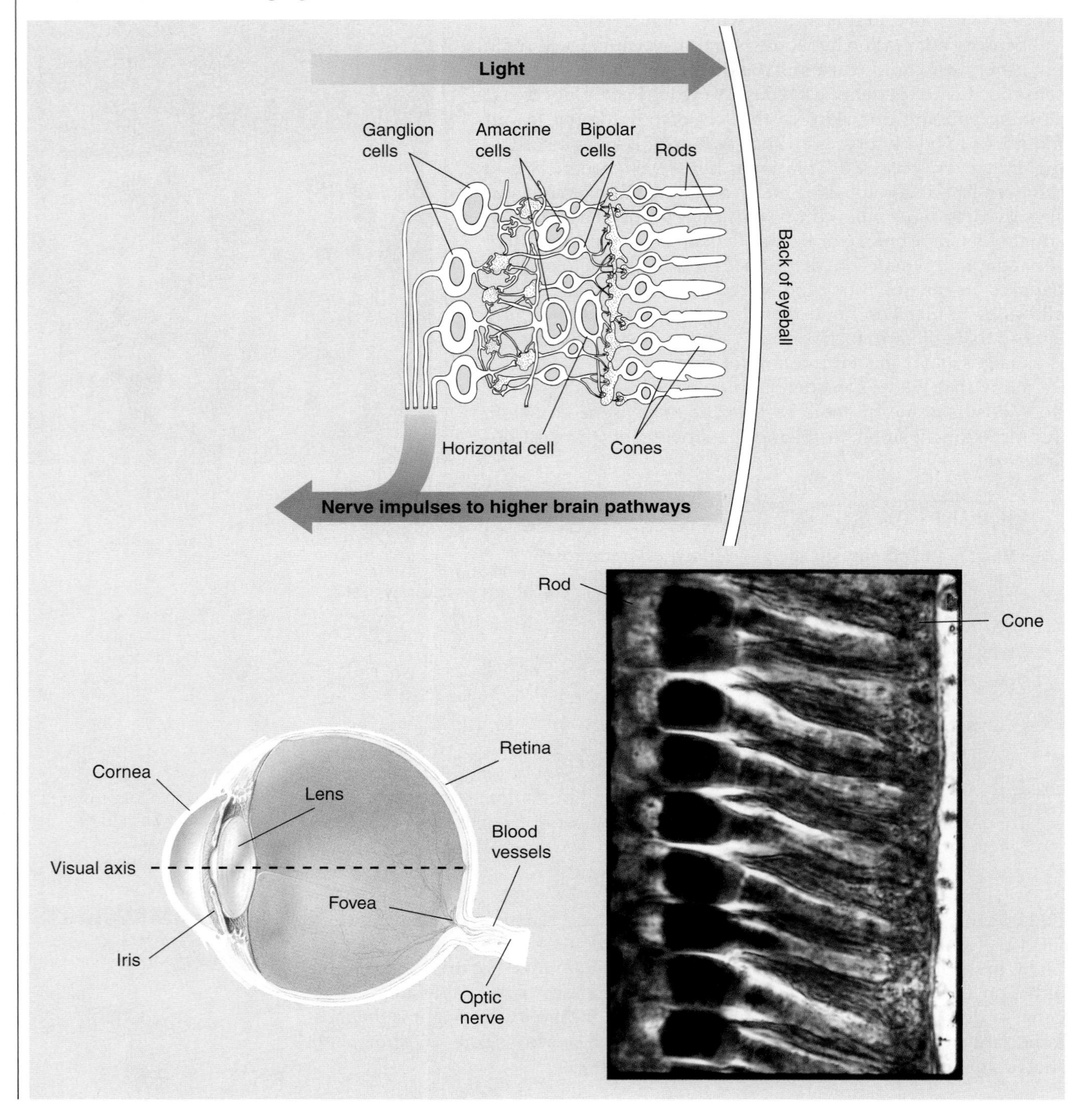


**Cornea:** The curved transparent layer through which light rays enter the eye.

a neural code understandable to our nervous system. Light rays first pass through a transparent protective structure called the **cornea** and then enter the eye through the **pupil,** a round opening whose size varies with lighting conditions: The less light

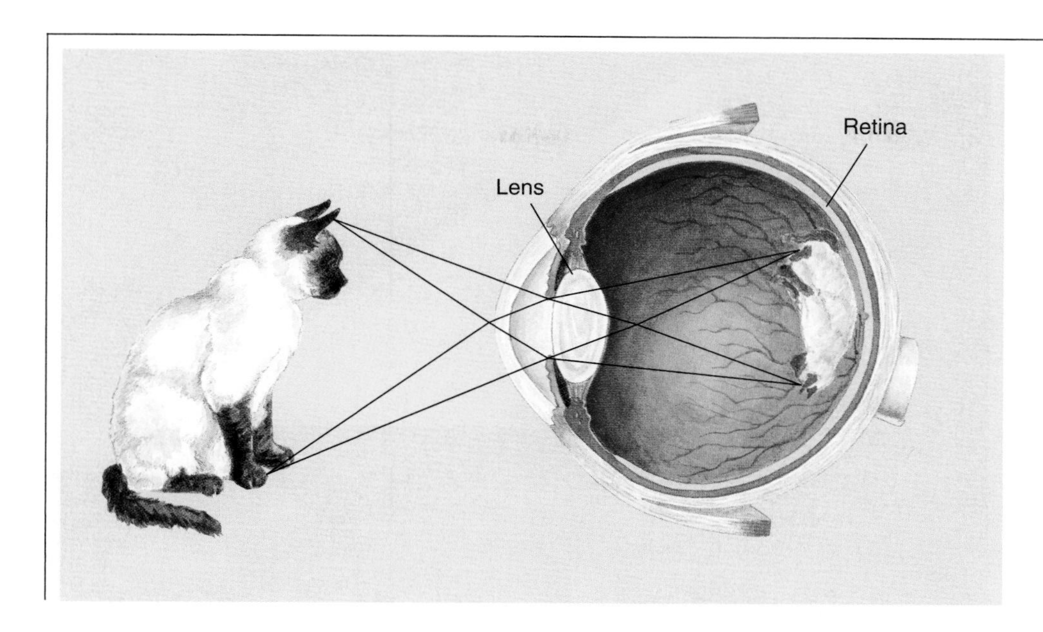


**Figure 3.7**
**The Upside-Down and Reversed Image Projected onto the Retina**

The lens bends light rays entering the eye so that the image projected onto the retina is upside down and reversed: Light rays from the top of an object are projected onto receptors at the bottom of the retina, and light rays from the left side of an object are projected onto receptors on the right side of the retina. Our brain rearranges this information and enables us to see the object correctly.

present, the wider the pupil opening (refer to Figure 3.6). These adjustments are executed by the **iris,** the colored part of the eye, which is actually a circular muscle that contracts or expands the pupil to let in varying amounts of light. After entering through the pupil, light rays pass through the **lens,** a clear structure whose shape adjusts to permit us to focus on objects at varying distances. When we look at a distant object, the lens becomes thinner and flatter; when we look at a nearby object, the lens becomes thicker and rounder. Light rays leaving the lens are projected on the **retina** at the back of the eyeball. As illustrated in Figure 3.7, the lens bends light rays in such a way that the image projected onto the retina is actually upside down and reversed; but the brain reverses this image, letting us see objects and people correctly.

The retina is a postage stamp–sized structure that contains two types of light-sensitive receptor cells: about 5 million **cones** and about 120 million **rods** (Coren, Ward, & Enns, 1999). Cones, located primarily in the center of the retina in an area called the **fovea,** function best in bright light and play a key role both in color vision and in our ability to notice fine detail. In contrast, rods are found only outside the fovea and function best under lower levels of illumination, so rods help us to see in a darkened room or at night. At increasing distances from the fovea, the density of cones decreases and the density of rods increases. Once stimulated, the rods and cones transmit neural information to other neurons called *bipolar cells.* These cells, in turn, stimulate other neurons, called *ganglion cells.* Axons from the ganglion cells converge to form the **optic nerve** and carry visual information to the brain. Interestingly, no receptors are present where this nerve exits the eye, so there is a **blind spot** at this point in our visual field.

**Pupil:** An opening in the eye, just behind the cornea, through which light rays enter the eye.

**Iris:** The colored part of the eye; adjusts the amount of light that enters by constricting or dilating the pupil.

**Lens:** A curved structure behind the pupil that bends light rays, focusing them on the retina.

**Retina:** The surface at the back of the eye containing the rods and cones.

**Cones:** Sensory receptors in the eye that play a crucial role in sensations of color.

**Rods:** One of the two types of sensory receptors for vision found in the eye.

**Fovea:** The area in the center of the retina in which cones are highly concentrated.

**Optic Nerve:** A bundle of nerve fibers that exit the back of the eye and carry visual information to the brain.

**Blind Spot:** The point in the back of the retina through which the optic nerve exits the eye. This exit point contains no rods or cones and is therefore insensitive to light.

**Wavelength:** The peak-to-peak distance in a sound or light wave.

**Hue:** The color that we experience due to the dominant wavelength of a light.

## Light: The Physical Stimulus for Vision

At this point we will consider some important facts about light, the physical stimulus for vision. First, the light that is visible to us is only a small portion of the electromagnetic spectrum. This spectrum ranges from radio waves at the slow or long-wave end to cosmic rays at the fast or short-wave end (refer to Figure 3.8 on page 94).

Second, certain physical properties of light contribute to our psychological experiences of vision. **Wavelength,** the distance between successive peaks and valleys of light energy, determines what we experience as **hue** or color. As shown in

**Figure 3.8**
**The Electromagnetic Spectrum**

Visible light occupies only a narrow band in the entire spectrum.

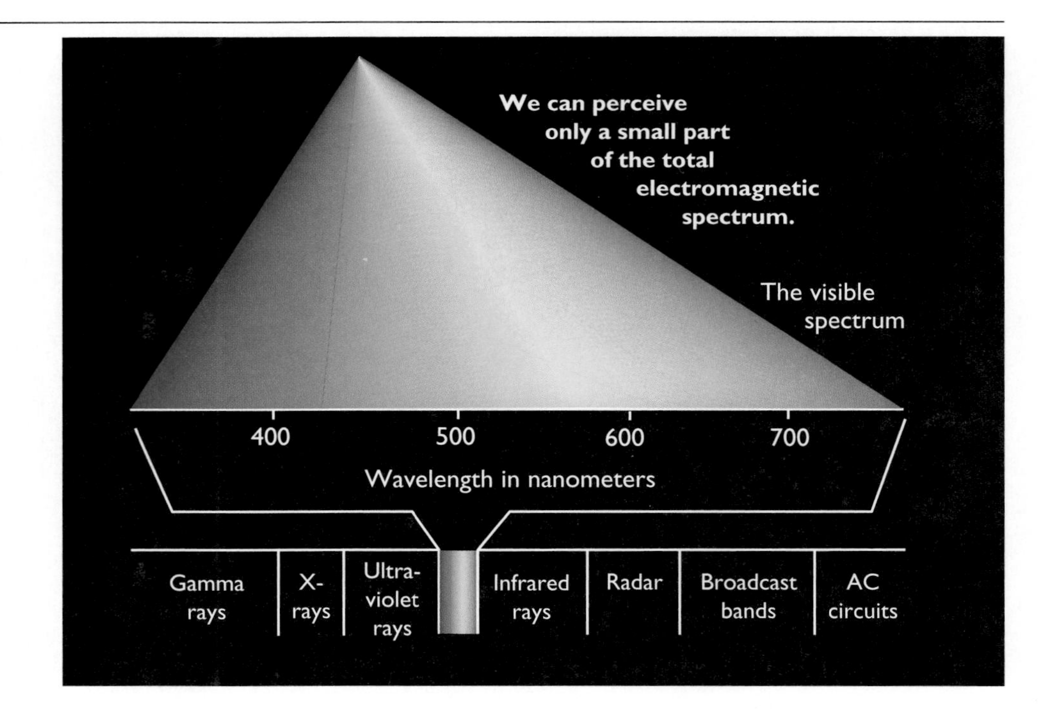

Web Link: *The Joy of Visual Perception: A Web Book*

Figure 3.8, as wavelength increases from about 400 to 700 nanometers (a nanometer is one billionth of a meter), our sensations shift from violet through blue (shorter wavelengths), green, yellow, orange (medium wavelengths), and finally red (longer wavelengths). The intensity of light, the amount of energy it contains, is experienced as **brightness.** The extent to which light contains only one wavelength, rather than many, determines our experience of **saturation;** the fewer the number of wavelengths mixed together, the more saturated or "pure" a color appears. For example, the deep red of an apple is highly saturated, whereas the pale pink of an apple blossom is low in saturation.

**Brightness:** The physical intensity of light.

**Saturation:** The degree of concentration of the hue of light. We experience saturation as the purity of a color.

**Acuity:** The visual ability to see fine details.

**Nearsightedness:** A condition in which the visual image entering our eye is focused slightly in front of our retina rather than directly on it. Therefore, near objects can be seen clearly, whereas distant objects appear fuzzy or blurred.

**Farsightedness:** A condition in which the visual image entering our eye is focused behind rather than directly on the retina. Therefore, close objects appear out of focus, whereas distant objects are in clear focus.

## Basic Functions of the Visual System: Acuity, Dark Adaptation, and Eye Movements

The human visual system is highly sensitive and can detect even tiny amounts of light. However, another important aspect of vision is **acuity,** the ability to resolve fine details. Two types of visual acuity are measured. The first is *static visual acuity (SVA),* our ability to discriminate different objects when they are stationary or static, as on the familiar chart at an eye doctor's office. The second measure of acuity is *dynamic visual acuity (DVA),* our ability to resolve detail when the test object and/or the viewer is in motion (Houfman, House, & Ryan, 1981). In general, our ability to discriminate objects decreases as the *angular velocity*—the speed at which an object's image moves across our retina—increases. This aspect of our visual capacity is important in, for example, the ability of baseball great Mark McGwire to detect a sizzling fastball on his way to hitting a grand slam home run.

If you wear eyeglasses or contact lenses designed to improve your visual acuity, chances are that your visual deficit stems from a slight abnormality in the shape of your eye or the cornea. If your eyeball is too long or the cornea is too stiffly curved, you suffer from **nearsightedness,** in which you see near objects clearly, but distant objects appear blurry. This occurs because the image entering your eye is focused slightly in front of the retina rather than directly on it. Similarly, in **farsightedness,** your eyeball is too short or the cornea too flat, and the lens focuses the image behind the retina. New surgical procedures have been developed to correct these problems. In one procedure, known as LASIK, a surgeon uses a motorized blade to create a hinged flap on the surface of the cornea, which is gently lifted up (please refer to Figure 3.9). A computer-controlled ultraviolet beam is then applied to reshape the underlying cornea. The flap is then returned to its original position, and healing begins. Most patients go home within an hour of the procedure, and nearly all experience improvement to their vision. In fact, according to one estimate, as many as 80 percent obtain perfect 20/20 vision (Rosenfeld, 1999).

**Figure 3.9**
**Applying Technology to Enhance Vision**

LASIX surgery is one of several emerging techniques used to reshape the cornea. After the eye is anesthetized with eyedrops, the surgeon uses a motorized blade to create a hinged flap on the surface of the cornea, which is gently lifted up. A computer-controlled ultraviolet beam is then used to reshape the underlying cornea. The flap is then returned to its original position.

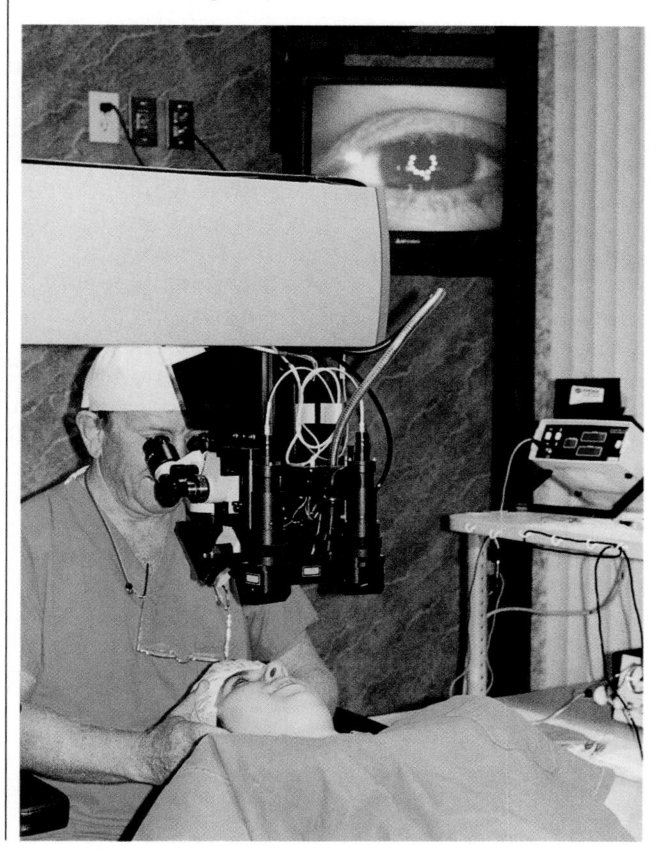

Another aspect of visual sensitivity is **dark adaptation,** the increase in sensitivity that occurs when we move from bright light to a dim environment, such as a movie theater. The dark-adapted eye is about 100,000 times more sensitive to light than the light-adapted eye. Actually, dark adaptation occurs in two steps. First, within five to ten minutes, the cones reach their maximum sensitivity. After about ten minutes, the rods begin to adapt; they complete this process in about thirty minutes (Matlin & Foley, 1997).

*Eye movements* also play a role in visual acuity. To appreciate the importance of the ability to move your eyes, just imagine how inefficient it would be to read a book or play your favorite sport if your eyes were stuck in one position. In order to change the direction of your gaze, you would have to move your entire head.

Eye movements are of two basic types: *version movements,* in which the eyes move together in the same direction, and *vergence movements,* in which the lines of sight for the two eyes converge or diverge. Three types of version movements are *involuntary movements, saccadic movements,* and *pursuit movements.* As we'll discover later in this chapter, vergence movements are crucial to our ability to perceive distance and depth.

At the end of this sentence, stop reading and stare at the last word for several seconds. Did your eyes remain motionless or did they tend to move about? The eye movements you probably experienced were *involuntary;* they occurred without your conscious control. These movements ensure that the stimuli reaching our rods and cones are constantly changing. Like other sensory receptors, those in our retina are subject to the effects of sensory adaptation; if involuntary movements did not occur, we would experience temporary blindness whenever we fixed our gaze on any object for more than a few seconds.

Web Link: *Blind Spot—Seeing More Than Your Eye Does*

**Saccadic movements** are fast, frequent jumps by the eyes from one fixation point to the next. Saccadic movements are apparent in reading or driving. Both the size of the jumps and the region seen during each fixation maximize the information we glean while reading (Just & Carpenter, 1987; McConkie & Zola, 1984). The saccadic movements of good readers move smoothly across the materials being read; those of poor readers are shorter and move backward as well as forward (Schiffman, 1990). Research suggests that characteristics of words tend to guide the location and duration of each fixation. Fixations tend to be shortest for short, predictable words that occur frequently (Reichle et al., 1998).

**Dark Adaptation:** The process through which our visual system increases its sensitivity to light under low levels of illumination.

**Saccadic Movements:** Quick movements of the eyes from one point of fixation to another.

**Trichromatic Theory:** A theory of color perception suggesting that we have three types of cones, each primarily receptive to different wavelengths of light.

**Negative Afterimages:** Sensations of complementary color that we experience after staring at a stimulus of a given hue.

**Opponent-Process Theory:** Theory that describes the processing of sensory information related to color at levels above the retina. The theory suggests that we possess six different types of neurons, each of which is either stimulated or inhibited by red, green, blue, yellow, black, or white.

Finally, *pursuit movements* are smooth movements used to track moving objects, as when you watch a plane fly overhead and out of sight.

## Color Vision

A world without color would be sadly limited; for color—vivid reds, glowing yellows, restful greens—is a crucial part of our visual experience. For many people, though, some degree of color deficiency is a fact of life. Nearly 8 percent of males and 0.4 percent of females are less sensitive than the rest of us either to red and green or to yellow and blue (Nathans, 1989). And a few individuals are totally color blind, experiencing the world only in varying shades of black and gray. Intriguing evidence on how the world appears to people suffering from color weakness has been gathered from rare cases in which individuals have normal color vision in one eye and impaired color vision in the other (e.g., Graham & Hsia, 1958). For example, one such woman indicated that to her color-impaired eye, all colors between red and green appeared yellow, while all colors between green and violet seemed blue.

There are two leading theories to explain our rich sense of color. The first, **trichromatic theory,** suggests that we have three different types of cones in our retina, each of which is maximally sensitive, though not exclusively so, to a particular range of light wavelengths—a range roughly corresponding to blue (400–500 nanometers), green (475–600 nanometers), or red (490–650 nanometers). Careful study of the human retina suggests that we do possess three types of receptors, although, as Figure 3.10 shows, there is a great deal of overlap among the three types' sensitivity ranges (DeValois & De Valois, 1975; Rushton, 1975). According to trichromatic theory, the ability to perceive colors results from the joint action of the three receptor types. Thus, light of a particular wavelength produces differential stimulation of each receptor type, and it is the overall pattern of stimulation that produces our rich sense of color. This differential sensitivity may be due to genes that direct different cones to produce pigments sensitive to blue, green, or red (Nathans, Thomas, & Hogness, 1986).

**Figure 3.10**
**Three Types of Receptors Contribute to Our Perception of Color**

Color vision appears to be mediated by three types of cones, each maximally (but not exclusively) sensitive to wavelengths corresponding to blue, green, or red.
(*Source:* Based on data from MacNichol, 1964.)

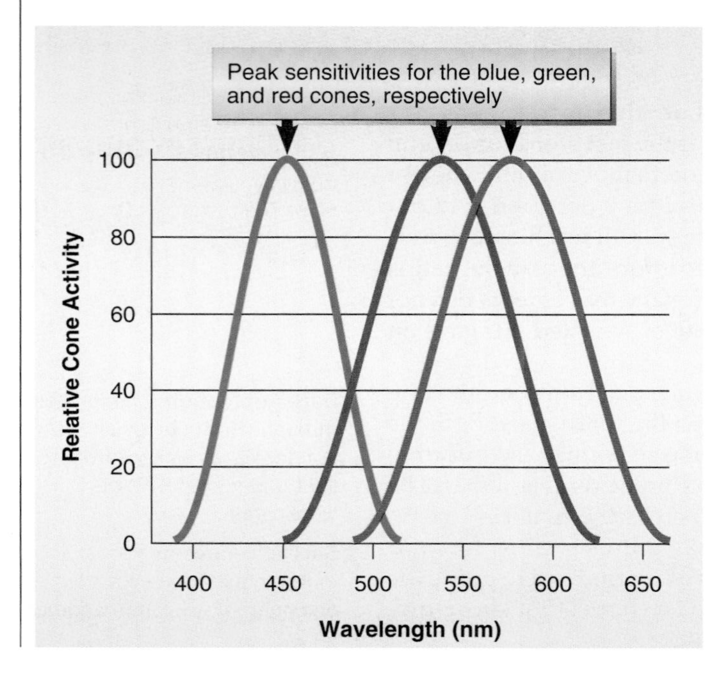


Trichromatic theory, however, fails to account for certain aspects of color vision, such as the occurrence of **negative afterimages**—sensations of complementary colors that occur after one stares at a stimulus of a given color. For example, after you stare at a red object, if you shift your gaze to a neutral background, sensations of green may follow. Similarly, after you stare at a yellow stimulus, sensations of blue may occur.

The **opponent-process theory** addresses these aspects more effectively by accounting for what happens after the cones in the retina transmit their information to the bipolar and ganglion cells, and to structures in the *visual cortex,* an area located at the back of the brain that processes visual information (Coren, Ward, & Enns, 1999). This theory suggests that we possess specialized cells that play a role in sensations of color (DeValois & DeValois, 1975). Two of these cells, for example, handle red and green: One is stimulated by red light and inhibited by green light, whereas the other is stimulated by green light and inhibited by red. This is where the phrase *opponent process* originates. Two additional types of cells handle yellow and blue; one is stimulated by yellow and inhibited by blue, while the other shows the opposite pattern. The remaining two types handle black and white—again, in an opponent-process manner. Opponent-process theory can help explain the occurrence of negative afterimages (Jameson & Hurvich, 1989). The idea is that when stimulation of one cell in an opponent pair is terminated, the other is automatically activated. Thus, if the original stimulus viewed was yellow, the afterimage seen would be blue. Each opponent pair is stimulated in different patterns by the three types of cones. It is the overall pattern of such stimulation that yields our complex and eloquent sensation of color.

Although these theories competed for many years, we now know that both are necessary to explain our impressive ability to respond to color. Trichromatic theory explains how color coding occurs in the cones of the retina, whereas opponent-process theory accounts for processing in higher-order nerve cells (Coren, Ward, & Enns, 1999; Hurvich, 1981; Matlin & Foley, 1997). We'll now turn to a discussion of how visual information is processed by the brain.

## Vision and the Brain: Processing Visual Information

Our rich sense of vision does not result from the output of single neurons, but instead from the overall pattern of our sensory receptors. In other words, there is more to vision than meets the eye. But how, then, do the simple action potentials of individual neurons contribute to our overall conscious experience? To help answer this question, let's consider how the brain "invents" our visual world.

The visual world we perceive results from a complex division of labor that only *begins* in the retina. In other words, it is only light that enters our eyes—we really see with our brains. Our understanding of the initial stages of this process was greatly advanced by the Nobel Prize–winning series of studies conducted by Hubel and Wiesel (1979). These researchers conducted studies on **feature detectors**—neurons at various levels in the visual cortex. Their work revealed the existence of three types of feature detectors. One group of neurons, known as **simple cells,** respond to bars or lines presented in certain orientations (horizontal, vertical, and so on). A second group, **complex cells,** respond maximally to moving stimuli, such as a vertical bar moving from left to right or a tilted bar moving from right to left. Finally, **hypercomplex cells** respond to even more complex features of the visual world, including length, width, and even aspects of shape such as corners and angles.

These findings led scientists to the intriguing possibility that the brain processes visual information hierarchically. According to this view, groups of neurons analyze simpler aspects of visual information and send their results to other groups of neurons for further analysis. At successive stages in this process, increasingly complex visual information is analyzed and compiled—eventually producing the coherent and flowing scenes that constitute our perception of the world around us (Zeki, 1992).

Consistent with this view, research using brain-imaging techniques (e.g., PET scans) has confirmed that various regions within the cortex are highly specialized to process only certain types of visual information—one region for color, another for brightness, yet another for motion, and so on. In fact, more than thirty distinct areas that process visual information have been identified (Felleman & Van Essen, 1991). Other studies have shown, however, that destruction of areas thought to be specialized for specific functions—for example, processing color information—doesn't necessarily eliminate color perception. Research now suggests another intriguing possibility: that cells in the visual cortex may play a dynamic role in processing visual information. In other words, the cells' function may not be fixed

**Feature Detectors:** Neurons at various levels within the visual cortex that respond primarily to stimuli possessing certain features.

**Simple Cells:** Cells within the visual system that respond to specific shapes presented in certain orientations (e.g., horizontal, vertical, etc.).

**Complex Cells:** Neurons in the visual cortex that respond to stimuli moving in a particular direction and having a particular orientation.

**Hypercomplex Cells:** Neurons in the visual cortex that respond to complex aspects of visual stimuli, such as width, length, and shape.

**Blindsight:** A rare condition resulting from damage to the primary visual cortex in which individuals report being blind, yet respond to certain aspects of visual stimuli as if they could see.

**Prosopagnosia:** A rare condition in which brain damage impairs a person's ability to recognize faces.

**Pinna:** The external portion of the ear.

but may change depending on what captures our attention or the personal relevance of a visual stimulus (Schiller, 1994).

Additional clues suggesting that the brain processes various aspects of visual information separately come from case studies of persons with visual disorders. For example, **blindsight** is a rare condition that results from damage to the primary visual cortex. Persons with blindsight are able to respond to certain aspects of visual stimuli, such as color or movement, as if they could see; yet, paradoxically, they are completely unaware of the stimuli and deny having "seen" anything (Gazzaniga, Fendrich, & Wessinger, 1994; Weiskrantz, 1995). A related disorder, termed **prosopagnosia,** provides further evidence that the visual system operates much like a computer, assembling bits of visual information at various locations in the brain. In prosopagnosia, persons lose the ability to recognize well-known persons by their faces but still retain relatively normal vision in other respects (Schweinberger, Klos, & Sommer, 1995). These disorders seem to confirm that a division of labor takes place in the visual system. This helps explain how we can lose certain visual abilities—such as recognizing faces—while others, including the ability to perceive form, motion, or color, remain largely unaffected (Barbur et al., 1993; Zeki, 1992).

Taken together, these findings have important implications for our understanding of visual perception. First, they suggest that the visual system is quite *selective;* certain types of visual stimuli stand a greater chance of reaching the brain and undergoing further processing. Second, because nature is rarely wasteful, the existence of cells specially equipped to detect certain features of the external world suggests that these features may be the building blocks for many complex visual abilities, including reading and identifying subtly varied visual patterns such as faces. Finally, as illustrated by disorders such as blindsight and prosopagnosia, "seeing" the world is a complex process—one that requires precise integration across many levels of our visual system.

**REVIEW QUESTIONS**

- What are the basic structures of the eye, and what is the physical stimulus for vision?
- What are the basic functions of the visual system?
- How do psychologists explain color perception?
- Why is visual perception a hierarchical process?
- What are the basic building blocks of visual perception?

# Hearing

The haunting melody of a beautiful song, the roar of a jet plane, the rustling of leaves on a crisp autumn day—clearly, we live in a world full of sound. And, as with vision, human beings are well equipped to receive many sounds in their environment. A simplified diagram of the human ear is shown in Figure 3.11; please refer to it as you proceed through the following discussion.

## The Ear: Its Basic Structure

Try asking a friend, "When did you get your pinna pierced?" The response will probably be a blank stare. **Pinna** is the technical term for the visible part of our hear-

**Figure 3.11**
**The Human Ear**

A simplified diagram of the human ear. Sound waves (alternating compressions and expansions in the air) enter through the external auditory canal and produce slight movements in the eardrum. This, in turn, produces movements in fluid within the cochlea. As this fluid moves, tiny hair cells shift their position, thus generating the nerve impulses we perceive as sound.

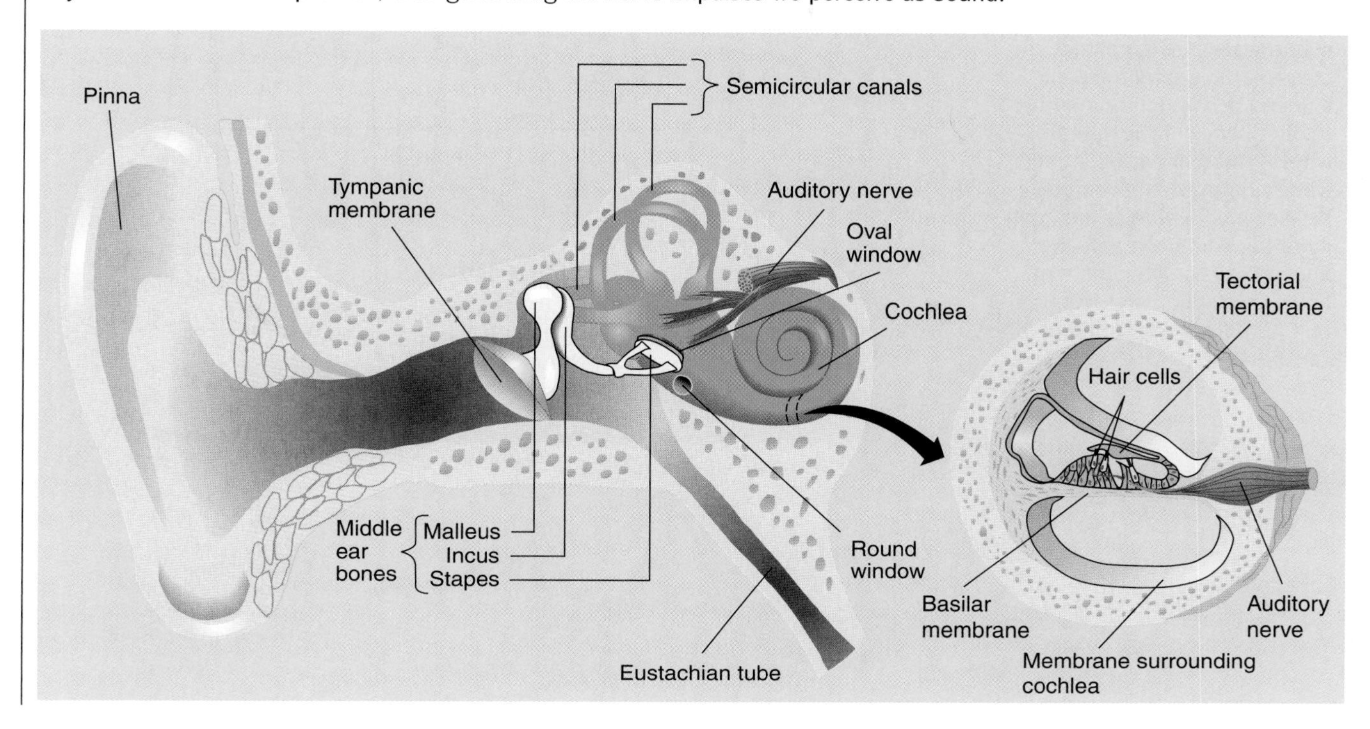


ing organ, the *ear.* However, this is only a small part of the entire ear. Inside the ear is an intricate system of membranes, small bones, and receptor cells that transform sound waves into neural information for the brain. The *eardrum,* a thin piece of tissue just inside the ear, moves ever so slightly in response to sound waves striking it. When it moves, the eardrum causes three tiny bones within the *middle ear* to vibrate. The third of these bones is attached to a second membrane, the *oval window,* which covers a fluid-filled, spiral-shaped structure known as the **cochlea.** Vibration of the oval window causes movements of the fluid in the cochlea. Finally, the movement of fluid bends tiny *hair cells,* the true sensory receptors of sound. The neural messages they create are then transmitted to the brain via the *auditory nerve.*

## Sound: The Physical Stimulus for Hearing

In discussing light, we noted that relationships exist between certain of its physical properties, such as wavelength and intensity, and psychological aspects of vision, such as hue and brightness. Similar relationships exist for sound, at least with respect to two of its psychological qualities: *loudness* and *pitch.*

Sound waves consist of alternating compressions of the air, or, more precisely, of the molecules that compose air. The greater the *amplitude* (magnitude) of these waves, the greater their loudness to us; see Figure 3.12 on page 100. The rate at which air is expanded and contracted constitutes the *frequency* of a sound wave, and the greater the frequency, the higher the **pitch.** Frequency is measured in terms

**Cochlea:** A portion of the inner ear containing the sensory receptors for sound.

**Pitch:** The characteristic of a sound that is described as high or low. Pitch is mediated by the frequency of a sound.

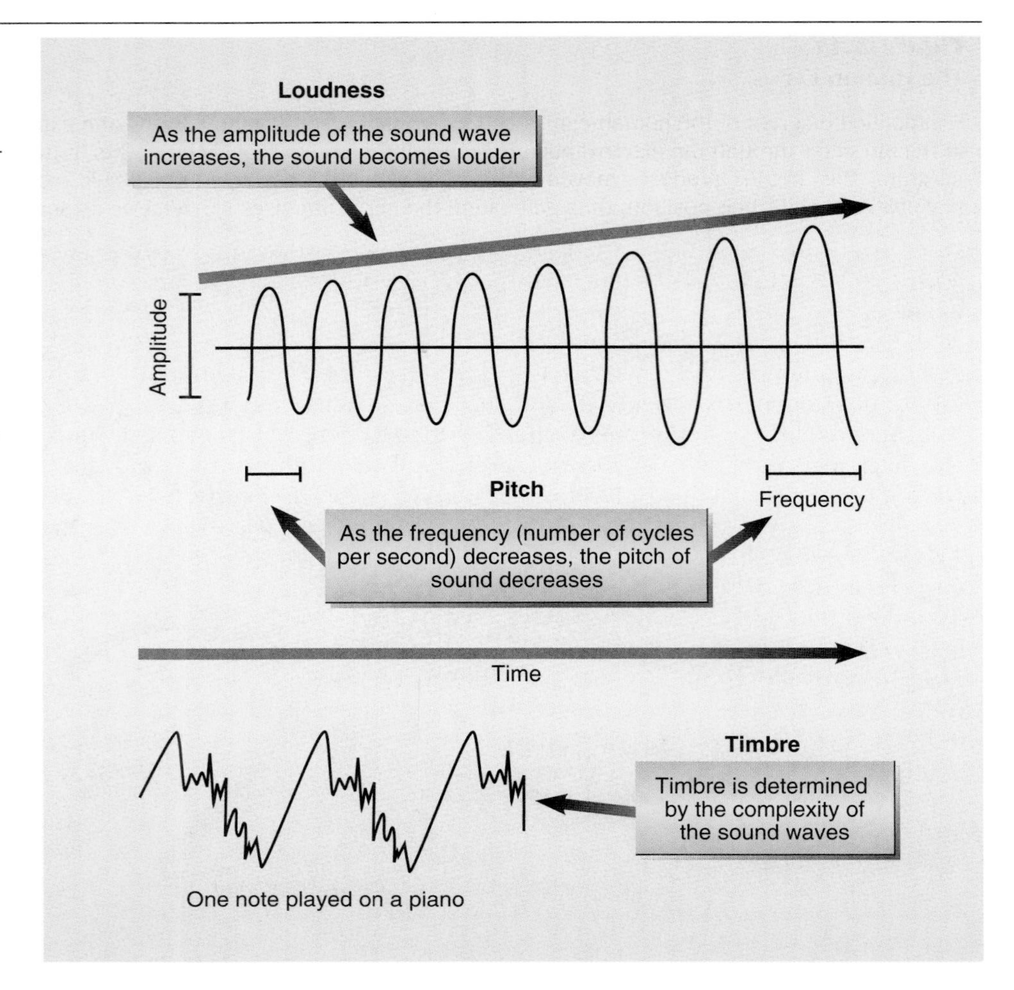


**Figure 3.12**
**Physical Characteristics of Sound**

Our perception of sounds is determined by three characteristics. *Loudness* depends on the amplitude, or height, of the sound waves; as amplitude increases, the sound appears louder. *Pitch* is determined by the frequency of the sound waves—the number of sound waves that pass a given point per second. *Timbre* is the quality of the sound we perceive and is the characteristic that helps us distinguish the sound of a flute from the sound of a saxophone.

of cycles per second, or hertz (Hz). Children and young adults can generally hear sounds ranging from about 20 Hz to about 20,000 Hz. Older adults progressively lose sensitivity, particularly for higher sound frequencies. The human ear is most sensitive to sounds with frequencies between 1,000 and 5,000 Hz (Coren, Ward, & Enns, 1999).

A third psychological aspect of sound is its **timbre,** or quality. This quality depends on the mixture of frequencies and amplitudes that make up the sound. For example, a piece of chalk squeaking across a blackboard may have the same pitch and amplitude as a note played on a clarinet, but it will certainly have a different quality. In general, the timbre of a sound is related to its complexity—how many different frequencies it contains. Other physical aspects of the source of the sound may be involved as well, however, so the relationship is not simple (refer to Figure 3.12).

**Timbre:** The quality of a sound, resulting from the complexity of a sound wave; timbre helps us to distinguish the sound of a trumpet from a saxophone.

**Place Theory:** A theory of pitch perception suggesting that sounds of different frequencies stimulate different areas of the basilar membrane, the portion of the cochlea containing sensory receptors for sound.

## Pitch Perception

When we tune a guitar or sing in harmony with other people, we demonstrate our ability to detect differences in pitch. Most of us can easily tell when two sounds have the same pitch and when they are different. But how do we manage to make such fine distinctions? Two explanations, based on two different mechanisms, seem to provide the answer.

**Place theory** (also called the *traveling wave theory*) suggests that sounds of different frequencies cause different places along the *basilar membrane* (the floor of the cochlea) to vibrate. These vibrations, in turn, stimulate the hair cells—the sensory receptors for sound. Actual observations have shown that sound does produce pressure waves and that these waves peak, or produce maximal displacement, at various distances along the basilar membrane, depending on the frequency of the sound (Békésy, 1960). High-frequency sounds cause maximum displacement at the narrow end of the basilar membrane near the oval window, whereas lower frequencies cause maximal displacement toward the wider, farther end of the basilar membrane. Unfortunately, place theory does not explain our ability to discriminate among very low-frequency sounds—sounds of only a few hundred cycles per second—because displacement on the basilar membrane is nearly identical for these sounds. Another problem is that place theory does not account for our ability to discriminate among sounds whose frequencies differ by as little as 1 or 2 Hz; for these sounds, too, basilar membrane displacement is nearly identical.

A second explanation, termed **frequency theory,** suggests that sounds of different pitch cause different rates of neural firing. Thus, high-pitched sounds produce high rates of activity in the auditory nerve, whereas low-pitched sounds produce lower rates. Frequency theory seems to be accurate up to sounds of about 1,000 Hz—the maximum rate of firing for individual neurons. Above that level, the theory must be modified to include the *volley principle*—the assumption that sound receptors for other neurons begin to fire in volleys. For example, a sound with a frequency of 5,000 Hz might generate a pattern of activity in which each of five groups of neurons fires 1,000 times in rapid succession—that is, in volleys.

Because our daily activities regularly expose us to sounds of many frequencies, both theories are needed to explain our ability to respond to this wide range of stimuli. Frequency theory explains how low-frequency sounds are registered, whereas place theory explains how high-frequency sounds are registered. In the middle ranges, between 500 and 4,000 Hz, the range that we use for most daily activities, both theories apply.

## Sound Localization

You are walking down a busy street, filled with many sights and sounds. Suddenly, a familiar voice calls your name. You instantly turn in the direction of this sound and spot one of your friends. How do you know where to turn? Research on **localization**—the ability of the auditory system to locate the source of a given sound—suggests that several factors play a role.

The first is the fact that we have two ears, placed on opposite sides of our head. As a result, our head creates a *sound shadow,* a barrier that reduces the intensity of sound on the "shadowed" side. Thus, a sound behind us and to our left will be slightly louder in our left ear. The shadow effect is strongest for high-frequency sounds, which have difficulty bending around the head, and may produce a difference in intensity of 30 decibels or more in the ear farthest away (Phillips & Brugge, 1985). The placement of our ears also produces a slight difference in the time it takes for a sound to reach each ear. Although this difference is truly minute—often less than one millisecond—it provides an important clue to sound localization.

What happens when sound comes from directly in front or directly in back of us? In such cases, we often have difficulty determining the location of the sound source, because the sound reaches our ears at the same time. Head movements can help resolve a problem like this. By turning your head, you create a slight difference in the time it takes for the sound to reach each of your ears—and now you can determine the location of the sound and take appropriate action (Moore, 1982).

In summary, our auditory system is ideally constructed to take full advantage of a variety of subtle cues. When you consider how rapidly we process and respond to such information, the whole system seems nothing short of marvelous in its

**Frequency Theory:** A theory suggesting that sounds of different frequencies (heard as differences in pitch) induce different rates of neural activity in the hair cells of the inner ear.

**Localization:** The ability of our auditory system to determine the direction of a sound source.

efficiency. Let's turn now to the **Beyond the Headlines** section below, which points out that the devices of modern living—tools and toys designed to make life easier—can actually decrease our quality of life by contributing to permanent hearing loss.

## BEYOND the HEADLINES: *As Psychologists See It*

## Premature Hearing Loss: The High Cost of Modern Living

### What'd you say? A High-Volume World Takes a Toll on Ever Younger Ears

U.S. NEWS & WORLD REPORT, APRIL 26, 1999. Like any loyal southerner, 42-year-old Marilynn Mobley grew up with the classic film *Gone with the Wind.* The only problem was that her impaired hearing had led to an interesting interpretation of the movie's ending. Until just recently—*after* she had read the book version—Marilynn thought Rhett Butler's famous line in the final scene of the movie was: "Frankly, I'm here and I wanna dig a dam," rather than "Frankly, my dear, I don't give a damn" (Kulman, 1999).

What was the cause of Marilynn's distorted perception of the movie's ending? A premature hearing loss induced by repeated exposure to gunfire. Because her father was a gunsmith, Marilynn had spent much of her youth target shooting on their farm. Unfortunately, she failed to wear ear protection, despite her father's urgings to do so. Marilynn's story highlights a growing problem in the United States: the fact that people are suffering significant permanent hearing loss at increasingly younger ages. Data from the National Health Interview Survey reveal that during the period 1971 to 1990, hearing problems increased 26 percent among people between the ages of 45 and 64 and 17 percent among those between the ages of 18 and 44. Even more alarming is the discovery of a similar trend among young persons between the ages of 6 and 19. Nearly 15 percent of persons in this age group showed evidence of premature hearing loss.

The cause appears to be noise from the toys and tools of modern living: car stereos and stereo headsets, electric blow-dryers, lawn mowers and leaf blowers, and even some children's toys. Although these devices are intended to offer convenience, enhance work performance, or heighten the pleasure we derive from recreational activities, there is growing concern that they may damage our hearing. Raging rock concerts, well known for their capacity to produce hearing loss among performing artists and their listeners, are being supplanted by advances in digital sound technologies that allow car owners to play their car stereos at more than 150 decibels. Another less well-known source of dangerous noise is air bags. Designed to lessen occupant injuries in the event of a vehicle crash, these devices can permanently damage hearing—because the sound that accompanies their deployment can reach levels up to 170 decibels!

Although very intense sounds like the ones just described can produce permanent damage following a single exposure, most of the damage appears to be the result of long-term exposure to moderately intense sounds, as occurs when people regularly crank up the volume of a stereo headset or work for long periods with or around noisy equipment (e.g., lawn mowers or industrial equipment; please refer to Figure 3.13).

To assess the effects of noise on hearing loss, psychologists measure hearing thresholds—the minimum level at which sounds are detected—at various sound frequencies before and after exposure to sounds of certain intensity. Three types of hearing loss are usually distinguished: *temporary threshold shift (TTS),* a short-term and reversible elevation of the level at which sounds are first heard; *permanent threshold shift (PTS),* nonreversible hearing loss from long-term exposure to noise; and *acoustic trauma,* permanent hearing loss stemming from brief exposure to extremely intense noise such as an explosion (Jones & Broadbent, 1987). How much sound is required to produce hearing loss? Much less than you might think. Exposure to 90-decibel sound levels—the level of noise that might be present in a crowded restaurant—can produce a TTS of nearly 20 decibels after only one and a half hours of sound exposure.

Hearing loss is actually the result of damage to the ear's sensory receptors, about 15,000 tiny hair cells that line the floor of the basilar membrane. The basilar membrane runs the length of the cochlea, a snail-shaped structure located deep within the inner ear (Coren, Ward, & Enns, 1999). There are actually two types of hair cell receptors: *inner hair cells* and *outer hair cells.* The inner hair cells (about 3,000 in each ear) detect mechanical vibrations on the basilar membrane and transform these vibrations into action potentials that are sent on to the brain. The outer hair cells, which are able to change their length in response to electrical or chemical stimulation, appear to help sharpen and amplify weak sounds (Moore & Oxenham, 1998).

Both types of hair cells bend in response to sound-induced mechanical vibrations relayed by the bones in the middle ear. Differential bending of the hair cells is converted to a neural code that is delivered to the brain and interpreted as sound. Initially, sound causes only temporary distortion of the hair cells; but over time hair cells lose their resilience, and the damage becomes permanent. Long-term exposure to moderately intense sound apparently speeds up the process.

Unfortunately, the public remains largely unaware of the damage that modern technologies can inflict on the sensitive organs that enable us to hear. This lack of awareness is due, at least in part, to the gradual nature of the decline. In other words, except in instances involving extremely intense sound, most hearing loss occurs only after years of exposure. So, the next time you get the urge to pump up the volume of your headset or think about not using protective equipment (e.g., ear plugs) before mowing the lawn or starting the weed-eater, consider the long-term advantages of making correct decisions. The hearing you save may be your own.

## CRITICAL THINKING QUESTIONS

1. Assuming that people tend to *under*estimate their susceptibility to hearing loss (which they do), do you feel that you are at risk for suffering permanent hearing loss? If so, what devices do you feel may contribute the most?
2. Why do you think people fail to take precautions to prevent hearing loss?

| Source of Sound | Sound Intensity (in decibels or dB) |
|---|---|
| A whisper | 30 dB |
| Normal conversation | 60 dB |
| Vacuum cleaner | 75 dB |
| Ringing telephone | 80 dB |
| City traffic | 85 dB |
| Hair dryer or power lawn mower | 90 dB |
| Chain saw and some children's toys | 110 dB |
| Stereo headset (turned to high setting) | 112 dB |
| Stadium football game | 117 dB |
| Ambulance siren | 120 dB |
| Noisy squeak toys | 135 dB |
| Firecrackers or jet engine at takeoff | 140 dB |
| Gunshot | 165 dB |
| Rocket launch | 180 dB |

Long-term exposure to sound intensities at or above these levels can produce permanent hearing loss.

**Figure 3.13**
**Decibels in Everyday Life**

Examples of sound intensities (in decibels) that are a part of modern daily life.

## REVIEW QUESTIONS

- What is the physical stimulus for hearing?
- How do psychologists explain pitch perception?
- How do we localize sound?
- How do psychologists measure hearing loss, and how much sound is required to produce it?

# Touch and Other Skin Senses

The skin is our largest sensory organ and produces the most varied experiences: everything from the pleasure of a soothing massage to the pain of an injury. Actually, there are several skin senses, including touch (or pressure), warmth, cold, and pain. As there are specific sensory receptors for vision and hearing, it seems reasonable to expect this also to be true for the various skin senses as well—one type of receptor for touch, another for warmth, and so on. And microscopic examination reveals several different receptor types, which led early researchers to suggest that each receptor type produced a specific sensory experience. However, the results of research conducted to test this prediction were disappointing; specific types of receptors were *not* found at spots highly sensitive to touch, warmth, or cold. Other studies have also shown that many different types of receptors often respond to a particular stimulus. Therefore, the skin's sensory experience is probably determined by the total pattern of nerve impulses reaching the brain (Sherrick & Cholewiak, 1986).

Have you ever wondered why certain areas on your body are more sensitive than others? As it turns out, the receptors in skin are not evenly distributed; the touch receptors in areas highly sensitive to touch, such as the face and fingertips, are much more densely packed than receptors in less sensitive areas, such as our legs. Additionally, areas of the skin with greater sensitivity also have greater representation in higher levels of the brain.

In most instances we discover the texture of an object through active exploration—using our fingertips or other sensitive areas of our body. Psychologists distinguish between *passive touch,* in which an object comes in contact with the skin, and *active touch,* in which we place our hand or other body part in contact with an object. We are considerably more accurate at identifying objects through active than through passive touch, in part because of feedback we receive from the movement of our fingers and hands when exploring an object (Matlin & Foley, 1997). Let's now turn to a discussion of how the sense of touch helps us experience pain.

Web Link: *Pain Library*

## Pain: Its Nature and Control

Pain plays an important adaptive role; without it, we would be unaware that something is amiss with our body or that we have suffered some type of injury. Determining the mechanisms for pain sensation has been particularly difficult, because unlike the other sensory processes that we have studied, pain sensation has no specific stimulus (Besson & Chaouch, 1987). However, sensations of pain do seem to originate in *free nerve endings* located throughout the body: in the skin, around muscles, and in internal organs (Carlson, 1998).

Actually, two types of pain seem to exist. One can best be described as quick and sharp—the kind of pain we experience when we receive a cut. The other is dull and throbbing—the pain we experience from a sore muscle or an injured back. The first type of pain seems to be transmitted through large myelinated sensory nerve fibers (Campbell & LaMotte, 1983). You may recall from Chapter 2 that impulses travel faster along myelinated fibers, and so it makes sense that sharp sensations of pain are carried via these fiber types. In contrast, dull pain is carried by smaller unmyelinated nerve fibers, which conduct neural impulses more slowly. Both fiber types synapse with neurons in the spinal cord that carry pain messages to the thalamus and other parts of the brain (Willis, 1985).

**Gate-Control Theory:** A theory of pain suggesting that the spinal cord contains a mechanism that can block transmission of pain to the brain.

**PAIN PERCEPTION: THE ROLE OF PHYSIOLOGICAL MECHANISMS** The discovery of the two pain systems described above led to the formulation of an influential view of pain known as the **gate-control theory** (Melzack, 1976). Gate-control theory suggests that there are neural mechanisms in the spinal cord that sometimes close, thus preventing pain messages from reaching the brain. Apparently, pain messages carried by the large fibers cause this "gate" to close, whereas messages carried by the smaller fibers—the ones related to dull, throbbing pain—do not. This may explain why sharp pain is relatively brief, whereas an ache persists. The gate-control theory also helps to explain why vigorously stimulating one area sometimes succeeds in reducing pain in another (Matlin & Foley, 1997). Presumably, countermeasures such as rubbing the skin near an injury, applying ice packs or hot-water bottles, and even acupuncture stimulate activity in the large nerve fibers, closing the spinal "gate" and reducing sensations of pain.

Gate-control theory has been revised to account for the importance of several brain mechanisms in the perception of pain (Melzack, 1993). For example, our current emotional state may interact with the onset of a painful stimulus to alter the intensity of pain we experience. The brain, in other words, may affect pain perception by transmitting messages that either close the spinal "gate" or keep it open. The result: When we are anxious, pain is intensified; when we are calm and relaxed, pain may be reduced. Gate-control theory has spurred the development of innovative treatment techniques, such as the use of neural stimulation devices to relieve pain (Abram, 1993). Additional factors, including culture, also play a role in the perception of pain, and we'll consider this important topic next.

**PAIN PERCEPTION AND CULTURE** Imagine the following scene: You are in the midst of an ancient tribal ceremony. Using an eagle's talon, an old man rips the skin above a younger man's chest, then inserts lengths of bone horizontally through each of the wounds. Amazingly, the young man's stoic expression remains unchanged. Loops of rope are secured around the bones, and the young man is hoisted into the air—where he is allowed to dangle until the bones tear through the skin or he becomes unconscious.

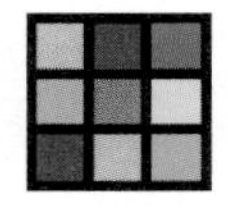

Sound like a sadistic late-night horror show? It's actually a description of "Swinging to the Pole," a ceremony practiced by the Lakota Sioux and Cheyenne tribes in which warriors demonstrate their courage and ability to withstand tremendous pain. This ceremony, and similar ones in other cultures, have led to intriguing questions about the nature of pain (Weisenberg, 1982). Although we commonly view pain as something automatic and universal, large cultural differences in the interpretation and expression of pain do exist. But what is the basis for these differences?

Web Link: *Questions and Answers about Pain Control*

At first glance, it is tempting to conclude that cultural differences in *pain threshold*—physical differences—are the cause. However, no consistent experimental evidence supports this view (Zatzick & Dimsdale, 1990). Instead, observed cultural differences in the capacity to withstand pain—or not—seem to be perceptual in nature and to reflect the powerful effects of social learning (Morse & Morse, 1988). For example, honor and social standing among the Bariba of West Africa are tied closely to stoicism and the ability to withstand great pain (Sargent, 1984). Thus, both Bariba men and women are expected to suffer pain silently. And, as you might expect, their language contains few words for the expression of pain.

In sum, the evidence suggests that pain may be universal—at least in some respects—and that differences in pain perception result from the powerful effects of social learning, not from physical differences among various groups of people.

**PAIN PERCEPTION: THE ROLE OF COGNITIVE PROCESSES** Emerging evidence seems to indicate that pain exerts its unpleasant effects by interrupting ongoing thought and behavior and redirecting our attention to the pain (Eccleston & Crombez, 1999). The extent to which we experience pain results from a dynamic interplay between two factors: characteristics related to the pain (e.g., its intensity, novelty, predictability) and the context in which the pain emerges. Cognition, or thought, appears to play a critical mediator role, determining the extent to which we focus on pain relative to these factors and the degree of threat they pose to us. This cognitive activity may help explain why procedures that redirect our attention are effective countermeasures for pain. Hypnosis, for example, has been shown to be effective in reducing the effects of pain, apparently by activating a supervisory attention-control system in the brain that shifts the focus of our attention away from the pain (Crawford, Knebel, & Vendemia, 1998). (Please refer to Chapter 4 for additional information on hypnosis.)

A group of therapies collectively termed *cognitive–behavioral procedures* have also been shown to be effective in counteracting the effects of pain (Novy et al., 1995; Turk, 1994). These procedures are based on the fact that our thoughts, feelings, and beliefs can dramatically influence our perceptions of pain (Sullivan, Bishop, & Pivik, 1995; Turk & Rudy, 1992). As mentioned earlier, for example, research suggests that a positive mood state can reduce our perception of pain. In one experiment, Weisenberg, Raz, and Hener (1998) had study participants watch one of three types of film (or no film): a humorous film intended to induce a positive mood; a Holocaust film to induce a negative mood; or a neutral film that was not expected to affect mood one way or the other. Participants were then exposed to a harmless but painful stimulus. As predicted, participants who viewed the humorous movie demonstrated greater pain tolerance than participants exposed to the other film types or participants who did not see a movie. These results suggest that maintaining a positive outlook can be an effective tool to counteract the effects of pain.

Our beliefs seem to also play an important role in pain perception. Montgomery and Kirsch (1996), for example, led participants in their study to believe they would be involved in testing a new topical anesthetic for its pain-reducing effect. The fictitious pain reliever (placebo) was actually a harmless but medicinal-smelling mixture dispensed from a bottle labeled "Trivaricane: Approved for research purposes only." The researchers applied the mixture to either the left or the right index finger of each participant. After waiting a brief period of time to allow the "medication" to take effect, the researchers applied equal intensities of a painful stimulus (pressure) to both the left *and* right fingers. As predicted, the placebo was effective in reducing the participants' perceptions of pain. These results illustrate the important role cognitive processes play in determining the extent to which we experience pain.

**REVIEW QUESTIONS**

- What is the physical stimulus for touch?
- Where does the sensation of pain originate?
- What is the basis for cultural differences in pain perception?
- What roles do cognitive processes play in the perception of pain?

## Smell and Taste: The Chemical Senses

Although smell and taste are separate senses, we'll consider them together for two reasons. First, both respond to substances in solution—substances that have been dissolved in a fluid or gas, usually water or air. That is why smell and taste are often referred to as the *chemical senses.* Second, in everyday life, smell and taste are interrelated.

### Smell and Taste: How They Operate

The stimulus for sensations of *smell* consists of molecules of various substances (odorants) contained in the air. Such molecules enter the nasal passages, where they dissolve in moist nasal tissues. This brings them in contact with receptor cells contained in the *olfactory epithelium* (see Figure 3.14). Human beings possess only about 50 million of these receptors. (Dogs, in contrast, possess more than 200 million receptors.) Nevertheless, our ability to detect smells is impressive. In a "scratch-and-sniff" smell survey distributed in *National Geographic* magazine, for example, six different odors were embedded separately onto panels about 1.75 by 1.25 inches in size. Less than one ounce of each odor was needed to place the smells onto 11 million copies of the survey (Gibbons, 1986; Gilbert & Wysocki, 1987). Yet, despite the tiny amounts deposited on each survey, people were easily able to detect the smells.

**Figure 3.14**
**The Receptors for Smell**

Receptors for our sense of smell are located in the olfactory epithelium, at the top of the nasal cavity. Molecules of odorous substances are dissolved in moisture present in the nasal passages. This brings them into contact with *receptor cells,* whose neural activity gives rise to sensations of smell.

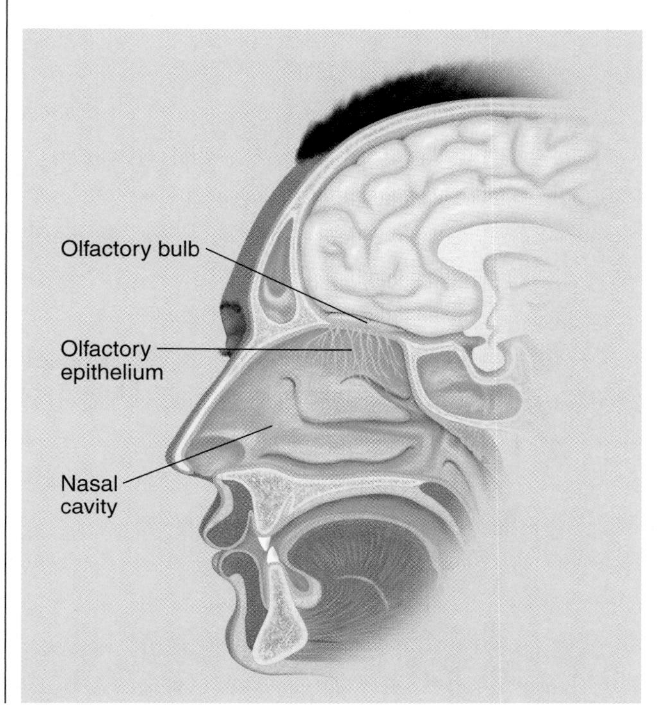


Our olfactory senses are restricted, however, in terms of the *range* of stimuli to which they are sensitive. Just as the visual system can detect only a small portion of the total electromagnetic spectrum, human olfactory receptors can detect only substances with molecular weights—the sum of the atomic weights of all atoms in an odorous molecule—between 15 and 300 (Carlson, 1998). This explains why we can smell the alcohol contained in a mixed drink, with a molecular weight of 46, but cannot smell table sugar, with a molecular weight of 342.

Several theories have been proposed for how smell messages are interpreted by the brain. *Stereochemical theory* suggests that substances differ in smell because they have different molecular shapes (Amoore, 1970, 1982). Unfortunately, support for this theory has been mixed; nearly identical molecules can have extremely different fragrances, whereas substances with very different chemical structures can produce very similar odors (Engen, 1982; Wright, 1982). Other theories have focused on isolating "primary odors," similar to the basic hues in color vision. But these efforts have been unsuccessful, because different individuals' perceptions of even the most basic smells often disagree.

One additional intriguing possibility is that the brain's ability to recognize odors may be based on the overall pattern of activity produced by the olfactory receptors (Sicard & Holley, 1984). According to this view, humans possess many different types of olfactory receptors, each one of which is stimulated to varying degrees by a particular odorant. Different patterns of stimulation may, in turn, result in different patterns of output that the brain recognizes as specific odors. How the brain accomplishes this task is not yet known.

We'll now turn to a discussion of the other chemical sense—*taste.* The sensory receptors for taste are located inside small bumps on the tongue known as *papillae.* Within each papilla is a cluster of *taste buds* (Figure 3.15 on page 108). Each taste bud contains several receptor cells. Human beings possess about 10,000 taste buds. In contrast, chickens have only 24, while catfish would win any "taste bud–counting contest"—they possess more than 175,000, scattered over the surface of their body. In a sense, catfish can "taste" with their entire skin (Pfaffmann, 1978).

People generally believe that they can distinguish a large number of flavors in foods. But in fact, there appear to be only four basic tastes: sweet, salty, sour, and bitter. Why, then, do we perceive many more? The answer lies in the fact that we are aware not only of the taste of the food but of its smell, its texture, its temperature, the pressure it exerts on our tongue and mouth, and many other sensations.

**Figure 3.15**
**Sensory Receptors for Taste**

Taste buds are located inside small bumps on the surface of the tongue known as papillae; within each taste bud are a number of individual receptor cells. Also shown are the areas of the tongue most sensitive to the four basic tastes: bitter, sour, salty, and sweet.

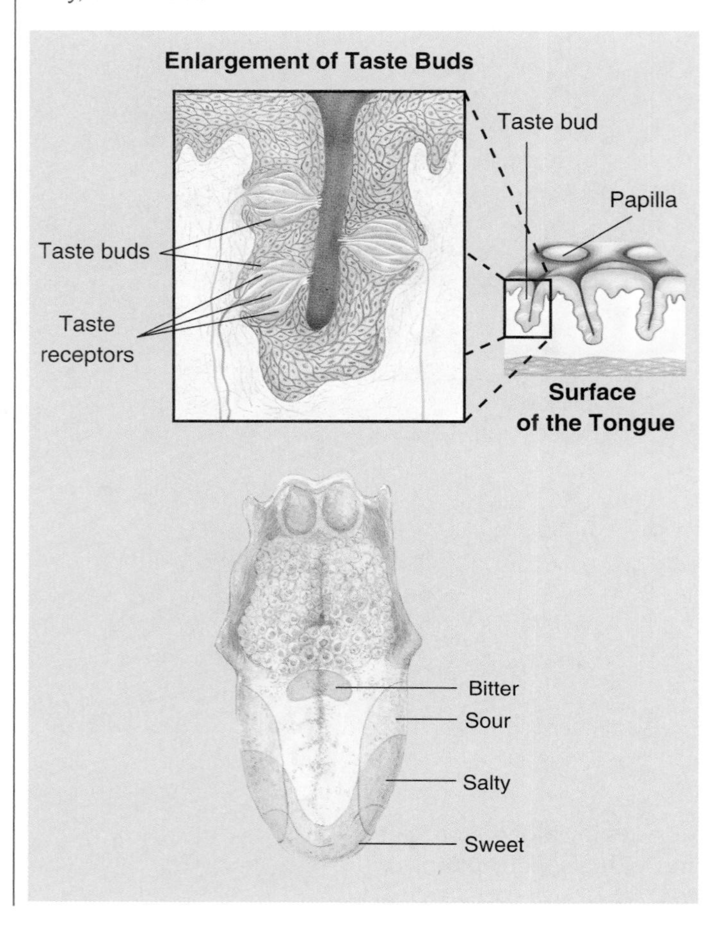


When these factors are removed from the picture, only the four basic tastes remain (see Figure 3.15).

## Smell and Taste: Some Interesting Facts

Perhaps because they are more difficult to study, smell and taste have received far less attention from researchers than vision and hearing. However, this does not imply that these senses are not important. Indeed, individuals who have lost their sense of smell (a state known as anosmia) often become deeply depressed; some even commit suicide (Douek, 1988).

Despite the relative lack of research effort, many interesting facts have been uncovered about smell and taste. For example, it appears that we are not very good at identifying different odors (Engen, 1986). When asked to identify thirteen common fragrances (such as grape, smoke, mint, pine, and soap), individuals were successful only 32 percent of the time. Even when brand-name products or common odors are used, accuracy is still less than 50 percent. Some research suggests that we lack a well-developed representational system for describing olfactory experiences (Engen, 1987). In other words, we may recognize a smell without being able to name the odor in question—a condition sometimes called the "tip-of-the-nose" phenomenon (Lawless & Engen, 1977; Richardson & Zucco, 1989). And some experiments have shown that when odorants are associated with experimenter-provided verbal and visual cues, participants' long-term ability to recognize odors is enhanced (Lyman & McDaniel, 1986, 1987).

CourseCompass
Audio 3.2: *Effects of Fragrance on Human Behavior*

Actually, although our ability to identify specific odors is limited, our memory of them is impressive (Schab, 1991). Once exposed to a specific odor, we can recognize it months or even years later (Engen & Ross, 1973; Rabin & Cain, 1984). This may be due, in part, to the fact that our memory for odors is often coded as part of memories of a more complex and significant life event (Richardson & Zucco, 1989). For example, the delicious aroma of freshly made popcorn may elicit images of your favorite movie theater.

Knowledge about the chemical senses—especially smell—can also have important practical implications, a fact that has not escaped manufacturers of scented products. Commercial success has led to numerous claims regarding the potential benefits of fragrance. For example, practitioners of a field called *aromatherapy* claim that they can successfully treat a wide range of psychological problems and physical ailments by means of specific fragrances (Tisserand, 1977). Supposedly, the fragrances yield a variety of benefits: Aromatherapists claim, for example, that fragrances such as lemon, peppermint, and basil lead to increased alertness and energy, whereas lavender and cedar promote relaxation and reduced tension after high-stress work periods (Iwahashi, 1992). Can fragrance influence human behavior in measurable ways? A growing body of evidence indicates that the answer is yes. But whether specific fragrances produce contrasting effects is still uncertain. Although some findings support this claim, others do not. A recent study by Diego and his colleagues (1998) provides some supporting evidence. Participants in this study were exposed to either lavender, supposedly a "relaxing" odor, or rosemary, presumably an "alerting" odor. Results showed that participants exposed to the rosemary fragrance were indeed more alert following the exposure, as gauged by self-report measures and changes in their EEG patterns. And although both fragrances led to *faster* performance on a math computation task, only participants exposed to the lavender fragrance showed improved *accuracy*.

Findings from other research, however, seriously question the claim that specific odors produce specific effects (e.g., Baron, 1997; Baron & Bronfen, 1994; Baron & Thomley, 1994). These studies suggest that *any* fragrance people find pleasant enhances their mood slightly, and that these positive feelings then influence their cognition and behavior (see Chapters 6 and 16). The specific fragrance doesn't seem to matter as long as it is one people find pleasant.

Nevertheless, even these more limited effects may have practical applications. For example, Baron and Kalsher (1998) tested the possibility that providing a pleasant ambient fragrance might be a cost-effective way to increase drivers' alertness and so combat drowsiness. To test this possibility they conducted a study in which participants performed a simulated driving task under varying conditions, including in the presence or absence of a pleasant lemon fragrance found to increase alertness in previous research (Baron & Thomley, 1994). Results indicated that performance on the task was significantly enhanced by the presence of a pleasant fragrance, thus suggesting that the use of fragrance may be an inexpensive but effective tool for maintaining alertness in persons engaged in potentially dangerous activities such as driving. So no, pleasant fragrances don't seem to have the powerful and highly specific effects aromatherapists claim; but yes, they do seem to influence behavior in interesting and potentially important ways.

**REVIEW QUESTIONS**

- What is the physical stimulus for smell, and where are the sensory receptors located?
- Where are the sensory receptors for taste located?
- What are the potential practical benefits of pleasant ambient fragrances?

## Kinesthesia and Vestibular Sense

Web Link: *The Vestibular Disorder Association Homepage*

One night while driving, you notice flashing lights on the roadside ahead. Because traffic has slowed to a crawl, you get a close look at the situation as you pass by. A state trooper is in the process of administering a sobriety test to the driver of the car he has pulled over. The driver's head is tilted back at an angle, and he is trying to touch each of his fingers to his nose but is having great difficulty doing so. This example illustrates the importance of our *kinesthetic* and *vestibular senses*—two critical but often ignored aspects of our sensory system.

**Kinesthesia:** The sense that gives us information about the location of our body parts with respect to one another and allows us to perform movement.

**Kinesthesia** is the sense that gives us information about the location of our body parts with respect to one another and allows us to perform movements—from simple ones like touching our nose with our fingertips to more complex movements required for gymnastics, dancing, or driving an automobile. Kinesthetic information

**Figure 3.16**
**The Structures Underlying Our Sense of Balance**

The sensory organs for the vestibular sense are located in the inner ear. Structures in the two *vestibular sacs* provide information about the positions of the head and body with respect to gravity by tracking changes in linear movement, whereas those in the *semicircular canals* provide information about *rotational acceleration* around three principal axes.

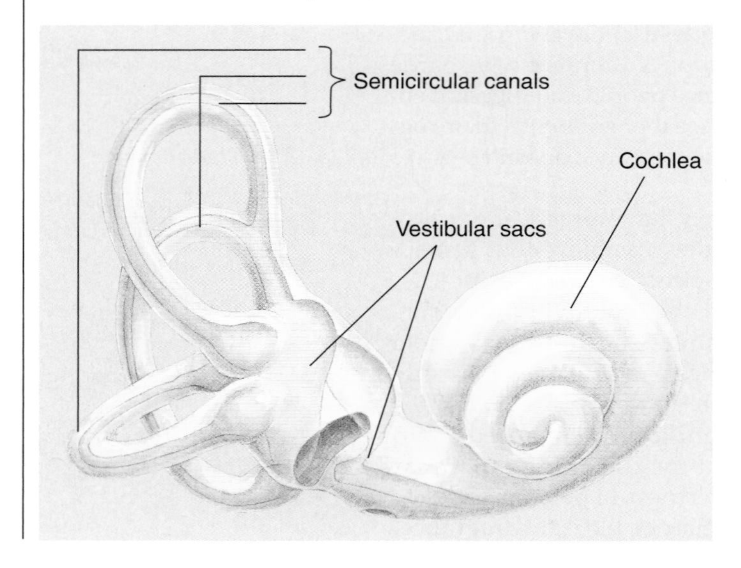


comes from receptors in joints, ligaments, and muscle fibers (Matlin & Foley, 1997). When we move our body, these receptors register the rate of change of movement speed as well as the rate of change of the angle of the bones in our limbs, then transform this mechanical information into neural signals for the brain. We also receive important kinesthetic information from our other senses, especially vision and touch. To demonstrate how your kinesthetic sense system draws on other senses, try the following experiment: Close your eyes for a moment and hold your arms down at your sides. Now, without looking, touch your nose with each of your index fingers—one at a time. Can you do it? Most people can, but only after missing their nose a time or two. Now try it again with your eyes open. Is it easier this way? In most instances it is, because of the added information we receive from our visual sense.

Whereas kinesthesia keeps our brain informed about the location of our body parts with respect to one another, the **vestibular sense** gives us information about body position, movement, and acceleration—factors critical for maintaining our sense of balance (Schiffman, 1990). We usually become aware of our vestibular sense after activities that make us feel dizzy, like the rides at amusement parks that involve rapid acceleration or spinning motions.

The sensory organs for the vestibular sense are located in the inner ear (see Figure 3.16). Two fluid-filled *vestibular sacs* provide information about the body's position in relation to the earth by tracking changes in linear movement. When our body accelerates (or decelerates) along a straight line, as when we are in a bus that is starting and stopping, or when we tilt our head or body to one side, hair cells bend in proportion to the rate of change in our motion. This differential bending of hair cells causes attached nerve fibers to discharge neural signals that are sent to the brain.

Three fluid-filled *semicircular canals,* also in the inner ear, provide information about rotational acceleration of the head or body along three principal axes. Whenever we turn or rotate our head, the fluid in these canals begins to move and causes a bending of hair cells. Because these structures are arranged at right angles to one another, bending is greatest in the semicircular canal corresponding to the axis along which the rotation occurs. Note that the vestibular system is designed to detect changes in motion rather than constant motion. For example, it helps us to perceive the change in acceleration that accompanies takeoff in an airplane, but not the constant velocity that follows.

We also receive vestibular information from our other senses, especially vision—a fact that can produce queasy consequences if the information from these senses is in conflict (Jefferson, 1993). During the early 1990s, developers of a realistic "Back to the Future" ride at Universal Studios in Florida discovered this fact when riders in their DeLorean simulator suffered from motion sickness. Apparently the visual effects were not synchronized with the movements the riders felt. Fortunately, scientists have learned from these early mistakes. Technologists can now combine an understanding of basic sensory systems with modern computer capabilities to create exciting—and useful—virtual environments, as we'll explore next in the **From Science to Practice** section on the opposite page.

**Vestibular Sense:** Our sense of balance.

**Telepresence:** A process in which a person's perceptual, cognitive, and psychomotor capabilities are projected virtually into simulated environments.

from SCIENCE to PRACTICE

## How a Basic Understanding of Sensory Processes Can Improve the Usefulness of Virtual Technologies

Consider each of the following situations:

- A woman lies dying in a hospital bed; the surgeon who can save her life is thousands of miles away at another hospital.
- Scientists wish to learn more about the surface of a distant planet. Although it is possible to reach the planet, exploration of the planet by humans may be unsafe.
- An explosion at a nuclear power plant ruptures a steam pipe, releasing a steady flow of radioactive steam. The pipe must be repaired to prevent further leakage, but the area surrounding the site of the explosion is contaminated by deadly radiation.

What do each of these fictitious, but plausible, incidents have in common? They all describe problems that can be solved through the use of **telepresence:** a process in which a person's perceptual, cognitive, and psychomotor capabilities are projected virtually into distant, dangerous, or simulated environments (Draper, Kaber, and Usher, 1998). Telepresence and the underlying virtual environments that support it are made possible through powerful computers that generate a steady stream of sensory information (e.g., visual, auditory, kinesthetic, vestibular) to the user. This information creates the perception that one is immersed in, or part of, the simulated environment.

Virtual environment (VE) technologies are finding numerous exciting new applications. They have, for example, given rise to a new generation of interactive video games that make participants feel as if they're actually a part of the virtual environment (see Figure 3.17). VE technologies are also effective training aids, particularly for people learning to perform dangerous or life-threatening tasks; for example, flying sophisticated aircraft or performing delicate surgical procedures (Christiansen, Alreu, & Huffman, 1996; Psotka, 1995). Why? Because these technologies allow learners to hone their skills through participation in realistic simulations—but spare them from expensive or life-threatening consequences should something go wrong.

How can psychologists help shape these rapidly advancing technologies? By applying their knowledge of basic sensory and perceptual processes to (1) enhance the realism of VEs and the extent to which people feel they are immersed; (2) determine the amount and type of sensory information that is necessary to facilitate performance in the simulated environment; and (3) design interfaces that improve people's ability to interact with and manipulate objects in the VE.

Initial research on VEs focused on the use of head-mounted visual displays. These devices permit people to participate visually in VEs, but they do not provide the cues from other senses that are necessary for people to feel immersed in, or part of, the VE. In addition, the disconnect between the cues

**Figure 3.17**
**Virtual Environments: Computer-Generated Worlds That Look and Feel Like the Real Thing**

New video games and amusement park rides incorporate virtual reality to give us the thrill of a lifetime.

people receive from head-mounted displays and those they receive from their other senses produces a mismatch that can lead to eyestrain, nausea, and disorientation (Bailey & Witmer, 1994). Systematic research has identified ways to enhance the realism of VEs that may help reduce the potential negative effects associated with their use (Barfield & Weghorst, 1995). These enhancements generally involve providing input to more than one sensory modality. For example, merely adding auditory cues has been shown to improve visual search performance in VEs (e.g., Flanagan et al., 1998; Nelson et al., 1998). Kinesthic and vestibular cues also seem to enhance the perceived realism of VEs.

Research also shows that the interfaces people use to interact with or manipulate objects in the VE can greatly affect performance. Werkhoven and Groen (1998), for example, compared people's ability to manipulate objects in a VE while using either a computer mouse or a virtual hand. The researchers predicted that performance might be better with the virtual hand. Why? Because virtual hands reproduce the movements of a real hand and permit people to grasp, rotate, and position objects in ways that mimic the use of a real human hand. The results indicated that participants who used the virtual hand were, in fact, faster and more accurate in completing the manipulation tasks than participants who used the mouse.

Although VE and telepresence are still in their infancy, it is clear they offer great potential for solving important problems in a world increasingly driven by technology. It is also clear that psychology will play a critical role as these exciting new technologies unfold.

REVIEW QUESTIONS

- What information does our kinesthetic sense provide to the brain?
- What information does our vestibular sense provide to the brain?
- How can psychology contribute to the development of virtual environments and telepresence?

Web Link: *Sensation and Perception Tutorials*

# Perception: Putting It All Together

Up to this point, we have focused on the sensory processes that convert raw physical stimulation into usable neural codes: vision, hearing, touch, taste, smell, and the kinesthetic and vestibular senses. But you may now be wondering how this array of action potentials contributes to the richness of conscious experience. Stop for a moment and look around you. Do you see a meaningless swirl of colors, brightnesses, and shapes? Probably not. Now turn on the radio and tune it to any station. Do you hear an incomprehensible babble of sounds? Certainly not (unless, of course, you've tuned to a foreign-language or heavy metal station). In both cases, you "see" and "hear" more than the raw sensations that stimulate the receptors in your eyes, ears, and other sense organs; you see recognizable objects and hear understandable words or music. In other words, transmission of sensory information from sensory receptors to the brain is only part of the picture. Equally important is the process of perception—the way in which we *select, organize,* and *interpret* sensory input to achieve a grasp of our surroundings. The remainder of this chapter concerns some basic principles that influence perception.

## Perception: The Focus of Our Attention

Based on the preceding discussion, you may realize that your attention, or mental focus, captures only a small portion of the visual and auditory stimuli available at a given moment, while ignoring other aspects. But what about information from our other senses? By shifting the focus of our attention, we may suddenly notice smells, tastes, and tactile sensations that were outside our awareness only moments ago. For example, if you're absorbed in a good book or watching a suspenseful movie, you may be unaware of the sound of someone knocking at the door, at least temporarily.

One thing is certain—we cannot absorb all of the available sensory information in our environment. Thus, we *selectively attend* to certain aspects of our environment while relegating others to the background (Johnston & Dark, 1986). Selective attention has obvious advantages, in that it allows us to maximize information gained from the object of our focus while reducing sensory interference from other irrelevant sources (Matlin & Foley, 1997). Unfortunately, selective attention to one thing may mean neglecting another. For a firsthand understanding of the power of selective attention, watch someone who is completely absorbed in a suspenseful novel or a thrilling sports event. Studies have shown that people can focus so intently on one task that they fail to notice other events occurring simultaneously—even very salient ones (Rensink, O'Regan, & Clark, 1997; Cherry, 1953). We are, however, faced with many everyday situations in which we must cope with multiple conflicting inputs. Think back to the last time you were at a crowded party with many conversations going on at once. Were you able to shut out all voices except for the voice of the person you were talking to? Probably not. Our attention often shifts to other aspects of our environment, such as a juicy bit of conversation or a mention of our own name (Moray, 1959). This is often referred to as the *cocktail party phenomenon* and illustrates one way in which we deal with the demands of divided attention.

Although we control the focus of our attention, at least to some extent, certain characteristics of stimuli can cause our attention to shift suddenly. Features such as contrast, novelty, stimulus intensity, color, and sudden change tend to attract our attention. As you might expect, the ability to shift the focus of our attention to detect such changes plays a crucial survival role in aspects of our everyday life by alerting us to immediate dangers in our environment—enabling us, for example, to leap back onto the curb when we catch a glimpse of a speeding car out of the corner of our eye. You can probably imagine hundreds of ways in which attentional processes help you to avoid peril.

**Gestalt Psychologists:** German psychologists intrigued by our tendency to perceive sensory patterns as well-organized wholes rather than as separate, isolated parts.

**Figure–Ground Relationship:** Our tendency to divide the perceptual world into two distinct parts—discrete figures and the background against which they stand out.

## Perception: Some Organizing Principles

Look at the illustrations in Figure 3.18. Instead of random bits of black and white, you can probably discern a familiar figure in each. But how does our brain allow us to interpret these confused specks as a dog and a horseback rider? The process by which we structure the input from our sensory receptors is called *perceptual organization.* Aspects of perceptual organization were first studied systematically in the early 1900s by **Gestalt psychologists**—German psychologists intrigued by certain innate tendencies of the human mind to impose order and structure on the physical world and to perceive sensory patterns as well-organized wholes rather than as separate, isolated parts (*Gestalt* means "whole" in German). These scientists outlined several principles that influence the way we organize basic sensory input into whole patterns (gestalts). Some of these are described below. You could say that the Gestalt psychologists changed our perceptions about the nature of perception.

**FIGURE AND GROUND: WHAT STANDS OUT?** By looking carefully at Figure 3.19 on page 114, you can experience a principle of perceptual organization known as the **figure–ground relationship.** What this means, simply, is that we

**Figure 3.18**
**Perceptual Organization**

Look carefully at each of these figures. What do you see? Our perceptual processes often allow us to perceive shapes and forms from incomplete and fragmented stimuli.

**Figure 3.19**
**A Demonstration of Figure–Ground**

What do you see when you look at this drawing? Probably, either a young woman or an old woman. Because this is an ambiguous figure, your perceptions may switch back and forth between these two possibilities.

tend to divide the world around us into two parts: *figure,* which has a definite shape and a location in space; and *ground,* which has no shape, seems to continue behind the figure, and has no definite location. The figure–ground relationship helps clarify the distinction between sensation and perception. Although the pattern of sensory input generated in our receptors remains constant, our perceptions shift between the two figure–ground patterns in Figure 3.19; thus, we may see either a young woman or an old woman, but not both. Note that the principles of perceptual organization apply to the other senses, too. For instance, consider how the figure–ground relationship applies to audition: During a complicated lecture, you become absorbed in whispered gossip between two students sitting next to you; the professor's voice becomes background noise. Suddenly you hear your name and realize that the professor has asked you a question; her voice has now become the sole focus of your attention, while the conversation becomes background noise.

**GROUPING: WHICH STIMULI GO TOGETHER?** The Gestaltists also called attention to a series of principles known as the **laws of grouping**—basic ways in which we group items together perceptually. Several of these laws are illustrated in Figure 3.20. As you can see from this figure, they do offer a good description of our perceptual tendencies.

The principles outlined by Gestalt psychologists are not, however, hard-and-fast rules. They are merely descriptions of ways in which we perceive the world around us. Whether these principles are innate, as the Gestaltists believe, or learned, as some newer evidence suggests, is still open to debate. In any case, principles of perceptual organization are readily visible in the natural world, and they are effective in helping us organize our perceptual world.

## Constancies and Illusions: When Perception Succeeds—and Fails

Perception, we have seen, is more than the sum of all the sensory input supplied by our eyes, ears, and other receptors. It is the active selection, organization, and interpretation of such input. It yields final products that differ from raw, unprocessed sensations in important ways. Up to now, this discussion has focused on the benefits of this process. But perception, like any other powerful process, can be a double-edged sword. On the one hand, perception helps us adapt to a complex and ever changing environment. On the other hand, perception sometimes leads us into error. To see how, let's consider *constancies* and *illusions.*

**Laws of Grouping:** Simple principles describing how we tend to group discrete stimuli together in the perceptual world.

**Constancies:** Our tendency to perceive physical objects as unchanging despite shifts in the pattern of sensations these objects induce.

**Size Constancy:** The tendency to perceive a physical object as having a constant size even when the size of the image it casts on the retina changes.

**PERCEPTUAL CONSTANCIES: STABILITY IN THE FACE OF CHANGE** Try this simple demonstration. Hold your right hand in front of you at arm's length. Next, move it toward and away from your face several times. Does it seem to change in size? Probably not. The purpose of this demonstration is to illustrate the principles of perceptual **constancies**—our tendency to perceive aspects of the world as unchanging despite changes in the sensory input we receive from them. The principle of **size constancy** relates to the fact that the perceived size of an object remains the same when the distance is varied, even though the size of the image it casts on the retina changes greatly. Under normal circumstances, such constancy is impressive. Consider, for example, seeing a friend you are meeting for lunch walking toward you, though still several blocks away. Distant objects—including cars, trees, and people—cast tiny images on your retina. Yet you perceive them as being of nor-

**Figure 3.20**
**Laws of Perceptual Grouping**

We seem to possess strong tendencies to group stimuli together in certain ways. Several of these *laws of grouping* are illustrated here.

**Laws of Similarity**

Tendency to perceive similar items as a group

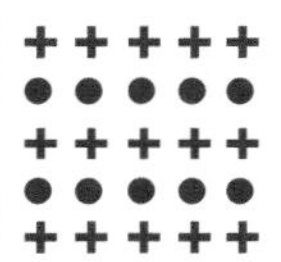

**Laws of Proximity**

Tendency to perceive items located together as a group

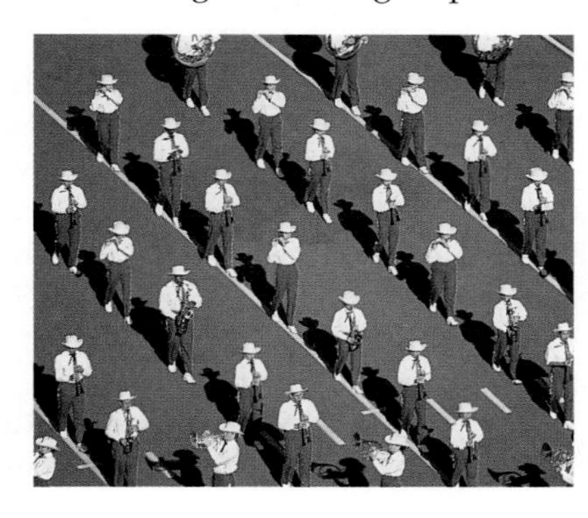

**Laws of Common Region**

Tendency to perceive objects as a group if they occupy the same place within a plane

**Law of Good Continuation**

Tendency to perceive stimuli as part of a continuous pattern

**Law of Closure**

Tendency to perceive objects as whole entities, despite the fact that some parts may be missing or obstructed from view

**Laws of Simplicity**

Tendency to perceive complex patterns in terms of simpler shapes

mal size. Two factors seem to account for this tendency: size–distance invariance and relative size.

The principle of *size–distance invariance* suggests that when estimating the size of an object, we take into account both the size of the image it casts on our retina and the apparent distance of the object. From these data we almost instantly calculate the object's size. Only when the cues that normally reveal an object's distance are missing do we run into difficulties in estimating the object's size (as we'll see in our discussion of illusions that follows). We also notice the **relative size** of an object compared to objects of known size. This mechanism is especially useful for estimating the size of unfamiliar things.

But size is not the only perceptual feature of the physical world that does not correspond directly with the information transmitted by our sensory receptors. The principle of **shape constancy** refers to the fact that the perceived shape of an object does not alter as the image it casts on the retina changes (refer to Figure 3.21 on page 116). For example, all of us know that coins are round; yet we rarely see them that way. Flip a coin into the air: Although you continue to perceive the coin as being round, the image that actually falls onto your retina constantly shifts from a circle to various forms of an ellipse.

The principle of **brightness constancy** refers to the fact that we perceive objects as constant in brightness and color, even when they are viewed under different

**Relative Size:** A visual cue based on comparison of the size of an unknown object to objects of known size.

**Shape Constancy:** The tendency to perceive a physical object as having a constant shape even when the image it casts on the retina changes.

**Brightness Constancy:** The tendency to perceive objects as having a constant brightness when they are viewed under different conditions of illumination.

**Figure 3.21**
**Shape Constancy: A Simple Example**

The principle of shape constancy allows us to recognize a coin as round, despite the fact that the shape of the image cast on the retina changes as the coin spins.

lighting conditions. Thus, we will perceive a sweater as dark green whether indoors or outdoors in bright sunlight. Brightness constancy apparently prevails because objects and their surroundings are usually lighted by the same illumination source, so changes in lighting conditions occur simultaneously for both the object and its immediate surroundings. As long as the changes in lighting remain constant for both object and surroundings, the neural message reaching the brain is unchanged. Brightness constancy breaks down, however, when changes in lighting are not equivalent for both the object and its surroundings (Sekuler & Blake, 1990).

Although most research on perceptual constancies has focused on size, shape, and brightness, constancy pervades nearly every area of perception, including our other senses. For example, imagine listening to background music while riding on an elevator. When one of your favorite oldies from the mid-1980s begins, but recorded by a different group, you can't believe what they've done to "your song." Nonetheless, you are still able to recognize it, despite differences in its loudness, tone, and pitch.

Whatever their basis, perceptual constancies are highly useful. Without them, we would spend a great deal of time and effort reidentifying sensory information in our environments each time we experienced the information from a new perspective. Thus, the gap between our sensations and the perceptions provided by the constancies is clearly beneficial.

**ILLUSIONS: WHEN PERCEPTION FAILS** We've seen that perception organizes sensory information into a coherent picture of the world around us. Perception can also, however, provide false interpretations of sensory information. Such cases are known as **illusions,** a term used by psychologists to refer to incorrect perceptions. Actually, there are two types of illusions: those due to physical processes and those due to cognitive processes (Matlin & Foley, 1997). Illusions due to distortion of physical conditions include *mirages,* in which you perceive things that aren't really there—such as the water you often seem to see on the dry road ahead of you. Our focus, however, will be on the latter type of illusion—those involving cognitive processes.

**Illusions:** Instances in which perception yields false interpretations of physical reality.

Countless illusions related to cognitive processes exist, but most fall into two categories; illusions of *size* and illusions of *shape* or *area* (Coren et al., 1976). Natural examples of two well-known size illusions are presented in Figure 3.22; as you can

**Figure 3.22**
**Powerful Illusions of Size**

Natural examples of two powerful illusions of size. The horizontal-vertical illusion stems from our tendency to perceive objects higher in our visual field as more distant. This illusion helps explain why the St. Louis Gateway *(left)* falsely appears taller than it is wide; its height and width are actually equal. In the Ponzo illusion *(right)* the line in the distance appears larger, although both lines are actually the same size.

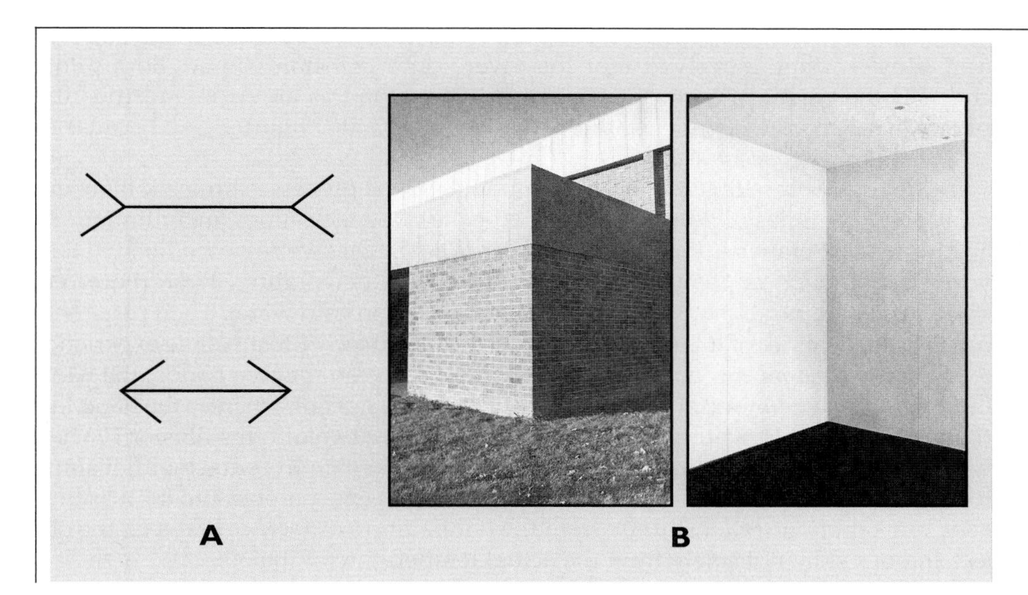


**Figure 3.23**
**The Müller–Lyer Illusion**

(A) In the Müller–Lyer illusion, lines of equal length appear unequal; the line with the wings pointing outward looks longer than the line with the wings pointing inward.
(B) Now carefully examine the vertical line in each of the photographs. Which line is longer? Most people perceive the vertical line in the photo on the right as longer, although careful measurement shows they are exactly the same length.

see, their effects are powerful. But why do illusions occur? What causes our interpretation of such stimuli to be directly at odds with physical reality? Some evidence suggests that illusions generally have multiple causes (Schiffman, 1990). However, one explanation is provided by the *theory of misapplied constancy.* This theory suggests that when looking at illusions, we interpret certain cues as suggesting that some parts are farther away than others. Our powerful tendency toward size constancy then comes into play, with the result that we perceptually distort the length of various lines (refer to Figure 3.23). Learning also plays an important role in illusions, as shown in the architectural examples of the *Müller–Lyer illusion* in Figure 3.23. Past experience tells us that the corner shown in the photo on the right is usually farther away than the corner in the photo on the left. Therefore, although the size of the retinal image cast by the vertical lines in both photos is identical, we interpret the vertical line as longer in the photo on the right. Moreover, learning seems to affect the extent to which our perception is influenced by illusions: Many visual illusions decline in magnitude following extended exposure—although they do not disappear altogether (Greist-Bousquet, Watson, & Schiffman, 1990).

Another type of illusion is that of *shape* or *area.* If you've ever wondered why the moon looks bigger at the horizon (about 30 percent bigger) than at its highest point in the sky, then you are familiar with the most famous area illusion—the *moon illusion.* Why does this illusion occur? In part, because when the moon is near the horizon, we can see that it is farther away than trees, houses, and other objects. When it is overhead at its zenith, such cues are lacking. Thus, the moon appears larger near the horizon because there are cues available that cause us to perceive that it is very far away. Once again, our tendency toward size constancy leads us astray.

Like illusions of size or area, shape illusions (see Figure 3.24) can influence perception—sometimes producing some unsettling consequences. Consider a real-world example involving the *Poggendorf illusion* (drawing A in Figure 3.24). In this illusion, a line disappears at an angle behind a solid figure, reappearing at the other side—at what seems to be an incorrect position. As reported by Coren and Girgus (1978), in 1965

**Figure 3.24**
**Illusions of Area or Shape**

Illusions of shape or area can be quite powerful. In drawing A, known as the Poggendorf illusion, which of the three lines on the right continues the line on the left? Check your answer with a ruler. In drawing B, are the horizontal lines straight or bent in the middle? Again, check for yourself. Finally, in drawing C, are the letters tilted or vertical? When you check, you'll see why sometimes you can't believe what you think you see.

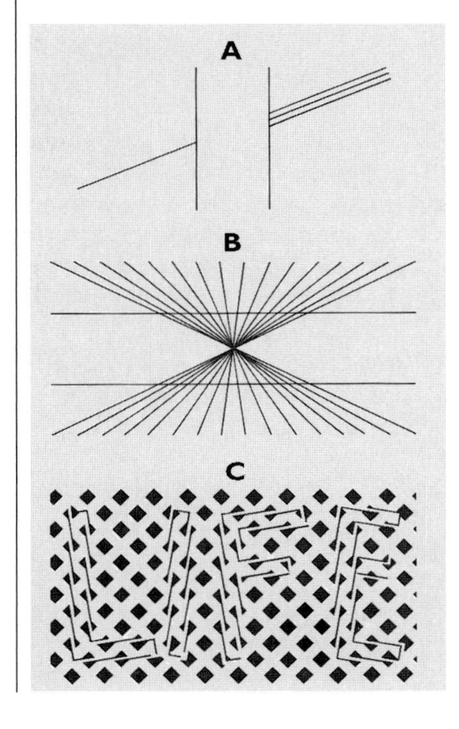

two airplanes were about to arrive in New York City, and because of the Poggendorf illusion, they perceived that they were on a collision course. Both pilots changed their path to correct for what they perceived as an error, and thus the planes collided. The result was four deaths and forty-nine injuries—all because of an illusion.

One final point: Illusions are not limited to visual processes. Indeed, there are numerous examples of illusions for our other sensory modalities, including touch and audition (Sekuler & Blake, 1990; Shepard, 1964). One well-known illusion that you can demonstrate for yourself is that of touch temperature. First, place one hand in a container of hot water and the other hand in cold water. Then place *both* hands in a container of lukewarm water. What do you feel? Most people experience a dramatic difference in perceived temperature between the two hands; the hand initially placed in hot water feels the lukewarm water as cool, whereas the hand initially placed in cold water feels it as hot. How do we explain this illusion? When we touch an object, the temperature of the area of our skin in contact with it shifts toward that of the object's surface. So when we perceive an object to be warm or cool, our experience stems partly from the temperature difference between the object and our skin, not solely from the actual temperature of the object.

**REVIEW QUESTIONS**

- Why is selective attention important?
- What role do the Gestalt principles play in perceptual processes?
- What are perceptual constancies?
- What are illusions?

## Some Key Perceptual Processes: Pattern and Distance

Perception is a practical process, for it provides organisms with information essential to survival in their normal habitat. The specific nature of this information varies greatly with different species. For example, frogs must be able to detect small moving objects in order to feed on insects, whereas porpoises require sensory input that enables them to navigate turbulent and murky ocean waters. Nonetheless, it is probably safe to say that virtually all living creatures need information concerning (1) what's out there and (2) how far away it is. Humans are no exception to this general rule, and we possess impressive perceptual skills in both areas.

**PATTERN RECOGNITION: WHAT'S OUT THERE?** Your ability to read the words on this page depends on your ability to recognize small black marks as letters and collections of such marks as words (Ittelson, 1996). How do we accomplish this task? Research on this issue suggests the following two possibilities, termed the bottom-up and top-down theories of pattern recognition.

As their names imply, these adopt somewhat opposite perspectives on the basic question of how we recognize patterns of visual stimuli. The *bottom-up approach* suggests that our ability to recognize specific patterns, such as letters of the alphabet, is based on simpler capacities to recognize and combine correctly lower-level features of objects, such as lines, edges, corners, and angles. Bottom-up theories suggest that pattern recognition is constructed from simpler perceptual abilities through a series of discrete steps (Hummell, 1994; Marr, 1982).

In contrast, the *top-down approach* emphasizes the fact that our expectancies play a critical role in shaping our perceptions. We often proceed in accordance with what our past experience tells us to expect, and therefore we don't always analyze every feature of most stimuli we encounter. Although top-down processing can be extremely efficient (think about the speed with which you can read this page), it can also lead us astray. Nearly everyone has had the experience of rushing over to another person who appears to be an old friend, only to realize he or she is actually a stranger. In such cases, our tendency to process information quickly from the top down can indeed produce errors.

**Figure 3.25**
**Dissociable Subsystems: A New Theory of Object Recognition**

According to one view, independent subsystems operate in each half of the brain. A features-based system in the left hemisphere identifies common features among objects, allowing us to conclude that the two objects in the photo are horses. The system in the right hemisphere processes visual information holistically and allows us to recognize specific ways in which the two images differ.

Which of these theories is correct? New evidence seems to indicate that *both* are involved in pattern recognition (Marsolek & Burgund, 1997). You may recall from our discussions in Chapter 2 that the brain is organized into two halves. Each half is specialized to perform certain functions more efficiently than the other. Marsolek (1999) suggests that this arrangement supports separate systems within each hemisphere that accommodate both the *features-based* processing that is characteristic of bottom-up processing and the *whole-based* processing characteristic of top-down processing. To illustrate how this system works, look carefully at the two objects in Figure 3.25. Immediately, you can recognize that they're the same in one respect (they're both horses) but different in other respects (they differ in color, size, and so on). How is the brain able to recognize their similarity at one level and differences at another? Apparently, independent systems, referred to as *dissociable subsystems,* operate simultaneously in each hemisphere. An *abstract-category subsystem,* located primarily in the left side of the brain, analyzes objects in terms of their features. This system allow us to recognize that the objects in Figure 3.25, while they differ in many ways, are both horses. In contrast, a *specific-exemplar subsystem,* located primarily in the right side of the brain, analyzes objects holistically. This system allows us to distinguish between exemplars within a single abstract category, explaining how we recognize the specific ways in which the two objects are different. Although additional research will be needed to verify the accuracy of this model, the dissociable subsystems theory does seem to provide a plausible explanation for our efficiency in making sense of the world around us.

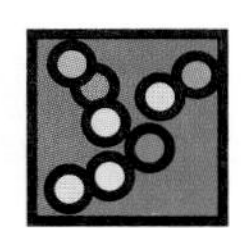

**DISTANCE PERCEPTION: HOW FAR AWAY IS IT?** Our impressive ability to judge depth and distance exists because we make use of many different cues in forming such judgments. These cues can be divided into two categories, *monocular* and *binocular,* depending on whether they can be seen with only one eye or require the use of both eyes.

Web Link: *Single Image (Random Dot) Stereograms*

**Monocular cues** to depth or distance include the following:

1. *Size cues.* The larger the image of an object on the retina, the larger it is judged to be; in addition, if an object is larger than other objects, it is often perceived as closer.
2. *Linear perspective.* Parallel lines appear to converge in the distance; the greater this effect, the farther away an object appears to be.
3. *Texture gradient.* The texture of a surface appears smoother as distance increases.

**Monocular Cues:** Cues to depth or distance provided by one eye.

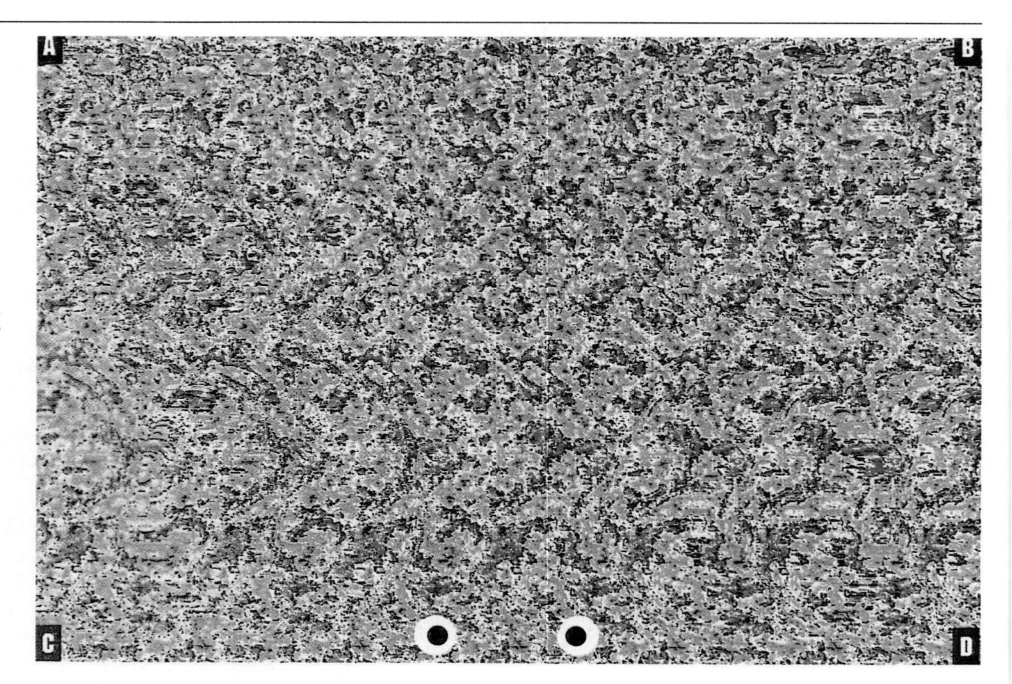


**Figure 3.26**
**Retinal Disparity and Stereograms**

Retinal disparity is the basis for our perception of 3-D images in stereograms. Hold the book right up to your nose; then very, very slowly pull the book away from your face. Look through the image, trying not to blink. A 3-D picture will magically appear. What do you see?

4. *Atmospheric perspective.* The farther away objects are, the less distinctly they are seen—smog, dust, haze get in the way.
5. *Overlap* (or interposition). If one object overlaps another, it is seen as being closer than the one it covers.
6. *Height cues* (aerial perspective). Below the horizon, objects lower down in our field of vision are perceived as closer; above the horizon, objects higher up are seen as closer.
7. *Motion parallax.* When we travel in a vehicle, objects far away appear to move in the same direction as the observer, whereas close objects move in the opposite direction. Objects at different distances appear to move at different velocities.

We also rely heavily on **binocular cues**—depth information based on the coordinated efforts of both eyes. Binocular cues for depth perception stem from two primary sources:

1. *Convergence.* In order to see close objects, our eyes turn inward, toward one another; the greater this movement, the closer such objects appear to be.
2. *Retinal disparity* (binocular parallax). Our two eyes observe objects from slightly different positions in space; the difference between these two images is interpreted by our brain to provide another cue to depth. Figure 3.26 contains a *stereogram*—a pattern of dots in which we can perceive 3-D images, partly because of retinal disparity.

These lists of monocular and binocular cues are by no means exhaustive. By using the wealth of information provided by these and other cues (Schiffman, 1990), we can usually perceive depth and distance with great accuracy.

**Binocular Cues:** Cues to depth or distance resulting from the fact that we have two eyes.

### REVIEW QUESTIONS

- What are the bottom-up and top-down theories of pattern recognition?
- What are dissociable subsystems? What is their role in object recognition?
- How are we able to judge depth and distance?

# The Plasticity of Perception: To What Extent Is It Innate or Learned?

Imagine a woman blind from birth whose sight is suddenly restored through a miraculous operation. Will her visual world be the same as yours or mine? Will it be orderly and consistent with her expectations? Or will she experience a chaotic swirl of colors, brightnesses, and meaningless shapes? This is an intriguing question that has often served as the basis for exploring the *nature–nurture controversy*, one of psychology's "grand issues" (see Chapter 1). In other words, to what extent are aspects of perception learned or hereditary? Although there is a growing consensus among behavioral scientists that most, if not all, aspects of perception involve *both* nature and nurture (e.g., Turkheimer, 1998), we'll consider their separate contributions in the sections below.

## Perception: Evidence That It's Innate

Evidence that perception is innate stems from two lines of research. The first involves people like the one described above—people born blind (or blinded soon after birth) whose sight is later restored through medical procedures. If perception is innate, then such persons should be able to see clearly immediately after recovery from surgery. Many of these individuals can, in fact, make at least partial sense out of the visual world soon after their sight is restored. For example, they can detect and follow moving objects, suggesting that some aspects of visual perception may indeed be innate (Von Senden, 1960). However, it is important to note that individuals who regain their vision later in life never seem to fully attain normal visual perception.

Additional evidence suggesting that perception is innate is provided by research with very young subjects, such as babies only a few hours or days old. These studies suggest that numerous perceptual abilities, particularly auditory and visual abilities, are present at birth or shortly afterward (Farah et al., 1998; Schiffman, 1990). In one study demonstrating this fact, Valenza and her colleagues (1996) exposed four-day-old babies to patterns prepared especially for the newborn visual system. The patterns either did or did not resemble a human face. The newborns were seated on the experimenter's lap in front of two screens onto which the images were projected. A video camera recorded the newborns' eye movements. As you can see in Figure 3.27, the infants showed a clear preference for the facelike pattern. Why do newborns demonstrate this preference? Valenza and her colleagues suggest that this behavior may be best explained in evolutionary terms: It may help newborns to focus on their primary source of care. Investigations involving monkeys show that neurons in certain areas of their brains respond differentially to faces. Because a high degree of similarity exists between the human and monkey visual systems, the identification of "face cells" in monkeys' brains suggests that the infant's preference for facelike stimuli may be

**Figure 3.27**
**Visual Perception in Newborns**

Babies looked significantly longer at a pattern that resembled a human face than at a nonfacelike pattern designed especially for the newborn visual system. These results suggest that some features of visual perception are present at birth, or shortly thereafter.

(*Source:* Based on data from Valenza et al., 1996.)

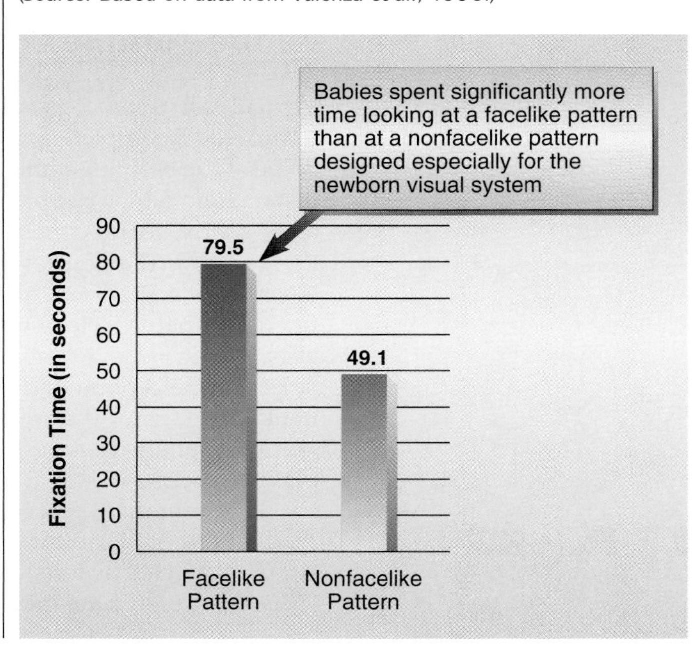

similarly hard-wired (Desimone, 1991; Farah et al., 1998). (See Chapter 8 for more information on the perceptual abilities of newborn infants.)

Audio 3.3: *Is Perception Learned?*

## Perception: Evidence That It's Learned

On the other hand, there is considerable evidence for the view that key aspects of perception are learned. In a famous series of studies, Blakemore and Cooper (1970) raised kittens in darkness except for brief periods, during which the kittens were exposed to either horizontal or vertical stripes. When later released from their restricted environment, the kittens showed what seemed to be permanent effects of their earlier experience. Those exposed only to vertical lines would respond to a long black rod when it was held in an upright position but ignored it when it was held horizontally. In contrast, kittens exposed only to horizontal lines would respond to a rod only when it was held in a horizontal position, ignoring it when presented vertically. Despite the fact that the kittens' visual systems were undamaged—at least in any measurable physical sense—their restricted visual experience appeared to produce permanent perceptual deficits. Please note, however, that more recent evidence shows that organisms may compensate for these deficits through enhanced abilities in their other senses. For example, in one study binocularly deprived cats seemed to show improved auditory localization abilities compared to normal control subjects. Apparently the brain, at least in cats, possesses the capacity to reorganize itself to compensate for a sensory loss (Rauschecker, 1995). Whether humans exhibit similar capabilities is still a topic of debate. However, it is common to hear of instances in which blind persons develop heightened capabilities in their other senses.

Additional evidence for the role of learning in perception comes from studies in which human volunteers wear special goggles that invert their view of the world and reverse right and left. Such persons initially experience difficulty in carrying out normal activities with their goggles on, but soon adapt and do everything from reading a book to flying a plane (Kohler, 1962). These findings, and others, suggest that we do indeed learn to interpret the information supplied by our sensory receptors.

## Must We Resolve the Nature–Nurture Controversy?

Virtually all psychologists accept that both innate factors *and* experience are needed to provide a complete account of our perceptual abilities (e.g., Turkheimer, 1998). Some of the best illustrations of how these processes work together come from rare instances in which people regain their sight after many years of blindness. In one case, a fifty-year-old man regained his sight after forty-five years of blindness (Sacks, 1993). Careful testing revealed that the man could detect visual features (such as letters, objects, and colors) and could perceive motion, suggesting the influence of nature. However, the man could not "see" in the true sense. Learning even simple visual relationships, such as those involved in recognition of common objects or perception of depth and distance, required great effort, because most of his knowledge of the world had come to him through the sense of touch. This graphic example clearly shows the integral roles that innate factors and experience play in perception.

To summarize, perception is plastic in the sense that it can be, and often is, modified by our encounters with physical reality. However, perception may also be strongly affected by innate tendencies and principles. So the answer to the question "Must we resolve the nature–nurture controversy?" is a resounding *no.* It is clear that learning *and* biology both play critical roles in perception. We'll now turn to a controversial topic in psychology—extrasensory perception.

## Extrasensory Perception: Perception without Sensation?

Have you ever wondered if we have a "sixth sense"? In other words, can we gain information about the external world without use of our five basic senses? Many persons believe we can and accept the existence of **extrasensory perception**—literally, perception without a basis in sensation. The first and most basic question we can ask about ESP is "Does it really exist?" This question has been recast by Bem and Honorton (1994) in terms of a hypothetical process known as **psi.** These researchers define psi as unusual processes of information or energy transfer that are currently unexplained in terms of known physical or biological mechanisms. What precisely is psi? And is there any evidence for its existence? In the section that follows, we will discuss some of the evidence regarding this intriguing topic.

### Psi: What Is It?

**Parapsychologists,** those who study psi and other *paranormal events,* or events outside our normal experience or knowledge, suggest there are actually several distinct forms of psi. One form of psi is *precognition,* the ability to foretell future events. Fortunetellers and psychics often make their livings from the supposed ability to make such predictions. *Clairvoyance,* the ability to perceive objects or events that do not directly stimulate your sensory organs, is another form of psi. While playing cards, if you somehow "know" which one will be dealt next, you are experiencing clairvoyance. *Telepathy,* a skill supposedly possessed by mind readers, involves the direct transmission of thought from one person to the next. Another phenomenon often associated with psi is *psychokinesis,* the ability to affect the physical world purely through thought. People who bend spoons or move objects with their mind or perform feats of levitation (making objects rise into the air) claim to have powers of psychokinesis.

### Psi: Does It Really Exist?

The idea of a mysterious sixth sense is intriguing, and many people are passionately convinced of its existence (Bowles & Hynds, 1978). But does psi really exist? Most psychologists are skeptical about the existence of psi for several reasons. The first, and perhaps the most important, reason for doubting its existence is the repeated failure to replicate instances of psi; that is, certain procedures yield evidence for psi at one time but not at others. Indeed, one survey failed to uncover a single instance of paranormal phenomena that could be reliably produced after researchers ruled out alternative explanations such as fraud, methodological flaws, and normal sensory functioning (Hoppe, 1988). Moreover, it appears that the more controlled studies of psi are, the less evidence for psi they have provided (Blackmore, 1986).

Second, present-day scientific understanding states that all aspects of our behavior must ultimately stem from biochemical events, yet it is not clear what physical mechanism could account for psi. In fact, the existence of such a mechanism would require restructuring our view of the physical world.

Third, much of the support for psi has been obtained by persons already deeply convinced of its existence. As we noted in Chapter 1, scientists are not immune to

**Extrasensory Perception:** Perception without a basis in sensory input.

**Psi:** Unusual processes of information or energy transfer that are currently unexplained in terms of known physical or biological mechanisms. Included under the heading of psi are such supposed abilities as telepathy (reading others' thoughts) and clairvoyance (perceiving distant objects).

**Parapsychologists:** Individuals who study ESP and other paranormal events.

being influenced in their observations by their own beliefs. Thus, while studies suggesting that psi exists may represent a small sample of all research conducted on this topic, perhaps only the few experiments yielding positive results find their way into print; perhaps the many "failures" are simply not reported.

**REVIEW QUESTIONS**

- How are the concepts *nature* and *nurture* related to perception?
- How do most psychologists view the possibility of extrasensory perception or psi?

# Making Psychology Part of Your Life

## Managing Your Pain: Some Useful Tips

As a longtime sports enthusiast, I am very familiar with the predictable muscular aches and pains that occasionally result from overdoing it. For instance, when I run too far or during the heat of the day, I can usually count on muscle soreness—or worse—the following day. And when I forget to stretch before exercising, there is a good possibility that I will experience lower back pain. Although these and other types of minor injuries definitely have a physical component, the degree to which we experience pain can be influenced by many factors, as we learned earlier in our discussion of pain perception. The context in which the injury occurs, our emotional state at the time, the way we interpret the injury, and the expectations of the culture in which we live all contribute to the perception of pain. Although you should do everything possible to avoid getting injured (e.g., stretching before you run or work out), there are several things you can do to lessen the impact of pain. Here are some useful tips.

- **Use counterirritants to relieve the pain.** The gate-control theory of pain proposes the existence of "gates," neural mechanisms in the spinal cord that sometimes close, thereby preventing pain messages from reaching the brain. The use of counterirritants, which stimulate or irritate a nearby area, can close the pain gate and thereby reduce pain. Deep massage, ice packs, or heat applied to the injured area can be effective in relieving the muscle pain people sometimes experience after strenuous exercise. People who experience chronic forms of pain sometimes find relief through other counterirritant techniques. *Acupuncture* is a pain-relief technique in which thin needles are inserted into various locations on the body. Stimulating specific points on the fingers, for example, seems to reduce dental and facial pain (Melzack, 1994). People also seek relief through electrical stimulation, accomplished by devices implanted either in the brain or spinal cord, or on the surface of the skin (*transcutaneous electrical nerve stimulation or TENS*). These techniques have been found to be particularly effective for back pain (Malzack, 1994).
- **Use cognitive–behavioral techniques to develop more adaptive reactions to pain.** Cognitive–behavioral techniques can change the way you think about pain. Research shows that dwelling on negative thoughts usually intensifies your perception of pain (Turk & Rudy, 1992). Substituting positive thoughts for negative ones can be an effective countermeasure. Distraction, too, can help alleviate pain, by shifting the focus of attention away from the pain. A good way to accomplish this is to select enjoyable activities that fully engage your attention, such as a good movie or activities with friends. Another technique to get your mind off the pain is to induce an emotional state incompatible with pain, such as laughter. You can readily use this technique: Simply expose yourself as quickly as possible to something—or someone—you find humorous. The pain you are experiencing may quickly abate.
- **Remember that pain serves a useful purpose, so don't ignore it completely!** Although the techniques just described are useful means for alleviating the effects of pain, remember that pain serves an important function that should definitely *not* be ignored. Indeed, it is essential that you use pain as a guide to hasten recovery from your injury.

# Summary and Review

## Sensation: The Raw Materials of Understanding

- **What is the primary function of our sensory receptors?** Sensory receptors transduce raw physical energy into neural impulses, which are then interpreted by our central nervous system.
- **What does the term *absolute threshold* refer to, and what are psychophysical methods?** The absolute threshold is the smallest magnitude of a stimulus that can be detected 50 percent of the time. Psychophysical methods are procedures researchers use to locate stimulus thresholds.
- **Why is signal detection theory important?** Signal detection theory helps to separate sensitivity from motivational factors.
- **What is a difference threshold?** *Difference threshold* refers to the amount of change in a stimulus required for a person to detect it.
- **Can subliminal messages affect our behavior?** Laboratory experiments using visual priming suggest that stimuli that stimulate the sensory receptors but remain outside conscious awareness can produce measurable effects on cognition and behavior. However, careful research fails to support the use of subliminal messages as tools of persuasion.
- **What is the role of sensory adaptation in sensation?** Sensory adaptation serves a useful function by allowing us to focus on important changes in our environment.

### Key Terms

sensation, p. 84, • perception, p. 85, • sensory receptors, p. 85, • transduction, p. 85, • absolute threshold, p. 87, • psychophysical methods, p. 87, • signal detection theory, p. 88, • difference threshold, p. 88, • just noticeable difference (jnd), p. 89, • subliminal perception, p. 89, • sensory adaptation, p. 91

## Vision

- **What are the basic structures of the eye, and what is the physical stimulus for vision?** Light rays first pass through the cornea and then enter the eye through the pupil. Adjustments to lighting conditions are executed by the iris. The lens is a clear structure whose shape adjusts to permit us to focus on objects at varying distances. Light rays leaving the lens are projected onto the retina at the back of the eyeball. The physical stimulus for vision is light: electromagnetic wavelengths that stimulate the rods and cones in the retina.
- **What are the basic functions of the visual system?** The basic functions of the visual system include not only perception of color and shape but acuity, dark adaptation, and eye movements. Acuity is the ability to see fine details. Dark adaptation is the increase in sensitivity that occurs when we move from bright light to a dim environment. Various types of eye movements are crucial to our ability to track moving objects and to perceive distance and depth.
- **How do psychologists explain color perception?** Our rich sense of color stems from mechanisms at several levels of our nervous system. Two leading theories that explain how we perceive color are trichromatic theory and opponent-process theory.
- **Why is visual perception a hierarchical process?** Visual perception is described as a hierarchical process because increasingly complex visual information is analyzed and compiled at successive stages—eventually yielding a coherent and flowing visual world.
- **What are the basic building blocks of visual perception?** The basic building blocks of visual perception begin with feature detectors—neurons in the visual cortex that respond when particular types of stimuli, with characteristic features, are detected.

### Key Terms

cornea, p. 92, • pupil, p. 93, • iris, p. 93, • lens, p. 93, • retina, p. 93, • cones, p. 93, • rods, p. 93, • fovea, p. 93, • optic nerve, p. 93, • blind spot, p. 93, • wavelength, p. 93, • hue, p. 93, • brightness, p. 94, • saturation, p. 94, • acuity, p. 94, • nearsightedness, p. 94, • farsightedness, p. 94, • dark adaptation, p. 95, • saccadic movements, p. 95, • trichromatic theory, p. 96, • negative afterimages, p. 96, • opponent-process theory, p. 96, • feature detectors, p. 97, • simple cells, p. 97, • complex cells, p. 97, • hypercomplex cells, p. 97, • blindsight, p. 98, • prosopagnosia, p. 98

## Hearing

- **What is the physical stimulus for hearing?** The physical stimulus for hearing consists of sound waves that stimulate tiny hair cells in the cochlea.
- **How do psychologists explain pitch perception?** Place theory and frequency theory help explain how we perceive pitch.
- **How do we localize sound?** The sound shadow created by our head causes sound to reach one ear at slightly greater intensity and slightly faster than it reaches the other. These small differences help us localize the source of sound.
- **How do psychologists measure hearing loss, and how much sound is required to produce it?** Psychologists assess hearing loss by measuring hearing thresholds—the minimum level at which sounds are detected—at various sound frequencies. Exposure to 90-decibel sound levels, the level of noise that might be present in a crowded restaurant, can produce significant hearing loss after only one and a half hours of sound exposure.

### Key Terms

pinna, p. 98, • cochlea, p. 99, • pitch, p. 99, • timbre, p. 100, • place theory, p. 100, • frequency theory, p. 101, • localization, p. 101

## Touch and Other Skin Senses

- **What is the physical stimulus for touch?** The physical stimulus for touch is a stretching of or pressure against receptors in the skin.
- **Where does the sensation of pain originate?** Sensations of pain originate in free nerve endings throughout the body.
- **What is the basis for cultural differences in pain perception?** Cultural differences in pain perception appear to be the result of learning, not physical differences.
- **What roles do cognitive processes play in the perception of pain?** Redirection of attention, positive or negative thoughts, and beliefs are among cognitive processes that can decrease or increase the perceived intensity of pain.

### Key Term

gate-control theory, p. 104

## Smell and Taste: The Chemical Senses

- **What is the physical stimulus for smell, and where are the sensory receptors located?** The physical stimulus for sensations of smell consists of molecules that stimulate receptors in the nose.
- **Where are the sensory receptors for taste located?** The sensory receptors for taste are located in papillae on the tongue.
- **What are the potential practical benefits of pleasant ambient fragrances?** The presence of pleasant fragrances can increase alertness among persons engaged in potentially dangerous activities such as driving.

## Kinesthesia and Vestibular Sense

- **What information does our kinesthetic sense provide to the brain?** Kinesthesia informs the brain about the location of body parts with respect to one another.
- **What information does the vestibular sense provide to the brain?** The vestibular sense provides information about body position, movement, and acceleration.
- **How can psychology contribute to the development of virtual environments and telepresence?** Psychologists' knowledge of basic sensory and perceptual processes can increase the realism of virtual environments and decrease potential negative effects such as dizziness and nausea.

### Key Terms

kinesthesia, p. 109, • vestibular sense, p. 110, • telepresence, p. 110

## Perception: Putting It All Together

- **Why is selective attention important?** Selective attention reduces the interference from irrelevant sensory sources.
- **What role do the Gestalt principles play in perceptual processes?** The Gestalt principles of perceptual organization help us to structure the input from our sensory receptors.
- **What are perceptual constancies?** Perceptual constancies are principles describing our ability to perceive aspects of the world as unchanging despite variations in the information reaching our sensory receptors, such as information about size, shape, or brightness.
- **What are illusions?** *Illusion* is a term used by psychologists to refer to errors in interpreting sensory information.
- **What are the bottom-up and top-down theories of pattern recognition?** The bottom-up theory suggests that pattern recognition stems from our ability to recognize and combine basic visual features. In contrast, top-down theory emphasizes the role that expectations play in shaping our perceptions.
- **What are dissociable subsystems? What is their role in object recognition?** Dissociable subsystems are specialized pattern-recognition systems that operate simultaneously in each brain hemisphere. An abstract-category system in the left hemisphere analyzes objects in terms of their features. A specific-exemplar system in the right hemisphere analyzes objects holistically.
- **How are we able to judge depth and distance?** Judgments of depth and distance are based on both binocular and monocular cues.

### Key Terms

Gestalt psychologists, p. 113, • figure–ground relationship, p. 113, • laws of grouping, p. 114, • constancies, p. 114, • size constancy, p. 114, • relative size, p. 115, • shape constancy, p. 115, • brightness constancy, p. 115, • illusions, p. 116, • monocular cues, p. 119, • binocular cues, p. 120

## The Plasticity of Perception: To What Extent Is It Innate or Learned?

- **How are the concepts *nature* and *nurture* related to perception?** Both nature and nurture are important determinants of the ways we perceive the world around us. *Nature* refers to genetic influences on perception, whereas *nurture* refers to the relative effects of the environment and learning.

## Extrasensory Perception: Perception without Sensation?

- **How do most psychologists view the possibility of extrasensory perception or psi?** Most psychologists remain highly skeptical about the existence of psi and await the results of further careful research.

### Key Terms

extrasensory perception, p. 123, • psi, p. 123, • parapsychologists, p. 123

# Critical Thinking Questions

## Appraisal

Many psychologists would agree that conscious experience is nothing more than the result of the brain's efforts to integrate information received from the senses. Do you agree? Why? If not, offer an alternative view.

## Controversy

Visual priming studies show that subliminal stimuli—stimuli that are registered by our sensory organs but that remain outside our conscious awareness—produce measurable effects on various aspects of cognition and behavior. Based on this evidence, do you think subliminal perception can be used as a powerful tool of persuasion?

## Making Psychology Part of Your Life

Now that you understand how we perceive pain, which techniques do you think might be most effective for reducing the effects of pain? Can you think of other ways in which you can benefit from such knowledge?

Chapter 4

# States of Consciousness

## CHAPTER OUTLINE


**BIOLOGICAL RHYTHMS: TIDES OF LIFE—AND CONSCIOUS EXPERIENCE 131**

Circadian Rhythms: Their Basic Nature
Longer-Term Biological Rhythms: Mechanisms That Govern Mating and Hibernation
Individual Differences in Circadian Rhythms: Are You a Morning Person or a Night Person?
Disturbances in Circadian Rhythms: Jet Lag and Shift Work

■ FROM SCIENCE TO PRACTICE *Counteracting the "Drowsy Driver" Syndrome: When Sounds—and Scents—Save Lives*

**WAKING STATES OF CONSCIOUSNESS 136**

Controlled and Automatic Processing: Two Modes of Thought
Self-Awareness: Some Effects of Thinking about Ourselves

**SLEEP: THE PAUSE THAT REFRESHES? 142**

■ RESEARCH METHODS *How Psychologists Study Sleep*

Sleep: What Functions Does It Serve?
Effects of Sleep Deprivation
Sleep Disorders: No Rest for Some of the Weary
Dreams: "Now Playing in Your Private, Inner Theater . . ."

**HYPNOSIS: ALTERED STATE OF CONSCIOUSNESS . . . OR SOCIAL ROLE PLAYING? 150**

Hypnosis: How It's Done and Who Is Susceptible to It
Hypnosis: Contrasting Views about Its Nature

**CONSCIOUSNESS-ALTERING DRUGS: WHAT THEY ARE AND WHAT THEY DO 154**

Consciousness-Altering Drugs: Some Basic Concepts
Psychological Mechanisms Underlying Drug Abuse: Contrasting Views
Consciousness-Altering Drugs: An Overview

■ BEYOND THE HEADLINES—As Psychologists See It: *Can You Buy the Fountain of Youth on the Internet? "Buyer Beware" Strikes Again*

■ MAKING PSYCHOLOGY PART OF YOUR LIFE *Are You High or Low in Private Self-Consciousness? A Self-Assessment*

I don't know what *you* think about when you're in the shower, but I know that my mind wanders all over the place while I'm soaping up and rinsing off; I think about anything and everything—current projects and things I have to do, people I've met, and even what's for dinner. One result of this mental activity is that several times a week I stop, just as I reach for the towel, and ask myself the following question: "Did I remember to wash my hair?" Unless I happened to leave the cap off the shampoo, I often don't know!

If you, too, have experiences like this (and I'm sure you do), you already realize that we all experience changing **states of consciousness** each day—varying levels of awareness of ourselves, our behavior, and the world around us. We shift from operating "on automatic" while driving a car, combing our hair, or brushing our teeth to full and careful attention to tasks we find challenging, either mentally or physically (see Figure 4.1). And when we go to sleep at night (perhaps to dream), or take some drug that affects the way we feel, we may also experience dramatic shifts in consciousness. The existence of these different states of consciousness raises many intriguing questions. Can we really do two or more things at once? Why are we more alert and energetic at some times during the day than at others? What causes jet lag? What happens when we fall asleep and dream?

Psychologists have studied states of consciousness for several decades—ever since the time, in the 1960s, when the field of psychology rejected the artificial constraints of extreme behaviorism and recognized that consciousness, like all aspects of our mental activity, is indeed a legitimate area of study. What have psychologists discovered in their research on consciousness? Many fascinating facts. To provide you with an overview of this body of knowledge, I'll focus on the following topics. First, I'll discuss *biological rhythms*—naturally occurring, cyclical changes in many basic bodily processes and mental states that occur over the course of a day or longer periods of time. These rhythms help explain why we feel so much more alert at some times than others, why we experience jet lag, and why working the "graveyard shift" (from midnight to 8:00 a.m.) is so difficult for many people. Next, we'll consider some aspects of *waking consciousness*—changes in consciousness that occur while we are awake. Here, we'll focus on two topics: (1) the distinction between *automatic* and *controlled* processing—the kind of "automatic" behavior I often show in the shower versus the kind of conscious behavior I'm demonstrating right now as I write these words; and (2) shifts in *self-awareness*—the extent to which we focus our attention inward on ourselves or outward on various aspects of the world around us. As we'll see, such shifts can have important effects on our social behavior, our psychological adjustment, and our performance of many tasks.

**States of Consciousness:** Varying degress of awareness of ourselves and the external world.

After examining changes in waking consciousness, we'll turn to what is perhaps the most profound shift in consciousness we experience: *sleep*. Here, we'll consider the nature of dreams and what functions, if any, they may serve. Our next topic will be *hypnosis* and the effects it produces. Finally, we'll examine *consciousness-altering drugs* and how they produce their effects.

**Figure 4.1**
**Changing States of Consciousness: A Part of Everyday Life**

During the course of each day, we experience several different states of consciousness—for instance, performing some tasks "on automatic" but others with our full attention and concentration.

# Biological Rhythms
## Tides of Life—and Conscious Experience

I've known for many years that I'm a "morning person": I rarely have trouble waking up, and I feel most alert and energetic early in the day. After lunch, though, I often experience a sharp drop in alertness from which I don't recover until late afternoon. What about you? When do *you* feel most alert and energetic? Whatever your answer, it's clear that most of us do experience regular shifts in these respects each day. Psychologists and other scientists refer to such changes as **biological rhythms**—regular fluctuations in our bodily processes and in consciousness over time. Many of these fluctuations occur over the course of a single day and are therefore known as **circadian rhythms** (from the Latin words for "around" and "day"). Other fluctuations occupy shorter periods of time; for instance, many people become hungry every two or three hours. And still other cycles occur over longer periods, such as the mating seasons shown by many animals—they mate only at certain times of the year (see Figure 4.2)—and the human female menstrual cycle, which is roughly twenty-eight days. Because circadian rhythms have been the subject of most research, however, we'll focus primarily on these.

**Figure 4.2**
**Longer-Term Biological Rhythms**

Many species mate only at certain times of the year; others hibernate during the winter months. These are examples of biological rhythms that are much longer in duration than a single day.

## Circadian Rhythms: Their Basic Nature

Web Link: *Society for Research on Biological Rhythms*

Web Link: *Society for Light Treatment and Biological Rhythms*

Most people are aware of fluctuations in their alertness, energy, and moods over the course of a day, and research findings indicate that such shifts are closely related to changes in underlying bodily processes (e.g., Moore-Ede, Sulzman, & Fuller, 1982). Daily cycles occur in the production of various hormones, core body temperature, blood pressure, and several other processes. For many persons, these functions are highest in the late afternoon and evening and lowest in the early hours of the morning. Large individual differences in this respect exist, however, so the pattern varies greatly for different persons. In addition, circadian rhythms seem to shift with age; as people grow older, their peaks often tend to occur earlier in the day.

As you might expect, these cyclic fluctuations in basic bodily functions—and in our subjective feelings of alertness—are related to task performance. In general, people do their best work when body temperature and other internal processes are at or near their personal peaks. However, this link appears to be somewhat stronger for physical tasks than for mental ones—especially tasks that require considerable cognitive effort (Daniel & Potasova, 1989).

If bodily processes, mental alertness, and performance on many tasks change regularly over the course of the day, it seems reasonable to suggest that we possess some internal biological mechanism for regulating such changes. In other words, we must possess one or more *biological clocks* that time various circadian rhythms. While there is not as yet total agreement on the number or nature of these internal clocks, existing evidence points to the conclusion that one structure—the **suprachiasmatic nucleus (SCN),** located in the hypothalamus—plays a key role in this respect (Lewy, Sack, & Singer, 1992; Moore & Card, 1985). Interestingly, it appears that individual cells in this structure "tick"—keep track of time. Welsh and his colleagues (1995) removed tissue from the SCN of rats and observed the activity of individual cells. Results indicated that each cell showed fairly regular cycles of activity.

**Biological Rhythms:** Cyclic changes in bodily processes.

**Circadian Rhythms:** Cyclic changes in bodily processes occurring within a single day.

**Suprachiasmatic Nucleus (SCN):** A portion of the hypothalamus that seems to play an important role in the regulation of circadian rhythms.

We should note, by the way, that the SCN is not a totally "sealed" clock, unresponsive to the outside world. On the contrary, it responds to light, which serves as a *zeitgeber* (German for "time giver"). Morning light resets our internal biological clock, synchronizing it with the outside world. Why is this necessary? Because left to its own devices, our biological clock (and that of many other species) seems to operate on a twenty-five-hour cycle; thus, if it were not reset each day, our internal biological rhythms would get farther and farther out of synch with the world around us. We know this from research studies in which volunteers have lived in caves where no sunlight can penetrate. Under these conditions, most persons seem to shift toward a "day" of about twenty-five hours (Moore-Ede, Sulzman, & Fuller, 1982).

CourseCompass
Web Link: *Seasonal Affective Disorder*

CourseCompass
Web Link: *Melatonin and Biological Rhythms*

## Longer-Term Biological Rhythms: Mechanisms That Govern Mating and Hibernation

What about longer-term biological rhythms, such as mating seasons and hibernation? Here another structure in the brain, the **pineal gland,** seems to play an important role. This gland, which sits on top of the midbrain, just in front of the cerebellum, secretes a hormone known as *melatonin*. The pineal gland is connected to the SCN and secretes melatonin in response to input from the SCN. Melatonin has far-reaching effects, influencing several structures in the brain (including the SCN), regulating the production of hormones, and affecting many basic physiological processes. Melatonin is secreted mostly at night; so when nights are long, larger amounts are secreted. Higher melatonin levels seem to play a role in triggering hibernation in many species. When days get longer, less melatonin is secreted, and many species enter their spring or summer phase; they become more active—and begin to seek a mate! As we'll soon see, melatonin also plays a role in circadian (twenty-four-hour) biological rhythms, and it may be useful in counteracting disturbances in these rhythms. (A historical note: As you may recall from Chapter 1, Descartes believed that the pineal gland is where the mind and body interact. The fact that this structure plays a role in circadian rhythms is interesting from this perspective.)

## Individual Differences in Circadian Rhythms: Are You a Morning Person or a Night Person?

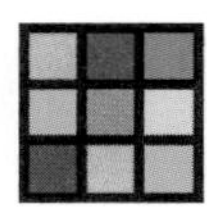

Before reading further, please answer the questions in Table 4.1. How did you score? If you answered "Day" to eight or more questions, the chances are good that you are a *morning person.* If, instead, you answered "Night" to eight or more questions, you are probably a *night person.* Morning people feel most alert and active early in the day, whereas night people experience peaks in alertness and energy in the afternoon or evening. Such differences are more than purely subjective. Studies comparing morning and evening persons indicate that the two groups differ in several important ways. Morning people have a higher overall level of adrenaline than night people; thus, they seem to operate at a higher overall level of activation (e.g., Akerstedt & Froberg, 1976). Similarly, morning people experience peaks in body temperature earlier in the day than night people (Wallace, 1993).

That these differences in alertness and bodily states translate into important effects on behavior is indicated by research demonstrating that students who are morning persons earn higher grades in early-morning classes, while those who are evening persons receive higher grades in classes offered later in the day (e.g., Guthrie, Ash, & Bendapudi, 1995). So, if you are a morning person, try to take your classes at that time; if you are an evening person, it's better to sign up for afternoon or evening classes. If you follow this strategy, the result may be higher grades.

**Pineal Gland:** A portion of the brain that secretes the hormone melatonin, and plays a role in biological rhythms.

**TABLE 4.1**

**Are You a Morning Person or a Night Person?**

If you answer "Day" to eight or more of these questions, you are probably a morning person. If you answer "Night" to eight or more, you are probably a night person.

| Answer each of the following items by circling either "Day" or "Night." | | |
|---|---|---|
| 1. I feel most alert during the | Day | Night |
| 2. I have most energy during the | Day | Night |
| 3. I prefer to take classes during the | Day | Night |
| 4. I prefer to study during the | Day | Night |
| 5. I get my best ideas during the | Day | Night |
| 6. When I graduate, I plan to find a job during the | Day | Night |
| 7. I am most productive during the | Day | Night |
| 8. I feel most intelligent during the | Day | Night |
| 9. I enjoy leisure-time activities most during the | Day | Night |
| 10. I prefer to work during the | Day | Night |

(*Source:* Based on items from Wallace, 1993.)

## Disturbances in Circadian Rhythms: Jet Lag and Shift Work

Under normal conditions, the existence of circadian rhythms poses no special problems; we simply adjust our activities to these daily fluctuations in energy and alertness. For instance, to take account of my "down" period around 2:00 p.m., I try to schedule less demanding tasks for that time of day. There are two situations, however, in which circadian rhythms may get badly out of phase with events in our lives—with potentially serious consequences.

The first of these occurs as a result of travel. When we fly across several time zones, we may experience considerable difficulty in adjusting our internal clock to the new location—an effect known as *jet lag.* Persons suffering from jet lag feel tired, dull, and generally out of sorts. Research on circadian rhythms indicates that in general it is easier to reset our biological clocks by delaying them than by advancing them. In other words, we experience less disruption when we fly to a time zone where it is *earlier* than the one in which we normally live, than when we fly to one where it is *later.* So, for instance, if you live on the East Coast of the United States and fly to California, where it is three hours earlier, you simply stay up a few extra hours, and then go to sleep. In contrast, if you live in California and fly to the East Coast, where it is three hours later, you may experience greater disruption, and take longer to adjust your internal clock.

Why is this so? One explanation is suggested by the fact that light acts as a zeitgeber, resetting our biological clock. If you travel from New York to, say, Paris, starting out in the evening (most flights depart at that time), you fly into darkness; but then, just when you are really tired and about to fall asleep, dawn occurs, and the cabin is filled with brilliant sunlight (see Figure 4.3 on page 134). Your SCN responds, and resets your biological clock to morning. But in fact, you

**Figure 4.3**
**Zeitgebers and Jet Lag: When Dawn Comes too Early!**

Passengers flying across several time zones to the east (e.g., from New York to Paris or London) often start their journey in the evening. Just when their biological clocks are signaling "Time to sleep," the plane flies into a new dawn. The bright light acts as a zeitgeber, resetting their biological clocks and contributing to their fatigue.

haven't had a night's sleep; you aren't really prepared for the start of a new day. As a result, you feel awful, and it may take you several days to get back to normal. If you fly to the west, however, you leave in daylight and arrive in daylight, so you don't experience the same unsettling effects. You "gain" several hours, and just stay up a little longer than usual.

A second cause of difficulties with respect to circadian rhythms is shift work, in which individuals must work at times when they would normally be sleeping (for instance, midnight to 8:00 a.m.). This is an important issue, because at the present time, about 20 percent of all employees in the United States and several other countries work at night (usually from 11:00 p.m. or midnight until 7:00 or 8:00 a.m.) (Fierman, 1995). To make matters worse, shift workers often face a schedule in which they work on one shift for a fairly short period (say a week), get two days off, and then work on another shift. The results of these "swing shifts" are, for many people, quite unsettling. The reason is clear: Such individuals have to reset their biological clocks over and over again, and this process is draining, both physically and psychologically (e.g., Czeisler, Moore-Ede, & Coleman, 1982). These effects, in turn, have been linked to poorer on-the-job performance, increased industrial and traffic accidents, and adverse effects on health (see Figure 4.4) (e.g., Lidell, 1982; Meijmann, van der Meer, & van Dormolen, 1993). In view of these findings, efforts have been made to develop procedures for minimizing such disruptions. One approach involves keeping employees on the same shift for several weeks rather than only one (e.g., Czeisler, Moore-Ede, & Coleman, 1982). This schedule gives individuals more opportunity to reset their biological clocks than do weekly changes in shift. Another procedure is to expose people who must stay awake at night to bright light just before they would normally go to sleep; this resets their circadian rhythm, so they have an easier time staying awake—and alert (e.g., Houpt, Boulos, & Moore-Ede, 1996).

**Figure 4.4**
**Shiftwork: Often, It Disturbs Biological Rhythms**

Tens of millions of employees work at night all around the world. This often disturbs their biological rhythms and can contribute to both reduced performance and the occurrence of industrial accidents.

Melatonin may also be useful in reducing the adverse effects of both jet lag and swing work shifts. Researchers report that taking melatonin just before going to bed helps people reset their biological clocks more quickly after jet travel or changing their work hours (Deacon & Arendt, 1996). However, the effects of melatonin are still somewhat uncertain, so it's best to treat this procedure as one of last resort—to be used when nothing else seems to work.

For information on another technique for helping people cope with the adverse effects of working at times when their biological rhythms are at a low ebb, please see the following **From Science to Practice** section.

from SCIENCE to PRACTICE

## Counteracting the "Drowsy Driver" Syndrome: When Sounds—and Scents—Save Lives

*It's late at night, and you have been driving for what seems to be an eternity. You have turned on the radio, lowered the window for fresh air, and you are drinking a cup of coffee as you drive—but nothing seems to work. You are tired and bored, and you have trouble keeping your eyes focused on the road ahead of you. Without your realizing it, your eyelids droop, your head drops, and suddenly you are off the road. Only a quick response—and luck—allow you to stop in time. A few more feet and you would have hit that tree. . . .*

Have you ever had an experience like this? I hope not, but most of us *have* become drowsy and mentally numb while driving on a dark road late at night. In fact, this "drowsy driver" effect has serious consequences. Each year, more than 500,000 people are killed and 15 million injured worldwide by traffic accidents, and it has been estimated that *driver fatigue* is responsible for more than 9 percent of these events (Evans, 1991; Knipling & Wang, 1994; Peters et al., 1995). This means that the drowsy driver syndrome may result in the deaths of more than 40,000 people each year!

In view of these findings, it seems reasonable to suggest that efforts to counter fatigue or drowsiness among drivers can yield important benefits (Haworth, Triggs, & Grey, 1988). How can this goal be attained? Many techniques exist, ranging from the use of caffeine and other drugs (see the discussion of these drugs later in this chapter) through use of various environmental stimuli to warn drivers that they are becoming fatigued and to restore them to an alert state. But what environmental stimuli work best in this respect? Research on this topic suggests that certain sounds—ones between 200 and 800 cycles per second (Hz) but consisting of a combination of tones and about 15 or 20 decibels stronger than background noise (e.g., wind noise, engine noise)—can be highly effective in this respect: They help restore drivers' alertness (e.g., Haas & Edworthy, 1996; Wierwille et al., 1994).

Another environmental variable that has proved useful in restoring drivers to an alert state is the release of various fragrances into the air. Fragrances people find pleasant have been found to put them in a good mood (e.g., Baron, 1997), and one aspect of being in a good mood is feeling alert and energized. To test this reasoning, Michael Kalsher and I (Baron & Kalsher, 1998) conducted research in which participants performed on a driving simulation task: They had to keep a moving target that simulated a vehicle on track on a computer screen (this is known as a *compensatory tracking task*). The task is analogous to keeping one's vehicle in lane on a road. To make the job more difficult, participants also performed the tracking task while responding to randomly occurring visual stimuli (STOP signs). They performed both versions of this task in the presence or absence of a pleasant fragrance. As shown in Figure 4.5, results indicated that performance on both versions was significantly enhanced by the presence of a pleasant fragrance in the air (a lemon scent, which had been found in previous research to be a fragrance most people liked and one that boosted their moods).

The story doesn't end there, however. Because we both strongly believe in applying the findings of psychological research to real-world problems, Michael and I have applied for a U.S. patent on a device that drivers can use to restore their

**Figure 4.5**
**Pleasant Fragrances: One Stimulus That Can Increase Drivers' Alertness**

As shown here, research participants performed better on two versions of a driving simulation task when a pleasant lemon fragrance was present in the room where they worked than when this fragrance was not present.
(*Source:* Based on data from Baron & Kalsher, 1998.)

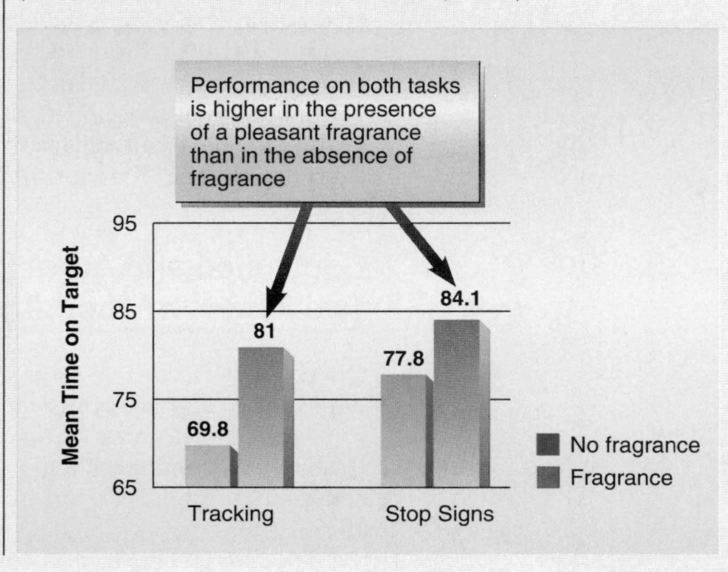

own alertness. This device would be mounted on the dashboard of any vehicle. When drivers felt themselves becoming drowsy, they would turn it on; it would then emit the kinds of sounds shown in basic research to restore alertness. In addition, because other research suggests that sounds that occur suddenly can startle drivers and cause them to have accidents (e.g., Haas, 1998; Haas & Schmidt, 1995), we have designed the device so that the sounds do not start at full intensity; rather, they ramp up to that level from a lower initial volume. The device also releases a pleasant lemon fragrance into the air. Finally, it contains a carbon monoxide detector, because this gas both endangers health and reduces alertness. Similar devices have been designed by other researchers (e.g., Richard Grace at Carnegie Mellon University; Bounds, 1996). Unfortunately, however, these devices were *not* designed by psychologists, so they don't seem to take account of the basic research findings concerning what kind of sounds or fragrances will be most helpful. Until our device is tested against these other products, we certainly can't claim that ours is necessarily better. We do feel, though, that any attempt to counter drowsiness among drivers should take careful account of what we know about biological rhythms and human perception—and this is what we have done in designing our new product.

**REVIEW QUESTIONS**

- What are biological rhythms? What are circadian rhythms?
- How do morning persons and night persons differ?
- What effects do jet lag and shift work have on circadian rhythms?
- What steps can be taken to counter "drowsy driver" syndrome?

**Food for Thought**

Suppose that you are an evening person but must make an important presentation early in the morning. What can you do to improve your own alertness—and your performance?

# Waking States of Consciousness

Each time I teach a class, I notice many students who are looking at me as I speak and who turn their heads to follow me as I move about the front of the room. They *seem* to be listening carefully to what I'm saying; but I know from past experience that if I call on some of these students and ask them a question, they will look totally blank: Their minds have been a million miles away, even as they looked at me and nodded their heads in response to what I have been saying. As such experiences suggest, even during our normal waking activities we often shift between various states of consciousness. One moment you are paying careful attention to a lecture; the next you are lost in a vivid daydream. Let's take a closer look at these everyday shifts in consciousness.

## Controlled and Automatic Processing: Two Modes of Thought

Often, we perform two tasks at the same time—for example, brushing our teeth while our thoughts wander far and wide, or talking to another person as we cook some dish. How can we do this? The answer involves the fact that we have two contrasting ways of controlling ongoing activities—different levels of attention to, or conscious control over, our own behavior (e.g., Folk & Remington, 1996; Logan, 1985, 1988).

The first level uses very little of our *information-processing capacity,* and seems to occur in an automatic manner with very little conscious awareness on our part.

**Figure 4.6**
**Automatic Processing Requires Less Effort than Controlled Processing—Unless We Think about It**

As Linus has just discovered, tasks we perform under automatic processing require little effort, unless we try to think about them! Directing attention to such tasks can actually interfere with their performance.

(*Source:* PEANUTS © Charles M. Schultz. Reprinted with permission of United Feature Syndicate, Inc.)

For this reason, psychologists refer to it as **automatic processing,** and it *does* seem, subjectively, to be automatic. Several different activities, each under automatic control, can occur at the same time (e.g., Shiffrin & Dumais, 1981; Shiffrin & Schneider, 1977). Every time you drive while listening to the radio, you demonstrate such automatic processing: Both activities can occur simultaneously, because both involve automatic processing.

In contrast, **controlled processing** involves more effortful and conscious control of thought and behavior. In controlled processing you direct careful attention to the task at hand and concentrate on it. Processing of this type consumes significant cognitive resources; as a result, only one task requiring controlled processing can usually be performed at a time.

Research on the nature of automatic and controlled processing suggests that these two states of consciousness differ in several respects. First, behaviors that have come under the control of automatic processing are performed more quickly and with less effort than ones that require controlled processing (Logan, 1988)—unless, like the character in Figure 4.6, we think about them! In addition, acts that have come under automatic processing—usually because they are well practiced and well learned—can be initiated without conscious intention; they are triggered in a seemingly automatic manner by specific stimuli or events (e.g., Norman & Shallice, 1985). In fact, it may be difficult to inhibit such actions once they are initiated. If you ever played Simple Simon as a child, you are well aware of this fact. After following many commands beginning "Simple Simon says do this," you probably also responded to the similar command, "Do this." Why? Because your imitation of the leader's actions was under automatic control, and you obeyed—without conscious thought—even when you should have refrained from doing so.

Because it requires less effort, automatic processing is very common in our everyday activities. Indeed, recent evidence suggests that it occurs even with respect to several aspects of perception—how we perceive the world around us (e.g., Lamb et al., 1998). Perhaps the most fascinating research on automatic processing, however, concerns our efforts to control our own mental processes and our own physical actions (e.g., Wegner, 1994, 1997). Often these efforts seem to backfire and produce precisely the thoughts, feelings, or actions we *don't* want. For instance, if you are on a diet and tell yourself, "Don't think about how good a juicy hamburger or a delicious dessert would taste," you may find yourself thinking precisely these thoughts. Similarly, if you are carrying a full cup of coffee and tell yourself, "Don't spill any!" you may find that this is exactly what happens—you *do* spill some! Daniel Wegner, a psychologist who has studied such effects for many years, suggests that these events occur because efforts to control our own thoughts and actions—to bring them under controlled processing—involve a system consisting of two parts. One, an *intentional operating process,* searches for mental contents that will produce the state we desire (avoiding thoughts of hamburgers, not spilling the coffee). The other, an *ironic monitoring process,* searches for mental contents that signal our *failure* to achieve the desired state. The intentional operating process is effortful and consciously guided—it involves controlled processing. The ironic

**Automatic Processing:** Processing of information with minimal conscious awareness.

**Controlled Processing:** Processing of information with relatively high levels of conscious awareness.

**Figure 4.7**
**Ironic Effects of Mental Control: Doing Precisely What We Don't Want to Do**

Individuals told to prevent a pendulum from moving sideways actually produced *more* movements of this kind than persons simply told to hold the pendulum steady. This was especially true when they experienced mental load (counting backwards by threes).
(*Source:* Based on data from Wegner, Ansfield, & Pilloff, 1998.)

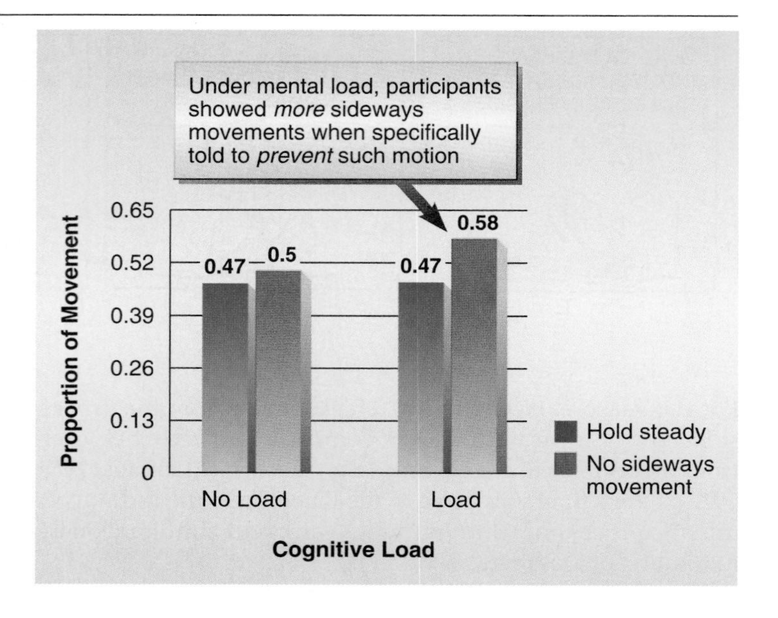


monitoring process, in contrast, is unconscious and less demanding; it involves automatic processing.

Usually the two processes work together—one to keep thoughts we want in mind, and the other to keep unwanted thoughts *out* of consciousness. But if there are extra demands on our information-processing capacity, the intentional operating process may be overloaded, with the result that the automatic monitoring process dominates, and we find ourselves thinking about, feeling, or doing precisely what we *don't* want to think, feel, or do. (Remember: This process is constantly searching for the thoughts or feelings we don't want to have, so it may have the ironic effect of actually bringing these to mind.)

Evidence for these suggestions has been obtained in many different studies (e.g., Wegner, 1997, Wegner, Broome, & Blumberg, 1997), but one of the most interesting was conducted by Wegner, Ansfield, and Pilloff (1998). These researchers asked male and female college students either to try to prevent a crystal suspended from a nylon rope from moving *sideways,* or simply to hold it steady. Within each of these two conditions, half the students were also asked to count backwards from 1,000 by threes (1,000, 997, 994, etc.) while performing this task; the other half were not. Wegner and his colleagues reasoned that counting backwards would use up information-processing capacity and so would interfere with the intentional (controlled) operating system. Thus, *more* sideways movement—precisely what the participants did *not* want—would occur under mental load than in its absence. However, more movement would not occur when students were simply told to hold the pendulum steady. As you can see from Figure 4.7, results confirmed these predictions. The students who tried to prevent sideways movement showed more of the unwanted movement than those merely told to hold it steady, and this difference was larger when they also counted backwards by threes. These results, and those of many other studies, suggests that automatic processing is indeed a ubiquitous aspect of human cognition.

The operation of the ironic monitoring process also helps explain why it is often so hard to pay attention to something—for instance, a lecture—even when we want to do so. Wegner (1994, 1997) suggests that operation of the ironic monitoring process causes us to lose the focus of our attention as it searches for signs that we aren't paying attention!

Is either of these types of processing superior? Not really. Automatic processing is rapid and efficient but can be relatively inflexible—precisely because it is so automatic. Controlled processing is slower but is more flexible and open to change. In sum, both play an important role in our efforts to deal with information from the external world. One final point: Automatic and controlled processing are not hard-and-fast categories, but rather ends of a continuous dimension. On any given task, individuals may operate in a relatively controlled or a relatively automatic manner.

## Self-Awareness: Some Effects of Thinking about Ourselves

What do you do when you pass a mirror? Probably, you stop—however briefly—and check your appearance. Is your hair messed up? Your hat on straight? Your makeup OK? When you engage in such activities, you are, in a sense, changing your current state of consciousness. Before you passed the mirror, you were probably thinking about something other than yourself; but while you stand in front of the glass, your thoughts are focused on yourself. Psychologists term this focus **self-awareness,** and they have found that entering this particular state of consciousness has interesting and widespread effects (e.g., Ingram, 1990; Trapnell & Campbell, 1999). Let's take a look at some of these.

**WHY DO WE BECOME SELF-AWARE, AND WHAT HAPPENS WHEN WE DO?** One question about self-awareness that comes readily to mind is, "Why do we enter this state to start with?" the answer seems to be that some situations induce us to do so. Passing a mirror is one, speaking to or performing in front of an audience is another, and having our picture taken is yet another. In these situations, we are induced to think about ourselves. And once we do, an interesting process is initiated. According to one theory of self-awareness, *control theory,* when we focus our attention on ourselves, we compare our current state (our feelings, thoughts, and performance) to internal standards—how we would *like* to feel, think, and perform (Carver & Scheier, 1981). If the gap between reality and these standards is small, everything is fine. If the gap is large, however, we have two choices: (1) We can "shape up," changing our thoughts or actions so that they fit more closely with our standards and goals; or (2) we can "ship out"—withdraw from self-awareness in some way. Such withdrawal can range from simple distraction (we can stop thinking about ourselves and how we are falling short of our own internal standards) to more dangerous actions, such as drinking alcohol, engaging in binge eating, or—in the extreme—ending our own existence through suicide (Baumeister, 1990).

What determines whether we try to change or try to escape from unpleasant self-awareness? Research findings suggest that a key factor is our beliefs concerning whether we *can* change successfully or not. If we believe that the chances we can change are good, we concentrate on meeting our internal standards and goals. But if we believe that we are unlikely to succeed in changing, then we may seek escape—with all the dangers this implies (e.g., Gibbons, 1990). In sum, self-awareness can have stronger and more far-reaching effects on behavior than you might at first guess (see Figure 4.8 on page 140).

Another factor that can strongly influence our tendency to focus on ourselves is our affective state—our current mood. Several studies suggest that we are more likely to turn our attention inward when we are in a negative mood than when we are in a positive one (e.g., Salovey, 1992; Wood, Saltzberg, & Goldsamt, 1990). However, more recent findings (Green & Sedikides, 1999) indicate that the situation may be more complex than this. Some affective states (e.g., sadness and contentment) tend to lead us to think about ourselves and why we are feeling as we do. Others, in contrast (e.g., being thrilled or angry) lead us to think about other persons. Anger, for instance, is often focused on someone who has annoyed or irritated us; when we experience such feelings, we tend to think about this other person rather

**Self-Awareness:** A state of consciousness in which we focus our attention inward, upon ourselves.

**Figure 4.8**
**Effects of Increased Self-Awareness**

When we experience heightened self-awareness, we compare our current states (our behavior, feelings, thoughts) to internal standards. If a large gap exists between reality and these standards, we assess the chances of closing this gap. If these seem good, we try to change so as to come closer to our internal standards. If the chances of closing the gap are poor, then we concentrate, instead, on trying to reduce our self-awareness.

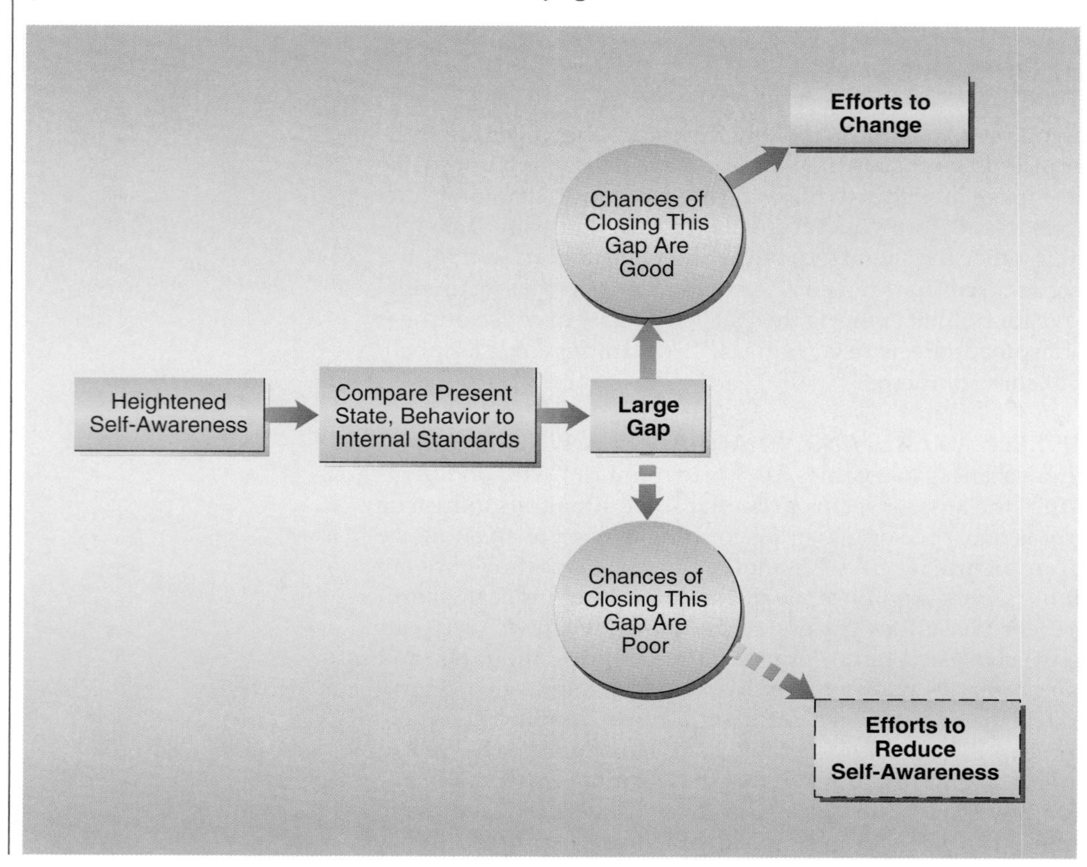


than about ourselves. So it's not necessarily the case that negative moods cause us to focus on ourselves and become self-aware; rather, this is true only when such moods are reflective in nature. Results of recent studies by Green and Sedikides (1999) offer support for these predictions: These researchers found that people show one kind of self-awareness (awareness of their own inner thoughts and feelings, known as *private self-consciousness*) when induced to experience reflective moods such as sadness or contentment, but do *not* experience increased self-awareness when induced to experience socially oriented moods such as being thrilled or being angry. Still another type of self-awareness involves the tendency to focus on our public image—how we appear to others; this is known as *public self-consciousness* (Fentstein, 1987).

Large individual differences exist in the tendency to become self-aware—to enter private self-consciousness or public self-consciousness. Some persons are very high in these dimensions, others are very low, and most are in between (e.g., Fentstein, 1987; Sedikides, 1992).

**EFFECTS OF SELF-AWARENESS: RUMINATION OR REFLECTION?** When we discuss psychological disorders and various forms of therapy in Chapters 14 and

15, we'll note that self-insight—understanding oneself—is often viewed as an important factor in good adjustment: People who know themselves well are less likely to go off the track psychologically. Yet, surprisingly, research on private self-consciousness (one of the two types of self-awareness we've considered) indicates that the higher people stand on this dimension, the *less* well adjusted they tend to be (Ingram, 1990). How can this be? One answer provided by recent research is as follows: When individuals focus on themselves, they may do so for two different motives. First, self-awareness can be motivated by curiosity—the desire to know oneself better; this is known as *reflection.* Second, self-awareness can be motivated primarily by *fear*—by concern over threats, perceived shortcomings, losses, or injustices one has experienced; this is known as *rumination.* Recent evidence indicates that rumination, but not reflection, is related to distress and several psychological problems. So thinking about ourselves can produce psychological benefits or psychological costs, depending on the motivation behind this activity and the topics on which we focus. To find out where *you* stand with respect to these aspects of self-awareness, see the **Making Psychology Part of Your Life** section at the end of the chapter.

**Choking under Pressure:** Reduced performance that occurs under conditions in which pressures to perform well are very high.

**EFFECTS OF SELF-AWARENESS: CHOKING UNDER PRESSURE** When I was in high school, I was on the track team. My specialty was the hundred-yard dash, and I was fast—one of the fastest males in my school. But my speed didn't do me much good when my high school competed against an arch-rival at a track meet. In the warm-up sessions I easily defeated all my opponents, so I approached the actual race with confidence. "Piece of cake," I thought. "I'll soon have another medal for my collection." But then I noticed lots of my friends, and a young woman I found very attractive, sitting in the stands. The pressure was on. I knew that I had to do my best—this was *important.* So what happened? I became so nervous and tried so hard that I was slow off the mark and lost the race. In short, I experienced **choking under pressure**—I performed *less* well when pressure for excellence was high than I had in the warm-up races, when pressure was low.

Why do such effects occur? One explanation involves arousal: In situations where pressures to do well are very strong, our arousal may be so high that it interferes with our performance. (We'll examine such effects in detail in Chapter 10.) Another explanation involves self-awareness and the automatic versus controlled processing distinction we discussed earlier (Baumeister, 1998). Many skilled actions we perform, from running to typing, are so well practiced that they are under automatic control. When pressures to perform well are very high, however, we may think about ourselves and our performance (i.e., become self-aware), thus interfering with the smooth, automatic control of these activities (see Figure 4.9). The result: Our performance drops from what it would be if we did *not* become self-aware.

**Figure 4.9**
**Choking under Pressure: Self-Awareness May Play a Role**

Sometimes, even skilled professional athletes such as those shown here choke under pressure—they perform more poorly when the stakes are high than when performance is less important. Heightened self-awareness may play a role in such effects.

Support for this reasoning is provided by an ingenious study carried out by Baumeister and Steinhilber (1984). They reasoned that although pressures for performance are high throughout World

**Sleep:** A process in which important physiological changes (e.g., shifts in brain activity, slowing of basic bodily functions) are accompanied by major shifts in consciousness.

**Electroencephalogram (EEG):** A record of electrical activity within the brain. EEGs play an important role in the scientific study of sleep.

**Electromyogram (EOM):** A record of electrical activity in various muscles.

**Electrooculogram (EOG):** A record of changes in electrical potentials in the eyes.

**Alpha Waves:** Brain waves that occur when individuals are awake but relaxed.

**Delta Activity:** Slow (3.5 Hz or less), high-amplitude brain waves that occur during several stages of sleep, but especially during Stage 4.

**REM Sleep:** A state of sleep in which brain activity resembling waking restfulness is accompanied by deep muscle relaxation and movements of the eyes. Most dreams occur during periods of REM sleep.

Series baseball games, they are especially intense during the final games (the ones that determine which team wins) and in games played at home, in front of the team's own fans. Thus, they predicted that choking would be most likely to occur under these conditions. To test this hypothesis, they examined the records of more than fifty years of World Series games. As predicted, teams actually lost a majority of the final games when they played at home—just the opposite of what the "home court advantage" concept would predict, but consistent with the view that choking under pressure involves, in part, the effects of heightened self-awareness. In short, turning our attention inward and entering a state of self-awareness can have positive or negative effects, depending on when and why we enter this state.

**REVIEW QUESTIONS**

- What is the difference between automatic processing and controlled processing?
- Why do we sometimes think or do precisely what we *don't* want to think or do?
- What is self-awareness, and why do we sometimes enter this state of consciousness?
- What are some of the effects of self-awareness on our adjustment and performance?

## Sleep: The Pause That Refreshes?

What single activity occupies more of your time than any other? You may be tempted to say "studying" or "working"—but think again. The correct answer is probably **sleep**—a process in which important physiological changes and slowing basic bodily functions are accompanied by major shifts in consciousness. In fact, most people spend fully one-third of their entire lives asleep (Dement, 1975; Webb, 1975). What is the nature of sleep? What functions does it serve? And what are dreams? These are key questions on which we'll focus. To get started, let's first consider the question of how psychologists study sleep in the **Research Methods** section that follows.

## Research methods: How Psychologists Study Sleep

Everyone would agree that when we sleep, we are in a different state of consciousness than when we are awake. But what is sleep really like? And how can we study it? Psychologists generally agree that the best way to study sleep in a scientific manner is in a *sleep laboratory*—a special facility, usually located in a university or a medical center, containing several small bedrooms next to an adjoining observation room. The bedrooms are occupied by volunteer research participants; the researchers remain in the observation room, monitoring the changes that occur as individuals fall asleep and remain asleep.

What changes do sleep researchers study? Primarily, three major types. Researchers study changes occurring in the electrical activity of the brain by means of the **electroencephalogram (EEG),** changes in electrical activity in various muscles with the **electromyogram (EMG),** and changes in electrical potentials in the eyes with the **electrooculogram (EOG).** It turns out that as individuals sleep, systematic changes occur in all these measures; and these changes, in turn, reveal much about the nature of sleep. In most sleep research involving humans, volunteers are fitted with electrodes on the scalp (to measure

EEG), the chin (to monitor EMG), and the eyes (to monitor EOG). In addition, changes in heart rate, respiration, and skin conductance are also measured. The result? A complex and revealing picture of the changes that occur in our nervous system and muscles as we sleep (see Figure 4.10).

What has research using these methods revealed about the nature of sleep? A picture of sleep that goes something like this. When you are fully awake and alert, your EEG contains many *beta waves:* relatively high-frequency (14–30 cycles per second or Hz), low-voltage activity. As you enter a quiet, resting state—for example, after getting into bed and turning out the light—beta waves are replaced by **alpha waves,** EEG activity that is somewhat lower in frequency (8–12 Hz) but slightly higher in voltage (amplitude). As you begin to fall asleep and enter what is known as Stage 1 sleep, *theta activity* occurs; this is EEG activity of 3.5–7.5 Hz (see Figure 4.10). Many researchers consider Stage 1 to be on the border between waking and sleep. After about ten minutes in Stage 1, many people enter Stage 2 sleep. This is marked by *sleep spindles* and *K complexes.* Sleep spindles are short bursts of waves of 12–14 Hz that occur two to five times per minute; they may represent the activity of a mechanism that reduces the brain's sensitivity to sensory input and so helps us to enter deeper stages of sleep. K complexes are sudden, sharp waveforms that occur about once each minute (refer to Figure 4.10). They can also be triggered by noises (Carlson, 1999), and may also be involved in helping us remain asleep.

The next stage, Stage 3, is marked by the appearance of **delta activity,** high-amplitude waves of less than 3.5 Hz. This is followed by Stage 4, in which the proportion of delta activity increases. Stage 3 shows 20 to 50 percent delta activity; Stage 4 is more than 50 percent delta activity. Some researchers believe that delta activity represents a synchronization of neurons in which increasingly large numbers of neurons fire together.

So far, the picture of sleep revealed by the EEG seems consistent with our subjective experience of sleep. About ninety minutes after the process begins, however, several dramatic changes occur, as individuals enter a distinctive phase known as **REM (rapid eye movement) sleep.** During this phase the electrical activity of the brain changes rapidly; it now closely resembles that shown when people are awake. Delta activity disappears, and fast, low-voltage activity returns. Sleepers' eyes begin to move about rapidly beneath their closed eyelids, and there is an almost total suppression of activity in body muscles.

These observable shifts in brain activity and bodily processes are accompanied, in many cases, by one of the most dramatic aspects of sleep: *dreams.* Individuals awakened during REM sleep often report dreaming. In some cases, eye movements during such sleep seem to be related to the content of dreams (Dement, 1975). It is as if dreamers are following the action in their dreams with their eyes. The relationship between rapid eye movements and dream content is uncertain, however, so it is best to view this as an intriguing but as yet unverified possibility.

**Figure 4.10**
**States of Sleep**

As shown here, there are four distinct stages of sleep, each characterized by changes in the electrical activity of our brains. In addition, another phase of sleep, REM sleep, is markedly different; during REM sleep activity in our brains closely resembles, in some respects, the activity that occurs when we are awake.

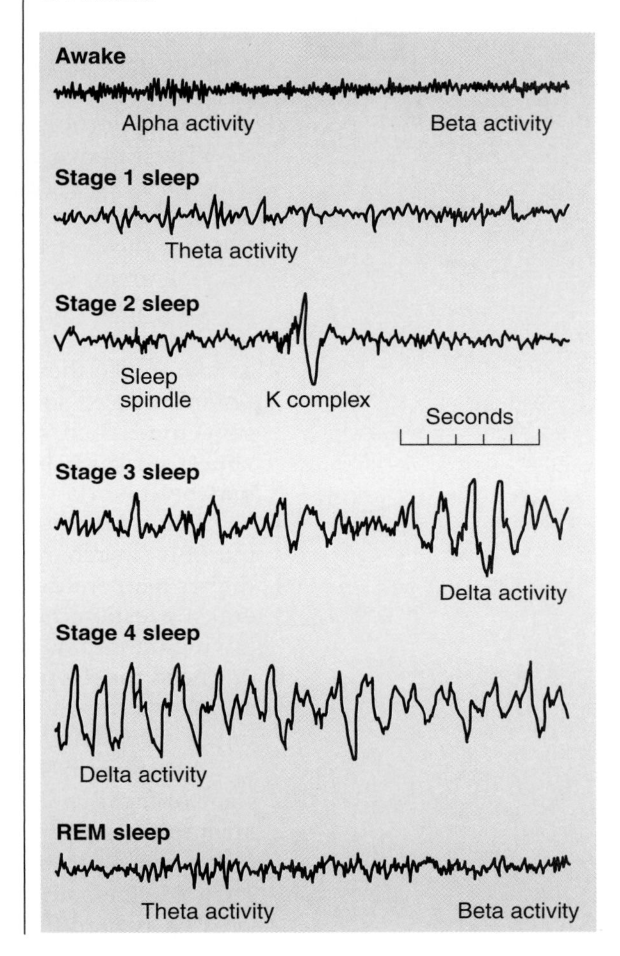


Periods of REM sleep continue to alternate with the other stages of sleep throughout the night. The duration is variable, but the REM periods tend to increase in length toward morning. Thus, while the first REM period may last only five to ten minutes, the final ones—from which many people awake—may last thirty minutes or more (Hartmann, 1973; Kelly, 1981). In addition, periods of non-REM sleep (Stages 1 through 4) contain an increasing proportion of Stage 2 sleep, and less and less of Stages 3 and 4 (which together are known as slow-wave sleep, for reasons obvious from Figure 4.10).

## Sleep: What Functions Does It Serve?

Any activity that fills as much of our lives as sleep must serve important functions. But what, precisely, are these? Several possibilities exist, and they may differ for slow-wave sleep (Stages 3 and 4) and REM sleep. Let's consider slow-wave sleep (Stages 3 and 4) first.

**POSSIBLE FUNCTION OF SLOW-WAVE SLEEP** Here, the most obvious possibility is that this kind of sleep serves mainly a restorative function, allowing us—and especially our brain—to rest and recover from the wear and tear of the day's activities. Several findings provide indirect evidence for this suggestion. First, if sleep allows our brain to rest, then we would expect to see more delta (slow-wave) activity in portions of the brain that have experienced intense activity during the day. The findings of several studies suggest that this is so (e.g., Kattler, Djik, & Borbely, 1994). PET scans of the brain (which reveal the level of activity in various areas) indicate that the portions of the brain most active during the day are indeed the ones showing most delta activity during the night. Second, some species of marine mammals show a pattern in which the two cerebral hemispheres take turns sleeping. This suggests that sleep does permit the brain to rest in some manner (Carlson, 1999). Why have these animals developed this pattern? Perhaps because, as mammals, they are not as well adapted to life in the water as other marine organisms and so simply can't afford to allow both hemispheres to sleep at the same time: There are too many dangers to permit that luxury, which is enjoyed by almost all land species of mammals. In short, adaptation to selection pressures may be at work.

Third, vigorous physical exercise seems to increase slow-wave, "resting" sleep, but only if such exercise raises the brain's temperature (Horne, 1988). Given that higher temperatures in the brain raise its metabolism, this, too, fits with the general suggestion that slow-wave sleep may be, at least in part, a mechanism for allowing our brains to rest after intense periods of activity. Incidentally, the fact that our need for sleep seems to increase after the brain's temperature has been raised suggests a reason why a hot bath may indeed be one effective technique for bringing on a good night's sleep.

A second possible function of slow-wave sleep emphasizes the relationship of sleep to circadian rhythms. According to this view, sleep is merely the neural mechanism that evolved to encourage various species, including our own, to remain inactive during those times of day when they do not usually engage in activities related to their survival. As one well-known sleep researcher (Webb, 1975) has put it, sleep is nature's way of keeping us quiet at night, a dangerous time for our ancestors—and for us—since we are not equipped with sensory capacities suited for nighttime activity.

**POSSIBLE FUNCTIONS OF REM SLEEP** Turning to REM sleep, some findings are consistent with the view that these special phases play a crucial role in learning—in allowing us to consolidate memories of the preceding day or, perhaps, to eliminate unnecessary memories and other mental clutter from our brains (e.g., Crick & Mitchison, 1995). If REM sleep performs functions related to learning, then two predictions follow: (1) Animals that undergo training of some kind but are then deprived of the opportunity to engage in REM sleep will show poorer performance than animals not deprived of such sleep; and (2) after intense learning, animals will show more REM sleep than at other times. Studies offer support for both predictions (e.g., Smith, 1996). For example, in one investigation, Block, Hennevin, and Leconte (1977) trained rats to run through a complex maze. As training on this task continued, the rats ran faster *and* spent an increasing proportion of their sleep in REM sleep. So there does seem to be some indication that REM sleep plays a role in learning.

REVIEW QUESTIONS

- How do psychologists study sleep?
- What are the major stages of sleep?
- What happens during REM sleep?
- What are the possible functions of slow-wave and REM sleep?

## Effects of Sleep Deprivation

Web Link: *American Academy of Sleep Medicine*

Everyone has had the experience of feeling completely miserable after a sleepless night, so it seems reasonable to focus on sleep deprivation as a possible source of useful information about the nature and functions of sleep. What, then, are the effects of sleep deprivation? Among humans, research results present a mixed picture. Even prolonged deprivation of sleep does not seem to produce large or clear-cut effects on behavior for many persons. For example, in one demonstration, seventeen-year-old Randy Gardner stayed awake for 264 hours and 12 minutes—eleven entire days! His motivation for doing this was simple: He wanted to earn a place in *The Guinness Book of Records*, and he did. Although Randy had some difficulty staying awake this long, he remained generally alert and active throughout the entire period. After completing his ordeal, Randy slept a mere 14 hours on the first day, 10 hours on the second, and less than 9 on the third. Interestingly, his sleep on these nights showed an elevated proportion of slow-wave sleep and REM sleep but did not show a rise in Stages 1 and 2. It was as if his brain focused on making up the deprivation in slow-wave and REM sleep, but could get along fine without compensating for the losses in Stages 1 and 2. Randy suffered no lasting physical or psychological harm from his long sleepless period—and, of course, his feat made him briefly famous. But don't consider trying to beat Randy's record. There are potential risks in long-term sleep deprivation, including an increased chance of serious accidents and harm to physical health.

That long-term deprivation of sleep *can* be harmful to human beings is suggested by a disorder known as **fatal familial insomnia** (e.g., Gallassi et al., 1996). In this disorder, individuals experience increasingly severe disturbances in sleep until, finally, slow-wave sleep totally disappears and only brief periods of REM sleep occur. The disease is fatal; but whether this is due to the sleep disturbances themselves, or whether the sleep disturbances are simply a sign of other neurological problems, remains uncertain.

Studies with animals also suggest that long-term deprivation of sleep can be harmful. For instance, Rechtschaffen and his colleagues (Rechtschaffen & Bergmann, 1995; Rechtschaffen et al., 1983) have used procedures such as those illustrated in Figure 4.11 on page 146 to study sleep deprivation effects. Two rats are placed on a platform surrounded by water. Whenever one (the experimental animal) begins to fall asleep, the platform is rotated, so the animal must wake up and move to avoid falling into the water. The other rat (the yoked-control animal) is also forced to move; but because this rat may or may not be asleep at the time, its sleep is not necessarily disturbed. In fact, these procedures reduce total sleep time by 87 percent for the experimental animal but by only 31 percent for the yoked-control animal. Results indicate that while the control animals remain in perfect health, the experimental animals become weak and uncoordinated and lose the ability to regulate their body temperature. Such findings suggest that sleep deprivation does indeed have serious consequences for health. Needless to say, similar experiments cannot be conducted with human beings, so we can't be certain that comparable results would be obtained. Still, there does seem to be sufficient evidence to suggest that sleep serves important functions for humans too.

**Fatal Familial Insomnia:** A genetic disorder in which individuals experience increasing disturbances in sleep; the disorder is, as its name suggests, fatal.

**Figure 4.11**
**Studying the Effects of Sleep Deprivation: One Technique**

As shown here, two animals are placed on a platform floating on water. Whenever one shows signs of falling asleep (e.g., as indicated by patterns of brain activity), the platform rotates, thus preventing the animal from sleeping. The other animal, too, is prevented from sleeping, but because this "yoked-control" animal may have been awake anyway, its sleep is disturbed to a much smaller degree.

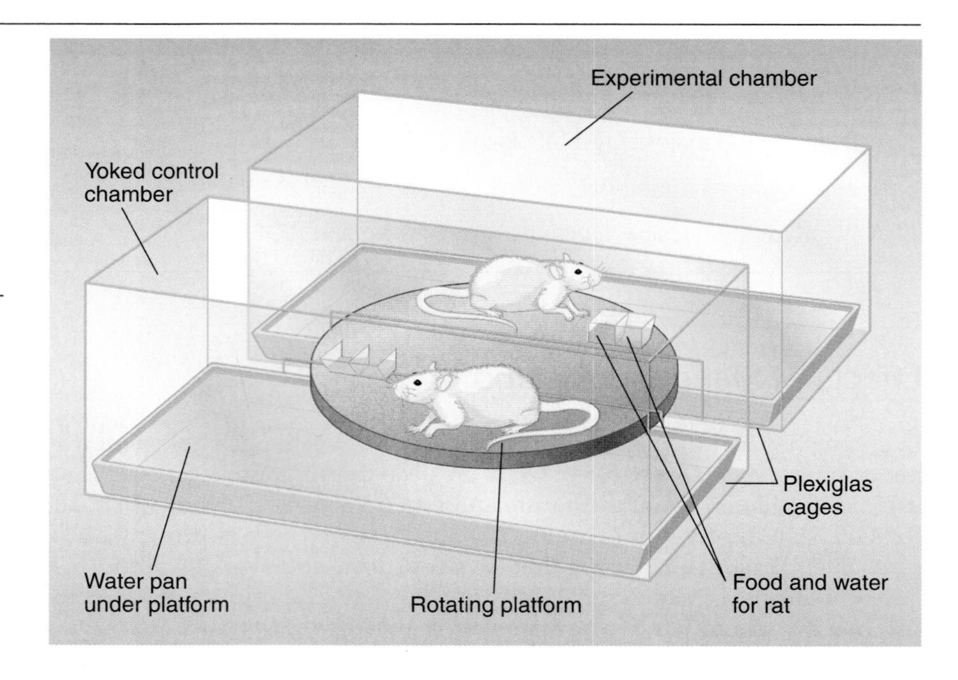

Web Link: *Pacific Sleep Medicine Services*

## Sleep Disorders: No Rest for Some of the Weary

Do you ever have trouble falling or staying asleep? If so, you are in good company: Almost 40 percent of adults report that they sometimes have these problems—known, together, as **insomnia** (Bixler et al., 1979). Such problems seem to increase with age and are somewhat more common among women than men. While many people report insomnia, however, it is not clear that the incidence of this problem is as high as these self-reports might suggest. When the sleep habits of people who claim to be suffering from insomnia are carefully studied, it turns out that many of them sleep as long as people who do not complain of insomnia (Empson, 1984). This does not mean that such persons are faking; rather, it is possible that although they attain an amount of sleep that falls within normal limits (6.5 hours or more per night), this is not enough to meet their individual needs. Further, the quality of their sleep may be disturbed in ways not yet measured in research. Still, such arguments aside, it does appear that many people who believe that their sleep is somewhat inadequate may actually be getting a normal amount.

On the other hand, insomnia is quite real for many persons, at least occasionally. What can you do if you encounter this problem? The following tactics may prove helpful:

- Read something pleasant or relaxing just before going to sleep.
- Arrange your schedule so you go to sleep at the same time each night.
- Take a warm bath or have a massage before going to sleep.
- Avoid coffee or tea late in the day.
- Exercise every day, but not just before going to sleep.
- Don't smoke.
- Don't nap during the day.
- Don't worry; almost everyone experiences difficulty falling asleep sometimes, so don't be overly concerned unless the problem persists for more than a few days.
- If, despite these measures, you find yourself tossing and turning, get up and read, work, or watch television until you feel drowsy. Lying in bed and worrying about your loss of sleep is definitely *not* the answer!

**Insomnia:** Disorder involving the inability to fall asleep or to maintain sleep once it is attained.

**Narcolepsy:** A sleep disorder in which individuals are overcome by sleep attacks—the uncontrollable urge to sleep during waking hours.

**Cataplexy:** A symptom of the sleep disorder narcolepsy; in cataplexy individuals fall down suddenly, like a sack of flour.

**Somnambulism:** A sleep disorder in which individuals actually get up and move about while still asleep.

**Night Terrors:** Extremely frightening dreamlike experiences that occur during non-REM sleep.

**Apnea:** A sleep disorder in which sleepers stop breathing, and thus wake up, many times each night.

By the way, despite the promises of advertisements, sleeping pills—prescription as well as nonprescription—are not usually an effective sleep aid. They may induce sleep at first, but tolerance to them develops quickly so that larger and larger doses are needed. The result is *drug-dependency insomnia*—insomnia caused by the side effects of ever larger doses of sleeping medicines. Further, some drugs used for this purpose interfere with REM sleep, and this can lead to other sleep disturbances.

Although insomnia is the most common sleep disorder, it is not the only one. Several other disorders, some related to REM sleep and some to slow-wave sleep, exist. Let's consider some in each category.

**DISORDERS ASSOCIATED WITH REM SLEEP** Perhaps the most dramatic disturbance of REM sleep is **narcolepsy,** a disorder in which sleep occurs at unexpected—and often inappropriate—times. Persons suffering from narcolepsy often have *sleep attacks* in which they experience an irresistible urge to sleep in the midst of waking activities. They sleep for two to five minutes, then awake refreshed. I once had a colleague who had sleep attacks in class. He would stop lecturing, put his head down on the desk, and—much to the amusement of his students, who made many jokes about his "putting himself under"—sleep.

Another symptom of narcolepsy is **cataplexy,** in which the individual falls down suddenly and without warning. Often, such persons remain fully conscious, but their muscles are paralyzed, as during REM sleep. And sometimes they experience vivid dreams while in this state; in other words, they are dreaming while awake!

Yet another disorder of REM sleep is REM sleep without *atonia*—REM sleep that occurs without muscle paralysis. Persons suffering from this disorder do something most of us are prevented from doing: They act out their dreams. While this might sound amusing, it can lead to serious injury as these persons move around and do whatever they are doing in their dreams.

**DISORDERS ASSOCIATED WITH SLOW-WAVE SLEEP** Perhaps the most dramatic disorder associated with slow-wave sleep is **somnambulism**—walking in one's sleep. This is less rare than you might guess; almost 25 percent of children experience at least one sleepwalking episode (see Figure 4.12) (Empson, 1984). A second, related disorder is **night terrors.** Here, individuals—especially children—awaken from deep sleep with signs of intense arousal and powerful feelings of fear. Yet they have no memory of any dream relating to these feelings. Night terrors seem to occur mainly during Stage 4 sleep. In contrast, *nightmares,* which most of us have experienced at some time, occur during REM sleep and often can be vividly recalled. Both somnambulism and night terrors appear to be linked to disturbances in the functioning of the autonomic system, which plays a key role in regulating brain activity during sleep.

Another disturbing type of sleep disorder is **apnea.** Persons suffering from sleep apnea actually stop breathing when they are asleep. This causes them to wake up, and since the process can be repeated hundreds of times each night, apnea can seriously affect the health of persons suffering from it.

The causes of sleep disorders are as varied as the complex neural and chemical systems that regulate sleep itself; detailing them here would lead us into topics well beyond the scope of this book. Suffice it to say that sleep disorders have their roots in the mechanisms and brain structures that regulate arousal, slow-wave sleep, and REM sleep.

**Figure 4.12**
**Sleepwalking: One Disorder of Slow-Wave Sleep**

About 25 percent of children go through one or more episodes of *somnambulism,* or sleepwalking. I remember having such experiences myself as a child; I'd suddenly awaken to find that I had gotten out of bed and walked into another room. These episodes stopped by the time I was about ten years old.

## Dreams: "Now Playing in Your Private, Inner Theater . . ."

What is the most dramatic aspect of sleep? For many persons, the answer is obvious: **dreams**—the jumbled, vivid, sometimes enticing, sometimes disturbing images that fill our sleeping minds. What are these experiences? Why do they occur? Let's first consider some basic facts about dreams, then turn to the answers to these questions provided by psychological research.

**DREAMS: SOME BASIC FACTS** Answer each of the following questions. Then consider the answers provided—which reflect our current knowledge about dreams.

1. *Does everybody dream?* The answer seems to be *yes.* Not all people remember dreaming, but EEG recordings and related data indicate that everyone experiences REM sleep.
2. *How long do dreams last?* Many people believe that dreams last only an instant, but in fact they seem to run on "real time": The longer dreams seem to last, the longer they really are (Dement & Kleitman, 1957).
3. *Can external events become part of dreams?* Yes, at least to a degree. For example, Dement and Wolpert (1958) sprayed water on sleepers who were in the REM stage of sleep. When they woke them up, more than half the sleepers reported water in their dreams.
4. *When people cannot remember their dreams, does this mean that they are purposely forgetting them, perhaps because they find the content disturbing?* Probably not. Research on why people can or cannot remember their dreams indicates that this is primarily a function of what they do when they wake up. If they lie quietly in bed, actively trying to remember the dream, they have a good chance of recalling it. If, instead, they jump out of bed and start the day's activities, the chances of remembering the dream are reduced. Although we can't totally rule out the possibility of some kind of repression—that is, motivated forgetting—there is little evidence for its occurrence.
5. *Do dreams foretell the future?* There is no scientific evidence for this widespread belief.
6. *Do dreams express unconscious wishes?* Again, there is no convincing scientific evidence for this view.

Now that we've considered some basic facts about dreams, let's turn to several views concerning their nature and function.

**DREAMS: THE PSYCHODYNAMIC VIEW** Let's begin with the idea that dreams express unconscious wishes or impulses. This view has existed for centuries, but its influence was greatly increased by Sigmund Freud, who felt that dreams provide a useful means for probing the unconscious—thoughts, impulses, and wishes that lie outside the realm of conscious experience. In dreams, Freud believed, we can give expression to impulses and desires we find unacceptable during our waking hours. Thus, we can dream about gratifying illicit sexual desires or about inflicting painful torture on persons who have made us angry—thoughts we actively repress during the day.

Freud carefully analyzed the dreams of his patients, and he reported that in this manner he frequently gained important insights into the causes of their problems. So fascinating were his reports of these experiences as a therapist, and so filled with conviction, that many people quickly accepted Freud's claims; and such beliefs about the meaning of dreams are definitely alive and well today. Despite this fact, they are *not* supported by convincing scientific evidence. On the contrary, Freud provided no clear-cut rules for interpreting dreams and no way of determining

**Dreams:** Cognitive events, often vivid but disconnected, that occur during sleep. Most dreams take place during REM sleep.

whether such interpretations are accurate. In view of these facts, few psychologists currently accept the view that dreams offer a unique means for exploring the unconscious. Instead, most accept one of the views we will now consider.

**DREAMS: THE PHYSIOLOGICAL VIEW** If dreams aren't reflections of hidden wishes or impulses, what are they? An answer is provided by what is sometimes known as the *physiological view* of dreams (Hobson, 1988). According to this perspective, dreams are simply our subjective experience of what is, in essence, random neural activity in the brain. Such activity occurs while we sleep simply because a minimal amount of stimulation is necessary for normal functioning of the brain and nervous system. Dreams then simply represent efforts by our cognitive systems to make sense out of this random neural activity (Foulkes, 1985; Hobson, 1988).

A logical extension of this view suggests that the activity of which we try to make sense is not actually random; rather, it occurs primarily in the two systems of the brain that are most active when we are awake—the visual system and the motor system. As this view suggests, dreams are usually silent but are filled with visual images. And although many dreams contain images of movement, few persons report experiencing smells, tactile (touch) sensations, or tastes in their dreams (Carlson, 1999).

**Dreams of Absent-Minded Transgression:** Dreams in which persons attempting to change their behavior, as in quitting smoking, see themselves slipping into the unwanted behavior in an absent-minded or careless manner.

Audio 4.1: *Significance of Dreams*

**DREAMS: THE COGNITIVE VIEW** Another, and closely related, explanation of dreams carries somewhat farther these suggestions concerning our cognitive systems' efforts to interpret neural activity while we sleep. This perspective, proposed by Antrobus (1991), suggests that two facts about REM sleep are crucial to understanding the nature of dreams: (1) During REM sleep, areas of the cerebral cortex that play a role in waking perception, thought, and regulation of motor processes are highly active; (2) yet at the same time, during REM sleep there is massive inhibition of input from sensory systems and muscles (these are suppressed). As a result, Antrobus (1991) reasons, the cortical structures or systems that normally regulate perception and thought have only their own activity as input. The result is that this activity forms the basis for the imagery and ideas in dreams.

Does this mean that dreams are meaningless? Not at all. Since they represent interpretations of neural activity by our own brain, dreams reflect aspects of our memories and waking experience—as the character in Figure 4.13 has discovered. Convincing evidence for this connection between dreams and important events in our lives is provided by the fact that many persons attempting to make important changes in their own behavior—for example, to quit smoking or drinking—report having **dreams of absent-minded transgression**—DAMIT dreams for short (e.g., Gill, 1985). In such dreams, people suddenly notice that they have carelessly or absent-mindedly slipped into the habit they wish to break—they are smoking or drinking without having planned to do so. This realization leads to feelings of

**Figure 4.13**
**Dreams: Sometimes They *Do* Reflect Aspects of Our Memories or Events in Our Daily Lives**

Memories of an old TV show have influenced the dreams of the character shown here; not surprisingly, his partner doesn't seem pleased with this apparently recurring dream!
(*Source:* ROBOTMAN reprinted by permission of United Feature Syndicate, Inc.)

panic or guilt in the dream. In many cases the dreamers awake at that point, feeling quite disturbed. Interestingly, having such dreams is positively related to success in breaking the habits in question (e.g., in giving up smoking) (Hajek & Belcher, 1991). So this kind of dream, at least, does seem to be related to important events in our daily lives.

**REVIEW QUESTIONS**

- What are the effects of sleep deprivation?
- What steps help promote a good night's sleep?
- What are important disorders of REM sleep? Of slow-wave sleep?
- How do the psychodynamic, physiological, and cognitive views of dreams differ?

## Hypnosis: Altered State of Consciousness . . . or Social Role Playing?

A few years ago I went to a local county fair. There were lots of attractions, but the one that drew the largest crowds by far was the hypnotism show. The hypnotist—who looked like anyone's grandfather—called for volunteers and quickly gathered about twenty people of all ages on the stage. Within a few minutes, he had put the volunteers into what he described as a "deep trance" and induced them to do some very strange things. He told one young woman to imagine that she was a rooster and it was dawn. She proceeded to crow at the top of her lungs. He told two young men that they were famous ballerinas and were dancing for the Queen of England; they took off doing circles around the stage. In his grand finale, he put everyone on the stage back into a deep trance just by snapping his fingers. (He had previously suggested to them, while they were under hypnosis, that they would react like this when he snapped his fingers.) Then he told them that whenever he said the word "turnip," they would fall deeply asleep. He woke them and engaged them in conversation. Then, suddenly, without warning, he uttered the magic word "turnip." Most of his subjects immediately slumped over in their chairs in what seemed to be deep, restful sleep.

Video 4.1: *Hypnosis*

After the show, everyone in our group turned to me, as the psychologist-in-residence, and asked what I thought. Is hypnotism real? Were the people on the stage really in a trance, or were they somehow faking? "Complicated," I replied. "Complicated." And now let me explain why I gave this answer—and how psychologists view the strange phenomenon of **hypnosis:** a special type of interaction between two persons in which one (the hypnotist) induces changes in the behavior, feelings, or cognitions of the other (the subject) through suggestions.

**Hypnosis:** An interaction between two persons in which one (the hypnotist) induces changes in the behavior, feelings, or cognitions of the other (the subject) through suggestions. Hypnosis involves expectations on the part of subjects and their attempts to conform to social roles (e.g., the role of the hypnotized person).

### Hypnosis: How It's Done and Who Is Susceptible to It

Let's start with two basic questions: (1) How is hypnotism performed? (2) Is everyone susceptible to it? With respect to the first, standard techniques for inducing hypnosis usually involve *suggestions* by the hypnotist that the person being hypnotized feels relaxed, is getting sleepy, and is unable to keep his or her eyes open. Speaking continuously in a calm voice, the hypnotist suggests to the subject that she or he is gradually sinking deeper and deeper into a relaxed state—not sleep, but a state in which the person will be highly susceptible and open to suggestions from the hypnotist, suggestions concerning the person's feelings, thoughts, and behavior. Another technique involves having the subject concentrate on a small object, often one that sparkles and can be rotated by the hypnotist. The result of such procedures, it seems, is that some people (emphasize the word *some*) enter what appears to be an altered state of consciousness that is definitely not sleep—EEG recordings from hypnotized persons resemble those of normal waking, not any of the sleep stages described earlier (Wallace & Fisher, 1987).

**Social–Cognitive or Role-Playing View:** A view suggesting that effects produced by hypnosis are the result of hypnotized persons' expectations about hypnosis and their social role as "hypnotized subject."

Now for the second question: Can everyone be hypnotized? The answer seems clear: Large individual differences in hypnotizability exist. About 15 percent of adults are highly susceptible (as measured by their response to a graded series of suggestions by the hypnotist); 10 percent are highly resistant; the rest are somewhere in between. In addition, it appears that people who are highly hypnotizable show several distinctive traits (Silva & Kirsch, 1992): They often have vivid fantasies; they are high in visual imagery; they are high in the trait of *absorption*, the tendency to become deeply involved in sensory and imaginative experiences; they often seek advice and direction from others; and—perhaps most important of all—they *expect* to be influenced by hypnotic suggestions. The greater the extent to which individuals possess these characteristics, the greater, in general, is their susceptibility to hypnosis.

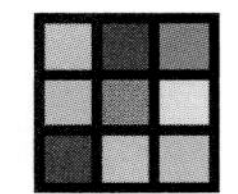

## Hypnosis: Contrasting Views about Its Nature

Web Link: *Hypnosis Online in the UK*

Now let's consider a more complex question: Is hypnosis real? Does it produce actual changes in consciousness? Systematic research on hypnosis has led to the formulation of several contrasting views concerning this issue.

**THE SOCIAL–COGNITIVE OR ROLE-PLAYING VIEW** The first of these approaches, the **social–cognitive or role-playing view,** suggests that in fact there is nothing strange or mysterious about hypnosis. On the contrary, the effects it produces are simply a reflection of a special type of relationship between the hypnotist and the subject. According to this perspective, persons undergoing hypnosis have seen many movies and read stories about hypnosis; they have clear ideas about what it involves and what, supposedly, will happen to them when hypnotized (see Figure 4.14). These views lead such persons to play a special *social role*—that of *hypnotic subject.* This role implies that they will be "in the hypnotist's power," unable to resist the hypnotist's suggestions. When they are then exposed to hypnotic inductions—instructions to behave in certain ways or to experience specific feelings—they tend to obey, because this is what the social role they are

**Figure 4.14**
**Hollywood: An Important Source of Our Beliefs about the Nature and Effects of Hypnotism**

After watching countless movies with scenes like the one shown here, many people form clear ideas about what hypnotism involves and what, supposedly, will happen to them if they are ever hypnotized.

enacting indicates *should* happen. Further, they often report experiencing the changes in perceptions and feelings that they *expect* to experience (e.g., Lynn, Rhue, & Weekes, 1990; Spanos, 1991).

It's important to note that this view does *not* imply that persons undergoing hypnosis are consciously faking. On the contrary, they sincerely believe that they are experiencing an altered state of consciousness and that they have no choice but to act and feel as the hypnotist suggests (Kinnunen, Zamansky, & Block, 1994). But these behaviors and experiences are due mainly to the subjects' beliefs about hypnosis and the role of hypnotic subject rather than to the special skills of the hypnotist or their entry into an altered state of consciousness.

**THE NEODISSOCIATION AND DISSOCIATED CONTROL VIEWS** Two additional views suggest, in contrast, that hypnosis does indeed produce an altered state of consciousness. The first of these, the **neodissociation theory of hypnosis,** contends that hypnosis induces a split or dissociation between two basic aspects of consciousness: an *executive or central control function,* through which we regulate our own behavior, and a *monitoring function,* through which we observe it. According to Hilgard (1986, 1993), the most influential supporter of this view, these two aspects of consciousness are normally linked. Hypnosis, however, breaks this bond and erects a cognitive barrier—referred to as *hypnotic amnesia*—that prevents some experiences during hypnosis from entering into normal consciousness. The result is that persons who are hypnotized are indeed in a special altered state of consciousness, in which one part of their mind accepts and responds to suggestions from the hypnotist, while the other part—which Hilgard terms "the hidden observer"—observes the procedures without participating in them. Because of this split in consciousness, these two cognitive mechanisms are no longer in direct contact with each other. So, for example, if hypnotized persons are told to put their arms into icy water but instructed by the hypnotist that they will experience no pain, they will obey and will indeed report no discomfort. However, if asked to describe their feelings in writing, they may indicate that they *did* experience intense cold (Hilgard, 1979). In other words, they have the experience of pain, but under hypnosis the pain is not available to their conscious thought as it would be normally.

Bowers and his associates (e.g., Bowers, 1992; Woody & Bowers, 1994) have modified this view by proposing what they describe as the **theory of dissociated control.** According to this theory, hypnotism does not necessarily involve a division of consciousness. Rather, it simply weakens control by the central function over other cognitive and behavioral subsystems. Thus, these subsystems can be invoked directly by the hypnotist's suggestions in an automatic manner that is not mediated by normal cognitive mechanisms.

Which approach is more accurate—the social–cognitive view or the theories emphasizing dissociation? Existing evidence offers a mixed and complex picture (e.g., Kirsch & Lynn, 1998; Noble & McConkey, 1995; Reed et al., 1996). Overall, though, it seems fair to say that strong support for the two views that emphasize dissociation (the neodissociation and dissociated control theories) is lacking (Green & Lynn, 1995; Kirsch & Lynn, 1998). However, as noted by Kihlstrom (1998), some findings do seem consistent with the splitting-of-consciousness idea so central to dissociation theories. For instance, although hypnotized persons told by the hypnotist to forget certain experiences can't report those experiences explicitly, they can show evidence that memories for these events are present implicitly. Such memories, for example, can influence their performance on various tasks (e.g., Barnier, 1997; Dorfman & Kihlstrom, 1994). But again, taking all available research into account, the evidence for theories suggesting that hypnosis represents a genuine altered state of consciousness is far from convincing.

In contrast, support for the social–cognitive view seems more convincing (e.g., Kirsch & Lynn, 1998; Spanos, 1991). Most of the unusual or bizarre effects observed

**Neodissociation Theory:** A theory of hypnosis suggesting that hypnotized individuals enter an altered state of consciousness in which consciousness is divided.

**Theory of Dissociated Control:** A theory of hypnosis suggesting that hypnotism weakens control by the central function over other cognitive and behavioral subsystems, thus permitting these subsystems to be invoked directly by the hypnotist's suggestions.

under hypnosis can readily be explained in terms of hypnotized persons' beliefs in the effects of hypnotism and their efforts—not necessarily conscious—to behave in accordance with these expectations. To see why I and many other psychologists have reached this conclusion, let's take a closer look at some of this evidence.

**EVIDENCE FOR THE SOCIAL-COGNITIVE VIEW** Perhaps evidence concerning the impact of hypnosis on perception is most informative. Under hypnosis, some persons seem to experience dramatic changes in their ability to perceive various stimuli. For example, they report little pain even when exposed to painful stimuli such as ice-cold water (Spanos et al., 1990). Further, when told by the hypnotist that they will not be able to perceive certain stimuli that are presented to them, or, alternatively, that they will "perceive" stimuli that are *not* actually there, many persons report such effects (e.g., Miller & Bowers, 1993). Are such effects real? Or are the hypnotized persons merely reporting what they think the hypnotist wants them to report, or what they expect to experience? Research findings offer support for the latter conclusion. For instance, in several studies, Spanos and his colleagues (Spanos, Burgess, & Perlini, 1992), have used the following procedures.

Individuals are exposed to a tone they can readily hear on three different occasions. After hearing it the first time, they rate its loudness. Then they are hypnotized and told that they will not be able to hear it. When the tone is presented again, they do tend to rate it as being less loud than on the first trial, as neodissociation theory would suggest. All participants are then awakened from hypnosis. Now comes the crucial part. Before the tone is presented the third time, some participants (those in a *demand instructions* group) are told that they have probably slipped back into hypnosis and probably won't be able to hear the tone very well. In contrast, those in a *control* group are not given these instructions. Spanos reasons that if persons in the demand instructions group (those who believe they have "slipped back into hypnosis") rate the tone as less loud than those in the control group, this provides strong evidence that hypnotized persons do *not* actually experience changes in perception; rather, they are simply reporting what they think the hypnotist wants to hear (they are responding to what psychologists term *demand characteristics*) or what they expect to happen. As shown in Figure 4.15, results

**Figure 4.15**
**Evidence for the Social-Cognitive View of Hypnosis**

Individuals who are hypnotized and told they will not be able to hear a tone rate it as lower in volume than they did initially. When some (those in a *demand instructions* group) are told that they have probably "slipped back into hypnosis" and probably won't be able to hear the tone again, they also rate it as less loud. In contrast, those in a control condition who are *not* told that they have "slipped back into hypnosis" rate the tone as louder. These findings suggest that some of the effects of hypnosis, at least, are due to individuals' expectations about what they will experience or what the hypnotist wants them to do. (*Source:* Based on findings reported by Spanos and his colleagues in several studies.)

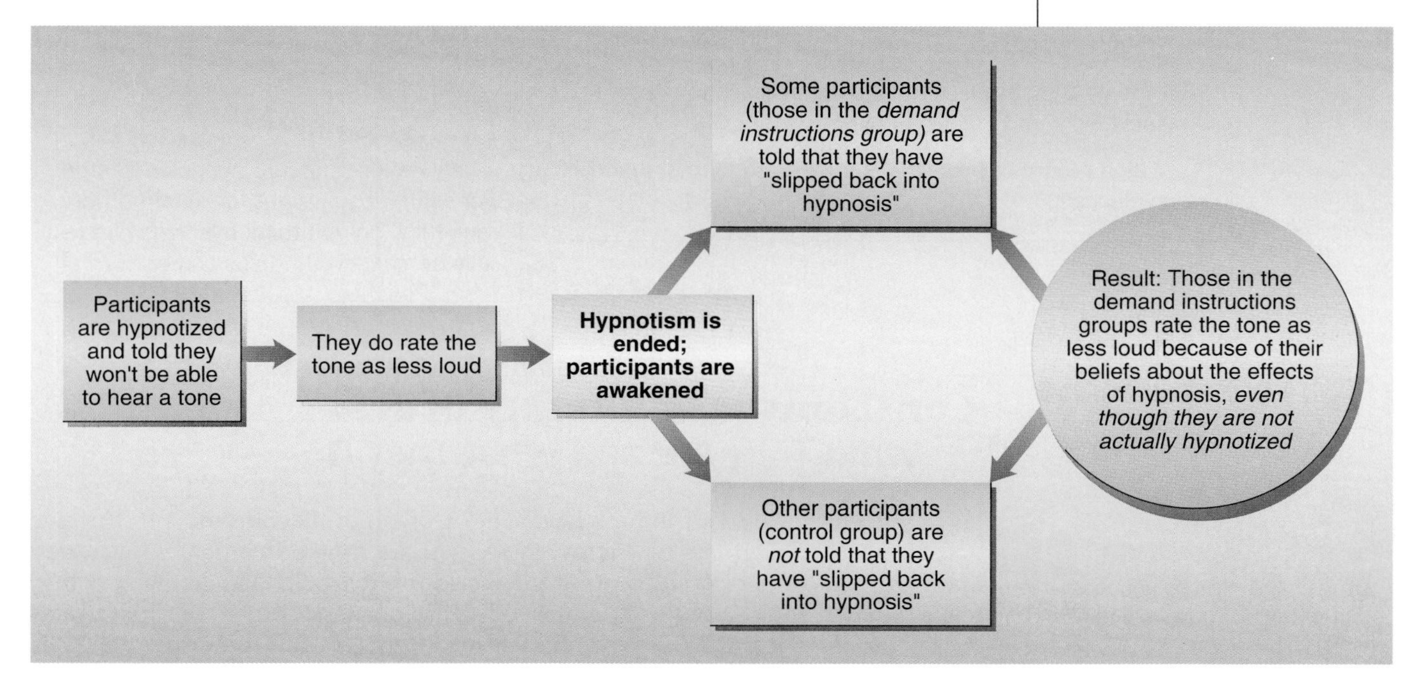

have strongly supported this latter conclusion. Thus, it appears that changes in perception under hypnosis do not represent actual changes in how people perceive the world; rather, they are the result of participants' expectations and of their desire to live up to the role of hypnotized subject.

In a similar manner, other effects attributed to hypnosis—for example, distortions in memory induced by a hypnotist's suggestions—have been found to be largely the result of hypnotized persons' expectations and their desire to do what the hypnotist wants them to do (Murray, Cross, & Whipple, 1992). Overall, then, most existing evidence seems to support the social–cognitive view of hypnosis: The effects of hypnotism stem primarily from hypnotized persons' beliefs about hypnotism, plus their tendency to meet the hypnotist's expectations (Green & Lynn, 1995).

**AND YET . . . SOME EVIDENCE FOR THE NEODISSOCIATION VIEW** Having emphasized that most scientific evidence argues *against* the view that hypnosis produces dramatic shifts in consciousness, I must, to be fair (and to practice critical thinking!), report that some findings do offer support for this position (e.g., Reed et al., 1996). Perhaps the most dramatic findings of this type involve studies in which researchers tell hypnotized persons, and persons who have *not* been hypnotized but who are instructed to simulate the effects of hypnotism, that they have undergone a sex change (e.g., McConkey, 1991; Noble & McConkey, 1995). Then the experimenters challenge this hypnotic suggestion in various ways; for instance, participants are told that a physician examined them and found no change in their sex, or they are shown their own image on television. Results indicate that a higher proportion of persons who have been hypnotized than persons who are merely simulating hypnosis maintain their belief that their sex has been changed even when that belief is strongly challenged. Findings such as these suggest that hypnotism can, perhaps, produce actual changes in perception and states of consciousness among some persons. However, it's important to note that such effects occur primarily among individuals who are exceptionally susceptible to hypnotism. For such persons, hypnotic suggestions may indeed induce changes in consciousness; for most persons, however, reactions to hypnosis seem to stem primarily from their beliefs and expectations about it, as social–cognitive theory predicts.

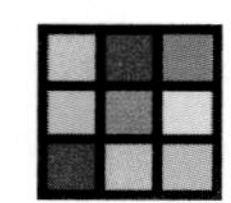

**REVIEW QUESTIONS**

- What is hypnosis?
- How do the social–cognitive, neodissociation, and dissociative control views of hypnosis differ?
- Which theory of hypnosis is supported by most current evidence?

**Food for Thought**

Many people undergo hypnosis to stop smoking, lose weight, or obtain other benefits. Do you think hypnosis can really be effective in these ways?

Web Link: *The National Clearinghouse for Alcohol and Drug Information*

## Consciousness-Altering Drugs: What They Are and What They Do

**Drugs:** Chemical compounds that change the functioning of biological systems.

Have you ever taken aspirin for a headache? Do you drink coffee or soft drinks to boost your own alertness or energy? If so, you are in good company: Each day, many millions of persons all around the world use drugs to change the way they feel—to alter their moods or states of consciousness. Much of this use of consciousness-altering drugs is completely legal—aspirin and soft drinks are freely available everywhere, and many other drugs are consumed under a doctor's supervision. In many other cases, however, people use drugs that are illegal, or use legal ones to excess. The effects of doing so can be both dramatic and tragic. In this final section, we'll consider several issues relating to the use of consciousness-altering drugs.

**Figure 4.16**
**Drugs at Home**

Does your own medicine cabinet look something like this? Probably it does; almost everyone uses a wide range of drugs—prescription and nonprescription.

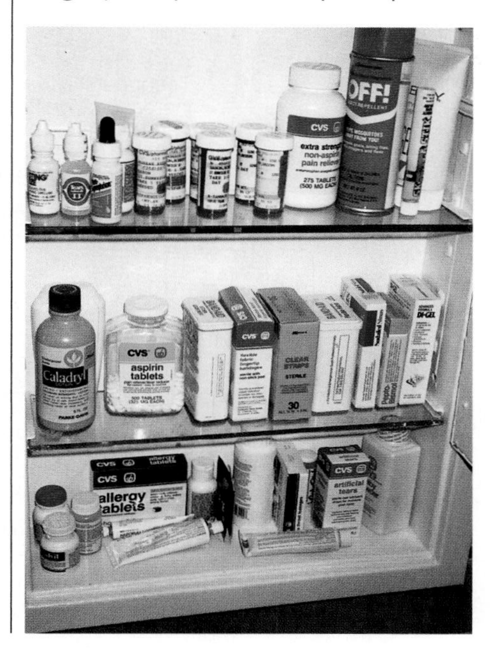


## Consciousness-Altering Drugs: Some Basic Concepts

Let's begin with some basic definitions. First, what are **drugs**? One widely accepted definition states that drugs are compounds that, because of their chemical structure, change the functioning of biological systems (Grilly, 1989; Levinthal, 1999). *Consciousness-altering drugs,* therefore, are drugs that produce changes in consciousness (Wallace & Fisher, 1987).

Suppose you went to your medicine cabinet and conducted a careful inventory of all the drugs present. How many would you find? Unless you are very unusual, quite a few (see Figure 4.16). Many of these drugs probably are perfectly legal and can be obtained in any pharmacy without a prescription (for example, aspirin). Others are probably ones prescribed by a physician. Using drugs in both categories is generally safe and appropriate. The term **drug abuse,** therefore, applies only to instances in which people take drugs purely to change their moods, and in which they experience impaired behavior or social functioning as a result of doing so (Wallace & Fisher, 1987).

Unfortunately, when people consume consciousness-altering drugs on a regular basis, they often develop **dependence**—they come to need the drug and cannot function without it. Two types of dependence exist. One, **physiological dependence,** occurs when the need for the drug is based on organic factors, such as changes in metabolism. This type of dependence is what is usually meant by the term *drug addiction.* However, people can also develop **psychological dependence,** in which they experience strong desires to continue using the drug even though, physiologically, their bodies do not need it. As we'll soon see, several psychological mechanisms probably contribute to such dependence. Physiological and psychological dependence often occur together and magnify individuals' cravings for and dependence on specific drugs.

Continued use of a drug over a prolonged period of time often leads to drug **tolerance**—a physiological reaction in which the body requires larger and larger doses in order to experience the same effects. For example, I once had a friend who drank more than twenty cups of coffee each day. He didn't start out this way; rather, he gradually increased the amount of coffee he consumed over the years until he reached the level where, we joked, he sloshed as he walked! In some cases, tolerance for one drug increases tolerance for another; this is known as **cross-tolerance.**

How widespread is drug use? Patterns vary greatly around the world and over time. In the United States, use of many consciousness-altering drugs by young people dropped during the 1980s but increased again during the 1990s. In fact, the results of one large survey (Johnston, O'Malley, & Bachman, 1997) indicated that teenagers' use of many drugs—including alcohol, cocaine, marijuana, and nicotine (in cigarettes)—had increased substantially (see Figure 4.17 on page 156). What factors were responsible for this rise? Many probably played a role, including greater availability of drugs; social factors (e.g., many teenagers consider it cool to use drugs, as we'll see shortly); and reduced parental supervision—both parents are working, and are so busy that they may have little time or energy to keep close tabs on their teenage children. Whatever the reasons, though, increased use of drugs poses many dangers to physical and psychological health, dangers I will describe below.

**Drug Abuse:** Instances in which individuals take drugs purely to change their moods and experience impaired behavior or social functioning as a result.

**Dependence:** Strong need for a particular drug and inability to function without it.

**Physiological Dependence:** Strong urges to continue using a drug based on organic factors such as changes in metabolism.

**Psychological Dependence:** Strong desires to coninue using a drug even though it is not physiologically addicting.

**Tolerance:** Habituation to a drug, causing larger and larger doses to be required to produce effects of the same magnitude.

**Cross-Tolerance:** Increased tolerance for one drug that develops as a result of taking another drug.

**Figure 4.17**
**Drug Use by Teenagers: Some Alarming Trends**

As shown here, teenagers' use of several drugs—including illegal ones—increased sharply in the 1990s. Will this trend continue or be reversed? Only time will tell, but the danger both for individuals and for society is obvious.

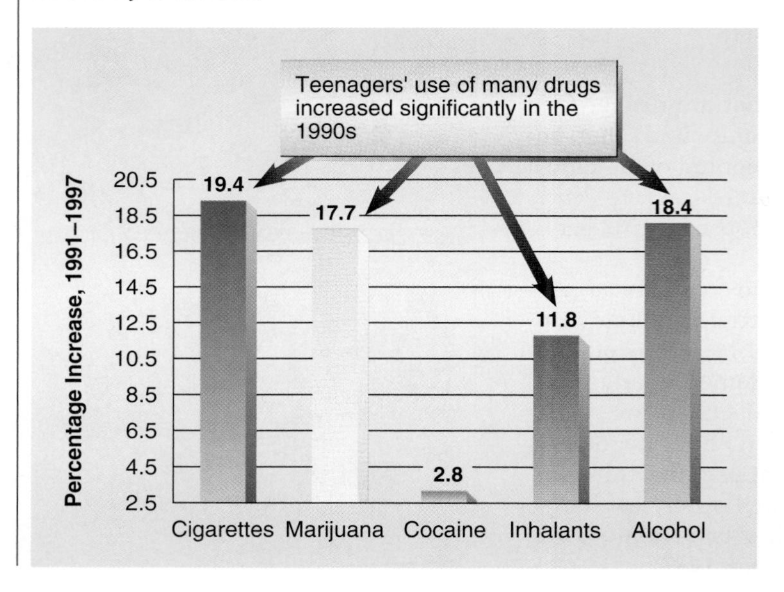


## Psychological Mechanisms Underlying Drug Abuse: Contrasting Views

Putting trends in drug use aside for the moment, a more basic question exists: Why do people take consciousness-altering drugs in the first place? Several psychological mechanisms seem to play a role.

**THE LEARNING PERSPECTIVE: REWARDING PROPERTIES OF CONSCIOUSNESS-ALTERING DRUGS** First, and perhaps most obvious, people often use such drugs because doing so feels good. In other words, the effects produced by the drugs are somehow rewarding (Wise & Bozarth, 1987); see our discussion of reinforcement in Chapter 5. Evidence supporting this view is provided by many studies indicating that animals will self-administer many of the same drugs that people abuse, presumably because they find the effects of these drugs rewarding (Young & Herling, 1986). The neural mechanisms responsible for such effects seem to involve a structure in the forebrain known as the **nucleus accumbens** (White, 1996). Many addictive drugs we'll consider below (alcohol, cocaine, nicotine, amphetamines) trigger the release of the neurotransmitter *dopamine* in this nucleus. That the nucleus accumbens plays a role in the "good feelings" produced by such drugs is suggested by the fact that if release of dopamine in this location is prevented, addictive drugs lose their reinforcing effects (e.g., Di Chiara, 1995).

On the other side of the coin, use of consciousness-altering drugs has also been attributed to the fact that these substances reduce *negative* feelings such as stress, anxiety, or physical discomfort. Thus, people take drugs to reduce negative feelings rather than simply to generate positive ones (Cooper, et al., 1995). This explanation is especially applicable when individuals have become dependent on a drug; the negative symptoms they experience when it is no longer consumed—known as *withdrawal*—may provide a powerful incentive to obtain the drug at all costs.

**THE SOCIAL PERSPECTIVE: DRUG ABUSE AND SOCIAL PRESSURE** Another perspective suggests that drug abuse can be understood largely in terms of social factors. According to this view, individuals, especially adolescents and young adults, use consciousness-altering drugs because it is the "in" thing to do. Their friends use these drugs, and they believe that if they do too, this will enhance their social image. Evidence for this view has been reported in many studies (e.g., Sharp and Getz, 1996), so it appears that social motivation is a powerful factor in drug abuse, especially by young people.

**Nucleus Accumbens:** A structure in the forebrain that plays an important role in the reinforcing effects of many addictive drugs.

**THE COGNITIVE PERSPECTIVE: DRUG ABUSE AS AUTOMATIC BEHAVIOR** The distinction between automatic and controlled behavior forms the basis for yet another perspective on drug abuse. According to this view, the cognitive systems controlling many aspects of obtaining and consuming various drugs may soon take on the character of automatic processes. To the extent that this occurs, drug use becomes quick and relatively effortless, occurs without conscious intention, is difficult to inhibit, and may even take place in the absence of conscious awareness.

Once individuals have used a drug on numerous occasions, then, they may find themselves responding almost automatically to external cues—for example, to a specific environment in which they have often enjoyed this drug, such as a bar, or to specific sights and smells, such as the aroma of a burning cigarette. In a similar manner, they may respond automatically to internal cues or emotions, such as wanting to celebrate or feeling tired or out of sorts. These cues may trigger people's tendencies to use drugs, and they may find themselves doing so before they realize it, even without any strong urge to take a drug (Tiffany, 1990).

Which of these perspectives is most accurate? Most psychologists favor a view that combines the learning, social, and cognitive perspectives. Drug abuse, it appears, stems from a combination of factors; and this—sadly—is one reason why it is so difficult to combat.

**REVIEW QUESTIONS**

- What are drugs? What is drug abuse?
- What are physiological and psychological dependence on drugs?
- How do the learning, social, and cognitive perspectives explain drug abuse?

## Consciousness-Altering Drugs: An Overview

Audio 4.2: *Alcohol and Human Aggression*

Web Link: *Institute of Alcohol Studies*

While many different drugs affect consciousness, most seem to fit under one of four major headings: *depressants, stimulants, opiates,* or *psychedelics and hallucinogens.*

**DEPRESSANTS** Drugs that reduce both behavioral output and activity in the central nervous system are called **depressants.** Perhaps the most important of these is *alcohol,* a likely candidate for the most widely consumed drug in the world. Small doses of alcohol seem, subjectively, to be stimulating—they induce feelings of excitement and activation. Larger doses, however, act as a depressant. They dull the senses so that feelings of pain, cold, and other forms of discomfort become less intense. Large doses of alcohol interfere with coordination and normal functioning of our senses, often with tragic results for motorists. Alcohol also lowers social inhibitions so that after consuming large quantities of this drug, people become less restrained in their words and actions and more likely to engage in dangerous forms of behavior such as aggression (e.g., Pihl, Lau, & Assaad, 1997). Alcohol seems to produce its pleasurable effects by stimulating special receptors in the brain. Its depressant effects may stem from the fact that it interferes with the capacity of neurons to conduct nerve impulses, perhaps by affecting the cell membrane directly.

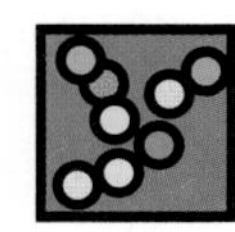

Growing evidence suggests that a tendency to abuse alcohol may have a strong genetic component. Two major patterns of alcohol abuse exist. One group of abusers drink consistently at high levels (steady drinkers), and people in this group usually have a history of antisocial acts—fighting, lying, and so on. In contrast, another group of abusers can resist drinking alcohol for long periods of time; but if they do drink, they cannot control themselves and go on true binges (see Figure 4.18 on page 158). The first of these patterns of alcohol abuse seems to be strongly influenced by heredity. For instance, one large-scale study carried out in Sweden (Sigvardsson, Bohman, & Cloninger, 1996) focused on people who were adopted early in life and raised in homes with or without an alcoholic parent; the researchers examined the behavior of the adoptees' biological parents, too, to see if *they* abused alcohol. Results indicated that men whose biological fathers were steady drinkers were about seven times more likely to become steady drinkers themselves than

**Depressants:** Drugs that reduce activity in the nervous system and therefore slow many bodily and cognitive processes. Depressants include alcohol and barbiturates.

**Figure 4.18**
**Steady Drinking: A Strong Genetic Basis**

Many people who abuse alcohol drink steadily—they consume alcohol at a high rate on a daily basis. This drinking pattern appears to stem to an important degree from genetic factors.

were men whose biological fathers did not show this pattern. Moreover—and crucially—this was true regardless of whether the *adoptive* fathers abused alcohol. These findings suggest that for this kind of alcohol abuse, hereditary factors are more important than environmental ones. In contrast, very few women become steady drinkers, even if their fathers show this pattern (few mothers do). Instead, they tend to develop a type of psychological disorder in which they complain of symptoms for which no physiological basis can be found (see Chapter 14 for discussion of this type of problem, known as *somatization disorder*).

Interestingly, the second pattern of alcohol abuse—binge drinking—seems to be influenced by both heredity and environment; in the same Swedish study, adopted persons with a biological parent who showed this pattern did not abuse alcohol themselves unless they were also placed in a family environment in which they were exposed to heavy drinking. This was true for both females and males.

**Barbiturates,** which are contained in sleeping pills and relaxants, constitute a second type of depressant. First manufactured in the late nineteenth century, these drugs depress activity in the central nervous system and reduce activation and mental alertness. How these effects are produced is not certain, but some evidence suggests that barbiturates may reduce the release of excitatory neurotransmitters by neurons in many different locations. Initially, high doses of barbiturates can produce feelings of relaxation and euphoria—a kind of drunkenness without alcohol. They often go on to produce confusion, slurred speech, memory lapses, and reduced ability to concentrate. Wide swings of emotion, from euphoria to depression, are also common. Extremely large doses can be fatal, because they result in paralysis of centers of the brain that regulate breathing. This is a real danger, because tolerance to barbiturates gradually develops, leading individuals to use larger and larger doses of these drugs.

Web Link: *Stop Drugs*

Because some barbiturates induce sleep, people often try to use them to treat sleep disorders such as insomnia. However, these drugs do not seem to produce normal sleep. They suppress REM sleep, and this sleep stage may rebound sharply after individuals stop taking the drugs.

**Barbiturates:** Drugs that act as depressants, reducing activity in the nervous system and behavior output.

**Stimulants:** Drugs that increase activity in the nervous system (e.g., amphetamines, caffeine, nicotine).

**Amphetamines:** Drugs that act as stimulants, increasing feelings of energy and activation.

**Cocaine:** A powerful stimulant that produces pleasurable sensations of increased energy and self-confidence.

**STIMULANTS** Drugs that produce the opposite effects of depressants—feelings of energy and activation—are known as **stimulants.** Included in this category are **amphetamines** and **cocaine.** Both of these stimulants inhibit the reuptake of the neurotransmitters dopamine and norepinephrine. As a result, neurons that would otherwise stop firing continue to respond. Such drugs raise blood pressure, heart rate, and respiration—signs of activation produced by the sympathetic nervous system. In addition, stimulants yield short periods of pleasurable sensations, twenty to forty minutes during which users feel extremely powerful and energetic. As these drugs wear off, however, users often experience an emotional crash involving anxiety, depression, and fatigue.

In the past, cocaine was widely praised as a valuable medical drug and was added to many patent medicines. Freud believed that it was useful in treating such illnesses as asthma, indigestion, and even addiction to alcohol or other drugs. But continued use of cocaine can produce harmful effects, including a loss of appetite and intense feelings of anxiety, so it is clearly a dangerous drug.

Was cocaine ever really present in Coca-Cola? Yes, but only prior to 1903 (Levinthal, 1999). Since that time, the Stephan Company has had the task of removing cocaine from the high-grade coca leaves used in Coca-Cola. The remainder, known as "decocanized flavor essence" is then sent to the Coca-Cola Company to flavor the world-famous drink. Many soft drinks do contain caffeine, however, often in doses as high as those found in coffee or tea. So you *can* get a lift from Coke or Pepsi, but not because these drinks contain cocaine.

Cocaine is usually consumed by *snorting,* a process in which it is inhaled into each nostril. There it is absorbed through the lining of the nose directly into the bloodstream. Cocaine can also be swallowed, usually in liquid form, but this produces weaker effects. When cocaine is heated and treated chemically, a form known as **crack** is produced. This can be smoked, and when it is, the drug affects the brain almost instantly. This produces a high during which individuals experience powerful feelings of energy, confidence, and excitement. While cocaine is not usually considered to be addicting, it often produces strong psychological dependence. And crack appears to have much stronger effects of this type. In order to obtain it, heavy users turn to prostitution, theft, and anything else they can think of that will provide enough money for the next dose (see Figure 4.19).

Other stimulants in common use include *caffeine,* found in coffee, tea, and many soft drinks, and *nicotine,* found in tobacco. Many experts view nicotine as highly addicting and it is difficult to argue with this view when more than 50 percent of persons who have been operated upon for lung cancer continue to smoke after their surgery (Carlson, 1999)!

**Figure 4.19**
**Crack Addiction: Descent into the Depths**

Crack cocaine is so addicting that individuals who become hooked on this drug will do anything to get it—prostitution, theft, swindles, anything that will get them the money they need to sustain their addiction.

**OPIATES** Among the most dangerous drugs in widespread use are the **opiates.** These drugs include opium, morphine, heroin, and related synthetic drugs. Opium is derived from the opium poppy—remember the scene in *The Wizard of Oz* in which Dorothy and the Cowardly Lion fall asleep in a field of beautiful poppies? Morphine is produced from opium, and heroin is derived from morphine. Opiates produce lethargy and a pronounced slowing of almost all bodily functions. These drugs also alter consciousness, producing a dreamlike state and, for some people, intensely pleasurable sensations. The costs associated with these thrills are high, however. Heroin and other opiates are extremely addicting, and withdrawal from them often produces agony for their users. Growing evidence indicates that the brain produces substances (opioid peptides or endorphins) closely related to the opiates in chemical structure and also contains special receptors for them (Phillips & Fibiger, 1989). This suggests one possible explanation for the pain experienced by opiate users during withdrawal. Regular use of opiates soon overloads endorphin receptors within the brain. As a result, the brain ceases production of these substances. When the drugs are withdrawn, endorphin levels remain depressed. Thus, an important internal mechanism for regulating pain is disrupted (Reid, 1990). To make matters worse, tolerance for opiates such as heroin increases rapidly with use, so physiological addiction can occur very quickly.

**PSYCHEDELICS AND HALLUCINOGENS** Perhaps the drugs with the most profound effects on consciousness are the **psychedelics,** drugs that alter sensory perception and so may be considered mind-expanding, and the **hallucinogens,** drugs that generate sensory perceptions for which there are no external stimuli. The most

**Crack:** A derivative of cocaine that can be smoked. It acts as a powerful stimulant.

**Opiates:** Drugs that induce a dreamy, relaxed state and, in some persons, intense feelings of pleasure. Opiates exert their effects by stimulating special receptor sites within the brain.

**Psychedelics:** Drugs that alter sensory perception and so may be considered mind-expanding (e.g., marijuana).

**Hallucinogens:** Drugs that generate sensory perceptions for which there are no external stimuli (e.g., LSD).

**Figure 4.20**
**Marijuana: From Medicine to Outlaw Drug and Back Again?**

Up until the 1920s, marijuana was legal and was widely used to treat several medical ailments. By the 1930s, however, it was seen as a sinister menace to society and was outlawed. Recently there have been efforts to make marijuana legal for medical use once again.

widely used psychedelic drug is *marijuana*. Use of this drug dates back to ancient times; indeed, it is described in a Chinese guide to medicines from the year 2737 B.C. Marijuana was widely used in the United States and elsewhere for medical purposes as late as the 1920s. It could be found in almost any drugstore and purchased without a prescription. It was often prescribed by physicians for headaches, cramps, and even ulcers. Starting in the 1930s, however, the tide of public opinion shifted, and by 1937 marijuana was outlawed completely in the United States (see Figure 4.20). When smoked or eaten—for example, in cookies—marijuana produces moderate physiological effects: increased heart rate (up to 160 beats per minute); changes in blood pressure (the direction seems to depend on whether the individual is sitting, standing, or lying down); and dilation of blood vessels in the eye, thus producing bloodshot eyes. Short-term psychological effects include heightened senses of sight and sound and a rush of ideas, which leads some individuals to conclude that marijuana increases their creativity. Unfortunately, marijuana also interferes with the ability to carry out tasks involving attention and memory, and reduces the ability to judge distances. This latter effect can lead to serious accidents when users of the drug drive a car or operate machinery. Other effects reported by some, but not all, users include reduced inhibitions, feelings of relaxation or drowsiness, and/or increased sexual pleasure. Most of these effects seem to vary strongly with expectations—with what marijuana users believe will happen to them. Thus, in the United States, many people believe that marijuana will turn them on sexually, and they report such effects. In India, in contrast, marijuana is believed to be a sexual depressant, and this is what users report. Similarly, in Jamaica, where marijuana is viewed as an appetite suppressant, users report that the drug reduces hunger. In North America, many people believe that marijuana will cause them to feel hungry, and especially to crave sweets, and this is what they experience. Clearly, then, the effects of marijuana are subtle and are shaped to an important degree by individuals' expectations.

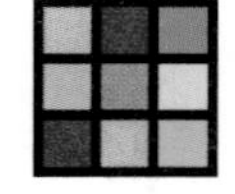

Marijuana is in widespread use throughout the world, mostly as a recreational drug. Unfortunately, there have been few studies of its long-term effects. The research that has been performed reports few adverse effects (e.g., Page, Fletcher, & True, 1988). Yet continued use of marijuana does pose certain dangers. First, the perceptual distortions it produces can result in tragedy when users drive or operate power machinery. Second, because it is an illegal drug in many nations, marijuana is sold by unreliable suppliers who frequently blend it with other substances; the result is that users never know exactly what they are getting. Third, there is some indication that long-term use of marijuana can impair the immune system, thus making long-term users more susceptible to various diseases. Finally, because marijuana users inhale deeply, they expose their lungs to damage from a wide range of contaminants. There is little evidence for theories on two other effects of marijuana that were once widely assumed to occur: (1) the concept of a drift toward an *amotivational syndrome* in which long-term users become increasingly passive and uninterested in their lives, or (2) the **gateway hypothesis,** which suggested that marijuana use was uniquely linked to subsequent use of other, more dangerous drugs (Levinthal, 1999). Neither of these effects appears to operate. However, the other potential risks of prolonged marijuana use do seem to be real and should be carefully considered by persons who consider using this drug.

**Gateway Hypothesis:** The view that use of marijuana is uniquely linked to the use of other drugs. This hypothesis is not supported by existing evidence.

**LSD:** A powerful hallucinogen that produces profound shifts in perception; many of these are frightening in nature.

More dramatic effects are produced by *hallucinogens*—drugs that produce vivid hallucinations and other perceptual shifts. Of these, the most famous drug is **LSD** (lysergic acid diethylamide), or *acid.* After taking LSD, many persons report profound changes in perceptions of the external world. Objects and people seem to change color and shape; walls may sway and move; and many sensations seem to be more intense than normal. There may also be a strange blending of sensory experiences so that colors produce feelings of warmth or cold or music yields visual sensations. Such effects may sound exciting, but many other sensations produced by LSD are quite negative. Objects, people, and even one's own body may seem distorted or threatening. Users may experience deep sorrow or develop intense fear of close friends and relatives. Perhaps worst of all, the effects of the drug are unpredictable; there is no way of knowing in advance whether LSD will yield mostly pleasant or unpleasant effects. In fact, the same person may experience radically different effects at different times. Unless you are willing to gamble with your own health, therefore, LSD is certainly a drug to avoid.

Recently many companies have begun to sell drugs over the Internet. Are such drugs safe? Are they legal? Do they work? For a discussion of these topics, see the following **Beyond the Headlines** section.

## BEYOND the HEADLINES: *As Psychologists See It*

## Can You Buy the Fountain of Youth on the Internet? "Buyer Beware" Strikes Again

### One Effect of a Law on Diet Supplements Is Leaner Regulation . . . One Man Scores on a "Stud Pill"

WALL STREET JOURNAL, JANUARY 27, 1999—EDINA, MINNESOTA: Wayne Josephson dreamed of starting his own business, but couldn't figure out what to sell. Then he realized the answer was in the tiny white capsules in his kitchen cabinet . . . the 49-year-old Mr. Josephson had begun taking androstenedione—the same substance that baseball hero Mark McGwire said he was using. . . . Mr. Josephson says it boosted his energy, built up his muscles, and even increased his sex drive. "I felt I'd found the fountain of youth," he says. Even better, Mr. Josephson believed he had discovered the perfect product. He called it "The Stud Pill for Men."

In October 1998, he began selling the substance as a dietary supplement for older men. He set up a Web site and issued a press release . . . that described the supplement as a "safe," "proven," "FDA legal" substance. He claimed that it reverses male aging, burns fat, builds muscle, and boosts strength, energy, and sex drive. . . . In his first month on the net, he sold 1,000 bottles or $30,000 worth of pills. Two months later, he began selling two more products: "The Passion Pill for Women," and "HerbalTrim," a dietary supplement he says promotes weight loss. . . .

Do these drugs really work? Are they safe? Have they actually been tested by the FDA (Food and Drug Administration)? In fact, we have no firm answers to the first two questions—because no, the FDA has *not* tested these drugs. Then how, you might wonder, can Mr. Josephson sell them? He can do so because of a 1994 law in the United States making it legal to sell "dietary supplements" without prior government testing. The law was designed to make dietary supplements easier for consumers to obtain, but it effectively did away with requirements for testing of the safety or effectiveness of these products before they are released for sale. So it is indeed legal for Mr. Josephson to offer them for sale.

But is it ethical for him to do so? Mr. Josephson himself claims that he believes in his products. He says that the day after he started taking androstenedione he "jumped out of bed" and felt years younger. Within days, he noticed that he wanted to exercise more and was less sore after his workouts. So he appears to be a true believer. As you already know, however, even strong personal convictions are no substitute for hard scientific data. My advice to you is simple: Beware of drugs sold over the Internet under the category of "dietary supplements." They may or not work, but given the very large loophole created by that 1994 law, you can't rely on any claims about their effectiveness—or their safety.

### CRITICAL THINKING QUESTIONS

1. How could the claimed effects of androstenedione and Mr. Josephson's other products be tested?
2. Do you think that the federal government should change the law so that "dietary supplements" must be tested carefully before being offered for sale? Why or why not?
3. Would *you* personally be willing to sell products like these? Or would you put ethical considerations ahead of the very real potential for large profits?

### REVIEW QUESTIONS

- What are the effects of depressants?
- What are the effects of stimulants? Opiates? Psychedelics? Hallucinogens?
- Why is it potentially dangerous to buy "dietary supplements" on the Internet?

# Making Psychology Part of Your Life

## Are You High or Low in Private Self-Consciousness? A Self-Assessment

In the sixth century B.C., the Chinese philosopher Lao-Tze wrote these lines: *"He who knows others is clever; he who knows himself has discernment."* This sentiment has been echoed over and over again down through the centuries, so there is widespread belief in the idea that knowing ourselves is beneficial. Yet, as we noted earlier in this chapter, a high level of *private self-consciousness*—awareness of our own inner feelings, thoughts, and values—is *not* always beneficial. When such self-reflection is motivated by the desire to know ourselves better, it can be both revealing and helpful: Self-understanding can contribute to personal adjustment and a happy life. But when it is motivated by concern over our possible shortcomings, or over losses, injustices, or regrets, a high level of self-awareness can be dangerous; it can lead to unhappiness, distress, and even depression (Trapnell & Campbell, 1999).

Where do you stand with respect to this dimension? Are you the kind of person who engages in reflection (simply trying to understand yourself better), or the kind who engages in rumination—searching for your own flaws and negative feelings? To find out, answer the questions below. For each item, indicate the extent to which it is true of you by entering a number from 1 to 5 in the blank space. 1 = It is definitely false about you. 2 = It is mostly false about you. 3 = It is neither true nor false about you. 4 = It is somewhat true about you. 5 = It is definitely true about you.

_____ 1. Often, I play back in my mind how I acted in a past situation.

_____ 2. I love exploring my inner self.

_____ 3. I always seem to be rehashing in my mind recent things I've said or done.

_____ 4. I love analyzing why I do things.

_____ 5. I often find myself reevaluating something I've done.

_____ 6. Contemplating myself is my idea of fun.

_____ 7. I often think deeply about myself, especially my flaws and or weaknesses.

_____ 8. People often say I'm a "deep" person.

_____ 9. I find it very hard to put unwanted thoughts out of my mind.

_____ 10. If I pass a mirror, my reflection in it causes me to think deeply about myself.

_____ 11. Long after an argument is over, I keep thinking about it.

_____ 12. I love to think about the nature and meaning of things.

To obtain your score, do the following:

Items 1, 3, 5, 7, 9, 11: Add the numbers you entered for these items. This is your score for the tendency to engage in *rumination.*

Items 2, 4, 6, 8, 10, 12: Add the numbers you entered for these items. This is your score for the tendency to engage in *reflection.*

If you scored 23 or higher on the first scale, you are relatively high in rumination. If you scored 23 or higher on the second scale, you are relatively high in reflection. It is possible to score high on both dimensions, low on both, or high on one and low on the other. Where do you stand? If you find that you are high in rumination, you may wish to ask yourself whether you think this is a characteristic you would like to change.

*A word of caution:* The items above are closely related to ones that have been found to provide reliable and valid measures of rumination and reflection. However, generally, a larger number of items are used to assess these aspects of self-consciousness, so you should interpret your scores with considerable caution; they may not be very accurate.

## Summary and Review

### Biological Rhythms: Tides of Life—and Conscious Experience

- **What are biological rhythms? What are circadian rhythms?** Biological rhythms are regular fluctuations in our bodily processes. Circadian rhythms are biological rhythms that occur within a single day.
- **How do morning persons and night persons differ?** Morning persons feel most alert and energetic early in the day. Night persons feel most alert and energetic late in the day.
- **What effects do jet lag and shift work have on circadian rhythms?** Both jet lag and shift work produce disturbances in circadian rhythms.
- **What steps can be taken to counter "drowsy driver" syndrome?** Research findings indicate that exposing drowsy drivers to certain sounds and to certain (pleasant) fragrances can make them more alert.

#### Key Terms

states of consciousness, p. 130 • biological rhythms, p. 131 • circadian rhythms, p. 131 • suprachiasmatic nucleus (SCN), 131 • pineal gland, p. 132

### Waking States of Consciousness

- **What is the difference between automatic processing and controlled processing?** In automatic processing, we perform activities without directing conscious attention to them. In controlled processing, we direct conscious attention to our activities.

- **Why do we sometimes think or do precisely what we *don't* want to think or do?** This happens when our conscious intentional operating process is overloaded, and our ironic monitoring process comes to dominate.
- **What is self-awareness, and why do we sometimes enter this state of consciousness?** Self-awareness is a state of consciousness in which we turn our attention inward, toward ourselves. We may enter this state because of situational factors (e.g., we pass a mirror), because of our affective states, or because we have a predisposition to enter this state.
- **What are some of the effects of self-awareness on our adjustment and performance?** If it takes the form of rumination (anxieties, worries, resentments), self-awareness can have negative effects on our adjustment. Heightened self-awareness can lead to choking under pressure.

### Key Terms

automatic processing, p. 137 • controlled processing, p. 137 • self-awareness, p. 139 • choking under pressure, p. 141

## Sleep: The Pause That Refreshes?

- **How do psychologists study sleep?** Researchers often study sleep by examining changes in the EEG, EMG, and EOG of volunteers in sleep laboratories.
- **What are the major stages of sleep?** There appear to be four major stages of sleep and a very different phase known as REM sleep.
- **What happens during REM sleep?** During REM sleep the EEG shows a pattern similar to that of waking, but the activity of body muscles is almost totally suppressed. Most dreams occur during REM sleep.
- **What are the possible functions of slow-wave and REM sleep?** Slow-wave sleep seems to provide an opportunity for the brain to rest. REM sleep may play a key role in learning and the consolidation of memories.
- **What are the effects of sleep deprivation?** Long-term sleep deprivation can adversely affect the health of both humans and animals.
- **What steps help promote a good night's sleep?** Among tactics that encourage sleep are the following: Read something pleasant or relaxing just before going to sleep; arrange your schedule so you go to sleep at the same time each night; take a warm bath or have a massage before going to sleep; avoid coffee or tea late in the day; exercise every day, but not just before going to sleep; don't smoke; don't nap during the day.
- **What are important disorders of REM sleep? Of slow-wave sleep?** Disorders of REM sleep include narcolepsy, cataplexy, and atonia. Disorders of slow-wave sleep include insomnia, somnambulism, night terrors, and apnea.
- **How do the psychodynamic, physiological, and cognitive views of dreams differ?** The psychodynamic view suggests that dreams reflect suppressed thoughts, wishes, and impulses. The physiological view suggests that dreams reflect the brain's interpretation of random neural activity that occurs while we sleep. The cognitive view holds that dreams result from the fact that in REM sleep many systems of the brain are active but input from muscles and sensory systems is inhibited.

### Key Terms

sleep, p. 142 • electroencephalogram (EEG), p. 142 • electromyogram (EMG), p. 142 • electrooculogram (EOG), p. 142 • alpha waves, p. 142 • delta activity, p. 142 • REM (rapid eye movement) sleep, p. 142 • fatal familial insomnia, p. 145 • insomnia, p. 146 • narcolepsy, p. 147 • cataplexy, p. 147 • somnambulism, p. 147 • night terrors, p. 147 • apnea, p. 146 • dreams, p. 148 • dreams of absent-minded transgression, p. 149

## Hypnosis: Altered State of Consciousness . . . or Social Role Playing?

- **What is hypnosis?** Hypnosis involves a special type of interaction between two persons in which one (the hypnotist) employs suggestions to induce changes in the behavior, feelings, or cognitions of the other (the subject).
- **How do the social–cognitive, neodissociation, and dissociative control views of hypnosis differ?** The social–cognitive view suggests that the effects of hypnosis stem from the hypnotized person's expectations and efforts to play the role of hypnotized subject. The neodissociation view suggests that the effects of hypnotism stem from a split in consciousness between the executive cognitive function and a monitoring function. Dissociative control theory suggests that hypnotism weakens control by the central function over other cognitive and behavioral subsystems.
- **Which theory of hypnosis is supported by most current evidence?** The social–cognitive view is supported by more evidence than the other views.

### Key Terms

hypnosis, 150 • social–cognitive or role-playing view, p. 151 • neodissociation theory, p. 152 • theory of dissociated control, p. 152

## Consciousness-Altering Drugs: What They Are and What They Do

- **What are drugs? What is drug abuse?** Drugs are substances that, because of their chemical structure, change the functioning of biological systems. Drug abuse involves instances in which people take drugs purely to change their moods, and in which drugs produce impaired behavior or social functioning.
- **What are physiological and psychological dependence on drugs?** Physiological dependence involves strong urges to continue using a drug based on organic factors, such as changes in metabolism. Psychological dependence involves strong desires to continue using a drug even though it is not physiologically addicting.

- **How do the learning, social, and cognitive perspectives explain drug abuse?** The learning perspective suggests that drugs are reinforcing (rewarding) and/or help to lessen stress, anxiety, and other negative feelings. The social perspective suggests that people abuse drugs because of strong social pressures to do so. The cognitive perspective suggests that drug abuse may be an automatic behavior triggered by the presence of external or internal cues.
- **What are the effects of depressants?** Depressants (e.g., alcohol) reduce both behavioral output and neural activity.
- **What are the effects of stimulants? Opiates? Psychedelics? Hallucinogens?** Stimulants produce feelings of energy and activation. Opiates produce lethargy and pronounced slowing of many bodily functions, but also induce intense feelings of pleasure in some persons. Psychedelics such as marijuana alter sensory perception, while hallucinogens such as LSD produce vivid hallucinations and other bizarre perceptual effects.
- **Why is it potentially dangerous to buy "dietary supplements" on the Internet?** This is potentially dangerous because laws exempt such drugs from government testing for safety and effectiveness.

### Key Terms

drugs, p. 154 • drug abuse, p. 155 • dependence, p. 155 • physiological dependence, p. 155 • psychological dependence, p. 155 • tolerance, p. 155 • cross-tolerance, p. 155 • nucleus accumbens, p. 156 • depressants, p. 157 • barbiturates, p. 158 • stimulants, p. 158 • amphetamines, p. 158 • cocaine, p. 158 • crack, p. 159 • opiates, p. 159 • psychedelics, p. 159 • hallucinogens, p. 159 • gateway hypothesis, p. 161 • LSD, p. 161

## Critical Thinking Questions

### Appraisal

Most psychologists believe that states of consciousness can be studied in a scientific manner. Do you agree? Or do you feel that this is stretching the definition of psychology, "the science of behavior," beyond the breaking point? Why do you hold the opinion that you do?

### Controversy

Hypnosis is one of the most controversial topics in the study of states of consciousness. Many psychologists doubt that hypnosis produces an altered state of consciousness. Yet there is some evidence consistent with the view that it does. What are your views? What kind of evidence would help to resolve this issue once and for all?

### Making Psychology Part of Your Life

Now that you have some basic understanding of states of consciousness, can you think of ways in which you can put this information to practical use? For example, how might you change your own daily schedule so as to take advantage of high points in your own circadian rhythms? Would it be beneficial for you to increase (or reduce) your level of self-awareness? What can you do to help improve your sleep? Will you be less willing to "experiment" with various drugs now that you know more about the risks these experiments may involve? List at least three ways in which you can put the information in this chapter to practical use in your own life.

# Chapter 5

# Learning: How We're Changed by Experience

## CHAPTER OUTLINE

**CLASSICAL CONDITIONING: LEARNING THAT SOME STIMULI SIGNAL OTHERS 169**

Pavlov's Early Work on Classical Conditioning: Does This Ring a Bell?
Classical Conditioning: Some Basic Principles
Classical Conditioning: The Neural Basis of Learning
Classical Conditioning: Exceptions to the Rules
Classical Conditioning: A Cognitive Perspective
Classical Conditioning: Turning Principles into Action

■ BEYOND THE HEADLINES—As Psychologists See It: *A New Approach to Teen Crime*

**OPERANT CONDITIONING: LEARNING BASED ON CONSEQUENCES 182**

The Nature of Operant Conditioning: Consequential Operations

■ FROM SCIENCE TO PRACTICE *"Horse Whispering": Applying Operant Conditioning to Treat Troubled Horses*

Operant Conditioning: Some Basic Principles
Operant Conditioning: A Cognitive Perspective

■ RESEARCH METHODS *How Psychologists Study Applications of Operant Conditioning*

Applying Operant Conditioning: Solving Problems of Everyday Life

**OBSERVATIONAL LEARNING: LEARNING FROM THE BEHAVIOR AND OUTCOMES OF OTHERS 200**

Observational Learning: Some Basic Principles
Observational Learning and Aggression
Observational Learning and Culture
Observational Learning: Some Practical Applications

■ MAKING PSYCHOLOGY PART OF YOUR LIFE *Getting in Shape: Using Principles of Learning to Get Fit and Stay Fit*

Some of the best opportunities to observe learning in action occur when one is watching young children. For example, I'll never forget teaching a friend's four-year-old to ride a bike. I vividly recall Ryan's squeals of delight as he climbed on board for the first time. After giving him some basic instruction on how to pedal, steer, and stop, I pushed the bike gently to get him started, then reluctantly stepped out of the way. The bicycle lurched forward, teetering back and forth, its upright position precariously maintained by training wheels mounted on either side of the back wheel. Much to my relief, Ryan was at first overly cautious: He pedaled the bicycle very slowly and made wide sweeping turns around the driveway to avoid tipping over. After a few weeks of practice, however, he became increasingly daring—occasionally taking a spill, usually after turning too sharply or bumping into something. Fortunately, because his parents insisted that he wear a helmet while riding, he suffered only minor injuries (usually a bruised ego). Following a crash, he became predictably cautious, riding more slowly and deliberately until his confidence was restored. It should be apparent that the learning in this example resulted from systematic trial and error. Actions that allowed Ryan to remain upright were repeated; ones that led to a crash were not. However, as you probably know from your own experience, not all learning proceeds in this way. Much of what we learn comes from observing the actions of others (see Figure 5.1). For instance, upon visiting my friend's home some time later, I heard Ryan shout, "Bob, watch this!" I looked up just in time to see him speed his bike down the driveway and jump off a crude dirt ramp he had constructed—all before I could get a word out of my mouth. Fortunately, he landed safely. I learned later that he had recently watched daredevil Robbie Knievel's motorcycle jump over the Grand Canyon on television and decided to try it himself!

As illustrated by the example above, the learning process is crucial to all organisms, including people, in that it helps us acquire important skills and adapt to changing conditions in the world around us. In this chapter we'll examine several basic principles that help to explain how experience affects many forms of behavior. Psychologists refer to these effects on behavior as learning. Specifically, they define **learning** *as any relatively permanent change in behavior, or behavior potential, produced by experience.* Several aspects of this definition are noteworthy. First, the term *learning* does not apply to temporary changes in behavior such as those stemming from fatigue, drugs, or illness. Second, it does not refer to changes resulting

**Learning:** Any relatively permanent change in behavior (or behavior potential) resulting from experience.

**Figure 5.1**
**Learning in Action: The Powerful Effects of Observing the Behavior of Others**

Although some learning occurs through systematic trial and error, much of what we learn results from watching other people's behavior.

from maturation—the fact that you change in many ways as you grow and develop. Third, learning can result from *vicarious* as well as from direct experiences; in other words, you can be affected by observing events and behavior in your environment as well as by participating in them (Bandura, 1986). Finally, the changes produced by learning are not always positive in nature. As you well know, people are as likely to acquire bad habits as good ones.

There can be no doubt that learning is a key process in human behavior. Indeed, it appears to play an important role in virtually every activity we perform. Although the effects of learning are diverse, many psychologists believe that learning occurs in several basic forms: *classical conditioning*, *operant conditioning*, and *observational learning*. We'll begin with *classical conditioning*, a form of learning in which two stimulus events become associated in such a way that the occurrence of one event reliably predicts the occurrence of the other. Classical conditioning is the basis for many learned fears and also helps explain how we acquire aversions to certain foods or beverages. Next, we'll turn to *operant conditioning*, a form of learning in which organisms learn associations between behaviors and stimuli that precede them (antecedents) or follow them (consequences). Here, we'll see how psychologists have applied basic operant principles to promote desirable behaviors, such as recycling and occupational safety, and to discourage inappropriate or dangerous ones. Finally, we'll explore *observational learning*, a form of learning in which organisms learn by observing the behaviors—and the consequences of the behaviors—of others around them.

## Classical Conditioning: Learning That Some Stimuli Signal Others

Imagine that during a very hectic semester, your class schedule leaves absolutely no time for lunch. After a few days, you lose your ability to concentrate during your afternoon classes because all you can think about is food. A friend tells you about a vending area where she buys microwaveable snacks, including popcorn. As it turns out, this solution works out well; you love popcorn, it is ready in only a few

**Figure 5.2**
**Classical Conditioning: A Simple Example**

At first, the sound of the microwave's beep may startle you and cause you to look toward its source, but it will probably not cause you to salivate. However, after the beep has been paired with the aroma and taste of the popcorn on several occasions, you may find that you salivate to the beep alone. This "mouthwatering" reaction is a result of classical conditioning.

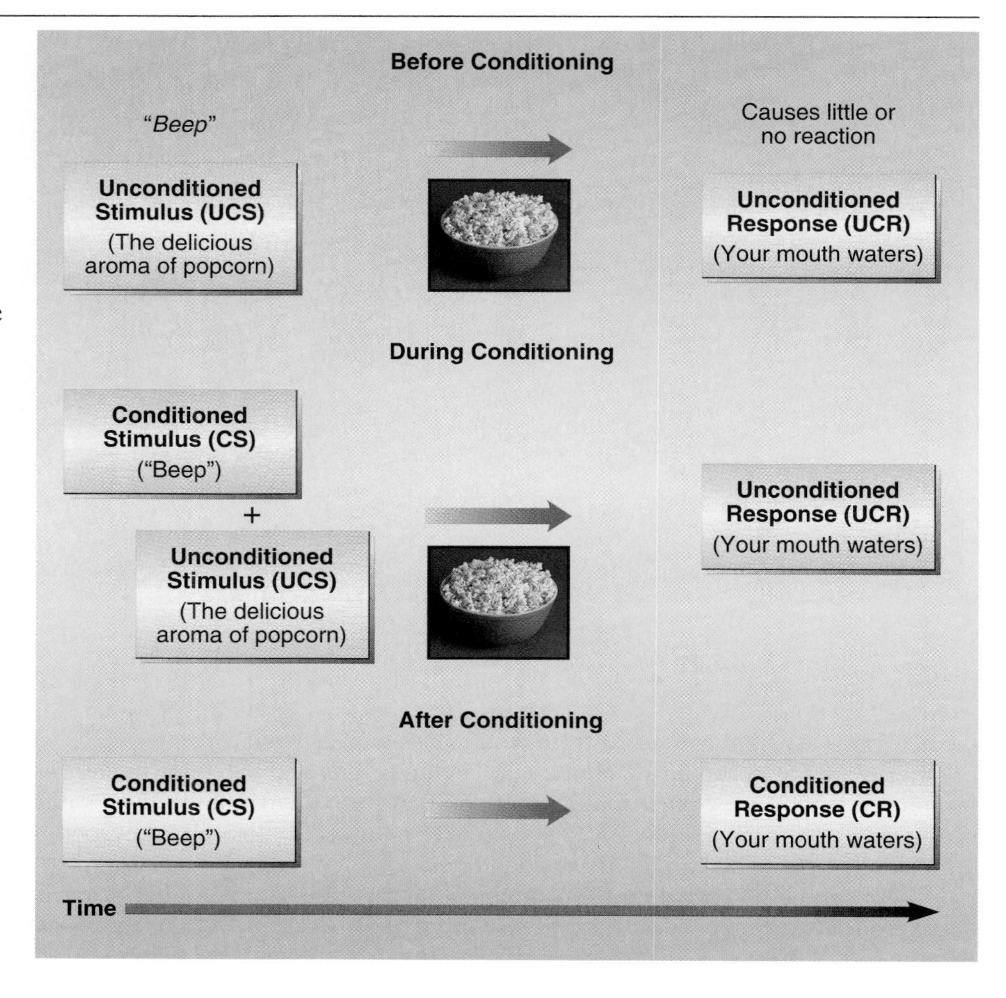


minutes, and you find that it is even possible to do other things while the popcorn is popping—like cram for tests—because a loud beep from the microwave signals when the popcorn is done. When you open the door of the microwave, the aroma of freshly popped popcorn rushes out, causing you to salivate in anticipation of eating it. After several days, however, your mouth waters immediately after the beep, before you actually open the door to the microwave. Why should this occur? After all, at this point you can neither see nor smell the popcorn. The reason is actually fairly simple: The beep is always followed by the aroma and taste of the popcorn, so the beep comes to serve as a signal. Just hearing the beep, you expect the smell and taste of the popcorn to follow, and you react accordingly (see Figure 5.2).

The situation just described is a common example of **classical conditioning,** the first type of learning that we will consider. In classical conditioning, a physical event—termed a **stimulus**—that initially does not elicit a particular response gradually acquires the capacity to elicit that response as a result of repeated pairing with a stimulus that *can* elicit a reaction. Learning of this type is quite common and seems to play a role in such varied reactions as strong fears, taste aversions, some aspects of sexual behavior, and even racial or ethnic prejudice (Baron & Byrne, 2000). Classical conditioning became the subject of careful study in the early twentieth century, when Ivan Pavlov, a Nobel Prize–winning physiologist from Russia, identified it as an important behavioral process.

**Classical Conditioning:** A basic form of learning in which one stimulus comes to serve as a signal for the occurrence of a second stimulus. During classical conditioning, organisms acquire information about the relations between various stimuli, not simple associations between them.

**Stimulus:** A physical event capable of affecting behavior.

**Figure 5.3**
**Early Research on Conditioning**

Ivan Pavlov, a Russian physiologist who won a Nobel Prize in 1904 for his work on digestion, is best known for his research on classical conditioning.

## Pavlov's Early Work on Classical Conditioning: Does This Ring a Bell?

Web Link: *Ivan Pavlov*

Pavlov did not actually set out to investigate classical conditioning. Rather, his research focused on the process of digestion in dogs (see Figure 5.3). During his investigations he noticed a curious fact: Similar to the popcorn example described above, the dogs in his studies often began to salivate when they saw or smelled food but *before* they actually tasted it. Some even salivated at the sight of the pan where their food was kept or at the sight or sound of the person who usually brought it. This suggested to Pavlov that these stimuli had somehow become signals for the food itself: The dogs had learned that when the signals were present, food would soon follow.

Pavlov quickly recognized the potential importance of this observation and shifted the focus of his research accordingly. The procedures that he now developed were relatively simple. On *conditioning trials,* a neutral stimulus that had previously been shown to have no effect on salivation—a bell, for example—was presented. This was immediately followed by a second stimulus known to produce a strong effect on salivation: dried meat powder placed directly into the dog's mouth. The meat powder was termed the **unconditioned stimulus (UCS),** because its ability to produce salivation was automatic and did not depend on the dog's having learned the response. Similarly, the response of salivation to the meat powder was termed an **unconditioned response (UCR);** it too did not depend on previous learning. The bell was termed a **conditioned stimulus (CS),** because its ability to produce salivation depended on its being paired with the meat powder. Finally, salivation in response to the bell was termed a **conditioned response (CR).**

The basic question was whether the sound of the bell would gradually come to elicit salivation in the dogs as a result of its repeated pairing with the meat powder. In other words, would the bell elicit a conditioned response when it was presented alone? The answer was clearly *yes.* After the bell had been paired repeatedly with the meat powder, the dogs salivated upon hearing it, even when the bell was not followed by the meat powder.

**Unconditioned Stimulus (UCS):** In classical conditioning, a stimulus that can evoke an unconditioned response the first time it is presented.

**Unconditioned Response (UCR):** In classical conditioning, the response evoked by an unconditioned stimulus.

**Conditioned Stimulus (CS):** In classical conditioning, the stimulus that is repeatedly paired with an unconditioned stimulus.

**Conditioned Response (CR):** In classical conditioning, the response to the conditioned stimulus.

## Classical Conditioning: Some Basic Principles

Let's turn now to the principles that govern the occurrence of classical conditioning.

**Acquisition:** The process by which a conditioned stimulus acquires the ability to elicit a conditioned response through repeated pairings of an unconditioned stimulus with the conditioned stimulus.

**Delay Conditioning:** A form of forward conditioning in which the onset of the unconditioned stimulus (UCS) begins while the conditioned stimulus (CS) is still present.

**Trace Conditioning:** A form of forward conditioning in which the onset of the conditioned stimulus (CS) precedes the onset of the unconditioned stimulus (UCS) and the presentation of the CS and UCS does not overlap.

**CourseCompass**
Audio 5.1: *Classical Conditioning in Social Contex*

**ACQUISITION: THE COURSE OF CLASSICAL CONDITIONING** In most instances, classical conditioning is a gradual process in which a conditioned stimulus gradually acquires the capacity to elicit a conditioned response as a result of repeated pairing with an unconditioned stimulus. This process—termed **acquisition**—proceeds quite rapidly at first, increasing as the number of pairings between conditioned and unconditioned stimulus increases. However, there is a limit to this effect; after a number of pairings of CS and UCS, acquisition slows down and finally levels off.

Although psychologists initially believed that conditioning was determined primarily by the number of conditioned–unconditioned stimulus pairings, we now know that this process is affected by other factors. As shown in Figure 5.4, one such factor is the *temporal arrangement* of the CS–UCS pairings. Temporal means time-related: the extent to which a conditioned stimulus precedes or follows the presentation of an unconditioned stimulus. The first two temporal arrangements shown, **delay conditioning** and **trace conditioning,** are examples of what is termed *forward conditioning,* because the presentation of the conditioned stimulus (light) always precedes the presentation of the unconditioned stimulus (shock). They differ, however, in that the CS and the UCS overlap to some degree in *delay* conditioning, but not in *trace* conditioning. Two other temporal arrangements are **simultaneous conditioning,** in which the conditioned and unconditioned stimuli begin and end at the same time; and **backward conditioning,** in which the unconditioned stimulus precedes the conditioned stimulus.

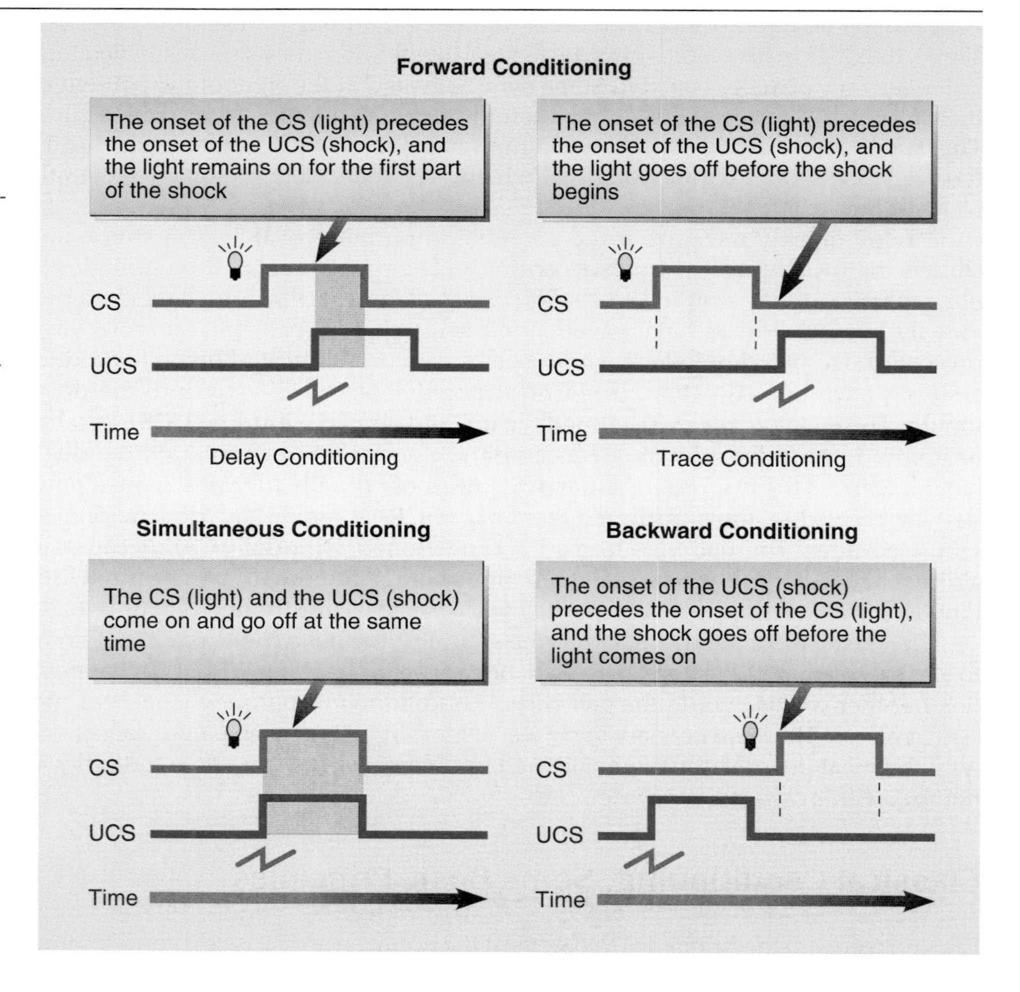


**Figure 5.4**
**Temporal Arrangement of the CS and UCS Affects the Acquisition of a Conditioned Response**

Four CS–UCS temporal arrangements commonly used in classical conditioning procedures are shown above. *Temporal* refers to timing: the extent to which a conditioned stimulus precedes or follows the presentation of an unconditioned stimulus. *Delay conditioning* generally produces the most rapid rate of learning. *Simultaneous* and *backward conditioning* are usually the least effective procedures.

Research suggests that *delay conditioning* is generally the most effective method for establishing a conditioned response. This is because the conditioned stimulus helps predict forthcoming presentations of the unconditioned stimulus (Lieberman, 1990). To illustrate this point, consider the following example: You are taking a shower when suddenly the water turns icy cold. Your response—a startle reaction to the cold water—is an unconditioned response. Now imagine that just before the water turns cold, the plumbing makes a slight grinding sound. Because this sound occurs just before and overlaps with the onset of the icy water, delay conditioning can occur. If this situation is repeated several times, you may acquire a startle reaction to the slight grinding sound; it serves as a conditioned stimulus. In contrast, suppose you do not hear the sound until after the water turns cold, as in backward conditioning, or until the precise instant at which it turns cold, as in simultaneous conditioning. In these cases you will probably not acquire a startle reaction to the grinding sound, because it provides no information useful in predicting the occurrence of the icy water.

Several additional factors also appear to affect conditioning. In general, conditioning is faster when the *intensity* of either the conditioned or unconditioned stimulus increases (Kamin, 1965). In other words, conditioning is more likely when conditioned stimuli stand out in relation to other background stimuli.

Second, conditioning also depends on the time interval between presentations of the two stimuli. Extremely short intervals—less than 0.2 second—rarely produce conditioning. In animal research, the optimal CS–UCS interval seems to be between 0.2 and 2 seconds; longer intervals make it difficult for animals to recognize the conditioned stimulus as a signal for some future event (Gordon, 1989).

Finally, *familiarity* can greatly affect conditioning. In contrast to the laboratory, where stimuli selected for study are often novel, many of the potential conditioning stimuli found in the environment are familiar to us. Thus, our day-to-day experiences often teach us that certain stimuli, such as the background noise usually present in an office setting or the odors ordinarily present in our homes, do not predict anything unusual. In other words, we learn that these stimuli are largely irrelevant, which makes it highly unlikely that these stimuli will come to act as conditioned stimuli in the future (Baker & Mackintosh, 1977).

**EXTINCTION: ONCE CONDITIONING IS ACQUIRED, HOW DO WE GET RID OF IT?** Suppose you are one of several executives in a large marketing firm. You and your coworkers have been working night and day to prepare a proposal crucial to the survival of the firm, and things are not going well. Over the past week the president of the company has chewed you out at least a dozen times. Now, when you hear the sound of his footsteps, your heart starts racing and your mouth gets dry, even though he has not yet reached your office. Fortunately, the company's directors are impressed by the proposal, and your boss is no longer angry when he enters your office. Will you continue to react strongly to his footsteps? In all likelihood, you won't. Gradually, his footsteps will cease to elicit the original conditioned response from you. The eventual decline and disappearance of a conditioned response in the absence of an *un*conditioned stimulus is known as **extinction.**

The course of extinction, however, is not always entirely smooth. Let's consider the behavior of one of Pavlov's dogs to see why this is true. After many presentations of a bell (conditioned stimulus) in the absence of meat powder (unconditioned stimulus), the dog no longer salivates in response to the bell. In other words, extinction has occurred. But if the conditioned stimulus (the bell) and the unconditioned stimulus (the meat powder) are again paired after the conditioned response of salivation has been extinguished, salivation will return very quickly—a process termed **reconditioning.**

Or suppose that after extinction, the experiment is interrupted: Pavlov is caught up in another project that keeps him away from his laboratory and the dog for several weeks. Now will the sound of the bell, the conditioned stimulus, elicit

**Simultaneous Conditioning:** A form of conditioning in which the conditioned stimulus (CS) and the unconditioned stimulus (UCS) begin and end at the same time.

**Backward Conditioning:** A type of conditioning in which the presentation of the unconditioned stimulus (UCS) precedes the presentation of the conditioned stimulus (CS).

**Extinction:** The process through which a conditioned stimulus gradually loses the ability to evoke conditioned responses when it is no longer followed by the unconditioned stimulus.

**Reconditioning:** The rapid recovery of a conditioned response (CR) to a CS–UCS pairing following extinction.

**Figure 5.5**
**Stimulus Generalization Can Sometimes Be Dangerous**

Young children may become trusting of *all* adults through the process of stimulus generalization. Unfortunately, this process can lead to unfortunate consequences if it extends to certain strangers.

salivation? The answer is yes, but the reaction will be in a weakened form. The reappearance of the reaction after a time interval is referred to as **spontaneous recovery.** If extinction is then allowed to continue—that is, if the sound of the bell is presented many times in the absence of meat powder—salivation to the sound of the bell will eventually disappear.

**GENERALIZATION AND DISCRIMINATION: RESPONDING TO SIMILARITIES AND DIFFERENCES** Suppose that because of several painful experiences, a child has acquired a strong conditioned fear of hornets: Whenever she sees one or hears one buzzing, she shows strong emotional reactions and heads for the hills. Will she also experience similar reactions to other flying insects, such as flies? She almost certainly will, because of a process called **stimulus generalization,** the tendency of stimuli similar to a conditioned stimulus to elicit similar conditioned responses (Honig & Urcuioli, 1981; Pearce, 1986). As you can readily see, stimulus generalization often serves a useful function. In this example, it may indeed save the girl from additional stings. The red lights that we encounter at certain intersections while driving also illustrate the important function served by stimulus generalization: Even though these signals often vary in brightness or shape, we learn to stop in response to all of them, and it's a good thing we do.

Many other species also turn the existence of stimulus generalization to their advantage. For example, some totally harmless insects resemble more dangerous species in coloring and so ward off would-be predators. Similarly, some frogs that would make a tasty mouthful for birds show markings highly similar to those of poisonous species, increasing their chances of survival.

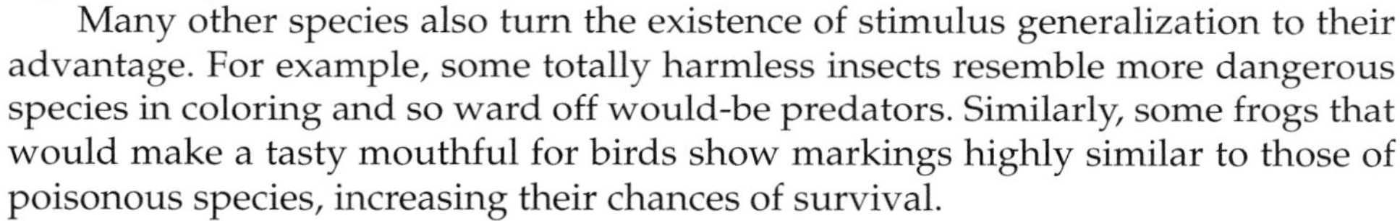

Although stimulus generalization can serve an important adaptive function, it is not always beneficial and in some cases can be dangerous. For example, because of many pleasant experiences with parents and other adult relatives, a young child may become trusting of all adults through stimulus generalization. Unfortunately, this process will not be beneficial if it extends to certain strangers. You can understand why stimulus generalization can be maladaptive—even deadly (see Figure 5.5). Fortunately, most of us avoid such potential problems through **stimulus discrimination**—a process of learning to respond to certain stimuli but not to others. A few years ago a friend was badly bitten by a dog. Until that incident she had no fear of dogs. Because she was so frightened by the attack, I was concerned that the incident would generalize to other breeds of dogs—perhaps even to her own dog. Fortunately, because of stimulus discrimination, this didn't happen; she becomes fearful only when she encounters the breed of dog that bit her.

**Spontaneous Recovery:** Reappearance of a weakened conditioned response to a conditioned stimulus after an interval of time following extinction.

**Stimulus Generalization:** The tendency of stimuli similar to a conditioned stimulus to evoke conditioned responses.

**Stimulus Discrimination:** The process by which organisms learn to respond to certain stimuli but not to others.

**REVIEW QUESTIONS**

- What is learning?
- What is classical conditioning?
- Upon what factors does acquisition of a classically conditioned response depend?
- What is extinction?
- What is the difference between stimulus generalization and stimulus discrimination?

## Classical Conditioning: The Neural Basis of Learning

CourseCompass
Web Link: *Computational Neuroscience Laboratory*

Now that we've discussed the basic principles of classical conditioning, let's turn to another question that has puzzled scientists for many years—what is the neural basis of this and other kinds of learning?

Psychologists have started to unravel this mystery, at least for relatively simple forms of behavior (Daum & Schugens, 1996; Woodruff-Pak, 1999). Systematic research with animals has resulted in nearly complete identification of the neural circuitry that underlies eye-blink classical conditioning (Steinmetz, 1996; Thompson et al., 1997). The evidence seems to indicate that the site essential to the acquisition and performance of this type of conditioned response is the cerebellum, a brain structure involved in balance and coordination. When the cerebellum of animals is surgically destroyed, previously learned associations can be severely disrupted, and the ability to learn new associations eliminated altogether (Thompson & Krupa, 1994). Other brain structures now known to be involved in eye-blink conditioning include the hippocampus, the amygdala, and brain-stem areas that project to or receive information from the cerebellum (Steinmetz, 1999).

Studies of humans who have sustained damage to the cerebellum or related structures reveal a similar pattern of results. Careful research indicates that it is extremely difficult to establish conditioned responses with these persons. They blink normally (UCR) in response to a puff of air to the eye (UCS), indicating that their motor functions and ability to respond to external stimulation remains intact. However, efforts to establish a conditioned eye-blink response to, say, a light or a tone are usually unsuccessful (Daum & Schugens, 1996; Topka et al., 1993).

Because the fundamental neural circuitry underlying eye-blink classical conditioning is so well known, behavioral researchers have begun to use this conditioning procedure to investigate a variety of basic processes in humans (e.g., Ivkovich et al., 1999; Clark & Squire, 1999), including the biological correlates of certain mental disorders. This research, in turn, may lead to more effective treatments. For example, psychologists have long known that the symptoms experienced by people with *obsessive–compulsive disorder* arise from learned associations that are maladaptive and particularly resistant to extinction. Obsessive–compulsive disorder is characterized by intrusive, unwanted, and uncontrollable thoughts, images, compulsions, or urges that are often accompanied by repetitive behaviors or mental acts that the person feels driven to perform (see Chapter 14 for additional information). A recent study by Tracy and colleagues (1999) suggests that eye-blink classical conditioning proceeds much more quickly in individuals who exhibit obsessive–compulsive tendencies than in those who do not—a finding suggesting that some people may be biologically predisposed to establish associations between feelings of fear and anxiety and otherwise neutral objects. Clearly, such findings will play an important role in the design of more effective treatments for obsessive–compulsive disorder or, conversely, in the discovery of ways to prevent the development of the maladaptive associations that characterize this disorder.

Scientists are just beginning to understand the complex relationship between brain functions and behavior, but it is clear that our knowledge of the neural basis of learning is expanding at a rapid pace.

## Classical Conditioning: Exceptions to the Rules

When psychologists began the systematic study of learning, around the turn of the twentieth century, they saw their task as that of establishing general principles of learning—principles that applied equally well to all organisms and to all stimuli. Beginning in the 1960s, however, some puzzling findings began to accumulate. These findings seemed to indicate that not all organisms learn all responses or all associations between stimuli with equal ease.

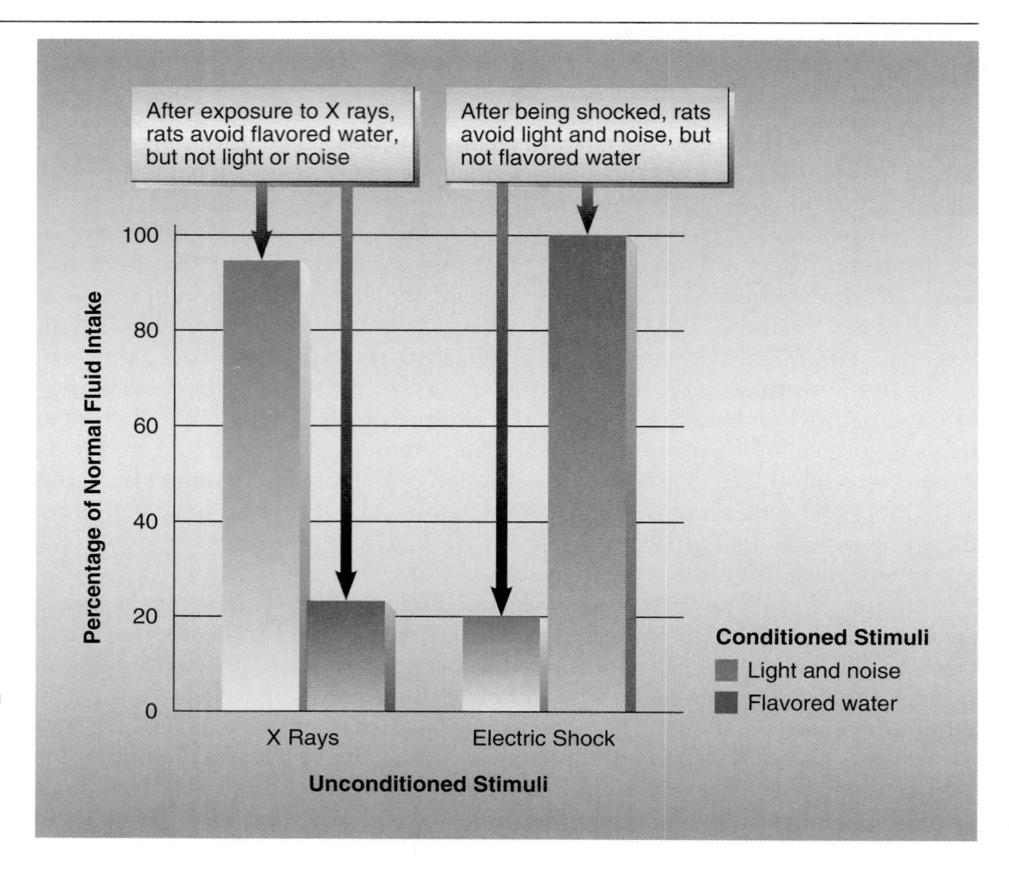


**Figure 5.6**
**Biological Constraints and Characteristics of the CS and UCS Affect the Acquisition of a Conditioned Response**

Rats quickly acquired an aversion to a flavored water when it was followed by X rays that made them ill, but they did *not* readily acquire an aversion to the flavored water when it was followed by an electric shock. In contrast, rats learned to avoid a light-noise combination when it was paired with shock, but *not* when it was followed by X rays. These findings indicate that classical conditioning cannot be established with equal ease for all stimuli and for all organisms.

(*Source:* Based on data from Garcia & Koelling, 1966.)

The most dramatic evidence pointing to such conclusions was reported by Garcia and his colleagues (Braverman & Bronstein, 1985; Garcia, Hankins, & Rusiniak, 1974). In perhaps the most famous of these studies, Garcia and Koelling (1966) allowed two groups of rats to sip saccharin-flavored water from a device that emitted a bright flashing light and a loud clicking noise (conditioned stimuli) whenever the rats licked the water. While both groups were drinking, one group of rats was exposed to X rays that later made them sick (an unconditioned stimulus); the other group received painful shocks to their feet (an unconditioned stimulus). Traditional principles of classical conditioning suggest that *both* groups of rats should have learned to avoid all three stimuli—the flavored water, the bright light, and the clicking noise. After all, for both groups, these stimuli were followed by a strong unconditioned stimulus (either sickness caused by X rays or a painful shock). But this was not what Garcia and Koelling found. Rats exposed to the painful shock learned to avoid the light and noise, but not the flavored water; rats that were made to feel ill learned to avoid the flavored water, but not the light or noise (see Figure 5.6). In short, it seems that rats—and other organisms—are predisposed to associate nausea and dizziness with something they've consumed (the flavored water) and to associate pain with something they've seen or heard (the bright light and clicking noise). Similar findings from many different studies (e.g., Braverman & Bronstein, 1985) suggest that acquisition of a conditioned response does not occur with equal ease for different stimuli.

Another intriguing outcome that emerged from Garcia and Koelling's study is also noteworthy: Although the rats who received the X rays did not get sick immediately, they still acquired an aversion to the taste of the flavored water. This finding contradicted the widely held belief that classical conditioning can occur only if the unconditioned stimulus follows the conditioned stimulus within a very short interval. I'll discuss learned taste aversions in greater detail shortly.

Further research has also shown that in regard to conditioning, important differences exist among species. Because of these **biological constraints on learning,** types of conditioning readily accomplished by some species are only slowly acquired by others. And often, the types of conditioning most readily accomplished by a species are the very ones it needs to survive in its normal habitat (Shettleworth, 1993). For example, rats eat a varied diet and are most active at night. Thus, it is especially useful for them to be able to associate specific tastes with later illness, because in many cases they can't see the foods they eat. In contrast, birds depend heavily upon vision for finding food. For a bird it is more useful to be able to form associations between visual cues and later illness (Wilcoxon, Dragoin, & Kral, 1971).

**CONDITIONED TASTE AVERSIONS: BREAKING ALL THE RULES?** As I've just noted, one of the clearest demonstrations of an exception to the rules of traditional classical conditioning involves what is termed **conditioned taste aversion.** Conditioned taste aversions are important for survival because they inhibit the repeated ingestion of dangerous and toxic substances in animals' natural environments. Surveys show that food or beverage aversions are very common among humans (Logue, Logue, & Strauss, 1983; Logue, Ophir, & Strauss, 1981). Such aversions are unusually strong and can occur despite our thoughts about the actual cause of our illness. For example, many people report that even though they are convinced that a particular food or beverage was not the cause of the illness that followed, they continue to experience a taste aversion to that substance (Seligman & Hager, 1972).

The way in which these powerful associations are formed differs from most classical conditioning in several important respects. First, a conditioned taste aversion can usually be established with a single CS–UCS pairing, termed *one-trial learning,* in contrast to the many pairings involved in most Pavlovian conditioning. Second, conditioned taste aversions have been reported when the conditioned stimulus was presented hours before the occurrence of the unconditioned stimulus. In contrast, most instances of conditioning require a CS–UCS interval of not more than a few seconds. Finally, conditioned taste aversions are extremely resistant to extinction; in fact, they may last a lifetime.

Conditioned taste aversions create serious problems for some people. For example, radiation and chemotherapy used to treat cancer often cause nausea or vomiting as a side effect (Burish & Carey, 1986). Thus, cancer patients may acquire taste aversions to food ingested before therapy sessions. Research shows that even thinking about the sight or smell of these foods can produce anticipatory nausea and vomiting in some patients. In one study, Redd and colleagues (1993) asked a group of women who had recently received chemotherapy to generate mental images of the smell of the treatment clinic, the sight of the chemotherapy equipment, and the food they had consumed before the chemotherapy. Results showed that merely thinking about these stimuli made these women feel sick.

Fortunately, patients receiving chemotherapy can take some steps to reduce their likelihood of developing a conditioned taste aversion. First, they should arrange their meal schedules to decrease the chances of establishing an association between ingestion of the food and illness; the interval between their meals and chemotherapy should be as long as possible. Second, patients should eat familiar food, avoiding new or unusual foods before therapy. Because familiar foods have already been associated with feeling good, it is less likely that cancer patients will acquire an aversion to them. Finally, because the strength of a conditioned response is related to the intensity of the conditioned stimulus, patients should eat bland foods and avoid strongly flavored ones.

Our knowledge regarding learned taste aversions has also been used in efforts to help Western ranchers reduce the loss of livestock to predators such as wolves and coyotes (Garcia, Rusiniak, & Brett, 1977; Gustavson et al., 1974). Ranchers have endeavored to establish a conditioned taste aversion for cattle and sheep and thus to save livestock without having to kill the predators. To create the taste aversion,

**Biological Constraints on Learning:** Tendencies of some species to acquire some forms of conditioning less readily than other species do.

**Conditioned Taste Aversion:** A type of conditioning in which the UCS (usually internal cues associated with nausea or vomiting) occurs several hours after the CS (often a novel food) and leads to a strong CS–UCS association in a single trial.

ranchers lace small amounts of mutton or beef with lithium chloride, a substance that causes dizziness and nausea. The idea is that the predators will eat the bait, become sick several hours later, and, as a result, learn to avoid sheep or cattle. Results have been mixed, however. Some research has shown that taste aversions may be limited to the contexts in which they were established (Bonardi, Honey, & Hall, 1990; Nakajima, Kobayashi, & Imada, 1995). Also, the degree of taste aversion appears to be dose-related (Houpt & Berlin, 1999). In other words, taste aversions established at one location may not extend to other places, and taste aversions established with weak doses of lithium chloride may decay over time. Thus, ranchers should take this information into account when planning interventions to control predators.

**REVIEW QUESTIONS**

- Where in the brain does classical conditioning take place?
- Is classical conditioning equally easy to establish with all stimuli for all organisms?
- How do we acquire conditioned taste aversions?

**Food for Thought**

Can you think of other ways in which principles of classical conditioning might be used to solve important problems of everyday life?

## Classical Conditioning: A Cognitive Perspective

There is a growing consensus among psychologists that classical conditioning involves more than just formation of a simple association. We now know, for example, that regular pairing of a conditioned stimulus with an unconditioned stimulus provides subjects with valuable *predictive* information; it indicates that whenever a conditioned stimulus is presented, an unconditioned stimulus will shortly follow. Thus, as conditioning proceeds, subjects acquire the *expectation* that a conditioned stimulus will be followed by an unconditioned stimulus; that is, a cognitive process takes place.

The idea that cognitive processes involving expectation play a role in classical conditioning is a thesis supported by several types of evidence (Rescorla & Wagner, 1972). First, conditioning fails to occur when unconditioned and conditioned stimuli are paired in a random manner. With random pairings, subjects cannot acquire any firm expectation that an unconditioned stimulus will indeed follow presentation of a conditioned stimulus. Therefore, for conditioning to occur, the CS–UCS pairing must be consistent.

Second, the cognitive thesis is supported by a phenomenon known as *blocking*—the fact that conditioning to one stimulus may be prevented by previous conditioning to another stimulus. For example, suppose that a dog is initially conditioned to a tone. After repeated pairings with presentation of meat powder, the tone becomes a conditioned stimulus, capable of causing the dog to salivate. Then a second stimulus, a light, is added to the situation. It too occurs just before the presentation of food. If classical conditioning occurs in an automatic manner, simply as a result of repeated pairings of a conditioned stimulus with an unconditioned stimulus, then the light too should become a conditioned stimulus: It should elicit salivation when presented alone. In fact, this does not happen. Why? Again, an explanation in terms of expectancies is helpful. Because the meat powder is already predicted by the tone, the light provides no new information. Therefore, it is of little predictive value to the subjects and fails to become a conditioned stimulus.

The idea that cognitive processes play a role in classical conditioning is also supported by studies of mental imagery (Dadds et al., 1997). The main question addressed by this research, of course, is whether mental images of stimuli can substitute for their physical counterparts in the conditioning process. The results of several converging lines of evidence indicate that the answer is yes. In a direct test of this possibility, Holzman and Levis (1991) assessed whether research participants could be conditioned to a mental image of a neutral stimulus if the image were paired with an electric shock (an unconditioned stimulus). One group of participants viewed the neutral stimulus before receiving the shock; another group did not see the actual stimulus, but instead were asked to imagine it before they received the shock. Physiological measures revealed that conditioning occurred in *both* conditions, although the conditioned response was larger among participants who actually saw the stimulus. Interestingly, both groups showed similar patterns of extinction when the CS (either the physical stimulus or a mental image of it) was no longer followed by the shock (US).

Why should a mental image of a physical stimulus be able to exert such effects? Research seems to indicate that the cognitive processes underlying the generation, manipulation, and scanning of mental images closely mirror the processes involved in perceiving actual physical stimuli (Kosslyn, 1994). Studies using brain-imaging techniques, for example, indicate that areas of the brain known to be involved in visual processing are also active during visual imagery tasks (Farah, 1988).

Mental images of physical stimuli also appear to elicit reactions that closely resemble the ones elicited by their physical counterparts. For example, asking people to *imagine* drinking a sour solution causes them to salivate as if they were actually drinking it; in contrast, asking people to drink a glass of water does not (Barber, Chauncey, & Winer, 1964). Mental imagery is also associated with relevant behavioral responses. Thus, when people are asked to mentally scan an object, their eye movements indicate that they process self-generated images as if they were processing the actual physical object. For example, when people are asked to mentally scan a tall building, observation of their eye movements reveals that they tend to move their eyeballs up and down, mirroring the type of movements that would occur if they were viewing the actual building.

Taken together, these findings suggest that classical conditioning involves much more than the formation of simple associations between specific stimuli. In short, both memory and active comparison processes play roles in what might at first seem to be an automatic function.

## Classical Conditioning: Turning Principles into Action

So far, this discussion has focused on basic principles of classical conditioning, many of them derived from laboratory research involving animals. Before concluding, however, I should call attention to the fact that knowledge of these principles has been put to many practical uses to help people. One of the earliest applications of classical conditioning was in the treatment of learned fears, or *phobias,* an issue we'll explore in greater detail in Chapters 14 and 15. These principles have also been applied to other important problems, which we'll consider next.

**CLASSICAL CONDITIONING AND DRUG OVERDOSE** Knowledge of conditioning processes has helped to explain some instances of drug overdose. For example, it is well known that certain drugs become less effective over time. But why does this occur? One possibility is that when a person uses drugs repeatedly in a particular context, the stimuli in that environment become conditioned stimuli and so elicit a conditioned response (Siegel, 1983, 1984). For certain addictive drugs, this conditioned response can be just the opposite of the unconditioned response (Siegel, 1975; Siegel et al., 1982).

An experiment conducted by Siegel and his colleagues (1982) may help illustrate this point. In the study, rats received injections of either heroin or placebo on alternating days, in alternating environments. Then all subjects received a single high—potentially fatal—dose of heroin. One group received this dose in the environment in which they'd previously received heroin, the other group in the environment in which they'd previously received the placebo. A control group that had previously received only placebo were also injected with the high dose of heroin. The results? First, more subjects with previous drug experience survived than control group subjects; apparently, tolerance resulted from the early nonlethal injections. Second, and more interesting, mortality differed between the other two groups: Mortality was highest among those receiving the injection in the environment previously associated with the placebo—*not* with heroin.

These facts suggest that environmental cues associated with the environment in which drugs are consumed served as conditioned stimuli and prepared the rats' bodies partially to counteract the effects of the lethal injection; the placebo environment did not provide such cues. Drug users who have nearly died following drug use commonly report something unusual about the environment in which they took the drug (Siegel, 1984). Often these environmental differences are quite subtle, a fact that emphasizes the powerful effects produced by conditioning. These results may also have implications for drug treatment: The environments to which former drug users return often contain cues that may produce drug-related conditioned responses, such as withdrawal symptoms and drug cravings (Ehrman et al., 1992). Health professionals can use this knowledge to arrange environments that minimize relapse among former drug users by eliminating the cues that trigger conditioned responses.

**CLASSICAL CONDITIONING AND THE IMMUNE SYSTEM** Research also seems to indicate that it may be possible to alter the immune system through classical conditioning (Ader et al., 1993; Husband et al., 1993). In one interesting study, Alvarez-Borda and her colleagues (1995) used classical conditioning to enhance specific immune functions in rats. On conditioning day, one group of rats was allowed to drink a distinctive beverage—saccharin-flavored water (the CS)—before receiving an injection of a substance (the UCS) known to raise the level of certain antibodies in their systems. A second group of rats received only water before receiving the same injection. As predicted, both groups showed an enhanced immune response (UCR) to the injection. Then, after the effects of the injection had faded (more than a month later), the researchers tested to see if conditioning had taken place. Half of the rats that had been exposed to saccharin-flavored water during conditioning were again exposed to saccharin-flavored water, while the other half received only water. The group that had received only water during conditioning also received water during the test trial. The researchers' predictions were supported: Reexposure to the saccharin-flavored water (the CS) resulted in a significant elevation of antibodies in these rats, despite the fact that no further injections (the UCS) were given. In contrast, there was no enhanced immune response in the other groups; measurements indicated that antibody levels in these rats were not significantly different from levels assessed before conditioning. Although these results are only preliminary, and require replication in additional studies and in different species, they clearly show that conditioning can exert powerful effects on the immune system—in the absence of the original substance that produced it. As you may have guessed already, the implications of these results are enormous. Indeed, they offer tremendous hope to people whose health is compromised because of depressed immune systems; for example, persons who are HIV positive or have AIDS (see Figure 5.7).

**Figure 5.7**
**Classical Conditioning and the Immune System**

Classical conditioning can exert powerful effects on the immune system, a discovery that may offer tremendous hope to people whose health is compromised because of depressed immune systems; for example, persons who are HIV positive or have AIDS.

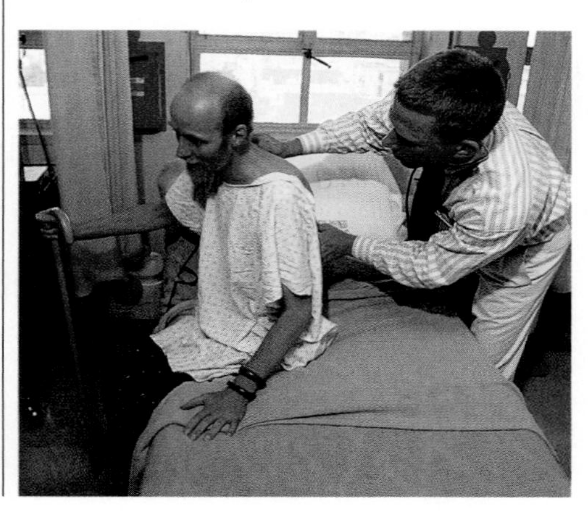

For additional information on applications of classical conditioning, please refer to the following **Beyond the Headlines** section.

## BEYOND the HEADLINES: *As Psychologists See It*

## A New Approach to Teen Crime

### Counteracting Teen Violence: Therapeutic Breakthrough?—Or New Application of Established Principles of Learning?

CBS *48 HOURS* (JUNE 10, 1999).—At first glance, the Giddings State School looks like an upscale high school campus; then you meet some of the kids. Outside Austin, Texas, Giddings is a fenced-in, secure institution that houses about four hundred armed robbers, rapists, murderers, and assorted other young criminals. The people who run Giddings reject what they view as an overly punitive mentality in America these days. Instead, they say they can turn bad kids around with a kinder, gentler approach. Their approach advocates talking, sharing feelings, and a controversial form of group therapy in which offenders are forced to reenact their crimes, often in gruesome detail! The idea is to make the teens take responsibility for what they did.

On this particular segment of *48 Hours,* a twenty-year-old named Elena is set to participate in a reenactment of her crime. Like many of the kids at Giddings, Elena had a troubled childhood. She came from a broken home and was sexually abused. When she was sixteen she left home and moved in with her best friend, a girl named Angela, who was living with her aunt and uncle. It was, by all accounts, a good home. But this fact did not stop Angela from convincing Elena to beat the aunt and uncle, with hammers, while they slept in their beds. The couple survived the attack, but just barely.

During the reenactment, Elena's therapists play the victims. At first nothing happens. Then all hell breaks loose. "Go after her, go after her," one of the therapists screams at Elena. "Keep hitting her. She doesn't know it's you. She doesn't know it's you." To help Elena fully comprehend the horror of her crime, she is physically forced to look at gruesome crime scene photos, ones she has never seen before. By the end of the session, Elena is sobbing and clearly shaken by the experience. She is adamant in claiming that she'll forever remember what she did to her victims.

In some cases, kids become physically ill when forced to re-create their offenses. Says the Giddings superintendent, "That's an excellent response and reaction. I want kids to feel sick to their stomachs when they think about what they've done to another human being." If Giddings officials deem Elena's treatment successful, she will be freed before she is twenty-one.

Critics have trouble believing that the Giddings approach really works and instead advocate harsh prison sentences. They argue that violent and repeat teen offenders should not be given a break because of their age and instead should face the same penalties as their adult counterparts. But is the program successful? Apparently so: Only 12 percent of the kids who complete the Giddings program end up back in trouble within a year, compared to the national average of more than 50 percent.

So, to what do we attribute the program's success? One possibility is that the reenactment procedure gives rise to *conditioned fear.* In other words, a strong association is forged between the offenders' violent act—or the mere thought of it—and the extreme discomfort the offenders experience during therapy. As we learned in a previous section, mental images can be powerful stimuli. In this case, mental images seem to help deter youthful offenders from committing similar violent acts in the future (Dadds et al., 1997). The moral: Basic principles of learning, including classical conditioning, can be effective tools to help solve important societal problems, including youth violence.

### CRITICAL THINKING QUESTIONS

1. Can you think of other explanations for the apparent success of the Giddings program?
2. The reenactment portion of the therapy appears to be very traumatic for the teens who experience it. Do you feel that forcing youngsters—even those who have committed violent acts—to undergo this controversial form of therapy is ethical?
3. Do you think this form of therapy would be useful if applied to adult violent offenders? If yes, why? If no, why not?

**REVIEW QUESTIONS**

- How do modern views of classical conditioning differ from earlier perspectives?
- What is blocking?
- How can classical conditioning principles be used to solve problems of everyday life?

## Operant Conditioning: Learning Based on Consequences

When a local politician started his campaign for state office, his speeches contained many remarks about the need for higher spending. He would note, with considerable passion, that the state's schools were in serious trouble, that its roads and bridges were falling apart, and that the salaries paid to its employees were below the national average. The crowds he addressed, however, weren't favorably impressed by these views. Whenever he mentioned raising taxes, many people would shake their heads, boo, or get up to leave. Now, several months later, his speeches have an entirely different flavor. He rarely if ever mentions the need for higher spending. Instead, he emphasizes efficiency—getting full value from every tax dollar spent. And when he makes such remarks, people smile, applaud, and cheer.

What happened here? Why did this politician change the nature of his speeches? The answer should be obvious: As many politicians do, he changed his remarks in response to the consequences they produced (see Figure 5.8). Statements that yielded hisses and boos from voters decreased in frequency, while those that yielded applause and cheers increased. In other words, he learned to perform behaviors that produced positive outcomes and to avoid behaviors that yielded negative ones. This process is known as *operant conditioning* and it is the second major form of learning we will consider.

**Figure 5.8**
**Operant Conditioning: Learning Based on Consequences**

Operant conditioning is a form of learning in which behavior is maintained, or changed, through consequences. The views politicians express are often shaped by the reactions of those who listen—or by the results of polls.

**Figure 5.9**
**Conditioned Reinforcers in Action**

Conditioned reinforcers acquire their capacity to act as positive reinforcers through association with primary reinforcers.

## The Nature of Operant Conditioning: Consequential Operations

In situations involving **operant conditioning,** the probability that a given behavior will occur changes depending on the consequences that follow it. Psychologists generally agree that these probabilities are determined through four basic procedures, two of which strengthen or increase the rate of behavior and two of which weaken or decrease the rate of behavior. Procedures that *strengthen* behavior are termed *reinforcement,* whereas those that *suppress* behavior are termed *punishment.*

**REINFORCEMENTS** There are two types of **reinforcement:** positive reinforcement and negative reinforcement. *Positive reinforcement* involves the impact of **positive reinforcers**—stimulus events or consequences that strengthen responses that precede them. In other words, if a consequence of some action increases the probability that the action will occur again in the future, that consequence is functioning as a positive reinforcer. Some positive reinforcers seem to exert these effects because they are related to basic biological needs. Such *primary reinforcers* include food when we are hungry, water when we are thirsty, and sexual pleasure. In contrast, other events acquire their capacity to act as positive reinforcers through association with primary reinforcers. As shown in Figure 5.9, such *conditioned reinforcers* include money, status, grades, trophies, and praise from others.

Preferred activities can also be used to reinforce behavior, a principle referred to as the **Premack principle.** If you recall hearing "You must clean your room before you can watch TV" or "You must eat your vegetables before you get dessert" when you were growing up, then you're already familiar with this principle. As you can guess, the Premack principle is a powerful tool for changing behavior.

Please note that a stimulus event that functions as a positive reinforcer at one time or in one context may have a different effect at another time or in another place. For example, food may serve as a positive reinforcer when you are hungry, but not when you are ill or just after you finish a large meal. Also, at least where people are concerned, many individual differences exist. Clearly, a stimulus that functions as a positive reinforcer for one person may fail to operate in a similar manner for another person. We will return to this important point later in this chapter.

**Operant Conditioning:** A process through which organisms learn to repeat behaviors that yield positive outcomes or permit them to avoid or escape from negative outcomes.

**Reinforcement:** The application or removal of a stimulus to increase the strength of a specific behavior.

**Positive Reinforcers:** Stimuli that strengthen responses that precede them.

**Premack Principle:** Principle stating that a more preferred activity can be used to reinforce a less preferred activity.

*Negative reinforcement* involves the impact of **negative reinforcers**—stimuli that strengthen responses that permit an organism to avoid or escape from their presence. Thus, when we perform an action that allows us to escape from a negative reinforcer that is already present or to avoid the threatened application of one, our tendency to perform this action in the future increases. Some negative reinforcers, such as intense heat, extreme cold, or electric shock, exert their effects the first time they are encountered, whereas others acquire their impact through repeated association.

There are many examples of negative reinforcement in our everyday lives. To illustrate this, imagine the following scene. On a particularly cold and dark winter morning, you're sleeping soundly in a warm, comfortable bed. Suddenly, the alarm clock across the room begins to wail. Getting out of your cozy bed is the last thing you want to do, but you find the noise intolerable. What do you do? If you get up to turn off the alarm—or, on subsequent mornings, get up early to avoid hearing the sound of the alarm altogether—your behavior has been negatively reinforced. In other words, your tendency to perform actions that allow you to escape from or avoid the sound of the alarm clock has increased. Another everyday example of negative reinforcement occurs when parents give in to their children's tantrums—especially in public places, such as restaurants and shopping malls. Over time, the parent's tendency to give in may increase, because doing so stops the screaming. To repeat, then, *both positive and negative reinforcement are procedures that strengthen or increase behavior.* Positive reinforcers are stimulus events that strengthen responses that precede them, whereas negative reinforcers are aversive (unpleasant) stimulus events that strengthen responses that lead to their termination or avoidance.

Audio 5.2: *Is Punishment an Effective Deterrent?*

**PUNISHMENT** In contrast to reinforcement, **punishment** refers to procedures that weaken or decrease the rate of behavior. As with reinforcement, there are two types of punishment: positive punishment and negative punishment. In *positive punishment,* behaviors are followed by aversive stimulus events termed *punishers.* In such instances, we learn not to perform these actions because aversive consequences—punishers—will follow. And this highlights a point about which there is often much confusion. Contrary to what common sense seems to suggest, punishment is *not* the same as negative reinforcement. Here is an example to illustrate the difference. Imagine that you are driving home in a hurry, exceeding the speed limit. A sick sensation creeps into your stomach as you become aware of flashing lights and a siren. A state trooper has detected your speeding. Your eyes bug out when you see how much the ticket will cost you; and after paying that fine, you obey the posted speed limit. This is an example of the impact of *punishment*—an unpleasant outcome follows your speeding, so the chances that you will speed in the future *decrease.* Now imagine that a year later you are again caught speeding. Apparently the punishment suppressed your speeding behavior only temporarily. Because you are a past offender, the judge handling your case gives you an interesting choice: either attend a monthlong series of driver education classes or lose your driver's license. In order to avoid losing your license, you attend every class. This is an example of *negative reinforcement:* You attend the driver education classes to *avoid* an aversive event—the loss of your license.

In *negative punishment,* the rate of a behavior is weakened or decreased because the behavior is linked to the loss of potential reinforcements (Catania, 1992; Millenson & Leslie, 1979). For example, parents frequently attempt to decrease the frequency of certain behaviors of their teenagers (e.g., hitting younger siblings or talking back to parents) by temporarily denying the teenagers access to positive reinforcers—such as driving the family car on weekend dates. Negative punishment is also commonly referred to as "time-out," a procedure you may have experienced as a youngster growing up. Thus, both positive and negative punishment are procedures that weaken or decrease behavior. Table 5.1 summarizes positive rein-

**Negative Reinforcers:** Stimuli that strengthen responses that permit the organism to avoid or escape from their presence.

**Punishment:** A procedure by which the application or removal of a stimulus decreases the strength of a behavior.

**TABLE 5.1**

## Reinforcement and Punishment: An Overview

Positive and negative reinforcement are both procedures that *strengthen* behavior. Positive and negative punishment are both procedures that *weaken* behavior.

| Procedure | Stimulus Event | Effects | Behavioral Outcomes |
|---|---|---|---|
| Positive reinforcement | Application of a desirable stimulus (e.g., food, sexual pleasure, praise) | Strengthens responses that precede occurrence of stimulus | Organisms learn to perform responses that produce positive reinforcers |
| Negative reinforcement | Application of an undesirable (aversive) stimulus (e.g., heat, cold, harsh criticism) | Strengthens responses that permit escape from or avoidance of stimulus | Organisms learn to perform responses that permit them to avoid or escape from negative reinforcers |
| Positive punishment | Application of an undesirable (aversive) stimulus | Weakens responses that precede occurrence of stimulus | Organisms learn to suppress responses that lead to unpleasant consequences |
| Negative punishment | Loss or postponement of a desirable stimulus | Weakens responses that lead to loss or postponement of stimulus | Organisms learn to suppress responses that lead to loss or postponement of desired stimulus |

forcement, negative reinforcement, positive punishment, and negative punishment. Please refer to the **From Science to Practice** section that follows for a concrete example of the principles of operant conditioning in action.

from SCIENCE to PRACTICE

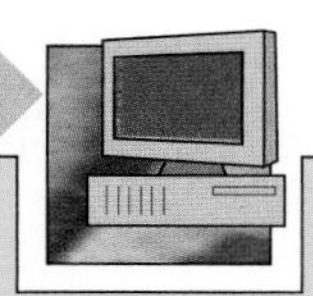

## "Horse Whispering": Applying Operant Conditioning to Treat Troubled Horses

Recently I noted that Monty Roberts, the well-known "horse whisperer," was scheduled to conduct a public demonstration in our area (see Figure 5.10 on page 186). Through a system of gentling horses called "join up," Roberts claims that he can train young horses or rehabilitate troubled ones in about twenty minutes (Roberts, 1997). I became aware of this method of training, as did much of the general public, after viewing Robert Redford's film adaptation of Nicholas Evans's best-selling novel, *The Horse Whisperer.*

To satisfy my curiosity, I attended the three-hour demonstration and watched intently as Roberts applied his methods to three local horses: one that reacted violently to its owner's attempts to load it onto a horse trailer; another that kicked wildly at people when they touched its legs or feet; and a third horse that reared and bucked when it was ridden.

"Join up" is based on two well-known facts about horses. First, horses are flight animals. When confronted with pressure or the threat of danger, they almost always choose to leave rather than fight, suggesting that their behavior is motivated through negative reinforcement. In other words, horses expend great effort to avoid or gain release from pain, fear, or otherwise uncomfortable situations. However, horses are also social animals, and with rare exceptions they prefer to be with other horses. In the wild, in fact, lead mares routinely force members away from the herd as punishment for misbehavior. Roberts's join-up method plays on these facts through the strategic use of *both* negative and positive reinforcement during training.

Roberts began the demonstration by leading the first troubled horse into a large, round pen, stopping briefly inside to rub its forehead gently. He then slowly moved behind and away from the horse and cast a thirty-foot length of nylon rope toward its flanks. In doing so, he sent the horse galloping away from him around the perimeter of the enclosure. Roberts

**Figure 5.10**
**Operant Conditioning in Action**

Monty Roberts, a noted "horse whisperer," uses the principles of positive *and* negative reinforcement to change the behavior of troubled horses. Roberts's system of mild pressure and release, termed "join up," has been taught to thousands of horse owners throughout the world.

maintained the pressure by periodically pitching the rope toward the horse whenever it slowed down. This is an example of *negative reinforcement* at work. According to Roberts, this step prepares the horse for the following message: Would you like to stop all of this work? After a few minutes, the horse signaled that it was willing to renegotiate; it tipped its ears toward Roberts, moved its head closer to the ground, and began to lick and chew—all signs that the horse was asking Roberts to remove the pressure.

At this point, Roberts coiled the line and assumed a submissive, nonthreatening posture. His eyes were cast toward the ground, and he did not face the horse directly, but instead maintained his shoulders at a 45-degree angle toward the horse. He turned and walked away from the horse, and amazingly, the horse began to follow him. When the horse moved within reach, Roberts quietly praised the horse and rubbed its forehead affectionately. This is an example of *positive reinforcement* at work.

According to Roberts, the gentle pressure and release that characterizes the join-up method tells the horse—in a language it understands—that "you would rather he did something" but not that he "must." This message was not lost on the three "problem" horses; they quickly learned that it was easier to work with Roberts than against him. By the end of the three-hour demonstration, all of the problem behaviors had vanished. During a final demonstration, the first horse repeatedly followed its owner in and out of the trailer without a hint of fuss; the second horse passively allowed its owner to touch and pick up each of its feet; and the third horse walked, trotted, and galloped around the circular enclosure with its owner aboard—without once rearing or bucking. Roberts and other horse whisperers have successfully applied this gentle method of training—based on basic principles of operant conditioning—to thousands of troubled horses.

**REVIEW QUESTIONS**

- What is operant conditioning?
- What are examples of primary reinforcers? Of conditioned reinforcers?
- Which operant techniques strengthen behavior? Weaken behavior?
- How do negative reinforcement and punishment differ?

**Food for Thought**

How do you think Monty Roberts's training methods are relevant to human behavior?

CourseCompass
Web Link: *Principles of Operant Conditioning*

CourseCompass
Video 5.1: *Military Teaches Morality*

## Operant Conditioning: Some Basic Principles

In classical conditioning, organisms learn associations between stimuli: Certain stimulus events predict the occurrence of others that naturally trigger a specific response. In addition, the responses performed are generally *involuntary.* In other words, they are *elicited*—pulled out of the organism—by a specific unconditioned stimulus in an automatic manner; for example, salivation to the taste of food, blinking of the eyes in response to a puff of air.

In operant conditioning, in contrast, organisms learn associations between particular *behaviors* and the consequences that follow them. Additionally, the responses involved in operant conditioning are more voluntary and are *emitted* by organisms in a given environment. In order to understand the nature of this form of conditioning, then, we must address two basic questions: (1) Why are certain behaviors emitted in the first place? (2) Once they occur, what factors determine the frequency with which they are repeated?

**Shaping:** A technique in which closer and closer approximations to desired behavior are required for the delivery of positive reinforcement.

**Chaining:** A procedure that establishes a sequence of responses, which lead to a reward following the final response in the chain.

Web Link: *Operant Conditioning and Behaviorism*

**SHAPING AND CHAINING: GETTING BEHAVIOR STARTED AND THEN PUTTING IT ALL TOGETHER** Many of the behaviors that we perform each day require little conscious effort on our part. But what about new forms of behavior with which we are unfamiliar? How are these behaviors initially established? The answer involves a procedure known as shaping.

In essence, **shaping** is based on the principle that a little can eventually go a long way. The organism undergoing shaping receives a reward for each small step toward a final goal—the target response—rather than only for the final response. At first, actions even remotely resembling the target behavior—termed *successive approximations*—are followed by a reward. Gradually, closer and closer approximations of the final target behavior are required before the reward is given. Shaping, then, helps organisms acquire, or construct, new and more complex forms of behavior from simpler behavior.

What about even more complex sequences of behavior, such as the routines performed by circus animals (see Figure 5.11)? These behaviors can be cultivated by means of a procedure called **chaining,** in which trainers establish a sequence, or chain, of responses, the last of which leads to a reward. Trainers usually begin chaining by first shaping the final response. When this response is well established, the trainer shapes responses earlier in the chain, then reinforces them by giving the animal the opportunity to perform responses later in the chain, the last of which produces the reinforcer. Shaping and chaining obviously have important implications for human behavior. For example, when working with a beginning student, a skilled dance teacher or ski instructor may use shaping techniques to establish basic skills, such as performing a basic step or standing on the skis without falling down, by praising simple accomplishments. As training progresses, however, the student may receive praise only when he or she successfully completes an entire sequence or chain of actions, such as skiing down a small slope.

Shaping and chaining techniques can produce dramatic effects. Indeed, noted columnist Calvin Trillin recently wrote an article about a chicken in New York City trained to play tic-tac-toe (Trillin, 1999). Apparently, the chicken plays so well that it never loses to its human challengers. After watching the bird in action, visitors that Trillin takes to play against the bird routinely complain, "But the bird gets to go first." Trillin calmly points out to them that "it's a chicken, and you're a human." Their typical reply? "But the chicken plays every day!"

This leads to the following question: Can shaping and chaining be used to establish virtually any form of behavior in any organism? If you recall our earlier discussion of *biological constraints* on classical conditioning, you can probably guess the answer: No. Just as there are biological constraints on classical conditioning, there are constraints on forms of learning based on consequences, or shaping. Perhaps this is most clearly illustrated by the experience of two psychologists, Keller and Marian Breland (1961), who attempted to put their expertise in techniques of operant conditioning to commercial use by training

**Figure 5.11**
**A Simple Demonstration of Shaping and Chaining**

The dual processes of shaping and chaining help to explain the development of complex behavior. Please note that *complex,* however, is a relative term—relative to the abilities and limitations of each organism.

animals to perform unusual tricks and exhibiting them at state fairs. At first, things went well. Using standard shaping techniques, the Brelands trained chickens to roll plastic capsules holding prizes down a ramp and then peck them into the hands of waiting customers; they taught pigs to deposit silver dollars into a piggy bank. As time went by, though, these star performers gradually developed some unexpected responses. The chickens began to seize the capsules and pound them against the floor, and the pigs began to throw coins onto the ground and root them about instead of making "deposits" in their bank. In short, despite careful training, the animals showed what the Brelands termed *instinctive drift*—a tendency to return to the type of behavior they would show under natural conditions. So operant conditioning, like classical conditioning, is subject to biological constraints. While the power of positive and negative reinforcers is great, natural tendencies are important, too, and can influence the course and results of operant conditioning in many cases.

**THE ROLE OF REWARD DELAY IN IMPULSIVENESS AND PROCRASTINATION: TWO SIDES OF THE SAME COIN?** Operant conditioning usually proceeds faster as the *magnitude* of the reward that follows each response increases. But the effectiveness of rewards can be dramatically affected by *reward delay*—the amount of time that elapses before the reward is delivered. In general, longer delays produce poorer levels of performance. A study by Capaldi (1978), for example, examined how reward delay affected running behavior in two groups of rats. Although both groups received the same amount and quality of food on each trial, one group received the reward immediately and the other group received it after a ten-second delay. As you might guess, subjects in the immediate-reward group performed better than subjects in the delayed-reward group.

The effects of reward delay are also evident in humans. For example, children will often choose smaller, immediate rewards over rewards of greater value that they must wait to receive, a tendency sometimes referred to as *impulsiveness* (Green, Fry, & Myerson, 1994; Logue, 1988). Please note, however that adults, too, frequently engage in impulsive behavior—even when the long-term consequences for their impulsiveness are deadly. Smokers and heavy drinkers, for instance, choose the immediate pleasures they derive from smoking or consuming alcoholic beverages over the potentially negative consequences they may suffer later on, such as cancer (Rachlin, 1995; Steele & Josephs, 1990).

This raises the following question: Why is it that some people seem to have amazing willpower, whereas others predictably succumb to temptation? Metcalfe and Mischel (1999) recently proposed a model to explain the processes that both enable and undermine self-control. They suggest that the ability to delay gratification effectively may be mediated through two interacting systems, which they refer to as the "know" and "go" systems. A cool, cognitive "know" system is viewed as the seat of rationality. It is complex and reflective, and it develops later in life. In contrast, a hot "go" system is specialized for quick emotional processing and action. It is simple and reflexive and is present shortly after birth. According to Metcalfe and Mischel, these systems, in conjunction with several other factors (such as the person's level of development, presence or absence of stress, and temperament), help explain individual differences in self-control.

Although the possibility of such systems is still speculative, the concept does seem to be consistent with what is known about the relative effects of human development, stress, and individual differences in temperament on self-control. We know, for example, that structures in the brain that control emotion (the "go" system) are present early in life, whereas brain structures that underlie rational thinking develop much later. Similarly, high levels of stress seem to erode self-control. However, the existence of the "know" and "go" systems proposed by Metcalfe and Mischel might be adaptive from an evolutionary standpoint. Under low levels of stress, the "know" system might predominate, allowing an organism to process information about the environment that might be useful later on—for example, the

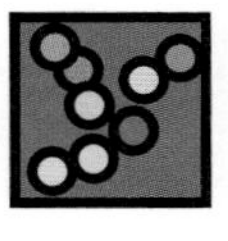

locations of sources of food, shelter, and clean water. Under stressful conditions, survival might instead depend on a reflexive "go" system that would allow the organism to escape immediate danger, such as a sudden attack by another animal.

According to Metcalfe and Mischel, viewing delay of gratification through the filter of the "know–go" model may help people boost their willpower by helping them avoid circumstances that trigger the "go" system, and helping them discover ways to enrich the functioning of the rational "know" system.

The processes underlying impulsive behavior just discussed also seem to describe another type of behavior you may be familiar with: *procrastination*—the tendency to put off until tomorrow what we should do today. The decision facing procrastinators is whether to perform a smaller, less effortful task now, or a larger, more effortful task later on. Although the most efficient decision in terms of time and effort is obvious—do the less effortful task now—research shows that people, and animals, often choose the more delayed alternative, even when it leads to more work (e.g., Mazur, 1996).

At first glance, it may seem obvious to you that the costs of procrastination outweigh any benefits it provides. It may therefore surprise you to learn that even the experts hold conflicting views regarding the effects of procrastination. Some psychologists point to evidence that procrastination leads to heightened levels of stress, which in turn can exert negative effects on task performance (Baumeister, 1984; Ferrari, Johnson, & McCown, 1995). Others, however, argue that procrastination may be beneficial in certain respects. Students who wait to the last minute to begin an assignment, for example, may benefit from the opportunity to incorporate new and critical information into their work. An impending deadline may also help certain people to focus their efforts and therefore work more efficiently. Finally, procrastination may actually reduce the overall amount of stress a person experiences by compressing the stress into a shorter period of time. This leads to the following question: What *are* the relative costs and benefits of procrastination?

Tice and Baumeister (1997) addressed this question directly in a semester-long study of college students. At the start of the term, students were told they would be required to write a term paper and were given a completion deadline. Procrastinators were identified by their scores on standardized measures designed to assess this tendency. The researchers also obtained several measures of stress, health, and performance at several points during the semester. As expected, students who were late in handing in the required paper scored much higher on the procrastination scales than students who handed their papers in on time. Moreover, procrastinators did not benefit from the extra time available to them to absorb course-related information, as they received significantly lower grades on the paper and on exams than did nonprocrastinators.

The results also revealed intriguing differences between procrastinators and nonprocrastinators in terms of their reported levels of stress and illness at the beginning and end of the semester. As shown in Figure 5.12 on page 190, procrastinators reported significantly fewer symptoms of illness at the beginning of the term than did nonprocrastinators. However, this relationship was reversed at the end of the term, when procrastinators reported significantly more stress and symptoms of illness than nonprocrastinators. These results seem to suggest that procrastination can be explained, at least in part, by people's tendency to follow the path of least resistance. In other words, we tend to procrastinate because of the short-term benefits that it provides to us. Unfortunately, as this study shows, these benefits are later outweighed by the negative effects that procrastinating exerts on many aspects of our performance and health.

**SCHEDULES OF REINFORCEMENT: DIFFERENT RULES FOR DELIVERY OF PAYOFFS** Through experience, you may already realize that under natural conditions reinforcement is often an uncertain event. Sometimes a given response yields a reward every time it occurs, but sometimes it does not. For example, smiling at

**Figure 5.12**
**The Potential Negative Effects of Procrastination**

The short-term benefits of procrastinating appear to be offset by the negative effects it exerts on our performance and health later on. Procrastinators reported fewer symptoms of illness at the beginning of the semester, compared to nonprocrastinators. Late in the semester, when procrastinators were faced with impending deadlines, this relationship switched.

(*Source:* Based on data from Tice & Baumeister, 1997.)

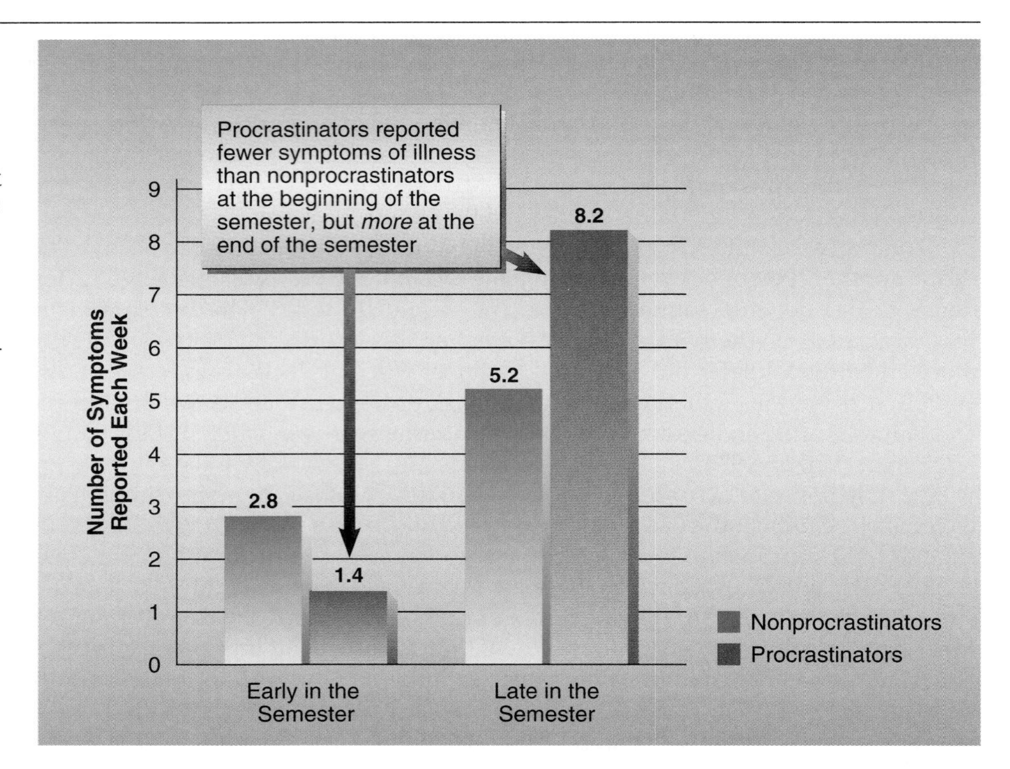


someone you don't know may produce a return smile and additional positive outcomes. On other occasions it may be followed by a suspicious frown or other rejection. Similarly, putting coins in a soda machine usually produces a soft drink. Sometimes, though, you merely lose the money.

In these cases, the occurrence or nonoccurrence of reinforcement seems to be random or unpredictable. In many other instances, though, it is governed by rules. For example, paychecks are given out on certain days of the month; free pizzas or car washes are provided to customers who have purchased a specific amount of products or services. Do such rules—known as **schedules of reinforcement**—affect behavior? Several decades of research by B. F. Skinner and other psychologists suggest that they do. Many different types of schedules of reinforcement exist (Ferster & Skinner, 1957; Honig & Staddon, 1977). We'll concentrate on several of the most important ones here.

**Schedules of Reinforcement:** Rules determining when and how reinforcements will be delivered.

**Continuous Reinforcement Schedule:** A schedule of reinforcement in which every occurrence of a particular behavior is reinforced.

**Fixed-Interval Schedule:** A schedule of reinforcement in which a specific interval of time must elapse before a response will yield reinforcement.

The simplest is called the **continuous reinforcement schedule (CRF),** in which every occurrence of a particular behavior is reinforced. For example, if a rat receives a food pellet each time it presses a lever, or a small child receives twenty-five cents each time he ties his shoes correctly, both are on a continuous reinforcement schedule. As you might imagine, continuous reinforcement is useful for establishing or strengthening new behaviors.

Other types of schedules, however, termed *partial* or *intermittent reinforcement,* are often more powerful in maintaining behavior. In the first of these, known as a **fixed-interval schedule,** the occurrence of reinforcement depends on the passage of time; the first response made after a specific period has elapsed brings the reward. When placed on schedules of this type, people generally show a pattern in which they respond at low rates immediately after delivery of a reinforcement, but then gradually respond more and more as the time when the next reward can be obtained approaches. A good example of behavior on a fixed-interval schedule is provided by students studying. After a big exam, little if any studying takes place. As the time for the next test approaches, the rate of such behavior increases dramatically.

Reinforcement is also controlled mainly by the passage of time in a **variable-interval schedule.** Here, though, the period that must elapse before a response will again yield reinforcement varies. An example of behavior on a variable-interval schedule of reinforcement is provided by employees whose supervisor checks their work at irregular intervals. Because the employees never know when such checks will occur, they must perform in a consistent manner in order to obtain positive outcomes, such as praise, or avoid negative ones, such as criticism. This is precisely what happens on variable-interval schedules: Organisms respond at a steady rate without the kind of pauses observed on fixed-interval schedules. An important procedure that is arranged according to a variable-interval schedule is random drug testing of individuals in safety-sensitive jobs—people whose impaired performance could endanger the lives of others, such as airline pilots, air-traffic controllers, or operators at nuclear reactor sites. Random drug testing is also common in many collegiate and professional sports. Because they cannot predict the day on which the next test will occur, these individuals may be more likely to refrain from using drugs that can either impair or unfairly enhance their performance.

Reinforcement is determined in a very different manner on a **fixed-ratio schedule.** Here, reinforcement occurs only after a fixed number of responses. Individuals who are paid on a piecework basis, in which a fixed amount is paid for each item produced, are operating according to a fixed-ratio schedule. Generally, such schedules yield a high rate of response, though with a tendency toward a brief pause immediately after each reinforcement. The pauses occur because individuals take a slight breather after earning each unit of reinforcement. People who collect beverage containers, office paper waste, and other recyclable materials for the money they bring are behaving according to a fixed-ratio schedule.

Finally, on a **variable-ratio schedule,** reinforcement occurs after completion of a variable number of responses. Since organisms confronted with a variable-ratio schedule cannot predict how many responses are required before reinforcement will occur, they usually respond at high and steady rates. The effect of such schedules on human behavior is readily apparent in gambling casinos, where high rates of responding occur in front of slot machines and other games of chance.

Variable-ratio schedules also result in behaviors that are highly resistant to extinction—ones that persist even when reinforcement is no longer available. In fact, resistance to extinction is much higher after exposure to a variable-ratio schedule of reinforcement than it is after exposure to a continuous reinforcement schedule. This phenomenon is known as the *partial reinforcement effect* and seems to occur for the following reason. Under a variable-ratio schedule, many responses are not followed by reinforcement. Many golfers are well acquainted with the partial reinforcement effect; for each great shot they hit, they hit many more poor ones, yet they continue to play the game. Suppose that a golfer fails to hit even one good shot over the course of an entire season—will she continue to play? The chances are good that she will. When reinforcement is infrequent and intermittent in its delivery, people or other organisms may continue to respond because it is difficult for them to recognize that reinforcement is no longer available. In short, they fail to realize that no amount of responding will do any good (Mowrer & Jones, 1945).

As summarized in Figure 5.13 on page 192 and evident throughout the preceding discussion, different schedules of reinforcement produce distinct patterns of responding. Each schedule helps describe how the delivery of consequences affects our behavior.

**CONCURRENT SCHEDULES OF REINFORCEMENT AND THE MATCHING LAW** Many psychologists readily admit that the schedules of reinforcement just described do not fully account for the complex forms of human behavior observed in everyday life (e.g., Hanisch, 1995; Pierce & Epling, 1994). Each day people are faced with alternatives and must choose one to the exclusion of others. For example, on a given evening, students must choose between doing homework and other activities they

**Variable-Interval Schedule:** A schedule of reinforcement in which a variable amount of time must elapse before a response will yield reinforcement.

**Fixed-Ratio Schedule:** A schedule of reinforcement in which reinforcement occurs only after a fixed number of responses have been emitted.

**Variable-Ratio Schedule:** A schedule of reinforcement in which reinforcement is delivered after a variable number of responses have been performed.

**Figure 5.13**
**Schedules of Reinforcement: A Summary of Their Effects**

Rates of responding vary under different schedules of reinforcement. Note that the steeper the line in each diagram, the higher the rate at which responses are performed.

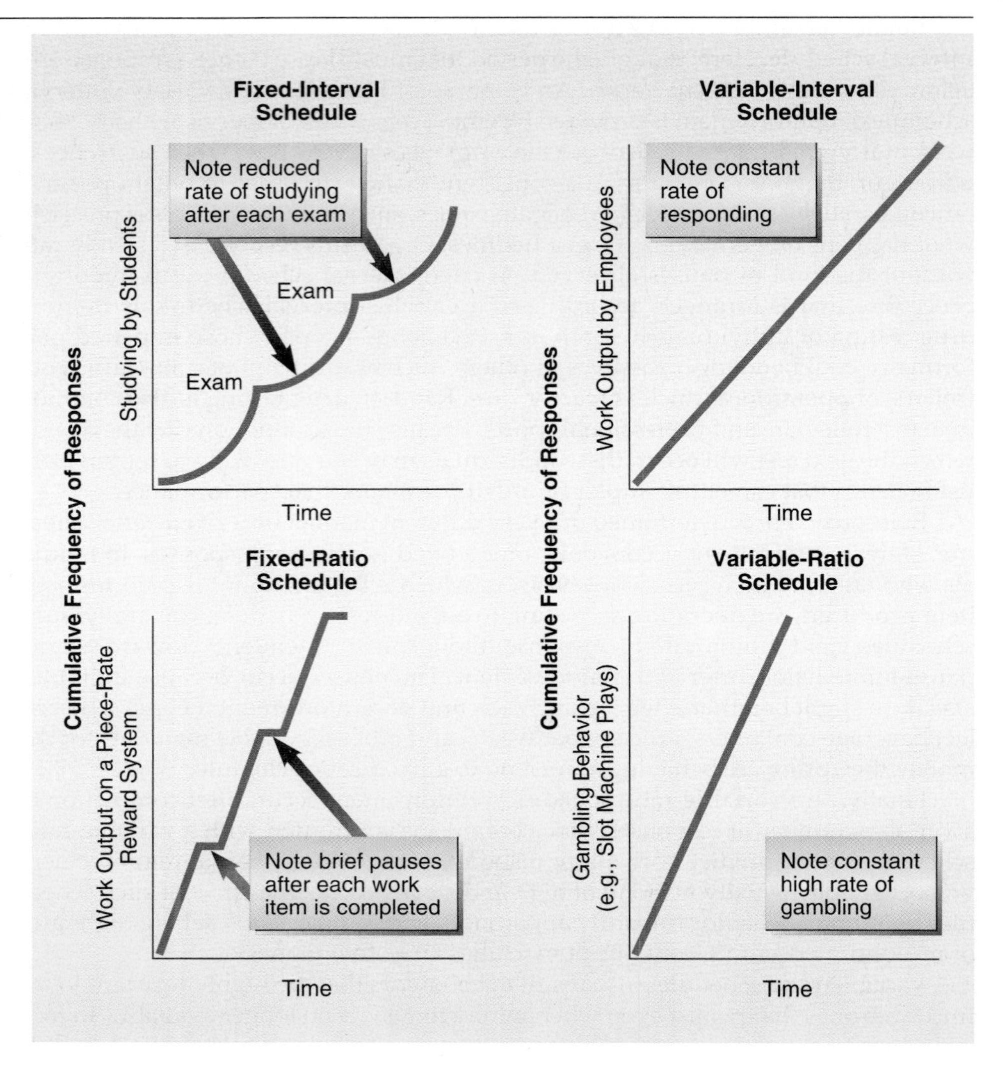


could do instead, such as going out with friends, talking on the telephone, doing their laundry, or watching TV. This describes a **concurrent schedule of reinforcement:** a situation in which a person's behavior is free to alternate continuously between two or more responses, each having its own schedule of reinforcement (Catania, 1992). This type of schedule has been used to study choice behavior in both animals and humans (e.g., Elsmore & McBride, 1994; Pierce & Epling, 1994).

To illustrate, let's consider a typical animal experiment involving a concurrent schedule of reinforcement in which a rat is free to press lever A or lever B at any time, or to press neither. Furthermore, the rat may distribute its presses between the two levers as it chooses. Now suppose the consequences of pressing each lever (e.g., food rewards) are arranged according to distinct variable-interval schedules of reinforcement. How will the rat distribute its lever presses? The rate of responding on each lever will tend to match the rate of reinforcement each lever produces. In other words, the rat will distribute its behavior between alternatives in such a way as to maximize the reinforcement it receives for its efforts. This phenomenon has been termed the *matching law* (Herrnstein, 1961).

**Concurrent Schedule of Reinforcement:** A situation in which two or more behaviors, each having its own reinforcement schedule, are simultaneously available.

Although this is a relatively simple example of choice behavior, the matching law can be extended to explain more complex forms of behavior, too. According to Herrnstein (1970), we don't usually choose between just two alternatives—A (doing homework) and B (going out with friends); instead, we choose between doing homework and all other available alternatives. Emerging evidence also seems to suggest that we evaluate these choices through the filter of our memory of these choices in the past (Dragoi & Staddon, 1999). This helps to explain why particular events are reinforcing at certain times and in certain contexts, but not others. For instance, on a particular Friday night, cleaning your room may not seem so bad if nothing else is going on. In contrast, the same chore may be unappealing if there is something better to do.

Please note that consequences are not the only determinants of behavior. As we'll see in the next section, stimuli that precede behavior and signal the availability of certain consequences are also important.

**Figure 5.14**
**Stimulus Control: A Humorous Example**

Stimulus control can be applied to solve important problems of everyday life—in this case, helping people to remain focused while at work.

(*Source:* CLOSE TO HOME. © John McPherson. Reprinted with permission of UNIVERSAL PRESS SYNDICATE. All rights reserved.)

**To stave off spring fever among employees on sunny days, Credmont Industries wisely installed rain-simulation devices above all windows.**

**STIMULUS CONTROL OF BEHAVIOR: SIGNALS ABOUT THE USEFULNESS (OR USELESSNESS) OF RESPONSES** People and other animals readily learn to pay attention to cues in the environment that reliably signal certain consequences for their actions. Children may learn, for example, that when their father whistles, it is an indication he is in a good mood and therefore more likely to respond favorably to requests for money or for permission to do something fun with their friends. Evidence of the father's mood, such as whistling or singing, actually function as signals: He is likely to agree to requests when he is in a good mood (e.g., when he is whistling), but unlikely to do so when he is in a bad mood or not feeling well. Over time, children learn to make requests only in the presence of these signals—termed **discriminative stimuli.** In short, their behavior has come under **stimulus control**—control by the sound of his whistling (or related cues): They are obeying the signal as to whether they should ask for something now or wait until he is in a better mood (Skinner, 1938) (see Figure 5.14).

Stimulus control has important practical applications, too. For example, one type of graphic discriminative stimulus, the *Mr. Yuk* sticker, has been used to prevent accidental poisonings among small children who can't yet read warning labels or understand the dangers of many household products. How do Mr. Yuk stickers work? Initially parents place the stickers on all poisonous products in their home and explain to their children that Mr. Yuk means "No, don't touch." Then, each time a child attempts to handle a product containing the sticker, he or she receives a scolding. Soon Mr. Yuk comes to signal the availability of unpleasant consequences, and children quickly learn to avoid products with Mr. Yuk stickers. In short, stimulus control has important implications for solving a variety of problems in everyday life.

**Discriminative Stimulus:** Stimulus that signals the availability of reinforcement if a specific response is made.

**Stimulus Control:** Consistent occurrence of a behavior in the presence of a discriminative stimulus.

**REVIEW QUESTIONS**

- What are shaping and chaining?
- How does reward delay affect operant conditioning? What are the effects of procrastination?
- What are schedules of reinforcement?

*Continued*

- When is the use of continuous reinforcement desirable?
- What are concurrent schedules of reinforcement and the matching law?
- What is a discriminative stimulus?

Food for Thought

Describe some examples of stimulus control in your own life.

## Operant Conditioning: A Cognitive Perspective

Do cognitive processes play a role in operant conditioning as they do in classical conditioning? This continues to be a point on which psychologists disagree. Operant psychologists (also referred to as behaviorists or Skinnerians) have contended that there is no need to introduce cognition into the picture: If we understand the nature of the reinforcers available in a situation and the schedules on which they are delivered, we can accurately predict behavior. But many other psychologists believe that no account of operant conditioning can be complete without attention to cognitive factors (e.g., Colwill, 1993). Several types of evidence support this conclusion.

**LEARNED HELPLESSNESS: THROWING IN THE TOWEL WHEN NOTHING SEEMS TO WORK** Perhaps the most dramatic evidence is the existence of a phenomenon known as **learned helplessness:** the lasting effects produced by exposure to situations in which nothing an organism does works—no response yields reinforcement or provides escape from negative events. After such experience, both people and animals seem literally to give up. And here is the unsettling part: If the situation changes so that some responses will work, they never discover this fact. Rather, they remain in a seemingly passive state and simply don't try (Seligman, 1975; Tennen & Eller, 1977). Although it is not yet clear why learned helplessness occurs, it seems impossible to explain it entirely in terms of contingent relations between individual responses and the consequences they produce. Rather, some evidence suggests that organisms learn a general expectation of helplessness that transfers across situations, even if they do gain control over their environment (Maier & Jackson, 1979). We will discuss the role of learned helplessness in depression in Chapter 14.

**Figure 5.15**
**Learned Helplessness: The Role of Individual Differences**

Learned helplessness seems to result from situations in which nothing a person does yields reinforcers or provides escape from aversive events. Recent evidence suggests that genetic predispositions may make some people more, or less, susceptible to learned helplessness.

Research on learned helplessness seems to suggest that its onset stems partly from our perceptions of control; when we begin to believe that we have no control over our environment or our lives, we stop trying to improve our situation (Dweck & Licht, 1980). For example, many children growing up in urban slums perceive that they have little control over their environment and even less hope of escaping it. As a result of learned helplessness, they may simply resign themselves to a lifetime of disenfranchisement, deprivation, and exclusion (see Figure 5.15). Please note, however, that not all people respond in this way. Indeed, a large number of studies show that even people whose early lives were ravaged by traumatic experiences such as the early death of a parent, divorce, war, or extreme poverty often grow up optimistic and resilient (e.g., Haggerty et al., 1994; Seabrook, 1995; Stewart et al., 1997). This suggests that other factors must also be involved.

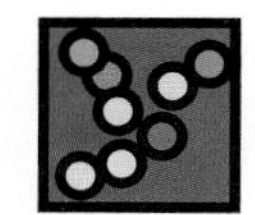

Researchers have begun to speculate that genetic factors may also play a role in learned helplessness. One such factor that has gained recent attention is a genetically inherited impairment in the ability to experience pleasure termed **hypohedonia** (Meehl, 1975). According to Hamburg (1998), this tendency may cause children who inherit it to interpret the feedback they receive for their actions quite differently from children who do not. Apparently these individuals experience the rewarding consequences they receive from their actions as if they were on an extinction schedule. This peculiar tendency to misinterpret rewarding feedback may, in turn, lead to perceptions of lack of control and helplessness.

To illustrate how this process might work, consider the following example. Two children of equal athletic ability are learning to play soccer. One of the children has hypohedonia; the other does not. Assume that they master the basic skills required to play soccer over the same period of time, and that they each make about the same number and similar types of mistakes during the learning process. How does each of them react, and what does each take away from the experience?

According to Hamburg, when normal children make mistakes while practicing a skill, it is typical for them to experience frustration, anger, and disappointment. However, when they eventually perform the skill correctly, it usually results in feelings of satisfaction and pride. Over time, the steady accumulation of positive experiences leads them to believe, for example, that they are good at soccer, that it is not as difficult as they initially thought, and that they will likely want to continue to play soccer. When children with inherited hypohedonia make the same mistakes, they are likely to experience similar negative feelings but to feel them more intensely than their unaffected counterparts. And unfortunately, when they eventually perform the skill successfully, they may not experience the same positive feelings enjoyed by their peers. They instead may experience a carryover of the frustration, anger, and disappointment elicited by previous mistakes. Over time, the steady accumulation of negative feelings may lead them to believe that they are not good at soccer, that soccer is hard, and that they will continue to perform poorly in the future. They may also generalize these expectations to other task domains. According to Hamburg, there is a strong likelihood that these children will eventually experience learned helplessness, particularly if they are faced with difficult circumstances later in life.

Apparently, the positive feelings that usually accompany successful performance are not experienced by people with hypohedonia. In other words, these individuals' correct responses may not feel very different from incorrect ones. If the sports example just described is extended to the learning of social skills, where there are fewer objective cues to signal that a response has been correct, the consistent failure to experience pleasure in response to one's own actions may be even more devastating. Please note that Hamburg's theory is just that—a theory. It has not yet been validated by empirical research, and it therefore requires further study. However, it does help explain why some people tend to give up in the face of adversity, while others remain resilient.

**EVIDENCE THAT IT'S ALL RELATIVE: THE CONTRAST EFFECT** Some evidence suggests that our behavior is influenced not only by the level of rewards we receive but by our evaluation of rewards relative to our experiences with previous rewards. Studies have shown that shifts in the amount of reward we receive can dramatically influence performance, a temporary behavior shift termed the *contrast effect* (e.g., Crespi, 1942; Flaherty & Largen, 1975; Shanab & Spencer, 1978). For example, when laboratory animals are shifted from a small reward to a larger reward, there is an increase in their performance to a level greater than that of subjects consistently receiving the larger reward. This increase is known as a *positive contrast*

**Learned Helplessness:** Feelings of helplessness that develop after exposure to situations in which no effort succeeds in affecting outcomes.

**Hypohedonia:** A genetically inherited impairment in the ability to experience pleasure.

*effect*. Conversely, when subjects are shifted from a large reward to a smaller reward, their performance decreases to a level lower than that of subjects consistently receiving only the smaller reward—a *negative contrast effect*. But positive and negative contrast effects are transient. Thus, the elevated or depressed performances slowly give way to performance levels similar to those of control animals that receive only one consistent level of reward.

The existence of contrast effects indicates that level of reward alone cannot always explain our behavior and that experience with a previous level of reward—and consequent expectancies—can dramatically affect our performance. Contrast effects also help explain certain instances of our everyday behavior. For example, following an unexpected raise in salary or a promotion, a person is initially elated, and his or her performance skyrockets—at least for a while. Then, after the novelty wears off, performance falls to a level equal to that of others already being rewarded at the same level.

**TOLMAN'S COGNITIVE MAP: A CLASSIC STUDY IN THE HISTORY OF PSYCHOLOGY** Finally, evidence suggests that cognitive processes play an important role in learning among animals, as well. In a classic study by Tolman and Honzik (1930), rats were trained to run through a complicated maze. One group, the reward group, received a food reward in the goal box at the end of the maze on each of their daily trials. A second group, the no-reward group, never received a reward. The third group, the no-reward/reward group, did not receive a food reward until the eleventh day of training. As illustrated in Figure 5.16, rats in the reward group showed steady improvement in performance, decreasing the number of errors they made in reaching the goal box. Rats in the no-reward group showed only a slight improvement in performance. Rats in the no-reward/reward group showed performance similar to those in the no-reward group—for the first ten days. However, their performance improved dramatically immediately after the in-

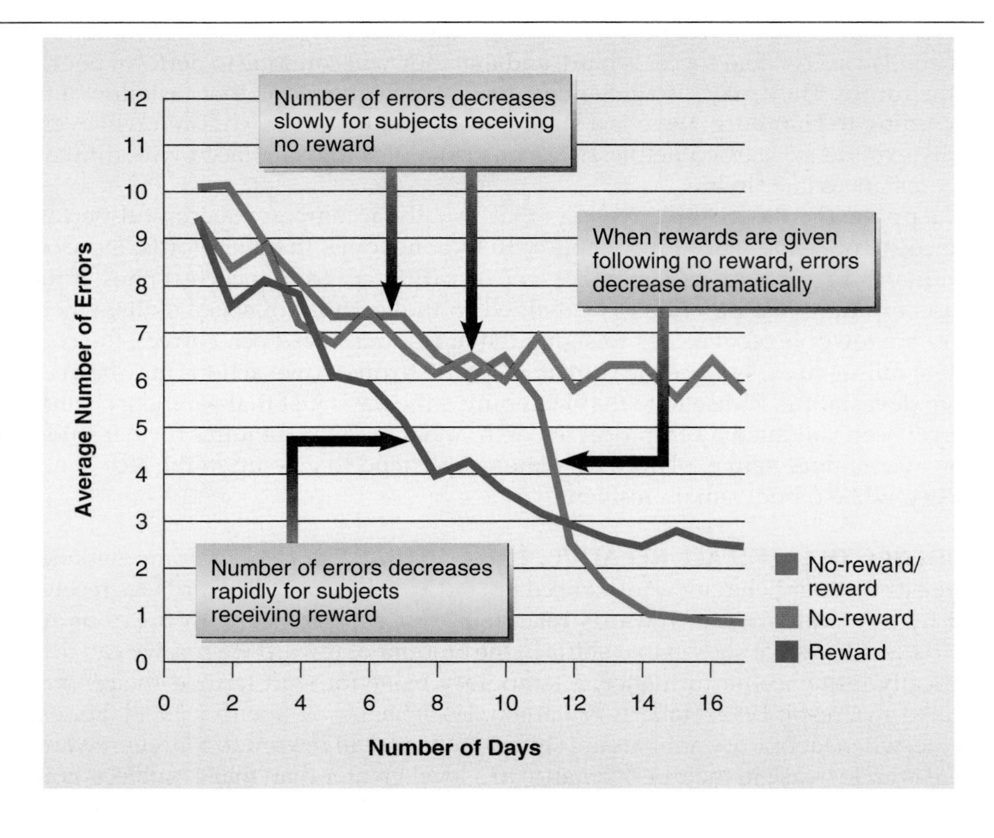


**Figure 5.16**
**The Role of Cognitive Processes in Learning**

Performance for rats in the no-reward/reward group improved dramatically immediately after the introduction of the food reward. Because the improvement was so dramatic, these data suggest that the animals had "learned" something during previous trials—even though they received no reward for their efforts. Tolman used this as evidence for the importance of cognitive processes in learning, suggesting that the rats may have formed a "cognitive map."
(*Source:* Based on data from Tolman & Honzik, 1930.)

troduction of the food reward. In fact, their performance was as good as that of rats who had been rewarded for their performance all along.

How do we account for these results? An explanation based on reinforcement alone is not sufficient; the improvement in the performance of the third group was too sudden. Obviously, the rats had learned something in the previous trials. Tolman and others point to these data, and to the results of other studies (e.g., Colwill & Rescorla, 1985, 1988), as evidence for the importance of cognitive processes in learning. In fact, Tolman theorized that the rats might have formed what he termed a *cognitive map*—a mental representation of the maze. Although the existence of such maps has not yet been clearly established (e.g., Dyer, 1991; Wehner & Menzel, 1990), a growing body of evidence supports the view that animals do, in fact, form mental representations of their environments—perhaps even memories of them.

Systematic research by Capaldi and his colleagues also points to the possibility that animals form memories of rewards they've received in the past (Capaldi, Alptekin, & Birmingham, 1997; Capaldi & Birmingham, 1998). According to this view, distinctive reward events produce distinctive reward memories. Reward event memories apparently serve two important purposes. First, they function as discriminative stimuli, directing the animal's behavior by signaling when, or if, future responses will lead to reinforcement. Second, reward memories serve a response-enhancing function. In other words, memories associated with bigger rewards lead to greater increases in responding than do memories of small rewards or nonreward. In sum, although we do not yet fully understand their precise nature, one thing is clear: Cognitive processes play an active and important role in animal learning. For additional details regarding how psychologists study operant conditioning in humans, see the **Research Methods** feature below.

**Applied Behavior Analysis:** A field of psychology that specializes in the application of operant conditioning principles to solve problems of everyday life.

## Research Methods: How Psychologists Study Applications of Operant Conditioning

You may have guessed by now that the principles of operant conditioning are powerful tools for changing many aspects of behavior. A major proponent of this approach to learning was B. F. Skinner (1904–90). Skinner is well known for his outspoken criticisms of cognitive psychology. Although Skinner never denied the existence of mental events, he felt that measuring these processes was irrelevant to accurate prediction and control of behavior (Skinner, 1938, 1971). He instead insisted that people could determine the causes of most forms of behavior by identifying environmental conditions, or contingencies, supporting the behavior and then manipulating these conditions to influence the behavior in desired directions. Skinner's views led to a distinct branch of psychology called **applied behavior analysis.** Research efforts in this area are directed primarily toward solving problems of everyday life. Before we review several significant contributions of applied behavior analysis, let's first examine how these researchers study behavior.

### How Applied Behavior Analysts Study Behavior

The research method used by applied behavior analysts is actually a four-step process. These steps can be summarized by the acronym *DO IT*, proposed by psychologist Scott Geller (1996b). As the primary focus here is on observable behavior or the outcomes of behavior, it is not surprising that the first step in the process is to clearly *Define* the target behaviors to be changed. Doing so allows researchers to develop procedures to *Observe* how often the behaviors occur under existing (or baseline) conditions. Once a stable measure of the behaviors has been obtained, researchers *Intervene* to change the target behavior in desired directions. For example, they may begin to reward behaviors they wish to increase, or withhold rewards following inappropriate behaviors they wish to decrease. Or they may alter aspects of the physical environment to encourage or discourage certain behaviors. Finally, it is important to *Test* the impact of the intervention by continuing to observe and record the target behavior(s) during the intervention, and beyond. Testing provides researchers with evidence of the intervention's impact and its effectiveness over time. By way of illustration, let's consider a study that used the DO IT process to investigate a widespread problem in this country—graffiti (Watson, 1996).

In their study, the researchers set out to reduce the amount of graffiti on the walls of three public bathrooms, each located in a different building on a university campus. The proliferation of graffiti had forced the university to repaint these rooms repeatedly. The researchers began by objectively defining graffiti; in this case, it was defined as the number of distinct markings on each wall. For example, each letter and punctuation mark counted as a separate mark; a happy face was counted as five marks—one for the circle depicting the head and one each for the two eyes, nose, and mouth.

Next, the researchers began making daily counts of graffiti to determine its baseline level of occurrence. Figure 5.17 shows the cumulative number of markings observed in each bathroom across consecutive observation days. Then the researchers introduced an intervention they felt might help reduce the proliferation of graffiti. The intervention consisted of a sign taped on the bathroom wall that read: "A local licensed doctor has agreed to donate a set amount of money to the local chapter of the United Way for each day this wall remains free of any writing, drawings, or other markings. Your assistance is greatly appreciated in helping to support your United Way."

As shown in Figure 5.17, the intervention was successful. After the posters were introduced, no further markings occurred on any of the walls. Moreover, they remained free of graffiti at each of three monthly follow-ups, suggesting that the posters were a cost-effective solution to this problem. Please note that the poster was introduced into the three bathrooms *sequentially*. The reason for this procedure was to ensure that any changes observed in the occurrence of graffiti were due to the intervention (the posting of the signs) and not to other unrelated factors. To illustrate this point, note that following the introduction of the poster into the first bathroom, graffiti ceased to occur there but continued to occur in the other two bathrooms. Similarly, following the introduction of the poster into the second bathroom, graffiti ceased to occur there but continued to occur in the third bathroom. In short, this procedure—termed a *multiple-baseline design*—increases our confidence that the poster was the cause of the abrupt change in the amount of graffiti observed.

Caution: The fact that the posters were useful in these three bathrooms does not ensure the same outcome elsewhere, such as in shopping malls or on subway cars. Nevertheless, the DO IT process remains a useful tool for systematically studying behavior and the effects of behavior-change interventions.

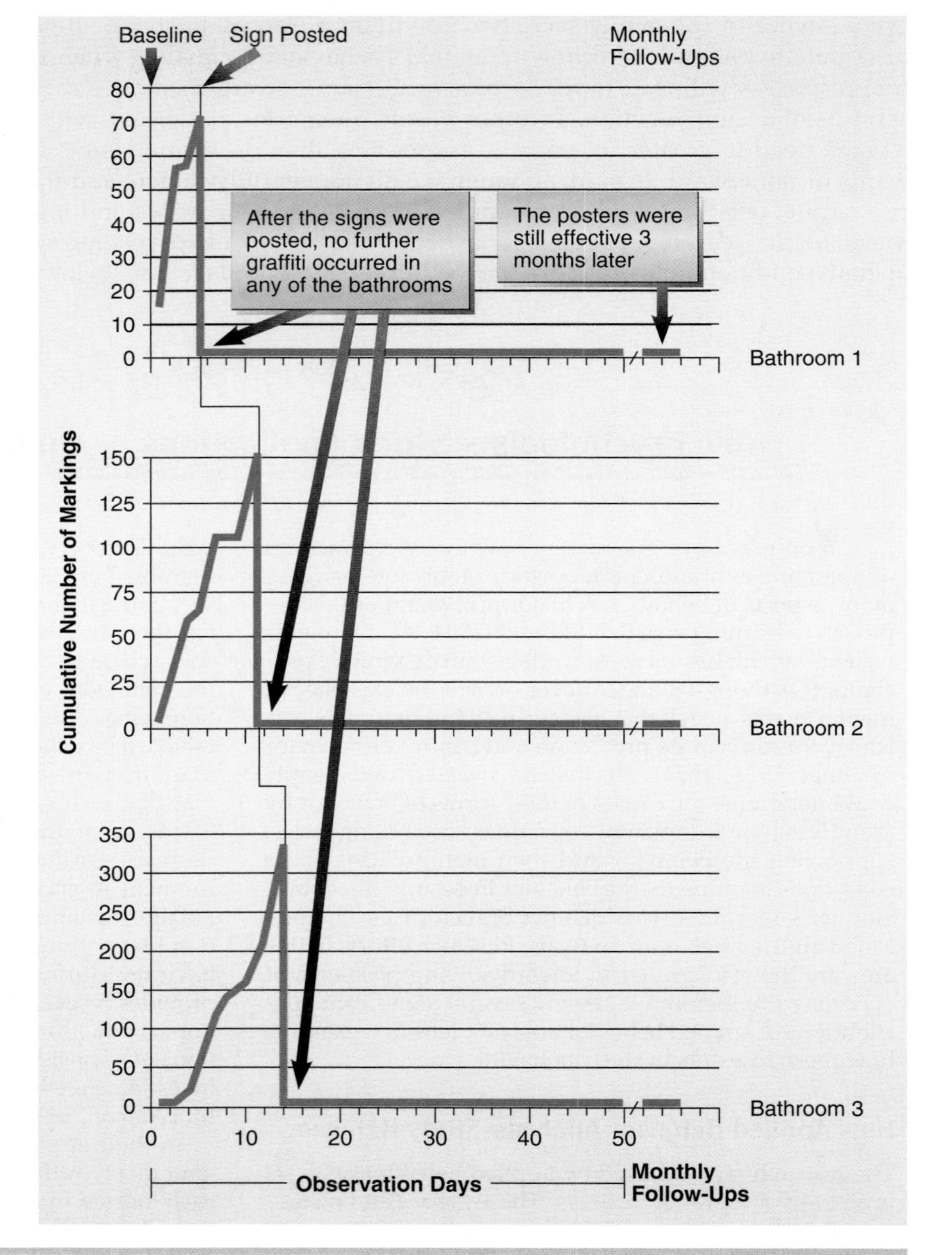


**Figure 5.17**
**Applied Behavior Analysis in Action**

This graph shows the cumulative number of graffiti markings across observation days in three public rest rooms. Before the intervention, a significant amount of graffiti was occurring in each of the bathrooms. After the intervention, however, no more graffiti occurred. Follow-up observations showed that the walls of the bathrooms remained graffiti-free three months later. Please note that the sequential introductions of the posters into the three bathrooms make it more likely that the reduction in graffiti resulted from the contents of the posters, not from other factors.

(Source: Based on data from Watson, 1996.)

## Applying Operant Conditioning: Solving Problems of Everyday Life

**Biofeedback:** A technique that enables people to monitor and self-regulate certain bodily functions through the use of specialized equipment.

Web Link: *Operant Conditioning and Marine Mammals*

Because positive and negative reinforcement exert powerful effects on behavior, procedures based on operant conditioning have been applied in many practical settings—so many that it would be impossible to describe them all here. An overview of some of these uses will suffice, though.

First, principles of operant conditioning have been applied to the field of education. One of the most impressive operant-based teaching techniques involves the use of computers in the classroom—often termed *computer-assisted instruction,* or *CAI.* In CAI students interact with sophisticated computer programs that provide immediate reinforcement of correct responses. With certain restrictions, these programs are paced according to each student's progress (Ross & McBean, 1995). CAI has recently been extended to enhance lecture-based distance education in which the instructor and learners are located at different sites throughout the world, but brought together through high-speed communication technologies (see Figure 5.18). Other emerging technologies such as desktop video conferencing and Web-based training also offer the ability to reach anybody, anywhere, at nearly any time (Wilson, 1999).

But does the use of technology in the classroom enhance teaching effectiveness beyond that afforded by more traditional instructional practices? Experts seem divided on this issue. Critics argue that the high costs of these technologies vastly outweigh any advantages they provide (Murray, 1999). Moreover, in terms of learning, critics argue that various approaches to education, including the use of computer-based technologies, fare equally well, particularly when evaluation criteria include comprehension or achievement. Viewed in this light, these different approaches to instruction are equally effective (e.g., Andrews et al., 1999; Boling & Robinson, 1999). However, if students' satisfaction with the learning experience is a major criterion, then the use of computer-based instruction is usually preferred.

A second intriguing area of application of operant conditioning is **biofeedback**—a technique in which sophisticated equipment allows people to monitor and then alter bodily responses not usually susceptible to voluntary control, such as skin temperature, muscle tension, blood pressure, and electrical activity of the brain. For example, ongoing increases or decreases in muscle tension are reflected by concomitant changes in a light or tone. A patient undergoing biofeedback then monitors this information and uses it to alter the tension in her muscles. Biofeedback has been used successfully to treat a broad range of ailments, including headaches (Arena et al., 1995; Hermann, Blanchard, & Flor, 1997), high blood pressure (Dubbert, 1995), muscle tics and chronic lower back pain (Newton et al., 1995; O'Connor, Gareau, & Borgeat, 1995), anxiety in patients recovering from traumatic brain injuries (Holland et al., 1999), depression in alcoholics (Saxby & Peniston, 1995)—and even sexual dysfunction (Palace, 1995).

Finally, principles of operant conditioning have been applied in interventions aimed at solving socially significant issues in our communities, such as crime, energy conservation and recycling, health care issues, consumer affairs, and safety promotion (Geller, 1995, 1996; Green et al., 1987; Topf, 1999).

**Figure 5.18**
**Infusing Technology into the Learning Process**

High-speed communication technologies now allow instructors and their students to come together even when they're located at many different places through the world. This has added considerable flexibility to the educational process. But are these new learning technologies any more effective than their traditional counterparts? Psychologists are currently conducting evaluation research to discover the answer to this question.

**Observational Learning:** The acquisition of new forms of behavior, information, or concepts through exposure to others and the consequences they experience.

REVIEW *QUESTIONS*

- What evidence supports the involvement of cognitive factors in operant conditioning?
- Why is knowledge of operant conditioning important?

CourseCompass
Audio 5.3: *Observational Learning*

CourseCompass
Web Link: *Biography of Albert Bandura*

# Observational Learning: Learning from the Behavior and Outcomes of Others

While at a formal dinner party, you notice five different forks placed next to your plate, including two of a shape you've never seen before. Which ones do you use for which dishes? You have no idea. In order to avoid making a complete fool of yourself, as the first course arrives, you watch the other guests. When several reach unhesitatingly for one of the unfamiliar forks, you do the same. Now, thank goodness, you can concentrate on the food.

You have probably encountered similar situations, in which you have acquired new information, forms of behavior, or even abstract rules and concepts from watching the actions of other people and the consequences they experience (see Figure 5.19). Such **observational learning** is a third major way we learn, and it is a common part of everyday life (Bandura, 1977, 1986). Indeed, a large body of research findings suggest it can play a role in almost every aspect of behavior.

More formal evidence for the existence of observational learning has been provided by hundreds of studies, many of them performed with children. Perhaps the most famous of these studies are the well-known "Bobo doll" experiments conducted by Bandura and his colleagues (e.g., Bandura, Ross, & Ross, 1963). In these studies one group of nursery-school children saw an adult engage in aggressive actions against a large inflated Bobo doll. The adult who was serving as a model knocked the doll down, sat on it, insulted it verbally, and repeatedly punched it in the nose. Another group of children were exposed to a model who behaved in a quiet, nonaggressive manner. Later, both groups of youngsters were placed in a room with several toys, including a Bobo doll. Careful observation of their behavior revealed that those who had seen the aggressive adult model often imitated this person's behavior: They too punched the toy, sat on it, and even uttered verbal comments similar to those of the model. In contrast, children in the control group rarely if ever demonstrated such actions. While you may not find these results surprising, they may be significant in relation to the enduring controversy over whether children acquire new ways of aggressing through exposure to violent television programs and movies. We'll return to this issue shortly. For the moment, let's consider the nature of observational learning itself.

**Figure 5.19**
**Acquiring New Skills through Observational Learning**

Acquiring new skills by observing the behavior of others is a common part of everyday life.

## Observational Learning: Some Basic Principles

Given that observational learning exists, what factors and conditions determine whether, and to what extent, we acquire behaviors, information, or concepts from others? The following four factors appear to be the most important (Bandura, 1986).

First, in order to learn through observation you must direct your *attention* to appropriate models—that is, to other persons performing an activity. And, as you might expect, you don't choose such models at random but focus most attention on people who are attractive to you; on people who possess signs that they know what they're doing, such as status or success; and on people whose behavior seems relevant to your own needs and goals (Baron, 1970).

Second, you must be able to *remember* what the persons have said or done. Only if you can retain some representation of their actions in memory can you perform similar actions at later times or acquire useful information from them.

Third, you need to be able to convert these memory representations into appropriate actions. This aspect of observational learning is termed *production processes.* Production processes depend on (1) your own physical abilities—if you can't perform the behavior in question, having a clear representation of it in memory is of little use; and (2) your capacity to monitor your own performance and adjust it until it matches that of the model.

Finally, *motivation* plays a role. We often acquire information through observational learning but do not put it into immediate use in our own behavior. You may have no need for the information, as when you watch someone tie a bow tie but have no plans to wear one yourself. Or the observed behaviors may involve high risk of punishment or be repugnant to you personally, as when you observe an ingenious way of cheating during an exam but don't want to try it yourself. Only if the information or behaviors acquired are useful will observers put them to actual use. Figure 5.20 summarizes factors affecting observational learning.

**Figure 5.20**
**Key Factors in Observational Learning**

Observational learning is affected by several factors or subprocesses. The most important of these are summarized here.

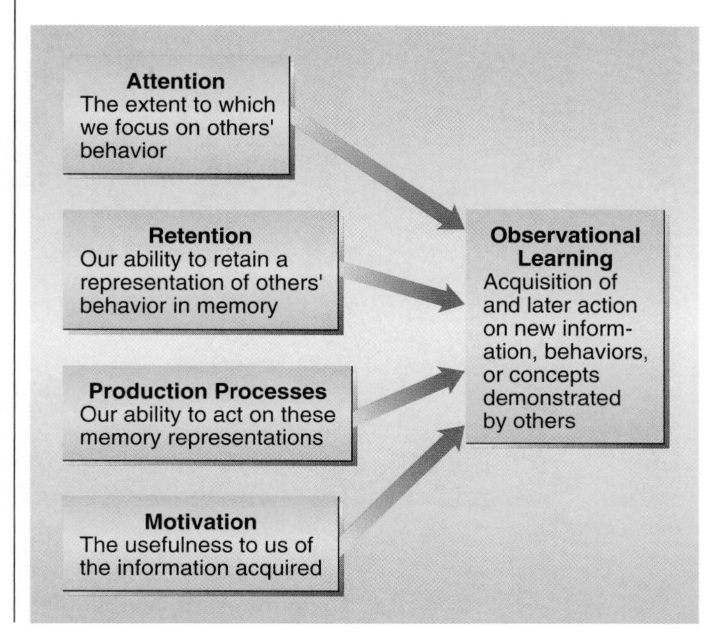


As you can see, observational learning is a complex process—far more complex than mere imitation—and plays an important role in many aspects of behavior. This point is perhaps most forcefully illustrated by a controversy that has persisted in psychology, and in society as a whole, since the early 1960s: the controversy over whether children, and perhaps even adults, are made more aggressive by long-term exposure to violence on television shows or in movies.

## Observational Learning and Aggression

Can young people learn aggression through watching the actions of others? This issue was recently brought sharply into focus when President Bill Clinton ordered a government study of how the entertainment industry markets violence to children. The president's order followed a series of school shootings, among them the one that occurred in April 1999 at Columbine High School in Littleton, Colorado (CNN Interactive, 1999). In that incident two student gunmen killed a dozen classmates and a teacher and wounded twenty-three other students before they committed suicide. Some experts attribute such incidents to the proliferation of violence depicted on television and in film. The *National Television Violence Study* (1996, 1997) analyzed nearly 4,500 hours of programming on cable and broadcast television and found that approximately 60 percent of these programs contained some form of violence. But does merely watching violence on television lead people to commit similar acts?

A large body of research indicates that aggression may indeed be learned through observation (Baron & Richardson, 1994; Centerwall, 1989; Snyder, 1991; Wood, Wong, & Chachere, 1991). Apparently, when children and adults are exposed to new ways of aggressing against others—techniques they have not previously seen—they may add these new behaviors to their repertoire (see Figure 5.21).

**Figure 5.21**
**Observational Learning and Aggression**

Experts continue to worry that exposure to violence on television and in movies may encourage children to perform violent acts.

Later, when angry, irritated, or frustrated, they may put such behaviors to actual use in assaults against others. Emerging evidence also seems to suggest that the negative effects of exposure to violence may be most pronounced for individuals who are highly aggressive by nature than for their nonaggressive counterparts. Bushman (1995), for example, showed that participants who scored higher on a measure of aggressive tendencies were more likely to choose a violent film to watch, were more likely to *feel* angry after watching it, and were more likely to commit aggressive acts after viewing videotaped violence than their less aggressive counterparts.

Of course, exposure to media violence, whether on the evening news or in movies or television programs, has other effects as well. It may convey messages that violence is an acceptable means of handling interpersonal difficulties; after all, if heroes and heroines can do it, why not viewers? It may elicit additional aggressive ideas and thoughts, convincing viewers, for example, that real-life violence is even more common than it is (Berkowitz, 1984). And it may also lessen emotional reactions to aggression and the harm it produces, so that such outcomes seem less upsetting or objectionable (Thomas, 1982). When these effects are coupled with new behaviors and skills acquired through observational learning, the overall impact may contribute to an increased tendency among many persons to engage in acts of aggression (Eron, 1987; Eron et al., 1996).

It is important to note that not all findings support such conclusions (Freedman, 1986; Widom, 1989) and that the effects of exposure to media violence, when they occur, seem to be modest in scope. In addition, some evidence suggests that those concerned about the effects of televised violence may begin getting help from companies that sponsor the shows. A recent study conducted by Bushman (1998) showed that the presence of violence decreased viewers' memories of brand names and commercial messages. Thus, sponsoring violent programs on television may not be profitable for advertisers; awareness of this could slow the proliferation of these types of shows.

Given the fact that many children spend more time watching television, playing violent video games, and, more recently, surfing the Web than they do in any other single activity, however, the potential influence of such experience on behavior seems worthy of careful attention. In Chapter 10 I'll return to the topic of aggression and discuss additional factors that seem to motivate aggressive behavior.

## Observational Learning and Culture

As we've already noted, observational learning plays an important role in many aspects of behavior. Much of our understanding of the world around us—including our language and customs—comes to us through our observation of the behaviors of others around us. Recently, psychologists have applied principles of observational learning to help meet a challenge of growing concern: preparing people to handle "culture shock."

As the United States and other countries move toward a global economy, companies throughout the world are faced with a difficult task. They must prepare their employees for the business environment of the twenty-first century—an environment that will require a broad range of skills and the ability to interact effectively with persons from other cultures (Adler & Bartholomew, 1992; Feldman & Tompson, 1993). Dramatic differences in language, customs, and lifestyle often lead to unintended misunderstandings between persons from different cultural backgrounds. Behaviors that are acceptable and in one country may be quite offensive to persons from another country (see Figure 5.22).

**Figure 5.22**
**Observational Learning: Adapting to Diversity**

Observing the behaviors of others can help us gain insight into cultures other than our own.

To soften the effects of culture shock, experts in the area of cross-cultural training have advocated an experiential approach based on behavioral modeling (Black & Mendenhall, 1990). Trainees first watch films in which models exhibit the correct behaviors in a problem situation. Then the trainees participate in a role-playing exercise to test their knowledge. Finally, they receive constructive feedback regarding their performance.

Some evidence suggests that this approach can be quite effective. In one study, Harrison (1992) compared the effectiveness of several approaches to cross-cultural training. One group of participants received culture-relevant information only; another received behavioral modeling training only; a third received both components; and a control group received no training. The results showed that participants who received both forms of training—information and behavioral modeling—performed best on measures of culture-specific knowledge and on a behavioral measure.

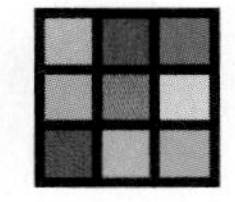

These findings illustrate the important role that observational learning plays in alleviating the effects of culture shock. Observation initially enables us to perform behaviors appropriate to our own cultures, but later can help us adapt to the demands of a rapidly changing world.

## Observational Learning: Some Practical Applications

As you can see from the previous discussions, the effects of observational learning on our behavior can indeed be powerful—and not always for the good. For example, observational learning may contribute to the development of unhealthy behaviors, including smoking, especially among adolescents (Hahn et al., 1990). Because acceptance by peers is so important to persons in this age group, it is possible that observing peers who smoke contributes to teenagers' own decisions to start smoking (Hawkins, Catalano, & Miller, 1992). Some evidence seems to indicate this is true. In one study, Aloise-Young, Graham, and Hansen (1994) surveyed several thousand seventh graders to assess their smoking habits and the smoking habits of their peers. They also asked participants if they cared how their friends would react if they used drugs or alcohol. Finally, they assessed whether each student was already a member of a social group ("group members") or not ("outsiders"). Then, during the following school year, they surveyed the students as eighth graders to determine their smoking status. Which of these students were most likely to have started smoking? Because peer acceptance is so important to twelve- and thirteen-year-olds, Aloise-Young and her colleagues predicted that the outsiders, teens who had not yet been accepted into a friendship group, would be influenced to a greater extent by the behavior of their peers than would teens already in a friendship group. These predictions were confirmed. The results showed that the outsiders were much more likely to emulate the behavior of others—and hence to begin smoking—than participants who were group members. In fact, outsiders whose best friend smoked in the seventh grade were twice as likely to begin smoking than outsiders whose friends did not smoke. In contrast, this pattern of

**Figure 5.23**
**Modeling Appropriate Behaviors Can Make a Difference**

People, particularly young persons, can often be influenced in positive ways when they have appropriate role models to emulate.

peer influence was not evident among teens who were already part of a group.

Although the results of this study highlight the potential negative effects of observational learning, there is a large body of evidence showing that peer influence can also be used to promote more productive behaviors (see Figure 5.23). In one interesting study, Werts, Caldwell, and Wolery (1996) examined whether mildly retarded children enrolled in a regular classroom could acquire skills by having their nonhandicapped peers model the skills for them. The skills included spelling their name, using a calculator to perform simple arithmetic, and sharpening a pencil. Each of the skills was broken down into simpler sets of tasks that the peer tutors learned to perform and describe accurately. The students were required to master performance on one set of tasks before moving on to the next step in the chain. Through this procedure, each participant acquired useful skills in a relatively short period of time (less than a month). It is noteworthy that the time the peers spent modeling the behaviors averaged about five minutes per day—suggesting that observational learning can be an efficient tool in the learning process. To summarize, then, observational learning plays an important role in many aspects of behavior.

**REVIEW QUESTIONS**

- What is observational learning?
- What factors determine the extent to which we acquire new information through observational learning?
- In what forms of behavior does observational learning play a role?
- In what ways can observational learning be used to solve problems of everyday life?

## Making Psychology Part of Your Life

### Getting in Shape: Using Principles of Learning to Get Fit and Stay Fit

Although it is well known that keeping fit is important to good health, a report from the U.S. Surgeon General suggests that staying in shape may help offset some less healthy behaviors—such as smoking, drinking alcohol, or overeating. Apparently, people who overindulge but exercise regularly may be less at risk for premature death than people who appear fit but are couch potatoes. Do you need to get back into shape? Lose a pound or twenty? Why not make learning principles a part of your fitness system—the *true* breakfast of champions. Indeed, establishing your fitness program using the learning principles we've discussed in this chapter will help you hit the diet and exercise trail running.

First, it is important to set realistic goals (see Chapter 10 for additional information on goal setting). Don't try to lose all twenty pounds in one week or to run ten miles the first time out. Why not? If you recall our discussion of reinforcement and punishment, you'll recognize that doing so will actually punish your efforts, making it even more difficult for you to stay with your program. If you've tried and failed to stick with a diet or exercise program in the past because of this, you can probably appreciate this point (see Figure 5.24).

Instead, remember that a little can go a long way. So set yourself up for small wins by taking advantage of the principle of *shaping*—rewarding yourself initially with modest rewards for successive approximations in the direction of your ultimate exercise and weight-reduction goals. Then slowly increase the amount of exercise you do or the amount of weight you lose, building on each of your previous successes. Also, take care in your selection of rewards—choose rewards that are desirable but consistent with your goals. For example, if you are trying to lose weight, reward yourself with a movie or clothes with a smaller waist size—not with a hot fudge sundae.

Third, specify the amount and intensity of the exercise you will do or the amount of weight you intend to lose—and write it down. Some people find that it is helpful to chart their progress in order to give themselves accurate and immediate feedback regarding their progress—feedback that will serve to reinforce or punish their behavior. Also, by placing the chart in a prominent place for yourself, your spouse, or other family members to see, you can take advantage of both *positive and negative reinforcement.* For example, you can work to receive the positive attention that will come your way when your chart shows progress. Negative reinforcement may also help keep you on track: Posting your progress publicly may motivate you to work to avoid the negative comments you may get if you are tempted to "take a day off . . . just because."

Fourth, *stimulus control* can help set the stage for healthy responses. So avoid situations in which you may be tempted to consume unhealthy food or beverages; instead, begin going to places and meeting people that are likely to occasion healthy responses. For example, by joining a health club, YMCA, or other *active* organization, you will be more likely to exercise and eat healthily.

Finally, take advantage of the principles of *observational learning* by identifying people with traits and skills that you admire. By observing and then emulating their behavior, you may become more efficient in reaching your goals. So make psychology a part of your fitness system—to get fit and stay fit!

**Figure 5.24**
**Applying Psychology to Stay Fit**

Martial arts champion Billy Blanks has developed a currently popular fitness program called Tae-Bo. Advertised as the "ultimate total body workout," Tae-Bo incorporates aspects of martial arts, dance, and boxing. Blanks has built into the program several features that may help people stick with it over the long run: It can be performed by nearly all persons; there are videotaped workouts of varying lengths and intensities to fit tight schedules and varying levels of fitness; and, perhaps most importantly, people who have tried Tae-Bo say it is fun!

# Summary and Review

## Classical Conditioning: Learning That Some Stimuli Signal Others

- **What is learning?** Learning is any relatively permanent change in behavior (or behavior potential) produced by experience.
- **What is classical conditioning?** Classical conditioning is a form of learning in which neutral stimuli—stimuli initially unable to elicit a particular response—come to elicit that response through their association with stimuli that are naturally able to do so.

- **Upon what factors does acquisition of a classically conditioned response depend?** Acquisition is dependent upon the temporal arrangement of the conditioned stimulus–unconditioned stimulus pairings, the intensity of the CS and UCS relative to other background stimuli, and the familiarity of potentially conditioned stimuli present.
- **What is extinction?** Extinction is the process through which a conditioned stimulus gradually ceases to elicit a conditioned response when it is no longer paired with an unconditioned stimulus. However, this response can be quickly regained through reconditioning.
- **What is the difference between stimulus generalization and stimulus discrimination?** Stimulus generalization allows us to apply our learning to other situations; stimulus discrimination allows us to differentiate among similar but different stimuli.
- **Where in the brain does classical conditioning take place?** Research shows that the cerebellum, a structure in the brain involved in balance and coordination, plays a key role in the formation of simple forms of classically conditioned responses.
- **Is classical conditioning equally easy to establish with all stimuli for all organisms?** Because of biological constraints that exist among different species, types of conditioning readily accomplished by some species are only slowly acquired—or not acquired at all—by others.
- **How do we acquire conditioned taste aversions?** Conditioned taste aversions are usually established when a food or beverage (conditioned stimulus) is paired with a stimulus that naturally leads to feelings of illness (unconditioned stimulus). Conditioned taste aversions can be established after a single CS–UCS pairing.
- **How do modern views of classical conditioning differ from earlier perspectives?** Modern views of classical conditioning emphasize the important role of cognitive processes. A large body of research suggests that conditioning is a complex process in which organisms form representations of the relationships among a variety of factors—including many aspects of the physical setting or context in which the conditioned and unconditioned stimuli are presented.
- **What is blocking?** In blocking, conditioning to one stimulus is prevented by previous conditioning to another stimulus.
- **How can classical conditioning principles solve problems of everyday life?** Basic principles of classical conditioning have been used to solve many everyday problems, including phobias (learned fears) and unexplained instances of drug overdose.

### Key Terms

learning, p. 168 • classical conditioning, p. 170 • stimulus, p. 170 • unconditioned stimulus (UCS), p. 171 • unconditioned response (UCR), p. 171 • conditioned stimulus (CS), p. 171 • conditioned response (CR), p. 171 • acquisition, p. 172 • delay conditioning, p. 172 • trace conditioning, p. 172 • simultaneous conditioning, p. 173 • backward conditioning, p. 173 • extinction, p. 173 • reconditioning, p. 173 • spontaneous recovery, p. 174 • stimulus generalization, p. 174 • stimulus discrimination, p. 174 • biological constraints on learning, p. 177 • conditioned taste aversion, p. 177

## Operant Conditioning: Learning Based on Consequences

- **What is operant conditioning?** In operant conditioning, organisms learn the relationships between certain behaviors and the consequences they produce.
- **What are examples of primary reinforcers? Of conditioned reinforcers?** Primary reinforcers include food, water, and sexual pleasure; conditioned reinforcers include money, status, and praise.
- **Which operant techniques strengthen behavior? Weaken behavior?** Both positive and negative reinforcement strengthen or increase behavior. In contrast, positive and negative punishment are procedures that suppress or weaken behavior.
- **How do negative reinforcement and punishment differ?** Both negative reinforcement and punishment involve aversive events. They differ, however, in terms of their effects on behavior: Negative reinforcement *strengthens* behaviors that allow an organism to avoid or escape from an aversive event, whereas in punishment an aversive event *weakens* the behavior it follows.
- **What are shaping and chaining?** Shaping is useful for establishing new responses by initially reinforcing behaviors that resemble the desired behavior, termed successive approximations. Chaining is a procedure used to establish a complex sequence or chain of behaviors. The final response in the chain is trained first; then, working backwards, earlier responses in the chain are reinforced by the opportunity to perform the last response in the chain, which leads to a reward.
- **How does reward delay affect operant conditioning? What are the effects of procrastination?** When asked to choose between a smaller-but-sooner and a larger-but-later reward, people often choose the latter option, a tendency termed impulsiveness. Avoiding circumstances that trigger the "go" system and enhancing the "know" system may facilitate more rational choices. People exhibit a similar tendency when faced with a choice between performing a smaller, less effortful task now and performing a larger, more effortful task later on: They *procrastinate,* choosing the more delayed alternative, even when it leads to more work. Procrastination has small benefits early on, but these advantages are outweighed later by costs to performance and health.
- **What are schedules of reinforcement?** Schedules of reinforcement are rules that determine the occasion on which a response will be reinforced. Schedules of reinforcement can be time based or event based, fixed or variable. Each schedule of reinforcement produces a characteristic pattern of responding.
- **When is the use of continuous reinforcement desirable?** A continuous reinforcement schedule is desirable for establishing new behaviors; partial or intermittent sched-

ules of reinforcement are more powerful in maintaining behavior.

- **What are concurrent schedules of reinforcement and the matching law?** In a concurrent schedule, an organism's behavior is free to alternate between two or more responses, each of which has its own schedule of reinforcement. The matching law suggests that an organism distributes its behavior between response alternatives in such a way as to maximize the reinforcement it receives from each alternative.
- **What is a discriminative stimulus?** Discriminative stimuli signal the availability of specific consequences if a certain response is made. When a behavior occurs consistently in the presence of a discriminative stimulus, it is said to be under stimulus control.
- **What evidence supports the involvement of cognitive factors in operant conditioning?** Studies of learned helplessness and the presence of a genetically inherited impairment in the ability to experience pleasure, contrast effects, and memory of reward events support the conclusion that cognitive factors play an important role in operant conditioning.
- **Why is knowledge of operant conditioning important?** Procedures based on operant conditioning principles can be applied to address many problems of everyday life—for example, in improving classroom instructional technology; in the application of biofeedback to various health problems; and in the development of interventions to solve community-based problems such as crime, health care, and safety.

#### Key Terms

operant conditioning, p. 183 • reinforcement, p. 183 • positive reinforcers, p. 183 • Premack principle, p. 183 • negative reinforcers, p. 184 • punishment, p. 184 • shaping, p. 187 • chaining, p. 187 • schedules of reinforcement, p. 190 • continuous reinforcement schedule, p. 190 • fixed-interval schedule, p. 190 • variable-interval schedule, p. 191 • fixed-ratio schedule, p. 191 • variable-ratio schedule, p. 191 • concurrent schedule of reinforcement, p. 192 • discriminative stimuli, p. 193 • stimulus control, p. 193 • learned helplessness, p. 195 • hypohedonia, p. 195 • applied behavior analysis, p. 197 • biofeedback, p. 199

### Observational Learning: Learning from the Behavior and Outcomes of Others

- **What is observational learning?** Observational learning is the acquisition of new information, concepts, or forms of behavior through exposure to others and the consequences they experience.
- **What factors determine the extent to which we acquire new information through observational learning?** In order for observational learning to be effective, we must pay attention to those modeling the behavior, remember the modeled speech or action, possess the ability to act on this memory, and have the motivation to do so.
- **In what forms of behavior does observational learning play a role?** Observational learning plays an important role in many types of behavior, including aggression.
- **In what ways can observational learning be used to solve problems of everyday life?** Observational learning can play an important role in work settings; for example, in helping workers interact more effectively with people from different cultural backgrounds. It can also play a role in the development of both appropriate and inappropriate forms of behavior.

#### Key Term

observational learning, p. 200

## Critical Thinking Questions

### Appraisal

Psychologists are moving increasingly toward a cognitive view of the learning process. Do you think this is appropriate, or is there still a role for the views of operant (behavioral) psychologists?

### Controversy

Therapies based on principles of learning, such as the one used by the Giddings program, have drawn mixed reactions from experts. Those who support the Giddings approach base their arguments on its apparent success in preventing teens from committing further violent acts. Critics, however, suggest that it may not be ethical to force juvenile offenders to endure the pain they experience when compelled to participate in reenactments of their crimes. Do you feel this approach to therapy with violent teen offenders is warranted? If so, why? If not, please explain your reasoning.

### Making Psychology Part of Your Life

Knowing something about principles of learning is very useful to persons who wish to get into shape or lose weight. But these are only two ways in which these principles can be applied to solve problems of everyday life. Can you think of others?

Chapter 6

# Memory:

## Of Things Remembered . . . and Forgotten

## CHAPTER OUTLINE

**HUMAN MEMORY: TWO INFLUENTIAL VIEWS 210**

The Atkinson and Shiffrin Model
Neural Network Models: Parallel Processing of Information

**KINDS OF INFORMATION STORED IN MEMORY 214**

Working Memory: The Workbench of Consciousness

■ RESEARCH METHODS *How Psychologists Study Memory*

Memory for Factual Information: Episodic and Semantic Memory
Memory for Skills: Procedural Memory

**FORGETTING: SOME CONTRASTING VIEWS 225**

Forgetting as a Result of Interference
Forgetting and Retrieval Inhibition

**MEMORY DISTORTION AND MEMORY CONSTRUCTION 226**

Distortion and the Influence of Schemas
Memory Construction: Remembering What Didn't Happen

**MEMORY IN EVERYDAY LIFE 230**

Repression: "What's Too Painful to Remember, We Simply Choose to Forget"
Autobiographical Memory: Remembering the Events of Our Own Lives
Memory for Emotionally Laden Events: Flashbulb Memories and the Effects of Mood on Memory

■ FROM SCIENCE TO PRACTICE *Mental Contamination and the Legal System: Can Jurors Really "Strike It from the Record"?*

**MEMORY AND THE BRAIN: EVIDENCE FROM MEMORY IMPAIRMENTS AND OTHER SOURCES 237**

Amnesia and Other Memory Disorders: Keys for Unlocking Brain–Memory Links
Memory and the Brain: A Modern View

■ BEYOND THE HEADLINES—As Psychologists See It: *Can Chewing Gum Improve Your Memory?*

■ MAKING PSYCHOLOGY PART OF YOUR LIFE *Improving Your Memory: Some Useful Steps*

Remember this: Memory is a very tricky thing. As I write these words, I have the feeling that I was supposed to do something before turning on my computer, but what it was I can't recall. And for the life of me, I can't remember the name of the bright young woman who sat next to me at dinner last night, despite the fact that I was introduced to her and heard her name several times. Yet with little or no effort, I can recall in vivid detail events that happened to me twenty, thirty, or even forty years ago. So yes indeed, the workings of memory are complex and, at first glance, somewhat mysterious (see Figure 6.1 on page 210).

**Figure 6.1**
**Memory: It Really *Is* Tricky!**

As shown here, we sometimes forget what we are about to do just as we are about to do it, but can remember events that happened many years ago with vivid clarity.

(*Source:* CALVIN AND HOBBS. © Watterson. Reprinted with permission of UNIVERSAL PRESS SYNDICATE. All rights reserved.)

If you stop for a moment and try to imagine life without **memory**—our cognitive system (or systems) for storing and retrieving information—you'll see at once that it is truly a crucial aspect of our cognition. If we did not possess memory, we would be unable to remember the past, retain new information, solve problems, or plan for the future. Recognizing the central role of memory, psychologists have studied it systematically for more than one hundred years. In fact, memory was the focus of some of the earliest research in psychology—studies conducted by Hermann Ebbinghaus in the late nineteenth century (1885). Using himself as a subject, Ebbinghaus memorized and then recalled hundreds of *nonsense syllables*—meaningless combinations of letters, such as *teg* or *bom.* Some of his findings about the nature of memory and forgetting have stood the test of time and are valid even today. For example, he found that at first we forget materials we have memorized quite rapidly, but that later, forgetting proceeds more slowly. And he found that *distributed practice,* in which we spread out our efforts to memorize materials over time, is often superior to *massed practice,* in which we attempt to do all our memorizing at once.

While early work by Ebbinghaus and other famous psychologists (e.g., Alfred Binet, who developed one of the first measures of intelligence; see Chapter 11) was quite ingenious, modern research on memory has gone far beyond these simple beginnings. In fact, it is probably correct to say that psychologists now know more about memory than about any other basic aspect of cognition. To provide you with an overview of this intriguing body of knowledge, this chapter will proceed as follows. First, we'll consider the picture of human memory that has emerged from psychological research—a picture suggesting that we possess several different kinds of memory rather than one. Next, we'll explore the nature and operation of each of these aspects of memory—working memory, memory for facts, memory for skills, and memory for events in our own lives. After this, we'll examine *forgetting*—how and why information is lost from memory. Then we'll examine *distortion and construction* in memory and the role these processes play in eyewitness testimony. Next, we'll focus on memory in *everyday life.* Here, we'll examine such topics as *autobiographical memory*—memory of events and experiences in our own lives—and memory for *emotional events.* We'll conclude by exploring memory *impairments* and what these disorders tell us about the biological basis of memory.

**Memory:** Our cognitive system(s) for storing and retrieving information.

**Encoding:** The process through which information is converted into a form that can be entered into memory.

**Storage:** The process through which information is retained in memory.

**Retrieval:** The process through which information stored in memory is located.

## Human Memory: Two Influential Views

Psychologists, like other scientists, often construct *models* of the processes they study. These models are overviews describing the nature and operation of the processes in question. In other words, models seek to meet two of the major goals of science described in Chapter 1: (1) accurate *description* and (2) *explanation*—clarification of *how* the processes being studied operate. Generally, a model is proposed after a large quantity of empirical data have been collected on some topic, and the purpose of the model is both to organize these research findings and to help researchers formulate predictions that can be tested in further studies. Following this standard scientific pattern, psychologists have proposed several models of human memory (e.g., Anderson, 1993; Baddeley & Hitsch, 1994; Raajimakers & Shiffrin, 1981). Here, we'll focus on two such models that have been very influential.

## The Atkinson and Shiffrin Model

Have you ever operated a personal computer? If so, you already know that computers, like people, have memories. In fact, most have two different types of memory: a temporary working memory (*random access memory*—what's open on your desktop at any given moment), and a larger and more permanent memory in which information is stored for longer periods of time (a hard drive). Do the memories of computers operate like those of human beings? Almost certainly not. Consider the following differences: Unless you correctly specify the precise nature and location of information you want to find—for instance, a specific file—computers are unable to recover it. In contrast, you can often find information in your own memory even on the basis of partial information ("I know his name . . . it rhymes with *sky*. . . . Oh yeah, *Frye*, that's it!") Similarly, if information is lost from a computer, it is often permanently gone—or, at least, can be recovered only with considerable difficulty. In contrast, you can fail to remember a fact or piece of information at one time but then remember it readily at another. And you can often remember part of the information you want, even if you can't remember all of it. So, clearly, human memory and computer memory are far from identical.

Yet many researchers have found computer memory to be useful as a working model for human memory—a way of thinking about it generally. And this basic analogy played a key role in a highly influential model of memory proposed by Atkinson and Shiffrin (1968), sometimes known as the *modal model* of memory. These researchers noted that both human memory and computer memory must accomplish three basic tasks: (1) **encoding**—converting information into a form that can be entered into memory; (2) **storage**—somehow retaining information over varying periods of time; and (3) **retrieval**—locating and accessing specific information when it is needed at later times. Taking note of this basic fact, Atkinson and Shiffrin went on to propose a model of human memory similar to the one shown in Figure 6.2.

Let's consider storage first. As you can see from Figure 6.2, the model proposed by Atkinson and

**Figure 6.2**
**Human Memory: One Influential View**

According to a model proposed by Atkinson and Shiffrin (1968), we possess three basic memory systems: sensory memory, short-term memory, and long-term memory. Each of these systems must deal with the tasks of encoding information, storing it, and retrieving it when needed.
(*Source:* Based on suggestions by Atkinson & Shiffrin, 1968.)

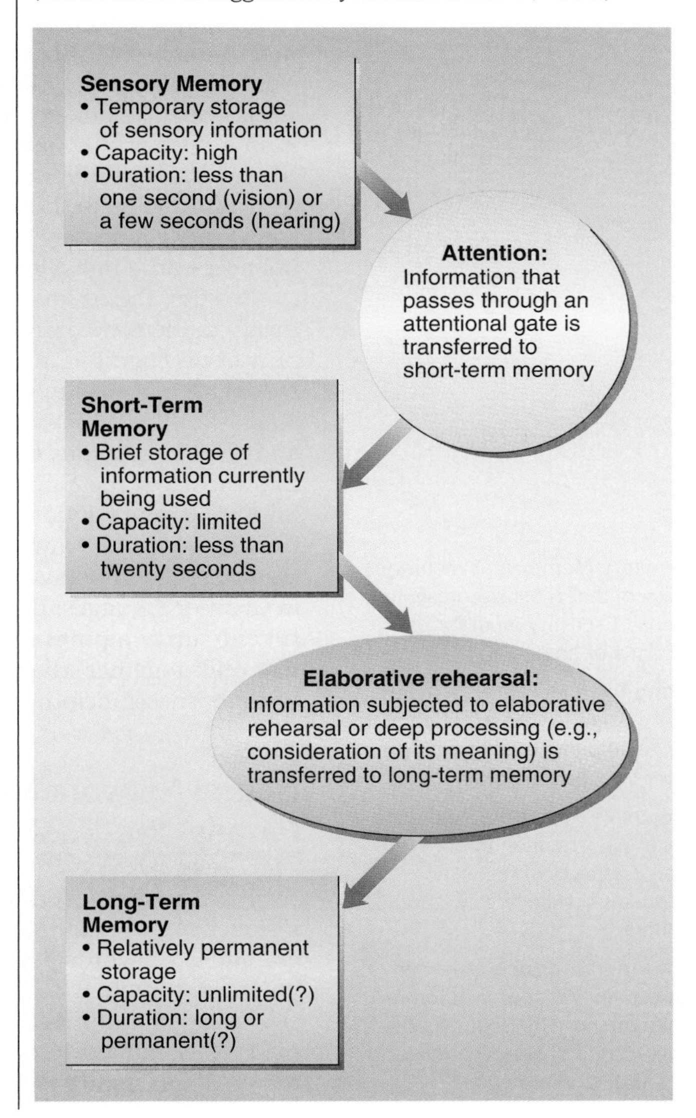

Shiffrin suggests that we possess three distinct systems for storing information. One of these, known as **sensory memory,** provides temporary storage of information brought to us by our senses. If you've ever watched someone wave a flashlight in a dark room and perceived trails of light behind it, you are familiar with the operation of sensory memory. A second type of memory is known as *short-term memory.* (As we'll soon see, psychologists now usually refer to this kind of memory as *working memory.*) Short-term memory holds relatively small amounts of information for brief periods of time, usually thirty seconds or less. This is the memory system you use when you look up a phone number and dial it.

Our third memory system, **long-term memory,** allows us to retain vast amounts of information for very long periods of time. It is this memory system that permits you to remember events that happened a few hours ago, yesterday, last month—or many years in the past. And it is long-term memory that allows you to remember factual information such as the capital of your state, the name of the president, and the information in this book.

How does information move from one memory system to another? Atkinson and Shiffrin proposed that this involves the operation of *active control processes* that act as filters, determining which information will be retained. Information in sensory memory enters short-term memory when it becomes the focus of our attention, whereas sensory impressions that do not engage attention fade and quickly disappear. So, where memory is concerned, **selective attention**—our ability to pay attention to only some aspects of the world around us while largely ignoring others—often plays a crucial role (Johnston, McCann, & Remington, 1995; Posner & Peterson, 1990). In contrast, information in short-term memory enters long-term storage through *elaborative rehearsal*—when we think about its meaning and relate it to other information already in long-term memory. Unless we engage in such cognitive effort, information in short-term memory, too, quickly fades away and is lost. In contrast, merely repeating information silently to ourselves (*maintenance rehearsal*) does not necessarily move information from short-term to long-term memory.

In sum, the Atkinson and Shiffrin model linked the study of human memory firmly to the general **information-processing perspective** that is an important aspect of all cognitive psychology today. Moreover, two of the basic ideas of this model have been supported by research findings and so remain influential: (1) the suggestion that memory involves encoding, storage, and retrieval of information; and (2) the basic idea that we possess several different kinds or types of memory. In these ways, the model proposed by Atkinson and Shiffrin clearly represents an important contribution to our understanding of memory, and that's why I have presented it here. However, recent advances in memory research, combined with the improved understanding of how the human brain functions, which I described in Chapter 2, suggest that the computer analogy can take us only so far and is useful only up to a point. Let's turn, therefore, to the modern view of memory—one that pulls together advances in memory research and in our understanding of how consciousness (including memory) emerges from the functioning of the brain.

**Sensory Memory:** A memory system that retains representations of sensory input for brief periods of time.

**Long-Term Memory:** A memory system for the retention of large amounts of information over long periods of time.

**Selective Attention:** Our ability to pay attention to only some aspects of the world around us while largely ignoring others.

**Information-Processing Perspective:** An approach to human memory that emphasizes the encoding, storage, and later retrieval of information.

## Neural Network Models: Parallel Processing of Information

As you read these words, you are performing some amazing feats of memory. For instance, you are able to recognize each word very quickly (most of us can read several hundred words per minute) and to understand its meaning. This means that you must somehow recognize each letter and the patterns these letters make (specific words), and must do this for literally thousands of different words as you read. How can we account for the speed with which we can accomplish this and many other cognitive tasks? The answer proposed by many psychologists is through the kind of *parallel processing* described in Chapter 2.

As I noted in that discussion, modern computers are *serial* devices: They work on information one step at a time. In contrast, our brains appear to process information in a *parallel* fashion; this means that many *modules*—collections of interconnected neurons—process information in different ways simultaneously. These modules may be scattered widely at different locations in the brain. Moreover, each may work on a different aspect of a task. The more complex the task, the greater the number of modules that are called into operation. The result is that even very complex tasks, such as reading the words on this page, can be handled very quickly, because different aspects of them are performed at the same time. In contrast, computers work in a serial manner, working on one step at a time, and this can result in slower performance, especially for complex tasks.

**Neural Network Models:** Models of memory that describe parallel (simultaneous) processing of information by numerous neural modules in the brain; each of these processing units is dedicated to a specific task, and all are interconnected.

What does this imply with respect to memory? First, that our memories don't operate in a sequential manner in which each letter and then each pattern of letters is compared with the contents of our memory for a match. This would be far too slow. Instead, we engage in parallel processing, in which all the letters, and many words too, are processed at the same time. How can we accomplish this? According to **neural network models** of memory, through the operation of large numbers of processing units (modules) in our brains. Each of these processing units is dedicated to a specific task. For instance, one neural network model (McClelland & Rumelhart, 1981), suggests that we possess processors for 26 different letters, 16 letter features, and more than 1,000 words. So when we encounter a string of letters such as *pen,* these neurons are activated in parallel—at the same time. The letter units recognize the letters, and the word units recognize the combination of letters, and all of this occurs simultaneously and at lightning speed (see Figure 6.3).

Neural network models suggest that it is the rich interconnectedness of our neural units that accounts for our ability to process information so quickly. These models also propose that information in memory is not located in a specific place within the brain; rather, it is represented by patterns of activation that spread over many processing units and by the strength of the activation across these various

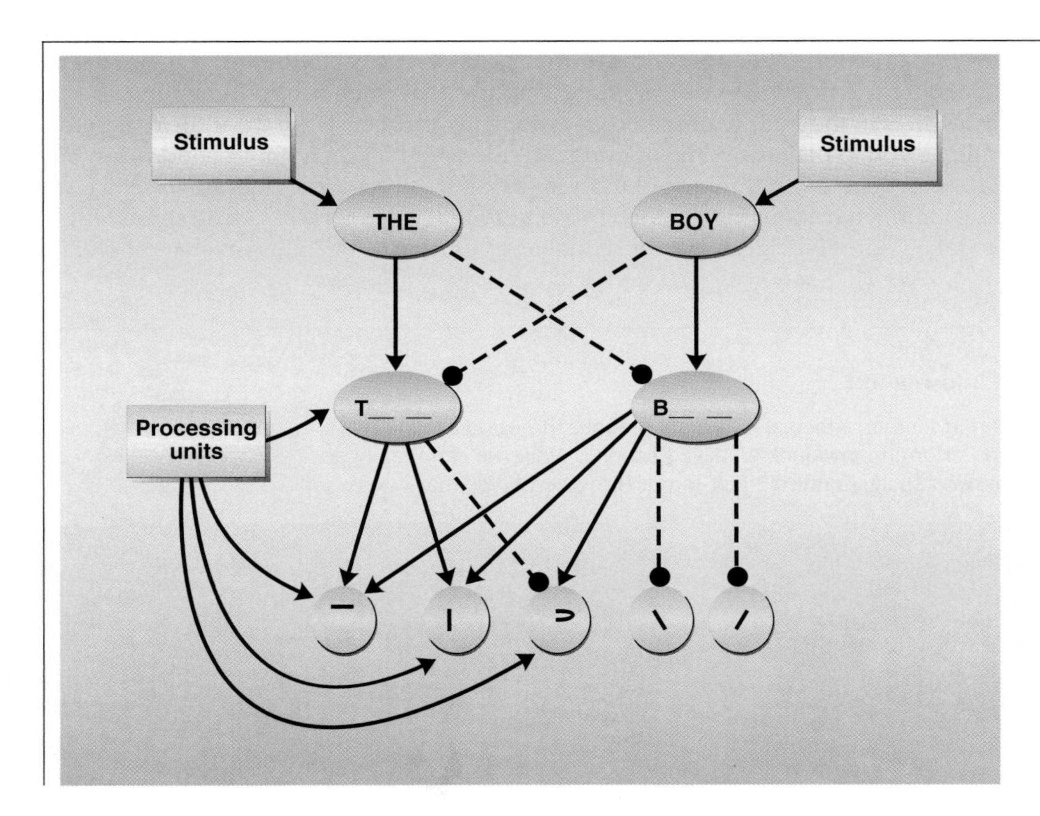


**Figure 6.3**
**Neural Network Models of Memory**

According to neural network models, we possess processing units (neurons or neuron-like units) that process incoming information in parallel, simultaneously. This permits us to handle information with impressive speed.
(*Source:* Adapted from Haberlandt, 1999.)

units. Perhaps the following analogy, offered by Lindsay and Reed (1995), will help: Think of neural networks as being like a spiderweb with millions of strands connecting various units. The tighter these strands, the stronger the connections among various units. Incoming information "pulls" on certain strands, thus activating other units, just as a fly that lands on a spider's web sends vibrations along the strands to other locations—including the center, where the spider is located. No analogy is perfect, and this one certainly isn't, but it may help you to grasp the nature of this model of memory.

**REVIEW QUESTIONS**

- According to the Atkinson and Shiffrin model, what basic tasks are carried out by memory?
- What are sensory memory, short-term memory, and long-term memory?
- What is parallel processing, and what role does it play in memory?

## Kinds of Information Stored in Memory

As you already know from your own experience, our memories hold many kinds of information. Some of it is factual; for instance, you heard today that one of your good friends is moving to another town, and you remember this information and think about it as you drive to work. Similarly, you have a vast store of information we might term "general knowledge"—everything from "The earth revolves around the sun" to "Hawaii is located in the Pacific Ocean, somewhere between California and China." But your memory holds much more than factual information. Can you play a musical instrument? Ride a bicycle? Type on a keyboard by touch? If so, you realize that you also have another, distinctly different type of information stored in memory—information that allows you to perform such activities. And here's the interesting point: While you can state verbally that your friend is moving or that Hawaii is in the middle of the ocean, you really can't describe the information that allows you to play the piano or guitar, to ride your bicycle without hands (don't do it!), or type without thinking of individual keys, as I'm doing right now (see Figure 6.4). And what about information in memory that tells you when to do something—to take your medicine, leave for school or work, and so on? This is yet another kind

**Figure 6.4**
**Memory for Different Kinds of Information**

We store many kinds of information in memory–factual information about the world around us, and information that permits us to perform many kinds of skilled actions. While we can readily describe the first type of information, we usually find it difficult to put the second type into words.

of information stored in memory until it is needed. So memory actually holds several kinds of information. Does this mean that we have several kinds of memory? Psychologists are still debating this issue. Some believe that in fact there are distinct systems, each specialized for storing a specific kind of information; others believe that there is only one system, capable of dealing with many types of information (see, e.g., Haberlandt, 1999). Putting that important issue aside, we'll now examine the kinds of information stored in memory. This, in turn, will help us develop a clearer picture of memory itself.

**Working Memory:** A memory system that holds information we are processing at the moment; formerly called *short-term memory.* Recent findings suggest that working memory involves more complex levels and forms of processing than was previously believed.

**Serial Position Curve:** The greater accuracy of recall of words or other information early and late in a list of information than of words or information in the middle of the list.

Web Link: *Human Memory Experiments*

## Working Memory: The Workbench of Consciousness

I like all kinds of food, so I purposely seek out restaurants serving dishes from around the world. Afghanistan, Iran, Ethiopia, Hungary—you name it, I've tried it. In these restaurants I often ask the waitpersons how to say "Thank you" or "Please" in their native languages. When they tell me, I repeat the word or phrase, and they usually say, "Good!" But here's the problem: A few minutes later, I have forgotten the information entirely and have to ask for it once again. What's going on here? How can I repeat the words I have heard immediately but be unable to do so a few minutes later? The answer involves the operation of what psychologists term **working memory.** Initially, this term and the phrase *short-term memory* were used interchangeably, but now memory experts generally distinguish between them. Short-term memory, as we saw earlier, refers to the temporary storage of information. In contrast, the term *working memory* involves both storage capacity *and* the capacity to transform (process) information held in this memory system. In a sense, working memory is the workbench of consciousness—the "place" where information we are using right now is held and processed. Let's take a look first at how working memory operates, and then at an influential model that describes its basic nature.

**EARLY RESEARCH ON WORKING MEMORY** Initial research on working memory focused on two questions: Does it exist, and how much can it hold? Evidence for the existence of this kind of memory system was soon provided by several findings, but the most important of these involved what is known as the **serial position curve.** The serial position curve has to do with the fact that when we memorize a list of words (or other stimuli), the words at the beginning *and* at the end of the list are remembered better than words in the middle (see Figure 6.5). Why does this effect occur? One possible answer, supported by the results of many studies, involves the existence of two memory systems—one that holds information for a few seconds and another that stores information for longer periods of time. You remember very well the last words you heard—a *recency effect*—because they are still present in working memory when you are asked to recall them. And you remember the words at the start of the list because they have already been entered into long-term memory. Words in the middle, in contrast, have vanished

**Figure 6.5**
**The Serial Position Curve**

When people try to recall a list of unrelated words, they usually remember more words from the beginning and end of the list than from the middle. This serial position curve provides evidence for the existence of two distinct memory systems, short-term (working) memory and long-term memory.

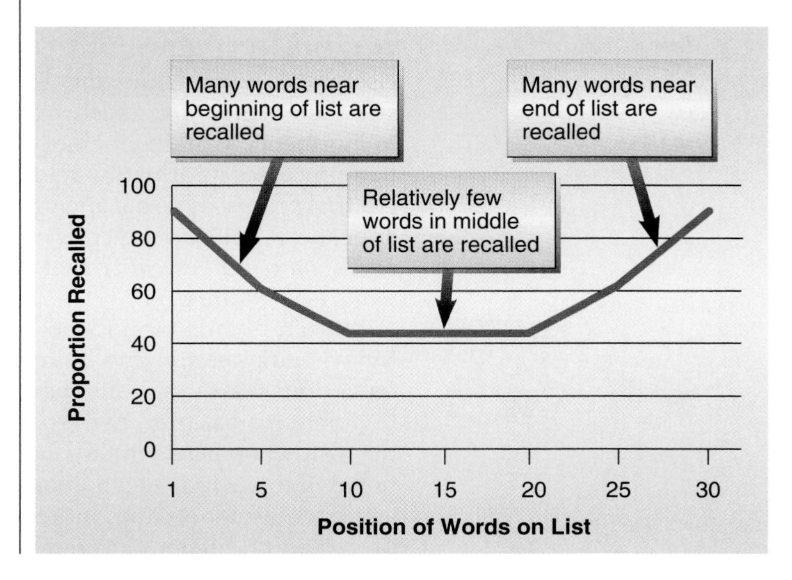

**Chunk:** Items containing several separate bits of information.

from working memory and are not present in long-term memory. The result? You remember few of them at this point in time.

But assuming that working memory exists, how much can it hold? Research findings again suggest a clear answer: As a storage system, working memory can hold only about seven (plus or minus two) discrete items. Beyond that point the system becomes overloaded, and if new information enters, existing information is lost (e.g., Miller, 1956). However, each of these "items " can contain several separate bits of information—bits that are somehow related and can be grouped together into meaningful units. When this is the case, each piece of information is described as a **chunk,** and the total amount of information held in chunks can be quite large. For example, consider the following list of letters: IBFIMBWBMATWIAC. After hearing or reading it once, how many could you remember? Probably no more than about seven. But imagine that instead, the letters were presented as follows: FBI, IBM, BMW, TWA, CIA. Could you remember more now? In all likelihood you could, because now the letters are grouped in meaningful chunks—the initials of famous organizations. Because of the process of *chunking,* working memory can hold a larger amount of information than you might guess, even though it can retain only seven to nine separate items at once.

**PROCESSING IN WORKING MEMORY: THERE'S A LOT GOING ON!** By the 1970s, psychologists were convinced that a short-term memory system exists, and that it is a system for holding small amounts of information for brief periods of time—period. Research conducted since then, however, points to the conclusion that our memory system for short-term storage is more than just a passive "holding area"; on the contrary, active processing of information occurs in it as well. This is why psychologists now use the term *working memory*—it suggests that something active is happening. And, in fact, it is. For example, it is clear that working memory can carry out simple computations, such as adding numbers (e.g., Anderson, Reder, & Lebiere, 1996; Posner & Rossman, 1965). Similarly, working memory plays a key role in sentence comprehension, allowing us, for instance, to tell what the word *it* refers to even in a long sentence like this: "*One example used to illustrate the function of working memory is the storage of a telephone number between the time it is looked up in a phone book and the time it is dialed.*" As you read this sentence, you know that the word *it* refers to the telephone number, and it is working memory that allows you to do this.

Other findings indicate that working memory performs many tasks through the kind of parallel processing described above—as information enters working memory, it is processed in several ways at once. In short, working memory is much more than a simple short-term holding place for limited amounts of information: It is where, in a sense, memory meets ongoing consciousness.

Web Link: *Spatial Short Term Memory Pinpointed in Human Brain*

**THE MULTIPLE COMPONENTS MODEL OF WORKING MEMORY** How, precisely, does working memory operate? While there's not total agreement on this issue, there is growing evidence for a model proposed by Baddeley (1992). According to this theory, working memory consists of three major parts: (1) a *phonological loop* that processes information relating to the sounds of words; (2) a *visuospatial sketch pad* that processes visual and spatial information (i.e., information about the visual appearance of objects, such as color and shape and where they are located in space); and (3) a *central executive* that supervises and coordinates the other two components (see Figure 6.6).

Several kinds of evidence offer support for this view of working memory. Many studies employing *neuroimaging*—scans of people's brains while they work on various tasks—indicate that spatial and phonological information is processed in different areas (e.g., Awh et al., 1996, 1999; Jonides, 1995). This finding supports the distinction between the phonological loop and visuospatial sketch pad. Additional findings indicate that the visuospatial sketch pad processes both visual and spatial information and, moreover, that these two kinds of information may be processed at different locations in the brain (e.g., Smith & Jonides, 1997). Finally, very recent research (e.g., Awh et al., 1999) has even, through brain-imaging techniques, been able to observe specific regions of the brain in which spatial information (e.g., the location of target stimuli within a visual field) is rehearsed, and so retained, in working memory.

What about the central executive—the component that regulates the other activities of working memory—how do we know that it exists too? One line of evidence supporting the existence of the central executive involves a *concurrent task paradigm* in which participants work on two tasks at the same time: a primary task such as adding digits (e.g., 13 + 18 + 13 + 21 + 13 + 25 = ?) *and,* at the same time, a distracting second task—for example, generating items at random from familiar item sets such as the alphabet or a set of ten numbers, or pushing buttons in a specific sequence (e.g., Logie, Gilhooly, & Wynn, 1994). The reasoning is that the more similar the distracting task is to the primary task, the more it will disrupt the planning and control functions of the central executive, and so the poorer the performance on the primary task will be. This is precisely what happens.

**Figure 6.6**
**The Multiple Components Model of Working Memory**

One modern model of working memory suggests that it consists of the distinct components shown here.
(*Source:* Based on suggestions by Baddeley, 1992.)

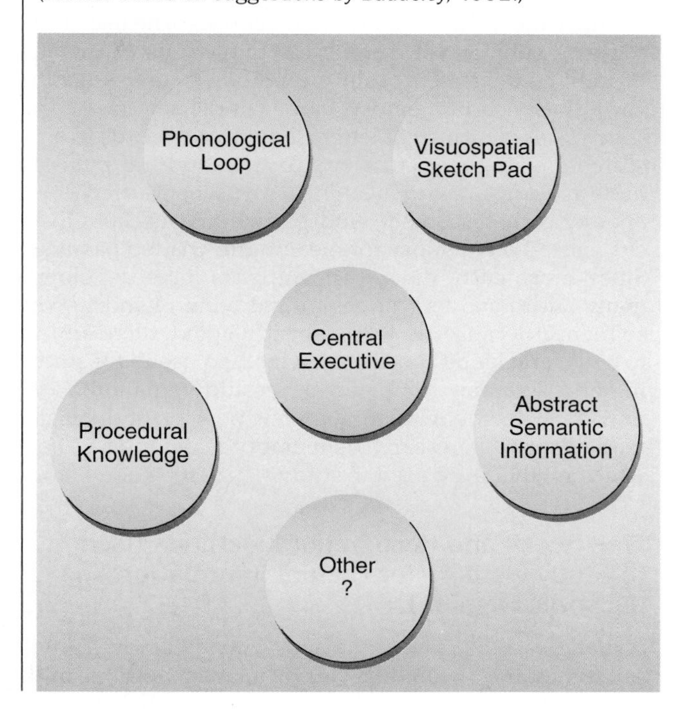


Other evidence for the existence of the central executive is provided by research on individuals who have suffered extensive injury to the frontal lobes—where the executive function is, presumably, centered. Such persons, described as suffering from the *dysexecutive syndrome,* are unable to make decisions: They sit for hours choosing a meal in a restaurant, are easily distracted, and show a tendency toward *perseveration*—they continue to pursue an initial goal instead of switching to other goals once the first one is met. All these effects are consistent with the view that working memory includes a central executive that plays a key role in coordinating a wide range of mental processes.

Where does all this leave us? With a view of working memory quite different from that accepted by psychologists ten years ago. At present, working memory is viewed as an aspect of memory capable of performing many different functions and of processing many kinds of information. It seems to contain at least the component systems proposed by Baddeley (1992), and possibly others as well (e.g., Romani & Martin, 1999). In a sense, our view of working memory has expanded so much that some experts now view it as involving all aspects of cognition (Shiffrin, 1993). Whether this is true or not, it is clear that working memory is a very important aspect of our ability to store, retrieve, and use information.

Before we go any farther, we should pause and address a question you may already have begun to ask: Just how do psychologists gather the kind of information we have just reviewed? How, in short, do they go about studying memory? For information on this issue, please see the following **Research Methods** section.

## REVIEW QUESTIONS

- What is the serial position curve, and why does it support the existence of working memory?
- What tasks does working memory perform?
- What is the multiple component model of working memory?

## Research Methods: How Psychologists Study Memory

When Ebbinghaus began the systematic study of memory more than one hundred years ago, he used himself as a subject; yet despite the limitations of this approach, he devised ingenious methods for investigating various aspects of memory—for example, the use of *nonsense syllables,* strings of letters that are not words in a researcher's language, to allow for the study of memory quite apart from word meanings. And when Alfred Binet, another early researcher, studied memory, he chose to focus instead on memory for meaningful written passages. Since those early days, psychologists have developed many additional techniques for studying memory. Why so many? Because, as we've already noted, there appear to be several kinds of memory; a method useful for studying one type may not be ideal for studying another. I'll now provide you with an overview of some of the major methods used in research on memory, explaining, as I do, which methods are used to study which type of memory.

### Free Recall and Recognition: Methods Used to Study Memory for Factual Information (Episodic Memory)

Sometimes, when I leave the house, my wife, Sandra, will say something like "While you're out, pick up some milk, bread, cheese, carrots—and, oh yes, some baking soda and some eggs." If I don't take the time to write these items down, I am faced with a *free recall* situation when I get to the store: I must try to remember the items I am supposed to buy (see Figure 6.7). This basic method is used by psychologists in many studies on memory for factual information. In these free-recall studies, participants are presented with some items (usually words) and later are asked to recall them in any order. The more they get right, the higher their performance.

A related method involves *recognition:* Instead of being asked to generate the items, research participants are shown stimuli they have seen before, plus other distractor items, and are asked to indicate which ones they have seen before—which ones are "old" items and which are "new." The more "old" items participants identify correctly, the better their memory score.

**Figure 6.7**
**Free Recall: One Measure of Memory**

Any time you go to a supermarket without a list and try to remember the items you are supposed to buy, you are engaging in *free recall.* This is one basic technique used by psychologists to measure episodic memory.

### Sentence Verification Task: A Technique for Studying Semantic Memory

We all have a vast store of information that we cannot remember acquiring at a specific time or place. For instance, when did you learn that the sun rises in the east, or that Coca-Cola and Pepsi-Cola are both soft drinks? Probably, you don't know: Such information is a part of a general store of knowledge we possess. To study memory for such general knowledge (termed *semantic memory*), psychologists use other methods designed to test how much information people retain—information gained through life experiences rather than studied in the laboratory. One technique for doing this is the *sentence verification task.* Here, participants are shown sentences and asked to indicate whether they are true or false. The faster people respond, it is reasoned, the better their memory for information relevant to these sentences. For instance, you would probably respond more quickly to "A Honda is a car" than to "Addis Ababa is the capital of Ethiopia." (It is.) Through this and related types of tests, psychologists assess semantic memory, or memory for general information.

### Priming: Measuring Memory for Information We Can't Report Verbally

As I noted earlier, we store in memory lots of information that we can't readily describe in words—for instance, information necessary for the performance of skilled actions such as riding a bicycle or playing the piano. Similarly, we often have information in memory of which we are quite unaware; it's there, but we don't know we possess it. Together, these kinds of memory are sometimes described as *implicit memory;* such memory is present, but we can't state it in words. (In contrast, we *can* state information in *explicit* memory in words; semantic memory is one kind of explicit memory.) How can we measure implicit memory? One technique involves *priming.* In this procedure, research participants are first exposed to some stimuli (e.g., a list of words, such as *hotel, river, stadium*). Then they are shown parts of these words (e.g., *hot, riv, stad*) along with parts of other words they have *not* seen, and are asked to complete the words. Generally, words they have seen previously have an advantage—participants complete them more quickly or accurately than the new words. Yet, if asked, participants are often unaware of this and believe they have simply guessed. So priming is one way of finding evidence that memory holds information we can't readily describe.

### Neuroimaging: Techniques for Studying the Biological Bases of Memory

I have already described some neuroimaging procedures in Chapter 2 and earlier in this chapter. These techniques involve forming images (scans) of people's brains as they work on various tasks. If the tasks are chosen carefully so as to involve certain aspects of memory, information can be obtained on which parts of the brain are involved in these aspects of memory. One commonly used procedure involves PET imaging. As we saw in Chapter 2, for a PET scan, technicians inject harmless radioactive substances into the bloodstream. Because areas of the brain that are busy working use more blood, this allows researchers to see which parts are involved in various mental tasks. As we'll see in later sections, psychologists have learned a great deal about the biological bases of memory through PET scans and other techniques for creating images of the brain as it works.

These are not the only methods used by psychologists to study memory—far from it. But they are among the most basic, and they play a role in much of the information I will present throughout this chapter.

## Memory for Factual Information: Episodic and Semantic Memory

Now that we've examined some of the techniques used by psychologists to study memory, let's return to our discussion of the different kinds of information stored in memory. One important type involves factual information. Memory for such information is sometimes termed *explicit* or *declarative memory,* because we can bring it into consciousness and report it verbally. It consists of two major types: **episodic memory** and **semantic memory.** Episodic memory holds information we acquired at a specific time and place; it is the kind of memory that allows you to go back in time and to remember specific thoughts or experiences you had in the past. This is the kind of memory studied by psychologists in experiments in which participants are presented with lists of words, numbers, and so on, and later are tested for memory of this information. Semantic memory, in contrast, holds information of a more general nature—information we do not remember acquiring at a specific time or place. Such memory includes the meaning of words, the properties of objects, typical events in everyday life, and the countless facts we all learn during our school years (e.g., $e = mc^2$; George Washington was the first president of the United States; there are about 6 billion people in the world). Let's take a closer look at memory for these two important kinds of information.

**EPISODIC MEMORY: SOME FACTORS THAT AFFECT IT** As a student, you have lots of firsthand experience with the functioning of episodic memory. Often, you must commit to memory lists of definitions, terms, or formulas. What can you do to improve such memory? Research on semantic memory suggests that many factors influence it, but that among these the most important are the *amount and spacing of practice.* The first finding seems fairly obvious; the more often we practice information, the more of it we can retain. However, the major gains occur at first, and then further improvements in memory slow down. For this reason, spacing (or distribution) of practice is important too. Spreading out your efforts to memorize information over time is helpful. For instance, two sessions of thirty minutes are often better, in terms of retaining information, than one session of sixty minutes. This suggests that memories somehow consolidate or grow stronger with the passage of time; we'll examine this idea and evidence relating to it shortly.

Another factor that has a powerful effect on retention is the kind of processing we perform. When we study a list of words, we can simply read them or listen to

Audio 6.1: *Levels of Processing View*

**Episodic Memory:** Memory for factual information that we acquired at a specific time.

**Semantic Memory:** A memory system that stores general, abstract knowledge about the world—information we cannot remember acquiring at a specific time and place.

them; or, alternatively, we can think about them in various ways. As you probably know from your own studying, it is possible to read the same pages in a text over and over again without remembering much of the information they contain. However, if you actively think about the material and try to understand it (e.g., its meaning, its relationship to other information), you stand a better chance of remembering it when the exam booklets are handed out.

Two psychologists, Craik and Lockhart (1972), took careful account of this fact in an influential theory of memory known as the **levels of processing view** (Craik & Lockhart, 1972). They suggested that the more deeply information is processed, the more likely it is to be retained. What are these levels of processing like? Shallow processing involves little mental effort and might consist of repeating a word or making a simple sensory judgment about it—for example, do two words or letters look alike? A deeper level of processing might involve more complex comparisons—for example, do two words rhyme? A much deeper level of processing would include attention to meaning—for instance, do two words have the same meaning? Does a word make sense when used in a specific sentence?

Considerable evidence suggests that the deeper the level of processing that takes place when we encounter new information, the more likely the information is to enter long-term memory (e.g., Craik & Tulving, 1975). However, important questions still exist with respect to this model. For example, it is difficult to specify in advance just what constitutes a deep versus a shallow level of processing. Second, it is not clear that a person can read a word over and over again and not be aware of, or think about, its meaning. In fact, several forms of processing may occur at once. So, because of these potential confusions, it is difficult to speak about discrete levels of processing.

Another, and very important, factor that influences episodic memory involves what are known as **retrieval cues**—stimuli that are associated with information stored in memory and so can help bring the information to mind at times when it cannot be recalled spontaneously. Many studies suggest that such cues can often help us remember. Indeed, the more retrieval cues we have, the better our ability to remember information entered into episodic memory (e.g., Tulving & Watking, 1973)—although, as Figure 6.8 suggests, even a large number of retrieval cues is no guarantee that we'll remember something we should remember! Perhaps the most intriguing research on this topic involves what is known as **context-dependent memory:** the fact that material learned in one environment or context is easier to remember in a similar environment or context than in a very different one. Many illustrations of this effect exist, but one of the most intriguing—and unusual—is a study conducted by Godden and Baddeley (1975).

In this experiment, participants were experienced deep-sea divers. They learned a list of words either on the beach or beneath fifteen feet of water. Then they tried to recall the words, either in the same environment in which they had learned them or in the other setting. Results offered clear support for the impact of context—in this case, physical setting. Words learned on land were recalled much better in this location than under water, and vice versa. Interestingly, additional findings suggest that it is not necessary to be in the location or context where information was first entered into long-term memory; merely imagining this setting may be sufficient (Smith, 1979). In other words, we seem capable of generating our own context-related retrieval cues. So, if you study for an exam in your room and then take the exam in a very different setting, it may be helpful to imagine yourself back in your room when you try to remember specific information; doing so may provide you with additional, self-generated retrieval cues.

External cues are not the only ones that can serve as aids to memory, however; a growing body of evidence indicates that our own internal states can sometimes play this role, too. The most general term for this kind of effect is **state-dependent retrieval,** which refers to the fact that it is often easier to recall information stored in long-term memory when our internal state is similar to that which existed when the information was first entered into memory. For example, suppose that while

**Levels of Processing View:** A view of memory suggesting that the greater the effort expended in processing information, the more readily the information will be recalled later.

**Retrieval Cues:** Stimuli associated with information stored in memory that can aid in its retrieval.

**Context-Dependent Memory:** Refers to the fact that information entered into memory in one context or setting is easier to recall in that context than in others.

**State-Dependent Retrieval:** Occurs when aspects of our physical states serve as retrieval cues for information stored in long-term memory.

**Figure 6.8**
**Retrieval Cues: Usually—But Not Always!—Helpful**

Retrieval cues, stimuli associated with information stored in memory, are often helpful in bringing such information to mind. As shown here, however, they don't always work!
(*Source:* CATHY. © Cathy Guisewite. Reprinted with permission of UNIVERSAL PRESS SYNDICATE. )

studying for an exam, you drink lots of coffee. Thus, the effects of caffeine are present while you memorize the information in question. On the day of the test, should you also drink lots of coffee? The answer appears to be yes—and not just for the boost in alertness this may provide. In addition, being in the same physical state may provide you with retrieval cues that may help boost your performance (Eich, 1985). The basic principle that underlies all these effects is sometimes described as the **encoding specificity principle,** which states that retrieval of information is successful to the extent that the retrieval cues match the cues the learner used during the study phase. The more these cues are similar, the more memory is facilitated.

**Encoding Specificity Principle:** Principle stating that retrieval of information is successful to the extent that the retrieval cues match the cues the learner used during the study phase.

**Concept:** A mental category for objects or events that are similar to one another in certain ways.

## SEMANTIC MEMORY: HOW INFORMATION IS ORGANIZED IN MEMORY

Now let's turn to semantic memory—memory of a general nature that we don't remember acquiring at a specific time or in a specific place. Because each of us already possesses a very large amount of information in semantic memory, psychologists have focused primarily on how such information is organized, rather than on how it is entered into memory in the first place. One important element of such organization consists of **concepts**—mental categories for objects or events that are similar to one another in certain ways. For instance, the words *bicycle, airplane, automobile,* and *elevator* are included in the concept for *vehicles* or *means of transportation.* The words *shoes, shirts, jeans,* and *jackets* are included in the concept *clothing.* We'll examine concepts and their role in cognition in detail in Chapter 7, so here we'll just briefly consider their role in semantic memory.

**Figure 6.9**
**Semantic Networks**

Semantic memory contains many concepts; these seem to exist in networks reflecting the relationships between them. One such network is shown here.

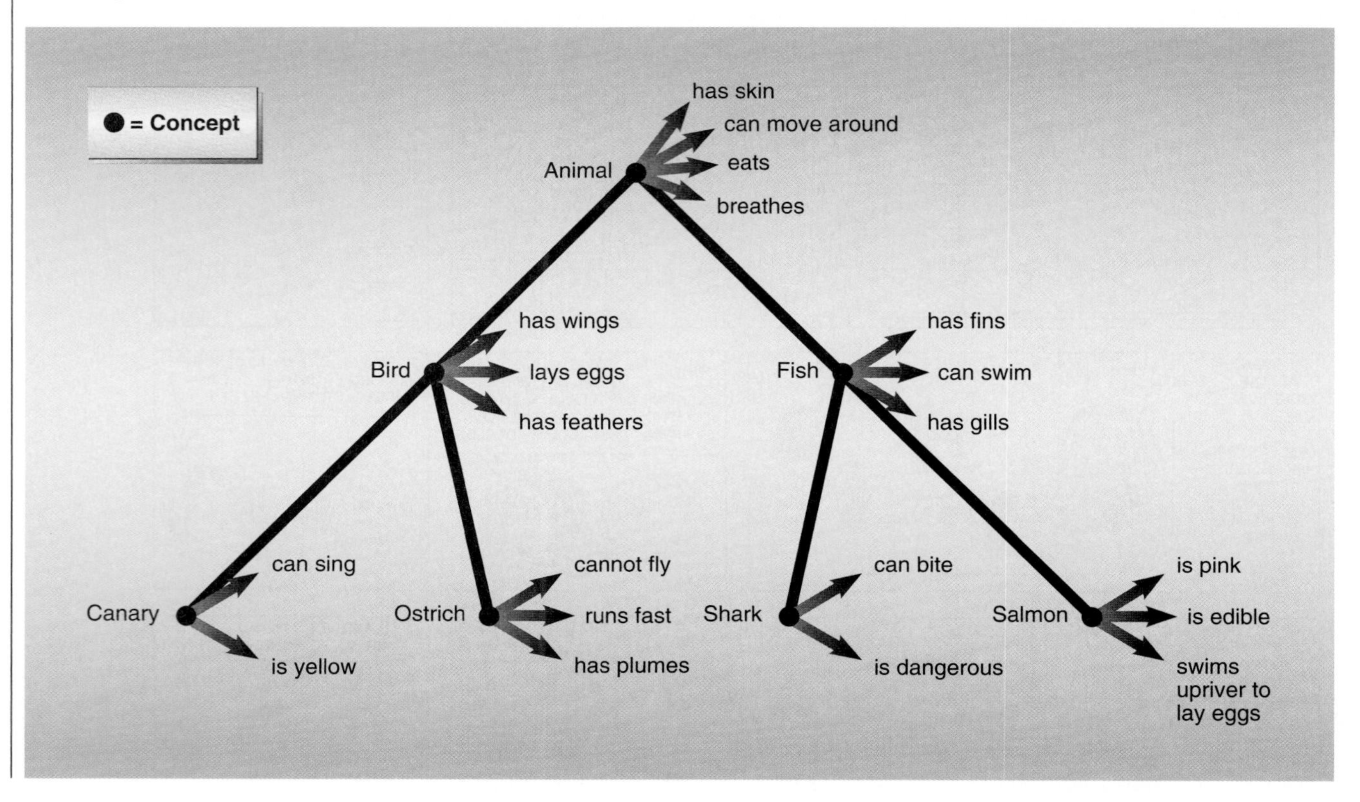


Concepts in semantic memory seem to exist in networks reflecting the relationships between them—semantic networks. One such network is shown in Figure 6.9. As you can readily see, this shows a hierarchy of concepts: *animals* includes both *birds* and *fish*, and *birds*, in turn, includes *ostriches* and *canaries*. Similarly, *fish* includes *sharks* and *salmon;* however, unless the person whose semantic memory is represented here is confused, it does *not* contain *porpoises*, because porpoises are mammals, not fish.

In the network model of semantic memory, the meaning of a concept reflects its links or associations with other, adjoining concepts. Another view is that the meaning of concepts derives from **prototypes**—abstract, idealized representations that capture an average or typical notion of members of the category. For instance, the prototype for *professor* in your semantic memory represents all the professors you have encountered and may suggest that professors are, on average, middle-aged, absent-minded, slightly rumpled looking, and so on. Still another view is that any given concept is represented in memory not in terms of an overall average (a prototype), but in terms of an **exemplar**—an example of the category that the individual can readily bring to mind. So for example, when you read the word *fruit*, what comes to mind? Probably an apple, a pear, or an orange. These are exemplars of the concept *fruit*, and in deciding whether a new object you encounter is a fruit, you may bring one or more of these exemplars to mind and compare the new object to them.

**Prototype:** Abstract, idealized representation that captures an average or typical member of a category of things.

**Exemplar:** An example of a category of things that is readily brought to mind.

One final question: Is there any concrete evidence that episodic memory and semantic memory, which both store factual information, actually differ? There definitely is. In some medical patients, diseases or operations that have damaged certain parts of the brain leave semantic memory intact while diminishing episodic memory, or vice versa (Schachter, 1996). In addition, other research using PET scans or recordings from individual brain cells indicate that different brain regions are active when individuals attempt to recall general information (from semantic memory) as opposed to information they acquired in a specific context (from episodic memory) (e.g., Kounious, 1996). So there do seem to be grounds for the distinction between semantic and episodic memory.

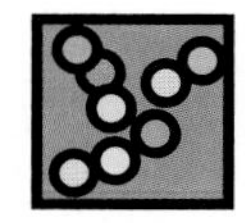

**REVIEW QUESTIONS**

- What are episodic memory and semantic memory?
- What is the level of processing view of memory?
- What are retrieval cues, and what role do they play in memory?
- What are concepts, and what role do they play in semantic memory?

## Memory for Skills: Procedural Memory

Audio 6.2: *Procedural Memory and Performance*

I like to bake bread, and I know from experience that it will turn out well *if* the dough has a certain consistency—not too wet, not too dry. But can I describe in words exactly how the dough has to look—and feel to my hands—in order to produce a delicious loaf? Not really. Similarly, woodworking is one of my hobbies, and when I begin to cut a piece of wood on my table saw, I can "feel" whether the saw will go all the way through or get stuck in the middle almost as soon as I start. Can I tell you how I reach this decision? Again, not really. These and countless other everyday experiences indicate that often we have information in our memories that we can't readily put into words. Our ability to store such information is known as **procedural memory,** or sometimes as *implicit memory.* Both terms are informative: We often know how to perform some action but can't describe this knowledge to others (e.g., can Mark McGwire tell me how he hits so many home runs?), and what we can't put into words is, in one sense, implicit.

Given that information stored in procedural memory can't be described verbally, how can we study it? As we noted in the **Research Methods** section on page 218, one way is through the *priming* effect: the fact that having seen or heard a stimulus once may facilitate our recognizing it on a later occasion, even if we are unaware that this is happening. Some experts on memory refer to the priming effect as a difference between remembering and knowing (Schachter, 1996). *Remembering* means being able to report an event and the circumstances under which it occurred; *knowing* is the familiarity we have with a stimulus even when we can't remember it explicitly—a familiarity that may strongly influence our behavior (e.g., Rajaram, 1993; Tulving, 1989, 1993).

Although priming was first identified by cognitive psychologists interested in memory, some of the most interesting demonstrations of its occurrence have been provided by social psychologists, who are interested in the role it may play in our reactions to other people. For example, consider an intriguing study by Erdley and D'Agostino (1989). These psychologists exposed one group of participants to adjectives related to the trait of honesty *(honorable, truthful, sincere).* The words were flashed on a screen so quickly, that participants were unaware of them—they merely saw a blur. Different words, unrelated to honesty *(what, little, many),* were flashed on the screen for another group of participants. Later, both groups read a description of an imaginary person—one that portrayed her in ambiguous terms. Finally, they rated this person on several dimensions, some of which were related to honesty. Results indicated that the participants exposed to the honesty-related words rated her higher on this trait than those exposed to the neutral words. So, even though participants

**Procedural Memory:** Memory system that retains information we cannot readily express verbally—for example, information necessary to perform skilled motor activities such as riding a bicycle. Also called *implicit memory.*

**Figure 6.10**
**Supermemory at Work**

A few people, such as the famous conductor Arturo Toscanini, seem to possess *supermemory*—they can remember amazing amount of information. Toscanini had memorized the entire musical scores for more than 350 symphonies and operas! For such persons, memory is indeed an impressive skill that they have developed—generally, through much hard work and practice.

were unaware of the words, they were still affected by them through a process of *automatic priming*.

Priming is not the only source of evidence for the existence of procedural memory, however. Additional evidence is provided by the way in which many skills are acquired. Initially, as we learn a skill, we think about what we are doing and can describe our actions and what we are learning verbally. As we master the skill, however, this declarative (explicit) knowledge is replaced by procedural knowledge, and we gradually become less and less able to describe precisely how we perform the actions in question (Anderson, 1993). (Recall our discussion of automatic processing in Chapter 4; procedural memory plays a role in such behavior.)

What about memory itself—can it be viewed as a skill that can be improved? Absolutely; and we'll examine some techniques for improving memory in the **Making Psychology Part of Your Life** section at the end of the chapter. But for now, we should note that memory does indeed improve with practice. For instance, consider the case of J. C., a waiter who was able to remember as many as twenty different orders without writing them down. How did he do this? Two psychologists who studied this individual (Ericsson & Polson, 1988) found that he had devised a scheme of encoding orders in terms of basic categories such as entrée (e.g., chicken, steak), temperature (rare, medium), and starches (e.g., rice, fries). He then used the initial letters of these and other food-related categories to form words and phrases that had meaning for him. Then he used these words or phrases as retrieval cues for the orders. For instance, if someone ordered steak cooked rare, with fries, he might form the phrase "Sue rarely fights." When he got to the kitchen, he translated this back into the order. The point is that over time, J. C. became so good at using this system that he no longer had to think about making up phrases; he did it automatically as he took orders without writing them down—and could concentrate on amusing customers by flaunting his skill before their eyes!

Other people who show what might be termed *supermemory* provide even more dramatic examples of procedural memory in action. For instance, consider this incident: Just before a concert, a musician in the orchestra came to the great conductor Arturo Toscanini and told him that one of the keys on his instrument was broken (see Figure 6.10). Toscanini thought for a moment and then said, "It is all right—that note does not occur in tonight's concert." In a flash, he had somehow examined all of the notes to be played and concluded that the broken key wouldn't matter! Could Toscanini explain how he did this? I doubt it, but instances like this demonstrate the amazing capacities of a well-developed procedural memory.

**REVIEW QUESTIONS**

- What is procedural memory?
- What is priming? Automatic priming?

**Food for Thought**

If stimuli of which we are unaware can sometimes serve as primes for information in memory, can such automatic priming be used by advertisers to induce us to remember—and buy—their products?

## Forgetting: Some Contrasting Views

**Retroactive Interference:** Interference with retention of information already present in memory by new information being entered into memory.

**Proactive Interference:** Interference with the learning or storage of current information by information previously entered into memory.

When are we most aware of memory? Typically, when it fails—when we are unable to remember information that we need at a particular moment. Often, memory seems to let us down just when we need it most—for instance, during an exam! Why does this occur? Why is information entered into long-term memory sometimes lost, at least in part, with the passage of time? Many explanations have been offered, so here we'll focus on the ones that have received most attention.

The earliest view of forgetting was that information entered into long-term memory fades or decays with the passage of time. While this seems to fit with our subjective experience, many studies indicate that the amount of forgetting is *not* simply a function of how much time has elapsed; rather, what happens during that period of time is crucial (e.g., Jenkins & Dallenbach, 1924). For instance, in one unusual study, Minami and Dallenbach (1946) taught cockroaches to avoid a dark compartment by giving them an electric shock whenever they entered it. After the subjects had mastered this simple task, they were either restrained in a paper cone or permitted to wander around a darkened cage at will. Results indicated that the insects permitted to move about showed more forgetting over a given period of time than those who were restrained. So what the roaches did between learning and being tested for memory was more important than the mere passage of time. Perhaps even more surprising, other studies indicated that recall sometimes *improves* over time (e.g., Erdelyi & Kleinbard, 1978). So, early on, psychologists rejected the notion that forgetting stems from passive decay of memories over time and turned instead to the views we'll consider next.

### Forgetting as a Result of Interference

Web Link: *Some Forgetting Curves*

If forgetting is not a function of the passage of time, then what *is* its source? One possibility is that it stems mainly from *interference* between items of information stored in memory. Such interference can take two different forms. In **retroactive interference,** information currently being learned interferes with information already present in memory. If learning how to operate a new computer program causes you to forget how to operate one you learned previously, this is an example of retroactive interference. In **proactive interference,** in contrast, previously learned information present in long-term memory interferes with information you are learning at present. Suppose you learned how to operate one VCR; now you buy a new one, which requires different steps for recording a television program. If you now make mistakes by trying to operate the new VCR in the same way as you did the old one, this constitutes proactive interference (see Figure 6.11).

**Figure 6.11**
**Retroactive and Proactive Interference**

In *retroactive interference,* information currently being learned interferes with the retention of information acquired previously. In *proactive interference,* information learned previously interferes with the retention of new information currently being acquired and entered into memory.

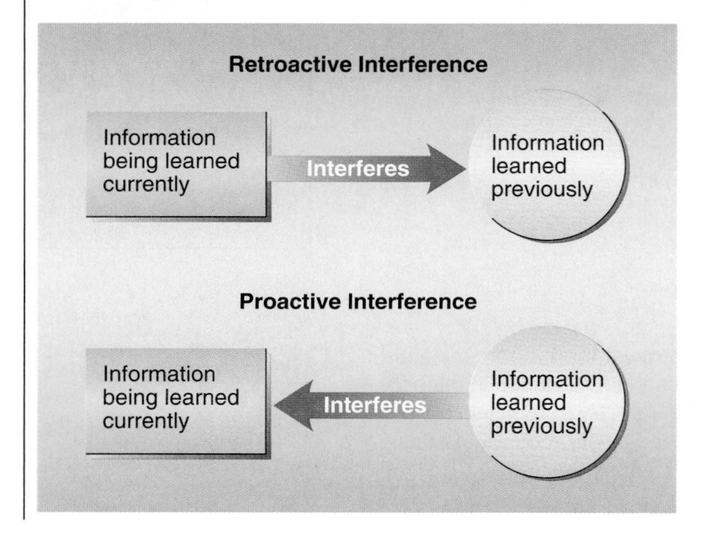


A large body of evidence offers support for the view that interference plays a key role in forgetting from long-term memory (e.g., Tulving & Psotka, 1971). For example, in many laboratory studies, the more similar the words or nonsense syllables participants learn from different lists, the more interference occurs among them, and the poorer their recall of these materials (Gruneberg, Morris, & Sykes, 1988). However, more recent research findings raise complex questions about the view that forgetting derives mainly from interference. First, while interference does seem to play a major role in the forgetting of meaningless materials such as nonsense syllables, it is far less important in forgetting of meaningful passages. Memory for the basic meaning, or *gist*, of such passages is often retained even if the passages are quite similar to one another and would be expected to produce interference (e.g., Haberlandt, 1999). Similarly, for interference to occur, something that is potentially interfering must occur in the period between original learning and testing for memory. Yet forgetting occurs even when research participants learn a single list or even a single item. Such forgetting might be due to interference from sources outside the experiment, but these have proved difficult to identify. Overall, then, interference, which was once viewed as *the* cause of forgetting, is no longer assigned this crucial role by most memory researchers. So what does cause forgetting? Research points to another intriguing possibility.

## Forgetting and Retrieval Inhibition

Suppose I asked you to remember the names of all fifty states in the United States. How many would you get right? Now, instead, imagine that I gave you the names of twenty-five of these states and let you study them. Would that help you remember the remaining ones? Common sense suggests that it would, but research using procedures similar to these indicates that you would actually do *worse;* studying half the states would actually reduce your overall performance (e.g., Brown, 1968). Why? Psychologists explain this seemingly paradoxical finding as follows: When we attempt to remember information in memory, we may recall the items we seek but at the same time generate *inhibition* of other items that we don't try to remember. As a result, these other items become more difficult to remember in the future. So when you study the names of twenty-five states, you generate inhibition that blocks recall of the other twenty-five states. In short, the act of retrieval itself can cause forgetting—not of the information you recall, but of other, related information. This phenomenon is known as **retrieval inhibition,** and its occurrence has been observed in several experiments (e.g., Anderson, Bjork, & Bjork, 1994; Anderson & Spellman, 1995). The results of these investigations suggest that inhibition produced when we actively try to retrieve information from memory may play an important role in forgetting.

In sum, at present psychologists believe that forgetting stems from several different factors. Interference may play a role, especially with respect to relatively meaningless materials; but other complex processes, such as inhibition generated by retrieval itself, may also contribute to our inability to recall information we would like to remember. We'll examine another view of forgetting—the idea that we *repress* memories we find painful or unpleasant—in a later discussion of memory for emotional events.

**REVIEW QUESTIONS**

- What are retroactive interference and proactive interference? What role do they play in forgetting?
- What is retrieval inhibition?

**Retrieval Inhibition:** The inhibition of information in memory we don't try to remember produced by our retrieval of other, related information.

## Memory Distortion and Memory Construction

What happens to information once it is stored in memory? Our discussion up to this point seems to suggest two possible outcomes: Information is stored in a permanent, unchanging form, or it is forgotten. This is not the entire story, however. A growing body of evidence suggests a third possibility: Information entered into memory is often altered in various ways over time—and these alterations can reduce its accuracy and change its meaning. Such changes take many different forms, but most fall under two major headings: Memory *distortion,* alterations in what is retained and later recalled, and memory *construction,* the addition of information that was not actually present.

## Distortion and the Influence of Schemas

Web Link: *Memory Distortion*

Almost everyone has had firsthand experience with memory distortion. For example, when we look back on our own behavior in various situations, we often tend to perceive it in a favorable light; we remember saying or doing the "right" thing, even if this wasn't quite what happened. Distortion in memory can also occur in response to false or misleading information provided by others. If someone's comments suggest a fact or detail that is not present in our memories, we may add that fact or detail (Loftus, 1992). Unfortunately, such effects often occur during trials, when attorneys pose *leading questions* to witnesses—questions that lead the witnesses to "remember" what the attorneys want them to remember. For example, during a trial, an attorney may ask a witness, "Was the getaway car a light color or a dark color?" The witness may not remember seeing a getaway car, but the question puts subtle pressure on this person to answer—to make a choice. And once the answer is given, it may be incorporated into the witness's memories and may tend to distort them. Unfortunately, such distortions seem to occur even if individuals are warned about them—and offered cash for resisting their influence (Belli & Loftus, 1996)! We'll return to such effects shortly in a discussion of eyewitness testimony.

What accounts for memory distortions? In many cases they seem to involve the operation of **schemas**—structures representing individuals' knowledge and assumptions about aspects of the world (Wyer & Srull, 1994). Schemas are developed through experience and act something like mental scaffolds, providing us with basic frameworks for processing new information and relating it to existing knowledge—including knowledge held in long-term memory.

Once schemas are formed, they exert strong effects on the way information is encoded, stored, and later retrieved. These effects, in turn, can lead to important errors or distortions in memory. Perhaps such effects are most apparent with respect to encoding. Current evidence suggests that when schemas are initially being formed—for example, when you are first learning about the activities, roles, and responsibilities of being a college student—information inconsistent with the newly formed schema is easier to notice and encode than information consistent with it. Such inconsistent information is surprising and thus seems more likely to become the focus of our attention. After the schema has been formed and is well developed, in contrast, information *consistent* with it becomes easier to notice and hence to remember (e.g., Stangor & Ruble, 1989). It is the operation of schemas that, in part, accounts for the fact that in many cases we are more likely to notice and remember information that supports our beliefs about the world than information that challenges them.

Another important cause of distortion in memory involves our motives: We often distort our memories in order to bring them in line with whatever goals we are currently seeking. For example, suppose that you like someone; this may lead you to want to remember positive information about him or her. Conversely, if you dislike someone, you want to remember negative information about this person. Effects of this kind were observed in a careful series of studies conducted by McDonald and Hirt (1997). These researchers had participants watch an interview between two students. The experiments varied participants' liking for one of the two individuals by having this stranger act in a polite, a rude, or a neutral manner. When later asked to recall information about this person's grades (information

**Schemas:** Cognitive frameworks representing our knowledge and assumptions about specific aspects of the world.

**Source Monitoring:** The process of identifying the origins of specific memories.

**Reality Monitoring:** The process of deciding whether specific memories are based on external (real) sources or on internal sources (e.g., imagination, thoughts).

**Eyewitness Testimony:** Information provided by witnesses to crimes or accidents.

that was provided during the interview), those participants who were induced to like the stranger distorted their memories so as to place this person in a more favorable light, whereas those induced to dislike the stranger showed the opposite pattern. In this and many other situations, then, our memories can be distorted by our current motives.

A final way in which memories can be distorted involves confusions concerning the sources of information in memory. We often make errors in **source monitoring**—the process of identifying the origins of specific memories (e.g., Johnson, Hashtroudi, & Lindsay, 1993). In other words, we remember information stored in memory, but we attribute it to the wrong source. For example, you may remember the quotation "Nostalgia is not what it used to be" but attribute it to someone who did not say it, or remember having read it in one source when in fact you read it in another.

A related effect involves **reality monitoring**—the process of deciding whether memories stem from external sources (events we actually experienced) or from internal sources (our imagination or thoughts). Both source monitoring and reality monitoring have important practical effects. For instance, errors in source monitoring may play a role in eyewitness testimony. Eyewitnesses, it turns out, aren't nearly as accurate as is widely believed, and one kind of error they make is attributing information they recall to one source—such as actions by a defendant—rather than to another, such as leading questions by lawyers or police. Errors with respect to reality monitoring have important implications for personal health. I've seen this problem at work with my own mother. She must take many different pills at different times of the day and often can't remember whether she actually took a particular pill or just "remembers" having taken it.

Web Link: *False Memory Syndrome Foundation*

## Memory Construction: Remembering What Didn't Happen

Not only can memories be distorted; they can also be constructed. In other words, people can recall events that did not actually occur, or experiences they never really had. As we'll soon see in a discussion of repression, constructed memories can have important effects; for instance, they can lead to false charges of child sexual abuse, when adults construct memories of such treatment even though it never actually occurred (e.g., Acocella, 1998). Unfortunately, a growing body of research evidence suggests that false memories are both persistent and convincing—people strongly believe that they are real (Brainerd & Reyna, 1998; Reyna & Titcomb, 1996). This, in turn, has important implications for several aspects of the legal system, including eyewitness testimony.

**EYEWITNESS TESTIMONY: IS IT AS ACCURATE AS WE BELIEVE?** **Eyewitness testimony**—evidence given by persons who have witnessed a crime—plays an important role in many trials. At first glance, this makes a great deal of sense: What better source of information about the events of a crime than the persons who actually saw them (see Figure 6.12)? After reading the previous discussions of distortion and construction in memory, however, you may already be wondering about an important question: Is such testimony really accurate?

The answer provided by careful research is clear: Eyewitnesses to crimes are far from infallible. In fact, they often falsely identify innocent persons as criminals (Wells, 1993), make mistakes about important details concerning a crime (Loftus, 1991), and even sometimes report "remembering" events they did not actually see (Haugaard et al., 1991). Why do such errors occur? Not, it appears, because the witnesses are purposely faking their testimony. On the contrary, most people really try to be as accurate as possible. Rather, these errors occur because of several factors that produce distortions in memory. One of these is *suggestibility*—witnesses are sometimes influenced by leading questions and similar techniques used by attorneys or police officers. Errors also occur with respect to *source monitoring*—eyewitnesses often attribute their memories to the wrong source. For instance, they identify a suspect in a police lineup as the person who committed a crime because they remember having seen this individual before and assume this was at the scene of the crime; in fact, the person's face may be familiar because they saw it in an album of mug shots. Another source of error is an effect known as the *illusion of outgroup homogeneity*—the fact that people outside our own group seem more similar in appearance and characteristics than people within our own group; because of this illusion it is easy to identify an outgroup individual incorrectly as the perpetrator of a crime (e.g., Rothgerber, 1997).

Given all these potential sources of error, it is not surprising that eyewitnesses are not nearly as accurate as our legal system assumes. And because jurors and even judges tend to place great weight on the testimony of eyewitnesses, such errors can have serious consequences: Innocent persons may be convicted of crimes they did not commit—or, conversely, persons guilty of serious crimes may be wrongly cleared of the charges against them. Indeed, recent evidence indicates that the single largest factor accounting for such miscarriages of justice is faulty eyewitness testimony (Wells, 1993).

Can anything be done to enhance eyewitnesses' accuracy? Fortunately, research on memory offers some answers, and these have been combined into suggestions for conducting improved interviews with witnesses—interviews that may enhance their ability to remember crucial information accurately (e.g., Geiselman & Fisher, 1997). In such *cognitive interviews* eyewitnesses are asked to report everything they can remember; this provides them with multiple retrieval cues and can increase accuracy of recall. In addition, they are sometimes asked to describe events from different perspectives and in several different orders—not just in the order in which the events actually occurred. These and other steps seem to increase the accuracy of eyewitness testimony, but they are far from a perfect solution, so the basic problem remains.

**Figure 6.12**
**Eyewitnesses: Do They Remember What They See?**

Growing evidence suggests that eyewitnesses are not nearly as accurate in remembering events they have seen as was once believed. Many factors (e.g., source confusion, suggestibility) can distort witnesses' memories and lead them to describe events inaccurately—or even to report seeing events that never took place.

What about hypnosis—can it help to improve eyewitness accuracy? You may have read in your local newspaper about instances in which eyewitnesses have undergone hypnosis in an attempt to increase their recall for the events they presumably saw. Unfortunately, there is little evidence that such procedures work. Eyewitnesses have occasionally reported new information while hypnotized, but it is unclear whether these effects stemmed from hypnosis or from differences in the way the witnesses were questioned while in this state. For example, while hypnotized, some witnesses have been forcefully instructed to "make a real effort" to remember. This kind of urging, rather than hypnosis itself, may have been responsible for improvements in memory—if improvements actually occurred.

To conclude: Existing evidence suggests that eyewitnesses are not as accurate a source of information as the public, attorneys, police, and juries often assume. Several techniques can assist such persons in remembering information they noticed and entered into memory; but if information was never entered into memory in the first place, such procedures will *not* prove helpful. In many cases, then, it is best to view eyewitness testimony as an imperfect and potentially misleading source of information about reality.

REVIEW QUESTIONS

- What are schemas, and what role do they play in memory distortion?
- What are constructed memories?
- What factors potentially reduce the accuracy of eyewitness testimony?

Food for Thought

If eyewitnesses to crimes are often inaccurate, why does the legal system continue to place so much emphasis on their testimony?

## Memory in Everyday Life

Many of the research studies mentioned so far have involved participants' performance of relatively artificial tasks: memorizing nonsense syllables or lists of unrelated words. While we do sometimes perform tasks like these outside the laboratory—for instance, as a student, you sometimes memorize lists of terms or definitions—we generally use memory for very different purposes in our daily lives. Let's see what psychologists have discovered about how memory functions in natural contexts. Three topics are of special interest: *repression* of emotionally traumatic events, *autobiographical memory,* and *memory for emotional events.*

Web Link: *False Memory*

### Repression: "What's Too Painful to Remember, We Simply Choose to Forget"

Do we really do what the words of one old song suggest—actively eliminate from consciousness memories of experiences we find threatening? In other words, do we engage in **repression?** As we'll see in Chapter 12, the concept of repression played a key role in Sigmund Freud's theory of human personality and in his view of the causes of psychological disorders. Freud contended that repressed memories are pushed into hidden recesses of the unconscious mind, where they remain, festering and causing many psychological problems, until they are brought back into consciousness by the efforts of a skilled therapist.

The existence of repression is widely accepted by psychologists and psychiatrists, as well as by society generally (Loftus & Herzog, 1991). Partly because of this fact, it has featured prominently in many dramatic trials focusing on charges of *early childhood sexual abuse.* In these trials, repression has sometimes been offered as an explanation for why the victims failed to remember their terrible experiences until many years later—and remembered them then only as a result of careful questioning, coupled with the application of suggestive techniques, by trained therapists.

Are such claims accurate? And, more to the point, are the "memories" reported by such persons during therapy real? Or, perhaps, are they suggested by the therapists' searching questions? This is a complex question. Many of the cases involved occurred so long ago that concrete, objective evidence is difficult, if not impossible, to obtain. In addition, as noted by Loftus (Loftus & Ketcham, 1994), a leading expert on memory, there are several reasons for viewing at least some of these claims with a healthy degree of skepticism.

**Repression:** The active elimination from consciousness of memories of experiences we find threatening.

First, despite its widespread acceptance, there is still very little scientific evidence to support the theory of repression. Most indications of the existence of repression derive from case studies. While case studies are often fascinating, they do not, as we saw in Chapter 1, provide conclusive scientific evidence on the issues they address. Second, the fact that many therapists believe strongly in the existence of repression and in its role in psychological disorders indicates that in some instances, at least, therapists may act in ways that lead clients to report repressed memories even if they don't really have them. In other words, therapists may *suggest* such memories, often in a subtle and unintentional manner (Bowers & Farvolden, 1996). For example, a therapist who believes in the powerful impact of repressed memories might say something like this to a client: "You know, in my experience, a lot of people who are struggling with the same kind of problems as you had painful experiences as children—they were beaten or even molested. I wonder if anything like that ever happened to you?" Faced with such questions and the *demand characteristics* they imply (subtle pressures to tell the therapist what she or he wants to hear), some clients may search their memories for traces of traumatic early events. And, unfortunately, this search may lead them to generate memories that weren't there or to distort ones that do exist so that they are consistent with what the therapist seems to be suggesting (Haugaard et al., 1991; Loftus & Coan, 1995).

Third, even if they are not undergoing therapy and do not hear their therapist talk about repressed memories, many people may be influenced by media reports indicating that both early sexual abuse and repressed memories of these experiences are quite common. As a result of exposure to such accounts, persons suffering from various psychological problems may begin to wonder if their own problems stem from such causes—and perhaps conclude that they do—even if this is *not* the case.

Finally, and perhaps most disturbing, growing evidence suggests that people often generate *false memories*—memories for events that never happened to them (e.g., Goodman et al., 1996). As you might guess, such effects may be especially likely to occur among young children, who readily show errors with respect to both source and reality monitoring: They often can't accurately identify the source of their memories or tell whether their memories are based on events that really happened or on something they imagined (e.g., Johnson, Hashtroudi, & Lindsay, 1993). Consider an intriguing study by Ceci and his colleagues (Ceci, 1995). This researcher worked with the parents of preschool children to identify real events the children had experienced (e.g., a bicycle accident) and fictitious but plausible events that the children had *not* experienced. One of the fictitious events was an accident involving a mousetrap: The children were asked about an incident in which they had caught their finger in a mousetrap and had to go to the hospital to have it removed. Once a week for ten weeks, each child was shown cards representing the actual and fictitious events (see Figure 6.13). The child would pick a card and the experimenter would ask whether the incident shown had occurred. For instance, when asking about the fictitious mousetrap incident, the interviewer would say, "Think real hard and tell me if this ever happened to you. Can you remember going to the hospital with the mousetrap on your finger?"

At the end of the ten-week period, procedures were changed so that a different interviewer met with the children and asked them more detailed questions about each of the situations—the real and the fictitious ones. Results provided dramatic evidence for the construction of false memories: Fully 58 percent of the children provided false accounts of the fictitious incident. Moreover, they provided great detail in these accounts of events that never happened. Perhaps worst of all, when videotapes of the children's accounts were shown to other psychologists, these experts could not tell the true events from the false ones—they performed at chance level in making such judgments.

Clearly, these results—plus those of many other studies conducted with both children and adults (e.g., Brainerd & Reyna, 1998; Goodman et al., 1996; Mazzoni et al.,

**Figure 6.13**
**Evidence for the Occurrence of False Memories**

When young children were shown drawings of fictitious events and asked whether they had experienced them, a majority reported that they had. Moreover, they provided detailed descriptions of these imaginary events. Even worse, trained psychologists who saw videotapes of the children describing both real and fictitious events could not accurately distinguish between the false memories and real ones. These findings suggest the need for considerable caution in the interpretation of supposedly repressed memories of early childhood abuse.

1999)—raise a serious flag of caution for researchers studying supposedly repressed memories of early childhood sexual abuse. Please don't misunderstand: I am certainly *not* suggesting that all such memories reported by individuals are false. There is no doubt that childhood sexual abuse is a disturbingly frequent occurrence (e.g., Keary & Fitzpatrick, 1994), and that some people who experience it do have difficulty in remembering it (Williams, 1994). However, there do seem to be sufficient questions about the nature of repression, and sufficient evidence that some "memories" of traumatic events can be unintentionally constructed, to suggest the need for caution (Koocher et al., 1995).

Can we ever succeed in distinguishing false memories from real ones? Recent findings suggest that PET scans may provide one key to this puzzle. In several studies (e.g., Hilts, 1996; Schachter, 1996) different patterns of brain activation have been observed when participants remember stimuli (e.g., words) that were actually presented during the study than when they "remember" stimuli that were not actually presented. Such methods are only in their infancy, and they must be viewed with considerable caution. The debate over these complex issues is certain to continue for some time to come. What is already clear, though, is this: We must be careful to avoid assuming that all reports of "repressed memories" of childhood abuse are accurate. If we make such assumptions, we run the risk of falsely convicting at least some innocent persons of crimes they never committed (Loftus, 1993; Roediger & McDermott, 1996).

## Autobiographical Memory: Remembering the Events of Our Own Lives

How do we remember information about our own lives? Such **autobiographical memory** (which falls under the more general heading of *episodic memory*) has long been of interest to psychologists. While autobiographical memory has been studied in several different ways—for example, by means of questionnaires in which individuals answer detailed questions about their lives (Baddeley, 1990)—perhaps the most dramatic approach has involved the use of *diary studies,* in which individuals keep detailed diaries of events in their own lives. (As I noted in Chapter 4, this method has also been used to study biological rhythms.)

In one well-known study using this approach, the Dutch psychologist Willem Wagenaar (1986) kept a diary for six years. Each day he recorded one or two incidents, carefully indicating who was involved, what happened, and where and when each event took place. He rated each incident in terms of whether it was something that happened often or rarely, and he also indicated the amount of emotional involvement he experienced. During the course of the study, he recorded a total of 2,400 incidents. Then he tested his own memory for each, over a period of twelve months. The results were complex, but generally indicated that autobiographical memory is affected by many of the same variables as other forms of memory—for example, by retrieval cues and emotional states. Since diary studies are conducted under more natural, if less controlled, conditions than typical laboratory studies of memory, and examine memory for everyday events rather than for lists of words or for nonsense syllables, diary studies are certainly useful in one crucial respect: They offer support for the view that the findings of research on memory can indeed be generalized beyond the confines of the psychological laboratory.

Using these and other methods, such as the ones discussed in the **Research Methods** section on page 218, psychologists have discovered quite a bit about autobiographical memory, including when it first occurs and how it is organized.

**Autobiographical Memory:** Memory for information about events in our own lives.

**INFANTILE AMNESIA: WHEN DO AUTOBIOGRAPHICAL MEMORIES BEGIN?** What is your earliest memory? Mine involves an incident during a heat wave, when my father and I went up to the roof of an apartment building where we lived. I can vividly remember asking him: "Daddy, when will it get cooler?" According to my parents, this incident must have occurred before I was four, because my father stopped going up to the roof after that time. (I still hate summer heat, by the way.) If you are like me—and most people—your earliest memory probably dates from your third or fourth year of life, although a few people report even earlier memories (Usher & Neisser, 1995). This fact raises several interesting questions: Can we remember events before this time—from the first two years of our lives? And if we can't, why not? Why does this inability to remember things early in life, termed **infantile amnesia** (Howe & Courage, 1993), exist?

**Infantile Amnesia:** Our supposed inability to remember experiences during the first two or three years of life.

Growing evidence suggests that in fact, we *can* remember events from very early periods in our lives. However, because we don't possess language skills in infancy, we can't report them in words (Bauer, 1996). For instance, consider a study by Myers, Clifton, & Clarkson (1987). These researchers allowed children six to forty weeks old to play with some toys in a laboratory room. Two years later, they brought the same children back to this room and again allowed them to play with the toys; a control group of the same age had never played with these toys in this room before. As expected, the behavior of the two groups differed: Those who had played with the toys two years earlier showed more interest in them and played with them more than did the control group. But when asked if they remembered ever having seen the toys before or having been in the room, the children almost unanimously said no. Clearly, the children showed evidence of having some kind of memory of their earlier experiences but could not put these into words.

Other factors, too, may contribute to our inability to report memories from the first two years of our lives. One possibility is that autobiographical memory is absent early in life because the brain structures necessary for such memory are not sufficiently developed at this time (Moscovitch, 1985). Another possibility, suggested by Howe & Courage (1993), is that we do not form a clear *self-concept* until sometime between our second and third birthdays. Without this concept, we lack the personal frame of reference necessary for autobiographical memory.

Whatever the precise mechanisms involved in our inability to verbally report memories from our early lives, growing evidence suggests that we can, indeed, store information from this period in memory. So, by and large, the term *infantile amnesia* is misleading; it suggests a lack of memory, while, in fact, certain types of memory ability are indeed present.

### ORGANIZATION OF AUTOBIOGRAPHICAL MEMORY

In order to study autobiographical memory, psychologists sometimes use the cue-word method. In this technique, individuals are presented with words and asked to associate autobiographical memories with them. For instance, they are given the words *fire, hospital, paper,* and *window* and are asked to describe memories from their own lives relating to these. The memories people bring to mind in this way show an interesting pattern. In general, most of the remembered events are recent, and the frequency of memories brought to mind drops off with increasing age: People recall fewer events from twenty years ago than from ten years ago, and so on. However, as shown in Figure 6.14, there is a "bump" in this function—people report more memories than we might expect from their early adult years (late teens to mid-twenties) (Rubin & Schulkind, 1997; Rubin, Wetzler, & Nebes, 1986). Why? Perhaps because a lot of important things happen at this time of life: People graduate from school, take a job, get married, start their careers, and so on. These events are personally important to the individuals who experience

**Figure 6.14**
**Autobiographical Memories: What We Remember Most**

As shown here, we tend to remember recent events in our lives more frequently than events that occurred longer ago. However, this function is interrupted by a "bump" for our early adult years: We remember more events from that period than from other periods.
(*Source:* Based on data from Rubin, 1982.)

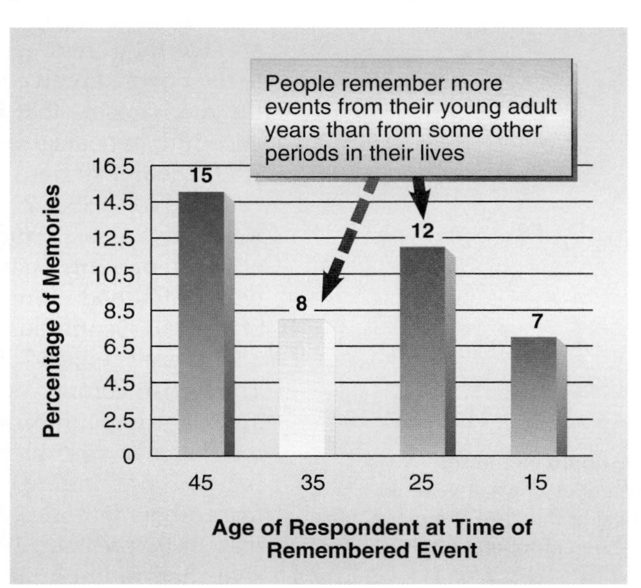

them, and also are linked to strong emotions. Thus, they may be encoded differently from events at other times in people's lives. In addition, individuals may use different techniques for retrieving events associated with landmarks in their lives, and this may aid their recall (Shum, 1998).

Whatever the reason, it is clear that we remember events from some periods of our life more vividly than events from other periods. In other words, autobiographical memories do not represent a random assortment of experiences. Rather, they appear to be organized around several major *lifetime periods,* periods of an individual's life lasting several years (e.g.,"my college years"). Below this level of organization are *general events* or *personal landmarks* most people remember, such as their first day at work, their first date with someone who played an important role in their life, and so on. Finally, there is information for specific, unique events (Conway, 1996). How do we know that such organization exists? Because when asked to think of various autobiographical memories, individuals usually respond faster when describing lifetime periods or personal landmarks than when describing other events, and respond slowest of all when describing memories for specific events that don't relate to larger themes. In sum, we do retain much information about events in our own lives; but this information is not all equally memorable, and, as noted above, our early adult years appear to be more memorable than other life periods.

## Memory for Emotionally Laden Events: Flashbulb Memories and the Effects of Mood on Memory

Can you remember where you were and what you were doing when you first learned about the massacre of fifteen faculty and students at Columbine High School, near Denver? If so, can you remember vividly both the event and what you were doing? If you can, you now have firsthand (although informal) evidence for what Brown and Kulik (1977) term **flashbulb memories**—vivid memories of what we were doing at the time of an emotion-provoking event. They are termed "flashbulb" memories because they seem to be preserved in autobiographical memory in considerable detail, almost like a photograph.

To study such memories, Brown and Kulik (1977) asked people whether they recalled the circumstances in which they first heard of ten major events (e.g., the assassination of President John F. Kennedy). They found that many respondents could report on their experience of such events in great detail—hence, the term "flashbulb memories." Additional research on such memories, however, has raised serious questions about whether they are really special after all (e.g., Shum, 1998). This research suggests that flashbulb memories *seem* to be especially vivid or strong because they are triggered by events that are surprising, distinctive, and important to the people involved. In other words, they can be understood largely in terms of the mechanisms that influence *all* autobiographical memories—elaborateness of encoding, rehearsal, and the emotionality of the event. A field study by Conway (1995) demonstrates the influence of such factors on flashbulb memories.

On November 22, 1990, the twenty-seventh anniversary of President John F. Kennedy's assassination, British Prime Minister Margaret Thatcher resigned. This occasion presented a unique opportunity for research on flashbulb memories. Conway (1995) had more than 200 volunteers in Great Britain and 150 in the United States and Denmark report their memories of the Thatcher resignation two weeks after it occurred, and about a year later. He found what you would probably expect: The British volunteers remembered the resignation much better than the American and Danish volunteers. This is not surprising, since the resignation of Prime Minister Thatcher was much more important and emotion-provoking for British participants. These findings suggest that flashbulb memories are not distinctly different from other memories. Moreover, contrary to popular belief, they are often also quite *in*accurate (Neisser, 1991); they do not provide individuals with perfect memory snapshots of important public events.

**Flashbulb Memories:** Vivid memories of what we were doing at the time of an emotion-provoking event.

**EFFECTS OF MOOD ON MEMORY** Earlier, in discussing retrieval cues, I noted that our own internal states can serve as cues for information stored in memory: It is often easier to recall information stored in long-term memory when our internal state is similar to that which existed when the information was first entered into memory. The effects of mood on memory are closely related to such state-dependent retrieval, because our moods are another internal state that can serve as a retrieval cue. How can mood influence memory? In two distinct but related ways. First, memory can be enhanced when our mood during retrieval is similar to that when we first encoded some information; this enhanced recall is known as **mood-dependent memory.** For instance, if you entered some information into memory when in a good mood, you are more likely to remember this information when in a similar mood once again; your current mood serves as a kind of retrieval cue for the information stored in memory. Note that you will remember this information whatever its nature—positive, negative, or unrelated to mood.

Second, we are more likely to store or remember positive information when in a positive mood and negative information when in a negative mood; in other words, we notice or remember information that is congruent with our current moods (Blaney, 1986); this is known as **mood congruence effects.** A simple way to think about the difference between mood-dependent memory and mood congruence effects is this: In mood-dependent memory, mood serves as a retrieval cue, helping us remember information we acquired when we were in that mood before—but this information may or may not be related to our current mood. In mood congruence effects, we tend to remember information consistent with our present mood—positive information when we feel happy, negative information when we feel sad (see Figure 6.15). Mood congruence effects are vividly illustrated by the case of an individual who suffered from periods of depression. She was asked at different times to remember trips to a swimming pool. When she felt depressed, she remembered painful aspects of those trips—how fat and unattractive she felt in her bathing suit. When she was happier, she remembered positive aspects of the same events—how much she enjoyed swimming (Baddeley, 1990).

**Figure 6.15**
**Effects of Mood on Memory**

Memory is enhanced when our mood at the time of retrieval is the same as that at the time information was first encoded, or entered into memory; this is *mood-dependent memory.* We also tend to notice and remember information consistent with our current mood; this is the *mood congruence effect.*

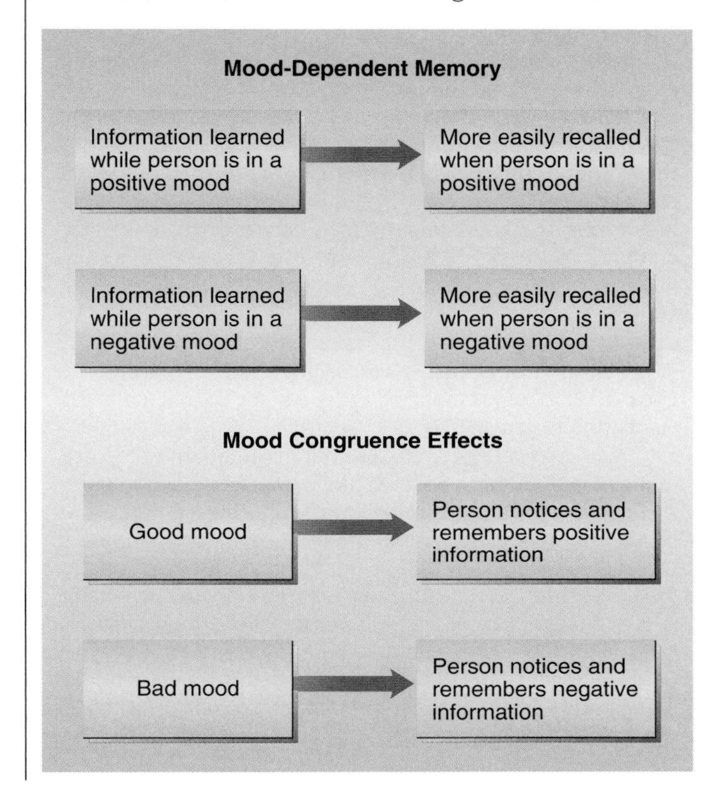


More systematic research confirms the existence of both kinds of mood effects (Eich, 1995); it also suggests that they may be quite important, especially with respect to depression, a very serious psychological disorder. Mood congruence effects help explain why depressed persons have difficulty in remembering times when they felt better (Schachter & Kihlstrom, 1989): Their current negative mood leads them to remember unhappy past experiences, and this information causes them to feel more depressed. In other words, mood congruence effects may push a person into a vicious circle in which negative feelings breed negative thoughts and memories, which result in even deeper depression. We'll discuss depression in detail in Chapter 14.

The effects of emotion-provoking stimuli or events often exert powerful effects on memory. For a discussion of such effects, and their practical implications, please see the **From Science to Practice** section on page 236.

**Mood-Dependent Memory:** Our enhanced ability, when we are in a given mood, to remember what we learned when previously in that same mood.

**Mood Congruence Effects:** Our tendency to notice or remember information congruent with our current mood.

from SCIENCE to PRACTICE

## Mental Contamination and the Legal System: Can Jurors Really "Strike It from the Record"?

In many trials, the following scene occurs: One attorney makes a remark and the opposing attorney objects. The judge then turns to the jury and says, "The jury will ignore that remark." Next, the judge tells the court stenographer to strike the comment from the record. The assumption is that this information—which is often dramatic or emotionally charged—can be ignored by the jury, just as it can be eliminated from the court records (see Figure 6.16). Is this assumption correct? A growing body of evidence gathered by psychologists suggests that it is on very shaky ground. Many studies suggest that information that evokes emotional reactions may be almost impossible to ignore or disregard (e.g., Edwards, Heindel, & Louis-Dreyfus, 1996; Wegner & Gold, 1995). For example, consider a study conducted by Edwards and Bryan (1997).

These researchers reasoned that information that is dramatic or evokes emotional reactions may be a potent source of what is known as **mental contamination**—a process in which our judgments, emotions, or behavior are influenced by mental processing that is not readily under our control (Wilson & Brekke, 1994). Specifically, they suggested that information that evokes emotional reactions may be especially likely to produce mental contamination because emotional reactions are diffuse in nature and tend to trigger thought that is *not* careful, rational, or analytic. The result: Once we are exposed to emotion-generating information, we can't ignore it, no matter how hard we try.

To test this reasoning, the researchers had the participants play the role of jurors. Each participant read a transcript of a murder trial that contained information about the defendant's previous criminal record. In one condition this information was presented in an emotion-generating manner (it described a vicious attack on a woman); in another condition it was presented in a more neutral manner (the transcript simply mentioned that the defendant was accused of a prior assault). For half the participants the transcript indicated that this information about the defendant was admissible and should be considered; for the other half the information was described as inadmissible, and jurors were specifically instructed to ignore it in reaching their verdict.

After reading the transcript, participants were asked to rate the guilt of the defendant and to recommend a sentence for him. Edwards and Bryan (1997) predicted that because of mental contamination, participants would not be able to ignore the emotion-generating information. In fact, when told to ignore it, they might find themselves thinking about it *more* often than when not told to ignore it—a kind of *rebound* effect observed in many other studies in which individuals are instructed not to think about something (e.g., Wegner, 1994). As a result, when exposed to emotion-generating information and told to ignore it, participants would view the defendant as more guilty and recommend a harsher sentence for him. Results strongly confirmed these predictions.

**Figure 6.16**
**Mental Contamination in Action**

Can jurors ignore emotion-provoking information if told to do so by the judge? Research findings indicate that this is extremely difficult. On the basis of such findings, psychologists have recommended changes in legal proceedings, and some of these changes are currently being instituted.

These findings have important implications for the legal system, in which jurors are often told to ignore emotion-provoking information. The results obtained by Edwards and Bryan (1997) and other psychologists suggest that this may be an impossible task. And in fact, there is growing recognition of this and related issues on the part of lawyers and judges. In recent years, legal systems in many states and countries have sought advice from *forensic psychologists* —psychologists who specialize in studying the cognitive and behavioral factors that influence legal proceedings and the law. On the basis of the psychologists' recommendations, changes have been made in the legal systems of many countries to improve their overall fairness. Clearly, this is one way in which the findings of psychology are contributing to human welfare.

**REVIEW QUESTIONS**

- What is repression? What role does it play in memory?
- What is autobiographical memory? When does it begin? How is it organized?
- What are flashbulb memories?
- What are mood-dependent memory and mood congruence effects?
- What is mental contamination? How may it influence legal proceedings?

# Memory and the Brain: Evidence from Memory Impairments and Other Sources

Web Link: *Memory Exploratorium*

Let's begin with a simple but necessary assumption: When information is entered into memory, *something* must happen in our brain. Given that memories can persist for decades, it is only reasonable to suggest that this "something" involves relatively permanent changes. But where, precisely, do these occur? And what kinds of alterations do they involve? These questions have fascinated—and frustrated—psychologists for decades. Thanks to the development of tools and methods such as those described in Chapter 2 and in the **Research Methods** section on page 218, however, answers to these questions appear be in sight (e.g., Paller, Kutas, & McIsaac, 1995). Let's see what research on these issues has revealed.

## Amnesia and Other Memory Disorders: Keys for Unlocking Brain–Memory Links

The study of **amnesia,** or loss of memory, has added greatly to our understanding of the biological bases of memory. Amnesia is far from rare. Among human beings it can stem from accidents that damage the brain, from drug abuse, from illness, or from operations performed to treat medical disorders. Two major types exist. In **retrograde amnesia,** memory of events prior to the amnesia-inducing event is impaired. Thus, persons suffering from such amnesia may be unable to remember events from specific periods in their lives. In **anterograde amnesia,** in contrast, individuals cannot remember events that occur *after* the amnesia-inducing event. For example, if they meet someone for the first time after the onset of amnesia, they cannot remember that person the next day—or even, in some cases, a few minutes after being introduced (see Figure 6.17 on page 238).

**Mental Contamination:** A process in which our judgments, emotions, or behavior are influenced by mental processing that is not readily under our control.

**Amnesia:** Loss of memory stemming from illness, injury, drug abuse, or other causes.

**Retrograde Amnesia:** Loss of memory of events that occurred prior to an amnesia-inducing event.

**Anterograde Amnesia:** The inability to store in long-term memory information that occurs after an amnesia-inducing event.

**S. P.: AN EXAMPLE OF THE DISSOCIATION BETWEEN WORKING MEMORY AND LONG-TERM MEMORY** One of the most important findings to emerge from studies of people with amnesia is this: Often, these persons retain factual information stored in memory but can no longer enter new information into long-term storage. S. P., a patient described by the Swiss psychologist Schnider (Schnider, Regard, & Landis, 1994), provides a vivid example of such effects. S. P. was sixty-six years old when he suffered a major stroke. Magnetic resonance imaging (an MRI scan) indicated that the stroke had affected S. P.'s medial temporal lobes, the left hippocampus, and many other adjoining areas. After the stroke, S. P. showed a pattern demonstrated by many other persons with damage to the hippocampus: He seemed unable to enter information into long-term memory. If he left a room for a few moments, he could not find his way back to it. He could not remember physicians who

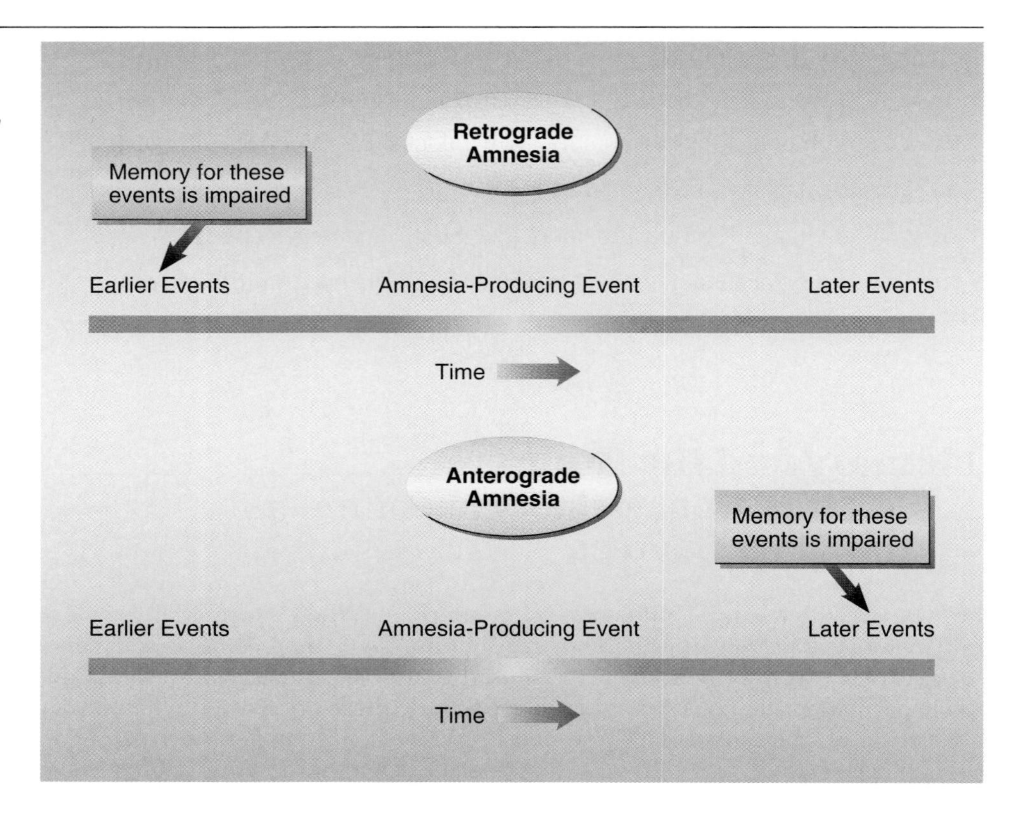


**Figure 6.17**
**Two Kinds of Amnesia**

In *retrograde amnesia,* memory of events prior to the amnesia-inducing event is impaired—people forget things that happened to them in the past. In *anterograde amnesia,* memory of events occurring after the amnesia-inducing event is impaired—people can't remember things that happened to them after the onset of their amnesia.

examined him or people he met for the first time. (He did, however, recognize his wife and children.) He could talk, read, and write, but he had difficulty naming some objects and experiences. He could repeat words on a list as they were read, but could not remember any after the list was completed. In short, S. P. showed profound anterograde amnesia. Interestingly, he retained the ability to acquire procedural knowledge: For example, his performance on tasks such as drawing geometric figures without directly looking at them improved with practice, although he couldn't remember performing the task or explain how he got better at it. This case, and many others like it, point to the importance of the *hippocampus,* a structure located on the inside edge of each brain hemisphere, adjacent to the temporal lobes. Damage to this structure seems to interfere with the ability to transfer information from working memory to a more permanent kind of storage. However, damage to the hippocampus does *not* eliminate the ability to acquire procedural knowledge (i.e., new skills), so this structure does not seem to be involved in procedural memory.

**CLIVE WEARING: THE TEMPORAL LOBES AND SEMANTIC MEMORY** Another dramatic case of amnesia was that of Clive Wearing, a musician and producer of considerable fame during the early 1980s. In 1985 Wearing caught infectious encephalitis. This disease caused extensive damage to both frontal lobes of his brain and to the hippocampus, resulting in profound memory deficits—many of which were recorded by Wearing's wife, Deborah. Most of these deficits involved semantic memory: Wearing could not distinguish between words such as honey, jam, and marmalade. He ate a lemon, including the peel, believing it was another kind of fruit. He mistook soap for toothpaste. His score on standard tests of semantic memory was very low—a major change, because before his illness he had been an expert at solving crossword puzzles and had had excellent semantic memory. Over time his memory impairments became worse, and he began to develop new, unique definitions for words. Researchers who studied his case concluded that his loss of semantic memory was due to damage to the temporal lobes (Wilson & Wearing, 1995); losses in the ability for new learning, which occurred later on, were attributed to growing damage to the hippocampus. On the basis of this and many other cases, psychologists have concluded that several parts of the brain play an important role in working memory, in the encoding of factual information (both episodic and semantic) in long-term memory, and in the retrieval of factual information from long-term memory.

**Korsakoff's Syndrome:** An illness caused by long-term abuse of alcohol; often involves profound retrograde amnesia.

**Alzheimer's Disease:** An illness primarily afflicting individuals over the age of sixty-five and involving severe mental deterioration, including severe amnesia.

**AMNESIA AS A RESULT OF KORSAKOFF'S SYNDROME** Individuals who consume large amounts of alcohol for many years sometimes develop a serious illness known as **Korsakoff's syndrome.** The many symptoms of Korsakoff's syndrome include sensory and motor problems as well as heart, liver, and gastrointestinal disorders. In addition, the syndrome is often accompanied by both anterograde amnesia and severe retrograde amnesia: Patients cannot remember events that took place many years before the onset of their illness. Careful medical examinations of such persons' brains after their death indicate that they have experienced extensive damage to portions of the thalamus and hypothalamus. This suggests that these portions of the brain play a key role in long-term memory.

**CourseCompass**

Web Link: *Alzheimer's Association*

Video 6.1: *Alzheimer's Disease*

**THE AMNESIA OF ALZHEIMER'S DISEASE** One of the most tragic illnesses to strike human beings in the closing decades of life is **Alzheimer's disease.** This illness occurs in 5 percent of all people over age sixty-five (see Figure 6.18). It begins with mild problems, such as increased difficulty in remembering names, phone numbers, or appointments. Gradually, though, patients' conditions worsen until they become totally confused, are unable to perform even simple tasks like dressing or grooming themselves, and experience an almost total loss of memory. In the later stages, patients may fail to recognize their spouse or children. In short, people suffering from Alzheimer's disease suffer a wide range of memory impairments: Working memory, semantic memory, episodic memory, memory for skills, and autobiographical memory are all disturbed. As one memory expert puts it: "Along with their memories, the patients lose their pasts and their souls" (Haberlandt, 1999, p. 266). Even worse, they are often aware of the progressive changes they are experiencing, and this is very disturbing to them (e.g., McGowin, 1993) (see Figure 6.18).

Careful study of the brains of deceased Alzheimer's patients has revealed that in most cases they contain tangles of *amyloid beta protein,* a substance not found in similar concentrations in normal brains. Research evidence (Yankner et al., 1990) suggests that this substance causes damage to neurons that project from nuclei in the basal forebrain to the hippocampus and cerebral cortex (Coyle, 1987). These neurons transmit information primarily by means of the neurotransmitter *acetylcholine,* so it appears that this substance may play a key role in memory. Further evidence that acetylcholine-based systems are important is provided by the fact that the brains of Alzheimer's patients contain lower than normal amounts of acetylcholine. In addition, studies with animal subjects in which the acetylcholine-transmitting neurons are destroyed suggest that this does indeed produce major memory problems (Fibiger, Murray, & Phillips, 1983). However, very recent evidence suggests that other neurotransmitters are also involved, so the picture is more complex than was previously assumed.

**Figure 6.18**
**Alzheimer's Disease: A Tragedy of Later Life**

Individuals suffering from Alzheimer's disease often realize that they are losing their memory and experiencing other effects of this illness. Former President Reagan is one such person: He held a formal ceremony to say good-bye to many friends and associates, because he realized that soon Alzheimer's disease would rob him of his memory and his personality.

## Memory and the Brain: A Modern View

So where does all this evidence leave us? With several major conclusions. First, memory functions do show some degree of localization within the brain: (1) The hippocampus plays a key role in converting information from temporary to more permanent memory, and in spatial learning; however, it does not seem to play a role in procedural memory, because damage to the hippocampus leaves such memory largely intact. (2) The frontal lobes play a role in working memory, in the executive functions in working memory, and in the encoding and retrieval of factual information in and from long-term memory. (3) The temporal lobes (or structures they contain) may play a role in semantic memory. Damage to these areas and structures disrupts these key functions but may leave other aspects of memory intact.

Why does damage to various brain structures produce amnesia and other memory deficits? Several possible explanations exist, and there is evidence consistent with each, so it is too early to choose between them. One possibility is that damage to these areas prevents consolidation of memories; memories are formed but cannot be converted to a lasting state (e.g., Squire, 1995). Another is that when information is stored in memory, not only the information itself but its context—when and how it was acquired—is stored; amnesia may result from an inability to enter this contextual information into memory (Mayes, 1996). Finally, it may be that amnesia stems from an inability to monitor errors (Baddeley, 1996); this may be one reason why amnesic patients often can't enter new information into memory, although their semantic memory remains intact (e.g., they can speak, read, and write).

What about the *memory trace* itself—the "something" within the brain that stores memories—where is it located and what is it? Over the years, the pendulum of scientific opinion concerning this issue has swung back and forth. One view holds that memories are highly localized within the brain—they exist in specific places. Another view is that memories are represented by the pattern of neural activity in many different brain regions; this is known as the distributed or equipotential view. At present, most experts on memory believe that both views are correct, at least to a degree. Some aspects of memory do appear to be represented in specific portions of the brain and even, perhaps, in specific cells. For instance, cells have been identified in the cortex of monkeys that respond to faces of other monkeys and humans but not to other stimuli (Desimone & Ungerleider, 1989). So there do appear to be "local specialists" within the brain. At the same time, however, networks of brain regions seem to be involved in many memory functions, as suggested by the distributed view. So the best available answer to the question "Where are memories located?" is that there is no single answer. Depending on the type of information or type of memory we are considering, memories may be represented in individual neurons, in the connections between neurons, in complex networks of structures throughout the brain, or in all of the above. Given the complexity of the functions memory involves, this is not surprising. After all, no one ever said that the task of understanding anything as complicated and wonderful as human memory would be easy!

Finally, what *is* the memory trace—what happens within the brain when we enter information into memory? Again, we are still far from a final, complete answer—although we are definitely getting there. The picture provided by current research goes something like this. The formation of long-term memories involves alterations in the rate of production or release of specific neurotransmitters (especially acetylcholine). Such changes increase the ease with which neural information can move within the brain and may produce *localized neural circuits.* Evidence for the existence of such circuits, or *neural networks,* is provided by animal research in which previously learned conditioned responses are eliminated when microscopic areas of the brain are destroyed—areas that, presumably, contain the neural circuits formed during conditioning (Thompson, 1989).

Long-term memory may also involve changes in the actual structure of neurons—changes that strengthen communication across specific synapses (Teyler & DiScenna, 1984). For instance, after learning experiences, the shape of dendrites in specific neurons may be altered, and these changes may increase the neurons' responsiveness to certain neurotransmitters. Some of these changes may occur very quickly, while others may require considerable amounts of time. This, perhaps, is one reason why newly formed memories are subject to disruption for some period after they are formed (Squire & Spanis, 1984).

In sum, it appears that we are now in an exciting period of rapid progress. Armed with sophisticated research techniques (e.g., PET scans), psychologists and other scientists may finally be able to unravel the mystery of the biological bases of memory. When they do, the potential benefits for persons suffering from amnesia and other memory disorders will probably be immense.

Can memory be improved by a pill? For a discussion of this topic, please see the following **Beyond the Headlines** section.

## BEYOND the HEADLINES: *As Psychologists See It*

## Can Chewing Gum Improve Your Memory?

### Can Brain Gum Save a Shrinking Memory? We Put It to the Test

WALL STREET JOURNAL (APRIL 10, 1999)—Michael Waldholz is a Pulitzer Prize–winning science reporter who can quickly grasp difficult concepts and analyze their scientific and business implications. But he sometimes can't remember where he left his car keys or, for that matter, his car. . . . Michael, 48 years old, is experiencing a nearly universal phenomenon of middle age: memory lapses. Like many people, Michael . . . has different strategies to compensate, such as taking careful notes and using a pocket calendar. . . . But many people go farther, looking for products to slow or reverse their memory decline. This is fueling a surging market for supplements such as vitamin E that some believe can help memory. . . . The latest product capturing the imagination—and dollars—of worried baby-boomers is Brain Gum. . . . Billed as the "mental alertness dietary supplement chewing gum," it contains phosphatidylserine, a nutrient the company claims improves concentration and name and face recognition, aids in recalling telephone numbers, and helps in learning and remembering information. . . . To test the effects of the gum, Michael had a friend give him a simple memory test of 20 words; he could recall six. After chewing the gum for three weeks, he was tested by a friend again on the same 20 words: he remembered 11, nearly doubling his previous score. . . . Mike realizes that the results of any one person may be due to chance. Still, he says he's thinking about continuing to use the gum. . . ."

Wow! I almost don't know where to begin in discussing this article. "Can drugs improve memory?" is certainly an interesting and important topic. But this article is truly a classic illustration of two things: (1) how *not* to do research on important questions relating to human behavior, and (2) what happens when people are misinformed about the findings of psychological research. The first point is obvious: We really can't learn anything much from a simple demonstration like this; after all, the single participant in this informal study may simply have rehearsed the words on the list in his own mind between the two tests. To the extent that he did, any improvements in memory might stem from that factor—not from the Brain Gum he chewed. And of course, differences in Michael's performance from the first to second memory test may simply have been a random fluctuation, due to chance alone. We would need data from a large number of participants before we could reach even tentative conclusions concerning the effectiveness of this gum.

Perhaps even worse, this article *assumes* that people begin to lose their memory functions in middle age. As we'll see in Chapter 9, this is absolutely false! Most aspects of memory remain unchanged throughout life, or at least until people enter their seventies or eighties. So the person who wrote this article either never took a course in psychology or, if he did, forgot what he learned in it.

The question does remain, though: Can drugs improve memory? Systematic research on this issue has yielded mixed results. It appears that some drugs may indeed increase the speed with which individual neurons store information (Hall, 1998). However, such effects are small and of short duration. Moreover, the drugs that seem to produce these gains in the ability to retain information often have negative side effects, producing dizziness, diarrhea, and so on. Also, there is some indication that if they do improve memory, such drugs may improve memory for irrelevant information as well as for information an individual wants to recall. For instance, if you took such a drug (e.g., UCB-6215, ampakines) before studying for a test, you might remember slightly more test-related information; but you might also have enhanced memory for the buzz of a fly that was in the room where you studied or for the smell of your neighbor's cooking. These stimuli would not be present during the test, however, so you might be lacking important retrieval cues and might do worse than you would have done without taking the drug. So as the cartoon in Figure 6.19 on page 242 suggests, at present, we don't really know about any drugs that can produce significant boosts in memory. But stay tuned: As our understanding of the biological bases of memory increases, such drugs may indeed be identified.

**Figure 6.19**
**Is There a Memory Pill?**

Although many products—including one called Brain Gum—are currently being sold as memory aids, there is really no convincing scientific evidence for the claim that specific drugs can produce improve memory.

(*Source:* Reprinted with special permission of King Features Syndicate.)



### CRITICAL THINKING QUESTIONS

1. How could Brain Gum's potential effects on memory be tested effectively?
2. If a drug that enhances memory is actually discovered, should it be given to all students in school? What if the drug has harmful side effects—who should take it then?
3. Why do so many people continue to believe that memory decreases with age, despite research findings indicating that such decrements do not occur?

### REVIEW QUESTIONS

- What are retrograde amnesia and anterograde amnesia?
- What role do the hippocampus frontal and temporal lobes play in memory?
- What are Korsakoff's syndrome and Alzheimer's disease? What do they tell us about the biological bases of memory?
- What does current research suggest about the location of the memory trace and its nature?

### Food for Thought

Suppose that someday we are able to identify all the changes that occur in the brain when memories are formed. What benefits would this offer? What potential dangers (e.g., threats to human freedom) might stem from such knowledge?

## Making Psychology Part of Your Life

### Improving Your Memory: Some Useful Steps

How good is your memory? If you are like most people, your answer is probably "Not good enough!" At one time or another, most of us have wished that we could improve our ability to retain facts and information. Fortunately, with a little work, almost anyone can improve her or his memory. Here are some tips for reaching this goal:

1. **Really think about what you want to remember.** If you wish to enter information into long-term memory, it is important to think about it. Ask questions about it, consider its meaning, and examine its relationship to information you already know. In other words, engage in elaboration or "deep processing." Doing so will help make the new information part of your existing knowledge frameworks—and will increase your chances of remembering it later.

2. **Pay careful attention to what you want to remember.** Unless you consciously *notice* information you want to remember, it stands little chance of really getting "in"—into long-term memory. So, be sure to direct your full attention to information you want to remember. True, this does involve a bit of work. But in the long run, it will save you time and effort.
3. **Minimize interference.** Interference is a major cause of forgetting; and, in general, the more similar materials are, the more likely they are to produce interference. In practical terms, this means that you should arrange your studying so that you don't study similar subjects one right after the other. Instead, work on subjects that are unrelated; the result may be less interference between them—and, potentially, better grades.
4. **Engage in distributed learning/practice.** Don't try to cram all the information you want to memorize into long-term storage at once. Rather, if at all possible, space your studying over several sessions—preferably, several days. This is especially important if you want to retain the information for a long period of time rather than just until the next exam!
5. **Use visual imagery and other mnemonics.** You've probably heard the saying "A picture is worth a thousand words." Where memory is concerned, this is sometimes true; it is often easier to remember information associated with vivid mental images (e.g., Gehring & Toglia, 1989). You can put this principle to use by adopting any one of several different *mnemonics*—tactics for improving memory. One of these, the *method of loci,* involves linking points you want to remember with visual images arranged in some familiar order. For instance, suppose you want to remember the points in a speech you will soon make. You can imagine walking through some familiar place, say your own home. Then form a series of images in which each item you wish to remember is placed in a specific location. Perhaps the first point is "The greenhouse effect is real." You might imagine a large, steamy greenhouse right outside your front door. The next point might be "Cutting down the rain forest is increasing the greenhouse effect." For this one, you might imagine a large cut-down tree in your living room. You'd form other images, in different locations, for the other points you want to make. Then, by taking an imaginary walk through your house, you can "see" each of these images and so remember the points in your speech.
6. **Give yourself extra retrieval cues.** Remember the concept of state-dependent retrieval? As I noted previously, you can use this principle to provide yourself with extra retrieval cues and so help to enhance your memory. For instance, if you studied for a test while in one physical state, try to be in the same state when you take the test. Similarly, use the principle of mood-dependent memory. If you learned some material while in a given mood and then want to remember it, try to put yourself in the same mood. This is not as hard as it sounds: You can often vary your own mood by imagining happy or sad events. To the degree that your mood matches the mood you were in when you learned some information, your memory for the information may be improved.
7. **Develop your own shorthand codes.** When I learned the names of the nine planets, I did so by the first-letter technique, in which the first letter of each word in a phrase stands for an item to be remembered. In this case, the phrase was "Mary's Violet Eyes Make John Stay Up Nights Pondering" (for Mercury, Venus, Earth, Mars, Jupiter, Saturn, Uranus, Neptune, and Pluto). This can be a very useful technique if you need to remember lists of items.

I could add additional techniques, but most would be related to the points already described. Whichever techniques you choose, you will learn that making them work does require effort. In memory training, as in any other kind of self-improvement, it appears that "No pain, no gain" holds true.

## Summary and Review

### Human Memory: Two Influential Views

- **According to the Atkinson and Shiffrin model, what basic tasks are performed by memory?** Encoding involves converting information into a form that can be entered into memory. Storage involves retaining information over time. Retrieval involves locating information when it is needed.
- **What are sensory memory, short-term memory, and long-term memory?** Sensory memory holds fleeting representations of our sensory experiences. Short-term memory holds a limited amount of information for short periods of time. Long-term memory holds large amounts of information for long periods of time.

- **What is parallel processing, and what role does it play in memory?** In neural network models of memory, *parallel processing* refers to simultaneous processing of information by many neural modules, each of which is dedicated to a specific job (e.g., recognizing a given letter of a particular word). Parallel processing greatly enhances the speed and efficiency of memory.

### Key Terms

memory, p. 210 • encoding, p. 210 • storage, p. 210 • retrieval, p. 210 • sensory memory, p. 212 • long-term memory, p. 212 • selective attention, p. 212 • information-processing perspective, p. 212 • neural network models, p. 213

## Kinds of Information Stored in Memory

- **What is the serial position curve, and why does it support the existence of working memory?** The serial position curve refers to the finding that items near the beginning and end of a list are remembered more accurately than items near the middle. The existence of this effect suggests that words early in the list are remembered because they have moved into long-term storage, while those near the end are recalled because they are still present in working memory.
- **What tasks does working memory perform?** Working memory stores and processes small amounts of information, performs simple computations, plays a role in sentence comprehension, and coordinates a wide range of mental processes.
- **What is the multiple component model of working memory?** The multiple component model of working memory suggests that working memory includes a phonological loop, a visuospatial sketch pad, and a central executive.
- **What are episodic memory and semantic memory?** Episodic memory contains factual information individuals can remember acquiring at a particular place and time. Semantic memory holds factual information of a more general nature.
- **What are the levels of processing view of memory?** This view suggests that the more deeply information is processed, the more likely it is to be retained.
- **What are retrieval cues, and what role do they play in memory?** These are stimuli that are associated with information stored in memory and so can help bring the information to mind at times when it cannot be recalled spontaneously.
- **What are concepts, and what role do they play in semantic memory?** Concepts are mental categories for objects or events that are similar to one another in certain ways. They seem to be arranged in hierarchical networks in semantic memory.
- **What is procedural memory?** Procedural memory is memory for information we cannot describe verbally—for instance, various skills.
- **What is priming? Automatic priming?** Priming refers to the fact having seen or heard a stimulus once may facilitate our recognizing it on a later occasion, even if we are unaware of this effect. Automatic priming occurs when we aren't even aware of the stimuli that serve as primes.

### Key Terms

working memory, p. 215 • serial position curve, p. 215 • chunk, p. 216 • episodic memory, p. 219 • semantic memory, p. 219 • levels of processing view, p. 220 • retrieval clues, p. 220 • context-dependent memory, p. 220 • state-dependent retrieval, p. 220 • encoding specificity principle, p. 221 • concept, p. 221 • prototype, p. 222 • exemplar, p. 222 • procedural memory, p. 223

## Forgetting: Some Contrasting Views

- **What are retroactive interference and proactive interference? What role do they play in forgetting?** Retroactive interference occurs when information currently being learned interferes with information already present in memory. Proactive interference occurs when information already present in memory interferes with the acquisition of new information.
- **What is retrieval inhibition?** Retrieval inhibition occurs when efforts to remember certain items of information in memory generate inhibition that blocks the recall of other, related items.

### Key Terms

retroactive interference, p. 225 • proactive interference, p. 225 • retrieval inhibition, p. 226

## Memory Distortion and Memory Construction

- **What are schemas, and what role do they play in memory distortion?** Schemas cognitive structures representing individuals' knowledge and assumptions about aspects of the world. Once formed, they strongly influence the ways in which we process new information—what we notice, what we store in memory, and what we can remember.
- **What are constructed memories?** Constructed memories are memories of events that never happened or experiences that we never had.
- **What factors potentially reduce the accuracy of eyewitness testimony?** Suggestibility, source-monitoring errors, and the illusion of outgroup homogeneity are among factors that can diminish the accuracy of the testimony of eyewitnesses to crimes.

### Key Terms

schemas, p. 227 • source monitoring, p. 228 • reality monitoring, p. 228 • eyewitness testimony, p. 228

## Memory in Everyday Life

- **What is repression? What role does it play in memory?** Repression is the active elimination from consciousness of memories of experiences we find threatening. There is little evidence that repression plays an important role in forgetting, although it has been suggested that it influences memories of sexual abuse early in life.

- **What is autobiographical memory? When does it begin? How is it organized?** Autobiographical memory contains information about our own lives. It begins very early in life, although most people can't describe memories from their first two years. It is organized around important lifetime periods (e.g., "my college years").
- **What are flashbulb memories?** Vivid memories of what we were doing at the time of an emotion-provoking event.
- **What are mood-dependent memory and mood congruence effects?** When our mood during retrieval is similar to that during encoding, memory may be enhanced; this is mood-dependent memory. We tend to remember information consistent with our current mood; this is mood congruence.
- **What is mental contamination? How may it influence legal proceedings?** Mental contamination occurs when our judgments, emotions, or behavior are influenced by mental processing that is not readily under our control. This effect may influence trials when jurors can't ignore emotion-provoking information presented by attorneys even if instructed to do so.

#### Key Terms

repression, p. 230 • autobiographical memory, p. 232 • infantile amnesia, p. 233 • flashbulb memories, p. 234 • mood-dependent memory, p. 235 • mood congruence effects, p. 235 • mental contamination, p. 237

### Memory and the Brain: Evidence from Memory Impairments and Other Sources

- **What are retrograde amnesia and anterograde amnesia?** Retrograde amnesia involves loss of memory of events prior to an amnesia-inducing event. Anterograde amnesia is loss of memory for events that occur after the amnesia-inducing event.
- **What roles do the hippocampus, frontal lobes, and temporal lobes play in long-term memory?** The hippocampus seems to play a crucial role in the consolidation of memory—the process of shifting new information from short-term to longer-term storage. The frontal lobes appear to be play a key role in various aspects of semantic memory.
- **What are Korsakoff's syndrome and Alzheimer's disease? What do they tell us about the biological bases of memory?** Korsakoff's syndrome, produced by long-term alcoholism, often involves severe forms of amnesia. It indicates that the hypothalamus and thalamus play important roles in memory. Alzheimer's disease produces increasingly severe deficits in memory. It calls attention to the role of the neurotransmitter acetylcholine in memory.
- **What does current research suggest about the location of the memory trace and its nature?** Current research suggests that the memory trace may involve individual neurons, connections between neurons, and complex networks of neurons and brain structures. It may involve changes in the structure and function of individual neurons, or of complex networks of neurons.

#### Key Terms

amnesia, p. 237 • retrograde amnesia, p. 237 • anterograde amnesia, p. 237 • Korsakoff's syndrome, p. 239 • Alzheimer's disease, p. 239

## Critical Thinking Questions

### Appraisal

Do you think that psychologists and other scientists will ever be able to determine precisely what happens in our brains when we enter information into memory? What if scientists cannot accomplish this—will that mean that research on memory has ultimately failed?

### Controversy

Public concern with childhood sexual abuse has increased greatly in recent years, as many people have come forward with claims that they were subjected to such treatment. Growing evidence indicates, however, that some charges of this type are false—that they are based on false memories suggested by therapists, attorneys, and others. What steps, if any, do you think should be taken to protect innocent persons against such charges, while also protecting the rights of persons who have actually suffered sexual abuse?

### Making Psychology Part of Your Life

Now that you know how fallible and prone to errors memory can be, can you think of ways in which you can put this knowledge to use? In other words, can you think of situations in your own life where you may be less willing to rely on your memory in making judgments or decisions than was true in the past? And if so, what steps can you take in those situations to improve the accuracy of your judgments or decisions?

Chapter 7

# Cognition:

## Thinking, Deciding, Communicating

## CHAPTER OUTLINE

**THINKING: FORMING CONCEPTS AND REASONING TO CONCLUSIONS 249**

Basic Elements of Thought: Concepts, Propositions, Images

■ RESEARCH METHODS *How Psychologists Study Cognitive Processes*

Reasoning: Transforming Information to Reach Conclusions

**MAKING DECISIONS: CHOOSING AMONG ALTERNATIVES 258**

Heuristics: Using Quick—but Fallible—Rules of Thumb to Make Decisions

Framing and Decision Strategy

Escalation of Commitment: Getting Trapped in Bad Decisions

Emotions and Decision Making: The Magnifying Effects of Unexpected Loss and Gain

■ BEYOND THE HEADLINES—As Psychologists See It: *Was It the Weather, or Did Faulty Reasoning Kill JFK Jr.?*

Naturalistic Decision Making: Making Choices in the Real World

**PROBLEM SOLVING: FINDING PATHS TO DESIRED GOALS 267**

Problem Solving: An Overview

Methods for Solving Problems: From Trial and Error to Heuristics

Facilitating Effective Problem Solving: The Role of Metacognitive Processing

Factors That Interfere with Effective Problem Solving

Artificial Intelligence: Can Machines Really Think?

■ FROM SCIENCE TO PRACTICE *Intelligent Agents: Just How Smart Are They?*

**LANGUAGE: THE COMMUNICATION OF INFORMATION 275**

Language: Its Basic Nature

The Development of Language

Language and Thought: Do We Think What We Say or Say What We Think?

Language in Other Species

■ MAKING PSYCHOLOGY PART OF YOUR LIFE *Making Better Decisions*

In many respects, the human mind is nothing short of amazing. It has given rise to cures for deadly diseases, to works of art and beautiful music, and to the development of the many conveniences of modern life. However, the human mind is also prone to many forms of error that can lead to faulty reasoning, poor decisions, ineffective problem solving, and, unfortunately, sometimes potentially tragic consequences. This last point was indelibly etched into my own mind a few years ago, when I was doing consulting work at a large medical center. One day I happened to be meeting with staff in the hospital's emergency department just as a young boy was brought in and rushed to surgery. Apparently he had been flown to the hospital by helicopter after falling out of the second story of a barn he had been playing in. Although the head injury he had sustained was quite serious, the medical staff in the trauma center was well versed in handling cases of this kind. A preliminary examination indicated that surgery would be necessary, but the surgeons were optimistic about the boy's chances of survival and recovery. The procedures undertaken, quite ordinary by trauma center standards, initially went ahead as planned. But then things began to go terribly wrong. Alarms on the monitoring equipment sounded, indicating that the patient was not receiving enough oxygen. Standard troubleshooting efforts failed to identify a problem with the ventilator (the machine that "breathes" for anesthetized patients), so members of the surgical team focused their efforts on other possible sources of the problem. But nothing they tried seemed to work. Within minutes, the patient's oxygen had plummeted to a dangerously low level. Finally, as a last resort, the doctors took the boy off the ventilator and began to ventilate him manually by means of a balloonlike device that, when squeezed, forces air into the lungs through a breathing tube inserted into the trachea or windpipe. Fortunately, the team's efforts were successful. The boy's oxygen level returned to normal, and the surgery proceeded without further incident. Subsequent investigation revealed a relatively simple solution to the ventilator problem—but a solution that would *not* have been revealed through the troubleshooting procedures the surgical staff had been trained to follow.

Why do I start this chapter with this particular event? Because for me it highlights the following irony. On the one hand, our cognitive abilities are impressive in many respects. On the other hand, we are prone to errors that frequently prevent us from recognizing even relatively simple solutions, such as the one in the ventilator example. It should also be clear from this example that even intelligent, highly trained people are not immune to errors that affect their ability to think and reason effectively.

In a sense, the chapter opening vignette team members' ability to solve the problem they faced had been limited by the training they had received. The high levels of stress they undoubtedly experienced during this episode may have also contributed to their inability to consider the problem from different perspectives (Vredenburgh et al., in press).

**Cognition** is a general term used to denote thinking and many other aspects of our higher mental processes. Let's begin our discussion of cognitive processes by examining the nature of *thinking,* an activity that involves the manipulation of mental representations of various features of the external world. Thinking includes *reasoning*—mental activity through which we transform available information in order to reach conclusions. Next, we'll turn to *decision making,* the process of choosing between two or more alternatives on the basis of information about them. Here we'll explore different factors that influence the decision-making process, as suggested by the humorous example in Figure 7.1. Third, we'll examine several aspects of *problem solving,* which typically involves processing information in various ways in order to move toward desired goals. Finally, we'll examine an aspect of cognition that provides the basis for much of the activity occurring in each of the processes listed so far: *language.* It is primarily through language that we can share the results of our own cognition with others and receive similar input from them. Language plays a crucial role in almost all aspects of daily life, and its possession and high degree of development is perhaps the single most important defining characteristic of our species. We'll also consider evidence suggesting the possibility that other species may also possess several basic elements of language.

**Figure 7.1**
**Decision Making: A Complex Process**

Decision making, the process of choosing between two or more alternatives on the basis of information about them, is often a difficult task. Based on the information available in this humorous scene, what would you decide?

(*Source:* DENNIS THE MENACE® used by permission of Hank Ketchum and © by North America Syndicate.)

DENNIS THE MENACE

"WOULD YOU HOLD THE NAIL, WHILE I HAMMER IT?"

One additional point: As I've already noted, our cognitive activities are subject to many forms of error and distortion. When we think, reason, make decisions, solve problems, and use language, we do not always do so in ways that would appear completely rational to an outside observer (Hawkins & Hastie, 1990; Johnson-Laird, Byrne, & Tabossi, 1989). As we examine each aspect of cognition, therefore, I'll call attention to these potential sources of distortion, because understanding the nature of such errors can shed important light on the nature of the cognitive processes they affect (Smith & Kida, 1991).

## Thinking: Forming Concepts and Reasoning to Conclusions

What are you thinking about right now? If you've answered the question, then it's safe to say that at least to some extent you are thinking about the words on this page. But perhaps you are also thinking about your dog, the movie you saw last night, the argument you had with a friend this morning—the list could be endless. At any given moment in time, consciousness contains a rapidly shifting pattern of diverse thoughts, impressions, and feelings. In order to try to understand this complex and ever changing pattern, psychologists have often adopted two main strategies. First, they have focused on the basic elements of *thought*—how, precisely, aspects of the external world are represented in our thinking. You may recall from Chapter 1 that Wilhelm Wundt investigated the basic elements of consciousness through *introspection,* a procedure in which trained subjects reported their conscious experiences in

**Cognition:** The mental activities associated with thought, decision making, language, and other higher mental processes.

response to various stimuli presented to them under carefully controlled conditions. Second, psychologists have sought to determine the manner in which we *reason*—how we attempt to process available information cognitively in order to reach specific conclusions.

Web Link: *About How Kids Think*

## Basic Elements of Thought: Concepts, Propositions, Images

What, precisely, does thinking involve? In other words, what are the basic elements of thought? While no conclusive answer currently exists, it appears that our thoughts consist largely of three basic components: *concepts, propositions,* and *images.*

**CONCEPTS: CATEGORIES FOR UNDERSTANDING EXPERIENCE** What do the following objects have in common: a dalmatian, a poodle, an Irish setter? Although they all look different, you probably have no difficulty in replying—they are all dogs. Now, how about these items: a tractor, a Jeep Grand Cherokee, an elevator? Perhaps it takes you a bit longer to answer, but soon you realize that they are all vehicles. The items in each of these groups look different from one another, yet in a sense you perceive—and think about—them as similar, at least in certain respects. The reason you find the task of answering these questions relatively simple is that you already possess well-developed concepts for both groups of items. As you will recall from Chapter 6, *concepts* are mental categories for objects, events, experiences, or ideas that are similar to one another in one or more respects. They allow us to represent a great deal of information about diverse objects, events, or ideas in a highly efficient manner.

***Logical and Natural Concepts.*** Psychologists often distinguish between logical and natural concepts. **Logical concepts** are ones that can be clearly defined by a set of rules or properties. Thus, an object's membership in a category is unambiguous: Any object or event either is or is not a member of a given concept category by virtue of whether or not it has the defining feature or features (Jahnke & Nowaczyk, 1998). For example, in geometry, a figure can be considered to be a triangle only if it has three sides whose angles add up to 180 degrees, and can be a square only if all four sides are of equal length and all four angles are 90 degrees. In contrast, **natural concepts** are fuzzy around the edges; they have no fixed or readily specified set of defining features. Yet natural concepts more accurately reflect the state of the natural world, which rarely offers us the luxury of hard-and-fast, clearly defined rules. Natural concepts are often based on *prototypes*—the best or clearest examples (Rosch, 1975). Prototypes emerge from our experience with the external world, and new items that might potentially fit within their category are then compared with them. The more attributes new items share with an existing prototype, the more likely they are to be included within the concept. For example, consider the following natural concepts: fruit and art. For fruit, most people think of apples, peaches, or pears. They are far less likely to mention avocados, tomatoes, or olives. Similarly, for art, most people think of paintings, drawings, and sculptures. Fewer think of works of art such as the example shown in Figure 7.2.

> **Logical Concepts:** Concepts that can be clearly defined by a set of rules or properties.
>
> **Natural Concepts:** Concepts that are not based on a precise set of attributes or properties, do not have clear-cut boundaries, and are often defined by prototypes.
>
> **Visual Images:** Mental pictures or representations of objects or events.

***Concepts: How They Are Represented.*** How are concepts represented in consciousness? No firm answer to this question exists, but several possibilities have been suggested. First, concepts may be represented in terms of their features or attributes. As natural concepts are formed, the attributes associated with them may be stored in memory. Then, when we encounter a new item, we compare its attributes with the ones we have already learned about. The closer the match, the more likely we are to include the item within the concept.

A second possibility is that natural concepts are represented, at least in part, through **visual images:** mental pictures of objects or events in the external world.

If asked whether chess is a sport, do you conjure up an image of two players bending intently over the board while an audience looks on? If so, you can readily see how visual images may play a role in the representation of natural concepts. I'll have more to say about the role of mental images in thought later in this section.

Finally, it is important to note that concepts are closely related to *schemas,* cognitive frameworks that represent our knowledge of and assumptions about the world (see Chapter 6). Like schemas, natural concepts are acquired through experience and also represent information about the world in an efficient summary form. However, schemas appear to be more complex than concepts; each schema contains a broad range of information and may include many distinct concepts. For example, each of us possesses a *self-schema,* a mental framework holding a wealth of information about our own traits, characteristics, and expectations. This framework, in turn, may contain numerous different concepts, such as intelligence, attractiveness, health, and so on. Some of these are natural concepts; so the possibility exists that natural concepts are represented, at least in part, through their links to schemas and other broad cognitive frameworks.

**Figure 7.2**
**Prototypes: An Unlikely Example**

When asked to think of art, most people think of paintings, drawings, or sculpture. Few think of examples like the light show at Disney World or the artwork depicted in this photo.

To summarize, concepts may be represented in the mind in several ways, and they play an important role in thinking and in our efforts to make sense out of a complex and ever changing external world.

**PROPOSITIONS: RELATIONS BETWEEN CONCEPTS** Thinking is not a passive process; it involves active manipulation of internal representations of the external world. As I have already noted, the representations that are mentally manipulated are often concepts. Frequently, thinking involves relating one concept to another, or one feature of a concept to the entire concept. Because we possess highly developed language skills, these cognitive actions take the form of **propositions**—sentences that relate one concept to another and can stand as separate assertions. Propositions such as "Bob kissed Sandra" describe a relationship between two concepts—in this case, affection expressed between the author and his wife. Others, such as "Polar bears have white fur," describe the relationship between a concept and its properties. Clusters of propositions are often represented as **mental models,** knowledge structures that guide our interactions with objects and events in the world around us (Johnson-Laird, Byrne, & Shaeken, 1992). For example, to understand how to invest your money wisely, you might use a mental model constructed from the following propositions: (1) "I should write down information about my current sources of income and debts"; (2) "I should schedule a meeting with a competent financial planner to review my current financial status and future goals"; (3) "I should work with this person to develop a financial plan and then stick with it." Please note, however, that if some aspect of a mental model is incorrect, or if we process information contained in the model incompletely or incorrectly, we may tend to make mistakes. Thus, if you hold an incorrect mental model of how prevailing economic conditions or interest rates affect certain investment vehicles (such as stocks and bonds), you may lose part or all of your money. Clearly, much of our thinking involves the formulation and consideration of propositions; therefore, propositions should be considered one of the basic elements of thought.

Web Link: *Mental Models Web Site*

**Propositions:** Sentences that relate one concept to another and can stand as separate assertions.

**Mental Models:** Knowledge structures that guide our interactions with objects and events in the world around us.

**IMAGES: MENTAL PICTURES OF THE WORLD** As I indicated earlier, thinking often involves the manipulation of visual images. Research seems to indicate that mental manipulations performed on images of objects are very similar to those that would be performed on the actual objects (Kosslyn, 1994). For example, if asked to conjure up a mental image of a winter scene in Yellowstone National Park, it would probably take you longer to think about whether any animals are present than about whether there is snow on the ground. Why? Because locating the animals requires more detailed scanning than finding the snow. Other research also seems to indicate that once we form a mental image, we perceive it and think about it just as we would if it actually existed. When instructed to imagine walking toward an object, for instance, people report that the mental image of the object gradually expands, filling their imaginary visual field just as a real object would. Similarly, when people are asked to estimate the distance between locations in a familiar place, the farther apart the places indicated, the longer respondents take to make such judgments (Baum & Jonides, 1979).

Whatever the precise mechanisms through which they are used, mental images serve important purposes in thinking. People report using images for understanding verbal instructions, by converting the words into mental pictures of actions; and for enhancing their own moods, by visualizing positive events or scenes (Kosslyn et al., 1991). New evidence also seems to indicate that mental imagery may have important practical benefits, including helping people change their behavior to achieve important goals, such as losing weight or enhancing certain aspects of their performance (Taylor et al., 1998). It appears that we derive the greatest benefits from mentally simulating the process or steps necessary to reach a desired outcome, *not* from visualizing the desired outcome itself. For example, in one recent study, Pham and Taylor (1999) assigned undergraduates studying for a midterm exam to one of three conditions. Students in the *process*-simulation condition were told to visualize themselves performing actions beneficial to studying, such as sitting at their desks, reviewing lecture notes, eliminating potential distractions (e.g., turning off the television or stereo), and declining invitations to go out. Students in the *outcome*-simulation condition were told to visualize themselves receiving an A on the exam and to imagine how they would feel upon learning the news. Finally, students in the control condition received no special visualization instructions. The results indicated that students who rehearsed the studying process studied more and received higher grades than students in the control group. Students who rehearsed the outcome of studying did somewhat worse (see Figure 7.3). Apparently, visualizing the process, as opposed to the outcome, forces people to identify and organize the specific activities that will enable them to reach their goals. Doing so also

**Figure 7.3**
**Practical Benefits of Mental Imagery**

Students who visualized the process of studying—picturing themselves sitting at their desks, reviewing their notes, and reducing distractions—studied more and received higher grades than did students in the control group, who received no visualization instructions. Students who merely imagined the outcome of studying performed worse.

(*Source:* Based on data from Pham & Taylor, 1999.)

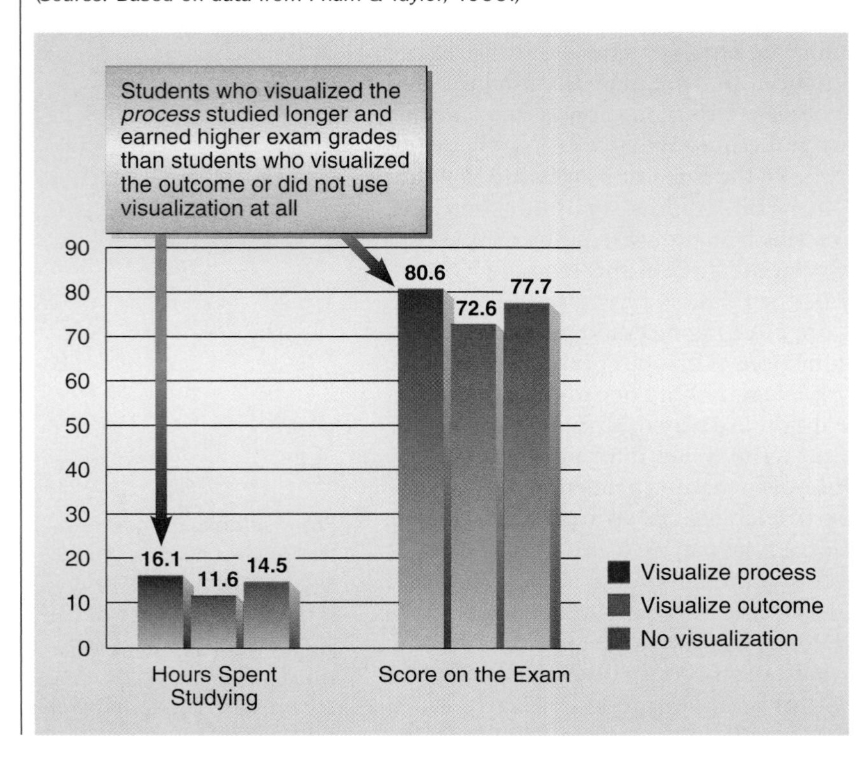

seems to help people avoid the *planning fallacy*—our tendency to underestimate the resources (such as time or money) necessary to achieve a goal, and to overestimate how easily the goal can be achieved (Buehler, Griffin, & Ross, 1994). (See the discussion of the "optimistic bias" in Chapter 16 for additional information on the planning fallacy.)

For more information on how psychologists study various aspects of thinking, please see the **Research Methods** section below.

**Reaction Time:** Time that elapses between the presentation of a stimulus and a person's reaction to it.

## Research Methods:
## How Psychologists Study Cognitive Processes

People think—that's obvious. But how do psychologists measure aspects of cognition since it is difficult to measure these processes directly? One of the earliest techniques used by psychologists to study cognitive processes is **reaction time:** the time that elapses between the presentation of a stimulus and a person's reaction to it. Why measure reaction time? If thinking involves distinct processes, then each process must take some time to complete. As I noted in Chapter 1, the development of computers has made it possible to measure the speed of people's reactions to specific stimuli with great precision. Researchers have used the information derived from reaction-time experiments as the basis for drawing inferences about underlying cognitive processes.

In a typical reaction-time experiment, participants are asked to respond verbally or press a button as quickly as possible following the presentation of a cue; say, a light, a tone, or the appearance of a particular stimulus on a computer screen. What can reaction time tell us about cognitive processes? Actually, plenty. Reaction time can be used to indicate how long it takes for a person to complete various types of perceptual tasks; for example, to react to the presentation of a visual stimulus, identify letters presented on a computer screen, or decide whether a letter is a vowel or a consonant. Researchers can then use the pattern of reaction times obtained on various tasks to determine the speed of the component mental processes involved; for example, the time required to detect a visual stimulus, reach a decision, or make a manual response to the stimulus.

Through the use of reaction-time measures, psychologists have gained tremendous insight into the timing of mental events. Still, an overreliance on reaction-time measures—or on any measure—can be limiting and, in certain respects, misleading. Why? One reason is that reaction time is an aggregate measure that represents only the final output of what is often a complicated series of cognitive events. As a result, important aspects of cognitive processing may not be revealed through reaction time.

To illustrate this point, let's consider the cognitive changes associated with old age. Among the most commonly observed of these are declines in memory, in attention, and in mental processing speed. These changes—usually gauged by measures of accuracy and reaction time—have led researchers to conclude that age-related changes in cognitive ability stem from an overall decline in mental processing, a decline that is magnified as the complexity of the task increases (Cerella, Poon, & Williams, 1980). But is this true? Recent findings using *event-related brain potentials,* or *ERPs,* cast doubt on this possibility (see Figure 7.4).

As we discussed in Chapter 2, ERPs reflect the momentary changes in brain electrical activity that occur as a person performs a cognitive task (Ashcraft, 1998). To measure ERPs, researchers place electrodes at standard locations on the scalp, and a computer analyzes the underlying neural patterns. The series of changes in brain electrical activity reflect different aspects of cognitive activity,

**Figure 7.4**
**Event-Related Brain Potentials: A Tool for Measuring Cognitive Processes**

Event-related brain potentials, or ERPs, are one of several high-tech tools psychologists use to measure aspects of cognitive processing.

as when a person detects and identifies a visual stimulus, or selects and executes the appropriate response to the stimulus. These changes are called components of the ERP and are named on the basis of the charge of the current flow (P for positive and N for negative) and the time at which they achieve their maximum amplitude following presentation of a stimulus. For example, the P300 component is so named because it achieves its maximum amplitude about 300 milliseconds after a stimulus is presented.

The use of ERPs in studies of aging appear to challenge the widely held notion of a general decline in cognitive functions as we get older (Bashore, Ridderinkhof, & van der Molen, 1997). Research findings suggest that age-related cognitive declines are *not* evident during older participants' initial processing of a visual stimulus; and about 200 milliseconds after the initial presentation of a stimulus, older participants actually process information faster than their younger counterparts. The major decline in performance among older people seems to occur at about 260 milliseconds, suggesting that the decline in cognitive performance typically observed in reaction-time studies may stem from a shift in the speed with which older persons are able to select and then executive the appropriate *response.*

The point of this section should be clear: Conclusions drawn from the use of a single measure can be limiting and can lead to incorrect conclusions about the nature of cognitive processes. Characterizing these processes may instead be best accomplished through the use of a variety of measures, including ERPs and other brain-imaging techniques such as PET scans (refer to Chapter 2 for additional information on brain-imaging tools).

Let's turn now to a discussion of another important aspect of cognition: reasoning.

REVIEW QUESTIONS

- What are concepts?
- What is the difference between logical and natural concepts?
- What are propositions and images?
- What are ERPs, and what can they tell us about cognition?

Food for Thought

Research shows a decline in the speed of cognitive processing in older persons as they select and execute the appropriate response to a stimulus, but not in the initial stages of processing. Could scientists use this information to slow the rate of such declines or prevent them from occurring altogether?

## Reasoning: Transforming Information to Reach Conclusions

One task we often face in everyday life is **reasoning:** drawing conclusions from available information. More formally, in reasoning we make cognitive transformations of appropriate information in order to reach specific conclusions (Galotti, 1989). How do we perform this task? And to what extent are we successful at it—in other words, how likely are the conclusions we reach to be accurate or valid?

First, it's important to draw a distinction between formal reasoning and what might be described as everyday reasoning. In *formal reasoning,* all the required information is supplied, the problem to be solved is straightforward, there is typically only one correct answer, and the reasoning we apply follows a specific method. In contrast to formal reasoning, *everyday reasoning* involves the kind of thinking we do in our daily lives: planning, making commitments, evaluating arguments. In such reasoning, important information may be missing or left unstated; the problems involved often have several possible answers, which may vary in quality or effectiveness; and the problems themselves are not self-contained—they relate to other issues and questions of daily life (Hilton, 1995). Everyday reasoning, then, is far more complex and far less definite than formal reasoning. But because it is the kind we usually perform, it is worthy of careful attention.

**Reasoning:** Cognitive activity in which we transform information in order to reach specific conclusions.

**REASONING: SOME BASIC SOURCES OF ERROR** How good are we at reasoning? Unfortunately, not as good as you might guess. Several factors, working together, seem to reduce our ability to reason effectively.

***The Role of Mood States.*** You may not be surprised to learn that the way we feel can reduce our ability to reason effectively (Forgas, 1995). Most of us have experienced situations in which we've lost our cool—and, unfortunately, our ability to reason effectively as well. You may be surprised to learn, however, that *positive* moods can also reduce our ability to reason effectively. In one study, Oaksford and colleagues (1996) used brief film clips to induce either positive, negative, or neutral moods in the participants. Following the mood induction, all participants attempted to solve several difficult reasoning tasks. For example, one task, referred to as the four-card problem, required them to turn cards over to verify a rule, such as "If there is a vowel on one side of a card, then there is an even number on the other side of the card." If the letter *A* appears on the first card, the letter *K* on the second card, the number 4 on the third card, and 7 on the fourth, which of these cards must be turned in order to verify the rule is being followed? The participants in the positive mood condition were less effective in solving problems like this one than participants in the other groups. Apparently, being in a positive mood makes more, and more diffuse, memories available to us. This is an asset for tasks requiring a creative solution. Solving problems like the ones used in this study, however, relies less on long-term memory retrieval and more on the ability to work through a series of discrete steps. In short, a positive mood state does not guarantee that our ability to reason effectively will be enhanced. (See Chapter 10 for additional information on the effects of mood on cognitive processes.)

***The Role of Beliefs.*** Reasoning is often influenced by emotion-laden beliefs. For example, imagine that a person with deeply held convictions against the death penalty listens to a speech favoring capital punishment. Suppose that the arguments presented by the speaker contain premises the listener can't readily refute, and thus point to the conclusion that the death penalty is justified for the purpose of preventing further social evil. Yet the listener totally rejects this conclusion. Why? Because of his or her passionate beliefs and convictions against the death penalty, the listener may alter the meaning of the speaker's premises or "remember" things the speaker never really said. This, of course, serves to weaken the speaker's conclusion. Such effects can arise in many ways. Whatever your views on this particular issue, the general principle remains the same: When powerful beliefs come face to face with logical arguments, it is often the latter that gives way. We'll consider the powerful effects of emotion again in Chapter 10.

***The Confirmation Bias: Searching for Positive Evidence.*** Imagine that over the course of several weeks, a person with deeply held convictions *against* the death penalty encounters numerous magazine articles; some report evidence confirming the usefulness of the death penalty, while others report evidence indicating that capital punishment is ineffective in terms of deterring crime. As you can readily guess, the individual will probably remember more of the information that supports the anti–death penalty view. In fact, there is a good chance that he or she will read only these articles, or will read these articles more carefully than ones arguing in favor of capital punishment. To the extent that this happens, it demonstrates the **confirmation bias**—our strong tendency to test conclusions or hypotheses by examining only, or primarily, evidence that confirms our initial views (Baron, 1988; Nickerson, 1998) (see Chapter 1 for additional information on the confirmation bias). Because of the confirmation bias, individuals often become firmly locked into flawed conclusions; after all, when this bias operates, it prevents people from even considering information that might call their premises, and thus their conclusions, into question (see Figure 7.5 on page 256).

**Confirmation Bias:** The tendency to pay attention primarily to information that confirms existing views or beliefs.

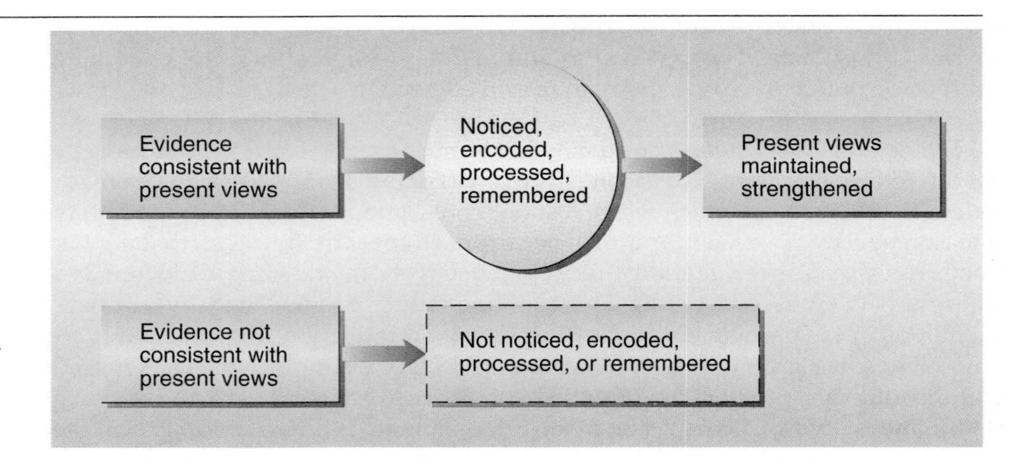


**Figure 7.5**
**The Confirmation Bias**

The confirmation bias leads individuals to test conclusions or hypotheses by examining primarily—or only—evidence consistent with their initial views. As a result, these views may be maintained regardless of the weight of opposing evidence.

***Hindsight: The "I knew it all along" Effect Revisited.*** Have you ever heard the old saying "Hindsight is better than foresight"? What it means is that after specific events occur, we often have the impression that we could have predicted or actually did predict them. This is known in psychology as the **hindsight effect** (Hawkins & Hastie, 1990). In many studies, conducted in widely different contexts, learning that an event occurred causes individuals to assume that they could have predicted it more accurately than is actually the case (Christensen-Szalanski & Willham, 1991; Dawson et al., 1988; Hawkins & Hastie, 1990).

Interestingly, most research on the hindsight effect has involved soliciting the opinions of observers of an event or decision outcome—not those of the participants or decision makers themselves. More recent research on this topic has examined whether decision makers themselves show hindsight bias (Mark & Mellor, 1991). Of particular interest to researchers is how individuals show the bias when their decisions reflect upon their ability or skill. Some evidence seems to indicate that hindsight may be influenced by whether outcomes reflect positively or negatively upon the decision maker (Dunning, Leuenberger, & Sherman, 1995). In the process of taking credit for outcomes that reflect well on them, people may show significant hindsight effects, as in "I knew the outcome would be favorable, because I made a wise decision." Similarly, if people deny responsibility for *un*successful outcomes, hindsight effects may be reduced or eliminated altogether, as in "The outcome was not foreseeable; and therefore, it was not my fault." This suggests that because of our tendency to act in ways that are self-serving, the hindsight effect may be most evident for events for which we receive favorable feedback for our actions.

To test this possibility, Louie (1999) asked participants to read a case study about a company that intended to market recycled motor oil for cars and other vehicles. Participants were then asked to assess the company's chance of succeeding and on that basis to decide whether it would be advantageous to buy shares of the company's stock. After making their decision, participants received either no information about the subsequent performance of the stock, information that the stock price had increased, or information that the stock price had dropped. They were then asked to rate what they had thought would happen to the stock price before they were informed. Results showed that the degree to which participants exhibited the hindsight bias depended on the favorableness of the match between their stock purchase decisions and the corresponding outcome information. Only participants who received favorable decision outcome information exhibited hindsight bias. These findings seem to point to the following tentative conclusion: In decision-making settings, individuals want to appear as if they "knew all along" what would occur—especially when it supports their self-serving tendencies.

**Hindsight Effect:** The tendency to assume that we would have been better at predicting actual events than is really true.

Please note, however, that the hindsight effect has impacts that go well beyond decision makers. Indeed, judgments influenced by the hindsight bias can often have serious consequences, both for decision makers and for those who depend on them. This can be illustrated by a tragic incident in which several hikers lost their lives during an ill-fated Mount Everest climb (Krakauer, 1997). Among those who died during the climb was the group's leader, by all accounts an experienced professional climbing guide. Bad weather appeared to play a role in the disaster, but a survivor also noted that the leader may have taken unnecessary risks motivated, at least in part, by hindsight bias. Previously, the guide had completed several successful climbs on Mount Everest. The favorable outcomes of prior climbs may have appeared to him to be more inevitable in hindsight that they did in foresight. This may have caused the leader to have more confidence in his abilities and in the probable outcome of the ill-fated expedition than was actually warranted. Unfortunately, focusing on the *actual* outcomes (success), and not on other possible outcomes (the many ways in which these expeditions could have failed), may have caused him to ignore factors responsible for his previous successes; for example, the fact that each of the previous climbs had taken place in good weather (Krakauer, 1997). In sum, it appears that we have a strong tendency to assume that we are better at predicting events than is truly justified, and this slant in our cognitions may be exaggerated by our self-serving tendencies. To the extent that we seek out ways to avoid these tendencies, our ability to reason more effectively may be enhanced.

**Physical Reasoning:** The ways in which people perceive physical objects and the cognitive processes that allow people to make predictions about events involving these objects.

**PHYSICAL REASONING: REASONING ABOUT OBJECTS IN THE PHYSICAL WORLD** Imagine a glass half full of water sitting on a table. If the top of the glass is now tipped slightly toward the table, will you be able to predict the resulting angle of the water? Now imagine that a person sitting on the roof of a house is set to let a ball roll down it. If asked, could you draw the path the ball will take as it falls to the ground? These simple problems illustrate a rapidly growing area of research within cognitive psychology: the study of **physical reasoning** (Pani, 1997). Psychologists who investigate physical reasoning are interested in how people perceive physical objects and their movement, and in the cognitive processes that allow people to make predictions about events involving these objects, as in the examples just described.

Emerging evidence suggests that the ability to reason effectively about the nature of physical objects depends on the fit between the information we gain through perception and our knowledge of fundamental properties of physical systems. Among the most important of these properties is *orientation*—how physical objects are aligned in three-dimensional space. To illustrate how objects' orientation can affect physical reasoning, let's consider a recent study by Pani, Zhou, and Friend (1997). Participants in this study viewed computer-simulated three-dimensional objects as they were slowly rotated around an imaginary vertical axis. The objects were oriented in one of two ways, as shown in Figure 7.6. Participants could study the objects as long as they wished. When they were sure that they could imagine a shape accurately, they were asked to imagine it superimposed onto a styrofoam sphere and then represent the shape physically by inserting pins into the sphere where the corners or surfaces of the shape would be. Results indicated that the way in which the objects were oriented had dramatic effects on participants' performance. Participants who viewed the objects depicted in the top part of Figure 7.6 on page 258 required much less time to study the shapes initially and were more accurate in representing the shapes than participants exposed to the objects in the bottom part.

Why should such differences occur? According to Pani and his colleagues, participants who viewed the vertically aligned objects perceived them as having symmetrical edges and surfaces and, therefore, as subjectively simple. In contrast, participants who viewed the same objects oriented differently perceived them to have nonuniform edges and surfaces, and therefore saw them as subjectively complex. Additional research involving object rotation has revealed similar findings (e.g., Pani, 1993). In short, research on physical reasoning has revealed important

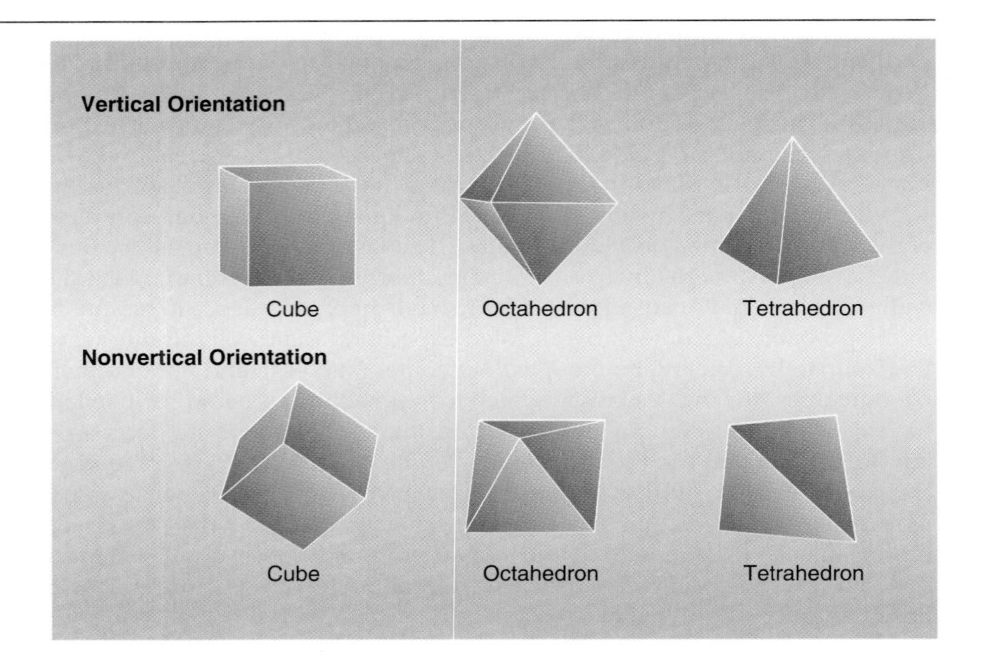


**Figure 7.6**
**Physical Reasoning: Reasoning about the Nature of Physical Objects**

Participants who viewed the objects oriented vertically required much less time to study the shapes initially and were more accurate in physically representing the shapes than participants exposed to the objects oriented nonvertically. Participants who viewed the vertically aligned objects perceived them as subjectively simple. In contrast, participants who viewed the same objects oriented differently perceived them as subjectively complex.
(*Source:* Adapted with permission from Pani, 1997.)

clues about the way people perceive aspects of the physical world and the cognitive processes that allow people to make predictions about events involving these objects. Let's turn next to another cognitive activity we perform many times each day: decision making.

**REVIEW QUESTIONS**

- What is the process of reasoning? How does formal reasoning differ from everyday reasoning?
- What forms of error and bias can lead to faulty reasoning?
- What is physical reasoning?

# Making Decisions: Choosing among Alternatives

Reasoning is hard work; in fact, it's an activity many people try to avoid. In some respects, though, reasoning is less difficult than another cognitive task you perform many times each day: **decision making.** Throughout our waking hours, life presents a continuous series of choices: what to wear, what to eat, whether to attend a class meeting, and so on—the list of everyday decisions is endless.

If you were a perfectly rational decision maker, you would make each of these choices in a cool, almost mathematical way, taking into consideration (1) the utility or value to you of the outcomes each alternative might yield and (2) the probability that such results would actually occur. As you know from your own life, though, people don't usually reason in such a systematic manner. Instead, we make decisions informally, on the basis of hunches, intuition, the information stored in our memories, and the opinions of others (Christenfeld, 1995; Dougherty, Gettys, & Ogden, 1999).

**Decision Making:** The process of choosing among various courses of action or alternatives.

Let's consider several factors that influence the decision-making process, making it less rational or effective than it might otherwise be.

## Heuristics: Using Quick—but Fallible—Rules of Thumb to Make Decisions

**Heuristics:** Mental rules of thumb that permit us to make decisions and judgments in a rapid and efficient manner.

**Availability Heuristic:** A cognitive rule of thumb in which the importance or probability of various events is judged on the basis of how readily they come to mind.

Audio 7.1: *Availability Heuristic and Ease Rule*

Where cognition is concerned, human beings often follow the path of least resistance. Making decisions is hard work, so it is only reasonable to expect people to take shortcuts in performing this activity. One group of cognitive shortcuts is known as **heuristics**—rules of thumb that reduce the effort required, though they may not necessarily enhance the quality or accuracy of the decisions reached (Kahneman & Tversky, 1982). Heuristics are extracted from past experience and serve as simple guidelines for making reasonably good choices quickly and efficiently. We'll focus on the three heuristics that tend to be used most frequently.

**AVAILABILITY: WHAT COMES TO MIND FIRST?** Let's start with the **availability heuristic:** the tendency to make judgments about the frequency or likelihood of events in terms of how readily examples of them can be brought to mind. This shortcut tends to work fairly well, because the more readily we can bring events to mind, the more frequent they generally are; but it can lead us into error as well. A good example of the availability heuristic in operation is provided by a study conducted by Tversky and Kahneman (1974). These researchers presented participants with lists of names like the one in Table 7.1 and then asked them whether the lists contained more men's or women's names. Although the numbers of male and female names were about equal, nearly 80 percent of the participants reported that women's names appeared more frequently. Why? Because the women named in the lists were more famous, so their names were more readily remembered and brought to mind. The availability heuristic also influences many persons to overestimate their chances of being a victim of violent crime, being involved in an airplane crash, or winning the lottery. Because such events are given extensive coverage in the mass media, people can readily bring vivid examples of them to mind. The result: They conclude that such outcomes are much more frequent than they really are (Tyler & Cook, 1984).

**TABLE 7.1**

### The Availability Heuristic in Operation

Does this list contain more men's or women's names? The answer may surprise you: There are fifteen male names and only fourteen female names. Because of the *availability heuristic,* however, most people tend to guess that female names are more numerous. The women listed are more famous than the men, so it is easier to bring their names to mind; this leads to overestimates of their frequency in the list.

| | | |
|---|---|---|
| Louisa May Alcott | Henry Vaughan | Allan Nevins |
| John Dickson Carr | Kate Millet | Jane Austen |
| Emily Dickinson | Eudora Welty | Henry Crabb Robinson |
| Thomas Hughes | Richard Watson Gilder | Joseph Lincoln |
| Laura Ingalls Wilder | Harriet Beecher Stowe | Emily Brontë |
| Jack Lindsay | Pearl Buck | Arthur Hutchinson |
| Edward George Lytton | Amy Lowell | James Hunt |
| Margaret Mitchell | Robert Lovett | Erica Jong |
| Michael Drayton | Edna St. Vincent Millay | Brian Hooker |
| Edith Wharton | George Jean Nathan | |

**REPRESENTATIVENESS: ASSUMING THAT WHAT'S TYPICAL IS ALSO LIKELY** Imagine that you've just met your next-door neighbor for the first time. On the basis of a brief conversation, you determine that he is neat in his appearance, has a good vocabulary, seems very well read, is somewhat shy, and dresses conservatively. Later, you realize that he never mentioned what he does for a living. Is he more likely to be a business executive, a dentist, a librarian, or a waiter? One quick way of making a guess is to compare him with your idea of typical members of each of these occupations. If you proceeded in this fashion, you might conclude that he is a librarian, because his traits might seem to resemble those of your image of the prototypical librarian more closely than those of waiters, dentists, or executives. If you reasoned in this manner, you would be using the **representativeness heuristic.** In other words, you would be making your decision on the basis of a relatively simple rule: The more closely an item—or event, object, or person—resembles the most typical examples of some concept or category, the more likely it is to belong to that concept or category.

Unfortunately, the use of this heuristic sometimes causes us to ignore forms of information that could potentially prove very helpful. The most important of these is information relating to *base rates*—the relative frequency of various items or events in the external world. Returning to your new neighbor, there are many more businessmen than male librarians. Thus, of the choices given, the most rational guess might be that your neighbor is a business executive. Yet because of the representativeness heuristic, you might falsely conclude that he is a librarian (Tversky & Kahneman, 1974).

**ANCHORING-AND-ADJUSTMENT: REFERENCE POINTS THAT MAY LEAD US ASTRAY** The day I received my driver's license, I began to shop for my first car. After a long search, I found the car of my dreams. The major question, of course, was "How much will it cost?" A totally rational person would have located this information in the *Blue Book,* which lists the average prices paid for various used cars in recent months. But did I proceed in this fashion? Absolutely not. I asked the seller what he wanted for the car, then proceeded to bargain from there. At first glance, this may seem like a reasonable strategy. But think again. If you adopt it, as I did when I purchased that car, you have allowed the seller to set a reference point—a figure from which your negotiations will proceed. In the case of a used car, if the reference point is close to the *Blue Book* price, all well and good. If it is much higher, though, you may end up paying more for the car than it is really worth—as I did.

Web Link: *Decision Research Center*

In such cases, decisions are influenced by what is known as the **anchoring-and-adjustment heuristic:** a mental rule of thumb for reaching decisions by making adjustments in information that is already available. The basic problem with the anchoring-and-adjustment heuristic is that the adjustments are often insufficient in magnitude to offset the impact of the original reference point. In this case, the reference point was the original asking price. In other contexts, it might be a performance rating assigned to an employee, a grade given to a term paper, or a suggested asking price for a new home (Diekmann et al., 1996; Northcraft & Neale, 1987).

**Representativeness Heuristic:** A mental rule of thumb suggesting that the more closely an event or object resembles typical examples of some concept or category, the more likely it is to belong to that concept or category.

**Anchoring-and-Adjustment Heuristic:** A cognitive rule of thumb for making decisions in which existing information is accepted as a reference point but then adjusted (usually insufficiently) in light of various factors.

## Framing and Decision Strategy

Imagine that a rare tropical disease has entered the United States and is expected to kill 600 people. Two plans for combating the disease exist. If plan A is adopted, 200 people will be saved. If plan B is adopted, the chances are one in three that all 600 will be saved but two in three that no one will be saved. Which plan would you choose?

Now consider the same situation with the following changes. Again, there are two plans. If plan C is chosen, 400 people will definitely die; if plan D is chosen, the chances are one in three that no one will die, but two in three that all 600 will die. Which would you choose now?

If you are like most respondents, you probably chose plan A in the first example but plan D in the second example (Tversky & Kahneman, 1981). Why? Plan D is just another way of stating the outcomes of plan B, and plan C is just another way of stating the outcome of plan A. Why, then, do you prefer plan A in the first example but plan D in the second? Because in the first example the emphasis is on lives saved, while in the second the emphasis is on lives lost. In other words, the two examples differ in what psychologists term **framing**—the presentation of information about potential outcomes in terms of gains or in terms of losses. When the emphasis is on potential gains (lives saved), research indicates that most people are *risk averse.* They prefer avoiding unnecessary risks. Thus, most choose plan A. In contrast, when the emphasis is on potential losses (deaths), most people are *risk prone;* they prefer taking risks to accepting probable losses. As a result, most choose plan D. The effects of framing have been demonstrated across a wide variety of contexts, including consumer purchases (Schul & Ganzach, 1995), medical decision making (McNeil, Pauker, & Tversky, 1988), and personal and career decisions (Gati, Houminer, & Aviram, 1998; Shafir, 1993).

**Framing:** Presentation of information concerning potential outcomes in terms of gains or in terms of losses.

Studies seem to indicate that the strength of framing effects may stem partly from the scenarios researchers use to induce them (Jou, Shanteau, & Harris, 1996; Wang, 1996). The disease example just described is arbitrary, in the sense that it does not provide a rationale for the relationships among the potential gains and losses. People usually have a general understanding about how events are related based on *schemas,* the cognitive frameworks we discussed in Chapter 6. When events we encounter cannot be fit into a schema, as in the disease scenario above, the relationship between the events may not be apparent. In one study, Jou and his colleagues (1996) asked participants to read either the original disease examples or the same ones revised to include a rationale that explained why a choice must be made. The rationale indicated that saving some proportion of lives would require sacrificing other lives because of limited resources. The researchers reasoned that including this rationale would clarify the relationship between lives saved and lives lost, which in turn might reduce the effects of framing. As shown in Figure 7.7, the researchers' predictions were confirmed: Framing effects were apparent for

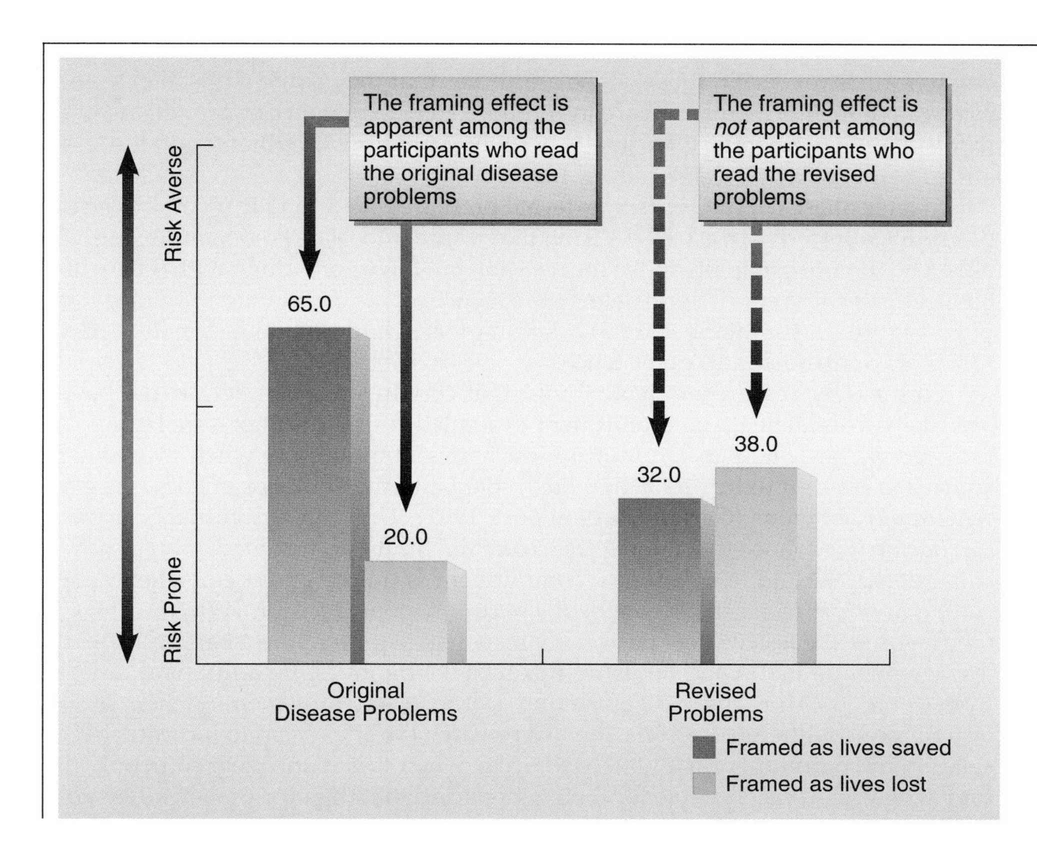


**Figure 7.7**
**Understanding the Effects of Framing**

The effects of framing are evident among participants who read the original disease problem: These participants were risk averse when the problem was framed positively (lives saved), but risk prone when it was framed negatively. The effects of framing disappeared, however, when participants were given a rationale that helped them understand the relationship between lives saved and lives lost.

(*Source:* Based on data from Jou et al., 1996.)

participants who read the original disease examples, but not for participants who read the revised examples. These results suggest that the effects of framing, though powerful, are not immutable; they are affected by people's attitudes and can be offset when people are given a more complete picture of the choices to be made (Rothman & Salovey, 1997).

CourseCompass

Web Link: *Errors of Judgment and Decision Making*

Video 7.1: *Marijuana Use and Decision Making*

## Escalation of Commitment: Getting Trapped in Bad Decisions

Have you ever heard the phrase "throwing good money after bad"? It refers to the fact that in many situations, persons who have made a bad decision tend to stick to it even as the evidence for its failure mounts. They may even commit additional time, effort, and resources to a failing course of action in order to turn the situation around. This tendency to become trapped in bad decisions, known as **escalation of commitment,** helps explain why many investors hold on to what are clearly bad investments and why people remain in troubled marriages or relationships (Brockner & Rubin, 1985). In these and many other situations, people do seem to become trapped in bad decisions with no simple or easy means of getting out.

**ESCALATION OF COMMITMENT: WHY DOES IT OCCUR?** Escalation of commitment is both real and widespread. But why, precisely, does it occur? Research suggests that escalation of commitment probably stems from several different factors (Staw & Ross, 1989). Early in the escalation process, initial decisions are based primarily on *rational* factors. People choose particular courses of action because they believe that these will yield favorable outcomes. When things go wrong and negative results occur, it is at first quite reasonable to continue. After all, temporary setbacks are common; and there may also be considerable costs associated with changing an initial decision before it has had a chance to succeed (Staw & Ross, 1987).

As negative outcomes continue to mount, however, *psychological* factors come into play. Persons responsible for the initial decision may realize that if they back away from or reverse it, they will be admitting that they made a mistake. Indeed, as negative results increase, these individuals may experience a growing need for *self-justification*—a tendency to justify both their previous judgments and the losses already endured (Bobocel & Meyer, 1994).

In later phases of the process, external pressures stemming from other persons or groups affected by the bad decision may come into play. For example, individuals who did not originally make the decision but have gone along with it may now block efforts to reverse it because they too have become committed to actions it implies. Figure 7.8 summarizes the escalation process and several factors that play a role in its occurrence and persistence.

Fortunately, researchers have found that certain steps can help make people less likely to escalate their commitment to a failed course of action (see Figure 7.8). First, people are likely to refrain from escalating commitment when available resources to commit to further action are limited and the evidence of failure is overwhelmingly obvious (Garland & Newport, 1991). Thus, an individual or a group can decide in advance that if losses reach certain limits, no further resources will be squandered. Second, escalation of commitment is unlikely to occur when people can *diffuse their responsibility* for being part of a poor decision (Whyte, 1991). In other words, the less we feel personally responsible for making a bad decision, the less we may be motivated to justify our mistake by investing additional time, efforts, or money. Thus, the tasks of making decisions and implementing them should be assigned to different persons. Finally, research findings seem to indicate that escalation of commitment is unlikely to occur when it is made clear to people that they will be held accountable for their actions and that they, or someone they work

**Escalation of Commitment:** The tendency to become increasingly committed to bad decisions even as losses associated with them increase.

**Figure 7.8**
**Escalation of Commitment: An Overview**

Early in the escalation-of-commitment process, there may be a rational expectation of a positive outcome. As losses occur, however, people are reluctant to admit their errors and seek self-justification. Later, external factors may strengthen tendencies to stick to the initial bad decision. However, other conditions may reduce the likelihood of escalation of commitment. (*Source:* Based on suggestions by Garland & Newport, 1991; and Staw & Ross, 1989.)

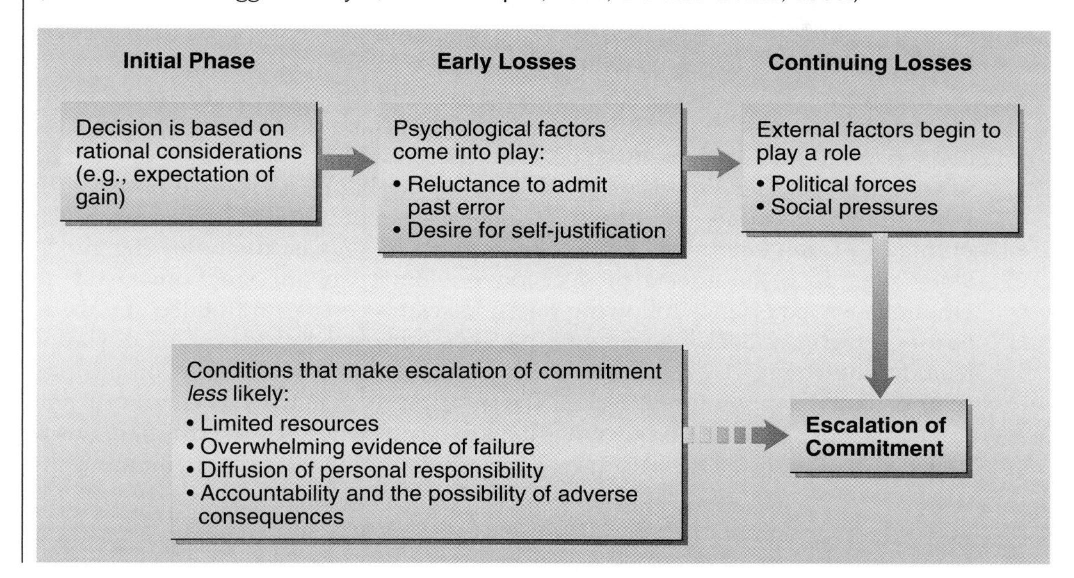


for, may be adversely affected by the consequences of their decisions (Kirby & Davis, 1998; Simonson & Staw, 1992). Together, these steps can help both individuals and groups avoid getting trapped in costly spirals that magnify the harmful effects of poor decisions. For additional information on escalation of commitment and other errors of reasoning, please see the **Beyond the Headlines** feature on page 264.

## Emotions and Decision Making: The Magnifying Effects of Unexpected Loss and Gain

Throughout our discussions of decision making, we have focused on various factors that influence the decision making process; for example, our inclination to rely on rules of thumb instead of careful reasoning and our tendency to be influenced by the powerful effects of framing. One aspect of decision making that we've not yet considered, though, is the role of emotions; in particular, how people feel about the outcomes of decisions they make. As you know from your own experience, our reactions to outcomes are often heavily influenced by the way decisions turn out. When desirable outcomes flow from a decision, we tend to feel happy. Conversely, undesirable outcomes may leave us feeling disappointed, perhaps even angry. However, other cognitive factors also seem to play a role. Our reactions to decision outcomes can also be influenced by our expectations—what we anticipate will happen—and by the comparisons we make between the actual outcome and other outcomes that could have occurred, a tendency referred to as *counterfactual thinking* (see Chapter 16 for additional information on counterfactual thinking).

To illustrate how these cognitive factors influence our emotional reactions to decision outcomes, let's consider an intriguing study conducted by Mellers and her colleagues (1997). Participants in this study were presented with a series of gambles in which they could either gain or lose money, and were told the probabilities associated with each gamble. After each gamble, they were informed of the outcome and then asked to indicate their feelings about it. The results were complex, but can be summarized as follows. As predicted, the results showed that participants' emotional reactions varied directly with the amount of money they won or lost. However, expectations also appeared to have a magnifying effect on individuals' emotional reactions. Surprising wins (those with a low probability of occurring) were more elating than expected wins (those with a high probability of occurring). Similarly, participants expressed greater disappointment in response to unexpected losses (those with a low probability of occurring) than expected ones.

Interestingly, counterfactual thinking also played a role in the participants' emotional reactions. In other words, their feelings about obtaining the same outcome differed greatly depending on what else could have occurred. For example, when participants avoided losing $50, they were happy to receive nothing. But when they missed an opportunity to *win* the same amount, they were disappointed to receive nothing. These results seem to suggest the following conclusions regarding the effects of decision outcomes on our emotions. First, the emotions we experience following decisions can be greatly influenced by the extent to which the decision outcome matches our expectations. Large deviations from the outcome we expect tend to amplify our joy (when the outcome is positive) or our disappointment (when the outcome is negative). Second, our emotional reactions to decision outcomes tend to be influenced by the comparisons we make with other possible outcomes: Depending on the comparison, the same outcome can be elating or disappointing.

## BEYOND the HEADLINES: *As Psychologists See It*

## Was It the Weather, or Did Faulty Reasoning Kill JFK Jr.?

### Limited Pilot Training, Weather among Variables, Experts Say

DALLAS MORNING NEWS (JULY 17, 1999)—Although John F. Kennedy Jr. had reportedly made the hop across the dark New England waters to Martha's Vineyard before, Friday night's flight held dangers that easily could have overcome a pilot with limited experience. Aviation experts say Kennedy had several things going against him: He was a relatively inexperienced pilot flying a slick new airplane that demanded lots of attention over water on a moonless night. It was technically legal for him to fly without the aid of instruments because visibility was still at least three miles. But other pilots reported that a thick summer haze hung off the coast like a fog, making it difficult to tell where the sky ended and the ocean began. Without a clear horizon, pilots must rely on their cockpit instruments to tell them whether their airplanes are flying levelly. It is easy for pilots to become disoriented as their inner ear tricks their sense of equilibrium. For example, decelerating while turning one direction can create the sensation of turning the opposite direction. Or an abrupt change from a climb to level flight can create the feeling of tumbling backward. Details of Kennedy's flight remain sketchy. But available evidence suggests that he was confident enough in his abilities that he decided not to take the precautions of filing a flight plan with the Federal Aviation Administration or asking air-traffic controllers to monitor his flight. Experts concede that it will probably be weeks—if ever—before investigators determine what caused the 38-year-old pilot's airplane to plunge into the ocean. There was no cockpit voice recorder or flight data recorder, but the absence of any distress calls before the crash suggests that whatever happened was sudden.

Veteran crash investigators say the most likely explanation for the plane crash that killed John F. Kennedy Jr., his wife, and her sister is that Kennedy may simply have been unable to tell which way was up. They contend that the airplane would have been descending in the dark toward an island that was nearly twenty miles away and almost certainly not visible. Kennedy had not received the training necessary to fly his airplane solely by the use of instruments, but without the use of instruments, he could have easily become disoriented (see Figure 7.9). Radar evidence showing a sudden unexpected dive, and inspection of the plane's wreckage revealing that the plane was intact as it hit the water, appear to support this possibility.

But were perceptual issues the only contributing factors to this tragedy? What about the series of flight-related decisions Kennedy had made prior to the crash? Had he exercised good judgment? Was the outcome of this ill-fated flight merely confirmation of his propensity to take risks, as some writers suggested afterwards? Although we will never have clear answers to these questions, the evidence seems to suggest the possibility that key decisions leading up to the flight may have been influenced by several errors of reasoning and decision making we have discussed in this chapter. Let's explore the following possibilities.

Interviews conducted after the plane crash indicate that John Kennedy and his passengers had intended to leave much earlier than their actual departure just before dark. Apparently a series of events, including congested traffic, contributed to the delay. Why is this relevant? As I've already noted, Kennedy was not an instrument-rated pilot. Therefore, the originally scheduled daylight departure time would have allowed him to complete the flight *before* dark. So why, when it became apparent that much of the flight would take place in darkness, didn't he postpone the flight until the following morning? One possibility is suggested by hindsight bias. Kennedy had already completed several successful flights to Martha's Vineyard. The favorable outcomes of these flights may have appeared to him more inevitable in hindsight than in foresight. This may have instilled in him more confidence in his abilities and in the probable outcome of the night flight than were actually warranted. Kennedy's focus on the actual outcomes of previous flights, and not on the ways in which they could have gone wrong, may have caused him to ignore factors that had allowed him to get there safely; in particular, the presence of an instructor who had accompanied him on these flights.

Escalation of commitment, too, may have played a role. How? Although Kennedy and his passengers had departed later than initially planned, we now know that Kennedy had received a preflight weather report indicating good visual-flight-rule conditions, with visibility from six to eight miles. Reports of hazy skies and limited visibility occurred only *after* the flight was under way. Thus, Kennedy's initial decision to proceed with a late departure was rational. Later, as he turned the airplane away from the coast and proceeded over the open sea—and away from critical visual cues—it might have seemed reasonable (at least to him) to continue, despite the inherent risks involved. After all, the flight was nearly over, and his destination was only minutes away. And perhaps, in Kennedy's estimation, the costs associated with turning back may have outweighed the risks of pressing on. For example, family members had been expecting him and his passengers to participate in festivities surrounding his cousin's wedding, so turning back would have meant disappointing the family. Moreover, if he turned back, he would be admitting that he had made a mistake in his earlier decision to attempt the flight.

Is it possible that hindsight and escalation of commitment played a role in John F. Kennedy Jr.'s flight-related decisions that night? Clearly, we will never know the true answer to this question. The possibilities described in this section merely speculate as to what may have occurred that night. However, based on evidence that emerged from the investigation of the crash and on a large body of research on cognitive processes, the involvement of these sources of error seems likely.

**Figure 7.9**
**Was It the Weather? Or a Tragic Outcome of Faulty Reasoning?**

The most likely explanation for the plane crash that killed John F. Kennedy Jr. is that he may have become disoriented as a result of the hazy conditions that existed that night. However, some evidence seem to indicate that several basic errors of reasoning may have also played a role in key decisions Kennedy made both before and during the ill-fated flight.

## CRITICAL THINKING QUESTIONS

1. Suppose that the cognitive biases discussed in this section did, in fact, affect key flight-related decisions JFK Jr. made with regard to his fatal flight. How could pilots and flight instructors use this information to prevent similar tragedies from happening in the future?
2. How could you design an experiment to test whether the reasoning errors discussed in this section affect pilot decisions in a way that does not jeopardize their own and their passengers' safety?
3. Suggest ways in which this tragic accident could have been prevented.

**Naturalistic Decision Making:** Decision making as it occurs in real-world settings.

## Naturalistic Decision Making: Making Choices in the Real World

In recent years, researchers who study decision making have begun to shift their efforts away from the laboratory and into applied settings. Decision making as it occurs in the real world has been termed **naturalistic decision making** (Orasanu & Connolly, 1993). The newer emphasis on this area contributes to the study of decision making in several ways (Cannon-Bowers, Salas, & Pruitt, 1996). First, it focuses attention on how people bring their experience to bear in making decisions. After all, people differ in many ways, and these differences contribute to the type and the quality of decisions they make. Second, research on naturalistic decision making broadens the focus from a single decision "event" to include elements of the decision context. Much of what is known about decision making is based on controlled laboratory studies in which participants read a brief story and then make a decision based on its contents. Some researchers question whether many of the findings of these studies bear any relationship to decision making in everyday life (Fischoff, 1996). Finally, work on naturalistic decision making emphasizes the dynamic nature of decision making and takes into account the complexity of modern decision environments—including the potentially enormous costs of making bad decisions, in terms of both money and loss of life.

Although research on naturalistic decision making is a relatively new development, its application has led to fuller, and perhaps more accurate, descriptions of the decision-making process as it unfolds in environments in which the accuracy of decisions is paramount (please refer to Figure 7.10). Examples of environments studied include military and health care settings, the courtroom, and even an oil-drilling platform in the North Sea (Flin, Slaven, & Stewart, 1996; Kaempf et al., 1996; Pennington & Hastie, 1993; Pierce, 1996).

The shift toward studying decision making in naturalistic settings has had another, unexpected effect as well. It has forced researchers to acknowledge that research findings derived from laboratory studies may not accurately depict decision making in real-life environments. A widely reported finding that has recently been called into question pertains to the tendency referred to as the *base-rate problem:* people's tendency to ignore the relative frequency of various events when making decisions and instead to opt for simpler heuristics. As we saw earlier, when given a general description of a person and asked to judge whether that person is a businessman or a librarian, many people in laboratory studies tend to rely on the representativeness heuristic—making their judgment merely on the basis of how closely the description matches the typical features of each occupation, and ignoring the fact that there are many more businessmen than male librarians. But evidence now seems to indicate that we've been oversold on the base-rate problem and that people do consider base rates in their decisions (e.g., Koehler, 1996). Some researchers have argued that laboratory tasks are often artificial and lack the kinds of contextual information that people have available to them when making judgments in everyday life. They add that experience may also play a role; as people gain experience with specific types of judgments, they are more likely to consider base rates in their decisions. Finally, in certain instances, it may actually be prudent to ignore base rates. Similar

**Figure 7.10**
**Naturalistic Decision Making: Making Choices in the Real World**

The study of naturalistic decision making involves decision making as it occurs in everyday life. The decisions required in many situations, such as the one depicted in this photo, often have serious ramifications for those who make the decisions—and for those affected by them.

criticisms have been leveled at other well-documented findings, including the effects of framing on decision making, a topic described earlier in this section. To summarize, then, research on naturalistic decision making represents a bold step toward discovering how people make decisions in real-world settings. Stay tuned for additional developments in this rapidly growing field—they are certain to come.

**REVIEW QUESTIONS**

- What are heuristics?
- What are the availability, representativeness, and anchoring-and-adjustment heuristics, and what role do they play in decision making?
- What is framing, and how does it relate to decision making?
- How does escalation of commitment affect decision making?
- What is naturalistic decision making?

# Problem Solving: Finding Paths to Desired Goals

Imagine that you are a parent whose son is attending college in another state. You've asked him to keep in touch, but long periods go by without a word—by either phone or mail. You phone him repeatedly, but all you get is his answering machine. What do you do? Several possibilities exist. You could call his friends and ask them to urge him to get in touch with you. You could leave a message that, you hope, will cause him to phone. Or—and here's the interesting one—you could try something like this: You write a letter to your son in which you mention that you've enclosed a check—but you don't enclose one. Is the problem solved? In all probability, yes. Your son will no doubt call to find out what happened to the check.

While you may not have any children, there is little doubt that you have encountered situations that resemble this one in basic structure: You would like to reach some goal, but there is no simple or direct way of doing so. Such situations involve **problem solving**—efforts to develop responses that permit us to attain desired goals. In this section we'll examine the nature of problem solving, techniques for enhancing its effectiveness, and factors that interfere with its successful execution. (Please note that we'll consider *creativity*—the ability to produce new and unusual solutions to various problems—in Chapter 11.)

## Problem Solving: An Overview

What does problem solving involve? Psychologists are not totally in agreement on this basic issue (e.g., Lipshitz & Bar-Ilan, 1996), but many believe that four major aspects, as summarized in Figure 7.11 on page 268, are central.

The first step is *problem identification:* We must recognize that a problem exists and then figure out just what issues, obstacles, and goals are involved. In the example above, the immediate problem boils down to this: You want to find some way of inducing your son to contact you. But understanding the nature of the problems we face is not always so simple. For example, suppose your car won't start. Why? Is it a bad battery? Bad ignition? Lack of fuel? Until you identify the problem and understand the issues involved, it is difficult to move ahead with a solution.

Second, we must *formulate potential solutions.* While this too might seem fairly simple, it is actually very complex (Treffinger, 1995). Solutions do not arise out of

**Problem Solving:** Efforts to develop or choose among various responses in order to attain desired goals.

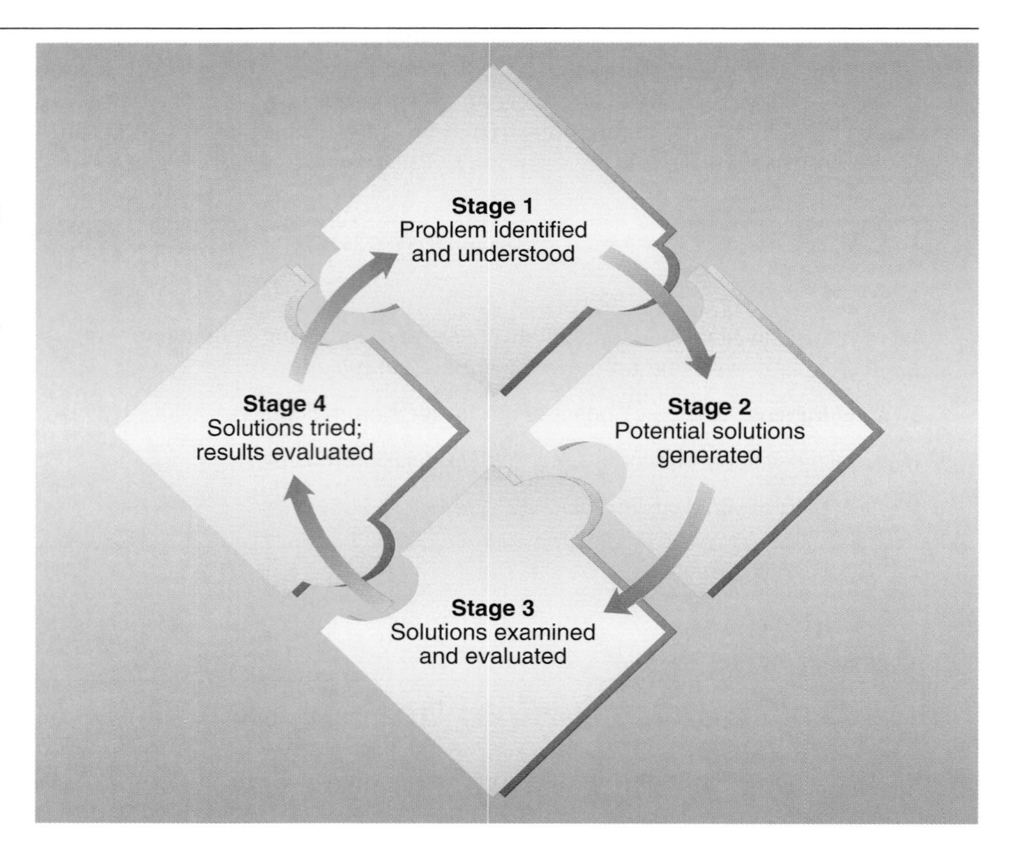


**Figure 7.11**
**Problem Solving: An Overview**

Effective problem solving involves four stages. First, the problem must be identified and understood. Next, potential solutions must be generated. Third, these must be examined and evaluated. Finally, the solutions must be tried and their results evaluated.

a cognitive vacuum; they require thinking critically about a problem, and they depend heavily on the information at our disposal—information stored in long-term memory that can be retrieved (see Chapter 6). The more information available, the greater the number and the wider the scope of potential solutions we can generate. Formulating a wide range of possible solutions is an extremely important step in effective problem solving.

Third, we must *evaluate* each alternative and the outcomes it will produce. Will a given solution work—bring us closer to the goal we want? Are there any serious obstacles to its use? Are there hidden costs that will make a potential solution less useful than it seems at first? These are considerations that must be taken into account.

Finally, we must *try* potential solutions and evaluate them on the basis of the effects they produce. All too often, a potential solution is only partially effective: It brings us closer to where we want to be but doesn't solve the problem completely or finally. The letter-without-a-check strategy illustrates this point. Yes, it may induce a response from the erring child on this occasion. But it does not guarantee that he will write or phone more frequently in the future. So it constitutes only a partial solution to the problem. In this case it is easy to recognize that the solution will be only a partial one. In many other situations, though, it is difficult to know how effective a potential solution will be until it is implemented. Thus, careful assessment of the effects of various solutions is another key step in the problem-solving process.

Web Link: *Tool Use in Animals*

## Methods for Solving Problems: From Trial and Error to Heuristics

**Trial and Error:** A method of solving problems in which possible solutions are tried until one succeeds.

Perhaps the simplest problem-solving approach is **trial and error,** a technique that you have no doubt used yourself. Trial and error involves trying different responses until, perhaps, one works. Sometimes this is all you can do—you don't have enough information to adopt a more systematic approach. But such an approach is not very efficient, and it offers no guarantee that a useful solution will be found.

A second general approach to solving problems involves the use of **algorithms.** These are rules for a particular kind of problem that will, if followed, yield a solution. For example, imagine that you are supposed to meet a friend at a restaurant. Try as you may, you can't remember the name of the place. What can you do? One approach is to get out the yellow pages and see if this refreshes your memory. If it doesn't, you can try calling all the restaurants listed to ask if your friend made a reservation (which you know she was planning to do). Following this algorithm—"Call every restaurant in the book"—will eventually work; but it is time-consuming and inefficient. A much more effective way of solving many problems is to use an appropriate *heuristic.*

Heuristics, as you'll recall, are rules of thumb we often use to guide our cognition. With respect to problem solving, heuristics involve strategies suggested by prior experience—ones we have found useful in the past. These may or may not work in the present case, so a solution is not guaranteed. But what heuristics lack in terms of certainty they gain in efficiency: They often provide useful shortcuts. In the case of the forgotten restaurant, you might begin by assuming that your friend probably chose a restaurant close to where she lives. This simple rule could eliminate many of the most distant restaurants and considerably simplify your task.

Finally, we sometimes attempt to solve problems through the use of **analogy**—the application of techniques that worked in similar situations in the past (Gentner & Holyoak, 1997; Holyoak & Thagard, 1997). For example, imagine that while driving through an unfamiliar town, you are suddenly seized by an uncontrollable desire for a Big Mac. You don't know your way around this town, but you know from past experience that many McDonald's restaurants are located near busy interstate highways. Applying this knowledge, you follow signs showing the way to the nearest interstate. If you are then rewarded by the sight of the famous golden arches, you have solved the problem through analogy. People frequently solve problems through the use of analogy—although they may remain unaware that they've done so (Burns, 1996; Schunn & Dunbar, 1996). To summarize, selecting an appropriate strategy is critical to effective problem solving.

**REVIEW QUESTIONS**

- How do psychologists define problem solving?
- What are two general approaches to problem solving?
- What role do heuristics play in problem solving?

## Facilitating Effective Problem Solving: The Role of Metacognitive Processing

Try to recall the last time you were faced with a difficult problem: solving a challenging math problem, determining why your car wouldn't start, finding an error in your checkbook. What steps did you follow in trying to solve the problem? Did you find it helpful to talk through the problem, either aloud or to yourself? People commonly report that talking things out hastens the process of finding a solution. But does doing so really help? Research on this topic suggests that talking through a problem helps divert attention away from irrelevant aspects of the problem and toward aspects that are important in the search for a solution. In other words, talking

**Algorithm:** A rule that guarantees a solution to a specific type of problem.

**Analogy:** A strategy for solving problems based on applying solutions that were previously successful with other problems similar in underlying structure.

**Metacognitive Processing:** An expanded level of awareness that allows us, in a sense, to observe ourselves in the problem-solving process.

through a problem may facilitate our ability to solve problems by expanding our level of awareness—in a sense, allowing us to observe ourselves engaged in the problem-solving process. This process has been termed **metacognitive processing** (Berardi-Coletta et al., 1995).

A study by Berardi-Coletta and her colleagues (1995) may help illustrate how metacognitive processing facilitates performance on problem-solving tasks. These researchers asked participants to practice solving progressively more difficult versions of a playing-card problem, then tested them on the most difficult one. The card problem involved ordering a set of playing cards so that when the cards were dealt, they would appear in a prescribed order. During the practice trials, participants were assigned to one of three groups: a group in which the researchers induced metacognitive processing by asking participants process-oriented questions as they practiced ("How are you deciding on a way to work out the order for the cards?"); a group in which participants were asked problem-focused questions ("What is the goal of the problem?"); or a control group in which participants worked on the problem with no additional instructions or discussion. As predicted, participants in the metacognitive condition performed best on the task, taking the least number of trials to obtain the correct solution. In contrast, participants in the problem-focused group performed worst, requiring the most trials to solve the problem. These results indicate that talking through a problem can be useful—especially when it leads to metacognitive processing and a focus on the problem-solving *process.* So the next time you're faced with a difficult problem—talk it out.

## Factors That Interfere with Effective Problem Solving

Sometimes, despite our best efforts, we are unable to solve problems. In many cases our failure stems from obvious causes, such as lack of necessary information or experience. Similarly, as we'll soon see, we may lack internal frameworks that allow us to represent the problem situation fully and effectively. As a result, we don't know which variables or factors are most important, and we spend lots of time "wandering about," using an informal type of trial and error (Johnson, 1985). In other cases, though, difficulties in solving problems seem to stem from more subtle factors. Let's consider some of these now.

**FUNCTIONAL FIXEDNESS: PRIOR USE VERSUS PRESENT SOLUTIONS** Suppose you want to use the objects shown in Figure 7.12 to attach the candle to a wall

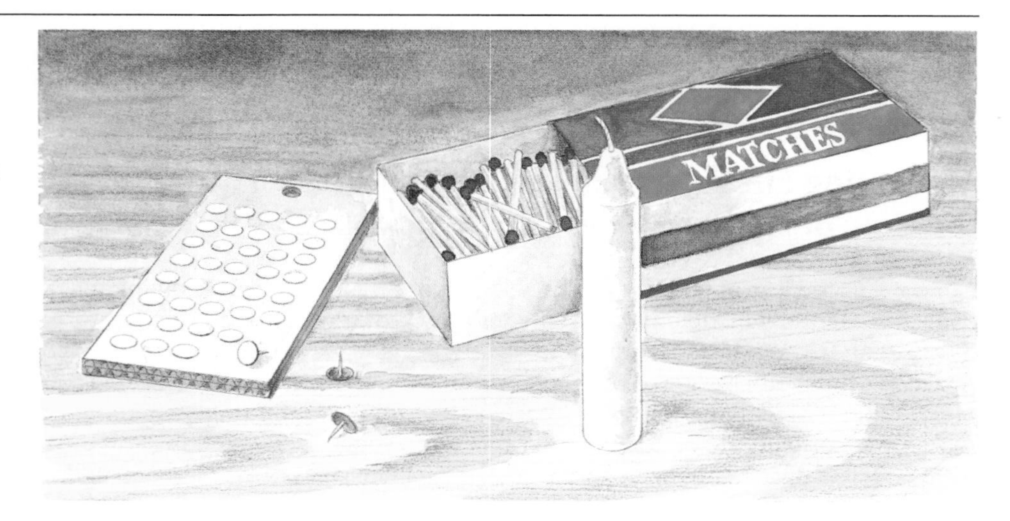


**Figure 7.12**
**Solving Complex Problems**

How can you attach the candle to a wall so that it stands upright and burns normally, using only the objects shown here?

so that it can stand upright and burn properly. What solution(s) do you come up with? If you are like most people, you may mention using the tacks to nail the candle to the wall or attaching it with melted wax (Duncker, 1945). While these techniques might work, they overlook a much more elegant solution: emptying the box of matches, attaching the box to the wall, and placing the candle on it (see Figure 7.13). Described like this, the solution probably sounds obvious. Then why don't most people think of it? The answer involves **functional fixedness**—our strong tendency to think of using objects only in ways they have been used before. Because most of us have never used an empty box as a candle holder, we don't think of it in these terms and so fail to hit upon this solution. Interestingly, if the matchbox in this problem is shown empty, people are much more likely to think of using it as a candle holder (Weisberg & Suls, 1973); it doesn't take much to overcome such mental blind spots. But unless we can avoid functional fixedness, our ability to solve many problems can be seriously impaired.

**Figure 7.13**
**Functional Fixedness: How It Interferes with Problem Solving**

Because of functional fixedness, surprisingly few people think of using the tacks to attach the box to the wall as a candle holder.

**MENTAL SET: STICKING TO THE TRIED AND TRUE** Another factor that often gets in the way of effective problem solving is **mental set.** This is the tendency to stick with a familiar method of solving a particular type of problem—one that has worked before. Given that past solutions have in fact succeeded, this tendency is certainly reasonable, at least up to a point. Difficulties arise, however, when mental set causes us to overlook other, more efficient approaches. The powerful impact of mental set was first demonstrated by Luchins (1942) in what is now a classic study. Luchins presented study participants with the problems shown in Table 7.2, which involve using three jars of different sizes to measure amounts of water. If you work through the first two or three items, you will soon discover that you can solve them all by following this simple formula: Fill jar B, and from it fill jar A once and jar C twice. The amount of water remaining in jar B is then the desired amount. Because this formula works for all items, participants in Luchins's study tended to stick with it for all seven problems. But look at item 6: It can be solved in a simpler way. Just fill jar A, then from it fill jar C. The amount remaining in jar A is precisely

**TABLE 7.2**

**Mental Set: Another Potential Impediment to Problem Solving**

How can you use three jars, A, B, and C, each capable of holding the amounts of liquid shown, to end up with one jar holding the exact amount listed in the right-hand column? See the text for two possible solutions.

| | Amount Held by Each Jar | | | |
|---|---|---|---|---|
| Problem | Jar A | Jar B | Jar C | Goal (amount of water desired) |
| 1 | 24 | 130 | 3 | 100 |
| 2 | 9 | 44 | 7 | 21 |
| 3 | 21 | 58 | 4 | 29 |
| 4 | 12 | 160 | 25 | 98 |
| 5 | 19 | 75 | 5 | 46 |
| 6 | 23 | 49 | 3 | 20 |
| 7 | 18 | 48 | 4 | 22 |

**Functional Fixedness:** The tendency to think of using objects only as they have been used in the past.

**Mental Set:** The impact of past experience on present problem solving; specifically, the tendency to retain methods that were successful in the past even if better alternatives now exist.

**Artificial Intelligence:** The capacity of computers to demonstrate performance that, if it were produced by human beings, would be described as showing intelligence.

what's required (20 units). A simple solution also exists for item 7; see if you can figure it out. Do you think many of the participants in Luchins's experiment noticed these simpler solutions? Absolutely not. When they reached item 6, almost all continued to use their old tried-and-true formula and overlooked the more efficient one. Similar effects occur in many other contexts. For example, commuters often continue to take the same crowded roads to work each day because they have always done so; they don't even consider alternate routes that might seem less direct but are easier to travel. In these and many other situations, sliding into mental ruts can indeed prove costly.

## Artificial Intelligence: Can Machines Really Think?

If we can someday hold ordinary conversations with computers, and if they can do many other things we usually attribute to human intelligence, an interesting question arises: Does it make sense to say that computers are intelligent? This question lies at the heart of the **artificial intelligence** field—an interdisciplinary branch of science in which psychologists study the capacity of computers to demonstrate performance that, if it were produced by human beings, would be described as showing intelligence. How much intelligence do computers show? Actually, quite a lot. Modern computers carry out complex computations at blinding speeds, often performing millions of computations per second—a capability far beyond that of mere mortals. It is therefore not surprising that computers are more proficient than people at doing repetitive tasks requiring speed and accuracy.

But is it possible to construct robots capable of interacting with humans in more meaningful ways? Ongoing research at the Massachusetts Institute of Technology (MIT), termed the Cog Project, suggests the answer may be yes. One product of this work is Kismet, an autonomous robot designed to engage in social interactions with humans (Breazeal & Scassellati, 2000). The development of Kismet was inspired by the way infants learn to communicate with adults. According to researcher Cynthia Breazeal, basic motivational factors play an important role in establishing meaningful social interactions between human infants and their caretakers. In an attempt to understand how these interactions develop, the MIT team has endowed Kismet with a motivational system that mirrors our own. This system works to maintain homeostasis and motivates the robot to learn behaviors that satisfy its needs. As shown in Figure 7.14, Kismet is capable of a wide range of facial expressions, which tell potential caregivers what needs must be tended to, allowing them to respond accordingly. An all too human feature built into Kismet is the capacity to become overwhelmed by too much stimulation. When overstimulated, Kismet is designed to terminate the interaction so it can restore homeostatic balance. To do so, Kismet shuts its eyes and "goes to sleep." When balance is achieved, Kismet wakes up ready to resume interaction. Through a series of such interactions, the robot learns how its actions influence the behavior of the caretaker, thus ultimately learning how to have its needs met.

**Figure 7.14**
**Social Interactions between Robots and Humans**

Kismet, a robot developed by researchers affiliated with the Cog Project at MIT, is capable of a wide range of facial expressions that can be interpreted by an untrained human observer.

(*Source:* © Sam Ogden Photography.)

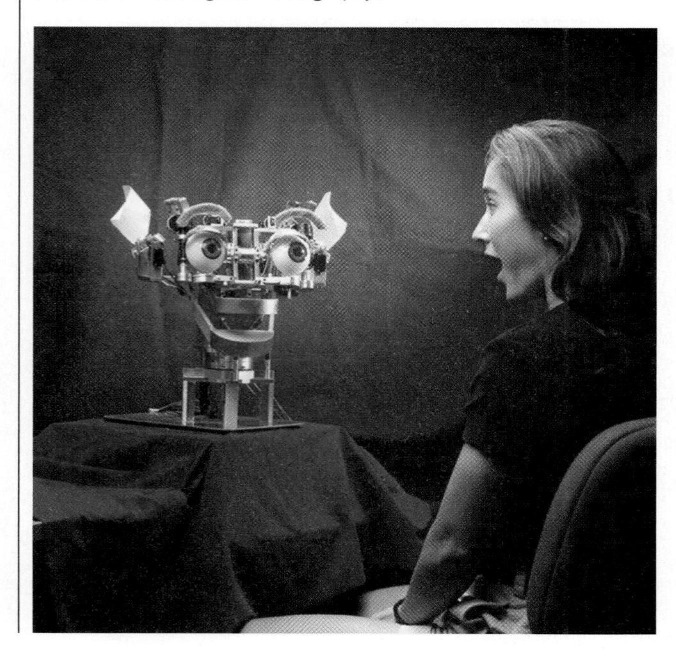

Efforts to demonstrate computer intelligence with regard to language—clearly an important human capability—have had somewhat mixed results, however. On one hand, the language abilities demonstrated by computers are remarkable. For example, banks, credit unions, and credit card companies now regularly use computerized voice recognition systems to handle certain business transactions, such as customer calls to check account balances. Even more impressive are computers that can converse with their owners and carry out a variety of tasks, including booking airline reservations. These complex machines possess large vocabularies, grasp syntax well enough to be able to understand normal sentences, and know when to ask relevant questions if they do not understand or do not have enough information to act (Rensberger, 1993).

**Neural Networks:** Computer systems modeled after the brain and made up of highly interconnected elementary computational units that work together in parallel.

On the other hand, though, it has proved frustratingly difficult to teach computers to comprehend many of the subtleties of human speech. And many ordinary activities that most people take for granted, such as understanding everyday conversation, exceed the capabilities of even the most powerful of today's computers. In response to these and related issues, researchers have designed computers that imitate the way in which the human brain—perhaps the most powerful computer in the universe—operates. As we discussed in Chapters 2 and 6, computers process information in a sequential fashion, one step at a time; in contrast, the brain processes the input from all of our senses simultaneously through a complex network of highly connected neurons. The new computer systems, called **neural networks,** are structures consisting of highly interconnected elementary computational units that work together in parallel (Denning, 1992; Levine, 1991). The primary advantage of neural networks comes not from the individual units themselves but from the overall pattern resulting from millions of these units working together. In addition, neural networks have the capacity to learn from experience by adjusting the strength of the output from individual units based on new information.

Where does all this leave us with respect to artificial intelligence? Most psychologists who specialize in this field would readily admit that early predictions about the capacities of computers to show such characteristics as intention, understanding, and consciousness were greatly overstated (Levine, 1991; Searle, 1980). However, these specialists note that computers are indeed exceptionally useful in the study of human cognition and can, in certain contexts, demonstrate performance that closely resembles that of intelligent human beings. For additional information on several intriguing applications of artificial intelligence, please refer to the following **From Science to Practice** section.

from SCIENCE to PRACTICE

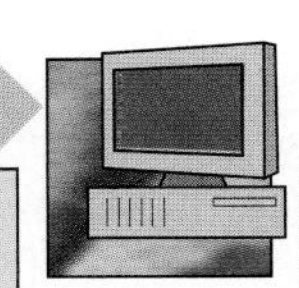

## Intelligent Agents: Just How Smart Are They?

Research on artificial intelligence has led to an amazing array of practical applications that would have seemed like science fiction as recently as ten years ago. Indeed, aspects of artificial intelligence have been incorporated into a broad range of applications, from on-board devices that help drivers navigate unfamiliar highways and city streets, to intelligent agents capable of learning Internet user preferences, to futuristic robots that will soon provide assistance, such as performing housework, to elderly and disabled persons (Johnstone, 1999). Perhaps one of the most intriguing of these applications, however, has been the development of *wearable computers,* the next generation of portable machines. Worn on the body, these devices provide their users with constant access to powerful computing and communications resources via satellite. One of the first such systems, termed WearComp, was developed by Steve Mann, a self-described *cyborg* (bionic man) who navigates the world with the aid of Internet-connected computers sewn into his clothing and opaque wraparound glasses he wears day and night, inside and outdoors (see Figure 7.15 on page 274). Through the use of WearComp, Mann claims that he can give himself eyes in the back of his head or the ability to "feel" the presence of vehicles and other objects at a distance when he's riding his bicycle in traffic. Mann suggests that WearComp also provides additional practical benefits; among the most important of these is staying connected to other people. For example, when shopping at the grocery store, cameras mounted in his glasses allow his wife—who may be located at home or at work—to see what he sees and help him shop.

**Figure 7.15**
**Wearable Computers: The Next Generation of Intelligent Tools**

These photographs illustrate the evolution of a wearable computer system invented by cognitive scientist Steve Mann. Wearable computers provide their users with constant access to powerful computing and communication resources.

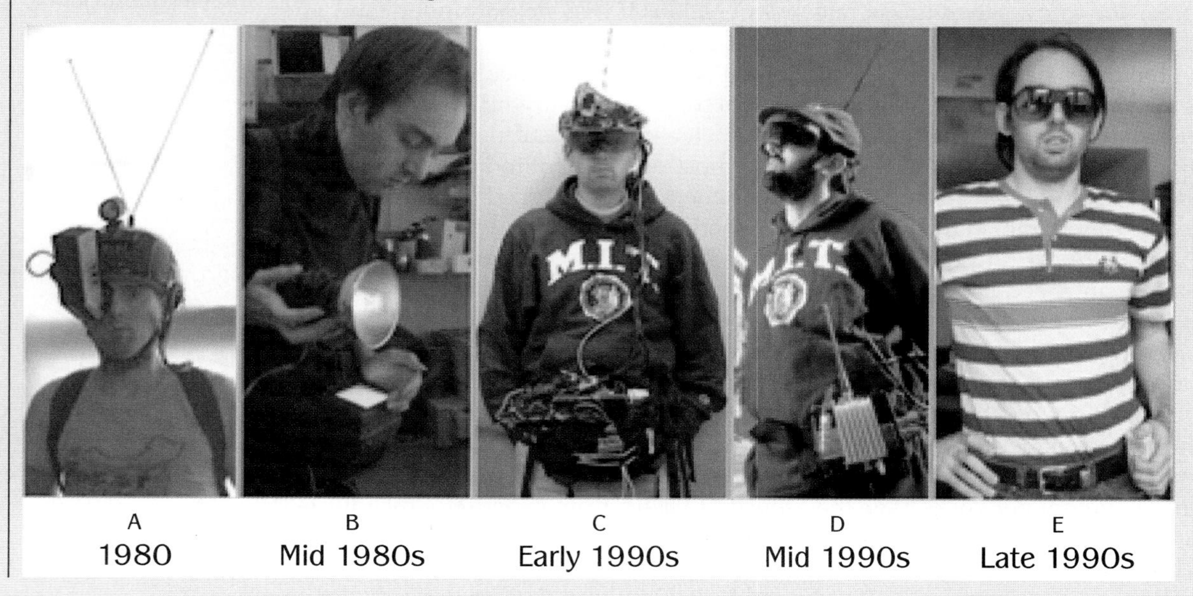


A 1980 | B Mid 1980s | C Early 1990s | D Mid 1990s | E Late 1990s

Critics have raised several ethical issues with regard to the use of wearable computers; in particular, the question of whether those who use these systems violate the rights of people with whom they interact. Most notable is the potential to violate people's right to privacy. Mann and others who support the use of these systems argue that given the widespread use of video surveillance in stores and in the workplace, the issue of privacy may already be largely settled. They also suggest that wearable computers will allow those who use them to maintain their own recorded memory of events, similar in some ways to a contract in which each party keeps a signed copy.

Still, although wearable computers and many of the other applications mentioned in this section are impressive in many respects, it could be argued that these devices do not really demonstrate intelligence, but instead merely facilitate the capabilities of the people who use them. This raises the following question: Is it possible to create computers that are truly intelligent? Cognitive scientists who believe that human thought is at its core algorithmic—and thus can be broken down into a series of mathematical operations—say the answer is yes. They argue that it is only a matter of time until cognitive scientists produce truly intelligent agents that think, learn, and create. The famous chess victory of IBM's Deep Blue computer over chess master Gary Kasparov, for example, seems to suggest that advocates of artificial intelligence could be right. Indeed, during interviews following his defeat, Kasparov said that he "sensed a new kind of intelligence" fighting against him. In general, while you may not soon meet a robot that can speak with you in a fluent manner like the ones in films, the chances are good that computers and other machines will continue to become more "intelligent" with the passage of time.

## REVIEW QUESTIONS

- What is metacognitive processing, and how does it contribute to more effective problem solving?
- What factors can interfere with effective problem solving?
- What is artificial intelligence?

### Food for Thought

Research conducted with Kismet, the autonomous robot, seems to indicate that it is able to engage in rudimentary forms of social communication with its caretakers. Do you think that robots can ever achieve true meaningful social interaction with humans? Why or why not?

# Language: The Communication of Information

CourseCompass
Web Link: *The Center for Research in Language (CRL)*

At present many experts agree that what truly sets us apart from other species of animals is our use of **language**—our ability to use an extremely rich set of symbols, plus rules for combining them, to communicate information. While the members of all species do communicate with one another in some manner, and while some may use certain features of language, the human ability to use language far exceeds that of any other organism on earth. We'll now examine the nature of language and its relationship to other aspects of cognition.

## Language: Its Basic Nature

Language uses symbols for communicating information. In order for a set of symbols to be viewed as a language, however, several additional criteria must be met. First, information must be transmitted by the symbols: The words and sentences must carry *meaning.* Second, although the number of separate sounds or words in a language may be limited, it must be possible to combine these elements into an essentially infinite number of sentences. Third, the meanings of these combinations must be independent of the settings in which they are used. In other words, sentences must be able to convey information about other places and other times. Only if all three of these criteria are met can the term *language* be applied to a system of communication.

## The Development of Language

Throughout the first weeks of life, infants have only one major means of verbal communication: crying. Within a few short years, however, children progress rapidly to speaking whole sentences and acquire a vocabulary of hundreds or even thousands of words. Some of the milestones along this remarkable journey are summarized in Table 7.3 on page 276. Although we'll consider other developmental issues in more detail in Chapter 8, this section will focus on two questions relating to the development of language: What mechanisms play a role in this process? And how, and at what ages, do children acquire various aspects of language skills?

### THEORIES OF LANGUAGE DEVELOPMENT: SOME CONTRASTING VIEWS

The *social learning view* suggests one mechanism for the rapid acquisition of language. This view proposes that speech is acquired through a combination of operant conditioning and imitation. Presumably, children are praised or otherwise rewarded by their parents for making sounds approximating those of their native language. Moreover, parents often model sounds, words, or sentences for them. Together, it is contended, these basic forms of learning contribute to the rapid acquisition of language.

A sharply different view has been proposed by the noted linguist Noam Chomsky (1968). According to Chomsky, language acquisition is at least partly innate. Human beings, he contends, have a *language acquisition device*—a built-in neural system that provides them with an intuitive grasp of grammar. In other words, humans are prepared to acquire language and do so rapidly for this reason.

Finally, a *cognitive theory* offered by Slobin (1979) recognizes the importance of both innate mechanisms and learning. This theory suggests that children possess certain information-processing abilities or strategies that they use in acquiring language. These are termed *operating principles* and seem to be present, or to develop, very early in life. One such operating principle seems to be "Pay attention to the

**Language:** A system of symbols, plus rules for combining them, used to communicate information.

TABLE 7.3

### Language Development: Some Milestones

Children develop language skills at an amazing pace. Please note: These approximate ages are only *averages;* individual children will often depart from them to a considerable degree.

| Average Age | Language Behavior Demonstrated by Child |
|---|---|
| 12 weeks | Smiles when talked to; makes cooing sounds |
| 16 weeks | Turns head in response to human voice |
| 20 weeks | Makes vowel and consonant sounds while cooing |
| 6 months | Progresses from cooing to babbling that contains all sounds of human speech. |
| 8 months | Repeats certain syllables (e.g., "ma-ma") |
| 12 months | Understands some words; may say a few |
| 18 months | Can produce up to fifty words |
| 24 months | Has vocabulary of more than fifty words; uses some two-word phrases |
| 30 months | Has vocabulary of several hundred words; uses phrases of three to five words |
| 36 months | Has vocabulary of about a thousand words |
| 48 months | Has mastered most basic elements of language |

ends of words"—children pay more attention to the ends than to the beginnings or middles of words. This makes sense, because in many languages suffixes carry important meanings. Another principle is "Pay attention to the order of words." And indeed, word order in children's speech tends to reflect that of their parents. As word order differs greatly from one language to another, this, too, is an important principle.

Which of these theories is correct? At present, all are supported by some evidence, but none seems sufficient by itself to account for all aspects of language development. For example, contrary to what the social learning view suggests, it appears that parental feedback may be too infrequent to account fully for the observed rapidity of language acquisition (Gordon, 1990; Pinker, 1989). Yet in every culture children's speech resembles that of their parents in many important ways, so imitation does seem to play an important role.

Turning to the possibility of an innate language acquisition device, some findings suggest that there may be a *critical period* for language development during which children find it easiest to acquire various language components (Elliot, 1981). If for some reason children are not exposed to normal speech at this time, they may find it increasingly difficult to master language (De Villiers & De Villiers, 1978). The possibility of a critical period for language development is also supported by research on adults who communicate via American Sign Language. Adults who acquire sign language early in life seem to be more proficient, on average, than those who learn to sign later in life.

Given this mixed pattern of evidence, it is probably safest to conclude that language development is the result of a complex process involving several aspects of learning, many cognitive processes, and perhaps various genetically determined mechanisms as well.

**BASIC COMPONENTS OF LANGUAGE DEVELOPMENT** Although the underlying mechanisms of language development remain to be clarified, much is known about how this process unfolds. Basically, it includes progress in three distinct but interrelated areas: **phonological development**—development of the ability to pronounce the sounds and words of one or more languages; **semantic development**—learning to understand the meaning of words; and acquisition of **grammar**—the rules by which words are arranged into sentences in a given language.

***Phonological Development: The Spoken Word.*** At some point between three and six months, babies begin babbling. At first **babbling** contains a rich mixture of sounds, virtually every sound used in human speech. Indeed, research suggests that babies only a few months old can distinguish sounds from many different languages (Werker & Desjardins, 1995). By nine or ten months, however, the range of babbling narrows and consists mainly of sounds used in the language of the child's native culture. From this point to the production of the first spoken word is a relatively short step, and most children accomplish it by their first birthday.

Between the ages of one and two, children's vocabularies increase rapidly; for instance, by the time they are eighteen months old, many toddlers have a vocabulary of fifty words or more. What are these words? Generally, they include the names of familiar objects important in the children's own lives—for instance, foods (*juice, cookie*), animals (*cat, dog*), toys (*block, ball*), body parts (*ear, eye*), clothing (*sock, hat, shoe*), and people (*momma, dadda*). Children make the most of these words, often using them as *holophrases*—single-word utterances that communicate much meaning, especially when combined with pointing and other gestures. For example, if a child wants some chocolate milk, she may point to the cupboard (in which the chocolate syrup is kept) while saying "milk," thus indicating that she wants some milk with syrup in it. Research seems to indicate that the use of gestures is an important component of early language development (Nicoladis, Mayberry, & Genesee, 1999). This may be due, at least in part, to the fact that at this stage children's pronunciation leaves much to be desired; many of their words take a simple form, consisting of a consonant and a vowel. So the child might say "mih" instead of "milk." Toddlers often have difficulty with clusters of two or more consonants. I remember, for instance, that when my daughter was in this age group (between one and two years old), she referred to the stairs in the house as "tairs" and to her blanket as "banky."

What about verbs—words describing action; when do children acquire these? Until recent years it was widely assumed that acquisition of such words follows the acquisition of nouns—words referring to specific objects (e.g., Gentner, 1982). However, some evidence suggests that in some cultures this order may be reversed. For instance, Tardif (1996) found that Chinese children twenty-two months old actually used more verbs than nouns in their everyday speech. Thus, the order in which children acquire nouns and verbs may vary somewhat from culture to culture, and further research is needed to determine precisely why this is so.

Web Link: *Language Comprehension*

**Phonological Development:** Development of the ability to produce recognizable speech.

**Semantic Development:** Development of understanding of the meaning of spoken or written language.

**Grammar:** Rules within a given language indicating how words can be combined into meaningful sentences.

**Babbling:** An early stage of speech development in which infants emit virtually all known sounds of human speech.

***Semantic Development: The Acquisition of Meaning.*** A child's vocabulary increases rapidly after age two, with many new words being learned each day. Thus, by the time children are six, most have a vocabulary of several thousand words. Children don't simply learn new words, however; they also learn new types of words—ones that allow them to communicate a much richer range of thoughts and ideas. Thus, they acquire understanding of negatives such as *no* and how to use these in sentences. Similarly, they acquire many adjectives and prepositions—words that allow them to be more specific in describing their own thoughts and the world around them. They start with simple adjectives such as *little, good,* and *bad,* but soon move on to ones with more specific meaning such as *high, low, narrow,* and *wide,* and prepositions such as *in front of* and *behind.* Children also learn to use question words—words that allow them to ask for information from others in efficient and specific ways: *Why? When? Who? Where?* These are key words children acquire between the ages of two and three.

While children increase their vocabulary very rapidly (they have to move fast to learn thousands of new words in just a few years!), they often demonstrate several interesting forms of error. One such error involves *overextensions*—a tendency to extend the meaning of a word beyond its actual usage. For instance, eighteen-month-olds may use the word *raisin* to refer to all small objects—flies and pebbles as well as raisins themselves. Similarly, they may use *meow* as a shorthand word for all small furry animals—dogs as well as cats. They also show *underextensions*—limiting the meaning of a word more than is appropriate. For instance, they may think that the word *cat* refers to the family's pet cat and to no others.

***The Development of Grammar.*** Every language has *grammar,* a set of rules dictating how words can be combined into sentences. Children must learn to follow these rules, as well as to utter sounds that others can recognize as words. At first grammar poses little problem; as noted earlier, children's earliest speech uses single words, often accompanied by pointing and other gestures. By the time most children are two, two-word sentences make their appearance—a pattern sometimes known as *telegraphic speech.* For instance, a child who wants a book may say "give book," and then—if this doesn't produce the desired action—switch to another two-word utterance: "Daddy give." Youngsters can pack quite a bit of meaning into these simple phrases by changing the inflection—"Go swim!" to indicate that they are going for a swim or "Go swim?" in order to ask permission for taking a swim.

Children's grasp of grammar continues to increase as they move to longer sentences of three words or more (generally between the ages of two and three). They add inflections to their words—endings that carry meaning, such as the letter *s* to indicate more than one object (plurals) and endings that change the tense of a verb (e.g., *ed* to indicate that something happened in the past, as in "He picked up the ball" rather than "He pick up the ball.").

From this, children move on to an increasing grasp of their language's grammar, and to the production of ever more complex sentences. They begin to link two or more ideas in a single utterance (e.g., Clark & Clark, 1977); and they gradually learn to understand, and use, sentences in which important ideas are implied or understood rather than directly stated. For instance, what does the following sentence mean to you? "Stacey promised Jason to bring the book." As an adult, you understand that Stacey will bring the book; she has promised to do so. Three-year-olds, however, may misinterpret it as meaning that Jason will bring the book because they don't fully understand that the word *promised* refers to Stacey. As they grow older, they learn to unravel this and other mysteries of grammar.

In sum, language development is definitely a continuing feature of cognitive development throughout childhood. Given the complexity it involves, and its central role in many aspects of cognition, this is far from surprising.

## Language and Thought: Do We Think What We Say or Say What We Think?

Although we often have vivid mental images, most of our thinking seems to involve words. This fact raises an intriguing question: What is the precise relationship between language and thought? One theory, known as the **linguistic relativity hypothesis,** suggests that language shapes or determines thought (Whorf, 1956). According to this view, people who speak different languages may perceive the world in different ways, because their thinking is determined, at least in part, by the words available to them. For example, the Inuit of Alaska, who have many different words for snow, may perceive this aspect of the physical world differently from English-speaking people, who have only one word.

**Linguistic Relativity Hypothesis:** The view that language shapes thought.

The opposing view is that thought shapes language. This position suggests that language merely reflects the way we think—how our minds work. Which position is more accurate? While the issue is far from resolved, a modified version of the linguistic relativity hypothesis has been advanced that suggests that structural characteristics of language may indeed influence the way people think about objects and relationships among objects in the physical world (Hunt & Agnoli, 1991; Lucy, 1992). Zhang and Schmitt (1998) recently explored this possibility by exploiting structural differences that often exist between languages; in this case, the use of words termed *classifiers* that exist in Mandarin Chinese but not in English. In a sense, classifiers answer the question, "What kind of category is this object a member of?" For example, the counterpart in Chinese for the English noun phrase "one bed" is "*yi–zhang–chuang.*" In this example, *zhang* (inserted between *yi,* meaning "one" and *chuang,* meaning "bed") is a classifier used for flat, extended objects such as beds, tables, desks, photos, and paper. The researchers predicted that this difference—the use of classifiers in one language but not in the other—would differentially affect both the way in which native speakers of these languages perceived relatedness between objects and their memory for these objects. The results showed that native Chinese speakers were more likely than native English speakers to perceive objects belonging to a common classifier as more similar than those belonging to different classifiers. Second, the Chinese-speaking participants were more likely to recall classifier-sharing objects in clusters than were their English-speaking counterparts. In short, these results seem to indicate that language may play an important role in shaping important aspects of cognition.

## Language in Other Species

Audio 7.2: *Language Ability in Animals*

Members of nonhuman species communicate with one another in many ways. Bees do a complex dance to indicate the distance to and direction of a food source; birds sing songs when seeking to attract a mate; seagoing mammals in the wild, such as whales, communicate with one another through complex patterns of sounds. But what about language? Are we the only species capable of using this sophisticated means of communication? Until the 1970s there seemed little question that this was so. Early efforts to teach chimpanzees to speak failed miserably. These disappointing results were due in part to the fact that researchers focused their efforts on teaching these animals to *speak.* Unfortunately, nonhuman primates (and other animals) lack the vocal control necessary to form words, and hence spoken language. But it may not be appropriate to ask animals to do what people do. The ability to speak is not essential for the use of language. For example, persons who have lost the power of speech through accident or illness can still communicate by writing or sign language. The fact that chimps cannot learn to speak, then, does not rule out the possibility that they or other animals can learn to use some form of language.

The findings reported by several teams of researchers seem to support this possibility. Beatrice and Allen Gardner succeeded in teaching Washoe, a female chimp, to use and understand almost two hundred signs in American Sign Language (ASL), which is used by many deaf persons (Gardner & Gardner, 1975). After several years of practice, Washoe learned to respond to simple questions and to request actions such as tickling and objects such as food. Research with gorillas, too, has yielded what some interpret as evidence for the ability to use language. Francine Patterson (1978) taught Koko, a female gorilla, a vocabulary of several hundred signs. Patterson reported that Koko showed great flexibility in using signs, constructing original sentences, remembering and describing past events, and even creating her own signs for new objects and events.

In what may be the most surprising evidence of all, Irene Pepperberg has trained an African gray parrot named Alex to use speech in what appear to be highly complex ways (Stipp, 1990). Alex can name more than eighty objects and events, frequently requests things he wants ("I want shower."), and has been known to give directions to his human trainers.

**Syntax:** Rules about how units of speech can be combined into sentences in a given language.

**ARE WE THE ONLY SPECIES CAPABLE OF USING LANGUAGE?** Based on the evidence presented thus far, you may now be ready to conclude that members of these species can indeed use language. Please note, however, that this conclusion has been the source of great controversy. Many psychologists believe that the animals in these studies, while exhibiting impressive learning, are not really demonstrating use of language (Davidson & Hopson, 1988; Terrace, 1985). For instance, close examination of the procedures used to train and test the animals suggests that their trainers may often unintentionally provide subtle cues that help animals respond correctly to questions. It also appears that in some cases trainers may have overinterpreted the animals' responses, reading complex meanings and intentions into relatively simple signs. Finally, it is still unclear whether animals are capable of mastering several basic features of human languages; for example, **syntax**—the rules by which words are arranged to form meaningful sentences—and *generativity*—the ability to combine a relatively limited number of words into unique combinations that convey a broad range of meanings.

Studies involving other species of animals, including bonobos (a rare type of chimpanzee) and dolphins, have addressed these and related issues. For example, consider the language abilities demonstrated by a bonobo named Kanzi (Savage-Rumbaugh et al., 1989). While attempting to teach Kanzi's mother to use an artificial language made up of abstract visual symbols, psychologist Sue Savage-Rumbaugh noticed that Kanzi (then an infant) had learned several symbols just by watching. Intrigued by the possibilities raised by this discovery, Savage-Rumbaugh and her colleagues continued to train Kanzi in this informal way—speaking to him throughout the day, while simultaneously pointing to the corresponding word symbols on portable language boards they carried with them. Kanzi quickly learned to combine the symbol-words to request tasty snacks and preferred activities, such as watching Tarzan movies. Since then, Kanzi has demonstrated a grasp of grammatical concepts, and he now comprehends several hundred spoken words (see Figure 7.16). More importantly, though, the use of strict control procedures ruled out the possibility that Kanzi was responding to subtle cues from his trainers, a criticism leveled against many early demonstrations of animal language. For instance, a one-way mirror prevented Kanzi from seeing who gave him the spoken commands, and persons recording his responses wore headphones to prevent them from hearing the requests. Psychologists are now more willing to accept that Kanzi was responding solely to the requests.

**Figure 7.16**
**Language in Other Species: Can We Talk to the Animals?**

A growing body of evidence suggests that certain species of animals, including bonobo chimpanzees such as Kanzi, can grasp many aspects of language, including comprehension of spoken language.

But what about more complex features of language? Are animals capable of grasping these concepts, too? Psychologist Louis Herman believes the answer is yes. Herman and his colleagues taught a female dolphin named Akeakamai—Ake for short—an artificial language in which sweeping hand gestures are the words (Herman, Richards, & Wolz, 1984). Each gesture symbolizes either an object, such as *Frisbee;* an action, such as *fetch;* or a description of position, such as *over* or *left.* Ake has learned more than fifty of these gesture-words. To test whether Ake is capable of comprehending complex features of language, the researchers established a set of rules on word order and the grammatical function of each type of gesture. They discovered that Ake comprehends word order and syntax in word sequences up to five gestures. For example, "Right basket left frisbee fetch" instructs Ake to take the Frisbee on her left to the basket on her right. More impressively, though, when familiar gestures are rearranged to form novel commands—ones Ake has never seen before—she continues to respond correctly.

Mounting evidence based on studies of several species of animals suggests that language may not be a uniquely human possession, but rather a continuum of skills that different species of animals exhibit to varying degrees. The results of further studies will undoubtedly shed additional light on this controversial issue. In the meantime, the question of whether we'll soon "talk with the animals" remains largely unresolved.

### REVIEW QUESTIONS

- What abilities are involved in the production of language, and how is language acquired in humans?
- What factors are involved in language acquisition?
- What is the linguistic relativity hypothesis?
- Do animals possess language?

## Making Psychology Part of Your Life

### Making Better Decisions

Have you ever made a bad decision—one that you later wished you could change? Such errors in judgment may prove quite costly. Here are some guidelines for increasing the chances that many of your decisions will be good ones—or at least as free from sources of error and bias as possible.

1. **Don't trust your own memory, or beware of availability.** When we make decisions, we can do so only on the basis of the information available to us. Be careful! The information that comes most readily to mind is not always the most useful or revealing (Kahneman & Tversky, 1982). When you face an important decision, therefore, jog your memory in several ways and, if time permits, consult written documents or sources before proceeding. As noted in Chapter 6, memory often plays tricks on us; relying on a quick scan of it when making an important decision can be risky.
2. **Don't take situations at face value, or question all anchors.** In many decision-making situations the stage is set long before we come on the scene. The asking price for a house or car is set by the seller, the number of meetings for a committee has been determined by its chair, and so on. While you can't always change such givens, you should at least recognize them for what they are and question whether they make sense. If you don't raise such questions, you will probably accept these "anchors" implicitly and then offer only minor adjustments to them (Northcraft & Neale, 1987).
3. **Remain flexible, or don't fall in love with your own decisions.** Making decisions is effortful, so once a decision is made we tend to heave a sigh of relief and to stick with it—through thick and thin. Then, before we know it, we may have too much invested to quit. In other words, we may be trapped in a situation where we ought to change our initial decision and cut our losses but where, instead, we continue down the path to ruin—or at least to negative outcomes (Brockner & Rubin, 1985). Don't let this happen! It's always difficult to admit a mistake, but doing so is often far better than sticking to a losing course of action.
4. **Consider all options.** When you make a decision, you must choose among the available options. But what, precisely, are your options? Start by gathering as much information as you can, then use it to generate as many potential options as possible. Doing so can often suggest choices or courses of action that you did not think of at first.

# Summary and Review

## Thinking: Forming Concepts and Reasoning to Conclusions

- **What are concepts?** Concepts are mental categories for objects, events, or experiences that are similar to one another in one or more respects.
- **What is the difference between logical and natural concepts?** Logical concepts can be clearly defined by a set of rules or properties. Natural concepts cannot; they are usually defined in terms of prototypes—the most typical category members.
- **What are propositions and images?** Propositions are sentences that relate one concept to another and can stand as separate assertions. Images are mental pictures of the world and are a basic element of thinking.
- **What are ERPs, and what can they tell us about cognition?** ERPs, or event-related brain potentials, reflect the momentary changes in electrical activity in the brain that occur as a person performs a cognitive task. They help clarify the relative speeds of different components of cognitive processes.
- **What is the process of reasoning? How does formal reasoning differ from everyday reasoning?** Reasoning involves transforming available information in order to reach specific conclusions. Formal reasoning derives conclusions from specific premises. In contrast, everyday reasoning is less clear-cut and more complex.
- **What forms of error and bias can lead to faulty reasoning?** Reasoning is subject to several forms of error and bias. It can be distorted by our emotions and/or beliefs; by our tendency to focus primarily on evidence that confirms our beliefs, or confirmation bias; and by our tendency to assume that we could have predicted actual events more successfully than is really the case, or the hindsight effect.
- **What is physical reasoning?** Physical reasoning has to do with how people perceive physical objects and their movement and with the cognitive processes that allow people to make predictions about events involving these objects.

### Key Terms

cognition, p. 249 • logical concepts, p. 250 • natural concepts, p. 250 • visual images, p. 250 • propositions, p. 251 • mental models, p. 251 • reaction time, p. 253 • reasoning, p. 254 • confirmation bias, p. 255 • hindsight effect, p. 256 • physical reasoning, p. 257

## Making Decisions: Choosing among Alternatives

- **What are heuristics?** Heuristics are mental rules of thumb that reduce the cognitive effort required for decision making. We often employ heuristics rather than carefully calculating the probability and the subjective value or utility of each possible outcome.
- **What are the availability, representativeness, and anchoring-and-adjustment heuristics, and what roles do they play in decision making?** The availability heuristic is our tendency to make judgments about the frequency or likelihood of various events in terms of how readily they can be brought to mind. The representativeness heuristic is the tendency to assume that the more closely an item resembles typical examples of some concept, the more likely it is to belong to that concept. The anchoring-and-adjustment heuristic is the tendency to reach decisions by making adjustments to reference points or existing information.
- **What is framing, and how does it relate to decision making?** Framing, the presentation of information about possible outcomes in terms of gains or losses, can strongly affect decisions.
- **How does escalation of commitment affect decision making?** People often become trapped in bad decisions through escalation of commitment, an effect that derives from reluctance to admit past mistakes and a desire to justify past losses.
- **What is naturalistic decision making?** Naturalistic decision making is decision making in real-world settings. Proponents argue that the study of naturalistic decision making has several advantages over laboratory research: It focuses attention on how decision makers bring their experience to bear in making a decision, it broadens the focus from a single decision event to include elements of the decision context, it emphasizes the dynamic nature of decision making, and it takes into account the complexity of modern decision environments.

### Key Terms

decision making, p. 258 • heuristics, p. 259 • availability heuristics, p. 259 • representativeness heuristic, p. 260 • anchoring-and-adjustment heuristic, p. 260 • framing, p. 261 • escalation of commitment, p. 262 • naturalistic decision making, p. 266

## Problem Solving: Finding Paths to Desired Goals

- **How do psychologists define problem solving?** Problem solving involves efforts to develop or choose among various responses in order to attain desired goals.
- **What are two general approaches to problem solving?** One common problem-solving technique is trial and error. Another is the use of algorithms—rules that will, if followed, yield solutions in certain situations.
- **What role do heuristics play in problem solving?** Heuristics, rules of thumb suggested by our experience, often provide useful shortcuts in problem solving.
- **What is metacognitive processing, and how does it contribute to more effective problem solving?** Metacognitive processing involves expanding our level of

awareness—in a sense, observing ourselves engaged in the problem-solving process. Metacognition seems to promote cognitive activities that lead to more effective problem solutions, such as a focus on the actual problem-solving process.

- **What factors can interfere with effective problem solving?** Both functional fixedness (the tendency to think of using objects only as they have been used before) and mental sets (tendencies to stick with familiar methods) can interfere with effective problem solving.
- **What is artificial intelligence?** Artificial intelligence is the focus of research in an interdisciplinary field concerned with the capacity of computers to demonstrate "intelligent" performance.

### Key Terms

problem solving, p. 267 • trial and error, p. 268 • algorithm, p. 269 • analogy, p. 269 • metacognitive processing, p. 270 • functional fixedness, p. 271 • mental set, p. 271 • artificial intelligence, p. 272 • neural networks, p. 273

## Language: The Communication of Information

- **What abilities are involved in the production of language, and how is language acquired in humans?** Language involves the ability to use a rich set of symbols, plus rules for combining these, to communicate information. Existing evidence on language development suggests that language is acquired by children through complex interactions among (1) social learning, (2) innate mechanisms, and (3) cognitive mechanisms.
- **What factors are involved in language acquisition?** Language acquisition involves phonological development—learning to produce the sounds of words; semantic development—learning to understand the meanings of words; and acquisition of grammar—the rules through which words can be combined into sentences in a given language.
- **What is the linguistic relativity hypothesis?** According to the linguistic relativity hypothesis, language shapes or determines thought. Existing evidence seems to support a revised version of the linguistic relativity hypothesis, suggesting that language does affect aspects of cognition.
- **Do animals possess language?** Growing evidence suggests that some species of animals, including bonobo chimpanzees and dolphins, are capable of grasping basic aspects of language, including word order and grammar; but these findings remain highly controversial.

### Key Terms

language, p. 275 • phonological development, p. 277 • semantic development, p. 277 • grammar, p. 277 • babbling, p. 277 • linguistic relativity hypothesis, p. 278 • syntax, p. 280

# Critical Thinking Questions

### Appraisal

Throughout this chapter, we've seen that human thought processes are less than optimal in several important respects. For instance, relying on heuristics frequently leads to flawed decision making. And we often fall prey to biases that lead us astray in our ability to think and reason effectively. How can psychology help people reduce or eliminate the effects of these errors?

### Controversy

The results of numerous studies demonstrate that animals are capable of grasping important aspects of language that many believed were beyond their capabilities. Do you think it is possible that in coming years scientists will discover ways to "talk with the animals"? If so, why? If not, why not?

### Making Psychology Part of Your Life

Now that you understand the basic nature of cognitive processes and the many factors that affect them, can you think of ways in which you can use this knowledge to improve your problem-solving abilities? Name several specific steps you could take to become more proficient in this regard.

Chapter 8

# Human Development I: The Childhood Years

## CHAPTER OUTLINE


**PHYSICAL GROWTH AND DEVELOPMENT 289**

The Prenatal Period
Prenatal Influences on Development

- BEYOND THE HEADLINES—As Psychologists See It: *Playpen Peril? The Potentially Harmful Effects of Plastic Toys*

Physical Development during Our Early Years

**PERCEPTUAL DEVELOPMENT 294**

- RESEARCH METHODS *How Psychologists Study Development*

**COGNITIVE DEVELOPMENT: CHANGES IN OUR ABILITY TO UNDERSTAND THE WORLD AROUND US 298**

Piaget's Theory: An Overview
Piaget's Theory: A Modern Assessment
Beyond Piaget: Children's Theory of Mind and Research on the Information-Processing Perspective

**MORAL DEVELOPMENT: REASONING ABOUT "RIGHT" AND "WRONG" 307**

Kohlberg's Stages of Moral Understanding
Evidence Concerning Kohlberg's Theory

**SOCIAL AND EMOTIONAL DEVELOPMENT: FORMING RELATIONSHIPS WITH OTHERS 311**

Emotional Development and Temperament
Attachment: The Beginnings of Love
School and Friendships: Key Factors in Social Development

- FROM SCIENCE TO PRACTICE *Making Playgrounds Safer: Some Concrete Steps*

Do Parents Really Matter? A Recent—and Continuing—Controversy

**FROM GENDER IDENTITY TO SEX-CATEGORY CONSTANCY: HOW CHILDREN COME TO UNDERSTAND THAT THEY ARE FEMALE OR MALE 321**

Children's Growing Sophistication with Respect to Gender
Gender Development: Contrasting Explanations of How It Occurs

- MAKING PSYCHOLOGY PART OF YOUR LIFE *Combating Childhood Obesity*

My maternal grandmother was a sweet person, but I really put her love for me to the test one day when I was about three and a half years old. My grandmother kept goldfish, and they gave her great pleasure. I too liked to watch the goldfish swim round and round in their large glass bowl; as I watched, however, the following thought took shape in my young mind: "What makes them move?" My grandfather had shown me the inner workings of the large clock he kept in the kitchen, and I wondered if the fish had works inside too. One morning, when my grandmother was outside in the garden, I decided to find out. So—I now admit with shame!—I reached into the tank, grabbed one of the fish, and performed surgery on it with a butter knife. To my disappointment, I couldn't see anything inside that explained how the fish were able to swim. So I grabbed another fish and was just about to send it off to goldfish heaven, too, when my grandmother walked into the room. I can still hear her cries of dismay as she saw what I was doing and what I had already done. She took the fish from my hand and scolded me loudly in two different languages; then she began to cry. I knew that I had done something bad, but I couldn't for the life of me figure out what it was. After all, didn't my father always praise me for asking questions and wanting to find out how things worked?

**Developmental Psychology:** The branch of psychology that focuses on the many ways we change throughout life.

**Childhood:** The years between birth and adolescence.

**Maturation:** Changes determined largely by our genes.

I hope that *you* never performed that kind of "experiment" as a child. But whether you did or not, I'm sure you can remember incidents from your own childhood in which you were puzzled by the world around you and simply could not understand certain aspects of it. Similarly, you can probably remember the frustration of being too short to reach the sink or a light switch; what it was like to enter your own magical world of play, in which everyday objects became whatever you wanted them to be; and the joys of learning—and friendship—you discovered in school. Such memories remind us that over the years, we all change tremendously in many ways—*physically, cognitively,* and *socially* (see Figure 8.1). Such *change* is the basic theme of this chapter and the next one, in which we'll review some of the major findings of the field of **developmental psychology**—the branch of psychology that focuses on the many ways we change throughout life. Here, we'll concentrate on changes during **childhood**—the years between birth and adolescence. In the next chapter, we'll examine change occurring during adolescence and adulthood. In both units, the general plan will be to consider changes in the three categories mentioned earlier—physical, cognitive, and social development. Given that these changes often occur together, however, this division is mainly for purposes of clarity and convenience—it is *not* a reflection of any clear boundaries between the categories.

One more point before we begin. In Chapter 1, I described two of psychology's "grand issues" as involving the *nature–nurture controversy* and *stability versus change.* While these issues relate to many areas of psychology (we've already discussed them in Chapters 2 and 3), they are especially relevant to the study of human development. To what extent do various aspects of our development represent **maturation**—changes determined largely by our genes? And to what extent, in contrast, do they reflect the impact of experience and the world around us? Developmental psychologists often grapple with these complex issues, so they'll arise at several points in this chapter.

**Figure 8.1**
**Change: The Central Aspect of Human Development**

As these photos suggest, we change tremendously—physically, cognitively, and socially—during our childhood years.

# Physical Growth and Development

When does human life begin? In one sense, this is a philosophical or religious issue, outside the realm of science. From a purely biological point of view, though, your life as an individual began when one of the millions of sperm released by your father during sexual intercourse fertilized an *ovum* deep within your mother's body. The product of this union was barely 1/175 of an inch in diameter—smaller than the period at the end of this sentence. Yet packed within this tiny speck were the genetic blueprints that guided all your subsequent physical growth. As you probably recall from our discussion of genetics in Chapter 2, each of us possesses twenty-three pairs of chromosomes, one member of each pair from our mother and one from our father. One of these pairs determines biological sex, with females possessing two X chromosomes (XX) and males possessing one X and one Y (XY).

## The Prenatal Period

After fertilization, the ovum moves through the mother's reproductive tract until it reaches the womb or *uterus*. This takes several days, and during this time the ovum divides frequently. Ten to fourteen days after fertilization, it becomes implanted in the wall of the uterus. For the next six weeks it is known as an **embryo** and develops rapidly. (If, instead, the ovum becomes implanted into the oviduct—the tube connecting the ovary with the uterus—an *ectopic pregnancy* results. This can be very serious for the mother and can even cause death if the condition is undetected; the oviduct can burst as the developing embryo grows larger.) By the third week the embryo is about one-fifth of an inch (one-half centimeter) long, and the region of the head is clearly visible. By the end of the eighth week the embryo is about one inch long, and a face as well as arms and legs are present. By this time, too, all major internal organs have begun to form; and some, such as the sex glands, are already active. The nervous system develops rapidly, and simple reflexes begin to appear during the eighth or ninth week after fertilization.

During the next seven months the developing child—now called a **fetus**—shows an increasingly human form. Different parts of the body grow at different rates during this period. At first, the head grows rapidly compared to the trunk and legs; later, the lower parts of the body grow more rapidly. The external genitals take shape, so the sex of the fetus is recognizable by the twelfth week. Fingernails and toenails form, hair follicles appear, and eyelids that open and close emerge. By the end of the twelfth week the fetus is 3 inches (7.6 centimeters) long and weighs

**Embryo:** The developing child during the second through the eighth week of prenatal development.

**Fetus:** The developing child during the last seven months of pregnancy.

**Figure 8.2**
**The Newborn: Starting Life's Journey**

Holding their newborn infant for the first time is one of the most profoundly moving experiences many parents ever have.

about ¾ ounce (21 grams). By the twentieth week it is almost 10 inches (25 cm) long and weighs 8 or 9 ounces (227–255 g). By the twenty-fourth week all the neurons that will be present in the brain have been produced. The eyes are formed and are sensitive to light by the end of the twenty-fourth to twenty-sixth week.

During the last three months of pregnancy, the fetus gains about eight ounces each week. By the seventh and eighth months, it appears to be virtually fully formed. However, if born prematurely, it may still experience difficulties in breathing. At birth, babies weigh more than 7 pounds (3.17 kilograms) on average and are about 20 inches (50.8 cm) long (see Figure 8.2).

## Prenatal Influences on Development

Under ideal conditions, development during the prenatal period occurs in an orderly fashion, and the newborn child is well equipped at birth to survive outside its mother's body. Unfortunately, however, conditions are not always ideal. Many environmental factors can damage the fetus and interfere with normal patterns of growth. Such factors are known as **teratogens,** and their impact can be devastating (e.g., Bookstein et al., 1996). We'll consider some of the most important teratogens here, but it's important to note that many others exist as well.

**INFECTIOUS AGENTS** The blood supply of the fetus and that of its mother come into close proximity in the **placenta,** a structure within the uterus that protects and nourishes the growing child. As a result, disease-producing organisms present in the mother's blood can sometimes infect the fetus. Tragically, diseases that exert only relatively minor effects on the mother can be very serious for the fetus. For example, *rubella,* or German measles, can cause blindness, deafness, or heart disease in the fetus if the mother contracts this illness during the first four weeks of pregnancy. Other diseases that can be transmitted to the fetus include chicken pox, mumps, tuberculosis, malaria, syphilis, and herpes (Samson 1988).

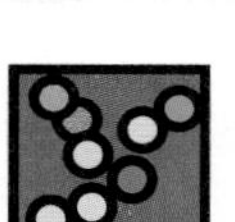

Since the early 1980s, two other illnesses, genital herpes and AIDS (acquired immune deficiency syndrome) have been added to this list. Genital herpes is usually transmitted during birth, when the newborn comes into contact with lesions present in the mother's genitals. When newborns contract this disease, they may suffer many harmful effects, ranging from paralysis and brain damage through deafness and blindness; the disease is fatal for many babies (Rosenblith, 1992). AIDS, in contrast, can be transmitted to the fetus prior to birth, as well as during the birth process. About 20 percent of women who carry the AIDS virus in their bodies transmit it to their infants (Mattheson et al., 1997), and growing evidence suggests that the disease can also be transmitted to infants during the birth process (Kuhn et al., 1994). Tragically, few babies born with AIDS survive until their first birthday.

**PRESCRIPTION AND OVER-THE-COUNTER DRUGS** The use of drugs by the mother can also have important effects on the fetus. Excessive use of aspirin, a drug most people take without hesitation, can result in harm to the fetus's circulatory system (Kelsey, 1969). Caffeine, the stimulant found in coffee, tea, and many soft drinks, can slow fetal growth, contribute to premature birth (Jacobson et al., 1984), and produce increased irritability in newborns whose mothers have consumed large amounts of this drug (Schickedanz et al., 1998).

**Teratogens:** Factors in the environment that can harm the developing fetus.

**Placenta:** A structure that surrounds, protects, and nourishes the developing fetus.

**COCAINE** While many illegal drugs taken by mothers during pregnancy can harm the developing fetus, there has been an alarming increase in the number of babies exposed to cocaine. Even if such babies are not born addicted to the drug, infants suffer many harmful effects from exposure to cocaine during the prenatal period: premature birth, brain lesions, impaired sensory functioning, increased irritability, and heart deformities, among others (e.g., Richardson, Day, & Goldschmidt, 1995; Volpe, 1992).

**Figure 8.3**
**Fetal Alcohol Syndrome**

As shown here, children suffering from the fetal alcohol syndrome often have a distinctive appearance. Sadly, this may be the least of the many problems they suffer.

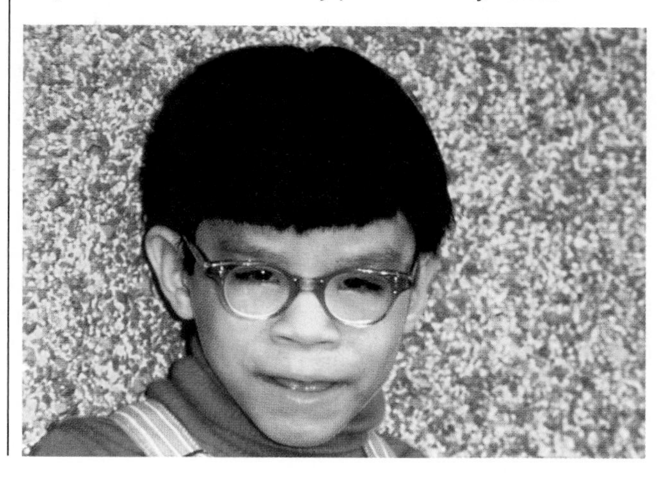

**ALCOHOL** In the past, it was widely believed that moderate consumption of alcohol by expectant mothers had no harmful effects on the fetus. Now, in contrast, it is widely recognized that virtually *any* alcohol consumption by expectant mothers can produce harmful effects. Because mothers who consume alcohol during pregnancy—especially in large amounts—often differ from mothers who do not in several ways (e.g., they may eat a poorer diet), it is difficult to say with certainty that it is alcohol alone that produces all the harmful effects. Yet existing data does point to the conclusion that alcohol consumption by pregnant mothers is linked to mental retardation, learning disorders, and retarded growth among their children (e.g., Streissguth et al., 1995; Williams, Howard, & McLaughlin, 1994).

If pregnant women consume large quantities of alcohol—and especially if they engage in binge drinking—their children may be born with a disorder known as the *fetal alcohol syndrome* (FAS) (Julien, 1995). This disorder includes a smaller than normal head size, deformities of the face (see Figure 8.3), irritability, hyperactivity, retarded motor and mental development, heart defects, limb and joint abnormalities, feeding problems, and short attention spans (e.g., Bookstein et al., 1996). These problems persist, and as children with FAS grow older, they have increasing difficulty interacting with others and may develop serious behavioral problems (e.g., Becker et al., 1994).

Web Link: *The National Organization on Fetal Alcohol Syndrome*

How much alcohol must a pregnant woman consume, and how often, before such effects are produced? This is a complex question; but, because alcohol has no benefits for the fetus and because even small amounts may be harmful, the safest answer seems to be: none. In other words, pregnant women should abstain from drinking *any* alcohol whatsoever.

**SMOKING** Although the proportion of adults who smoke has decreased in the United States and several other nations, this figure is increasing in many parts of the world (see Chapter 13). Moreover, the proportion of *women* who smoke is definitely on the rise. From the point of view of fetal development, this is unfortunate, for smoking by pregnant women is related to many harmful effects on the fetus and newborn child. These include decreased birth weight and size and increased risk for miscarriage and stillbirth (Wen et al., 1990). Maternal smoking may also interfere with cognitive development in early childhood (Cunningham, Dockery, & Speizer, 1994), perhaps in part because smoking raises the level of carbon monoxide in the mother's blood, and this harmful substance, rather than oxygen, is carried across the placenta to the fetus. Still other findings suggest that even if a nonsmoking mother is merely in an environment containing cigarette smoke, the infant can be harmed (Dreher, 1995). So, not only should pregnant women not smoke themselves—they should avoid locations in which other people are smoking.

In sum, many factors can adversely affect development during the prenatal period, and prospective mothers should carefully consider the potential risks before engaging in actions that may put their unborn children at risk. And the harmful effects of teratogens don't end when babies are born; for information on how these factors can influence newborns, please see the following **Beyond the Headlines** section.

# BEYOND the HEADLINES: As Psychologists See It

## Playpen Peril? The Potentially Harmful Effects of Plastic Toys

### Toy Makers Say Bye-Bye to "Plasticizers"

WALL STREET JOURNAL (MARCH 10, 1999)—A wave of big companies plan to stop using vinyl in teething rings, bathtub toys and other playthings as a war over chemicals in kids' toys escalates. The alleged culprit: chemical additives known as "phthalate esters," a kind of plasticizer that makes polyvinyl chloride soft and pliable. Some environmentalists say that when ingested in large quantities, plasticizers may cause cancer or interfere with hormonal development. . . . The toy makers say their products are safe, but they are taking action largely as a public-relations measure. . . . The chemicals industry is assuring retailers and consumers that no health problem exists. "It's clear to us that this is a completely harmless substance," says Dean Finney, member of a special panel commissioned by the industry . . . to study the additive's safety. Phthalates have been shown to cause cancer only in rats and only at "heroic dosages," says Mr. Finney. So far, science hasn't found the same effects in humans.

I really felt a chill down my spine when I noticed this article, because I can remember my own daughter, Jessica, sucking happily on her pacifier (made out of nipple-shaped plastic) and then chewing merrily away on her teething rings (see Figure 8.4). Did she ingest harmful substances while demonstrating her sucking reflex and other related forms of behavior? I don't know, but there is mounting evidence that, far from being inert and harmless, many types of plastic release small amounts of harmful chemicals as they are used—whether in drinking cups, plastic bottles, or infants' teething rings and other toys (Warren, 1999). What do these chemicals do? Some seem to mimic the effects of human hormones, binding with sites in the nervous system that are normally stimulated by these hormones. The result may be disturbances in the delicate balance of hormones within the body—a balance that plays a key role in normal growth and development.

Unfortunately, substances that have such effects are not present only in plastic toys; they are also being pumped into the food supply at an alarming rate. For instance, one chemical, *DES* (diethylstilbestrol), is used by the ton in animal feed because it increases growth rates. DES mimics the effects of important hormones, binding sites throughout the body that are normally responsive to *estrogen,* an important naturally occurring hormone found in much higher levels in females than males. Not only does DES occupy such sites—it appears to stimulate them more strongly than estrogen does. There is also growing concern over the effects of foods from genetically engineered plants and animals. While there is little direct evidence concerning this issue, companies that manufacture baby food are playing it safe: They recently announced that they would no longer use foods from genetically modified organisms.

**Figure 8.4**
**Plasticizers: A Potential Risk to Infants**

Recent findings suggest that plasticizers—chemicals added to plastic toys to make them softer—may act as carcinogens (causes of cancer) and may also disrupt infants' hormonal systems.

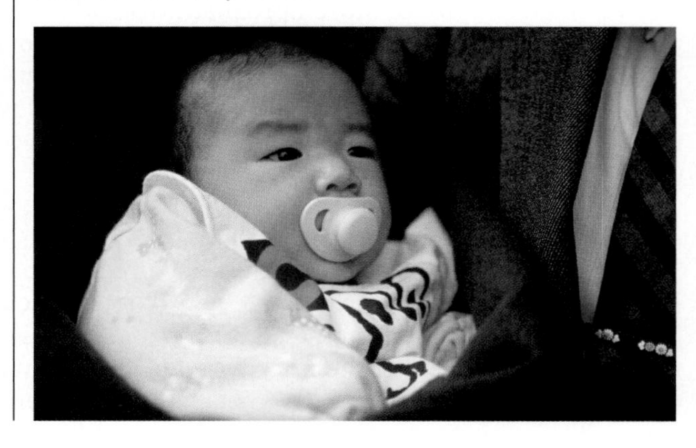

What do hormone-disrupting chemicals do to infants—or to the developing fetus? Research on this issue is just beginning; but in animals, substances such as DES appear to produce several kinds of cancer and several kinds of reproductive-system problems, ranging from undescended testicles to abnormal sperm and reduced fertility (e.g., Colborn, Dumanoski, & Myers, 1996). In humans, some findings suggest that DES and related chemicals may be linked to vaginal cancers and to a decline in human sperm counts that may be occurring throughout the world (it is not certain that this is actually occurring, however).

If all this scares you, you are in good company: A growing number of scientists have sounded a warning against the continued use of hormone-disrupting compounds. They are concerned that these substances are producing nothing short of "hormonal sabotage" where the human population is concerned and are having especially adverse effects on the health of infants and young children. Are these scientists correct? And if so, will their warnings have any impact on the use of such chemicals? Only time will tell; but in the meantime it does seem clear that by using a growing number of exotic chemicals, we are truly gambling with our own future as a species.

### CRITICAL THINKING QUESTIONS

1. At present, we don't know for certain whether plasticizers are actually harmful to children. What kind of research could be conducted to find out if they really cause cancer or interfere with hormonal development?
2. Suppose that such research indicates that plasticizers—and perhaps various kinds of plastic—are harmful to children; would it be possible to ban their use? Could we remove all such substances from the environment? (Literally billions of plastic bottles are produced each year, so this would be a massive undertaking.)
3. Should governments require more careful testing of new chemicals before they are used in large quantities? What role could psychologists play in such testing?

## Physical Development during Our Early Years

Audio 8.1: *Parent's Conflict in Size of Offspring*

Web Link: *Newborns' Growth and Development*

Physical growth is rapid during infancy. Assuming good nutrition, infants almost triple in weight (to about 20 pounds or 9 kilograms) and increase in body length by about one-third (to 28 or 29 inches, 71 to 74 cm) during the first year alone. Although infants are capable of eating immediately, they have limited capacity for what they can consume at one time—their stomachs will not hold very much. They compensate for this by eating small amounts frequently, about every 2.5 to 4 hours. Should parents try to put their babies on a feeding schedule, or let them eat whenever they are hungry? Most adopt a compromise in which they gradually try to establish some regularity in the baby's feeding schedule, but learn to distinguish between crying that means "I'm hungry! Feed me!" and crying that suggests, "I'm hungry, but not so hungry that I can't wait if you play with me." Most experts believe that this compromise approach is a reasonable one. However, they do warn against putting babies on a very rigid schedule, because this may lead to a situation in which babies eat when they are not experiencing the internal cues of hunger. The result? They don't learn to respond to hunger cues; this can lead to obesity—a growing problem among children in many countries. (See the **Making Psychology Part of Your Life** section at the end of this chapter.)

At birth, babies have little ability to regulate their own temperature; in fact, they can't maintain a normal body temperature by themselves until they are about eight or nine weeks old. So it's important to keep them warm—but not too warm! I have often seen babies dressed in heavy sweaters or snow suits at a nearby shopping mall, even though the temperature inside the mall is high, and the babies were obviously experiencing discomfort. So the best course is for parents to take account of what they themselves are wearing and how they feel in a given environment.

**REFLEXES** At birth newborns possess several simple **reflexes**—inherited responses to stimulation in certain areas of the body. If these reflexes are present, the baby's nervous system is assumed to be intact and working normally; if they are not, this is often a sign that something is seriously wrong. One such reflex, the *Moro reflex,* is triggered by a loud sound or a sudden dropping back of the infant's head. It involves a series of actions in which the baby first throws out his or her arms, then fans his or her fingers and lets out a cry before bringing the arms back over his or her chest. Another is the *palmar grasping reflex,* which is elicited by pressing or stroking the palms of the newborn's hands. The baby closes its hand and holds tight; in fact, infants can be lifted up from a flat surface by their grip. This reflex might well be useful in helping a baby cling to its mother as the mother moves

**Reflexes:** Inherited responses to stimulation in certain areas of the body.

TABLE 8.1

**Reflexes in the Newborn**

Newborns show all the reflexes described here at birth or very shortly thereafter.

| Reflex | Description |
| --- | --- |
| Blinking | Baby closes eyes in response to light |
| Rooting | When cheek is touched or stroked, baby turns toward touch; moves lips and tongue to suck |
| Sucking | When nipple or other object is placed in mouth, baby sucks |
| Tonic neck | When baby is placed on back with head turned to one side, baby stretches out arm and leg on side baby is facing |
| Moro | Baby throws out arms and fans fingers, extends neck, and cries in response to loud noise or sudden drop of head |
| Babinski | When baby's foot is stroked from heel to toe, toes fan out |
| Grasping | When palms of hands are stroked, baby closes fingers around the object in a strong grasp |
| Stepping | Baby makes stepping motions if held upright so one foot just touches a surface |

about. Babies also possess a *rooting reflex,* in which stroking the baby's cheek causes the baby to turn toward the stimulation and move its lips and tongue, and a *sucking reflex,* involving a combination of pressure and suction. These and other reflexes are summarized in Table 8.1.

**LOCOMOTOR DEVELOPMENT** As anyone who has observed newborns well knows, infants have limited ability to move around at birth. This situation changes quickly, however, and within a few months they become quite mobile. Within about five to ten months, babies can sit and crawl; and most begin to walk by the time they are fourteen or fifteen months old. Motor development proceeds from the head toward the limbs, so that at first babies can hold up their head, then lift their chest, then sit, and so on. Figure 8.5 summarizes several milestones of motor development. It's important to keep in mind that the ages shown are *merely averages.* Departures from them are of little importance unless they are quite extreme.

After the initial spurt of the first year, the rate of physical growth slows considerably; both boys and girls gain about 2 to 3 inches (5 to 10 cm) and 4 to 7 pounds (2 to 4 kg) per year. The rate accelerates during adolescence, when both sexes experience a *growth spurt* lasting about two years. These outward changes are accompanied by important inner ones, too. For instance, the brain expands rapidly through the first eighteen months of life, reaching more than half of the adult brain weight by the end of this period; by the time children are only five years old, the brain is almost full-sized. During this period there is a rapid growth of dendrites and axons within the brain; and *glial cells,* which supply nutrients to neurons, remove waste materials, and produce the myelin sheath that speeds neural impulses (see Chapter 2), increase rapidly in number.

Interestingly, motor development does not seem to be a function solely of maturation; cross-cultural studies indicate that it can be speeded or slowed by various

**Figure 8.5**
**Milestones of Locomotor Development**

As shown here, infants make rapid progress in their ability to move around. Please note that the ages shown are only *averages*. Most children will depart from them to some extent, and such variations are of little importance unless they are extreme.
(*Source:* From Schickedanz et al., 1998.)

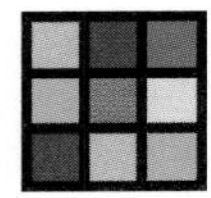

child-rearing practices. For instance, in Uganda and Kenya, mothers start early to teach their babies to sit, and the babies learn to do so at an earlier age than children in several Western countries such as the United States (Super, 1981). Similarly, mothers in the West Indies massage their babies and exercise their motor skills frequently (e.g., they throw them up in the air, hold them upside down by the heels, and frequently hold them upright with their feet touching a solid surface, which encourages stepping motions). These practices seem to speed motor development. In contrast, infants living in nomadic tribes in Paraguay are carried everywhere and prevented from exploring their environments; as a result, they show delayed motor development and don't begin to walk until they are more than two years old.

**LEARNING ABILITIES OF NEWBORNS** Can newborns show the kinds of learning discussed in Chapter 5? Evidence indicates that they can be *classically conditioned,* but primarily with respect to stimuli that have survival value for babies. For example, infants only two hours old readily learn to associate gentle stroking on the forehead with a sweet solution, and after these two stimuli have been paired repeatedly, they will show sucking responses to the stroking (the conditioned stimulus) (Clarke-Stewart, Friedman, & Koch, 1985). In contrast, human infants do not readily acquire conditioned fears (refer to Chapter 5) until they are at least eight months old.

Turning to *operant conditioning,* there is evidence that newborns can readily show this basic kind of learning. For example, they readily learn to suck faster, to see visual designs, or to hear music and human voices (Sansavini, Bertoncini, & Giovanelli, 1997). By the time infants are two months old, they can learn to turn their heads to the side on which their cheek is gently brushed to gain access to a bottle of sugar water (e.g., Siquelande & Lipsitt, 1966).

**REVIEW QUESTIONS**

- What environmental factors (teratogens) can adversely affect the developing fetus?
- What are plasticizers, and how can they adversely affect the development of children?
- What are reflexes, and which ones do infants possess at birth?
- What learning abilities are shown by newborns?

Audio 8.2: *Research Experience with Stimuli on Infants*

## Perceptual Development

How do infants perceive the world around them? Do they recognize form, see color, and perceive depth in the same manner as adults? Infants can't talk, so it is necessary to answer such questions through indirect methods, such as observing changes in behaviors infants *can* perform when exposed to various stimuli—for instance, differences in sucking responses, in bodily functions such as heart rate, or in the amount of time they spend looking at various stimuli. Developmental psychologists reason that if infants show different reactions to different stimuli, then they can indeed distinguish between them, at some level. For example, it has been found that after infants have seen a visual stimulus several times, they spend less time looking at it when it is presented again than they do looking at a new stimulus they have never seen before. This fact provides a means for determining whether infants can detect a difference between two stimuli. If they can, then after seeing one stimulus repeatedly, infants should spend less time looking at it than at a new stimulus. If they cannot tell the two stimuli apart, then they should look at both equally.

Studies based on this reasoning have found that newborns can distinguish between different colors (Adams, 1987), odors (Balogh & Porter, 1986), tastes (Granchrow, Steiner, & Daher, 1983), and sounds (Morrongiello & Clifton, 1984). Moreover, infants as young as two or three days old have been found to show differential patterns of sucking in response to what seem to be quite subtle differences in the sounds of human speech. Even at this tender age, infants show more vigorous sucking to words that are spoken with changing patterns of stress—for instance, "ma*ma*" versus "*ma*ma"—than to the same words when they are spoken with a constant pattern of stress (Sansavini, Bertoncini, & Giovanelli, 1997). Infants as young as three days old will turn their eyes and heads in the direction of a sound (Bargones & Werner, 1994; Eimas & Tarter, 1979). One sound to which infants are especially attentive is—not surprisingly—that of their own names. Apparently, by the time they are only a few months old, they can tell the difference between their own name and other names—even ones that have the same number of syllables (e.g., Mandel, Jusczyk, & Pisoni, 1995).

Web Link: *Evaluation of Speech Perception Development*

Perhaps most surprising of all, newborns can tell the difference between the sound of their own cry and that of another newborn infant. That they can do so is indicated by the results of research conducted by Dondi, Simion, and Caltran (1999). These researchers observed infants only one to three days old while they were exposed either to the sound of their own prerecorded cry, or to the crying of another infant of the same age. This was done both when the infants were awake and alert, and when they were sleeping. Both the infants' facial expressions and their amount of sucking on a pacifier (without plasticizers, I hope!) were observed both before the sounds were presented and while they were present. Results were clear: Both when awake and sleeping, the infants showed greater responsiveness to the sound of another infant crying than to the sound of their own crying (see Figure 8.6). Specifically, they showed reduced sucking and more expressions of distress in response to the other infants' cries. This study, of course, not only provides information on the impressive sensory abilities of newborns; it also suggests that even at this tender age, infants show the foundations of important forms of social behavior such as *empathy*—emotional reactions to the emotions of others. We'll return to social development in a later section, but this is a good moment to emphasize the fact that physical, cognitive, and social development do *not* occur in isolation from one another; rather, they proceed together, in an intricately interwoven pattern. They are separated in this chapter solely to facilitate discussion.

Web Link: *How Babies Learn to Listen*

**Figure 8.6**
**Newborns' Reactions to the Cries of Another Infant: The Beginnings of Empathy**

Infants showed significant reductions in sucking (a sign of distress) when they listened to the cry of another infant. In contrast, they showed smaller changes in behavior in response to the sound of their own cries.

(*Source:* Based on data from Dondi, Simion, & Caltran, 1999.)

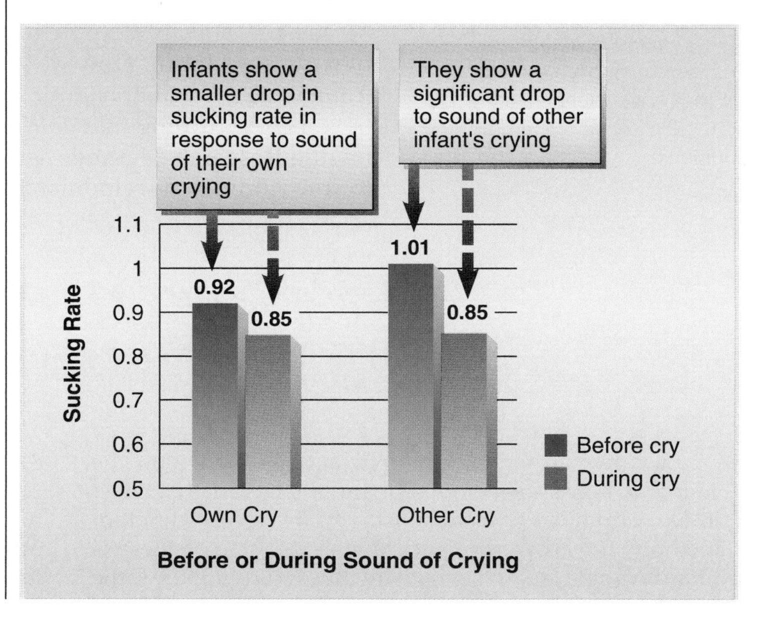


Infants also show impressive abilities with respect to recognizing *form* or *pattern*. Although they can't see very clearly at birth (their vision is about 20/400, which means that they can see an object 20 feet away only as clearly as an adult could see it at 400 feet), they show marked preferences for patterns and contrasts in visual stimuli. In now classic research on this topic, Fantz (1961) showed babies six months old a variety of visual patterns. By observing how long they looked at each, he determined that the babies had a clear preference for patterned as opposed to plain targets and that they seemed to prefer the human face over all other stimuli tested. Later research indicated that recognition

**Figure 8.7**
**The Visual Cliff: Apparatus for Testing Infant Depth Perception**

Infants six or seven months old will not crawl out over the "deep" side of the visual cliff. This indicates that they can perceive depth. Even two-month-old infants show changes in heart rate when placed over the "deep" side, so perception of depth may be present even at this young age.

of faces may develop even earlier. By two months of age, infants prefer a face with features in normal locations over one with scrambled features (Maurer & Barrera, 1981).

Many mothers and fathers have the impression that their newborns can recognize them soon after birth. Is this correct? Growing evidence suggests that it is. Even infants two days old can distinguish their mother's face from the face of a female stranger (Field et al., 1984). For instance, in one study on this issue, Walton, Bower, and Bower (1992) videotaped infants' mothers' faces and a stranger's face, then used a computer to control for changes in facial expressions over time (it is difficult to sit for a long period with a totally blank look). When the infants sucked on a pacifier, this turned on the video of the mother, and when they stopped sucking, this switched on the video of the stranger. What did the infants do? They sucked to see their mother's face. But how can infants this young recognize their mothers? Not, it appears, from facial features; in fact, newborns don't look at faces the way other children or adults do—that is, at the eyes first. Rather, they fixate on high-contrast areas, such as the hairline or the outer edge of the head. Evidence for this conclusion is provided by studies in which mothers and strangers wear head scarves that cover their hairline. Under these conditions, infants did not look longer at their mothers, because the scarves prevented them from recognizing their unique hairline or shape of their heads.

The ability to perceive depth, too, seems to develop rapidly. Early studies on *depth perception* employed an apparatus known as the *visual cliff* (Gibson & Walk, 1960). As you can see in Figure 8.7, the patterned floor drops away on the deep side of the "cliff," but a transparent surface continues across this drop, so there is no drop in the surface—and no real danger. Yet human infants six or seven months old refuse to crawl across the "deep" side to reach their mothers, thus indicating that they perceive depth by this time. Does this ability appear even before six months? Because younger infants can't crawl across the cliff even if they want to, this research method can't answer that question. But other research, using different methods, indicates that depth perception may first appear when infants are only two months old—infants of this age show a change in heart rate when presented with the visual cliff (e.g., Campos, Langer, & Krowitz, 1970; Yonas, Arterberry, & Granrud, 1987).

In sum, shortly after birth, infants have sophisticated abilities to interpret complex sensory input. How do they then integrate such information into cognitive frameworks for understanding the world? This is the question we will consider next. Before turning to *cognitive development*, however, let's take a look, in the following **Research Methods** section, at the basic procedures used by psychologists to study human development.

**Longitudinal Research:** Research in which the same individuals are studied across relatively long periods of time.

**Cross-Sectional Research:** Research comparing groups of persons of different ages in order to determine how certain aspects of behavior or cognition change with age.

**Cohort Effects:** Differences between persons of different ages stemming from the fact that they have experienced contrasting social or cultural conditions.

## Research Methods: How Psychologists Study Development

How can we obtain systematic evidence on the course of human development and the factors that affect it? Developmental psychologists employ several different methods for answering such questions. One of these is **longitudinal research,** which involves studying the same individuals for an extended period of time (see Figure 8.8). For example, suppose that a psychologist wanted to investigate the effects on children's later development of being bullied—of being victimized in some way by another child (Hodges et al., 1999; Olweus, 1995). Using the longitudinal method, the researcher could first identify two groups of children—ones who were currently being bullied and ones who were not. The psychologist would compare the two groups' behavior now—for instance, their level of confidence, the number of friends they have, their school performance. Then the researcher would study the same children on several future occasions—for example, midway through each of the next five school years. In this way, the psychologist could obtain evidence on the effects of being bullied.

Longitudinal research offers several important advantages. Because the same people are studied over long periods of time, it may be possible to draw conclusions about how specific events influence the course of subsequent development. For instance, if the youngsters being bullied showed decrements in their confidence over time, whereas those not being bullied did not show such reductions, these findings would suggest that bullying has harmful effects on self-assurance. However, this method, like all other research methods, is far from perfect. For instance, there is the problem of *subject attrition*—the loss of participants over the course of time. Families may move, children may be transferred to a different school; in such cases, the children are no longer available to participate in the study. Another problem is *practice effects.* Children who are tested or observed repeatedly may become very familiar with the kind of tasks used in the research, or may even be affected by them. As a result, the findings may be difficult to interpret.

A very different approach to studying human development is known as **cross-sectional research.** Here, children of different ages are compared at one point in time, to see if they differ in certain ways. Returning to our study of the effects of being bullied, a psychologist might study the behavior of children who are six years old, eight years old, and ten years old, comparing, for each age group, youngsters who are being bullied and those who are not.

Such research offers several advantages. It can be conducted much more quickly than longitudinal research; all the children are studied at one time, so we don't have to wait months or years to see what happens as they grow older. However, cross-sectional research also suffers from certain disadvantages. Perhaps the most important of these involve what are known as **cohort effects.** That is, differences between groups of persons of different ages

**Figure 8.8**
**Basic Methods of Developmental Research**

Developmental psychologists often use the two methods of research shown here to study many aspects of human development. In longitudinal research (upper panel), the same persons are studied repeatedly over time. In cross-sectional research (lower panel), persons of different ages are studied at the same point in time.

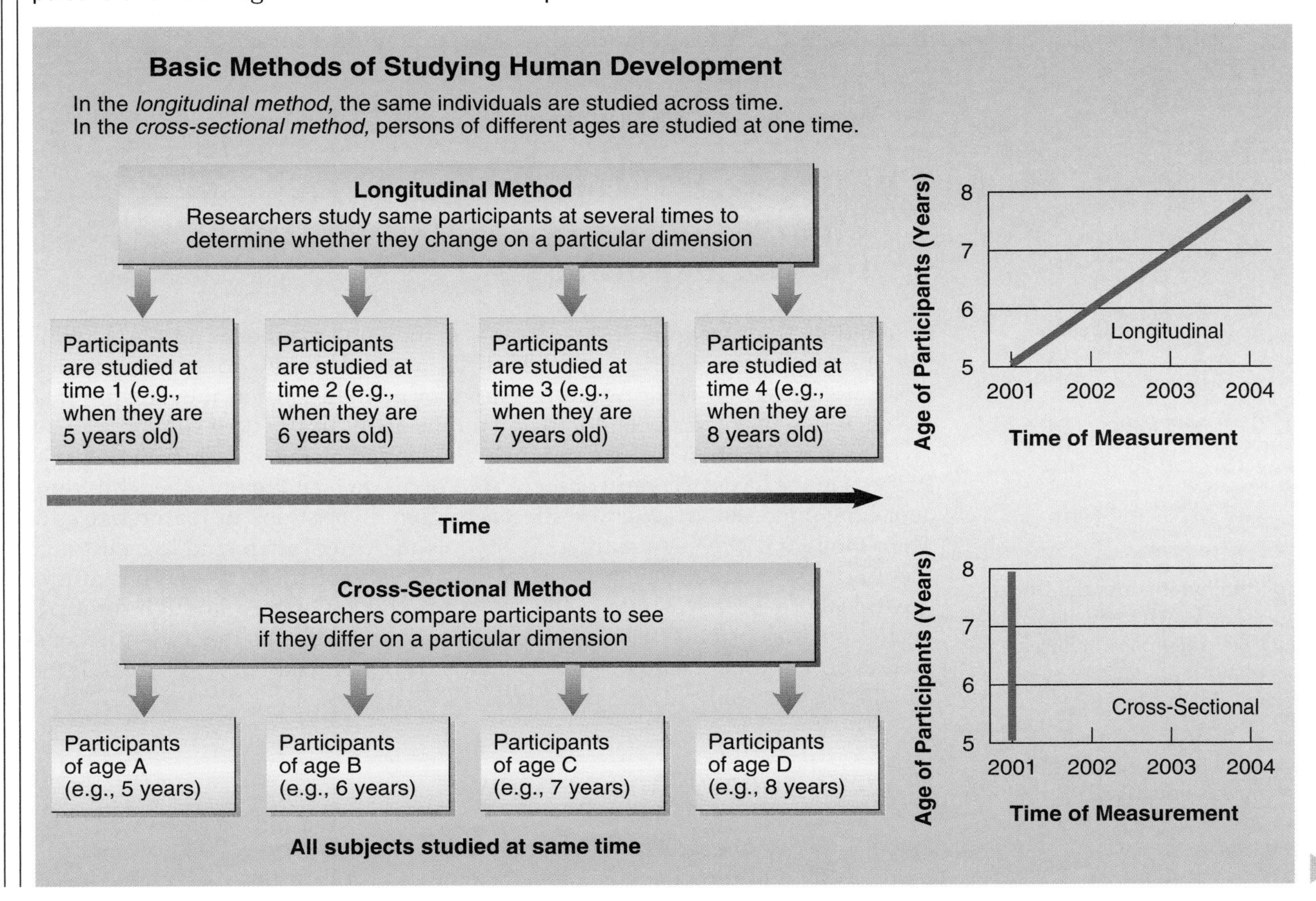

may derive not only from differences in age and changes in development related to age, but also from the fact that the groups were born at different times and have been exposed to contrasting life experiences or cultural conditions. Such differences may be small among children who are currently six, eight, and ten years old. But suppose we are comparing people who are sixty-five, forty-five, and twenty-five? Clearly, the life experiences of these groups may differ greatly; and these differences, not increasing age, may be responsible for differences among the groups.

Faced with the mixed picture of advantages and disadvantages I have outlined, developmental psychologists have tried to devise approaches that combine the advantages of longitudinal and cross-sectional research while minimizing the disadvantages of both. One such approach is known as the **longitudinal–sequential design.** It involves studying several samples of people of different ages over a prolonged period of time—months or even years. In other words, this technique combines major aspects of both longitudinal and cross-sectional research. Because each sample of participants is studied across time, changes within each can be attributed to development. But because several such samples are studied, researchers can also assess the impact of cohort effects, by comparing persons born in different years with one another *when they are the same age.* Any differences among them can then reasonably be attributed to cohort effects—to the fact that participants were born in different years and have, as a result, had different life experiences. Another advantage of such designs is that they allow for both longitudinal and cross-sectional comparisons. If the results for both are the same, then we can be quite confident about the validity of these. While the longitudinal–sequential design still faces problems of participant attrition and practice effects, it does offer an additional means for untangling some of the interwoven strands of culture and individual change. In this respect, it constitutes another useful research tool for developmental psychologists.

### REVIEW QUESTIONS

- What perceptual abilities are shown by infants?
- At what age can infants recognize their mother's face? How do they do this?
- What are the three basic methods psychologists use to study human development?

## Cognitive Development: Changes in Our Ability to Understand the World around Us

Do children think, reason, and remember in the same manner as adults? Until well into the twentieth century, it was widely assumed that they do. In many societies, it was assumed that while adults are superior mentally, just as they are physically, the cognitive processes of children and adults are basically very similar.

These assumptions were vigorously challenged by the Swiss psychologist Jean Piaget. On the basis of careful observations of his own and many other children, Piaget concluded that in several respects children do *not* think or reason like adults: Their thought processes are different not only in degree but in kind as well. Piaget's theory of *cognitive development* contains many valuable insights and has guided a great deal of research. Thus, we'll consider it in detail here. Although some of Piaget's conclusions have been questioned in recent years, his theory is still considered to be a uniquely valuable one by many developmental psychologists. For this reason, we'll consider it carefully here.

Web Link: *The Jean Piaget Society*

**Longitudinal–Sequential Design:** A research method in which several groups of individuals of different ages are studied across time.

**Stage Theory:** Any theory proposing that all human beings move through an orderly and predictable series of changes.

### Piaget's Theory: An Overview

Piaget's theory of cognitive development is a **stage theory**—a type of theory suggesting that all human beings move through an orderly and predictable series of changes. We'll have reason to examine other stage theories in our discussions of adult development (Chapter 9) and personality (Chapter 12). Currently, however, many psychologists question the ideas, basic to such theories, that (1) all human beings move through a set series of stages; (2) they move from one stage to another at specific ages; and (3) the order of such progress is unchanging (Flavell, 1985). There simply seems to be too much variability among individuals to enable us to assume such a high degree of orderliness in human development.

Having clarified this point, let's return to Piaget's theory, and begin by noting that central to it is the assumption—often known as *constructivism*—that children are active thinkers who are constantly trying to construct more accurate or advanced understanding of the world around them (e.g., Siegler & Ellis, 1996). In other words, from this perspective, children *construct* their knowledge of the world by interacting with it. How do children build such knowledge? According to Piaget, through two basic processes. The first of these is **assimilation,** which involves the incorporation of new information or knowledge into existing knowledge structures known as **schemas.** As discussed in Chapter 6, a schema is a kind of "cognitive scaffold"—a framework for holding knowledge and organizing it. The second process is **accommodation;** it involves modifications in existing knowledge structures (schemas) as a result of exposure to new information or experiences. Here's a concrete example of how, in Piaget's theory, these processes operate.

**Assimilation:** In Piaget's theory of cognitive development, incorporation of new information into existing mental frameworks (schemas).

**Accommodation:** In Piaget's theory, the modification of existing knowledge structures (schemas) as a result of exposure to new information or experiences.

**Sensorimotor Stage:** In Piaget's theory, the earliest stage of cognitive development.

A two-year-old child has seen many different kinds of cats and, on the basis of such experience, has built up a schema for cats: relatively small four-legged animals. Now she sees a squirrel for the first time and through assimilation includes it in this schema. As she encounters more and more squirrels, however, she begins to notice that they differ from cats in several respects: They move differently, climb trees, have much bushier tails, and so on. On the basis of this new experience, she gradually develops another schema for squirrels. This illustrates accommodation—changes in our existing knowledge structures resulting from exposure to new information (see Figure 8.9). Piaget believed that it is the tension between these two processes that encourages cognitive development. But don't lose sight of the key fact: According to Piaget, as these changes occur, children are constantly trying to make better and more accurate sense out of the complex world around them. Let's now take a closer look at the discrete stages of cognitive development Piaget described.

### THE SENSORIMOTOR STAGE: FIGURING OUT WAYS TO MAKE THINGS HAPPEN

Piaget suggested that the first stage of cognitive development lasts from birth until somewhere between eighteen and twenty-four months. During this period, termed the **sensorimotor stage,** infants gradually learn that there is a relationship between their actions and the external world. They discover that they can manipulate objects and produce effects. In short, they acquire a basic grasp of the concept of *cause and effect.* For example, they learn that if they make certain movements—for instance, shaking their leg—specific effects follow (for instance, toys suspended over their crib also move), and they begin to experiment with various actions to see what effects they will produce.

Throughout the sensorimotor period, Piaget contended, infants seem to know the world only through motor activities and

**Figure 8.9**
**Assimilation and Accommodation**

According to Piaget, children build increasing knowledge of the world through two processes: *assimilation,* in which new information is incorporated into existing schemas, and *accommodation,* in which existing schemas are modified in response to new information and experiences.

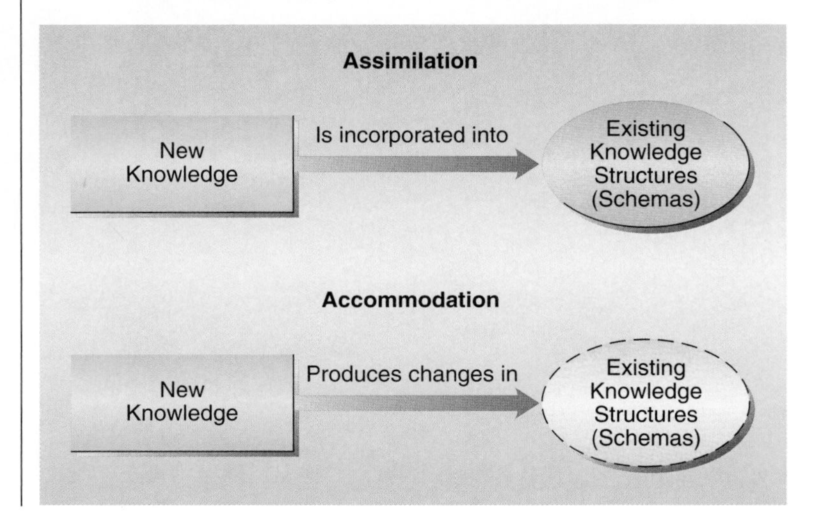

**Object Permanence:** The fact that objects continue to exist when they pass from view.

**Preoperational Stage:** In Piaget's theory, a stage of cognitive development during which children become capable of mental representations of the external world.

**Symbolic Play:** Play in which children pretend that one object is another object.

**Egocentrism:** The inability of young children to distinguish their own perspective from that of others.

sensory impressions. They have not yet learned to use mental symbols or images to represent objects or events. This results in some interesting effects. For example, if an object is hidden from view, four-month-olds will not attempt to search for it. For such infants, "out of sight" is truly "out of mind." By eight or nine months of age, however, they *will* search for the hidden objects. They have acquired a basic idea of **object permanence**—the idea that objects continue to exist even when they are hidden from view. (But see our discussion of this topic below; recent findings suggest that here, as in many other cases, Piaget underestimated the abilities of infants.)

**THE PREOPERATIONAL STAGE: GROWTH OF SYMBOLIC ACTIVITY** Sometime between the ages of eighteen and twenty-four months, Piaget suggested, toddlers acquire the ability to form mental images of objects and events. At the same time, language develops to the point at which they begin to think in terms of verbal symbols—words. These developments mark the transition to Piaget's second stage—the **preoperational stage.** This term reflects Piaget's view that at this stage, children don't yet show much ability to use logic and mental operations.

During the preoperational stage, which lasts until about age seven, children are capable of many actions they could not perform earlier. For instance, they demonstrate **symbolic play,** in which they pretend that one object is another—that a pencil is a rocket or a wooden block is a frog, for example. Such play is marked by three shifts that afford unique insights into how children's cognitive abilities change during this period. One is *decentration,* in which children gradually begin to make others rather than themselves the recipients of their playful actions—for instance, they begin to feed their dolls or dress them. The second shift is *decontextualization:* Objects are made to substitute for each other, as when a child pretends that a twig is a spoon. The third change involves *integration*—combining play actions into increasingly complex sequences. For instance, when I was a little boy, I had a collection of toy cars; and I now realize that as I grew older, I played with them in ever more intricate ways: I had them compete in imaginary races, brought them into a toy service station for more and more elaborate "servicing," and so on (see Figure 8.10). Can you see how children's abilities to engage in more and more complex forms of play indicate that they are growing cognitively? After all, in order to imagine that one object is another and to conduct long play sessions in which dolls are treated as though they had thoughts and feelings of their own, a child must have a growing ability to think in terms of words.

**Figure 8.10**
**Symbolic Play: A Sign of Children's Growing Cognitive Abilities**

By the time they are five or six, most children can engage in *symbolic play,* in which they pretend that one object is another object, and in which they imagine increasingly complex sequences of events and actions.

While the thought processes of preoperational children are more advanced than those in the preceding stage, Piaget emphasized that these children are still immature in several respects. True, they can use mental symbols; but their thinking remains somewhat inflexible, illogical, fragmented, and tied to specific contexts. One way in which the thinking of preoperational children is immature involves what Piaget termed **egocentrism**—children's inability to understand that others may perceive the world differently than they do (Piaget, 1975). For example, if two-year-olds are shown a card with a picture of a dog on one side and a cat on the other, and the card is placed between the child and the researcher, many do not seem to realize that they and the adult see different pictures. (Again, however, Piaget seems to have underestimated the abilities of young children; we'll discuss this point shortly.)

Children in the preoperational stage also seem to lack understanding of relational terms such as *lighter, larger, softer.* Further, they lack *seriation*—the ability to arrange objects in order along some dimension. Finally, and most important, they lack a grasp of what Piaget terms the principle of **conservation**—knowledge that certain physical attributes of an object remain unchanged even though the outward appearance of the object is altered. For example, imagine that a four-year-old is shown two identical lumps of clay. One lump is then flattened into a large pancake as the child watches. Asked whether the two lumps still contain the same amount of clay, the child may answer no.

**THE STAGE OF CONCRETE OPERATIONS: THE EMERGENCE OF LOGICAL THOUGHT** By the time they are six or seven (or perhaps even earlier, as we'll soon discuss), most children can solve the simple problems described above. According to Piaget, a child's mastery of conservation marks the beginning of a third major stage known as the stage of **concrete operations.**

During this stage, which lasts until about the age of eleven, many important skills emerge. Children gain understanding of relational terms and seriation. They come to understand *reversibility*—the fact that many physical changes can be undone by a reversal of the original action. Children who have reached the stage of concrete operations also begin to engage in what Piaget described as *logical thought.* If asked, "Why did you and your mother go to the store?" they reply, "Because my mother needed some milk." Younger children, in contrast, may reply "Because afterwards, we came home."

**THE STAGE OF FORMAL OPERATIONS: DEALING WITH ABSTRACTIONS AS WELL AS REALITY** At about the age of twelve, Piaget suggested, most children enter the final stage of cognitive development—the stage of **formal operations.** During this period, major features of adult thought make their appearance. While children in the earlier stage of concrete operations can think logically, they can do so only about concrete events and objects. In contrast, those who have reached the stage of formal operations can think abstractly; they can deal not only with the real or concrete but with possibilities—events or relationships that do not exist, but can be imagined.

During this final stage, children become capable of what Piaget termed **hypothetico–deductive reasoning.** This involves the ability to generate hypotheses and to think logically about symbols, ideas, and propositions. Children at the stage of formal operations also became capable of engaging in **interpropositional thinking**—thinking in which they seek to test the validity of several propositions. (Children at the level of concrete operations can sometimes test single propositions.)

While the thinking of older children or adolescents closely approaches that of adults, however, Piaget, believed that still falls short of the adult level. Older children, and especially adolescents, often use their new powers of reasoning to construct sweeping theories about human relationships, ethics, or political systems. The reasoning behind such views may be logical, but the theories are often false, because the young persons who construct them don't have enough experience or information to do a more sophisticated job.

One final—but crucial—point: Even though people who have reached the stage of formal operations are *capable* of engaging in advanced forms of thought, there is no guarantee that they will actually do so. Such thinking requires lots of cognitive effort, so it is not surprising that adolescents, and adults too, often slip back into less advanced modes of thought. Table 8.2 on page 302 provides a summary of the major stages in Piaget's theory.

**Conservation:** The fact that certain physical attributes of an object remain unchanged even though its outward appearance changes.

**Concrete Operations:** In Piaget's theory, a stage of cognitive development occurring roughly between the ages of seven and eleven. It is at this stage that children become aware of the permanence of objects.

**Formal Operations:** In Piaget's theory, the final stage of cognitive development, during which individuals may acquire the capacity for deductive or propositional reasoning.

**Hypothetico–Deductive Reasoning:** In Piaget's theory, a type of reasoning first shown by individuals during the stage of formal operations. It involves formulating a general theory and deducing specific hypotheses from it.

**Interpropositional Thinking:** In Piaget's theory, thinking in which a child seeks to test the validity of several propositions.

TABLE 8.2

**Major Stages in Piaget's Theory**

According to Piaget, we move through the stages of cognitive development described here.

| Stage | Age | Major Accomplishments |
|---|---|---|
| Sensorimotor | 0–2 years | The child develops basic ideas of cause and effect and object permanence. |
| Preoperational | 2–6 or 7 years | The child begins to represent the world symbolically. |
| Concrete Operations | 7–11 or 12 years | The child gains understanding of principles such as conservation; logical thought emerges. |
| Formal Operations | 12–adult | The adolescent becomes capable of several forms of logical thought. |

Audio 8.3: *Problems with Piaget's Theory*

## Piaget's Theory: A Modern Assessment

All theories in psychology are subject to careful scientific testing, but grand theories such as Piaget's require especially careful assessment, because they are so sweeping in nature. What do the results of research on Piaget's theory reveal? Briefly, that it is highly insightful in many ways—but that, like virtually every theory, it should be revised in the light of new evidence. In particular, developmental psychologists have suggested revisions in Piaget's theory with respect to three important issues: (1) the cognitive abilities of infants and preschoolers (these turn out to be considerably greater than Piaget believed); (2) the discreteness of stages of cognitive development; and (3) the importance of social interactions between children and caregivers in the children's cognitive development.

**THE CASE OF THE COMPETENT PRESCHOOLER** With respect to the first of these issues, growing evidence indicates that Piaget seriously underestimated the cognitive abilities of infants and young children in many respects (e.g., Siegal & Peterson, 1996). Why did this happen? Apparently, because some of the research methods Piaget used, although ingenious, made it difficult for infants and preschool children to demonstrate cognitive abilities they actually possessed. Let's take a brief look at two of these abilities—*object permanence* and *egocentrism.*

As you will recall, Piaget concluded that infants below the age of eight or nine months did not realize that objects have an existence that continues even when they are removed from sight. However, it now appears that these findings may have stemmed from the fact that children this young don't understand the concept "under." Thus, when an object is placed under a cover, they are stumped, because they don't realize that one object can be underneath another. So if objects are placed *behind* a screen, rather than under a cover, infants as young as four or five months of age *do* act as if they know it is still there.

And infants seem to understand far more about physical objects than this; they even seem to have a basic understanding of how physical objects will behave under various conditions. Insight into babies' impressive skills in this respect is provided by tasks involving what Baillargeon (1987) terms *impossible events.* For instance, in one ingenious study using such tasks (Baillargeon, Needham, & DeVos, 1992), infants 6.5 months old watched while a gloved hand pushed an object along a platform. In the *possible event* condition, the hand stopped while the object was still on the platform. In the *impossible event* condition, it pushed the object until it was off the edge of the platform (see Figure 8.11). Would the children look longer at the impossible event than the possible event? They did indeed, thus indicating that they understood that physical objects can't stay suspended in empty space! In other conditions, the

**Figure 8.11**
**Infants' Reactions to Impossible Events**

Infants only 6.5 months olds showed signs of surprise when confronted with impossible events such as the one shown in the lower pair of drawings. In contrast, they did not show surprise at various kinds of possible events such as those shown in the upper drawings. These findings suggest that infants possess considerable understanding of the nature and properties of physical objects. (*Source:* Adapted from drawings in Baillargeon, 1994, and Schickedanz et al., 1998.)

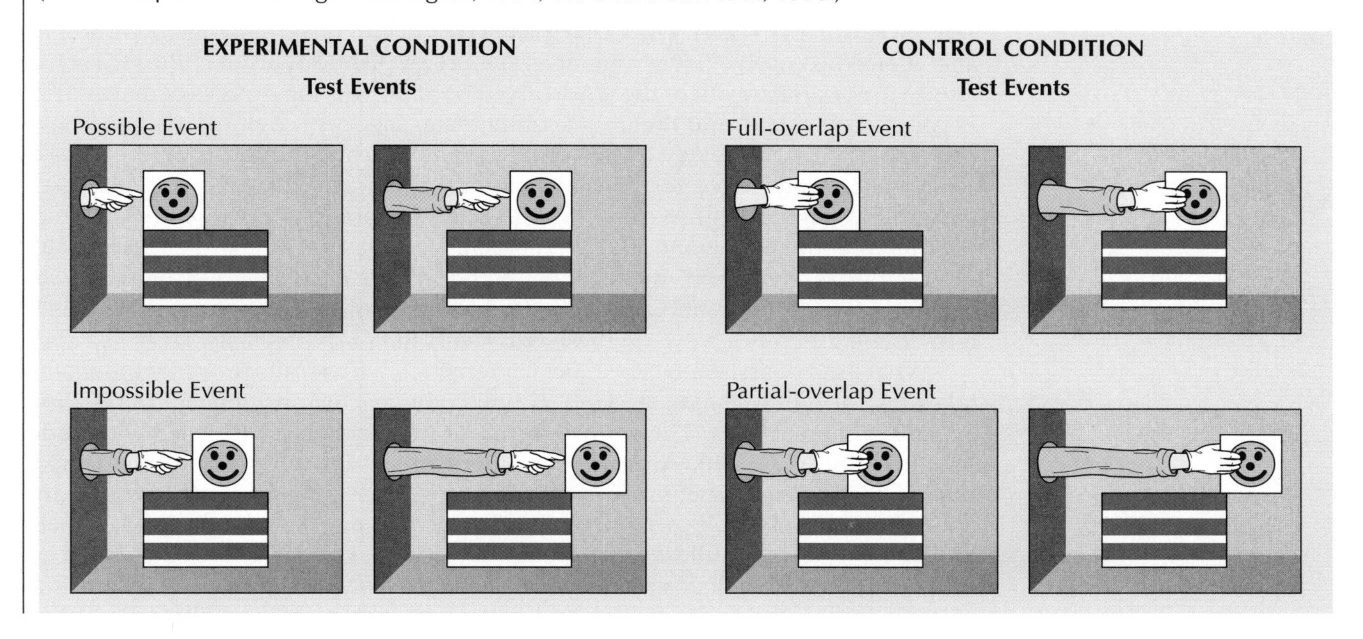


gloved hand grasped the object and held it while pushing it along the platform. When the object was pushed beyond the edge of the platform *but was still held by the gloved hand,* the children did not seem surprised, and did not look at this any longer than at the event in which the object stopped before reaching the edge (refer to Figure 8.11). This and other studies suggest that infants as young as 3.5 months old understand much about the physical nature of objects—much more, in fact, than Piaget believed.

Now let's consider *egocentrism*—young children's inability to understand that others may perceive the world differently than they do. To study egocentrism, Piaget showed children a model of a mountain with various features (e.g., a path, a small stream) visible only from certain sides. He had children walk about the mountain, looking at it from all angles. Then he placed a doll at various positions around the mountain and asked children to describe what the doll saw or to choose the photo that showed what the doll could see. He found that children could not perform this task accurately until they were six or seven years old. However, once again, it appears that the task Piaget used may have led him astray. When, instead, this task involves more distinctive and familiar objects—for instance, people and trees—even children as young as three or four can respond accurately (e.g., Borke, 1975; Newcombe & Huttenlocher, 1992). Indeed, even infants fourteen to eighteen months old show some awareness of the fact that others may not see what they see; for instance, they will look back and forth between objects and adults as they point to objects they want the adults to notice (Schickedanz et al., 1998). Piaget also underestimated young children's understanding of *conservation,* both of number and of physical attributes such as size; their ability to classify objects (e.g., Mandler, Bauer, & McDonough, 1991); and their understanding of what it means to be alive (e.g., Bullock, 1985). So, in sum, it is reasonable to conclude that although he certainly called attention to important aspects of young children's thought, Piaget significantly underestimated children's abilities in several of these respects.

**DISCRETE STAGES IN COGNITIVE DEVELOPMENT** Piaget proposed that cognitive development passes through discrete stages and that these are *discontinuous*—children must complete one stage before entering another. Most research findings, however, indicate that cognitive changes occur in a more gradual manner. Rarely does an ability entirely absent at one age appear suddenly at another. Further, these changes are often *domain specific*—children may be advanced with respect to some kinds of thinking, but far less advanced with respect to others (Gopnik, 1996).

**THE SOCIAL CONTEXT OF COGNITIVE DEVELOPMENT** As noted earlier, Piaget viewed cognitive development as stemming primarily from children's active efforts to make sense out of the world around them, plus the process of maturation. In contrast, **sociocultural theory**—another major theory of cognitive development, proposed by Lev Vygotsky (1987)—placed much greater emphasis on the roles of social factors and language, especially among school-aged children. Vygotsky suggested that cognitive growth occurs in an interpersonal, social context in which children are moved beyond their *level of actual development* (what they are capable of doing unassisted) and toward their *level of potential development* (what they are capable of achieving with assistance from older—and wiser!—tutors). Vygotsky termed the difference between these two levels the *zone of proximal development.*

What kind of assistance does social interaction with adults provide? Often, this takes the form of *reciprocal teaching,* in which the teacher and the child take turns engaging in an activity. This allows the adult (or other tutor) to serve as a model for the child. In addition, during their interactions with children, adults provide *scaffolding*—mental structures the children can use as they master new tasks and new ways of thinking. A growing body of evidence suggests that the kind of social interactions between children and older tutors Vygotsky emphasized do indeed enhance cognitive development, helping children to acquire specific skills such as reading ability, and new insights and improvements in inferential thinking (e.g., Azmitia, 1988). Children can also learn from other children—for instance, classmates—in this manner (e.g., Astington, 1995). And being socially skilled (being able to get along well with peers and others) seems to be an important plus in this process: The more socially skilled children are, the more advanced they are in their understanding of how other people think—an important aspect of cognitive development we'll soon consider (Watson et al., 1999).

In sum, there is now general agreement among developmental psychologists that in certain respects Piaget's theory is in need of revision. Despite its shortcomings, however, there is no doubt that this theory has profoundly altered our ideas about how children think and reason (e.g., Brainerd, 1996). In this sense, certainly, Piaget's work has made a lasting contribution to psychology.

**REVIEW QUESTIONS**

- What are the major stages in Piaget's theory, and what cognitive abilities do infants, children, and adolescents acquire as they move through these stages?
- In what respects does Piaget's theory appear to be in need of revision?

## Beyond Piaget: Children's Theory of Mind and Research on the Information-Processing Perspective

**Sociocultural Theory:** Vygotsky's theory of cognitive development, which emphasizes the role of social factors and language.

Piaget is truly a giant in the history of psychology; in an important sense, his theory and insights set the agenda for research by developmental psychologists for decades. In recent years, however, researchers have investigated topics and perspectives that were not included in Piaget's work, but which appear to be important for understanding cognitive development. One of these areas of study involves children's

**theory of mind**—their growing understanding of their own mental states and those of others. A second involves the application of an *information-processing perspective* to various aspects of cognitive development. We'll now consider both topics.

**Theory of Mind:** Refers to children's growing understanding of their own mental states and those of others.

**CHILDREN'S THEORY OF MIND: THINKING ABOUT THINKING** As adults, we possess a sophisticated understanding of thoughts and the process of thinking. We realize that our own thoughts may change over time and that we may have false beliefs or reach false conclusions. Similarly, we realize that other people may have goals or desires that differ from our own and that they may sometimes try to conceal these from us; further, we realize that given the same information, others may reason to conclusions that differ from our own. In other words, we understand quite a bit about how we and other people think. But what about children? When—and how—do they acquire such understanding? This has been a major focus of recent research on cognitive development, and this work has yielded some surprising findings.

Let's begin with what might seem to be a fairly simple aspect of such thinking—children's ability to recognize that others can hold beliefs different from their own, and that these beliefs can be false. Do children understand this basic fact? Not, it appears, until they are about four years old. This fact has been established by the following kind of research: Children are shown drawings of a story in which a boy named Maxi puts some candy in a box (see Figure 8.12). Then, while Maxi is out of

**Figure 8.12**
**Children's Theory of Mind: Their Understanding that Others Can Hold Different Beliefs Than They Do**

If young children (e.g., three-year-olds) are told the story depicted here, they predict that the character in the story will look for the candy where his mother left it; they don't understand that what *they* know can be different from what the story character knows, or that he can hold mistaken beliefs. Four-year-olds, however, predict that the character will look where *he* left the candy, thus demonstrating their growing understanding of how others, and they, think.
(*Source:* Schickedanz et al., 1998, p. 335.)

**Figure 8.13**
**Children's Understanding of Others' Wishes**

Even two-year-olds were able to determine what another person wanted from the direction of his gaze. However, both two-year-olds and three-year-olds did even better at guessing another's wishes when additional cues were also present; for instance, this person turned toward the object he wanted and also pointed to it.
(*Source:* Based on data from Lee et al., 1998.)

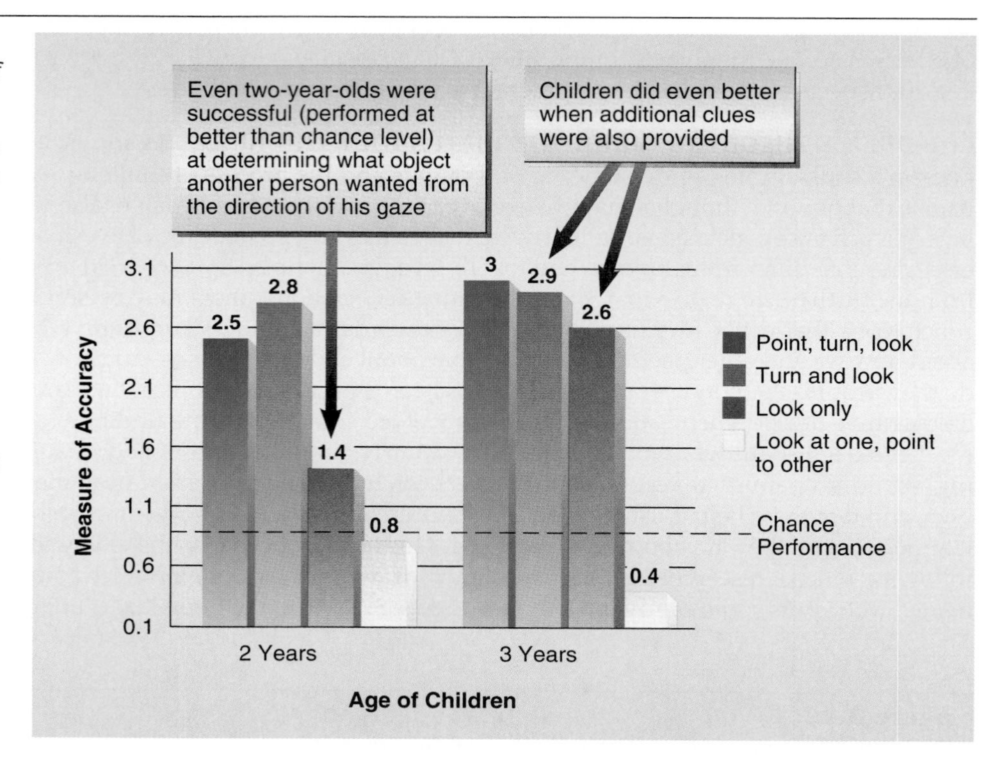


the room, his mother moves it to another box. Maxi then returns and wants to find his candy. When asked, "Where will Maxi look for the candy?" three-year-olds indicate that he will look in the box where his mother put it. In other words, they don't seem to realize that Maxi will have the mistaken belief that the candy is where *he* left it. *They* know where it is, so they assume he will too (e.g., Naito, Komatsu, & Fuke, 1994). By the time children are four, however, they realize that Maxi will look in the wrong box.

Here's another illustration of how children's theory of mind becomes more sophisticated over time. Infants as young as two or three months of age can tell whether an adult is looking at them or away (e.g., Vecra & Johnson, 1995). But at what age will they follow another's gaze to determine what that other person is looking at, and so, perhaps, the other's desires or intentions (e.g., Baron-Cohen et al., 1995)? Recent studies suggest that under some conditions, even two-year-olds can accomplish this task. For instance, in one study on this topic, Lee and his colleagues (1998) showed children two and three years old a televised image of Giggles the clown; the children's task was to indicate what object Giggles wanted. In one condition, Giggles looked at one of several objects (teacup, figurine, ball), turned toward it, pointed, and said: "I want that!" Then, a few seconds later, Giggles was shown holding the object and saying "That is what I wanted!" In another condition, only Giggles's head and eyes were shown, so no pointing cues were available. In still another condition, Giggles looked at the object he wanted but did not turn his head toward it. Finally, in another condition, he pointed to one object but looked at another while saying "I want that." Results were clear: The three-year-olds generally outperformed the two-year-olds, but even the younger children were successful in identifying what Giggles wanted at an above-chance level in all conditions *except* the one in which he looked at one object and pointed to another (see Figure 8.13). These findings indicate that even very young children possess considerable understanding of others' thoughts.

I should quickly add, however, that although young children are surprisingly accomplished in this respect, they do lack important insights into the nature of thought. For instance, they have difficulty recognizing *when* another person is thinking; they know thinking is different from talking or seeing, but don't fully understand that it is a private mental event (Flavell, Green, & Flavell, 1995). Similarly, young children know when they know something, but they are often unclear about the *source* of this knowledge: Did they obtain it themselves? Did someone tell them? Did they draw an inference? This may be one reason why, as we saw in Chapter 6, young children are often unreliable witnesses, even to traumatic events they have personally experienced. They know that they have knowledge of various events but are unsure how they acquired it—whether through direct experience or from the comments and suggestions of an adult. So, although young children have a surprisingly complex theory of mind, it is incomplete in several important respects.

**COGNITIVE DEVELOPMENT: AN INFORMATION-PROCESSING PERSPECTIVE** Another way in which recent research on cognitive development has moved beyond the framework described by Piaget involves application of an *information-processing perspective.* This perspective seeks insights into cognitive development in terms of children's growing abilities with respect to basic aspects of cognition such as attention, memory, and metacognition (thinking about thinking and being able to control and use one's own cognitive abilities strategically). For instance, as they grow older, children acquire increasingly effective strategies for retaining information in working (short-term) memory. Five- and six-year-olds are much less likely than adults to use *rehearsal*—the tactic of repeating information to oneself to try to memorize it. By the time children are eight years old, however, they can do this much more effectively. Similarly, older children are better able than younger ones to use *elaboration,* a strategy in which new information is linked to existing knowledge.

In a similar manner, children acquire increasingly effective strategies for focusing their attention; strategies for using scripts and other mental frameworks (schemas) (Fivush, Kuebli, & Clubb, 1992); and greater understanding of metacognition—for instance, how to regulate and control problem-solving processes and memory (Frederiksen, 1994). Research conducted from an information-processing perspective has helped link the process of cognitive development more closely to basic research on cognition, so it too has proved very useful.

**REVIEW QUESTIONS**

- What is the focus of research on children's theory of mind?
- According to the information-processing perspective, what does cognitive development involve?

**Food for Thought**

Do you think that young children's inability to understand that other people may have different thoughts or motives from themselves is one reason why children are sometimes vulnerable to child molesters?

## Moral Development: Reasoning about "Right" and "Wrong"

Is it ever right to cheat on an exam? To mislead consumers through false advertising (see Figure 8.14 on page 308)? To claim exaggerated deductions on your income taxes? As adults we often ponder such *moral questions*—issues concerning what is right and what is wrong in a given context. And as adults, we realize that such matters are often complex. Whether a given action is acceptable or unacceptable may depend on many factors, including the specific circumstances involved, legal considerations, and our own personal code of ethics.

**Figure 8.14**
**Moral Judgment: Is It Ever Right to Deceive Consumers?**

Most adults would agree that the kinds of actions suggested here are morally wrong. But what about young children—would they reach the same conclusion? Research on moral development suggests that they might well have difficulty in understanding the meaning of such situations—and what is right or wrong in them.
(*Source:* DILBERT reprinted by permission of UNITED FEATURE SYNDICATE, Inc.)

But how do children deal with such issues? They, too, must make moral judgments. Is their reasoning about such matters similar to that of adults? This is the key question addressed in research on **moral development**—changes in the ability to reason about what is right and what is wrong in a given situation (e.g., Carlo et al., 1996; Carpendale & Krebs, 1995). While many different views of moral development have been proposed, the most famous is a theory offered by Lawrence Kohlberg (1984).

CourseCompass
Web Link: *Kohlberg's Theory of Moral Development*

## Kohlberg's Stages of Moral Understanding

Building on earlier views proposed by Piaget (1932/1965), Kohlberg studied boys and men and suggested that human beings move through three distinct levels of moral reasoning, each divided into two separate phases. In order to determine the stage of moral development participants had reached, Kohlberg asked them to consider imaginary situations that raised moral dilemmas for the persons involved. Participants then indicated the course of action they would choose, and explained why. According to Kohlberg, it is the explanations, *not* the decisions themselves, that are crucial, for it is the reasoning displayed in these explanations that reveals individuals' stage of moral development. One such dilemma is as follows:

> A man's wife is ill with a special kind of cancer. There is a drug that may save her, but it is very expensive. The pharmacist who discovered this medicine will sell it for $2,000, but the man has only $1,000. He asks the pharmacist to let him pay part of the cost now and the rest later, but the pharmacist refuses. Being desperate, the man steals the drug. Should he have done so? Why?

Let's consider the kinds of reasoning that would reflect several of the major stages of moral reasoning described by Kohlberg; see Table 8.3 for an overview of all the stages he described.

**THE PRECONVENTIONAL LEVEL** At the first level of moral development, the **preconventional level,** children judge morality largely in terms of consequences: Actions that lead to rewards are perceived as good or acceptable; ones that lead to punishments are seen as bad or unacceptable. For example, a child at this stage might say, "The man should not steal the drug, because if he does, he'll be punished."

**THE CONVENTIONAL LEVEL** As children's cognitive abilities increase, Kohlberg suggests, they enter a second level of moral development, the **conventional level.** Now they are aware of some of the complexities of the social order and judge morality in terms of what supports and preserves the laws and rules of their society. Thus, a child at this stage might reason: "It's OK to steal the drug, because no one will think you are bad if you do. If you don't, and let your wife die, you'll never be able to look anyone in the eye again."

**Moral Development:** Changes in the capacity to reason about the rightness or wrongness of various actions that occur with age.

**Preconventional Level** (of morality)**:** According to Kohlberg, the earliest stage of moral development, in which individuals judge morality in terms of the effects produced by various actions.

**Conventional Level** (of morality)**:** According to Kohlberg, a stage of moral development during which individuals judge morality largely in terms of existing social norms or rules.

**TABLE 8.3**

**Kohlberg's Theory of Moral Development: An Overview**

According to Kohlberg, we move through the stages of moral development described here.

| Level/Stage | Description |
|---|---|
| ***Preconventional Level*** | |
| *Stage 1:* Punishment-and-obedience orientation | Morality judged in terms of consequences |
| *Stage 2:* Naive hedonistic orientation | Morality judged in terms of what satisfies own needs or those of others |
| ***Conventional Level*** | |
| *Stage 3:* Good boy–good girl orientation | Morality judged in terms of adherence to social rules or norms with respect to personal acquaintances |
| *Stage 4:* Social order–maintaining orientation | Morality judged in terms of social rules or laws applied universally, not just to acquaintances |
| ***Postconventional Level*** | |
| *Stage 5:* Legalistic orientation | Morality judged in terms of human rights, which may transcend laws |
| *Stage 6:* Universal ethical principle orientation | Morality judged in terms of self-chosen ethical principles |

**THE POSTCONVENTIONAL LEVEL** Finally, in adolescence or early adulthood many, though by no means all, individuals enter a third level known as the **postconventional level,** or principled level. At this stage, people judge morality in terms of abstract principles and values rather than in terms of existing laws or rules of society. Persons who attain this stage often believe that certain obligations and values transcend the laws of society. The rules they follow are abstract and ethical, not concrete like the Ten Commandments, and are based on inner conscience rather than on external sources of authority. For example, a person at this stage of moral development might argue for stealing the drug as follows: "If the man doesn't steal the drug, he is putting property above human life; this makes no sense. People could live together without private property, but a respect for human life is essential." In contrast, if they argue for not stealing the drug, they might reason: "If the man stole the drug he wouldn't be blamed by others, but he would probably blame himself, since he has violated his own standards of honesty and hurt another person for his own gain."

## Evidence Concerning Kohlberg's Theory

Do we really pass through the series of stages described by Kohlberg, becoming increasingly sophisticated in our judgments of morality? Some findings are consistent with this view, at least in its broad outlines. As suggested by Kohlberg, individuals do generally seem to progress through the stages of moral reasoning he described, moving from less sophisticated to increasingly sophisticated modes of thought (e.g.,

**Postconventional Level** (of morality)**:** According to Kohlberg, the final stage of moral development, in which individuals judge morality in terms of abstract principles.

**Gender Differences:** Differences in the behavior of females and males. Often, these are exaggerated by *gender stereotypes.*

Walker, 1989). Other findings, however, suggest that Kohlberg's theory, while providing important insights, requires major revisions in several respects.

**GENDER DIFFERENCES IN MORAL DEVELOPMENT** Soon after Kohlberg presented his theory, one psychologist—Carol Gilligan—criticized it strongly on the grounds that it was biased against women (e.g., Gilligan, 1982). She noted that many women do not base moral judgments on the principles of justice emphasized by Kohlberg; rather, they base them on what she termed *care-based principles*—concerns over relationships, caring, and the promotion of others' welfare. Because moral reasoning based on such considerations is scored as relatively immature in Kohlberg's theory, Gilligan charged that Kohlberg's approach undervalued the moral maturity of females.

Are such charges accurate? Evidence on this issue is mixed but, overall, fails to provide clear support for Gilligan's suggestions. Several studies comparing the moral development of males and females have failed to uncover the differences predicted by Gilligan; indeed, if anything, females have tended to score *higher,* not lower, than males (e.g., Thoma, 1986; Walker, 1991). Further, it appears that contrary to Gilligan's suggestions, females do *not* seem to base their moral reasoning solely, or even primarily, on care-based concerns. While females do show a tendency to make more care-based judgments than males, this occurs primarily for personal moral dilemmas they have experienced themselves, and does *not* appear for other types of questions, including the ones used originally by Kohlberg (e.g., Wark & Krebs, 1996). So, overall, there is little evidence for important differences between males and females with respect to moral development or moral reasoning. Instead, it appears that if such differences exist, they are quite subtle and restricted in scope, occurring only with respect to specific kinds of moral dilemmas.

**CONSISTENCY OF MORAL JUDGMENTS** Kohlberg's theory, like other stage theories, suggests that as people grow older, they move through a series of successive discrete stages. If that were true, then it would be predicted that individuals' moral reasoning across a wide range of moral dilemmas should be consistent—it should reflect the stage they have reached. Do people show such consistency? The answer appears to be no. For example, in one revealing study on this issue, Wark and Krebs (1996) asked college students to respond to the moral dilemmas developed by Kohlberg and also to describe real-life dilemmas they had experienced or witnessed—dilemmas that affected them personally, and dilemmas they knew about but which had not affected them personally. For these real-life dilemmas, the students also described their moral reasoning—their thoughts about the issues, what they felt was the right course of action, and so on. Results indicated that contrary to Kohlberg's theory, participants showed little consistency across the various types of moral dilemmas. In fact, only 24 percent obtained the same global stage score (e.g., Stage 3, Stage 4) across all three types of dilemmas. A large majority, fully 85 percent, made judgments that ranged across three different stages. So, contrary to what Kohlberg's theory suggests, people do not show a high degree of consistency reflecting a specific stage of moral reasoning.

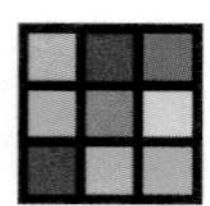

**CULTURAL DIFFERENCES AND MORAL DEVELOPMENT** Finally, it's important to note that the stages described by Kohlberg, and steady movement through them, do not appear in all cultures. In cross-cultural studies carried out in many countries (Taiwan, Turkey, Mexico), it has sometimes been found that persons from tribal or rural village backgrounds are less likely to reach Stage 5 reasoning than persons from more advantaged backgrounds (e.g., Nisan & Kohlberg, 1982; Simpson, 1974). These findings suggest that Kohlberg's work may, to an extent, be "culture bound": It may be biased against persons from ethnic groups and populations different from the ones he originally studied. Whether and to what degree this is true remains uncertain, but it *is* clear that cultural factors play an important role in shaping moral development and should be taken fully into account in our efforts to understand this important topic.

**REVIEW QUESTIONS**

- What are the major stages of moral development described by Kohlberg's theory?
- What do research findings indicate with respect to gender differences in moral reasoning?
- Do cultural factors have any impact on moral development?

Web Link: *Erik Erikson—The Father of Psychosocial Development*

Web Link: *An Erik Erikson Tutorial*

Web Link: *Encouraging Social Skills in Young Children*

# Social and Emotional Development: Forming Relationships with Others

Cognitive development is a crucial aspect of human growth, but it does not occur in a social vacuum. As infants and children are acquiring the capacities to think and reason, they are also gaining the basic experiences, skills, and emotions that permit them to form close relationships and to interact effectively with others in many settings. In this section we'll examine several aspects of such *social and emotional development.*

## Emotional Development and Temperament

At what age do infants begin to experience and demonstrate discrete emotions? They can't describe their subjective feelings, of course, so efforts to answer these questions have focused mainly on discrete *facial expressions*—outward signs of distinct emotions. Research on emotional development has documented that such expressions appear within the first few months of life (Izard, 1991). Infants as young as two months old demonstrate *social smiling* in response to human faces. They show laughter by the time they are three or four months old (Sroufe & Waters, 1976). And other emotions, such as anger, sadness, and surprise, also appear quite early and are readily recognizable to adults.

Interestingly, some expressions appear before others, or at least are more common at early ages. For example, following medical inoculations, two-month-old infants show pain expressions more frequently than anger expressions (Izard, Hembree, & Huebner, 1987). A few months later, however, they show anger expressions more often than pain. These findings, and many others, underscore an important point: *Emotional development and cognitive development occur simultaneously, and there are many connections between them.* The finding that anger expressions in response to painful experiences become more common during the first eighteen months of life can be interpreted, for instance, as reflecting infants' growing ability to understand who or what has caused their discomfort.

As they grow older, infants also acquire increasing capacities to "read" the emotional expressions of others. At three months, they become upset when their mothers show an immobile facial expression (Tronick, 1989). By eight or ten months, they actively seek information about other people's feelings and begin to demonstrate growing understanding of their own mental states and those of others (an increasingly sophisticated theory of mind). Thus, after a fall, one-year-olds will often look at their caregivers and, depending on *their* reactions, will cry or laugh—that is, they engage in *social referencing* (Walden & Ogan, 1988) (see Figure 8.15 on page 312).

**Figure 8.15**
**Social Referencing in Action**

Toddlers often look at their caregivers in order to determine how they should react, emotionally, to a new situation or experience.

Finally, children also grow in ability to regulate their own emotional reactions and to express their emotions to others. Infants have very little capacity to do this, but within a few years they begin to engage in active efforts to understand and regulate their own feelings. If you have ever seen a four-year-old cover his ears or eyes while watching a frightening television show or film, you have witnessed such efforts directly: The child involved is trying to regulate his own feelings by preventing exposure to something he doesn't like! Children's abilities to regulate their emotions increase through the grade-school years, as does the range of strategies available to them for expressing these feelings—for communicating them to others (e.g., Saarni, 1993). By the time they are ten, therefore, most children are quite adept at these tasks. For instance, they have learned to express sadness, both verbally and nonverbally, in order to gain sympathy and support, and to withhold or disguise anger in order to avoid adult disapproval for such reactions (e.g., Zeman & Shipman, 1996). Progress in both these tasks—regulating and expressing emotions—plays a key role in children's ability to form increasingly complex social relationships—a topic to which we'll soon return.

**TEMPERAMENT: INDIVIDUAL DIFFERENCES IN EMOTIONAL STYLE** Do you know anyone who is almost always bouncy, cheerful, and upbeat? And what about the other extreme—someone who is usually reserved, quiet, and gloomy? Psychologists refer to such stable individual differences in characteristic mood, activity level, and emotional reactivity as **temperament** (e.g., Guerin & Gottfried, 1994; Plomin et al., 1993). Growing evidence suggests that these differences are present very early in life—perhaps at birth (e.g., Kagan & Snidman, 1991; Seifer et al., 1994). What are the key dimensions of temperament? Most experts agree that they involve *positive emotionality*—the extent to which an infant shows pleasure and is typically in a good, happy mood; *distress–anger*—the extent to which an infant shows distress and the emotion of anger; *fear*—the extent to which an infant shows fear in various situations; and *activity level*—an infant's overall level of activity or energy.

Web Link: *Keirsey Temperament Sorter*

Large individual differences occur in these dimensions, and these are sometimes easy to spot even during brief interactions with infants. On the basis of such differences, some researchers (Thomas & Chess, 1989) have suggested that many infants can be divided into three basic groups. *Easy children* (about 40 percent) are infants who are generally cheerful, adapt readily to new experiences, and quickly establish routines for many activities of daily life. *Difficult children* (about 10 percent) are irregular in daily routines, are slow to accept new situations or experiences, and show negative reactions more than other infants. *Slow-to-warm-up children* (15 percent) are relatively inactive and apathetic and show mild negative reactions when exposed to unexpected events or new situations. The remaining 35 percent of infants cannot be readily classified under one of these headings.

How stable are such differences in temperament? Research findings suggest that they are only moderately stable early in life—from birth until about twenty-four months. After that time, however, they appear to be highly stable (e.g., Lemery et al., 1999). Growing evidence suggests that individual differences in temperament are at least partially genetic in origin (e.g., Lytton, 1990). However, different aspects of temperament may be influenced by genetic and environmental factors to varying degrees (e.g., Magai & McFadden, 1995). Whatever the relative contribution of genetic and environmental factors to temperament, individual differences in emotional style have important implications for social development. For example, a much higher proportion of difficult than easy children experience behavioral problems later in life (Chess & Thomas, 1984). They find it more diffi-

**Temperament:** Stable individual differences in the quality and intensity of emotional reactions.

cult to adjust to school, to form friendships, and to get along with others. In addition, many high-reactive children demonstrate *shyness* as they grow older and enter an increasingly broad range of social situations. Finally, there is growing evidence for the view that some aspects of temperament can influence attachment—the kinds of bonds infants form with their caregivers—and hence important aspects of children's personality and even their abilities to form close relationships with other persons when they are adults (Shaver & Brennan, 1992; Shaver & Hazan, 1994). We'll return to attachment shortly; but first, let's consider another aspect of emotional and social growth—the development of *empathy*.

**Figure 8.16**
**The Beginnings of Empathy—and of Prosocial Behavior**

By the time they are eighteen months old, toddlers will try to comfort another child who is crying; and by the time they are two, they may offer the child a toy or go to seek help from an adult. Such actions mark the beginnings of empathy and prosocial behavior.

**EMPATHY: RESPONDING TO OTHERS' EMOTIONS** Earlier, I noted that even newborns show more distress in response to the cry of another infant than to the sound of their own cries (Dondi et al., 1999). Does such responsiveness mark the beginnings of **empathy**—our ability to recognize the emotions of others, to understand these feelings, and to experience them ourselves, at least to a degree? Many psychologists believe that it does, and that our capacity for empathy then increases during the first two years of life. During those years our cognitive development permits us, first, to distinguish ourselves clearly from others—to form a concept of our *self*—and then to construct an ever more sophisticated theory of mind, which allows us to understand that others have feelings that may differ from our own.

Infants as young as eighteen months old attempt to do something comforting when another child is distressed—for instance, touching or patting that child. And by the time they are two, they may offer an object (e.g., a teddy bear) or go to seek adult help (e.g., Zahn-Waxler et al., 1992) (see Figure 8.16). At age four, most children can understand why others are upset and have a grasp of the kinds of situations that can cause people emotional distress. Ultimately, empathy develops to the point where individuals experience guilt if they view themselves as the cause of another's distress; empathy also serves as one important source of *prosocial behavior*—actions designed to help another in some way that do not necessarily benefit the person who performs them. Clearly, then, the development of empathy represents an important aspect of emotional and social development.

## Attachment: The Beginnings of Love

Do infants love their parents? They can't say so directly, but by the time they are six or seven months old, most appear to have a strong emotional bond with the persons who care for them (Ainsworth, 1973; Lamb, 1977). This strong affectional tie between infants and their caregivers is known as **attachment** and is, an important sense, the first form of love we experience toward others. What are the origins of this initial form of love? How can it be measured? These are among the questions developmental psychologists have sought to answer in their research on attachment.

**Empathy:** Our ability to recognize the emotions of others, to understand these feelings, and to experience them ourselves, at least to a degree.

**Attachment:** A strong affectional bond between infants and their caregivers.

**THE MEASUREMENT AND ORIGINS OF ATTACHMENT** That infants form strong attachments to the persons who care for them is obvious to anyone who has ever watched what happens when babies are separated from their caregivers. I remember my daughter Jessica's reactions when her mother and I had to leave her with some friends in order to travel to another state to search for a new home. She was only six months old at the time. To this day, I can still hear her anguished, heartbreaking cries as we left. I also vividly recall her reactions when we returned after an absence of several days. She refused to come to either of us, even though we were both very eager to hug her. It took several days before Jessica forgave us.

Actually, infants' reactions to such separations play a central role in one way psychologists measure attachment. This is known as the **strange situation test:** a procedure in which a caregiver leaves a child alone with a stranger for a few minutes and then returns. This test is based on a theory proposed by Bowlby (1969), suggesting that attachment involves a balance between infants' tendencies to seek to be near to their caregivers and their willingness to explore new environments. The quality of attachment, Bowlby contended, is revealed by the degree to which the infant behaves as if the caregiver, when present, serves as a secure base of operations—provides comfort and reassurance; and by the effectiveness of infant–caregiver interactions when the caregiver returns after a separation. Do babies cry when their mother leaves the room? How do they react when she returns? Do they appear more confident in her presence despite the presence of the stranger?

Research using the strange situation test has found that infants differ in the quality or style of their attachment to their caregivers (remember: all people who care for infants are not mothers). In fact, most show one of four distinct patterns of attachment. Most infants show **secure attachment:** They freely explore new environments, touching base with their caregiver periodically to assure themselves that she is present and will respond if needed. They may or may not cry on separation from this person, but if they do, it is because of her absence; and when she returns, they actively seek contact with her and stop crying very quickly. Another, smaller group of infants show **insecure/avoidant attachment.** They don't cry when their caregiver leaves, and they react to the stranger in much the same way as to their caregiver. When the caregiver returns they typically avoid her or are slow to greet her. A third group of infants show a pattern known as **insecure/ambivalent attachment.** Before separation, these infants seek contact with their caregiver. After she leaves and then returns, however, they first seek her but then resist or reject her offers of comfort—hence the term *ambivalent.* A fourth pattern, containing elements of both avoidant and ambivalent patterns, has sometimes been suggested; it is known as **disorganized attachment** (or **disoriented attachment**). However, it is not clear that such a pattern exists and is distinct from the others. Interestingly, the relative frequency of the three major patterns of attachment (secure, insecure/avoidant, and insecure/ambivalent) differs across cultures. These differences probably reflect contrasting approaches to child rearing in these cultures. For instance, the rate of insecure/avoidant attachment is relatively high in Germany, perhaps reflecting the fact that German parents often emphasize independence. In any case, it seems clear that studying such differences in attachment patterns across cultures may provide important clues concerning the effects of various child-rearing practices on infant attachment.

**Strange Situation Test:** A procedure for studying attachment in which a caregiver leaves a child alone with a stranger for several minutes and then returns.

**Secure Attachment:** A pattern of attachment in which infants actively seek contact with their caregiver and take comfort from her presence when she returns in the strange situation test.

**Insecure/Avoidant Attachment:** A pattern of attachment in which children don't cry when their caregiver leaves in the strange situation test, and are slow to greet their caregiver when this person returns.

**Insecure/Ambivalent Attachment:** A pattern of attachment in which infants seek contact with their caregiver children before separation but then, after she leaves and then returns, first seek her but then resist or reject her offers of comfort.

**Disorganized or Disoriented Attachment:** A pattern of attachment in which infants show contradictory reactions to their caregiver after being reunited with her in the strange situation test.

The existence of these distinct patterns of attachment raise an intriguing—and important—question: What factors influence attachment and the particular form it takes? One factor that was long assumed to play a central role is *maternal sensitivity*—a caregiver's alertness to infant signals, appropriate and prompt responses to these, flexibility of attention and behavior, appropriate level of control over the infant, and so on. It was long assumed that caregivers who showed a high degree of sensitivity would be more likely to produce secure attachment in their infants than caregivers who did not, and some research findings offered support for this view (e.g., Isabella, 1993). However, more recent evidence suggests that maternal sensitivity may actually play a somewhat smaller role in determining infants' attachment, and that other factors, such as infant temperament, may actually be more important (e.g., Rosen & Rothbaum, 1993; Seifer et al., 1996).

**THE LONG-TERM EFFECTS OF ATTACHMENT STYLE** Do differences in patterns of attachment have effects that persist beyond infancy? A growing body of evidence indicates that they do. During childhood, youngsters who are securely attached to their caregivers are more sociable, better at solving certain kinds of problems, more tolerant of frustration, and more flexible and persistent in many situations than children who are insecurely attached (Belsky & Cassidy, 1995; Pastor, 1981). Further, securely attached children seem to experience fewer behavioral problems during later childhood (Fagot & Kavanagh, 1990).

Perhaps even more surprising, some findings suggest that differences in attachment style in infancy may have strong effects on the kinds of relationships individuals form when they are adults (e.g., Hazan & Shaver, 1990). People who were avoidantly attached to their caregivers as infants seem to worry constantly about losing their romantic partners; they didn't trust their caregivers as infants, and they don't trust spouses or lovers when they are adults. Similarly, persons who showed ambivalent attachment in infancy seem to be ambivalent about romantic relationships, too: They want them, but they also fear them, because they perceive their partners as distant and unloving. In contrast, persons who were securely attached to their caregivers as infants seek closeness in their adult relationships and are comfortable with having to depend on their partners (Shaver & Hazan, 1994). In a sense, then, it seems that the pattern of our relationships with others is set—at least to a degree—by the nature of the very first relationship we form, attachment to our caregiver (see Figure 8.17).

**CONTACT COMFORT AND ATTACHMENT: THE SOFT TOUCH OF LOVE** Before concluding, it's important to consider an additional factor that seems to play a key role in attachment. This is *close physical contact* between infants and their

Web Link: *Harry Harlow*

**Figure 8.17**
**Childhood Attachment and Adult Adjustment: Links Appear to Exist**

Growing evidence suggests that the kind of attachments we form with our caregivers as children exert long-term effects on our subsequent relationships, including romantic ones. People who were insecurely (avoidantly or ambivalently) attached early in life seem to have more difficulty with adult romantic relationships than persons who were securely attached.

**Figure 8.18**
**Harlow's Studies of Attachment**

Although the wire "mothers" used in Harlow's research provided monkey babies with nourishment, the babies preferred the soft, cloth-covered mothers that provided contact comfort.

caregivers. Such contact—known as *contact comfort*—involves the hugging, cuddling, and caresses infants receive from their caregivers, and it seems to be an essential ingredient in attachment. The research that first established this fact is a classic in the history of psychology; it was conducted by Harry Harlow and his coworkers.

When Harlow began his research, infant attachment was the farthest thing from his mind. He was interested in testing the effects of brain damage on learning. Since he could not perform such experiments with humans, he chose to work with rhesus monkeys. To prevent the baby monkeys from catching various diseases, Harlow raised them alone, away from their mothers. This led to a surprising observation. Many of the infants seemed to become quite attached to small scraps of cloth present in their cages. They would hold tightly to these "security blankets" and protest loudly when they were removed for cleaning. This led Harlow to wonder whether the babies actually needed contact with soft materials.

To find out, he built two artificial "mothers." One consisted of bare wire, while the other possessed a soft terry-cloth cover. Conditions were then arranged so that the monkey babies could obtain milk only from the wire mother. According to principles of conditioning, they should soon have developed a strong bond to this cold wire mother; after all, she was the source of all their nourishment. To Harlow's surprise, this did not happen. The infants spent almost all their time clinging tightly to the soft cloth-covered mother and left her to visit the wire mother only when driven by pangs of hunger (see Figure 8.18).

Additional and even more dramatic evidence that the infants formed strong bonds to the soft mothers was obtained in further research (e.g., Harlow & Harlow, 1966), in which monkey babies were exposed to various forms of rejection by their artificial mothers. Some of the mothers blew them away with strong jets of air; others contained metal spikes that suddenly appeared from inside the cloth covering and pushed the infants away. None of these actions had any lasting effects on the babies' attachment. They merely waited until the periods of rejection were over and then clung to their cloth mother as tightly as before.

On the basis of these and related findings, Harlow concluded that a monkey baby's attachment to its mother rests, at least in part, on her ability to satisfy its need for contact comfort—direct contact with soft objects. Satisfying other physical needs, such as that for food, is not enough.

Do such effects occur among human babies as well? Some studies seem to suggest that they may. For example, two- and three-year-old children placed in a strange room play for longer periods of time without becoming distressed when they have a security blanket present than when it is absent (Passman & Weisberg, 1975). In fact, they play almost as long as they do when their mother is in the room. These findings suggest that for blanket-attached children, the presence of this object provides the same kind of comfort and reassurance as that provided by their mothers. So human infants, too, may have a need for contact comfort; and the gentle hugs, caresses, and cuddling they obtain from their mothers and other caregivers may play a role in the formation of attachment.

## School and Friendships: Key Factors in Social Development

Audio 8.4: *Siblings' Effect on Social Development*

Once they pass their fifth or sixth birthday, children in many different countries spend more of their time in school than anywhere else. As a result, their experiences in this setting play an important role in their social and emotional development. In school, children do not merely acquire information that contributes to their cognitive growth; they also have the opportunity to acquire, and practice, many social skills. They learn to share, to cooperate, to work together in groups to solve problems. And, perhaps most important of all, they acquire growing experience in forming and maintaining **friendships**—relationships involving strong affective (emotional) ties between two persons.

How do friendships differ from other relationships children have with their peers? A recent review of many studies dealing with this topic indicates that children's friendships (Newcomb & Bagwell, 1995) are marked by the following characteristics:

- Friends have stronger affective ties to each other than they have to other peers.
- Friends cooperate with and help each other more than they do other peers.
- Friends may have conflicts with each other, but are more concerned with resolving such disputes than is true with respect to other peers.
- Friends see themselves as equals, and engage in less intense competition and fewer attempts at domination than is true for other peers.
- Friends are more similar to each other than to other peers, and also express more mutual liking, closeness, and loyalty.

What role do friendships play in social and emotional development? Apparently, an important one. Friendships give children an opportunity to learn and practice social skills—skills needed for effective interpersonal relationships; and, as noted earlier, growing evidence suggests that such skills play an important role in children's developing theory of mind (Watson et al., 1999). In other words, the better their social skills, the more friendships children form; and friendships, in turn, facilitate children's growing understanding of the fact that others may have thoughts quite different from their own. Friendships also contribute to emotional development, by giving children opportunities to experience intense emotional bonds with persons other than their caregivers and to express these feelings in their behavior.

**Friendships:** Relationships involving strong affective (emotional) ties between two persons.

When you were in school, did you ever encounter a *bully*—someone who liked to push other children around either physically or verbally? If you were ever the victim of such a person, or even if you only witnessed bullies doing their thing, you probably realize that being a bully's victim can have devastating effects. In fact, research findings indicate that being victimized by bullies produces anxiety, depression, loneliness, and low self-esteem in children (e.g., Boivin & Hymel, 1997; Egan & Perry, 1998). And here is where friendship enters the picture: Recent findings indicate that children who have close friends are less likely to be victimized in this way. In fact, having a friend may prevent bullies from picking even on children who show behaviors that would otherwise make them prime candidates for being bullied—*internalizing behaviors* such as being worried and fearful, working alone, or appearing sad or close to tears (Hodges et al., 1999). How does having a close friend help such children avoid being victimized by bullies? Apparently, close friends play a protective role—telling the teacher when bullies swing into action, or even fighting back to protect their friends.

One thing children do with their friends—obviously!—is play with them; and this, unfortunately, sometimes leads to injuries. Can anything be done to reduce the frequency of play-related accidents? This issue is discussed in the following **From Science to Practice** section.

from SCIENCE to PRACTICE

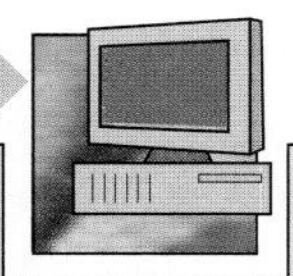

## Making Playgrounds Safer: Some Concrete Steps

When I was in elementary and junior high school, I went around most of the time with Band-Aids on both knees. Why? The playgrounds in which I played with my friends were paved with asphalt, so every minor fall seemed to result in a painful scrape—not to mention damage to my clothes. What kind of playground did you play in? Did it, too, have a paved surface? Or was the one you played in kinder to your knees?

Looking back, it now seems ridiculous to me that anyone would choose asphalt or concrete as the surface for a children's playground; but in fact, these were once the materials of choice. It is not surprising, then, that more than 150,000 children per year in the U.S. alone are hurt so badly while playing that they require treatment in hospital emergency rooms. Of course, such injuries stem not only from hard surfaces but from swing sets that do not have a safety zone around them (I once got hit with a flying swing and it almost knocked me out), or from slides and monkey bars that are simply too high. Can anything be done to reduce such hazards? Absolutely. Studies by psychologists and others indicate that injuries to children are substantially reduced when playground builders take the following steps (see Figure 8.19):

- Use sand 8 to 10 inches deep as the surface (an alternative: rubber mats more than 1 inch thick).

**Figure 8.19**
**Building Safer Playgrounds**
As you can readily tell, the playground on the left is much safer than the one on the right.

- Reduce the height of slides, seesaws, and climbing apparatus to less than 4 feet. (Some are as high as 12 or 13 feet, and the chances of injury in a fall from these heights are several times as great as in a fall from lower heights.)
- Carefully inspect all surfaces for exposed bolts, rough or rusty surfaces, or deteriorated parts—these are a major cause of cuts and bruises.
- Carefully inspect the ground for crushed soda cans, broken glass, and other hazardous materials.
- Never allow children to play barefoot in playgrounds.
- Create safety zones around swings (e.g., build fences that protect persons not on the swings from being hurt by them).

Programs that have implemented such steps have resulted in drops of up to 50 percent in the number of children treated for injuries in local hospitals (e.g., Fisher, Harris, & VanGuren, 1980; Sachs et al., 1990). So, clearly, this is a case in which careful research on how and why children are injured while playing has yielded important practical benefits for those communities wise enough to pay attention.

In sum, through a wide range of experiences in school—and especially through the formation of friendships—children expand their social and emotional skills and acquire the skills needed for forming close and lasting relationships with others. How important are such friendships? One psychologist, Judith Harris, has suggested that friends play a more important role in children's social development than parents! This suggestion has stirred a heated controversy among developmental psychologists, so we'll pause here to take a closer look at it.

## Do Parents Really Matter? A Recent—and Continuing—Controversy

Web Link: *A Discussion with Judith Rich Harris*

In 1998, Judith Rich Harris published a book titled *The Nurture Assumption: Why Children Turn Out the Way They Do.* The major thesis of this book was captured by the statement on its cover: "Parents Matter Less Than You Think and Peers Matter More." In other words, Harris contended, contrary to the prevailing view, that parents have little if any impact on their children's development; rather, it is peers, friends, teachers, and others outside the home that exert the major effects. As you can imagine, Harris's book stirred heated debate. On one side of the controversy, some psychologists applauded her efforts to shift the weight of responsibility for children's behavior away from their parents. Some parents, after all, raise their children with all the love and affection they can provide, only to see them turn out to be unpleasant, unethical, or even dangerous people. If, as was widely believed in the past, parents are *the* major influence on their children, then a burden of guilt for such outcomes falls on the shoulders of parents.

As evidence for her conclusions, Harris points to many studies indicating that identical twins reared in the same homes are no more similar to each other in personality and in other respects than are identical twins reared in different homes by different parents. Similarly, she notes that siblings (brothers and sisters) raised by the same parents are no more similar than are brothers and sisters raised in different homes—and even no more similar to one another than to unrelated persons. On the contrary, she suggests that any similarities between children of the same parents are due *not* to the parents' influence but to genetic factors. In this context, Harris cites growing evidence that many traits such as impulsivity, aggressiveness, thrill-seeking tendencies, neuroticism, intelligence, friendliness, and shyness are due in part to genetic factors. So even if children *do* resemble their parents in some respects, it is because of their inherited tendencies, not because of the parents' efforts at child rearing. In fact, Harris notes, because of these built-in differences, parents can't really use the same techniques with all of their children. Rather, they adjust their parenting style to each child and are, in fact, "different parents" for each child. What

**Figure 8.20**
**Peers or Parents: Which Matter More?**

According to Judith Harris, peers exert much stronger effects on children's development than do their parents. Many psychologists disagree with this theory and assign an important role to both parents and peers. The characters in this cartoon, however, seem to agree with Professor Harris!

(*Source:* Reprinted with special permision of King Features Syndicate)

really counts, Harris suggests, is peers and friends: These influence children throughout their development and produce effects that persist into adulthood (see Figure 8.20); in contrast, parents' influence, if it exists, occurs only within the home and dissipates as children grow up and lead increasingly independent lives.

Is Harris correct in these provocative assertions? Some findings seem to offer support for her view—for instance, research evidence that whether children are raised by their parents or in day-care centers makes relatively little difference to their cognitive development, behavior problems, or self-esteem (Harvey, 1999). If parents really mattered, wouldn't their presence make a larger difference? On the other side of the coin, however, is a very large body of findings suggesting that parents do indeed matter—tremendously. First, recent findings from a large-scale research program (the NICHD Study of Early Child Care) suggest that whether children receive care from their mothers or from other persons in child-care centers *does* make a difference: Careful observation of interactions between mothers and their children during the first three years of life indicate that mothers who care for their infants themselves show greater sensitivity to their youngsters while their youngsters, in turn, show more positive engagement with their mothers, than is true for children who receive nonmaternal child care (NICHD Early Child Care Research Network, 1999). The effects are small, but given that they were observed in a sample of more than twelve hundred children, they do seem to be real; and to the extent they are, they suggest that contrary to what Harris suggests, parents do indeed matter.

Similarly, studies of shyness indicate that although this trait is indeed influenced by genetic factors, parents play a key role in determining whether and to what extent children actually become shy (e.g., Kagan & Snidman, 1991). Shy children whose parents encourage them to try new things become less shy, while those whose parents do not make this effort often become painfully shy and withdrawn. Similarly, when parents change their parenting style, children's behavior often changes too. For instance, when parents learn and then practice skills such as being sensitive to their children's emotions and actively work to help them solve emotional problems, the children often become more socially competent (e.g., Schickedanz et al., 1998).

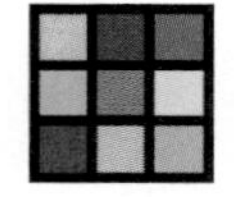

Finally, consider the excellent adjustment and achievement of children from many immigrant families in the United States (Fuligni, 1998). Despite the fact that they have moved to a new country and must learn a new language and a whole new style of life, such children tend to do extremely well; indeed, they often show fewer behavioral problems, higher self-esteem, and better school achievement than many native-born youngsters (Harris, 1999). What accounts for these surprisingly positive results? Many experts attribute them to the impact of parents who emphasize the value of education, stress family members' obligations to one another ("Don't do anything to shame the family!"), and instill values promoting hard work and achievement. Do parents have any effect on such children? It seems absurd to suggest that they do not.

So where does all this leave us? With the following conclusions: By calling attention to the fact that parental influence is not all important, and by emphasizing the crucial role of peers and friends, Harris has indeed made an important contribution. But her contention that parents play no significant role in their children's development—that parents don't matter—is too extreme and rests on foundations far too weak to be accepted by most psychologists or, I hope, by you.

**REVIEW QUESTIONS**

- At what age do infants first show recognizable facial expressions?
- Children's abilities to regulate their own emotions develop?
- What is temperament, and what role does it play in later development?
- What is attachment, and how is it measured?
- What factors affect attachment between infants and their caregivers?
- How does attachment style influence later social development?
- What role do children's friendships play in their social and emotional development?
- Do parents have an important impact on their children's social and emotional development—or very little impact, as one psychologist has suggested?

**Food for Thought**

People who were securely attached to their parents as children seem to form more successful adult relationships. Does this imply that we should look for such secure attachment patterns in potential lovers or spouses?

## From Gender Identity to Sex-Category Constancy:

### How Children Come to Understand That They Are Female or Male

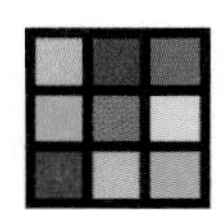

When I was about four years old, my mother decided that I would benefit from dance classes. My reaction? I hated them! I liked music, but almost every other student in the class was a girl, and I already had pretty firm ideas about things boys did—and dancing with a bunch of girls wasn't one of them! By the age of four, in short, I not only had a clear idea that I was a boy—what psychologists term **gender identity.** I also believed that I would remain a boy for life—what psychologists term **gender stability.** What I probably did not yet fully understand was the fact that I would remain a boy even if I had to wear fancy dance costumes and engage in activities that, in my mind, boys didn't usually do, such as dancing with girls. That is, I was less certain about **gender consistency**—understanding that sex identity remains the same even if one dresses or behaves like members of the opposite sex. Such gender consistency often doesn't fully develop until children are six or even seven (e.g., Ruble & Martin, 1998).

Recently, Ruble and her colleagues (e.g., Ruble & Martin, 1998; Szkrybalo & Ruble, 1999) have proposed that complete understanding of one's sexual identity involves all three components and centers around a biologically based categorical distinction between males and females; they term this understanding **sex-category constancy** (SCC), and the SCC concept emphasizes the fact that one's gender is, ultimately, linked to one's biological sex.

In the remainder of this section I'll first focus on the question of when children acquire each aspect of sex-category constancy, and then turn to theories that attempt to explain how this process occurs. Before beginning, however, it's important

**Gender Identity:** Understanding of the fact that one is male or female.

**Gender Stability:** Children's understanding that gender is stable over time.

**Gender Consistency:** Children's understanding that their gender will not change even if they adopted the behavior, dress, or hairstyles of the other gender.

**Sex-Category Constancy:** Complete understanding of one's sexual identity, centering around a biologically based categorical distinction between males and females.

to clarify the meaning of two terms: *gender* and *biological sex*. Biological sex is straightforward: It has to do with whether an individual is, biologically speaking, male or female (e.g., does this person possess two X chromosomes or one X and one Y? Are the genitalia of this person male or female?). **Gender,** in contrast, is a much more complex term. Gender relates to a given society's beliefs about the traits and behaviors supposedly characteristic of males and females. Thus, the concept of gender incorporates what psychologists term **gender stereotypes**—beliefs, often exaggerated, about traits possessed by males and females and differences between them (e.g., Eagly & Wood, 1999; Unger & Crawford, 1992) and **gender roles:** expectations concerning the roles males and females should fill and the ways they should behave (e.g., Deaux, 1993). Such expectations come into play as soon as a nurse or physician announces, "It's a boy!" or "It's a girl!" And beliefs about gender roles continue to influence us and our behavior throughout life. So gender is clearly an important aspect of development, one worthy of our special attention.

## Children's Growing Sophistication with Respect to Gender

The first step on the path toward a grasp of sex-category constancy is children's recognition that they belong to one sex or the other—that they are a boy or a girl. *Gender identity* is established quite early in life; by the time they are two, many children have learned to label themselves appropriately and consistently. At this time, however, they are uncertain as to whether they will always be a boy or a girl. Understanding of *gender stability* is usually in place by the time children are four. At this age they can answer correctly such questions as "When you grow up, will you be a mother or a father?" or "Could you change into a girl/boy from what you are now?"

It is not until they are about six or even seven, however, that children acquire *gender consistency*—the understanding that even if they adopted the clothing, hairstyles, and behaviors associated with the other sex they would still retain their current sexual identity. At this time they can answer correctly questions such as: "If Jack were gentle and cooked dinner, would Jack be a boy or a girl?"

Additional evidence suggests that these shifts toward increasing understanding of gender stem, at least in part, from the child's growing understanding of *why* an individual's gender will normally remain stable throughout life. In a recent study on this issue, Szkrybalo and Ruble (1999) asked children ranging from four to eight years of age a series of questions about their identity as a boy or a girl—questions similar to the ones mentioned above. After answering each question, children were asked *why* they had answered as they did. Their responses were intriguing. When preschoolers answered correctly (e.g., indicated that their sex would not change), they explained such gender stability largely in terms of gender norms: They and others would remain male or female because they would continue to behave like a male or a female. Older children, in contrast, made increasing reference to the fact that people cannot change their gender because one's sex is an unchanging, biologically determined characteristic. These findings suggest that children's growing appreciation of sex-category constancy is based, at least in part, on increasingly sophisticated forms of reasoning.

**Gender:** A society's beliefs about the traits and behavior of males and females.

**Gender Stereotypes:** Cultural beliefs about differences between women and men.

**Gender Roles:** Expected behaviors of males and females in many situations.

## Gender Development: Contrasting Explanations of How It Occurs

That children move toward full understanding of sex-category constancy as they grow older is clear. But how, precisely, do they acquire such knowledge? Several contrasting—but not necessarily competing—explanations have been offered. One of these, *social learning theory,* emphasizes the role of learning—especially the im-

**Figure 8.21**
**The Social Learning Theory of Gender Development**

According to the social learning view, children have a preference for imitating the behavior and dress of their same-sex parent. As they become increasingly aware of these similarities, they conclude that they are "a boy like Daddy" or "a girl like Mommy." However, other factors have also been found to play a role in gender development, so this is only part of the total story.

pact of *modeling* and *operant conditioning* (see Chapter 5). According to this theory, children are rewarded (e.g., with verbal praise) for behaving in accordance with gender stereotypes and gender roles—for behaving as boys and girls are expected to behave. Further, because children have a tendency to imitate models they perceive as being similar to themselves, they tend to adopt the behaviors shown by their same-sex parents (e.g., Bandura, 1986; Baron, 1970).

As children become increasingly aware of these similarities and of their own behavior, the idea that they belong to one gender or the other emerges with growing clarity. It is as if they reason, "I act like Daddy, so I'm a boy," or "I act like Mommy, so I'm a girl" (see Figure 8.21).

A second view of gender development, *cognitive development theory,* suggests that children's increasing understanding of gender is just one reflection of their steady cognitive growth. For instance, below the age of two, children lack a clear concept of self, so they can't identify themselves consistently as a boy or a girl. Once they acquire a concept of self, they can do this and begin to show gender constancy. Later, as they acquire increasing ability to classify things as belonging to specific categories, they begin to form an idea of gender stability: They realize that they belong to one category and won't shift to the other. Gradually, then, children acquire the understanding that they belong to one sex or the other and, as a result of this understanding, strive to adopt behaviors they view as consistent with this identity. As you can see, this is the opposite of what social learning theory proposes; that theory suggests that children first imitate the behavior of same-sex models and *then* develop sexual identity. Cognitive development theory suggests that they first develop their gender identity and then adopt behaviors consistent with this identity.

A third, and highly influential, view known as **gender schema theory** has been proposed by Bem (1984, 1989). Bem noted that knowledge of one's sex or gender is far more important than knowledge that one has blue or brown eyes, or even that one belongs to a particular race or religious group. This reasoning led her to propose that children acquire *gender schemas*—cognitive frameworks reflecting children's experiences with their society's beliefs about the attributes of males and females, such as instructions from their parents, observations of how males and females typically behave, and so on. Gender schemas develop, in part, because adults call attention to gender even in situations where it is irrelevant; for instance, teachers say, "Good morning, boys and girls!"

**Gender Schema Theory:** Theory that children develop a cognitive framework reflecting the beliefs of their society about the characteristics and roles of males and females; this gender schema then strongly affects the processing of new social information.

Once a gender schema forms, it influences children's processing of many kinds of social information (Martin & Little, 1990). For example, children with firmly established gender schemas tend to categorize the behavior of others as either masculine or feminine. Similarly, they may process and recall behaviors consistent with their own gender schema more easily than ones not consistent with it. In short, for children possessing such schemas, gender is a key concept or dimension, one they often use in attempts to make sense out of the social world, and one that becomes linked in important ways to their self-concept. This link between gender and one's self-concept is also emphasized in other, related views about gender identity.

While these three theories emphasize different aspects of gender development, all seem to provide important insights into this process. Thus, as is true of other aspects of development, several interrelated processes appear to influence children's progress toward full sex-category constancy.

### REVIEW QUESTIONS

- What is gender identity? Gender stability? Gender consistency?
- What is sex-category constancy?
- How do social learning theory, cognitive development theory, and gender schema theory explain gender development?

# Making Psychology Part of Your Life

## Combating Childhood Obesity

Every time I visit a nearby shopping mall, I'm amazed at the number of people who are seriously overweight. Obesity has increased to virtually epidemic proportions in the United States and many other countries. And children, alas, are not immune from this problem (see Figure 8.22). In fact, it is estimated that 50 per-

**Figure 8.22**
**Childhood Obesity: A Serious and Growing Problem**

The proportion of children who are obese has increased greatly in the United States in recent years. Psychologists are working to develop techniques for combating this serious problem.

cent of obese adults were obese as school-age children (Williams et al., 1992). So the problem seems to start early, and it is then carried over to adulthood. Given that obese children are at risk for the same physical illnesses as obese adults (see Chapter 10), this is a serious issue. Can anything be done to "reduce" this disturbing problem? (Sorry, that just slipped out!) Fortunately, research by psychologists suggests that several steps can be helpful, including the ones below.

- **Acquiring healthy eating habits.** This may be easier to accomplish with children than with adults. One program involves identifying various foods: "Go" foods can be eaten in unlimited quantities (e.g., salads; raw fruits and vegetables); "Caution" foods can be eaten only in moderate amounts; and "Stop" foods should be avoided (you can guess what these are—high-calorie fast foods and rich, sweet desserts). Children can understand these categories readily, and knowing which foods to avoid seems to help.
- **Contracting.** In a contracting program, parents and children pay money into the program when it begins; they receive it back as they attend the sessions—and make progress in weight control.
- **Self-monitoring.** Children are taught to self-monitor by keeping a log of foods they eat; they earn points for holding their total number of calories down.
- **Exercise.** Buring calories through exercise is the other side of the weight-loss equation, and many studies indicate that obese children exercise less than others. Teaching children new ways to expend calories (new games, new activities) can be a big plus in helping them shed extra pounds.

Through a combination of the steps outlined above, children with a weight problem can be helped to reduce the calories they consume, to burn more energy, and so to attain a happier and healthier life.

# Summary and Review

## Physical Growth and Development

- **What environmental factors (teratogens) can adversely affect the developing fetus?** Infectious agents, drugs, alcohol, and smoking by prospective mothers are all among teratogens that can harm the developing fetus.
- **What are plasticizers, and how can they adversely affect the development of children?** Plasticizers are chemicals added to plastic toys, pacifiers, and teething rings to make then softer. As infants chew on these objects, they can absorb chemicals that adversely affect their hormonal system and may act as carcinogens.
- **What are reflexes, and which ones do infants possess at birth?** Reflexes are inherited responses to stimulation in certain areas of the body. Newborn infants possess several reflexes, including the Moro reflex, the palmar grasping reflex, and the sucking reflex.
- **What learning abilities are shown by newborns?** Newborns seem capable of basic forms of learning, including classical conditioning and operant conditioning.

### Key Terms

developmental psychology, p. 286 • childhood, p. 286 • maturation, p. 286 • embryo, p. 287 • fetus, p. 287 • teratogens, p. 288 • placenta, p. 288 • reflexes, p. 291

## Perceptual Development

- **What perceptual abilities are shown by infants?** Infants can distinguish among different colors, sounds, and tastes, and they prefer certain patterns, such as the human face. They can distinguish the cries of another newborn from their own cries, and can recognize their mothers.
- **At what age can infants recognize their mother's face? How do they do this?** Newborns a few days old can recognize their mother's face, primarily by focusing on high-contrast areas such as her hairline or the outline of her head.
- **What are the three basic methods psychologists use to study human development?** In longitudinal research, the same individuals are studied for extended periods of time. In cross-sectional research, persons of different ages are studied at the same time. In longitudinal–sequential research, persons of different ages are studied over extended periods of time.

### Key Terms

longitudinal research, p. 296 • cross-sectional research, p. 296 • cohort effects, p. 296 • longitudinal–sequential design, p. 298

## Cognitive Development: Changes in Our Ability to Understand the World around Us

- **What are the major stages in Piaget's theory, and what cognitive abilities do infants, children, and adolescents acquire as they move through these stages?** During the sensorimotor stage, infants acquire basic understanding of the links between their own behavior and the effects it produces—cause and effect. During the preoperational stage, infants can form mental representations of the external world but show egocentrism in their thinking. During the stage of concrete operations, children are capable of logical thought and show understanding of conversation. During the stage of formal operations, children and adolescents can think logically.

- **In what respects does Piaget's theory appear to be in need of revision?** Piaget's theory is inaccurate in that it underestimates the cognitive abilities of young children, overstates the importance of discrete stages, and underestimates the importance of language and social interactions in cognitive development.
- **What is the focus of research on children's theory of mind?** This research investigates children's growing understanding of their own mental states and those of others.
- **According to the information-processing perspective, what does cognitive development involve?** It involves children's growing abilities with respect to basic aspects of cognition (e.g., attention, memory, metacognition).

### Key Terms

stage theory, p. 298 • assimilation, p. 299 • accommodation, p. 299 • sensorimotor stage, p. 299 • object permanence, p. 300 • preoperational stage, p. 300 • symbolic play, p. 300 • egocentrism, p. 300 • conservation, p. 301 • concrete operations, p. 301 • formal operations, p. 301 • hypothetico–deductive reasoning, p. 301 • interpropositional thinking, p. 301 • sociocultural theory, p. 304 • theory of mind, p. 305

## Moral Development: Reasoning about "Right" and "Wrong"

- **What are the major stages of moral development described by Kohlberg's theory?** At the first, or preconventional, level, moral behavior is judged largely in terms of its consequences. At the conventional level, morality is judged in terms of laws and rules of society. At the third, or postconventional, level, morality is judged in terms of abstract principles and values.
- **What do research findings indicate with respect to gender differences in moral reasoning?** Contrary to suggestions by Gilligan, there is no evidence that males and females differ in moral reasoning or attain different levels of moral development.
- **Do cultural factors have any impact on moral development?** Cultural factors do appear to influence moral development. Depending on the society in which they live, individuals learn to make moral judgments on the basis of different criteria.

### Key Terms

moral development, p. 308 • preconventional level, p. 308 • conventional level, p. 308 • postconventional level, p. 309 • gender differences, p. 310

## Social and Emotional Development: Forming Relationships with Others

- **At what age do infants first show recognizable facial expressions?** Infants show discrete facial expressions as early as two months of age.
- **How do children's abilities to regulate their own emotions develop?** As they grow older, children acquire increasing abilities to avoid disturbing stimuli and to adjust and express their emotional reactions.
- **What is temperament, and what role does it play in later development?** Temperament consists of to stable individual differences in the quality or intensity of emotional reactions. It plays a role in shyness and in several kinds of behavioral problems, and may even influence attachment and thus the nature of adult romantic relationships.
- **What is attachment, and how is it measured?** Attachment, or infants' strong emotional bonds with their caregivers, is measured by the *strange situation test,* in which infants' reactions to being separated from their caregiver are studied, as well as through observation of infants' behavior in their own homes.
- **What factors affect attachment between infants and their caregivers?** Attachment is influenced by infants' temperament and by several other factors, including contact comfort and parents' responsiveness to children's needs.
- **How does attachment style influence later social development?** Children who are securely attached to their caregivers are more sociable, better at solving some problems, more tolerant of frustration, and more flexible and persistent in many situations than children who are insecurely (avoidantly or ambivalently) attached. In addition, adults who were securely attached to their caregivers as infants seem more capable of forming close, lasting relationships than do persons who were insecurely attached.
- **What role do children's friendships play in their social and emotional development?** Friendships help children to develop socially and emotionally, and often provide them with protection against bullies.
- **Do parents have an important impact on their children's social or emotional development—or very little impact, as one psychologist has suggested?** Existing evidence suggests that parents do play an important role in their children's development.

### Key Terms

temperament, p. 312 • empathy, p. 313 • attachment, p. 313 • strange situation test, p. 314 • secure attachment, p. 314 • insecure/avoidant attachment, p. 314 • insecure/ambivalent attachment, p. 314 • disorganized or disoriented attachment, p. 314 • friendships, p. 317

## From Gender Identity to Sex-Category Constancy: How Children Come to Understand That They Are Female or Male

- **What is gender identity? Gender stability? Gender consistency?** Gender identity refers to children's ability to label their own sex and that of others accurately. Gender stability is children's understanding that sex identity is stable over time. Gender consistency is children's understanding that sex identity won't change even if they adopt the clothing, hairstyles, and activities of the other sex.

- **What is sex-category constancy?** An awareness of sex-category constancy is children's understanding that sex identity is a biologically based categorical distinction.
- **How do social learning theory, cognitive development theory, and gender schema theory explain gender development?** Social learning theory emphasizes the role of operant conditions and modeling. Cognitive development theory emphasizes the role of children's growing cognitive abilities. Gender schema theory emphasizes the role of gender schemas.

### Key Terms

gender identity, p. 321 • gender stability, p. 321 • gender consistency, p. 321 • sex-category constancy, p. 321 • gender, p. 322 • gender stereotypes, p. 322 • gender roles, p. 322 • gender schema theory, p. 323

## Critical Thinking Questions

### Appraisal

Physical, cognitive, and emotional/social development occur simultaneously. Given this fact, can we really study them separately?

### Controversy

Do you agree with Judith Harris's contention that parents actually have little impact on the development of their children's personalities? Or do you feel that her conclusions are wrong, and that parents *are* important? Why do you hold the view that you do?

### Making Psychology Part of Your Life

Events such as the murders in a Littleton, Colorado high school during 1999 cause parents to worry about the effects on their children of television, movies, and other media. Do you think that such concerns are justified? And if so, what should be done about such effects?

Chapter 9

# Human Development II:

## Adolescence, Adulthood, and Aging

## CHAPTER OUTLINE


**ADOLESCENCE: BETWEEN CHILD AND ADULT 330**

Physical Development during Adolescence
Cognitive Development during Adolescence
Social and Emotional Development during Adolescence
Adolescence in the New Millennium: A Generation at Risk?

- BEYOND THE HEADLINES—As Psychologists See It: *Preventing Teen Pregnancies: Should Adolescents Decide?*

**DEVELOPMENT DURING OUR ADULT YEARS 343**

Contrasting Views of Adult Development: Stage Theories versus the Contextual Approach
Physical Change during Our Adult Years
Cognitive Change during Adulthood
Social and Emotional Development during Adulthood

**AGING, DEATH, AND BEREAVEMENT 359**

Theories of Aging: Contrasting Views about Why We Grow Old

- FROM SCIENCE TO PRACTICE *Living Longer—and Healthier—Lives: Some Concrete Steps*

Meeting Death: Facing the End of Life
Bereavement: Coming to Terms with the Death of Loved Ones

- MAKING PSYCHOLOGY PART OF YOUR LIFE *Helping Others Cope with Bereavement: Effective Condolence Behavior*


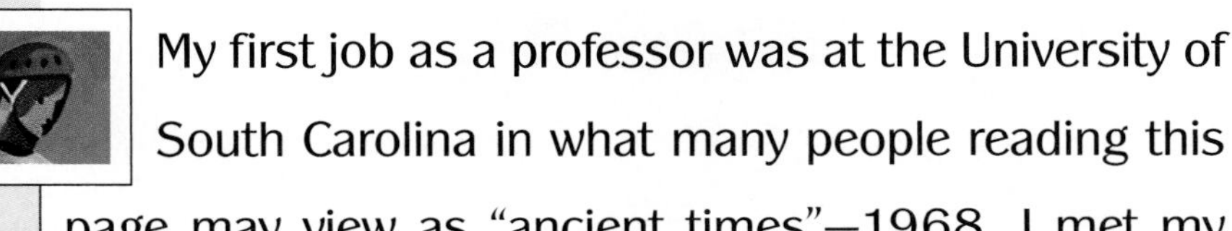

My first job as a professor was at the University of South Carolina in what many people reading this page may view as "ancient times"—1968. I met my wife there, so it was a true nostalgia trip to return there recently to attend a conference. The university decided long ago to retain the central part of campus in an unchanged state, so it looked just as I remembered it: the same giant live oak trees and lush Southern foliage, the same sweet smell of blossoms in the air. As we strolled hand in hand down familiar brick-paved paths, it seemed to me that the intervening thirty years were just the blink of an eye, and that I was still the same person now that I was then. This illusion was quickly shattered when I returned to the conference and passed a mirror at the entrance to the building. Reflected there was physical reality: not the young assistant professor I was thirty years ago, but the graying, middle-aged person I have become.

**Figure 9.1**
**Development: A Continuous Process**

As this cartoon suggests, we continue to change throughout our lives.

(*Source:* © The New Yorker Collection. 1983. Charles Addams from cartoonbank.com. All rights reserved.)

But are these obvious physical changes the whole story? Am I still really *me* on the inside—or is this, too, something of an illusion? In other words, have I changed in many other, less visible ways, too? These are intriguing questions, and they relate to one of psychology's grand themes—*stability versus change.* Back in 1968, most psychologists studying human development would probably have emphasized *stability* in their answer. "Yes," they would have said, "we do change physically throughout life. But our major traits, our cognitive abilities, and basic aspects of our social behavior remain relatively stable throughout our adult years." Now, however, many would give a somewhat different answer; they would emphasize the fact that, as the character in Figure 9.1 recognizes, change is indeed a constant of life, and that the physical alterations we all recognize as part of growing older are only the highly visible signs of much broader changes (e.g., Duncan & Agronick, 1995; Friedman et al., 1995).

We'll examine these changes in this chapter, where we'll focus on human development in the years after childhood—during *adolescence,* the period between puberty (sexual maturation) and entry into adult life, and during *adulthood,* the remaining decades of our lives. As in Chapter 8, we'll examine changes during these periods under three major headings: *physical, cognitive,* and *social and emotional* development. In addition, because *aging, death,* and *bereavement* (mourning for loved ones who have died) are basic facts of human life, these topics, too, will be considered. (I won't include a special **Research Methods** in this chapter, because the methods used by psychologists to study development during adolescence and adulthood are very similar to those used to study development during childhood.)

## Adolescence: Between Child and Adult

Video 9.1: *Attention Deficit Hyperactivity Disorder*

When does childhood end and adulthood start? Since development is a continuous process, there are no hard-and-fast answers to these questions. Rather, every culture decides for itself just where the dividing line falls. Many cultures mark this passage with special ceremonies, like those shown in Figure 9.2. In many countries, however, the transition from child to adult takes place more gradually during a period known as **adolescence.**

Adolescence has traditionally been viewed as beginning with the onset of **puberty,** a rapid spurt in physical growth accompanied by sexual maturation, and as ending when individuals assume the responsibilities associated with adult life—marriage, entry into the workforce, and so on (Rice, 1992).

**Adolescence:** A period beginning with the onset of puberty and ending when individuals assume adult roles and responsibilities.

**Puberty:** The period of rapid growth and change during which individuals reach sexual maturity.

### Physical Development during Adolescence

The beginning of adolescence is signaled by a sudden increase in the rate of physical growth. While this *growth spurt* occurs for both sexes, it starts earlier for girls (at about age ten or eleven) than for boys (about age twelve or thirteen). Before this

**Figure 9.2**
**Adolescent to Adult: Marking the Transition**

In many cultures the transition from adolescent to adult is marked by special rituals or ceremonies such as these.

spurt, boys and girls are similar in height; in its early phases, girls are often taller than boys; after it is over, males are several inches taller, on average, than females.

This growth spurt is just one aspect of *puberty,* the period of rapid change during which individuals of both genders reach sexual maturity. During puberty the *gonads,* or primary sex glands, produce increased levels of sex hormones, and the external sex organs assume their adult form. Girls begin to *menstruate* and boys start to produce sperm. In addition, both sexes undergo many other shifts relating to sexual maturity. Boys develop facial and chest hair and their voices deepen. Girls' breasts develop, and their hips widen; both sexes develop pubic hair. There is great individual variability in all these respects. Most girls begin to menstruate by the time they are thirteen, but for some this process does not start until considerably later, and for others it may begin as early as age seven or eight. Most boys begin to produce sperm by the time they are fourteen or fifteen; but again, for some the process may start either earlier or later (see Figure 9.3 on page 332).

Facial features, too, often change during puberty. Characteristics associated with childhood, such as large eyes, a high forehead, round cheeks, and a small chin, give way to a more adult appearance (Berry, 1991; Berry & McArthur, 1986). As we'll see in a later discussion of what makes people physically attractive (Chapter 16), some members of both genders retain relatively childlike facial features; for females such "baby-faced" appearance can be a plus, because many males find it attractive (Cunningham et al., 1995). Being baby-faced does not confer such advantages on males, however. In fact, recent findings indicate that adolescent males who are baby-faced may attempt to compensate for this by behaving in antisocial ways (e.g., committing crimes) (Zebrowitz et al., 1998).

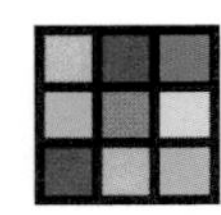

Gender differences also exist with respect to the effects of early sexual maturation. Early-maturing boys seem to have a definite edge over those who mature

**Figure 9.3**
**Individual Variation in the Onset of Puberty**

As shown by this photo, puberty starts much earlier for some children than for others. Thus, some sixth graders may look quite mature, while others are still essentially children.

later. They are stronger and more athletic and often excel in competitive sports. Partly as a result of these advantages, they tend to be more self-assured and popular and are often chosen for leadership roles (Blyth, Bulcroft, & Simmons, 1981). In contrast, early sexual maturation can have negative implications for females. Early-maturing girls are taller than their classmates—frequently taller than boys their own age—and their increased sexual attractiveness may invite unwanted sexual advances from older persons (Peterson, 1987). In short, the timing of puberty can play an important role in adolescents' developing self-identities and so in their later social development.

Web Link: *Homepage for the National Attention Deficit Disorder Association*

## Cognitive Development during Adolescence

As we saw in Chapter 8, adolescents become capable of logical thought. However, this does not mean that they necessarily demonstrate such thinking. In fact, only about 40 percent of adolescents can solve the kind of problems used by Piaget to test for formal operational thinking (e.g., Stanovich, 1993). Moreover, if they do show such logical thought, it may be restricted to topics or types of problems with which they have had direct experience (Rogoff & Chavajay, 1995).

In addition, adolescents' *theory of mind*—their understanding of how they and others think—continues to change and develop. Younger children take what has been described as a *realist approach* to knowledge; they believe that knowledge is a property of the real world and that there are definite facts or truths that can be acquired. In contrast, older children and preadolescents become aware of the fact that experts often disagree; this leads them to develop a *relativist approach,* which recognizes that different people may interpret the same information in contrasting ways.

Preadolescents go a bit farther, adopting a *defended realism approach,* which recognizes the difference between facts and opinions. Yet they continue to believe that there is a set of facts about the world that are completely true, and that differences in opinion stem from differences in available information. Still later, adolescents come to realize that there is no secure basis for knowledge or for making decisions; at this point, they adopt an approach described as *dogmatism–skepticism,* in which they alternate between blind faith in some authority and doubting everything. Finally, some adolescents, at least, realize that while there are no absolute truths, there are better or worse reasons for holding certain views—an approach described as *postskeptical rationalism.* This, of course, is the kind of thinking democratic societies wish to encourage among their citizens, because only people capable of thinking in this way can make the kind of informed judgments necessary for free elections.

In sum, cognitive development does not stop in childhood; on the contrary it continues throughout adolescence and results, ultimately, in more mature modes of thought (Klaczynski, 1997).

**REVIEW QUESTIONS**

- What physical changes occur during puberty?
- How does thinking change during adolescence?

CourseCompass

Web Link: *Social and Emotional Development*

Audio 9.1: *Siblings' Effect on Social Development*

## Social and Emotional Development during Adolescence

It would be surprising if the major physical and cognitive changes occurring during adolescence were not accompanied by corresponding changes in social and emotional development. What are these changes like? Let's see what research has revealed.

**EMOTIONAL CHANGES: THE UPS AND DOWNS OF EVERYDAY LIFE** It is widely believed that adolescents are wildly emotional—that they experience huge swings in mood and turbulent outbursts of emotion. Is this belief correct? To a degree, it is. In several studies on this issue, large numbers of teenagers wore beepers and were signaled at random times throughout an entire week. When signaled, they entered their thoughts and feelings in a diary. Results indicated that they did show more frequent and larger swings in mood than those shown by older persons (e.g., Csikszentmihalyi & Larson, 1984). Moreover, these swings occurred very quickly, sometimes within only a few minutes. Older people also show shifts in mood, but these tend to be less frequent, slower, and smaller in magnitude.

Other widely accepted views about adolescent emotionality, however, do not appear to be correct. For instance, it is often assumed that adolescence is a period of great stress and unhappiness. In fact, most adolescents report feeling quite happy and self-confident, *not* unhappy or distressed (Diener & Diener, 1996). Moreover, and again contrary to prevailing views, most teenagers report that they enjoy relatively good relations with their parents. They agree with them on basic values, on future plans, and on many other matters (Bachman, 1987). There are some points of friction, of course. Teenagers often disagree with their parents about how they should spend their leisure time and how much money they should have or spend; and to some extent parents and teenagers disagree about sexual behavior, although the gap is not nearly as large as you might believe. In general, though, teenagers are happier and get along better with their parents than is widely assumed.

**PARENTING STYLES AND THEIR EFFECTS ON ADOLESCENTS** The fact that most adolescents get along well with their parents is, in one sense, surprising; after all, there are growing sources of conflict between parents and children during these years. In particular, parents must come to terms with the fact that their children are turning rapidly into adults, and this means giving them the increasing freedom they seek—at least up to a point. How should parents react to these changes? Growing evidence suggests that while there is no single "best" parenting style, some broad patterns or styles of parenting have more beneficial effects than others.

**Figure 9.4**
**Styles of Parenting**

Two key dimensions seem to underlie differences in parenting styles: parental demandingness and parental responsiveness. Together, these yield the four distinct patterns of parenting shown here.

| | | Parental Demandingness | |
|---|---|---|---|
| | | Low | High |
| Parental Responsiveness | Low | ***Rejecting/Neglecting*** | ***Authoritarian*** |
| | High | ***Permissive*** | ***Authoritative*** |

Two key dimensions seem to underlie differences in parenting styles. One has to do with **parental demandingness**—the extent to which parents are strict or controlling. Parents high on this dimension seek to control their children through status and power, and confront them (often angrily) when they do not meet the parents' expectations. A second dimension is that of **parental responsiveness**—the extent to which parents are involved in and supportive of their children's activities. Parents high on this dimension listen actively to their children, respond to their requests, show warmth, and focus on their children's concerns and interests during conversations with them. Together, these two dimensions yield the parenting styles shown in Figure 9.4. *Authoritarian parents* are high in demandingness (controlling) and low in responsiveness. They establish strict rules for their children and don't give them much say in decisions. *Authoritative parents,* in contrast, are high in both demandingness and responsiveness: They establish rules for their children but show great interest in, and responsiveness to, them. *Permissive parents* are high in responsiveness but low in demandingness: They are warm and responsive, but they set no rules or standards for their children and don't hold them accountable for their actions. Finally, *rejecting/neglecting* parents are low in both responsiveness and demandingess—they just don't seem to care what children do or what they become.

Not surprisingly, these contrasting styles have strong and lasting effects. Growing evidence (e.g., Baumrind, 1991) suggests that an authoritative style may yield the most beneficial effects: Adolescents whose parents adopt this approach are generally competent both socially and cognitively. That is, they are confident yet friendly and cooperative, and they tend to do well in school. In contrast, adolescents whose parents show a rejecting/neglecting style tend to be lower on both dimensions. Moreover, they often show unsettled patterns of behavior, rejecting their parents and engaging in various forms of antisocial behavior that can get them into serious trouble. Children whose parents adopt an authoritarian or permissive style tend to fall in between. So, again, contrary to what Harris (1998) suggested (see Chapter 8), parents do indeed seem to matter where the adjustment of adolescents is concerned.

**SOCIAL DEVELOPMENT: FRIENDSHIPS AND THE QUEST FOR IDENTITY** Important as they are, parents are only part of the total picture in the social development of adolescents. *Friendships,* primarily with members of their own gender, but also with members of the other gender, become increasingly important. In fact, most adolescents are part of extensive *social networks* consisting of many friends and acquaintances. Girls tend to have somewhat larger networks than boys, and these networks tend to become smaller and more exclusive as adolescents grow older (Urberg et al., 1995)—a trend that continues throughout life (e.g., Fung, Carstensen, & Lutz, in press).

One motive for forming friendships during adolescence seems to be the developing *need to belong*—the need to have frequent positive interactions within ongoing relationships. This need strengthens during early adolescence and leads many preteens and teenagers to reject parental influence and to identify with their peers. Thus, they adopt the dress, style of speech, and overall style of their chosen peer group, sometimes to the point where parents worry that their offspring have entirely sur-

**Parental Demandingness:** The extent to which parents are strict or controlling and confront their children (often angrily) when they do not meet the parents' expectations.

**Parental Responsiveness:** The extent to which parents are involved in and supportive of their children's activities.

rendered their unique identity (see Figure 9.5). Within a few years, however, this tendency subsides, and teenagers begin to conform less and less to their peer group.

Friendships and social success also play an important role in another key aspect of social development during adolescence—the quest for a *personal identity.* This process is a key element in a famous theory of psychosocial development proposed by Erik Erikson (1950, 1987), a theory well worthy of a closer look.

**Figure 9.5**
**The Need to Belong: One Reason for Adolescent Conformity**

Because adolescents have a strong need to belong—to be part of a friendship group—they often show a high level of conformity, adopting whatever styles of dress, grooming, and speech are popular among their friends.

### ERIKSON'S EIGHT STAGES OF LIFE

Erikson's theory deals with development across the entire life span, so I could have introduced it in Chapter 8. But adolescence is in some ways a bridge between childhood and adulthood, so it makes sense to examine the theory here; we can look back to topics we covered previously and ahead to ones we'll discuss later.

Erikson's theory is, like Piaget's, a *stage* theory: It suggests that all human beings pass through specific stages or phases of development. In contrast to Piaget's theory, however, Erikson's is concerned primarily with social rather than cognitive development. Erikson believed that each stage of life is marked by a specific crisis or conflict between competing tendencies. Only if individuals negotiate each of these hurdles successfully can they continue to develop in a normal, healthy manner.

The stages in Erikson's theory are summarized in Table 9.1 on page 336. The first four occur during childhood; one takes place during adolescence; and the final three occur during our adult years. The initial stage, which occurs during the first year of life, centers on the crisis of *trust versus mistrust.* Infants must trust others to satisfy their needs. If these needs are not met, infants fail to develop feelings of trust in others and remain forever suspicious and wary.

The next crisis occurs during the second year of life and involves *autonomy versus shame and doubt.* During this time, toddlers are learning to regulate their own bodies and to act in independent ways. If they succeed in these tasks, they develop a sense of autonomy. But if they fail, or if they are labeled as inadequate by the persons who care for them, they may experience shame and may doubt their abilities to interact effectively with the external world.

The third stage unfolds during the preschool years, between the ages of three and five. The crisis at this time involves what Erikson terms *initiative versus guilt.* During these years, children are acquiring many new physical and mental skills. Simultaneously, however, they must develop the capacity to control their impulses, some of which lead to unacceptable behavior. If they strike the right balance between feelings of initiative and feelings of guilt, all is well. However, if initiative overwhelms guilt, children may become too unruly for their own good; if guilt overwhelms initiative, they may become too inhibited.

The fourth and final stage of childhood occurs during the early school years, when children are between six and eleven or twelve years of age. This stage involves the crisis of *industry versus inferiority.* During these years, children learn to make things, use tools, and acquire many of the skills necessary for adult life. Children who successfully acquire these skills form a sense of their own competence; those who do not may compare themselves unfavorably with others and suffer from low self-esteem.

**TABLE 9.1**

## Erikson's Eight Stages of Psychosocial Development

According to Erikson, we move through eight stages of psychosocial development during our lives. Each stage centers around a specific crisis or conflict between competing tendencies.

| Crisis/Phase | Description |
|---|---|
| Trust versus mistrust | Infants learn either to trust the environment (if needs are met) or to mistrust it. |
| Autonomy versus shame and doubt | Toddlers acquire self-confidence if they learn to regulate their bodies and act independently. If they fail or are labeled as inadequate, they experience shame and doubt. |
| Initiative versus guilt | Preschoolers (aged 3–5) acquire new physical and mental skills but must also learn to control their impulses. Unless a good balance is struck, they become either unruly or too inhibited. |
| Industry versus inferiority | Children (aged 6–11) acquire many skills and competencies. If they take pride in these, they acquire high self-esteem. If they compare themselves unfavorably with others, they may develop low self-esteem. |
| Identity versus role confusion | Adolescents must integrate various roles into a consistent self-identity. If they fail to do so, they may experience confusion over who they are. |
| Intimacy versus isolation | Young adults must develop the ability to form deep, intimate relationships with others. If they do not, they may become socially or emotionally isolated. |
| Generativity versus self-absorption | Adults must take an active interest in helping and guiding younger persons. If they do not, they may become preoccupied with purely selfish needs. |
| Integrity versus despair | In the closing decades of life, individuals ask themselves whether their lives had any meaning. If they can answer *yes,* they attain a sense of integrity. If they answer *no,* they experience despair. |

Now we come to the crucial stage in Erikson's theory for this discussion of adolescence: the crisis of *identity versus role confusion.* At this time of life, teenagers ask themselves, "Who am I?" "What am I *really* like?" "What do I want to become?" In other words, they seek to establish a clear *self-identity*—to understand their own unique traits and what is really of central importance to them. These, of course, are questions individuals ask themselves at many points in life. According to Erikson, though, during adolescence it is crucial that these questions be answered effectively. If they are not, individuals may drift, uncertain of where they want to go or what they wish to accomplish.

Adolescents adopt many different strategies to help them resolve their own personal identity crises. They try out many different roles—the good girl/boy, the rebel, the dutiful daughter/son, the athlete, the supercool operator—and join many different social groups. They consider many possible *social selves*—different kinds of persons they might potentially become (Markus & Nurius, 1986). Out of these experiences they gradually piece together a cognitive framework for understanding themselves—a *self-schema.* Once formed, this framework remains fairly constant and serves as a guide for adolescents in many contexts.

**Identity Fusion:** A pattern in which bicultural or multicultural children combine their different cultural identities into one.

Many psychologists other than Erikson have focused on the importance of forming a clear personal identity (e.g., Noller, 1994). For instance, Marcia (1991) suggests that adolescents can be categorized in terms of whether they have explored alternative selves and whether they have actually chosen one. These two dimensions yield four possible patterns: adolescents who have gone through their identity crisis and made a commitment to one clear alternative (they are described as showing *identity achievement*); adolescents who are still searching for an identity *(identity moratorium);* adolescents who have chosen an identity suggested to them by their parents or other authority figures *(identity foreclosure);* and adolescents who haven't begun the process *(identity diffusion).* Marcia (1988, 1991) suggests that resolving the identity crisis is an important aspect of development during adolescence, and that completing this task helps individuals to plan their adult lives (Wallace-Broscious, Serafica, & Osipow, 1994) and, ultimately, to attain personal happiness (Diener & Suh, 1997).

Web Link: *Gender Identity Disorders Standards of Care*

The remaining three stages in Erikson's theory (refer to Table 9.1) relate to crises we face as adults. We'll return to them in our later discussions of adult development.

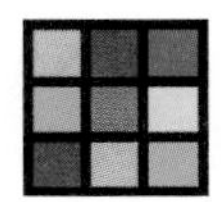

**LIVING IN TWO WORLDS: IDENTITY FORMATION AMONG BICULTURAL ADOLESCENTS** What about adolescents whose parents are immigrants or whose parents come from two different ethnic or cultural groups? Do they experience special problems in forming a clear identity? Growing research on this issue suggests that they do. After all, such children must understand not merely one culture and their place in it, but *two* cultures, which may differ in many respects. How do they cope with this situation? One possibility is that they achieve separate identities in both cultures, then alternate between these depending on the social situation; this is known as the *alternation model.* So, for instance, children with one African American parent and one European parent, or with one Hispanic parent and one European parent, may act differently depending on whether they are interacting with relatives or friends from each group.

Another pattern is known as **identity fusion.** Here, the children combine the different cultural identities into one. There is a growing tendency for people in the United States, where the number of biracial or multiracial children is increasing rapidly, to do this. Such adolescents describe themselves not as belonging to either group but as "biracial" or of "mixed race" (see Figure 9.6). A third pattern is for such adolescents to reject one of their cultural heritages and to identify entirely with the other. This pattern is especially likely in children who recognize that adopting a social identity linked to one of the two cultures may lead to discrimination against them—and therefore choose the other.

**Figure 9.6**
**Bicultural Adolescents: Fusing Two Cultures**

In the United States and many other countries, the number of adolescents with a biracial or multiracial background is increasing rapidly. These young people often fuse their two cultures into a new identity and do not view themselves as belonging wholly to either group.

**REVIEW QUESTIONS**

- What are parental demandingness and parental supportiveness? What styles of parenting do they yield?
- According to Erikson, what is the most important crisis faced by adolescents?
- How do bicultural adolescents cope with belonging to two cultural groups?

## Adolescence in the New Millennium: A Generation at Risk?

Recently I reread a book by the famous novelist Pearl S. Buck—a book I first read when I was an adolescent. This book *(Dragon Seed)* describes the Japanese invasion of China during the 1930s. The story focuses on one family and tells how the invasion brought death and suffering, in one form or another, to all of its members. For instance, the youngest son, aged fifteen, was brutally raped by Japanese soldiers when they failed to find any women in the family's house (the women had already fled to the relative safety of a nearby Christian mission). After this horrendous experience, he left home to join rebels in the nearby hills. Why do I mention this book? To emphasize the fact that there have been—and continue to be—many periods in the world's history when adolescents have been placed at great risk by war, revolution, plagues, and other tragic and frightening events. (Recent events in Kosovo and in several African nations are examples; see Figure 9.7.)

Yet, despite this fact, many experts believe that today's adolescents face a unique set of dangers. The following statistics relate to the United States, but some of the trends are also present in many other countries:

- Adolescents living in the United States are fifteen to twenty times more likely to die from homicide than adolescents living in other developed countries (Baron & Richardson, 1994). Armed assaults in high schools have become increasingly common, as in the case of the murders of students by fellow students in Littleton, Colorado.

**Figure 9.7**
**Adolescents at Risk**

Wars, revolutions, natural disasters, and, more recently, "ethnic" cleansing put adolescents at risk for great harm. Although such events have always occurred, many experts believe that adolescents living today face an especially long list of potential dangers.

- Between 1960 and 1997, the proportion of adolescents suffering from sexually transmitted disease increased more than fourfold. And it is estimated that more than ten million young women in the United States in their teens and early twenties have active *papilloma* infections—a sexual disease that can be transmitted even when couples do not have sexual intercourse, because the virus that causes it lives in outer layers of the skin and can pass from one person to another during foreplay (Groopman, 1999). Frighteningly, this disease has been linked to cervical cancer—a form of cancer that can be fatal.
- Although teenage birth rates dropped in the late 1990s, they remain at levels much higher than those of previous decades.
- The number of children being raised in fatherless homes has quadrupled since 1950 (Burrell, 1996).

These and related statistics suggest that today's adolescents face a new set of dangers—ones different from those faced by previous generations, and perhaps harder to defend against. Let's take a closer look at some of the factors that seem to threaten the welfare of teenagers.

**DIVORCED, PARENT-ABSENT, AND BLENDED FAMILIES** At present, more than half of all marriages in the United States and many other countries end in divorce. This means that a large proportion of children and adolescents will spend at least part of their lives in a one-parent family—typically, with their mothers (Norton & Moorman, 1987). Adolescents react to divorce with fear, anxiety, and guilt. They become angry at the remaining parent, wondering, "What did she/he do to make my father/mother leave?" And sometimes they blame themselves: "Why doesn't he love me anymore?"

The effects of divorce on adolescents' emotional well-being depend on many different factors, including the quality of the care they received before the divorce (Raphael et al., 1990) and the nature of the divorce itself—whether amicable or filled with anger and resentment. The more negative the feelings of parents toward each other, the more likely is emotional harm to the adolescent (e.g., McCall, 1994). One lasting effect of divorce that has emerged in recent years is this: Children whose parents divorced seem to be significantly less likely to marry than those whose parents did not (Lemme, 1999).

Adolescents living in *parent-absent* families face another set of problems. A growing percentage of children are being born to unmarried mothers, and many of these youngsters never even know their fathers. What are the risks of growing up in a parent-absent (typically, *father-absent*) family? Research findings suggest that they include the following: increased risk for delinquent (externalizing) behaviors and for depression and anxiety, impaired cognitive and school performance, and difficulties in forming meaningful relationships, including stable romantic ones (e.g., Sommers et al., 1993). As you might expect, the magnitude of such effects is even greater when the mothers of the children are themselves little more than children. This is a serious problem, because in the United States alone, several hundred thousand babies are born each year to mothers seventeen years old or younger. What are the effects of having an unmarried teenage mother? Certainly, they are negative; but just *how* negative seems to depend to an important extent on the degree to which adolescent mothers are ready, emotionally and cognitively, for the burdens of motherhood. The less ready they are in these respects, the poorer the outlook for their babies (e.g., C. L. Miller et al., 1996).

What can be done to reduce the number of unplanned births among teenagers? Most psychologists would emphasize such steps as providing teenagers with information about the risks and personal costs of pregnancy, or even, perhaps, making birth control information and devices available to them. For information on another approach to the problem of unplanned teenage pregnancies, please see the **Beyond the Headlines** section on page 340.

# BEYOND the HEADLINES: As Psychologists See It

## Preventing Teen Pregnancies: Should Adolescents Decide?

### Why teenage girls love "the shot": Why others aren't so sure

WALL STREET JOURNAL (OCTOBER 14, 1998)—At a clinic run by Planned Parenthood, 17-year-old Kisha Louis tells a nurse that she had an abortion last July after she forgot to take her birth-control pills. Now she wants to try a method she calls "the shot." . . . "With the shot, I'll just need to come here every three months. There's no hassle," Ms. Louis says. Moments later, she gets her first injection of a contraceptive that goes by the brand name Depo-Provera. . . .

Though little known among older, married contraceptive users, "the shot" is a major presence among teens in America's inner cities and other poor communities. Simple to use and nearly 100% effective, it has quietly emerged as a driving force behind a recent dramatic decline in teen pregnancies, especially among blacks. U.S. teen pregnancy rates, though, are still among the highest in the developed world. . . .

An injection that, taken once every three months, prevents unwanted pregnancy? At first glance, this sounds like major help for teenage girls who are sexually active but who find it difficult to use other methods of contraception—because their boyfriends won't use condoms, because they don't want their parents to find their pills, or because they simply can't afford to buy contraceptives. The injection, given by a trained nurse, is very safe and virtually 100 percent effective. Yet its use is highly controversial. In fact, legislation has been proposed in several states, requiring that publicly funded women's health clinics get the consent of the teens' parents before giving them the Depro-Provera shot. Critics feel that teenagers, who are still minors, should not be making such decisions for themselves. Further, critics argue that making it so easy to avoid pregnancy removes one important barrier to teenage promiscuity: If girls know they can get the shot and not get pregnant, then why should they refrain from sexual relations? In addition, the shot offers no protection whatsoever against sexually transmitted diseases.

A final factor in the equation is cost: The shot is produced by only a single company, and that company has taken advantage of its monopoly by raising the price to the point where the shot is several times as expensive as birth control pills. Some state officials object to using this more expensive form of contraception when cheaper methods are readily available.

What would psychologists say about this question? Clearly, it involves religious, ethical, and moral issues that are largely outside the realm of science. But psychologists recognize two key facts: (1) Once adolescents become sexually active, they tend to remain sexually active; and (2) children born to teenage mothers are at great risk in many ways (e.g., C. L. Miller et al., 1996). Psychologists also recognize the tremendous costs involved in trying to overcome the many disadvantages faced by such children. In view of these and other factors, many would conclude that *anything* that helps prevent unwanted births to teenage parents is worth considering very carefully.

But again, this is largely an ethical and moral issue. Psychologists can contribute their perspective and findings to the debate, but only informed and concerned citizens like *you* can ultimately decide the issue.

### CRITICAL THINKING QUESTIONS

1. Do you think it is ethical for women's health clinics to give "the shot" to teenage girls who request it, even if they are still minors?
2. If use of the shot continues or increases, do you think this will interfere with efforts to prevent the spread of sexually transmitted diseases such as AIDS and herpes?

**DYSFUNCTIONAL FAMILIES: THE INTIMATE ENEMY** During the 1950s, television shows in the United States painted a glowing picture of family life. A caring, loving mother; a kind and wise father; considerate siblings—even as a teenager I knew that there was a sizable gap between these images and reality. For many of today's adolescents, however, it's not so much a gap as a chasm. Many teenagers find themselves in what are known as **dysfunctional families**—families that do not meet children's needs and which, in fact, may do them serious harm (Amato, 1990; McKenry, Kotch, & Browne, 1991). Some dysfunctional families are neglectful of or even mistreat children. For example, consider what it is like for adolescents growing up in homes where one or both parents abuse alcohol or other drugs. And try to imagine what it is like for youngsters who must deal with parents who suffer from serious psychological problems—problems that may cause them to act in unpredictable, abusive, or even physically threatening ways (e.g., Ge et al., 1995). Clearly such parents do not provide the kind of guidance, consistent control, and support children need for successful development. Research findings indicate that when these factors are lacking, children and adolescents are at increased risk for a wide range of problems, such as drug abuse and *externalizing behaviors* (e.g., stealing, disobedience at home and at school, and overt aggression) (Stice & Barrera, 1995).

An even more disturbing form of maltreatment is **sexual abuse**—sexual contact or activities forced on children or adolescents. Unfortunately, sexual abuse is far from rare (Kendall-Tackett, Williams, & Finkelhor, 1993), and it may have truly traumatic effects on at least some of its victims. Common among adolescent victims of sexual abuse are depression, withdrawal, running away, and substance abuse (Morrow & Sorell, 1989). The likelihood and magnitude of these harmful effects increase with the frequency and duration of such abuse; when the perpetrator is a close family member, such as father, mother, or sibling; and when overt force is involved (Kendall-Tackett, 1991). Clearly, then, sexual abuse is a very serious problem requiring both energetic efforts at prevention and compassionate, effective treatment for its victims.

**ADOLESCENT PERSONALITY: ANOTHER FACTOR THAT PREDICTS FUTURE PROBLEMS** While the environments in which adolescents live are certainly important, it's crucial to note that these environments interact with characteristics of adolescents themselves to generate contrasting levels of adjustment. In other words, not all of the blame for antisocial behavior and other problems shown by adolescents can be attached to dysfunctional families, rejecting parenting styles, and other factors. Growing evidence suggests that certain adolescents are at high risk for being rejected by their peers and for engaging in various kinds of antisocial behavior. These adolescents are those who show high levels of aggression; who are disruptive or hyperactive; and, especially, who show what has been termed *irritable–inattentive behavior*—they complain a lot, "act like a baby," and don't pay attention to others (e.g., French, Conrad, & Turner, 1995).

For example, consider recent research by Pope and Bierman (1999). These investigators conducted a longitudinal study in which they examined the behavior of boys in grades 3 through 6, and then again four years later when the same children were in grades 7 through 10. Pope and Bierman (1999) obtained peer ratings of these boys (ratings by other children in their classes) with respect to several kinds of behavior previously shown to be related to peer rejection and antisocial behavior: aggression; irritable–inattentive behavior; disruptive–hyperactive behavior (fidgety, excitable; acts before thinking); and withdrawn behavior (shy, bashful, unhappy; seems sad, puts self down). They found that withdrawn behavior and aggression by the boys in grades 3 to 6 predicted negative outcomes for them in grades 7 to 10: rejection by their peers, victimization by others. In addition, aggression accompanied by irritable–inattentive behaviors, and irritable–inattentive behaviors alone, predicted the boys' tendencies to engage in both confrontational antisocial behaviors (stealing, vandalism) and nonconfrontational antisocial behaviors (truancy, alcohol abuse); see Figure 9.8 on page 342.

In sum, certain personal characteristics on the part of preteenagers and adolescents contribute to poor adjustment. So, as is almost always the case where complex aspects of behavior are concerned, both individual factors (including, perhaps, temperament) and environmental factors play important roles.

**Dysfunctional Families:** Families that do not meet the needs of children and in fact do them serious harm.

**Sexual Abuse:** Sexual contact or activities forced on children or adolescents by other persons, usually adults.

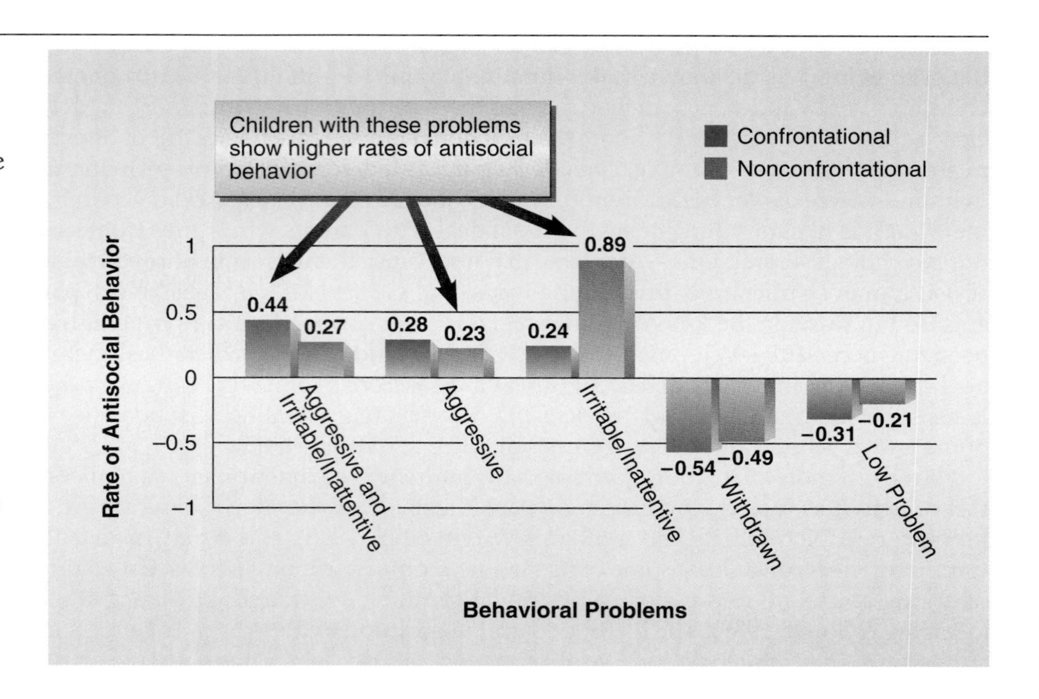


**Figure 9.8**
**Behaviors that Predict Problems in Adolescence**

As shown here, boys who were highly aggressive and showed irritable–inattentive behavior (e.g., complaining a lot, "acting like a baby") when in elementary school were more likely to get into serious trouble as adolescents than were boys who did not show these problems or who were simply withdrawn (e.g., shy, unhappy, easily hurt).

(*Source:* Based on data from Pope & Bierman, 1999.)

**OVERCOMING THE ODDS: RESILIENT ADOLESCENTS** Children, it has sometimes been said, are like weeds: They can grow and flourish even in very harsh environments. Some support for this view is provided by studies of children and adolescents who, despite their exposure to truly devastating conditions, develop into competent, confident, healthy adults (Jessor, 1993; Taylor, 1991). Such persons are described as showing **resilience in development:** somehow, they manage to buck the odds and rise far above the harmful environments they must confront. How do they manage to accomplish this task? Research findings point to the conclusion that they do so because of several *protective factors*—factors that, together, serve to buffer resilient individuals against conditions that would ordinarily be expected to undermine their chances. What are these factors? Research findings (e.g., Werner, 1995) point to the following conclusions.

First, resilience in development stems from protective factors within the individuals themselves. Careful study of such youngsters suggests that they possess traits and temperament that elicit positive responses from many caregivers. They are active, affectionate, good-natured, and easy to deal with. In short, they have an "easy" temperament, and this allows them to recruit the help of many competent adult caregivers who contribute willingly to their development. In addition, such youngsters are often highly intelligent and have good communication and problem-solving skills. The result: They get along well with others and form friendships easily; these factors, too, contribute to their resilience.

Second, such children and adolescents also benefit from protective factors within their families. Even in a dysfunctional environment, they have the opportunity to establish a close bond with at least one competent and emotionally stable person. This gives them the sense of trust Erikson views as so crucial to healthy growth. In many cases these bonds are formed not with mothers or fathers but with other persons in an extended family. What is crucial is not the biological relationship between the adolescent and the adult or adults in question, but rather the fact that these adults serve as models and provide encouragement.

**Resilience in Development:** The capacity of some adolescents raised in harmful environments to somehow rise above these disadvantages and achieve healthy development.

Finally, resilient youngsters often benefit from protective factors relating to their community. Favorite teachers are often positive role models for them. Caring neighbors, youth workers, clergy, and others—all can give adolescents the boost

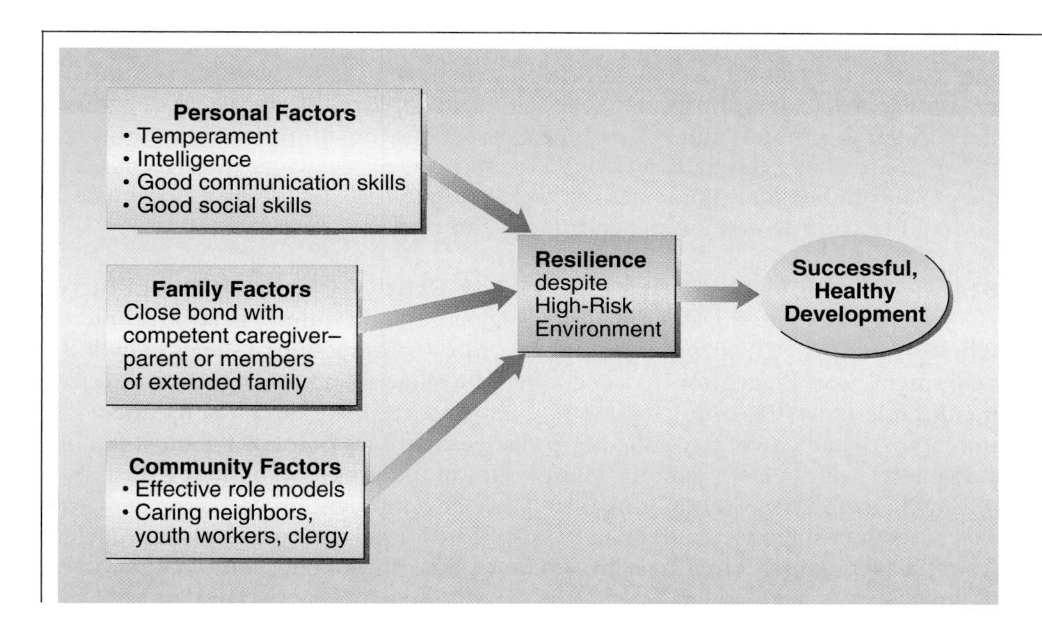


**Figure 9.9**
**Factors Contributing to Adolescent Resilience**

The factors summarized here have been found to contribute to adolescent resilience—the ability to develop normally even in potentially harmful environments.
(*Source:* Based on suggestions by Werner, 1995.)

they need to rise above the poverty, shattered homes, and parental instability that mark their early lives. (See Figure 9.9 for a summary of these factors.) When children and adolescents benefit from these and perhaps other protective factors, they can beat the odds and develop into competent, confident, responsible, and caring adults—good parents and role models for their own children (Werner, 1995).

**REVIEW QUESTIONS**

- What are some of the major threats to the well-being of adolescents at the present time?
- What characteristics of adolescents themselves can put them at risk for behavioral problems?
- What factors contribute to adolescent resilience?

*Food for Thought*

What factors do you think contribute to rising violence in high schools in the United States? Can anything be done to reduce such violence?

# Development during Our Adult Years

If you live an average number of years, you will spend more than 70 percent of your life as an adult. How will you change during that period? Obviously, in many different ways. Before turning to these changes, however, let's first pause to consider two contrasting views concerning the nature of adult development as a process.

## Contrasting Views of Adult Development: Stage Theories versus the Contextual Approach

How—and why—does change occur during our adult years? Is it purely the result of biological processes—alterations in our bodies and brains as we grow older? Certainly, such changes must play a role, but are they the entire story? Could it be, perhaps, that some of the changes we experience have their roots in our life experience, or in the specific society or time in which we live? Perhaps ideas about aging and about what is appropriate behavior for people of different ages depend on the social or historical context surrounding us. These are important questions, and psychologists have generally answered them in one of two ways: through *stage theories* or through what is known as the *contextual approach.* Let's take a closer look at both of these influential views of adult development.

CourseCompass

Web Link: *Erik Erikson: The Father of Psychosocial Development*

### STAGE THEORIES: DEVELOPMENT AS THE RESULT OF INNER BLUEPRINTS

As I noted in Chapter 8, stage theories suggest that all human beings, no matter where or when they live, move through an orderly progression of stages in their development. Jean Piaget, for instance, offered a stage theory of cognitive development; and, as we'll see in Chapter 12, Sigmund Freud offered a stage theory of human personality. We have already considered what is perhaps the most famous stage theory of development: the eight stages of life proposed by Erik Erikson. As you will recall, Erikson (1987) suggested that development proceeds through a series of distinct stages, each defined by a specific crisis. These crises, in turn, result from the fact that as individuals grow older, they confront new combinations of biological drives and societal demands. The biological drives reflect individual growth and physical change, while the societal demands reflect the expectations and requirements of society for people at different ages.

During adulthood, Erikson suggests, we pass through three major crises. The first of these is the crisis of *intimacy versus isolation.* During late adolescence and early adulthood, Erikson suggests, individuals must develop the ability to form deep, intimate relationships with others. This does not mean simply sexual intimacy; rather, it involves the ability to form strong emotional attachments to others. In short, this first crisis of adult life centers in the capacity to *love*—to care deeply and consistently for others. People who fail to resolve it successfully will live in isolation, unable to form truly intimate, lasting relationships.

Erikson labeled the second crisis of adult life the crisis of *generativity versus self-absorption:* the need for individuals to overcome selfish, self-centered concerns and to take an active interest in helping and guiding the next generation. For parents, such activities are focused on their children. After the children are grown, however, the tendency toward generativity may involve serving as a *mentor* or guide for members of the younger generation, helping them in their careers and lives. People who do not become parents can express generativity by providing help and guidance to young people—students, younger coworkers, nieces and nephews, and so on. Individuals who successfully resolve this crisis and turn away from total absorption with their own lives discover new meaning. People who do not resolve this crisis successfully become absorbed in their own lives and gradually cut themselves off from an important source of growth and satisfaction.

Erikson termed the final crisis of adult development *integrity versus despair.* As people reach the final decades of life, they look back and ask, "Did my life have any meaning?" "Did my being here really matter?" If they are able to answer *yes,* and to feel that they reached many of their goals, they attain a sense of integrity. If, instead, they find their lives to be lacking on such dimensions, they may experience intense feelings of despair. Successful resolution of this final crisis can have important effects on how individuals come to terms with their own mortality—the inevitable fact of death—and on their psychological and physical health during the final years of life.

In sum, according to Erikson and others who view adult development in terms of discrete phases or stages, development during our adult years follows an orderly plan, reflecting the fact that at different times in our lives, we all experience the same problems, events, challenges, or—as he puts it—crises. The way in which we deal with each of these turning points then determines the course and nature of our lives from that point on. Several other influential stage theories of adult development exist (e.g., Kotre, 1984), and we'll consider one of them in a later section (Levinson, 1986, 1996). Now, however, let's turn to a sharply different approach.

**Ecological Systems Theory:** Bronfenbrenner's theory suggesting that in order to fully understand human development, we must focus on relationships between individuals and their environments—ecology.

**Social Age Clocks:** Internalized calendars telling us when certain events should occur in our lives and what we should be doing at certain ages.

**CONTEXTUAL APPROACHES: DEVELOPMENT IN RESPONSE TO THE ENVIRONMENT** What would it have been like to live and grow old in ancient Rome? India? Egypt? Life expectancy was shorter in these societies, especially for people who did not belong to the privileged or ruling classes. Consequently, ideas about when people became "old" were quite different from the views we hold today. On the other hand, however, all of these societies offered great respect to their older citizens, who were viewed as important sources of wisdom and good judgment. Contrast that to present-day attitudes: In many societies today, *ageism*—negative stereotyped views about older persons—is widespread.

Contextual theories of development take careful account of such differences. Specifically, these theories suggest that because life events and conditions may vary from culture to culture and over time, adult development must be viewed against this backdrop of social and historical factors. A notable example of such contextual theories is Urie Bronfenbrenner's **ecological systems theory** (Bronfenbrenner, 1989). This theory suggests that in order to fully understand human development, we must focus on relationships between individuals and their environments—*ecology.* Such relationships exist at several levels. First, the *microsystem:* settings in which the developing person interacts directly with people and objects—at home, at work, in school, in the neighborhood, and so on. In addition, we must consider what Bronfenbrenner describes as the *mesosystem*—relationships between settings in which the individual participates. For instance, what happens to people at work is often influenced by events in their home life, and vice versa. Above this is the *exosystem,* settings the individual doesn't experience directly but which still influence her or his life—for instance, the company in which the person's spouse works, the local school board (whose decisions influence the person's children and taxes!), and so on. Finally, there is the *macrosystem*—widely shared cultural values, beliefs, and laws, which influence all of the inner systems, and hence the person's life and development. (See Figure 9.10 for an overview of these aspects of the environment.)

According to Bronfenbrenner, it makes no sense to try to understand how people change over the course of their lives without considering the ways in which they interact with, and are affected by, these aspects of their environments. And because environments differ from one another and change radically over time, the course of adult development, too, may vary; it will *not* necessarily follow the orderly sequence of events suggested by stage theories.

Perhaps a concrete example illustrating the difference between these two approaches will help. Consider the meaning of age. In stage theories such as Erikson's, various life crises and changes occur at specific ages, or at least within clearly defined age ranges. Contextual theories, in contrast, suggest that the links between chronological age and various aspects of development are much more fluid and can vary greatly in response to varying environmental conditions. Consider, for instance, the meaning of chronological age. All societies have what Neugarten (1987) describe as **social age clocks**—internalized calendars telling us when certain events should occur in our lives and what we should be doing at certain ages. When should we finish

**Figure 9.10**
**Bronfenbrenner's Ecological Systems Theory**

According to ecological systems theory, in order to fully understand human development, we must focus on interactions between individuals and the environments that influence them.

(*Source:* Adapted from Lemme, 1999.)

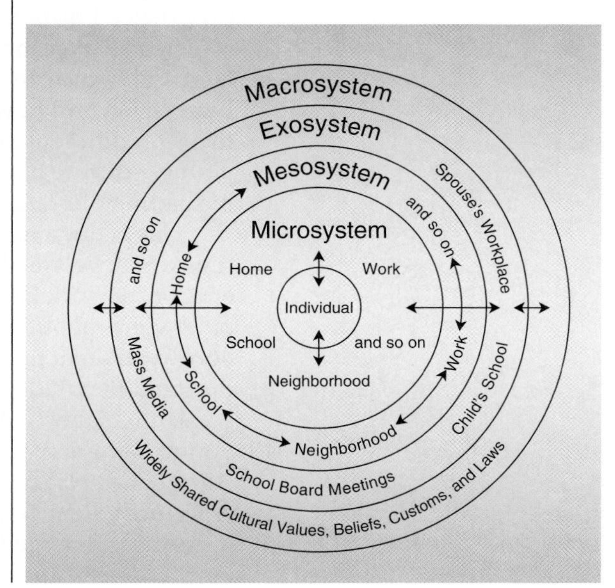

school? Get married? Have children? Retire? The social age clock of our society tells us. And here's the important point: This clock is really many different clocks (Schroots & Birren, 1990), which can vary greatly depending on our occupation, socioeconomic status, and when and where we live. For instance, Olympic gymnasts are considered "old" at sixteen or seventeen; professional baseball players aren't viewed as "old" until they are over thirty or even thirty-five. And what about professors—when are they viewed as old? (I don't know the answer to that one—*you* provide it!) Similarly, persons with college degrees tend to get married and have children several years later than persons without college degrees (Lemme, 1999). In short, the social context in which we live determines when various events are supposed to occur in our lives; these do not take place solely on the basis of our chronological age or in response to the orderly unfolding of specific stages.

One additional point: In Western societies in recent years, there has been a blurring of the social clock, and the link between chronological age and specific life events has become increasingly fluid. Why? In part because, in many countries, people are living longer than ever before and are often postponing the time at which they enter the labor force or the age at which they have their first child. In the United States, for example, this latter event used to occur primarily when women were in their early twenties; but many women now wait until they are well into their thirties to have their first child. This change is vividly illustrated for me by my mother's comment when, at age thirty, she gave birth to my brother Randy: "I'm too old to have a baby!" How times have changed! Interestingly, people seem to *feel* younger at various ages, too. When asked to indicate how old they feel, both men and women above the age of twenty-five show a gap between how old they are and how old they report feeling: They report feeling younger than they actually are, and this gap widens with the passing years (Montepare & Lachman, 1989) (see Figure 9.11). In a sense, then, many societies are becoming ones in which chronological age matters less and less. So, as contextual theories suggest, adult development is more a function of social definitions and beliefs than it is of specific age-linked stages.

Web Link: *High School Reunion Memories*

**ARE WE STRONGLY SHAPED BY THE EVENTS OF OUR YOUTH?** Before turning to the specific physical, cognitive, and social changes we experience during our adult years, it's important to consider one additional question, which is related to contextual theories of development: Are we influenced strongly, perhaps in a unique way, by events that occur in our societies when we are young and in what have been termed our "formative years"? My own life experience suggests that this is true. During my childhood my parents told me many stories about events they experienced during World War II: My father was in the air force, and my mother traveled all over the United States in order to be with him until he was sent to England and France. In contrast, my grandparents often told me stories about the Great Depression and how it affected their lives. Why did my parents and grandparents focus on different events? Perhaps because the experiences we have when we are young—during adolescence and early adulthood—play an especially crucial role in shaping our later development.

This is not a new idea; it is closely related to Erikson's belief that events occurring when we are about seventeen to twenty-five years old have a profound influence on our social identity—our views about who we are. And this idea also fits with other views about the origins of *cohort effects*—differences between groups of people born at different times who had contrasting life experiences as a result of being raised during different decades (e.g., Braungart & Braungart, 1990; Mannheim, 1972).

Is this view really accurate? Do events in our society that occur when we are young play a special role in our later development? A study by Duncan and Agronick (1995) suggests that they do. These researchers reasoned that if this idea is accurate, then women who were adolescents or young adults when the women's movement emerged in the late 1960s would view this movement as more important, and be influenced by it to a greater extent, than women who were somewhat older at that time. To test this hypothesis, Duncan and Agronick asked women of

**Figure 9.11**
**Subjective Age: Feeling Younger than We Are**

Until they are about twenty-five, most people report perceiving themselves as older than they are. Above this age, however, most report that they feel *younger* than they actually are. (*Source:* Based on data from Montepare & Lachtman, 1989.)

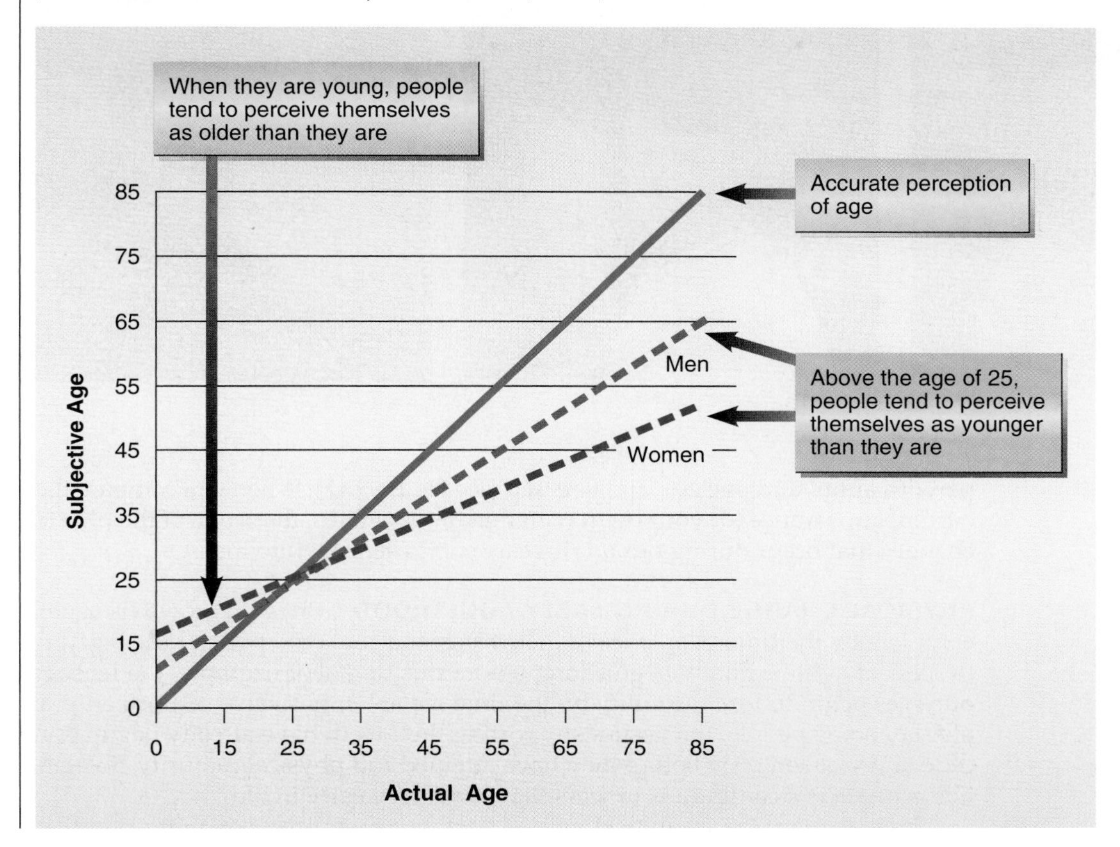


different ages to describe the societal events that were most important in their own lives. As expected, participants generally mentioned events that occurred when they were adolescents or young adults as the most influential. The nature of these events varied with the age of the women: Those who graduated from college in the 1940s chose the Depression and World War II. Those who graduated during the 1950s mentioned the Civil Rights movement and the Kennedy presidency; and those who graduated during the 1960s mentioned the women's movement, AIDS, and issues relating to the environment. Regardless of the specific issues they identified, in almost all cases the participants pointed to events occurring during their early adult years as the most influential.

In sum, it appears that what happens to us when we are young really does matter: Events occurring in our society at this time exert lasting effects on our later development. Perhaps such effects, to a much greater extent than mere differences in age, help explain why persons belonging to different generations sometimes see the world through very different eyes.

## Physical Change during Our Adult Years

Looking through a family photo album—one that spans several decades—can be very revealing. There, staring out at you with youthful faces, are your grandparents,

**Figure 9.12**
**Physical Change: It Occurs Throughout Life**

As these photos of the author at ages four, twenty-nine, and fifty-five suggest, our appearance changes greatly over the course of our lives.

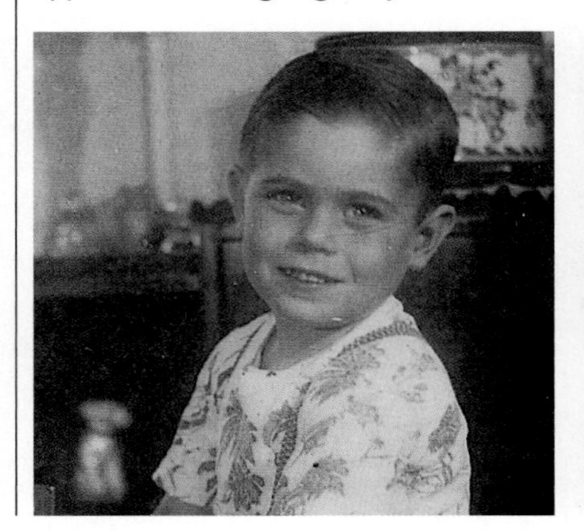

parents, aunts, and uncles—and yourself (see Figure 9.12). When you compare their current appearance (or your own) with that in the photos, the scope of the physical changes that occur during our adult years comes sharply into focus.

**PHYSICAL CHANGE DURING EARLY ADULTHOOD** Physical growth is usually complete by the time people leave their teens; but for some parts of the body, the process of aging actually begins long before this time. For example, the lenses in our eyes begin to lose flexibility by the time we are only twelve or thirteen years old. For some people, the tissues supporting their teeth have already begun to recede and weaken even before they have attained full physical maturity. So aging, like growth, is a continuous process that starts very early in life.

Such change occurs quite slowly at first, but then proceeds more rapidly in later decades. Muscular strength, reaction time, sensory acuity, and heart action and output are all at or near their peaks through the mid-twenties and then decline—slowly—through the mid-thirties. Many members of both genders do experience considerable weight gain during early adulthood, and some men undergo significant hair loss. By and large, however, physical change is relatively slow during this period of life.

**PHYSICAL CHANGE DURING MIDLIFE** By the time they are in their forties, most people are all too aware of the age-related changes occurring in their bodies. *Cardiac output*, the amount of blood pumped by the heart, decreases noticeably, and the walls of the large arteries lose some degree of flexibility. As a result, less oxygen can be delivered to working muscles within a given period of time, and even people who exercise regularly become aware of some decline in this respect. They simply can't do quite as much as they once could. The performance of other major organ systems, too, declines, and an increasing number of people experience difficulties with digestion. Other changes are readily visible when middle-aged people look in the mirror: thinning and graying hair, bulges and wrinkles in place of the sleek torso and smooth skin of youth. Huge individual differences exist in the rate at which such changes occur, however. While some persons in their forties and fifties closely match common stereotypes concerning middle age, others retain much of their youthful appearance and vigor during this period of life.

**Climacteric:** A period during which the functioning of the reproductive system and various aspects of sexual activity change greatly.

Among the most dramatic changes occurring during middle adulthood is the **climacteric**—a period of several years during which the functioning of the reproductive system and various aspects of sexual activity change greatly. Although both sexes experience the climacteric, its effects are more obvious for females, most of whom experience **menopause**—cessation of the menstrual cycle—in their late forties or early fifties. During menopause the ovaries stop producing estrogens, and many changes in the reproductive system occur: thinning of the vaginal walls, reduced secretion of fluids that lubricate the vagina, and so on. Once females stop releasing ova, pregnancy is no longer possible. In the past, menopause was considered in some Western societies to be a stressful process. Some women do find *hot flashes*—bursts of heat and perspiration that occur in what seems to be an unpredictable manner—somewhat unpleasant. However, many women do not experience such symptoms at all or experience them to a minimal degree. There is growing recognition of the fact that cultural factors play a key role in reactions to menopause and its effects, and that for most women it is definitely *not* a disturbing or anxiety-provoking event (e.g., Datan, Antonovsky, & Moaz, 1984).

After menopause women become more susceptible to *osteoporosis,* a decrease in bone mass and strength. To avoid such effects, an increasing number of women in developed nations undergo *hormone replacement therapy (HRT),* which supplements estrogen and progesterone, usually through daily pills or transdermal (skin) patches. Such treatment may reduce a woman's risk of osteoporosis and heart disease, but it may also be related to increased risk of breast cancer; so debate continues as to whether the benefits of HRT more than offset its potential costs.

Among men the climacteric involves reduced secretion of testosterone and reduced functioning of the *prostate gland,* which plays a role in semen formation. In many men the prostate gland becomes enlarged, and this may interfere not only with sexual functioning but with urination. Men often experience reduced sexual drive at this time of life; but although sperm production decreases, many can still father children.

So far, this picture of physical change during midlife may sound discouraging; strength, beauty, and vigor all decline during this period. But remember: While some physical decline is inevitable during the middle decades of life, both the magnitude and the rate of such decrements are strongly influenced by individual lifestyle. In fact, growing evidence suggests that while we can't stop the clock of aging altogether, we *can* slow it down appreciably. In other words, we can achieve **successful aging**—experience minimal physiological losses in many functions when compared to younger persons (Arking, 1991). How can we attain this goal? I'll return to this topic in more detail in a special **From Science to Practice** section later in this chapter. Here, I'll simply note that factors such as physical exercise, personal nutrition, and effective stress management play important roles. Thus, a fifty-year-old who exercises regularly, eats a balanced diet, doesn't smoke, and avoids weight gain may score higher on many tests of physical fitness than a twenty-five-year-old who gets no exercise, lives on fast food, smokes heavily, and is very overweight. So yes, aging is a fact of life; but no, it's not necessary to say good-bye to vigor, health, and energy in one's thirties or forties. We can maintain health and well-being much longer than was once believed—provided we are willing to make the effort to do so.

**PHYSICAL CHANGES IN LATER LIFE** Average age in many Western countries is currently rising at a steady pace. In the United States, for example, the proportion of the population sixty-five or older has risen from about 4 or 5 percent in 1900 to about 12 or 13 percent now; and this figure will increase to almost 20 percent when the baby-boom generation born during the 1950s and 1960s turns sixty-five. Similar trends are occurring in many other developed countries (see Figure 9.13 on page 350). These trends make it particularly important to understand physical changes during the later decades of life.

What picture emerges from research concerning such changes? A mixed but somewhat encouraging one. Stereotypes suggesting that people in their sixties,

**Menopause:** Cessation of the menstrual cycle.

**Successful Aging:** Aging with minimal physiological losses in many bodily functions relative to younger persons; results from a healthy lifestyle.

**Figure 9.13**
**The Graying of the Developed World's Population**

As shown here, the proportion of the population over age sixty-five will increase considerably in many countries in the coming decades.
(*Source:* Based on data from United States Senate Special Committee on Aging, 1991.)

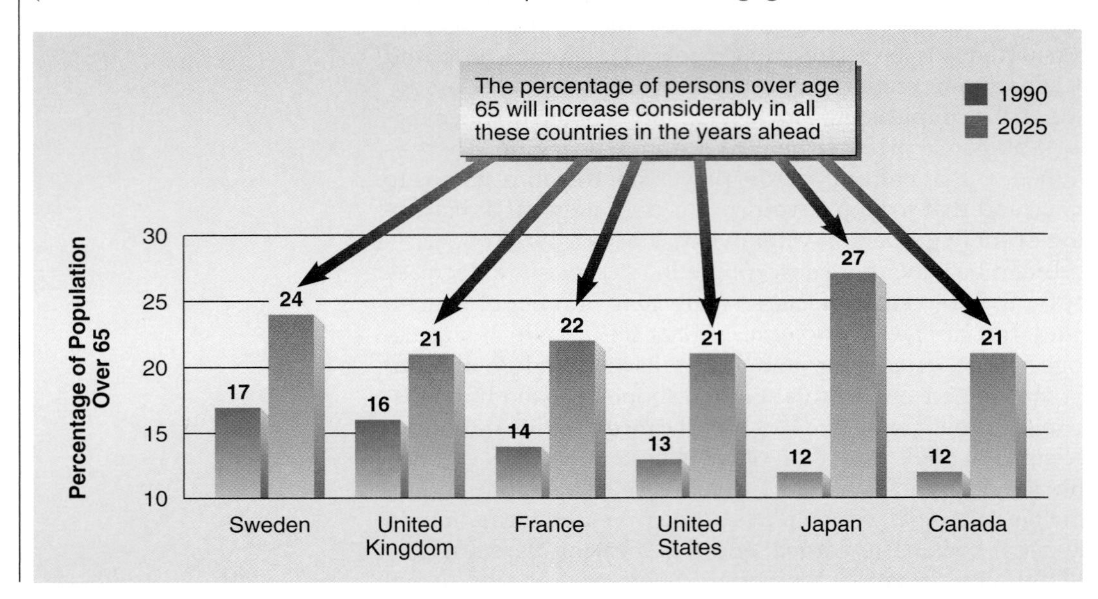


seventies, and eighties are generally frail, in poor health, and unable to take care of themselves turn out to be largely false. In the United States a very large proportion of people in these age groups report good or excellent health. And these are not simply overoptimistic self-reports. It appears that most people below the age of eighty *are* in reasonably good health and are not much more likely than middle-aged people to suffer from *chronic illnesses*—ones that are long-term, progressive, and incurable (United States Department of Health and Human Services, 1989). Further, even in their seventies and eighties, a large majority of people do not receive hospital care during any given year (Thomas, 1992). In short, the picture of older persons that emerges, at least in developed countries such as the United States, is quite encouraging.

One additional point should not be overlooked: While many physical changes do occur with increasing age, it is crucial to distinguish between those that are the result of **primary aging**—changes caused by the passage of time and, perhaps, genetic factors—and those that result from **secondary aging**—changes due to disease, disuse, or abuse of our bodies. Let's briefly examine some of the physical changes that are the result of primary aging.

**Primary Aging:** Changes in our bodies caused by the passage of time and, perhaps, by genetic factors.

**Secondary Aging:** Changes in our bodies due to disease, disuse, or abuse.

Several of these involve decrements in *sensory abilities.* As people age, they experience decline with respect to vision, hearing, smell, taste, and other senses. *Visual acuity,* as measured by the ability to read letters on a standard eye examination chart, drops off sharply after age seventy. In addition, many people experience such changes as slower *dark adaptation* and reduced ability to notice moving targets, such as cars on a highway (Long & Crambert, 1990). Similarly, auditory sensitivity decreases with age, especially among persons who have worked in noisy environments (Corso, 1977). Declines also occur in abilities to identify specific tastes and smells, although these declines do not become noticeable until after age seventy-five (Spence, 1989). There is also a general slowing in reflexes and in the speed of responding generally, so *reaction time* increases with age (Spirduso & Macrae, 1990).

Again, however, there are large individual differences: A specific seventy-year-old may still respond more quickly than a specific forty-year-old.

Many of these changes have important implications for everyday activities. For example, consider driving. Accident rates are high among young drivers—perhaps because of a youth-related tendency toward recklessness—and then fall to much lower levels through much of adult life. However, accident rates rise sharply again above the age of seventy-five or eighty (Cerelli, 1989).

Hearing, too, decreases with age. By age fifty many people can notice slightly reduced ability to hear high-frequency sounds—although, as we saw in Chapter 3, such changes may now be occurring at even earlier ages, because of increased exposure to very loud sounds (e.g., rock music played through earphones). By the time they are in their sixties or seventies, many people experience some difficulty in understanding others' speech, especially if it is rapid or occurs against background noise. Indeed, older people have a decreased ability to block out background noise—to detect signal against noise (refer to Chapter 3).

**REVIEW QUESTIONS**

- How do stage theories and contextual theories account for adult development?
- At what age are we most influenced by the events occurring in our society?
- What physical changes occur during early and middle adulthood?
- What physical changes occur in later life?

## Cognitive Change during Adulthood

That people change physically across the life span is obvious: We can see such changes with our own eyes. But what about *cognition?* Do adults change in this respect as well? Our cognitive abilities rest ultimately on biological processes—events occurring within our brains (see Chapters 2 and 6)—so it is reasonable to expect some declines in cognitive functioning with age. On the other hand, as we grow older, we also gain in experience, practice with various tasks, and our overall knowledge base. Can these changes compensate for inevitable biological decline? The issue of whether, and how, our cognitive functioning changes with age is more complex than you might at first guess.

**AGING AND MEMORY** First, let's consider the impact of aging on memory. Research on working (short-term) memory indicates that older people seem able to retain about as much information in this limited-capacity system as young ones—seven to nine separate items (Poon & Fozard, 1980). Some findings, however, suggest that the ability to transfer information from working memory to long-term memory may decrease with age (Hunt, 1993). A related finding is that older persons perform more poorly than younger ones if they must carry out several working memory tasks in a row; in such cases, older persons show a greater decline on later tasks than young persons (e.g., Shimamura & Jurica, 1994). This suggests that as we grow older, our ability to deal with the effects of *proactive interference*—interference with materials we are currently entering into working memory from materials we entered earlier—declines (e.g., Shimamura et al., 1995). However, such effects may also stem from a general slowing in cognitive systems that occurs with increasing age (e.g., Park et al., 1996).

Audio 9.3: *Does Memory Decline with Age?*

Turning to long-term memory, it appears that with increasing age there may be some declines in episodic memory (memory for events experienced by an individual and associated with a particular time and place), while semantic memory (general knowledge) remains largely intact. Procedural memory—the information necessary for performing many skilled actions—seems to be the most stable of all. I saw a demonstration of this fact one day about ten years ago when my father, who was then 72, tried to ride a bicycle for the first time in forty years. He was a little wobbly, but did just fine.

Other findings indicate that memory for relatively meaningless information such as nonsense syllables or paired associates does decline with age (Hultsch & Dixon, 1990). But when the information being committed to memory is meaningful—for instance, has some connection to an individual's everyday life—differences between younger and older persons are much smaller and in some studies do not appear at all (e.g., May, Hasher, & Stoltzfus, 1993). Overall, then, it appears that unless we experience serious illness (e.g., Alzheimer's disease), we retain many of our cognitive abilities largely intact. Further, and perhaps even more encouraging, it appears that even modest declines in memory can be avoided through "mental exercise"—engaging in activities that require us to think, reason, and remember (Shimamura et al., 1995).

Why do declines in certain aspects of memory occur with increasing age? Partly, it seems, because of changes in the brain. As we age, total brain weight decreases—5 percent by age seventy, 10 percent by age eighty, and 20 percent by age ninety (Wisniewski & Terry, 1976). Further, the *frontal lobes,* a region of the brain that plays a key role in working memory, seem to experience greater loss of neurons than other areas of the brain (Parkin & Walter, 1992). The *hippocampus,* too, shows increasing damage over time; and, as we saw in Chapter 6, this region of the brain also plays an important role in memory.

Interestingly, women seem to experience smaller changes than men in brain structure as they age (e.g., Gur et al., 1991). This suggests that female sex hormones may protect women's brains from age-related changes.

**AGING AND INTELLIGENCE: DECLINE OR STABILITY?** In the past it was widely believed that intelligence increases into early adulthood, remains stable through the thirties, but then begins to decline as early as the forties. This view was based largely on cross-sectional research that compared the performance of persons of different ages on standard tests of intelligence. Results indicated that in general, the older persons were, the lower their scores tended to be (Schaie, 1974; Thomas, 1992). Unfortunately, such cross-sectional research suffers from a serious drawback. Differences among various groups of participants can stem from factors other than their respective ages, such as differences in education or health. In order to eliminate such problems, more recent research on aging and intelligence has often employed a longitudinal design. In such research, as you probably recall, the same persons are tested at several different times over a period of years to see whether there are consistent changes in their performance.

The results of studies using longitudinal procedures have yielded a more positive picture than the earlier cross-sectional studies. Instead of declining sharply with age, many intellectual abilities seem to remain quite stable across the entire life span. In fact, they show relatively little change until persons are well into their sixties, seventies, or beyond. Moreover, some abilities even seem to increase. For example, Schaie and his colleagues (Schaie, 1986, 1990, 1994) have tested thousands of people ranging in age from twenty-five to eighty-one at seven-year intervals. Results clearly indicate that various aspects of cognitive functioning (as measured by one standard test of intelligence) remain remarkably stable throughout adult life. Indeed, even at age eighty, fewer than half of the persons studied showed any declines during the preceding seven years. Only on tasks involving speed of reasoning do there appear to be consistent declines in performance. In

**Figure 9.14**
**Age-Related Changes in Intelligence: Cohort Effects**

In tests administered over a nine-year period, declines in intelligence seemed to occur only among the oldest participants. These findings suggest that such declines may not be a function of aging; rather, they may result from *cohort effects*—the fact that older persons had different life experiences (e.g., less formal education, poorer nutrition) than younger persons. To the extent that this is true, declines in intelligence with increasing age may disappear in the years ahead.
(*Source:* Based on data from Finkel et al., 1998.)

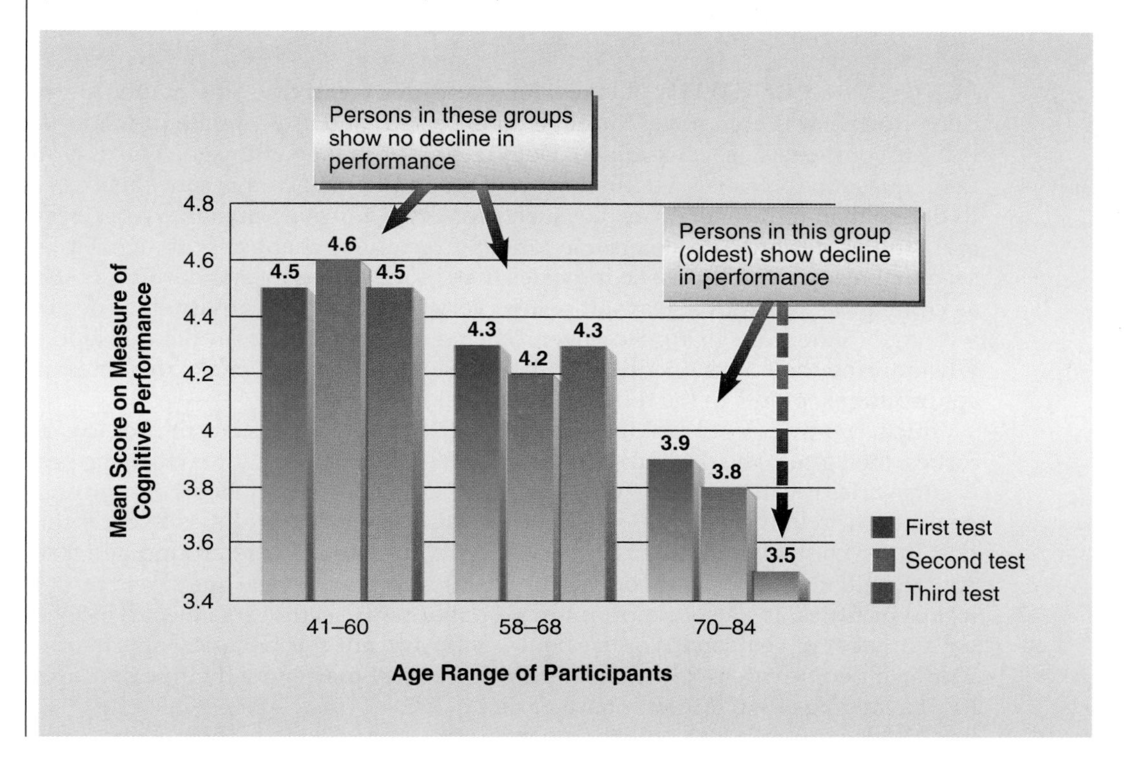


view of the fact that drops in performance may reflect slower reaction time—which is known to occur with age (e.g., Shimamura et al., 1995)—there is little if any indication of a general decrease in intelligence with age.

Additional findings reported recently by Finkel and others (1998) indicate that important *cohort effects* may be involved in age-related changes in intelligence (or in general cognitive performance). These researchers studied several hundred twins in Sweden—individuals ranging in age from their early forties to their mid-eighties. They found that for the younger samples (cohorts), there was little evidence of change in various aspects of cognitive performance over a nine-year period. For the oldest samples (people in their seventies and eighties), however, some declines did occur (see Figure 9.14). Why? Many researchers would point to the fact that these persons, as compared to younger ones, probably had poorer nutrition and had less formal education as they grew up. If such factors are equated, then, as Schaie (1994) has found, little or no decrements in performance are evident.

While such findings are encouraging, they are not the entire story. As I'll explain in Chapter 11, standardized intelligence tests may not capture all aspects of adult intelligence. The distinction between *crystallized* and *fluid intelligence* is especially relevant here. **Crystallized intelligence** consists of those aspects of intelligence that draw on previously learned information—our accumulated knowledge. Classroom tests, vocabulary tests, and many social situations in which we must

**Crystallized Intelligence:** Aspects of intelligence that draw on previously learned information—our accumulated knowledge.

**Fluid Intelligence:** Our abilities (largely inherited) to think and reason.

**Creativity:** The ability to produce work that is both novel (original, unexpected) and appropriate.

**Social Network:** A group of people with whom one interacts regularly.

**Convoy Model:** A model of social networks suggesting that from midlife on, we tend to maintain close relationships with a small number of people.

make judgments or decisions about other persons draw on crystallized intelligence. In contrast, **fluid intelligence** includes our abilities (at least in part inherited) to think and reason. Research focusing on these two types of intelligence suggests that fluid intelligence increases into the early twenties and then gradually declines. In contrast, crystallized intelligence tends to increase across the entire life span (e.g., Lerner, 1990; Willis & Nesselroade, 1990). Similarly, there may be little or no decline in *practical intelligence*—the ability to solve everyday problems. In fact, it seems possible that such intelligence, which is very important, may actually *increase* with age (e.g., Sternberg et al., 1995) (see Chapter 11). In sum, while there may be some declines in intelligence with age, these are smaller in both magnitude and scope than age-related stereotypes suggest.

**AGING AND CREATIVITY** Finally, let's consider **creativity**—the ability to produce work that is both novel (original, unexpected) and appropriate (it works—it is useful or meets task constraints). Does creativity change with age? This is a difficult question to answer, because, as we'll see in Chapter 11, this concept is easier to define than to measure. Despite such problems, however, there have been several studies designed to determine whether creativity changes with age. Cross-sectional research on this issue indicates that, as measured by standard tasks such as coming up with novel ways of using everyday objects, creativity does decline with age (Simonton, 1990). However, other research, focused on the question of when during their lives scientists, authors, poets, and painters make their creative contributions, points to the following conclusions.

First, creativity rises rapidly to a peak, usually in a person's late thirties to early forties, then gradually declines (Simonton, 1988). Second, the age at which the peak occurs varies greatly by field. In poetry, pure mathematics, and theoretical physics, peaks occur relatively early—when people are in their late twenties to early thirties. In psychology and other fields of science, the peak occurs around age forty. And in still other fields—history, writing, philosophy—the peak may be in the late forties or fifties. It's also important to note that what seems crucial is an individual's number of years in his or her field—*career age,* not chronological age. In other words, if people enter a given field later in life, they may show their peak creativity at a later age than if they enter it earlier in life.

It's also important to note that many famous people made their major contributions when they were in their sixties, seventies, or eighties. Cervantes wrote *Don Quixote* at age sixty, Monet produced many of his most famous paintings in his seventies, and Michelangelo was designing and painting until his death at eighty-three (see Figure 9.15). Finally, many famous people show a secondary peak in creativity near the end of their lives—the *swan-song phenomenon* (Simonton, 1990). These works of old age are often shorter and more restrained than the creators' earlier works, but they often win critical acclaim precisely for this reason: They do it all with less complexity.

**Figure 9.15**
**Creativity: Not the Sole Property of Youth**

Many famous artists, inventors, and composers completed major works very late in their lives. This suggests that creativity does not necessarily decline with age. Julia Child, world-famous chef *(left);* Michelangelo *(right).*

Where does all this leave us? With, I believe, an overall pattern of evidence suggesting that few intellectual abilities decline sharply with age. Some do decrease—especially ones closely related to speed of responding. But others remain quite stable over many years, and still others may actually increase as individuals gain in experience. My conclusion: Aging is inevitable, but our minds can, and often do, remain active until the very end of life.

**REVIEW QUESTIONS**

- What changes in memory occur as we age?
- How do intelligence and creativity change over the life span?

**Food for Thought**

Does the fact that crystallized intelligence increases throughout life provide a strong rationale for entrusting important decisions to older, more experienced persons?

## Social and Emotional Development during Adulthood

My grandfather lived until he was ninety-two, and he was alert and energetic right until the end. Over the years he told me many things that I'll always remember, but one comment he made with increasing frequency as the years passed sticks in my mind: "Bobby," he said, "I feel as though I'm losing my past. . . . So many people I knew and cared about are gone." He wasn't grieving for these people when he made this remark (I'll discuss *bereavement* in a later section); rather, he was expressing the fact that he felt increasingly alone, because most of his lifelong friends were gone. How important are friends during our adult years? Do our emotional reactions change as we grow older? And what changes and transitions do we experience with the passing years? Let's see what psychologists have discovered about these aspects of social and emotional development during our adult years.

**FRIENDSHIPS: THE CONVOY MODEL** I mentioned friendship a moment ago, so let's begin with this topic. The reasons why we form and maintain friendships are clear: We seem to have a strong need to affiliate—to interact in positive ways with others; and we gain much help, information, and social support from friendships. So being part of what psychologists term a **social network**—a group of people with whom one interacts regularly (friends, neighbors, relatives)—can be very beneficial as we age. Given that we continue to meet people throughout life, you might guess that we would expand these networks as we grow older. However, the opposite seems to be true. Early in our adult years, we interact with a large number of people and have many casual friends. As we enter our middle years, though, we tend to reduce the size of our social networks—down to something like ten people. And then we tend to maintain these close ties through the remainder of our lives, moving through the decades like a convoy of ships sailing the ocean. This **convoy model** of adult social networks seems to offer an accurate description of the pattern of our friendships throughout much of our lives (Kahn & Antonucci, 1980) (see Figure 9.16).

**Figure 9.16**
**Friends for Life: The Convoy Model**

One model of friendship during our adult years suggests that beyond midlife, we reduce the size of our social networks to about ten persons with whom we are especially close. We then maintain social contacts with these persons throughout the remainder of our lives—like a convoy of ships crossing the ocean together.

Why do we gradually reduce the number of friends we have? Research by Carstensen and her colleagues (e.g., Carstensen & Charles, 1998; Carstensen, Isaacowitz, & Charles, 1999) suggests that this tendency may stem in part from our growing realization that time is limited and that we should therefore invest most of our effort in a relatively small number of social partners. Time available for interacting with various people may be limited by many factors—increasing age, impending retirement, physical relocations. And recent findings indicate that the more time is perceived as limited, the greater the preference of all persons—young and old—for interacting with close friends or relatives (e.g., Fung, Carstensen, & Lutz, in press). Because older persons feel that time is indeed running out for them, however, they generally show a stronger preference than younger persons, overall, for interacting with a small number of close friends or relatives.

CourseCompass
Web Link: *Demographics of Divorce*

**EMOTIONAL EXPERIENCES. DO WE FEEL EMOTIONS LESS INTENSELY AS WE AGE?** Older people are often viewed as being calmer than younger ones. Does this imply that they experience a reduced range of emotions? Growing evidence suggests that this is not the case. Older adults report experiencing emotional experiences as rich and intense as younger ones (Carstensen & Charles, 1998), and when experiencing specific emotions they show facial expressions and patterns of physiological reactions that are virtually identical to those of younger adults (e.g., Levenson et al., 1991). However, older people do differ from younger ones in certain respects: While they report experiencing positive emotions such as happiness and joy just as frequently as younger people, they report experiencing negative emotional experiences such as anger or sorrow *less* frequently (Carstensen, Pasupathi, & Mary, 1998). Further, older persons report greater control over their emotions and greater stability of mood than younger persons. In short, there seems to be some truth to the view that older persons are calmer and less excitable emotionally than younger ones, but no truth to the view that they live an impoverished emotional existence.

**LEVINSON'S STAGES OF ADULT LIFE** Before concluding this discussion of social development during our adult years, I'll briefly describe one theory that considers the changes and transitions we experience during our adult lives—the controversial theory proposed by Levinson (1986). Because it is a stage theory, I could have described it when we discussed that topic. However, Levinson's theory deals in part with aspects of social development, so it makes sense to consider it here.

Let's begin with a crucial aspect of Levinson's theory—a concept he terms the **life structure.** This term refers to the underlying patterns of a person's life at a particular time, an evolving cognitive framework reflecting an individual's views about the nature and meaning of his or her life. Work and family are usually central to the life structure, but it may include other components as well—for example, a person's racial or ethnic background, or important external events that provide a backdrop for life, such as an economic boom or depression. According to Levinson, individuals have different life structures at different times during their adult years and move from one to another through *transition periods* lasting about five years.

Levinson divides our adult years into four major *eras,* each separated from the next by a transition period. These eras are summarized in Figure 9.17. As you can see, the first transition occurs between the *preadult era,* the time before we are adults, and early adulthood. Taking place between the ages of seventeen and twenty-two, this transition involves establishing one's independence, both financial and emotional. It is marked by such events as establishing a separate residence and learning to live on one's own.

**Life Structure:** In Levinson's theory of adult development, then underlying patterns or design of a person's life.

**Dream:** In Levinson's theory of adult development, a vision of future accomplishments—what a person hopes to achieve in the years ahead.

**Mentor:** Older and more experienced individual who helps guide a young adult.

Once this first transition is complete, individuals enter *early adulthood.* Two key components of their life structure at this time are what Levinson terms the **dream** and the **mentor.** The dream is a vision of future accomplishments—what the person hopes to achieve in the years ahead. Mentors are older and more experienced individuals who help guide young adults. Both the dream and the mentor play an important part in our early adult years.

At about age thirty, Levinson suggests, many people experience what he terms the *age thirty transition.* At this time individuals realize that they are nearing the point of no return: If they remain in their present life course, they will soon have too much

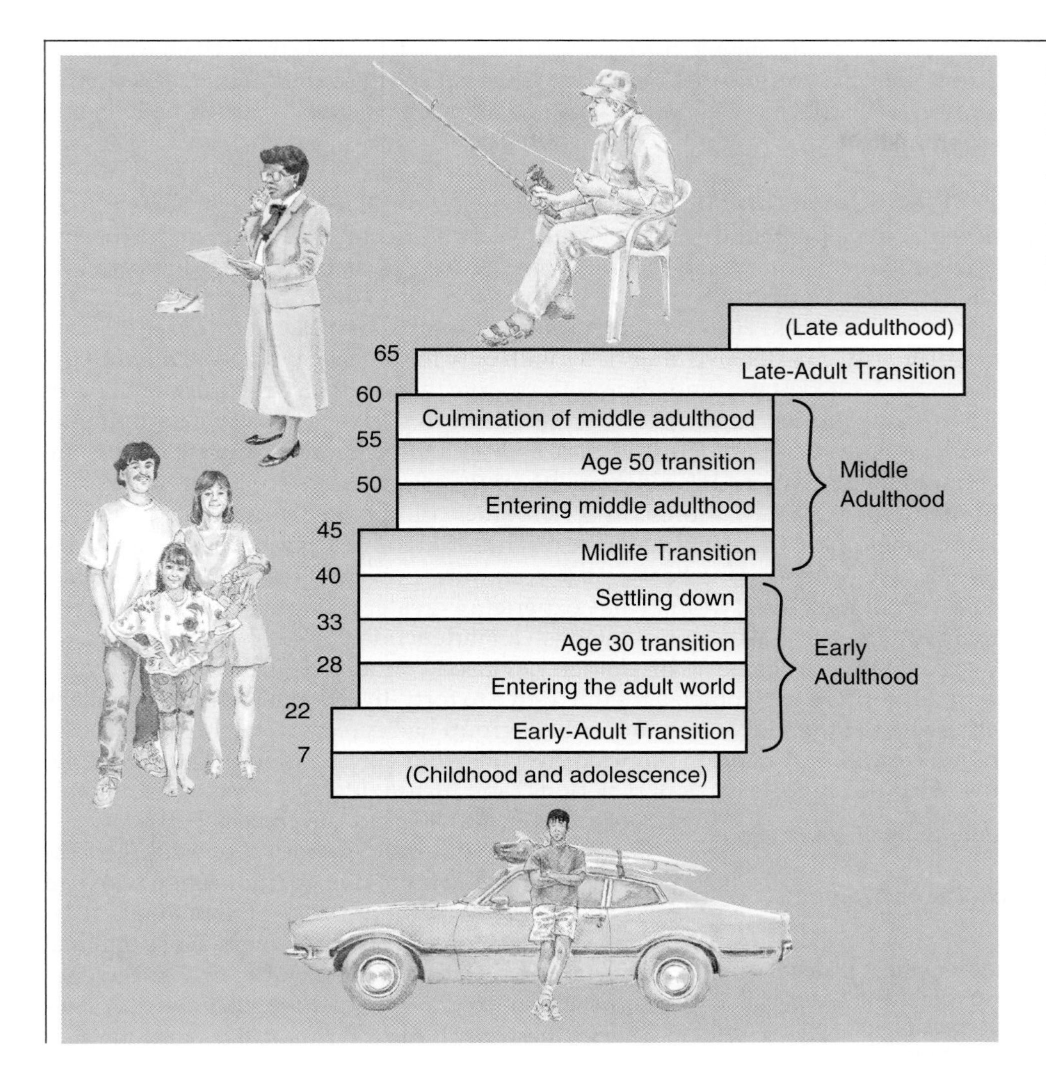


**Figure 9.17**
**Levinson's Theory of Adult Development**

According to Levinson (1986), individuals move through distinct eras of life, each separated from the next by a turbulent transition period.

invested to change. Faced with this fact, they reexamine their initial choices and either make specific changes or conclude that they have indeed chosen the best course.

Now, after the relative calm of the closing years of early adulthood, individuals move into another potentially turbulent transitional period—the **midlife transition.** For most people this occurs somewhere between the ages of forty and forty-five. It is a time when many people must come to terms for the first time with their own mortality. Up until this period, most people view themselves as "still young." After age forty, however, many come to view themselves as the older generation. Levinson's findings suggest that for many persons this realization leads to a period of emotional turmoil. They take stock of where they have been, the success of their past choices, and the possibility of reaching their youthful dreams. This leads to the formation of a new life structure, one that takes account of the individual's new position in life and may involve new elements such as a change in career direction, divorce, or a redefinition of one's relationship with one's spouse.

Many persons experience another period of transition between ages fifty and fifty-five, a transition in which they consider modifying their life structure once again—for example, by adopting a new role in their career or by coming to view themselves as a grandparent as well as a parent. However, this transition is often less dramatic than one that occurs somewhere between the ages of sixty and sixty-five. This **late-adult transition** marks the close of the middle years and the start of late adulthood. During this transition, individuals must come to terms with their impending retirement and the major life changes it will bring. As they move through

**Midlife Transition:** In Levinson's theory of adult development, a turbulent transitional period occurring between the ages of forty and forty-five.

**Late-Adult Transition:** In Levinson's theory of adult development, a transition in which individuals must come to terms with their impending retirement.

this period of readjustment, their life structure shifts to include these changes. For example, they may come to see themselves as persons whose working career is over, or almost over, and who will now have much more leisure time to pursue hobbies and other interests.

**LEVINSON'S THEORY: IS IT ACCURATE?** In several respects Levinson's picture of social development during our adult years seems to match our commonsense ideas about this process. Relatively long periods of stability are punctuated by shorter, turbulent periods in which we come to terms with changes in our goals, status, and outlook. However, it's important to note that Levinson based his theory primarily on extensive interviews with only forty participants—all men, all living in the United States, and all ages thirty-five to forty-five. Critics argue that this is too small and too restricted a sample on which to base such a sweeping framework (Wrightsman, 1988). In addition, and perhaps even more important, it is uncertain whether Levinson's suggestions apply to women as well as men. Women in many societies face a different set of issues and problems as they age. For instance, they, more than men, have the responsibility of *caring for their elderly parents;* also, if they have remained at home to concentrate on child rearing during at least a portion of their lives, women may experience greater changes than men do when their youngest child sets out to establish an independent life.

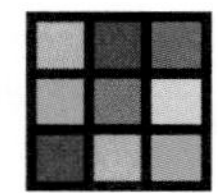

To deal with the issue of gender, Levinson conducted further research on a sample of forty-five women ages thirty-five to forty-five. Some were homemakers, others had academic careers, and a third group had careers in the business world (Levinson, 1996). Levinson reported that the women in his sample went through the same sequence of eras and periods, and at roughly the same ages, as men. However, he did find differences between men and women in several respects. For example, during the midlife transition, many women who had chosen the traditional role of homemaker expressed strong regrets about their choice and had what he described as a "rock-bottom" experience in which they questioned whether the sacrifices they had made for their marriages and families were justified.

This finding has been further explored by Stewart and Vandewater (1999) in a longitudinal study of women at two ages: thiry-six and forty-seven. When they were thirty-six, the women were asked whether they had any regrets about having chosen to marry and become homemakers rather than pursue a career and whether they wished to make a change. When they were forty-seven, the same women were asked these questions again, and were also asked to indicate whether they had made a career-relevant change—entered a new career, taken courses, and so on. In addition, the women provided information on their physical and psychological well-being.

The researchers found that many of the women in the study expressed regret over their earlier choice to become a homemaker, and many stated the desire to change their lives and careers. Further, those who expressed regret and a desire to change and then *actually made changes* in their lives reported higher physical and psychological adjustment than those who also expressed regrets but had *not* made such changes (see Figure 9.18).

**Figure 9.18**
**Regrets and Midlife Change: Effects on Women's Well-Being**

Women who had regrets about choosing the traditional homemaker role rather than a career, and who made changes in their lives in response to these regrets, showed higher adjustment and greater physical well-being than women who also had such regrets but did *not* make life changes to address them. These findings were obtained for two different samples.
(*Source:* Based on data from Stewart & Vandewater, 1999.)

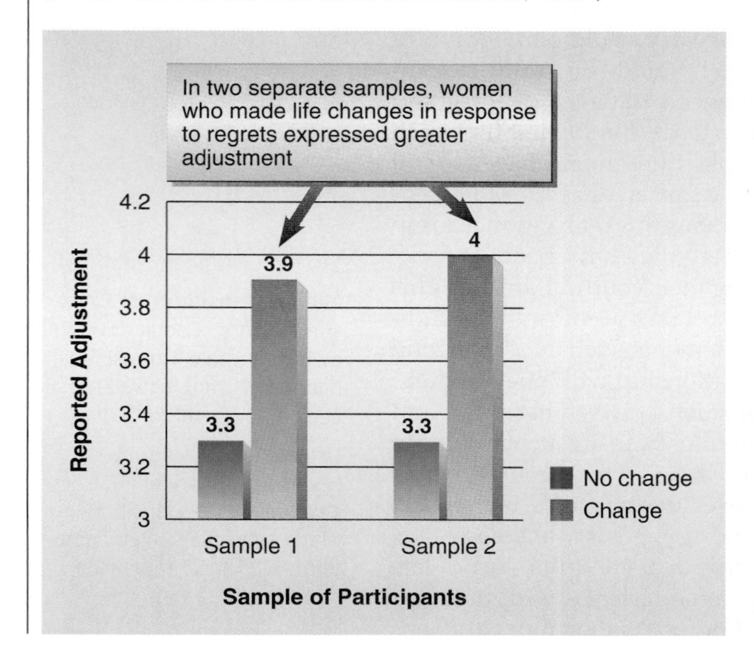

These findings suggest that as Levinson proposed, many women review their lives in midlife and both seek and make important changes, especially if they regret their earlier lifestyle choices.

What, then, can we conclude about Levinson's theory? That some findings offer support for his conclusion that "There is . . . a single human life cycle through which all our lives evolve" (Levinson, 1996, p. x), but that we must take careful note of gender, race, and socioeconomic factors that may strongly affect various aspects of this cycle.

**REVIEW QUESTIONS**

- In Levinson's theory, what is the life structure, and what are the major eras of adult life?
- What criticisms have been directed against Levinson's theory?
- What does recent research suggest about gender differences in adult development?

**Food for Thought**

Why, in your opinion, do many women who have chosen traditional roles express regret over this decision? Do you think this will change in the future?

# Aging, Death, and Bereavement

Since ancient times, human beings have searched for the "fountain of youth"—some means of prolonging youth, and life, indefinitely. Sad to relate, such dreams have remained only illusions: Life and health *can* be prolonged (see Chapter 13 and the **From Science to Practice** section on page 360), but there is no way to live forever. In fact, current estimates suggest that the upper limit of the human life span may be in the neighborhood of 120 years. In this section we'll consider several questions relating to the close of life: (1) What are the causes of aging and death? (2) How do terminally ill people react to their own impending death? And (3) How do survivors cope with the loss of their loved ones?

Web Link: *Senior Net: Bringing Wisdom to the Information Age*

## Theories of Aging: Contrasting Views about Why We Grow Old

Audio 9.4: *Genetic Wear and Tear Theories*

Many different views about the causes of aging have been proposed, but most fall under one of two major headings: *stochastic theories* and *programmed theories.*

**STOCHASTIC THEORIES: "GROWING OLD IS THE RESULT OF LIVING."** The first group, **stochastic theories,** also known as **wear-and-tear theories of aging,** suggest that we grow old because of cumulative damage to our bodies from both external and internal sources. Because such damage is not completely repaired, we simply "wear out" over time. One such theory emphasizes the role of *free radicals*—atoms that are unstable because they have lost electrons. According to this theory, these highly unstable particles are continuously produced by body metabolism; once formed, they react violently with other molecules in cells, thus producing damage. When this damage affects DNA, free radicals can interfere with basic aspects of cell maintenance and repair. The theory proposes that this damage cumulates over time, thus producing the declines associated with aging.

**Stochastic Theories of Aging:** Theories suggesting that we grow old because of cumulative damage to our bodies from both external and internal sources; also known as *wear-and-tear theories of aging.*

**Wear-and-Tear Theories of Aging:** Theories suggesting that aging results from the continuous use of cells and organs in our bodies.

Another stochastic theory stresses the effects of damage to our DNA—damage produced either because cell division somehow "goes wrong," or by external causes such as viruses or toxins in the environment. As the number of cells

**Programmed Theories of Aging:** Theories that attribute physical aging primarily to genetic programming.

**Teleomeres:** Caps consisting of DNA that cover the ends of chromosomes and seem to regulate the number of times a cell can divide.

damaged by DNA deterioration increases, we age and our internal systems gradually decline.

Indirect evidence for wear-and-tear theories of aging is provided by individuals who repeatedly expose their bodies to harmful conditions or substances—for instance, large doses of alcohol, various drugs, or harsh environments. Such persons often show premature signs of aging, presumably because they have overloaded their bodies' capacity for internal repairs.

**PROGRAMMED THEORIES** A second group of theories attributes physical aging primarily to genetic programming. According to the these **programmed theories of aging,** every living organism contains a kind of built-in biological clock that regulates the aging process. Where is this clock located? Very recent findings suggest that it may involve, at least in part, strips of DNA that cap the ends of our chromosomes—**teleomeres** (Gladwell, 1996). Each time a cell divides, the teleomere becomes shorter; when this shortening reaches some critical point, the cell can no longer divide, and this may contribute to the aging process. For instance, in skin cells, when the teleomeres are shortened to a critical length, the cells cannot divide, and normal repair processes that keep the skin healthy and young looking begin to break down.

Other programmed theories stress the fact that our immune system seems to "wind down" over time and that our endocrine system, and the neural areas that control it, declines with increasing age. These systems regulate many basic processes (e.g., our metabolism); so as they decline, our vitality drops too.

Support for programmed theories is provided by several observations. First, each species has a characteristic maximum life span; this suggests that length of life is somehow built into different species' genetic codes. Second, longevity appears to be an inherited trait; one rough indicator of how long *you* will live is the life span of your parents and grandparents. This, too, suggests an important role of genetic factors in the aging process. Third, age-related changes in our bodies show a regularity that is hard to explain without reference to genetic factors. Finally, some findings suggest that certain cells do indeed divide only a set number of times before dying. Moreover, no environmental conditions seem capable of altering this set number.

Which group of theories is the most accurate? No one theory is supported by sufficient evidence to be viewed as conclusive. The best scientific guess at present is that aging is caused by several different mechanisms and results from a complex interplay between environmental and genetic factors.

Whatever its cause, aging is a fact of life. What steps can we take to slow it down? For information on this issue, please see the following **From Science to Practice** section.

from SCIENCE to PRACTICE

## Living Longer—and Healthier—Lives: Some Concrete Steps

Every so often, newspapers carry accounts of populations—usually living in some remote corner of the world—that appear to be especially long-lived. According to such stories, large proportions of these people live beyond one hundred; moreover, they are described as being vigorous and healthy. On closer examination, unfortunately, such stories appear to be exaggerated. Birth records for these populations are generally scarce or nonexistent, so we really don't know how old the people are. And it often turns out to be the case that the proportions of very old people in such groups are far lower than initially claimed.

Yet the search for some kind of "fountain of youth" continues, and not without considerable success. The goal of research on this topic is what has been termed *optimal* or *successful aging*—aging that involves minimal physiological losses across a number of functions (Arking, 1991). What steps can help individuals reach this goal? Here are some of the most important:

- **Eat a healthy diet.** Growing evidence suggests that eating a healthy, balanced diet—one high in fruits, vegetables, and whole grains but low in cholesterol-promoting foods such as animal fat—can be a big step in the right direction. People who eat a healthy diet often have stronger immune systems, and this can help slow the effects of aging.
- **Exercise regularly.** Exercise means three things: cardiovascular exercise (jogging, walking, running, swimming—anything that makes your heart work harder), calisthenics (for flexibility), and weight training (for strength). How much do you have to do? Growing evidence suggests that a little can go a long way: Cardiovascular training three times a week for twenty minutes will give you much of the benefits of such exercise; five minutes of vigorous calisthenics can help you avoid stiffness, and mild weight training twice a week will significantly increase your strength. The important point is to engage in such activities *regularly*—not just when guilt or worry spurs you to do so!
- **Minimize exposure to the sun.** One of the most visible outward signs of aging is wrinkling of the skin, and this can be slowed greatly if we avoid exposure to the sun. This guideline is especially important for fair-skinned persons, but it applies to everyone of all skin shades. If you do go out into the sun, be sure to wear sun block, and limit exposure between 11:00 a.m. and 4:00 p.m., the hours when damaging rays from the sun are most intense.
- **Reduce stress.** No one can live a stress-free life; but, as we'll see in Chapter 13, there are many steps you can take to reduce the level of stress to which you are exposed. Stress undermines the immune system and weakens our bodies in many ways, so it is very important to keep it down.
- **Don't smoke or abuse alcohol and other drugs.** This step is so obvious it needs no further comment. But in light of growing evidence suggesting that inhaling secondary smoke—smoke from others' cigarettes—can be almost as harmful as smoking itself, you may want to change some aspects of your lifestyle so as to avoid exposure to smokers (e.g., by avoiding crowded bars or other night spots).
- **Avoid prolonged exposure to loud noise.** Having noted the dangers of smoky bars, I should add that such places are also very noisy, and loud noise can speed the decline in hearing that occurs as a function of age. Loud music may be stimulating, but it has a serious cost where hearing is concerned.
- **Cultivate certain aspects of your personality.** Here comes the surprise: Personality, too, seems to be linked to longevity in important ways. Evidence for this conclusion is provided by the results of one of the most famous studies in psychology—a longitudinal study of 1,528 bright California boys and girls that began in 1921 (Friedman et al., 1995). These individuals, who were about eleven years old when the study began, have been tested repeatedly for more than seventy-eight years. The length of this study provides a unique opportunity to determine whether aspects of personality, and many other factors, are related to longevity. In a report summarizing findings through the mid 1990s, Friedman and his colleagues (Friedman et al., 1995) noted that one significant predictor of longevity was an aspect of personality known as *conscientiousness*—the tendency to be neat, orderly, and dependable (see Chapter 12). Conscientious children, for instance, get their homework done on time and keep their rooms neat. They set goals and fulfill them, and generally don't take many risks. Persons high in this characteristic were fully *30 percent less likely to die in any given year than persons low in this trait.* Why should conscientiousness be related to living a long time? At present we don't know for sure. But whatever the cause, developing this trait (it *can* be enhanced with sufficient effort) may be an important means for lengthening your own life.
- **Consider the benefits of faith:** A growing body of evidence suggests that people who hold religious beliefs (*any* religious beliefs) live longer, happier lives than those who don't (e.g., Kim, Nesselroade, & Feaherman, 1996). Why? In part, apparently, because these beliefs lead them to adopt healthier lifestyles (e.g., to limit smoking and drinking), provide them with social support, and offer hope and a sense of meaning and purpose in life. Again, the particular faith or religion does not seem to matter; but having some kind of faith or religious belief does seem to offer important benefits in terms of living a long life.

In sum, while there's clearly no fountain of youth, research by psychologists does provide useful guidelines for making our lives healthier and longer. The information already exists; whether and to what extent you use it is, of course, up to you.

## Meeting Death: Facing the End of Life

CourseCompass
Web Link: *The Kevorkian Verdict*

What is death? The answer to this question is more complex than you might suspect. First, there are several kinds of death. *Physiological death* occurs when all

**Figure 9.19**
**Fighting for the Right to Die**

Dr. Jack Kevorkian, shown here, has long campaigned for legislation that would permit terminally ill persons to die at a time of their own choosing. In 1999 Kevorkian was convicted of manslaughter for helping one such person die.

physical processes that sustain life cease. *Brain death* is defined as a total absence of brain activity for at least ten minutes. *Cerebral death* means cessation of activity in the cerebral cortex. And *social death* refers to a process through which other people relinquish their relationships with the deceased (Thomas, 1992).

Second, there are complex ethical issues connected with death. Should individuals have the right to die when they choose? Should physicians be allowed to help such individuals die? As you may know, these issues have received a great deal of attention in the United States, partly because of the efforts of one physician, Dr. Jack Kevorkian (sometimes known as "Doctor Death"). He has campaigned long and hard for laws that guarantee terminally ill patients the right to choose when to die (see Figure 9.19), and recently was sentenced to jail for assisting one such person to die. These are complex questions, only partly within the realm of science. I raise them here simply to remind you that death involves much more than a biological event.

But given that death is the inevitable end of life, how do persons confronted with their own impending death react? Perhaps the most famous study on this subject was conducted in the late 1960s by Elizabeth Kübler-Ross (1969). She studied terminally ill cancer patients and, on the basis of extensive interviews with them, concluded that they pass through five distinct stages.

The first is *denial*. In this phase, patients refuse to believe that the end is in sight. "No, it can't be true," they seem to say. This stage is soon replaced by a second—*anger*. "Why me?" dying persons ask. "It isn't fair." In the third stage, patients show what Kübler-Ross terms *bargaining*. They offer prayer, good behavior, or other changes in lifestyle in exchange for a postponement of death. Unfortunately, such efforts cannot alter medical realities, so when it becomes apparent that their best efforts to make a deal with death have failed, many dying persons enter a stage of *depression*.

That's not the end of the process, however. According to Kübler-Ross, many people ultimately move into a final stage she labels *acceptance*. At this stage, dying persons are no longer angry or depressed. Instead, they seem to accept their impending death with dignity; they concentrate on saying good-bye to important persons in their lives and putting their affairs in good order.

Although these findings are comforting and appealing, they have not been confirmed by other researchers. For example, Aronoff and Spilka (1984–1985) videotaped terminally ill patients at various points during their illness and examined their facial expressions for evidence of Kübler-Ross's five stages. They found an increase in sad expressions over time, but no evidence that these persons became calmer or happier as their deaths approached. Other researches have found somewhat different patterns, such as expressions of hope throughout a terminal illness (Metzger, 1980). It is also important to note that Kübler-Ross worked with a special group of individuals: people who were middle-aged and had suddenly learned that their lives would be cut off prematurely by cancer. This raises important questions about whether her findings can be generalized to other persons—especially older individuals for whom death is a less unexpected event. In view of these points, it seems best to view Kübler-Ross's conclusions with caution. They are intriguing, and they certainly hold out hope that many of us can meet death in a dignified manner. However, they cannot be viewed as scientifically valid unless they are confirmed by further research.

"Look, I'm dying. Gotta go."

**Figure 9.20**
**An Unusual Attitude Toward Death**

Few persons could face their own deaths with the composure shown by the woman in this cartoon. Yet many people do believe that they should have the right to end their lives with dignity and without being a burden to others.

(*Source:* © The New Yorker Collection. 1995. Bruce Eric Kaplan from cartoonbank.com. All rights reserved.)

**LEGAL ISSUES RELATING TO DEATH: LIVING WILLS AND DURABLE POWERS OF ATTORNEY FOR HEALTH CARE** Additional research on reactions to the idea of death suggests that while many persons express anxiety over the end of their own lives, most are more concerned with the *process* of dying—what will happen to them as they die—rather than with death itself. This concern has led a growing number of persons to take steps to enable them to die with dignity and without needless suffering. One legal procedure for reaching this goal involves preparing a *living will:* a will in which an individual expresses his or her desires about the use of life-prolonging technology. Usually, such wills state that if recovery is not possible, the individual prefers to die rather than be kept alive artificially. Another procedure involves executing a *durable power of attorney for health care;* in this kind of legal instrument, individuals identify the person or persons who will have the authority to make health care decisions for them if they are no longer able to do so. The main goal of these and related techniques is to ensure that individuals can leave their lives with dignity, without becoming a burden to others, and without needless suffering. While few of us could be as nonchalant about our own deaths as the character in Figure 9.20, most people *do* care about how their lives will end and want some choice in this important matter.

## Bereavement: Coming to Terms with the Death of Loved Ones

Web Link: *The Mourner's Corner*

Until a few years ago, I had little personal experience with **bereavement**—grieving for the loss of persons who are dear to us. But then my mother-in-law, a wonderful person in every way, was diagnosed with pancreatic cancer; she died, as do most people with this disease, within a few months. My wife was very close to her mother, and watching my wife's intense pain and suffering taught me several lessons about love and bereavement.

Because bereavement is an experience most adults have, it has been studied in detail by psychologists (Norris & Murrell, 1990). This research suggests that bereavement is a process in which individuals move through a series of discrete stages. The first is *shock*—a feeling of numbness and unreality. This is followed by stages of *protest* and *yearning,* in which bereaved persons resent the loss of their loved one and fantasize about this person's return. These reactions are often followed by deep *despair,* which can last a year or more—a period when bereaved

**Bereavement:** The process of grieving for the persons we love who die.

**Figure 9.21**
**Funerals: Definitely for the Living**

Almost all societies have funerals—formal rituals in which grieving persons take final leave of their deceased loved ones. Funerals permit grieving persons to express their sorrow and also keep these persons occupied at a time when they are experiencing intense emotions.

persons feel that life is not worth living. Finally, bereaved persons usually enter a state of *detachment and recovery,* in which they gradually separate themselves psychologically from the loved person who has died (e.g., Hart et al., 1995) and go on with their lives. Even during this stage, however, painful bouts of grieving may recur on birthdays, anniversaries, and other occasions that remind the bereaved person of his or her loss. I observed such reactions in my wife, who experienced new waves of grief each time her mother's birthday or a special holiday such as Christmas approached.

Bereavement is especially strong in cases like that of my mother-in-law: She was in excellent health, and we all expected her to live many more years. The unexpected nature of her death made it a *high-grief* experience for all of us. When death is expected, in contrast, grief may be less pronounced (*low-grief* death). One type of death seems to leave especially deep and long-lasting scars: the death of a child. Parents who go through this agonizing experience may never recover from it entirely; they continue to experience what is known as *shadow grief* for their entire lives (Knapp, 1987).

Have you ever heard the phrase "Funerals are for the living"? In an important sense, it is correct. Funerals and other rituals relating to death are designed to help grieving people take final leave of the person who has died, and to assist them in seeing the death as a part of the continuing story of life. These ceremonies also provide an opportunity for grieving persons—family and friends alike—to demonstrate publicly both their grief and their love and respect for the deceased individual (see Figure 9.21). Finally, they serve to distract the people who are most touched by the death by keeping them occupied during the initial stages of bereavement. All too soon, however, these leave-taking rituals are over, and the grieving persons are left alone with their feelings of loss and despair. This is why it is especially important for friends and relatives to come forward, not simply to offer their sympathy but to help those most affected to reenter a normal life as soon as possible.

Fortunately, a large majority of grieving persons do ultimately recover from the pain of their loss and go on to resume their lives. The loss of persons we love is truly one of the deepest sorrows of human life; but, as one Italian saying puts it, "La vita continua"—"Life goes on"—as it must. (For steps you can take to help grieving persons cope with their grief, see the following **Making Psychology Part of Your Life** section.)

**REVIEW QUESTIONS**

- How do stochastic theories and programmed theories account for aging and death?
- According to Kübler-Ross, what stages do terminally ill persons pass through when confronting their own death?
- What are the major stages of bereavement?

## Making Psychology Part of Your Life

### Helping Others Cope with Bereavement: Effective Condolence Behavior

After the funeral is over and relatives have returned home, and after the cards, flowers, and letters stop coming, persons who have lost a loved one must pick up the pieces of their lives and face day-to-day reality once again. Yet bereavement, as we have seen, is a lengthy process, often taking years. As a result, grieving persons are often left without help just when they need it most. Can you do anything to help such persons? Research by psychologists suggests that engaging in certain *condolence behaviors*—actions designed to offer comfort to grieving persons—can be very helpful. Here are some points to keep in mind.

- **Continue your contacts with the grieving person.** Phone calls, social invitations, notes—signs that you are thinking of the grieving person—can all help. They indicate to grieving persons that they are not alone and do have friends and relatives who care about them and their problems.
- **Sometimes, just be present.** Often, it appears, the best thing you can do for a grieving person is to be there, physically, while remaining silent. This evidence that you care about the person can be very comforting.
- **Listen: Let grieving people express their grief.** When you are present, it is often best to remain silent and to *listen.* Grieving people often find that it consoles them to express their grief to a sympathetic audience—someone who hears them, understands them, and cares about them.
- **Don't tell them that things will get easier.** While this is true, research findings indicate that many grieving persons react to such statements with resentment: They interpret them as a sign that you don't really understand, because to them it seems as though their loss is irreparable—one they can never get over.
- **Keep in touch.** As I noted above, this seems to be what grieving people appreciate most; so do call them, write to them, and visit them as often as you can.

Through such sensitive condolence behaviors, you can help make the bereavement process a bit more bearable for persons you care about. In short, others' bereavement is a time for you to express your own friendship or love for them and to help them deal with one of life's most painful experiences.

## Summary and Review

### Adolescence: Between Child and Adult

- **What physical changes occur during puberty?** Puberty, the most important feature of physical development during adolescence, is a period of rapid change and growth during which individuals attain sexual maturity.

- **How does thinking change during adolescence?** During adolescence individuals come to realize that others can hold views different from theirs, and that while there are no absolute truths in many areas of life, there are better or worse reasons for holding certain views.
- **What are parental demandingness and parental supportiveness? What styles of parenting do they yield?** Demandingness is parents' tendency to set firm rules for their children. Supportiveness is parents' tendency to be supportive of and interested in their children's activities. Differences on these dimensions yield the following parenting styles: authoritarian, authoritative, permissive, and rejecting/neglecting.
- **According to Erikson, what is the most important crisis faced by adolescents?** Erikson suggests that this is the crisis of identity versus role confusion, which concerns establishment of a clear self-identity.
- **How do bicultural adolescents cope with belonging to two cultural groups?** They do this by establishing a separate identity in each culture and alternating between these, by fusing their different cultural identities into one, or by rejecting one cultural heritage and identifying with the other.
- **What are some of the major threats to the well-being of adolescents at the present time?** These threats include the effects of growing up in families in which the parents are divorced, in families with one or both parents absent, or in dysfunctional families that expose youngsters to various forms of abuse.
- **What characteristics of adolescents can put them at risk for behavioral problems?** These include high levels of aggression, withdrawn behavior, and especially irritable–inattentive behaviors.
- **What factors contribute to adolescent resilience?** Factors contributing to resilience include personal characteristics that make adolescents easy to get along with; family-based factors, including a close bond with one or more competent, emotionally stable caregivers; and community-based factors such as supportive teachers, neighbors, or clergy.

### Key Terms

adolescence, p. 330 • puberty, p. 330 • parental demandingness, p. 334 • parental responsiveness, p. 334 • identity fusion, p. 337 • dysfunctional families, p. 341 • sexual abuse, p. 341 • resilience in development, p. 342

## Development during Our Adult Years

- **How do stage theories and contextual theories account for adult development?** Stage theories propose that we move through distinct stages that occur in an orderly manner during our adult years. In contrast, contextual theories suggest that in order to understand development we must consider the environments (social, cultural) in which people live.
- **At what age are we most influenced by the events occurring in our society?** We are most influenced by events occurring when we are adolescents or young adults.
- **What physical changes occur during early and middle adulthood?** Reduced physical functioning, decreased vigor, and changes in appearance appear during middle adulthood. In addition, both women and men experience changes in their reproductive systems during midlife.
- **What physical changes occur in later life?** Among the many physical changes occurring in later life are declines in sensory abilities and a slowing of reflexes.
- **What changes in memory occur as we age?** Working memory does not decline with age, but moving information from it to long-term storage may become somewhat slower. Recall of information from long-term memory does decline somewhat, but such effects are greater for meaningless information than for meaningful information.
- **How do intelligence and creativity change over the life span?** There may be some declines in some aspects of intelligence with age, but these are smaller and more limited in scope than was once widely believed. Crystallized intelligence may increase throughout life, while fluid intelligence may decline as we age. Creativity appears to decline somewhat in later life, but the age at which creativity peaks is highly variable.
- **In Levinson's theory, what is the life structure, and what are the major eras of adult life?** The life structure is an underlying pattern or design individuals follow in their lives. It often changes as individuals move through four major life eras: preadult, early adulthood, middle adulthood, and late adulthood.
- **What criticisms have been directed against Levinson's theory?** Levinson's theory is based on a small sample of men living in the United States, so it is unclear whether his findings apply to women as well.
- **What does recent research suggest about gender differences in adult development?** Recent research on Levinson's theory suggests that women and men move through similar stages of development but that at midlife, women who chose the traditional role of homemaker may experience strong regret over this choice and seek to make important changes in their subsequent lives.

### Key Terms

ecological systems theory, p. 345 • social age clocks, p. 345 • climacteric, p. 348 • menopause, p. 349 • successful aging, p. 349 • primary aging, p. 350 • secondary aging, p. 350 • crystallized intelligence, p. 353 • fluid intelligence, p. 354 • creativity, p. 354 • social network, p. 354 • convoy model, p. 354 • life structure, p. 356 • dream, p. 356 • mentor, p. 356 • midlife transition, p. 357 • late-adult transition, p. 357

## Aging, Death, and Bereavement

- **How do stochastic theories and programmed theories account for aging and death?** Stochastic theories suggest that aging results from the process of living: Cells and organs in our bodies wear out with continued use. Programmed theories suggest that we possess biological clocks that limit longevity.

- **According to Kübler-Ross, what stages do terminally ill persons pass through when confronting their own death?** Kübler-Ross reported five stages: denial, anger, bargaining, depression, and acceptance.
- **What are the major stages of bereavement?** The stages of bereavement include shock, protest and yearning, despair, and finally detachment and recovery.

### Key Terms

stochastic theories of aging, p. 359 • wear-and-tear theories of aging, p. 359 • programmed theories of aging, p. 360 • teleomeres, p. 360 • bereavement, p. 363

## Critical Thinking Questions

### Appraisal

The changes we experience during childhood are truly huge. Do you think that the changes we experience during our adult years are as great?

### Controversy

Some psychologists believe that today's adolescents face a unique set of risks and dangers. Do you agree? Or do you think that adolescents have always been exposed to many factors that can adversely influence their development—and their future lives?

### Making Psychology Part of Your Life

On the basis of what you've learned from this chapter, can you think of actions *you* can take to increase the chances that your adult life will be happy, productive, and healthy? What about the possibility of taking various steps to increase your own longevity—can you formulate several of these, too?

# Chapter 10

# Motivation and Emotion

## CHAPTER OUTLINE

**MOTIVATION: THE ACTIVATION AND PERSISTENCE OF BEHAVIOR 371**

Theories of Motivation: Some Major Perspectives

■ FROM SCIENCE TO PRACTICE *Using Goal Setting to Increase Occupational Safety—and Save Lives*

Hunger: Regulating Our Caloric Intake
Sexual Motivation: The Most Intimate Motive
Aggressive Motivation: The Most Dangerous Motive

■ RESEARCH METHODS *How Psychologists Study Aggression*

Achievement Motivation: The Desire to Excel

■ BEYOND THE HEADLINES—As Psychologists See It: *The Need for Stimulation . . . and How It Can Get Out of Hand*

Intrinsic Motivation: How, Sometimes, to Turn Play into Work

**EMOTIONS: THEIR NATURE, EXPRESSION, AND IMPACT 395**

The Nature of Emotions: Some Contrasting Views
The Biological Basis of Emotions
The External Expression of Emotion: Outward Signs of Inner Feelings
Emotion and Cognition: How Feelings Shape Thought and Thought Shapes Feelings
Subjective Well-Being: Some Thoughts on Personal Happiness

■ MAKING PSYCHOLOGY PART OF YOUR LIFE *Some Tips on Winning the Battle of the Bulge*

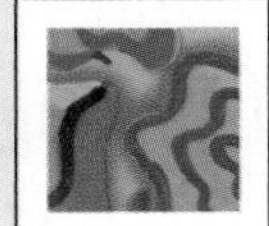

Do you exercise? I didn't until about twenty years ago. Then, after a period of intense stress, I decided to see if running could help. I was working at the National Science Foundation at the time, and the program for which I was responsible suddenly experienced a budget cut of 75 percent. This meant that I had to phone many colleagues and tell them that their research grants would not be renewed. Talk about stress! Each day I came home feeling like a zombie—totally drained emotionally. So I decided to start exercising. I had been on the track team in high school, so running was a logical choice. To this day, I remember how much harder it was than I imagined. We lived about half a mile from the zoo, but it was all uphill. On the first day, I thought I'd make it to the zoo, but was badly out of breath after only a couple of blocks. On top of that, the weather turned hot and humid—and stayed that way. I'm no quitter, though, so I kept at it. After a couple of weeks, I managed to reach my goal. I was elated—real progress! All through the summer I kept raising my goals with respect to distance and speed, and reached them. By the fall I was ready to try running all the way to my office—about 2.5 miles, all downhill. I made it, carrying a backpack. But still I wasn't satisfied. "I can do better," I thought. So I began working up to running home from the office—all *up*hill. By the winter I had reached that goal, too, and I clearly remember the sense of accomplishment I felt when, not even breathing hard, I walked into our apartment and announced my success to my wife. I've kept exercising, and although I use a treadmill or an exercise bicycle now part of the time, I still exercise four or five times a week.

Why do I begin with this experience from my own life? Because it illustrates two important topics we'll consider in this chapter: *motivation* and *emotion*. Psychologists define *motivation* as internal processes that activate, guide, and maintain behavior, so motivation is clearly visible in my efforts to take up running. Why, after all, would I subject myself to so much pain and discomfort? No one offered me any rewards for doing so—not even encouragement. (My wife was so sure I would hurt myself that she actively *discouraged* me.) The answer clearly involves *internal* processes—for instance, my desire to reduce my stress, to get in shape, and, once started, to reach the various goals I set for myself. Understanding motivation often helps us answer the question "Why?" as in "Why do people behave as they do?" or "Why do people persist in certain courses of action even when these don't seem to yield any obvious or immediate rewards?" As we'll soon see, motivation is relevant to many important forms of behavior, ranging from the regulation of body weight to sex and aggression, so it is clearly worthy of our careful attention (see Figure 10.1).

*Emotion,* in contrast, refers to complex reactions consisting of (1) physiological responses such as changes in blood pressure and heart rate; (2) the subjective feelings we describe as happiness, anger, sorrow, disgust, and so on; and (3) expressive reactions that reflect these internal states, such as changes in facial expression or posture. Such reactions are apparent in the elation I felt when I managed to run all the way home from work, and in the annoyance I felt on days when hard rain pre-

**Figure 10.1**
**Motivation: Useful in Answering the Question "Why?"**

We often wonder why other people behave as they do. The concept of motivation is often helpful in answering such questions. Can you guess why the "guru" in this cartoon founded his new religion?

(*Source:* © Tribune Media Services, Inc. All rights reserved. Reprinted with permission.)

vented me from exercising. Emotions, of course, play a crucial role in many aspects of behavior, including personal health (see Chapter 13) and psychological disorders (see Chapter 14). In addition, emotions exert strong effects on many aspects of cognition, coloring or even determining our judgments and decisions in important ways (e.g., Forgas, 1995a, 1998a).

This chapter will provide you with an overview of what psychologists currently know about these two important topics. Starting with *motivation,* we'll consider contrasting theories about its basic nature. Next, we'll examine several important forms of motivation: *hunger, sexual motivation,* and *aggressive motivation.* In addition, we'll consider a motive that, as far as we can tell, is unique to human beings: *achievement motivation*—the desire to excel.

After these discussions, we'll turn to the topic of *emotion.* Again, we'll start by examining several theories about its nature. Then we'll turn to the biological bases of emotion, an area in which research has made many recent advances. Third, we'll consider the expression and communication of emotion—how emotional reactions are reflected in external behavior. We'll then shift focus somewhat, turning to *affect,* or affective states—relatively mild subjective feelings and moods. Here, we'll consider the complex relationships between emotion and cognition: how feelings shape thought and thought shapes feelings. Finally, we'll examine one important kind of affective state—personal happiness, or what psychologists describe as *subjective well-being.*

## Motivation: The Activation and Persistence of Behavior

Consider the following events:

*A group of young women and men hurl themselves out of a plane. Then, as they fall toward earth, they join hands and form a circle. After that, they divide into pairs and swing round and round each other in a kind of dance. Only at the last minute do they open their parachutes and glide safely to the ground.*

*Employees of a large company remain on strike for many weeks, despite the fact that no matter how large the settlement they ultimately win, it will not be enough to compensate them for the wages and benefits they have lost during the strike.*

*An individual spends long hours working on complex word puzzles that require a great deal of concentration. He receives no rewards for solving these puzzles; in fact, he is often frustrated by being unable to solve them.*

How can these actions, and actions such as those shown in Figure 10.2 on page 372, be explained? On the face of it, they are puzzling. Why would people—including

**Figure 10.2**
**Motivation in Action**

People have a wide range of motives, and their behavior often stems from these internal processes.

former President Bush—voluntarily jump out of planes and risk their lives playing games as they fall toward earth? Why would workers remain on strike even though their action offers no chance of real economic gains? Why would someone exert so much effort to solve puzzles? One answer to such questions is this: These actions occur because the persons involved are *motivated* to perform them. In other words, they are responding to their own **motivation**—internal processes that can't be directly observed in the situation but which are real, nevertheless, and which serve to activate, guide, and maintain people's actions. Whenever the causes of a specific form of behavior can't be readily observed in the immediate situation, many psychologists believe that it is reasonable to explain them in terms of various motives. But what, precisely, are these motives? And how do they influence behavior? Let's see what psychologists have to say about these issues.

Web Link: *Theories of Motivation*

## Theories of Motivation: Some Major Perspectives

Over the years, many different theories of motivation have been proposed—more theories than we could possibly examine here. The views I will describe, however, are the ones that have received the most attention.

**Motivation:** Internal processes that activate, guide, and maintain behavior over time.

**DRIVE THEORY: MOTIVATION AND HOMEOSTASIS** What do being hungry, thirsty, too cold, and too hot have in common? One answer is that they are all un-

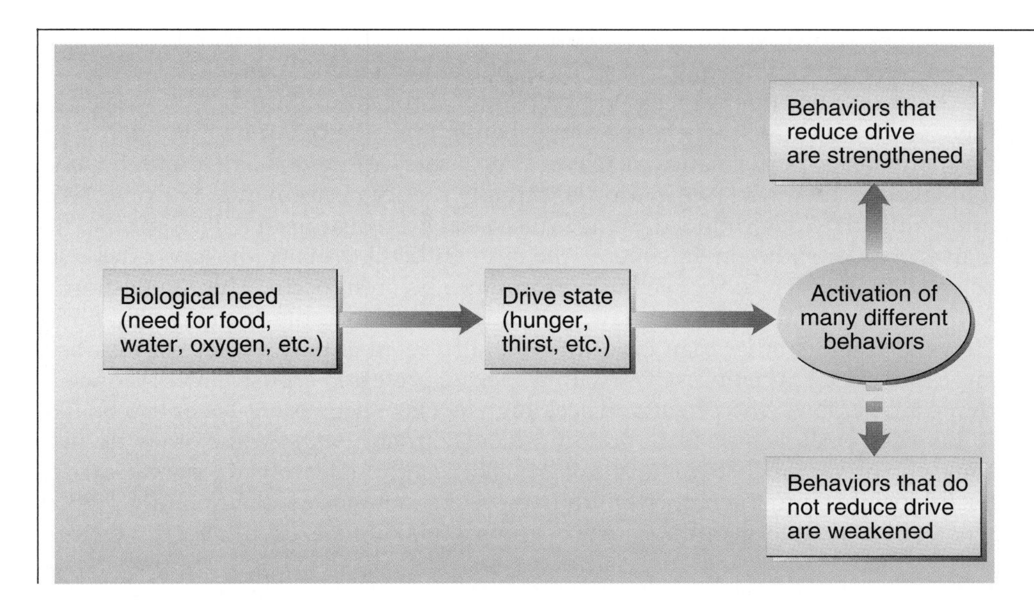


**Figure 10.3**
**Drive Theory: An Overview**

According to drive theory, biological needs lead to the arousal of *drives,* which activate efforts to reduce them. Behaviors that succeed in reducing a drive are strengthened and are repeated when the drive is aroused again. Behaviors that fail to reduce the drive are weakened and are less likely to recur when the drive is aroused once again.

pleasant states and cause us to do something to reduce or eliminate them. This basic fact provides the basis for a major approach to motivation known as **drive theory.** According to drive theory, biological needs arising within our bodies create unpleasant states of arousal—the feelings we describe as hunger, thirst, fatigue, and so on. In order to eliminate such feelings and restore a balanced physiological state, or **homeostasis,** we engage in certain activities (Winn, 1995). Thus, according to drive theory, motivation is basically a process in which various biological needs *push* (drive) us to actions designed to satisfy these needs (see Figure 10.3). Behaviors that work—ones that help reduce the appropriate drive—are strengthened and tend to be repeated (see Chapter 5). Those that fail to produce the desired effects are weakened and will not be repeated when the drive is present once again.

In its original form, drive theory focused primarily on biological needs and the drives they produce. Soon, though, psychologists extended this model to other forms of behavior not so clearly linked to basic needs, such as drives for stimulation, status, achievement, power, and forming stable social relationships (e.g., Baumeister & Leary, 1995).

Drive theory persisted in psychology for several decades; indeed, it has not been totally discarded even today. However, most psychologists believe that this approach suffers from several major drawbacks. Contrary to what drive theory suggests, human beings often engage in actions that *increase* rather than reduce various drives. For example, people sometimes skip snacks when hungry in order to lose weight or to maximize their enjoyment of a special dinner. Similarly, many people watch or read erotic materials in order to increase their sexual excitement, even when they don't anticipate immediate sexual gratification. In view of such evidence, most psychologists now believe that drive theory, by itself, does not provide a full explanation of human motivation.

Web Link: *Reversal Theory*

**Drive Theory:** A theory of motivation suggesting that behavior is "pushed" from within by drives stemming from basic biological needs.

**Homeostasis:** A state of physiological balance within the body.

**Arousal Theory:** A theory of motivation suggesting that human beings seek an optimal level of arousal, not minimal levels of arousal.

**AROUSAL THEORY: SEEKING OPTIMUM ACTIVATION** When it became clear that people sometimes seek to increase rather than reduce existing drives, an alternative theory of motivation known as **arousal theory** was formulated (Geen, Beatty, & Arkin, 1984). This theory focuses on *arousal,* our general level of activation. Arousal varies throughout the day, from low levels during sleep to much higher ones when we are performing strenuous tasks or activities we find exciting. Arousal theory suggests that what we seek is not minimal levels of arousal, but rather *optimal arousal*—the level that is best suited to our personal characteristics and to whatever activity we are currently performing. So, for example, if you are knitting, whittling, or performing similar activities, a low level of arousal will be optimal and will be preferred. If you are competing in a sports event, a much higher one will be best.

Many studies offer at least indirect support for arousal theory. For example, there *is* often a close link between arousal and performance (Weiner, 1989). In fact, for many tasks, performance increases as arousal rises, up to some point; beyond that level, further increases in arousal actually reduce performance. However, it is often difficult to determine in advance just what level of arousal will be optimal for a given task or situation. In general, the more difficult the task, the lower the level of arousal at which reductions in performance begin to occur. This suggestion is known as the **Yerkes–Dodson law,** and it does seem to apply in many situations. However, factors other than task difficulty also seem to play a role. For instance, large individual differences exist with respect to preferred arousal level. At one extreme are persons who prefer and seek high levels of activation—people who like to sky dive or parachute from buildings (Zuckerman, 1990). At the other are persons who prefer much lower levels of arousal. So although arousal theory provides useful insights into the nature of motivation, the fact that we can't readily predict what will constitute an optimal level of arousal does limit its usefulness to a degree.

**EXPECTANCY THEORY: A COGNITIVE APPROACH** Why are you reading this book? Not, I'd guess, to reduce some biological need. Rather, you are probably reading it because doing so will help you to reach important goals: gaining useful and interesting knowledge, earning a high grade on the next exam, graduating from college. In short, your behavior is determined by your thoughts about future outcomes and about how your current actions can help you get wherever it is that you want to go in life. This basic point forms the basis for another major theory of motivation, **expectancy theory.**

This theory suggests that motivation is not primarily a matter of being pushed from within by various urges or drives; rather, it is more a question of being *pulled* from without by expectations of attaining desired outcomes. Such outcomes, known as **incentives,** can be almost anything we have learned to value—money, status, the approval of others, to name just a few. In other words, while drive theory focuses mainly on the factors that push (drive) us toward certain actions, expectancy theory focuses more on the outcomes we wish to obtain. Why do people engage in complex, effortful, or even painful behaviors such as working many hours on their jobs, studying long into the night, or performing exercises that are, at least initially, painful? Expectancy theory answers: Because they believe that doing so will yield the outcomes they wish to attain.

Expectancy theory has been applied to many aspects of human motivation, but perhaps it has found its most important applications as an explanation of *work motivation*—the tendency to expend energy and effort on one's job (Locke & Latham, 1990). Research findings in the field of *industrial/organizational psychology* indicate that people will work hard at their jobs only when they believe that doing so will improve their performance (known as *expectancy* in the theory), that good performance will be recognized and rewarded (known as *instrumentality* in the theory), and that the rewards provided will be ones they want (known as *valence*).

**GOAL-SETTING THEORY** Another theory of motivation that emphasizes the importance of cognitive factors rather than drives or arousal is known as *goal-setting theory,* and it can be illustrated by the following example. Suppose that you are studying for a big exam. Do you ever tell yourself, in advance, that you won't stop until you have read a certain number of pages, memorized some specific number of definitions, or solved a fixed number of problems? The chances are good that you do, because most people realize that they often accomplish more when they have a concrete goal than when they do not. This basic fact is central to **goal-setting theory** (e.g., Locke & Latham, 1990), which suggests that motivation can be strongly influenced by goals.

**Yerkes–Dodson Law:** The suggestion that the level of arousal beyond which performance begins to decline is a function of task difficulty.

**Expectancy Theory:** A theory of motivation suggesting that behavior is "pulled" by expectations of desirable outcomes.

**Incentives:** Rewards individuals seek to attain.

**Goal-Setting Theory:** The view that motivation can be strongly influenced by goals.

**Figure 10.4**
**Goal Setting: How Not to Do It**

As shown here, setting goals can actually backfire and *reduce* motivation if the persons involved are not committed to reaching them.

(*Source:* Reprinted with special permission of King Features Syndicate)

Actually, goal-setting theory did not begin as a theory. Rather, this was one of those cases in which an interesting finding occurred first, and then a theory was constructed to help explain it. The finding was simple but impressive: On a wide variety of tasks, people performed better when they were given specific goals than when they were simply told to "do your best" (e.g., Wood & Locke, 1990). The term "impressive" is appropriate, because people often did *much* better when working toward specific goals than when such goals were absent (see the **From Science to Practice** section below for a concrete example).

Additional findings, however, indicated that goal setting works best under certain conditions. It is most effective in boosting performance when the goals set are highly *specific* (people know just what they are trying to accomplish); the goals are *challenging* (meeting them requires considerable effort); but the goals are perceived as *attainable* (people believe they can actually reach them). Finally, goal setting is most successful when people receive feedback on their progress toward meeting the goals and when they are truly and deeply committed to reaching them. This last point is quite important: If goals are set by someone else and the people who are expected to meet these goals aren't committed to doing so, then goal setting can be totally ineffective; it may even backfire and produce effects such as those shown in Figure 10.4. When the required conditions *are* met, though, goal setting is a highly effective way of increasing motivation and performance (e.g., Mento, Locke, & Klein, 1992; Wright et al., 1994).

from SCIENCE to PRACTICE

## Using Goal Setting to Increase Occupational Safety—and Save Lives

That goal setting is an effective technique for increasing motivation—your own and that of others—is a well-established fact (e.g., Phillips & Gully, 1997). As a result, goal setting has been used to increase employees' performance in many businesses (e.g., Donovan & Radosevich, 1998). But goal setting has many other practical—and beneficial—uses, too. For instance, it has been used to increase employees' compliance with safety regulations, and so to reduce serious injuries. That goal setting can be highly effective in this respect is illustrated by the results of many studies (e.g., Hofmann & Morgeson, 1999), but one study conducted by Chokar and Wallin (1984) provides an especially clear example of such effects.

These researchers began by observing the extent to which employees in various departments of a large manufacturing plant complied with safety regulations—for instance, wore hard hats when these were required, cleaned up spills immediately, wore safety gear to protect their eyes and ears. They found that employees engaged in such safe behaviors only about 65 percent of the time.

The researchers then met with employees and established a clear goal: 95 percent compliance with safety regulations. This goal was highly specific; it was perceived as difficult but attainable; and it was chosen in discussions with employees, so that these persons were committed to it. As shown in Figure 10.5, the establishment of this goal had an immediate effect: Compliance with safety regulations soon rose to more than 80 percent. But this was still shy of the goal of 95 percent compliance. At this point, the researchers added another factor to their efforts to improve safety: They began posting large charts each week showing the performance of each department. With such visible feedback, safety behavior improved further and soon reached the 95 percent goal. The result? The frequency of accidents was significantly and sharply reduced.

These findings, and those of many other studies, suggest that goal setting is indeed a powerful tool for increasing motivation, and so for changing behavior. Moreover, once goals have been reached, performance tends to remain at the new, higher levels. Why? In part because this higher level of performance becomes the *norm*—the expected level of performance. So goal setting produces lasting beneficial effects that do not fade away over time. Rather, when used with skill and care, goal setting can be a powerful tool not simply for improving performance and profits, but for saving lives as well.

**Figure 10.5**
**Goal Setting, Feedback, and Safety on the Job**

When employees were committed to the goal of increasing compliance with safety regulations, their performance in this respect improved. When they also received feedback in the form of charts showing how well they were doing, performance improved still further.

(*Source:* Based on data from Chokar & Wallin, 1984.)

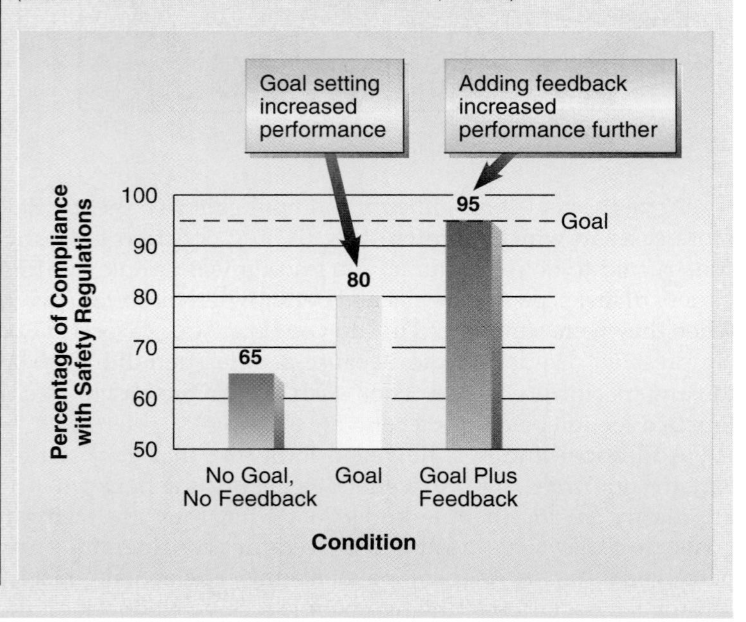


**MASLOW'S NEEDS HIERARCHY: RELATIONS AMONG MOTIVES** Suppose that you were very hungry and very cold; could you study effectively under these conditions? Probably not. Your hunger and feelings of cold would probably prevent you from focusing on the task of learning new materials, even if these were quite interesting to you. Observations like this suggest that human motives may exist in a *hierarchy,* so that we must satisfy those that are more basic before moving on to ones that are less linked to biological needs. This point is central to a theory of motivation proposed by Maslow (1970). Maslow places *physiological needs* such as those for food, water, oxygen, and sleep at the base of the **hierarchy of needs.** One step above these are *safety needs:* needs for feeling safe and secure in one's life. Above the safety needs are *social needs,* including needs to have friends, to be loved and appreciated, and to belong—to fit into a network of social relationships (e.g., Baumeister & Leary, 1995).

Maslow refers to physiological, safety, and social needs as *deficiency needs.* They are the basics and must be satisfied before higher levels of motivation, or *growth needs,* can emerge. Above the social needs in the hierarchy he proposes are *esteem needs,* the needs to develop self-respect, gain the approval of others, and achieve success. Ambition and the need for achievement, to which we'll return later, are closely linked to esteem needs. Finally, at the top of the hierarchy are *self-actualization needs.* These involve the need for self-fulfillment—the desire to become all that one is capable of being. Figure 10.6 provides an overview of Maslow's theory.

**Figure 10.6**
**Maslow's Needs Hierarchy**

According to Maslow (1970), needs exist in a hierarchy. Only when lower-order needs are satisfied can higher-order needs be activated and serve as sources of motivation.

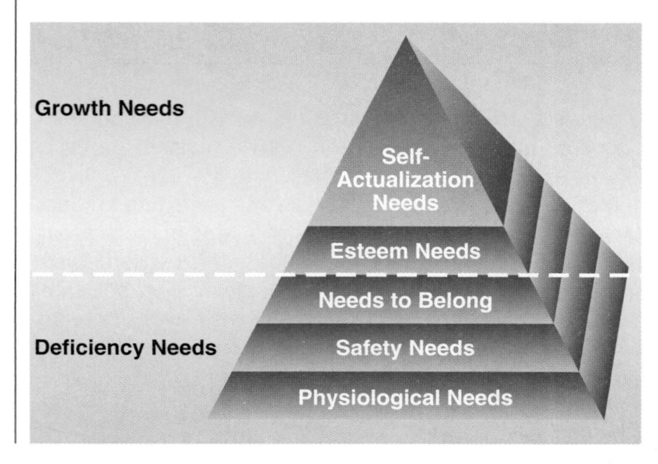

**TABLE 10.1**

**Theories of Motivation: An Overview**

The theories summarized here are among the ones that have been most influential in psychology.

| Theory of Motivation | Key Assumptions | Strengths/Weaknesses |
|---|---|---|
| Drive Theory | Biological needs produce unpleasant states of arousal which people seek to reduce. | People sometimes try to *increase* their drives, not reduce them. |
| Arousal Theory | Arousal (general level of activation) varies throughout the day and can motivate many forms of behavior; people seek *optimal* arousal, not low arousal. | Arousal is only one of many factors that influence motivated behavior. |
| Expectancy Theory | Behavior is "pulled" by expectations of desired outcomes rather than "pushed" from within by biologically based drives. | Focus on cognitive processes in motivation is consistent with modern psychology; widely used to explain *work motivation*. |
| Goal-Setting Theory | Setting specific and challenging but attainable goals can boost motivation and performance, especially when individuals are committed to reaching the goals and receive feedback on their progress. | Goal setting is highly effective in increasing performance, but mechanisms that explain these effects are still somewhat uncertain. |

Maslow's theory is intuitively appealing, but research designed to test it has yielded mixed results. Some results suggest that growth needs do come into play only after people have satisfied lower-level needs (e.g., Betz, 1982). But other findings indicate that people sometimes seek to satisfy higher-order needs even when ones lower in the hierarchy have not been met (e.g., Williams & Page, 1989). So the idea that needs arise and are satisfied in a particular order has not been confirmed. For this reason, Maslow's theory should be viewed mainly as an interesting but unverified framework for understanding motivation. (See Table 10.1 for an overview of the theories of motivation discussed in this section.)

**REVIEW QUESTIONS**

- According to drive theory, what is the basis for various motives?
- How does arousal theory explain motivation?
- According to expectancy theory, why do people engage in tasks requiring effort?
- Under what conditions will goal setting increase motivation and performance?
- What are the basic ideas behind Maslow's needs hierarchy theory?

**Hierarchy of Needs:** In Maslow's theory of motivation, an arrangement of needs from the most basic to those at the highest levels.

Audio 10.1: *Growing Problem of Overweight Americans*

## Hunger: Regulating Our Caloric Intake

A Greek proverb states: "You cannot reason with a hungry belly; it has no ears." This statement suggests—eloquently!—that **hunger motivation,** the urge to obtain and consume food, is a powerful one. If you have ever had the experience of going without food for even a single day, you know how strong feelings of hunger can be, and what a powerful source of motivation they can provide. But where do such feelings come from? And how do we manage to regulate the amount of food we consume? Why is it that for many persons body weight remains fairly stable over long periods of time, whereas for others the "battle of the bulge" is quickly lost? Let's see what psychologists have discovered about these and related questions.

**THE REGULATION OF EATING: A COMPLEX PROCESS** Consider the following fact: If you consume just twenty extra calories each day (less than the number in a single small carrot), you will gain about two pounds a year—twenty pounds in a decade. How do people keep caloric input and output closely balanced and so avoid such outcomes? One answer, of course, is that in many cases they don't: People do gain weight despite their best efforts to avoid doing so. Indeed, we are living in the midst of what seems to be an epidemic of obesity. Since the early 1960s the percentage of people in the United States who are obese has risen from 17 percent to 32.3 percent (some recent surveys suggest that this figure may be even higher); and over that period the proportion of people who are too overweight to fit into an airplane seat has more than tripled, to approximately 4 percent. We'll return shortly to several factors that may be contributing to these trends. Now, though, let's focus on the question of why, for most people, around the world, a balance *is* struck between needs and caloric intake so that weight remains relatively stable. What mechanisms contribute to this balance? As we saw in Chapter 2, part of the answer involves the *hypothalamus,* which plays a role in both eating and satiety (knowing when we've had enough) and also, through its links with portions of the cerebral cortex, in our ability to adapt to changing environmental conditions such as shifts in the foods available to us (Winn, 1995).

The regulation of eating involves much more than this, however. In fact, it seems to involve a complex system of regulatory mechanisms located not only in the hypothalamus but in the liver and other organs of the body as well. These systems contain special *detectors,* cells that respond to variations in the concentration of several nutrients in the blood. One type of detector responds to the amount of *glucose* or blood sugar. Other detectors respond to levels of *protein,* and especially to certain amino acids. This is why we feel full after eating a meal high in protein, such as a steak, even though the level of glucose in our blood remains relatively low. Finally, other detectors respond to *lipids,* or fats. Again, even if glucose levels are low, when the amount of lipids circulating in the blood is high, we do not feel hungry.

Complex as this may sound, it is still not the entire picture. In addition, eating and hunger are also strongly affected by the smell and taste of food and by feedback produced by chewing and swallowing. As we consume food, information from taste and smell receptors, and from muscles in our mouth and throat, provide feedback that helps us determine when we have eaten enough (e.g., Stellar, 1985).

The sight of food, too, is important. Foods that are attractive in appearance are hard to resist and may overwhelm the regulatory mechanisms described above, leading us to overeat. Cultural factors also play a major role in determining what, when, and how much we eat. Would you munch on fried grasshoppers? Sea urchin? Octopus cooked in its own ink? How about snake? Depending on the culture in which you have been raised, the thoughts of such items may induce hunger pangs or feelings of disgust (Rozin, 1996).

Cognitive factors, too, play a role. Recent findings reported by Rozin and his colleagues (1998) indicate that memories about when we last ate can influence whether we decide to eat and how much we consume at any given time, quite apart

**Hunger Motivation:** The motivation to obtain and consume food.

**Figure 10.7**
**Image Versus Reality**

Even as the emphasis on being slim has increased in many cultures, people have been gaining weight. The result? A growing gap between how people would like to be and how they actually are with respect to body weight.

from what internal cues from our bodies may be telling us. In this research, Rozin and his colleagues (1998) offered several meals in a row to two individuals who had suffered extensive bilateral damage to the hippocampus and amygdala—structures that, as we saw in Chapter 6, play a role in memory. As a result of their brain injuries, these persons could not remember recent events. Both individuals were offered a meal at lunchtime. A few minutes after eating it, they were offered a second meal; then, a few minutes after eating that one, they were offered yet a third meal. Both persons consumed the second meal, and one of them ate part of the third meal as well. Yet both rated their hunger as lower after consuming the first meal than before it. Why, then, did they eat again? Apparently because they could not remember that they had just eaten! Findings such as these underscore the main point I wish to make: Many mechanisms operating together influence hunger motivation and eating.

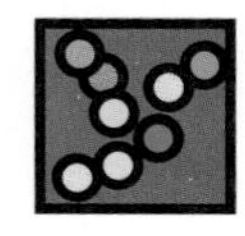

**FACTORS IN WEIGHT GAIN: WHY MANY PERSONS EXPERIENCE DIFFICULTY IN THE LONG-TERM REGULATION OF BODY WEIGHT** There can be little doubt that thin is in, at least in most Western cultures. Every year, consumers in many countries spend huge sums on books and other products related to weight loss. Despite these efforts, however, many people can't seem to prevent their weight from increasing. As a result, there is an increasing gap between people's desired weight (most want to be slim) and their actual weight (see Figure 10.7). What factors are responsible for this trend? Research findings point to several.

First, part of the problem involves the effects of learning. Many people acquire eating habits that are very likely to generate excess pounds. They learn to prefer high-calorie meals that are rich in protein and fats—Big Macs and Whoppers, for instance. Further, they learn to associate the act of eating with many different contexts and situations. If you feel a strong urge to snack every time you sit down in front of the television set or movie screen, you already know about such effects. The desire to eat can be classically conditioned (see Chapter 5); cues associated with eating when we are hungry can acquire the capacity to prompt eating when we are *not* hungry.

Second, genetic factors interact with these changes in diet and can, for many persons, intensify them. Consider the situation faced by our early ancestors: periods of plenty alternated with periods of famine. Under these conditions, people who were efficient at storing excess calories as fat during times of plenty gained an important advantage: These individuals were more likely to survive during famines and to have children. As a result, almost all of us living today have some

**Figure 10.8**
**The Pima: A Culture in the Grip of an Obesity Epidemic**

Because the Pima (a Native American group who live in Arizona) once faced harsh environmental conditions, only those who could gain weight readily in times of plenty survived. As a result, the Pima, who now eat a normal North American diet, are experiencing an epidemic of obesity that seriously threatens their health.

tendency to gain weight when we overeat. However, genetic factors determine the strength of this tendency. For some groups the tendency is so strong that it poses a severe threat to their health. The Pima, a Native American group living in Arizona, are a prime example of such effects.

Because the Pima lived for many centuries in a harsh desert environment, they apparently possess a powerful genetically inherited tendency to gain weight readily. But in recent decades they have shifted from their traditional diet, consisting mainly of vegetables and grain, to the "normal" North American diet, which is high in fat and fast foods. As a result, the Pima are currently suffering an epidemic of obesity (Gladwell, 1998). A high proportion of adults are seriously overweight (see Figure 10.8), and the rate of diabetes, a disease closely linked with obesity, is fully *eight times the national average:* Fifty percent of the Pima suffer from this disease. Many adults weigh more than 500 pounds, and even many children as young as six or seven years old are already obese. That these disturbing effects stem from an interaction between environmental and genetic factors is suggested by the fact that other Pima living in Mexico, who have stuck to their traditional diet, are quite slim and show no signs of growing heavier. Findings such as these suggest that genetic factors do indeed play an important role in weight regulation—especially in combination with environmental variables.

Speaking of environmental factors, it's important to note that in recent years, the size of portions of many foods has increased dramatically. When I was a teenager, a Coke or Pepsi was eight ounces; now, one-liter bottles (about a quart!) are being offered as a single serving. Similarly, the original McDonald's hamburgers were small and thin and contained about 200 calories; now, most people purchase double cheeseburgers or Big Macs containing 400 or 500 calories. Since people tend to eat their entire portion of food, no matter how big it is, this, too, may be a factor in the rising rate of obesity.

Yet another factor that seems to contribute to unwanted weight gain involves an intriguing difference between people who are obese and those who are not. Several studies indicate that overweight persons respond more strongly to external cues relating to food (Rodin & Slochower, 1976). They report feeling hungrier in the presence of food-related cues—the sight or smell of foods—than do persons of normal weight, and they find it harder to resist eating when tasty foods are available (Rodin, 1984). And, of course, modern societies expose such individuals to many food cues all day long.

One final factor, and perhaps the most discouraging of all, involves our own bodies' reaction to weight gain. Common sense might suggest that when we gained weight, internal mechanisms might spring into action to return us to our initial healthy weight. In fact, the opposite seems to be true. Such mechanisms do exist, and normally serve to regulate our weight within a specific range (our current *set point*). Unfortunately, growing evidence suggests that once we gain a significant amount of weight, our sensitivity to *leptin* (a chemical produced by our own bodies that reduces appetite and speeds metabolism) actually *decreases.* The result: Once we start to gain weight, it becomes harder and harder to stop (Gladwell, 1998). The process *can* be halted if we lose weight and maintain the weight loss for several years; but this requires more willpower and discipline than many people seem to possess.

Taking all these factors together, it is not surprising that many persons experience difficulties in regulating their own weight over the long term. There are simply too many variables or conditions that, acting together, overwhelm the mechanisms that establish and maintain a balance between our internal needs and the food we consume. I don't want to end on a pessimistic note, however, so I should quickly emphasize that there *are* several techniques that can help. These are summarized in the **Making Psychology Part of Your Life** section at the end of this chapter. If your own weight has increased, please read this section carefully: The health you protect will be your own! (We'll examine two serious eating disorders—*anorexia nervosa,* in which individuals starve themselves and lose dangerous amounts of weight, and *bulimia,* a condition involving repeated binging and purging—in Chapter 14.)

**REVIEW QUESTIONS**

- What factors play a role in the regulation of eating?
- What factors override this regulatory system, causing many people to fail to maintain a stable weight?

**Food for Thought**

Do you think that the percentage of people who are overweight will continue to rise in the future? What could reverse this trend?

## Sexual Motivation: The Most Intimate Motive

Audio 10.2: *Sexual Behavior and Health*

Suppose that voyagers from another planet arrived on Earth and visited large cities in many different countries. What would they see? Among other things, many advertisements designed to attract attention through the use of sex-related images (see Figure 10.9 on page 382). In fact, so common are such displays that the alien visitors might quickly conclude that human beings are obsessed with sex. Even though advertisements may well exaggerate our interest in sex, it is clear that **sexual motivation**—our motivation to engage in sexual activity—is a powerful one. Let's see what psychologists have discovered about this topic.

**Sexual Motivation:** Motivation to engage in various forms of sexual activity.

**Gonads:** The primary sex glands.

**HORMONES AND SEXUAL BEHAVIOR** As we saw in Chapter 9, the onset of puberty involves rapid increases in the activity of the sex glands, or **gonads.** The hormones produced by these glands have many effects on the body, and in many species they strongly affect sexual motivation. In fact, sex hormones exert what are usually termed *activation effects*—in their presence sexual behavior occurs, while in their absence sexual behavior does not occur or takes place with very low frequency.

**Figure 10.9**
**Sex Sells**

Judging from ads in magazines and on billboards—and virtually everywhere else!—sexual motivation is very powerful in human beings.

For example, in rats, the species in which the link between sex hormones and sexual behavior has been most extensively studied, females show receptivity to males only at times during their menstrual cycle when concentrations of certain sex hormones are high. Once these levels drop—regardless of whether mating has resulted in fertilization—the females are no longer receptive. Additional evidence for a link between sex hormones and mating is also provided by the fact that in many species removal of the ovaries totally eliminates female sexual receptivity to males. Removal of the testes in males produces similar though somewhat less clear-cut results. In many species, then, hormones produced by the gonads play a key role in sexual motivation (Rissman, 1995).

Human beings, and to some degree other primates, are an exception to this general pattern. Although research findings indicate that many women report rises in sexual desire at certain times over the course of their menstrual cycle, these changes do *not* occur at times when hormones such as estrogen are at peak levels (Zillmann, Schweitzer, & Mundorf, 1994). On the contrary, peaks of sexual desire or interest seem to occur when such hormones are at relatively low levels. Further, many women continue to engage in and enjoy sexual relations after menopause, when the hormonal output of their ovaries drops sharply. And in men, there is little evidence of a clear link between sexual responsiveness and blood levels of sex hormones such as testosterone (Byrne, 1982).

This is not to say, however, that sex hormones play no role in human sexual motivation. Among males, there is some evidence that testosterone levels are associated with differences in sexual arousal. For example, men with high levels of testosterone become aroused more quickly by erotic films than those with relatively low levels of this hormone (Lange et al., 1980). In general, though, the link between sex hormones and sexual motivation appears to be far less clear-cut and less compelling for human beings than is true for many other species.

Other chemical substances within the body, however, may play a role. Recent findings suggest that when human beings are sexually attracted to another person, their brain produces increased amounts of several substances chemically related to *amphetamines*. As you may recall from Chapter 4, amphetamines are stimulants, and the increased production of amphetaminelike substances such as phenylethylamine (PEA) may account for the fact that many people describe strong sexual attraction—the first stage in falling in love—as a feeling that "sweeps them away." As one researcher puts it, "love is a natural high" (Walsh, 1993).

In sum, while sex hormones are not as clearly linked to sexual motivation in humans as in other species, there is some evidence that other substances produced by our bodies do play a role in such motivation, and even in romantic love. Thus, there does appear to be a biochemical side to love, but we are only just beginning to understand it.

**HUMAN SEXUAL BEHAVIOR: SOME BASIC FACTS** Until the 1960s the only source of scientific information about human sexual motivation was surveys: Large samples of individuals were asked to report on their sexual behavior and experiences (e.g., Kinsey, Pomeroy, & Martin, 1984; Kinsey et al., 1953). Results were varied, but such surveys generally pointed to the conclusion that where sexual behavior is concerned, individual differences are enormous. Some people reported little or no interest in sex and indicated that they had been celibate for years; at the other extreme, some reported engaging in sexual relations with a large number of partners and having three or more orgasms every day.

Starting in the 1960s, however, another source of information about human sexual motivation became available: direct and systematic observation of actual sexual activities. The first and still most famous project of this kind was conducted by Masters and Johnson in the mid-1960s (Masters & Johnson, 1966). These researchers observed and recorded the reactions of several hundred volunteers of both sexes as they engaged in sexual intercourse or masturbation. More than ten thousand cycles of arousal and satisfaction were studied. The results yielded important insights into the nature of human sexuality. Perhaps the clearest finding was that both males and females move through four distinct phases during sexual behavior. The *excitement phase* involves physiological changes indicative of growing sexual excitement (e.g., the penis and clitoris become enlarged, vaginal lubrication increases). In the *plateau phase* the size of the penis increases still further, and the outer third of the vagina becomes engorged with blood, reducing its diameter. The *orgasmic phase* consists of several contractions of the muscles surrounding the genitals, along with intense sensations of pleasure (the pattern of contractions, including their timing and length, is virtually identical in females and males). In the *resolution phase*, in males, orgasm is followed by a reduction in sexual and physiological arousal. Among females, in contrast, two distinct patterns are possible: They too may experience a reduction in sexual and physiological arousal; or, if stimulation continues, women may experience additional orgasms.

The basic pattern just described seems to apply to all human beings. However, practically everything else varies from one society to another. Different cultures have widely different standards about such matters as (1) the age at which sexual behavior should begin, (2) the frequency with which it should occur, (3) physical characteristics considered attractive or sexy, (4) the particular positions and practices that are acceptable, (5) the proper time and setting for sexual relations, (6) the persons who are appropriate partners, and (7) the number of partners individuals should have at one time or in succession. So, to repeat: Where human sexuality is concerned, *variability* is definitely the central theme.

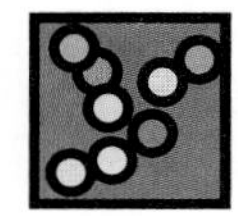

**HUMAN SEXUAL BEHAVIOR: AN EVOLUTIONARY PERSPECTIVE ON MATING STRATEGIES** Consider the following two quotations: "I don't think I was constructed to be monogamous. I don't think it's the nature of *any* man to be monogamous" (Marlon Brando, 1994); "To sleep around is absolutely wrong for a woman; it's degrading and it completely ruins her personality" (Barbara Cartland, British novelist, 1978). Together, these two comments suggest that women and men show contrasting patterns of sexual behavior, at least where choosing potential mates is concerned. Most men, according to Brando and many other observers, seek variety: They want to have sex with as many women as possible. Women, on the other hand, are more selective: They don't necessarily seek many different lovers but tend to prefer quality to quantity. Are these suggestions accurate? To a degree, they are. For instance, when asked how long they would have to know someone before consenting to sexual relations with them, men on average name much shorter periods of time than women (Buss & Schmitt, 1993). Similarly, as shown in Figure 10.10 on page 384, men generally indicate that they would like to have more sexual partners in the future than would women (Buss & Schmitt, 1993). In short, there seem to be some differences between males and females where short-term sexual strategies are concerned (Buss, 1999). Why is this the case?

Evolutionary psychology offers the following answer. By having sex with many different women, men can father a large number of children—many more than if

**Figure 10.10**
**Gender Differences In Short-Term Mating Strategies**

As shown by this graph, males indicate that they would like to have more sexual partners than would females. Evolutionary psychology offers intriguing explanations for why this may be so. (*Source:* Buss & Schmitt, 1993.)

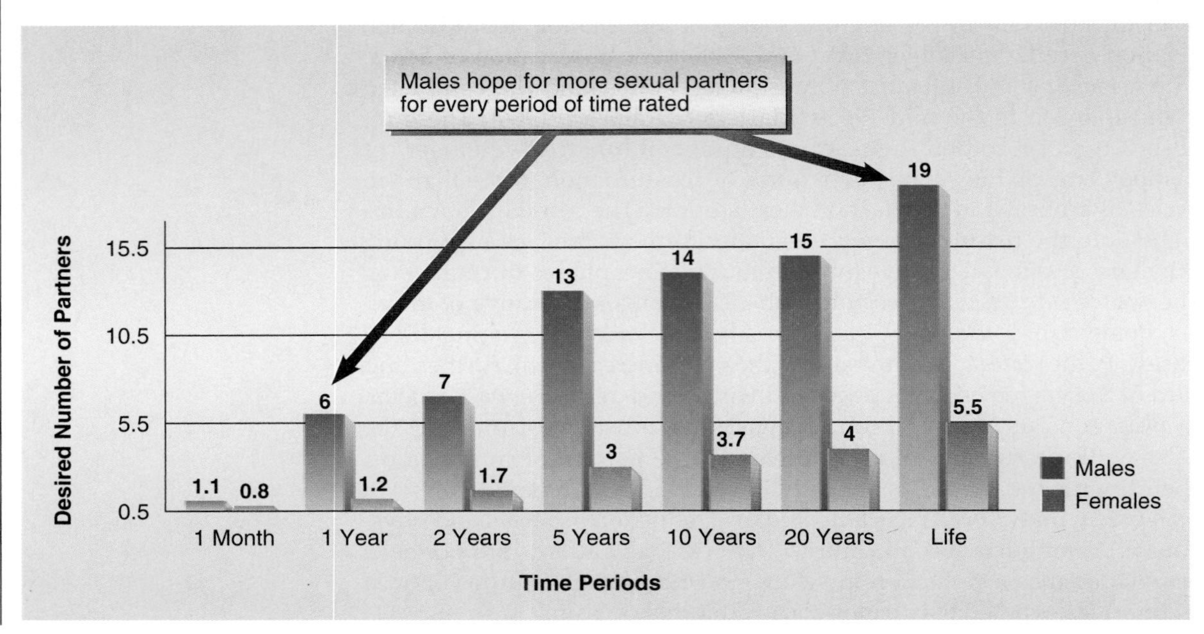


they had sex with only one woman. In contrast, no matter how many lovers a woman has, she can only have one pregnancy at a time. Moreover, the investment in having a child is much greater for women than men: Women are the ones who are pregnant for nine months and must care for the child after it is born. Evolutionary psychology suggests that because of these facts, natural selection has tended to produce a stronger preference for sexual variety among males than among females. The reasoning behind this suggestion is as follows. Men who prefer many different mates produce more offspring than men with a weaker preference for sexual variety. As a result, a preference for variety has become widespread among males. In contrast, women who prefer sexual variety do not necessarily produce more children, so a preference for sexual variety is not as strongly favored by natural selection.

It is also clear, though, that men could never have evolved a strong desire for sexual variety if no women ever showed an interest in such behavior. After all, making love requires two partners. Throughout the evolution of our species, therefore, *some* women, at least, must have been interested in variety, too. Why would this be the case? Evolutionary psychology suggests explanations such as these: By having multiple partners, women could gain valuable resources from them (e.g., food, gifts); alternatively, by having many lovers a woman could perfect her love-making skills and so, perhaps, replace her current mate with a more desirable one. As noted by Buss (1999), there is some support for both of these hypotheses.

Biological evidence also suggests that some women have sought variety in their sexual partners. One such piece of evidence is the fact that human sperm are not all alike. Most are what can be described as "egg getters"—they race toward the egg to fertilize it. But other sperm have a different shape and can be described as "blockers"—their function seems to be that of blocking the sperm of other men. There would be no need for such sperm if all females were monogamous; so the fact that these "blockers" exist suggests that in the past, as now, some women did indeed have more than one lover at a time (Baker & Bellis, 1995). Interestingly, the proportion of such "blocker" sperm rises when a man has been separated from his mate for a long period of time, during which perhaps the woman has had other lovers (Baker & Bellis, 1995).

In sum, differences between males and females do seem to exist where mating strategies are concerned: In general, men seek variety to a greater degree than women. However, this difference, like many other differences between men and women, is often exaggerated by literature, films, and folklore; it may not be as large or as universal as many people seem to believe.

**Heterosexual** (Sexual Orientation): A sexual orientation in which individuals prefer sexual relations with members of the other sex.

**Bisexual:** Motivated to engage in sexual relations with members of both sexes.

**Homosexual** (Sexual Orientation): A sexual orientation in which individuals prefer sexual relations with members of their own sex.

**HUMAN SEXUAL BEHAVIOR: WHAT'S AROUSING AND WHY** Clearly, sexual motivation plays an important role in human behavior. But what, precisely, stimulates sexual arousal? In certain respects, the same events or stimuli that produce arousal in other species: direct physical contact, in the form of various kinds of touching and foreplay. In addition, however, human beings can also be sexually aroused by real or imagined erotic stimuli and images (Leitenberg & Henning, 1995). Because there is no evidence that other species respond in these ways, our highly developed cognitive capacities seem to play an important role in human sexual motivation. In many cases, in fact, they may play the *most* important role in human sexual arousal. As one famous researcher put it, "The mind is the only true erogenous zone" (D. Byrne, personal communication, 1992).

**SEXUAL ORIENTATION** A large majority of human beings are exclusively **heterosexual**—they engage in sexual relations only with members of the opposite sex. Some people, however, are **bisexual**—they seek partners of their own as well as the other sex; and still others are exclusively **homosexual,** seeking partners only of their own sex (Laumann et al., 1994). What factors influence or determine sexual orientation? In other words, why are some persons exclusively homosexual while most others are exclusively heterosexual? This is a very complex question and one to which no one, psychologists included, can yet offer a complete answer. Initially, emphasis was on environmental factors. For example, psychodynamic theory (see Chapter 15) suggested that people became homosexual as a result of having an overprotective mother and a distant, ineffectual father. Other views emphasized factors ranging from separation from members of the opposite sex during childhood (e.g., attending all-boy or all-girl schools) to sexual abuse by parents or other adults. Decades of research have failed to yield clear support for *any* of these suggestions (Storms, 1983). Indeed, large-scale studies of thousands of homosexuals have failed to find any consistent differences between them and heterosexuals in terms of early life experiences.

On the other hand, there is growing evidence for the role of genetic and other biological factors in homosexuality. For example, Green (1987) followed fourty-four extremely "feminine"-acting boys for fifteen years—from early childhood until they were young adults. Fully three-fourths of the boys turned out to be homosexual or bisexual. In contrast, only one boy from a group of typically "masculine" boys was homosexual. Moreover, efforts by parents or professionals (psychologists, psychiatrists) to alter the behavior of the feminine boys made little or no difference. Such findings point to the possibility that some individuals have a biological predisposition toward homosexuality or bisexuality.

Other findings indicate that there may be subtle differences between the brains of heterosexual and homosexual individuals. For instance, the *anterior commissure,* a bundle of nerve fibers that allows communication between the two hemispheres of the brain, is larger in homosexual men than in heterosexual men or women (Allen & Gorski, 1992). Similarly, the hypothalamus is smaller in homosexual men than in heterosexual men (LeVay, 1991). Twin studies, too, point to the role of genetic and biological factors in homosexuality. If one identical twin is homosexual, there is a greater than 50 percent chance that the other twin, too, will be homosexual. Among

**Aggressive Motivation:** The desire to harm or injure others in some manner.

**Aggression:** Behavior directed toward the goal of harming another living being that wishes to avoid such treatment.

fraternal twins this figure drops to only 22 percent (Bailey & Pillard, 1991). Finally, homosexuals differ from heterosexual men in some cognitive abilities, falling in between heterosexual men and heterosexual women in their performance on tests of visual/spatial ability (Witelson, 1991).

But how, precisely, do genetic and biological factors shape sexual orientation? Perhaps, as Bem (1996) suggests, they contribute to differences in temperament, which in turn cause individuals to prefer gender-typical or gender-atypical activities and friends. These preferences then lead the children to experience attraction to whichever gender differs from themselves in terms of such behavior. So boys who show behavior defined by their society as feminine find males attractive, and girls who show behavior defined as masculine find females attractive. This is only one possibility, however, and at present there is no conclusive evidence on precisely how genetic factors influence sexual preference. It does seem clear, though, that sexual orientation is not simply a matter of preference or "free will"; rather, it may stem, at least in part, from biological and genetic factors that are not directly under individuals' control and which operate outside their conscious awareness.

**REVIEW QUESTIONS**

- What role do hormones play in human sexual motivation?
- What are the major phases of sexual activity?
- What is a key difference between human beings and other species with respect to sexual arousal?
- According to evolutionary psychology, why do males and females differ with respect to short-term mating strategies?
- What factors appear to play a role in determining sexual orientation?

**Figure 10.11**
**Aggressive Motivation: Often, the Results Are Tragic**

Human beings often have powerful desires to harm others; such aggressive motivation can produce truly tragic consequences.

## Aggressive Motivation: The Most Dangerous Motive

Atrocities in Kosovo, mass murder in high schools, alarming rates of child abuse, a seemingly rising tide of workplace violence—the alarming frequency of such events suggests that **aggressive motivation,** or the desire to inflict harm on others, plays an all too common role in human behavior (see Figure 10.11). While human beings don't always express aggressive motivation overtly (often, they simply fantasize about such behavior), they often do engage in various forms of **aggression** against others—efforts to harm them in some manner (Baron & Richardson, 1994). Here, we'll examine some contrasting perspectives concerning the origins of aggression, and some of the factors that influence its occurrence.

**THE ROOTS OF AGGRESSION: INNATE OR LEARNED?** Is aggression an inherited human tendency? After witnessing the horrible carnage of World War I, Freud concluded that human beings possess a powerful built-in tendency to harm others. While this view has been shared by many other scientists—for example, Konrad Lorenz, the famous *ethologist*—it is not widely accepted by psychologists at the present time (e.g., Anderson, Anderson, & Deuser, 1996; Berkowitz, 1993). Most believe that aggression is elicited by a wide range of external events and stimuli. In other words, it is often "pulled" from without rather than "pushed" or driven from within by irresistible, perhaps inherited, tendencies. Why do psychologists hold this view? Partly because several findings argue strongly against the existence of universal, innate human tendencies toward aggression. Perhaps the most telling of these is the finding that rates of violent crime differ tremendously in different cultures. For instance, in many developed countries rates of violent crime are much lower than those reported in the United States, whereas in some developing nations rates are even higher (Kutchinsky, 1992; Osterman et al., 1994). In fact, murder rates are more than one hundred times higher in some countries than in others (Scott, 1992). These huge differences in the incidence of aggression suggest that such behavior is strongly influenced by social and cultural factors, and that even if it stems in part from innate tendencies, these are less important than social conditions and other factors. This is not to imply that biological or genetic factors play no role in human aggression; on the contrary, they probably do—see the discussion of hormonal influences later in this section (e.g., Buss & Shackelford, 1997). But in the case of human beings, most experts agree that aggression is influenced more strongly by a wide range of situational factors that evoke its occurrence and shape its form and targets than by inherited tendencies or mechanisms.

**Frustration:** The blocking of ongoing, goal-directed behavior.

**Workplace Violence:** Violent outbursts in which employees attack and even kill other persons with whom they work.

If aggression does not stem primarily from inherited tendencies, the next question is obvious: What factors *do* influence its occurrence? Decades of careful research have yielded increasingly clear answers (e.g., Geen & Donnerstein, 1998). While it would be impossible to summarize the results of all this research here, we can at least take a brief look at several factors that have been found to play an important role in eliciting overt aggression.

**SOCIAL FACTORS** Try to remember the last time you lost your temper. What made you blow your cool? The chances are good that your aggressive motivation stemmed from the actions of another person. For instance, the other person may have done something that blocked or thwarted you from reaching your goals—in other words, this person may have *frustrated* you. For many years psychologists viewed **frustration** as *the* major cause of aggression (Dollard et al., 1939). Research findings indicate, however, that in fact frustration is just one of many different social causes of aggression, and perhaps not the strongest one. First, when exposed to severe frustration, many people become depressed rather than aggressive (e.g., Berkowitz, 1989). Thus, contrary to one famous view known as the *frustration–aggression hypothesis*, frustration does not always produce aggression. Second, aggression does not always stem from frustration; often, individuals aggress against others because it is part of their role or job, *not* because they are feeling frustrated (see Figure 10.12).

**Figure 10.12**
**Aggression: Clearly, It Does Not Always Stem from Frustration**

As suggested by this cartoon, individuals often aggress against others when they are *not* frustrated—for example, because it is their job or role to do so.

(*Source:* The Far Side. © 1980 Farworks, Inc. Used by permission. All rights reserved.)

Now over here, Mom and Dad, is what we call "The Rack," and I'll show you how it works.

So, does frustration play any role in aggression? The answer seems to be yes. When individuals feel that their interests have been thwarted, *and* that such thwarting is unfair, frustration can indeed be a powerful cause of aggression. In fact, feelings of injustice have recently been found to play an important role in instances of **workplace violence**—violent outbursts in which employees attack and even kill other persons with whom they work (e.g., Baron, Neuman, & Geddes, 1999; Folger & Baron, 1996).

Another social factor that often plays a role in aggression is direct provocation from another person. Verbal insults or physical actions interpreted as aggressive in nature often lead the party on the receiving end to reciprocate, with the result that a powerful spiral of aggression—counter-aggression can develop (e.g., Ohbuchi & Ogura, 1984).

Finally, I should note that a large body of evidence indicates that exposure to *violence in the media*—television, movies, and so on—has been found to increase aggression on the part of viewers (e.g., Huesmann, 1994). Such results have been obtained in literally hundreds of studies, so this is one of the most consistent findings of research on aggression. Apparently, when viewers witness scenes in which characters assault one another, they can acquire new and often ingenious ways of assaulting others. Further, they learn that such actions are an appropriate response to provocation or frustration—and that, moreover, aggression often succeeds. In addition, they may experience reductions in their own restraints against such behavior. Perhaps most alarming of all, exposure to a steady diet of media violence can lead individuals to become *desensitized* to the harm produced by violence: Scenes in which others are harmed no longer have any emotional impact on them. As you can see, the implications of such findings are frightening for any society in which large numbers of people are regularly exposed to scenes of violence in films and on television.

If exposure to violence in the mass media has harmful effects on society, why, you may be wondering, is there so much of it? One answer is that the advertisers who pay for television programs believe that violence sells—that violence is one way to increase audience size. Although this may be true, findings reported by Bushman (1998) also suggest that television violence may actually backfire from the point of view of increasing the sales of products advertised on the shows. Bushman found that audiences who watch violent programs are significantly *less* likely to remember the content of commercials shown during these programs than audiences who watch nonviolent programs. Apparently, violent images on the television screen trigger memories of other violent scenes, and such thoughts distract viewers from paying attention to commercials. These findings suggest that sponsoring violent television programs is not just questionable from a moral point of view; it may also make little economic sense for sponsors!

Audio 10.3: *High Temperatures and Aggression*

**ENVIRONMENTAL FACTORS** While social factors seem to be among the most important causes of aggression, I should note that such behavior sometimes stems from other causes as well. Especially important here are any conditions in the physical environment that cause individuals to experience discomfort—for instance, uncomfortably high temperatures (e.g., Anderson, Deuser, & DeNeve, 1995; Cohn & Rotton, 1997) disagreeable crowding, or unpleasant, irritating noise (e.g., Baron, 1994). The negative feelings produced by such conditions can increase aggressive motivation in several ways. First, they may trigger aggression directly: When we feel bad—whatever the cause—we tend to lash out against others (e.g., Berkowitz, 1993). Alternatively, such unpleasant feelings may trigger negative thoughts and memories, or may lead us to attribute others' actions to hostile intentions even when this is not the case. In other words, unpleasant feelings may lead us to think in ways that tend to activate aggressive motives (e.g., Anderson, Anderson, & Deuser, 1996). Whatever the precise mechanism involved, research findings do offer strong support for the view that environmental conditions that we find uncomfortable or unpleasant can sometimes increase our tendencies to aggress—something to keep firmly in mind the next time you are caught in traffic on a sweltering day and feel your temper beginning to fray around the edges! (For information on how psychologists study aggression, please see the **Research Methods** section on page 389.)

**HORMONAL INFLUENCES** Finally, some recent findings suggest that sex hormones, especially the male sex hormone *testosterone,* may play a role in aggression. Drugs that reduce testosterone levels in violent human males seem to reduce their aggression; and research on prisoners indicates that testosterone levels tend to be higher in those who have committed unprovoked violent crimes than among those who have committed nonviolent crimes (Dabbs, 1992; Dabbs et al., 1995). Also, testosterone levels seem to be related not only to aggression but to prosocial (helpful) behaviors. One study demonstrating such relationships was conducted by Harris and her colleagues (1996). Participants completed questionnaires that measured their tendencies to behave aggressively and also to behave in a helpful, nurturant manner in a wide range of situations (Harris et al., 1996). Two measures of participants' level of testosterone were also obtained. Results indicated for both males and females, the higher the testosterone levels, the higher the tendency to engage in aggression and the lower the tendency to engage in helpful, nurturant behaviors reported by participants. Although these findings were based on correlations, further analyses indicated that the relationship between testosterone and aggression was a direct one: Increments in testosterone appeared to cause increased tendencies to aggress.

**Aggression Machine:** A device used in the laboratory study of human aggression.

In sum, aggressive motivation, and the overt aggression it produces, stem from many different factors (e.g., Baron & Richardson, 1994). Identifying these factors, of course, is an essential first step toward the goal of reducing the frequency of human violence. However, the number of variables involved does suggest that achieving this objective will not be easy.

## Research Methods: How Psychologists Study Aggression

Whether we like it or not, aggression is an important part of the human experience. At one time or another, almost everyone experiences anger and the intense desire to aggress against others. It is not surprising, then, that psychologists have studied aggression for many years. But *how,* precisely, can such behavior be investigated? As you can readily see, researchers who want to study human aggression face a dilemma: On the one hand, they wish to examine a form of behavior that is, by definition, potentially dangerous. On the other, they cannot expose research participants to the risk of harm. How can this predicament be resolved? One answer—which remains somewhat controversial even today—emerged during the 1960s: It involves placing research participants in a situation where they are told that they can harm another person in some manner although in fact they cannot.

In actual practice, this approach, which was first developed by Arnold Buss (1961), involved the following procedures. Research participants (all men in Buss's initial studies) were told that they were participating, along with another person, in a study dealing with the effects of punishment on learning. One participant would serve as a *teacher,* the other as a *learner.* The teacher would present various materials to the learner, and on occasions when the learner made a correct response, the learner would reward this person by flashing a light indicating "Correct." When the learner made an error, however, the teacher would deliver an electric shock as punishment for this mistake. These shocks would be delivered by means of a device like the one shown in Figure 10.13, which soon came to be known as the **aggression machine.** Participants were told that the higher the number of the button they pushed, the stronger the shock to the learner, and that the longer they held it down, the longer this pulse would last.

That is what participants were told. In reality, however, the "learner" was an assistant working with the researcher, and this person *never received any electric shocks,* no matter

**Figure 10.13**
**The Aggression Machine**

The device shown here has been used to study aggression under safe laboratory conditions. Participants are told that they can deliver shocks (or other unpleasant stimuli such as heat) to another person by pushing numbered buttons on the machine. The higher the number of the button pushed, the stronger the "shock." In fact, however, there is no victim, and no shocks (or heat) are ever delivered.

what the participants did. During the course of the session, the learner made many prearranged errors. On each of these occasions, then, participants faced a choice: They could inform the learner of his error by choosing the mildest shock button on the aggression machine—a shock so weak that, as the experimenter explained, "almost no one can even feel it." Or they could choose higher-numbered buttons that, presumably, delivered very intense shocks. (Participants received a fairly mild but slightly unpleasant sample shock from button number 3; given the strength of this shock, those from buttons 8, 9, and 10 would be strong indeed.) On each occasion when the learner made an error, the participants' choice was theirs: They could aggress or not, as they wished.

What did they do? As you can guess, this depended very much on other conditions in the study. For instance, if the accomplice had acted in a rude or condescending manner toward participants, they tended to choose higher-numbered shocks than if this person had behaved in a courteous and pleasant manner. Similarly, if the study took place under uncomfortably hot temperatures, participants sometimes tended to choose higher-numbered buttons. I could go on, but by now you probably get the picture: The *aggression machine* appeared to be a tool that could be used to investigate the potential effects of many different variables on aggression.

Now for a key question: Did these procedures really measure human aggression? This question has never been totally resolved, but several lines of evidence suggest that Buss's procedures—or ones similar to them (e.g., participants are told they can deliver heat or even hot sauce [!] to the supposed victim)—do indeed provide a useful measure of human aggression. First, many studies have found that people with a prior history of real aggressive behavior—for instance, violent criminals—chose stronger shocks than persons without such a history (e.g., Cherek et al., 1996; Gully & Dengerink, 1983; Wolfe & Baron, 1971). Second, variables found to influence aggression in real-life settings have also been found to influence aggression in laboratory studies using the procedures devised by Buss and others (e.g., Taylor, 1967). For instance, Anderson and Bushman (Anderson & Bushman, 1997; Anderson, Lindsay, & Bushman, 1999) have found that aggression in laboratory studies is strongly increased by such factors as direct provocation, exposure to media violence, high temperatures, and the consumption of alcohol—variables that have also been found to influence aggression outside the laboratory.

Together, such findings seem to indicate that the method devised by Buss provides one useful means for studying aggression—or, at least, aggressive intent, which is the heart of aggressive motivation. Certainly this method is far from perfect: Some participants probably don't really believe that they can deliver painful stimuli to the victim. However, if nothing else, Buss's procedures gave psychologists a new tool for studying aggression; and this tool led researchers to investigate many variables that had previously been ignored—everything from the impact of uncomfortable heat (the "long hot summer" effect) through the effects of exposure to erotic materials (e.g., Anderson, Anderson, & Deuser, 1996; Baron & Richardson, 1994). In this respect, these procedures did contribute to our understanding of an important form of behavior. And that, of course, is the central task of modern psychology.

**REVIEW QUESTIONS**

- Why do psychologists generally reject the view that aggression stems from innate tendencies?
- What social factors facilitate aggression?
- What environmental factors contribute to aggression?
- What is the aggression machine, and how is it used to study aggression?

**Food for Thought**

Do you think that studying aggression in the laboratory makes sense? Would it be better to study such behavior in natural environments?

## Achievement Motivation: The Desire to Excel

**Achievement Motivation:** The desire to accomplish difficult tasks and to meet standards of excellence.

Hunger, sex, aggression—these are motives we share with many other forms of life. There are some motives, however, that appear to be unique to our own species. In this section we'll focus on one such motive: **achievement motivation** (often termed *need for achievement*), or the desire to accomplish difficult tasks and to excel.

That individuals differ greatly in the desire for achievement is obvious. For some persons, accomplishing difficult tasks and meeting high standards of excellence are extremely important. For others, just getting by is quite enough. How can differences in this motive be measured? What are their effects? Psychologists have studied both issues.

**Figure 10.14**
**Measuring Achievement Motivation**

One measure of achievement motivation is the TAT (Thematic Apperception Test). Persons taking the test make up stories about ambiguous scenes; the amount of achievement-related imagery in these stories is then scored.

**MEASURING ACHIEVEMENT MOTIVATION** While several different methods have been used to measure achievement motivation, most are based on the **Thematic Apperception Test (TAT).** This test consists of a series of ambiguous pictures similar to the one shown in Figure 10.14. Other drawings used for this purpose show a boy at a desk, an engineer at a drawing board, a couple sitting on a bench, two women in a laboratory, a couple engaged in a trapeze act. Persons taking the test are asked to make up stories about them. These are then scored for the presence of achievement-related content according to carefully developed scoring manuals (e.g., Smith, 1992). The result is a score for achievement motivation and, if this is of interest to the researchers, scores for several other motives as well (e.g., *power motivation,* the desire to exert influence over others; *affiliation motivation,* the desire for close, friendly relations with others). The TAT continues to be used in its original form, but Winter (1983) has also developed a technique for scoring achievement motivation directly from any type of verbal material, without the need for ambiguous pictures or story construction. Winter's technique can be applied to books, speeches, or any other written material. This has permitted psychologists to study the achievement motivation of political and military leaders and to compare achievement motivation across many different societies—with some fascinating results, as I'll describe shortly.

**EFFECTS OF ACHIEVEMENT MOTIVATION ON INDIVIDUALS** Do individual differences in achievement and power motivation really matter? In other words, do persons high and low in these motives have contrasting life experiences? Existing evidence suggests that they do. As you might expect, individuals high in achievement motivation tend to get higher grades in school, earn more rapid promotions, and attain greater success in running their own businesses than persons low in such motivation (Andrews, 1967; Raynor, 1970). Interestingly, additional findings suggest that achievement motivation, in combination with several other factors, may affect success in school and elsewhere in the same manner across various ethnic and cultural groups (Rowe, Vazsonyi, & Flannery, 1995). In other words, success may stem from much the same factors regardless of one's ethnic or cultural background.

Persons high in achievement motivation differ from persons low in this motive in other respects, too. First, persons high in achievement motivation tend to prefer tasks that are moderately difficult and challenging. The reason why they tend to avoid very easy tasks is obvious: Such tasks don't pose enough challenge for persons high in achievement motivation. But why do they prefer tasks that are moderately challenging to ones that are extremely difficult? Because the chances of failing on extremely difficult tasks is too high, and such persons want success above everything else (e.g., McClelland, 1985).

**Thematic Apperception Test (TAT):** A psychological test used to assess individual differences in several different motives (e.g., achievement motivation, power motivation).

Another characteristic of persons high in achievement motivation is that they have a stronger-than-average desire for feedback on their performance: They want to know how well they are doing so they can adjust their goals to make these challenging—but not impossible. Because of this desire for feedback, persons high in achievement motivation tend to prefer jobs in which rewards are closely related to individual performance—*merit-based pay systems.* They generally don't like working in situations where everyone receives the same across-the-board raises regardless of their performance (e.g., Turban & Keon, 1993).

Finally, as you might expect, persons high in achievement motivation tend to excel under conditions in which their achievement motive is activated (e.g., McClelland, 1995). Situations in which they are challenged to do their best, are confronted with difficult goals, or in which they compete against others are "grist for the mill" of high-achievement persons, and they generally rise to the occasion in terms of excellent performance.

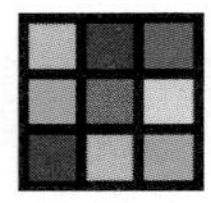

**EFFECTS OF ACHIEVEMENT ON SOCIETIES: ACHIEVEMENT MOTIVATION AND ECONOMIC GROWTH** That the economic fortunes of nations rise and fall over time is obvious. When I took high school economics in the late 1950s, our teacher showed us many graphs indicating that the United States was truly the dominant economic power in the world: it accounted for a majority of the world's output of steel, automobiles, and electricity, to name just a few important items. Today, of course, such graphs tell a very different story. The United States no longer accounts for most of the world's production in these areas, and throughout the 1980s and early 1990s, its rate of growth was exceeded by that of several Asian countries. In the late 1990s this situation reversed again; the economies of many Asian countries went into a sharp tailspin from which they are only now recovering, while that of the United States boomed. What factors contribute to such trends? Most persons (including economists) would list such factors as the price of natural resources, labor costs, and government policies that encourage growth. To this list psychologists would add another factor: national differences in achievement motivation.

While achievement motivation is certainly an individual process, some evidence points to the conclusion that average levels of this motive vary sharply across cultures. For example, in classic research on this topic, McClelland (1985) analyzed children's stories in twenty-two different cultures with respect to the degree to which they showed themes of achievement motivation. He then related these levels of achievement motivation to two measures of economic development: average income per person in each society, and electrical production per person. The major finding was clear: Achievement motivation scores were highly correlated with economic growth. In other words, the greater the emphasis placed on achievement in the stories told to children in various nations, the more rapid the economic growth in these nations as the children grew up.

While you may find these results surprising, they have been confirmed repeatedly. For example, in a massive study involving more than 12,000 participants in forty-one different countries, Furnham, Kirkcaldy, and Lynn (1994) examined the relationship between a wide range of attitudes closely related to achievement motivation, and two indicators of economic growth: gross domestic product (the amount of income produced by a country) and growth rate (percentage of increase in economic output from year to year). Results showed a significant relationship between achievement-related attitudes and economic growth. For instance, across all countries studied, attitudes toward competitiveness were a significant predictor of economic growth: The stronger these attitudes, and therefore the higher the achievement motivation, the greater the rate of growth (see Figure 10.15).

These findings, and those reported in several earlier studies, support McClelland's original conclusion that a nation's economic success is related, at least in part, to the level of achievement motivation among its citizens. Of course, such research is correlational in nature, so we can't be certain that differences in achievement motivation across various cultures *cause* differences in economic growth. However, the fact that achievement motivation does influence *individual* perfor-

**Figure 10.15**
**Achievement Motivation and Economic Growth**

Growing evidence suggests that countries in which achievement motivation is strong tend to experience more rapid economic growth than countries in which such motivation is relatively weak.

mance and success suggests that investigating cultural differences with respect to this motive may indeed provide us with insights into why certain countries suddenly rise to economic prominence at particular times in their history.

For a discussion of another, and somewhat unsettling human motive, see the following **Beyond the Headlines** section.

## BEYOND the HEADLINES: *As Psychologists See It*

### The Need for Stimulation . . . and How It Can Get Out of Hand

**"Fainting Game" Death Alarms Top Schools**

*REUTERS* (MARCH 18, 1999)—LONDON: A thrill-seeking "fainting game" that killed a boy at Britain's elite Eton College has set worried school authorities on a search into how widespread the practice is and why privileged youth needs the buzz of dicing with death. Masters at Eton, where the two sons of Prince Charles are pupils, were amazed by the revelations at an inquest into why 15-year-old Nicholas Taylor hanged himself in his room with a dressing gown rope.... An Eton pupil told the court how two boys would tie a cord round the neck of a third pupil. When the boy being "fainted" stopped tapping his thigh the others would release him. When others lost interest in the game, Taylor tried it alone....

"Why?... what on earth were they thinking of?" coroner Robert Wilson said in announcing a verdict of death by misadventure Tuesday...."You probably would have been regarded as a wimp if you didn't take part," said a spokeswoman for the British Association for Counseling. "It's an example of young boys' desire to experiment," Stuart Westley, a boarding-school master in Southern England told Reuters.... The fainting game tragedy was seized on by Britain' s press, which loves to portray an image of bizarre goings on at schools like Eton, where students wear stiff white collars and black gowns to lessons and parents pay about $24,420 a year in tuition....

What's going on here? Why would teenagers engage in such dangerous, even potentially deadly games? While we can't know for certain, psychologists would point to a motive (or aspect of personality) known as **sensation seeking**—the desire to seek out novel and intense experiences (e.g., Zuckerman, 1990). As we'll see in Chapter 12, people differ greatly with respect to the need for such stimulation, and those who are high on this dimension often engage in behaviors most of us would view as dangerous or downright reckless. Persons high in sensation seeking want lots of excitement and stimulation in their lives and become intensely bored when they don't get it. This, in turn, leads them to engage in high-risk behaviors such as driving fast, experimenting with drugs, and taking risks where sex is concerned. Research on sensation seeking indicates that compared to low sensation seekers, high sensation seekers are more likely to engage in substance abuse (Teichman, Barnea, & Rahav, 1989) and more likely to participate in high-risk sports such as skydiving (Humbaugh & Garrett, 1974). In short, persons high in sensation seeking often engage in behaviors that put their safety and health at risk—a high price to pay for the excitement they crave!

It seems possible, then, that the boys who played the "fainting game" were high in the need for such intense, exciting stimulation. Bored with their classes and with the strict discipline at their school, too young to drive, and denied access to members of the opposite sex most of the time, they came up with a uniquely dangerous way of obtaining the stimulation they craved. The results, of course, proved tragic—as is often the case when people give free rein to a strong motivation for intense stimulation.

### CRITICAL THINKING QUESTIONS

1. What, if anything, could Eton or other boarding schools do to prevent such dangerous actions by students in the future?
2. Can you think of any other explanation(s) for why the boys engaged in this dangerous game? Could motives other than the desire for excitement and stimulation be involved?

### REVIEW QUESTIONS

- What is achievement motivation, and how is it measured?
- What are the effects of achievement motivation on individual behavior and on the economic fortunes of countries?
- What is sensation seeking, and how can this motive be dangerous to the persons who possess it?

## Intrinsic Motivation: How, Sometimes, to Turn Play into Work

Individuals perform many activities simply because they find them enjoyable. Hobbies, gourmet dining, lovemaking—these are a few of the actions that fit within this category. Such activities may be described as stemming from **intrinsic motivation**—we perform them because of the pleasure they yield, not because they lead to external rewards. But what happens if people are given external rewards for performing these activities—if, for example, they are paid for sipping vintage wines or for pursuing their favorite hobby? Research findings suggest that they may then actually experience reductions in intrinsic motivation. In other words, they may become *less* motivated to engage in such activities. Why? One explanation goes something like this. When people consider their own behavior, they now conclude that they chose to perform the activities in question partly to obtain the external reward provided—not simply because they enjoyed these activities. To the extent that they reach that conclusion, they may then view their own interest in these activities as lower than was previously the case. In short, when provided with an external reward for performing some activity they enjoy, people shift from viewing their own behavior as stemming from intrinsic motivation ("I do it because I enjoy it") to perceiving it as stemming from external rewards ("I do it partly because of the external rewards I receive").

**Sensation Seeking:** The desire to seek out novel, intense, experiences.

**Intrinsic Motivation:** Motivation to perform activities because they are rewarding in and of themselves.

Many studies support this reasoning. In such research, some participants were provided with extrinsic rewards for engaging in a task they initially enjoyed, while others were not. When later given an opportunity to perform the task, those who received the external rewards showed reduced motivation to do so (Deci, 1975; Lepper & Green, 1978). These results have important implications for anyone seeking to motivate others by means of rewards—parents, teachers, managers. If the target persons already enjoy various activities, then offering them rewards for performing these activities may lower their intrinsic motivation and so actually *reduce* rather than enhance their performance!

**Emotions:** Reactions consisting of subjective cognitive states, physiological reactions, and expressive behaviors.

Fortunately, additional evidence suggests that this is not always the case, and that intrinsic and extrinsic motivation are not necessarily incompatible (Deci & Ryan, 1985; Rigby et al., 1992). If external rewards are viewed as signs of recognition rather than as bribes (Rosenfeld, Folger, & Adelman, 1980), and if the rewards provided are large and satisfying, intrinsic motivation may be enhanced rather than reduced (Lepper & Cordova, 1992; Ryan, 1982).

In addition, research findings indicate that individuals can "buffer" themselves against reductions in intrinsic motivation by engaging in a strategy known as *self-handicapping* (Berglas & Jones, 1978; Rhodewalt & Fairfield, 1991). In this strategy, individuals provide themselves with ready explanations for poor performance—explanations they offer *before* performing some task. If you've ever said, before beginning some activity, "I really didn't sleep well last night," or "I'm really not feeling too great today," you have used self-handicapping. The goal is to be able to explain away poor performance—which, most of us realize, could reduce our intrinsic motivation (Deppe & Harackiewicz, 1996). Since most of us are quite expert at self-handicapping, it appears that we have at least one effective technique for protecting our intrinsic motivation when we wish to do so.

### REVIEW QUESTIONS

- What is intrinsic motivation?
- Why is intrinsic motivation sometimes reduced when individuals receive external rewards for performing activities they enjoy?
- What is self-handicapping, and how can it protect against reductions in intrinsic motivation?

Web Link: *How Do We Study Emotions?*

## Emotions: Their Nature, Expression, and Impact

Can you imagine life without **emotions**—without joy, anger, sorrow, or fear? What would such an existence be like—a life without any feelings? If you've seen any of the *Star Trek* movies, you know that Mr. Spock, who prided himself on being completely lacking in emotions, often suffered greatly from this deficit—thus proving, of course, that he was *not* totally devoid of human feelings! (See Figure 10.16.) So, while we can imagine a life without emotions, few of us would choose such an existence.

But what, precisely, are emotions? The closer we look, the more complex these reactions seem to be. There is general agreement among scientists who study emotions, however, that they involve three major components: (1) physiological changes within our bodies—shifts in heart rate, blood pressure, and so on; (2) subjective cognitive states—the personal experiences we label as emotions; and (3) expressive

**Figure 10.16**
**Mr. Spock: A Person without Emotions?**

Mr. Spock, science officer of the *USS Enterprise* in the *Star Trek* series, claimed to have no emotions. In many episodes, however, he seemed to suffer greatly from this lack–thus indicating that he did have emotions after all!

**Cannon–Bard Theory:** A theory of emotion suggesting that various emotion-provoking events simultaneously produce physiological arousal and subjective reactions labeled as emotions.

**James–Lange Theory:** A theory of emotion suggesting that emotion-provoking events produce various physiological reactions and that recognition of these is responsible for subjective emotional experiences.

Video 10.1: *Heat and Hostility*

behaviors—outward signs of these internal reactions (Tangney et al., 1996; Zajonc & McIntosh, 1992).

In this discussion, therefore, we'll first look at several contrasting theories of emotion. Then we'll consider the biological basis of emotions. Third, we'll examine how emotions are expressed. Next, we'll turn to *affect,* or affective states (Russell & Carroll, 1999), examining the complex interplay between affect and cognition. We'll conclude with a brief look at what psychologists have discovered about *subjective well-being,* or personal happiness.

## The Nature of Emotions: Some Contrasting Views

Many different theories of emotions have been proposed, but among these, three have been most influential. These are known, after the scientists who proposed them, as the *Cannon–Bard, James–Lange,* and *Schachter–Singer* theories. A fourth theory—the *opponent-process theory*—offers additional insights into the nature of emotion.

**THE CANNON–BARD AND JAMES–LANGE THEORIES: WHICH COMES FIRST, ACTION OR FEELING?** Imagine that in one of your courses, you are required to make a class presentation. As you walk to the front of the room, your pulse races, your mouth feels dry, and you can feel beads of perspiration on your forehead. In short, you are terrified. What is the basis for this feeling? Contrasting answers are offered by the Cannon–Bard and James–Lange theories of emotion.

Let's begin with the **Cannon–Bard theory,** because it is consistent with our own commonsense beliefs about emotions. This theory suggests that various emotion-provoking events induce *simultaneously* the subjective experiences we label as emotions and the physiological reactions that accompany them. In the situation just described, the sight of the audience and of your professor, pen poised to evaluate your performance, causes you to experience a racing heart, a dry mouth, and other signs of physiological arousal *and,* at the same time, to experience subjective feelings you label as fear. In other words, this situation stimulates various portions of your nervous system so that both arousal, mediated by your *autonomic nervous system* (discussed in Chapter 2), and subjective feelings, mediated by your cerebral cortex and other portions of the brain, are produced.

In contrast, the **James–Lange theory** offers a more surprising view of emotion. It suggests that subjective emotional experiences are actually the *result* of physiological changes within our bodies. In other words, you feel frightened when making your speech *because* you notice that your heart is racing, your mouth is dry, and so on. As William James himself put it (1890, p. 1066): "We feel sorry because we cry, angry because we strike, and afraid because we tremble." (See Figure 10.17 for a comparison of these two theories.)

Which of these theories is most accurate? Until recently, most evidence seemed to favor the Cannon–Bard approach: Emotion-provoking events produce both physiological arousal and the subjective experiences we label as emotions. Now, however, the pendulum of scientific opinion has moved toward greater acceptance of the James–Lange approach—the view that we experience emotions because of our awareness of physiological reactions to

**Figure 10.17**
**Two Major Theories of Emotion**

According to the Cannon–Bard theory, emotion-provoking stimuli simultaneously evoke physiological reactions and the subjective states we label as emotions. According to the James–Lange theory, emotion-provoking events produce physiological reactions, and it is our awareness of these changes in bodily states that we label as emotions.

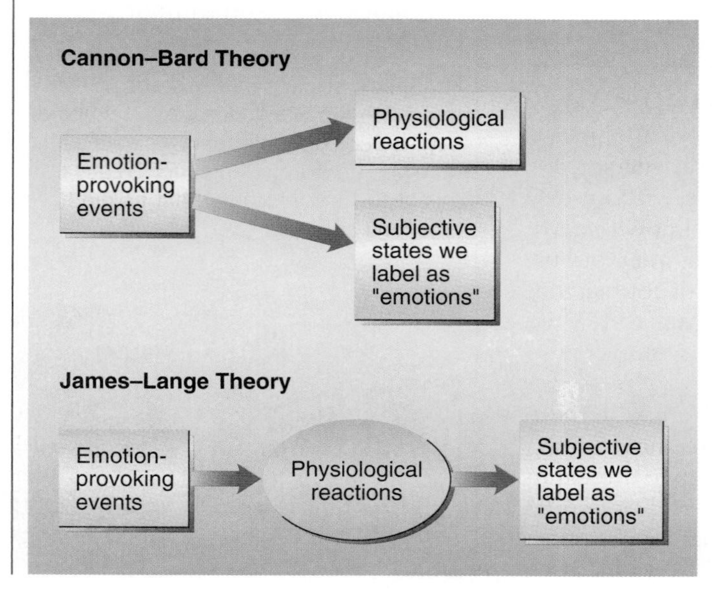

various stimuli or situations. Several lines of evidence point to this conclusion. First, studies conducted with modern equipment indicate that different emotions are indeed associated with different patterns of physiological activity (Levenson, 1992). Not only do various emotions *feel* different, it appears; they also result in somewhat different patterns of bodily changes, including contrasting patterns of brain and muscle activity (Ekman, Davidson, & Friesen, 1990; Izard, 1991).

Second, support for the James–Lange theory is also provided by research on the **facial feedback hypothesis** (Laird, 1984; Zajonc & McIntosh, 1992). This hypothesis suggests that changes in our facial expressions sometimes produce shifts in our emotional experiences rather than merely reflecting them. In addition, other research suggests that changing our bodily postures (e.g., Flack, Laird, & Cavallero, 1999) or even the tone of our voices (e.g., Siegman & Boyle, 1993) may influence emotional experiences. In view of such findings, the facial feedback hypothesis has been renamed the *peripheral feedback effect*, to indicate that emotions can be influenced by more than simply facial expressions. While there are many complexities in examining this hypothesis, the results of several studies offer support for its accuracy (e.g., Ekman et al., 1990). These findings suggest that there may be a substantial grain of truth in the James–Lange theory (Zajonc, Murphy, & Inglehart, 1989). While subjective emotional experiences *are* often produced by specific external stimuli, as the Cannon–Bard view suggests, emotional reactions can also be generated by changes in and awareness of our own bodily states, as the James–Lange theory contends (Ekman, 1992).

**SCHACHTER AND SINGER'S TWO-FACTOR THEORY** Strong emotions are a common part of daily life, but how do we tell them apart? How do we know that we are angry rather than frightened, sad rather than surprised? One potential answer is provided by a third theory of emotion. According to this view, known as the **Schachter–Singer theory** or, sometimes, as the *two-factor theory*, emotion-provoking events produce increased arousal (Schachter & Singer, 1962). In response to these feelings, we then search the external environment in order to identify the causes behind them. The factors we then select play a key role in determining the label we place on our arousal, and so in determining the emotion we experience. If we feel aroused after a near miss in traffic, we will probably label our emotion as "fear" or perhaps "anger." If, instead, we feel aroused in the presence of an attractive person, we may label our arousal as "attraction" or even "love." In short, we perceive ourselves to be experiencing the emotion that external cues tell us we *should* be feeling. This contrasts with the James–Lange theory, which suggests that we focus on internal physiological cues to determine whether we are experiencing an emotion and what this emotion is. The Schachter–Singer theory is a two-factor view because it considers both arousal and the cognitive appraisal we perform in our efforts to identify the causes of such arousal.

Many studies provide support for the Schachter–Singer theory (Reisenzein, 1983; Sinclair et al., 1994). For example, in one field study, Dutton and Aron (1974) arranged conditions so that male hikers encountered an attractive female research assistant while crossing a swaying suspension bridge high above a rocky gorge, or while on solid ground. Later, the researchers asked the men to rate their attraction to the assistant. The Schachter–Singer theory predicts that those who met the assistant on the swaying bridge would be more aroused and would—to the extent they attributed this arousal to the assistant—report finding her more attractive. This is precisely what was found. In fact, not only did the hikers who met her on the bridge rate the assistant as more attractive, they were also more likely to call her for a date! Findings such as these suggest that the Schachter–Singer theory provides important insights into the process through which we label our own emotions.

**Facial Feedback Hypothesis:** A hypothesis indicating that facial expressions can produce changes in emotional states.

**Schachter–Singer Theory:** A theory of emotion suggesting that our subjective emotional states are determined, at least in part, by the cognitive labels we attach to feelings of arousal; also known as *two-factor theory.*

**OPPONENT-PROCESS THEORY: ACTION AND REACTION TO EMOTION** Have you ever noticed that when you experience a strong emotional reaction, it is soon followed by the opposite reaction? Elation is followed by a letdown, and anger is

TABLE 10.2

**Theories of Emotion: An Overview**

The theories summarized here are among the ones that have received most attention from researchers.

| Theory of Emotion | Basic Assumptions |
|---|---|
| Cannon–Bard Theory | Emotion-provoking events induce simultaneously the subjective experiences we label as emotions and the physiological reactions that accompany them. |
| James–Lange Theory | Subjective emotional experiences result from physiological changes within our bodies (e.g., we feel sorry because we cry, frightened because we run away from something, etc.). |
| Schachter–Singer (Two-Factor) Theory | Emotion-provoking events produce increased arousal; in response to the arousal, we search the external environment in order to identify the causes behind it. The factors we identify then determine the label we place on our arousal and the emotion we experience. |
| Opponent-Process Theory | Emotional reactions to a stimulus are followed automatically by an opposite reaction; repeated exposure to a stimulus causes the initial reaction to weaken and the opponent process (opposite reaction) to strengthen. |

often followed by calm, or even by regret over one's previous outbursts. This relationship is the focus of the **opponent-process theory of emotion** (Solomon, 1982). The theory suggests that (1) an emotional reaction to a stimulus is followed automatically by an opposite reaction, and (2) repeated exposure to a stimulus causes the initial reaction to weaken and the opponent process, or opposite reaction, to strengthen.

For example, consider a surgeon who initially experiences very positive emotions each time she successfully completes a lifesaving operation. Later, however, she experiences a sharp emotional letdown. Over time, her positive reactions decrease, while the letdown intensifies or occurs sooner after each medical procedure. The result: She may gradually reduce the number of operations she performs or, at least, become increasingly bored with and indifferent to her work.

Opponent-process theory provides important insights into drug addiction. For instance, heroin users initially experience intense pleasure followed by unpleasant sensations of withdrawal. With repeated use of the drug, the pleasure becomes less intense and the unpleasant withdrawal reactions strengthen (Marlatt et al., 1988). In response, addicts begin to use the drug not for the pleasure it provides, but to avoid the negative feelings that occur when they *don't* use it.

In sum, opponent-process theory suggests that a law of physics—every action produces a reaction—may apply to emotions as well. Every emotional action produces a reaction, and such cycles can have important effects on many aspects of our behavior. (An overview of the theories of emotion discussed in this section is provided in Table 10.2.)

**Opponent-Process Theory of Emotion:** A theory suggesting that an emotional reaction is followed automatically by an opposite reaction.

REVIEW QUESTIONS

- How do the Cannon–Bard and James–Lange theories of emotion differ?
- What is the Schachter–Singer theory of emotion?
- What is the opponent-process theory of emotion?

## The Biological Basis of Emotions

As I noted earlier, emotions are complex reactions, involving not only the intense subjective feelings we label as "joy," "anger," "sorrow," and so on, but also outward emotional expressions and the ability (or abilities) to understand emotional information (e.g., the ability to "read" the emotional reactions of others). Research on the biological and neural bases of emotions indicates that different portions of the brain play a role in each of these components. Research concerning the neural basis of emotion is complex, so here I'll simply try to summarize a few of the key findings.

First, it appears that the right cerebral hemisphere plays an especially important role in emotional functions (e.g., Harrington, 1995). The right hemisphere seems to be specialized for processing emotional information. Individuals with damage to the right hemisphere have difficulty in understanding the emotional tone of another person's voice or in correctly describing emotional scenes (Heller, 1997; Heller, Nitschke, & Miller, 1998). Similarly, among healthy persons with no damage to their brains, individuals do better at identifying others' emotions when such information is presented to their right hemisphere rather than to their left hemisphere (it is exposed to one part or the other of the visual field; see the discussion of the visual system in Chapter 3) (e.g., Ladavas, Umilta, & Ricci-Bitti, 1980). The right hemisphere also seems to be specialized for the expression of emotion; for instance, patients with damage to the right hemisphere are less successful at expressing emotions through the tone of their voice than persons without such damage (Borod, 1993).

In addition, there appear to be important differences between the left and right hemispheres of the brain with respect to two key aspects of emotion: *valence*—the extent to which an emotion is pleasant or unpleasant; and *arousal*—the intensity of emotion. Activation of the left hemisphere is associated with approach, response to reward, and positive affect (i.e., positive feelings), whereas activation of the right hemisphere is associated with avoidance, withdrawal from aversive stimuli, and negative affect (Heller, Nitschke, & Miller, 1998). Further, anterior regions of the hemispheres are associated primarily with the valence (pleasant–unpleasant) dimension, while posterior regions are associated primarily with arousal (intensity). These findings have important implications for our understanding of the neural basis of various psychological disorders. Consider, for instance, depression and anxiety—disorders we'll examine in detail in Chapter 14. Both disorders involve negative feelings or emotions, but depression is usually associated with low arousal (depressed people lack energy), while anxiety is associated with high arousal (if you've ever experienced anxiety right before an exam, you know this very well!). This leads to interesting predictions: Persons suffering from depression should show reduced activity in the right posterior region, while persons suffering from anxiety should show increased activity in that brain region (see Figure 10.18 on page 400). These predictions have been confirmed in several studies (e.g., Heller, Etienne, & Miller, 1995). Insight into the neural mechanisms that underlie such disorders can be an important first step toward developing effective treatments for them, so our growing knowledge of the neural bases of emotions has important practical as well as scientific implications.

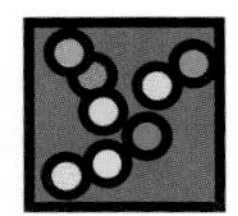

Additional research indicates that structures deep within the brain, too, play an important role in emotions. In particular, the *amygdala* (see Chapter 2) seems to be involved in our ability to judge the intensity, although not the valence, of others' emotions (Adolphs, in press). For instance, consider an intriguing study by Adolphs, Russell, and Tranel (1999). These researchers studied a woman who had damage to her amygdala resulting from a hereditary disease. This patient was shown slides of faces demonstrating various emotions (surprise, happiness, fear, anger, sadness) and also heard sentences describing various actions or events (e.g., "Jody giggled and laughed," "Tom's wife and children all died in the car crash"). For both sets of stimuli, the patient and a group of control participants who had

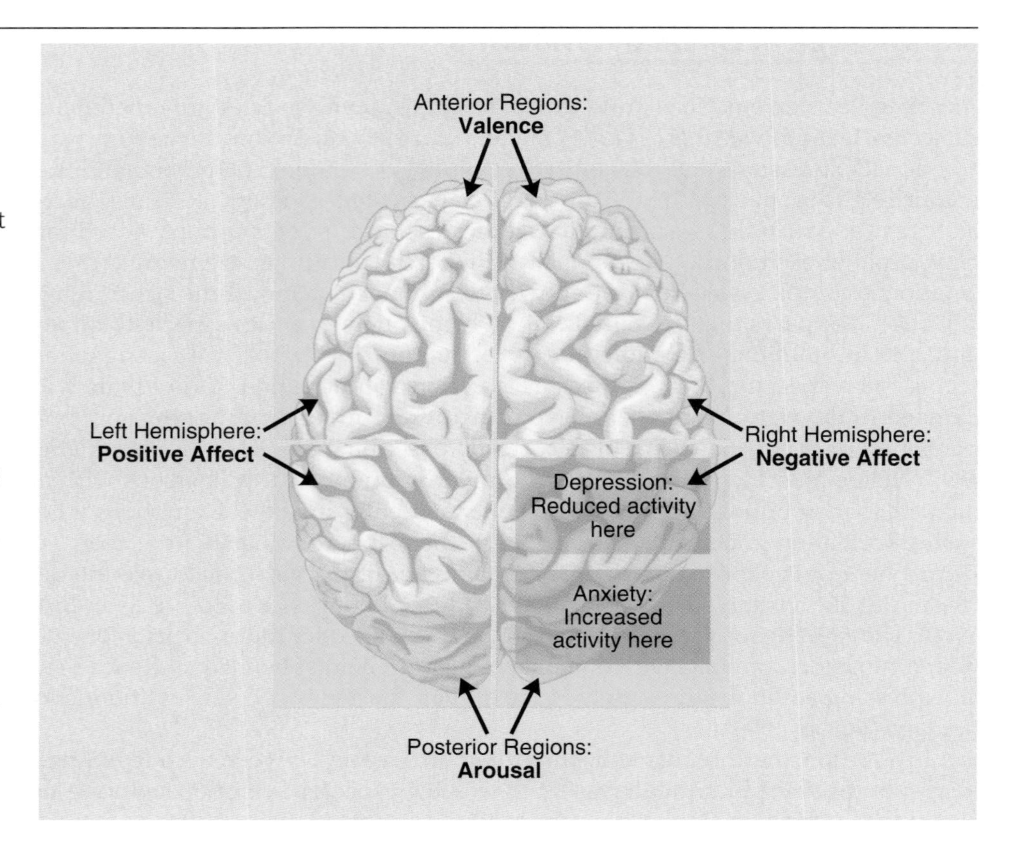


**Figure 10.18**
**Role of the Cerebral Hemispheres in Emotion—and in Psychological Disorders**

Growing evidence indicates that activation of the left cerebral hemisphere is associated with positive affect, while activation of the right hemisphere is associated with negative affect. Further, activation of anterior portions of both hemispheres is associated with the valence (pleasantness/unpleasantness) of emotions, while activation of the posterior portions of the hemispheres is associated with arousal—the intensity of emotions. Together, these findings suggest that depressed persons should show reduced activity in the right posterior regions, while anxious persons should show increased activity in these regions. These results have been confirmed in recent studies.

no brain damage were asked to rate how the persons shown or described were feeling with respect to both arousal and valence. Results were clear: The patient's responses were quite similar to those of the control participants in terms of valence—she could readily tell which emotions were pleasant and which were unpleasant. However, she showed impaired performance relative to the control group in recognizing arousal, especially for negatively valenced emotions (fear and anger). For positively valenced emotions (e.g., happiness) her ratings were within the normal range. What do these findings mean? They seem to suggest that the amygdala plays a key role in our interpretation of emotional information relating to threat or danger—for instance, signs of fear or anger on the part of other persons. From an evolutionary perspective, the existence of systems within the brain that focus on expressions of fear or anger makes considerable sense: Being able to respond quickly to such stimuli can mean the difference between survival and death.

## REVIEW QUESTIONS

- What roles do the left and right cerebral hemispheres play in emotions?
- What is the role of the amygdala in emotions?

### Food for Thought

Suppose that in the future we learn enough about the brain to be able to produce specific emotions by stimulating certain portions of it. Would these emotions be "real"? Why or Why not?

## The External Expression of Emotion: Outward Signs of Inner Feelings

Emotions are a private affair. No one, no matter how intimate with us they are, can truly share our subjective inner experiences. Yet we are able to recognize the presence of various emotions in others, and we are able to communicate our own feelings to them as well. How does such communication occur? A large part of the answer involves **nonverbal cues**—outward signs of others' internal emotional states shown in their facial expressions, body posture, and other behaviors (see Figure 10.19).

**Figure 10.19**
**Nonverbal Cues: External Guides to Internal Reactions**

People often reveal their emotions through *nonverbal cues*—facial expressions, body movements or postures, and other observable actions.

### NONVERBAL CUES: THE BASIC CHANNELS

Decades of research on nonverbal cues suggest that this kind of communication occurs through several different *channels* or paths simultaneously. The most revealing of these involve *facial expressions* and *body movements and posture.*

***Unmasking the Face: Facial Expressions as Clues to Others' Emotions.*** More than two thousand years ago, the Roman orator Cicero stated that "the face is the image of the soul." By this he meant that feelings and emotions are often reflected in the face and can be read there from specific expressions. Modern research suggests that Cicero was correct: It *is* possible to learn much about others' current moods and feelings from their facial expressions. In fact, it appears that six different basic emotions are represented clearly, and from an early age, on the human face: anger, fear, sadness, disgust, happiness, and surprise (Ekman, 1992). In addition, some findings suggest that another emotion—contempt—may also be quite basic (e.g., Rosenberg & Ekman, 1995). However, agreement on what specific facial expression represents this emotion is less consistent than that for the other six emotions just mentioned.

Until fairly recently, it was widely assumed that basic facial expressions such as those for happiness, anger, or disgust are universal—that they are recognized as indicating specific emotions by persons all over the world (e.g., Ekman & Friesen, 1975). Some research findings, however, have called this assumption into question (e.g., Russell, 1994). The findings of several studies indicate that although facial expressions may indeed reveal much about others' emotions, interpretations of such expressions are also affected by the context in which the expressions occur, and by various situational cues. For instance, if participants in a study are shown a photo of a face showing what would normally be judged as fear but are also read a story suggesting that the person is actually showing anger, many describe the face as showing *this* emotion—not fear (Carroll & Russell, 1996). Findings such as these suggest that facial expressions may not be as universal in terms of providing clear signals about underlying emotions as was previously assumed. These findings are somewhat controversial, however, so at present it would be unwise to reach firm conclusions about this issue.

***Gestures, Posture, and Movements.*** Try this simple demonstration: First, remember some incident that made you angry—the angrier the better. Think about it for a minute. Now try to remember another incident—one that made you feel happy—the happier the better. Did you change your posture or move your hands, arms, or legs as your thoughts shifted from the first incident to the second? The chances are good that you did, for our current mood or emotion is often reflected

**Nonverbal Cues:** Outward signs of others' emotional states, such as facial expressions, eye contact, and body language.

**Figure 10.20**
**Gestures: Body Language that Communicates**

Can you guess what the persons shown are trying to communicate? Probably you can, because within a given culture, *gestures* often carry highly specific meanings.

in the posture, position, and movement of our body. Together, such nonverbal behaviors are sometimes termed **body language** or, more scientifically, *kinesics;* and they can provide several kinds of information about others' emotions.

First, frequent body movements, especially ones in which a particular part of the body does something to another part, such as touching, scratching, or rubbing, suggest emotional arousal. The greater the frequency of such behavior, the higher a person's level of arousal or nervousness seems to be (Harrigan et al., 1991).

Larger patterns of movements involving the whole body can also be informative. Such phrases as "she adopted a *threatening posture*" and "he greeted her with *open arms*" suggest that different body orientations or postures can be suggestive of contrasting emotional reactions (Aronoff, Woike, & Hyman, 1992).

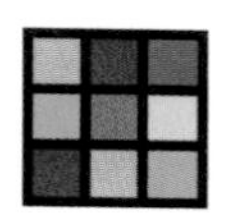

Finally, more specific information about others' feelings is often provided by **gestures**—body movements carrying specific meanings in a given culture. Do you recognize the gestures shown in Figure 10.20? In the United States and several other countries, these movements have clear and definite meanings. In other cultures, however, they might have no meaning or a different meaning. For this reason, it is wise to be careful about using gestures while traveling in cultures different from your own: You may offend the people around you without intending to do so!

**REVIEW QUESTIONS**

- What emotions are shown by clear facial expressions? What do research findings indicate about the universality of such expressions?
- What information about others' emotions is conveyed by body language?

**CourseCompass**
Audio 10.4: *Affective States and Cognition*

**Body Language:** Nonverbal cues involving body posture or movement of body parts.

**Gestures:** Movements of various body parts that convey specific meanings in a given culture.

## Emotion and Cognition: How Feelings Shape Thought and Thought Shapes Feelings

Earlier, I asked you to recall incidents that made you feel angry and happy. When you thought about these events, did your mood also change? The chances are good that it did. In many instances, our thoughts seem to exert strong effects on our emotions. And this relationship works in the other direction as well: Being in a happy mood often causes us to think happy thoughts, while feeling sad tends to bring negative memories and images to mind. In short, there are important links between *emotion* and *cognition*—between the way we feel and the way we think. Let's take a brief look at some of the evidence for such links (e.g., Forgas, 1995a; Forgas & Fiedler, 1996).

I should clarify one important point before beginning: Throughout this discussion, I'll be focusing on **affect**—relatively mild feelings and moods—rather than on intense emotions. The boundary between emotions and affective reactions is somewhat fuzzy; but because most research has focused on the effects of relatively modest shifts in mood—the kinds of changes we experience many times each day as a result of run-of-the-mill experiences—these will be the focus here. For many years it was assumed that affective reactions are *bipolar* in nature; that is, that positive affect and negative affect represent opposite ends of a single dimension, and that our moods fall somewhere along this dimension at any point in time. However, in recent years this assumption has been challenged by the suggestion that perhaps positive affect and negative affect are actually independent dimensions—so that we can be high in one, low in the other, high in both, or low in both. This issue has not yet been resolved, although recent findings seem to offer fairly strong support for the idea that positive and negative affect are indeed two ends of a single dimension (e.g., Barrett & Russell, 1999; Russell & Carroll, 1999). But remember, this conclusion is tentative; the scientific jury is still out on this one.

**HOW AFFECT INFLUENCES COGNITION** The findings of many studies indicate that our current moods can strongly influence several aspects of cognition. In Chapter 6 we examined the influence of affect on memory (mood-dependent memory), so here we'll focus on other ways in which moods or feelings influence cognition. One such effect involves the impact of our current moods, or *affective states,* on our perception of ambiguous stimuli. In general, we perceive and evaluate these stimuli more favorably when we are in a good mood than when we are in a negative one (Isen, 1993; Isen & Baron, 1991). For example, when asked to interview applicants whose qualifications for a job are ambiguous—neither very strong nor very weak—research participants assign higher ratings to applicants when they (the interviewers) are in a positive mood than when they are in a negative mood (e.g., Baron, 1987, 1993a).

Another way in which affect influences cognition is through its impact on the style of information processing we adopt. A growing body of research findings indicate that a positive affect encourages us to adopt a flexible, fluid style of thinking, while negative affect leads us to engage in more systematic and careful processing (e.g., Stroessner & Mackie, 1992). Why? Perhaps because we interpret negative affect as a kind of danger signal, indicating that the current situation requires our full attention (e.g., Edwards & Bryan, 1997).

Our current moods also influence another important aspect of cognition—creativity. The results of several studies suggest that being in a happy mood can increase creativity—perhaps because being in a happy mood activates a wider range of ideas or associations than being in a negative mood, and creativity consists, in part, of combining such associations into new patterns (e.g., Estrada, Isen, & Young, 1995).

A fourth way in which affect can influence cognition involves its impact on our plans and intentions in a wide range of social situations. For instance, recent findings reported by Forgas (1998b) suggest that negotiators who are in a good mood adopt more cooperative strategies and expect better outcomes than ones who are in a bad mood.

**HOW COGNITION INFLUENCES AFFECT** Most research on the relationship between affect and cognition has focused on how feelings influence thought. However, there is also compelling evidence for the reverse—the impact of cognition on affect. I mentioned one aspect of this relationship in discussing the two-factor theory of emotion proposed by Schachter and Singer (1962). As you may recall, their theory suggests that often we don't know our own feelings or attitudes directly.

**Affect:** Relatively mild feelings and moods.

Rather, because these internal reactions are often somewhat ambiguous, we look outward—at our own behavior or at other aspects of the external world—for clues about the nature of our feelings. In such cases the emotions or feelings we experience are strongly determined by the interpretation or cognitive labels we select.

A second way in which cognition can affect emotions is through the activation of schemas containing a strong affective component. For example, if we label an individual as belonging to some group, our schema for this social category may suggest what traits he or she probably possesses. In addition, it may also tell us how we feel about such persons. Thus, activation of a strong racial, ethnic, or religious schema or stereotype may exert powerful effects upon our current feelings or moods. (Please see Chapter 16 for more information on this topic.)

Third, our thoughts can often influence our reactions to emotion-provoking events. For example, anger and resulting aggressive motivation can often be reduced by apologies and other information that helps explain why others have treated us in a provocative manner (Ohbuchi, Kameda, & Agarie, 1989). Further, anger can sometimes be reduced—or even prevented—by techniques such as thinking about events *other* than those that generate anger (Zillmann, 1993). In such instances, the effects of cognition on feelings can have important social consequences.

In sum, as our everyday experience suggests, there are indeed many links between affect and cognition. The way we feel—our current mood—influences the way we think, and our thoughts, in turn, often shape our moods and emotions.

**REVIEW QUESTIONS**

- In what ways do our affective states influence cognition?
- In what ways does cognition influence our affective states?

CourseCompass
Web Link: *The EQ Factor*

## Subjective Well-Being: Some Thoughts on Personal Happiness

Suppose you were asked the following questions: "How happy are you?" and "How satisfied are you with your life?" Suppose that in both cases your answer could range from 1 (very unhappy; very unsatisfied) to 7 (very happy; very satisfied). How would you reply? If you are like most people—a large majority, in fact—you would probably indicate that you are quite happy and quite satisfied with your life. In fact, research findings (e.g., Diener & Diener, 1996; Diener & Lucas, in press; Myers & Diener, 1995) suggest that something like 80 percent of all people who answer this question report being satisfied. In other words, they report relatively high levels of what psychologists term **subjective well-being**—individuals' global judgments of their own life satisfaction (Diener et al., 1999). Moreover, this seems to be true all over the world, across all age groups, at all income levels above grinding poverty, among relatively unattractive persons as well as among attractive ones (Diener, Wolsic, & Fujita, 1995), and in all racial and ethnic groups (e.g., Myers & Diener, 1995).

**Subjective Well-Being:** Individuals' global judgments of their own life satisfaction.

Does this mean that everyone is happy, no matter what their life circumstances? Not at all; in fact, as I'll soon explain, several factors have been found to influence subjective well-being. But overall, most people report being relatively happy and satisfied with their lives. Why? We don't know for certain, but it appears that overall, human beings have a strong tendency to look on the bright side of things—to be optimistic and upbeat in a wide range of situations (e.g., Diener & Suh, in press). For instance, as we'll see in Chapter 16, they often show a strong *optimistic bias*—a powerful tendency to believe that they can accomplish more in a given period of time than they really can (Baron, 1998).

But given that most people report being happy, what factors influence just how happy they are? A recent review of research on this question by Diener and his colleagues (Diener et al., 1999) points to the following variables. First, genetic factors seem to play a role. Some people, it appears, have an inherited tendency to have a pleasant, easygoing temperament, and this contributes to their personal happiness (e.g., Lykken & Tellegen, 1996). Because of this tendency they get along well with others, and this can help pave the way to happiness.

Second, personality factors are important. People who are emotionally stable (low on what is sometimes termed *neuroticism;* see Chapter 12), who are high in affiliation (the tendency to want to relate to other people), and in percieved control (they feel that they are "in charge" of their own lives), tend to be happier than those who are not emotionally stable, who are lower in affiliation, and low in percieved control (DeNeve, 1999). In addition, some findings suggest—not surprisingly—that people who are optimistic, extraverted, and avoid undue worrying also tend to be happier than those who are pessimistic, introverted, and prone to worry excessively (e.g., DeNeve & Cooper, 1998).

A third factor involves having goals—and the resources (personal, economic, and otherwise) needed to reach them. Many studies indicate that people who have concrete goals, especially goals that they have a realistic chance of reaching, and who feel (realistically or otherwise) that they are making progress toward these, are happier than persons lacking such goals (Cantor & Sanderson, in press).

Finally, external conditions over which individuals have varying degrees of influence also play a role in personal happiness. Not surprisingly, people living in wealthy countries are happier than those in poor nations. In general, married people tend to be happier than single people—although this finding varies with how the particular culture views marriage (Diener et al., 1998). Also, people who are satisfied with their jobs and careers tend to be happier than those who are not (e.g., Weiss & Cropanzano, 1996).

Perhaps much more surprising than these findings are ones indicating that several factors we might expect to be related to personal happiness do *not* seem to affect it. For instance, contrary to widespread beliefs, wealthy people are not significantly happier than those who are less wealthy (e.g., Clark & Oswald, 1994). Similarly, personal happiness does not decline with age, despite the fact that both income and the proportion of people who are married drop as people grow older (see Figure 10.21 on page 406). Finally, there appear to be no substantial gender differences in terms of personal happiness (e.g., White, 1992). This is true despite the fact that women seem to experience wider swings in affective states than men (e.g., Nolen-Hoeksema & Rusting, in press). Apparently, women's "lows" are lower than those experienced by men, but their "highs" are also higher; so overall, the two genders do not differ significantly in subjective well-being (Diener et al., 1999).

In sum, although many factors can have an impact on personal happiness, most people report relatively high levels of subjective well-being and are quite satisfied with their lives. Despite the many negative events that occur during our adult years, we tend to retain a degree of optimism and a positive outlook on life. So the poet Theodosia Garrison was correct about most of us when she wrote: "The hardest habit of all to break is the terrible habit of happiness."

**REVIEW QUESTIONS**

- Why do a high proportion of individuals all over the world report a realtively high level of subjective well-being—satisfaction with their own lives?
- What factors influence subjective well-being?

**Figure 10.21**
**Subjective Well-Being and Age**

Contrary to what you might expect, subjective well-being does *not* decline with age, despite the fact that income and other resources do tend to drop beyond midlife. (*Source:* Based on data from Diener & Suh, 1998.)

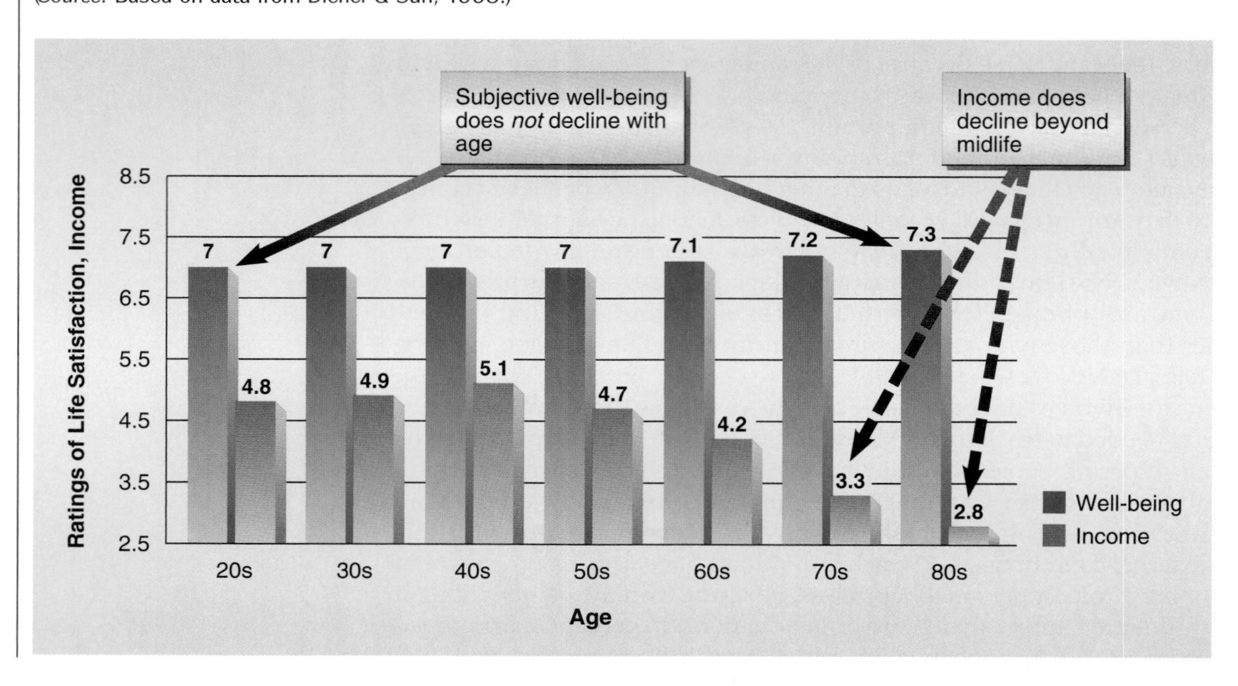


# *Making* Psychology *Part of Your Life*

## Some Tips on Winning the Battle of the Bulge

The old saying "You can never be too rich or too thin" may be an exaggeration, but most people do want to remain—or become—slim if they can. Below are some steps suggested by research on factors related to weight gain that may help *you* achieve this goal.

- **Avoid high-calorie snack foods.** A handful of potato chips or a small order of fries can contain hundreds of calories. Yet these high-fat snacks don't tend to make you feel full. Avoid such foods as much as possible.
- **Don't eat when you aren't hungry, out of habit.** It's all too easy to get into the habit of eating whenever you watch TV, study, or sit down to talk with friends. If you must munch on something, eat a piece of fruit, or drink some coffee or tea (preferably decaf). These drinks contain natural substances that tend to reduce appetite.
- **Avoid temptation.** President Clinton, who often gains weight, has often been described as a "see food eater"—when he sees food, he eats it! And the same principle holds for many of us. Thus, if you want to avoid gaining weight, try to avoid temptation. If you encounter attractive, appetizing foods, look the other way and get out of there fast! The waistline you save will be your own.
- **Exercise!** I'm one of the lucky ones: I never gain weight. So I started exercising for health reasons, not to lose weight. But exercising vigorously *will* help you burn calories while it improves your health. Losing weight, after all, is a simple formula: You lose if the number of calories you burn exceeds

the number you eat. So exercise regularly—it can be a tremendous help.

- **Drink water with your meals.** During the past two decades, the consumption of soft drinks in the United States and many other countries has soared. From the point of view of weight gain, that's unfortunate, because each glass of Coke, Pepsi, or whatever contains almost 200 calories. So ignore the ads and sip water when you are thirsty.
- **Don't give up.** If you have succeeded in losing weight—most people on diets do—don't quit. Managing your weight is a lifelong process. And if you persist, you will eventually lower your body's set point so that keeping the extra pounds off will actually become easier.
- **Don't succumb to fad diets.** Diet books are perpetual best-sellers and usually claim to offer new approaches for losing weight quickly and effortlessly. Don't be fooled by such claims! There is really no scientific evidence for these diets; the only thing they accomplish, in general, is to make their authors rich and famous. You *can* lose weight, and fairly quickly, too, but the best way to do it is by reducing the amount you eat while increasing your exercise. That formula is 100 percent certain to yield the results you want, with minimum risk to your health.
- **Good luck!**

## Summary and Review

### Motivation: The Activation and Persistence of Behavior

- **According to drive theory, what is the basis for various motives?** Drive theory suggests that motivation is a process in which various biological needs push (drive) us to actions designed to satisfy them.
- **How does arousal theory explain motivation?** According to arousal theory, our arousal (general level of activation) varies throughout the day, and we tend to seek the level of arousal that is optimal for us as individuals and for the activities we perform.
- **According to expectancy theory, why do people engage in tasks requiring effort?** Expectancy theory suggests that people exert effort on tasks because they believe doing so will yield results they want to attain.
- **Under what conditions will goal setting increase motivation and performance?** Goal setting will increase motivation and performance when the goals are specific and challenging yet attainable, and when individuals are committed to them and receive feedback on their progress.
- **What are the basic ideas behind Maslow's needs hierarchy theory?** Maslow's theory suggests that needs exist in a hierarchy and that higher-level needs cannot serve as motivators until lower-level ones are satisfied.
- **What factors play a role in the regulation of eating?** Eating is regulated by complex biochemical systems within the body involving detector cells in the hypothalamus and elsewhere; it is also affected by external food cues, feedback from chewing and swallowing, cognitive factors (e.g., memories about when we ate last), and cultural factors.
- **What factors override this regulatory system, causing many people to fail to maintain a stable weight?** Many factors tend to override this system, including the impact of learning, responses to food-related cues, genetic factors (a predisposition to gain weight), the growing size of food portions, and reduced sensitivity to leptin once we gain significant amounts of weight.
- **What role do hormones play in human sexual motivation?** Sex hormones play only a subtle and relatively minor role in human sexual motivation. However, other chemicals produced within the body may play a more important role.
- **What are the major phases of sexual activity?** During sexual activity both males and females move through a series of distinct phases: excitement, plateau, orgasm, and resolution.
- **What is a key difference between human beings and other species with respect to sexual arousal?** In contrast to other species, human beings can be sexually aroused by self-generated fantasies and by exposure to erotic stimuli.
- **According to evolutionary psychology, why do males and females differ with respect to short-term mating strategies?** Evolutionary psychology suggests that males can have more offspring by having many sexual partners, whereas women cannot increase their offspring by having many sexual partners and must make a major investment in each child.
- **What factors appear to play a role in determining sexual orientation?** The weight of available evidence suggests that genetic and biological factors play some role in determining sexual orientation.

- **Why do psychologists generally reject the view that aggression stems from innate tendencies?** Huge variations in the incidence of aggression across different cultures suggest that social and cultural factors play a key role in aggression.
- **What social factors facilitate aggression?** Social factors that facilitate aggression include some forms of frustration, direct provocation from others, and exposure to media violence.
- **What environmental factors contribute to aggression?** Environmental factors such as uncomfortably high temperatures, irritating noise, and crowding may promote aggression.
- **What is the aggression machine, and how is it used to study aggression?** The aggression machine is a device used to measure aggression under laboratory conditions. It contains a series of buttons that supposedly deliver shocks (or other unpleasant stimuli) of varying intensity to another person. In fact, no shocks or other unpleasant stimuli are ever delivered.
- **What is achievement motivation, and how is it measured?** Achievement motivation is the desire to meet standards of excellence or outperform others. It is measured by the Thematic Apperception Test and by the content of verbal materials.
- **What are the effects of achievement motivation on individual behavior and on the economic fortunes of countries?** Individuals high in achievement motivation tend to excel in school and in running their own businesses. The higher the level of achievement motivation in a given society, the greater its economic success.
- **What is sensation seeking, and how can this motive be dangerous to the persons who possess it?** Sensation seeking involves the desire to seek out novel and intense experiences. People high on this dimension often engage in risky or dangerous behavior to obtain such stimulation.
- **What is intrinsic motivation?** Intrinsic motivation is motivation to perform some activity simply because it is enjoyable.
- **Why is intrinsic motivation sometimes reduced when individuals receive external rewards for performing activities they enjoy?** When individuals receive rewards for performing activities they enjoy, they conclude that they perform these activities not solely because they like them, but also because of the external rewards they receive.
- **What is self-handicapping, and how can it protect against reductions in intrinsic motivation?** In self-handicapping individuals provide themselves—in advance—with good excuses for poor performance. This can protect against reductions in intrinsic motivation resulting from poor performance.

### Key Terms

motivation, p. 372 • drive theory, p. 373 • homeostasis, p. 373 • arousal theory, p. 373 • Yerkes–Dodson law, p. 374 • expectancy theory, p. 374 • incentives, p. 374 • goal-setting theory, p. 374 • hierarchy of needs, p. 377 • hunger motivation, p. 378 • sexual motivation, p. 381 • gonads, p. 381 • heterosexual, p. 385 • bisexual, p. 385 • homosexual, p. 385 • aggressive motivation, p. 386 • aggression, p. 386 • frustration, p. 387 • workplace violence, p. 387 • aggression machine, p. 389 • achievement motivation, p. 390 • Thematic Apperception Test (TAT), p. 391 • sensation seeking, p. 394 • intrinsic motivation, p. 394

## Emotions: Their Nature, Expression, and Impact

- **How do the Cannon–Bard and James–Lange theories differ?** The Cannon–Bard theory suggests that emotion-provoking stimuli simultaneously elicit physiological arousal and the subjective cognitive states we label as emotions. The James–Lange theory suggests that emotion-provoking stimuli induce physiological reactions and that these form the basis for the subjective cognitive states we label as emotions.
- **What is the Schachter–Singer theory of emotion?** The Schachter–Singer theory, or two-factor theory, suggests that when we are aroused by emotion-provoking stimuli, we search the external environment for the causes of our feelings of arousal. The causes we select then determine our emotions.
- **What is the opponent-process theory of emotion?** The opponent-process theory suggests that every strong emotional reaction is followed by an opposite reaction (opponent process), and that as a result our reactions to emotion-provoking stimuli tend to decrease over time.
- **What roles do the left and right cerebral hemispheres play in emotions?** Activation of the left hemisphere plays a role in positive emotions; activation of the right hemisphere plays a role in negative emotions. Anterior regions of the hemispheres are associated primarily with the valence (pleasantness or unpleasantness) of emotions, while posterior regions are associated primarily with arousal (intensity).
- **What is the role of the amygdala in emotions?** The amygdala seems to contain neural mechanisms specialized in interpreting emotional information relating to threat or danger, such as signs of fear or anger on the part of others.
- **What emotions are shown by clear facial expressions? What do research findings indicate about the universality of such expressions?** Clear facial expressions have long been believed to exist for anger, fear, sadness, disgust, happiness, and surprise. Research findings indicate, however, that such expressions, though informative, may not be as universal in meaning as was previously assumed.
- **What information about others' emotions is conveyed by body language?** Body language provides information about others' overall level of arousal as well as about specific emotional reactions they may be having.
- **In what ways do our affective states influence cognition?** Affective states can influence our perception of ambiguous stimuli, our memory, our plans and intentions, the style of information processing we adopt, and our creativity.

- **In what ways does cognition influence our affective states?** Cognition can influence the labels we place on emotional states, activate schemas containing strong affective components, and shape our interpretations of emotion-provoking events.
- **Why do a high proportion of individuals all over the world report a relatively high level of subjective well-being—satisfaction with their own lives?** A high proportion report being relatively happy because of a strong human tendency to be optimistic and look on the bright side of things.
- **What factors influence subjective well-being?** Subjective well-being is influenced by genetic factors (e.g., a pleasant, easygoing temperament), several aspects of personality (e.g., optimism, extraversion), having reasonable goals coupled with a realistic chance to reach them, and favorable external conditions (e.g., being satisfied with one's job or career).

### Key Terms

emotions, p. 395 • Cannon–Bard theory, p. 396 • James–Lange theory, p. 396 • facial feedback hypothesis, p. 397 • Schachter–Singer theory, p. 397 • opponent-process theory of emotion, p. 398 • nonverbal cues, p. 401 • body language, p. 402 • gestures, p. 402 • affect, p. 403 • subjective well-being, p. 404

## Critical Thinking Questions

### Appraisal

Motivation is, by definition, a hidden, internal process: We can measure its effects, but we can't "see" it directly. Given this fact, do you think that the concept of motivation is a useful one?

### Controversy

Research findings suggest that exposure to violence in the media is one factor contributing to increased aggression. In view of this fact, would it be appropriate for the government to pass laws designed to reduce the amount of violence included in films and television shows? Or would this be a violation of basic civil rights?

### Making Psychology Part of Your Life

Now that you know more about the factors that contribute to personal happiness, can you use this information to increase your own level of subjective well-being?

Chapter 11

# Intelligence:
## Cognitive, Practical, Emotional

## CHAPTER OUTLINE


**INTELLIGENCE: CONTRASTING VIEWS OF ITS NATURE 413**

Intelligence: Unitary or Multifaceted?
Gardner's Theory of Multiple Intelligences
Sternberg's Triarchic Theory: The Value of Practical Intelligence
Cattell's Theory of Fluid and Crystallized Intelligence

**MEASURING INTELLIGENCE 416**

IQ: Its Meaning Then and Now
The Wechsler Scales
Individual Tests of Intelligence: Measuring the Extremes

- BEYOND THE HEADLINES—As Psychologists See It: *Williams Syndrome: Mentally Challenged Persons with Music in Their Souls*

Group Tests of Intelligence

- RESEARCH METHODS *How Psychologists Evaluate Their Own Assessment Tools: Basic Requirements of Psychological Tests*

The Cognitive Basis of Intelligence: Processing Speed
The Neural Basis of Intelligence: Intelligence and Neural Efficiency

- FROM SCIENCE TO PRACTICE *Predicting Career Success: Competency Assessment*

**HUMAN INTELLIGENCE: THE ROLE OF HEREDITY AND THE ROLE OF ENVIRONMENT 428**

Evidence for the Influence of Heredity
Evidence for the Influence of Environmental Factors
Environment, Heredity, and Intelligence: Summing Up

**GROUP DIFFERENCES IN INTELLIGENCE TEST SCORES: WHY THEY OCCUR 434**

Group Differences in IQ Scores: Evidence for the Role of Environmental Factors
Group Differences in IQ Scores: Is There Any Evidence for the Role of Genetic Factors?
Gender Differences in Intelligence

**EMOTIONAL INTELLIGENCE: THE FEELING SIDE OF INTELLIGENCE 439**

Major Components of Emotional Intelligence
Emotional Intelligence: Evidence on Its Existence and Effects

**CREATIVITY: GENERATING THE EXTRAORDINARY 442**

Contrasting Views of Creativity
Research on Creativity: Evidence for the Confluence Approach

- MAKING PSYCHOLOGY PART OF YOUR LIFE *Managing Your Own Anger: A Very Useful Skill*

When I was in high school, one student stood out as the "superbrain" of our entire school: Paul Kronen. He was so smart it was scary. I was in several classes with him, and it didn't matter what the subject was—he was light-years ahead of the rest of us. In math he would get into conversations with the teacher about equations and concepts we couldn't begin to understand. In English he would quote Shakespeare and poetry. And in science all of his experiments worked—every one. What Paul wasn't so good at, though, was getting along with people; far from it. So although everyone agreed that he was brilliant, he wasn't very popular, and I don't recall ever seeing him at parties or dances.

After I graduated and went to college, I lost touch with Paul and many other people I knew in high school. One day, however, I was visiting the neighborhood where I grew up and happened to step into a shoe store. The clerk looked vaguely familiar, and he seemed to recognize me too. When I heard his voice, I knew who it was at once: Paul Kronen. I was shocked. What was he doing here, in this job? I had imagined him as a professor at some prestigious school or as the top scientist at a major laboratory. Paul told me that he had dropped out of college because he found it dull and a waste of time. As we talked, I could see that he was still—how can I put it—a little strange, just as he was in high school. He never looked directly at me, and he jumped from topic to topic so quickly that I had trouble having a conversation with him. I left the store feeling slightly melancholy. There's absolutely nothing wrong with selling shoes, of course. But Paul was so bright that it seemed as though he had wasted some wonderful talents. . . .

Why do I start with this incident? Because it illustrates two points I want to emphasize at the very beginning: (1) Intelligence, the major topic of this chapter, is indeed an important human characteristic. (2) By itself, though, it is *not* a guarantee of success, accomplishment, or personal happiness. But what, precisely, *is* intelligence? Can it be measured, and if so, how? Is there only one kind of intelligence, or are there many? And to what extent is intelligence influenced by genetic factors and by environmental factors, such as each person's unique life experience? These are among the questions psychologists have sought to answer in their research on human intelligence, and we'll address all of them in this chapter. Specifically, our discussion will proceed as follows.

First, we'll examine several different perspectives on the nature of intelligence—contrasting views about what it is and how it operates. Next, we'll consider some of the ways in which intelligence is measured—psychological tests, measures of basic cognitive processes, and even measures of neural functioning. As part of this discussion, we'll examine three basic requirements of any psychological test: *reliability, validity,* and *standardization.* After that, we'll focus on a very basic question concerning intelligence: To what extent do individual differences in intelligence stem from genetic factors and from environmental factors? This same question also applies to *group differences* in intelligence, so we'll examine that highly controversial topic, too. Then we'll briefly examine *emotional intelligence*—our ability to deal effectively with the emotional side of life (Mayer & Salovey, in press). Finally, we'll focus on *creativity*—a characteristic that is related to, but not identical, with intelligence (e.g., Sternberg & Lubart, 1996).

**Intelligence:** Individuals' abilities to understand complex ideas, to adapt effectively to the environment, to learn from experience, to engage in various forms of reasoning, to overcome obstacles by careful thought.

# Intelligence: Contrasting Views of Its Nature

Intelligence, like love, is one of those concepts that are easier to recognize than to define. We often refer to others' intelligence, describing people as *bright, sharp,* or *quick* on the one hand, or as *slow, dull,* or even *stupid* on the other. And slurs on one's intelligence are often fighting words where children—and even adults—are concerned. But again, what, precisely, *is* intelligence? Psychologists don't entirely agree, but as a working definition we can adopt the wording offered by a distinguished panel of experts (Neisser et al., 1996): The term **intelligence** refers to *individuals' abilities to understand complex ideas, to adapt effectively to the environment, to learn from experience, to engage in various forms of reasoning, to overcome obstacles by careful thought.*

Why do we place so much importance on evaluating others' (and our own) intelligence? Partly because we believe that intelligence is related to many important outcomes: how quickly individuals can master new tasks and adapt to new situations, how successful they will be in school and in various kinds of jobs, and even how well they can get along with others (e.g., Goleman, 1998). To some extent, our commonsense ideas in this respect are correct. For instance, the person shown in Figure 11.1 is not acting in a way most of us would describe as intelligent—he is insulting the interviewer! The result? He probably won't get the job. But although intelligence *is* related to important life outcomes, this relationship is far from perfect. Many other factors, too, play a role, so predictions based on intelligence alone can be wrong—as they were with respect to my classmate Paul.

## Intelligence: Unitary or Multifaceted?

Is intelligence a single characteristic, or does it involve several different components? In the past, psychologists who studied intelligence often disagreed sharply on this issue. In one camp were scientists who viewed intelligence as a single

**Figure 11.1**
**Intelligence: We Need It in Everyday Life!**

The person being interviewed here is *not* behaving in a way most people would describe as intelligent: He has insulted the interviewer!

(*Source:* DILBERT reprinted by permission of United Feature Syndicate, Inc.)

characteristic or dimension along which people vary. One early supporter of this view was Spearman (1927), who believed that performance on any cognitive task depended on a primary *general* factor (which he termed *g*) and one or more *specific* factors relating to particular tasks. Spearman based this view on the following finding: Although tests of intelligence often contain different kinds of items designed to measure different aspects of intelligence, scores on these items often correlate highly with one another. This fact suggested to him that no matter how intelligence was measured, it was related to a single, primary factor.

In contrast, other researchers believed that intelligence is composed of many separate abilities that operate more or less independently. According to this *multifactor* view, a given person can be high on some components of intelligence but low on others and vice versa. One early supporter of this position was Thurstone (1938), who suggested that intelligence is composed of seven distinct primary mental abilities. Included in his list were *verbal meaning*—understanding of ideas and word meanings; *number*—speed and accuracy in dealing with numbers; and *space*—the ability to visualize objects in three dimensions.

Which of these views of intelligence has prevailed? Most modern theories of intelligence adopt a position somewhere in between these extremes. They recognize that intelligence may involve a general ability to handle a wide range of cognitive tasks and problems, as Spearman suggested, but also that intelligence *is* expressed in many different ways, and that persons can be high on some aspects of intelligence but low on others. As examples of this modern approach, let's briefly consider three influential views of intelligence.

CourseCompass
Web Link: *Who Owns Intelligence?*

## Gardner's Theory of Multiple Intelligences

In formulating their views of intelligence, most researchers have focused primarily on what might be described as "normal" children and adults: persons who neither greatly exceed nor fall far below what most of us would view as "average" levels of intelligence. Howard Gardner (1983) argued that this approach was limiting psychology's view of intelligence. A better tactic, he suggested, would be to study not only persons in the middle of the intelligence dimension, but also ones at the extremes—acclaimed geniuses and those whose cognitive functioning is impaired, as well as experts in various domains and those who might be described as possessing special mental "gifts." For instance, consider the young athletes who compete in the Olympics. Watching these young people, I am often truly amazed by the feats they can perform. Is their ability to execute complex maneuvers like those shown in Figure 11.2 simply the result of extensive training? Or does their performance also show a special kind of intelligence—something very different from the verbal fluency we usually associate with the term *intelligence,* but perhaps just as important?

**Figure 11.2**
**Great Athletic Skill: A Kind of Intelligence?**

Gardner's theory of multiple intelligences views performance such as that shown here as involving a high level of *bodily–kinesthetic intelligence.*

Gardner would argue strongly for the latter view. In fact, to aspects of intelligence most of us readily recognize, such as the verbal, mathematical, and spatial abilities studied by Thurstone, Gardner added such components as *musical intelligence*—the kind of intelligence shown by one of my friends who, without any formal training, can play virtually any tune on the piano; *bodily–kinesthetic intelligence*—the kind shown by the Olympic athletes shown in Figure 11.2; and *personal intelligence*—for instance, the ability to get along well with others. (I'll return to this latter topic in detail in the discussion of *emotional intelligence.*)

In sum, as its name suggests, Gardner's theory of multiple intelligences proposes that there are several important types of intelligence, and that we must understand each in order to get the big picture where this important human characteristic is concerned.

**Triarchic Theory:** A theory suggesting that there are three basic forms of intelligence: componential, experiential, and contextual.

**Practical Intelligence:** Intelligence useful in solving everyday problems.

Web Link: *Creating the Future: Perspectives on Educational Change*

## Sternberg's Triarchic Theory: The Value of Practical Intelligence

Another important modern theory of intelligence is one proposed by Robert Sternberg (Sternberg, 1985; Sternberg et al., 1995). According to this theory, known as the **triarchic theory** of intelligence, there are actually three basic types of human intelligence. The first, called *componential* or *analytic* intelligence, involves the abilities to think critically and analytically. Persons high on this dimension usually excel on standard tests of academic potential and make excellent students. It's a good bet that your professors are high on this aspect of intelligence. The second type of intelligence, *experiential* or *creative* intelligence, emphasizes insight and the ability to formulate new ideas. Persons who rate high on this dimension excel at zeroing in on what information is crucial in a given situation, and at combining seemingly unrelated facts. This is the kind of intelligence shown by many scientific geniuses and inventors, such as Einstein, Newton, and—some would say—Freud. For example, Johannes Gutenberg, inventor of the printing press, combined the mechanisms for producing playing cards, making wine, and minting coins in his invention; thus, he showed a high level of creative intelligence.

Sternberg terms the third type of intelligence *contextual* or **practical intelligence,** and in some ways, it is the most interesting of all. Persons high on this dimension are intelligent in a practical, adaptive sense—they have what many would term "street smarts" and are adept at solving the problems of everyday life. For example, consider the following incident, cited by Sternberg and his colleagues as an example of high practical intelligence.

The Florida city of Tallahassee (home of Florida State University) provides trash containers to all residents. Garbage collectors used to retrieve each full container from the resident's backyard, bring it to the truck, empty it, and then return it to its original location. This system continued until one day a newly hired employee considered this situation—and realized that the amount of work involved could be cut almost in half through one simple but ingenious change. Can you guess the solution he devised? Here it is: After emptying each trash can, the collectors would take it to the next yard instead of returning it to its original location. There, it would replace the full container that would then be brought to the truck. All the city trash cans were identical, so it made no difference to each resident which trash can they received back; but this simple step *saved one entire trip to each backyard for the trash collectors.* According to Sternberg, solving practical problems like this requires a kind of different intelligence from that required for success in school or other intellectual pursuits. And, as this example suggests, practical intelligence can be valuable in many contexts (see Figure 11.3).

**Figure 11.3**
**Practical Intelligence in Action**

The person shown here has solved a practical problem in an ingenious manner, demonstrating what Sternberg describes as *practical* (contextual) *intelligence.*

## Cattell's Theory of Fluid and Crystallized Intelligence

In their efforts to determine whether intelligence consists of one or several different components, psychologists in past decades often made use of a statistical technique known as *factor analysis.* This technique identifies clusters of items on a test that seem to be related to one another and so can be viewed as measuring a common underlying *factor*—a specific aspect of intelligence. This technique was used by many researchers; Spearman, for instance, employed it as basis for his conclusion that there is a general or *g* factor that underlies all the others. Somewhat different conclusions were reached by Cattell (1963), who concluded that two major clusters of mental abilities exist: what he termed *fluid* and *crystallized intelligence.* As we saw in Chapter 9, *fluid intelligence* refers to our largely inherited abilities to think and reason—in a sense, the hardware of our brains that determines the limits of our information-processing capabilities. In contrast, *crystallized intelligence* refers to accumulated knowledge—information we store over a lifetime of experience, plus the application of skills and knowledge to solving specific problems. In a sense, then, crystallized intelligence is the outcome of experience acting on our fluid intelligence. The speed with which one can analyze information is an example of fluid intelligence, while the breadth of one's vocabulary—how many words one can put to use—illustrates crystallized intelligence.

As I noted in Chapter 9, fluid intelligence seems to decrease slowly with age, but crystallized intelligence stays level or even increases (e.g., Baltes, 1987). This is why older, more experienced individuals can sometimes outperform younger ones on cognitive tasks ranging from scientific research to chess: Declines in older persons' fluid intelligence are more than offset by the vast store of knowledge in their crystallized intelligence.

**REVIEW QUESTIONS**

- What is intelligence?
- What is Gardner's theory of multiple intelligences?
- What is Sternberg's triarchic theory of intelligence?
- What is fluid intelligence? Crystallized intelligence?

Audio 11.1: *Questionable Validity of Research*

## Measuring Intelligence

In 1904, when psychology was just emerging as an independent field, members of the Paris school board approached Alfred Binet with an interesting request: Could he develop an objective method for identifying the children who, in the language of that era, were described as being mentally retarded, so that they could be given special education? Binet was already at work on related topics, so he agreed, enlisting the aid of his colleague, Theodore Simon.

In designing this test Binet and Simon were guided by the belief that the items used should be ones children could answer without special training or study. They felt that this was important because the test should measure the ability to handle intellectual tasks—*not* specific knowledge acquired in school. To attain this goal, Binet and Simon decided to use items of two basic types: ones so new or unusual that none of the children would have prior exposure to them, and ones so familiar that almost all youngsters would have encountered them in the past. Children were asked to perform the following tasks: Follow simple commands or imitate simple gestures; name objects shown in pictures; repeat a sentence of fifteen words; tell how two common objects are different; complete sentences begun by the examiner.

The first version of Binet and Simon's test was published in 1905 and contained thirty items. Much to the two authors' pleasure, it was quite effective: With it, schools could readily identify children in need of special help. Encouraged by this success, Binet and Simon broadened the scope of their test to measure variations in intelligence among all children. The revised version, published in 1908, grouped items by age, with six items at each level from three to thirteen years. Items were placed at a particular age level if about 75 percent of children of that age could pass them correctly.

Binet's tests were soon revised and adapted for use in many countries. In the United States, Lewis Terman, a psychologist at Stanford University, developed the **Stanford–Binet test**—a test that was soon put to use in many different settings. Over the years the Stanford–Binet has been revised several times. One of the features of the Stanford–Binet that contributed to its popularity was the fact that it yielded a single score assumed to reflect an individual's level of intelligence—the now famous (some would say *infamous*) IQ.

## IQ: Its Meaning Then and Now

Originally, the letters **IQ** stood for *intelligence quotient,* and a "quotient" is precisely what the scores represented. To obtain an IQ score, an examiner divided a student's mental age by his or her chronological age, then multiplied this number by 100. For this computation, mental age was based on the number of items a person passed correctly on the test: Test takers received two months' credit of "mental age" for each item passed. If an individual's mental and chronological ages were equal, an IQ of 100 was obtained; this was considered to be an average score. IQs above 100 indicated that a person's intellectual age was greater than her or his chronological age—in other words, that the individual was more intelligent than typical students of the same age. In contrast, numbers below 100 indicated that the individual was less intelligent than her or his peers.

Perhaps you can already see one obvious problem with this type of IQ score: At some point, mental growth levels off or stops, while chronological age continues to grow. As a result, IQ scores begin to decline after the early teen years! Partly because of this problem, IQ scores now have a different definition. They simply reflect an individual's performance relative to that of persons of the same age who have taken the same test. Thus, an IQ above 100 indicates that the person has scored higher than the average person in her or his age group, while a score below 100 indicates that the person has scored lower than average.

## The Wechsler Scales

As noted earlier, the tests developed by Binet and later adapted by Terman and others remained popular for many years. They do, however, suffer from one major drawback: All are mainly verbal in content. As a result, they pay little attention to the fact that intelligence can be revealed in nonverbal activities as well. For example, an architect who visualizes a majestic design for a new building is demonstrating a high level of intelligence; yet no means for assessing such abilities was included in early versions of the Stanford–Binet test.

To overcome this and other problems, David Wechsler devised a set of tests for both children and adults that include nonverbal, or *performance,* items as well as verbal ones, and that yield separate scores for these two components of intelligence. Thus, Wechsler began with the view that intelligence is *not* a unitary characteristic,

**Stanford–Binet Test:** A widely used individual test of intelligence.

**IQ:** Originally, "intelligent quotient," a number that examiners derived by dividing an individual's mental age by his or her chronological age. Now IQ simply indicates an individual's performance on an intelligence test relative to those of other persons.

**TABLE 11.1**

## Subtests of the Wechsler Adult Intelligence Scale

This widely used test of adult intelligence includes the subtests described here.

| Test | Description |
|---|---|
| ***Verbal Tests*** | |
| Information | Examinees are asked to answer general information questions, increasing in difficulty. |
| Digit Span | Examinees are asked to repeat series of digits read out loud by the examiner. |
| Vocabulary | Examinees are asked to define thirty-five words. |
| Arithmetic | Examinees are asked to solve arithmetic problems. |
| Comprehension | Examinees are asked to answer questions requiring detailed answers; answers indicate their comprehension of the questions. |
| Similarities | Examinees indicate in what way two items are alike. |
| ***Performance Tests*** | |
| Picture Completion | Examinees indicate what part of each picture is missing. |
| Picture Arrangement | Examinees arrange pictures to make a sensible story. |
| Block Design | Examinees attempt to duplicate designs made with red and white blocks. |
| Object Assembly | Examinees attempt to solve picture puzzles. |
| Digit Symbol | Examinees fill in small boxes with coded symbols corresponding to a number above each box. |

shown only through verbal and mathematical reasoning. However, he developed these tests at a time when the multifaceted nature of intelligence was not yet well understood, and it is not clear that Wechsler's various subtests actually do measure different aspects of intelligence. Despite such problems, the Wechsler tests are currently among the most frequently used individual tests of intelligence. An overview of the subtests that make up one of the Wechsler scales, the *Weschsler Adult Intelligence Scale–Revised* (WAIS–3 for short) is presented in Table 11.1.

Wechsler believed that differences between scores on the various subtests could be used to diagnose serious psychological disorders (see Chapter 14). However, research on this possibility has yielded mixed results at best.

A Wechsler test for children, the *Wechsler Intelligence Scale for Children* (WISC), has also been developed; it too is in widespread use. Patterns of scores on the subtests of the WISC are sometimes used to identify children suffering from various *learning disabilities.* Some findings indicate that children who score high on certain subtests, such as Picture Completion and Object Assembly, but lower on others, such as Arithmetic, Information, and Vocabulary, are more likely to suffer from learning disabilities than children with other patterns of scores (Aiken, 1991). Once again, however, not all findings point to such conclusions, so the value of the WISC (now in its third revision, WISC–3) for this kind of diagnosis remains somewhat uncertain.

**Aptitude Tests:** Tests designed to measure the ability to acquire new information; used primarily to predict future performance.

**Achievement Tests:** Tests designed to measure current knowledge—the results of previous learning.

**Mental Retardation:** Considerably below-average intellectual functioning combined with varying degrees of difficulty in meeting the demands of everyday life.

**Down Syndrome:** A genetically caused condition that results in mental retardation.

One more point: Tests such as the WAIS are designed to measure the ability to acquire new information or skills, an ability implied by our definition of intelligence. Psychologists describe such tests as **aptitude tests,** and scores on these tests are often used to predict future performance. In contrast, **achievement tests** are designed to measure what you have already learned; for example, the tests you take in this class are designed to be achievement tests. The distinction between these two types of tests is not precise, however. For instance, many aptitude tests (including college entrance examinations) include measures of vocabulary, which, to a degree, reflect past learning. But in general it is useful to think of aptitude tests as ones designed to predict future performance and achievement tests as ones that reflect current performance and the results of past learning.

## Individual Tests of Intelligence: Measuring the Extremes

Web Link: *Introduction to Mental Retardation*

Individual tests of intelligence such as the Stanford–Binet or WISC are costly: They must be administered one-on-one by a psychologist or other trained professional. Why, then, do these tests continue in widespread use? The answer is that these tests have several practical uses and provide benefits that help to offset these costs. The most important of these uses involves identification of children at the extremes with respect to intelligence—those who are mentally challenged (i.e., who suffer from some degree of *mental retardation*), and those who are *intellectually gifted.*

The term **mental retardation** refers to intellectual functioning that is considerably below average combined with varying degrees of difficulty in meeting the demands of everyday life (Aiken, 1991; Wielkiewicz & Calvert, 1989). As shown in Figure 11.4, persons with mental retardation are typically described according to four broad categories of retardation: mild, moderate, severe, and profound (American Psychiatric Association, 1994). Individuals' level of retardation is determined by at least two factors: their test scores *and* their success in carrying out activities of daily living expected of persons their age. As you can guess, persons whose retardation is in the "mild" category can usually learn to function quite well.

What causes mental retardation? In some cases it can be traced to genetic abnormalities such as **Down syndrome,** which is caused by the presence of an extra chromosome; persons with Down syndrome usually have IQs below 50. Mental retardation can also result from environmental factors, such as inadequate nutrition or use of drugs or alcohol by expectant mothers, infections, toxic agents, and traumas resulting from a lack of oxygen during birth. Most cases of mental retardation, however, cannot readily be traced to specific causes.

Intelligence tests have also been used to identify the *intellectually gifted*—persons whose intelligence is far above average (Friedman et al., 1995; Terman, 1954). I mentioned the most comprehensive study on such persons in Chapter 9,

**Figure 11.4**
**Degrees of Mental Retardation**

As shown here, persons with mild retardation can acquire many basic academic skills and become self-supporting. Those with profound retardation, however, generally require constant supervision; they can't perform simple tasks without assistance.

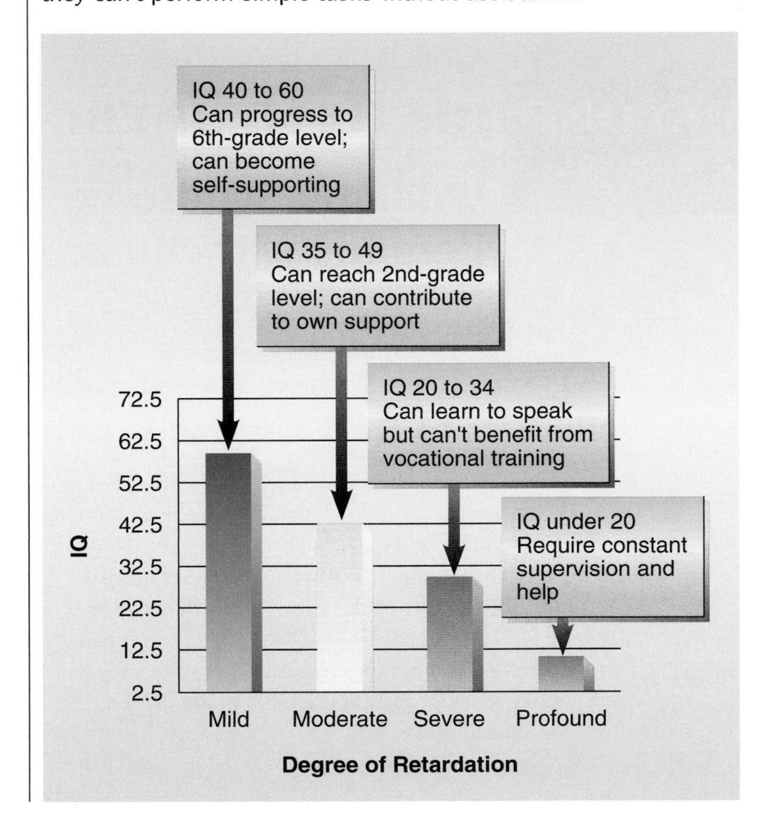

**Figure 11.5**
**Billionaires Don't Necessarily Have High IQs**

People who start successful businesses don't necessarily have high IQs. They may possess other skills or abilities that contribute to their great success. Shown here is Jeff Bezos, who founded Amazon.Com (the on-line bookstore) and quickly became a billionaire. He may or may not have high IQ, but whether he does or not, he is certainly high in *practical intelligence*.

where I briefly described the results of a study on exceptionally bright persons first begun by Lewis Terman in 1925. This study has followed the lives of about 1,500 children with IQs of 130 or above to determine the relationship between high intelligence and occupational success and social adjustment. As a group, these gifted persons have experienced high levels of success. They have earned more degrees, attained higher occupational status and salaries, experienced better personal and social adjustment, and were healthier, at each age, than the average adult.

As you can readily guess, Paul, the "superbrain" from my high school class, was intellectually gifted; in fact, rumor had it that his IQ was 185. But remember, as his later career showed, even a very high level of intelligence is not a guarantee of success or happiness. By the same token, an average level of intelligence is definitely not a sentence to low levels of success or achievement. In fact, as I'll note in a later section, many people who attain great success in business—for instance, *entrepreneurs* who start companies that make them billionaires—are not necessarily far above average in the kind of intelligence measured by the Stanford–Binet, WISC, and other "IQ" tests (see Figure 11.5). On the contrary, they may excel in other aspects of intelligence, or in *creativity*, instead (e.g., Baron, 2000).

Some persons who are classified as mentally retarded show amazing mental abilities in specific areas. For a dramatic example of this surprising pattern, please see the following **Beyond the Headlines** section.

## the HEADLINES: *As Psychologists See It*

## Williams Syndrome: Mentally Challenged Persons with Music in Their Souls

### A Mysterious Musical Gift Leads Scientists to Re-Examine Intelligence

ORANGE COUNTY REGISTER (SEPTEMBER 22, 1998): From birth, something was clearly wrong. The puffy eyes. The elfin nose. The tiny chin. "Williams syndrome," the doctors said. "Mentally retarded," the parents heard. So imagine Kristine Hendryx's surprise when baby Mary's gift surfaced while she was still in the crib.

"I would sing a few notes to her and she would sing them right back, and she always had perfect pitch" Hendryx says. Other parents of Williams kids tells similar stories. When Meghan Flynn was 2, she began picking out harmonies on the piano. When Gloria Lenhoff was a toddler, she toddled in time to the music. "Gloria had a short attention span for everything except music," father Howard Lenhoff says. "She could listen to music for hours." The mysterious musicality of these girls—and thousands like them—is forcing science to rethink its definition of intelligence.

Persons with Williams syndrome are indeed a puzzle. Although they have IQs that classify them as mildly to moderately retarded and can't accomplish simple tasks such as making change for a dollar or adding two numbers together, they show incredible musical talents. For instance, Gloria Lenhoff, whose IQ is 60, can sing opera in German, entirely from memory. And Mary Hendryx, who has a similar low IQ, can compose original ballads for the piano. How can individuals who score so low on standard tests of intelligence accomplish their amazing feats? The answer, most psychologists would suggest, is one we've stated before: Intelligence involves much more than the reasoning and thinking capacities measured by standard IQ tests. Intelligence is truly like a multifaceted jewel, and some people who do not shine in one aspect can dazzle in others.

Research on persons with Williams syndrome—and on other mentally challenged individuals who show unusual abilities—also calls to our attention the fact that genetic factors play a major role in human intelligence, and perhaps even in personality as well. Not only do persons with this syndrome show similar physical characteristics (they look like pixies in children's books; see Figure 11.6) and share remarkable musical talents; they also show similar personality traits (e.g., they are exceptionally warm, compassionate, and outgoing). So persons with Williams syndrome add one more piece of evidence to the ever growing body of scientific data suggesting that everything from our thought processes to our personalities may be rooted, at least to a degree, in genetic factors. Consistent with this suggestion, recent findings point to the loss of a tiny piece of genetic material from chromosome number 7 as the genetic basis for Williams syndrome.

Does this mean that intelligence, personality, and other important human characteristics can't be changed? As I've said before: Far from it. Intelligence, as we'll soon see, is influenced by environmental as well as genetic factors and can be enhanced by, for example, enriched early experience (Ramey & Ramey, 1998). But recognizing that genetic factors play a role in many aspects of human behavior assists us in our efforts to unravel the mysteries of intelligence, personality, and many other topics, and that, in essence, is what psychology is all about.

### CRITICAL THINKING QUESTIONS

1. Parents' observations of their children's behavior are open to many forms of bias. Do you think this might be so in reports of the musical abilities of persons with Williams syndrome?
2. What about reports that all persons with Williams syndrome have similar personalities? How could we test this assertion systematically?
3. Do you think that their pixielike appearance might play a role in shaping the personality—and perhaps the intelligence—of persons with Williams syndrome?

**Figure 11.6**
**Williams Syndrome: Low IQ Paired with Exceptional Musical Talent**

Persons who have Williams syndrome have low IQ but often demonstrate unusual musical talents. In addition, they are often described as having a very warm and friendly personality and a distinctive facial appearance.

## Group Tests of Intelligence

Both the Stanford–Binet and the Wechsler scales are *individual* tests of intelligence: They are designed for use with one person at a time. Obviously, it would be much more efficient if *group* tests could be administered to large numbers of people at once. The need for such tests was driven home at the start of World War I, when the armed forces in the United States suddenly faced the task of screening several million recruits. In response to this challenge, psychologists such as Arthur Otis developed two tests: *Army Alpha* for persons who could read (remember, this was back in 1917), and *Army Beta* for persons would could not read or who did not speak

Web Link: *Test Reliability*

Web Link: *Test Validity*

English. These early group tests proved highly useful. For example, the tests were used to select candidates for officer training school, and they did accurately predict success in such training.

In the succeeding decades many other group tests of intelligence were developed. Among the more popular of these are the *Otis tests,* such as the Otis–Lennon School Ability Test (Otis & Lennon, 1967); the *Henmon–Nelson Tests* (Nelson, Lamke, & French, 1973); and the *Cognitive Abilities Test* (CAT) (Thorndike & Hagen, 1982). All are available in versions that can be administered to large numbers of persons. The advantages offered by such tests soon made them very popular, and they were put to routine use in many school systems—especially in schools in large cities, such as the one I attended. During the 1960s, however, this practice was called into serious question and became the focus of harsh criticism. While there were many reasons for this controversy, the most serious was the charge that such tests were unfair to children from disadvantaged backgrounds—especially youngsters from certain minority groups. We'll return to these objections in a later section. Here, however, we'll pause briefly to address the following question: What are the basic requirements for a useful test of intelligence? For information on this crucial issue, please see the following **Research Methods** section.

## Research Methods: How Psychologists Evaluate Their Own Assessment Tools: Basic Requirements of Psychological Tests

One of my hobbies is woodworking, and there is an old saying in that field: "Measure twice, cut once." This means that it is *crucial* to measure carefully before cutting any piece of wood. Unless the measurements are precise, the project won't turn out well. A similar principle applies to all psychological tests, including ones designed to measure intelligence: Unless the tests do a good job of measuring what they are designed to measure, they are useless. Briefly, a test must meet three crucial requirements before we can conclude that it provides an accurate and useful measure of intelligence: The test must be carefully *standardized,* it must be *reliable,* and it must be *valid.* This discussion will focus on intelligence tests, but please remember that the basic principles discussed here apply to *any* psychological test.

### Test Standardization: A Sound Basis for Comparison

Suppose you take an exam in one of your classes and learn that you got 70 percent of the items correct. What does this tell you? Very little, by itself, because in a class that is "graded on a curve," you don't know whether that equals an A, a B, or a C. Unless you also know the *average* score for all members of the class and how the scores are distributed (e.g., did most people get 40 percent right? 60 percent right? 80 percent right?), you can't really evaluate your performance.

The same principle is true for tests of intelligence. In order for the scores to be useful, the tests must be carefully *standardized.* This means that a large group of persons representative of the population for whom the test is designed must take it. Then the mean and the distribution of their scores is carefully examined. If the test is well constructed, the distribution of scores will approach the *normal curve* in shape—a bell-shaped function with most scores in the middle and fewer scores as we move toward the extremes (very low scores or very high scores; see Figure 11.7). The normal curve is very useful because, as we'll note in more detail in the Appendix, it helps us determine just where an individual stands relative to other persons who also took the test. Specifically, using the normal curve, we can tell what percentage of all people who took the test scored as high as this person. This information then helps us to interpret each individual's performance as being relatively low, average, or high. For instance, if only 2 percent of all persons who take an intelligence test score as high as a specific person does, we can conclude that she is very high in intelligence. If 50 percent score as high as she does, we can conclude that she is average in intelligence. And if 98 percent score higher than she does, we can conclude that she is very low in intelligence. Most widely used intelligence tests are designed to yield an average score of about 100, so the score of each test taker can be compared with this value to determine just where the person stands, in a relative sense, with respect to intelligence.

### Reliability: The Importance of Consistency

Suppose that in preparation for a summer at the beach, you decide to go on a diet to lose 10 pounds. Your current weight is 135, and for two weeks you skip desserts and engage in extra exercise. Then you step onto your bathroom scale to see how you've done. Much to your surprise, the needle reads 139; you've actually *gained* 4 pounds! How can this be? Perhaps you made a mistake. So you step

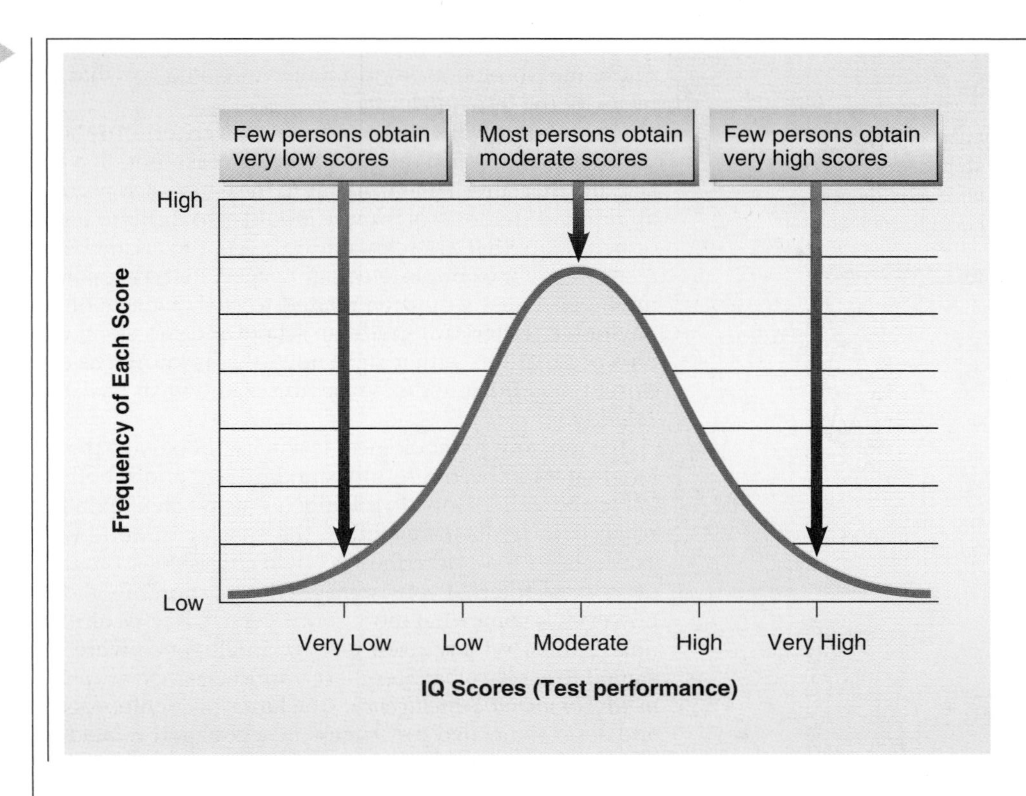


**Figure 11.7**
**Test Standardization and the Normal Curve**

Tests that are well constructed show a normal distribution of scores: Most scores fall near the middle, and fewer and fewer scores occur at the extremes. Because of certain mathematical properties, the normal curve can be used to describe an individual's relative standing with respect to intelligence (or whatever psychological characteristic is being measured) with great precision.

back on the scale. Now it reads 134. You get off and try again; the needle swings to 131. At this point, you realize the truth: Your scale is *unreliable*—the numbers it shows change even though your weight, obviously, doesn't change from one instant to the next.

This is a simple illustration of a very basic but important point: In order to be of any use, measuring devices, whether they are bathroom scales or psychological tests, must have high **reliability:** They must yield the same result each time they are applied to the same quantity. If they don't, they are essentially useless. Two basic forms of reliability are important. First, tests must possess what psychologists call *internal consistency:* All the items on the test must actually measure intelligence (or whatever the test is designed to measure). One way to assess such internal consistency involves dividing the test in two equivalent parts, such as the first and second halves or odd- and even-numbered items, and then comparing people's scores on each part. If the test measures intelligence reliably, then the correlation between the two parts should be positive and high. If it is, then the test is said to be high in **split-half reliability.** If it is not, then some of the items may be measuring different things, and the test may be unreliable in one important sense.

Second, to be viewed as reliable, tests of intelligence must yield scores that are stable over time—unlike the bathroom scale described above! Psychologists measure such **test–retest reliability** by having the same persons take the test at different times. The more similar a given person's scores on these occasions are, the higher is the test–retest reliability. Because intelligence is a characteristic that would not be expected to change over time—unless, of course, something fairly dramatic happened to the persons involved—high test–retest reliability is an important requirement of all tests of human intelligence.

### Validity: Do Tests Measure What They Claim to Measure?

On a recent visit to one of our local malls, I noticed a new machine outside one of the stores. A sign on the front read, "Test Your Sex Appeal!" I was fascinated, so I read further. According to the instructions, if I inserted a quarter and pushed some buttons, the machine would rate my appeal to members of the opposite sex (see Figure 11.8 on page 424). Do you think the machine was really capable of measuring sex appeal? The answer is obvious, if a little disappointing: No way! After all, how could this device tell persons who used it how they would be perceived by others? Psychologists would say that machines such as this one—and any other measuring devices that claim to measure something they do not—are low in **validity:** the ability to measure what they are supposed to measure.

**Reliability:** The extent to which any measuring device (including psychological tests) yields the same result each time it is applied to the same quantity.

**Split-Half Reliability:** The correlation between scores on two parts of a test.

**Test–Retest Reliability:** A measure of the extent to which scores on a test remain stable over time.

**Validity:** The extent to which a test actually measures what it claims to measure.

**Figure 11.8**
**Low Validity: An Example**

Devices like this one really can't help you find your "perfect match," so the scores they provide have no validity; that is, the devices do not measure what they claim to measure.

The same principle applies to psychological tests: They are useful only to the extent that they really measure the characteristics they claim to measure. Thus, an intelligence test is useful only to the extent that it really measures intelligence. How can we determine whether a test is valid? Through several different methods. One of these, known as **content validity,** has to do with the extent to which items on a test are related in a straightforward way to the characteristic we wish to measure. For example, if an intelligence test consisted of measurements of the length of people's ears or the sharpness of their teeth, we would probably conclude that it was low in content validity: These measurements seem totally unrelated to what we mean by the term *intelligence.*

Another type of validity is known as **criterion-related validity** and is based on the following reasoning: If a test actually measures what it claims to measure, then persons attaining different scores on it should also differ in terms of behaviors that are relevant to the characteristic being measured. For example, we might expect that scores on an intelligence test would be related to such aspects of behavior (i.e., criteria) as grades in school and success in various occupations, either right now (this is known as *concurrent validity*) or in the future (this is known as *predictive validity*).

In sum, any psychological test is useful only to the extent that it has been carefully standardized and is both reliable and valid. How do intelligence tests stack up in this respect? In terms of reliability, the answer is: quite well. The tests we have described do yield consistent scores and do possess internal consistency. The question of validity, however, is somewhat more controversial. As I've already noted, most widely used tests of intelligence were designed to assess what Sternberg would describe as *componential* or *analytic intelligence*—the kinds of cognitive skills and abilities needed for success in school and related activities. These tests were *not* designed to measure practical intelligence; indeed, as we saw earlier, persons high in practical intelligence do not necessarily score high on standard tests of academic intelligence. As a result, tests such as the Stanford–Binet and the Wechsler scales have high validity where predictions of performance in school are concerned. In addition, intelligence test scores are moderately related (perhaps "modestly" is a better word) to success in such fields as medicine, law, science, and engineering—fields in which the kind of academic intelligence they measure can be useful (e.g., Gottfredson, 1987). Why aren't these relationships stronger? Perhaps because many factors other than intelligence play a role in success in these complex fields. For instance, successful physicians need more than high intelligence—they must be good with people, too. Finally, the tests are even less useful in predicting success in other areas of life—for instance, in predicting who will become a successful musician, a successful executive, or a successful politician (e.g., McClelland, 1998). In sum, the tests are valid, but only for certain limited uses. We'll return to this issue below, in a discussion of group differences in intelligence test scores. Now, however, let's briefly consider some techniques other than tests that are also used by psychologists to measure intelligence.

**Content Validity:** The extent to which items on a test are related in a straightforward way to the characteristic the test aims to measure.

**Criterion-Related Validity:** The extent to which scores on a test are related to behaviors (criteria) that are relevant to the characteristics the test purports to measure.

## The Cognitive Basis of Intelligence: Processing Speed

"Quick study," "quick-witted," "fast learner"—phrases such as these are often used to describe people who are high in intelligence, both academic and practical. They suggest that being intelligent

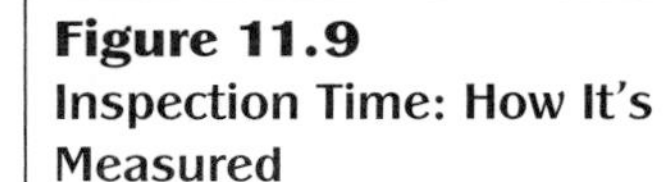

involves being able to process information quickly. Is there any scientific evidence to support this idea? In fact, there is. Psychologists interested in studying intelligence have moved beyond tests such as the Stanford–Binet and Wechsler scales in an attempt to try to identify the basic cognitive mechanisms and processes that underlie intelligence—and that enable people to score high on intelligence tests (e.g., Deary, 1995). This work has led to two major developments. First, several tests have been constructed that are based on the findings of cognitive psychology and on our growing understanding of many aspects of cognition (Naglieri, 1997). Among these the most noteworthy are the *Kaufman Assessment Battery for Children* and the *Kaufman Adult Intelligence Test* (e.g., Kaufman & Kaufman, 1993), and the *Woodcock–Johnson Test of Cognitive Abilities* (Woodcock & Johnson, 1989). The Woodcock–Johnson Test, for instance, attempts to measure important aspects of both fluid and crystallized intelligence.

Second, a growing body of research has focused on the finding that the speed with which individuals perform simple perceptual and cognitive tasks (processing speed) is often correlated with scores on intelligence tests (Neisser et al., 1996; Vernon, 1987). For example, significant correlations (on the order of –.30 to –.40) have often been found between various measures of *reaction time* (one measure of processing speed) and scores on intelligence tests (see, e.g., Deary & Stough, 1996; Fry & Hale, 1996).

Another and even more promising cognitive measure of intelligence is a measure known as **inspection time.** This measure reflects the minimum amount of time a particular stimulus must be exposed for individuals to make a judgment about it that meets some preestablished criterion of accuracy. The shorter the duration time necessary for a given individual to attain a given level of accuracy, presumably, the faster the speed of important aspects of that person's cognitive (mental) operations. To measure inspection time, psychologists often use procedures in which individuals are shown simple drawings like the one in Figure 11.9 and are asked to indicate whether the longer side occurs on the left or right. Participants are *not* told to respond as quickly as possible. Rather, they are instructed to take their time and to be accurate. Inspection time is measured by the time they take to make such decisions at a prespecified level of accuracy—for example, 85 percent.

**Figure 11.9**
**Inspection Time: How It's Measured**

To measure inspection time, psychologists ask research participants to indicate whether the long side of a stimulus *(left)* is on the left or the right. Immediately after a participant sees each stimulus, it is masked by another one in which both sides are long *(right)*. Participants are not told to respond as quickly as possible; rather, they are instructed to take their time and be accurate. Inspection time is measured in terms of the time they require in order to make such decisions at some predetermined level of accuracy.

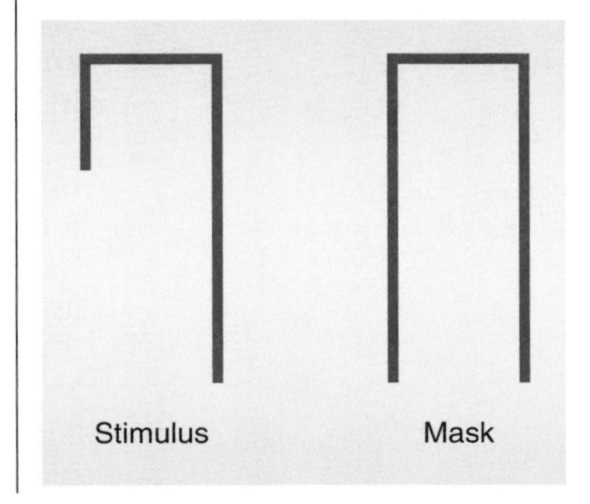


**Inspection Time:** The minimum amount of time a particular stimulus must be exposed for individuals to make a judgment about it that meets some preestablished criterion of accuracy.

What does inspection time measure? Presumably, the amount of time individuals require for the intake of new visual information. Supporters of this measure argue that this task—perceiving new information—is basic to all higher-level mental operations in human thought (e.g., Deary, 1995; Deary & Stough, 1996). Further, they note that this measure is closely related to current theories of perception and decision making, theories emphasizing that new visual information is perceived in discrete samples and then combined into judgments such as "I see it" or "I don't see it." Growing evidence indicates that inspection time is indeed closely related to intelligence, as measured by standard tests. In fact, inspection time and scores on such tests correlate –.50 or more (e.g., Kranzler & Jensen, 1989).

In sum, inspection time appears to be a very promising measure for probing the nature of human intelligence—for understanding the basic cognitive processes that underlie this important characteristic. And since understanding a process is often an essential first step to being able to change it in beneficial ways, this is valuable progress.

## The Neural Basis of Intelligence: Intelligence and Neural Efficiency

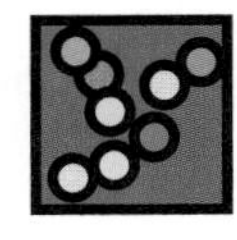

In Chapter 2, and again in discussing memory in Chapter 6, I noted that everything we do, think, or feel rests, in an ultimate sense, on neurochemical events occurring

**Competency Assessment:** A technique for predicting future performance; involves identifying key differences between persons who are currently showing outstanding performance and those showing average performance.

in our brains. If that is indeed true—and virtually all psychologists believe that it is—then an intriguing possibility arises: Can we trace individual differences in intelligence to differences in neural functioning? The answer suggested by a growing body of evidence is *yes* (e.g., Matarazzo, 1992; Vernon, 1993). Such research suggests, first, that *nerve conduction velocity*—the speed with which nerve impulses are conducted in the visual system—correlates significantly with measures of intelligence (e.g., the Raven Progressive Matrices test) (Reed & Jensen, 1993).

Other, and related, research has examined metabolic activity in the brain during cognitive tasks (e.g., Haier et al., 1993). Presumably, if intelligence is related to efficient brain functioning, then the more intelligent people are, the less energy their brains should expend while working on various tasks. This prediction, too, has been confirmed: The brains of persons scoring highest on written measures of intellectual ability *do* expend less energy when these individuals perform complex cognitive tasks. The data in these studies have been gathered using the PET technique of brain imaging described in Chapters 2 and 6.

Finally, some findings suggest that there is a link between brain structure and intelligence (Andreason et al., 1993). Specifically, scores on standard measures of intelligence such as the Wechsler Adult Intelligence Scale are related to the size of certain portions of the brain, including the left and right temporal lobes and the left and right hippocampus. Moreover, this is true even when corrections are made for individuals' overall physical size.

In sum, it appears that the improved methods now available for studying the brain and nervous system are beginning to establish the kind of links between intelligence and physical structures that psychologists have long suspected to exist. Such research is very recent, so it is still too soon to reach firm conclusions. It does appear, though, that we are on the verge of establishing much firmer links between intelligence—a crucial aspect of mind—and body than has ever been true before.

For a discussion of yet another technique used by psychologists to measure cognitive abilities—and to make important predictions about future success—please see the following **From Science to Practice** section.

from SCIENCE to PRACTICE

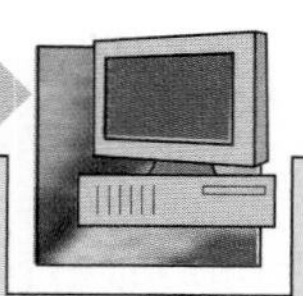

## Predicting Career Success: Competency Assessment

Earlier, I noted that standard intelligence tests are not very effective in predicting success outside academic circles. They are moderately related to achievement in fields that require skills similar to those needed for success in school (e.g., science, law, medicine) but are quite ineffective in predicting success in other contexts, including the one in which most people spend much of their adult lives: the business world (e.g., Whitla, 1975). Is there a better way to predict success in such settings? Fortunately, there is.

This approach is known as **competency assessment,** and it is based on the following reasoning: If we start with two groups—one known to be highly successful and the other known to be only average in terms of career success—and then search for differences between them, the differences we identify may be useful in predicting success in other groups of persons. But how do we go about identifying the key differences between highly successful and less successful persons? One useful procedure involves what are known as *behavioral-event interviews* (e.g., Spencer & Spencer, 1993). In these interviews persons rated by others who know them well as being outstanding at their jobs, and persons rated as being only average, describe what they said, thought, felt, and did in various work-related situations (e.g., how they reached decisions, how they dealt with sudden emergencies, and so on). Their answers are then carefully examined for patterns of differences. Such differences, when identified, are labeled *competencies:* Presumably, these are the key skills or abilities that distinguish outstanding performers from average ones. Using such interviews, researchers have identified several competencies that seem to play a key role in success in several fields, such as being a business executive. These include skill at several kinds of thinking, such as inductive reasoning and analytical thinking; a strong desire for success; flexibility; wanting to have an impact on others; willingness to take initiative; self-confidence; and good understanding of others (a cluster of skills psychologists often describe as *social skills*).

Are *all* these skills necessary for success? Not necessarily; further studies indicate that being highly successful seems to require only that individuals possess several of them—for instance, five of the competencies listed (e.g., Nygren & Ukeritis, 1993).

Now for the most important question: Does possession of these competencies do a good job of predicting career success? Research findings suggest that they do. For instance, in one major project, McClelland (1998) studied the executives in a large corporation. On the basis of behavioral-event interviews, the researchers classified the executives as being highly qualified or average in potential. They then followed the executives' performance for several years. As expected, those classified as being highly qualified were rated by their bosses as doing a better job, and received significantly higher bonuses, in two different years (see Figure 11.10). Another important finding was this: Although almost half of the executives hired in the usual way by the company quit within a year, none of those hired on the basis of competency assessment (having been rated as outstanding in potential) quit. Hiring and training each new executive cost the company more than $250,000, so by using competency assessment the organization saved more than $4 million in a single year!

In sum, competency assessment appears to provide a useful technique for predicting success in the world of work. So although standard intelligence tests don't seem to do a very good job in this respect, psychologists have used their understanding of human behavior and their knowledge of human cognition and intelligence to devise other, more effective procedures. Clearly, this represents an important contribution by the science of psychology to the solution of important practical problems.

**Figure 11.10**
**Evidence for the Usefulness of Competency Assessment**

Executives who were classified as being outstanding in potential on the basis of behavioral-event interviews were rated higher by their bosses and earned significantly larger bonuses than executives who were rated as being average in potential. Findings such as these suggest that competency assessment can be a useful technique for predicting career success.
(*Source:* Based on data from McClelland, 1998.)

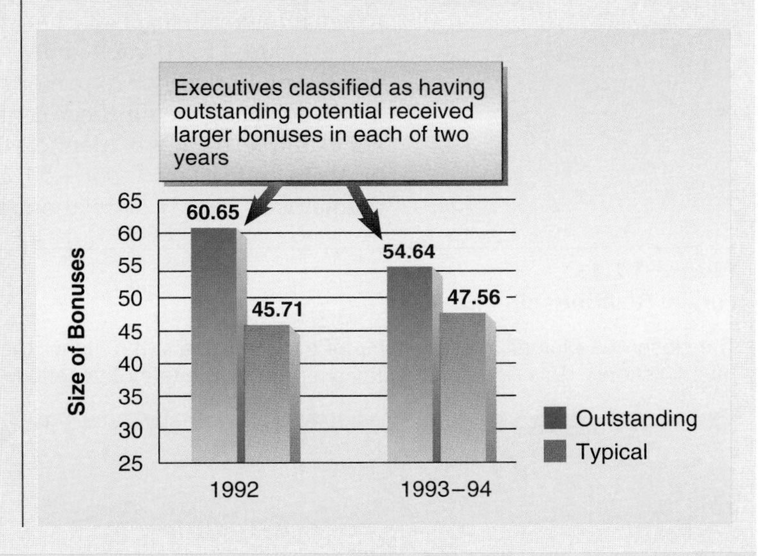


## REVIEW QUESTIONS

- What was the first individual test of intelligence, and what did scores on it mean?
- What are the Wechsler scales?
- What are standardization, reliability, and validity?
- What is inspection time, and what does it measure?
- What findings suggest that intelligence is related to neural functioning or brain structure?
- What is competency assessment, and how is it used?

### Food for Thought

Suppose that a highly reliable technique for measuring intelligence through brain activity could be determined. Would it be necessarily more valid than other techniques? Could it be put to practical use?

# Human Intelligence: The Role of Heredity and the Role of Environment

That people differ in intelligence is obvious. *Why* such differences exist is quite another matter. Are they largely a matter of heredity—differences in the genetic materials and codes we inherit from our parents? Or are they primarily the result of environmental factors—conditions in the world around us that affect our intellectual development? I'm sure you know the answer: Both types of factors are involved. Human intelligence is clearly the result of the complex interplay between genetic factors and a wide range of environmental conditions (e.g., Plomin, 1997). Let's now consider some of the evidence pointing to this conclusion.

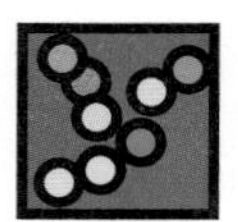

## Evidence for the Influence of Heredity

Several lines of research offer support for the view that heredity plays an important role in human intelligence. First, consider findings with respect to family relationship and measured IQ. If intelligence is indeed determined by heredity, we would expect that the more closely two persons are related, the more similar their IQs will be. This prediction has generally been confirmed (e.g., McGue et al., 1993; Neisser et al., 1996). For example, the IQs of identical twins raised together correlate almost +.90, those of brothers and sisters about +.50, and those of cousins about +.15 (see Figure 11.11). (Remember: Higher correlations indicate stronger relationships between variables.)

**Figure 11.11**
**Family Relationship and IQ**

The closer the biological relationship of two individuals, the higher the correlation between their IQ scores. This finding provides support for the role of genetic factors in intelligence.

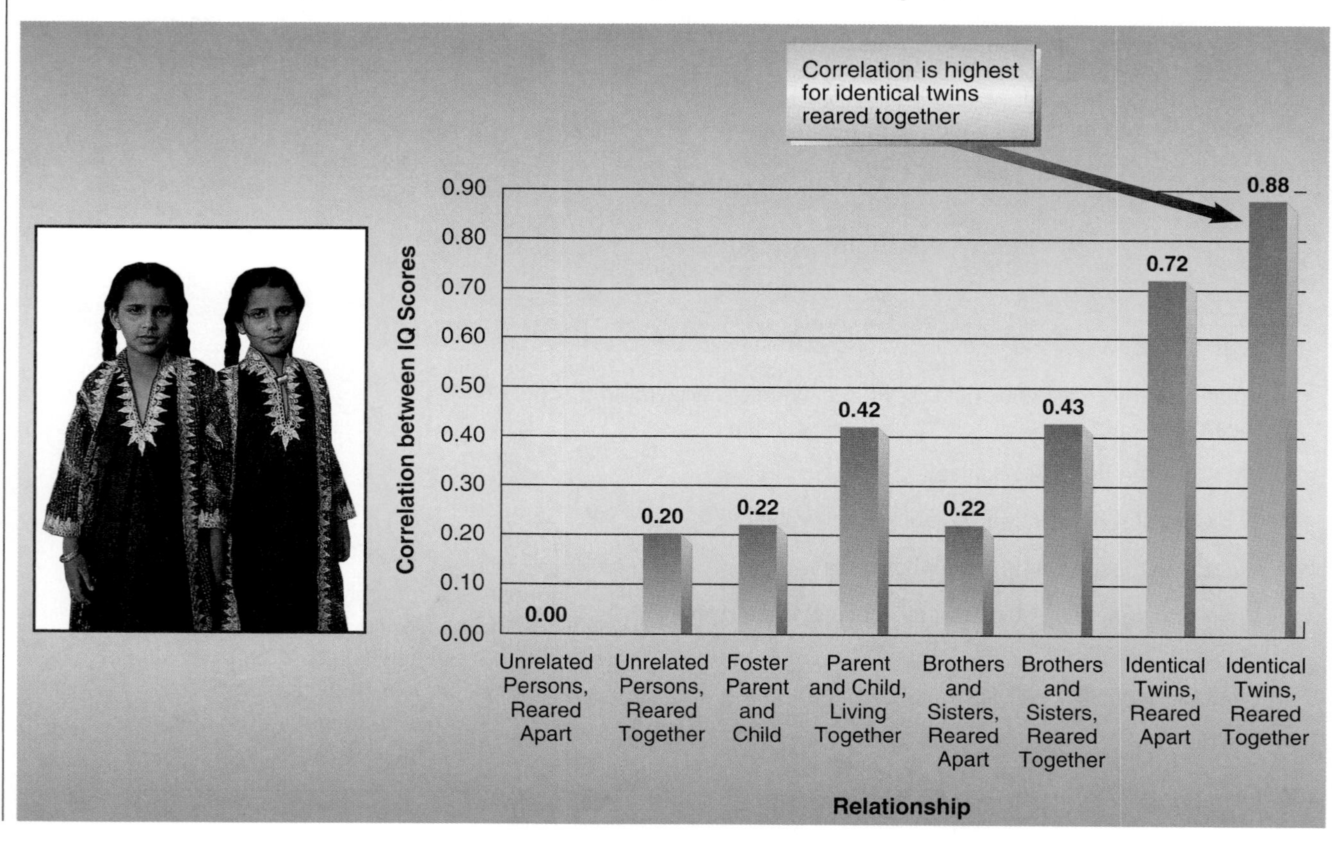

Additional support for the impact of heredity on intelligence is provided by studies involving adopted children. If intelligence is strongly affected by genetic factors, the IQs of adopted children should resemble those of their biological parents more closely than those of their adoptive parents. In short, the children should be more similar in IQ to the persons from whom they received their genes than to the persons who raised them. This prediction, too, has been confirmed (Jencks, 1972; Munsinger, 1978). For example, consider a long-term study conducted by Plomin and his colleagues (Plomin et al., 1997).

In this investigation (the Colorado Adoption Project), the researchers studied 245 children who were placed for adoption by their mothers shortly after birth (on average, when they were twenty-nine days old) until they were teenagers. Measures of the children's intelligence were obtained when they were one, two, three, four, seven, twelve, and sixteen years old. In addition, measures were obtained of their biological mothers' intelligence and of their adoptive parents' intelligence. A comparison group of children who were living with their biological parents was tested in the same manner. As you can see from Figure 11.12, results showed a clear pattern: The correlation between the adopted children's intelligence and that of their biological parents increased over time, as did the correlation between the intelligence of the control group (children living with their biological parents) and that of their parents. In contrast, the correlation between the intelligence of the adopted children and that of their adoptive parents *decreased*

**Figure 11.12**
**Evidence for the Role of Heredity in Intelligence**

As shown here, correlations between the intelligence of adopted children and that of their biological parents (biological curve), and between the intelligence of children living at home and that of their biological parents (control curve), increased over time. In contrast, correlations between the intelligence of adopted children and that of their adoptive parents (adoptive curve) decreased over time.
(*Source:* Based on data from Plomin et al., 1997.)

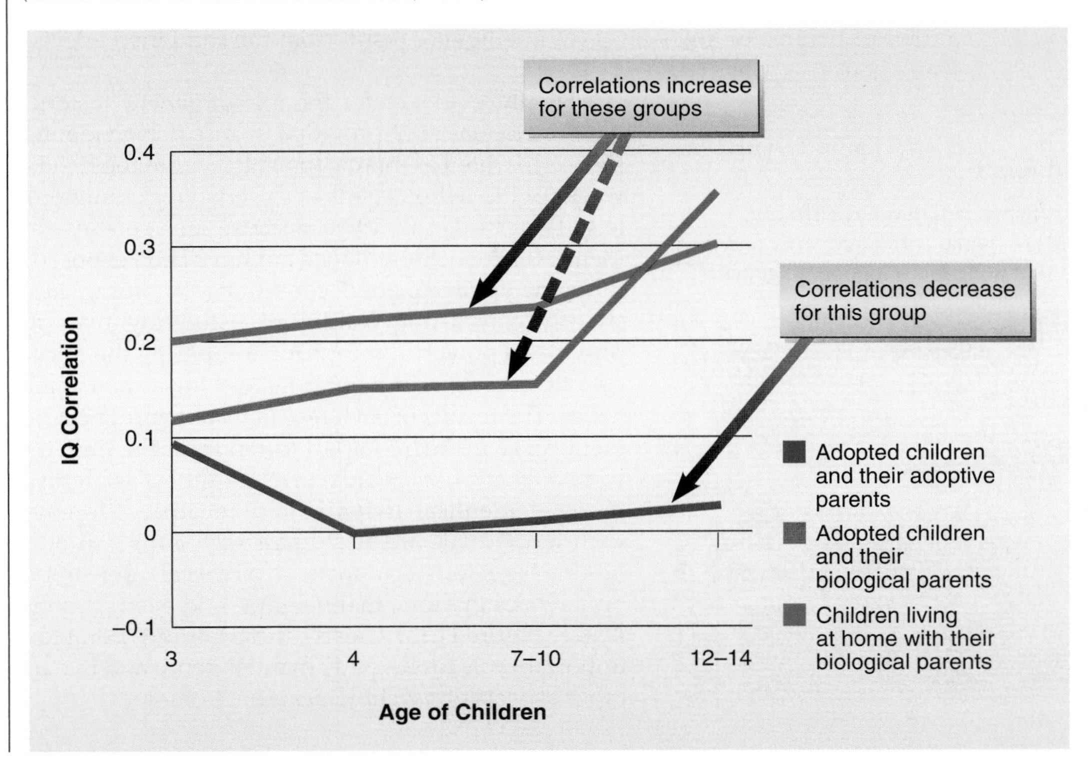

over time. Similar patterns were found for specific components of intelligence, as well as for general cognitive abilities—for instance, for verbal and spatial abilities. In other words, the adopted children came to resemble their biological parents, but not their adoptive parents, more closely in intelligence over time. As Plomin and his colleagues (1997) note, these findings suggest that genetic factors play an important role in intelligence and may indeed outweigh environmental factors in this respect. However, the authors are also quick to add that the children studied were placed in homes above average in socioeconomic status; thus, they were *not* exposed to environmental extremes of poverty, disadvantage, or malnutrition. As we'll note below, such extreme conditions can strongly affect children's intelligence. In addition, somewhat different measures of intelligence were employed at different ages, especially for the youngest children; this too may have played some role in the pattern of findings obtained.

Additional evidence for the role of genetic factors in intelligence is provided by recent studies focused on the task of identifying the specific genes that influence intelligence (e.g., Rutter & Plomin, 1997; Sherman et al., 1997). These studies have adopted as a working hypothesis the view that many genes, each exerting relatively small effects, probably play a role in general intelligence—that is, in what many aspects of mental abilities (e.g., verbal, spatial, speed-of-processing, and memory abilities) have in common (e.g., Plomin, 1997). In other words, such research has not attempted to identify *the* gene that influences intelligence, but rather has sought *quantitative trait loci* (QTLs): genes that have relatively small effects and that influence the likelihood of some characteristic in a population. The results of such studies suggest that certain genes are indeed associated with high intelligence. For instance, Chorney and his colleagues (1998) compared individuals with IQ scores greater than 160 and a control group of persons average in intelligence (with mean IQ scores of about 100). They found that persons in the very high-IQ group were more likely to possess a specific gene (actually, a particular form of this gene) than were persons in the average group: About 34 percent of the high-IQ group possessed this form of the gene, but only 17 percent of those in the average group did. It's important to note again, however, that the effects of this gene were small; the researchers estimated that it accounted for only 2 percent of the variance in general intelligence. Thus, as suggested earlier, many different genes working together play a role, and high—or low—levels of intelligence result from the combined effects of many genes.

Finally, evidence for the role of genetic factors in intelligence has been provided by research on identical twins separated as infants (usually, within the first few weeks of life) who were then raised in different homes (e.g., Bouchard et al., 1990). Because such persons have identical genetic inheritance but have been exposed to different environmental conditions—in some cases, sharply contrasting conditions—studying their IQs provides a powerful means for comparing the roles of genetic and environmental factors in human intelligence. The results of such research are clear: The IQs of identical twins reared apart (often from the time they were only a few days old) correlate almost as highly as those of identical twins reared together. Moreover, such individuals are also amazingly similar in many other characteristics, such as physical appearance, preferences in dress, mannerisms, and even personality (see Figure 11.13). Clearly, these findings point to an important role for heredity in intelligence and in many other aspects of psychological functioning.

**Figure 11.13**
**Identical Twins Reared Apart**

The IQ scores of identical twins separated at birth and raised in different homes are highly correlated. This provides evidence for the impact of genetic factors on intelligence.

On the basis of these and other findings, some researchers have estimated that the **heritability** of intelligence—the proportion of the variance in intelligence within a given population that is attributable to genetic factors—ranges from about 35 percent in childhood to as much as 75 percent in adulthood (McGue et al., 1993), and may be about 50 percent overall (Plomin et al., 1997). Why does the contribution of genetic factors to intelligence increase with age? Perhaps because as individuals grow older, their interactions with their environment are shaped less and less by restraints imposed on them by their families or by their social origins and are shaped more and more by the characteristics they bring with them to these environments. In other words, as they grow older, individuals are increasingly able to choose or change their environments so that these permit expression of their genetically determined tendencies and preferences (Neisser et al., 1996). Whatever the precise origin of the increasing heritability of intelligence with age, there is little doubt that genetic factors do indeed play an important role in intelligence throughout life.

**Heritability:** The proportion of the variance in any trait within a given population that is attributable to genetic factors.

## Evidence for the Influence of Environmental Factors

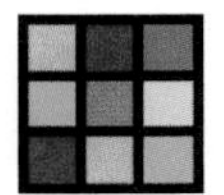

Genetic factors are definitely *not* the entire picture where human intelligence is concerned, however. Other findings point to the conclusion that environmental variables, too, are important. One such finding is that performance on IQ tests has risen substantially around the world at all age levels in recent decades. This phenomenon is known as the *Flynn effect* after the psychologist who first reported it (Flynn, 1987, 1996). Such increases have averaged about 3 IQ points per decade worldwide; but, as shown in Figure 11.14, in some countries they have been even larger. As a result of these gains in performance, it has been necessary to restandardize widely used tests so that they continue to yield an average IQ of 100; what is termed "average" today is actually a higher level of performance than was true in the past.

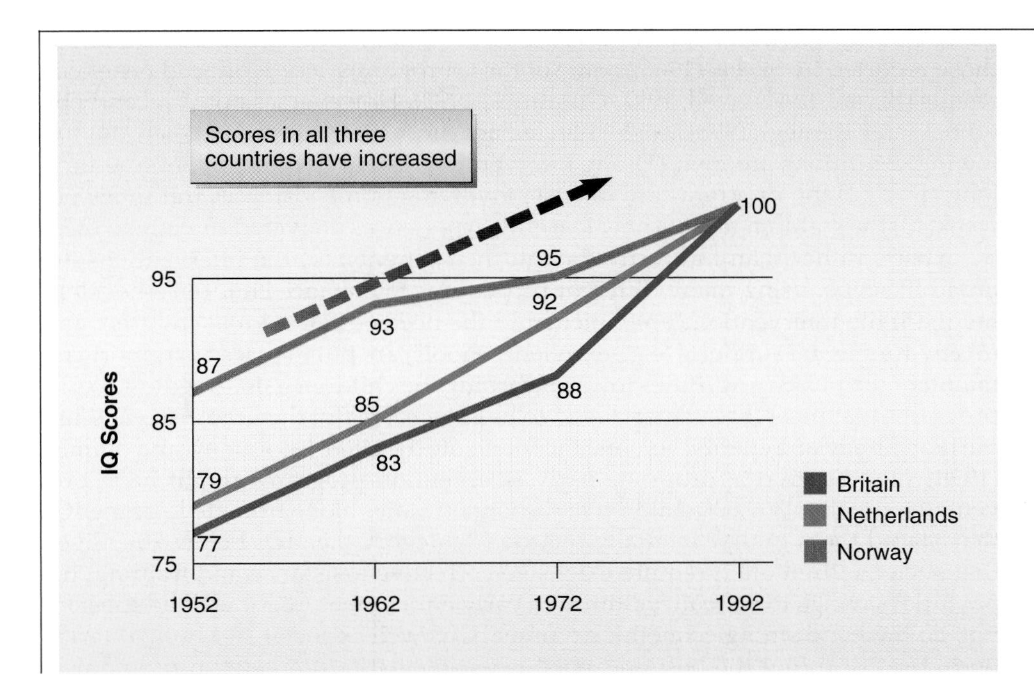


**Figure 11.14**
**Worldwide Gains in IQ: Evidence for the Role of Environmental Factors in Intelligence**

Performance on intelligence tests has risen sharply around the world in recent decades. Because it is very unlikely that genetic factors have changed during this period, these higher scores must be due to environmental factors. Current average IQ is set at 100; in this graph the gain is shown by the fact that average scores in previous years would, by current test standards, be lower than 100. (*Source:* Based on data from Flynn, 1999.)

What accounts for these increases? It seems unlikely that massive shifts in human heredity occur from one generation to the next. A more reasonable explanation, therefore, focuses on changes in environmental factors. What factors have changed in recent decades? The following variables have been suggested as possible contributors to the continuing rise in IQ (e.g., Flynn, 1999; Williams, 1998): better nutrition, increased urbanization, the advent of television, more and better education, more cognitively demanding jobs, and even exposure to computer games! Many of these changes are real and seem plausible as explanations for the rise in IQ; but, as noted recently by Flynn (1999), there is as yet not sufficient evidence to conclude that any or all of these factors have played a role. In any case, whatever the specific causes involved, the steady rise in performance on IQ tests points to the importance of environmental factors in human intelligence.

Additional evidence for the role of environmental factors in intelligence is provided by the findings of studies of *environmental deprivation* and *environmental enrichment*. With respect to deprivation, some findings suggest that intelligence can be reduced by the absence of key forms of environmental stimulation early in life (Gottfried, 1984). In terms of enrichment, removing children from sterile, restricted environments and placing them in more favorable settings seems to enhance their intellectual growth. For example, in one of the first demonstrations of the beneficial impact on IQ of an enriched environment, Skeels (1938, 1966) removed thirteen children, all about two years old, from an orphanage in which they received virtually no intellectual stimulation—and virtually no contact with adults—and placed them in the care of a group of retarded women living in an institution. After a few years, Skeels noted that the children's IQs had risen dramatically—29 points on average (although later corrections reduced this figure to about 10 to 13 points; Flynn, 1993). Interestingly, Skeels also obtained IQ measures of children who had remained in the orphanage and found that these had actually dropped by 26 points on average—presumably as a result of continued exposure to the impoverished environment at the orphanage. Twenty-five years later, the thirteen children who had experienced the enriched environment were all doing well; most had graduated from high school, found a job, and married. In contrast, those in the original control group either remained institutionalized or were functioning poorly in society.

While more recent—and more carefully controlled—efforts to increase intelligence through environmental interventions have not yielded gains as dramatic as those reported by Skeels (1966), some of these programs *have* produced beneficial results (Bryant & Maxwell, 1997; Guralnick, 1997). However, as noted recently by Ramey and Ramey (1998), such changes are most likely to occur when the following conditions are met: (1) The interventions begin early and continue for a long time; (2) the programs are intense, involving home visits several times per week; (3) the children receive new learning experiences delivered directly to them by experts rather than indirectly though their parents; (4) the interventions are broad in scope, using many different procedures to enhance children's development; (5) the interventions are matched to the needs of individual children; and (6) environmental supports (e.g., excellent schools) are put in place to support and maintain the positive attitudes toward learning the children gain. Needless to say, programs that meet these criteria tend to be expensive. But they can also yield important financial benefits; for instance, one study cited by Ramey and Ramey (1998) suggests that appropriate early intervention programs might have prevented more than 300,000 children in the United States alone from developing IQs that placed them in the "mentally retarded" category (i.e., IQs below 70). Given that such children often require extensive corrective assistance and training, the potential savings to be realized through early enrichment might well be substantial. So there are strong economic arguments, as well as social and humanitarian ones, for instituting the best and most extensive early intervention programs a given society can afford.

Additional support for the role of environmental factors in intelligence is provided by the finding that many biological factors that children encounter while growing up can affect their intelligence. Prolonged malnutrition can adversely affect IQ (e.g., Sigman, 1995), as can exposure to lead—either in the air or in lead-based paint, which young children often eat because it tastes sweet (e.g., Baghurst et al., 1992). We have already examined the adverse effects on the health of developing fetuses of exposure to such factors as alcohol and drugs; here I simply want to add that research findings indicate that these factors can also adversely affect intelligence (e.g., Neisser et al., 1996). In sum, therefore, many forms of evidence support the view that intelligence is determined, at least in part, by environmental factors. Especially when these are extreme, they may slow—or accelerate—children's intellectual growth; and this effect, in turn, can have important implications for the societies in which those children will become adults.

## Environment, Heredity, and Intelligence: Summing Up

There is considerable evidence that *both* environmental and genetic factors play a role in intelligence. This is the view accepted by almost all psychologists, and there is little controversy about it. Greater controversy continues to exist, however, concerning the *relative* contribution of each of these factors. Do environmental or genetic factors play a stronger role in shaping intelligence? As I noted earlier, existing evidence seems to favor the view that genetic factors may account for more of the variance in IQ scores within a given population than environmental factors (e.g., Plomin, 1997; Neisser et al., 1996). Many people, including psychologists, are made somewhat uneasy by this conclusion, in part because they assume that characteristics that are heritable—ones that are strongly influenced by genetic factors—cannot readily be changed. *It's important to recognize that this assumption is false.* For instance, consider height: This is a characteristic that is highly heritable—one that is influenced by genetic factors to a greater extent than by intelligence. Yet despite this fact, average heights have increased in many countries as nutrition has improved (and, perhaps, as young persons have been exposed to the growth hormones used to increase food production). So the fact that a trait is strongly influenced by genetic factors does *not* imply that it cannot also be affected by environmental factors.

The same thing is almost certainly true for intelligence. Yes, existing evidence suggests that it is affected by genetic factors. But this in no way implies that it cannot be influenced by environmental conditions, too—and, as we've seen, it certainly is. The recognition that genetic factors play an important role in intelligence in no way implies that intelligence is etched in stone—and definitely does *not* constitute an excuse for giving up on children who, because of poverty, prejudice, or neglect, are seriously at risk.

### REVIEW QUESTIONS

- What evidence suggests that intelligence is influenced by genetic factors?
- What evidence suggests that intelligence is influenced by environmental factors?
- Can characteristics that are highly heritable be influenced by environmental factors?

### Food for Thought

Suppose several genes that influence intelligence are identified. Would it be ethical to alter these genes so as to produce higher levels of intelligence in many persons? What might be the effects on society of doing so?

# Group Differences in Intelligence Test Scores: Why They Occur

Audio 11.2: *Social Skills of Successful Entrepreneurs*

Earlier, I noted that there are sizable differences among the average IQ scores of various ethnic groups. In the United States and elsewhere, members of some minority groups score lower, on average, than members of the majority group. Why do such differences occur? This has been a topic of considerable controversy in psychology for many years, and currently there is still no final, universally accepted conclusion. However, it seems fair to say that at present, most psychologists attribute such group differences in performance on standard intelligence tests largely to environmental variables. Let's take a closer look at the evidence that points to this conclusion. I'll then present some findings that argue *against* the view that group differences in intelligence derive from genetic factors. Finally, I'll turn to a different category of group differences in intelligence test scores—gender differences.

## Group Differences in IQ Scores: Evidence for the Role of Environmental Factors

I have already referred to one form of evidence suggesting that group differences in performance on intelligence tests stem primarily from environmental factors: the fact that the tests themselves may be biased against test takers from some minority groups. Why? In part because the tests were standardized largely on middle-class white persons; thus, interpreting the test scores of persons from minority groups in terms of these norms is not appropriate. Even worse, some critics have suggested that the tests themselves suffer from **cultural bias:** Items on the tests are ones that are familiar to middle-class white children and so give them an important edge in terms of test performance. Are such concerns valid? Careful examination of the items used on intelligence tests suggests that they may indeed be culturally biased, at least to a degree. Some items do seem to be ones that are less familiar—and therefore more difficult to answer—for minority test takers. To the extent that such cultural bias exists, it is indeed a serious flaw in IQ tests.

On the other hand, though, it's important to note that the tests are generally about as successful in predicting future school performance by children from all groups. So while the tests may be biased in terms of content, this in itself does not make them useless from the point of view of predicting future performance (e.g., Rowe, Vazsonyi, & Flannery, 1994). However, as noted by Steele and Aronson (1996), because minority children find at least some of the items on these tests unfamiliar, they may feel threatened by the tests; and this, in turn, may reduce their scores.

In an effort to eliminate cultural bias from intelligence tests, psychologists have attempted to design *culture-fair* tests. Such tests attempt to include only items to which all groups, regardless of ethnic or racial background, have been exposed. Because many minority children are exposed to languages other than standard English, these tests tend to be nonverbal in nature. One of these, the **Raven Progressive Matrices** (Raven, 1977), is illustrated in Figure 11.15. This test consists of sixty matrices of varying difficulty, each containing a logical pattern or design with a missing part. Individuals select the item that completes the pattern from several different choices. Because the Raven test and ones like it focus primarily on *fluid intelligence*—our basic abilities to form concepts, reason, and identify similarities—these tests seem less likely to be subject to cultural bias than other kinds of intelligence tests. However, it is not clear that these tests, or any others, totally eliminate the problem of subtle built-in bias.

**Cultural Bias:** The tendency of items on a test of intelligence to require specific cultural experience or knowledge.

**Raven Progressive Matrices:** A popular test of intelligence that was designed to be relatively free of cultural bias.

Additional evidence for the role of environmental factors in group differences in test performance has been divided by Flynn (1999), one expert on this issue, into

**An Example of a Test Item on a Culture-Fair Test**

This culture-fair test does not penalize test takers whose language or cultural experiences differ from those of the urban middle or upper classes. Subjects are to select, from the six samples on the right, the patch that would complete the pattern. Patch number 3 is the correct answer. (Adapted from the Raven Standard Progressive Matrices Test.)

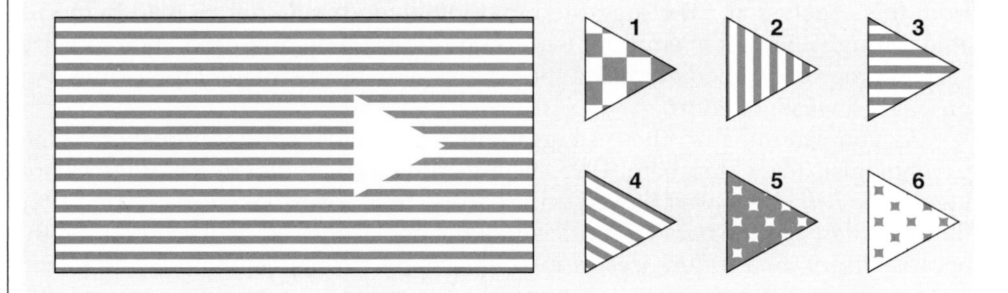


**Figure 11.15**
**An Example of a Test Item on a Culture-Fair Test**

Items on this test are designed to avoid penalizing test takers whose language or cultural experience differs from that of persons in the urban middle class. Persons taking the test select, from the six samples on the right, the patch that would complete the pattern. (Correct answer for this item: number 3.) (*Source:* Adapted from the Raven Standard Progressive Matrices Test.)

two categories: indirect and direct. *Indirect evidence* is evidence from research in which efforts are made to equate environmental factors for all test takers—for instance, by eliminating the effects of socioeconomic status through statistical techniques. The results of such studies are mixed; some suggest that the gap between minority groups and whites is reduced by such procedures (e.g., Flynn, 1993), but other studies indicate that between-group differences still remain (e.g., Loehlin, Lindzey, & Spuhle, 1975; Lynn, 1996). These findings suggest that while socioeconomic factors contribute to group differences in IQ scores, other factors, as yet unknown, may also play some role.

*Direct evidence* for environmental factors, in contrast, involves actual life changes that take many minority persons out of the disadvantaged environment they often face and provide them with an environment equivalent to that of other groups. Obtaining such evidence is, of course, very difficult; many minority persons do grow up in environments quite distinct from those of other groups. According to Flynn (1999), however, one compelling piece of direct evidence for the role of environmental factors in group differences does exist. During World War II, African American soldiers fathered thousands of children in Germany (much of which was occupied by U.S. troops after the war). These children have been raised by white mothers in what is essentially a white environment. The result? Their IQs are virtually identical to those of white children matched to them in socioeconomic status (e.g., Flynn, 1980). Given that the fathers of these children scored very similarly to other African American soldiers, these findings suggest that environmental factors are in fact the key to group differences in IQ: When such factors are largely eliminated, differences between the groups, too, disappear.

## Group Differences in IQ Scores: Is There Any Evidence for the Role of Genetic Factors?

Web Link: *Two Views of The Bell Curve*

Now for the other side of the story—the suggestion that group differences in intelligence stem largely from genetic factors. In 1994 this issue was brought into sharp focus by the publication of a highly controversial book entitled *The Bell Curve.* Because the book was written by two well-known psychologists, Richard Herrnstein and Charles Murray, it received immediate attention in the popular press and soon became a best-seller. The book focused on human intelligence and covered many aspects of this topic. The most controversial portions, however, dealt with what is known as the **genetic hypothesis**—the view that group differences in intelligence are due, at least in part, to genetic factors.

In *The Bell Curve* Herrnstein and Murray (1994) voiced strong support for the genetic hypothesis. They noted, for instance, that there are several converging sources of evidence for "a genetic factor in cognitive ethnic differences" (p. 270) between African American and other ethnic groups in the United States. Proceeding from this conclusion, they suggested that intelligence may not be readily modifiable through changes in environmental conditions. They proposed, therefore, that special programs aimed at raising the IQ scores of disadvantaged minorities were probably a waste of effort.

As you can imagine, these suggestions were challenged vigorously by many psychologists (e.g., Sternberg, 1995). These critics argued that much of the reasoning in *The Bell Curve* was flawed and that the book overlooked many important findings. Perhaps the harshest criticism of the book centered on its contention that because individual differences in intelligence are strongly influenced by genetic factors, group differences are, too. Several researchers took strong exception to this logic (e.g., Schultze, Kane, & Dickens, 1996; Sternberg, 1995). They contended that this reasoning would be accurate only if the environments of the various groups being compared were identical. Under those conditions, it could be argued that differences between the groups stemmed, at least in part, from genetic factors. In reality, however, the environments in which the members of various ethnic groups exist are *not* identical. As a result, it is false to assume that group differences with respect to IQ scores stem from genetic factors, even if we know that individual differences in such scores *are* strongly influenced by these factors. (And, as we saw earlier, when environmental differences are removed or minimized, group differences in intelligence, too, disappear.) Perhaps this point is best illustrated by a simple analogy.

Imagine that a farmer plants a batch of seeds that are known to be genetically identical. The farmer plants the seeds in two different fields; one is known to contain all the nutrients needed for good plant growth, but the other lacks these nutrients. Several months later, there are large differences between the plants growing in the two fields, *despite the fact that their genetic makeup is identical.* Why? Probably because of the contrasting soil fertility. So differences *between* the two fields are due to this environmental factor, whereas *within* each field, any differences among the plants are due to genetic factors (see Figure 11.16). In a similar manner, it is entirely possible that differences in the IQ scores of various groups occur because of contrasting life environments and that genetic factors play little if any role in such differences. In fact, the worldwide gains in IQ I discussed earlier are directly analogous to this example. Here we have a case in which variation in intelligence *within* each generation is strongly influenced by genetic factors—we know that this is so. Yet differences *between* the generations must be due to environmental factors: No one would argue that one generation is genetically different from the next. Such reasoning argues powerfully against a genetic basis for group differences in performance on tests of intelligence.

So where does all this leave us? With the conclusion that although individual differences in IQ scores are certainly influenced by genetic factors, there are no strong grounds for assuming that such factors also contribute to group differences. While some researchers continue to insist that sufficient evidence exists to conclude that genetic factors play a role (e.g., Rushton, 1997), most take strong exception to this view and contend that the evidence for this view is relatively weak (e.g., Neisser, 1997). As I like to put it, *The Bell Curve* has certainly "rung," at least in an economic sense—the book sold tens of thousands of copies and received a great deal of public attention—but from the standpoint of scientific knowledge, it definitely does *not* ring true.

**Genetic Hypothesis:** The view that group differences in intelligence are due, at least in part, to genetic factors.

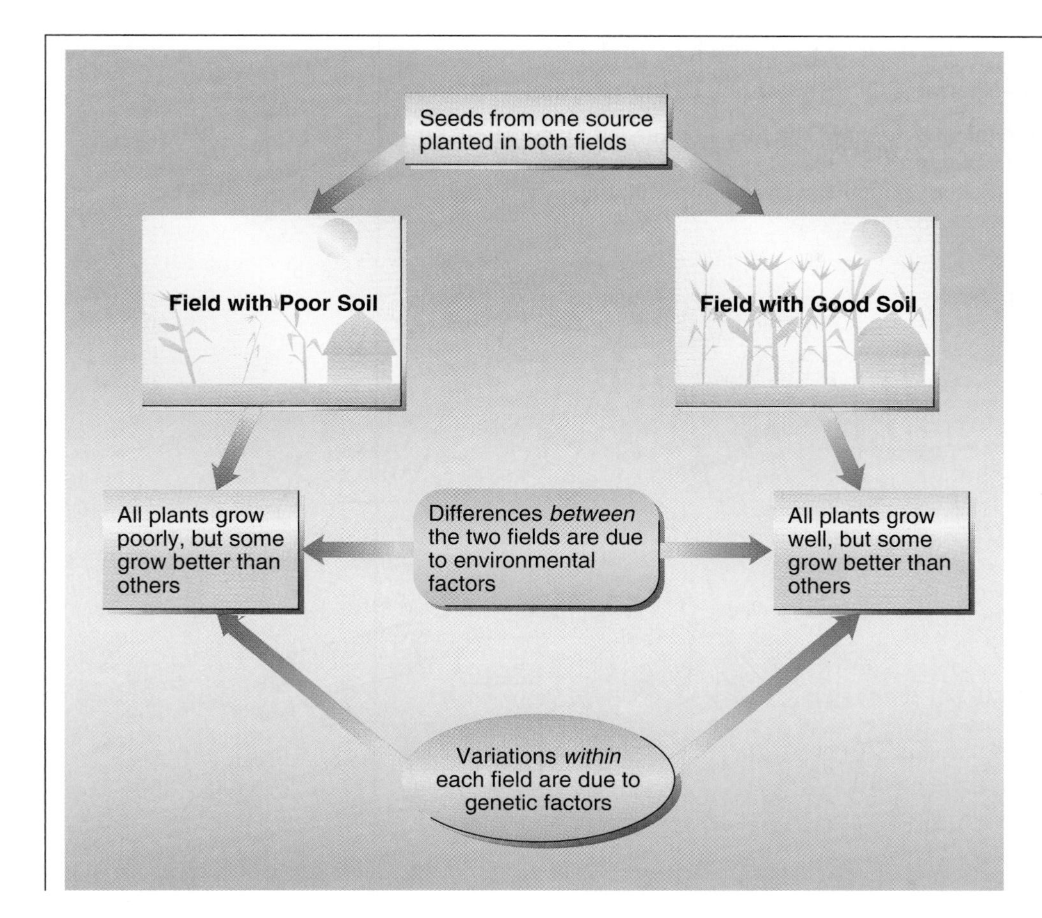


**Figure 11.16**
**Genetic and Environmental Components of Group Differences in IQ**

If seeds from the same source are planted in two fields, differences in growth *within* each field may be due to genetic factors. But if the fields differ in terms of soil fertility, differences *between* the fields are probably due to environmental factors. In a similar manner, differences in IQ between groups of people who live in contrasting environments can be due to these environmental differences, even if differences *within* each group stem from genetic factors.

## Gender Differences in Intelligence

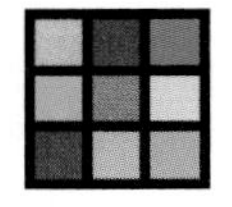

Do males and females differ in intelligence? Overall, they score virtually identically on standard tests of this characteristic (e.g., Lynn, 1994). However, a few subtle differences do seem to exist with respect to certain components of intelligence. First, females tend to score higher than males with respect to verbal abilities—such tasks as naming synonyms (words with the same meaning) and verbal fluency (e.g., naming words that start with a given letter). Females also score higher than males on college achievement tests in literature, spelling, and writing (e.g., Stanley, 1993). Such differences are relatively small and seem to be decreasing (Feingold, 1992), but they do appear, even in very careful meta-analyses performed on the results of many different studies.

In contrast, males tend to score somewhat higher than females on visual–spatial tasks such as mental rotation or tracking a moving object through space (Law, Pellegrino, & Hunt, 1993). You may be able to demonstrate such differences for yourself by following the instructions in Figure 11.17 on page 438. Ask several male and female friends to try their hand at the task it involves. You may discover that the males find this slightly easier (and perhaps more enjoyable) than the females. However, gender differences in performing visual–spatial tasks, like almost all gender differences, are far smaller than gender stereotypes suggest; so if you do observe any difference, it is likely to be a small one.

Additional findings suggest that other subtle differences may exist between males and females with respect to various aspects of intelligence. For instance, consider the following study by Silverman and Eals (1992). These researchers asked female and male participants to perform several tasks in a small office. In one condition

**Figure 11.17**
**Gender Differences in Visual–Spatial Abilities: A Quick Demonstration**

Which figure (or figures) on the right shows (show) the figure on the left in a different position? Males tend to score slightly higher than females on tasks such as this one. Try it with your friends. Do the males do better or find it easier (or more fun) than the females? Answers: Top row: 1, 3; bottom row: 2, 3.

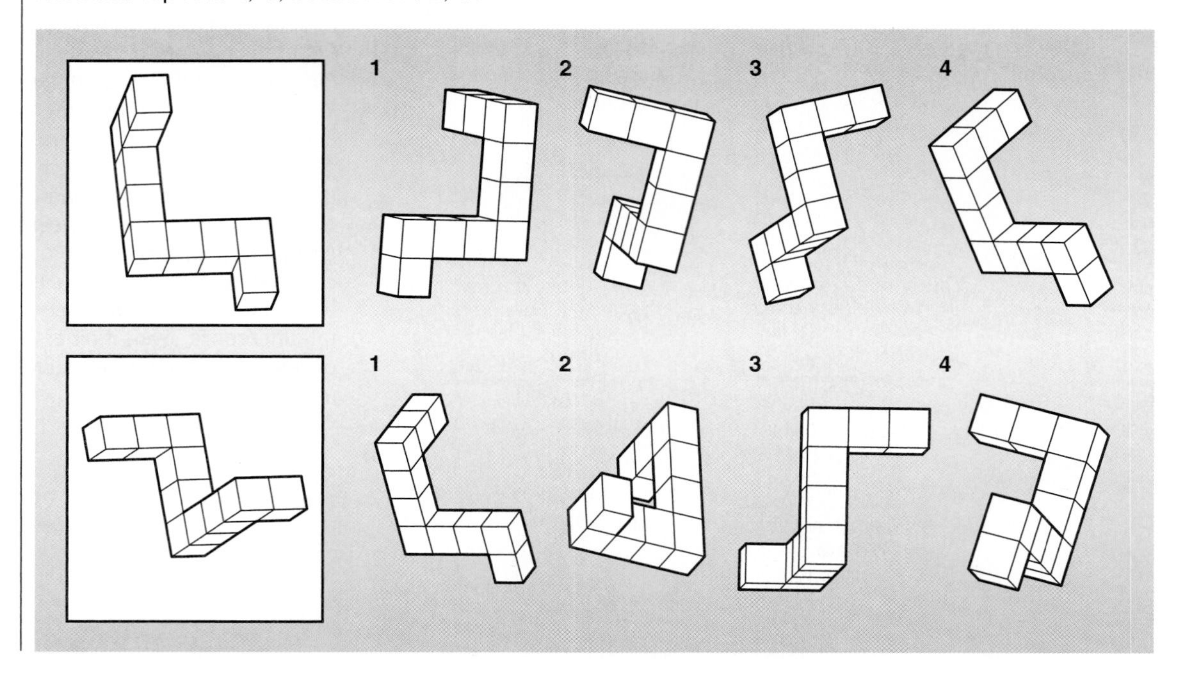


participants were told to try to remember the location of various objects in the room; in another no mention was made of this task. When later asked to name the objects and indicate their locations, women outperformed men in both conditions. However, the difference was larger in the condition in which participants were *not* told to remember the information (Azar, 1996).

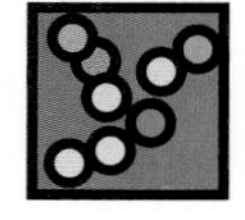

Other studies, in contrast, indicate that men are better at finding their way back to some physical location after taking a complex route away from it. What accounts for these observations? Silverman and Eals suggest that such gender differences may reflect different kinds of tasks performed by females and males during the evolution of our species. Before the development of civilization, humans lived by hunting and gathering. Men hunted and women foraged for edible plants. Silverman and Eals suggest that these tasks required different spatial abilities. Gatherers (primarily females) needed to be able to notice edible plants and to pinpoint their location so that they could find them again in the future. In contrast, hunters (mainly males) needed to be able to find their way back home after crossing large distances. The result, the two psychologists suggest, is that men are better at tasks such as rotating objects in their minds, while women are better at noticing and remembering specific objects and their locations. Perhaps this is one reason why when I can't find something—socks, my keys, my glasses—my wife is able to locate the missing object with ease in a matter of seconds! We can't do experiments on the evolution of our species, however, so we can't know for certain. In any case, it is clear that a few differences do exist between males and females where certain components of intelligence are concerned, but that these differences are small in size and subtle in nature.

**REVIEW QUESTIONS**

- What evidence suggests that group differences in intelligence stem largely from environmental factors?
- Is there any evidence for the role of genetic factors in group differences in intelligence?
- Do any gender differences in intelligence exist? If so, what is the possible origin of such differences?

# Emotional Intelligence: The Feeling Side of Intelligence

Do you remember Paul, my brilliant but unsuccessful high school classmate? I mentioned before that he was not very good with people, but in fact that was an understatement. Many things he did rubbed people the wrong way. First, he was arrogant. He was smart, he knew it, and he made sure that *you* knew it too. In addition, Paul was what I'd now describe as *emotionally unstable.* His moods swung widely and quickly from one extreme to another. Even more important, he seemed incapable of restraining his temper or his impulses: He would get into angry exchanges with teachers because he just didn't know when to quit—when to stop contradicting them and making them look bad in front of the class. Taking all this into account, I'm not really surprised that Paul didn't live up to his initial promise. He was brilliant, all right, but only in certain respects; in others, he was truly backward.

These memories of my childhood friend suggest that there is another kind of intelligence, quite distinct from that measured by IQ tests. In fact, one psychologist—Daniel Goleman (1995, 1998)—has argued strongly that this other kind of intelligence is more important for a happy, productive life than IQ. Goleman terms this kind of intelligence **emotional intelligence** (or **EQ** for short) and defines it as a cluster of traits or abilities relating to the emotional side of life. Let's take a closer look at the major components of emotional intelligence and then examine current evidence concerning its existence and effects.

## Major Components of Emotional Intelligence

Goleman (1995) suggests that emotional intelligence consists of five major parts: (1) knowing our own emotions, (2) managing our emotions, (3) motivating ourselves, (4) recognizing the emotions of others, and (5) handling relationships. Each of these elements, he contends, plays an important role in shaping the outcomes we experience in life.

**Emotional Intelligence (EQ):** A cluster of traits or abilities relating to the emotional side of life—abilities such as recognizing and managing one's own emotions, being able to motivate oneself and restrain one's impulses, recognizing and managing others' emotions, and handling interpersonal relationships in an effective manner.

**KNOWING OUR OWN EMOTIONS** As I noted in Chapter 10, emotions are often powerful reactions, so it would seem at first glance that everyone ought to be able to recognize their own feelings. In fact, however, this is not always the case. Some persons are highly aware of their own emotions and their thoughts about them, but others seem to be almost totally oblivious to these. What are the implications of such differences? First, to the extent individuals are not aware of their own feelings, they cannot make intelligent choices. How can they tell whom to date or marry, what job to take, which house or car to buy, or even what to order in a restaurant? Second, because such persons aren't aware of their own emotions, they are often low in *expressiveness*—they don't show their feelings clearly through facial expressions, body language, or other cues most of use to recognize others' feelings (Malandro, Barker, & Barker, 1994). This can have adverse effects on their interpersonal relationships, because other people find it hard to know how they are feeling or reacting. For these reasons, this first component of emotional intelligence seems to be quite important.

**MANAGING OUR OWN EMOTIONS** Have you ever lost your temper or cried when you didn't want to show such reactions? Have you ever done something to cheer yourself up when you felt anxious or depressed? If so, you are already aware of the fact that we often try to *manage* our emotions—to regulate their nature, intensity, and expression (e.g., Zillmann, 1996). Doing so is very important both for our own mental health and from the point of view of interacting effectively with others (see Figure 11.18). For instance, consider persons who simply cannot control their temper; are they bound for success and a happy life? No. They will probably be avoided by many people and will *not* get the jobs, promotions, or lovers they want.

**MOTIVATING OURSELVES** Thomas Edison, the famous inventor, once remarked: "Success is two percent inspiration and ninety-eight percent perspiration." Do you agree? While inspiration or creativity is certainly important (see the next section of this chapter), I'm inclined to believe that Edison was right. By "perspiration," however, I mean more than simply hard work: I also include aspects of emotional intelligence, such as being able to motivate oneself to work long and hard on a task, remaining enthusiastic and optimistic about the final outcome, and being able to delay gratification—to put off receiving small rewards now in order to get larger ones later on (e.g., Shoda, Mischel, & Peake, 1990). Being high in such skills can indeed contribute to success in many different contexts.

**Figure 11.18**
**Regulating Our Own Emotions (or Expressions of Them)**

As suggested by this cartoon, the ability to regulate our emotions—for instance, to hold our temper in check—is very helpful in many situations.

(*Source:* The New Yorker Collection. 1986. Lee Lorenz from cartoonbank.com. All rights reserved.)

**RECOGNIZING AND INFLUENCING OTHERS' EMOTIONS** Another aspect of emotional intelligence, as described by Goleman, is the ability to "read" others accurately—to recognize the mood they are in and what emotion they are experiencing. This skill is valuable in many practical settings. For instance, if you can accurately gauge another person's current mood, you can tell whether it's the right time to ask her or him for a favor. Similarly, persons who are skilled at generating strong emotions in others are often highly successful in such fields as sales and politics: They can get other people to feel what *they* want them to feel.

**HANDLING RELATIONSHIPS** Some people seem to have a knack for getting along with others: most people who meet these people like then, and as a result they have many friends and often enjoy high levels of success in their careers. In contrast, others seem to make a mess of virtually all their personal relationships. According to Goleman (1995), such differences are another reflection of differences in emotional intelligence or, as some researchers would phrase it, differences in *interpersonal intelligence* (Hatch, 1990).

What does interpersonal intelligence involve? Such skills as being able to coordinate the efforts of several people and to negotiate solutions to complex interpersonal problems, being good at giving others feedback that doesn't make them angry or resentful (e.g., Baron, 1993a), and being a team player. Again, these skills are clearly distinct from the ones needed for getting good grades or scoring high on tests of intelligence, but they often play a key role in important life outcomes.

## Emotional Intelligence: Evidence on Its Existence and Effects

Web Link: *Road Rage and Emotional Intelligence*

Goleman's (1995, 1998) books on emotional intelligence have been best-sellers, so you may well have heard about the concept before taking this course. Unfortunately, though, most of the evidence Goleman offers concerning the existence and impact of emotional intelligence is anecdotal or indirect in nature. Psychologists, of course, strongly prefer more concrete kinds of evidence. Accordingly, researchers have put the concept of emotional intelligence to the test, trying to determine whether the distinct skills described by Goleman cluster together as a single (if multifaceted) factor, and whether this factor influences important life outcomes.

With respect to the first of these issues, evidence is mixed. While some researchers (Mayer, Caruso, & Salovey, 1998; Salovey & Mayer, 1994) have reported findings consistent with Goleman's suggestions and with their own, similar definitions of emotional intelligence, others have obtained less encouraging results. For example, in a recent and carefully conducted study, Davies, Stankov, and Roberts (1998) focused on two important questions: (1) Are the methods currently used to measure emotional intelligence adequate—that is, are they reliable and valid? And (2) is emotional intelligence really different from other seemingly related concepts—for instance, social intelligence and several aspects of personality (e.g., empathy)? To answer these basic questions, they conducted several studies in which hundreds of participants varying in age, education, gender, and nationality completed measures designed to assess each aspect of emotional intelligence and several other variables as well. Results indicated that only one of the components emphasized by Goleman and other advocates of emotional intelligence emerged as clear and independent: *emotion perception*—the ability to accurately read others' emotions.

Does this mean that the theory of emotional intelligence is useless and that discussing it has been a waste of time—yours as well as mine? I don't believe so. Another interpretation of existing evidence concerning emotional intelligence is this: At present, we don't have adequate methods for measuring all aspects of emotional intelligence. Further, these components may, in fact, be somewhat independent of each other. Thus, we may not be able to assign individuals a single overall EQ score comparable to the single IQ score yielded by many intelligence tests. In a sense, though, this is not surprising. After all, the more psychologists study intelligence, the more they recognize that it probably consists of a number of distinct components—verbal, spatial, speed-of-processing, and perhaps many others. So the fact that we also possess distinct and perhaps largely independent abilities relating to the emotional side of life simply mirrors this pattern. One point *is* clear, however: At present, we do not possess fully adequate tests for measuring emotional intelligence. Until we do, we will not be able to fully determine its role in important aspects of our lives.

And yet, having said that, I should add that other research offers support for the view that some of the components included in emotional intelligence—especially emotion perception—can indeed have measurable effects. For instance, in

**Creativity:** The ability to produce work that is both novel (original, unexpected) and appropriate (it works—it is useful or meets task constraints).

recent studies, Gideon Markman and I (e.g., Baron, 2000; Baron & Markman, 2000) have focused on the following question: Why is it that some entrepreneurs are so successful in starting new businesses, while others fail? This is an important question, because in recent years it is the companies started by entrepreneurs that have created most new jobs around the world (e.g., Shane & Venkataraman, in press). We've used several different methods to study this issue, and what we've found, repeatedly, is this: Entrepreneurs who are adept at "reading" others accurately and who adapt easily to new social situations (what we describe as "social adaptability") are significantly more successful, financially, than entrepreneurs who score lower in these skills. To the extent that these two traits are related to emotional intelligence, our findings can be viewed as offering indirect support for the view that EQ influences the outcomes people experience in practical contexts. But stay tuned: The idea of emotional intelligence is an appealing one with important implications, so it is certain to be the topic of research by psychologists in the years ahead.

**REVIEW QUESTIONS**

- What is emotional intelligence?
- What does evidence to date suggest about the existence of emotional intelligence? Its effects?

CourseCompass
Web Link: *The Creativity Web Homepage*

## Creativity: Generating the Extraordinary

Suppose you were asked to name people high in creativity: Who would be on your list? When faced with this question, many people name such famous figures as Albert Einstein, Leonardo da Vinci, Thomas Edison, Sigmund Freud. What do these individuals have in common? All were responsible for producing something—a theory, inventions—viewed by other people as unexpected and *new.* More formally, as we saw in Chapter 9, psychologists generally define **creativity** as involving the ability to produce work that is both novel (original, unexpected) and appropriate (it works—it is useful or meets task constraints) (e.g., Lubart, 1994). By this definition, does the work shown in Figure 11.19 illustrate creativity? Probably not, because while it is certainly original, it really isn't practical! The United States Patent Office—and patent offices in other countries, too—apply the same criteria to patent applications: Not only must an idea be new, but it must be practical too.

**Figure 11.19**
**Creativity: Something Novel that Works**

The "invention" shown here does not meet the definition of creativity accepted by most psychologists: It may be new, but is not exactly practical!
(*Source:* © The New Yorker Collection. 1999. Christopher Weyant from cartoonbank.com. All rights reserved.)

*"That's just great. I discover the cure for the common cold and all you can do is criticize."*

Clearly, creativity is important; after all, it provides us with new knowledge and new inventions that can improve the quality of human life. It is somewhat surprising to learn, therefore, that until recently it was *not* the subject of extensive study by psychologists. Why was this so? One important reason was that although several methods for measuring creativity existed—for instance, asking individuals to come up with as many uses for everyday objects as possible (known as the Unusual Uses Test; Guilford, 1950), or to formulate as many ways of improving a product as possible (Torrance, 1974)—none of these seemed to be completely satisfactory. They did not seem to capture all aspects of creativity as it occurs in real-life situations (Sternberg & Lubart, 1996). Another problem was the fact that the concept of creativity was associated, in many people's minds, with forces outside the realm of science—for instance, with vague notions of "the creative spirit." This made psychologists somewhat reluctant to study this topic.

During the past two decades, however, this situation has changed and rapid advances have been made in our understanding of creativity. Because creativity is clearly related to certain aspects of intelligence, and because it is an important topic in its own right, I'll now describe what psychologists have discovered about this fascinating topic.

## Contrasting Views of Creativity

A basic question about creativity is "What factors produce it?" Several contrasting answers have been proposed. Cognitive psychologists, for example, have tended to focus on the basic processes that underlie creative thought. Research findings indicate that such processes as retrieval of information from memory, association, synthesis, transformation, and categorical reduction (mentally assigning objects to basic categories) may all play a role in creativity (e.g., Ward, Smith, & Vaid, 1997). Moreover, a cognitive approach to creativity calls attention to the fact that creativity is part of our everyday lives: Each time we utter a new sentence or understand a new concept we are showing creativity. Thus, a key task in the study of creativity is that of distinguishing between this kind of everyday creativity (termed *mundane creativity*) and *exceptional creativity*—the emergence of something dramatically new, such as the idea of integrated circuits, which made modern computers possible.

What differentiates these two kinds of creativity? According to Perkins (1997), one psychologist who has focused on this issue, the difference may lie in the fact that everyday creativity occurs with respect to problems for which our past knowledge and experience give us valuable clues: We know where to look for a solution. In contrast, exceptional creativity may arise in what he describes as *Klondike spaces*—in areas where, like the miners of long ago who searched for gold in the Klondike, we don't know even where to begin looking. When we do find a solution in such situations, it is likely to be dramatic and to require thinking that is "outside the box"—thinking that breaks out of what I often describe as "mental ruts."

The cognitive approach to creativity has been dominant in psychology, but other approaches exist as well. For instance, social psychologists have often focused on the personality traits that make people creative and the environmental conditions that either encourage or discourage creativity (e.g., Simonton, 1994). And still other researchers have focused on the motivation behind exceptional creativity—the kind of intrinsic motivation we described in Chapter 10, which can be sustained from within in the absence of external rewards.

While all of these approaches have certainly added to our understanding of creativity, a view known as **confluence approach** has gained considerable acceptance. This view suggests that in order for creativity to occur, multiple components must converge (Amabile, 1983). For example, according to Lubart (1994), creativity requires a confluence of six distinct resources:

- *Intellectual abilities:* The ability to see problems in new ways, the ability to recognize which of one's ideas are worth pursuing, and persuasive skills—the ability to convince others of these new ideas.
- *Knowledge:* Enough knowledge about a field to move it forward.

**Confluence Approach:** An approach suggesting that for creativity to occur, multiple components must converge.

**Figure 11.20**
**Creativity: A Confluence Approach**

According to modern *confluence theories*, creativity can emerge only when several different conditions are present or converge.

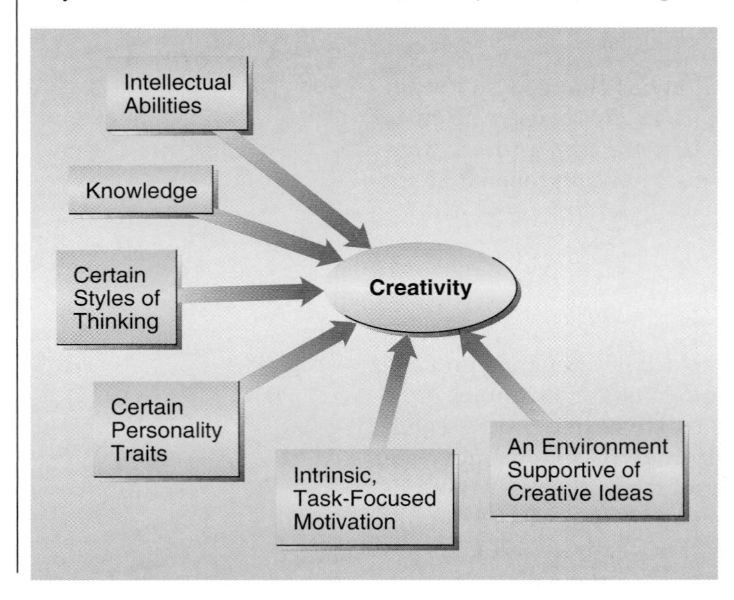


- *Certain styles of thinking:* A preference for thinking in novel ways and an ability to see the big picture—to think globally as well as locally.
- *Personality attributes:* Such traits as willingness to take risks and to tolerate ambiguity.
- *Intrinsic, task-focused motivation:* Creative people usually love what they are doing and find intrinsic rewards in their work.
- *An environment that is supportive of creative ideas.*

Only when all of these conditions are present, Lubart and others argue, can a high level of creativity emerge (see Figure 11.20) (Sternberg & Lubart, 1996).

## Research on Creativity: Evidence for the Confluence Approach

A growing body of evidence offers support for the confluence approach. For example, consider one creative (!) study by Lubart and Sternberg (1995). In this study, forty-eight adults ranging in age from eighteen to sixty-five were asked to produce creative products in each of four domains: writing, art, advertising, and science. In the art category, for example, they were asked to produce drawings showing "hope" and "rage" and "the earth from an insect's point of view." With respect to advertising, they were asked to design television ads for bow ties and the Internal Revenue Service. All the products participants created were rated for overall creativity, novelty, and perceived effort. Participants also completed a measure of fluid intelligence, a measure of thinking style, and two personality measures.

Results indicated, first, that there was considerable agreement among raters: They agreed on what was creative and what was not creative. This is an important finding, because it indicates that creativity can be studied scientifically. Second, it was found that creativity in one domain (art, writing, and so on) was only moderately related to creativity in other domains. Thus, as common sense suggests, people can be creative in one area but not in another. Third, intellectual ability, thinking style, and personality were all significantly related to creativity.

Taken together, these findings, and those of other recent studies, offer support for the confluence approach. Creativity, it appears, requires the convergence of many factors for its emergence. None of these factors are unusual in and of themselves, but together they produce outcomes and results that are, in some cases, extraordinary.

### REVIEW QUESTIONS

- What is creativity?
- What are confluence theories, and what factors do they view as essential to creativity?
- What evidence offers support for the confluence approach?

# *Making* Psychology *Part of Your Life*

## Managing Your Own Anger: A Very Useful Skill

In discussing emotional intelligence, I noted that one suggested aspect of such intelligence is the ability to manage our own emotions. Perhaps the most difficult emotion of all to manage is anger, which all too often erupts into open rage. You probably know from your own experience that once it starts, anger tends to be self-perpetuating—and sometimes self-amplifying, too. What begins as mild irritation can quickly move into strong anger and then, if we don't take active steps to stop it, a virtual emotional explosion. What can you do to avoid such outcomes—to manage your own anger more effectively? Here are some useful steps.

- **Stop the process early.** Because anger is self-amplifying, it is easier to break the annoyance–anger–rage cycle early on. So if you feel yourself getting angry and suspect that this emotion might get out of hand, take one of the actions described below as soon as possible. Delay can be quite costly in terms of your ability to break this cycle.
- **Try a cooling-off period.** If possible, leave the scene, change the subject, or at least stop interacting with the other person. Doing so can give your emotional arousal a chance to dissipate, *as long as you don't use this time to mull over the causes of your anger.* So if you do try a cooling-off period, it's important to also use the next step.
- **Do something to get yourself off the anger track.** As I just noted, if you think angry thoughts, you will remain angry—and perhaps become even angrier. So it's important to do something to get your mind *off* the causes of your anger. Here's where the *incompatible response* approach, a technique I developed some years ago (e.g., Baron, 1983, 1993a), can come in handy. This technique suggests that it is difficult, if not impossible, to remain angry in the presence of stimuli that cause us to experience some incompatible emotion—for example, humorous materials that make us laugh. You can readily use this technique to control your own anger: Just expose yourself as quickly as possible to stimuli you know will induce pleasant feelings incompatible with anger. Your anger may quickly vanish.
- **Seek positive explanations for the things others say or do that make you angry.** When others make us angry, we usually attribute their actions to insensitivity, selfishness—or worse. If, instead, you try to come up with other explanations for the words or actions that have made you angry, this may greatly reduce your annoyance. Did the other person mean to say something that hurt your feelings? Perhaps she or he didn't realize the implications of what they said. If you concentrate on interpretations like this, your anger may quickly dissipate.
- **Whatever you do, don't rely on "catharsis"—on getting it out of your system.** A large body of research findings indicates that giving vent to anger does *not* usually reduce it. On the contrary, such actions tend to fan the flames of annoyance, not drown them (e.g., Bushman, Baumeister, & Stack, 1999). So, whatever else you do, *don't follow your impulse to give the other person a dirty look, to shout, or to pound your fist.* Doing so will only make the situation worse. A little restraint is definitely in order.

# Summary and Review

### Intelligence: Contrasting Views of Its Nature

- **What is intelligence?** The term *intelligence* refers to individuals' abilities to understand complex ideas, to adapt effectively to the environment, to learn from experience, to engage in various forms of reasoning, and to overcome obstacles by careful thought.
- **What is Gardner's theory of multiple intelligences?** Gardner's theory suggests that there are several different kinds of intelligence, such as verbal, mathematical, musical, and bodily–kinesthetic.
- **What is Sternberg's triarchic theory of intelligence?** Sternberg's theory suggests that there are three basic kinds of intelligence: componential, experiential, and contextual (practical).

- **What is fluid intelligence? Crystallized intelligence?** Fluid intelligence has to do with our inherited abilities to think and reason. Crystallized intelligence consists of accumulated knowledge—information and skills stored over a lifetime.

### Key Terms

intelligence, p. 413 • triarchic theory, p. 415 • practical intelligence, p. 415

## Measuring Intelligence

- **What was the first individual test of intelligence, and what did scores on it mean?** The first individual test of intelligence was devised by Binet and Simon. It yielded a "mental age," and testers then derived an IQ (intelligence quotient) score obtained by dividing mental by chronological age and multiplying by 100.
- **What are the Wechsler scales?** The Wechsler scales are individual tests of intelligence for children and adults that seek to measure several aspects of intelligence—performance components as well as verbal components of intelligence.
- **What are standardization, reliability, and validity?** Standardization is the process of establishing the average score and distribution of scores on a test so that the scores of persons taking the test can be meaningfully interpreted. Reliability is the extent to which a test yields consistent results. Validity is the extent to which a test measures what it is supposed to measure.
- **What is inspection time, and what does it measure?** Inspection time is the minimum amount of time a stimulus must be exposed for individuals to make a judgment about it that meets some preestablished criterion of accuracy.
- **What findings suggest that intelligence is related to neural functioning or brain structure?** Research findings indicate that scores on standard tests of intelligence are correlated with nerve conduction velocity, with efficiency in brain functioning, and with the size of certain parts of the brain.
- **What is competency assessment and how is it used?** Competency assessment is a procedure used for identifying the key skills or competencies that distinguish outstanding performers from average ones. It is often used to predict success in business careers.

### Key Terms

Stanford–Binet test, p. 417 • IQ, p. 417 • aptitude tests, p. 418 • achievement tests, p. 418 • mental retardation, p. 418 • Down syndrome, p. 418 • reliability, p. 423 • split-half reliability, p. 423 • test–retest reliability, p. 423 • validity, p. 423 • content validity, p. 424 • criterion-related validity, p. 424 • inspection time, p. 425 • competency assessment, p. 426

## Human Intelligence: The Role of Heredity and the Role of Environment

- **What evidence suggests that intelligence is influenced by genetic factors?** Evidence for the role of genetic factors is provided by the findings that the more closely related persons are, the higher the correlation in their IQ scores; by research on adopted children; and by research on identical twins separated early in life and raised in different homes.
- **What evidence suggests that intelligence is influenced by environmental factors?** Evidence for the role of environmental factors is provided by the worldwide rise in IQ scores in recent decades (the Flynn effect), studies of environmental deprivation and enrichment, and the finding that many environmental factors can affect children's intelligence.
- **Can characteristics that are highly heritable be influenced by environmental factors?** Traits that are highly heritable can be strongly influenced by environmental factors. For example, height is highly heritable, yet average height has increased in many countries as a result of improved nutrition and other factors.

### Key Term

heritability, p. 431

## Group Differences in Intelligence Test Scores: Why They Occur

- **What evidence suggests that group differences in intelligence stem largely from environmental factors?** There is some indication that many intelligence tests suffer from cultural bias. Other sources of evidence include the Flynn effect—worldwide rises in IQ over time—and direct evidence indicating that when minority children are raised in enhanced environments, their IQ matches that of nonminority children.
- **Is there any evidence for the role of genetic factors in group differences in intelligence?** Very little if any evidence indicates that group differences in intelligence have a genetic basis.
- **Do any gender differences in intelligence exist? If so, what is the possible origin of such differences?** Females tend to score higher than males with respect to verbal abilities, while males tend to score higher in visual–spatial abilities (e.g., mental rotation of objects). These differences may reflect the evolutionary history of our species.

### Key Terms

cultural bias, p. 434 • Raven Progressive Matrices, p. 434 • genetic hypothesis, p. 436

## Emotional Intelligence: The Feeling Side of Intelligence

- **What is emotional intelligence?** Emotional intelligence is a cluster of traits or abilities relating to the emotional side of life—abilities such as recognizing and managing one's own emotions, being able to motivate oneself and restrain one's impulses, recognizing and managing others' emotions, and handling interpersonal relationships in an effective manner.
- **What does evidence to date indicate about the existence of emotional intelligence? Its effects?** Research evidence

provides clear support for only one of the components of emotional intelligence—emotion perception. However, some findings indicate that this component, and perhaps others as well, can influence the outcomes people experience in important practical contexts.

#### Key Term

emotional intelligence (EQ), p. 439

### Creativity: Generating the Extraordinary

- **What is creativity?** Creativity involves the ability to produce work that is both novel (original, unexpected) and appropriate (it works—it is useful or meets task constraints).
- **What are confluence theories, and what factors do they view as essential to creativity?** Confluence theories suggest that for creativity to occur, multiple components must converge. Among the factors such theories view as crucial for creativity are certain intellectual abilities, knowledge of a given field, certain styles of thinking, personality traits, intrinsic motivation, and an environment supportive of creative ideas.
- **What evidence offers support for the confluence approach?** Research findings indicate that all of the factors mentioned by confluence theories are significant predictors of creativity across many different domains (e.g., writing, art, science).

#### Key Terms

creativity, p. 442 • confluence approach, p. 443

## Critical Thinking Questions

### Appraisal

Ultimately, intelligence must be related to events occurring within our brains. Do you think we will ever reach the stage where we can pinpoint the differences in brain function or activity that distinguish highly intelligent persons from less intelligent ones? If so, how could this knowledge be put to use?

### Controversy

At present, existing evidence suggests that group differences in intelligence are due primarily to environmental factors. What kind of evidence would be needed before we could conclude that genetic factors, too, play a role?

### Making Psychology Part of Your Life

Now that you understand some of the basic requirements of all psychological tests, do you think you will be more skeptical of the questionnaires published in many magazines that claim to measure various traits? Why should you view these "tests" with caution? Under what conditions could you view them as useful or informative?

# Chapter 12

# Personality:

## Uniqueness and Consistency in the Behavior of Individuals

## CHAPTER OUTLINE


**PERSONALITY: IS IT REAL? 450**

**THE PSYCHOANALYTIC APPROACH: MESSAGES FROM THE UNCONSCIOUS 452**

Freud the Person
Freud's Theory of Personality
Research Related to Freud's Theory: Probing the Unconscious
Freud's Theory: An Overall Evaluation
Other Psychoanalytic Views: Freud's Disciples . . . and Defectors

**HUMANISTIC THEORIES: EMPHASIS ON GROWTH 463**

Rogers's Self Theory: Becoming a Fully Functioning Person
Maslow and the Study of Self-Actualizing People
Research Related to Humanistic Theories: Studying the Self-Concept

- BEYOND THE HEADLINES—As Psychologists See It: *What's In a Name? Ask the People Who Have Unusual Ones*

Humanistic Theories: An Evaluation

**TRAIT THEORIES: SEEKING THE KEY DIMENSIONS OF PERSONALITY 468**

The Search for Basic Traits: Initial Efforts by Allport and Cattell
The "Big Five" Factors: The Basic Dimensions of Personality?
Trait Theories: An Evaluation

**LEARNING APPROACHES TO PERSONALITY 472**

Social Cognitive Theory: A Modern View of Personality
Research on the Learning Perspective

- FROM SCIENCE TO PRACTICE *The Potential Benefits of Boosting Self-Efficacy: Helping Unemployed Persons to Help Themselves*

Evaluation of the Learning Approach

**MEASURING PERSONALITY 476**

Self-Report Tests of Personality: Questionnaires and Inventories
Projective Measures of Personality
Other Measures: Behavioral Observations, Interviews, and Biological Measures

**MODERN RESEARCH ON PERSONALITY: APPLICATIONS TO PERSONAL HEALTH AND BEHAVIOR IN WORK SETTINGS 479**

Personality and Health: The Type A Behavior Pattern, Sensation Seeking, and Longevity
Personality and Behavior in Work Settings: Job Performance and Workplace Aggression

- MAKING PSYCHOLOGY PART OF YOUR LIFE *Are You a Type A?*

Several years ago, I attended the thirtieth reunion of my high school class. I had never been to a reunion before, so I knew I was in for some interesting experiences—and some surprises. At first, when I entered the room and looked around, I could not recognize a single person in the large crowd. This was not surprising; after all, thirty years does produce a lot of change in the way people look. Then, suddenly, a large smiling face appeared in front of me and I heard a voice say, "Bob! It's me . . . Joe!

Don't you know me?" I stared at the unfamiliar face, and gradually something I recognized began to emerge. "Yes, I *do* know that smile . . . and that nose. . . . Hey, it *is* Joe!" True, he had gained fifty pounds and lost most of his hair, but I could see that he was still the same friendly, happy person he had been thirty years earlier. The evening continued in much the same way. Ina, the cool blonde for whom I had longed as a junior, was there, and still as cool—and sexy—as ever. And my high school hero, David, still exuded confidence plus that familiar touch of arrogance; he was now a successful attorney, and I would hate to have to face *him* in court!

Looking back over that experience, the thought that stands out most in my mind is this: Almost everyone I saw that night had changed physically, but underneath these changes, many were still easily recognizable as the same persons I had known thirty years before. It is this kind of stability that is the central topic of the present chapter, which focuses on **personality**—an individual's unique and relatively stable patterns of behavior, thoughts, and emotions (e.g., Nelson & Miller, 1995; Zuckerman, 1995) or, as Friedman and Schustack (1999) have recently put it, the psychological forces that make people uniquely themselves.

Web Link: *What Makes Us Who We Are?*

Web Link: *Personality Processes*

## Personality: Is It Real?

Interest in personality is as old as civilization: Ancient philosophers and poets often speculated about why individuals were unique and why they differed from each other in so many ways. It was not until the emergence of a scientific field of psychology, however, that personality became the focus of systematic research. Yet although the study of personality now has a long history in psychology, it's important to note that there has been a continuing discussion among psychologists about whether personality is actually *real*—whether individuals show enough consistency in their behavior over time and across situations to make studying personality worthwhile. On one side of this issue, Walter Mischel (1985) argued that people show so much variability across situations that we can't make any useful predictions about their behavior from personality; moreover, he noted, various traits generally show only modest correlations with overt behavior (+.20 to +.30).

In reply to such criticisms, other psychologists called attention to a growing body of evidence suggesting that in fact people *do* show a considerable degree of consistency in their behavior across situations—more than Mischel suggested (e.g., Heatherton & Weinberger, 1994; Steel & Rentsch, 1997). Further, even when an in-

**Personality:** Individuals' unique and relatively stable patterns of behavior, thoughts, and feelings.

dividual shows contrasting patterns of behavior in different situations, these actions may be *functionally equivalent* for that person—in other words, the behaviors may have the same meaning for the individual. For instance, consider a woman who is very kindhearted. In most situations, she gives help to others whenever they request it. In some cases, though, she refuses. Why? Not because she no longer has an underlying and lasting tendency to be kind, but because she firmly believes that it is better in the long run for the persons in question if she refuses. In other words, from her point of view, these contrasting behaviors (saying yes and saying no to requests for help) actually serve the same purpose: assisting the people in question. Finally, researchers who believe that personality is well worth studying note that correlations of .20 to .30 between aspects of personality and behavior can be quite useful and are just as high as correlations between almost *any* factors and behavior (Friedman & Schustack, 1999). Indeed, correlations much lower than .20 to .30 are often viewed as quite important—for instance, the correlation between amount of carbon dioxide in the earth's atmosphere and increases in temperature (the greenhouse effect).

**Interactionist Perspective:** The view that behavior in any situation is a function of both personality and external factors.

Weighing all these points in the balance, most psychologists have reached the conclusion that personality is indeed real and worth studying. Indeed, even Mischel, perhaps the arch-critic of studying personality, has focused on what he terms *personal styles* or *strategies*—individual differences in the meanings people assign to various situations and events (e.g., Mischel & Shoda, 1995). According to Mischel, individuals show considerable consistency in this respect, and such consistency, in turn, becomes a kind of *behavioral signature* of their personalities. So, as my high school reunion illustrated, people do show a considerable degree of consistency with respect to certain aspects of their behavior, even over many years. But please take note: This in no way implies that people are *entirely* consistent in their behavior, either across situations or across time. On the contrary, as you know from your own experience, our behavior at any given time is also strongly affected by situational (external) factors. For instance, consider an individual who has a very bad temper; she gets angry easily and usually tells people exactly what she thinks of them. Imagine that one day she is stopped by a state trooper for speeding. Will she blow up and shout at the trooper for wasting her time? Perhaps; but the situational pressures toward being polite are so strong that she may well hold her temper in check for once and behave in a mild and polite manner.

In short, our behavior in any given situation is usually a complex function of both our personality (the stable internal factors that make us unique individuals) *and* situational factors in the world around us. This **interactionist perspective** is the one currently accepted by most psychologists, so please keep it in mind as you read further in this chapter (see Figure 12.1) (Vansteelandt & Van Mechelen, 1999).

What have psychologists learned about personality from their research? Is this information of any practical value? And how can you use it to gain insight into your own personality and the personalities of others? These are the questions we'll address in the present chapter.

**Figure 12.1**
**The Interactionist Perspective: Behavior as Function of Personality and Situational Factors**

Even drivers with a short temper usually manage to act politely when stopped by a state trooper. In situations like this, situational factors exert a stronger impact on behavior than personality.

To acquaint you with what psychologists have discovered about personality, we'll proceed as follows. First, I'll describe several major *theories of personality*—sweeping frameworks for understanding personality offered by some of the true giants in the history of psychology. These theories represent different perspectives on personality—contrasting views about the origins and nature of human uniqueness. As you'll see, they differ greatly; but please don't take this as a sign that they are competing or contradictory. Rather, each offers a point of view and insights that have added to our understanding of personality—that's why they are covered here. It's also important to note, however, that none of these theories are currently accepted as completely accurate by psychologists, and that modern research on personality has gone well beyond them in many respects. For each theoretical framework, I'll first describe the theory, then present some research evidence relating to it, and finally offer an evaluation of its current status.

After examining these famous theories, we'll turn to another basic question: How is personality measured? Finally, I'll provide you with the flavor of modern research on personality by examining recent findings concerning the roles of various aspects of personality in *personal health* and in behavior in *work settings*. (Because research methods used to study each of the theories covered are discussed along with each theory, I have not included a separate **Research Methods** section in this chapter.)

**REVIEW QUESTIONS**

- What is personality?
- What evidence suggests that personality is real?
- What is the interactionist perspective currently adopted by most psychologists?

**Food for Thought**

Can you formulate a list of the characteristics that make *you* a unique person? If so, how do you know what belongs on this list and what does not?

Web Link: *Psychoanalysis*

## The Psychoanalytic Approach: Messages from the Unconscious

Quick: Before you took this course, whom would you have named as the most famous psychologist in history? If you are like most students I have known, your answer would probably be *Freud*. Sigmund Freud is, by far, the most famous figure in the history of psychology—even though he was a medical doctor. Why is this so? The answer lies in several provocative and influential theories he proposed—theories that focus on personality and the origins of psychological disorders. Before turning to his theories, let's consider Freud as an individual—*his* personality, if you will (see Figure 12.2).

### Freud the Person

Freud was born in what is now part of the Czech Republic, but when he was four years old, his family moved to Vienna, and he spent almost his entire life in that city. As a young man, Freud was highly ambitious and decided to make a name for himself as a medical researcher. He became discouraged with his prospects in this respect, however, and soon after receiving his medical degree, he entered private practice. It was during this period that he formulated his theories of human personality and psychological disorders.

Freud's mother was his father's third wife, and she was twenty years younger than her husband. In fact, she was only twenty-one when Freud was born. She had several other children, but Sigmund was the first and always remained her favorite—although Freud later reported that he was often jealous when his stepbrothers, who were much older than he was, flirted with his young mother. Among the Freud children, only Sigmund had his own room, and when his sister's piano practice disturbed his study, her lessons were stopped and the piano sold. Freud's relationship with his father, in contrast, was cold and distant, Indeed, he even arrived late at his father's funeral and missed most of the service (although he did express sorrow over his parent's death). At the age of twenty-six, Freud married Martha Bernays. The marriage was a happy one and produced six children. Freud had a powerful personality and, as he developed his theories, he attracted numerous followers. In many cases they began as ardent disciples but then came to question some aspects of Freud's work. Freud was intolerant of such criticism and often had angry breaks with once cherished students. One disciple, however, never broke with him: his daughter Anna, who became famous in her own right.

**Figure 12.2**
**Freud: The Source of Many Insights about Personality**

Although he was a physician, not a psychologist, Freud's views about personality had strong and lasting effects on the study of personality.

Like many people of Jewish descent, Freud found it necessary to flee the Nazis, and in 1938 he left Vienna for England. (Freud's native language was German, but he spoke and wrote English quite fluently.) He died in England of throat cancer the next year. Many biographies of Freud have been written, and several draw connections between his theories and his personal life experiences—for example, his close relationship with his mother and distant relationship with his father. Whether such links actually exist remains open to debate. What *is* certain, however, is that this complex, brilliant, and dominating man exerted a powerful impact on many of our ideas about personality and psychological disorders.

## Freud's Theory of Personality

Freud entered private medical practice soon after graduating from medical school. A turning point in his early career came when he won a research grant to travel to Paris to observe the work of Jean-Martin Charcot, who was then using hypnosis to treat several types of mental disorders. When Freud returned to Vienna, he worked with Joseph Breuer, a colleague who was using hypnosis in the treatment of *hysteria*—a condition in which individuals experienced physical symptoms such as blindness, deafness, or paralysis of arms or legs for which there seemed to be no underlying physical cause. Out of these experiences and his growing clinical practice, Freud gradually developed his theories of human personality and mental illness. His ideas were complex and touched on many different issues. With respect to personality, however, four topics are most central: *levels of consciousness*, the *structure of personality*, *anxiety and defense mechanisms*, and *psychosexual stages of development*.

**LEVELS OF CONSCIOUSNESS: BENEATH THE ICEBERG'S TIP** Freud viewed himself as a scientist, and he was well aware of research on sensory thresholds (see Chapter 3). In fact, he believed that his psychological theories were just a temporary measure and would ultimately be replaced by knowledge of underlying biological and neural processes (Zuckerman, 1995). In any case, Freud applied to the task of understanding the human mind some of the then emerging ideas about sensory thresholds and the possibility of responding to stimuli we can't report perceiving. He soon reached the startling conclusion that most of the mind lies below the surface—below the threshold of conscious experience. Above this boundary is the realm of the *conscious*. This includes our current thoughts: whatever we are thinking about or experiencing at a given moment. Beneath this conscious realm is the much larger *preconscious*. This contains memories that are not part of current thought but can readily be brought to mind if the need arises. Finally, beneath the preconscious, and forming the bulk of the human mind, is the *unconscious:*

**Figure 12.3**
**Freud's Views about Levels of Consciousness and the Structure of Personality**

Freud believed that the human mind has three distinct levels: the conscious, preconscious, and unconscious. He also believed that personality involves three basic structures: id, ego, and superego, which correspond very roughly to desire, reason, and conscience.

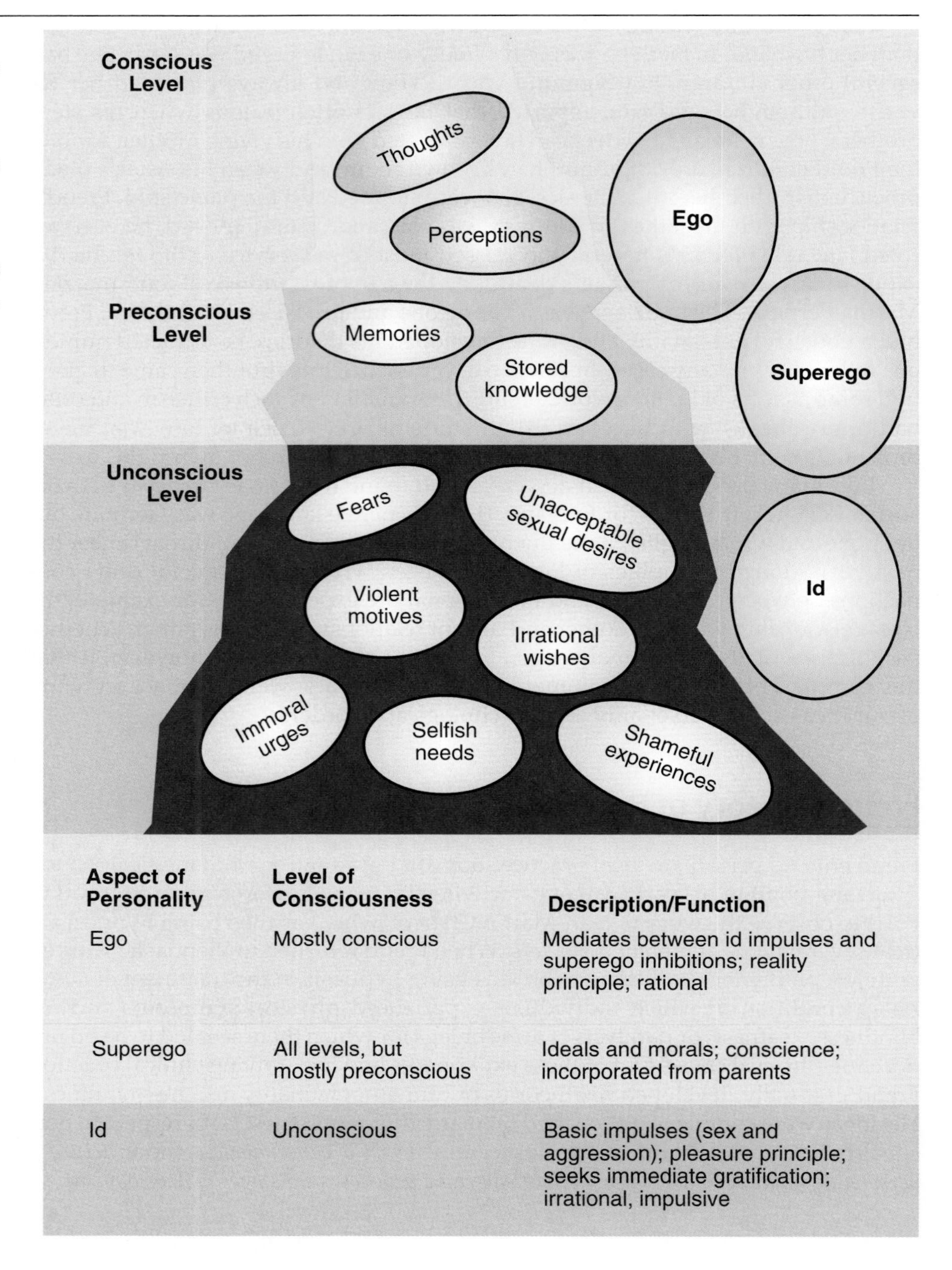


| Aspect of Personality | Level of Consciousness | Description/Function |
|---|---|---|
| Ego | Mostly conscious | Mediates between id impulses and superego inhibitions; reality principle; rational |
| Superego | All levels, but mostly preconscious | Ideals and morals; conscience; incorporated from parents |
| Id | Unconscious | Basic impulses (sex and aggression); pleasure principle; seeks immediate gratification; irrational, impulsive |

thoughts, desires, and impulses of which we remain largely unaware (see Figure 12.3). Although some of this material has always been unconscious, Freud believed that much of it was once conscious but has been actively *repressed*—driven from consciousness because it was too anxiety-provoking. For example, Freud contended that shameful experiences or unacceptable sexual or aggressive urges are often driven deep within the unconscious. The fact that we are not aware of them, however, in no way prevents them from affecting our behavior. Indeed, Freud believed that many of the symptoms experienced by his patients were disguised and indirect reflections of repressed thoughts and desires. This is why one major goal of **psychoanalysis**—the method of treating psychological disorders devised by

**Psychoanalysis:** A method of therapy based on Freud's theory of personality, in which the therapist attempts to bring repressed unconscious material into consciousness.

Freud—is to bring repressed material back into consciousness. Presumably, once such material is made conscious and patients gain insight into the early life experiences that caused them to repress it in the first place, important causes of mental illness are removed.

As we saw in Chapter 4, Freud believed that one way of probing the unconscious was through the *interpretation of dreams.* In dreams, Freud believed, we can give expression to impulses and desires we find unacceptable during our waking hours. Unfortunately, as I explained in that earlier discussion, there is little scientific evidence for this view.

**THE STRUCTURE OF PERSONALITY: ID, EGO, AND SUPEREGO** Do you know the story of Dr. Jekyll, the good, kind doctor, and Mr. Hyde, his evil side? If so, you already have a basic idea of some of the key structures of personality described by Freud. He suggested that personality consists largely of three parts: the *id,* the *ego,* and the *superego* (refer again to Figure 12.3). As we'll soon see, these correspond, roughly, to *desire, reason,* and *conscience.*

The **id** consists of all our primitive, innate urges. These include various bodily needs, sexual desire, and aggressive impulses. According to Freud, the id is totally unconscious and operates in accordance with what he termed the **pleasure principle:** It demands immediate, total gratification and is not capable of considering the potential costs of seeking this goal. In short, the id is the Mr. Hyde of our personality—although, in contrast to this character, it is more appropriately described as *unrestrained* rather than evil.

Unfortunately, the world offers few opportunities for instant pleasure. Moreover, attempting to gratify many of our innate urges would soon get us into serious trouble. It is in response to these facts that the second structure of personality, the **ego,** develops. The ego's task is to hold the id in check until conditions allow for satisfaction of its impulses. Thus, the ego operates in accordance with the **reality principle:** It takes into account external conditions and the consequences of various actions and directs behavior so as to maximize pleasure *and* minimize pain. The ego is partly conscious but not entirely so; thus, some of its actions—for example, its eternal struggle with the id—are outside our conscious knowledge or understanding.

The final aspect of personality described by Freud is the **superego.** It too seeks to control satisfaction of id impulses; but, in contrast to the ego, it is concerned with *morality*—with whether various ways that could potentially satisfy id impulses are right or wrong. The superego permits us to gratify such impulses only when it is morally correct to do so—not simply when it is safe or feasible, as required by the ego. So, for example, it would be the superego, not the ego, that would prevent a stockbroker from altering a computer program and thereby transferring funds from his clients' accounts into his own account, even though he knew he could get away with this action.

The superego is acquired from our parents and through experience and represents our internalization of the moral teachings and norms of our society. Unfortunately, such teachings are often quite inflexible and leave little room for gratification of our basic desires—they require us to be good all the time, like Dr. Jekyll. Because of this fact, the ego faces another difficult task: It must strike a balance between our primitive urges (the id) and our learned moral constraints (the superego). Freud felt that this constant struggle among id, ego, and superego plays a key role in personality and in many psychological disorders. Moreover, he suggested that the struggle was often visible in everyday behavior in what have come to be known as **Freudian slips**—errors in speech that actually reflect unconscious impulses that have "gotten by" the ego or superego. An example: "She was tempting . . . I mean attempting to. . . ." According to Freud, the word *tempting* reveals an unacceptable sexual impulse.

**Id:** In Freud's theory, the portion of personality concerned with immediate gratification of primitive needs.

**Pleasure Principle:** The principle on which the id operates, according to which immediate pleasure is the sole motivation for behavior.

**Ego:** In Freud's theory, the part of personality that takes account of external reality in the expression of instinctive sexual and aggressive urges.

**Reality Principle:** The principle according to which the ego operates, in which the external consequences of behavior are considered in the expression of impulses from the id.

**Superego:** According to Freud, the portion of human personality representing the conscience.

**Freudian Slips:** Errors in speech that in fact betray unconscious thoughts or impulses.

**ANXIETY AND DEFENSE MECHANISMS: SELF-PROTECTION BY THE EGO** In its constant struggle to prevent the eruption of dangerous id impulses, the ego faces a difficult task. Yet for most people, most of the time, the ego succeeds. Sometimes, though, id impulses grow so strong that they threaten to get out of control. For example, consider the case of a middle-aged widow who finds herself strongly attracted to her daughter's boyfriend. She hasn't had a romantic attachment in years, so her sexual desire quickly rises to high levels. What happens next? According to Freud, when her ego senses that unacceptable impulses are about to get out of hand, it experiences **anxiety**—intense feelings of nervousness, tension, or worry. These feelings occur because the unacceptable impulses are getting closer and closer to consciousness, as well as closer and closer to the limits of the ego to hold them in check.

At this point, Freud contended, the ego may resort to one of several different **defense mechanisms.** These are all designed to keep unacceptable impulses from the id out of consciousness and to prevent their open expression. Defense mechanisms take many different forms. For example, in **sublimation,** the unacceptable impulse is channeled into some socially acceptable action. Instead of trying to seduce the young man, as Freud would say the widow's id wants to do, she might "adopt" him as a son and provide financial support to further his education. Other defense mechanisms are described in Table 12.1. While they differ in form, all serve the function of reducing anxiety by keeping unacceptable urges and impulses from breaking into consciousness.

**TABLE 12.1**

**Defense Mechanisms: Reactions to Anxiety**

Freud believed that when the ego feels it may be unable to control impulses from the id, it experiences anxiety. To reduce such feelings, the ego uses various *defense mechanisms* such as those described here.

| Defense Mechanism | Its Basic Nature | Example |
|---|---|---|
| Repression | "Forgetting"—or pushing from consciousness into unconsciousness—unacceptable thoughts or impulses | A woman fails to recognize her attraction to her handsome new son-in-law. |
| Rationalization | Conjuring up socially acceptable reasons for thoughts or actions based on unacceptable motives | A young woman explains that she ate an entire chocolate cake so that it wouldn't spoil in the summer heat. |
| Displacement | Redirecting an emotional response from a dangerous object to a safe one | A man redirects anger from his boss to his child. |
| Projection | Transferring unacceptable motives or impulses to others | A man who feels strong hostility toward a neighbor perceives the neighbor as being hostile to him. |
| Regression | Responding to a threatening situation in a way appropriate to an earlier age or level of development | A student asks a professor to raise his grade; when she refuses, the student throws a temper tantrum. |

**Anxiety:** In Freudian theory, unpleasant feelings of tension or worry experienced by individuals in reaction to unacceptable wishes or impulses.

**Defense Mechanisms:** Techniques used by the ego to keep threatening and unacceptable material out of consciousness, and so to reduce anxiety.

**Sublimation:** A defense mechanism in which threatening unconscious impulses are channeled into socially acceptable forms of behavior.

**PSYCHOSEXUAL STAGES OF DEVELOPMENT** Now we come to what is perhaps the most controversial aspect of Freud's theory of personality: his ideas about its formation or development. Freud's views in this respect can be grouped under the heading **psychosexual stages of development:** innately determined stages of sexual development through which, presumably, we all pass, and which strongly shape the nature of our personality. Before turning to the stages themselves, however, we must first consider two important concepts relating to them: *libido* and *fixation*.

**Libido** refers to the instinctual life force that energizes the id. Release of libido is closely related to pleasure, but the focus of such pleasure—and the expression of libido—changes as we develop. In each stage of development, we obtain different kinds of pleasure and leave behind a small amount of our libido—this is the normal course of events. If an excessive amount of libido energy is tied to a particular stage, however, **fixation** results. This can stem from either too little or too much gratification during this stage, and in either case the result is harmful. Because the individual has left too much "psychic energy" behind, less is available for full adult development. The outcome may be an adult personality reflecting the stage or stages at which fixation has occurred. To put it another way, if too much energy is drained away by fixation at earlier stages of development, the amount remaining may be insufficient to power movement to full adult development. Then an individual may show an immature personality and several psychological disorders.

Now back to the actual stages themselves. According to Freud, as we grow and develop, different parts of the body serve as the focus of our quest for pleasure. In the initial **oral stage,** lasting until we are about eighteen months old, we seek pleasure mainly through the mouth. If too much or too little gratification occurs during this stage, an individual may become fixated at it. Too little gratification results in a personality that is overly dependent on others; too much, especially after the child has developed some teeth, results in a personality that is excessively hostile, especially through verbal sarcasm.

The next stage occurs in response to efforts by parents to toilet train their children. During the **anal stage,** the process of elimination becomes the primary focus of pleasure. Fixation at this stage, stemming from overly harsh toilet-training experiences, may result in individuals who are excessively orderly or *compulsive*—they can't leave any job unfinished and strive for perfection and neatness in everything they do (see Figure 12.4 on page 458). In contrast, fixation stemming from very relaxed toilet training may result in people who are undisciplined, impulsive, and excessively generous. Freud himself might well be described as compulsive; even when he was seriously ill, he personally answered dozens of letters every day—even letters from total strangers asking his advice (Benjamin & Dixon, 1996).

At about age four, the genitals become the primary source of pleasure, and children enter the **phallic stage.** Freud speculated that at this time we fantasize about sex with our opposite-sex parent—a phenomenon he termed the **Oedipus complex,** after Oedipus, a character in ancient Greek literature who unknowingly killed his father and then married his mother. Fear of punishment for such desires then enters the picture. Among boys the feared punishment is castration, leading to *castration anxiety.* Among girls the feared punishment is loss of love. In both cases, these fears bring about resolution of the Oedipus complex and identification with the same-sex parent. In other words, little boys give up sexual desires for their mothers and come to see their fathers as models rather than as rivals; little girls give up their sexual desires for their father and come to see their mothers as models.

Perhaps one of Freud's most controversial suggestions is the idea that little girls experience *penis envy* stemming from their own lack of a male organ. Freud suggested that because of such envy, girls experience strong feelings of inferiority and envy—feelings they carry with them in disguised form even in adult life. As you can readily imagine, many psychologists object strongly to these ideas, and there is virtually no evidence for them.

**Psychosexual Stages of Development:** According to Freud, an innate sequence of stages through which all human beings pass. At each stage, pleasure is focused on a different region of the body.

**Libido:** According to Freud, the psychic energy that powers all mental activity.

**Fixation:** Excessive investment of psychic energy in a particular stage of psychosexual development; this results in various types of psychological disorders.

**Oral Stage:** In Freud's theory, the stage of psychosexual development during which pleasure is centered in the region of the mouth.

**Anal Stage:** In Freud's theory, the psychosexual stage of development in which pleasure is focused primarily on he anal zone.

**Phallic Stage:** In Freud's theory, an early stage of psychosexual development during which pleasure is centered in the genital region. It is during this stage that the Oedipus complex develops.

**Oedipus Complex:** In Freud's theory, a crisis of psychosexual development in which children must give up their sexual attraction to their opposite-sex parent.

**Figure 12.4**
**The Compulsive Personality in Action**

Freud believed that people who don't obtain enough satisfaction during the anal stage develop a compulsive personality. Like the person shown here, they are excessively neat and orderly.
(*Source:* © The New Yorker Collection. 1999. Robert Weber from cartoonbank.com. All rights reserved.)

*"I'm sorry, dear, but you knew I was a bureaucrat when you married me."*

After resolution of the Oedipus conflict, children enter the **latency stage,** during which sexual urges are, according to Freud, at a minimum. Finally, during puberty adolescents enter the **genital stage.** During this stage pleasure is again focused on the genitals. Now, however, lust is blended with affection, and people become capable of adult love. Remember: According to Freud, progression to this final stage is possible only if serious fixation has *not* occurred at earlier stages. If such fixation exists, development is blocked and various disorders result. Major stages in Freud's theory are summarized in Figure 12.5.

CourseCompass
Audio 12.1: *The Unconscious Mind*

## Research Related to Freud's Theory: Probing the Unconscious

Freud's theories contain many intriguing ideas; and, as you probably know, several of these have entered into world culture—people everywhere talk about the unconscious, repressed impulses, the id and ego, and so on. It's not surprising, therefore, that psychologists have investigated several of these ideas—at least, the ones that *can* be studied through scientific means. We have already discussed the scientific status of Freud's ideas about dreams (Chapter 4); here, let's consider his ideas about the unconscious.

**Latency Stage:** In Freud's theory, the psychosexual stage of development that follows resolution of the Oedipus complex. During this stage, sexual desires are relatively weak.

**Genital Stage:** In Freud's theory, the final stage of psychosexual development—one in which individuals acquire the adult capacity to combine lust with affection.

Freud contended that our feelings and behavior can be strongly affected by information we can't bring to mind and can't describe verbally. Research in many fields of psychology suggests that to some extent this is true (e.g., Bornstein, 1992), although psychologists refer to such information as *nonconscious* rather than as "unconscious" in order to avoid assuming that such information has been repressed. (It may be nonconscious for other reasons—for instance, because it was presented so quickly that it couldn't be recognized.) Do you recall our discussion of *procedural memory* in Chapter 6? This kind of memory allows you to perform many skilled

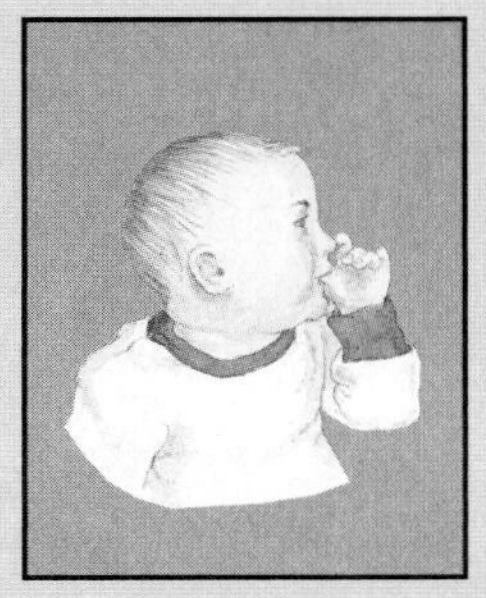

**Oral 0–2**
Infant achieves gratification through oral activities such as feeding, thumb sucking, and babbling.

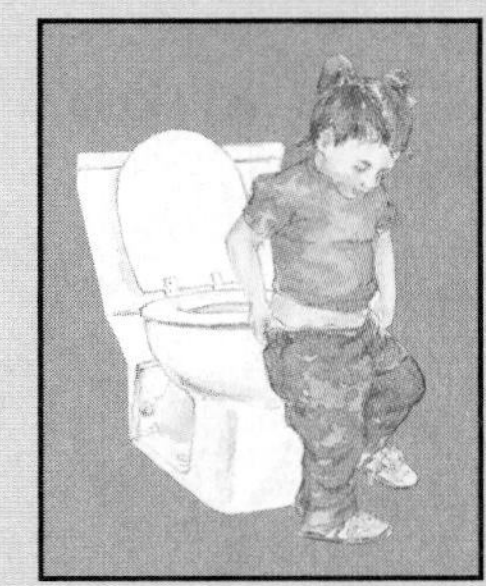

**Anal 2–3**
The child learns to respond to some of the demands of society (such as bowel and bladder control).

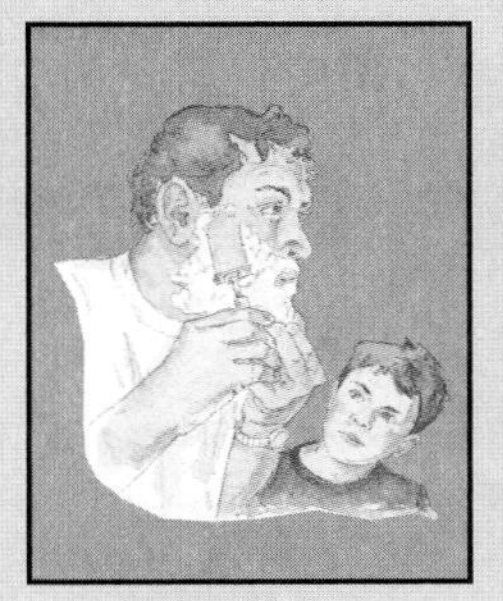

**Phallic 3–7**
The child learns to realize the differences between males and females and becomes aware of sexuality.

**Latency 7–11**
The child continues his or her development but sexual urges are relatively quiet.

**Genital 11–adult**
The growing adolescent shakes off old dependencies and learns to deal maturely with the opposite sex.

**Figure 12.5**
**The Psychosexual Stages of Development Described by Freud**

According to Freud, all human beings pass through a series of discrete psychosexual stages of development. At each stage, pleasure is focused on a particular part of the body. Too much or too little gratification at any stage can result in *fixation* and can lead to psychological disorders.

physical actions, such as tying your shoelaces, playing a musical instrument, or doing the complex steps of swing dancing (see Figure 12.6 on page 460). Although such information is obviously present in memory, you can't readily describe it or put it into words. Thus, when someone asks you to explain how you do a certain dance step, you may say, "Just watch, I'll show you." So the existence of procedural memory suggests that often we do possess information we can't describe verbally.

Additional evidence for the impact of nonconscious thoughts or feelings on our behavior is provided by recent research on the nature of prejudice. Several studies show that persons who describe themselves as totally unprejudiced still sometimes demonstrate signs of negative feelings or emotions about members of minority groups—feelings of which they appear to be largely unaware. For instance, consider an ingenious study by Vanman and his colleagues (Vanman et al., 1997).

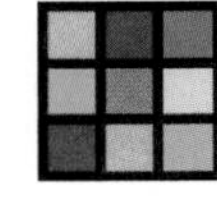

In this investigation, white participants of both genders were asked to imagine working on several cooperative tasks (e.g., a team running race, a debate team competition, a team research project) with a partner who was either white or African American. They were further told to imagine that their outcomes in each situation would be determined either by their joint efforts or by their own individual performance. While participants were imagining these situations, the researchers made recordings of electrical activity in participants' facial muscles—muscles related to smiling and to frowning.

**Figure 12.6**
**Procedural Memory: Information that Can't Be Put into Words**

Could the dancers here describe in words how they perform each step? Perhaps, but they might also prefer to say "Let me show you!" Situations like this indicate that in one sense Freud was correct: Our minds *do* hold information we can't readily put into words. Freud described this as the unconscious, but modern psychologists would say that information used in performing complex physical actions is stored in *procedural memory.*

The researchers predicted that although participants would not *report* more negative attitudes toward black than toward white partners, their facial muscles would show more activity indicative of negative emotional reactions when their imagined partner was black than when this person was white. Moreover, they reasoned that that this would occur under both the independent and joint reward conditions. As you can see from Figure 12.7, results offered clear support for these predictions: Participants did indeed show greater signs of negative emotional reactions to the thought of an African American partner. Moreover, this was true despite the fact that participants actually reported *more positive* attitudes toward their partners when these persons were supposedly black than when they were supposedly white. Were they simply concealing their prejudiced views? Additional evidence suggests that they were not: The research participants truly *believed* that they were unprejudiced, and at a purely verbal level, they were. Yet underneath they seemed to harbor residual negative feelings toward African Americans.

**Figure 12.7**
**Prejudice: Based in Part on Nonconscious Thoughts?**

White participants who expressed positive feelings about a black partner on a questionnaire showed facial muscle activity indicative of *negative* reactions to this person when they imagined working with him or her. Thus, at a conscious level (what they could report), participants were not prejudiced; at a nonconscious level, however, they seemed to harbor hidden prejudice.

(*Source:* Based on data from Vanman et al., 1997.)

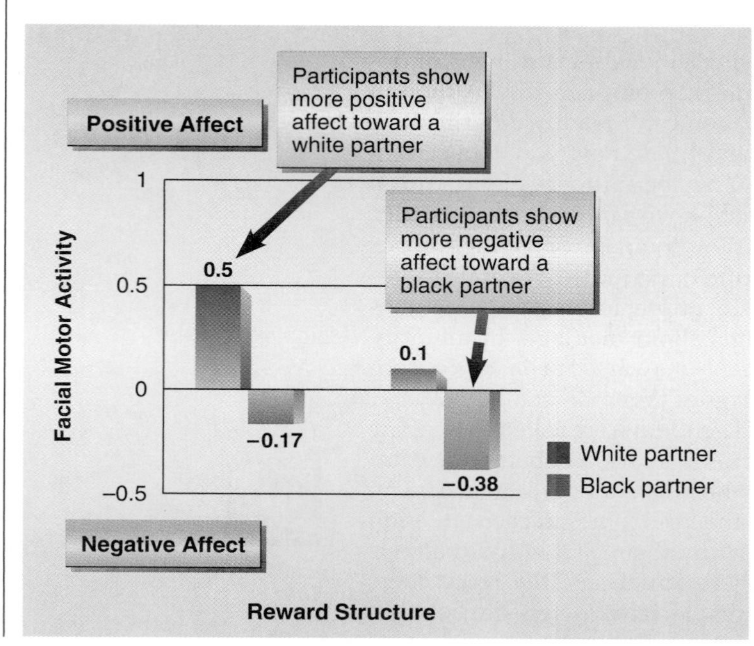


Additional support for the existence of nonconscious information is provided by *subliminal perception*—a topic we discussed in Chapter 3. As you may recall, claims for subliminal perception have been overstated, especially with respect to its supposed value as a learning aid or marketing technique. Yet there is no doubt that sometimes we can be influenced by stimuli of which we are unaware

(Reder & Gordon, 1997). So, once again, there is some support in research findings for Freud's suggestion that we can be influenced by information or feelings we can't describe—although, as noted in Chapter 6, there is little or no support for his suggestion that repression is responsible for driving such thoughts out of consciousness in the first place.

## Freud's Theory: An Overall Evaluation

Freud's place in history is assured: His ideas and writings have exerted a profound impact on society. But what about his theory of personality? Is it currently accepted by most psychologists? As you can probably guess from my earlier comments, the answer is *definitely not.* The reasons are clear. First, many critics have pointed out that Freud's theory is not really a scientific theory at all. True, as we just saw, some of his ideas, or hypotheses derived from them, can be tested. But many concepts in his theory cannot be measured or studied systematically. How, for instance can one go about observing an *id,* a *fixation,* or the psychic energy contained in the *libido*? As I noted in Chapter 1, a theory that cannot be tested is largely useless, and this criticism does apply to many of Freud's ideas.

Second, as we have already seen, several of Freud's proposals are not consistent with the findings of modern research—for instance, his ideas about the meaning of dreams. Third, in constructing his theory, Freud relied heavily on a small number of case studies—no more than a dozen at most. Almost all of these persons came from wealthy backgrounds and lived in a large and sophisticated city within a single culture. Thus, they were not representative of human beings generally.

Finally, and perhaps most important of all, Freud's theories contain so many different concepts that they can explain virtually any pattern of behavior in an after-the-fact manner. If a theory can't be disconfirmed—shown to be false—then, once again, it is largely useless; and this does seem to be the case with Freud's views.

For these and other reasons, Freud's theory of personality is not currently accepted by most psychologists. Yet several of his insights—especially his ideas about levels of consciousness and about the importance of anxiety in psychological disorders—*have* contributed to our understanding of human behavior and personality. So although his theories don't measure up to the rigorous standards of science required by modern psychology, there is no doubt that Freud has a profound and lasting impact on modern thought.

### REVIEW QUESTIONS

- According to Freud, what are the three levels of consciousness?
- In Freud's theory, what are the three basic components of personality?
- According to Freud, what are the psychosexual stages of development?
- Do research findings support Freud's views about the unconscious?

## Other Psychoanalytic Views: Freud's Disciples . . . and Defectors

Whatever else Freud was, he was certainly an intellectual magnet. Over the course of several decades, he attracted as students or colleagues many brilliant people. Most of them began by accepting Freud's views. Later, however, they often disagreed with

**Figure 12.8**
**The Young Hero: An Archetype**

According to Jung, all human beings possess a *collective unconscious.* Information stored there is often expressed in terms of *archetypes*—representations of key aspects of human experience, such as the hero (shown here), mother, father, and so on.

some of his major assumptions. Let's see why these individuals, often termed **neo-Freudians,** broke with Freud, and what they had to say about the nature of personality.

**JUNG: THE COLLECTIVE UNCONSCIOUS** Perhaps the most bitter of all the defections Freud experienced was that of Carl Jung—the follower Freud viewed as his heir apparent. Jung shared Freud's views concerning the importance of the unconscious, but contended that there is another part to this aspect of personality that Freud overlooked: the **collective unconscious.** According to Jung, the collective unconscious holds experiences shared by all human beings—experiences that are, in a sense, part of our biological heritage. The contents of the collective unconscious, in short, reflect the experiences our species has had since it originated on earth. The collective unconscious finds expression in our minds in several ways, but among these, **archetypes** are the most central to Jung's theory. These are manifestations of the collective unconscious that express themselves when our conscious mind is distracted or inactive; for example, during sleep, in dreams, or in fantasies (e.g., Neher, 1996). The specific expression of archetypes depends in part on our unique experience as individuals, but in all cases such images are representations of key aspects of the human experience—*mother, father, wise old man, the sun, the moon, God, death,* and *the hero* (see Figure 12.8). It is because of these shared innate images, Jung contended, that the folklore of many different cultures contains similar figures and themes.

Web Link: *Carl Jung Hompage*

**Neo-Freudians:** Personality theorists who accepted basic portions of Freud's theory but rejected or modified other portions.

**Collective Unconscious:** In Jung's theory, a portion of the unconscious shared by all human beings.

**Archetypes:** According to Jung, inherited images in the collective unconscious that shape our perceptions of the external world.

**Animus:** According to Jung, the archetype representing the masculine side of females.

**Anima:** According to Jung, the archetype representing the feminine side of males.

**Introverts:** In Jung's theory, individuals who are hesitant and cautious and do not make friends easily.

**Extroverts:** In Jung's theory, individuals who are open and and confident and make friends readily.

Two especially important archetypes in Jung's theory are known as **animus** and **anima.** The animus is the masculine side of females, while the anima is the feminine side of males. Jung believed that in looking for a mate, we search for the person onto whom we can best project these hidden sides of our personality. When there is a good match between such projections and another person, attraction occurs.

Another aspect of Jung's theory was his suggestion that we are all born with innate tendencies to be concerned primarily either with our inner selves or with the outside world. Jung labeled persons in the first category **introverts** and described them as being hesitant and cautious; introverts do not make friends easily and prefer to observe the world rather than become involved in it. He labeled persons in the second category **extroverts.** Such persons are open and confident, make friends readily, and enjoy high levels of stimulation and a wide range of activities. Although many aspects of Jung's theory have been rejected by psychologists—especially the idea of the collective unconscious—the dimension of introversion–extroversion appears to be a basic one of major importance; it is included in several *trait theories* we'll consider in a later section (although in these theories the term is spelled extr*a*version).

**KAREN HORNEY AND ALFRED ADLER** Two other important neo-Freudians are Karen Horney and Alfred Adler. Horney was one of the few females in the early psychoanalytic movement, and she disagreed with Freud strongly over his view that differences between men and women stemmed largely from innate factors—for example, from anatomical differences resulting in penis envy among females. Horney contended that although women often do feel inferior to men (remember, she was writing in Germany in the 1920s), this is a result not of penis envy but of how women are treated by society. She argued that if women were raised in a different type of environment, they would see themselves more favorably. In other words, it was not the male penis women envied, but rather the *power* and *autonomy* associated with maleness. In addition, she maintained that psychological disorders stem not from fixation of psychic energy, as Freud contended, but rather from disturbed interpersonal relationships during childhood and what she termed **basic anxiety**—children's fear of being left alone, helpless, and insecure. She suggested that in reaction to excessive levels of such anxiety, which stem from poor relations with their parents, children adopt one of three styles: a *passive* style, in which they try to cope by being agreeable and compliant; an *aggressive* style, in which they fight to get attention; or a *withdrawn* style, in which they repress their emotions. All three patterns can lead to serious psychological disorders. By emphasizing the importance of children's relationships with their parents, then, Horney called attention to the importance of social factors in shaping personality—a view echoed by modern psychology.

Alfred Adler also disagreed with Freud very strongly, but over somewhat different issues. In particular, he emphasized the importance of feelings of inferiority, which he believed we experience as children because of our small size and physical weakness. He viewed personality development as stemming primarily from our efforts to overcome such feelings through what he termed **striving for superiority.** If these efforts go too far, we may develop a *superiority complex* and become a braggart or a bully (Sutton & Smith, 1999). Under the surface, however, persons who show this pattern still feel inferior: They are merely covering up with an outward show of strength. Like Horney and other neo-Freudians, Adler also emphasized the importance of social factors in personality; for instance, he called attention to the importance of birth order. Only children, he suggested, are spoiled by too much parental attention, while firstborns are "dethroned" by a second child. Second-borns, in contrast, are competitive because they have to struggle to catch up with an older sibling.

By now the main point of this discussion should be clear: neo-Freudians, while accepting many of Freud's basic ideas, rejected his emphasis on innate patterns of development. On the contrary, they perceived personality as stemming from a complex interplay between social factors and the experiences we have during childhood, primarily in our own families. The theories proposed by neo-Freudians are not widely accepted by psychologists, but they did serve as a kind of bridge between the provocative views offered by Freud and more modern conceptions of personality. In this respect, at least, they made an important lasting contribution.

**REVIEW QUESTIONS**

- According to Jung, what is the collective unconscious?
- In Horney's theory, what is basic anxiety?
- According to Adler, what is the role of feelings of inferiority in personality?

**Basic Anxiety:** According to Karen Horney, children's fear of being left alone, helpless, and insecure.

**Striving for Superiority:** Attempting to overcome feelings of inferiority. According to Adler, this is the primary motive for human behavior.

**Humanistic Theories:** Theories of personality emphasizing personal responsibility and innate tendencies toward personal growth.

## Humanistic Theories: Emphasis on Growth

Id versus ego, Jekyll versus Hyde—on the whole, psychoanalytic theories of personality take a dim view of human nature, contending that we must struggle constantly to control our bestial impulses if we are to function as healthy, rational adults. Is this view accurate? Many psychologists doubt it. They believe that human strivings for growth, dignity, and self-determination are just as important, if not more important, in the development of personality than the primitive motives Freud emphasized. Because of their more optimistic ideas about human nature, such views are known as **humanistic theories** (Maslow, 1970; Rogers, 1977, 1982).

These theories differ widely in the concepts on which they focus, but they share the following characteristics.

First, humanistic theories emphasize *personal responsibility.* Each of us, these theories contend, is largely responsible for what happens to us. Our fate is mostly in our own hands; we are not merely chips driven here and there by dark forces within our personalities. Second, while these theories don't deny the importance of past experience, they generally *focus on the present.* True, we may be influenced by traumatic events early in life. Yet these do not have to shape our entire adult lives, and the capacity to overcome them and to go on is both real and powerful. Third, humanistic theories stress the importance of *personal growth.* People are not content with merely meeting their current needs. They wish to progress toward "bigger" goals such as becoming the best they can be. Only when obstacles interfere with such growth is the process interrupted. A key goal of therapy, therefore, should be the removal of obstacles that prevent natural growth processes from proceeding. As examples of humanistic theories, we'll now consider the views proposed by Carl Rogers and Abraham Maslow.

Web Link: *Carl Rogers*

Web Link: *Carl Rogers—Core of Personality*

## Rogers's Self Theory: Becoming a Fully Functioning Person

Carl Rogers planned to become a minister, but after taking several courses in psychology, he changed his mind and decided instead to focus on human personality. The theory Rogers formulated played an important role in the emergence of humanistic psychology and remains influential even today.

One central assumption of Rogers's theory was this: Left to their own devices, human beings show many positive characteristics and move, over the course of their lives, toward becoming **fully functioning persons.** What are such persons like? Rogers suggested that they are people who strive to experience life to the fullest, who live in the here and now, and who trust their own feelings. They are sensitive to the needs and rights of others, but they do not allow society's standards to shape their feelings or actions to an excessive degree. Fully functioning people aren't saints; they can—and do—act in ways they later regret. But throughout life, their actions are dominated by constructive impulses. They are in close touch with their own values and feelings and experience life more deeply than most other persons.

If all human beings possess the capacity to become fully functioning persons, why don't they all succeed? Why aren't we surrounded by models of health and happy adjustment? The answer, Rogers contends, lies in the anxiety generated when life experiences are inconsistent with our ideas about ourselves—in short, when a gap develops between our **self-concept** (our beliefs and knowledge about ourselves) and reality or our perceptions of it. For example, imagine a young girl who is quite independent and self-reliant, and who thinks of herself in this way. After her older sibling dies in an accident, however, her parents begin to baby her and to convey the message, over and over again, that she is vulnerable and must be sheltered from the outside world. This treatment is highly inconsistent with her self-concept. As a result, she experiences anxiety and adopts one or more psychological defenses to reduce it. The most common of these defenses is *distortion*—changing our perceptions of reality so that they *are* consistent with our self-concept. For example, the girl may come to believe that her parents aren't being overprotective; they are just showing normal concern for her safety. Another defense process is *denial;* she may refuse to admit to herself that as a result of being babied, she is indeed losing her independence.

In the short run, such tactics can be successful; they help reduce anxiety. Ultimately, however, they produce sizable gaps between an individual's self-concept and reality. For instance, the girl may cling to the belief that she is independent when in fact, as a result of her parents' treatment, she is becoming increasingly helpless.

**Fully Functioning Persons:** In Rogers's theory, psychologically healthy persons who live life to the fullest.

**Self-Concept:** All the information and beliefs individuals have about their own characteristics and themselves.

The larger such gaps, Rogers contends, the greater an individual's maladjustment—and personal unhappiness (see Figure 12.9). Rogers suggested that distortions in the self-concept are common, because most people grow up in an atmosphere of *conditional positive regard.* That is, they learn that others, such as their parents, will approve of them only when they behave in certain ways and express certain feelings. As a result, many people are forced to deny the existence of various impulses and feelings, and their self-concepts become badly distorted.

How can such distorted self-concepts be repaired so that healthy development can continue? Rogers suggests that therapists can help accomplish this goal by placing individuals in an atmosphere of **unconditional positive regard**—a setting in which they will be accepted by the therapist *no matter what they say or do.* Such conditions are provided by *client-centered therapy,* a form of therapy we'll consider in detail in Chapter 15.

**Figure 12.9**
**Gaps between Our Self-Concept and Our Experience: A Cause of Maladjustment in Rogers's Theory**

According to Rogers, the larger the gap between an individual's self-concept and reality, the poorer this person's psychological adjustment.

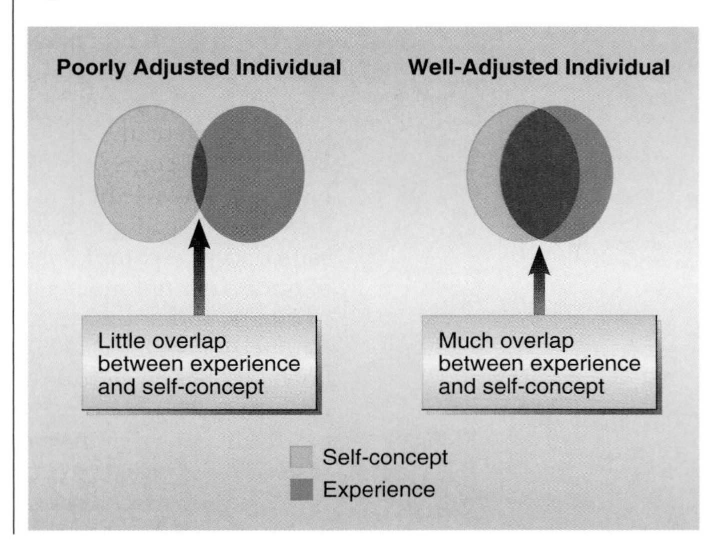


## Maslow and the Study of Self-Actualizing People

Another influential humanistic theory of personality was proposed by Abraham Maslow (1970). We have already encountered a portion of Maslow's theory, his concept of a *needs hierarchy,* in Chapter 10. As you may recall, this concept suggests that human needs exist in a hierarchy, ranging from *physiological needs,* on the bottom, through *safety needs, social needs, esteem needs,* and finally *self-actualization needs* at the top. According to Maslow, lower-order needs must be satisfied before we can turn to more complex, higher-order needs (Neher, 1991). Presumably, higher-order needs can't serve as motives until lower-level needs have been satisfied. Thus, a hungry person won't be very interested in self-actualizing; and one whose safety is threatened won't focus on gaining others' approval—unless, of course, this helps to meet her or his more basic safety needs.

The needs hierarchy, however, is only part of Maslow's theory of personality. Maslow has also devoted much attention to the study of people who, in his terms, are *psychologically healthy.* These are individuals who have attained high levels of **self-actualization**—a state in which they have reached their fullest true potential. What are such people like? In essence, much like the fully functioning persons described by Rogers. Self-actualized people accept themselves for what they are; they recognize their shortcomings as well as their strengths. Being in touch with their own personalities, they are less inhibited and less likely to conform than most of us. Self-actualized people are well aware of the rules imposed by society, but feel greater freedom to ignore them than most persons. Unlike most of us, they seem to retain their childhood wonder and amazement with the world. For them, life continues to be an exciting adventure rather than a boring routine. Finally, self-actualized persons sometimes have what Maslow describes as **peak experiences**—instances in which they have powerful feelings of unity with the universe and feel tremendous waves of power and wonder. Such experiences appear to be linked to personal growth, for after them individuals report feeling more spontaneous, more appreciative of life, and less concerned with the problems of everyday life. Examples of people Maslow describes as fully self-actualized are Thomas Jefferson, Albert Einstein, Eleanor Roosevelt, and George Washington Carver.

**Unconditional Positive Regard:** In Rogers's theory, a therapeutic atmosphere that communicates that a person will be respected or loved regardless of what he or she says or does.

**Self-Actualization:** In Maslow's theory, the stage of personal development in which individuals reach their maximum potential.

**Peak Experiences:** According to Maslow, intense emotional experiences during which individuals feel at one with the universe.

## Research Related to Humanistic Theories: Studying the Self-Concept

At first glance it might seem that humanistic theories, like psychoanalytic ones, would not be readily open to scientific test. In fact, however, the opposite is true. Humanistic theories were proposed by psychologists, and a commitment to empirical research is one of the true hallmarks of modern psychology. For this reason, several concepts that play a key role in humanistic theories have been studied quite extensively. Among these, the one that has probably received most attention is the idea of the *self-concept,* which is so central to Rogers's theory.

Research on the self-concept has addressed may different issues—for instance, how our self-concept is formed (e.g., Sedikides & Skowronski, 1997), how it influences the way we think (e.g., Kendzierski & Whitaker, 1997), and what information it contains (e.g., Rentsch & Heffner, 1994). Together, such research suggests that the self-concept is complex and consists of many different parts, including knowledge of our own traits and beliefs, understanding of how we are perceived by and relate to others, and knowledge of how we are similar to and different from others (e.g., Baumeister & Leary, 1995). One of the most interesting lines of research on the self, however, has focused on cultural influences—the question of whether our self-concept is shaped, in part, by the culture to which we belong.

Such research indicates that part of our self-concept does indeed reflect our culture. For instance, in Western cultures, which are often described as *individualistic* because they place great emphasis on individuality (e.g., individual accomplishments and self-expression), people often express unrealistically optimistic self-evaluations: They think (or at least report) that they are better than they actually are. To demonstrate this for yourself, ask ten of your friends to rate their own intelligence, leadership ability, and social skills on the following scale: 1 = poor; 2 = below average; 3 = average; 4 = above average; 5 = excellent. Almost all of them will rate themselves as average or above on all these dimensions. Needless to say, we can't all be above average on everything! In contrast, in Eastern cultures, which are often described as *collectivistic,* greater emphasis is placed on cooperation and maintaining social harmony. The result? Persons from such cultures do *not* express overoptimistic self-evaluations (see Figure 12.10) (e.g., Yik, Bond, & Paulhus, 1998).

**Figure 12.10**
**Culture and the Self-Concept**

In Western cultures, which are *individualistic* in nature, many persons express unrealistically high evaluations of their own abilities. In Asian cultures, which are *collectivistic,* these tendencies toward overoptimistic self-evaluations are less apparent.

Together, these and other findings indicate that Rogers and other humanistic theorists were correct in assigning the self-concept an important role in personality, and their interest in this topic helped to call it to the attention of other psychologists, too. Many factors influence the development of our self-concept; but for one that is especially thought-provoking, please see the following **Beyond the Headlines** section.

## BEYOND the HEADLINES: *As Psychologists See It*

### What's in a Name? Ask the People Who Have Unusual Ones

#### Could Your Name Be Your Destiny? Just Ask Mr. Roach

WALL STREET JOURNAL (JUNE 14, 1997)—The undertaker in York, Pa., isn't merely being friendly when he tells the bereaved to call him by his first name. He doesn't want to seem stiff. Cramer J. Stiff is a licensed cemeterian . . . for Mount Rose Cemetery . . . Today, business ought to be brisk for a hairdresser named Barbara Trimmer, for a chef named Susan Spicer . . . and life should be a song for Daniel Harp, who teaches music. Benjamin Franklin is professor of early American literature at the University of South Carolina. C. Martin Lawyer, a legal-aid attorney in Tampa, Fla., tries to deflect the inevitable question before clients can even ask it: "My name is Martin Lawyer. Yes, I am an attorney. And yes, Lawyer is my real name."

Chris Roach, an inspector in Sterling, Va., with Terminix, the pest-control company, gets tired of people asking "Did you bring the problem with you?" And Bonnie Glass-Coffin, a Utah anthropologist, wonders if people take her seriously enough. R. Bruce Money, a former banker and now a business professor . . . says his first name is actually Richard, but he doesn't use it because people might start calling him Rich Money. . . .

Are people with unusual monikers drawn to professions that suit their names? Or are they more likely to reject such jobs, to avoid these connections? Mr. Roach, the termite inspector, says the name–job connection might seem fishy, but still, both his mother and his brother also work for Terminix. "Destiny," he says, "works in strange ways."

What do you think? Are people whose last names are related to various occupations actually drawn to them? Can a person's last name shape his or her self-concept, and so a choice of occupations? Psychologists are divided on this issue. Professor Lewis P. Lipsitt, a child psychologist at Brown University, believes that *something* is at work, perhaps unconsciously. Having an unusual last name, he reasons, "could easily become a repeated reminder of an interest area that could eventually become yours," he says. Dr. Neal Goldsmith, a New York City psychologist, goes one step farther. He speculates that people with job-related names may "either grow into or grow in opposition" to their names. Thus, would a man named Crook be more likely than other people to become either a police officer or a criminal? When asked, most people with job-related names state emphatically that their names had nothing to do with their choice of jobs. But as I've noted before (see Chapters 6 and 7), people are not always aware of the factors that shape their behavior; so perhaps there *is* something to the name–choice of occupation link. In any case, given that our self-concept is strongly influenced by our last names, which do often reflect our ethnic and cultural heritage, and also by our occupations, this is certainly a topic worth considering. It may provide additional insights into the nature of the self-concept, and so of personality.

#### CRITICAL THINKING QUESTIONS

1. Do you think that people's last names really play a role in their choice of occupations?
2. How could psychologists study this topic? Through what kind of research methods?
3. Suppose research findings indicate that last names *do* influence our choice of occupations. What would be the practical implications (if any) of this finding?

## Humanistic Theories: An Evaluation

The comments above suggest that humanistic theories have had a lasting impact on psychology, and this is definitely so. Several of the ideas first proposed by Rogers, Maslow, and other humanistic theorists have entered into the mainstream of psychology. But humanistic theories have also been subject to strong criticism. Many psychologists are uncomfortable with the strong emphasis, in these theories, on personal responsibility or *free will.* Humanistic theories propose that individuals are responsible for their own actions and can change these if they wish to do so. To an extent, this is certainly true. Yet it conflicts with *determinism,* the idea that behavior is determined by numerous factors and can be predicted from them. Such determinism is a basic assumption of all science, so questioning it makes many psychologists uneasy.

Second, many key concepts of humanistic theories are loosely defined. What, precisely, is self-actualization? A peak experience? A fully functioning person? Until such terms are clearly defined, it is difficult to conduct systematic research on them. Despite such criticisms, the impact of humanistic theories has persisted, and does indeed constitute a lasting contribution to our understanding of human personality.

### REVIEW QUESTIONS

- How does the view of human beings proposed by humanistic theories of personality differ from that of psychoanalytic theories?
- According to Rogers, why do many individuals fail to become fully functioning persons?
- In Maslow's theory, what is self-actualization?
- What is the self-concept, and how is it influenced by cultural factors?

### Food for Thought

In recent years, schools in the United States have focused on raising students' self-esteem (positive feelings about themselves). What benefits might stem from this approach? Is there a potential downside to it, too?

## Trait Theories: Seeking the Key Dimensions of Personality

When we describe other persons, we often do so in terms of specific **personality traits**—stable dimensions of personality along which people vary, from very low to very high. This strong tendency to think about others in terms of specific characteristics is reflected in **trait theories** of personality. Such theories focus on identifying key dimensions of personality—the most important ways in which people differ. The basic idea behind this approach is as follows: Once we identify the key dimensions along which people differ, we can measure how *much* they differ and can then relate such differences to many important forms of behavior.

**Personality Traits:** Specific dimensions along which individuals differ in consistent, stable ways.

**Trait Theories:** Theories of personality that focus on identifying the key dimensions along which people differ.

Unfortunately, this task sounds easier than it actually is. Human beings differ in an almost countless number of ways. How can we determine which of these are most important and stable (i.e., lasting)? One approach is to search for *clusters*—groups of traits that seem to go together. We'll now take a brief look at two theories that adopted this approach. Then we'll turn to evidence suggesting that in the final analysis, the number of key traits or dimensions of personality is actually quite small—perhaps no more than five.

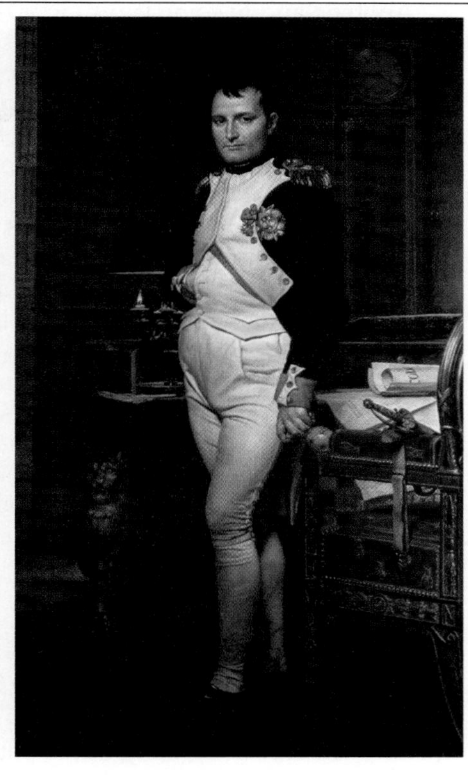

**Figure 12.11**
**Cardinal Traits: Dominant Aspects of Personality**

According to Allport, some people are dominated by a single, cardinal trait—for example, the desire to help others (Florence Nightingale) or the lust for power (Napoleon).

## The Search for Basic Traits: Initial Efforts by Allport and Cattell

One of the first efforts to identify key human traits—the most important dimensions along which personalities vary—was the work of Gordon Allport. On the basis of his studies, Allport concluded that personality traits could be divided into several categories that varied in their importance. The least important are **secondary traits;** these are traits that exert relatively weak and limited effects on behavior. More important are **central traits**—five to ten traits that together account for the uniqueness of an individual's personality. Such traits are stronger and more resistant to situational forces. Finally, Allport noted that a few people are dominated by a single all-important **cardinal trait.** A few examples of such persons and the cardinal traits that seemed to drive their personalities: Napoleon (ambition), Florence Nightingale (empathy), Alexander the Great (lust for power), and Don Juan (just plain lust) (see Figure 12.11).

Perhaps an even more important aspect of Allport's theory of personality is his concept of **functional autonomy** (Allport, 1965)—the idea that patterns of behavior that are initially acquired under one set of circumstances, and which satisfy one set of motives, may later be performed for very different reasons. For example, initially a child may learn to read because this pleases his teachers and parents and because failure to do so is punished. Later in life, however, the same person may read because he has come to enjoy this activity in and of itself—it is, in terms of our discussion in Chapter 10, intrinsically motivated. Notice how this contrasts with Freud's view that the roots of adult personality are planted firmly in the soil of childhood—that, as Freud put it, "The child is the father [mother] of the man [woman]." For Allport, such connections are not necessarily present, and our adult behavior may spring from roots entirely different from those that gave rise to our childhood behavior.

**Secondary Traits:** According to Allport, traits that exert relatively specific and weak effects on behavior.

**Central Traits:** According to Allport, the five or ten traits that best describe an individual's personality.

**Cardinal Trait:** According to Allport, a single trait that dominates an individual's entire personality.

**Functional Autonomy:** In Allport's theory, maintenance of patterns of behavior by motives other than the ones originally responsible for the behavior's occurrence.

**Source Traits:** According to Cattell, key dimensions of personality that underlie many other traits.

**Extraversion:** One of the "big five" dimensions of personality; ranges from sociable, talkative, and enthusiastic at one end to sober, reserved, and cautious at the other.

**Agreeableness:** One of the "big five" dimensions of personality; ranges from good-natured, cooperative, trusting at one end to irritable, suspicious, uncooperative at the other.

**Conscientiousness:** One of the "big five" dimensions of personality; ranges from well-organized, careful, and responsible at one end to disorganized, careless, and unscrupulous at the other.

Another, and in some ways more sophisticated, trait theory was proposed by Raymond Cattell. He and his colleagues focused on the task described earlier: identifying the basic dimensions of personality. Instead of beginning with hunches or insights, however, Cattell used a very different approach. He conducted extensive research in which literally thousands of persons responded to measures designed to reflect individual differences on hundreds of traits. These responses were then subjected to a statistical technique known as *factor analysis.* This technique reveals patterns in the extent to which various traits are correlated. In this manner, it can help to identify important clusters of traits—groups of traits that seem to be closely linked to one another. As such clusters are identified, Cattell reasoned, the number of key traits in human personality can be reduced until we are left with those that are truly central.

Using this approach, Cattell and his associates (e.g., Cattell & Dreger, 1977) identified sixteen **source traits**—dimensions of personality that underlie differences in many other, less important *surface traits.* A few of the source traits identified by Cattell: cool versus warm, easily upset versus calm and stable, not assertive versus dominant, trusting versus suspicious, and undisciplined versus self-disciplined. It is not yet clear whether Cattell's list is actually valid, but at least this list is considerably briefer than previous ones.

## The "Big Five" Factors: The Basic Dimensions of Personality?

Web Link: *The Five-Factor Model*

By now, you may be running out of patience. "OK, Professor Baron," I can almost hear you saying, "how many basic traits or dimensions of personality *are* there?" This is one time when I can offer you a fairly definite answer, because research conducted during the past twenty years has converged on the following conclusion: In fact, there may be only five key or central dimensions of personality (e.g., Costa & McCrae, 1994; Zuckerman, 1994). These are sometimes labeled the "big five," and they can be described as follows:

1. **Extraversion:** A dimension ranging from energetic, enthusiastic, sociable, and talkative at one end to retiring, sober, reserved, silent, and cautious at the other.
2. **Agreeableness:** A dimension ranging from good-natured, cooperative, trusting, and helpful at one end to irritable, suspicious, and uncooperative at the other.
3. **Conscientiousness:** A dimension ranging from well-organized, careful, self-disciplined, responsible, and precise at one end to disorganized, impulsive, careless, and undependable at the other.
4. **Emotional stability** (sometimes labeled *neuroticisim*): A dimension ranging from poised, calm, composed, and not hypochondriacal at one end to nervous, anxious, high-strung, and hypochondriacal at the other.
5. **Openness to experience:** A dimension ranging from imaginative, witty, and having broad interests at one end to down-to-earth, simple, and having narrow interests at the other. (See Figure 12.12 for an illustration of people who would probably be classified as *low* on this dimension.)

**Figure 12.12**
**Openness to Experience: One of the "Big Five" Dimensions of Personality**

The persons shown here are almost certainly low on the dimension of openness to experience; they are reluctant to try something new!

(*Source:* Reprinted by permission of Richard Guindon.)

How basic, and therefore how important, are the "big five" dimensions? Although there is far from complete agreement on this point (e.g., Friedman & Schustack, 1999), many researchers believe that these dimensions are indeed very basic ones. This is indicated, in part, by the fact that these dimensions are ones to which most people in many different cultures refer in describing themselves (Funder &

Colvin, 1991), and by the fact that we can often tell where individuals stand along at least some of these dimensions from an initial meeting with them that lasts only a few minutes (e.g., Zebrowitz & Collins, 1997). How do we know this is true? From several studies in which strangers meet and interact briefly with each other, then rate each other on measures of the big five dimensions. When these ratings by strangers are then compared with ratings by other people who know the participants in the study very well (e.g., their parents or best friends), substantial agreement is obtained for at least some of the big five dimensions (e.g., Funder & Sneed, 1993; Watson, 1989). For instance, strangers who meet each other for a few minutes are quite accurate in rating each other with respect to the dimensions of extraversion and conscientiousness. This may seem surprising, but it actually fits quite well with our informal experience. Think about it; if someone met *you* for the first time, could they tell right away whether you are friendly and outgoing or shy and reserved? Whether you are neat and orderly or impulsive and disorganized? The answer offered by research findings is clear: they probably could.

Audio 12.2: *"Big Five" Dimensions of Personality*

Web Link: *The Five-Factor Model: Is the Theory Good?*

Why are we so good at recognizing where others stand on these dimensions? Evolutionary psychology suggests that this is because such information is very useful to us from the point of view of survival: We need to know quickly whether others will cooperate with us (i.e., be agreeable), whether they will be dependable (i.e., high in conscientiousness), whether they will make a good leader (e.g., by being high in extraversion and low in neuroticism), and so on. Of course, this is just speculation, but it is interesting food for thought.

If the big five dimensions of personality are really so basic, then it is reasonable to expect that they will be related to important forms of behavior. And in fact, many studies indicate that this is the case. Where people stand on the big five dimensions is closely linked to important outcomes, such as their success in performing many jobs (e.g., Hogan, Hogan, & Roberts, 1996). We'll return to the practical applications of the big five dimensions in work settings in a later section. The main point here is that there is a large and growing body of evidence suggesting that these dimensions are indeed very basic ones where personality is concerned.

One final point: Although many psychologists now view the big five dimensions as truly basic, there is *not* total consensus on this point. For example, Eysenck (1994), one expert on personality, believes that there are only three basic dimensions—extraversion, neuroticism (emotional instability and apprehensiveness), and psychoticism (a tendency toward psychopathology, especially impulsivity and cruelty). Other psychologists (e.g., Block, 1995) believe that the methods on which the big five dimensions are based (largely the statistical technique known as factor analysis) are inadequate. By and large, though, many psychologists view the big five as providing important insights into the key dimensions of personality.

## Trait Theories: An Evaluation

At present, most research on personality by psychologists occurs within the context of the trait approach. Instead of seeking to propose and test grand theories such as the ones offered by Freud, Jung, and Rogers, most psychologists currently direct their effort to the task of understanding specific traits (Kring, Smith, & Neale, 1994). This trend is due both to the success of the trait approach and to the obvious shortcomings of the theories described in earlier sections of this chapter.

This is not to imply that the trait approach is perfect, however. On the contrary, it too can be criticized on several grounds. First, the trait approach is largely *descriptive* in nature. It seeks to describe the key dimensions of personality but does not attempt to determine *how* various traits develop, *how* they influence behavior, or *why* they are important. This is true with respect to the "big five" model, which was based, initially, on the fact that when asked to describe others, most people use these dimensions. Fully developed theories of personality must, of

**Emotional Stability:** One of the "big five" dimensions of personality; ranges from poised, calm, and composed at one end to nervous, anxious, and excitable at the other; also called *neuroticism.*

**Openness to Experience:** One of the "big five" dimensions of personality; ranges from imaginative, witty, and intellectual at one end to down-to-earth, simple, and narrow in interests at the other.

course, address such issues in more detail. Second, despite several decades of careful research, there is still no final agreement concerning the traits that are most important or most basic. The big five dimensions are widely accepted, but they are far from *universally* accepted, and some psychologists feel that they are far from the final answer to these issues (e.g., Bandura, 1999; Block, 1995; Goldberg & Saucier, 1995).

As you can readily see, these criticisms relate primarily to what the trait approach has not yet accomplished rather than to its findings or proposals. All in all, we can conclude that this approach to personality has generally been a very valuable one. Attempting to understand how people differ appears to be a useful strategy for understanding the uniqueness and consistency of key aspects of human behavior.

**REVIEW QUESTIONS**

- What are central traits? Source traits?
- What are the "big five" dimensions of personality?
- What are the strengths and weaknesses of the trait approach?

Video 12.1: *Learning Approaches to Personality*

## Learning Approaches to Personality

Whatever their focus, all personality theories must ultimately come to grips with two basic questions: What accounts for the *uniqueness* and *consistency* of human behavior? Freud's answer focused on *internal* factors—hidden conflicts among the id, ego, and superego and the active struggle to keep unacceptable impulses out of consciousness. At the other end of the continuum are approaches to personality that emphasize the role of learning and experience. Although such views were not originally presented as formal theories of personality, they are often described as *learning theories of personality* to distinguish them from other perspectives (Bandura, 1986, 1997; Rotter, 1982; Skinner, 1974).

How can a learning perspective account for the uniqueness and consistency of human behavior? Very readily. Uniqueness, the learning approach contends, merely reflects the fact that we all have distinctive life (and learning) experiences. Similarly, the learning approach can explain consistency in behavior over time and across situations by noting that the responses, associations, or habits acquired through learning tend to persist. Moreover, because individuals often find themselves in situations very similar to the ones in which they acquired these tendencies, their behavior, too, tends to remain quite stable. As I noted earlier, Mischel, a strong advocate of the learning approach, has suggested that individuals acquire personal strategies or styles through experience, and that these cognitive aspects of personality influence their behavior across many different situations (Mischel & Shoda, 1995).

Early learning-oriented views of personality took what now seems to be a somewhat extreme position: They denied the importance of *any* internal causes of behavior—motives, traits, intentions, goals (Skinner, 1974). The only things that matter, these early theorists suggested, are external conditions determining patterns of reinforcement (recall the discussion of *schedules of reinforcement* in Chapter 5). At present, few psychologists agree with this position. Most now believe that internal factors—especially many aspects of *cognition*—play a crucial role in behavior. A prime example of this modern approach is provided by Bandura's *social cognitive theory* (e.g., Bandura, 1986, 1997).

## Social Cognitive Theory: A Modern View of Personality

In his **social cognitive theory,** Bandura places great emphasis on what he terms the **self-system**—the cognitive processes by which a person perceives, evaluates, and regulates his or her own behavior so that it is appropriate in a given situation. Reflecting the emphasis on cognition in modern psychology, Bandura calls attention to the fact that people don't simply respond to reinforcements; rather, they think about the consequences of their actions, anticipate future events, and establish goals and plans. In addition, they engage in **self-reinforcement,** patting themselves on the back when they attain their goals. For example, consider the hundreds of amateur runners who participate in major marathons. Few believe that they have any chance of winning and obtaining the external rewards offered—status, fame, cash prizes. Why, then do they run? Because, Bandura would contend, they have *self-set goals,* such as finishing the race, or merely going as far as they can. Meeting these personal goals allows runners to engage in self-reinforcement, and this is sufficient to initiate what is obviously very effortful behavior.

Another important feature of Bandura's theory is its emphasis on *observational learning* (which I described in Chapter 5), a form of learning in which individuals acquire both information and new forms of behavior through observing others (Bandura, 1977). Such learning plays a role in a very wide range of human activities—everything from learning how to dress and groom in the style of one's own society (see Figure 12.13) through learning how to perform new and difficult tasks. In essence, any time that human beings observe others, they can learn from this experience, and such learning can then play an important part in their own behavior. Such *models* don't have to be present in the flesh for observational learning to occur; as we saw in Chapter 5 and in our discussion of the effects of media violence on aggression in Chapter 10, human beings can also acquire new information and new ways of behaving from exposure to models who are presented symbolically, in films, on television, and so on.

Perhaps the aspect of Bandura's theory that has received most attention in recent research is his concept of **self-efficacy**—an individual's belief that he or she can perform some behavior or task successfully. If you sit down to take an exam in your psychology class and expect to do well, your self-efficacy is high; if you have doubts about your performance, then your self-efficacy is lower. Self-efficacy has been found to play a role in success on many tasks (e.g., Maurer & Pierce, 1998); in health—people who expect to handle stress effectively or to get better quickly often actually do (Bandura, 1992); and in personal happiness and life satisfaction (Judge, Martocchio, & Thorsen, 1998). Although self-efficacy as described by Bandura was related to performance of specific tasks and is not, strictly speaking, an aspect of personality, recent findings indicate that people form *general* expectations about their abilities to succeed at many tasks or to exert control over the events in their lives. Such generalized beliefs about their task-related capabilities are stable over time, and these can be viewed as an important aspect of personality. We'll return to research on self-efficacy's important effects in a later section.

I should note that other learning-oriented approaches to personality have much in common with Bandura's views. For example, the *social learning theory* proposed by Julian Rotter (1954, 1982) suggests

**Social Cognitive Theory:** A theory of behavior suggesting that human behavior is influenced by many cognitive factors as well as by reinforcement contingencies, and that human beings have an impressive capacity to regulate their own actions.

**Self-System:** In Bandura's social cognitive theory, the set of cognitive processes by which a person perceives, evaluates, and regulates his or her own behavior.

**Self-Reinforcement:** A process in which individuals reward themselves for reaching their own goals.

**Self-Efficacy:** Individuals' expectations concerning their ability to perform various tasks.

CourseCompass

Audio 12.3: *Difference Between Self-Efficacy and Self-Esteem*

CourseCompass

Web Link: *Albert Bandura*

**Figure 12.13**
**Observational Learning: One Aspect of Fashion**

How do fashions spread so quickly? People who adopt them notice how people they see in the flesh or in the media present themselves, and this influences them to adopt the same styles of dress or grooming. The trends change, but the process at work—observational learning—remains the same.

**Internals:** In Rotter's theory, individuals who believe that they exert considerable control over the outcomes they experience.

**Externals:** In Rotter's term, individuals who believe that they have little control over the outcomes they experience.

that the likelihood that a given behavior will occur in a specific situation depends on individuals' *expectancies* concerning the outcomes the behavior will produce and on the *reinforcement value* they attach to such outcomes—the degree to which they prefer one reinforcer over another. According to Rotter, individuals form *generalized expectancies* concerning the extent to which their own actions determine the outcomes they experience. Rotter terms persons who strongly believe that they can shape their own destinies **internals** and those who believe their outcomes are largely the result of forces outside their control **externals.** As you can probably guess, internals are often happier and better adjusted than externals. Note again how in this theory, internal factors such as subjective estimates concerning the likelihood of various outcomes, subjective reactions to these outcomes, and generalized expectancies of personal control all combine to influence behavior. Certainly, such suggestions contrast very sharply with the view, stated in early learning approaches to personality, that only external reinforcement contingencies should be taken into account.

CourseCompass
Web Link: *Why Positive Reinforcement Works*

## Research on the Learning Perspective

Because they are based on well-established principles of psychology, learning theories of personality have been the subject of a great deal of research attention (e.g., Friedman & Schustack, 1998). Indeed, as we'll see in Chapter 15, efforts to test these theories have led to the development of several new and highly effective techniques for treating psychological disorders. For an example of research on the learning (or social cognitive) approach, please see the following **From Science to Practice** section.

from SCIENCE to PRACTICE

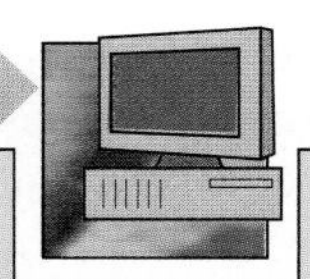

### The Potential Benefits of Boosting Self-Efficacy: Helping Unemployed Persons to Help Themselves

In recent years large companies in many countries have engaged in *downsizing*—they have reduced the size of their workforce greatly, often by 50 percent or more. What does losing one's job after ten, twenty, or more years with a single company do to one's general sense of self-efficacy? As you might expect, the results of such an experience can be shattering. I observed this myself when, some years ago, I was hired by a large corporation to conduct stress-management workshops with employees who were scheduled to lose their jobs. The pay was very good, but after a few sessions I regretted taking on this task: The level of stress *I* experienced was extremely high as I tried to help these people cope with a life experience that threatened to destroy their sense of self-efficacy.

Shattered self-efficacy is certainly a personal calamity in itself; but it has other effects, too. Once people begin to doubt their ability to succeed in many situations, they may become less effective at finding another job. In other words, a vicious circle may be set up in which losing a job undermines generalized self-efficacy, and this in turn makes it harder to obtain another job, thus reducing self-efficacy still further. Can anything be done to help individuals escape from this psychological trap? Research by Eden and Aviram (1993) indicates that in fact psychologists can do much to help.

Recognizing the impact of the kind of vicious circle that can develop, these researchers developed two techniques designed to help restore individuals' crushed self-efficacy. One of these involved teaching people how to be effective as job seekers—for instance, how to make a convincing presentation of their skills during an interview. The other involved exposing individuals who had recently lost their jobs to models of people who successfully searched for and found a good job; presumably, exposure to such models would help them acquire useful job-seeking skills through observational learning.

Participants in the study were Israeli workers who had been unemployed for 2 to 18 weeks, who enrolled in special workshops designed to help them seek reemployment. The workshops, conducted over a 2½-week period, began with presentation of four- to five-minute videotapes showing people successfully performing various job-search behaviors. These behaviors were then discussed by the group; followed by role-playing sessions in which each participant rehearsed the behaviors shown in the tapes. Feedback was provided to each individual about how effectively he or she practiced the behaviors, and strong verbal encouragement was also given. To determine the effectiveness of the workshops, the investigators compared persons who participated in them with a control group, a comparable group of workers who did *not* participate.

Results were highly encouraging. First, the workshops did raise levels of self-efficacy: Measures of self-efficacy rose among those who participated in the workshops but did not increase for the control group. Second, and perhaps even more important, these gains in self-efficacy helped participants in conducting their job search and, ultimately, in getting a new job. Among persons who were initially low in self-efficacy, fully 62 percent of those who took part in the workshops later reported that they were reemployed; in contrast, only 23 percent of those who had not participated reported having a new job. Why did increased self-efficacy help individuals to obtain a new job? Apparently, because such persons engaged in more active job searches. In other words, once their self-efficacy was restored, they actively and confidently sought another job—and often found one (see Figure 12.14). In contrast, persons whose self-efficacy remained low were discouraged and tended to search for a new job in a halfhearted way.

These findings, which have been confirmed in other studies (e.g., Wanberg, Kanfer, & Rotundo, 1999), point to two important conclusions. First, self-efficacy is definitely *not* an unchangeable characteristic; rather, it can be significantly raised even by short-term interventions. Second, providing persons who have lost their jobs with self-efficacy-boosting experiences can be highly beneficial: It can increase their chances of obtaining another job. Given the fact that millions of persons throughout the world have been or soon will be downsized out of their jobs, it is clear that knowledge of this aspect of personality can be put to excellent practical use.

**Figure 12.14**
**Self-Efficacy and Job Search**

In recent research, unemployed persons who participated in a workshop designed to enhance their self-efficacy took a more active approach to finding a job than persons who did not receive such help. The result? They were more successful in actually finding new jobs.

## Evaluation of the Learning Approach

Do all human beings confront an Oedipus conflict? Are peak experiences real, and do they in fact constitute a sign of growing self-actualization? Considerable controversy exists with respect to these and many other aspects of psychoanalytic and humanistic theories of personality. In contrast, virtually all psychologists agree that behaviors are acquired and modified through basic processes of learning. Moreover, there is general agreement among psychologists about the importance of cognitive factors in human behavior. Thus, a key strength of the learning approach is obvious: It is based on widely accepted and well-documented principles of psychology. Another positive feature of this framework is its practical usefulness in efforts to modify maladaptive forms of behavior. I'll return to such efforts in detail in Chapter 15.

Turning to criticisms, most of these have focused on older approaches rather than on the more sophisticated theories proposed by Bandura (1986, 1997) and others. Those early behaviorist theorists generally ignored the role of cognitive factors in human behavior, but this is certainly *not* true of the modern theories. A related criticism has to do with the fact that learning theories generally ignore inner conflicts and the influence of unconscious thoughts and impulses on behavior. However, while such issues are not explicitly addressed by theories such as Bandura's, their existence and possible impact is not in any way denied by these theories. Rather, learning theories would simply insist that such effects be interpreted within the context of modern psychology.

As you can readily see, these are *not* major criticisms. Thus, it seems fair to state that at present, social cognitive theories of personality are more in tune with the eclectic, sophisticated approach of modern psychology than were earlier theories. Along with the trait approach, learning approaches are certain to play an important role in continuing efforts to understand the uniqueness and consistency of human behavior—the issues that led us to consider personality in the first place.

**REVIEW QUESTIONS**

- How do learning theories of personality explain the uniqueness and consistency of human behavior?
- In Bandura's social cognitive theory, what is the self-system? Self-efficacy?
- According to Rotter's social learning theory, what is the key difference between internals and externals?

**Food for Thought**

In your own everyday life, do you think that your behavior is more strongly influenced by external events such as reinforcements or punishments, or by your own plans, expectations, and goals?

Web Link: *Buros Institute of Mental Measurement*

Web Link: *Keirsey Temperament Sorter*

## Measuring Personality

To study personality scientifically, we must first be able to measure it. How do psychologists deal with this issue? As we'll soon see, in several different ways.

### Self-Report Tests of Personality: Questionnaires and Inventories

One way of measuring personality involves asking individuals to respond to a *self-report* inventory or questionnaire. Such measures (sometimes known as *objective* tests of personality) contain questions or statements to which individuals respond in various ways. For example, a questionnaire might ask respondents to indicate the extent to which each of a set of statements is true or false about themselves, the extent to which they agree or disagree with various sentences, which of a pair of activities they prefer. By way of illustration, here are a few items that are similar to those appearing on one widely used measure of the "big five" dimensions of personality. (I'll describe this measure below.) Persons taking the test simply indicate the extent to which they agree or disagree with each item (1 = strongly disagree, 2 = disagree, 3 = neutral, 4 = agree, and 5 = strongly agree).

I am very careful and methodical.

I generally get along well with others.

I cry easily.

Sometimes I feel totally worthless.

I have a lot of trust in other people.

Answers to the questions on these objective tests are scored by means of special keys. The score obtained by a specific person is then compared with those obtained by hundreds or even thousands of other people who have taken the test previously. In this way, an individual's relative standing on the trait being measured can be determined.

For some objective tests, the items included have what is known as *face validity:* Reading them, it is easy to see that they are related to the trait or traits being measured. For instance, the first item above seems to be related to the *conscientiousness* dimension of personality; the second is clearly related to the *agreeableness* dimension. On other tests, however, the items do not necessarily appear to be related to the traits or characteristics. Rather, a procedure known as *empirical keying* is used. The items are given to hundreds of persons belonging to groups known to differ from one another—for instance, psychiatric patients with specific forms of mental illness and normal persons. Then the answers given by the two groups are compared. Items answered differently by the groups are included on the test, *regardless of whether these items seem to be related to the traits being measured.* The reasoning is as follows: As long as a test item differentiates between the groups in question—groups we know to be different—then the specific content of the item itself is unimportant.

One widely used test designed to measure various types of psychological disorder, the **MMPI,** uses precisely this method. The MMPI (short for *Minnesota Multiphasic Personality Inventory*) was developed during the 1930s but underwent a major revision in 1989 (Butcher, 1990). The current version, the MMPI–2, contains ten *clinical scales* and several *validity scales.* The clinical scales, which are summarized in Table 12.2, relate to various forms of psychological disorder. Items included in each of these scales are ones that are answered differently by persons who have been diagnosed as having this particular disorder and by persons in a comparison group who do *not* have the disorder. The validity scales are designed to determine whether and to what extent people are trying to fake their answers—for instance, whether they are trying to seem bizarre or, conversely, to give the

Web Link: *The Minnesota Multiphasic Personality Inventory-2 (MMPI-2)*

**TABLE 12.2**

**Clinical Scales of the MMPI–2**

The MMPI–2 is designed to measure many aspects of personality related to psychological disorders.

| Clinical Scale | Description of Disorder |
|---|---|
| Hypochondriasis | Excessive concern with bodily functions |
| Depression | Pessimism; hopelessness; slowing of action and thought |
| Hysteria | Development of physical disorders such as blindness, paralysis, and vomiting as an escape from emotional problems |
| Psychopathic Deviance | Disregard for social customs; shallow emotions |
| Masculinity–Femininity | Possession of traits and interests typically associated with the opposite sex |
| Paranoia | Suspiciousness; delusions of grandeur or persecution |
| Psychasthenia | Obsession; compulsions; fears; guilt; indecisiveness |
| Schizophrenia | Bizarre, unusual thoughts or behavior; withdrawal; hallucinations; delusions |
| Hypomania | Emotional excitement; flight of ideas; overactivity |
| Social Introversion | Shyness; lack of interest in others; insecurity |

**MMPI:** A widely used objective test based on empirical keying.

**Millon Clinical Multiaxial Inventory (MCMI):** An objective test of personality specifically designed to assist psychologists in diagnosing various psychological disorders.

**NEO Personality Inventory (NEO–PI):** An objective measure of personality designed to assess individuals' relative standing on each of the "big five" dimensions of personality.

**Rorschach Test:** A widely used projective test of personality in which individuals are asked to describe what they see in a series of inkblots.

Web Link: *Classical Rorschach*

impression that they are extremely "normal" and well-adjusted. If persons taking the test score high on these validity scales, their responses to the clinical scales must be interpreted with special caution.

Another widely used objective measure of personality is the **Millon Clinical Multiaxial Inventory (MCMI)** (Millon, 1987, 1997). Items on this test correspond more closely than those on the MMPI to the categories of psychological disorders currently used by psychologists (we'll discuss these in detail in Chapter 14). This makes the test especially useful to clinical psychologists, who must first identify individuals' problems before recommending specific forms of therapy for them.

A third objective test, the **NEO Personality Inventory (NEO–PI)** (Costa & McCrae, 1989), is used to measure aspects of personality that are *not* directly linked to psychological disorders. Specifically, it measures the "big five" dimensions of personality. Because these dimensions appear to represent basic aspects of personality, the NEO Personality Inventory has been widely used in research. (The sample items listed earlier in this section are similar to the items on this inventory.)

## Projective Measures of Personality

In contrast to questionnaires and inventories, *projective tests* of personality adopt a very different approach. They present individuals with ambiguous stimuli—stimuli that can be interpreted in many different ways. For instance, these can be inkblots such as the one shown in Figure 12.15, or ambiguous scenes of the type described in Chapter 10 in our discussion of achievement motivation. Persons taking the test are asked to indicate what they see, to make up a story about the stimulus, and so on. Since the stimuli themselves are ambiguous, it is assumed that the answers given by respondents will reflect various aspects of their personality. In others words, different persons will see different things in these stimuli because these persons differ from one another in important ways.

Do such tests really work—do they meet the criteria of reliability and validity discussed in Chapter 11? For some projective tests, such as the *TAT,* which is used to measure achievement motivation and other social motives (see Chapter 10), the answer appears to be *yes;* such tests do yield reliable scores and do seem to measure what they are intended to measure. For others, such as the famous **Rorschach test,** which uses inkblots such as the one in Figure 12.15, the answer is more doubtful. Responses to this test are scored in many different ways. For instance, one measure involves responses that mention *pairs* of objects or a *reflection* (e.g., the inkblot is interpreted as showing two people, or one person looking into a mirror). Such responses are taken as a sign of self-focus—excessive concern with oneself. Other scoring involves the number of times individuals mention movement, color, or shading in the inkblots. The more responses of this type they make, the more sources of stress they supposedly have in their lives.

Are such interpretations accurate? Psychologists disagree about this point. The Rorschach test, like other projective tests, has a standard scoring manual (Exner, 1993) that tells psychologists precisely how to score various kinds of responses. Presumably, this manual is based on careful research designed to determine just what the test measures. More recent research, however, suggests that the scoring advice provided by the Rorschach manual may be flawed in several respects and does not rest on the firm scientific foundation psychologists prefer (Wood, Nezworski, & Stejskal, 1996). Thus, projective tests of personality, like objective tests, may vary with respect to validity. Only tests that meet high standards in this respect can provide us with useful information about personality.

**Figure 12.15**
**The Rorschach Test: One Projective Measure of Personality**

Persons taking the *Rorschach test* describe what they see in a series of inkblots. Supposedly, individuals' responses reveal much about their personality. However, recent findings cast doubt on the validity of this test.

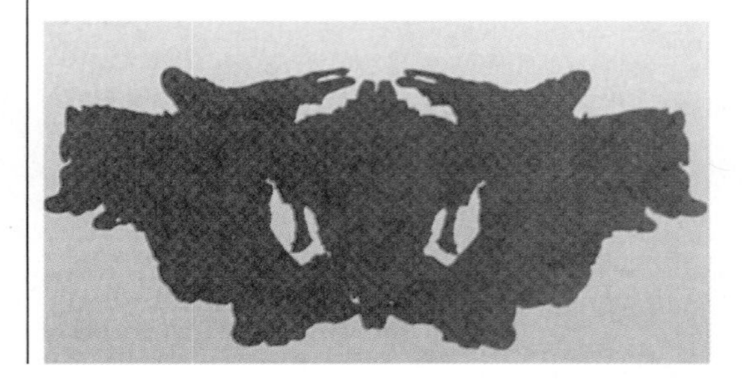

## Other Measures: Behavioral Observations, Interviews, and Biological Measures

While self-report questionnaires and projective techniques are the most widely used measures of personality, several other techniques exist as well. For instance, the advent of electronic pagers now allows researchers to beep individuals at random (or preestablished) times during the day in order to obtain descriptions of their behavior at these times. This *experience sampling method* (e.g., Stone, Kessler, & Haythornthwaite, 1991) can often reveal much about stable patterns of individual behavior; and these, of course, constitute an important aspect of personality.

*Interviews* are also used to measure specific aspects of personality. Psychoanalysis, of course, uses one type of interview to probe supposedly underlying aspects of personality. But in modern research special types of interviews, in which individuals are asked questions assumed to be related to specific traits, are often used instead. For instance, interviews are used to measure the *Type A behavior pattern,* an important aspect of personality closely related to personal health. As we'll see shortly, persons high in this pattern are always in a hurry—they hate being delayed. Thus, questions asked during the interview focus on this tendency; for instance: "What do you do when you are stuck on the highway behind a slow driver?"

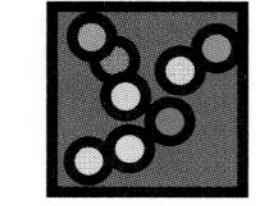

In recent years several *biological measures* of personality have also been developed. Some of these use positron emission tomography (PET) scans to see if individuals show characteristic patterns of activity in their brains—patterns that are related to differences in their overt behavior. Other measures focus on hormone levels—for instance, the question of whether highly aggressive persons have different levels of certain sex hormones than other persons. Some results suggest that this may indeed be the case (Harris et al., 1996).

In sum, many tools for measuring personality exist. None are perfect, but together they provide psychologists with many useful techniques for investigating the stable patterns of behavior that make each of us a unique human being.

**REVIEW QUESTIONS**

- What are self-report tests of personality?
- What are projective tests of personality?
- What other measures of personality do psychologists currently use?

## Modern Research on Personality: Applications to Personal Health and Behavior in Work Settings

Web Link: *Psychological, Educational, and Health Tests and Measurements: Selected Sources*

Once again, I can almost hear your comments: "OK, so there are lots of theories of personality and lots of ways of measuring personality. So what? Is any of this information practical? Can we *do* anything with it?" My answer is: absolutely. As psychologists have learned more and more about personality, they have largely stopped constructing grand theories about this topic and have turned at least part of their efforts to the task of applying this knowledge to practical problems. Here, I'll acquaint you with the flavor of this modern research by examining applications of our growing understanding of personality to two important topics: personal health and behavior in work settings.

**Type A Behavior Pattern:** A cluster of traits that includes competitiveness, impatience, and hostility; related to important aspects of health, social behavior, and task performance.

## Personality and Health: The Type A Behavior Pattern, Sensation Seeking, and Longevity

Back in the 1960s, two cardiologists, Meyer Friedman and Ray Rosenman (1974) noticed an interesting fact: When a worker came to reupholster the furniture in their office, the fronts of the cushions on the chairs were worn down, as if their patients had sat on the very edge of the seats. They followed up on this observation, and soon realized that many of the people they treated for heart attacks seemed to show a similar cluster of personality traits: They were always in a hurry, highly competitive, and hostile or easily irritated. Even during medical examinations they looked at their watches repeatedly; and if they had to wait to see the doctor, they tended to express their annoyance openly.

These observations led the physicians, and soon psychologists too, to develop the concept of the **Type A behavior pattern**—a cluster of traits that predispose individuals toward having heart attacks. Indeed, researchers soon noted that Type As (as they are termed) are more than twice as likely to suffer serious heart attacks as Type Bs (persons who are *not* always in a hurry, irritable, or highly competitive). In short, one cluster of personality traits seemed to be strongly linked to an important aspect of personal health—in fact, to a life-threatening aspect of health.

Why do Type As experience more heart attacks than other persons—especially, than Type Bs? For several reasons. Type As seem to seek out high levels of stress: They take on more tasks and more responsibilities than other persons (see Figure 12.16) (Kirmeyer & Biggers, 1988). They experience higher physiological arousal when exposed to stress than other persons (Holmes, McGilley, & Houston, 1984), and they are reluctant to take a rest after completing a major task; on the contrary, they view this as a signal to start the next one (Schauabroeck, Ganster, & Kemmerer, 1994). These and other tendencies shown by Type As (especially their irritability) seem to ensure that they are always stirred up emotionally; and this, in turn, may increase the chances that they will become the victims of heart attacks.

CourseCompass
Web Link: *Youth Risk Behavior Surveillance System (YRBSS)*

Interestingly, additional research suggests that it is the *cynical hostility* of Type As—their suspiciousness, resentment, anger, and distrust of others—that is most directly linked to their cardiac problems (e.g., Miller et al., 1996). Whatever specific components are most central, though, it seems clear that this is one aspect of personality with important implications for individuals' health and well-being.

Fortunately, individuals can learn to reduce their tendency toward Type A behavior; they can learn to be more patient, less competitive, and less irritable or suspicious (Nakano, 1990). Having the characteristics of a Type A is *not* necessarily a death sentence. Unless individuals take active steps to counter their own tendencies toward the Type A pattern, however, they do appear to be at risk. (Are *you* a Type A? Please see the **Making Psychology Part of Your Life** section at the end of the chapter to find out.)

**Figure 12.16**
**Type As: They Create Their Own Stress!**
Individuals who show the Type A behavior pattern take on many jobs and responsibilities at the same time, thus exposing themselves to high levels of stress.

**SENSATION SEEKING** Now, let's consider another aspect of personality that can strongly influence personal health: *sensation seeking*, or the desire to seek out novel and intense experiences (e.g., Zuckerman, 1990). As we saw in Chapter 10, persons high on this characteristic want lots of excitement and stimulation in their lives, and become intensely bored when they don't get it. This, in turn, leads them to engage in many high-risk behaviors, such as driving fast, experimenting with drugs, climbing mountains, and taking risks where sex is concerned. An extreme example of such high-risk behavior is provided by people who engage in BASE jumping—they jump off high buildings, bridges, and cliffs with a small parachute (see Figure 12.17). For instance, Thor Axel Kappfjell jumped off the World Trade Center in New York in 1998, floating safely to the bottom of the 110-story building. However, his luck ran out in 1999, when he was killed by smashing into a 3,300-foot cliff in his native Norway.

**Figure 12.17**
**High Sensation Seekers: People Who Like to Take Risks**
Persons high in sensation seeking crave high levels of stimulation and excitement. This often leads them to engage in high-risk behaviors that can be harmful to their health.

What accounts for this preference for high levels of stimulation? Marvin Zuckerman (1990, 1995), the psychologist who first called attention to sensation seeking as an aspect of personality, believes that it has important roots in biological processes. High sensation seekers, he suggests, are persons whose nervous systems operate best at high levels of arousal. Zuckerman (1995) notes that high sensation seekers may have a high optimal level of activity in what is known as the *catecholamine system,* a system within the brain that plays a role in mood, performance, and social behavior. In a sense, the "thermostat" for activity in this neurotransmitter system is set higher in such persons than in most others, and they feel better when they are receiving the external stimulation that plays a role in activation of this system. Whatever the precise roots of high sensation seeking, though, it is clear that persons showing this characteristic do often engage in behaviors that expose them to danger. Sensation seeking has survived as a trait, which suggests that the benefits it yields more than offset these potential costs; but the costs are real, nonetheless.

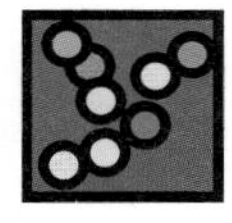

**PERSONALITY AND LONGEVITY** So far, this discussion has focused on aspects of personality that can adversely affect personal health and perhaps even shorten one's life. Are there characteristics that have opposite, beneficial effects? In fact, research findings suggest that there are. The results of one of psychology's longest-running studies—research first begun in 1921—indicate that people high in *conscientiousness,* one of the "big five" dimensions of personality, may well live longer than persons lower on this dimension (Friedman et al., 1995). This study, which was also discussed in Chapter 9, focused on 1,528 bright California boys and girls who were about eleven years old when the research began. (Because the study was started by Lewis Terman, participants referred to themselves as "Termites.") The same persons have been tested repeatedly for almost eighty years, thus providing psychologists with an opportunity to learn whether aspects of personality are related to how long people live. When the study began, of course, the big five dimensions had not yet been identified. However, the children were rated on characteristics closely related to this concept, including carefulness, dependability, and orderliness. Results have indicated that participants rated high on such traits were *fully 30 percent less likely to die in any given year than persons low in these traits.* Why has this been the case? The study is correlational in nature, so we can't tell for sure, but part of the answer seems to involve health-related behaviors: Persons high in conscientiousness are found to be less likely to abuse alcohol, to smoke, and to engage in other behaviors that put their own health at risk. This is not the entire story, though, because even when such differences are held constant statistically, persons high in conscientiousness still seem to live longer. This suggests that conscientiousness itself may reflect some underlying biological factor; what that is, however, remains to be determined. In any case, the findings of this study suggest that certain aspects of personality can contribute to living a long and healthy life.

## Personality and Behavior in Work Settings: Job Performance and Workplace Aggression

What activity occupies more of your waking time than any other? The answer for most adults is simple: *work.* Once we leave school and launch our careers, we spend more time on work-related activities than on any others. Further, for many of us, our jobs or occupation become a key part of our self-concept. When asked, "Who are you?" many people respond in terms of their job or career: "I'm an engineer," "I'm a professor," or "I'm a salesperson." And although many people complain about the necessity of working, most can't imagine life without a job or some kind of productive work. Psychologists have long recognized the importance of work in our lives, and in fact, **industrial/organizational psychologists** specialize in studying all aspects of behavior in work settings—everything from how people actually perform their jobs and the attitudes they hold about them (i.e., job satisfaction) through factors that increase or decrease their motivation to work and their willingness to help—or harm—other people in their work settings (e.g., Neuman & Baron, 1998). Does personality play a role in such processes? A growing body of evidence indicates that it does, and that knowledge about personality can be applied in important ways to enhance people's experiences at work. Let's look briefly at two of these applications: personality and job performance and the role of personality in workplace aggression.

**PERSONALITY AND JOB PERFORMANCE** Suppose you were faced with the task of choosing someone to be a salesperson; would you look for a person with certain personality traits—for instance, someone who was high in friendliness and who would be comfortable around strangers? And what if your task was that of hiring someone to be a tax collector? Would you search for different traits—someone like the person in Figure 12.18? In all likelihood you would assume that individuals with somewhat different personalities would be most suited to these contrasting jobs. Industrial/organizational psychologists, too, make this assumption: They believe that people will be happiest, and do their best work, when *person–job fit* is high: when the individuals who hold various jobs have personal characteristics (personality traits or other attributes) that suit them for the work they do. Systematic research offers clear support for this view (e.g., Day, Bedeian, & Conte, 1998). In particular, several aspects of the big five dimensions of personality seem to be linked to the performance of many different jobs (e.g., Barrick & Mount, 1993).

For example, in one large-scale study, Salgado (1997) reviewed previous research conducted with literally tens of thousands of participants that examined the relationship between individuals' standing on the big five dimensions and job performance. Many different occupational groups were included (professionals, police, managers, salespersons, skilled laborers), and several kinds of performance measures (e.g., ratings of individuals' performance by managers or others, performance during training programs, personnel records) were examined. In addition, participants came from several different countries within the European Economic Community. Results were clear: *Conscientiousness* and *emotional stability* were both significantly related to job performance across all occupational groups and across all measures of performance. In other words, the higher individuals scored on these dimensions, the better their job performance. The other dimensions of the big five also predicted performance, but only for some occupations and some kinds of measures. For example, openness to experience was related to performance during training, but not after training was completed; and extraversion was related to job performance for managers and police—two occupational groups that must interact with many other persons during the course of the day and for whom being friendly and sociable might come in very handy.

Many other studies have confirmed and extended these results. For example, consider these findings: Individuals high in conscientiousness are less likely to be absent from work than those low on this dimension, while the opposite is true for

**Industrial/Organizational Psychologists:** Psychologists who study all aspects of behavior in work settings.

**Figure 12.18**
**Personality and Job Performance: Choosing the Right Person for the Job**

Research findings indicate that people are happiest and do their best work when their personal characteristics suit them for the work they do—when *person-job fit* is high. The king in this cartoon seems to be well aware of this fact.

(*Source:* Reprinted with special permission of King Feature Syndicate, Inc.)

persons high in extraversion (Judge, Martocchio, & Thorsen, 1998); the higher the average scores of members of work teams on conscientiousness, agreeableness, extraversion, and emotional stability, the higher the teams' performance (Barrick et al., 1998). In sum, it seems clear that the big five dimensions of personality are related to the performance of many different jobs, and that careful attention to these aspects of personality when choosing employees might well be beneficial.

**PERSONALITY AND WORKPLACE AGGRESSION** *Atlanta (August, 1999)—After murdering his wife and children, Mark Barton marched into two securities firms—Momentum Securities and All-Tech Investment Group—and calmly shot more than a dozen people; eight died. When he was finally cornered by police at a gas station, he turned his weapons on himself and committed suicide. Barton, who had previously done business with both firms, had recently experienced large losses as a result of his day-trading activities. . . .*

Incidents like this one have appeared in newspapers and the evening news with increasing frequency in recent years, and they seem to suggest that we are in the midst of an epidemic of workplace violence. Closer examination of this issue by psychologists, however, points to somewhat different conclusions. Yes, an alarming number of persons are indeed killed at work each year—more than 800 in the United States alone (National Institute for Occupational Safety and Health, 1993). In fact, however, a large majority of these victims (more than 82 percent) are murdered by outsiders during robberies or other crimes. (Barton fits this pattern; he was *not* employed by either firm, although he had done business with them.) Further, threats of physical harm or actual assaults between employees are actually quite rare. In reality, the odds of being physically attacked while at work are less than 1 in 450,000 for most persons, although this number is considerably higher in some high-risk occupations such as those of taxi drivers or police (Leonard & Sloboda, 1996).

While actual *violence* is indeed something of a rarity in work settings, other forms of aggression (e.g., spreading damaging rumors about someone, interfering with someone's work in various ways) are much more common (see Figure 12.19) (e.g., Baron & Neuman, 1996, 1998). Are some persons more likely to engage in such behavior than others? In other words, do some aspects of personality play a role in workplace aggression? The findings of recent research suggest that they do. For instance, Type A persons report being both the victims and the perpetrators of workplace aggression significantly more frequently than

**Figure 12.19**
**Workplace Aggression: It Takes Many Forms**

While overt violence is the most dramatic form of aggression in workplaces, such behavior is relatively rare. Research indicates that other, more subtle forms of aggression (e.g., spreading false rumors about someone, talking behind someone's back) are much more common. Additional findings indicate that persons possessing certain traits (e.g., Type As) are more likely to get involved in workplace aggression than other persons.

Type B persons (e.g., Baron, Neuman, & Geddes, 1999). Similarly, as you might expect, persons high in agreeableness—one of the big five dimensions of personality—are less likely to engage in retaliation against others for real or imagined wrongs than persons low in agreeableness (Skarlicki, Folger, & Tesluk, 1999).

Please don't misunderstand: Many factors other than personality also seem to play a strong role in determining whether, and with what intensity, workplace aggression occurs—factors such as feelings of having been treated unfairly by others (e.g., Greenberg & Alge, 1999) and unsettling changes in workplaces such as downsizing (e.g., Baron & Neuman, 1996). But personal characteristics do seem important too. This suggests that paying careful attention to these aspects of personality when hiring new employees, or offering assistance to existing employees, could help organizations reduce the incidence of workplace aggression. Clearly, this would be beneficial both to employees and to the companies where they work.

**REVIEW QUESTIONS**

- What is the Type A behavior pattern, and what effects does it have on personal health?
- What is sensation seeking, and how does it influence personal health?
- What aspects of personality are related to longevity?
- Are there any aspects of personality related to job performance?
- Does personality play any role in workplace aggression?

## Making Psychology Part of Your Life

### Are You a Type A?

The Type A behavior pattern is one aspect of personality related to many important outcomes—personal health, task performance, even how frequently individuals become involved in aggression. Are *you* high or low on this dimension? To find out, complete the items below. For each, circle the number of the answer that is true for you.

1. Is your daily life filled mainly with:
   a. problems needing solution
   b. challenges needing to be met
   c. a predictable routine of events
   d. not enough things to keep me busy
2. When you are under pressure, do you usually:
   a. do something about it at once
   b. plan carefully before taking action
3. How rapidly do you eat?
   a. very fast—I'm usually finished before others are finished
   b. faster than average
   c. about average
   d. more slowly than average
4. Has your best friend ever told you that you eat too fast?
   a. yes, often
   b. yes, occasionally
   c. no
5. When you listen to someone speaking, do you feel like hurrying him/her along?
   a. frequently
   b. sometimes
   c. never
6. How often do you "put words in his/her mouth" to speed things up?
   a. frequently
   b. sometimes
   c. never

7. When you make an appointment, how often are you late?
   a. sometimes
   b. rarely
   c. never
8. Do you consider yourself to be:
   a. very competitive
   b. somewhat competitive
   c. relatively easygoing
   d. very easygoing
9. How would a close friend rate you?
   a. very competitive
   b. somewhat competitive
   c. relatively easygoing
   d. very easygoing
10. How would others describe your general level of activity?
    a. slow and inactive; should do more
    b. about average
    c. too active; should slow down
11. Would people who know you well say that you have less energy than most people?
    a. definitely yes
    b. probably yes
    c. probably no
    d. definitely no
12. How often do you face deadlines in your work?
    a. every day
    b. once a week
    c. once a month
    d. rarely
13. Do you ever set deadlines for yourself?
    a. no
    b. sometimes
    c. often
14. Do you ever work on two or more projects at once?
    a. never
    b. occasionally
    c. often
15. Do you work during vacation periods such as Thanksgiving, Christmas, spring break?
    a. yes
    b. no
    c. sometimes

To calculate your score, give yourself one point for each of the following answers:

(1) a or b; (2) a; (3) a or b; (4) a; (5) a; (6) a; (7) c; (8) a or b; (9) a or b; (10) c; (11) d; (12) c; (13) c; (14) c; (15) a

If your total score is 12 or higher, you show some of the same tendencies as Type A persons; if your score is 5 or lower, you show the tendencies characteristic of Type B persons. But please view these results as only a very rough guide to where you fall on this dimension. The items above, while similar to the ones used to measure the Type A behavior pattern, have not been carefully validated. So use these results simply as a way of gaining some initial, preliminary insight into your own personality. Also remember that if you *are* a Type A, this does *not* mean you can't change. On the contrary, research findings indicate that even extreme Type As can modify their behavior so that they are less at risk for the harmful effects of this pattern. If you feel that you are indeed an extreme Type A and do want to change—for instance, if you are concerned about the health risks associated with this pattern—speak to your professor. She or he can probably help you to find a psychologist or other professional who can help you attain this goal. But of course, if you are happy with your current status as a Type A (or a Type B, or something in between), then just view this exercise as a source of increased self-insight.

## Summary and Review

### Personality: Is It Real?

- **What is personality?** Personality consists of the unique and stable patterns of behavior, thoughts, and emotions shown by individuals.
- **What evidence suggests that personality is real?** Existing evidence suggests that people do show consistency in their behavior, so personality definitely exists.

- **What is the interactionist perspective currently adopted by most psychologists?** The interactionist perspective holds that behavior in any situation is a complex function of both personality and external factors.

### Key Terms

personality, p. 450 • interactionist perspective, p. 451

## The Psychoanalytic Approach: Messages from the Unconscious

- **According to Freud, what are the three levels of consciousness?** These levels are the conscious, the preconscious, and the unconscious.
- **In Freud's theory, what are the three basic parts of personality?** The three basic parts of personality are id, ego, and superego, which correspond roughly to desire, reason, and conscience.
- **According to Freud, what are the psychosexual stages of development?** Freud believed that all human beings move through a series of psychosexual stages during which the id's search for pleasure is focused on different regions of the body: the oral, anal, phallic, and latency stages, and finally the genital stage.
- **Do research findings support Freud's views about the unconscious?** Research findings indicate that our behavior is sometimes influenced by stimuli or information we can't describe verbally, although theres no support for his view that such information has been driven from consciousness by repression.
- **According to Jung, what is the collective unconscious?** Jung believed that all human beings share memories of our collective experience as a species. These are expressed when our conscious mind is distracted or inactive, often through archetypes.
- **In Horney's theory what is basic anxiety?** Basic anxiety is the child's fear of being alone, helpless, and insecure.
- **According to Adler, what is the role of feelings of inferiority in personality?** Adler believed that human beings experience strong feelings of inferiority during early life and must struggle in various ways to overcome these.

### Key Terms

psychoanalysis, p. 454 • id, p. 455 • pleasure principle, p. 455 • ego, p. 455 • reality principle, p. 455 • superego, p. 455 • Freudian slips, p. 455 • anxiety, p. 456 • defense mechanisms, p. 456 • sublimation, p. 456 • psychosexual stages of development, p. 457 • libido, p. 457 • fixation, p. 457 • oral stage, p. 457 • anal stage, p. 457 • phallic stage, p. 457 • Oedipus complex, p. 457 • latency stage, p. 458 • genital stage, p. 458 • neo-Freudians, p. 462 • collective unconscious, p. 462 • archetypes, p. 462 • animus, p. 462 • anima, p. 462 • introverts, p. 462 • extroverts, p. 462 • basic anxiety, p. 463 • striving for superiority, p. 463

## Humanistic Theories: Emphasis on Growth

- **How does the view of human beings proposed by humanistic theories of personality differ from that of psychoanalytic theories?** Humanistic theories of personality suggest that people strive for personal development and growth; in contrast, psychoanalytic theory views human beings as constantly struggling to control the sexual and aggressive impulses of the id.
- **According to Rogers, why do many individuals fail to become fully functioning persons?** Rogers believed that many individuals fail to become fully functioning persons because distorted self-concepts interfere with personal growth.
- **In Maslow's theory, what is self-actualization?** Self-actualization is a stage in which an individual has reached his or her maximum potential and becomes the best human being she or he can be.
- **What is the self-concept, and how is it influenced by cultural factors?** The self-concept consists of all of our beliefs and knowledge about ourselves. Research findings indicate that cultural factors can influence several aspects of the self-concept, including our self-evaluations.

### Key Terms

humanistic theories, p. 463 • fully functioning persons, p. 464 • self-concept, p. 464 • unconditional positive regard, p. 465 • self-actualization, p. 465 • peak experiences, p. 465

## Trait Theories: Seeking the Key Dimensions of Personality

- **What are central traits? Source traits?** Allport suggested that human beings possess a small number of central traits that account for much of their uniqueness as individuals. According to Cattell, there are sixteen source traits that underlie differences between individuals on many specific dimensions.
- **What are the "big five" dimensions of personality?** Research findings point to the conclusion that there are only five basic dimensions of personality: extraversion, agreeableness, conscientiousness, emotional stability, and openness to experience.
- **What are the strengths and weaknesses of the trait approach?** Strengths of the trait approach include the fact that as the basis for most current research on personality, this approach has uncovered traits that are related to important aspects of behavior. Weaknesses include the fact that the trait approach offers no comprehensive theory for *how* certain traits develop or *why* they are so important.

### Key Terms

personality traits, p. 468 • trait theories, p. 468 • secondary traits, p. 469 • central traits, p. 469 • cardinal trait, p. 469 • functional autonomy, p. 469 • source traits, p. 470 • extraversion, p. 470 • agreeableness, p. 470 • conscientiousness, p. 470 • emotional stability, p. 471 • openness to experience, p. 471

## Learning Approaches to Personality

- **How do learning theories of personality explain the uniqueness and consistency of human behavior?** Learning theories of personality suggest that uniqueness derives from the unique pattern of learning experiences each individual has experienced. These theories explain consistency by noting that patterns of behavior, once acquired, tend to persist.

- **In Bandura's social cognitive theory, what is the self-system? Self-efficacy?** The self-system is the set of cognitive processes by which individuals perceive, evaluate, and regulate their own behavior. Self-efficacy refers to individual's beliefs concerning his or her ability to perform various tasks; it can affect many aspects of behavior, such as efforts to obtain a new job.
- **According to Rotter's social learning theory, what is the key difference between internals and externals?** Internals believe that they can control the outcomes they experience, while externals do not.

### Key Terms

social cognitive theory, p. 473 • self-system, p. 473 • self-reinforcement, p. 473 • self-efficacy, p. 473 • internals, p. 474 • externals, p. 474

## Measuring Personality

- **What are self-report tests of personality?** These are questionnaires containing questions individuals answer about themselves. Examples are the MMPI and MCMI tests.
- **What are projective tests of personality?** Projective tests present individuals with ambiguous stimuli. The test takers' responses to these stimuli are assumed to reflect various aspects of their personalities.
- **What other measures of personality do psychologists currently use?** Other measures include behavioral observations (including experience sampling), interviews, and biological measures.

### Key Terms

MMPI, p. 477 • Millon Clinical Multiaxial Inventory (MCMI), p. 478 • NEO Personality Inventory (NEO–PI), p. 478 • Rorschach test, p. 478

## Modern Research on Personality: Applications to Personal Health and Behavior in Work Settings

- **What is the Type A behavior pattern, and what effects does it have on personal health?** The Type A behavior pattern involves a cluster of traits—impatience, competitiveness, and hostility. Persons high in the Type A behavior pattern are more likely than others to experience heart attacks.
- **What is sensation seeking, and how does it influence personal health?** Persons high in sensation seeking desire a great deal of stimulation and excitement in their lives. This leads them to engage in behaviors that can be dangerous.
- **What aspects of personality are related to longevity?** Persons high in conscientiousness seem to live longer than persons low in conscientiousness.
- **Are there any aspects of personality related to job performance?** Several aspects of the "big five" dimensions of personality are related to job performance (e.g., conscientiousness, emotional stability). Openness to experience is related to performance during job training.
- **Does personality play any role in workplace aggression?** Type As and persons low in agreeableness seem to become involved in workplace aggression more often than Type Bs and persons high in agreeableness.

### Key Terms

Type A behavior pattern, p. 480 • industrial/organizational psychologists, p. 482

# Critical Thinking Questions

### Appraisal

While many people do tend to show consistency in their behavior, some do not. Also, people may be consistent in some ways but inconsistent in others. Does this mean that the concept of personality is applicable only to people who show consistency in their behavior over time and across situations?

### Controversy

Growing evidence indicates that some aspects of personality are influenced by genetic factors. Does this mean that personality can't be changed? Or, even if genetic factors *do* play a role, do you think that personality remains open to change throughout life?

### Making Psychology Part of Your Life

Different jobs or careers seem to require different traits for success. Taking your own personality into account, can you think of careers for which you are, or are not, personally suited? How do your current career plans fit with these conclusions?

Chapter 13

# Health, Stress, and Coping

# CHAPTER OUTLINE


**HEALTH PSYCHOLOGY: AN OVERVIEW 490**

■ RESEARCH METHODS *How Psychologists Study Health Behavior*

**STRESS: ITS CAUSES, EFFECTS, AND CONTROL 494**

Stress: Its Basic Nature
Stress: Some Major Causes
Stress: Some Major Effects

**UNDERSTANDING AND COMMUNICATING OUR HEALTH NEEDS 504**

Health Beliefs: When Do We Seek Medical Advice?
Doctor–Patient Interactions: Why Can't We Talk to Our Doctors?

■ FROM SCIENCE TO PRACTICE *Surfing for Solutions to Medical Problems on the Internet: Using Information Technologies to Diagnose Our Illnesses*

**BEHAVIORAL AND PSYCHOLOGICAL CORRELATES OF ILLNESS: THE EFFECTS OF THOUGHTS AND ACTIONS ON HEALTH 509**

Smoking: Risky for You and Everyone around You

■ BEYOND THE HEADLINES—As Psychologists See It: *A New Weapon in the Antismoking Arsenal*

Diet and Nutrition: What You Eat May Save Your Life
Alcohol Consumption: Here's to Your Health?
Emotions and Health
AIDS: A Tragic Assault on Public Health

**PROMOTING WELLNESS: DEVELOPING A HEALTHIER LIFESTYLE 521**

Primary Prevention: Decreasing the Risks of Illness
Secondary Prevention: The Role of Early Detection in Disease and Illness

■ MAKING PSYCHOLOGY PART OF YOUR LIFE *Managing Stress: Some Useful Tactics*


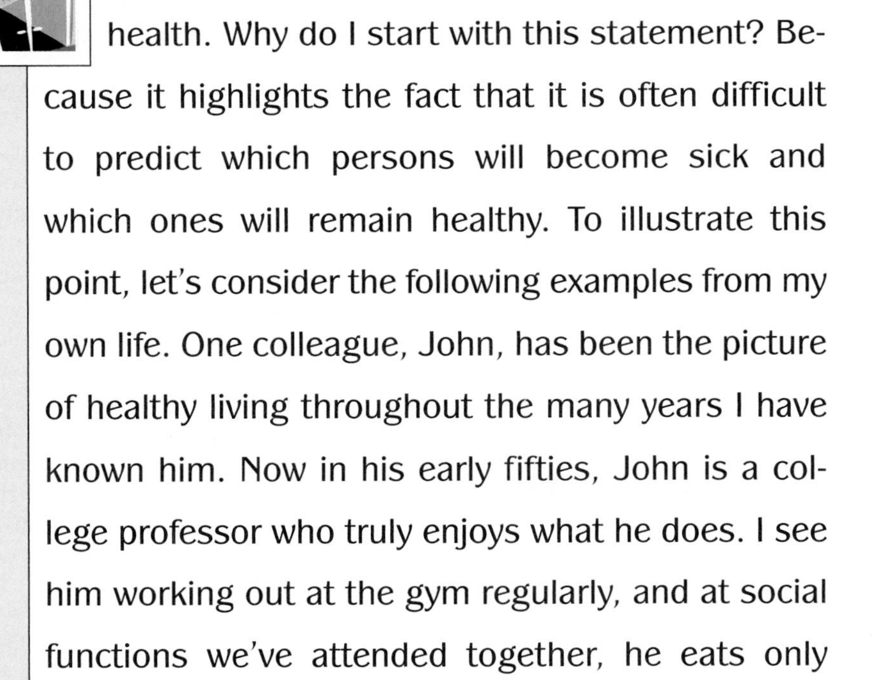

Life is full of ironies, particularly in the realm of health. Why do I start with this statement? Because it highlights the fact that it is often difficult to predict which persons will become sick and which ones will remain healthy. To illustrate this point, let's consider the following examples from my own life. One colleague, John, has been the picture of healthy living throughout the many years I have known him. Now in his early fifties, John is a college professor who truly enjoys what he does. I see him working out at the gym regularly, and at social functions we've attended together, he eats only fruits, whole grains, and vegetables. He is happily married and has two healthy daughters. He doesn't smoke and drinks only an occasional glass of wine. Based on this brief description of his lifestyle, one might predict that John would enjoy good health. Unfortunately, he recently learned from his doctor that he has an advanced case of pancreatic cancer, one of the deadliest forms of this disease. Let's contrast John's lifestyle with the health practices of another person I've known about the same length of time. Paul is a banker and always seems to be highly stressed. About the same age as John, Paul works long hours, often works weekends, and rarely takes a break from his work. He is divorced, smoked cigarettes for about twenty years, and is a heavy drinker. Yet, he is in excellent health and hasn't missed a day of work in years.

**Health Psychology:** The study of the relation between psychological variables and health, which reflects the view that both mind and body are important determinants of health and illness.

What's going on here? Why is it that some people who clearly take good care of themselves get sick, whereas others, who do not, remain healthy? Research conducted over several decades now suggests the following answer: that good health is determined not only by our lifestyle but also by a complex interaction among genetic, psychological, and social factors. Throughout this chapter, we'll encounter findings that show how these factors combine to produce good—and poor—health.

We'll begin by describing the exciting branch of psychology known as *health psychology.* The primary aim of health psychology is to identify important relationships between psychological variables and health. We'll also discuss the methods health psychologists use to study these relationships. Second, we'll consider the nature of *stress,* a major health-related problem as we begin the new millennium. We'll focus on both the causes of stress and some of its major effects—how it influences health and performance. Next, we'll consider how some of our *beliefs and attitudes* influence the way in which we interpret certain health symptoms, and thus affect our willingness to seek necessary medical assistance. Fourth, we'll look at *behaviors* that can directly affect our risk of contracting certain lifestyle-related illnesses, such as cancer, cardiovascular diseases, and AIDS. Finally, we'll consider various ways in which psychologists work to promote personal health by encouraging healthy lifestyles.

Web Link: *National Institutes of Health Homepage*

Video 13.1: *The Changing Definition of Health from a Historical Perspective*

## Health Psychology: An Overview

**Health psychology,** the branch of psychology that studies the relation between psychological variables and health, reflects the view that both mind and body are important determinants of health and illness (Taylor, 1999). Specifically, health psychologists believe that our beliefs, attitudes, and behavior contribute significantly to the onset or prevention of illness (Baum & Posluszny, 1999). A closely related field, known as *behavioral medicine,* combines behavioral and biomedical knowledge for the prevention and treatment of disorders ordinarily thought of as being within the domain of medicine (Compas et al., 1998; Epstein, 1992).

**Lifestyle:** In the context of health psychology, the overall pattern of decisions and behaviors that determine health and quality of life.

Health psychology and behavioral medicine have experienced tremendous growth since their beginnings in the early 1970s. Perhaps the most fundamental reason for the increased interest in health psychology and behavioral medicine is the dramatic shift observed in the leading causes of death during this century. In 1900, many of the leading causes of death could be traced to infectious diseases, such as influenza, pneumonia, and tuberculosis. However, the development of antibiotics and vaccines and improved sanitation practices have significantly reduced these health threats, at least in this country.

As shown in Table 13.1, the current leading causes of death are attributable to a significant degree to characteristics that make up each person's **lifestyle:** the overall pattern of decisions and behaviors that determines a person's health and quality of life. This fact suggests that psychologists, now more than ever, can make a difference in people's quality of life by helping them to eliminate behaviors that lead to illness and to adopt behaviors that lead to wellness. Indeed, a majority of the conditions that now constitute the leading causes of death could be prevented if people would eat nutritious foods, reduce their alcohol consumption, practice safe sex, eliminate smoking, and exercise regularly.

How much progress have we actually made in getting people to adopt healthier lifestyles? Actually, plenty. One encouraging sign comes from a recent progress report of the *Healthy People 2000 Initiative,* a large-scale program, begun in 1979, whose aim is to promote good health among citizens of the United States by identifying the most significant preventable threats to health and then focusing public

Web Link: *National Center for Health Statistics Homepage*

**TABLE 13.1**

**Leading Causes of Death in the United States in 1996**

Many of the important causes of death shown here are related to lifestyle. Thus, they can be prevented by changes in behavior.

| Causes of Death | Number of Yearly Deaths |
|---|---|
| Heart disease | 733,361 |
| Cancer | 539,533 |
| Stroke | 159,942 |
| Chronic lung disease | 106,027 |
| Accidents | 94,948 |
| Pneumonia/influenza | 83,727 |
| Diabetes | 61,767 |
| HIV/AIDS | 31,130 |
| Suicide | 30,903 |
| Chronic liver disease and cirrhosis | 25,047 |

(*Source:* National Vital Statistics Reports, Vol. 47, No. 9, 1998.)

Web Link: *Health Psychology and Rehabilitation: Promoting Mental and Physical Health*

**TABLE 13.2**

**Priority Areas of the *Healthy People 2000* Initiative**

A recent review of each of twenty-two targeted priority areas indicates that the Healthy People 2000 Initiative either is on track toward or has already reached more than half of its health-related objectives.

1. Physical Activity and Fitness
2. Nutrition
3. Tobacco
4. Substance Abuse: Alcohol and Other Drugs
5. Family Planning
6. Mental Health and Mental Disorders
7. Violent and Abusive Behavior
8. Educational and Community-Based Programs
9. Unintentional Injuries
10. Occupational Safety and Health
11. Environmental Health
12. Food and Drug Safety
13. Oral Health
14. Maternal and Infant Health
15. Heart Disease and Stroke
16. Cancer
17. Diabetes and Chronic Disabling Conditions
18. HIV Infection
19. Sexually Transmitted Diseases
20. Immunization and Infectious Diseases
21. Clinical Preventive Services
22. Surveillance and Data Systems

(*Source:* National Center for Health Statistics, 1999.)

and private resources to address those threats effectively. The three primary goals of the program are to (1) increase the span of healthy life; (2) reduce disparities in health in different population groups, such as children, the poor, and the elderly; and (3) make preventive health services available to everyone in the country. These goals provide a general framework for measuring the results of efforts to meet specific health-related goals. Progress reviews are conducted periodically on each of twenty-two targeted priority areas, which are presented in Table 13.2.

The most recent progress report on this project, entitled "Healthy People 2000 Review, 1998–99," reveals that the project either is on track to reach or has already reached more than half of its health objectives. Areas in which target objectives have already been met include maternal and infant health, heart disease, oral and breast cancer, and mental health. Significant progress has also been made toward meeting other important objectives, including increases in the number of children receiving immunizations and women receiving mammography screening, an increase in consumption of fruits and vegetables, and a reduction in infant mortality rates. Unfortunately, however, there are several areas in which we have actually lost ground. For example, a significant percentage of U.S. adults and children continue to be overweight, and little progress has been made in increasing their level of physical activity and fitness. Planning is currently under way to identify specific objectives for the next phase of this ambitious project, termed *Healthy People 2010* (http://www.health.gov/healthypeople/).

**Epidemiological Studies:** Large-scale research conducted to identify risk factors that lead to the development of certain diseases.

Let's now turn to the following **Research Methods** section to see how health psychologists study important aspects of health-related behaviors.

## Research Methods: How Psychologists Study Health Behavior

Much of the basic knowledge that we have obtained about the factors that lead to good or poor health has emerged from **epidemiological studies**—large-scale attempts to identify *risk factors* that predict the development of certain diseases and premature death (Winett, 1995). Why are epidemiological studies important? There are actually several reasons. One has to do with the complexity of causality; certain forms of illness often have multiple causes. For example, a large body of evidence has confirmed that the development of heart disease—currently the leading cause of death among people in the United States and in many countries throughout the world (The World Health Report, 1999)—results from a combination of biological, behavioral, and environmental factors.

A second reason epidemiological studies are important has to do with their scope. Epidemiological studies often involve the study of thousands of people across lengthy periods of time. Data obtained through this approach help explain why certain groups are at greater risk for acquiring some diseases, or more likely to die prematurely, than others. For example, epidemiological studies first alerted scientists that the groups most likely to engage in unprotected sex and intravenous drug use are also most at risk of acquiring HIV, the virus that causes AIDS.

Finally, and perhaps most importantly, the results of epidemiological studies have highlighted patterns that exist between various aspects of people, their behavior, their environments, and their health outcomes. The clues provided by these patterns are useful for developing interventions that promote both good health and longevity.

To illustrate how epidemiological research is performed, let's consider a classic decade-long study conducted in Alameda County, California. The researchers asked a large group of adults whether they followed certain health practices, including sleeping seven to eight hours each night, eating breakfast regularly, refraining from smoking, drinking alcohol in moderation or not at all, maintaining their weight within normal limits, and exercising regularly (Wiley & Camacho, 1980). The results revealed that participants who reported practicing all or most of these behaviors were much less likely to die during the study period than those who practiced few or none of these behaviors. These results highlight the intimate connection between lifestyle and good health.

Epidemiological studies have also revealed that other factors, including aspects of our personality and certain life experiences, also play an important role in determining health and longevity. To illustrate this link, let's return to the intriguing study conducted by Howard Friedman and his colleagues (1995), building upon the famous study initiated by psychologist Lewis Terman in 1921 to investigate his theories of intelligence. As described in Chapters 9 and 12, Terman recruited the 856 boys and 672 girls now referred to as the "Termites"; intensively studied many aspects of their psychological, social, and intellectual development; and then followed them into adulthood. Quite apart from Terman's initial goals for the study, Friedman and his colleagues have used the extensive database of information that has accrued on the Termites since 1921 to examine whether the various measures obtained from the Termites as young children, and at several points since then, are predictive of health and well-being later in life. Moreover, because about half of the Termites have now died, and because the cause of most of these deaths is known, Friedman and his colleagues have been able to examine how aspects of the Termites' personality and early life experiences contribute to longevity. (Refer to Chapter 12 for additional information on personality.)

Can childhood personality measures and early life experiences actually predict health-related outcomes later in life? Friedman's findings seem to suggest the answer is yes. One of the most striking discoveries is that, as we saw in Chapter 12, the Termites, especially boys, who had been rated as conscientious and dependable by their parents and teachers tended to live longer than Termites who received lower ratings on these dimensions. Why would these children outlive their less conscientious counterparts? Archival data on the Termites suggests that the protective effects of conscientiousness may stem from the fact that these individuals were less likely to take risks or engage in unhealthy behaviors such as smoking and heavy drinking. Conversely, children who were rated high on cheerfulness and optimism—usually viewed as buffers against the detrimental effects of stressful life experiences—were more prone to die early. Why would this be so? Again, a review of archival data reveals that these individuals were *more* likely to engage in unhealthy behaviors. Friedman and his colleagues suggest that the risky patterns of behavior they practiced may have offset the potential buffering effects of these Termites' optimistic outlook on life.

Also of interest are findings related to differences in the Termites' early life experiences, especially the effects of divorce. Termites whose parents divorced during their childhood (before they were twenty-one) were significantly more likely to die prematurely than their counterparts whose parents either did not divorce or divorced after the children had reached adulthood. A large number of studies have shown that children of divorce, especially boys, are at greater risk for observable behavior and adjustment problems (e.g., Amato & Keith, 1991; Zill, Morrison, & Coiro, 1993); but this study is among the first to establish a link between having experienced parental divorce and premature death. Analysis of the Termites' own marital history yielded similar results: Termites who were either separated, divorced, widowed, or remarried were at higher risk for premature death than either the Termites who were steadily married or those who never married.

One important caution is in order: Please note that the results of this study, and of the Alameda County study described earlier in this section, are based on correlations and therefore are *not* conclusive (see Chapter 1). However, they are important because they highlight the intimate connection that exists between lifestyle and good health. As you proceed through this chapter, I hope that you'll note that many of the findings you'll encounter are based on the results of basic epidemiological research.

REVIEW QUESTIONS

- What is health psychology?
- What is the field of behavioral medicine?
- To what can we attribute today's leading causes of premature death?
- What are epidemiological studies?

*Food for Thought*

Research with the Termites seems to indicate that certain early life experiences such as experiencing the divorce of one's parents are linked to detrimental effects on health. Why do you think that such events might contribute to premature death?

CourseCompass
Web Link: *The Medical Basis of Stress*

# Stress: Its Causes, Effects, and Control

Have you ever felt that you were right at the edge of being overwhelmed by negative events in your life? Or felt so overwhelmed that you just gave up? If so, you are already quite familiar with **stress,** our response to events that disrupt, or threaten to disrupt, our physical or psychological functioning (Lazarus & Folkman, 1984; Taylor, 1999). Unfortunately, stress is a common part of life as we begin the new millennium—something few of us can avoid altogether. Partly for this reason, and partly because it seems to exert negative effects on both physical health and psychological well-being, stress has become an important topic of research in psychology. Let's examine the basic nature of stress and some of its major causes.

## Stress: Its Basic Nature

Stress is a many-faceted process that occurs in reaction to events or situations in our environment termed **stressors.** An interesting feature of stress is the wide range of physical and psychological reactions that different people have to the same event; some may interpret an event as stressful, whereas others simply take it in stride. Moreover, a particular person may react quite differently to the same stressor at different points in time.

**Stress:** Our response to events that disrupt, or threaten to disrupt, our physical or psychological functioning.

**Stressors:** Events or situations in our environment that cause stress.

**STRESSORS: THE ACTIVATORS OF STRESS** What are stressors? Although we normally think of stress as stemming from negative events in our lives, positive events such as getting married or receiving an unexpected job promotion can also produce stress (Brown & McGill, 1989). Despite the wide range of stimuli that can potentially produce stress, it appears that many events we find stressful share several characteristics: (1) They are so intense that they produce a state of overload—we can no longer adapt to them. (2) They evoke incompatible tendencies in us, such as tendencies both to approach and to avoid some object or activity. (3) They are uncontrollable—beyond our limits of control. Indeed, a great deal of evidence suggests that when people can predict, control, or terminate an event or situation, they perceive it to be less stressful than when they feel less in control (Karasek & Theorell, 1990; Rodin & Salovey, 1989).

**PHYSIOLOGICAL RESPONSES TO STRESSORS** When exposed to stressors, we generally experience many physiological reactions. If you've been caught off-guard by someone who appears out of nowhere and grabs you while yelling "Gotcha," then you are probably familiar with some common physical reactions to stress (see Figure 13.1). Initially, your blood pressure soars, your pulse races, and you may even begin to sweat. These are part of a general pattern of reactions referred to as the *fight-or-flight syndrome,* a process controlled through the sympathetic nervous system. As we saw in Chapter 2, the sympathetic nervous system prepares our bodies for immediate action. Usually these responses are brief, and we soon return to normal levels. When we are exposed to chronic sources of stress, however, this reaction is only the first in a longer sequence of responses activated by our efforts to adapt to a stressor.

**Figure 13.1**
**Physiological Reactions to Stressors**

When we encounter stressors that frighten or surprise us, we experience a wave of physiological reactions, as illustrated in the photo below. These are part of a general pattern of reactions referred to as the fight-or-flight syndrome, a process controlled through the sympathetic nervous system.

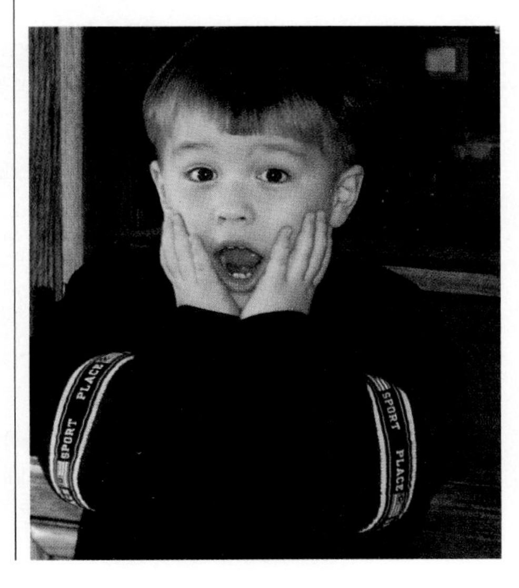


This sequence, termed by Hans Selye (1976) the **general adaptation syndrome (GAS),** consists of three stages. The first is the *alarm* stage, in which the body prepares itself for immediate action; arousal of the sympathetic nervous system releases hormones that help prepare our body to meet threats or dangers (Selye, 1976). If stress is prolonged, however, the *resistance* stage begins. During this second stage, arousal is lower than during the alarm stage, but our bodies continue to draw on resources at an above-normal rate in order to cope effectively with the stressor. Continued exposure to the same stressor or additional stressors drains the body of its resources and leads to the third stage, *exhaustion.* During this stage our capacity to resist is depleted, and our susceptibility to illness increases. In severe cases of prolonged physical stress, the result can be death.

**COGNITIVE APPRAISAL OF OUR STRESSORS** Selye's general adaptation syndrome provides a framework for understanding our physiological responses to stressful events and suggests at least one reasonable explanation for the relation between stress and illness. Few experts would disagree that chronic stress can lead to a lowered resistance to disease. However, a critical weakness with Selye's model is that it fails to consider the importance of cognitive processes in determining whether we interpret a specific event as stressful. The importance of these processes is made clear by the following fact: When confronted with the same potentially stress-inducing situation, some persons experience stress, whereas others do not. Why? One reason involves individuals' cognitive appraisals (see Figure 13.2 on page 496). In simple terms, stress occurs only to the extent that the persons involved perceive (1) that the situation is somehow threatening to their important goals (often described as *primary appraisal*) and (2) that they will be unable to cope with these dangers or demands (often described as *secondary appraisal*) (Croyle, 1992; Lazarus & Folkman, 1984).

**General Adaptation Syndrome (GAS):** A three-step profile of response to stress: (1) alarm, a nonspecific mobilization phase that promotes sympathetic nervous system activity; (2) resistance, during which the organism makes efforts to cope; and (3) exhaustion, which occurs if the organism fails to overcome the threat and depletes its coping resources.

A study of the cognitive appraisal process by Tomaka and his colleagues (1993) may help illustrate this point. Participants in this study were told that the researchers were interested in measuring their physiological responses (heart rate, pulse) while they performed a mental task: counting backward from 2,737 by sevens—that is, 2,730, 2,723, 2,716, and so on. Just before the participants began counting, the researchers assessed their primary and secondary appraisals of the task. They assessed primary appraisals by asking them, "How threatening do you expect

**Figure 13.2**
**Stress: The Role of Cognitive Appraisals**

The amount of stress you experience depends in part on your cognitive appraisals of the event or situation—the extent to which you perceive it as threatening and perceive that you will be unable to cope with it.
(*Source:* Based on data from Hingson et al., 1990.)

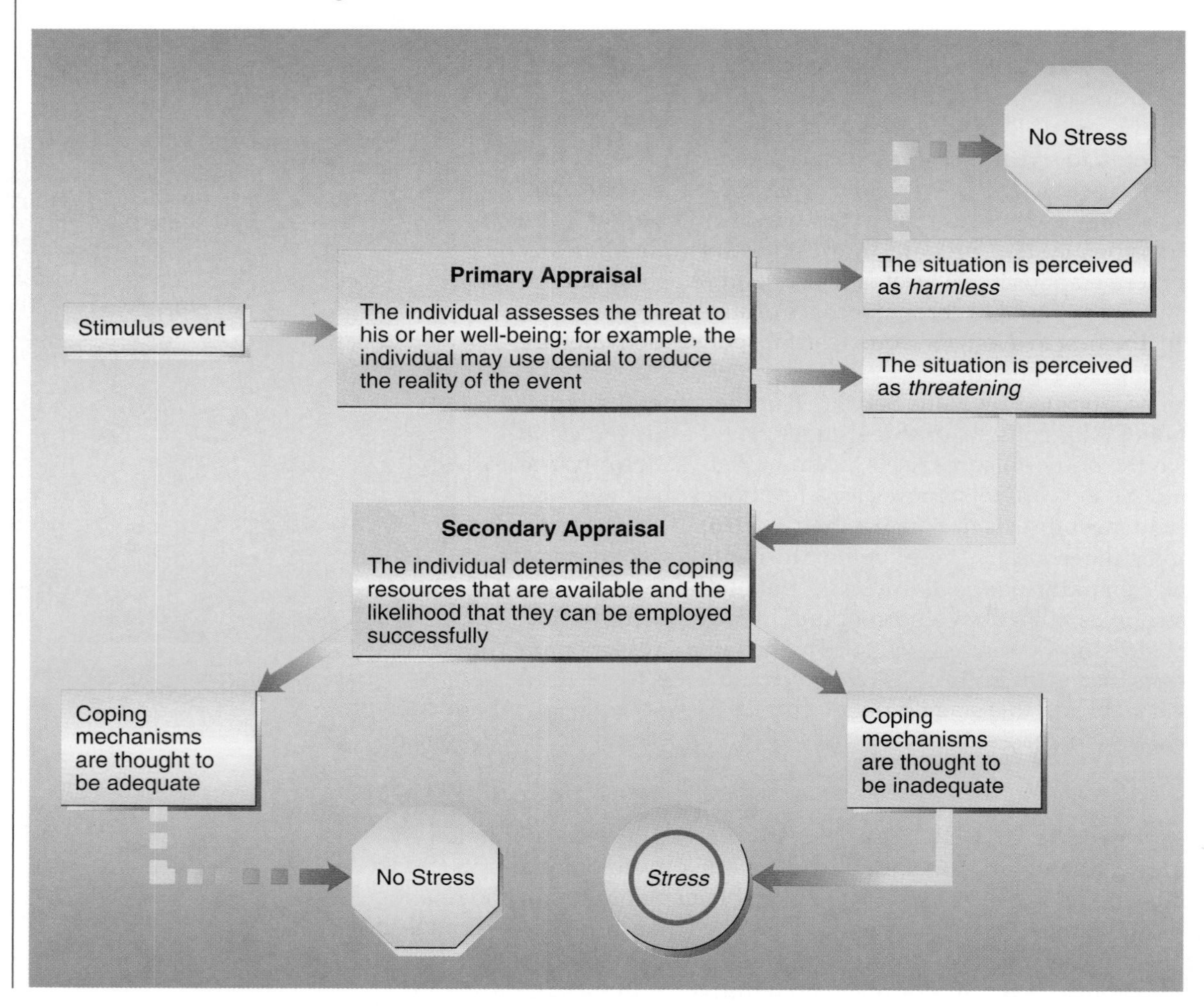


the upcoming task to be?" They assessed secondary appraisals by asking, "How able are you to cope with this task?" The researchers predicted that persons who felt they could *not* successfully perform the task would perceive it as threatening ("threat group") and would therefore experience stress. In contrast, they reasoned, persons who were more confident in their abilities might perceive the task as a challenge ("challenge group"); while these persons would not experience stress, they would in fact exhibit greater physiological arousal as they prepared to meet the challenge. All predictions were confirmed. Participants in the threat group reported *feeling* greater stress, while participants in the challenge group actually showed greater physiological arousal. Moreover, the challenge group scored higher on both perceived and actual measures of performance.

In short, these results and the results of related research provide evidence for the important role of cognitive and social processes in shaping our responses to stress. We'll turn next to some of the causes of stress.

**REVIEW QUESTIONS**

- What is stress?
- What is the GAS model?
- What determines whether an event will be interpreted as stressful or as a challenge?

## Stress: Some Major Causes

What factors contribute to stress? Unfortunately, the list is a long one. A wide range of conditions and events seem capable of generating such feelings. Among the most important of these are major stressful life events, such as the death of a loved one or a painful divorce; the all-too-frequent minor hassles of everyday life; conditions and events relating to one's job or career; and certain aspects of the physical environment.

**STRESSFUL LIFE EVENTS** Death of a spouse, injury to one's child, war, failure in school or at work, an unplanned pregnancy—unless we lead truly charmed lives, most of us experience traumatic events and changes at some time or other. What are their effects on us? This question was first investigated by Holmes and Rahe (1967), who asked a large group of persons to assign arbitrary points (to a maximum of one hundred) to various life events according to how much readjustment each had required. It was reasoned that the greater the number of points assigned to a given event, the more stressful it was for the persons experiencing it.

As you can see from Table 13.3 on page 498, participants in Holmes and Rahe's study assigned the greatest number of points to such serious events as death of a spouse, divorce, and marital separation. In contrast, they assigned much smaller values to such events as change in residence, vacation, and minor violations of the law, such as a parking ticket.

Holmes and Rahe (1967) then related the total number of points accumulated by individuals during a single year to changes in their personal health. The results were dramatic—and did much to stir psychologists' interest in the effects of stress. The greater the number of "stress points" people accumulated, the greater was their likelihood of becoming seriously ill.

Newer research has put a finer point on the relationship between stress and illness. For example, in one recent study, Cohen and his colleagues (1998) asked a group of volunteers to describe stressful events they had experienced during the previous year and to indicate the temporal course (the onset and cessation) of each event. The stressful events participants described ranged from acute stressors that were brief in duration (e.g., a severe reprimand at work or a fight with a spouse) to more chronic ones that typically lasted a month or more and involved significant disruption of everyday routines (e.g., ongoing marital problems or unemployment). Then the researchers gave these persons nose drops containing a low dose of a virus that causes the common cold. The results showed that volunteers who reported chronic stressors (those lasting longer than a month) were more likely to develop a cold than volunteers who had experienced only acute stressors. Moreover, the longer the duration of the stressor, the greater was the risk for developing a cold. These results suggest that chronic stressors may be a more important determinant of disease risk than are short-term stressful events.

This picture is complicated, however, by the existence of large differences in individuals' ability to withstand the impact of stress (Oulette-Kobasa & Puccetti, 1983). While some persons suffer ill effects after exposure to a few mildly stressful events, others remain healthy even after prolonged exposure to high levels of

TABLE 13.3

**Life Events, Stress, and Personal Health**

When individuals experience stressful life events, such as those near the top of this list, their health often suffers. The greater the number of points for each event, the more stressful it is perceived as being.

| Life Event | Points |
|---|---|
| 1. Death of spouse | 100 |
| 2. Divorce | 73 |
| 3. Marital separation | 65 |
| 4. Jail term | 63 |
| 5. Death of close family member | 63 |
| 6. Personal injury or illness | 53 |
| 7. Marriage | 50 |
| 8. Getting fired at work | 47 |
| 9. Marital reconciliation | 45 |
| 10. Retirement | 45 |
| 11. Change in health of family member | 44 |
| 12. Pregnancy | 40 |
| 13. Sex difficulties | 39 |
| 14. Gain of new family member | 39 |
| 15. Business readjustment | 39 |
| 16. Change in financial state | 38 |
| 17. Death of close friend | 37 |
| 18. Change to different line of work | 36 |
| 19. Change in number of arguments with spouse | 35 |
| 20. Taking out morgage for major purchase (e.g., home) | 31 |
| 21. Foreclosure of mortgage or loan | 30 |
| 22. Change in responsibilites at work | 29 |
| 23. Son or daughter leaving home | 29 |
| 24. Trouble with inlaws | 29 |
| 25. Outstanding personal achievement | 28 |
| 26. Wife beginning or stopping work | 26 |
| 27. Beginning or ending school | 26 |
| 28. Change in living conditions | 25 |
| 29. Revision of personal habits | 24 |
| 30. Trouble with boss | 23 |
| 31. Change in work hours or conditions | 20 |
| 32. Change in residence | 20 |
| 33. Change in schools | 20 |
| 34. Change in recreation | 19 |
| 35. Change in church activities | 19 |
| 36. Change in social activities | 18 |
| 37. Taking out a loan for a lesser purchase (e.g., car or TV) | 17 |
| 38. Change in sleeping habits | 16 |
| 39. Change in number of family get-togethers | 15 |
| 40. Change in eating habits | 15 |
| 41. Vacation | 13 |
| 42. Christmas | 12 |
| 43. Minor violation of the law | 11 |

(*Source:* Based on data from Holmes & Masuda, 1974.)

stress; these individuals are described as being *stress-resistant* or *hardy*. I'll return to such differences later in this chapter. For the moment, I wish merely to emphasize the fact that in general, the greater the number of stressful life events experienced by an individual, and the longer these events are in duration, the greater the likelihood that the person's subsequent health will be adversely affected.

Web Link: *Lifestyle Management*

Audio 13.1: *Hassles of Daily Life*

**Hassles:** Annoying minor events of everyday life that cumulatively can affect psychological well-being.

**THE HASSLES OF DAILY LIFE** While certain events, such as the death of someone close to us, are clearly stressful, they occur relatively infrequently. Does this mean that people's lives are mostly a serene lake of tranquillity? Hardly. As you know, daily life is filled with countless minor annoying sources of stress—termed **hassles**—that seem to make up for their relatively low intensity by their much higher frequency. That such daily hassles are an important cause of stress is suggested by the findings of several studies by Lazarus and his colleagues (DeLongis, Folkman, & Lazarus, 1988; Kanner et al., 1981; Lazarus et al., 1985). These researchers developed a Hassles Scale on which individuals indicate the extent to which they have been "hassled" by common events during the past month. The items included in this scale deal with a wide range of everyday events, such as having too many things to do at once, shopping, and concerns over money.

Although such events may seem relatively minor when compared with the life changes studied by Holmes and Rahe (1967), they appear to have important effects. When scores on the Hassles Scale are related to reports of psychological symptoms, strong positive correlations are obtained (Lazarus et al., 1985). In short, the more stress people report as a result of daily hassles, the poorer their psychological well-being. Let's turn now to a discussion of the effects of work-related stress.

Web Link: *Workplace Stress*

**WORK-RELATED STRESS** Most adults spend more time at work than in any other single activity. It is not surprising, then, that jobs or careers are a central source of stress. Some of the factors producing stress in work settings are obvious; for example, blatant sexual harassment, discrimination, or extreme *overload*—being asked to do too much in too short a time. Interestingly, being asked to do too little can also cause stress. Such *underload* produces intense feelings of boredom, and these, in turn, can be very stressful.

Several other factors that play a role in work-related stress may be less apparent. One of these is *role conflict*—being the target of conflicting demands or expectations from different groups of people. For example, consider the plight of many beginning managers. Their subordinates often expect such persons to go to bat for them with the company to improve their work assignments, pay, and conditions. In contrast, the managers' own bosses often expect them to do the opposite: somehow to induce the employees to work harder for fewer rewards. The result: a stressful situation for the managers.

Another work-related factor that can sometimes generate intense levels of stress involves *performance appraisals,* procedures used for evaluating employees' performance. If employees perceive these as fair, employee stress tends to be low; if employees view them as arbitrary or unfair, it is almost certain to be high. After all, no one wants to feel that rewards such as raises, promotions, or bonuses are being distributed in an unjust manner (Vredenburgh, McLeod, & Nebeker, 1999). Additional factors that have been found to contribute to stress at work are summarized in Figure 13.3.

Can anything be done to reduce such effects? Fortunately, several lines of research suggest that the answer is yes. First, employers can reduce workplace

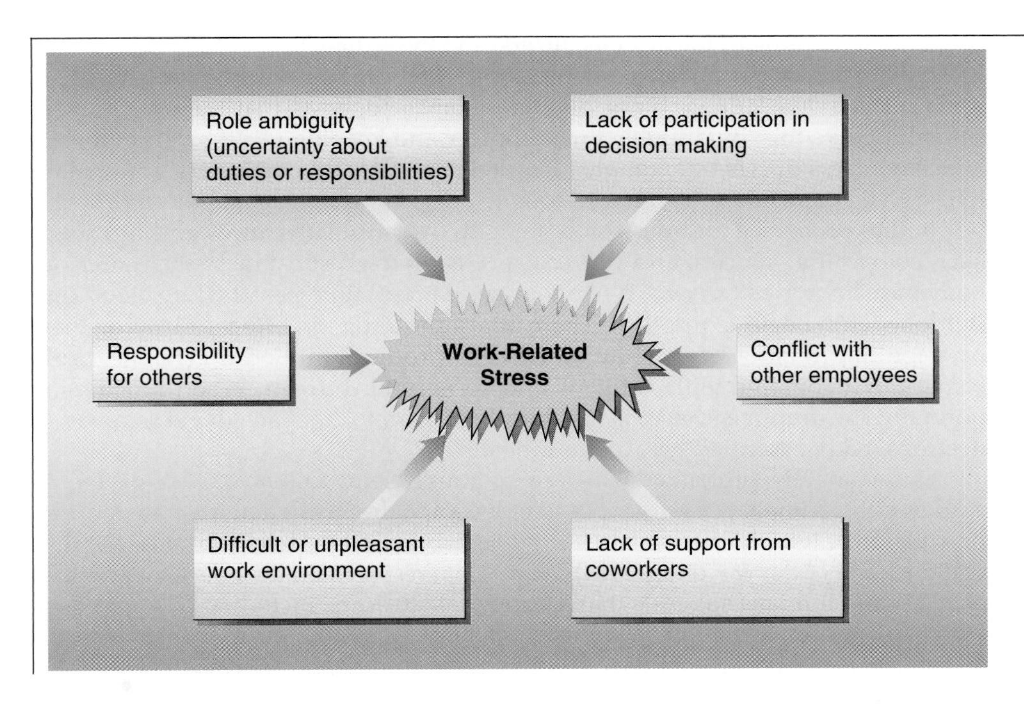


**Figure 13.3**
**Sources of Work-Related Stress**

Many factors contribute to stress at work. Several of the most important are summarized here.

stress by considering the **person–environment (P–E) fit** (Edwards & Harrison, 1993). Mismatches between characteristics of workers and characteristics of their jobs or work environments are associated with increases in stress-related illnesses (Harrison, 1985). Second, sources of social support, both on and off the job, can serve as a buffer against stressful events that occur at work (Frese, 1999; Uchino, Cacioppo, & Kiecolt-Glaser, 1996). Finally, companies can help reduce the potential negative effects of workplace stress by implementing interventions that improve their employees' ability to cope with workplace stress and change unhealthy practices that can intensify the effects of stress (Maturi, 1992).

**REVIEW QUESTIONS**

- What are stressors?
- What are some sources of work-related stress?
- What is the person-environment fit, and why is it important?

CourseCompass
Video 13.2: *Stress Prevention*

## Stress: Some Major Effects

By now you may be convinced that stress stems from many different sources and exerts important effects on persons who experience it. What is sometimes difficult to grasp, though, is just how far-reaching these effects can be. Stress can influence our physical and psychological well-being, our performance on many tasks, and even the ultimate course of our careers.

**STRESS AND HEALTH: THE SILENT KILLER** The link between stress and personal health, according to medical experts, is very strong (Kiecolt-Glaser & Glaser, 1992). Some authorities estimate that stress plays some role in 50 to 70 percent of all physical illness (Frese, 1985). Moreover, included in these percentages are some of the most serious and life-threatening ailments known to medical science. To list just a few, stress has been implicated in the occurrence of heart disease, high blood pressure, hardening of the arteries, ulcers, and even diabetes.

How does stress produce such effects? The precise mechanisms involved remain to be determined, but growing evidence suggests that the process goes something like this: By draining our resources and keeping us off balance physiologically, stress upsets our complex internal chemistry. In particular, it may interfere with efficient operation of our *immune system*—the mechanism through which our bodies recognize and destroy potentially harmful substances and intruders, such as bacteria, viruses, and cancerous cells. Foreign substances that enter our bodies are known as *antigens*. When they appear, certain types of white blood cells (lymphocytes) begin to multiply. These attack the antigens, often destroying them by engulfing them. Other white blood cells produce antibodies, chemical substances that combine with antigens and so neutralize them. When functioning normally, the immune system is nothing short of amazing: Each day it removes or destroys many potential threats to our health.

Unfortunately, prolonged exposure to stress seems to disrupt this system. In studies with animals, subjects exposed to inescapable shocks demonstrate reduced production of lymphocytes relative to subjects exposed to shocks from which they could escape (Ader & Cohen, 1984). Additional research on the effects of stress on animals and humans suggests that a variety of stressors, including disruptions in interpersonal relationships, loneliness, academic pressure, daily hassles, and the lack of social support, can interfere with our immune systems (Cohen et al., 1992; Miller et al., 1999).

**Person–Environment (P–E) Fit:** The appropriateness of the fit, or match, between a person and his or her work environment; a poor P–E fit may produce stress.

For example, in one study, Cohen and his colleagues (1992) assessed the effects of social stability on the immune systems of monkeys. During the year preceding the study, a group of monkeys lived in stable (unchanging) social conditions. When the study began, however, they were randomly assigned to live in either a stable or an unstable social condition for the next twenty-six months. Monkeys in the stable group lived in the same environment through the entire study period. In the unstable condition, however, social groups were reorganized frequently. The researchers then observed and assessed the amount of time the monkeys in each group spent in various forms of social interaction, including affiliative behaviors such as engaging in passive physical contact and grooming with other group members. Why were the researchers interested in observing affiliative behaviors? They reasoned that if social support serves as a stress buffer, then the monkeys in the unstable group that engaged in the least amount of affiliative behaviors would experience the greatest negative impact on measures of immune functions. The results of the experiment confirmed these predictions. In short, social support may be an important buffer against the adverse effects of chronic stress.

These results are relevant to people, too. Persons who are divorced or separated from their spouses often experience reduced functioning in certain aspects of their immune system, compared to individuals who are happily married (Kiecolt-Glaser et al., 1987, 1988). Additionally, some recent evidence suggests that the effects of stress on the immune system may be less potent for people who have effective ways of dealing with their stressors than for those who do not. Some research shows that optimism, regular exercise, and feelings of control over stressful events are associated with reduced suppression of the immune system under stress (Taylor, 1999). Such findings are both unsettling and encouraging. On the one hand, they suggest that our complex, high-stress lifestyles may be undermining, at least to a degree, our ability to resist many serious forms of illness. On the other hand, these findings indicate that reductions in such stress may be beneficial to our health.

Audio 13.2: *Effects of Burnout*

**STRESS AND TASK PERFORMANCE** Psychologists once believed that stress actually improves performance on a wide range of tasks. They held that the relationship between stress and task performance takes the form of an upside-down U: at first, performance improves as stress increases, presumably because the stress is arousing or energizing. Beyond some point, though, stress becomes distracting, and performance actually drops.

While this relationship may hold true under some conditions, growing evidence suggests that even low or moderate levels of stress can interfere with task performance (Motowidlo, Packard, & Manning, 1986; Steers, 1984). There are several reasons why this is so. First, even relatively mild stress can be distracting. People experiencing stress may focus on the unpleasant feelings and emotions it involves, rather than on the task at hand. Second, prolonged or repeated exposure to even mild levels of stress may exert harmful effects on health, and health problems may interfere with effective performance. Finally, as we saw in Chapter 10, a large body of research indicates that as arousal increases, task performance may rise at first, but that at some point it falls (Berlyne, 1967). The precise location of this turning, or *inflection,* point seems to depend to an important extent on the complexity of the task performed. The greater the complexity, the lower the level of arousal at which the downturn in performance occurs. Many observers believe that the tasks performed by today's working people are more complex than those in the past. For this reason, even relatively low levels of stress may interfere with performance in today's complex work world.

Together, these factors help explain why even moderate levels of stress may interfere with many types of performance. However, stress does not always produce adverse effects. For example, people sometimes do seem to rise to the occasion and turn in sterling performances at times when stress is intense (see Figure 13.4 on page 502). Perhaps the most reasonable conclusion, then, is that although stress can interfere with task performance in many situations, its precise effects depend on many

**Figure 13.4**
**The Effects of Stress on Performance**

Even relatively low levels of stress may interfere with performance in today's complex work world. These effects are often most evident among people who are under tremendous pressure to perform well. Still, some people are able to rise to the occasion at times when stress is intense.

different factors, such as the complexity of the task being performed and personal characteristics of the individuals involved. As a result, generalizations about the impact of stress on work effectiveness should be made with considerable caution.

**INDIVIDUAL DIFFERENCES IN RESISTANCE TO STRESS: OPTIMISM AND PESSIMISM** As I noted earlier, it is clear that individuals differ in their resistance to stress. Some people seem to be disease prone—they suffer ill effects from even mild levels of stress. Other people, sometimes referred to as *self-healers,* are able to function effectively even in the face of intense ongoing stress (Friedman, Hawley, & Tucker, 1994). How do such persons differ?

One answer involves the dimension of *optimism–pessimism.* Optimists are people who see the glass as half full; pessimists are those who see it as half empty. Some evidence indicates that optimists—people who have general expectancies for good outcomes (Scheier & Carver, 1988)—are much more stress-resistant than pessimists—people who have general expectancies for poor outcomes. Research seems to indicate that this resistance stems from beneficial changes that occur in their immune system. For example, in one recent study, Segerstrom and her colleagues (1998) examined the effects of optimism on mood and immune changes among law students in their first semester of study. The results showed that optimism was associated with better mood, higher numbers of helper T cells (involved in immune reactions to infections), and higher natural killer cell activity (thought to be important in fighting viral infections and some types of cancers). Additional evidence helps explain why this is the case. Briefly, optimists and pessimists seem to adopt different tactics for coping with stress (Scheier & Carver, 1992). Optimists focus on problem-focused coping: making and enacting specific plans for dealing with sources of stress. They also seek to obtain social support—the advice and help of others (Carver et al., 1993). In contrast, pessimists tend to adopt different strategies, such as giving up the goal with which stress is interfering or denying that the stress exists (Scheier, Weintraub, & Carver, 1986). Needless to say, the former strategies are often more effective than the latter, although *flexibility* seems to be the key: Problem-focused coping is associated with positive outcomes when the source of the stress is controllable, but with poorer outcomes when it is not (Lester, Smart, & Baum, 1994). In short, success in dealing with stress is best accomplished through the use of a wide variety of coping strategies. Table 13.4 presents a summary of strategies adopted by optimists and pessimists.

Web Link: *How to Deal with Stress*

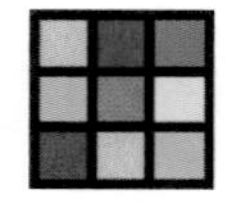

Some evidence also indicates that men and women differ in terms of their choice of coping strategies. Studies have reported that men tend to engage in more problem-focused coping and that females tend to seek social support from friends or to engage in emotion-focused strategies. These findings have been attributed to the different ways men and women are taught to cope with stress (Ptacek, Smith, & Dodge, 1994). A study by Porter and Stone (1995), however, seems to cast doubt on these conclusions. Their results instead indicate that men and women differ very little in the amount of stress they report or in the coping strategies they use to

TABLE 13.4

**Optimists and Pessimists: Contrasting Strategies for Coping with Stress**

Optimists and pessimists employ different strategies in coping with stress. The strategies used by optimists seem to be more effective than those adopted by pessimists.

| Strategies Preferred | Description |
|---|---|
| **By Optimists** | |
| Problem-focused coping | Making specific plans for dealing with the source of stress; implementing such plans |
| Suppressing competing activities | Refraining from other activities until the problem is solved and stress is reduced |
| Seeking social support | Obtaining the advice of others; talking the problem over with others |
| **By Pessimists** | |
| Denial/distancing | Ignoring the problem or source of stress; refusing to believe that it exists or is important |
| Disengaging from the goal | Giving up on reaching the goal that is being blocked by the stressor |
| Focusing on the expression of feelings | Letting off steam instead of working on the problem directly |

cope with the stress. They do differ, however, in terms of the content of their respective problems—men are more likely to report work-related problems, whereas women tend to report problems relevant to themselves, parenting, and interactions with others.

People from different cultures may also differ in this regard. In one study, Chang (1996) examined whether Asian students and students of European descent differed in terms of optimism, pessimism, and their preferences for coping strategies. The results indicated that the Asian students were more pessimistic and tended to use more problem avoidance and social withdrawal as coping strategies.

These and other findings indicate that individuals differ greatly in terms of their ability to deal with stress. Understanding the reasons for such differences can be of considerable practical value. We'll return to various techniques for coping with stress in **Making Psychology Part of Your Life** at the end of this chapter.

**REVIEW QUESTIONS**

- Does stress play a role in physical illness?
- What are the effects of exposure to low levels of stress? High levels?
- Why are some people better able to cope with the effects of stress than others?

**Food for Thought**

Research indicates that access to strong sources of social support can be beneficial. Why do you think this factor reduces the effects of stress?

Web Link: *Go Ask Alice*

# Understanding and Communicating Our Health Needs

There is no doubt that modern medicine has provided us with the means to alleviate many types of disease and illness considered incurable until this century. Yet all the available medicine and technology still does not ensure that we will seek proper treatment when necessary, or that we possess the knowledge or skills necessary to realize when help is required. Moreover, because of the beliefs and attitudes we hold, it's often difficult for health professionals to get us to comply with health-promoting advice.

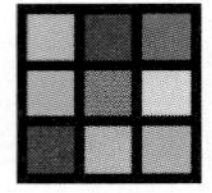

Consider, for example, the results of an Australian study in which people were asked to identify the behavior patterns responsible for health problems in their country (Hetzel & McMichael, 1987). The most frequently cited examples were alcohol and drug abuse, poor diet, lack of exercise, and smoking—a clear indication that respondents were aware of the health risks associated with these behaviors. Similarly, when asked to name the changes that would most likely improve their own health, the respondents cited better diet, more exercise, stopping or reducing smoking, reducing alcohol consumption, and coping better with their worries—again proof that they knew what they were supposed to do to improve their health. Yet when they were asked why they had not made changes in the behaviors they considered most essential to improving their own health, their answers—including "laziness," "lack of time," "not worthwhile," "too difficult or expensive," or "lack of social support"—suggested that sufficient motivation to change was simply not there. This seems to indicate an important role for health psychologists: not only to help people achieve a better understanding of their health needs and to inform them about the risks of specific unhealthy behaviors, but also to identify techniques to reduce or eliminate unhealthy behaviors and to promote the adoption of healthy lifestyles.

CourseCompass
Web Link: *Testing Four Competing Theories of Health-Protective Behavior*

## Health Beliefs: When Do We Seek Medical Advice?

As we discovered in Chapter 3, we all experience bodily sensations, such as the steady beating of our heart or the rush of air flowing in and out of our lungs as we breathe. But certain sensations—like irregularities in heartbeat, tiny aches and pains, a slight queasiness, or a backache—are often termed *symptoms,* because they may reflect an underlying medical problem. How do we decide that a symptom is severe enough to require medical attention? Many different factors may help determine the conditions under which we actually go to a doctor, clinic, or emergency room. People sometimes report symptoms or seek out medical attention when something is clearly wrong. Frequently, however, they do *not* seek appropriate help, even when they know that something is seriously wrong (Locke & Slaby, 1982). Why is this so?

The **health belief model,** initially developed to help explain why people don't use medical screening services, may help us to understand the reasons. This model (see Figure 13.5) suggests that our willingness to seek medical help depends on (1) the extent to which we perceive that a threat to our health exists, and (2) the extent to which we believe that a particular behavior will effectively reduce that threat (Rosenstock, 1974). The perception of a personal threat is influenced by our health values, our specific beliefs about our susceptibility to a health problem, and our beliefs concerning the seriousness of the problem. For example, we may decide to stop engaging in unprotected sex or sex with multiple partners if we value our health, if we feel that our risky behavior might lead to contracting HIV, and if we don't like what we hear about death from AIDS.

**Health Belief Model:** A theory of health behaviors; the model predicts that whether or not a person practices a particular health behavior may depend on the degree to which the person perceives a personal health threat and believes that practicing the behavior will reduce that threat.

Our perceptions as to whether our behavior will be effective in reducing a health threat—in this case the risk of contracting the virus that causes AIDS—depend on whether we believe that a particular practice will reduce the chances we will contract a particular illness and whether we feel the potential benefits of the practice are worth the effort. For example, a person concerned about contracting AIDS may actually practice safe sex if that person believes that the use of condoms will reduce the risk of exposure to the HIV and that the benefits of using condoms so will outweigh the pleasures of high-risk unprotected sex (Kelly & Kalichman, 1998).

The health belief model helps explain why certain people, especially young persons and adults who have never experienced a serious illness or injury, often fail to engage in actions that would be effective in preventing illness or injury—such as wearing a condom during sexual intercourse or using a safety belt when driving a car (Taylor & Brown, 1988). They don't engage in such preventive health-protecting actions because, in their minds, their likelihood of experiencing illness or injury is very low—so why bother?

The health belief model also suggests that if people believe that their actions will be ineffective in changing their health status, they will be less likely to seek help or engage in healthy behaviors. For example, suppose you are overweight and have a family history of high blood pressure. Because you do not believe that anything can be done to lessen your genetic predisposition for heart attacks, you may refuse to adhere to a recommended diet and exercise program, even when you begin to experience symptoms.

**Figure 13.5**
**When Do People Seek Out Medical Treatment?**

According to the health belief model, our willingness to seek medical help depends on the extent to which we (1) perceive a threat to our health and (2) believe that a particular behavior will effectively reduce that threat.

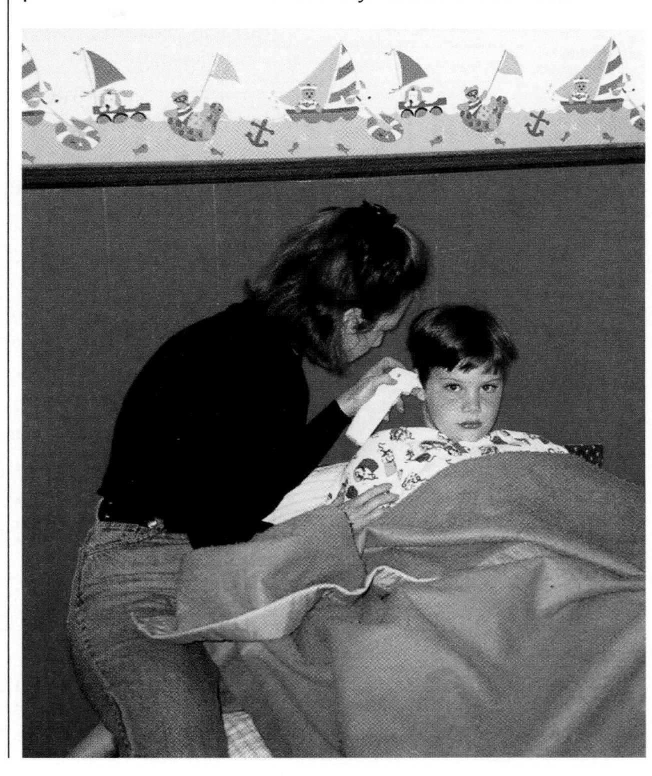

## Doctor–Patient Interactions: Why Can't We Talk to Our Doctors?

Audio 13.3: *Doctor-Patient Relationships*

Web Link: *From Intimidation to Participation*

Imagine the following situation: You have been waiting in a crowded doctor's office for forty-five minutes beyond your scheduled appointment time. Just before you reach the end of your rope, the nurse finally calls your name. Relieved finally to get away from the congestion of the waiting room, you swallow the choice words you've been saving for the doctor. But then, adding insult to injury, she sticks her head in the door of the examining room, says, "Please be seated, I'll be right back"—and leaves! Fully twenty minutes pass before she returns. She offers no apology for the delay. After a rapid succession of questions, pokes, and prods, the doctor scribbles a prescription onto a piece of paper and says, "Take two of these four times a day, and call my office in a week if you have further problems." Then she promptly leaves once more.

If aspects of the preceding example sound familiar, then you may recognize the frustration that stems from ineffective doctor–patient interactions. Research has shown that the most frequently observed communication skills exhibited by doctors during actual medical examinations are those dealing with the mechanics of a patient's illness; for example, direct physical examination of relevant areas of the body and explanation of the nature of prescribed medication and therapy (Duffy, Hamerman, & Cohen, 1980). In contrast, the skills observed least frequently are those related to the psychosocial aspects of patients' problems, such as asking patients what they know or how they feel about their illnesses.

A study by Ford, Fallowfield, and Lewis (1996) found similar results during "bad news" consultations between physicians and newly referred cancer patients in a London hospital. These researchers observed that the doctor–patient interactions were typically clinician-dominated rather than patient-centered. For example, the physicians tended to use closed questions—ones that require only a yes-or-no response—rather than open questions, and patients were seldom given the opportunity to initiate discussion or offer comments. In addition, discussions of psychosocial issues were rare. This was surprising, given the fact that these conversations typically centered on the painful nature of cancer treatments and the possibility that the patients might die.

A rapidly growing body of evidence on this topic suggests that patient–doctor rapport and the quality of information communicated are critical factors both in the successful treatment of disease and in patients' satisfaction with the treatment they receive (Hall, Roter, & Milburn, 1999). Why is patient satisfaction important? Research shows that patients who are more satisfied are more likely to adhere to their treatment regiments and less likely to change physicians, thereby ensuring continuity of their treatment (DiMatteo & Di Nicola, 1982). Greater patient satisfaction is also associated with additional beneficial outcomes, including better emotional health and fewer hospitalizations (Hall et al., 1999).

What do doctors perceive as their role during medical examinations? The results of a study by Wechsler and his colleagues (1996) suggest that even among doctors, opinions seem to change over time. In 1994 these researchers surveyed physicians to learn their opinions regarding (1) the forms of health-promoting behavior they felt were important to convey to their patients, and (2) the extent to which they considered certain health-promotion responsibilities as part of their job. Then the researchers compared the results of the survey to one administered

**Figure 13.6**
**The Changing Role of Physicians in Health Promotion: Then and Now**

Physicians surveyed in 1994 were more likely to endorse medically relevant tasks as "definitely" part of their role than were physicians surveyed in 1981. In contrast, physicians in the 1981 sample were more likely to endorse psychosocial, or supportive, behaviors as "definitely" part of their role.
(*Source:* Based on data from Wechsler et al., 1996.)

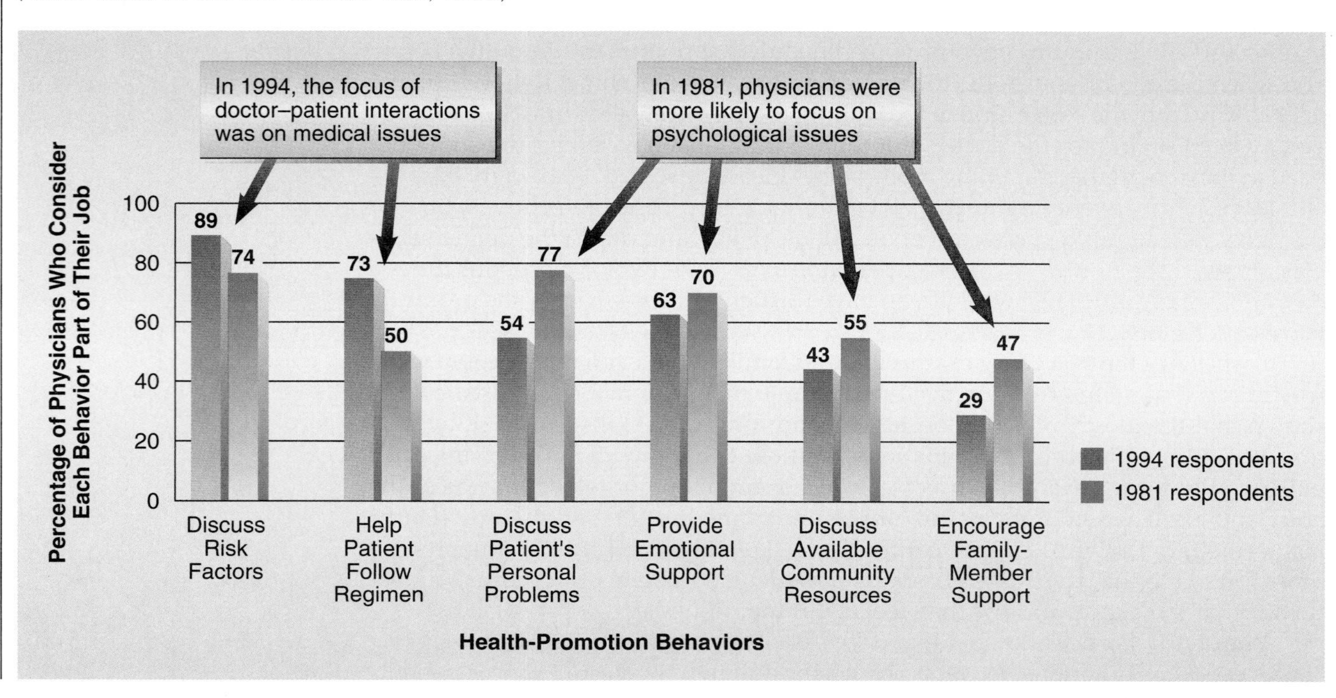

thirteen years earlier. The results showed, first, that compared to the physicians surveyed in 1981, a greater percentage of those surveyed in 1994 felt that discussing health risk factors with their patients, such as the dangers of smoking or the risk of fatty foods, was an important part of their job. Second, when asked which of several responsibilities physicians considered to be "definitely" part of their job, an interesting pattern emerged: The 1994 respondents were more likely to endorse medically relevant tasks as "definitely" part of their role than were the 1981 respondents (see Figure 13.6). In contrast, the 1981 respondents were more likely to endorse psychosocial, or supportive, behaviors as "definitely" part of their role.

Together, these studies underscore the importance of training in communication skills for health care professionals. In order to be effective in treating patients and promoting their wellness, doctors, nurses, and other health professionals need to know how to get their message across—how to communicate effectively with the persons who come to them for help.

For information on how the availability of medical information on the Internet has begun to change the nature of doctor–patient interactions, please see the **From Science to Practice** section that follows.

from SCIENCE to PRACTICE

## Surfing for Solutions to Medical Problems on the Internet: Using Information Technologies to Diagnose Our Illnesses

Imagine that a college student is awakened in the middle of the night by a throbbing headache and achy muscles. Suspecting that she might have contracted the flu that's been going around, she heads for the medicine cabinet to get some aspirin. She switches on the bathroom light—and gasps at the sight of her image in the mirror. Red blotches, ones she's never seen before, have erupted on her face and neck; further inspection reveals that her body is covered with them. What will she do? One possibility is to head straight to the nearest emergency room. But such visits are expensive, and her health plan doesn't cover them, so she decides against this course of action. Another option is to return to bed and phone a doctor in the morning, but there is no guarantee that the doctor will be able to see her right away. A third option—and one that an increasing number of people would choose—is to search the Internet for information that will help her to diagnose the problem herself. She walks quickly to her computer, turns it on, and begins to surf the Net for clues that may shed some light on her illness.

Going to the doctor for our health concerns used to be a highly predictable ritual: You would show up, be told what was wrong and what needed to be fixed, and then obey the doctor's instructions. But recent developments have greatly changed this picture for many people. Frustrated by busy doctors and the cumbersome managed-care system, many people are quietly taking matters into their own hands: They consult the vast array of health-related information that is now available from sources other than physicians. Newspapers and television news programs dedicate more space and time to health news than ever before. Bookstore shelves sag under the weight of health-related books and audiotapes. And a growing number of superstar doctors, from psychologist Laura Schlessinger to Dr. Dean Edell, host radio talk shows that offer on-the-spot advice on a wide range of health-related issues.

But the information source that is quickly becoming the most ubiquitous—and potentially the most dangerous—is the Internet. Patients anxious to participate in decisions about their own treatment are turning increasingly to the Internet to obtain confirmation of diagnoses, validate physician-recommended treatment, or seek alternative therapies (Bader & Braude, 1998). The World Wide Web has become a clearinghouse of information where, with the click of a mouse, people can get instant access to medical and mental health advice (see Figure 13.7 on page 508).

Unfortunately, this practice can prove to be risky business. Why? One reason is that the Internet is largely unpoliced; the quality and accuracy of the information contained there varies considerably. Some of the nation's top medical research facilities have created publicly accessible Web sites, but so too have unethical individuals and businesses trying to sell drugs or therapies that do not have scientific evidence to support their use.

Another reason is that the information patients find on the Internet can have unpredictable effects on them. Web sites that hype new, untested cures for deadly diseases may fill patients with false hope, prompting them to abandon treatments already under way or to delay urgently needed procedures that could save their life. Conversely, sites that offer accurate but graphic details about an illness may cause people already anxious about their health to avoid seeking medical treatment altogether. In other words, for people who do

**Figure 13.7**
**Surfing for Medical Advice on the World Wide Web**

Patients are using the Internet to find their way to the best doctors, confirm diagnoses, validate physician-recommended advice, and obtain important sources of social support at times when they need it the most.

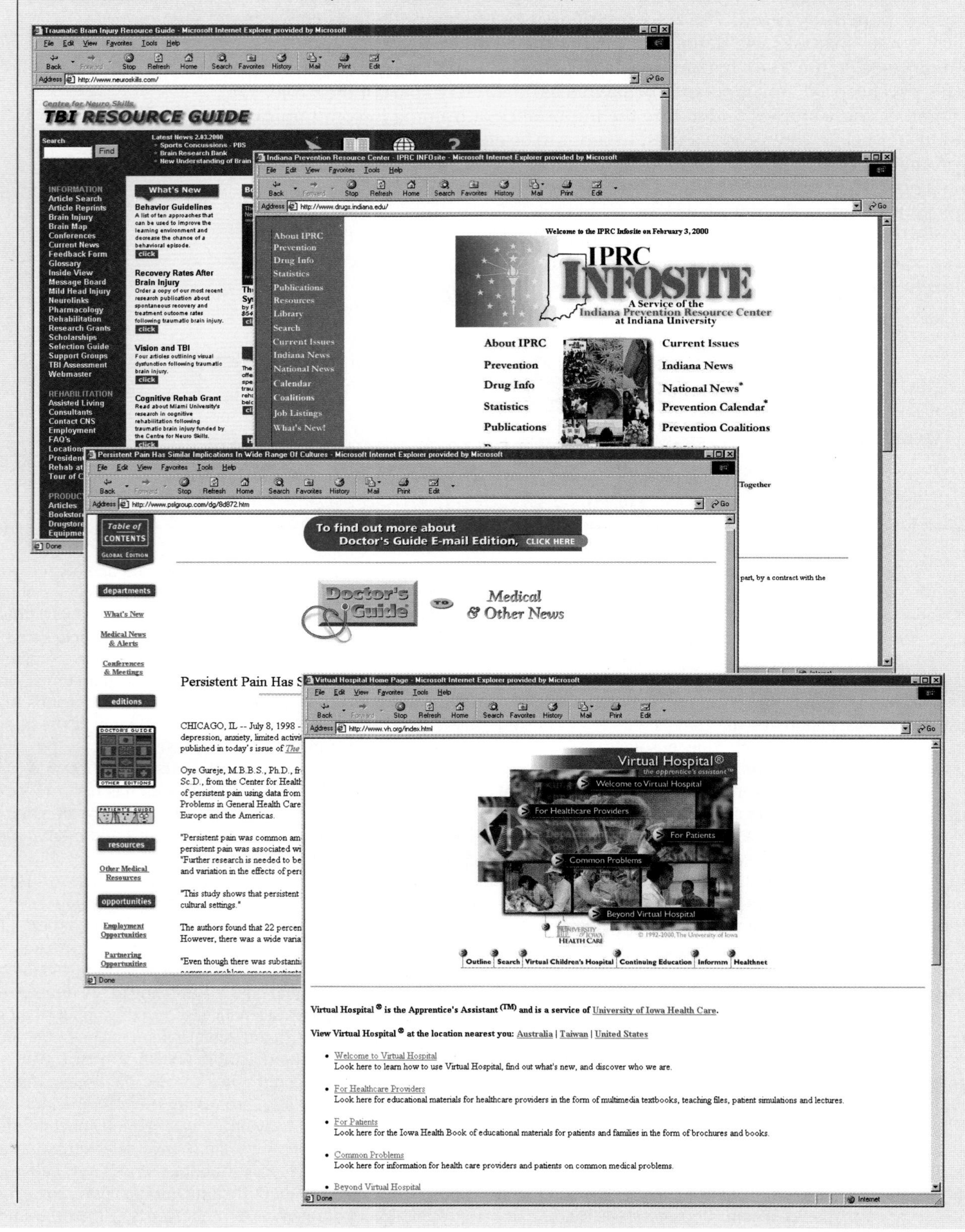

not have specialized medical training or someone so trained to guide them, a little knowledge can be a dangerous thing.

Still, with all its problems, the Internet is a useful medical tool. With a little effort, patients can find their way to excellent doctors, cutting-edge research, and sources of social support at the time when they need it the most (Landro, 1998). Although some physicians are reportedly put off by patients who try to second-guess them with information gleaned from the Internet, others say that Internet-savvy patients actually make their lives easier. Patients quickly develop a working knowledge of their illness and, as a result, take a more informed and active role in their treatment—including soliciting a second opinion if their physician's assessment varies dramatically from what they've uncovered through their research. Patient education via the Internet can also save valuable time that can be used for more productive communication between doctor and patient, such as discussions of treatment options and the advantages and disadvantages associated with each one. Finally, the Internet may eventually lead to better treatment outcomes by providing both patients and their doctors with increased access to information that will enable them to work together to make more informed medical decisions.

**REVIEW QUESTIONS**

- Why are symptoms and sensations important?
- What is the health belief model?
- What factors determine our willingness to make lifestyle changes or to seek medical help?
- Why is it important for psychologists to study aspects of doctor–patient interactions?

**Food for Thought**

Do you think it is wise for people to use medical information they find on the Web to self-diagnose their health problems? Why or why not?

## Behavioral and Psychological Correlates of Illness: The Effects of Thoughts and Actions on Health

Web Link: *Coping with Cancer*

We are frequently exposed to media accounts of miraculous cures of cancer or other serious illnesses. Although one should be extremely skeptical of such reports, a possible basis for these events is becoming clear. **Cancer,** a group of illnesses in which proliferating abnormal cells overwhelm normal tissue, is often viewed as a physical illness with a definite genetic component; but mounting evidence suggests that psychological variables interact in important ways with physical conditions to determine cancer's progression (McGuire, 1999). In other words, aspects of our behavior, perceptions, and personality can affect the onset and course of this often life-threatening illness.

One common characteristic among individuals from families with high cancer rates is a diminished efficiency of their *natural killer cells*—cells designed specifically for the surveillance and destruction of cancerous tumor cells (Kiecolt-Glaser & Glaser, 1992). In most cases, however, whether we actually develop a cancer or other illness is moderated by **risk factors**—aspects of lifestyle that affect our chances of developing or contracting a particular disease, within the limits established by our genes (American Cancer Society, 1989).

A deadly class of risk factors are behaviors within our lifestyle that increase our exposure to **carcinogens**—cancer-producing agents in our environment. Tobacco and the smoke it produces, chemicals in the food we eat and the air we breathe,

**Cancer:** A group of illnesses in which abnormal cells proliferate, invade, overwhelm normal tissues, and spread to distant sites in the body.

**Risk Factors:** Aspects of our environment or behavior that influence our chances of developing or contracting a particular disease, within the limits established through our genetic structure.

**Carcinogens:** Cancer-producing agents in our environment.

**Cardiovascular Disease:** All diseases of the heart and blood vessels.

alcohol in the beverages we drink, and the radiation we receive from overexposure to the sun have all been implicated to some extent as carcinogens. It was because of concerns about exposure to such substances that in 1994 many people in the United States protested plans to sell milk from cows fed large amounts of growth hormones; the protesters didn't want such substances in their milk. A more recent example has been the public's response to genetically modified crops. Some of these products, such as corn, have been altered to produce their own pesticides. Consumers worry about the possible effects these products may have on their health and on the ecology in general.

Are such concerns warranted? Even the experts cannot agree. On the one hand, a large body of research demonstrates that long-term exposure to carcinogens increases the risk of getting cancer. Critics point out, however, that conclusions about certain environmental carcinogens are often based on animal studies that use concentrations of substances that are many times greater than their occurrence under natural conditions.

Still, because people create some cancer risks through their own behaviors, psychologists can play a crucial role in preventing cancer and other health problems by developing interventions that reduce individuals' exposure to potential carcinogens and promote healthy behaviors such as exercise and a proper diet. We'll now consider several behavioral risk factors that may contribute to the development of certain illnesses.

Web Link: *Action on Smoking Health*

Video 13.3: *Effects of Smoking*

Audio 13.4: *Tobacco Companies Pay*

Audio 13.5: *Smokeless Tobacco*

## Smoking: Risky for You and Everyone around You

Smoking is the largest preventable cause of illness and premature death (death before age sixty-five) in the United States, accounting for about 430,000 deaths annually in the United States alone (Centers for Disease Control, 1997). It is the leading cause of several types of cancer, including cancers of the lung, larynx, bladder, and cervix (Fry, Menck, & Winchester, 1996). Smoking also causes **cardiovascular disease** (disease of the heart and blood vessels). But despite the numerous risks associated with smoking—and the numerous health benefits of quitting—more than 25 percent of adults in the United States, some 47 million individuals, currently smoke (Centers for Disease Control, 1996a); and the figure is even higher elsewhere in the world. Unfortunately, the harmful effects of smoking do not end with the smoker. Smoking during pregnancy can have harmful effects on the developing fetus. And exposure to secondhand smoke causes an estimated 3,000 nonsmokers to die of lung cancer and up to 300,000 children to suffer from respiratory tract infections annually in the United States (Centers for Disease Control, 1999).

Public health officials are particularly concerned about recent changes in smoking trends. One concern stems from the fact that the regular annual declines in the percentages of smokers observed since the mid-1960s began to stall around 1990. The percentage of people who smoke decreased from about 50 percent in 1965 to about 25 percent in 1990. However, the percentage of smokers has remained fairly constant since then. Another concern is that smoking is actually rising among certain groups, especially among high school students and pregnant teens in the United States, and people in developing nations (Centers for Disease Control, 1999; National Center for Health Statistics, 1999; Rothenberg & Koplan, 1990). Federal lawmakers are hopeful that legislation restricting both the sale of tobacco products to teens and advertising campaigns that target persons in these groups will reverse this trend. (Please refer to the **Beyond the Headlines** feature on page 512 for additional information on antismoking campaigns.)

Given the overwhelming evidence against smoking, then, why do people smoke? Genetic, psychosocial, and cognitive factors all seem to play a role. Individual differences in our reaction to **nicotine,** the addictive substance in tobacco, suggest that some people are biologically predisposed to become addicted to nicotine, whereas others remain unaffected—evidence that our genes play a role in determining who will become a smoker (Pomerleau, 1995; Pomerleau & Kardia, 1999). Nicotine enhances the availability of certain neurotransmitter substances, including acetylcholine, norepinephrine, dopamine, and endogenous opioids. As you may recall from Chapter 2, these substances produce temporary improvements in concentration, recall, alertness, arousal, and psychomotor performance that can be extremely pleasurable for some people. Perhaps the best evidence for a genetic association for cigarette smoking behavior comes from recent studies of genes involved in dopamine transmission (Lerman et al., 1999; Sabol et al., 1999). These studies show that individuals with a particular gene characteristic—termed SLC6A3-9—are significantly less likely to be smokers. Moreover, smokers with the SLC6A3-9 gene type are also significantly less likely to start smoking before sixteen years of age and are more likely to quit smoking than smokers without the gene type.

Other evidence suggests that psychosocial factors play a role in establishing smoking behavior, especially among young persons. Adolescents are more likely to begin smoking if their parents or other role models smoke, or if they experience peer pressure to do so (Aloise-Young et al., 1994). A 1994 report by the U.S. Surgeon General also suggests that about 90 percent of smokers report having smoked their first cigarette by age eighteen—and that very few people begin to smoke after age twenty (U.S. Department of Health and Human Services, 1994). These data highlight the urgent need for prevention programs targeting young people.

Finally, cognitive factors appear to influence people's tendency to continue smoking. Research suggests, for example, that smokers frequently hold inaccurate perceptions about the risks of smoking (Weinstein, 1998). Smokers consistently acknowledge that smoking increases their health risks; but compared to nonsmokers, smokers tend to underestimate these risks. Smokers also tend to minimize the personal relevance of the risks of smoking. For example, they tend not to believe that they are as much at risk as other smokers of becoming addicted or of suffering negative health effects. Please note, however, that some research reveals cultural differences in the degree of risk associated with smoking. In one study, Vrendenburgh and Cohen (1995) found that Asian participants perceived smoking to be less risky than African American, White, or Hispanic American participants.

Unfortunately, efforts to get people to quit smoking have not been very effective. Although more than 40 percent of adult smokers, on average, make an attempt to quit each year, only a small percentage of them are able to maintain abstinence even for short periods of time (Centers for Disease Control, 1993). What makes a treatment program effective? A recent review of smoking-cessation programs revealed that certain key characteristics are associated with better treatment outcomes (Wetter et al., 1998). First, interventions delivered by trained health care providers tend to be more effective than self-help programs (e.g., videotapes, audiotapes, pamphlets). Second, the content of smoking-cessation interventions and the specific behavior-change programs used also seem to make a difference (see Table 13.5 on page 512). Most effective appear to be aversive procedures, ones designed to associate smoking stimuli with feeling ill (e.g., rapid smoking), followed by interventions that include either a supportive component or training in problem solving to help smokers identify and cope with situations or problems that increase the likelihood of smoking. Third, the intensity of the person-to-person contact, as measured by the amount of time the clinician spends with smokers, has a direct influence on treatment effectiveness: More contact leads to higher cessation rates. Finally, the use of nicotine replacement therapies (e.g., patch, gum), especially when combined with an intensive psychosocial intervention tailored to the needs of individual smokers, tends to improve smoking-cessation rates considerably (Silagy et al., 1994; Tang, Law, & Wald, 1994).

**Nicotine:** The addictive substance in tobacco.

**TABLE 13.5**

**Relative Effectiveness of Smoking-Cessation Interventions**

A comparison of different types of smoking-cessation interventions shows they differ in their ability to help smokers kick the habit.

| Type of Intervention | Estimated Smoking-Cessation Rates |
|---|---|
| No-intervention comparison group | 8.8% |
| Aversive smoking | 17.5% |
| Social support (providing support or encouragement as a component of treatment) | 15.2% |
| General problem solving | 13.7% |
| Quit smoking on a specific date | 11.5% |
| Motivational programs | 9.8% |
| Weight, diet, or nutrition management | 9.8% |
| Exercise or fitness programs | 9.6% |
| Contingency contracts (rewards for compliance; costs for noncompliance) | 9.1% |
| Relaxation or breathing techniques | 7.5% |
| Cigarette fading (gradually reducing cigarettes smoked or amount of nicotine) | 6.4% |

(*Source*: Based on data from Wetter et al., 1998.)

## the HEADLINES: *As Psychologists See It*

## A New Weapon in the Antismoking Arsenal

### Smoking Not So Sexy, New Campaigns Say

WALL STREET JOURNAL (NOVEMBER 29, 1998)—A potent new weapon is surfacing in the battle against smoking: impotence! Scientists have known about links between smoking and sexual problems for several years. Smoking can harm a man's sexual function because it constricts blood vessels, compromising blood flow. But doctors and health-advocacy groups—in some cases emboldened by the global publicity for the drug Viagra—are just now beginning to trumpet the warnings. The State of California has been running a $21 million antismoking campaign featuring a TV commercial in which a man's efforts at flirtation fail when his cigarette goes limp. "Cigarettes," says the spokesperson, "Still think they're sexy?" Similarly, in Thailand, where 90 percent of all smokers are male, cigarette packs are now required to carry the following warning: "Cigarette smoking causes sexual impotence." That message, one of a series of tough warnings to be printed in rotation, must be plastered in white letters on a black background covering one-third of each pack. "If men are not concerned about their heart or their lungs, maybe they will be concerned about their sex life," says Prakit Vathirsathojkit, secretary-general of the National Committee for Control of Tobacco Use, who provided the impetus for the Thai package warning, believed to be the first in the world. Other Asian countries—which have half the world's smokers—are watching the Thai program closely. Cigarette makers, who have devoted huge sums to strengthen smoking's macho, sexy image, are mum on the subject.

Despite their obvious appeal to consumers, will marketing efforts such as the ad shown in Figure 13.8 succeed where many other approaches to get people to kick the smoking habit have failed? Experts have their doubts. Why? One reason, as we saw earlier, is that some people may be biologically predisposed to nicotine addiction, making quitting especially difficult for these smokers (Pomerleau, 1995). Another reason is that ads that attempt to persuade people to stop smoking by playing on their fears, in this case the fear of impotence, typically don't work, or work only for some people (Keller, 1999). A third reason is that for the most part the new ads are targeted at men. Unfortunately, some of the most significant increases in cigarette smoking in the world over the past decade have occurred among women (Boyle, 1993). A fourth reason pertains to the powerful forces that continue to promote smoking. Cigarette makers have invested huge sums of money in campaigns designed to portray smoking as macho or sexy, and these efforts may be difficult to overcome. Added to this have been the emergence of discount brands of cigarettes that cost only a dollar a pack and the tobacco industry's use of discount coupons on cigarettes that lower the real price of premium brands.

**Figure 13.8**
**A New Weapon in the Antismoking Arsenal**

Although scientists have known about the link between smoking and sexual problems for several years, doctors and health advocacy groups have only recently incorporated this theme into antismoking campaigns.

A more recent threat that has not yet been the subject of antismoking campaigns is a tobacco product currently popular among teenagers: candy-flavored cigarettes called bidis. Despite containing less tobacco than a U.S. cigarette, an unfiltered bidi releases two to three times more tar and nicotine, making them potentially more addictive. Additionally, the leaves used to wrap the tobacco in bidis are not porous, which means smokers must inhale often and deeply to keep them lit; this results in the absorption of especially large quantities of nicotine and toxins. Besides the candy-flavored taste contained in the wrapper, observers cite several other reasons for bidis' appeal to teenagers: Teens tend to view smoking bidis as exotic and hip; bidis are often sold in health food stores, so teenagers perceive them as more "natural" and therefore less harmful than regular cigarettes; and finally, bidis tend to be cheaper than other cigarettes.

Where does all of this leave us? Smoking continues to be this country's largest preventable cause of death, and interventions designed to help people quit smoking—including ad campaigns and cigarette warnings—have not been effective. Still, psychologists and other health care professionals remain optimistic. In light of recent advances in our understanding of the genetic, psychosocial, and cognitive factors that contribute to smoking, they remain convinced that the development of effective interventions to enable people to kick the habit—or avoid it altogether—may be right around the corner.

### CRITICAL THINKING QUESTIONS

1. What factors do you believe contribute most heavily to people's decision to start smoking?
2. Do you believe the impotence ad campaign described in this section will be effective in getting men to stop smoking? Why or why not?
3. Given that bidis are especially popular among teenagers, do you think the government should develop ads to inform teens of the dangers they pose? Should the government take steps to ban the sale of bidis in the United States? Why or why not?

## Diet and Nutrition: What You Eat May Save Your Life

Audio 13.6: *Nutritional Advice*

Poor dietary practices can dramatically increase individuals' risk of developing chronic diseases. A poor diet has been most closely linked with cancers of the colon and rectum. Colorectal cancer is one of the leading causes of cancer deaths in the United States, killing more than 56,000 people annually (Landis et al., 1998). Fortunately, regular consumption of certain foods, particularly fresh fruits and vegetables, may *reduce* a person's risk of developing these cancers. Regular exercise has also

Web Link: *Fat and Cholesterol*

been shown to have a protective effect against the development of colorectal cancer (Harvard Center for Cancer Prevention, 1996; World Cancer Research Fund, 1997).

Diet is also a significant risk factor in the development of *cardiovascular disease*, a term used to describe all diseases of the heart and blood vessels, including arteriosclerosis (hardening of the arteries), coronary heart disease (reduced blood flow to the heart muscle), and stroke (bursting of a blood vessel in the brain) (McGinnis & Meyers, 1995). Most cardiovascular diseases affect the amount of oxygen and nutrients that reach organs and other tissues; prolonged oxygen and nutrition deficiency can result in permanent damage to the organs or tissues and even death. *Arteriosclerosis,* the major cause of heart disease in the United States, is caused by the buildup of cholesterol and other substances on arterial walls, which leads to a narrowing of those blood vessels.

High levels of a certain type of **serum cholesterol,** or blood cholesterol, are strongly associated with increased risk of cardiovascular diseases (Allred, 1993; Klag et al., 1993). "Bad" or *LDL cholesterol* clogs arteries, and is therefore the kind that places us most at risk of heart disease. *HDL cholesterol* helps clear LDL from the arteries and escorts it to the liver for excretion. In other words, the more LDL you have, the more HDL you need. The amount of cholesterol in our blood is affected by the amount of fat, especially saturated fat, and cholesterol in our diets. Serum cholesterol can be greatly reduced, however, through a diet that is low in fats, cholesterol, and calories, and high in fiber, fruits, and vegetables.

Although the link between dietary practices and good health is clear, it is difficult to get people to adhere to a healthy diet (Brownell & Cohen, 1995). One reason stems from the fact that people generally tend to prefer the taste of high-fat foods over healthier alternatives. They enjoy the oral sensations they experience when they eat foods such as pizza or french fries. But why would such preferences for these foods exist? Research seems to indicate that both genetic and learned factors play a role. Apparently, people and other animals readily learn associations between the sensory properties of food—tastes, textures, and smells—and their nutritional effects on the body (Warwick & Schiffman, 1992). High-fat foods are energy dense—they contain more calories than foods high in carbohydrate or protein—and tend to elevate natural opiate levels in the body. If you recall our discussion in Chapter 2, natural opiates have pain-killing properties that can be extremely pleasurable for some people. Thus, because of these effects, it is not surprising that people learn to prefer eating high-fat foods. Interestingly, when people are given a drug that blocks the effects of opiates and are allowed to choose between different foods, they tend to reduce their intake of fat relative to carbohydrates (Schiffman et al., 1998).

Although getting people to eat the right foods is important, many Americans simply eat *too much.* As I noted in Chapter 10, more than a third of the adults in the United States are too heavy. Most interventions designed to help people lose weight do work initially, but the weight loss achieved through these programs typically does not last (Garner & Wooley, 1991). Why is maintaining weight loss a continuous struggle for some people? As we saw in Chapter 10, a variety of genetic, behavioral, and environmental factors have been shown to play a role (Grilo & Pogue-Geile, 1991). One factor we did not discuss previously, however, involves the *type* of motivation behind the decision to begin dieting (Williams et al., 1996).

According to **self-determination theory** (Deci & Ryan, 1985), long-term maintenance of weight loss depends on whether the motivation for dietary restraint is perceived by the dieter as autonomous or controlled. Overweight persons frequently begin dieting on the advice of their doctor or at the insistence of concerned family members. Under these circumstances, people may feel coerced into losing weight; this is an example of *controlled motivation.* On the other hand, persons who begin a weight-loss program because they want to do it for themselves may experience the same activity (dieting) quite differently; this is an example of *autonomous motivation.* Self-determination theory predicts that autonomously motivated weight

**Serum Cholesterol:** The cholesterol in our blood.

**Self-Determination Theory:** In relation to health and lifestyle, theory suggesting that motivation for health-promoting behaviors is highest when it is autonomous and lowest when these behaviors are prompted by others.

loss will be maintained over time, whereas long-term maintenance of weight loss achieved at the urging of others is less likely. In one study, Williams and his colleagues (1996) explored whether self-determination theory would predict long-term success among a group of overweight persons entering a six-month weight-loss program. The results of their study provided support for the theory: Participants who reported entering the program for themselves (autonomous motivation) attended the program more regularly, lost more weight during the program, and were more likely to maintain the weight loss nearly two years later than persons who reported joining the program because of other people's wishes (controlled motivation). These results indicate that the type of motivation underlying a decision to lose weight may be an important predictor of weight loss and, more importantly, of success in keeping those extra pounds off permanently.

**REVIEW** *QUESTIONS*

- What is cancer?
- What determines who will become addicted to smoking?
- What are the potential consequences of smoking and exposure to secondhand smoke?
- What are the effects of poor dietary practices?
- What is self-determination theory?

## Alcohol Consumption: Here's to Your Health?

Web Link: *Fetal Alcohol Syndrome*

Some evidence shows that moderate alcohol consumption—typically defined as a daily glass of an alcoholic beverage—may be associated with significant health benefits (Hennekens, 1996). The results of several large-scale studies indicate that moderate alcohol consumption can reduce the risk of coronary heart disease. Some of the health-protective effects of alcohol, in particular those conferred by drinking red wine, appear to stem from compounds called *phenolic antioxidants,* so named because these substances slow the damaging cell-oxidation process. These compounds are found in high concentrations in grape skins, seeds, and stems and seem to exert their protective effects by reducing LDL (bad) cholesterol, inhibiting blood clotting, and producing a more favorable HDL–LDL (good-to-bad) cholesterol ratio. Some evidence indicates that moderate alcohol consumers may even live longer than nondrinkers (e.g., Dufour, 1996; Wannamethee & Shaper, 1998).

On the other hand, too much alcohol is harmful and can have damaging effects on our health. Chronic excessive alcohol consumption can lead to deficits in many different cognitive abilities, including learning and memory, perceptual–motor skills, visual–spatial processing, and problem solving (e.g., Evert & Oscar-Berman, 1995; Oscar-Berman et al., 1997). Newer research also suggests that the effects of chronic alcohol exposure may be more diffuse, perhaps leading to an overall reduction in the efficiency of our cognitive functions (Nixon, 1999). One manifestation of this general decline is an inability to tune out irrelevant information in order to focus on the critical aspects of a task. For example, in studies in which participants are asked to focus their attention on only one aspect of a task, say speed *or* accuracy, alcoholics have a difficult time ignoring the irrelevant part of the task, whereas nonalcoholics do not (Nixon, Paul, & Phillips, 1998).

The negative effects of excessive drinking also extend to other aspects of our health. Drinking can lead to stomach disease; cirrhosis of the liver; cancer; impaired sexual functioning; cognitive impairment; and, as we saw in Chapter 8, *fetal alcohol syndrome*, a condition of retardation and physical abnormalities that occurs in children of mothers who are heavy drinkers. Heavy drinking has also been implicated as a risk factor for suicide and suicide attempts (e.g., Borges & Rosovsky, 1996). It also appears to promote the transmission of the virus that causes AIDS, both by interfering with aspects of our immune system and by increasing the likelihood that people will engage in unprotected sex (Dingle & Oei, 1997).

Given the many negative health effects associated with excessive alcohol consumption, why do people continue to drink? Research conducted with both animals and humans seems to indicate that genetic factors play an important role. New findings from animal studies show that genetically engineered "knockout" mice—so named because they lack the gene responsible for production of a brain chemical called neuropeptide Y—drink more alcohol than normal mice and appear to have a greater tolerance for its effects (Thiele et al., 1998). Because neuropeptide Y also appears to calm anxiety, at least in animals, these findings suggest that some alcoholics may drink excessively to relieve stress and help explain the high rates of alcoholism among people with anxiety disorders.

Studies with humans also highlight the role of genetic factors in drinking. Some of the most direct evidence comes from adoption studies investigating rates of alcoholism among adopted children raised apart from their biological parents (refer to Chapter 4 for additional information on the role of genetic factors in alcohol abuse). Such studies show, for example, that biological sons of male alcoholics raised in adoptive homes have higher rates of alcoholism than biological sons of nonalcoholics who grow up under similar circumstances (McGue, 1999). Twin studies that have compared the concordance rate for alcoholism among genetically identical (monozygotic) twins and fraternal (dizygotic) twins—ones who share on average only about half of their genes—also provide support for a genetic link. The term *concordance* refers to the probability of co-occurrence of a condition—in this case, the probability of co-occurrence of alcoholism among pairs of twins. Kendler and his colleagues (1997) examined concordance rates in groups of Swedish male twins born between the years 1902 and 1949. As shown in Figure 13.9, the concordance rates among each group of identical twins always exceeded concordance rates among fraternal twins.

**Figure 13.9**
**Genetic Influences on Drinking**

Research results show that the *concordance* (probability of co-occurrence) rate for alcoholism among identical twins was always higher than the concordance rate among fraternal, or nonidentical, twins.

(*Source:* Based on data from Kendler et al., 1997.)

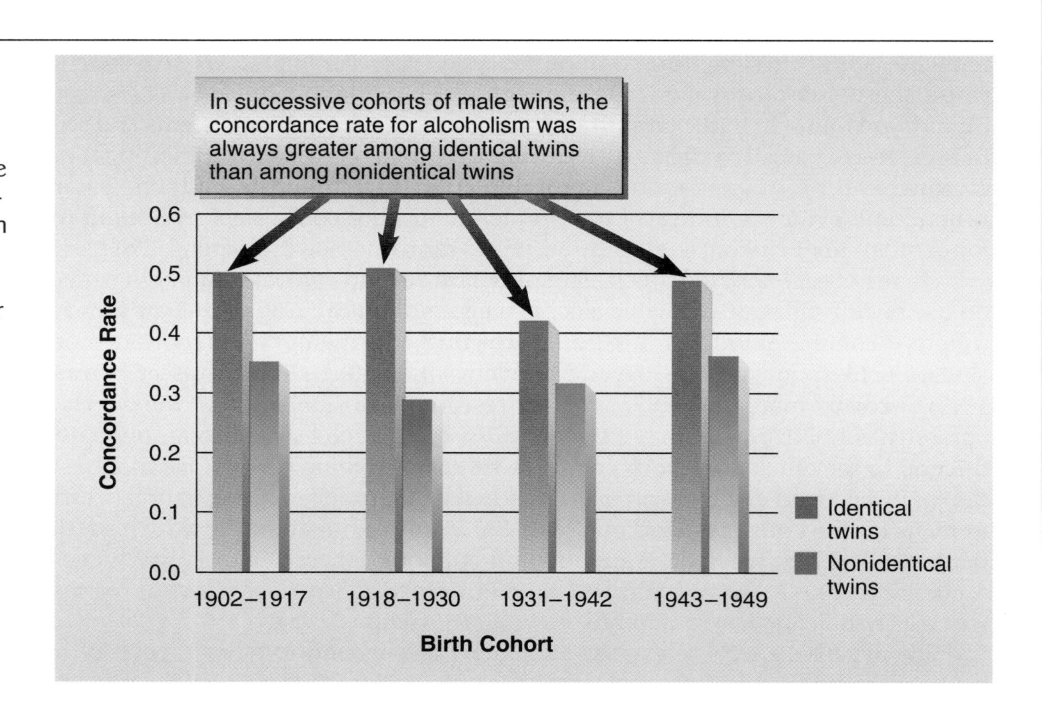

But genetic factors are definitely *not* the only determinants of excessive drinking. The concordance rates just described are substantially less than 100 percent, which means that environmental factors must also be involved. Ironically, the strongest evidence for the role of environmental factors in drinking also comes from studies of adoption. For example, research has shown that children reared in an adoptive family containing an alcoholic member are at significant risk of becoming alcoholics themselves (Cadoret, Troughton, & O'Gorman, 1987). The effects of this source of influence appear to be strongest when the alcoholic family member is a same-sex sibling of about the same age. Related research has also shown that unrelated siblings who are raised together eventually exhibit similar drinking practices (McGue, Sharma, & Benson, 1996). Together, these studies provide evidence that environmental factors also play a significant role in drinking. Let's now turn to a discussion of the effects of emotions on health.

## Emotions and Health

Inadequate emotional expression—especially of negative feelings—can have an adverse effect on the progression of certain types of illness, such as cancer (Levy et al., 1985, 1988). People who tend to experience negative emotions and who also inhibit self-expression in their social interactions are exhibiting a pattern of behavior recently termed the **Type D**—for *distressed*—personality type (Denollet, 1999). Individuals who cope with stress by keeping their negative emotions to themselves are likely to experience suppressed immune systems, greater recurrence of cancer, and higher mortality rates. In contrast, patients who demonstrate positive affect—especially joy, well-being, and happiness—increase the likelihood of recovery.

An intriguing finding is the relation between expression of distress and treatment outcome. Open expression of negative affect and a willingness to fight illness are sometimes associated with greater immune function, decreased recurrence rates, and increased survival time, even among patients at advanced stages of cancer. For example, combative individuals—those who express anger about getting cancer and hostility toward their doctors and family members—often live longer than patients who passively accept their fate and quietly undergo treatment (Levy, 1990).

Emotion can also play a role in the progression of **hypertension,** or high blood pressure, a condition in which the pressure within the blood vessels is abnormally high. Prolonged hypertension, when untreated, can result in extensive damage to the entire circulatory system. Indeed, about 30 percent of cardiovascular disease deaths each year are attributable to hypertension. Some evidence suggests that emotional stressors can affect the regulation of blood pressure through neurohormonal mechanisms (Krakoff et al., 1985). For example, anxiety and hostility can increase general arousal and facilitate the release of *catecholamines*—a class of neurotransmitters that play an important role in the sympathetic nervous system. The release of the catecholamine epinephrine has the effect of boosting a person's overall readiness to act; a rise in blood pressure is part of this overall readiness. Although the effects of emotional stressors are usually brief, extreme reactivity to anxiety, hostility, and anger may indicate a predisposition to develop hypertension (Rosenman, 1988). Not surprisingly, the strongest relations between emotions and blood pressure have been found for unexpressed anger and hostility. Fortunately, as Chapter 12 explained, research has shown that people *can* learn to reduce such tendencies. In one study, Gidron and Davidson (1996) identified a group of participants who scored high on measures of cynical hostility, the harmful component of the *Type A* behavior pattern (refer to Chapter 12 for additional information on Type A behavior). Half of these persons were assigned to an eight-week intervention specifically designed to modify cynical hostility; the other half (the control group) received information about the link between hostility and heart disease and about ways to reduce hostility. Participants assigned to the intervention condition attended weekly meetings,

**Type D:** A personality type characterized by a general tendency to cope with stress by keeping negative emotions to oneself. People who exhibit this behavior pattern are more likely to experience suppressed immune systems and health-related problems.

**Hypertension:** High blood pressure, a condition in which the pressure within the blood vessels is abnormally high.

**AIDS (Acquired Immune Deficiency Syndrome):** A viral infection that reduces the immune system's ability to defend the body against the introduction of foreign substances (antigens).

monitored their hostility daily, and received instruction in the use of specific coping skills; for example, they learned to use relaxation exercises and practiced ways to vent their angry feelings. The results indicated that the intervention was effective: Participants in the intervention group showed significant improvement on measures of cynical hostility, whereas participants assigned to the control group did not. Although these results are preliminary and require confirmation by additional research, they do offer hope to persons who exhibit these tendencies and are therefore at risk for developing health problems later in life.

CourseCompass
Audio 13.7: *Living with AIDS*

## AIDS: A Tragic Assault on Public Health

**AIDS (acquired immune deficiency syndrome)** is a viral disease that reduces the immune system's ability to defend the body against the introduction of foreign substances (antigens). The process by which *HIV (human immunodeficiency virus)* produces AIDS symptoms is complex, but essentially involves the devastation of aspects of the infected person's immune system; this makes the person extremely vulnerable to diseases such as tuberculosis, pneumonia, and several forms of cancer. The first cases of AIDS in the United States were reported in 1981, although it was not until 1984 that the cause of AIDS—the HIV virus—was isolated and an antibody test was developed to detect infection.

CourseCompass
Audio 13.8: *Antibody Testing*

**ACQUIRED IMMUNE DEFICIENCY SYNDROME: THE FACTS ABOUT AIDS** Since 1981 researchers have discovered a number of frightening facts about AIDS. First, the estimated incubation period—the time it takes for the disease to develop—can be as long as ten years. This means that infected individuals can spread the disease to others without even realizing that they are infected. It is estimated that more than 33 million people worldwide are currently infected with HIV and that nearly 14 million people have died from AIDS (UNAIDS, 1998).

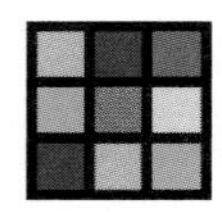

AIDS is most prevalent in parts of Africa, although the spotlight has recently shifted to the Asian continent, particularly in India and China, where HIV is spreading rapidly. Interestingly, in 1996, after more than a decade of continuous increases, the overall number of deaths from AIDS finally declined in the United States (Mann & Tarantola, 1998). But this reduction has not occurred across all groups of people. The incidence of AIDS has actually increased among African

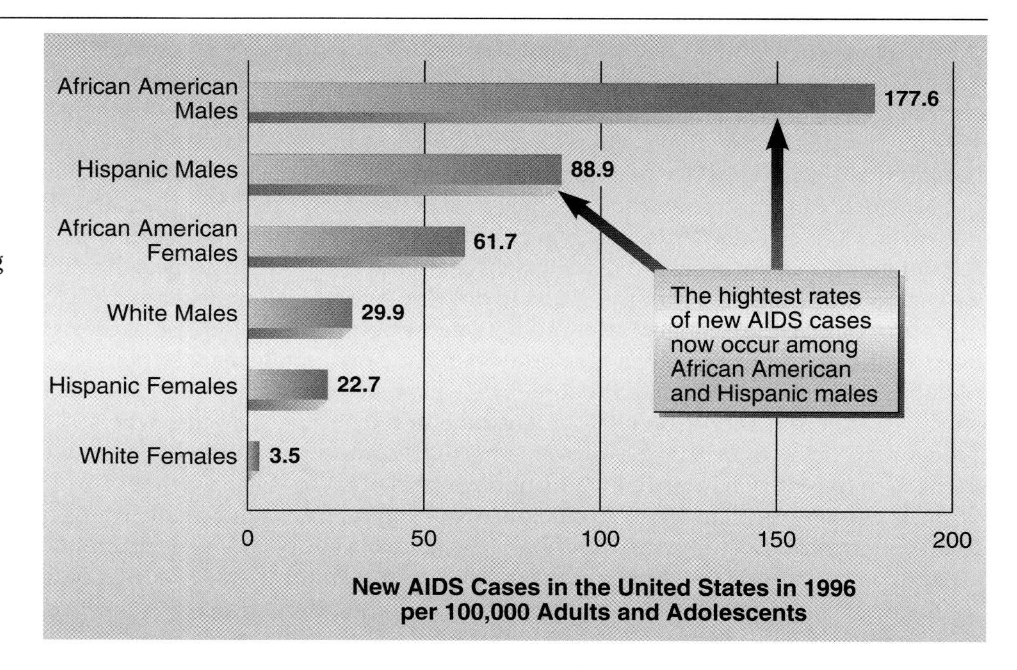


**Figure 13.10**
**Distribution of AIDS in the United States**

The incidence of AIDS among different groups in the United States has shifted during the past decade. The highest rates of new cases now occur among African American and Hispanic males.

(*Source:* Centers for Disease Control, 1997.)

American and Hispanic males as shown in Figure 13.10; these groups now account for most of the new cases of AIDS in this country.

Second, an individual can be infected only if the virus is introduced directly into the bloodstream. This means that the disease cannot be contracted through such actions as shaking hands with or hugging an infected person. Most HIV infections are acquired through unprotected sexual intercourse and infected blood or blood products. Unfortunately, this means that women can pass the disease to their unborn children during pregnancy or delivery or through breast feeding. It is estimated that about 1.2 million children are currently infected with HIV worldwide (UNAIDS, 1998).

Third, until only a few years ago, HIV infection was a virtual death sentence, since it was almost always fatal. Since late 1995, however, several related advances have led to a profound shift in the outlook for some people who are infected with HIV. Scientists have gained a better understanding of how HIV behaves in the body and, as a result, have developed more effective drugs to attack it. Two classes of potent drugs, *protease inhibitors* and *transcriptase inhibitors,* block the HIV from replicating once it has invaded certain cells of the immune system (Bartlett and Moore, 1998). Also, tests developed to monitor viral levels directly have enabled physicians to accurately gauge a therapy's effectiveness (Mellors, 1998). These advances have significantly prolonged the lives of many AIDS patients and reduced the number of deaths from AIDS, at least in industrialized nations and among people who can afford the drug therapies. Currently, the annual costs of the drugs needed to treat the disease exceeds $10,000 (Bartlett & Moore, 1998). Experts are also quick to point out two additional limitations of the new drug therapies: First, it is extremely difficult to get people to comply with the complex regimens they must follow; and second, because HIV readily mutates, drugs that are effective today may not work tomorrow (Richman, 1998). Therefore, the need for interventions that help prevent the spread of AIDS is crucial. We'll consider this issue next.

**HOW PSYCHOLOGISTS CAN HELP PREVENT THE SPREAD OF AIDS** Why are psychologists relevant to the AIDS epidemic? One reason, aside from the tragic consequences of this disease, is that most people contract HIV as a result of certain behaviors. Although AIDS was initially believed to be restricted to homosexuals and intravenous drug users, AIDS is currently being spread worldwide mainly through unprotected *heterosexual* rather than homosexual intercourse (Centers for Disease Control, 1996b). Psychologists are interested in this problem, then, because the only effective means of combating AIDS are prevention programs that focus on changing the behaviors that place people most at risk for acquiring HIV—behaviors such as injecting drugs with previously used needles, engaging in unprotected sex, and having sex with multiple partners (Reinecke, Schmidt, & Ajzen, 1996).

Health psychologists recognize that developing effective AIDS prevention programs is a complicated business. They know, for example, that information campaigns alone—merely teaching people the facts about HIV and AIDS—are often ineffective in changing the behaviors that place people at risk for contracting HIV (Helweg-Larsen & Collins, 1997). They also recognize that techniques effective for a particular target group are not necessarily effective for all groups of people (Coates & Collins, 1998). One model that is useful in developing interventions that accommodate individual and group differences is the *information–motivation–behavioral skills (IMB)* model (Fisher et al., 1994) (see Figure 13.11). According to the IMB model, people are more likely to perform HIV-preventive behaviors to the extent that they (1) know how HIV is acquired and the specific actions they must take to avoid it; (2) are motivated to perform HIV-preventive behaviors and omit risky ones; and (3) possess the skills necessary to perform relevant HIV-preventive behaviors, such as the ability to communicate with and to be appropriately assertive with a potential sexual partner.

The IMB model serves as a framework in which to conduct *elicitation research.* The purpose of this kind of research is to attain specific information about a target group, including their current knowledge of HIV and AIDS, the factors that determine their

**Figure 13.11**
**AIDS-Preventive Behaviors: A Model**

Growing evidence suggests that prevention programs are more effective when they are tailored to meet the needs of specific target groups and when they provide people with the knowledge, motivation, and behavioral skills necessary to perform AIDS-preventive behaviors.
(*Source:* Based on Fisher et al., 1996.)

motivation to reduce their personal risk, and their existing HIV-preventive behavioral skills (Fisher et al., 1994). Elicitation research and the IMB model are useful tools for developing effective behavior-change programs that are specific to the needs of particular target groups. Why? Because they can help researchers uncover the reasons why certain groups of people do not perform AIDS-preventive behavior.

One group that is currently at risk with regard to HIV and AIDS is women. Growing evidence shows that HIV infection rates among women are growing at a rapid rate (UNAIDS, 1998). What is the reason for this increase? The results of elicitation research suggest that several factors play a role. First, the mode of transmission of HIV differs between men and women in ways that place women at significantly greater risk (Amaro, 1995). Most women (67 percent) acquire HIV as a result of intravenous drug use. Women who use drugs add to their risk of contracting HIV if they have unprotected sex with male partners who may also use drugs or have multiple sexual partners. Finally, research has uncovered another risk factor unique to women: The chances of male-to-female transmission of HIV are about twelve times greater than those of female-to-male transmission (Padian, Shiboski, & Jewell, 1990).

Second, gender role differences between men and women may also be involved. For example, adherence to traditional gender roles may increase the chances that some women will succumb to pressure to engage in unprotected sex (Amaro, 1995). A related problem involves differences in the skills required to ensure safe sex. Consider, for example, the skills necessary to ensure the use of a condom during sex. For the man, this simply means putting on the condom. For the woman, however, it means persuading her partner to use a condom or, perhaps, withholding sex if he refuses.

Finally, fear may be an important factor, especially among inner-city women and women in abusive relationships marked by physical violence (Hobfoll et al., 1994). Under conditions like these, in which the potential for personal injury is high, it is understandable that women are reluctant to negotiate safe sex with their partners, let alone refuse to have sex with them.

Can anything be done to reverse this trend? The results of one study suggest the answer is yes. Hobfoll and his colleagues (1994) compared the relative impact of two training programs on measures of HIV-preventive behaviors. Participants in the study, a group of inner-city women, were assigned randomly to one of the programs or to a no-training control group. The interventions differed in terms of their content (HIV-specific information versus general health information) but were otherwise identical. Consistent with the IMB model I described earlier, the HIV-prevention training program was designed to (1) increase the women's knowledge of HIV transmission and prevention; (2) motivate the women to perform HIV-preventive behaviors by highlighting their specific risks of acquiring HIV; and (3) provide them with the behavioral skills necessary to convince their sexual partner to adopt HIV-preventive behaviors, such as wearing a condom during sex. The results showed that the HIV-preventive group outperformed both the health-promotion group and the no-treatment control group on knowledge measures and in terms of self-reported HIV-preventive behaviors. Most importantly, these results highlight the value of models like IMB in guiding the development of more effective interventions.

## REVIEW QUESTIONS

- What are the consequences of heavy consumption of alcohol?
- How is the way in which we express our emotions related to our health?
- What is AIDS? How is HIV transmitted?

## Promoting Wellness: Developing a Healthier Lifestyle

Web Link: *Med Web*

Have you ever wondered why some individuals live to be more than one hundred years old, whereas most people live only sixty or seventy years? Studies of persons who live to be more than one hundred indicate that several factors may play a role in their extended life spans. One of these factors is diet: Long-lived persons often show a pattern involving greater-than-average consumption of grains, leafy green and root vegetables, fresh milk, and fresh fruits; and they tend to eat low to moderate amounts of meat and animal fat. In addition, they maintain low to moderate levels of daily caloric intake (1,200 to 3,000 calories) and consume only moderate amounts of alcohol each day. Physical activity is perhaps the most important factor contributing to longevity and good health among long-lived people. Many work outdoors and walk a great deal. That is, regular physical activity is an integral part of their lives, continuing well into old age. Additional factors that may contribute to their extended life span are continued sexual activity, personality characteristics, family stability, and continued involvement in family and community affairs during advanced years. (Chapter 9 provides additional information on older adults.)

In sum, while genetic factors certainly play a role in determining life span, research suggests that people may be able to extend their lives significantly by adhering to a lifestyle that includes a balanced, low-fat, low-calorie diet; regular exercise; and continued activity during later years (Pelletier, 1986).

On the basis of such findings, a growing number of health professionals and psychologists have adopted an approach to health and wellness that is based on **prevention strategies**—techniques designed to reduce the occurrence of illness and other physical and psychological problems. *Primary prevention* is considered the optimal prevention approach. Its goal is to reduce or eliminate the incidence of preventable illness and injury. Primary prevention strategies usually involve one or more of the following components: educating people about the relation between their behaviors and their health, promoting motivation and skills to practice healthy behaviors, and directly modifying poor health practices through intervention.

*Secondary prevention* focuses on decreasing the severity of illness that is already present by means of early detection. Thus, individuals learn about their health status through medical tests that screen for the presence of disease. Although early detection of certain diseases is traditionally carried out by health professionals and often requires sophisticated medical tests, exciting research is under way to teach patients methods of self-examination, especially for early detection of breast and testicular cancer.

### Primary Prevention: Decreasing the Risks of Illness

In most instances, our initial attempts to change our health behaviors are unsuccessful. Typically, we become aware of the need to change behaviors; we initiate change—and we experience a series of failed attempts at change. Only sometimes do we actually succeed in changing our behaviors. The nature of this process indicates that we need help; a variety of intervention programs to meet our varied needs and purposes.

**Prevention Strategies:** Techniques designed to reduce the occurrence of disease and other physical and psychological problems.

**HEALTH-PROMOTION MESSAGES: MARKETING HEALTHY LIFESTYLES** We are constantly bombarded with messages about health risks. Numerous nonprofit organizations use television commercials, newspaper articles, magazine ads, radio advertising, and now the Internet to warn us about unhealthy behaviors such as smoking, unprotected sex, and alcohol and drug abuse, and to tell us about their associated risks, including cancer, heart disease, and AIDS. These campaigns typically provide information about symptoms that may indicate the presence of a health problem, such as shortness of breath or chest pains in the case of heart attacks, and information about the relation between specific behaviors and disease; for example, "Smoking is the number one cause of heart disease."

But can mass media campaigns alone produce widespread changes in behavior? There is little evidence that they can (Meyer, Maccoby, & Farquhar, 1980). One reason for the limited success of these programs may be the media's depiction and promotion of unhealthy habits, which counteract health-promotion messages (Winett, 1995). For example, Story and Faulkner (1990) computed the frequency of commercials advertising healthy versus unhealthy food and beverages. Most of the prime-time commercials were for unhealthy foods and beverages. The clearest example was the large difference in numbers of commercials for fast-food versus family-style restaurants.

Another reason for the limited success of these programs is that they ignore important individual differences that exist among people, such as different degrees of readiness to change (Prochaska, 1996). As you might expect, interventions tailored to meet the interests and needs of individuals or specific target groups are significantly more effective than general, one-size-fits-all interventions. For example, as part of one smoking-cessation intervention, researchers mailed out birthday cards and other materials that were designed specifically for each of several specific target groups (Azar, 1999). A birthday card tailored for African American participants in the study included the following message:

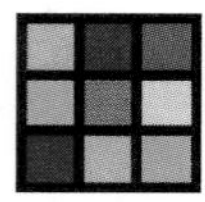

> "Each year, more black Americans die from smoking than from car crashes, AIDS, alcohol, murder, heroin, cocaine, and other drugs put together. If we count the number of people it kills, smoking is the number one problem facing the black community."

The results showed that 32 percent of the participants who received the tailored prevention materials quit smoking, compared to 12 percent among participants who did not. Velicer and Prochaska (1999) found similar results using a computer-based expert system to select intervention components on the basis of individual participants' specific needs and an assessment of their readiness to change.

Third, research suggests that the effectiveness of health-promotion messages depends on the way they are framed (Rothman & Salovey, 1997). Some health-promotion messages seem to work best when they emphasize the benefits of a certain health practice (gain framing), whereas others work best when they emphasize the costs of risky behaviors (loss framing). The relative effectiveness of a gain-framed or loss-framed message depends, at least in part, on whether the function of the recommended behavior is prevention or detection. Research seems to indicate that gain framing works best for *prevention behaviors* that help people to avert the onset or development of a health problem, such as using sunscreen consistently or refraining from smoking cigarettes (Detweiler et al., 1999). In contrast, loss framing seems to work best for messages intended to motivate *detection behaviors*, such as performing regular breast self-examinations or obtaining a yearly mammography screening (Banks et al., 1995).

Finally, some evidence suggests that fear may also play a role in our responses to health-promotion messages. For example, individuals with high fear of contracting AIDS rate advertisements about AIDS as more effective than people with low fear of contracting AIDS (Struckman-Johnson et al., 1990). These findings suggest that ad campaigns regarding deadly diseases such as cancer or AIDS may be able to enhance their effectiveness by playing to people's fear of contracting the disease (see Figure 13.12).

**Figure 13.12**
**Encouraging Health-promoting Behaviors through Fear Messages**

Fear-based messages have been used to encourage health-promoting behaviors among people at risk for serious illnesses such as cancer and AIDS. Research indicates that the people most likely to change their behavior in response to this type of message are those who believe they are susceptible to a disease.

**THE WORK OF STAYING HEALTHY: MOTIVATING THE COUCH POTATO** Research indicates that only one in five U.S. citizens exercises regularly and intensely enough to reduce his or her risk for chronic disease and premature death (Dubbert, 1992). This is surprising, since it is now very well known that regular and vigorous exercise can significantly reduce individuals' risk of cancer and cardiovascular disease, even in the presence of other health risk factors, including smoking, obesity, high blood pressure, and high blood cholesterol (Dishman, 1988). A 1996 U.S. Surgeon General's Report on Physical Activity and Health concluded that even less vigorous forms of activity can be beneficial if done consistently (http://www.cdc.gov/nccdphp/sgr/prerep.htm). According to this report, healthful benefits can be obtained from modest levels of exercise, if performed regularly. What does this mean? Some research seems to indicate that fifteen minutes of running or thirty minutes of walking can produce healthful benefits, although newer evidence suggests that better outcomes, in terms of overall fitness and strength, may be achieved through shorter, more intense aerobic workouts (Winett, 1998) (see Figure 13.13).

Exercise can affect mental health, too. A recent study by Kramer and his colleagues (1999), for example, showed that modest exercise—defined as walking briskly for an hour, three to four days per week—significantly improved the cognitive functioning of a group of older adults who had previously been sedentary for most of their lives. Exercise has also been found to improve self-concept, alleviate feelings of depression, and reduce anxiety (Dubbert, 1992). These effects are particularly apparent just after a workout, but there may also be some long-term mental health benefits from participation in exercise. Changes in mood following exercise may result from socializing and being involved with others (Plante & Rodin, 1990); running with a friend may improve mood because of the companionship the exercise provides. Mood may also improve because of exercise's effect on our self-efficacy—our enhanced confidence in our ability to perform a behavior such as running a mile or completing an aerobics workout (Rodin & Plante, 1989).

**Figure 13.13**
**Exercise and Health: Intensity Seems to Matter**

New evidence indicates that optimal health outcomes, in terms of overall fitness and strength, may be achieved through shorter, more intense aerobic workouts—though perhaps not *quite* as intense as the workout depicted here. Healthful benefits *can* be derived from more moderate forms of exercise, such as walking, if these activities are performed consistently.

(*Source:* CLOSE TO HOME. © John McPherson. Reprinted with permission of UNIVERSAL PRESS SYNDICATE. All rights reserved.)

"Here's the problem! The workout tape has been on fast-forward the whole time!"

So how can we get the rest of the couch potatoes off the couch? Some research suggests that starting and then maintaining an exercise program requires that people arrange their environment so that it supports the desired exercise behavior and weakens competing behaviors. First, it is important to arrange effective cues that become a signal to exercise. Working out in the same location, doing a similar warm-up routine, and recording and posting the results of one's physical activity can be effective in cueing future exercise behavior. It is also important to arrange when exercise occurs, to minimize the effects of the cues for competing behaviors. For example, individuals who have a tendency to work late should establish a morning training routine to minimize competition with a busy work schedule. An increasing number of businesses have helped to minimize schedule conflicts by building on-site exercise facilities for their employees. Second, it is also important to arrange for consequences that maintain exercise behavior. Initially, it is critical for new exercisers to seek out sources of rewards for their exercise behavior and to avoid potential sources of punishment, including muscle soreness, fatigue, and injury. Paradoxically, those most in need of consistent exercise, such as obese or extremely out-of-shape persons or older individuals, may be those most subject to punishing consequences—including the risk of heart attack—if they overdo it (Curfman, 1993; Knapp, 1988). Finally, the presence of a strong social support network can greatly increase adherence to a lifelong exercise habit. Many people find they enjoy exercise more when it is incorporated into social activities they find pleasurable; for example, organized sports or group-based activities such as aerobics or dancing.

## Secondary Prevention: The Role of Early Detection in Disease and Illness

Psychologists are taking an increasingly active role in developing motivational strategies to get people to take part in *early detection* procedures—techniques used to screen for the presence of high blood pressure, high blood cholesterol, and some forms of cancer. The identification of these conditions at an early stage can make an enormous difference in the chances for treatment success—in some cases the difference between life and death.

**SCREENING FOR DISEASE: SEEKING INFORMATION ABOUT OUR HEALTH STATUS** The fact that early detection and treatment of an illness is more effective than later detection and treatment is the foundation for screening programs. Research evidence suggests that the widespread use of available screening techniques could decrease the incidence of cardiovascular disease through the early detection of high blood pressure and cholesterol, and could significantly reduce the number of cervical, colon, and prostate cancer deaths (Murray, 1999; Rothenberg et al., 1987).

Many companies, colleges, community organizations, and hospitals have screening programs to test for high blood pressure and serum cholesterol. Unfortunately, many people either do not take advantage of screening programs at all or fail to get screened regularly. Forgetting and underestimating the time since the last test are the primary reasons people wait too long between screenings. Interventions that heighten awareness or serve a reminder function, such as physician reminder systems and local advertising campaigns, can increase the frequency of screening visits (Mitchell, 1988). As with educational messages used to promote primary prevention, researchers also believe that educational messages used to promote screening procedures need to be tailored to people's varying levels of knowledge and screening frequency; for example, a person who has never had a screening will require a different motivational message than the person who believes that a single screening is enough (Murray, 1999).

The most significant factors that predict an individual's use of screening, as indicated by the health belief model, are the person's beliefs about the possible benefits of screening, perceptions of the severity of possible illnesses, perceptions of his or her vulnerability to disease, and beliefs about what other people (friends, family) think about screening (Hennig & Knowles, 1990).

**SELF-EXAMINATION: DETECTING THE EARLY SIGNS OF ILLNESS** Self-examination can be instrumental in the early detection of both testicular and breast cancer. The cure rate for testicular cancer is extremely high—over 90 percent—if the cancer is detected early. Unfortunately, in nearly half of the testicular cancers diagnosed, the presence of the disease is not detected until it has spread from the testes to the abdomen and other organs, and in these cases the chances of a full recovery are significantly less. Despite the fact that testicular self-examination techniques are available and are effective in revealing the early signs of cancer, many males remain unaware of these procedures or do not know how to perform them correctly (Finney, Weist, & Friman, 1995; Steffen, 1990).

It is noteworthy that public awareness of testicular cancer increased dramatically following cyclist Lance Armstrong's victory in the grueling Tour de France in July 1999 (see Figure 13.14). Why would this capture the public's attention? Just three years earlier, Armstrong was diagnosed with an advanced form of testicular cancer that nearly killed him. By the time he was diagnosed, the cancer had already spread to his abdomen, lungs, and brain. Although given a mere 50 percent chance of survival, Armstrong miraculously survived a year of painful treatment, going on to win the Tour de France, one of sport's biggest challenges.

The dangers associated with breast cancer pose similar challenge for females. Some researchers suggest that breast cancers detected early through secondary prevention programs, such as breast self-examination, clinical breast examination, and mammography, have an 85 to 90 percent chance of being cured (American Cancer Society, 1989). Women are most likely to obtain mammography screening when their physician recommends it, a fact that highlights the critical role these professionals play in promoting early detection. Programs designed to change certain beliefs are also effective in getting women to obtain mammography screening; for example, beliefs concerning their susceptibility to breast cancer, the severity of breast cancer, and the potential benefits of mammography screening (Aiken et al., 1994; Miller, Shoda, & Hurley, 1996).

**Figure 13.14**
**Battling Back from Cancer**

Cyclist Lance Armstrong gained instant fame following his victory in the 1999 Tour de France. Why? One reason was that several years earlier he had nearly died from an advanced case of testicular cancer. Armstrong's dramatic comeback significantly raised the public's awareness of this form of cancer and highlighted the importance of regular cancer self-examinations for detection of the disease at an earlier—and more curable—stage.

### REVIEW QUESTIONS

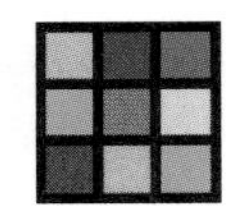

- What role do the mass media play in our health?
- What are the effects of regular exercise on our health?
- What is primary prevention? Secondary prevention?

## Making Psychology Part of Your Life

### Managing Stress: Some Useful Tactics

Stress is a fact of life. Stressors are all around us: at work, in our environment, and in our personal lives. Because stress arises from so many different factors and conditions, it's probably impossible to eliminate it completely. But we can apply techniques to lessen its potentially harmful effects. Let's consider several of these

**TABLE 13.6**

## Getting the Most Out of Your Day: Psychology in Action

One behavioral coping strategy is time management. Here are some tips to help you get the most out of your day.

**Basic Principles of Time Management**

1. Each day, make a list of things you want to accomplish.
2. Prioritize your list. Plan to do the toughest things first, and save the easier tasks for later in the day when you are low on energy.
3. Arrange your work schedule to take best advantage of the hours when you work best.
4. Always set aside a block of time when you can work without any interruptions.
5. Be flexible about changes in your schedule so that you can handle unexpected events.
6. Set aside time in your daily schedule for exercise such as jogging, aerobics, or brisk walking. You'll find that the time spent is well worth it and may even increase your productivity.
7. Set aside some times each day or week in which you always do some planned leisure activity—everybody needs a break.

stress-management techniques, dividing them into three major categories: physiological, cognitive, and behavioral.

**Physiological Coping Techniques** Common physiological responses to stress include tense muscles, racing pulse, pounding heart, dry mouth, queasy stomach, and sweating. But several coping techniques can be effective.

One of the most effective procedures is learning to reduce the tension in our own muscles through **progressive relaxation.** To use this technique, begin by alternately flexing and relaxing your muscles to appreciate the difference between relaxed and tense muscles. Next, you might shake out your arms and then let them flop by your sides. Then relax your shoulders by slowly rolling them up and down. Now relax your neck. Step by step, extend this process until your body is completely relaxed from head to toe. Controlled breathing is also important. When you are tense, you tend to take in relatively short, shallow breaths. However, as your body slows down during relaxation, notice that your breathing changes to deeper, longer breaths. Relaxation procedures are effective in reducing emotional as well as physical tension. A related technique that is often effective for achieving a relaxed state is *meditation.*

Regular vigorous exercise is another important technique for reducing stress. I've been using this technique myself for many years, mainly in the form of running. Although exercise does not eliminate the problems that sometimes lead to stress, it certainly increases my capacity to cope with the stress, and it definitely makes me feel better.

**Progressive Relaxation:** A stress-reduction technique in which people learn to relax by alternately flexing and relaxing, one by one, muscle groups throughout the body.

**Cognitive Restructuring:** A method of reducing stress by adjusting cognitive appraisals of stressors; clients learn to monitor and modify their self-talk and coping strategies.

**Behavioral Coping Techniques** We're all guilty of behaving in ways that bring stress on ourselves. We overload our schedules with too many responsibilities; we procrastinate; it all adds up to stress. There are plenty of things we can do to reduce the stressors in our lives. One method is *time management:* learning how to make time work for us instead of against us. Adhering to a well-planned schedule can help us make more efficient use of our time and eliminate behaviors that interfere with our main goals. An important—though often ignored—principle of time management is to balance work time and play time. Table 13.6 offers several time-management tips to help you get the most out of your day.

**Cognitive Coping Techniques** We don't always have control over all the stressors in our lives. We can, however, gain some control over our cognitive reactions to them. In other words, when exposed to a stressful situation, we can think about it in different ways—and some of these are much more beneficial than others. The process of replacing negative appraisals of stressors with more positive ones is called **cognitive restructuring** (Meichenbaum, 1977). To use this technique successfully, begin by monitoring what you say to yourself during periods of stress. Begin to modify these thoughts by thinking more adaptive thoughts. For example, try to discover something humorous about the situation, or imagine creative ways to reduce or eliminate the source of stress. Also, social support is important. Family, friends, or associates can often help you to "restructure" stressors (Bruhn & Phillips, 1987); that is, these persons can help you to perceive stressful events as less threatening and more under control than you might otherwise do. As you may recall, cognitive appraisal plays a crucial role in the way we interpret stressors. It's a good idea to be in contact with people who can suggest strategies for dealing with the sources of stress that you might not generate yourself. Such strategies can help reduce the negative feelings that often accompany stressful events or situations.

# Summary and Review

## Health Psychology: An Overview

- **What is health psychology?** Health psychology is the study of the relation between psychological variables and health.
- **What is the field of behavioral medicine?** Behavioral medicine, a field closely related to health psychology, combines behavioral and biomedical science knowledge to prevent and treat disorders.
- **To what can we attribute today's leading causes of premature death?** Many of today's leading causes of premature death can be attributed to people's lifestyles.
- **What are epidemiological studies?** Epidemiological studies are large-scale research efforts that focus on identifying the risk factors that predict development of certain diseases, such as heart disease and cancer, and premature death.

### Key Terms

health psychology, p. 490 • lifestyle, p. 491 • epidemiological studies, p. 492

## Stress: Its Causes, Effects, and Control

- **What is stress?** Stress is the process that occurs in response to situations or events (stressors) that disrupt, or threaten to disrupt, our physical or psychological functioning.
- **What is the GAS model?** The general adaptation syndrome (GAS), first reported by Hans Selye, describes how our bodies react to the effects of stress and includes three distinct stages: alarm, resistance, and finally, exhaustion.
- **What determines whether an event will be interpreted as stressful or as a challenge?** Cognitive appraisals play an important role in determining whether we interpret potentially stressful events as stressful or as a challenge.
- **What are stressors?** Stressors can be major life events, such as the death of a spouse, or daily hassles of everyday life, such as receiving a minor traffic ticket or having to wait in a line at the grocery store.
- **What are some sources of work-related stress?** Sources of work-related stress include work overload and underload, role conflict, and performance appraisals.
- **What is the person–environment fit, and why is it important?** The person–environment (P–E) fit is the match between characteristics of workers and characteristics of their jobs or work environments. Mismatches between these characteristics can lead to increases in stress-related illnesses.
- **Does stress play a role in physical illness?** Stress may play a role in 50 to 70 percent of all physical illness, primarily through its effect on the immune system.
- **What are the effects of exposure to low levels of stress? High levels?** Even relatively low levels of stress may interfere with task performance. Prolonged exposure to high levels of stress may lead to illness.
- **Why are some people better able to cope with the effects of stress than others?** Individual differences in optimism help explain the ability of some people to cope with stress better than others. Optimists generally focus on problem-focused ways of coping with stress and actively seek out social support.

### Key Terms

stress, p. 494 • stressors, p. 494 • general adaptation syndrome (GAS), p. 495 • hassles, p. 498 • person–environment (P–E) fit, p. 500

## Understanding and Communicating Our Health Needs

- **Why are symptoms and sensations important?** Symptoms and sensations, such as irregularities in heartbeat, are useful because they may help alert us to underlying health problems.

- **What is the health belief model?** The health belief model, initially developed to help explain why people don't use medical screening services, suggests that willingness to seek medical help depends on the extent to which we perceive a threat to our health and the extent to which we believe that a particular behavior will effectively reduce that threat.
- **What factors determine our willingness to make lifestyle changes or to seek medical help?** According to the health belief model, our willingness to make lifestyle changes or to seek medical help depends on our beliefs concerning our susceptibility to an illness, the severity of the illness, and the effectiveness of steps taken to deal with the illness.
- **Why is it important for psychologists to study aspects of doctor–patient interactions?** Physicians are often more effective in dealing with the technical aspects of medicine than in handling the psychosocial aspects. Because of this fact, psychologists have begun to develop interventions aimed at improving doctor–patient interactions; better interactions, in turn, can have a beneficial impact on important medical outcomes.

#### Key Term

health belief model, p. 504

### Behavioral and Psychological Correlates of Illness: The Effects of Thoughts and Actions on Health

- **What is cancer?** Cancer is actually a group of diseases characterized by a loss of some cells' ability to function normally. Cancerous cells multiply rapidly, generating tumors.
- **What determines who will become addicted to smoking?** Genetic, psychosocial, and cognitive factors all seem to play a role in determining who will become addicted to smoking.
- **What are the potential consequences of smoking and exposure to secondhand smoke?** Both smoking and exposure to secondhand smoke have been implicated in many types of cancer, in cardiovascular disease, and in a host of pathologies in children and in the developing fetus.
- **What are the effects of poor dietary practices?** Poor dietary practices can increase the risks of colon and rectal cancer, breast cancer, and cardiovascular disease.
- **What is self-determination theory?** Self-determination theory predicts that autonomously motivated health-promoting behavior is more likely to be maintained over time than behavior achieved at the urging of others.
- **What are the consequences of heavy consumption of alcohol?** Heavy drinking can cause a variety of health problems including stomach disease, liver disease, and intestinal cancer. It can also impair mental and sexual functioning, and it can result in fetal alcohol syndrome.
- **How is the way in which we express our emotions related to our health?** Failure to express our emotions can adversely affect the progression of cancer and other illnesses. Emotions can also lead to an increase in a person's blood pressure.
- **What is AIDS? How is HIV transmitted?** AIDS (acquired immune deficiency syndrome) is a reduction in the immune system's ability to defend the body against invaders. The disease is caused by the HIV virus. HIV is transmitted primarily through unprotected sex and infected blood.

#### Key Terms

cancer, p. 509 • risk factors, p. 509 • carcinogens, p. 509• cardiovascular disease, p. 510 • nicotine, p. 511 • serum cholesterol, p. 514 • self-determination theory, p. 514 • Type D, p. 517 • hypertension, p.517 • AIDS (acquired immune deficiency syndrome), p. 518

### Promoting Wellness: Developing a Healthier Lifestyle

- **What role do the mass media play in our health?** The mass media, when combined with other health promotion programs, can have a beneficial impact on health behaviors.
- **What are the effects of regular exercise on our health?** Regular, moderately intense exercise promotes both physical and psychological health. Starting and maintaining an exercise habit requires that people arrange their environment in a way that supports the desired exercise behaviors and weakens competing behaviors.
- **What is primary prevention? Secondary prevention?** Primary prevention emphasizes disease prevention and includes educating people about the relation between their behavior and their health, promoting healthy behavior, and directly modifying poor health practices. Secondary prevention emphasizes early detection of disease to decrease the severity of illness that is already present.

#### Key Terms

prevention strategies, p. 521 • progressive relaxation, p. 526 • cognitive restructuring, p. 526

## Critical Thinking Questions

### Appraisal

Throughout this chapter we've seen that lifestyle factors—what we choose to eat, drink, or smoke, and whether we choose to exercise regularly—greatly influence our health. If one can achieve good health simply by changing one's own behaviors, then why aren't more people doing so?

## Controversy

The amount of health-related information present on the Internet has exploded in recent years. People are increasingly using this information for a variety of useful purposes, such as locating doctors, confirming diagnoses, verifying physician-recommended treatments, and identifying sources of social support. Still, experts worry that people may get into trouble if they use this unpoliced source of information to perform self-diagnosis without also consulting their doctors. What are your views? What can be done to ensure the accuracy of health-related information on the Web?

## Making Psychology Part of Your Life

Now that you know something about the many practices that can improve physical and psychological health, will you be more likely to follow these practices yourself? Why or why not?

Chapter 14

# Mental Disorders:

## Their Nature and Causes

## CHAPTER OUTLINE


**MODELS OF ABNORMALITY: CHANGING CONCEPTIONS OF MENTAL DISORDERS 533**

From the Ancient World to the Age of Enlightenment
Modern Perspectives: Biological, Psychological, Sociocultural, and Diathesis–Stress Models

**ASSESSMENT AND DIAGNOSIS: THE DSM–IV AND OTHER TOOLS 537**

■ RESEARCH METHODS *How Psychologists Assess Mental Disorders*

**DISORDERS OF INFANCY, CHILDHOOD, AND ADOLESCENCE 541**

Disruptive Behavior

■ FROM SCIENCE TO PRACTICE *Preventing Conduct Disorder—or Worse!*

Attention-Deficit/Hyperactivity Disorder (ADHD)
Feeding and Eating Disorders
Autism: A Pervasive Developmental Disorder

**MOOD DISORDERS: THE DOWNS AND UPS OF LIFE 549**

Depressive Disorders: Probing the Depths of Despair
Bipolar Disorders: Riding the Emotional Roller Coaster
The Causes of Depression: Its Biological and Psychological Roots
Suicide: When Life Becomes Unbearable

**ANXIETY DISORDERS: WHEN DREAD DEBILITATES 553**

Phobias: Excessive Fear of Specific Objects or Situations
Panic Disorder and Agoraphobia
Obsessive–Compulsive Disorder: Behaviors and Thoughts outside One's Control
Posttraumatic Stress Disorder

**DISSOCIATIVE AND SOMATOFORM DISORDERS 558**

Dissociative Disorders
Somatoform Disorders: Physical Symptoms without Physical Causes

**SEXUAL AND GENDER IDENTITY DISORDERS 561**

Sexual Dysfunctions: Disturbances in Desire and Arousal
Paraphilias: Disturbances in Sexual Object or Behavior
Gender Identity Disorders

**PERSONALITY DISORDERS: TRAITS THAT HARM 563**

■ BEYOND THE HEADLINES—As Psychologists See It: *Life without a Conscience: The Antisocial Personality Disorder in Action*

**SCHIZOPHRENIA: LOSING TOUCH WITH REALITY 567**

The Nature of Schizophrenia
The Onset and Course of Schizophrenia
Causes of Schizophrenia

**SUBSTANCE-RELATED DISORDERS 571**

■ MAKING PSYCHOLOGY PART OF YOUR LIFE *Preventing Suicide: How You Can Help*

When I was nineteen, I had one of the most frightening experiences of my life. I was working at a summer job where I struck up an acquaintance with Luis, one of the full-time employees. Luis was a recent immigrant from the Dominican Republic, and I was very interested in learning about his country, so we began taking breaks and occasional lunches together. I thought we were becoming good friends—but suddenly Luis changed. He avoided my company and soon stopped talking to me altogether unless our jobs required it. Even worse, I could sometimes see him staring at me from across the room in a very cold and unfriendly way; and when I passed his desk, he would glance at me and then begin muttering angrily under his breath. I couldn't figure out what was wrong, so I asked Luis if I had offended him in some way. "*You* know what you have done!" he grumbled between clenched teeth; and he wouldn't say another word. When I asked other employees what was wrong, they told me Luis was sure that I was trying to steal his girlfriend, Maria, and that I had been saying nasty things about him to the boss. These ideas were completely false: Maria didn't like him and was definitely *not* his girlfriend, and I was going steady and was not interested in another romance. Also, I knew for a fact that I had never said anything negative about him to anyone. The situation grew more and more tense until one day Luis actually followed me home on the subway. He kept fingering some heavy object in his pocket, and I was sure it was a gun. When I got off the train, I turned to face him, hoping that the crowd would prevent him from doing anything violent. Luckily, a police officer was standing close by on the platform, so Luis never got off the train. Next day, he was not at work and I learned that he had been arrested for assaulting a neighbor; I never saw him again.

At the time these events took place (almost forty years ago), I was a biology major; and I've often wondered whether that close brush with violence—and with a person showing signs of serious mental illness—influenced my decision to become a psychologist. I'll never know for sure, but one thing *is* clear: Such problems are as fascinating as they are disturbing.

At this point, I should note that several different terms have been used to describe problems such as the ones shown by Luis—terms such as *abnormal behavior, mental illness,* and *psychopathology,* to mention just a few. At present, though, the term *mental disorders* is the one used most frequently by psychologists and other mental health professionals, so that's the term I'll use from now on (Nietzel et al., 1998). But what, precisely, are mental disorders? This question is much harder to answer than you might at first assume, because in fact there is no hard-and-fast dividing line between behavior that is normal and behavior that is somehow abnormal; rather, these are simply end points on an unbroken dimension. Most people—and most psychologists—would describe Luis's actions as falling toward the "abnormal" or "disturbed" end of the continuum, but even in a fairly extreme case such as this, there is room for interpretation. For example, suppose that in Luis's culture, a part-time employee like me would be expected to show a great deal of deference to a full-time employee like Luis. In this context, his anger toward me would be somewhat more understandable. Of course, I'm not suggesting that even in another culture Luis's behavior would be seen as appropriate; I simply wish to emphasize the fact that deciding what is "normal" and what is "abnormal" or "disturbed" can be a complex task.

That said, most psychologists do agree that mental disorders include the following features. First, they involve patterns of behavior or thought that are judged to be unusual or *atypical* in the society. People with these disorders don't behave or think like most others, and these differences are often apparent to the people around them. Second, such disorders usually generate *distress*—negative feelings and reactions—in the persons who experience them. Third, mental disorders are *maladaptive*—they interfere with individuals' ability to function normally and meet the demands of daily life. Combining these points, we can define **mental disorders** as *disturbances of an individual's behavioral or psychological functioning that are not culturally accepted and that lead to psychological distress, behavioral disability, and/or impaired overall functioning* (Nietzel et al., 1998).

In the remainder of this chapter, we'll examine a number of different mental disorders and some of the factors that lead to their occurrence; in the next chapter, we'll turn to procedures for treating or alleviating such disorders. Before turning to these disorders, however, we'll focus on two preliminary tasks. First, we'll take a brief look at how ideas concerning the nature of mental disorders have changed over the centuries and gradually evolved into the science-based view held by psychologists today. Second, we'll examine the question of how psychologists seek to identify various mental disorders; such identification is a necessary first step toward choosing or devising effective treatments, so this is truly a crucial process.

Web Link: *Psychiatry Information for the General Public*

## Models of Abnormality: Changing Conceptions of Mental Disorders

**Mental Disorders:** Disturbances of an individual's behavioral or psychological functioning that are not culturally expected and that lead to psychological distress, behavioral disability, and/or impaired overall functioning.

**Models of Abnormality:** Frameworks that provide comprehensive accounts of how and why mental disorders develop and how they can best be treated.

The pendulum of history swings, and like other pendulums, it does not move in only one direction. Over the course of the centuries and in different societies, mental disorders have been attributed to natural factors or forces—for example, to imbalances within our bodies—or, alternatively, to supernatural ones, such as possession by demons or gods. Let's take a look at a few of these historical shifts, then turn to the modern view of mental disorders: **models of abnormality** that provide comprehensive accounts of how and why mental disorders develop and how they can best be treated.

### From the Ancient World to the Age of Enlightenment

The earliest views of abnormal behavior emphasized supernatural forces. In societies from China to ancient Babylon, unusual behavior was attributed to possession by evil spirits or other forces outside our everyday experience. Ancient Greece, however, provided an exception to this picture. Several centuries before the start of the common era, Hippocrates, a famous Greek physician, suggested that all forms of disease, including mental illness, had natural causes. He attributed psychological disorders to physical factors such as brain damage, heredity, and the imbalance of *humors* within the body—four essential fluids that, he believed, influenced our health and shaped our behavior. He even suggested treatments for these disorders that sound impressively modern: rest, solitude, and good food and drink. The Romans generally accepted this view of psychological disorders, and because the Romans spread their beliefs all around what was then the known world, the idea of psychological disorders as the result of natural rather than supernatural causes enjoyed widespread acceptance, too. These views, of course, provided the foundations for what is known as the *medical view* of mental disorders—the idea that such disturbances stem from natural biological causes and should be treated as forms of illness.

After the fall of Rome, however, this picture changed radically, at least in the Western world. While other cultures maintained the view that mental disorders stemmed from natural causes, religion came to dominate Western societies. The result was that mental disorders were once again attributed largely to supernatural forces. This was not always the case; some physicians suggested that strange behavior might stem from natural causes, but they were generally ignored, or worse. The result of this shift in views was that persons with serious psychological disorders were seen as being punished for their sins by demons and devils. Thus, they were subjected to often painful *exorcisms*—efforts to remove these demons—and were often beaten, starved, or worse.

With the start of the Renaissance in the 1400s, however, the pendulum swung once again. The Swiss physician Paracelsus (1493–1541) suggested that abnormal behavior might stem, at least in part, from the influence of natural forces such as the moon, which, he believed, influenced the brain and induced madness or lunacy. A few decades later, the physician John Weyer (1515–1588) emphasized the role of natural, physical causes in mental disorders and was, in a sense, the first *psychiatrist* (medical doctor specializing in the treatment of mental disorders). As the Renaissance continued, and as knowledge of anatomy and biology increased, Weyer's view that abnormal behavior was a kind of illness gained acceptance.

Weyer also objected strongly to the brutal way in which people with mental disorders were treated. Because these people were viewed as possessed by evil spirits, they were kept in *asylums* where they were beaten and tortured. Patients were shackled to walls in dark, damp cells, were never permitted outside, and were often abused by their guards. Indeed, tickets were sold to the public to view them, just as individuals would pay to visit zoos.

Change, however, was in the wind. During the 1700s reformers called attention to these problems, and in 1793 Philippe Pinel (1745–1826), a French physician in charge of a large mental hospital in Paris, unchained the patients, arguing that they would do much better if treated in a kinder fashion (see Figure 14.1). These changes did produce beneficial effects, so Pinel's ideas soon spread and did much to reduce the suffering of patients in such "hospitals." The result, ultimately, was the development of the *moral treatment* or *mental hygiene movement,* and during the nineteenth century reformers secured improved conditions for many persons experiencing mental disorders. However, the movement soon produced results its supporters did not foresee: It led to establishment of new state hospitals (mainly in the early decades of the twentieth century) that were so understaffed that they could offer only custodial care to the large number of patients they housed (refer to Figure 14.1). However, these facilities did allow psychiatrists to study and compare the symptoms of many patients; this work led, ultimately, to the development of improved ways for describing and classifying mental disorders. We'll return to this important topic shortly.

**Figure 14.1**
**Moral Treatment—and Its Unexpected Effects**

The moral treatment movement, which began in the late eighteenth century, focused on humane treatment for mental patients *(left)*. However, it ultimately led to the establishment of huge state-run mental hospitals *(right)* in which patients received only minimal custodial care.

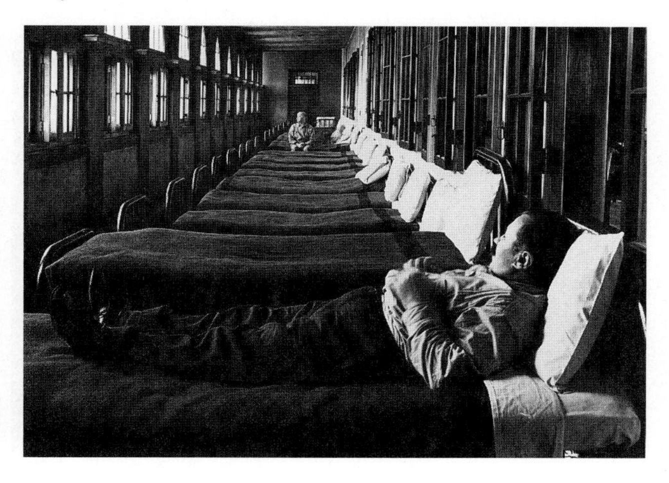

## Modern Perspectives: Biological, Psychological, Sociocultural, and Diathesis–Stress Models

Web Link: *Psychiatric Disorders—Internet Mental Health*

So how are mental disorders viewed today? The answer involves several perspectives that should be viewed as *complementary* to one another: Together, these approaches provide a more accurate and complete picture of how such disorders arise and how they can be treated than any single perspective does alone.

One of these approaches, the *biological model,* emphasizes the role of the nervous system in mental disorders. This approach seeks to understand such disorders in terms of malfunctioning of portions of the brain, imbalances in various neurotransmitters (recall our discussion of these in Chapter 2), and genetic factors. For example, as we'll see in later discussions, many mental disorders show a high degree of *concordance* among close relatives: If one family member develops a disorder, then others are at increased risk for developing it too. The biological model has become increasingly influential in recent years as advances in neuroscience have revealed more and more about the role of various portions of the brain in many aspects of behavior, and as techniques for observing the functioning of the brain (e.g., magnetic resonance imaging, PET scans) have improved.

It is clear, however, that biological factors are not the entire story where mental disorders are concerned. Often, such disorders occur without any apparent underlying biological cause. This suggests that *psychological factors,* too, can be important. The psychological perspective emphasizes the role of basic psychological processes in the occurrence of mental disorders. For instance, many psychologists believe that *learning* plays a key role in many disorders. An example: *phobias,* or excessive fears of objects or situations. According to the psychological view, a boy who is humiliated in front of classmates by an insensitive teacher may acquire a fear of all social situations in which he is the center of attention, and may avoid them on future occasions. The psychological perspective also emphasizes the role of cognitive factors in mental disorders. For instance, many theories of *depression* suggest that long-lasting negative feelings often stem from faulty patterns of thoughts. For example, individuals may attribute positive events and accomplishments to luck and other factors beyond their control, but negative outcomes to internal factors

**Figure 14.2**
**Sociocultural Factors Play a Role in Mental Disorders**

Psychologists recognize that *sociocultural factors* relating to the environments in which people live, including racial prejudice and cultural values, often play an important role in mental disorders. How do you think living in environments such as these would influence *your* psychological health?

such as their own flaws or failings. Finally, the psychological perspective also takes account of unconscious forces and conflicts within individuals—the factors so vividly emphasized by Freud and his followers (as discussed in Chapter 12).

What about *sociocultural factors*—do they too play a role in mental disorders? Psychologists and other mental health professionals believe that they do, and point to the important role of such social variables as poverty, unemployment, inferior education, and prejudice as potential causes of at least some mental disorders. In other words, the sociocultural perspective emphasizes the fact that external factors such as negative environments, a disadvantaged position in society, and cultural traditions can play a role in mental disorders (see Figure 14.2).

A third modern perspective on mental disorders is the **diathesis–stress model.** This view suggests that mental disorders result from the joint effects of two influences: (1) a predisposition for a given disorder, termed a *diathesis,* and (2) stressors in an individual's environment that tend to activate or stimulate the predisposition or vulnerability. In other words, the diathesis–stress model suggests that for various reasons—genetic factors, early traumatic experiences, specific personality traits—individuals show varying degrees of vulnerability to specific mental disorders. Whether and to what extent an individual actually experiences such a disorder, however, depends on the environment in which the person lives. If the environment is favorable, the vulnerability (diathesis) may never be activated, and the person may never experience a mental disorder. If environmental factors are unfavorable, the diathesis may be activated, and one or more mental disorders may result (see Figure 14.3). For instance, consider *posttraumatic stress disorder* (*PTSD*). As I'll discuss later in this chapter, PTSD is a disorder in which individuals reexperience traumatic events in vivid flashbacks while awake, or in repeated nightmares while asleep, and attempt to avoid stimuli associated with the traumatic event. This disorder is often seen in soldiers returning from combat, and in the survivors of tornadoes, hurricanes, or floods. But in all these cases, only some of the persons exposed to traumatic events develop PTSD. Why? The diathesis–stress model suggests that only some persons possess factors that make them vulnerable to this disorder; thus, only such persons experience PTSD when actually exposed to traumatic events. And if these individuals never experience such events, they may never show this disorder (see Figure 14.3).

**Diathesis–Stress Model:** A model suggesting that genetic or other factors may predispose an individual to develop a mental disorder but that the disorder will develop only if the person is exposed to certain kinds of stressful environmental conditions.

The diathesis–stress model has also played an important role in the emergence of a new perspective in the study of mental disorders, one that emphasizes the *development* of such disorders over time. This approach, often known as the **developmental psychopathology perspective,** emphasizes the fact that problems that first appear during childhood or adolescence often are linked to and serve as precursors for disorders that occur later in life. For example, shyness early in childhood may be a forerunner of a later social phobia—intense fear of social situations that can adversely affect an individual's personal adjustment. Such progression from relatively mild to more intense disorders seems to occur, at least in part, because individuals encounter new forms of stress as they move into new and increasingly complex environments, and these stressors, in turn, serve to activate existing vulnerabilities. Many psychologists believe that a developmental perspective can shed important light on how mental disorders develop, so I'll call attention to such factors at several points in this chapter.

**Figure 14.3**
**The Diathesis–Stress Model**

According to the diathesis–stress model, some individuals possess a predisposition (diathesis) to develop certain mental disorders. However, the disorders will occur only if the vulnerable individuals are also exposed to stressors that trigger or activate such predispositions.

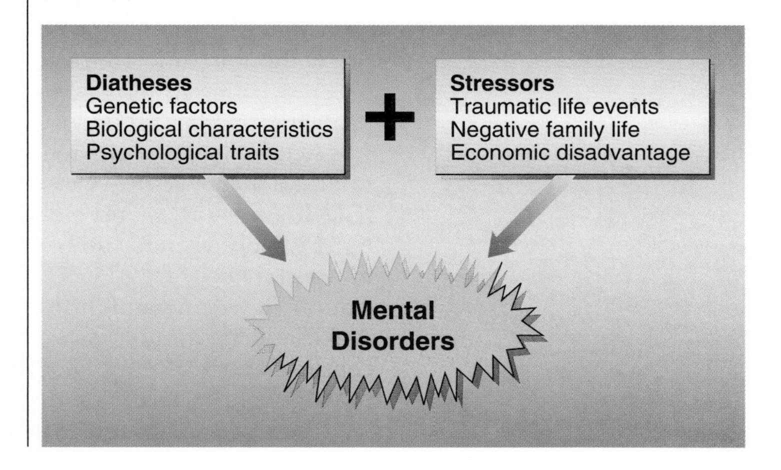


As I noted earlier, these modern models of abnormality—the biological, psychological, and sociocultural perspectives and the diathesis–stress model—are complementary rather than competing. Each identifies an important piece of the puzzle where mental disorders are concerned, and most psychologists believe that all these models must be included as part of our efforts to gain full understanding of the nature and origins of such disorders.

**REVIEW QUESTIONS**

- What are mental disorders?
- To what factors were such disorders attributed in the past?
- What is the modern perspective on such disorders?

## Assessment and Diagnosis: The DSM-IV and Other Tools

Suppose that one day your car won't start. What do you do? The first step is probably to gather information that will help you figure out *why* nothing happens when you turn the key. You might check to see if the headlights were left on. You might try switching on the radio; if it plays, then the battery is not totally dead. Next, you might open the hood and check the connections to the battery. After gathering such information, you would make an initial decision about what's wrong: The battery is bad, the starter isn't working, and so on.

In a similar manner, a psychologist might go through a comparable set of steps when seeing a new patient for the first time. The psychologist would first gather information on the kind of problems the person is experiencing, inquire about conditions in her or his current life, examine the person's responses to various psychological tests (see Chapter 11), and so on. These information-gathering steps

**Developmental Psychopathology Perspective:** A view emphasizing the fact that problems that first appear during childhood or adolescence are often precursors for disorders that occur later in life.

are known as *assessment,* and they are directed toward the goal of formulating an accurate *diagnosis*—identification of the person's problem(s). Diagnosis is a crucial step, because identifying the problem often determines what the psychologist should do next—how she or he can best help the individual.

But how does the psychologist identify the specific disorder or disorders a given person is experiencing? In general, by comparing the information gathered through assessment to standard definitions of various mental disorders. In other words, psychologists and other mental health professionals have an agreed-upon system for describing and classifying mental disorders. Such a system is very useful; without it, different psychologists or psychiatrists might refer to the same disorder in different terms or might use the same terms to describe very different problems (Millon, 1991).

Actually, several different systems for classifying mental disorders exist (e.g., the International Statistical Classification of Diseases, Injuries, and Causes of Death, or ICD-10 for short; World Health Organization, 1992). However, the one that is the most widely used in the United States is the **Diagnostic and Statistical Manual of Mental Disorders–IV (DSM–IV),** published by the American Psychiatric Association (1994). Although this manual is published by the American Psychiatric Association, psychologists have long contributed to its development—and increasingly so in recent years. Thus, the manual is designed to help all mental health practitioners correctly identify (diagnose) specific disorders.

The major diagnostic categories of the DSM–IV are shown in Table 14.1, and among them are all the major kinds of disorders covered in this chapter. In fact, the manual describes hundreds of specific disorders—many more than we'll consider here. These descriptions focus on observable features and include *diagnostic features*—symptoms that must be present before an individual is diagnosed as suffering from a particular problem. In addition, the manual also provides much additional background information on each disorder; for instance, information about biological factors associated with the condition and about variations in each disorder that may be related to age, cultural background, or gender.

An important feature of the DSM–IV is that it classifies disorders along five *axes* rather than merely assigning them to a given category. This means that a person is described along several different dimensions (axes) rather than only one. Different axes relate to mental disorders, physical health, and social and occupational functioning. For our purposes, two of these axes are most important: Axis I, which relates to major disorders themselves, and Axis II, which relates to *mental retardation* (recall our discussion of this topic in Chapter 11) and to *personality disorders*—extreme and inflexible personality traits that are distressing to the person or that cause problems in school, work, or interpersonal relationships. The third axis pertains to general medical conditions relevant to each disorder; the fourth axis considers psychosocial and environmental factors, including specific sources of stress. Finally, the fifth axis relates to a global assessment of current functioning. By providing a system for evaluating people along each of these various axes, the DSM–IV helps clinicians gain a fuller picture of each patient's current state and psychological functioning.

Another important feature of the DSM–IV is that it reflects efforts to take greater account of the potential role of cultural factors in mental disorders. For example, in the DSM–IV the description of each disorder contains a new section that focuses on *culturally related features*—aspects of each disorder that are related to, and may be affected by, culture. For instance, some disorders seem to occur only in some cultures. A disorder known as *koro* occurs only in Southeast Asia; this involves strong beliefs on the part of some men that their penis is about to retract into their stomach and kill them. Similarly, a disorder known as *Windigo,* found only among Native Americans in North America, involves intense anxieties that the victims will turn into monsters who literally devour other human beings! Symptoms specific to a given culture and unique ways of describing distress in various cultures are included whenever available. This information is designed to

**Diagnostic and Statistical Manual of Mental Disorders–IV (DSM–IV):** A manual designed to help all mental health practitioners to recognize and correctly diagnose specific disorders; known as DSM–IV.

**TABLE 14.1**

**Major Diagnostic Categories of the DSM–IV**

The DSM–IV classifies mental disorders according to the categories shown here.

| Diagnostic Category—Axis I | Examples |
|---|---|
| Disorders usually first diagnosed in infancy, childhood, or adolescence | Learning disorders, pervasive developmental disorders, attention-deficit and disruptive behavior disorders, feeding and eating disorders |
| Delirium, dementia, and amnesic and other cognitive disorders | Delirium, dementia, amnesic disorders |
| Substance-related disorders | Alcohol-related disorders, cocaine-related disorders, opioid-related disorders |
| Schizophrenia and other psychotic disorders | Schizophrenia, schizoaffective disorder, brief psychotic disorder |
| Mood disorders | Depressive disorders, bipolar disorders |
| Anxiety disorders | Panic disorder, specific phobias, posttraumatic stress disorder, generalized anxiety disorder |
| Somatoform disorders | Somatization disorder, conversion disorder, hypochondriasis |
| Factitious disorders | With predominantly psychological signs and symptoms, with predominantly physical signs and symptoms |
| Dissociative disorders | Dissociative amnesia, dissociative fugue, dissociative identity disorder |
| Sexual and gender identity disorders | Sexual dysfunctions, paraphilias, gender identity disorders |
| Eating disorders | Anorexia nervosa, bulimia nervosa |
| Sleep disorders | Primary sleep disorders, sleep disorders related to another mental disorder |
| Impulse-control disorders not elsewhere classified | Kleptomania, pyromania, pathological gambling |
| Adjustment disorders | With depressed mood, with anxiety |
| Other conditions that may be a focus of clinical attention | Medication-induced movement disorders, relational problems, problems related to abuse or neglect |
| **Diagnostic Category—Axis II** | **Examples** |
| Personality disorders | Paranoid personality disorder, schizotypal personality disorder, antisocial personality disorder |
| Mental retardation | Mild mental retardation, moderate mental retardation, severe mental retardation, profound mental retardation |

help professionals recognize the many ways in which an individual's culture can influence the form of psychological disorders.

Is the DSM–IV a useful tool for psychologists? In several ways, it is. Strenuous efforts were made by the psychiatrists and psychologists who developed the DSM–IV to improve it over previous versions (e.g., the DSM–III–R), and in many respects these efforts succeeded: The DSM–IV appears to be higher in *reliability* than earlier versions, and it rests more firmly on careful empirical research. However, it's important to note that it is still largely *descriptive* in nature: It describes psychological disorders, but it makes no attempt to explain them. This is deliberate; the DSM–IV was specifically designed to assist in diagnosis. It remains neutral with respect to various theories about the origins of psychological disorders. Because psychology as a science seeks *explanation*, not simply description, however, many psychologists view this aspect of the DSM–IV as a shortcoming that limits its value. In addition, the DSM–IV attaches specific *labels* to people, and this may activate stereotypes about them. Once a person is labeled as showing a particular mental disorder, psychologists and mental health professionals may perceive the person largely in terms of that label; and this may lead them to overlook important information about the person.

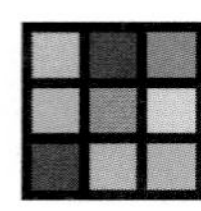

A third criticism is that the DSM–IV may be gender-biased. Females are diagnosed as showing certain disorders much more frequently than males, and some critics suggest that this is due to the fact that the DSM–IV descriptions of these disorders seem to reflect society's views about women (sex-role stereotypes).

Finally, the DSM–IV has been criticized because mental disorders occur on a continuum, not in discrete categories. People don't necessarily simply have or not have a disorder; they may have the disorder to various degrees, and may show different aspects of it in varying proportions. For this reason, many psychologists prefer a *dimensional approach,* in which individuals are not simply assigned to specific categories but rather are rated on many different dimensions, each relevant to a specific mental disorder. Still, although many psychologists might prefer a dimensional approach, and although they recognize the other potential problems with the DSM–IV already noted, they continue to use the manual because of the benefits of having a single widely used framework for describing and discussing mental disorders. Reflecting this fact, the DSM–IV will serve as the basis for our discussions of various disorders throughout this chapter.

**Assessment Interviews:** Interviews conducted by psychologists in which they seek information about individuals' past and present behaviors, current problems, interpersonal relations, and personality.

What other tools do psychologists use for purposes of assessment? See the **Research Methods** section below for more information on this issue.

## Research Methods: How Psychologists Assess Mental Disorders

Earlier, I noted that assessment—systematic collection of information—is a necessary first step to *diagnosis,* or accurate identification of mental disorders. But how, specifically, do psychologists gather such information? The answer involves several different tools that together can help psychologists decide what disorder or disorders are shown by specific patients. Before turning to these, however, it's important to emphasize the following point: Psychologists want to accomplish much more than simply identifying (diagnosing) various mental disorders. In addition, they want to understand the causes of such disorders—why they occur in the first place. This is one important reason why psychologists conduct research: This is the way scientists attempt to answer "Why?" questions. So unlike psychiatrists, who concentrate on treating mental disorders, psychologists often view accurate assessment as the first step in conducting valuable research, as well as in choosing the best form of treatment for specific persons. Now, back to the specific assessment tools psychologists use for this purpose.

***Life Records.*** One source of such information is *life records*—basic information on an individual's past life (e.g., school grades, police reports, medical records). This information can get the process started by indicating when a problem may have originated, how long it has persisted, and how it has affected the individual's life. Unfortunately, life records are often hard to obtain and may be distorted by patients who attempt to put themselves in a favorable light. Still, they can sometimes be helpful as an initial step.

***Assessment Interviews.*** As experts in human behavior, psychologists realize that much can be learned from direct interactions with individuals who seek their help. Thus, they often conduct **assessment interviews** in which they seek information about individuals' past and present behaviors, current problems, interpersonal relations, and personality (see Figure 14.4). Such interviews can be *structured,* in which case psychologists follow a detailed set of questions prepared in advance and known to get at the information they want, or *semistructured,* in which psychologists follow an outline of major topics but do not have a list of specific questions. Through such procedures a psychologist can learn a great deal about a person and can formulate hypotheses concerning the origins of the individual's problems.

***Psychological Tests.*** As noted in Chapter 11, psychological tests involve standardized procedures for observing and describing a person's behavior. Such tests can provide information on cognitive functioning (e.g., intelligence), personality, interests, and attitudes; and all of this information can help psychologists understand the problems being experienced by individuals who seek their help.

Some psychological disorders are linked to, or are the result of, damage to the brain or other portions of the nervous system. Thus, in their research psychologists sometimes use *neuropsychological tests*—measures specifically designed to assess nervous-system damage and brain functioning generally. One such measure is the **Halstead–Reitan Neuropsychological Battery.** This consists of many tests of auditory, visual, and psychomotor functioning (e.g., eye–hand coordination). The pattern of scores obtained by an individual can point to the presence of specific forms of brain damage.

***Observations of Behavior.*** Another source of assessment information used by psychologists is observation of individuals' behavior—especially behavior relevant to problems suggested by other assessment tools. This often involves observing individuals in natural situations: at school, at work, in interactions with spouses and other family members, and so on. Alternatively, it can involve observing their reactions in a standardized situation—for instance, reactions to a video showing objects or situations they strongly fear (see our later discussion of phobias). Still another observational technique involves *self-monitoring* by patients themselves, who keep records of the frequency, duration, and quality of their own behaviors and moods (e.g., Nietzel et al., 1998).

***Biological Measures.*** Revealing information is often provided by various *neuroimaging techniques* discussed in Chapter 2—*computerized tomography (CT)* scans, *magnetic resonance imaging (MRI)*, and *positron emission tomography (PET)* scans. These tools are often used by psychologists to study the biological bases of various psychological disorders. In addition, various *biological markers*—biological changes associated with specific mental disorders—have been identified. Such markers include changes in liver enzymes (a useful marker for alcoholism) (e.g., Allen & Litten, 1993) and elevations in heart rate, blood pressure, and muscle tension, which are often a sign of anxiety disorders.

In sum, psychologists use many different tools to gather information helpful in identifying psychological disorders. Indeed, the development of reliable and valid assessment tools is one of psychology's unique contributions to the study of mental disorders. We'll encounter many examples of the use of these tools as we discuss various mental disorders and efforts by psychologists to identify their causes.

**Figure 14.4**
**Assessment Interviews: One Technique for Gathering Information about Potential Psychological Disorders**

Psychologists often conduct assessment interviews with individuals seeking their help. These interviews provide information that helps psychologists identify the psychological disorders being experienced by these persons.

**REVIEW QUESTIONS**

- What is the DSM-IV?
- In what ways is the DSM-IV an improvement over earlier versions?
- What assessment tools other than the DSM-IV are used by psychologists in their efforts to accurately identify mental disorders?

**Halstead–Reitan Neuropsychological Battery:** A battery of tests of auditory, visual, and psychomotor functioning (e.g., eye–hand coordination). The pattern of scores obtained by a given individual can point to the existence of specific forms of brain damage.

# Disorders of Infancy, Childhood, and Adolescence

Freud once stated that the child is the parent of the adult, and where mental disorders are concerned, he was correct: The problems people experience as adults are

**Disruptive Behaviors:** Childhood mental disorders involving poor control of impulses, conflict with other children and adults, and, in some cases, more serious forms of antisocial behavior.

often visible much earlier in life. Recognition of this basic fact is one reason behind the increasing importance of a developmental perspective on mental disorders—the view that problems and difficulties experienced during childhood or adolescence can play an important role in the emergence of various disorders during adulthood. The DSM–IV takes note of this fact, and lists many disorders that first emerge during childhood or adolescence. We'll consider several of these here. Before doing so, however, I should note that many psychologists feel that a dimensional approach is especially useful in describing these disorders. In particular, they note that many childhood problems can be described in terms of two basic dimensions: *Externalizing problems* are disruptive behaviors that are often a nuisance to others, such as aggression, hyperactivity, impulsivity, and inattention; in contrast, *internalizing problems* are ones in which children show deficits in desired behaviors, such as difficulty in interacting with peers or problems with expressing their wishes and needs to others (e.g., Achenbach, 1997). Children show these difficulties to varying degrees, so considering where a child falls along these dimensions can be very revealing. For purposes of this discussion, however, I'll stick closely to the disorders described by the DSM–IV.

## Disruptive Behavior

**Disruptive behaviors** are the most common single reason why children are referred to psychologists for diagnosis and treatment. And in fact disruptive behaviors are quite common: As many as 10 percent of children may show such problems at some time or other. Disruptive behaviors are divided by the DSM–IV into two major categories: *oppositional defiant disorder* and *conduct disorder.*

Oppositional defiant disorder involves a pattern of behavior in which children have poor control of their emotions or have repeated conflicts with parents, teachers, and other adults (see Figure 14.5). Consider this description of Nick, a nine-year-old boy brought by his mother to a mental health center:

> "Within the past month, Nick has been sent to the principal's office three times for swearing at his teacher in front of other children. At home . . . he is argumentative and spiteful. He has to be told again and again to do the smallest chore, and complains about all the work expected of him. . . . His mother says she is fed up with Nick, claiming, 'It's just one battle after the next with him. . . .' "

Children showing this pattern have problems getting along with others and as a result may start on a road that leads them to more serious difficulties later in life—one of which may be *conduct disorder,* or CD. Oppositional defiant disorder usually starts when children are quite young (ages three to seven), but conduct disorder begins somewhat later, often when children enter puberty. CD involves more serious antisocial behaviors that go beyond throwing tantrums or disobeying rules; these are behaviors that are potentially harmful to the child, to others, or to property.

**Figure 14.5**
**Oppositional Defiant Disorder**

Disruptive behaviors—although not usually as severe as the one shown here!—are the most common reason why children are referred to psychologists for diagnosis and treatment.

(*Source:* © The New Yorker Collection. 1996. Edward Koren from cartoonbank.com. All rights reserved.)

*"Never, ever do that again!"*

What are the causes of these disruptive patterns of behavior? Biological factors appear to play a role. Boys show such problems much more often than girls, a pattern that suggests a role for sex hormones. Also, some findings suggest that children who develop CD have unusually low levels of general arousal—and thus seem to crave the excitement that accompanies their disruptive behaviors (e.g., Raine, Venebles, & Williams, 1990). But psychological factors, too, play a role. Children with conduct disorder often show insecure attachment to their parents and often live in negative environments that may involve poverty, large family size, and being placed in foster care (Biederman et al., 1990). In addition, their parents often use coercive child-rearing practices, which may actually encourage disruptive behavior (e.g., Campbell et al., 1986). Whatever the precise causes, it is clear that CD is a serious problem that can well pave the way to additional problems during adulthood. Can CD be prevented? For a discussion of this topic, see the **From Science to Practice** section below.

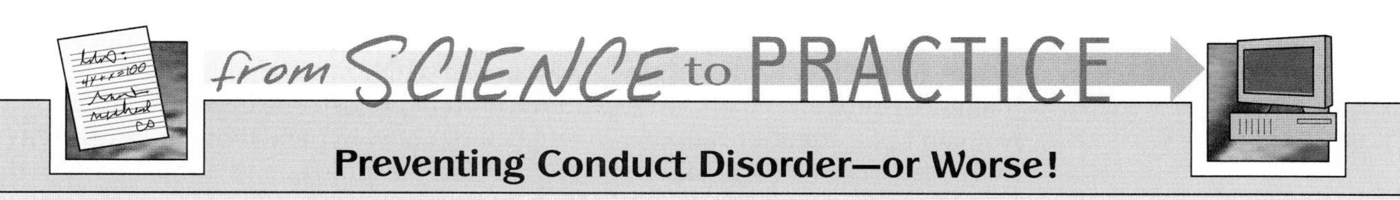


## Preventing Conduct Disorder—or Worse!

Because I haven't said it explicitly yet, let me begin by noting that *prevention* of mental disorders is a major theme of *clinical psychology*—the branch of psychology that specializes in the diagnosis and treatment of such disorders. In fact, most psychologists firmly believe that preventing mental disorders is at *least* as important as dealing with them once they appear. Consistent with this view, much attention has been focused, in recent years, on efforts to prevent oppositional defiant disorder from developing into conduct disorder and then—as often happens—into even more serious problems (see the discussion of *antisocial personality disorder* on pages 564).

Can this progression from disruptive behaviors to increasingly serious antisocial actions be prevented? The findings of several studies are at least promising in this respect. For instance, one well-conducted longitudinal investigation studied the effects of specific interventions on kindergarten boys living in an inner-city neighborhood in Montreal. The boys had been identified by their teachers as showing disruptive behavior; thus, they were at high risk for developing conduct disorder in the years ahead (Tremblay et al., 1995). Some of the boys were assigned to a prevention program in which they were taught new social skills designed to help them form friendships and solve social conflicts, and in which their parents were given training in more effective child discipline and behavior-management techniques. The intervention lasted for two years. In contrast, the rest of the boys were assigned to a no-treatment control condition.

The boys were followed for ten years, until they were about fifteen, and the results were encouraging. Those in the treatment condition reported a lower level of engaging in delinquent acts (e.g., vandalism, truancy, theft, assaults on others) than those in the control group (see Figure 14.6). Moreover, there was some indication

**Figure 14.6**
**Preventing Conduct Disorder**

Boys who received training in social skills and whose parents were trained in effective discipline techniques later reported fewer instances of delinquent behavior (e.g., vandalism, truancy, theft, assaults on others) than those who did not receive such treatment. These findings suggest that early intervention can be effective in preventing conduct disorders. (*Source:* Based on data from Tremblay et al., 1995.)

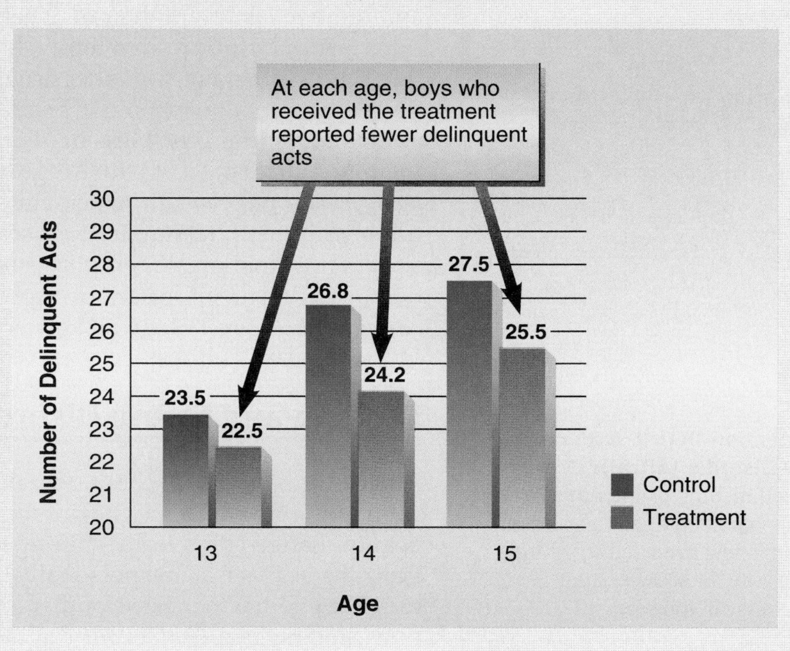

that the size of this difference in favor of the treatment group increased over time, and that the magnitude of these beneficial effects would have been even greater if the intervention procedures had continued even longer. These results were based largely on self-reports by the boys themselves and thus are open to question on several grounds. Still, findings such as these suggest that appropriate interventions *can* be helpful in preventing conduct disorder and—as we'll see in later sections—in preventing many other mental disorders as well.

## Attention-Deficit/Hyperactivity Disorder (ADHD)

When you were in school, did you ever have a classmate who couldn't sit still and who interrupted the class repeatedly by getting up and wandering around? I did, and I remember how our teacher struggled to get Joseph to stay in his seat and pay attention to the lesson. Looking back, I'm now convinced that Joseph suffered from **attention-deficit/hyperactivity disorder (ADHD),** another important childhood mental disorder. Actually, three patterns of ADHD exist: one in which children simply can't pay attention; another in which they show hyperactivity or impulsivity—they really *can't* sit still and can't restrain their impulses; and a third pattern that combines the two. Unfortunately, ADHD is *not* a problem that fades with the passage of time: Seventy percent of children diagnosed with ADHD in elementary school still show signs of it when they are sixteen (Barkley, DuPaul, & McMurray, 1990). Moreover, by this time it is often accompanied by conduct disorder.

The causes of ADHD appear, again, to be both biological and psychological. For instance, such factors as low birth weight, oxygen deprivation at birth, and alcohol consumption by expectant mothers have all been associated with ADHD (Streissguth, 1994). In addition, deficits in the reticular activating system and in the frontal lobes may be linked to ADHD. With respect to psychological factors, risk factors seem to include parental intrusiveness and overstimulation—parents who just can't seem to let their infants alone.

Fortunately, ADHD can be treated successfully with several drugs, all of which act as stimulants. *Ritalin* is the most frequently used, and it amplifies the impact of two neurotransmitters—norepinephrine and dopamine—in the brain. While taking this drug, children are better able to pay attention and often become calmer and more in control of their own behavior. The effects of Ritalin and other medications last only four to five hours, however, so the drugs must be taken quite frequently. Also, Ritalin and other drugs produce potentially harmful side effects (e.g., decreased appetite, insomnia, headaches, increased blood pressure); they are definitely *not* an unmixed blessing. For this reason, many psychologists recommend treating ADHD not just with drugs (a purely medical approach), but with *behavioral management programs* in which children are taught to listen to directions, to continue with tasks, to stay in their seat while in class, and other important skills. I should note that greater emphasis on changing behavior rather than on giving patients drugs is an important feature of modern psychology and is one of the unique contributions psychology makes, as a field, to the treatment of all mental disorders.

Web Link: *The Academy for Eating Disorders*

Audio 14.1: *Who's at Risk for Eating Disorders*

**Attention-Deficit/Hyperactivity Disorder (ADHD):** A childhood mental disorder in which children simply can't pay attention, show hyperactivity or impulsivity, or show both of these symptoms.

## Feeding and Eating Disorders

When I was in high school, female figures that can only be described as well-rounded were in vogue. Beginning in the mid-1960s, however, this standard of beauty changed drastically, shifting toward a much slimmer shape (see Figure 14.7). Puzzling as this is to me personally (I have my own preferences!), the "thin is beautiful" image has persisted and is emphasized over and over again by television, films, and magazines. Despite this fact, a growing proportion of adults in the United

**Figure 14.7**
**Changing Ideals of Feminine Beauty: One Factor in the Growing Incidence of Eating Disorders**

Until the 1960s, well-rounded female figures such as that of Marilyn Monroe were considered to be the most attractive. After that time, however, a trend toward being thin developed and grew stronger (as typified by today's supermodels). Research findings suggest that this shift is one factor that has contributed, along with many others, to the rising incidence of eating disorders in recent decades.

States and other countries are actually overweight, a fact I noted in Chapters 10 and 13. Given this increasing gap between physical reality and the image of personal beauty portrayed by the mass media, it is not surprising that **feeding and eating disorders**—disturbances in eating behavior that involve maladaptive and unhealthy efforts to control body weight—are increasingly common. Although these obviously occur among adults (indeed, most people think of these as adult disorders), eating disorders often begin in childhood or adolescence; so it makes sense to consider them here, even though adult forms of these disorders are also classified separately in the DSM–IV. In addition, the trend in recent decades has been for these disturbing disorders to start at earlier and earlier ages—as young as age eight (Nietzel et al., 1998). Two eating disorders, *anorexia nervosa* and *bulimia nervosa,* have received most attention.

**ANOREXIA NERVOSA: PROOF THAT YOU *CAN* BE TOO SLIM** **Anorexia nervosa** involves an intense and excessive fear of gaining weight coupled with refusal to maintain a normal body weight. In other words, people with this disorder relentlessly pursue the goal of being thin, no matter what this does to their health. They often have distorted perceptions of their own bodies, believing that they are much heavier than they really are. As a result of such fears and distorted perceptions, they starve themselves to the point where their weight drops to dangerously low levels.

Video 14.1: *Anorexia*

Why do persons with this disorder have such an intense fear of becoming fat? Important clues are provided by the fact that anorexia nervosa is far more common among females than males. This has led researchers to propose that because many societies emphasize physical attractiveness for females far more than for males, adolescents and young women feel tremendous pressure to live up to the images of beauty shown in the mass media—to be as thin as the models who are held up as paragons of female desirability. If they are not this thin, they reason, they will be viewed as unattractive. Actually, such assumptions appear to be false: Research findings indicate that few men prefer the extremely thin figures that anorexics *believe* men admire (e.g., Williamson, Cubic, & Gleaves, 1993); rather, men find a fuller-figured, more rounded appearance much more attractive.

That intense social pressures do indeed play a role in anorexia nervosa is suggested by the findings of a recent study by Paxton and her colleagues (1999). These researchers found that among fifteen-year-old girls, the greater the pressure from their friends to be thin, the more likely the teens were to be unhappy with their current bodies and to be greatly restricting their food intake. Whatever its precise origins, anorexia nervosa poses a serious threat to the physical as well as the psychological health of the persons who experience it.

**Feeding and Eating Disorders:** Disturbances in eating behavior that involve maladaptive and unhealthy efforts to control body weight.

**Anorexia Nervosa:** An eating disorder involving intense fears of gaining weight coupled with refusal to maintain normal body weight.

**BULIMIA: THE BINGE–PURGE CYCLE** If you found anorexia nervosa disturbing, you may find a second eating disorder, **bulimia nervosa,** even more unsettling. In this disorder individuals engage in recurrent episodes of binge eating—eating huge amounts of food within short periods of time—followed by some kind of compensatory behavior designed to prevent weight gain. This can involve self-induced vomiting, the misuse of laxatives, fasting, or exercise so excessive that it is potentially harmful to the person's health. Amazing as it may seem, persons suffering from bulimia nervosa—again, mainly young women—report purging about twelve times per week, and many purge even more often than this. My daughter once had a roommate who was a recovered bulimic. She was no longer trapped in the binge–purge cycle and was of normal weight, as are most bulimics; but her repeated binge–purge cycles had done permanent harm to her digestive system, and she had to stick to a bland diet of boiled or steamed foods.

The causes of bulimia nervosa appear to be similar to those of anorexia nervosa: Once again, the "thin is beautiful" ideal seems to play an important role (e.g., Thompson, 1992; Williamson, Cubic, & Gleaves, 1993). Another, and related, factor is the desire to be perfect in all respects, including those relating to physical beauty. Research findings indicate that women who are high on this trait are at risk for developing bulimia, especially if they perceive themselves to be overweight (Joiner et al., 1997). And, in fact, bulimics—like anorexics—do tend to perceive themselves as much heavier than they really are. This fact is illustrated clearly by a study conducted by Williamson, Cubic, and Gleaves (1993). These researchers asked three groups of young women—ones diagnosed as showing bulimia, ones diagnosed as showing anorexia, and ones who had no eating disorder—to rate silhouettes of women ranging from ones that were very skinny to ones that were very obese. First, participants selected the silhouette that most accurately matched their own *current* body size; then they rated the silhouette that represented the body size they most preferred (their *ideal*). The results: When current body size was held constant statistically, both bulimic and anorexic persons rated their current body size as larger than did control participants, and both rated their ideal as smaller than did controls (see Figure 14.8). In other words, when current body weight was taken into account (anorexics were, of course, the thinnest), both groups with eating disorders viewed themselves as farther from their ideal than did persons who did not suffer from an eating disorder.

Fortunately, it appears that the frequency of eating disorders tends to decrease with age, at least for women (Heatherton et al., 1997). Men, in contrast, may be more at risk for such problems as they get older: The percentage of men who diet increases somewhat with age, and dieting can sometimes lead to excessive efforts to reduce one's weight (Heatherton et al., 1997).

## Autism: A Pervasive Developmental Disorder

Of all the childhood disorders, the ones that may be most disturbing of all are those described in the DSM–IV as **pervasive developmental disorders.** Such disorders involve lifelong impairment in mental or physical functioning; among these, the one that has received most attention is *autistic disorder,* or *autism.* This term is derived from the Greek word *autos* (self) and is an apt description for children with this disorder, for they seem to be preoccupied with themselves and to live in an almost totally private world. Children with autism show three major characteristics: marked impairments in establishing social interactions with others (e.g., they don't use nonverbal behaviors such as eye contact, don't develop peer relationships, and don't seem to be interested in other people); nonexistent or poor language skills; and stereotyped, repetitive patterns of behavior. Consider the following description of one such child:

**Bulimia Nervosa:** An eating disorder in which individuals engage in recurrent episodes of binge eating followed by some form of purging.

**Pervasive Developmental Disorders:** Disorders involve lifelong impairment in mental or physical functioning.

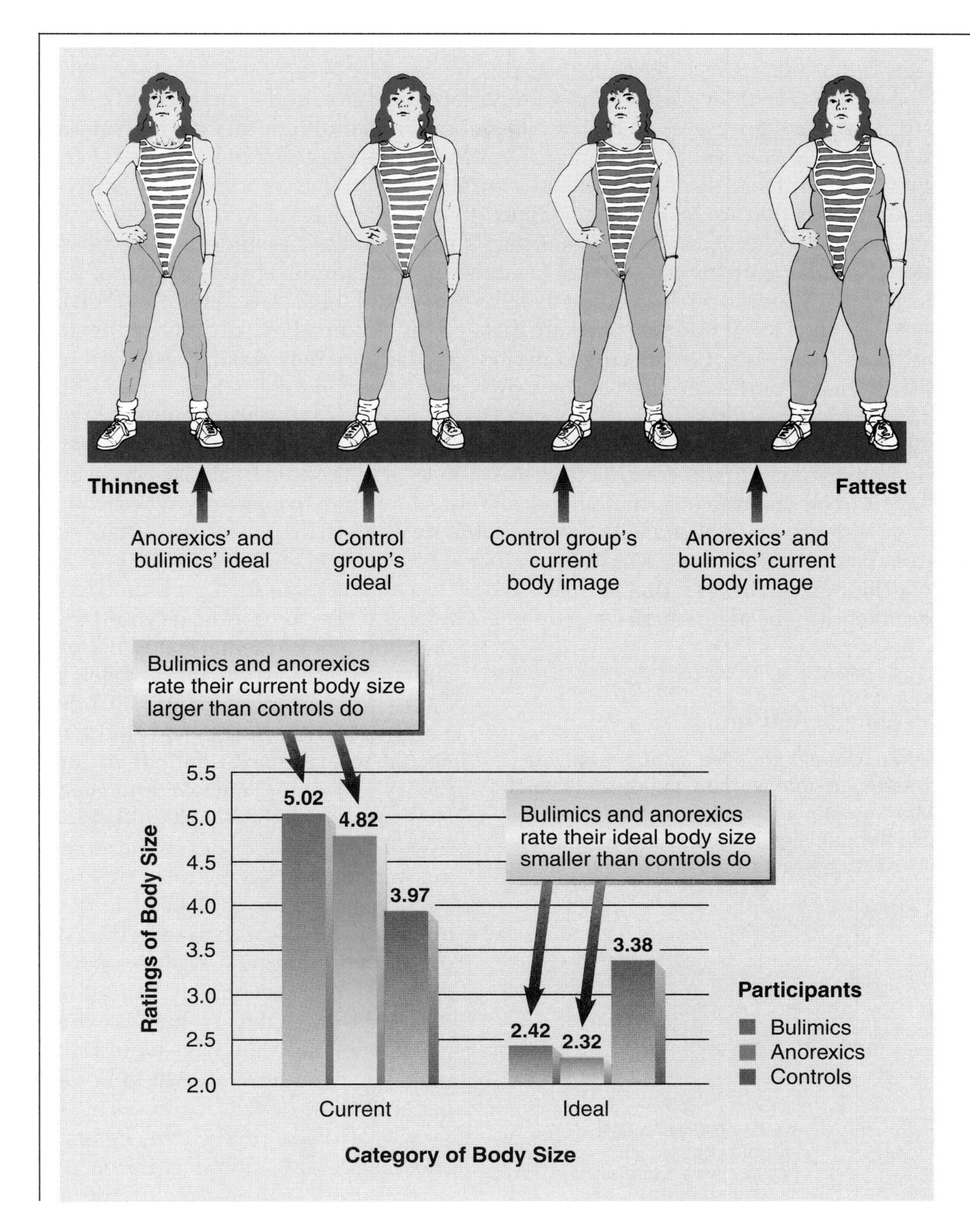


**Figure 14.8**
**Distorted Perceptions of One's Own Body: An Important Factor in Eating Disorders**

When actual body size was held constant statistically, both anorexics and bulimics rated their own current body size as larger than did controls (persons not suffering from these disorders). Moreover, both groups showing eating disorders rated their ideal body size as smaller than did controls.

(*Source:* Based on data from Williamson, Cubic, & Gleaves, 1993.)

> "Kathy Mills sits at her kitchen table, watching her three-year-old son, Devon, play in the den. For the last hour, Devon has been sitting on the floor staring at his right hand, which he holds over his head as he opens and closes his fingers. Devon is looking at changes in the lighting that he makes by waving his fingers in front of the ceiling light. He has been doing this every day for months. . . . Before Devon was a year old, Kathy had begun to notice all sorts of problems. Devon would never reach out for toys or babble like other babies. He wouldn't even splash around in the water when she gave him a bath. . . . Perhaps most upsetting of all, Devon didn't use language and didn't seem to notice other people. If another child walked over to him, he would shrink back and begin to cry. If his mother called his name, he would ignore her. . . . The only time Devon seemed to notice other people was when he got upset. . . ."

Truly, children with autistic disorder seem to live in a world of their own. They make little contact with others, either through words or nonverbal gestures; show little interest in others; and, when they do notice them, often seem to treat them as objects rather than people. How truly sad.

Autistic disorder seems to have important biological and genetic causes. Twin studies, for instance, show a higher concordance rate for identical than for fraternal twins (e.g., Rutter et al., 1990). Similarly, other studies suggest that the brains of children with autistic disorder have structural or functional abnormalities, such as frontal lobes that are less well developed than in normal children (e.g., Gaffney et al., 1989). Psychological factors that play a role in autistic disorder include attentional deficits: Autistic children fail to attend to social stimuli such as their mother's face and voice, or to others' calling their names (Osterling & Dawson, 1994). Perhaps the most intriguing findings of all are that autistic children have deficits in their *theory of mind,* a concept we discussed in Chapter 8. As you may recall, this term refers to children's understanding of their own and others' mental states. Apparently, autistic children show serious deficits in this respect (e.g., Shulman, Yirmiya, & Greenbaum, 1995). They are unable to realize that other people can have access to different sources of information than themselves, and they are unable to predict the beliefs of others from information that should allow them to make such predictions.

Evidence that deficits with respect to theory of mind do play an important role in autism is provided by research conducted by Peterson and Siegal (1999). These psychologists reasoned that in order to develop an adequate theory of mind, children require social interactions with others in which they communicate about their own and others' mental states. Because autistic children show marked deficits in the use of language and in interacting with others, they would be expected to experience deficits in their theory of mind. Peterson and Siegal (1999) reasoned that this would also be true, to a degree, for deaf children living in homes where no one else knew the sign language they used to communicate: Such children would be deprived of opportunities to develop their theory of mind adequately. In contrast, deaf children living in homes where others knew sign language would have such opportunities and would not experience these deficits.

To test these predictions, Peterson and Siegal had autistic children and several groups of deaf children (ones who could use sign language at home and ones who could not) perform tasks that measure children's theory of mind. In one task, for instance, children were shown a box that usually contained candy but in this case contained pencils. After discovering the unexpected contents, the children were asked what another child would expect to find in the box. A correct reply was that this other child would expect candy, because she or he wouldn't know, as the child did, that the box contained pencils. As shown in Figure 14.9, results confirmed the prediction

**Figure 14.9**
**The Role of Children's Theory of Mind in Autism**

Both autistic children and deaf children who did not have an opportunity to converse with others about mental states performed more poorly on tests of theory of mind than did children who were not deaf and deaf children who *did* have the opportunity to converse through sign language. These findings offer support for the view that deficits with respect to theory of mind play an important role in childhood autism.

(*Source:* Based on data from Peterson & Siegal, 1999.)

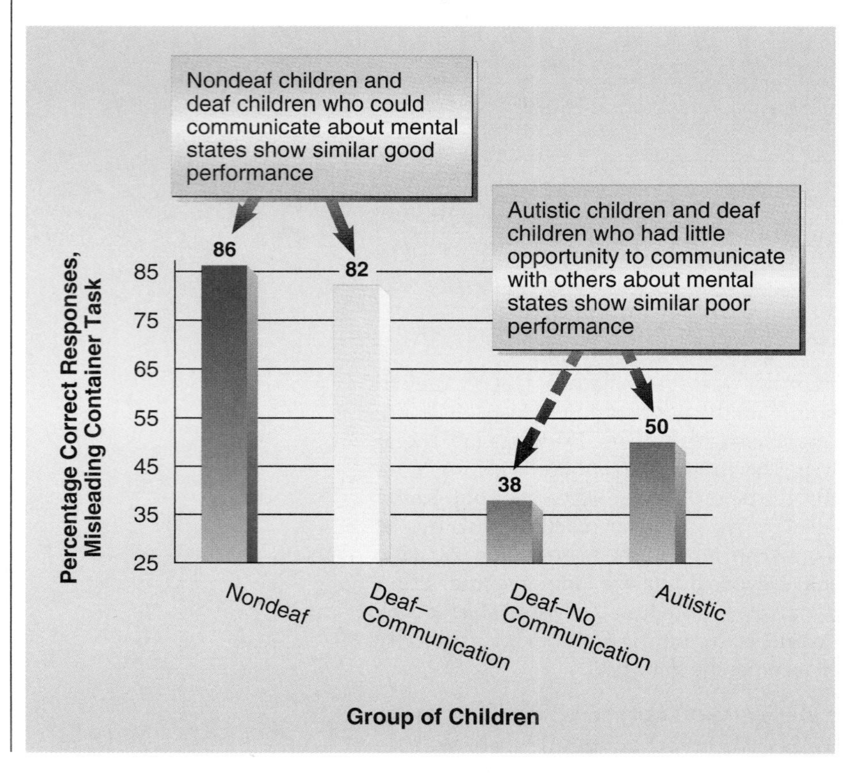

that both autistic children and deaf children who did not have an opportunity to converse with others about mental states would perform more poorly than would nondeaf children or deaf children who *did* have the opportunity to converse. These findings suggest that deficits with respect to theory of mind do indeed play a role in autistic disorder.

**REVIEW QUESTIONS**

- What is oppositional defiant disorder? Conduct disorder?
- What is attention-deficit/hyperactivity disorder?
- What are anorexia nervosa and bulimia nervosa?
- What is autistic disorder?

**Food for Thought**

Do you think efforts should be undertaken to discourage the media from overemphasizing thinness as a sign of female beauty?

# Mood Disorders: The Downs and Ups of Life

Have you ever felt truly "down in the dumps"—sad, blue, and dejected? How about "up in the clouds"—happy, elated, excited? Probably you can easily bring such experiences to mind, for everyone has swings in mood or emotional state. For most of us, these swings are usually moderate in scope; periods of deep despair and wild elation are rare. Some persons, however, experience swings in their emotional states that are much more extreme and prolonged. Their highs are higher, their lows are lower, and they spend more time in these states than most people. Such persons are described as suffering from **mood disorders.** Among the most important of these are *depressive disorders* and *bipolar disorders.*

**Mood Disorders:** Psychological disorders in which individuals experience swings in their emotional states that are much more extreme and prolonged than is true of most people.

**Depression:** A mood disorder in which individuals experience extreme unhappiness, lack of energy, and several related symptoms.

Web Link: *Homepage of the National Foundation for Depressive Illness, Inc.*

## Depressive Disorders: Probing the Depths of Despair

Unless we lead a truly charmed existence, our daily lives bring some events that make us feel sad or disappointed. A poor grade, breaking up with one's romantic partner, failure to get a promotion—these and many other events tip our emotional balance toward sadness. When do such reactions constitute depression? Most psychologist agree that several criteria are useful for reaching this decision.

First, persons suffering from **depression** experience truly profound unhappiness, and they experience it much of the time. Second, persons experiencing depression report that they have lost interest in all the usual pleasures of life. Eating, sex, sports, hobbies—all fail to provide the enjoyment they once did. Third, persons suffering from depression often experience significant weight loss (when not dieting) or gain. Depression may also involve fatigue, insomnia, feelings of worthlessness, a recurrent inability to think or concentrate, and recurrent thoughts of death or suicide. An individual who experiences five or more of these symptoms at once during the same two-week period is classified by the DSM–IV as undergoing a *major depressive episode* (see Figure 14.10 on page 550).

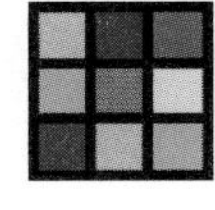

Depression is very common. In fact, it is experienced by 21.3 percent of women and 12.7 percent of men at some time during their lives (Kessler et al., 1994). This nearly two-to-one gender difference in depression rates has been reported in many studies (e.g., Culberton, 1997), especially in studies conducted in wealthy, developed countries; so it appears to be a real one. Why does it exist? As noted by Strickland

**Figure 14.10**
**Depression: The Emotional Sinkhole of Life**

A person experiencing a *major depressive episode* shows such symptoms as an intensely negative mood, loss of interest in all the things that usually give pleasure, significant loss or gain of weight, intense feelings of fatigue, and insomnia. Truly, such a person is in the depths of despair.

CourseCompass
Video 14.2: *Bipolar Disease*

(1992), several factors account for this finding, including the fact that females have traditionally had lower status, power, and income than males; must worry more than males about their personal safety; and are the victims of sexual harassment and assaults much more often than males. Gender differences in rates of depression may also stem, at least to a degree, from the fact that females are more willing to admit to such feelings than males, or from the fact that women are more likely than men to remember such episodes (Wilhelm & Parker, 1994).

Unfortunately, episodes of major depression are not isolated events; most people who experience one such episode also experience others during their lives—an average of five or six (Winokur, 1986). And others experience what is known as *double depression*—they recover from major depression but continue to experience a depressed mood (*dysthymic disorder*) or, in some cases, unusual irritability.

## Bipolar Disorders: Riding the Emotional Roller Coaster

If depression is the emotional sinkhole of life, **bipolar disorder** is life's emotional roller coaster. People suffering from bipolar disorder experience wide swings in mood. They move, over varying periods of time, between deep depression and an emotional state known as *mania,* in which they are extremely excited, elated, and energetic. During manic periods such persons speak rapidly, show a sharply decreased need for sleep, jump from one idea or activity to another, and show excessive involvement in pleasurable activities that have a high potential for harmful consequences. For example, they may engage in wild buying sprees or make extremely risky investments. Clearly, bipolar disorders are very disruptive not only to the individuals who experience them but to other people in their lives as well.

**Bipolar Disorder:** A mood disorder in which individuals experience very wide swings in mood, from deep depression to wild elation.

## The Causes of Depression: Its Biological and Psychological Roots

Depression tends to run in families (Egeland et al., 1987) and is about four times more likely to occur in both members of identical-twin pairs than in both members of nonidentical-twin pairs (Bowman & Nernberger, 1993). Overall, however, existing evidence suggests that genetic factors play a stronger role in bipolar than in unipolar depression. Other findings suggest that mood disorders may involve abnormalities in brain biochemistry. For example, it has been found that levels of two neurotransmitters, *norepinephrine* and *serotonin,* are lower in the brains of depressed persons than in those of nondepressed persons. Similarly, levels of these neurotransmitters are higher in the brains of persons showing mania. Further, when persons who have recovered from depression undergo procedures that reduce the levels of serotonin in their brains, their depressive symptoms return within twenty-four hours (Delgado et al., 1990).

Unfortunately, this relatively neat picture is complicated by the following facts: Not all persons suffering from depression show reduced levels of norepinephrine or serotonin, and not all persons demonstrating mania have increased levels of these neurotransmitters. A current hypothesis is that low levels of serotonin may allow other neurotransmitters such as dopamine and norepinephrine to swing out of control and that this, in turn, may lead to extreme changes in mood. However, this is just one possibility; at present, the precise nature of the neurochemical mechanisms that play a role in depression remains uncertain.

Several psychological factors have been found to play a role in depression. One of these is a pattern we encountered in Chapter 5: *learned helplessness* (Seligman, 1975), or beliefs on the part of individuals that they have no control over their own outcomes. Such views often develop after exposure to situations in which such lack of control is present, but then generalize to other situations where individuals' fate *is* at least partly in their hands. One result of such feelings of helplessness seems to be depression (e.g., Seligman et al., 1988).

Another psychological mechanism that plays a key role in depression involves negative views about oneself (Beck, 1976; Beck et al., 1979). Individuals suffering from depression often possess negative *self-schemas*—negative conceptions of their own traits, abilities, and behavior. As a result, they tend to be highly sensitive to criticism from others (Joiner, Alfano, & Metalsky, 1993). Because such persons are more likely to notice and remember negative information, their feelings of worthlessness strengthen; and when they are exposed to various stressors (e.g., the breakup of a romantic relationship, a failure at work), their thinking can become distorted in important and self-defeating ways. Depressed persons begin to see neutral or even pleasant events in a negative light—for instance, they may interpret a compliment from a friend as insincere, or someone's being late for an appointment as a sign of rejection. These distortions in thinking make it difficult for depressed people to make realistic judgments about events, and they begin to engage in *primitive thinking*—thinking characterized by global judgments that are absolute, invariant, and irreversible (for example, "I am basically weak, and can never be strong," or "I am always a coward in every situation I encounter"). Ultimately, depressed persons come to show what Beck describes as the *negative cognitive triad* in which they have automatic, repetitive, and negative thoughts about the self, the world, and the future. In sum, depressed persons see themselves as inadequate and worthless, feel that they can't cope with the demands made on them, and dread the future which, they believe, will bring more of the same.

Another cognitive factor that plays a role in depression is heightened *self-awareness*. Persons experiencing depression often focus their attention inward, on themselves. When they do, they often notice gaps between what they would like to be or what they'd like to accomplish, and what they are or where they are in life. Most people handle such gaps by adjusting their goals or standards: They realize they can't be perfect or attain every goal, so they adjust their hopes to be more in line with reality. Persons who become depressed, however, don't make such adjustments; they begin to torture themselves with self-criticism and feelings of worthlessness. This generates negative feelings, which lead to more self-criticism, and eventually to deep depression. Figure 14.11 on page 552 summarizes the role of the cognitive factors we have discussed—learned helplessness, negative self-schemas, and self-focused attention—in the development of depression. Fortunately, as we'll see in Chapter 15, several effective procedures for countering these factors have been developed (e.g., Zuroff et al., 1999) and together, these offer considerable hope for persons who experience depression.

## Suicide: When Life Becomes Unbearable

Web Link: *NIMH—In Harm's Way: Suicide in America*

Hopelessness, despair, negative views about oneself—these are some of the hallmarks of depression. Given such reactions, it is not surprising that many persons suffering from this disorder seek a drastic solution—**suicide,** or the taking of their own lives. In the United States, for instance, about 40,000 people commit suicide each year. This figure may actually be an underestimate, because many people who die because of high-risk behaviors, such as speeding on the highway or using dangerous drugs, may have intended to end their own lives. In addition, more than 300,000 people attempt suicide but don't succeed (Andreason & Black, 1995). More than two times as many women as men attempt suicide, but men are three to four times more likely to succeed when they take this course of action, mainly because men use no-fail methods such as jumping from high places, guns, or hanging; women tend to use less certain tactics such as poison or drug overdose (Kaplan &

**Suicide:** The voluntary taking of one's own life.

**Figure 14.11**
**Cognitive Mechanisms in Depression**

Extensive research indicates that the cognitive mechanisms and factors shown here often play a role in depression.

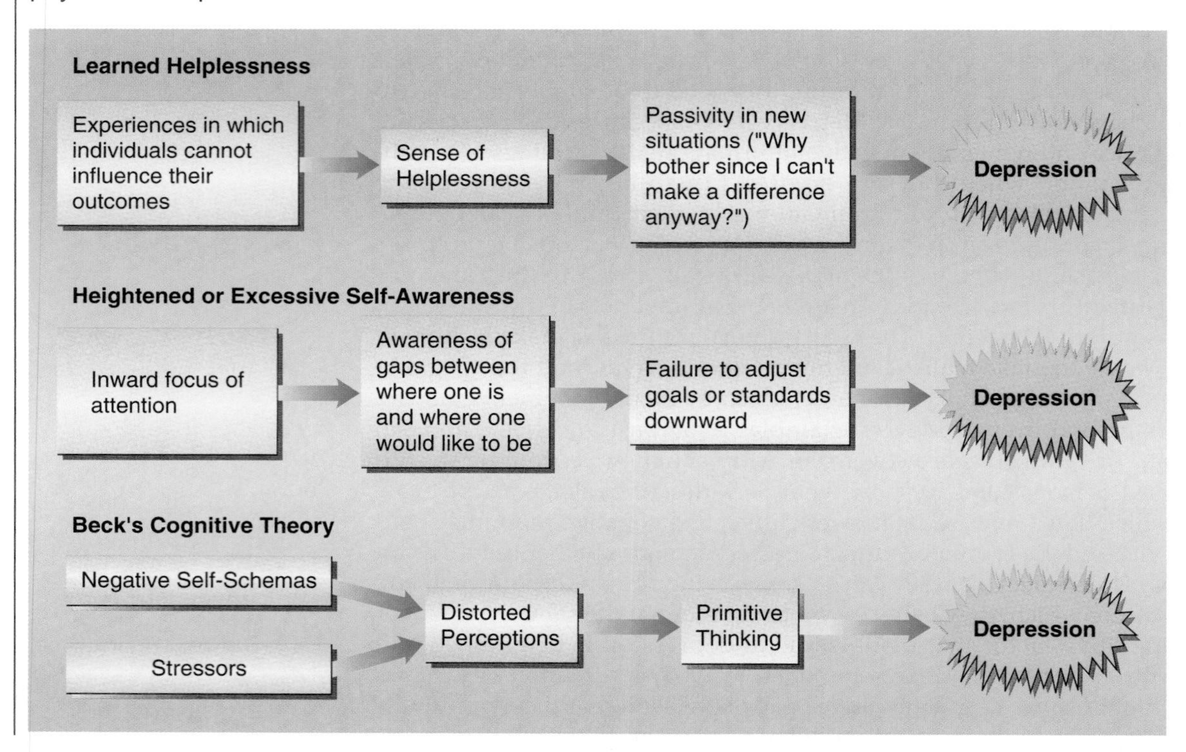


Sadock, 1991). Suicide is the tenth or eleventh most frequent cause of death in the United States. Suicide rates vary with age; the highest rates occur among older people, but suicide has been on the rise among young people and is now, disturbingly, high even among teenagers. Why do people turn to suicide? Notes left by persons who have killed themselves and information provided by suicide attempters suggest that there are many different reasons. However, problems with relationships seem to head the list.

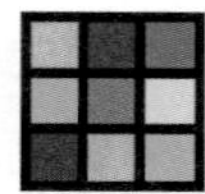

Suicide varies across different cultures. In some northern European countries and in Japan, the suicide rate is as high as 25 per 100,000 inhabitants. In countries with strong religious prohibitions against suicide, such as Greece and Ireland, the rate is about 6 per 100,000. In the United States it is about 12 per 100,000. Suicide in the United States is more common among persons of European descent than among those of African descent, but this gap narrowed in the late twentieth century (Bongar, 1991). Suicide rates are low among U.S. citizens of Hispanic descent but high among Native American males—as high as 24 per 100,000. Perhaps most disturbing of all, suicide rates have increased sharply among U.S. adolescents in recent decades and are now about 15 per 100,000 for boys and 3 per 100,000 for girls (Robins & Rutter, 1990). Indeed, suicide is the third leading cause of death for adolescents fifteen to nineteen years old, accounting for fully 14 percent of all deaths in this age group (Garland & Zigler, 1993).

Adolescents who commit suicide often do so impulsively, soon after a highly stressful event—for instance, after being dumped by a boyfriend or girlfriend, being humiliated in some other way in public, or failing a major exam in school. Suicide pacts, too play a role: Teen lovers sometimes agree to kill themselves if they can't be together, and the two young men who killed more than a dozen of their teachers and classmates in a Colorado high school in 1999 had agreed in advance to take their own lives. As you might guess, most adolescents who commit suicide—about 80 percent—have long-standing mental health problems (Shaffer, 1990) such as depression, externalizing behavior disorders, or substance abuse.

**SUICIDE PREVENTION** Can suicide be prevented? Evidence on this issue suggests that three steps may be helpful: (1) accurately assessing individuals' risk for suicidal behavior—identifying those most at risk for such actions; (2) helping resolve the immediate crises that surround and lead to most suicide attempts; and (3) providing treatment to help persons at risk for suicide recover from feelings of hopelessness and despair, and to equip such persons with more effective skills for solving the life problems they face. Of course, it is one thing to state these steps, and quite another to implement them effectively. Persons at risk for committing suicide often are *not* readily identified, and they are frequently too depressed to expend the effort—cognitive and otherwise—needed to produce real change. In short, there is no simple or totally reliable procedure for preventing suicide. However, appropriate treatment *can* help in at least some cases, and using every available technique is certainly well justified, given that every successful intervention represents a life saved. For some suggestions about what you yourself can do to prevent suicide by people you know, see the **Making Psychology Part of Your Life** section at the end of this chapter.

**REVIEW QUESTIONS**

- What are the major symptoms of depression? Of bipolar disorder?
- What factors play a role in the occurrence of mood disorders?
- What steps can be taken to prevent suicide?

## Anxiety Disorders: When Dread Debilitates

Web Link: *Anxiety Disorders Association of America*

At one time or another, we all experience **anxiety**—a diffuse or vague concern that something unpleasant will soon occur. If such feelings become intense and persist for long periods of time, however, they can constitute another important form of mental disorder. Such **anxiety disorders** take several different forms, and we'll consider the most important of these here (e.g., Zinberg & Barlow, 1995).

Audio 14.2: *Effects of Social Phobia*

### Phobias: Excessive Fear of Specific Objects or Situations

Most people express some fear of snakes, heights, violent storms, and buzzing insects such as bees or wasps. Because all of these can pose real threats to our safety, such reactions are adaptive, up to a point. But if such fears become excessive, in that they cause intense emotional distress and interfere significantly with everyday activities, they constitute **phobias,** one important type of anxiety disorder. The effects of one type of phobia are vividly illustrated by the following case:

> "At nine years old, Jessica's fear of heights was so strong she was unable to attend schools with more than one story. She panicked when her class went on field trips where there were steps. She was both frightened and embarrassed in front of her classmates on their trip to a museum; she was able to climb the stairs to the second floor, but then she had to lie down and slide on her stomach to get back down."

**Anxiety:** Increased arousal accompanied by generalized feelings of fear or apprehension.

**Anxiety Disorders:** Psychological disorders that take several different forms, but which are all related to a generalized feeling of anxiety.

**Phobias:** Intense, irrational fears of objects or events.

**Figure 14.12**
**Social Phobias: Cultural Differences in Their Focus**

Social phobias exist all around the world, but their content or focus varies across cultures. In individualistic cultures such as that of the United States, such phobias tend to focus on fear of being evaluated negatively by others. In collectivistic cultures such as that of Japan, social phobias focus on individuals' fear that they will do something to offend other members of their social group (e.g., say something offensive, have a displeasing appearance, or emit an offensive odor).

While many different phobias exist, most seem to involve fear of animals (e.g., bees, spiders, snakes); the natural environment (e.g., thunder, darkness, wind); illness and injections (e.g., blood, needles, pain, contamination); and various specific situations (e.g., enclosed places, travel, empty rooms). The most common phobia of all is *social phobia*—excessive fear of situations in which a person might be evaluated and perhaps embarrassed. It is estimated that fully 13 percent of people living in the United States have had a social phobia at some time in their lives, and almost 8 percent report having experienced such fears during the past year (Kessler et al., 1994). Social phobias appear to exist all around the world, but they take different forms in different cultures (see Figure 14.12). In collectivistic cultures such as Japan, social phobias seem to focus on individuals' fear that they will do something to offend other members of their social group (e.g., say something offensive, have a displeasing appearance, emit an offensive odor) (Takahashi, 1989). In individualistic cultures such as those in Europe or North America, social phobias tend to focus on the fear of being evaluated negatively by others in public situations.

What are the causes of phobias? One possibility involves the process of *classical conditioning,* described in Chapter 5. Through such learning, stimuli that do not initially elicit strong emotional reactions can often come to do so. For example, an individual may acquire an intense fear of buzzing sounds such as those made by bees after being stung by a bee or wasp. In the past, the buzzing sound was a neutral stimulus that produced little or no reaction. The pain of being stung, however, is an unconditioned stimulus; and as a result of being closely paired with the pain, the buzzing sound acquires the capacity to evoke strong fear (e.g., Mulkens, deJong, & Merckelbach, 1996). Genetic factors, too, may play a role. Some findings suggest that persons who develop phobias are prone to excessive physiological arousal in certain situations, perhaps because portions of their brain (e.g., the limbic system, the amygdala) are overactive (Merkelbach et al., 1996). This intense arousal can serve as the basis for classical conditioning and other forms of learning, and so can result in phobias.

## Panic Disorder and Agoraphobia

**Panic Disorder:** Condition characterized by periodic, unexpected attacks of intense, terrifying anxiety known as panic attacks.

**Agoraphobia:** Intense fear of specific situations in which individuals suspect that help will not be available should they experience an incapacitating or embarrassing event.

The intense fears associated with phobias are triggered by specific objects or situations. Some individuals, in contrast, experience intense, terrifying anxiety that is *not* activated by a specific event or situation. Such *panic attacks* are the hallmark of **panic disorder,** a condition characterized by periodic, unexpected attacks of intense, terrifying anxiety. Panic attacks come on suddenly, reach peak intensity within a few minutes, and may last for hours (e.g., Barlow, 1988). They leave the persons who experience them feeling as if they are about to die or are losing their minds. Among the specific symptoms of panic attacks are a racing heart, sweating, dizziness, nausea, trembling, palpitations, pounding heart, feelings of unreality, fear of losing control, fear of dying, numbness or tingling sensations, and chills or hot flashes.

Although panic attacks often seem to occur out of the blue, in the absence of any specific triggering event, they often take place in specific situations. In such cases panic disorder is said to be associated with **agoraphobia,** or fear of situations in which the individual suspects that help will not be available if needed. Agoraphobia often takes the form of intense fear of open spaces, fear of being in public, fear of traveling—or, commonly, fear of having a panic attack while away from home! Persons suffering from panic disorder with agoraphobia often experience anticipatory anxiety—they are terrified of becoming afraid. I have a friend who suffers from one form of agoraphobia: He is totally unwilling to travel by airplane. Because he has an active career, this condition causes him great difficulties. He has to drive or take trains even to distant locations. Yet he resists all suggestions that he seek professional help. Apparently the mere thought of discussing his problems is too anxiety-provoking for him to contemplate.

What causes panic attacks? Existing evidence indicates that both biological factors and cognitive factors play a role. With respect to biological factors, it has been found that there is a genetic component in this disorder: About 50 percent of people with panic disorder have relatives who have it too (Barlow, 1988). In addition, PET scans of the brains of persons who suffer from panic attacks suggest that even in the nonpanic state, their brains may be functioning differently from those of other persons (e.g., Reiman et al., 1989). A portion of the brain stem, the *locus coeruleus* (LC), may play a key role in panic experiences. This area seems to function as a primitive "alarm system," and stimulating it artificially in animals results in paniclike behavior (Gorman et al., 1989). It seems possible that in persons who experience panic attacks, the LC may be hypersensitive to certain stimuli (e.g., lactic acid, a natural by-product of exercise); as a result, these persons may experience intense fear in situations in which others do not (e.g., Papp et al., 1993). No conclusive evidence on this possible mechanism yet exists, but it seems worthy of further study.

**Figure 14.13**
**Barlow's Model of Panic Disorders**

According to one influential model of panic disorders, such reactions stem from the effects of stress coupled with the tendencies to perceive relatively harmless stressors as signs of mortal danger and to remain vigilant and "on guard" against such imagined dangers.
(*Source:* Based on suggestions by Barlow, 1988, 1993.)

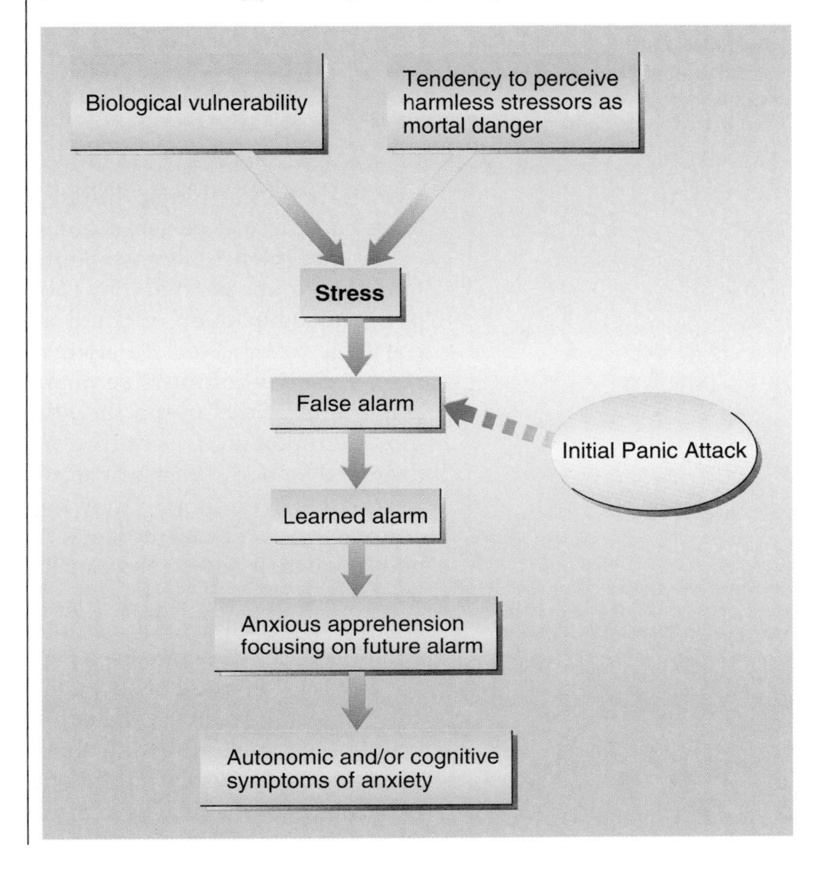


With respect to cognitive factors, persons suffering from panic disorder tend to show a pattern of interpreting bodily sensations as being more dangerous than they really are—for instance, they perceive palpitations as a sign of a heart attack—and so experience anxiety, which itself induces further bodily changes and sensations. A diathesis–stress model proposed by Barlow (1988, 1993) suggests that panic disorder combines biological vulnerability with cognitive factors such as the tendency to perceive relatively harmless stressors as signs of mortal danger and the tendency to then remain vigilant and "on guard" against such imagined dangers. This model is summarized in Figure 14.13.

CourseCompass
Web Link: *Obsessive-Compulsive Foundation*

Video 14.3: *Obsessive-Compulsive Disorder*

Audio 14.3: *Gender and Obsessive-Compulsive Disorder*

## Obsessive–Compulsive Disorder: Behaviors and Thoughts outside One's Control

Have you ever left your home, gotten halfway down the street, and then returned to see if you really locked the door or turned off the stove? And have you ever

**Figure 14.14**
**Obsessive–Compulsive Disorder: A Humorous Example**

Although obsessive–compulsive disorder is far from a laughing matter, the repetitive, ritualistic behaviors shown by compulsive individuals are a favorite theme of cartoonists.

(*Source:* ROBOTMAN reprinted by permission of United Feature Syndicate, Inc.)

worried about catching a disease by touching infected people or objects? Most of us have had these experiences, and they are completely normal. But some persons experience intense anxiety about such concerns. These individuals have disturbing thoughts or images that they cannot get out of their minds *(obsessions)* unless they perform some action or ritual that somehow reassures them and helps to break the cycle *(compulsions).* Persons who have such experiences may be experiencing **obsessive–compulsive disorder,** another important type of anxiety disorder. What kind of disturbing thoughts or images do such persons have? Among the most common are fear of dirt or germs or of touching infected people or objects; disgust over body wastes or secretions; undue concern about not having done a job adequately even though they know quite well that they have; and fear of having antireligious or sexual thoughts. Common compulsions—actions people perform to neutralize their obsessions—include repetitive hand washing, checking doors, windows, water, or gas repeatedly; counting objects a precise number of times or repeating an action a specific number of times; and hoarding old mail, newspapers, and other useless objects (see Figure 14.14).

What is the cause of such reactions? We all have repetitious thoughts occasionally. For example, after watching a film containing disturbing scenes of violence, we may find ourselves thinking about these over and over again. Most of us soon manage to distract ourselves from such unpleasant thoughts. But individuals who develop obsessive–compulsive disorder are unable to do so. They are made anxious by their obsessive thoughts, yet they can't dismiss them readily from their minds. Moreover, they have had past experiences—for instance, embarrassments—that suggest to them that some thoughts are so dangerous they must be avoided at all costs. As a result, they become even more anxious, and the cycle builds. Only by performing specific actions can these individuals ensure their "safety" and reduce their anxiety. Therefore, they engage in complex repetitive rituals that can gradually grow to fill most of their day. Because these rituals do help reduce anxiety, the tendency to perform them grows stronger. Unless such persons receive effective outside help, they have little chance of escaping from their self-constructed, anxiety-ridden prisons.

**CourseCompass**
Web Link: *Posttraumatic Stress Disorder*

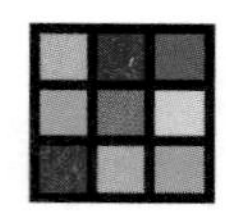

Some intriguing gender differences exist with respect to obsessive–compulsive disorder. Although the rate of this disorder is about equal for females and males, females are much more likely to be compulsive "washers" than males. In contrast, there are no gender differences with respect to other compulsive behaviors such as checking items repeatedly or counting (Emmelkamp, 1982). These findings emphasize the fact that sociocultural factors often influence not only the incidence of mental disorders, but their specific form as well.

**Obsessive–Compulsive Disorder:** An anxiety disorder in which individuals have recurrent, disturbing thoughts (obsessions) they can't prevent unless they engage in specific behaviors (compulsions).

## Posttraumatic Stress Disorder

Imagine that you are sleeping peacefully in your own bed when suddenly the ground under your home heaves and shakes, and you are thrown to the floor. Once awakened, you find yourself surrounded by the sounds of objects, walls, and even entire buildings crashing to the ground—accompanied by shrieks of fear and pain from your neighbors or perhaps even your own family. This is precisely the kind of experience reported by many persons following earthquakes.

Such experiences are described as *traumatic* by psychologists because they are extraordinary in nature—and extraordinarily disturbing. It is not surprising, then, that some persons exposed to them experience **posttraumatic stress disorder,** or PTSD—a disorder in which people persistently reexperience the traumatic event in their thoughts or dreams; feel as if they are reliving the event from time to time; persistently avoid stimuli associated with the traumatic event (places, people, thoughts); and persistently experience symptoms of increased arousal such as difficulty falling asleep, irritability, outbursts of anger, or difficulty in concentrating. Posttraumatic stress disorder can stem from a wide range of traumatic events—natural disasters, accidents, rape and other assaults, torture, or the horrors of wartime combat (see Figure 14.15) (Basoglu et al., 1996; Layman et al., 1996; Vernberg et al., 1996).

**Figure 14.15**
**Traumatic Events: One Cause of Psychological Disorders**

Some individuals who experience traumatic events develop posttraumatic stress disorder, in which they persistently reexperience the traumatic event in their thoughts or dreams and show signs of increased arousal such as difficulty falling asleep, irritability, and difficulty in concentrating.

Not all persons exposed to traumatic events experience PTSD, so a key question is this: What factors lead to PTSD's occurrence? Research on this question suggests that many factors play a role. The amount of social support trauma victims receive after the traumatic event seems crucial (e.g., Vernberg et al., 1996): The more support, the less likely are such persons to develop PTSD. Similarly, the coping strategies chosen by trauma victims are important. Effective strategies such as trying to see the good side of things (e.g., "I survived!") help to prevent PTSD from developing, whereas ineffective strategies such as blaming oneself for the traumatic event ("I should have moved away from here!") increase its likelihood. Individual differences, too, play a role; PTSD is more likely among persons who are passive, inner-directed, and highly sensitive to criticism and who exhibited social maladjustment before the trauma (e.g., legal difficulties, irresponsibility) than among persons who don't show these traits (Schnurr, Friedman, & Rosenberg, 1993). In sum, it appears that whether individuals experience posttraumatic stress disorder after exposure to a frightening event depends on several different factors.

**Posttraumatic Stress Disorder:** A disorder in which people persistently reexperience a traumatic event in their thoughts or dreams, feel as if they are reliving this event from time to time, persistently avoid stimuli associated with the traumatic event, and may experience several other symptoms.

**REVIEW QUESTIONS**

- What are phobias?
- What is panic disorder?
- What is obsessive-compulsive disorder?
- What is posttraumatic stress disorder?

# Dissociative and Somatoform Disorders

As we have just seen, traumatic events sometimes result in posttraumatic stress disorder. This is not the only mental disorder that can result from such events, however. Two other major types of disorder seem to involve dramatic, unexpected, and involuntary reactions to traumatic experiences: *dissociative disorders* and *somatoform disorders.* Dissociative disorders involve disruptions in a person's memory, consciousness, or identity—processes that are normally integrated. In contrast, somatoform disorders involve physical symptoms for which there is no apparent physical cause. Although these disorders are classified separately in the DSM–IV, I'll cover them together here, because historically they have been viewed as stemming from similar causes and involving similar symptoms. As will soon be apparent, though, they are distinct in many ways.

CourseCompass
Web Link: *Multiple Personality Disorder*

CourseCompass
Web Link: *The Spectrum of Dissociative Disorders*

CourseCompass
Web Link: *Commentary on "Multiple Personality and Moral Responsibility"*

## Dissociative Disorders

Have you ever awakened during the night and, just for a moment, been uncertain about where you were or even who you were? Such temporary disruptions in our normal cognitive functioning are far from rare; many persons experience them from time to time as a result of fatigue, illness, or the use of alcohol or other drugs. **Dissociative disorders,** however, go far beyond such experiences. They involve much more profound losses of identity or memory, intense feelings of unreality, a sense of being depersonalized (i.e., separate from oneself), and uncertainty about one's own identity.

Dissociative disorders take several different forms. In **dissociative amnesia,** individuals suddenly experience a loss of memory that does not stem from medical conditions or other mental disorders. Such losses can be localized, involving only a specific period of time, or generalized, involving memory for the person's entire life. In another dissociative disorder, **dissociative fugue,** an individual suddenly leaves home and travels to a new location where he or she has no memory of his or her previous life. In *depersonalization disorder* the individual retains memory but feels like an actor in a dream or movie.

As dramatic as these disorders are, they pale when compared with the most amazing—and controversial—dissociative disorder, **dissociative identity disorder.** This was known as *multiple personality disorder* in the past, and it involves a shattering of personal identity into at least two—and often more—separate but coexisting personalities, each possessing different traits, behaviors, memories, and emotions. Usually, there is one *host personality*—the primary identity that is present most of the time, and one or more *alters*—alternative personalities that appear from time to time. *Switching,* the process of changing from one personality to another, often seems to occur in response to anxiety brought on by thoughts or memories of previous traumatic experiences.

Until the 1950s, cases of dissociative identity disorder were rare. Starting with the book *The Three Faces of Eve* (Thigpen & Cleckley, 1957), however, both interest in this disorder and its reported frequency skyrocketed. In 1973 a book describing one case, *Sybil* (Schreiber, 1973), became a best-seller and was soon made into a TV program. *Sybil* offered an interpretation of the causes of this disorder that soon became famous—and highly controversial. This explanation suggested that dissociative identity disorder occurs as a response to traumatic events early in life, especially sexual abuse. In order to deal with such events, the theory contended, children create alternate personalities that can cope with such experiences more effectively than they, and may also be able to protect them from further harm.

In the years that followed, thousands of new cases of dissociative identity disorder were diagnosed by psychiatrists and some psychologists. The overwhelming majority of these cases were women who, during therapy sessions (and often under hypnosis), developed dozens or even hundreds (!) of alters, and who also suddenly

**Dissociative Disorders:** Disorders involving disruptions in a person's memory, consciousness, or identity.

**Dissociative Amnesia:** Profound amnesia stemming from the active motivation to forget specific events or information.

**Dissociative Fugue:** A sudden and extreme disturbance of memory in which individuals wander off, adopt a new identity, and are unable to recall their own past.

**Dissociative Identity Disorder:** A condition previously called *multiple personality disorder,* in which a single person seems to possess two or more distinct identities or personality states and these take control of the person's behavior at different times.

had "recovered memories" of having endured horrible sexual abuse and satanic rituals while children. These "memories" led many to bring legal charges against their parents (mothers as well as fathers) and other relatives, thus shattering families. For example, consider the case of Elizabeth Carlson. Suffering from depression, Ms. Carlson sought help from psychiatrist Dr. Diane Humenansky (Acocella, 1998). Dr. Humenansky asked her to read *Sybil* and *The Three Faces of Eve* and instructed her to think about scenes of childhood sexual abuse. Ms. Carlson did, and soon "recalled" instances in which she was abused by as many as fifty relatives, including both parents, both sets of grandparents, aunts, uncles, and even great-grandparents (see Figure 14.16). Dr. Humenansky used hypnosis and "guided imagery" to awaken Ms. Carlson's supposedly buried memories of early abuse, urging her to imagine herself in scenes involving satanic rituals, robed figures, candles, and cannibalism. Primed in this way, Ms. Carlson reported vivid memories of all these events. She also identified several different alters—Little Miss Fluff, a hussy named Nikita, two nuns, two male alters, and a scared, depressed Old Lady. Needless to say, the mass media had a field day with this and many other equally dramatic cases.

**Figure 14.16**
**Dissociative Identity Disorder: Fraud, Suggestion, or Reality?**

In response to repeated suggestions from her therapist (psychiatrist Dr. Diane Humenansky), Elizabeth Carlson "remembered" sexual abuse by more than fifty relatives and developed several alters. Later, however, she realized that none of these experiences were real. She sued Dr. Humenansky and won damages of $2.5 million for malpractice. Cases such as these cast doubt on some of the more extreme claims concerning dissociative identity disorder. (*Source:* © Sally Savage.)

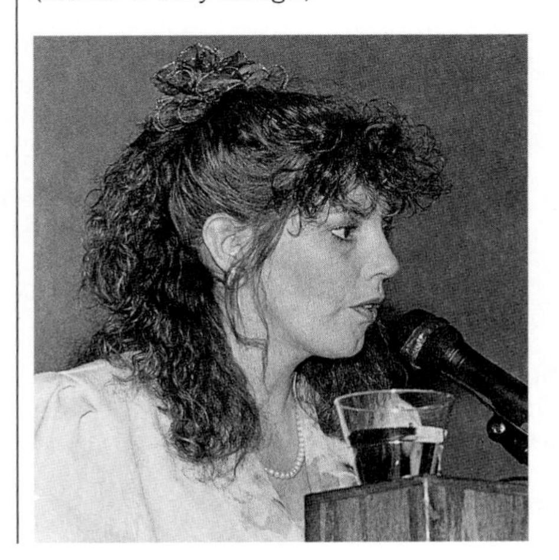

Does all of this cause warning bells to sound in your head? It should, because, as we saw in Chapter 6, memory is often a tricky thing. We often forget information we'd prefer to remember and sometimes "remember" experiences we never had or information we never encountered. And unfortunately, the procedures used by Dr. Humenansky and many other psychiatrists who specialized in treating dissociative identity disorder were ones that might well prime such false memories. Indeed, Ms. Carlson and many other patients gradually realized that this was the case—that they had never actually been abused and that their alternative personalities, too, were the result of strong suggestions from their therapists. Ultimately, Ms. Carlson sued Dr. Humenansky for malpractice and won damages of $2.5 million! (As you can probably guess, psychologists rarely if ever use the kind of procedures used by Dr. Humenansky to treat dissociative identity disorder.)

Now for the key question: Do cases like this suggest that dissociative identity disorder is a complete fraud? Not necessarily. Many mental health professionals believe that this disorder does indeed exist, and it *is* included in the DSM–IV. Several kinds of evidence offer support for its reality. First, persons with dissociative identity disorder sometimes show distinctive patterns of brain activity when each of their supposedly separate personalities appears (Kaplan & Sadock, 1991). Similarly, alters sometimes differ in ways that are hard to fake: Some are right-handed and others left-handed; some show allergic reactions to various substances and others do not; and some alters may be color blind while others are not (Kluft, 1995). Findings such as these suggest that this disorder may indeed be real in at least some cases. However, this evidence itself is somewhat controversial; so at present the best approach is one of considerable caution. This is in no way to suggest that the potentially harmful effects of early traumatic experiences should be ignored—if these are severe, many psychologists believe, they may indeed lead to some kind of dissociation (splitting of identity or consciousness). But accepting exaggerated claims about dissociative identity disorder does seem unjustified.

**REVIEW QUESTIONS**

- What are dissociative disorders such as dissociative amnesia?
- What is dissociative identity disorder?

*Food for Thought*

What do *you* think—is dissociative identity disorder real?

## Somatoform Disorders: Physical Symptoms without Physical Causes

Several of Freud's early cases, ones that played an important role in his developing theory of personality, involved the following puzzling situation. An individual would show some physical symptom (such as deafness or paralysis of some part of the body); yet careful examination would reveal no underlying physical causes for the problem. Such disorders are known as **somatoform disorders**—disorders in which individuals have physical symptoms in the absence of identifiable physical causes for these symptoms.

One such disorder is **somatization disorder,** a condition in which an individual has a history of many physical complaints, beginning before age thirty, that occur over a period of years and result in treatment being sought for significant impairments in social, occupational, or other important areas of life. The symptoms reported may include pain in various parts of the body (e.g., head, back, abdomen), gastrointestinal problems (e.g., nausea, vomiting, bloating), sexual symptoms (e.g., sexual indifference, excessive menstrual bleeding), and neurological symptoms not related to pain (e.g., impaired coordination or balance, paralysis, blindness).

Another somatoform disorder is **hypochondriasis**—preoccupation with fear of disease. Hypochondriacs do not actually have the diseases they fear, but they persist in worrying about them, despite repeated reassurance by their doctors that they are healthy. Many hypochondriacs are not simply faking; they feel the pain and discomfort they report and are truly afraid that they are sick or will soon become sick.

Other persons who seek medical help *are* faking. For instance, persons with **Munchausen's syndrome** devote their lives to seeking—and often obtaining—costly and painful medical procedures they realize they don't need. Why? Perhaps because they relish the attention, or because they enjoy fooling physicians and other trained professionals. In any case, such persons waste precious medical resources and often run up huge bills that must be paid by insurance companies or government programs; so Munchausen's syndrome, no matter how strange, is definitely no laughing matter.

Yet another somatoform disorder is known as **conversion disorder.** Persons with this disorder actually experience physical problems such as *motor deficits* (poor balance or coordination, paralysis, or weakness of arms or legs) or *sensory deficits* (loss of sensitivity to touch or pain, double vision, blindness, deafness). While these disabilities are quite real to the persons involved, there is no medical condition present to account for them.

What are the causes of somatoform disorders? As is true with almost all mental disorders, several factors seem to play a role. Individuals who develop such disorders seem to have a tendency to focus on inner sensations—they are high in *private self-consciousness.* In addition, they tend to perceive normal bodily sensations as being more intense and disturbing than do most people. Finally, they have a high level of negative affectivity—they tend to be pessimistic, fear uncertainty, experience guilt, and have low self-esteem (Nietzel et al., 1998). Together, these traits create a predisposition or vulnerability to stressors (e.g., intense conflict with others, severe trauma); operating together, in a diathesis–stress model, these factors then contribute to the emergence of somatoform disorders.

In addition, of course, persons who develop such disorders learn that their symptoms often yield increased attention and better treatment from family members: These persons are reluctant to give the patient a hard time, bcause he or she is already suffering so much! In short, these patients gain important forms of reinforcement from their disorder.

**Somatoform Disorders:** Disorders in which individuals experience physical symptoms for which there is no apparent physical cause.

**Somatization Disorder:** A condition in which an individual has a history of many physical complaints, beginning before age thirty, that occur over a period of years and result in treatment being sought for significant impairments in social, occupational, or other important areas of life.

**Hypochondriasis:** A disorder involving preoccupation with fears of disease or illness.

**Munchausen's Syndrome:** A syndrome in which individuals pretend to have various medical problems in order to get attention from health practitioners.

**Conversion Disorder:** A somatoform disorder in which individuals experience actual physical impairment such as blindness, deafness, or paralysis for which there is no underlying medical cause.

**REVIEW QUESTIONS**

- What are somatoform disorders?
- What factors contribute to the occurrence of somatoform disorders?

**Sexual Desire Disorders:** Disorders involving a lack of interest in sex or active aversion to sexual activity.

**Sexual Arousal Disorders:** The inability to attain or maintain an erection (males) or the absence of vaginal swelling and lubrication (females).

# Sexual and Gender Identity Disorders

As we saw in Chapter 12, Freud believed that many psychological disorders can be traced to disturbances in *psychosexual development.* While Freud's theory is not widely accepted by psychologists today, there is little doubt that individuals experience many problems relating to sexuality and gender identity. Several of these are discussed below.

## Sexual Dysfunctions: Disturbances in Desire and Arousal

Sexual dysfunctions include disturbances in sexual desire and/or sexual arousal, disturbances in the ability to attain orgasms, and disorders involving pain during sexual relations. **Sexual desire disorders** involve a lack of interest in sex or active aversion to sexual activity. Persons experiencing these disorders report that they rarely have the sexual fantasies most persons generate, that they avoid all or almost all sexual activity, and that these reactions cause them considerable distress.

In contrast, **sexual arousal disorders** involve the inability to attain or maintain an erection (males) or the absence of vaginal swelling and lubrication (females). *Orgasm disorders* include the delay or absence of orgasms in both sexes as well as *premature ejaculation* (reaching orgasm too quickly) in males. Needless to say, these problems cause considerable distress to the persons who experience them (e.g., Rowland, Cooper, & Slob, 1996).

**Figure 14.17**
**Paraphilias for Sale?**

Many men find alluring lingerie to be sexually arousing. Such reactions, however, are not a sign of a sexual disorder (a paraphilia) unless these objects *must* be present for sexual arousal to occur.

## Paraphilias: Disturbances in Sexual Object or Behavior

What is sexually arousing? For most people, the answer involves the sight or touch of another human being. But many people find other stimuli arousing, too. The large volume of business done by Victoria's Secret and other companies specializing in alluring lingerie for women stems, at least in part, from the fact that many men find such garments mildly sexually arousing (see Figure 14.17). Other persons find that inflicting or receiving some slight pain during lovemaking increases their arousal and sexual pleasure. Do such reactions

**Paraphilias:** Disorders in which sexual arousal cannot occur without the presence of unusual imagery or acts.

constitute sexual disorders? According to most psychologists, and the DSM–IV, they do not. Only when unusual or bizarre imagery or acts are *necessary* for sexual arousal (that is, when arousal cannot occur without them) do such preferences qualify as a disorder. Such disorders are termed **paraphilias,** and they take many different forms.

In *fetishes,* individuals become aroused exclusively by inanimate objects. Often these are articles of clothing; in more unusual cases they can involve animals, dead bodies, or even human waste. *Frotteurism,* another paraphilia, involves fantasies and urges focused on touching or rubbing against a nonconsenting person. The touching, not the coercive nature of the act, is what persons with this disorder find sexually arousing. The most disturbing paraphilia of all is *pedophilia,* in which individuals experience sexual urges and fantasies involving children, generally ones younger than thirteen. When such urges are translated into overt actions, the effects on the young victims can, as I noted in Chapter 9, be devastating (e.g., Ambuel, 1995). Two other paraphilias are *sexual sadism* and *sexual masochism.* In the former, individuals become sexually aroused only by inflicting pain or humiliation on others. In the latter, they are aroused by receiving such treatment. See Table 14.2 for a description of these and other paraphilias.

**TABLE 14.2**

## Paraphilias

Paraphilias are sexual disorders in which unusual or bizarre imagery or acts are necessary for sexual arousal. Some of the more common types of paraphilias are described here.

| Description | Symptoms |
|---|---|
| Exhibitionism | Sexual urges or arousing fantasies involving exposure of one's genitals to an unsuspecting stranger |
| Voyeurism | Recurrent sexual urges or arousing fantasies involving the act of observing an unsuspecting person who is naked, disrobing, or engaging in sexual activity |
| Fetishism | Sexual arousal or persistent fantasies about or actual use of nonliving objects |
| Sadism and Masochism | Sadism: Sexual arousal or fantasies about or from engaging in actions of dominating or beating another person<br>Masochism: Sexual arousal or fantasies about or from engaging in the act of being dominated, humiliated, or even beaten |
| Transvestic Fetishism | Intense sexual urges and arousing fantasies involving cross-dressing (dressing in the clothing of the other sex) |
| Other Paraphilias | Frotteurism: Sexual urges involving touching or rubbing against a nonconsenting person<br>Necrophilia: Sexual obsession with corpses<br>Klismaphilia: Sexual excitement from having enemas<br>Coprophilia: Sexual interest in feces<br>Zoophilia: Sexual gratification from having sexual activity with animals |

## Gender Identity Disorders

Have you ever read about a man who altered his gender to become a woman, or vice versa? Such individuals feel, often from an early age, that they were born with the wrong sexual identity. They identify strongly with the other sex and show preferences for cross-dressing (wearing clothing associated with the other gender). They are displeased with their own bodies and request—again, often from an early age—that they receive medical treatment to alter their primary and secondary sex characteristics. In the past, there was little that medicine could do satisfy these desires on the part of persons suffering from **gender identity disorder.** Advances in surgical techniques, however, have now made it possible for such persons to undergo *sex-change operations,* in which their sexual organs are actually altered to approximate those of the other gender. Several thousand individuals have undergone such operations, and existing evidence indicates that most report being satisfied with the results and happier than they were before (Green & Blanchard, 1995). However, it is difficult to evaluate such self-reports. Perhaps after waiting years for surgery and spending large amounts of money for their sex-change operations, such persons have little choice but to report positive effects. Clearly, such surgery is a drastic step and should be performed only when the would-be patient fully understands all potential risks.

**REVIEW QUESTIONS**

- What are sexual dysfunctions and paraphilias?
- What is gender identity disorder?

## Personality Disorders: Traits That Harm

Web Link: *Personality Disorders*

Web Link: *Mental Health Net—Borderline Personality Disorder*

Have you ever known someone who was highly suspicious and mistrustful of others in virtually all situations? How about someone who seemed to believe that the world revolved around him or her—that he or she was the most important individual on earth? Someone who seemed to have no conscience whatsoever, never experiencing guilt or regret no matter how much he or she hurt others? These may well have been people with what psychologists term **personality disorders.** These disorders are defined by the DSM–IV as extreme and inflexible personality traits that are distressing to the persons who have them or cause them problems in school, work, or interpersonal relations. The emphasis should probably be on "cause them problems" rather than on "are distressing," because many people with these kinds of traits are *not* disturbed by them: They view their behavior, strange as it may seem to others, as perfectly normal and beneficial, at least to them.

The DSM–IV divides personality disorders into three distinct clusters, so let's take a look at some of the traits that fit under these categories. The first group involves *odd, eccentric* behavior or traits and includes three personality disorders: *paranoid, schizoid,* and *schizotypal.* Persons suffering from *paranoid personality disorders* believe that everyone is out to get them, deceive them, or take advantage of them in some way. Luis, the employee who came close to attacking me many years ago, certainly acted in this way. In contrast, the *schizoid personality disorder* involves a very different pattern. Persons with this disorder show little or no sign of emotion and lack basic social skills. As a result, they form few if any social relationships. Often they end up existing on the fringes of society, living isolated lives in cheap hotels or run-down boardinghouses. The third type, *schizotypal personality disorder,*

**Gender Identity Disorder:** A disorder in which individuals believe that they were born with the wrong sexual identity.

**Personality Disorders:** Disorders involving extreme and inflexible personality traits that are distressing to the persons who have them or cause them problems in school, at work, or in interpersonal relations.

**Antisocial Personality Disorder:** A personality disorder involving deceitfulness, impulsivity, callous disregard for the safety or welfare of others, and a total lack of remorse for actions that harm others.

also involves a pattern of social isolation and avoidance of close relationships. However, persons with this disorder are highly anxious in social situations and often act in bizarre or strange ways; for instance, they may wear strangely out-of-date or mismatched clothes, or may show up in a wool sweater in August. Recent findings suggest that such persons may have deficits in working memory and in the ability to shift from automatic to controlled processing (Raine et al., 1999). This may account, in part, for their strange behavior in many contexts.

The second major cluster of personality disorders described by the DSM–IV includes disorders involving *dramatic, emotional, and erratic* forms of behavior. In one of these, the *borderline personality disorder,* people show tremendous instability in their interpersonal relationships, self-image, and moods. Did you ever see the movie *Fatal Attraction?* It depicts a very unstable woman who has a brief affair with a married man. When he indicates that he does not want to continue the relationship, she goes off the deep end and behaves in very erratic and dangerous ways. That is the kind of pattern shown by persons with this personality disorder. For these persons, mood swings are huge, love often changes quickly to hate, and best friends become enemies overnight.

In contrast, people with the *histrionic personality disorder* show a tremendous need for attention from others. They want to be the center of attention, and they will do almost anything to attain this goal—often dressing in unusual ways or using physical beauty or sex appeal to attract attention. On the surface these persons show confidence and seem socially skilled; but inside, they are lacking in confidence and have powerful needs for acceptance and approval from others. Yet another pattern is the *narcissistic personality disorder* shown by people who have grandiose ideas about their own abilities and importance. Such persons think they are exceptional and react with rage or humiliation if others don't recognize this fact.

Also included in this cluster of personality disorders is the one that is in some ways the most important and the most disturbing—the **antisocial personality disorder.** Individuals with this disorder are chronically callous and manipulative toward others, ignore social rules and laws, behave impulsively and irresponsibly, fail to learn from punishment, and lack remorse or guilt over their misdeeds. Such persons often become criminals or confidence artists—and some may even become politicians. In the film *The Grifters,* for example, several characters show a total lack of concern with laws and social norms and a total lack of remorse for harm they have done to others (see Figure 14.18). Sometimes the total disregard for the rights of others shown by persons with the antisocial personality disorder leads them to perform brutal acts, including murder. For an especially grisly example of such behavior, see the **Beyond the Headlines** section on page 566.

What are the origins of this disorder? Many factors seem to play a role. The impulsivity and aggression it involves may be linked to deficits in the ability to delay gratification—a skill most people acquire during childhood (e.g., Sher & Trull, 1994). Biological factors, too, may play a role. Some findings suggest that persons with the antisocial personality disorder show disturbances in brain function, including abnormalities in the neurotransmitter serotonin (Lahey et al., 1993). Additional evidence indicates that such persons show re-

**Figure 14.18**
**Hollywood Portrayals of the Antisocial Personality Disorder**

Persons who are chronically callous and manipulative toward others, ignore social rules and laws, behave impulsively and irresponsibly, and lack remorse or guilt over their misdeeds demonstrate the antisocial personality disorder—and are often featured in popular films.

duced reactions to negative stimuli—for instance, ones that are related to unpleasant experiences such as punishment (Patrick, Bradley, & Lang, 1993). This finding suggests that persons with the antisocial personality disorder may be less capable than others of experiencing negative emotions and less responsive to stimuli that serve as warnings to most people to "back off"—for example, angry facial expressions on the part of others (Ogloff & Wong, 1990). Whatever the origins of this disorder, one point is clear: Persons with the antisocial personality disorder often pose a serious threat to themselves and to others.

The third major cluster described by the DSM–IV includes disorders involving *anxious* and *fearful* behavior; the disorders in this group, as well as those in the two previous clusters, are described in Table 14.3.

**TABLE 14.3**

**Personality Disorders**

The DSM–IV divides personality disorders into three major clusters. Personality disorders in each cluster are described here.

| Disorder | Description |
|---|---|
| **Odd and Eccentric Personality Disorders** | |
| Paranoid Personality Disorder | Pervasive distrust and suspiciousness of others |
| Schizoid Personality Disorder | Pervasive pattern of detachment from social relationships and restricted range of emotions |
| Schizotypal Personality Disorder | Intense discomfort in interpersonal relationships, cognitive or perceptual distortions, and eccentric behavior |
| **Dramatic, Emotional, Erratic Personality Disorders** | |
| Antisocial Personality Disorder | Deceitfulness, impulsivity, irritability, reckless disregard for safety and welfare of others, lack of remorse |
| Borderline Personality Disorder | Pervasive pattern of instability in interpersonal relationships, self-image, moods |
| Histrionic Personality Disorder | Pervasive pattern of excessive emotionality and attention seeking |
| Narcissistic Personality Disorder | Pervasive pattern of grandiosity in fantasy or behavior, plus lack of empathy |
| **Anxious and Fearful Personality Disorders** | |
| Avoidant Personality Disorder | Pervasive pattern of social inhibition, feelings of inadequacy, hypersensitivity to negative evaluation |
| Obsessive-Compulsive Personality Disorder | Preoccupation with orderliness, perfectionism, and need for mental and interpersonal control |
| Dependent Personality Disorder | Pervasive and excessive need to be taken care of |

**REVIEW QUESTIONS**

- What are personality disorders?
- What characteristics are shown by persons who have the antisocial personality disorder?

## BEYOND the HEADLINES: As Psychologists See It

### Life without a Conscience: The Antisocial Personality Disorder in Action

**Teenage 'vampire' sentenced to death: 17-year-old killed couple in Florida with a crowbar**

*MIAMI TIMES* (FEBRUARY 28, 1998)—A 17-year-old youth who proclaims he is a vampire and admitted murdering a middle-aged couple with a crowbar was sentenced to die in Florida's electric chair. In handing down the sentence Judge Jerry T. Lockett called him a "disturbed young man" who proves "there is genuine evil in the world." Rodrick Ferrell, of Murray, Kentucky, admitted killing Richard Wendorf and Naoma Queen in their home in Eustis, Florida, on November 25, 1996. The letter "V," apparently for vampire, was burned into Wendorf's body.

Ferrell said he and three friends who also called themselves vampires traveled to Eustis after Heather Wendorf, whom he had met when both were students in Eustis, asked him to help steal her parents' sport utility vehicle so she could run away from home. Prosecutors said she intended to join a group headed by Ferrell that engaged in group sex and drank blood as part of what members considered vampire rituals. Six hours before the murders Ferrell, then 16, and Heather Wendorf, then 15, sat in a cemetery and drank each other's blood so she could become a vampire in his group and so that he could fortify himself to kill. . . .

Teenage vampires who drink each other's blood and murder for the sake of a joyride—shocking, to say the least. But what's going on here? How could teenagers behave in such bizarre and appalling ways? From the point of view of psychology, the judge in this case has it right: The defendant and his friends are seriously disturbed. In fact, it seems clear that Rodrick Ferrell and Heather Wendorf, daughter of the murdered couple, probably have one or more psychological disorders. Diagnosis without sufficient assessment is always risky (and unethical, too), so consider this to be more of a guess than diagnosis; but to me, at least, it seems possible that both these young people have the *antisocial personality disorder.* Both showed the impulsive, irresponsible behavior that is part of this pattern, and neither seemed to feel regret or remorse over murdering two persons simply to get their vehicle so that it would be easier for Wendorf to run away from home. But this case also illustrates another important point about personality disorders: They often occur together with other mental disorders. So, for instance, it is possible that Ferrell, who really seemed to believe that he was a vampire, was also showing signs of *schizophrenia*—another very serious form of mental disorder we'll discuss shortly. Among the features of schizophrenia are delusions and bizarre forms of behavior, and Rodrick Ferrell certainly showed such symptoms.

Again, it is inappropriate to diagnose mental disorders without careful assessment, and I certainly don't mean to do that here. We do not know what mental disorders, if any, these young persons may have. My main reason for discussing this frightening episode is simply to emphasize the following point: Human beings in the grip of serious mental disorders often engage in behavior that, to the rest of us, is as incomprehensible as it is disturbing.

#### CRITICAL THINKING QUESTIONS

1. Can you think of any other mental disorders that may have played a role in Rodrick Ferrell's horrifying behavior?
2. If Ferrell is indeed suffering from one or more mental disorders, is this any excuse for his actions? Should he be viewed as a "sick" person in need of help rather than as a criminal who should be punished?
3. Is there any hope for someone like Ferrell? That is, do you think he can be successfully treated?

# Schizophrenia: Losing Touch with Reality

Web Link: *Schizophrenia.com*

We come now to what many experts consider to be the most devastating mental disorder of all: **schizophrenia.** This can be defined as a complex disorder (or, as many psychologists believe, a cluster of disorders) characterized by fragmentation of basic psychological functions (attention, perception, thought, emotions, and behavior). As a result of such fragmentation, persons with schizophrenia have serious problems in adjusting to the demands of reality. They misperceive what's happening around them, often seeing or hearing things that aren't there. They have trouble paying attention to what is going on around them, and their thinking is often so confused and disorganized that they cannot communicate with others. They often show bizarre behavior and blunting of emotion and motivation that makes them unable to move or take action. And when they do show emotion, it is often inappropriate in a given situation. Schizophrenia is so serious and so disruptive that often persons who develop it must be removed from society, at least temporarily, for their own protection and to undergo treatment. Let's take a closer look at this extremely serious and disturbing form of mental disorder.

## The Nature of Schizophrenia

Let's begin with a closer look at the major symptoms of schizophrenia—the criteria presented in the DSM–IV for diagnosing this disorder. These are often divided into *positive* and *negative* symptoms. As these terms suggest, positive symptoms involve adding something that isn't normally there—excessive and bizarre behaviors, seeing and hearing things that don't exist. Negative symptoms, in contrast, involve absence or reduction of normal functions. Persons showing mainly positive symptoms are sometimes described as having Type I schizophrenia, while those showing negative symptoms are described as having Type II schizophrenia.

**POSITIVE SYMPTOMS OF SCHIZOPHRENIA** Positive symptoms include *delusions, hallucinations, disordered thought processes,* and *disordered behaviors.* **Delusions** are misinterpretations of normal events and experiences—misinterpretations that lead schizophrenics to hold beliefs with little basis in reality. Delusions can take many different forms. One common type is *delusions of persecution*—the belief that one is being plotted against, spied on, threatened, or otherwise mistreated. I believe that Luis, my potentially violent fellow employee, had such delusions: He really believed that I was out to get him! Another common type is *delusions of grandeur*—belief that one is extremely famous, important, or powerful. Persons suffering from such delusions may claim that they are the president, a famous movie star, or even Jesus, Mohammed, or Buddha. A third type of delusion involves *delusions of control*—the belief that other people, evil forces, or even beings from another planet are controlling one's thoughts, actions, or feelings. Delusions, like most of the positive symptoms of schizophrenia, are *phasic*—they come and go. Thus, at any given time, they may be present to varying degrees. When delusions are strong, however, persons with schizophrenia have truly tenuous ties to reality.

About 70 percent of schizophrenics experience **hallucinations:** They see or hear things that aren't really there. These hallucinations often take the form of voices telling them what to do, as illustrated by this case:

> "Mark reported hearing the voices of a man, a woman and a child all telling him that he was Harry Truman and that he was responsible for killing thousands of Japanese. They warned him that if he 'was ever out of his house after 11 PM,' he would be set on fire and burned to death" (Nietzel et al., 1998, p. 337).

In addition, persons with schizophrenia do not think or speak like other persons. Their words jump about in a fragmented and disorganized manner. There is

**Schizophrenia:** A complex disorder characterized by hallucinations (e.g., hearing voices), delusions (beliefs with no basis in reality), disturbances in speech, and several other symptoms.

**Delusions:** Firmly held beliefs that have no basis in reality.

**Hallucinations:** Vivid sensory experiences that have no basis in physical reality.

**Figure 14.19**
**Disturbed Movements and Postures: One Symptom of Schizophrenia**

Some persons who have schizophrenia show *catatonia*—they remain immobile in fixed, awkward postures for hours at a time.

a loosening of associations so that one idea does not follow logically from another; indeed, ideas often seem totally unconnected. Schizophrenics often create words of their own—words that resemble real words but do not exist in their native language, such as "littlehood" for childhood or "crimery" for bad actions. Their sentences often begin with one thought and then shift abruptly to another (e.g., Barch & Berenbaum, 1996). In extreme cases, their words seem to be totally jumbled into what is sometimes termed a *verbal salad.*

These problems, and several others, seem to stem from a breakdown in the capacity for *selective attention.* Normally, we can focus our attention on certain stimuli while largely ignoring others. This is not true for schizophrenics. They are easily distracted. Even the sound of their own words may disrupt their train of thought and send them wandering off into a mysterious world of their own creation.

The behavioral disorders shown by schizophrenics are even more bizarre. For instance, they may make odd movements or strange gestures, or may remain immobile in an awkward position for long periods of time—a condition called *catatonia* (see Figure 14.19). They may also show disorganized behavior that makes it impossible for them to dress themselves, prepare food, or perform other daily chores.

**NEGATIVE SYMPTOMS OF SCHIZOPHRENIA** As noted above, negative symptoms involve the absence of functions or reactions that most persons show. One such symptom is *flat affect*—many persons with schizophrenia show no emotion. Their faces are like emotionless masks, and they stare off into space with a glazed look. Is this because they feel nothing, or merely because they show no emotion outwardly? Some findings suggest that in fact schizophrenics do experience emotional reactions, but don't show any sign of them on the outside (e.g., Berenbaum & Oltmanns, 1992). Some schizophrenics do show emotion, but their reactions are inappropriate: They may giggle when describing a painful childhood experience, or cry after hearing a joke.

Another negative symptom of schizophrenia is *avolition*—a seemingly total lack of motivation or will. Persons showing this symptom may sit doing nothing hour after hour; if they do start to do something, they will often stop in the middle of the activity and wander off. A third, related symptom is *alogia:* a lack of speech. Schizophrenics often have little or nothing to say; they may answer direct questions but otherwise tend to remain silent, withdrawn into their own private worlds.

## The Onset and Course of Schizophrenia

Schizophrenia is a *chronic* disorder, as defined by the DSM–IV: it lasts at least six months. For most people, however, this disorder lasts far longer, and symptoms come and go. People with schizophrenia have periods when they appear almost normal, and long periods when their symptoms are readily apparent. Schizophrenia can occur among adolescents, but it generally begins in the early twenties; males show the onset of this disorder at earlier ages than females (Remschmidt et al., 1994). Although schizophrenia occurs all over the world, specific symptoms differ across cultures. For instance, the content of hallucinations varies; in Western societies hallucinations often include high-tech features (computers, neon lights, etc.), whereas in less developed countries they often focus on ghosts, demons, or animals (Al-Issa, 1977).

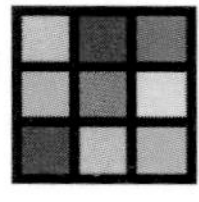

TABLE 14.4

**Major Types of Schizophrenia**

The DSM-IV divides schizophrenia into the types shown here. Each is marked by a different pattern of symptoms.

| Type | Symptoms |
|---|---|
| Catatonic | Unusual patterns of motor activity, such as rigid postures; also speech disturbances such as repetitive chatter |
| Disorganized | Absence of affect, poorly developed delusions, verbal incoherence |
| Paranoid | Preoccupation with one or more sets of delusions, often centering on the belief that others are "out to get" the schizophrenic in some way |
| Undifferentiated | Many symptoms, including delusions, hallucinations, incoherence |
| Residual | Withdrawal, minimal affect, and absence of motivation; occurs after prominent delusions and hallucinations are no longer present |

Schizophrenia is often divided into five distinct types. The most dramatic of these is the **catatonic type,** in which individuals show marked disturbances in motor behavior. Many alternate between total immobility—sitting for days or even weeks frozen in a single posture—and wild, excited behavior in which they rush madly about. Other types of schizophrenia are described in Table 14.4.

## Causes of Schizophrenia

Schizophrenia is one of the most bizarre, and most serious, psychological disorders. It is also more common that you might guess: Between 1 and 2 percent of all people in the United States suffer from this disorder (Wilson et al., 1996). What are the causes of schizophrenia? Research findings point to the roles of many factors.

**GENETIC FACTORS** Schizophrenia, like several other psychological disorders, tends to run in families. The closer the family tie between two individuals, the higher the likelihood that if one develops schizophrenia, the other will show this disorder too (e.g., Gottesman, 1993). Schizophrenia does not appear to be traceable to a single gene, however; on the contrary, research findings suggest that many genes and many environmental factors operate together to produce a tendency toward this disorder (e.g., Fowles, 1994). Other evidence for the role of genetic factors in schizophrenia is provided by adoption studies. For instance, in one large-scale study conducted in Finland (Tiernari, 1991), 144 children born to schizophrenic mothers and adopted shortly after birth were compared with adopted children born to nonschizophrenic mothers. Results indicated that fully 9 percent of those with schizophrenic mothers showed this mental disorder; in contrast, fewer than 1 percent of those born to nonschizophrenic mothers were diagnosed as schizophrenic.

**BRAIN DYSFUNCTION** Additional evidence suggests that several types of brain dysfunctions occur in persons with schizophrenia. For instance, some findings indicate that some ventricles (fluid-filled spaces within the brain) are larger in schizophrenics than in other persons, and this increased size may produce abnormalities in the cerebral cortex (e.g., Weinberger, 1994). In fact, the decreased brain

**Catatonic Type** (of schizophrenia): A dramatic type of schizophrenia in which individuals show marked disturbances in motor behavior; many alternate between total immobility and wild, excited behavior in which they rush madly about.

volume resulting from enlarged ventricles has been found, in research using magnetic resonance imaging, to be related to increased hallucinations and reduced emotion among schizophrenics (e.g., Gur & Pearlson, 1993; Klausner et al., 1992). Schizophrenics also show reduced activity in the frontal lobes relative to other persons during tasks involving memory or abstract thought (Gur & Pearlson, 1993). Together, these findings suggest that schizophrenia is related to cognitive deficits and several types of abnormalities in brain functioning.

A new and especially fascinating theory concerning the causes of schizophrenia relates the onset of this disorder to a natural "pruning" of neural circuits in the brain that seems to occur as individuals leave adolescence and become adults. This removal of unessential circuits seems to help the brain function more efficiently, so it provides important benefits. According to the *prodromal pruning* theory, however, this process goes astray in some persons, whose brains "prune" too aggressively. The result is that crucial neural links are eliminated, thus making such persons susceptible to the disordered thought processes and behaviors that are key symptoms of schizophrenia (e.g., Tanouye, 1999a). (The term *prodromal* refers to the earliest stage of schizophrenia, a time when major symptoms are not present or are only beginning to appear.) This theory is very new, but some findings offer support for it, so it is certain to receive increased attention from researchers in the years ahead.

**BIOCHEMICAL FACTORS** Several findings point to the possibility that disturbances in the functioning of certain neurotransmitters may play a role in schizophrenia. For instance, consider these facts: (1) Drugs that increase dopamine activity in the brain tend to intensify schizophrenic symptoms (e.g., Lieberman & Koreen, 1993); (2) drugs that block the action of dopamine in the brain are effective in reducing many symptoms of schizophrenia, especially positive symptoms (Syvalahti, 1994). Together, these and other findings point to the possibility that excessive activity in the dopamine system may lead to positive symptoms of schizophrenia and that deficits in dopamine activity may lead to negative symptoms (e.g., Julien, 1995). Although this suggestion is intriguing, additional findings are not entirely consistent with it; for instance, direct comparisons of dopamine levels in schizophrenic patients and other persons do not always reveal the expected differences (Lieberman & Koreen, 1993). As a result, it seems clear that dopamine is not *the* crucial biochemical factor in schizophrenia. Rather, growing evidence suggests that many neurotransmitters, and perhaps other chemicals in the brain as well (e.g., glutamate), play roles in its occurrence. This is why the newest drugs used in the treatment of schizophrenia target not one neurotransmitter or chemical, but many (see Chapter 15 for more information) (Tanouye, 1999b).

**PSYCHOLOGICAL FACTORS** The fact that schizophrenia seems to run in families raises the possibility that some families create social environments that place their children at risk for this disorder. What are such environments like? Intriguing clues are provided by research on *relapses* among schizophrenic patients—recurrences of the disorder after periods of relative normality. It appears that patients are more likely to suffer relapses when their families adopt certain patterns of expressing emotion. Specifically, patients are more likely to suffer relapses when their families engage in harsh criticism ("You are nothing but trouble!"), express hostility toward them ("I'm sick and tired of taking care of you!"), and show too much concern with their problems ("I'm trying so hard to help you!"). The relapse rate in families showing this pattern over the course of a year is fully 48 percent, while in families that do not show this pattern it is only about 20 percent (Kavanagh, 1992). Do these patterns of communication also contribute to the onset of schizophrenia as well? We don't know for sure; but other studies, including research I have conducted myself, suggest that harsh criticism induces emotional turmoil in those who receive it—and this, in turn, may serve as one source of stress that pushes vulnerable persons closer to the brink of this serious mental disorder (Baron, 1993a).

One final comment: Reading about the disorders covered in this chapter can, I realize, be somewhat discouraging—together, they provide a seemingly endless list of different forms of human suffering. But take heart: Psychologists have developed effective procedures for treating virtually all of these disorders. These procedures are described in Chapter 15, so please read that chapter as soon as possible for the rays of optimism I—and I'm sure you, too—strongly prefer.

**REVIEW QUESTIONS**

- What is schizophrenia?
- What are positive and negative symptoms of schizophrenia?
- What factors play a role in the occurrence of schizophrenia?

**Food for Thought**

It has been suggested that many homeless persons are schizophrenic. Do you think that's so? And if it is, why?

## Substance-Related Disorders

Web Link: *Why Are People Homeless?*

Before concluding, we should consider a group of disorders that are extremely common—**substance-related disorders,** or disorders related to the use of psychoactive drugs (see Chapter 4). Do you know a heavy smoker who has tried over and over again to quit this habit? Or do you know someone who can't get through the day without several drinks or beers? If so, you already have firsthand experience with some of the obvious effects of substance-related disorders. Such disorders are further divided by the DSM–IV into two categories: *substance-induced disorders,* or impaired functioning as a direct result of the physiological effects of the substance in question, and *substance-use disorders*—repeated frequent use of substances resulting in harmful behaviors or impairments in personal, social, and occupational functioning.

According to the DSM–IV, then, **substance abuse** is a maladaptive pattern of substance use that results in repeated, significant adverse effects and maladaptive behaviors: failure to meet obligations at work, in school, or at home; repeated use of a psychoactive substance in hazardous ways (e.g., while driving); recurrent legal problems related to the substance; and continued use of the substance despite its negative effects on social relationships. (See Chapter 4 for further discussion of psychoactive substances.)

Substance abuse is far from rare. Many different substances are involved (amphetamines, nicotine, opioids), but the one that is most frequently abused by far is alcohol. It is estimated that more than 7 percent of the U.S. population shows alcohol abuse or dependence (Grant et al., 1994). And the costs of such abuse are appalling. More than half of all fatal traffic accidents involve alcohol, and 25 to 50 percent of deaths due to fires, falls, and drowning involve this substance (Institute of Medicine, 1989). The bottom line is this: The average life expectancy of people who abuse alcohol is more than ten years shorter than that of people who do not. Such statistics are totally ignored by advertising, which, of course, presents alcohol consumption in a totally favorable light. The reality is something else (see Figure 14.20 on page 572). These comments, I should quickly add, refer to *abuse* of alcohol; many persons use alcohol without abusing it; and there is no implication in the DSM–IV that such drinking constitutes a mental disorder.

Statistics suggest that alcohol abuse among teenagers is increasing, so this is a special area of concern. Why do so many teens start down this potentially dangerous path? Research findings suggest that a combination of factors play a role, including these: high levels of stress in teenagers' lives; a tendency to cope with problems in maladaptive ways (e.g., by avoiding them or using substances to feel

**Substance-Related Disorders:** Disorders related to the use of psychoactive substances.

**Substance Abuse:** A maladaptive pattern of substance use that results in repeated, significant adverse effects and maladaptive behaviors: failure to meet obligations at work, in school, or at home; repeated use of a psychoactive substance in hazardous ways; recurrent legal problems related to the substance; and continued use of the substance despite its negative effects on social relationships.

**Figure 14.20**
**The Two Faces of Alcohol**

Ads often link alcohol consumption to having a wonderful time, and for many persons alcohol *is* a part of enjoyable social occasions. When it is abused, however, alcohol can lead to tragic consequences; in fact, more than half of all fatal traffic accidents involve alcohol consumption.

better); exposure to peers who smoke, drink, or use drugs; a low level of support from parents; and positive expectancies about the effects of alcohol (e.g., belief that alcohol will reduce tension, increase social competence, or enhance sexual performance) (Smith et al., 1995; Wills et al., 1996). An understanding of the factors that induce teenagers to abuse alcohol and other substances in the first place is an important part of programs to help teens avoid the risks of substance-related disorders.

Unfortunately, alcohol is not the only psychoactive substance that is abused. Hundreds of millions of persons smoke cigarettes, and as we saw in Chapter 13, smokers often develop nicotine dependence, which makes it extremely difficult for them to give up the drug. The social costs of addiction to heroin, cocaine, crack, and other drugs are perhaps even higher. These harmful effects, coupled with the very large numbers of persons involved, make substance-abuse disorders among the most damaging of all the disorders described in the DSM–IV. Moreover, because they stem from many different factors—biological, social, and personal—substance-related disorders are often very difficult to treat. However, several forms of therapy do seem at least moderately effective in treating such problems; we'll examine several of these in Chapter 15.

**REVIEW QUESTIONS**

- What is substance abuse?
- What factors place teenagers at risk for abusing alcohol?

## Making Psychology Part of Your Life

### Preventing Suicide: How You Can Help

When terminally ill persons choose to end their lives rather than endure continued pain, their actions seem understandable, even if we disapprove of them on moral or religious grounds. But when young persons whose lives have just begun follow this route, nearly everyone would agree that their death is tragic. Can *you* do anything to help prevent suicides among people you know? Research findings suggest that you can, if you pay careful attention to several warning signs.

- **Take all suicide threats seriously.** One common myth about suicide is that people who threaten to kill themselves rarely do—only those who tell no one about their plans commit suicide. *This is untrue!* Approximately 70 percent of all suicides tell others about their intentions. So when someone talks about suicide, *take it seriously.*

- **If someone mentions suicide, don't be afraid to discuss it.** Another common myth about suicide is that this topic should never be discussed with another person—talking about it will only make matters worse. This, too, is false. Encouraging people to talk about suicidal thoughts gets their problems out into the open and can be helpful. So don't ignore it if someone you know mentions suicide; talking about it is usually better.
- **Recognize the danger signs.** These include *(a)* statements by someone that he or she has no strong reasons for living; *(b)* agitation or excitement followed by a period of calm resignation; *(c)* sudden efforts to give valued possessions away to others; *(d)* direct statements such as "I don't want to be a burden anymore"; *(e)* revival from a deeply depressed state, coupled with apparent leave-taking. If you observe these changes in someone, they may well be danger signs worth considering carefully.
- **Discourage others from blaming themselves for failure to reach unrealistic goals.** Many people who attempt suicide do so because they feel they have failed to measure up to their own standards—even if these are unrealistically high. If you know someone who is prone to this pattern, try to get the person to focus on his or her good points and to realize that overly high standards *are* unrealistic—that no one could hope to measure up to them.
- **If a friend or family member shows the danger signs described above, don't leave this person alone.** With rare exceptions, suicide is a solitary act. So if you are concerned that someone might attempt suicide, don't leave this person alone. If you can't stay with the individual, get others to help—or bring the depressed friend or relative along wherever you go.
- **Most important of all: Get help!** Remember signal detection theory (Chapter 3)? Where preventing suicide is concerned, many false alarms are better than one miss—it's far better to get worried or concerned for nothing than to look the other way while a tragedy occurs. So if you are concerned about someone you know, *get professional help.* Call a local suicide hot line, discuss your concerns with someone in the campus counseling center, see a physician or a member of the clergy. Help *is* available. If you have any concerns at all, seek it!

# Summary and Review

## Models of Abnormality: Changing Conceptions of Mental Disorders

- **What are mental disorders?** Mental disorders are disturbances of an individual's behavioral or psychological functioning that are not culturally expected and that lead to psychological distress, behavioral disability, and/or impaired overall functioning.
- **To what factors were such disorders attributed in the past?** At different times in the past, psychological disorders were attributed to supernatural causes (e.g., evil spirits) or natural causes (e.g., injuries to the brain).
- **What is the modern perspective on such disorders?** The modern psychological view suggests that mental disorders involve biological, psychological, and sociocultural factors as well as the joint effects of individual vulnerabilities (diatheses) and stressors.

### Key Terms

mental disorders, p. 533 • models of abnormality, p. 533 • diathesis–stress model, p. 536

## Assessment and Diagnosis: The DSM–IV and Other Tools

- **What is the DSM–IV?** The DSM–IV—Diagnostic and Statistical Manual of Mental Disorders—is a widely used guide to mental disorders. It provides descriptions of these disorders, plus information about biological factors associated with them.
- **In what ways is the DSM–IV an improvement over earlier versions?** The DSM–IV rests on a firmer basis of published research than did earlier versions and directs increased attention to the role of cultural factors.
- **What assessment tools other than the DMS–IV are used by psychologists in their efforts to accurately identify mental disorders?** Psychologists also use life records, assessment interviews, psychological tests, observations of behavior, and biological measures.

### Key Terms

developmental psychopathology perspective, p. 537 • Diagnostic and Statistical Manual of Mental Disorders–IV (DSM–IV), p. 538 • assessment interviews, p. 540

• Halstead–Reitan Neuropsychological Battery, p. 541

## Disorders of Infancy, Childhood, and Adolescence

- **What is oppositional defiant disorder? Conduct disorder?** Oppositional defiant disorder involves behavior in which children have poor control of their emotions and/or have repeated conflicts with parents and other adults (e.g., teachers). Conduct disorder (CD) involves more serious antisocial behaviors that are potentially harmful to the child, to others, or to property.
- **What is attention-deficit/hyperactivity disorder?** ADHD is a childhood disorder in which children show inattention or hyperactivity and impulsivity, or a combination of these behaviors.
- **What are anorexia nervosa and bulimia nervosa?** Anorexia nervosa involves excessive fear of becoming fat coupled with inability to maintain normal weight. Bulimia nervosa involves repeated cycles of binging and purging.
- **What is autistic disorder?** Autism is a disorder in which children show marked impairments in establishing social interactions with others, have nonexistent or poor language skills, and show stereotyped, repetitive patterns of behavior or interests.

### Key Terms

disruptive behaviors, p. 542 • attention-deficit/hyperactivity disorder (ADHD), p. 544 • feeding and eating disorders, p. 545 • anorexia nervosa, p. 545 • bulimia nervosa, p. 546 • pervasive developmental disorders, p. 546

## Mood Disorders: The Downs and Ups of Life

- **What are the major symptoms of depression? Of bipolar disorder?** Major symptoms of depression include negative mood, reduced energy, feelings of hopelessness, loss of interest in previously satisfying activities, difficulties in sleeping, and significant changes in weight. Bipolar disorders involve wide swings in mood between deep depression and mania.
- **What factors play a role in the occurrence of mood disorders?** Mood disorders are influenced by genetic factors and by disturbances in brain activity. Psychological factors also play a role, including learned helplessness, negative perceptions of oneself, and a tendency to focus inward on one's shortcomings.
- **What steps can be taken to prevent suicide?** Steps that can help prevent suicide include (1) accurately assessing individuals' risk for suicidal behavior, (2) helping resolve the immediate crises that surround and lead to most attempts, and (3) providing treatment to help persons at risk for suicide recover from feelings of hopelessness and despair.

### Key Terms

mood disorders, p. 549 • depression, p. 549 • bipolar disorder, p. 550 • suicide, p. 551

## Anxiety Disorders: When Dread Debilitates

- **What are phobias?** Phobias are excessive and unrealistic fears focused on specific objects or situations.
- **What is panic disorder?** Panic disorder is intense, terrifying anxiety that is not triggered by any specific situation or event; in many cases it is associated with *agoraphobia*—fear of open spaces or of being away from home.
- **What is obsessive–compulsive disorder?** In obsessive–compulsive disorder individuals have uncontrollable, unwanted, disturbing thoughts or mental images (obsessions) and engage in repetitious behaviors (compulsions) to neutralize such thoughts.
- **What is posttraumatic stress disorder?** PTSD is a disorder in which people persistently reexperience a traumatic event in their thoughts or dreams, feel as if they are reliving the event from time to time, persistently avoid stimuli associated with the traumatic event, and experience symptoms such as difficulty falling asleep, irritability, and difficulty in concentrating.

### Key Terms

anxiety, p. 553 • anxiety disorders, p. 553 • phobias, p. 553 • panic disorder, p. 554 • agoraphobia, p. 554 • obsessive–compulsive disorder, p. 556 • posttraumatic stress disorder, p. 557

## Dissociative and Somatoform Disorders

- **What are dissociative disorders such as dissociative amnesia?** Dissociative disorders are profound disruptions in a person's memory, consciousness, or identity—processes that are normally integrated.
- **What is dissociative identity disorder?** Dissociative identity disorder, formerly called multiple personality disorder, is a shattering of identity into at least two—and often more—separate but coexisting personalities, each possessing different traits, behaviors, memories, and emotions.
- **What are somatoform disorders?** In somatoform disorders individuals have physical symptoms in the absence of identifiable physical causes for these symptoms.
- **What factors contribute to the occurrence of somatoform disorders?** Individuals who develop somatoform disorders focus on inner sensations, perceive normal bodily sensations as more intense and disturbing than do other people, and have a high level of negative affectivity. In addition, they obtain important forms of reinforcement from their symptoms.

### Key Terms

dissociative disorders, p. 558 • dissociative amnesia, p. 558 • dissociative fugue, p. 558 • dissociative identity disorder, p. 558 • somatoform disorders, p. 560 • somatization disorders, p. 560 • hypochondriasis, p. 560 • Munchausen's syndrome, p. 560 • conversion disorder, p. 560

## Sexual and Gender Identity Disorders

- **What are sexual dysfunctions and paraphilias?** Sexual dysfunctions involve disturbances in sexual desire and/or sexual arousal, problems with attaining orgasm, or pain during sexual relations. In paraphilias, unusual imagery or acts are necessary for sexual arousal.

- **What is gender identity disorder?** Individuals with gender identity disorder feel that they were born with the wrong sexual identity and strongly desire to change this identity through medical treatment or other means.

### Key Terms

sexual desire disorders, p. 561 • sexual arousal disorders, p. 561 • paraphilias, p. 562 • gender identity disorder, p. 563

## Personality Disorders: Traits That Harm

- **What are personality disorders?** Personality disorders are extreme and inflexible personality traits that are distressing to the persons who have them or cause them problems in school, work, or interpersonal relations.
- **What characteristics are shown by persons with the antisocial personality disorder?** Persons with the antisocial personality disorder are chronically callous and manipulative toward others, ignore social rules and laws, behave impulsively and irresponsibly, fail to learn from punishment, and lack remorse or guilt for their misdeeds.

### Key Terms

personality disorders, p. 563 • antisocial personality disorder, p. 564

## Schizophrenia: Losing Touch with Reality

- **What is schizophrenia?** Schizophrenia is a very serious mental disorder characterized by hallucinations (e.g., hearing voices), delusions (beliefs with no basis in reality), and disturbances in speech, behavior, and emotion.
- **What are positive and negative symptoms of schizophrenia?** Positive symptoms involve the presence of something that is normally absent, such as hallucinations and delusions. Negative symptoms involve the absence of something that is normally present and include withdrawal, apathy, absence of emotion, and so on.
- **What factors play a role in the occurrence of schizophrenia?** Schizophrenia has complex origins that include genetic factors, brain dysfunction, biochemical factors, and certain aspects of family environment.

### Key Terms

schizophrenia, p. 567 • delusions, p. 567 • hallucinations, p. 567, catatonic type, p. 569

## Substance-Related Disorders

- **What is substance abuse?** Substance abuse is a maladaptive pattern of substance use that results in repeated, significant adverse effects and maladaptive behavior (e.g., failure to meet obligations at work, in school, or at home; repeated use of a psychoactive substance in hazardous ways).
- **What factors place teenagers at risk for abusing alcohol?** Factors that can lead teenagers to abuse alcohol include high levels of stress, a tendency to cope with problems in maladaptive ways, exposure to peers who drink or use drugs, a low level of parental support, and positive expectancies about the effects of alcohol.

### Key Terms

substance-related disorders, p. 571 • substance abuse, p. 571

# Critical Thinking Questions

### Appraisal

Suppose that in a given society cannibalism is viewed as fully acceptable, is practiced by most members of the culture, and causes persons who engage in it no distress. Would it still constitute a mental disorder? Why? Why not?

### Controversy

Research on stereotypes suggests that when people are labeled in some way (e.g., "blacks," "whites," "gays," etc.), strong stereotypes relating to these labels may be activated. Such stereotypes may then exert a powerful influence on subsequent judgments and decisions about these people. This has led some psychologists to criticize the DSM–IV, since one of the results of its use is the assignment of labels to individuals (e.g., "schizophrenic," "autistic," or "depressed"). Do you think that assigning such descriptive labels to people could have negative effects? If so, what would these be?

### Making Psychology Part of Your Life

Now that you know about the major kinds of mental disorders, do you think this knowledge will help you recognize these problems in yourself or in other persons? And if you do, will your knowledge increase the chances that you will seek professional help yourself or recommend to others that they seek such assistance?

# Chapter 15

# Therapies:

## Techniques for Alleviating Mental Disorders

## CHAPTER OUTLINE


**PSYCHOTHERAPIES: PSYCHOLOGICAL APPROACHES TO MENTAL DISORDERS 579**

Psychodynamic Therapies: From Repression to Insight
Phenomenological/Experiential Therapies: Emphasizing the Positive
Behavior Therapies: Mental Disorders and Faulty Learning
Cognitive Therapies: Changing Disordered Thought

**ALTERNATIVES TO INDIVIDUAL PSYCHOTHERAPY: GROUP THERAPY, MARITAL THERAPY, FAMILY THERAPY, AND PSYCHOSOCIAL REHABILITATION 589**

Group Therapies: Working Together to Solve Personal Problems
Marital and Family Therapies: Therapies Focused on Interpersonal Relations
■ BEYOND THE HEADLINES—As Psychologists See It: *Is Better Sex the Key to a Happier Marriage? Don't Bet on It!*
Self-Help Groups: When Misery Derives Comfort from Company
Psychosocial Rehabilitation

**BIOLOGICAL THERAPIES 597**

Drug Therapy: The Pharmacological Revolution
Electroconvulsive Therapy
Psychosurgery

**PSYCHOTHERAPY: IS IT EFFECTIVE? 603**

■ RESEARCH METHODS *How Psychologists Study the Effectiveness of Psychotherapy*
The Effectiveness of Psychotherapy: An Overview of Key Findings
Are Some Forms of Therapy More Successful Than Others?
Culturally Sensitive Psychotherapy

**THE PREVENTION OF MENTAL DISORDERS: COMMUNITY PSYCHOLOGY AND ITS LEGACY 608**

**LEGAL AND ETHICAL ISSUES RELATING TO MENTAL DISORDERS 610**

The Rights of Individuals and the Rights of Society
Ethical Issues in the Practice of Psychotherapy
■ MAKING PSYCHOLOGY PART OF YOUR LIFE *How to Choose a Therapist: A Consumer's Guide*


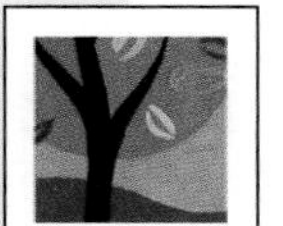

It was the spring of 1954 when my grandmother began acting strangely. Before that time, she had been lively, energetic, and humorous; I loved going to see her, because she always made a big fuss over me (I was her first grandchild) and always cooked great meals. But now she was . . . different. She seemed so sad, and she spent a lot of time in bed. When I asked her what was wrong, she just shook her head and cried. I loved my grandmother and wanted to help, but my parents refused to discuss her problems with me; I guess they assumed that there was nothing an eleven-year-old could do. Things got worse, and then my grandmother suddenly went away for what my parents described as a "vacation." I wondered how this could be, because my grandfather stayed home. My grandmother was gone several weeks, and when she returned, she seemed much better. She didn't stay in bed all day, and she cooked my favorites when I came to see her. But somehow she wasn't quite the same. She didn't make any jokes, and she didn't seem to have the zest for living she showed before. Also, she seemed to have forgotten many things that had happened during the past year. One day I asked her where she had been and whether she had enjoyed her vacation. A look of terror came into her eyes, and she left the room. I was persistent, though, and kept asking her from time to time until she told me. "I went to a place where I could rest and get better," she said. And then, in response to my unrelenting questions, she admitted that it was a "rest home" where she had been treated by doctors for her sadness. But when I asked her what they did to her, she again showed that look of terror. All she would say, no matter how many times I asked, was this: "I can't describe it to you—you wouldn't understand. But I only pray that *you* never have to experience it!"

**Psychotherapies:** Procedures in which persons with mental disorders interact with a trained psychotherapist who helps them change certain behaviors, thoughts, or emotions so that they feel and function better.

I realize now that my grandmother suffered from severe depression and that what happened to her on her "vacation" was a form of treatment known as *electroconvulsive shock therapy* (ECT for short), in which she received powerful jolts of electricity. As I'll explain later in this chapter, ECT often does seem to help people with depression, but it produces side effects such as loss of memory (e.g., Janicak et al., 1991). Fortunately, ECT is just one of many different procedures for alleviating mental disorders, and in this chapter I'll describe a broad range of such therapies (e.g., Seligman, 1995). We'll begin with several **psychotherapies**—procedures in which persons with mental disorders interact with a trained psychotherapist who helps them change certain behaviors, thoughts, or emotions so that they feel and function better (Nietzel et al., 1998). Many forms of psychotherapy exist, ranging from the famous procedures devised by Freud through modern techniques that rest firmly on basic principles of learning and cognition. Next, we'll explore alternatives to individual psychotherapy—*group therapies,* in which several persons interact with a therapist and with each other; *marital therapies,* which focus on problems experienced by couples (married or otherwise); and *family therapies,* which focus on changing patterns of family interaction to correct family disturbances or conflicts. In addition, we'll examine *self-help groups,* in which individuals who share specific problems attempt to assist one another, and a new approach known as *psychosocial rehabilitation,* which focuses on teaching individuals with serious mental disorders how to cope better with these disorders and the crises they often produce. After examining these varied types of psychotherapy, we'll turn to several *biological therapies:* efforts to treat mental disorders through surgery, ECT, or—most importantly—drugs. After that, we'll consider two central questions relating to psychotherapy: How effective is therapy, and are some kinds more effective than others? Two final sections will examine efforts to *prevent* mental disorders and some of the complex *legal and ethical issues* relating to such disorders and efforts to treat them. (Because this entire chapter reflects psychology's commitment to the use of science as a basis for practice, no separate **From Science to Practice** section is included.)

## Psychotherapies: Psychological Approaches to Mental Disorders

Say the word *psychotherapy,* and many people quickly imagine a scene in which a patient lies on a couch in a dimly lit room while a therapist sits in the background. The therapist urges the patient to reveal the deepest secrets of her or his mind—hidden urges, traumatic early experiences, and especially anything relating to sex! As these painful thoughts and images are dredged out of the unconscious, the patient suffers emotional turmoil, but also moves toward improved mental health (see Figure 15.1).

Actually, this popular image has little to do with many modern forms of psychotherapy. In fact, it applies primarily to only one type, an approach developed by Freud that is rarely used by psychologists and is even fading rapidly from psychiatry, in which it was a mainstay for many years (e.g., Hymowitz, 1995). Psychotherapy, as it is currently practiced by psychologists and other professionals, actually takes many different forms, uses a tremendously varied range of procedures, and can be conducted with groups as well as with individuals. Let's take a

**Figure 15.1**
**The Popular View of Psychotherapy**

As suggested by this cartoon, when many people hear the word *psychotherapy,* they think of scenes like this one, in which individuals are urged by the therapist to reveal their deepest secrets—especially anything relating to sex! (*Source:* Reprinted with special permission of King Features Syndicate.)

**Psychodynamic Therapies:** Therapies based on the idea that mental disorders stem primarily from the kind of hidden inner conflicts first described by Freud.

**Free Association:** A verbal reporting by persons undergoing psychoanalysis of everything that passes through their minds, no matter how trivial it may appear to be.

**Resistance:** In psychoanalysis, a patient's stubborn refusal to report certain thoughts, motives, and experiences or overt rejection of the analyst's interpretations.

Web Link: *About Psychoanalysis*

closer look at several important forms of psychotherapy—including, of course, the methods used by Freud.

## Psychodynamic Therapies: From Repression to Insight

**Psychodynamic therapies** are based on the idea that mental disorders stem primarily from the kind of hidden inner conflicts first described by Freud—for instance, conflicts between our primitive sexual and aggressive urges (id impulses) and the ego. More specifically, psychodynamic therapies assume that mental disorders occur because something has gone seriously wrong in the balance between these inner forces. Several forms of therapy are based on these assumptions, but the most famous is *psychoanalysis,* the approach developed by Freud.

**PSYCHOANALYSIS** As you may recall from Chapter 12, Freud believed that personality consists of three major parts: *id, ego,* and *superego,* which correspond roughly to desire, reason, and conscience. Freud believed that mental disorders stem from the fact that many impulses of the id are unacceptable to the ego or the superego and are therefore *repressed*—driven into the depths of the unconscious. There these urges persist, and individuals must devote a considerable portion of their psychic energy to keeping them in check and out of consciousness. In fact, people often use various *defense mechanisms* to protect the ego from feelings of anxiety generated by these inner conflicts and clashes.

How can such problems be relieved? Freud felt that the crucial task was for people to overcome repression and recognize—and confront—their hidden feelings and impulses. Having gained such insight, he believed, they would experience a release of emotion known as *abreaction;* then, with their energies at last freed from the task of repression, they could direct these energies into healthy growth. Figure 15.2 summarizes these views.

**Figure 15.2**
**Psychoanalysis: How, Supposedly, It Works**

Psychoanalysis, the kind of therapy developed by Freud, focuses on helping individuals gain insight into their hidden inner conflicts and repressed wishes. Freud believed that once awareness of these conflicts penetrated patients' *defense mechanisms* and moved into consciousness, disorders would fade away. In fact, there is little support for this view.

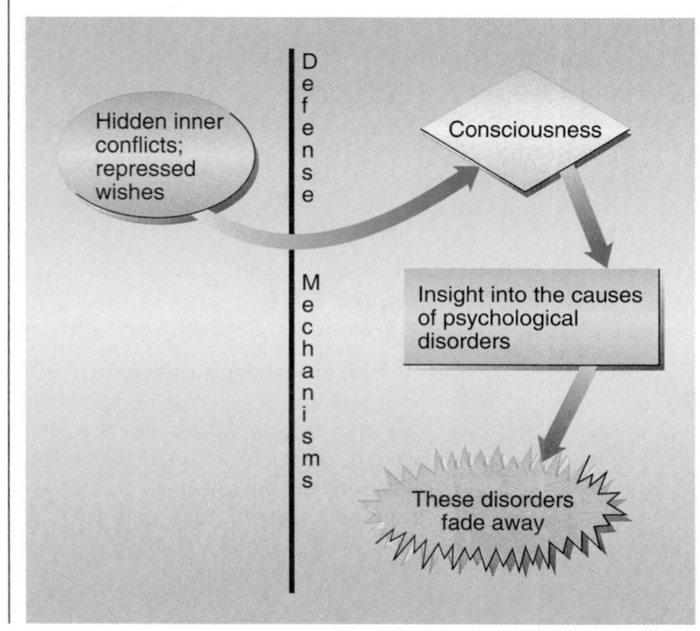


These ideas concerning the causes and cure of mental illness are reflected in *psychoanalysis,* the type of therapy developed by Freud. As popular images suggest, the patient undergoing psychoanalysis lies on a couch in a partly darkened room and engages in **free association**—he or she reports *everything* that passes through his or her mind. Freud believed that the repressed impulses and inner conflicts present in the unconscious would ultimately be revealed by these mental wanderings, at least to the trained ear of the analyst. As we saw in Chapter 4, Freud felt that dreams were especially useful in this respect, because they often represented inner conflicts and hidden impulses in disguised form. But everyday events, too, could be revealing. Slips of the tongue (such as "I hurt you" rather than "I heard you") and seemingly accidental events (e.g., spilling a drink on someone or dropping papers into the mud) could aid the analyst in making interpretations concerning the patient's hidden inner conflicts.

Freud noted that during psychoanalysis several intriguing events often occur. The first of these is **resistance**—a patient's stubborn refusal to report certain thoughts, motives, and experiences or overt rejection of the analyst's interpretations (Strean, 1985). Presumably, resistance occurs because patients wish to avoid the anxiety they experience as threatening or painful thoughts come closer and closer to consciousness.

Another aspect of psychoanalysis is **transference**—intense feelings of love or hate toward the analyst on the part of the patient. Often, patients react toward their analyst as they did to someone who played a crucial role in their early lives—for example, one of their parents. Freud believed that transference could be an important tool for helping individuals work through conflicts regarding their parents, this time in a setting where the harm done by disordered early relationships could be effectively countered. As patients' insight increased, Freud believed, transference would gradually fade away.

**PSYCHOANALYSIS: AN EVALUATION** Psychoanalysis is probably the most famous form of psychotherapy (Hornstein, 1992). What accounts for its fame? Certainly not its proven effectiveness. It is fair to say that the reputation of psychoanalysis far exceeds its success in alleviating mental disorders. In the form proposed by Freud, psychoanalysis suffers from several major and obvious weaknesses that lessen its value. First, it is a costly and time-consuming process. Several years and large amounts of money are usually required for its completion—assuming it ever ends. Second, psychoanalysis is based largely on Freud's theories of personality and psychosexual development. As I noted in Chapter 12, these theories are provocative but difficult to test scientifically, so psychoanalysis rests on shaky scientific ground. Third, Freud designed psychoanalysis for use with highly educated persons with impressive verbal skills—persons who could describe their inner thoughts and feelings with ease. Finally, and perhaps most important, psychoanalysis has often adopted the posture of a closed logical system. You don't believe in psychoanalysis? That's a clear sign that you are showing resistance—or are suffering from serious mental disorders that prevent you from seeing the truth!

Audio 15.1: *Does Psychoanalysis Work?*

Finally, this theory's major assumption—that once insight is acquired, mental health will follow automatically—is contradicted by research findings. Over and over again, psychologists have found that insight into one's thoughts and feelings does *not* necessarily change those thoughts or feelings or prevent them from influencing behavior (e.g., Rozin, 1996). In fact, as we'll see in a later discussion of cognitive therapies, changing distorted or maladaptive modes of thought often requires great effort and persistence.

**BEYOND PSYCHOANALYSIS: PSYCHODYNAMIC THERAPY TODAY** Because of such problems, classical psychoanalysis is rarely practiced today. However, modified (and less lengthy) versions introduced by Freud's students and disciples, including the neo-Freudians we discussed in Chapter 12, are used more frequently. For instance, in *psychoanalytically oriented psychotherapy,* client and therapist sit facing each other, and conversations focus on current problems rather than on the distant past. The therapist attempts to help the client reexperience old conflicts so that they can be resolved in a more adaptive manner.

Web Link: *Contrasts in Approaches to Psychotherapy*

Alfred Adler, one famous neo-Freudian, emphasized the importance of feelings of inferiority in mental disorders. He believed that people often show **basic mistakes** in their thinking—false beliefs that interfere with their mental health, such as "Life is very dangerous" or "I have to please everybody" (Mosak, 1995). Adler developed procedures for changing these beliefs that are similar in some ways to more modern forms of therapy we'll consider shortly.

A third example of alternative forms of psychodynamic therapy is the type devised by Henry Stack Sullivan. Sullivan felt that mental disorders stem not from unconscious conflicts but rather from disturbances in *interpersonal relationships*—problems that develop out of early interactions between children and their parents or peers. Sullivan's approach to therapy focuses on helping the client identify his

**Transference:** Intense emotional feelings of love or hate toward the analyst on the part of a patient undergoing psychoanalysis.

**Basic Mistakes:** False beliefs held by individuals that interfere with their mental health; a concept in psychotherapy devised by Adler.

or her maladaptive interpersonal styles—actions that provoke others into treating the person in ways that reinforce maladaptive behaviors. In sum, psychoanalysis is just one of several types of psychodynamic therapy, and today it is practiced by a relatively small number of therapists, primarily psychiatrists.

**REVIEW QUESTIONS**

- What is psychoanalysis, and what are its major assumptions?
- What is the role of free association in psychoanalysis?
- How are psychodynamic therapies practiced today?

## Phenomenological/Experiential Therapies: Emphasizing the Positive

Freud was something of a pessimist about basic human nature. He felt that we must struggle constantly with primitive impulses from the id. As we saw in Chapter 12, however, many psychologists reject this view. They contend that people are basically good and that our strivings for growth, dignity, and self-control are just as strong as the powerful aggressive and sexual urges Freud described. According to such psychologists, mental disorders do not stem from unresolved inner conflicts. Rather, they arise because the environment we live in somehow interferes with personal growth and fulfillment.

The **phenomenological/experiential therapies** (often known as **humanistic therapies**) are based on this view and on the following three principles: (1) Understanding other people requires trying to see the world through their eyes (a phenomenological approach); (2) clients should be treated as equals; and (3) the therapeutic relationship with the client is central to the benefits of therapy. The goal of phenomenological/experiential therapy is to help *clients* (not "patients") to become more truly themselves—to find meaning in their lives and to live in ways truly consistent with their own traits and values. Unlike psychoanalysts, humanistic therapists believe that clients, not they, must take essential responsibility for the success of therapy. The therapist is mainly a guide and facilitator, *not* the one who runs the show. Let's take a closer look at two forms of humanistic therapy.

**Phenomenological/Experiential Therapies (Humanistic Therapies):** Therapies based on the view that understanding people requires trying to see the world through their eyes (a phenomenological approach) and on the belief that the therapist's therapeutic relationship with the client is central to the benefits of therapy.

**Conditions of Worth:** In Rogers's client-centered therapy, individuals' beliefs that they must be something other than what they really are in order to be loved and accepted by others.

**Client-Centered Therapy:** Carl Rogers's approach to psychotherapy, which seeks to eliminate irrational "conditions of worth" in the client's mind by providing unconditional positive regard in a caring, empathetic environment.

**Gestalt Therapy:** A humanistic therapy that focuses on helping individuals to acknowledge hidden aspects of their thoughts and feelings.

**CLIENT-CENTERED THERAPY: THE BENEFITS OF BEING ACCEPTED** Perhaps the most influential humanistic approach is *client-centered therapy*, developed by Carl Rogers (1970, 1980). Rogers strongly rejected Freud's view that mental disorders stem from conflicts over the expression of primitive, instinctive urges. On the contrary, he argued, such problems arise mainly because clients' efforts to attain self-actualization—growth and development—are thwarted early in life by judgments and ideas imposed by other people. According to Rogers, these judgments lead individuals to acquire what he terms unrealistic **conditions of worth.** That is, they learn that they must be something other than what they really are in order to be loved and accepted—to be worthwhile as a person. For example, children may come to believe that they will be rejected by their parents if they are not always neat and submissive or if they do not live up to various parental ideals. Such beliefs block people from recognizing large portions of their experience and emotions. This, in turn, interferes with normal development of the self and causes people to experience maladjustment.

**Client-centered therapy** focuses on eliminating such unrealistic conditions of worth through creation of a psychological climate in which clients feel valued as persons. Client-centered therapists offer *unconditional positive regard,* or *unconditional acceptance,* of the client and her or his feelings; a high level of *empathetic understanding;* and accurate reflection of the client's feelings and perceptions. In this warm, caring environment, freed from the threat of rejection, individuals can come to understand their own feelings and accept even previously unwanted aspects of their own personalities. As a result, they come to see themselves as unique human beings with many desirable characteristics. To the extent such changes occur, Rogers suggests, many mental disorders disappear and individuals can resume their normal progress toward self-fulfillment (see Figure 15.3).

**Figure 15.3**
**Client-Centered Therapy: An Overview**

Rogers believed that mental disorders stem from unrealistic *conditions of worth* acquired early in life. Client-centered therapy seeks to change such beliefs, primarily by placing individuals in an environment where they receive *unconditional acceptance* from the therapist.

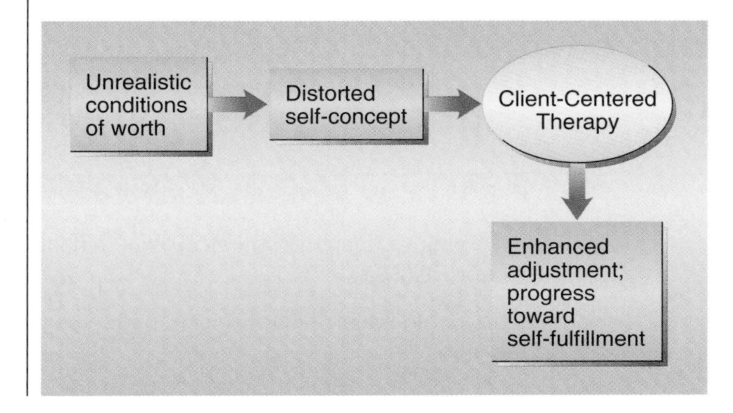


**GESTALT THERAPY: BECOMING WHOLE** The theme of incomplete self-awareness—especially of gaps in clients' awareness of their genuine feelings—is echoed in a second humanistic approach, **Gestalt therapy.** According to Fritz Perls, originator of this type of therapy, many people have difficulties in directly experiencing and expressing emotions such as anger or the need for love. As a result, they develop manipulative social games or phony roles to try (usually without success) to satisfy their needs indirectly. Playing these games, in turn, leads people to believe that they are not responsible for their own behavior; they blame others and come to feel powerless. Gestalt therapy, therefore, aims to help clients to become aware of the feelings and needs they have disowned, to recognize that these are a genuine part of themselves, and so to attain psychological "wholeness" (the meaning of *Gestalt*).

Web Link: *Gestalt Theory*

How can clients reach these goals? Only by reexperiencing old hurts, jealousies, fears, and resentments. To help clients do this, Gestalt therapists often use the *empty chair* technique (see Figure 15.4). The client imagines that an important person from his or her past—a parent, child, spouse—is sitting in the chair; then, perhaps for the first time, the client expresses his or her true feelings to this person (feelings about the imaginary person or about events or conflicts in which this person played a part). As a result, clients gain insight into their true feelings. This may actually help to reduce the emotional turmoil that brought clients to therapy in the first place—an important benefit in itself (Greenberg, Elliott, & Lietaer, 1994).

**Figure 15.4**
**The Empty Chair Technique Used in Gestalt Therapy**

In the *empty chair* technique, clients are asked to imagine that an important person from their past–a parent, child, spouse–is sitting in the chair. Then clients hold a conversation with this person. As a result, they presumably gain increased insight into their true inner feelings.

**HUMANISTIC THERAPIES: AN OVERVIEW** Phenomenological/experiential therapies certainly have a much more optimistic flavor than psychoanalysis; they don't assume that human beings must constantly struggle to control dark internal forces. In this sense, they cast bright sunshine into the shadowy world envisioned by psychoanalysis. In addition, several techniques devised by humanistic therapists are now widely used, even by psychologists who do not share this perspective. For instance, Carl Rogers was one of the first therapists to tape-record therapy sessions so that therapists could study the tapes at a later time. This tactic not only helps therapists to assist their clients; it also provides information about which techniques are most effective during therapy. Finally, some of the assumptions underlying humanistic therapies have been subjected to scientific test and found to be valid. For instance, research findings tend to confirm Rogers's view that the gap between an individual's self-image and his or her "ideal self" plays a crucial role in maladjustment (e.g., Bootzin, Acocella, & Alloy, 1993). In these ways, then, humanistic therapies have made lasting contributions to the practice of psychotherapy.

On the other side of the coin, such therapies have been criticized for their lack of a unified theoretical base and for being vague about precisely what is supposed to happen between clients and therapists. So although they are more widely used at present than psychoanalysis, they are subject to important criticisms.

**REVIEW QUESTIONS**

- According to phenomenological/experiential therapies, what is the cause of mental disorders?
- What is the major goal of Rogers's client-centered therapy?
- What is the major goal of Gestalt therapy?

**Food for Thought**

In view of the fact that clients come to therapy seeking help from an "expert," do you think the goal of equality between client and therapist can actually be attained?

## Behavior Therapies: Mental Disorders and Faulty Learning

Although psychodynamic and phenomenological/experiential therapies differ in many ways, they both place importance on early events in clients' lives as a key source of current disturbances. In contrast, another major group of therapies, known collectively as **behavior therapies,** focus primarily on individuals' current behavior. These therapies are based on the belief that many mental disorders stem from faulty learning. Either the persons involved have failed to acquire the skills and behaviors they need for coping with the problems of daily life, or they have acquired *maladaptive* habits and reactions. Within this context, the key task for therapy is to change current behavior, not to correct faulty self-concepts or to resolve inner conflicts. What kinds of learning play a role in behavior therapy? As we saw in Chapter 5, there are several basic kinds of learning. Reflecting this fact, behavior therapies employ techniques based on three major kinds of learning.

**THERAPIES BASED ON CLASSICAL CONDITIONING** *Classical conditioning,* as you will remember, is a process in which organisms learn that the occurrence of one stimulus will soon be followed by the occurrence of another. As a result, reactions that are at first produced only by the second stimulus gradually come to be evoked by the first as well. (Remember the popcorn example in Chapter 5?)

What does classical conditioning have to do with mental disorders? According to behavior therapists, quite a bit. Behavior therapists suggest, for example, that many *phobias* are acquired in this manner. Stimuli that happen to be present when real dangers occur may acquire the capacity to evoke intense fear because of this association. As a result, individuals experience intense fears in response to these conditioned stimuli, even though they pose no threat to their well-being. To eliminate such reactions, behavior therapists sometimes use the technique of *flooding.* This involves exposure to the feared stimuli, or to mental representations of them,

**Behavior Therapies:** Therapies based on the belief that many mental disorders stem from faulty learning.

**Figure 15.5**
**Systematic Desensitization: A Behavioral Technique for Eliminating Phobias**

In systematic desensitization, individuals with phobias first learn how to induce a relaxed state in their own bodies—often by learning how to relax their muscles. Then, while in this state, they are exposed to stimuli that elicit fear. Because relaxation is incompatible with fear, the conditioned link between these stimuli and fear is weakened and the phobias are reduced.

under conditions in which the person with the phobias can't escape from them. These procedures encourage *extinction* of such fears; the phobias may soon fade away (Levis, 1985).

Another technique based in part on principles of classical conditioning is known as **systematic desensitization.** In systematic desensitization, individuals first learn how to induce a relaxed state in their own bodies—often by learning how to relax their muscles. Then, while in a relaxed state, they are exposed to stimuli that elicit fear. Because they are now experiencing relaxation, which is incompatible with fear, the conditioned link between these stimuli and fear is weakened (see Figure 15.5).

**THERAPIES BASED ON OPERANT CONDITIONING** Behavior is often shaped by the consequences it produces; actions are repeated if they yield positive outcomes or if they permit individuals to avoid or escape from negative ones. In contrast, actions that lead to negative results are suppressed. These basic principles of learning are incorporated in several forms of therapy based on *operant conditioning*. These therapies differ considerably in their details, but all include the following steps: (1) clear identification of undesirable or maladaptive behaviors currently shown by individuals, (2) identification of events that reinforce and maintain such responses, and (3) efforts to change the environment so that these maladaptive behaviors are no longer followed by reinforcement.

Operant principles have sometimes been used in hospital settings, where a large degree of control over patients' reinforcements is possible (Kazdin, 1982). Several projects have involved the establishment of **token economies**—systems under which patients earn tokens they can exchange for various rewards, such as television-watching privileges, candy, or trips to town. These tokens are awarded for various forms of adaptive behavior, such as keeping one's room neat, participating in group meetings or therapy sessions, coming to meals on time, and eating neatly. The results have often been impressive. When individuals learn that they can acquire rewards by behaving in adaptive ways, they often do so, with important benefits to them as well as to hospital staff (e.g., Paul, 1982; Paul & Lentz, 1977).

**Systematic Desensitization:** A form of behavior therapy for phobias in which individuals first learn how to induce a relaxed state in their own bodies. Then, while in a relaxed state, they are exposed to stimuli that elicit fear.

**Token Economies:** A form of behavior therapy in which patients in hospital settings earn tokens they can exchange for various rewards by engaging in desirable forms of behavior.

**Figure 15.6**
**Poor Social Skills: An Important Factor in Many Mental Disorders**

As suggested by this cartoon, people lacking in basic *social skills* encounter serious difficulties in many life situations. These difficulties, in turn, can leave them feeling helpless, depressed, anxious, and resentful, and so plant the seeds for the development of mental disorders.
(*Source:* © The New Yorker Collection. 1997. Robert Mankoff from cartoonbank.com. All rights reserved.)

"I insist."

**OBSERVATIONAL LEARNING: BENEFITING FROM EXPOSURE TO OTHERS** Many people who come to psychologists for help appear to be lacking in basic *social skills*—they don't know how to interact with others in an effective manner. They don't know how to make a request without sounding pushy, or how to refuse one without making the requester angry. They don't know how to express their feelings clearly, how to hold their temper in check, or how to hold an ordinary conversation with others. As a result, such individuals experience difficulties in forming friendships or intimate relationships, and they encounter problems in many everyday situations (see Figure 15.6 for an example). These difficulties, in turn, can leave them feeling helpless, depressed, anxious, and resentful. Behavior therapists have developed techniques for helping people improve their social skills through observational learning. These often involve *modeling*—showing individuals live demonstrations or videotapes of how people with good social skills behave in many situations (e.g., Wilson et al., 1996). For instance, modeling (as well as other techniques) is often used in *assertiveness training,* which focuses on helping clients learn how to express their feelings and desires more clearly and effectively. Being assertive doesn't mean being aggressive; rather, it means being able to state one's preferences and needs rather than simply surrendering to those of others. Have you ever seen the television show *Keeping Up Appearances?* In it, a very pushy character (Hyacinth Bucket) insists over and over again that her kind and unassertive neighbor Elizabeth come to her house for coffee. Elizabeth wants to refuse but can't. Clearly, she—and millions of other persons—could benefit from assertiveness training.

Modeling techniques have also been used, with impressive success, in the treatment of phobias. Many studies indicate that individuals who experience intense fear of relatively harmless objects can be helped to overcome these fears through exposure to appropriate social models who demonstrate lack of fear and show that no harm occurs as a result of contact with these objects (e.g., Bandura, 1977). Such procedures have been found to be effective in reducing a wide range of phobias—excessive fears of dogs, snakes, and spiders, to mention just a few (Bandura, 1986). In sum, behavioral therapies have been shown to be useful in alleviating many types of mental disorders.

**REVIEW QUESTIONS**

- According to behavior therapies, what is the primary cause of mental disorders?
- On what basic principles of learning are behavior therapies based?
- What is modeling, and how can it be used in treating mental disorders?

**Food for Thought**

Some critics argue that behavior therapies treat symptoms of mental disorders without addressing their underlying causes. Do you think this is a valid criticism? Why? Why not?

## Cognitive Therapies: Changing Disordered Thought

CourseCompass
Video 15.1: *Cognitive Therapy*

CourseCompass
Audio 15.2: *Effectiveness of Cognitive Therapies*

CourseCompass
Web Link: *Rational Emotive Behavior Therapy*

At several points in this book, I've noted that cognitive processes often exert powerful effects on emotions and behavior. In other words, what we *think* strongly influences how we *feel* and what we *do.* This principle underlies another major group of approaches to psychotherapy, **cognitive therapies.** The basic idea behind all cognitive therapies is this: Many mental disorders stem from faulty or distorted modes of thought. Change these, and the disorders, too, can be alleviated. Let's examine several forms of therapy based on this reasoning.

### RATIONAL-EMOTIVE THERAPY: OVERCOMING IRRATIONAL BELIEFS

Everyone I meet should like me.

I should be perfect (or darn near perfect) in every way.

Because something once affected my life, it will always affect it.

I can't bear it when things are not the way I would like them to be.

I can't help feeling the way I do about certain things or in certain situations.

Be honest: Do such views ever influence *your* thinking? While you may strongly protest that they do not, one psychologist, Albert Ellis (1987), believes that they probably *do* influence your thinking to some extent. Moreover, he contends that such *irrational thoughts* often play a key role in many mental disorders. According to Ellis, the process goes something like this. Individuals experience *activating events*—things that happen to them that can potentially trigger upsetting emotional reactions. If they actually experience these strong emotional reactions, then mental disorders such as anxiety or depression may develop. The key factor determining whether this happens, however, is the way people *think* about the activating events. If people allow irrational beliefs to shape their thoughts, they are at serious risk for experiencing psychological problems.

Here's an example: Suppose that one day, your current romantic partner dumps you. This is certainly an unpleasant event—but does it undermine your self-esteem and cause you to become deeply depressed? Ellis argues that this depends on how you think about it. If you fall prey to irrational beliefs such as "Everyone must love me!" or "I can't control my emotions—I must feel totally crushed by this rejection!" you may well become depressed. If, instead, you reject these modes of thought and think, instead, "Some people will love me and others won't, and love itself isn't always constant," or "I can deal with this—it's painful, but not the end of the world"—then you will bounce back and will *not* experience depression. In essence, Ellis is saying this: You can't always change the world or what happens to you, but you *can* change the ways in which you think about your experiences. *You* can decide whether, and how much, to be bothered or upset by being dumped by a romantic partner, losing a job, getting a lower-than-expected grade on a test, and so on.

CourseCompass
Web Link: *Beck Institute for Cognitive Therapy and Reasearch*

To help people combat the negative effects of irrational thinking, Ellis developed **rational–emotive therapy (RET).** During RET, the therapist first attempts to identify irrational thoughts and then tries to persuade clients to recognize them for what they are. By challenging the irrationality of their clients' beliefs, therapists practicing RET get them to see how ridiculous and unrealistic some of their ideas are; in this way, they can help them stop being their own worst enemies.

**Cognitive Therapies:** Forms of therapy focused on changing distorted and maladaptive patterns of thought.

**Rational–Emotive Therapy (RET):** A form of therapy that focuses on persuading individuals to recognize and change irrational assumptions that underlie their thinking.

**Cognitive Behavior Therapy:** A form of cognitive therapy that focuses on changing illogical patterns of thought that underlie depression.

**BECK'S COGNITIVE BEHAVIOR THERAPY FOR DEPRESSION** In discussing depression in Chapter 14, I noted that this extremely common but serious mental disorder has an important cognitive component: It stems, at least in part, from distorted and often self-defeating modes of thought. Recognizing this important fact, Aaron Beck (1985) devised a **cognitive behavior therapy** for alleviating depression. Like Ellis, Beck assumes that depressed individuals engage in illogical thinking and

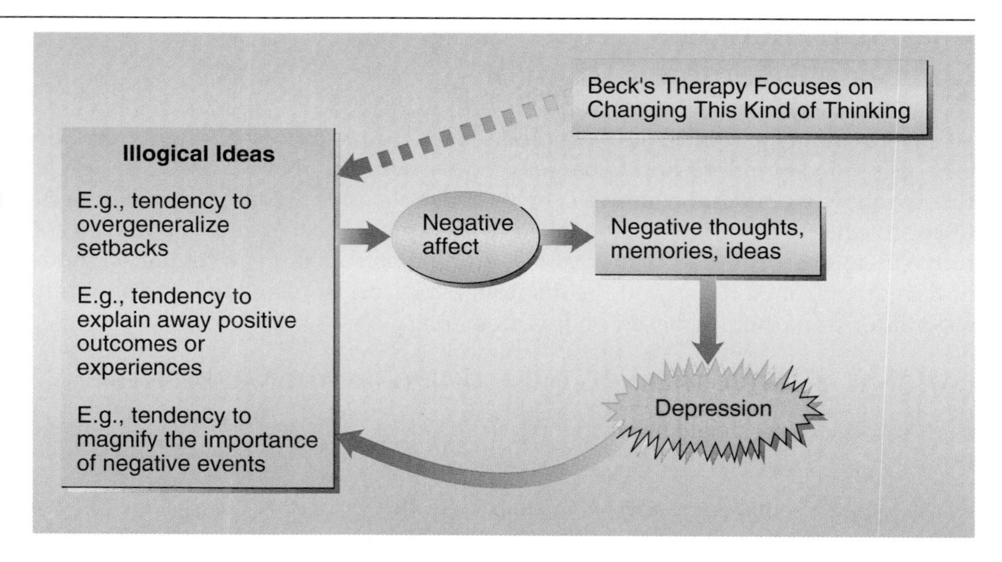


**Figure 15.7**
**Beck's Cognitive Behavior Therapy**

Beck's cognitive behavior therapy is designed to change cognitive tendencies (e.g., distorted thinking) that contribute to depression. Such patterns of thought often produce negative affect (mood), which then increases the likelihood of further negative thoughts. Cognitive behavior therapy attempts to break this cycle.

that this underlies their difficulties. Such individuals hold unrealistically negative beliefs and assumptions about themselves, the future, and the world (e.g., "I'm a worthless person no one could ever love," "If good things happen to me, it's just blind luck," "My life is a mess and will never improve"). Moreover, Beck contends, people cling to these illogical ideas and assumptions no matter what happens.

According to Beck, such distorted thinking leads individuals to have negative moods—which, in turn, increase the probability of more negative thinking (see Figure 15.7). In other words, Beck emphasizes the importance of mood-dependent memory—how our current moods influence what we remember and what we think about (see Chapters 6 and 14). How can this vicious circle be broken? In contrast to rational–emotive therapy, Beck's cognitive approach does not attempt to disprove the ideas held by depressed persons. Rather, the therapist and client work together to identify the individual's assumptions, beliefs, and expectations and to formulate ways of testing them. For example, if a client states that she is a total failure, the therapist may ask how she defines failure, and whether some experiences she defines this way may actually be only partial failures. If that's so, the therapist inquires, aren't they also partial successes? Continuing in this manner, the therapist might then ask the client whether there are any areas of her life in which she *does* experience success and has succeeded in reaching goals. Research findings indicate that as a result of these procedures, individuals learn to reinterpret negative events in ways that help them cope with such outcomes without becoming depressed (e.g., Bruder et al., 1997). So although the specific techniques used are different from those used in RET, the major goal is much the same: helping people to recognize, and reject, the false assumptions that are central to their difficulties.

**COGNITIVE THERAPIES: AN EVALUATION** An essential question about any form of therapy is "Does it work?" Cognitive therapies pass this test with flying colors: Many studies indicate that changing or eliminating irrational beliefs can be very effective in countering depression and other personal difficulties (e.g., Blatt et al., 1996). Similarly, the procedures outlined by Beck have been found to be highly effective in treating depression (e.g., Bruder et al., 1997). Perhaps even more important, the effects of cognitive therapy tend to be longer-lasting than those produced by other forms of therapy for depression—for instance, antidepressant drugs (which we'll examine in a later section). For instance, consider a study conducted by Segal, Gemar, and Williams (1999).

These psychologists exposed two groups of persons who had recently recovered from depression to procedures designed to induce negative moods: Participants listened to sad music and were also asked to remember a time in their lives

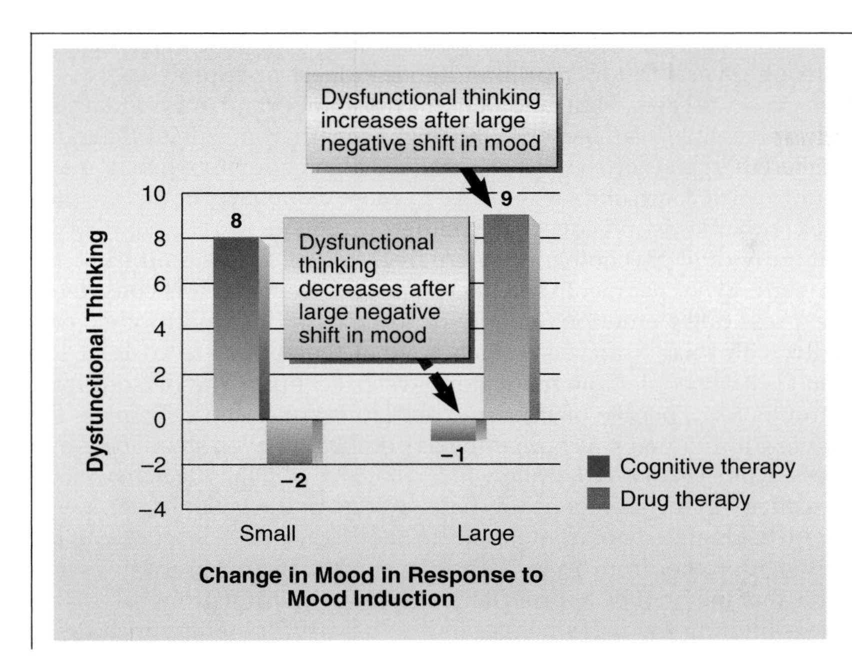


**Figure 15.8**
**Relative Effectiveness of Two Kinds of Therapy**

Following strong induction of a negative mood (large induction condition), persons who had recovered from depression as a result of drug therapy showed a stronger tendency to engage in dysfunctional, depression-inducing patterns of thought than did persons who had recovered as a result of cognitive behavior therapy. These findings suggest that cognitive behavior therapy may produce longer-lasting protection against the recurrence of depression than drug therapy.

(*Source:* Based on data from Segal, Gemar, & Williams, 1999.)

when they had felt sad. One of the groups had recovered from depression as a result of cognitive therapy, whereas the other had been treated only with drugs. Both groups of participants completed measures of the kinds of cognitions that often accompany depression (the kinds of negative self-evaluations highlighted by Beck and others as playing a key role in depression) on two separate occasions: before the negative mood induction and after it. The researchers predicted that persons who had recovered from depression as a result of cognitive behavior therapy would show lower levels of dysfunctional (i.e., depression-inducing) thoughts than would those who had recovered as a result of drug therapy. As you can see from Figure 15.8, this is precisely what happened. Moreover, follow-up research over a four-year period indicated that the kind of dysfunctional thinking shown by the drug-treated group was indeed predictive of a recurrence of depression. Findings such as these suggest that not only is cognitive therapy for depression effective—it may offer longer-lasting protection against the recurrence of this serious psychological disorder than other forms of therapy.

**REVIEW QUESTIONS**

- According to cognitive therapies, what is the primary cause of mental disorders?
- What is the major goal of rational–emotive therapy?
- What is the major goal of Beck's cognitive therapy for depression?

## Alternatives to Individual Psychotherapy: Group Therapy, Marital Therapy, Family Therapy, and Psychosocial Rehabilitation

As we'll see in a later section, growing evidence suggests that individual psychotherapy works: Many of the kinds of therapy we have already considered *are* effective in alleviating mental disorders (e.g., American Psychological Association, 1995). But there are several factors that limit the usefulness or appropriateness of such procedures in some cases. First, and perhaps most important, individual psychotherapy is not accessible to all persons who might benefit from it. It is often quite expensive—skilled therapists often receive $200 or $300 per hour! Obviously, many people can't afford such costs; and, as we'll see in more detail later in this chapter, their insurance companies won't cover them either.

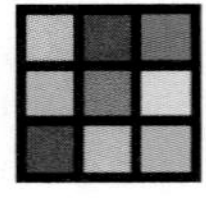

But even if individual psychotherapy were free, *cultural factors* limit its accessibility for some groups of people. In many cultures, for example, it is considered unseemly to express one's emotions openly or to discuss them with other persons—especially with total strangers (which is what therapists are, at least initially). The result is that people from many non-Western cultures and persons from some ethnic groups (e.g., people of Hispanic or Native American descent in the United States) view individual psychotherapy as pointless or even shameful—as a sign of weakness. This situation is definitely not helped by what has been described as *cultural insensitivity* in the mental health field, at least in the past (Rogler, 1999). Such insensitivity has resulted not from prejudice or other negative reactions on the part of therapists, but rather from an insistence on using standard procedures and assessment tools that may not be appropriate for various cultural groups.

Other factors limiting the usefulness of individual psychotherapy include its emphasis on individuals, a focus that overlooks the fact that social factors (e.g., conflicts and relationships with others) often play an important role in mental disorders, and its emphasis on *treatment* rather than on *prevention.* As we'll soon see, preventing mental disorders has become an important theme in psychology, just as preventing physical illness has become an important aspect of modern medicine.

Largely in response to these and other limitations, alternative forms of treatment for mental disorders have been developed. Several of these are described below.

## Group Therapies: Working Together to Solve Personal Problems

**Group therapies** involve procedures in which several people discuss their problems with one another under the guidance of a trained therapist. In some cases the procedures followed in group therapies are derived from specific forms of individual psychotherapy. For instance, techniques developed by Freud for individual therapy have also been modified for use in *psychodrama*—a form of group therapy in which group members act out their problems in front of one another, often on an actual stage. Psychodrama also involves such techniques as *role reversal,* in which group members switch parts, and *mirroring,* in which they portray one another on the stage. In each case the goal is to show clients how they actually behave and to help them understand *why* they behave that way—what hidden inner conflicts lie behind their overt actions (Olsson, 1989).

In contrast, *behavioral group therapies* are derived from the basic principles of learning that underlie behavior therapies. Such therapy has been found to be especially useful in teaching people basic *social skills,* such as how to communicate their wishes to others and how to stand up for their rights without being aggressive (the kind of *assertiveness training* described earlier). It has also proved helpful in teaching people *self-control*—the ability to regulate their own behavior.

**Group Therapies:** Procedures in which several people discuss their problems with one another under the guidance or leadership of a trained therapist.

Psychologists who practice phenomenological/experiential therapies have perhaps been the most enthusiastic about adapting their techniques to group therapy. In fact, interest in group therapy first originated among humanistic therapists, who developed two forms of such therapy—*encounter groups* and *sensitivity-training groups.* Both of these techniques focus on the goal of fostering personal growth through clients' increased understanding of their own behavior and through increased honesty and openness in personal relations. In both kinds of groups, members are encouraged to talk about the problems they encounter in their lives. The reactions they receive from other group members then help them understand their own responses to these problems. The major difference between encounter groups and sensitivity-training groups lies in the fact that encounter groups carry the goal of open exchange of views to a greater extreme: Members in these groups are encouraged to yell, cry, touch each other, and generally to act in a completely uninhibited manner. Sensitivity-training groups, in contrast, are somewhat more subdued.

In practice, most group therapy involves six to twelve persons, plus a therapist. Sessions last about two hours—twice as long as most sessions of individual psychotherapy. Yet costs can be relatively low, because group members, in essence, share the therapist's fee. Do such groups really produce beneficial changes? Growing evidence suggests that they can indeed be helpful, primarily because they provide the following benefits (Bednar & Kaul, 1994): (1) People participating in these groups learn that their problems are not unique but that in fact they are shared by many other persons. (2) Group therapy sessions encourage hope—when group members see others coping with their problems, they realize that they too can do the same. (3) Persons in group therapy sessions share information with one another—suggestions on how to cope with specific problems and insights into these problems. (4) Group therapy sessions give members a chance to practice altruism—to offer help to others; and this can boost their self-esteem. And (5) group therapy sessions offer a supportive environment in which to practice basic social skills. When these potential benefits are combined, it is not surprising that group therapies can sometimes be very beneficial for the persons who participate in them (see Figure 15.9).

**Figure 15.9**
**Group Therapy: It Can Sometimes Be Effective**

In group therapy, people with similar problems work together under the direction of a trained therapist to reduce these problems. For several reasons—people learn that their problems are not unique, group members share information and insights, the group provides a supportive environment for practicing social skills—such therapy can often be beneficial.

**REVIEW QUESTIONS**

- Why are alternatives to individual psychotherapy needed?
- What are group therapies?

## Marital and Family Therapies: Therapies Focused on Interpersonal Relations

Web Link: *Why Use a Family and Marriage Therapist*

Although group therapies take place in settings where several people are present, these therapeutic approaches often search for the roots of mental disorders in processes operating largely *within* individuals—for instance, in inner conflicts, faulty habits, distorted self-concepts, faulty learning. In contrast, two other kinds of therapy—*marital therapy* and *family therapy*—focus on the potential role of *interpersonal relations* in mental disorders and psychological problems (Gurman, Kniskern,

**Figure 15.10**
**Marital Therapy: Not for Everyone!**

Marital therapy is *not* designed to keep mutually destructive relationships like this one alive. Rather, it focuses on helping couples who believe that their relationships are truly worth saving, even if this requires a lot of work. (*Source:* © The New Yorker Collection. 1977. Joseph Mirachi from cartoonbank.com. All rights reserved.)

*"Let's face it, Ron. The only time we meet each other's needs is when we fight."*

& Pinsof, 1986). In other words, therapies in this category assume that individuals experience personal problems because their relations with important persons in their lives are ineffective, unsatisfying, or worse. Let's now examine two important forms of therapy that adopt this interpersonal perspective.

**MARITAL THERAPY: SPOUSES AS THE INTIMATE ENEMY** In the United States and many other countries, more than 50 percent of all marriages now end in divorce. Moreover, the marriage rate has dropped sharply in recent years; it seems that young people may see these odds in increasingly unfavorable terms (Popenoe & Whitehead, 1999). Of course, keeping people in joyless marriages or mutually destructive relationships like the one shown in Figure 15.10 is definitely *not* a goal of therapy. Rather, **marital therapy** (sometimes termed *couples therapy*) is designed to help couples who feel that their marriage is worth saving. In addition, marital problems are related to several mental disorders, including depression, anxiety, and drug dependency (Gotlieb & McCabe, 1990); so marital therapy can be beneficial in helping people avoid these problems.

Web Link: *How Do Therapists Threaten Marriages?*

Before turning to the procedures used in such therapy, however, let's first consider a very basic question: What, in your opinion, is the number one reason why couples seek professional help in the first place? If you guessed "sexual problems," guess again; such difficulties are a distant second on the list (see Figure 15.11). Problems relating to *communication* are far and away the number one cause of difficulties. People entering marital therapy often state that their partner "never talks to them" or "never tells them what she/he is thinking." Or they report that all their partner ever does is *complain.* "He/she never tells me that he/she loves me," they remark. "All he/she does is tell me about my faults and what I'm doing wrong." Given that couples begin their relationships with frequent statements of mutual esteem and love, the pain of such faulty communication patterns is doubled: Each person wonders what went wrong—and then generally blames his or her partner!

Now, back to the specific goals and procedures of marital therapy. One type, *behavioral* marital therapy, focuses on the communication problems I have just emphasized. Therapists work to foster improved communication in many ways, including having each partner play the role of the other person so as to see their relationship as the other does. Other techniques involve having couples watch videotapes of their own interactions. This procedure is often a real eye-opener: "Wow, I never realized that's how I come across!" is a common reaction. As communication between members of a couple improves, many other beneficial changes occur; for instance, the partners stop criticizing each other in destructive ways (e.g., Baron, 1993a), express positive sentiments toward each other more frequently, and stop assuming that everything the other person does that annoys or angers them is done on purpose (e.g., Kubany et al., 1995). Once good communication is established, couples may also find it easier to resolve other sources of friction in their

**Marital Therapy:** Therapy designed to help couples improve the quality of their relationship.

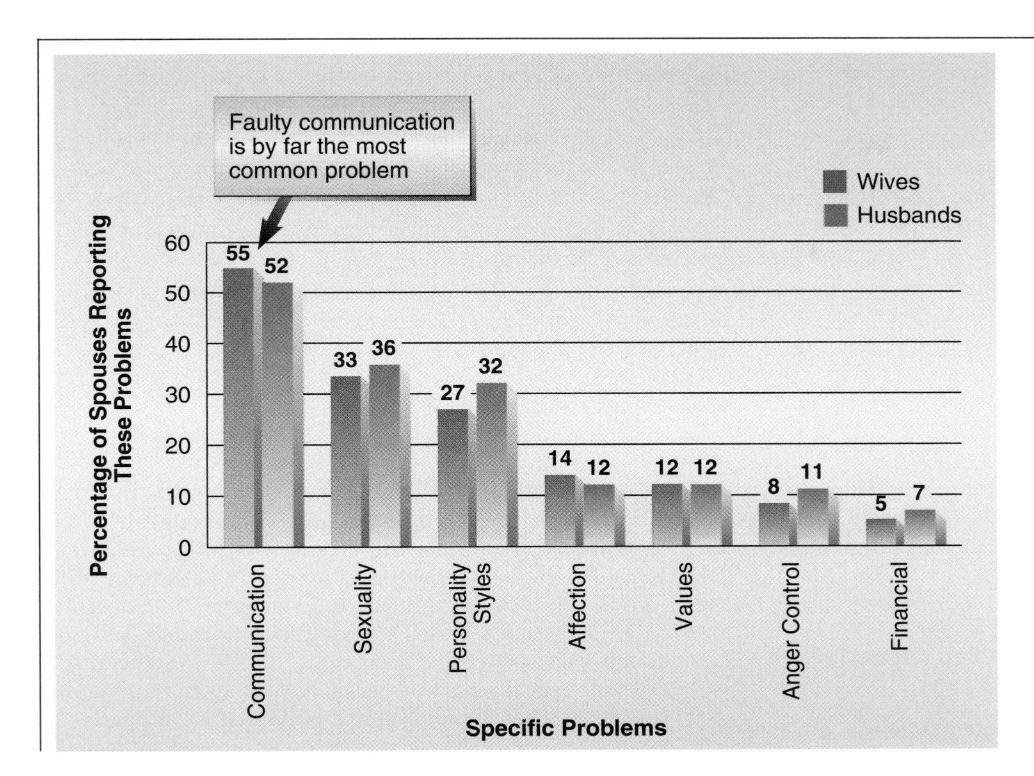


**Figure 15.11**
**Why Couples Seek Marital Therapy**

The number one reason why couples enter marital therapy is faulty communication—*not*, as you might have guessed, difficulties relating to sex. (*Source:* Based on data from O'Leary, Vivian, & Malone, 1992.)

relationships. The result may then be a happier and more stable relationship—a relationship that increases, rather than reduces, the psychological well-being of both partners.

Other forms of marital therapy focus not on specific skills that can help people get along better but on gaining insight into the causes of couples' problems. Such *insight* marital therapy and behavioral marital therapy have both been found to be helpful: Couples who undergo such therapy are more likely to stay together and report being happier than couples who do not. For information on an additional form of marital therapy—one involving drugs—see the following **Beyond the Headlines** section.

## the HEADLINES: *As Psychologists See It*

## Is Better Sex the Key to a Happier Marriage? Don't Bet on It!

### Viagra's Other Side Effect: Upsets in Many a Marriage

NEW YORK TIMES (JUNE 23, 1998)—On the surface, the couple from Queens seemed like perfect candidates for Viagra. The woman, 53, has been married to her husband, 59, for 30 years. A few years ago he started to have trouble achieving an erection. . . .Viagra, the popular new drug for impotence, would appear to be their ticket back to a more conventional sex life. But like many other couples contemplating Viagra, the two are starkly divided about whether to try it: while he is looking for a medical panacea for a physical problem . . . she has long wondered whether the problem might be better addressed on a therapist's couch than in a doctor's office. . . .

A few months ago, Viagra was being promoted by everyone from urologists to drug companies as the new miracle drug destined to help solve millions of couples' sexual problems. The drug flew off pharmacy shelves. But experts on sexuality and therapists are finding that Viagra and other impotence aids may actually throw into chaos relationships that have fallen into their own routine, sexual dysfunction and all. The most common problem, they say, is that men hope to treat their impotence as a simple mechanical issue, while women want to address the emotions related to impotence. In other cases, a man and woman are forced to confront their divergent views about what it means to have sex and how often they want to have it—issues that impotence had rendered moot. The result is that many couples are finding that a solution to what they thought was a medical problem may uncover many other issues in the relationship. . . .

Viagra, it seems, it not the miracle drug many believed it to be. True, it seems to help some men attain erections. But, as I noted earlier, sexual problems are *not* the most common difficulties faced by couples. Relationships—especially long-term ones—are complex; and many other factors, ranging from communication and interests to values and styles of expressing affection, enter into the equation where marital happiness is concerned. Changing men's sexual performance does not, in itself, address any of these other issues. Besides, renewed sexual vigor on the part of the male partner may upset the delicate balance of a relationship that has developed over years or decades. Most couples experience a gradual decline in frequency of sexual relations over time; thus, a sudden increase in the sexual appetite of one partner may not necessarily be welcomed by the other. In fact, it may simply bring other problems in the relationship—such as contrasting views about intimacy or expressive styles—sharply into focus.

**Figure 15.12**
**Better Sex Does Not Always Equal a Better Relationship**

Drugs like the one being promoted in this ad may help some men perform better in the bedroom, but—given the complexity of intimate relationships—this is no guarantee of increased happiness.

So becoming a star in the bedroom is definitely *not* always the answer to having a better relationship. Viagra, in short, is not the magic bullet for marital problems that ads like the one in Figure 15.12 seem to suggest.

## CRITICAL THINKING QUESTIONS

1. Do you think that male impotence might stem from problems in a relationship itself? If so, would treating the impotence help solve these problems, or would the problems tend to persist even if the impotence were overcome?
2. According to many experts on human sexuality, "the mind is the only erogenous zone"—sexual desire involves much more than physical reactions. If that's true, can *any* pill really be helpful in improving sexual relations?

**FAMILY THERAPY: CHANGING ENVIRONMENTS THAT HARM** Let's begin with a disturbing fact: When individuals who have been hospitalized for the treatment of serious mental disorders and who have shown improvements return home, they often experience a relapse. All the gains they have made through individual therapy vanish. This fact points to an unsettling possibility: Perhaps the problems experienced by such persons stem, at least in part, from their families—from disturbed patterns of interaction among family members (Hazelrigg, Cooper, & Borduin, 1987). To the extent that this is true, attempting to help one member of a family is not sufficient; unless changes are made in the family environment, too, any benefits they have experienced may disappear once they return home.

Recognition of this important fact spurred the development of several types of **family therapy**—therapy designed to change the relationships among family members in constructive ways. Such therapies differ in form, but most are based on the following concepts suggested by *systems theory,* an approach that views families as social systems: (1) *circular causality*—events within a family are interrelated and cause one another in reciprocal fashion; (2) *ecology*—families are integrated systems, so change in one member will affect all other members; and (3) *subjectivity*—each family member has her or his personal view of family events. Together, these ideas emphasize the importance of working with all family members: Family members are in constant contact with one another and create an environment in which all exist.

**Family Therapy:** Therapy designed to change the relationships among family members in constructive ways.

**Family Systems Therapy:** A form of family therapy in which therapists treat families as dynamic systems in which each member has an important major role.

**Self-Help Groups:** Groups of persons who are experiencing the same kinds of problems and who meet regularly, without professionally trained leaders, to help one another in their efforts to cope with these difficulties.

Web Link: *Alcoholics Anonymous*

What specific techniques does family therapy involve? **Family systems therapy**—an approach closely linked to the concepts mentioned above—assumes that relations among family members are more important in producing mental disorders than aspects of personality or other factors operating largely within individuals (Minuchin & Fishman, 1981). This approach also assumes that all members of the family influence one another through the complex network of their relationships. How does family systems therapy work? Here's an example. Consider a highly aggressive boy who is getting into lots of trouble in school and elsewhere. A family systems approach would assume that this youngster's difficulties stem, at least in part, from disturbed relationships between him and other family members. Close observation of interactions among the family members might reveal that the parents are locked in bitter conflict, with each trying to recruit the boy to their side. The result: He experiences tremendous stress and anger and directs this outward toward schoolmates and others. Understanding the dynamics of this family, in short, can provide insights into the causes of the boy's problem. Changing these dynamics, in turn, could help to reduce his difficulties.

In contrast, *behavioral approaches* (sometimes known as *problem-solving therapy*) emphasize teaching family members improved, noncoercive ways of communicating their needs and ways of acting that prevent or reduce conflicts (e.g., Robbin & Foster, 1988).

Does family therapy work? Research findings indicate that in many cases it is quite successful. After undergoing such therapy, family members are rated by therapists, teachers, and other observers as showing more adaptive behavior and better relations with one another than was true before the therapy (Hazelrigg, Cooper, & Borduin, 1987). And family therapy does seem to help reduce problems experienced by individual members (e.g., Henggler, Melton, & Smith, 1992). However, as has been the case with many forms of therapy involving several persons, most research on the effectiveness of family therapy has been somewhat informal in nature.

## Self-Help Groups: When Misery Derives Comfort from Company

When we are anxious, upset, or otherwise troubled, we often seek comfort and support from others. Long before there were psychologists and psychiatrists, people sought informal help with personal difficulties from family members, friends, or clergy. This tendency to seek help from people we know, even if they are not professionals, has taken a new form in **self-help groups** (Christensen & Jacobson, 1994). These are groups of persons who are experiencing the same kinds of problems and who meet regularly, without professionally trained leaders, to help one another in their efforts to cope with these difficulties (see Figure 15.13). Self-help

**Figure 15.13**
**Self-Help Groups: Are They Really Beneficial?**

Self-help groups have become increasingly popular in recent years. In them, groups of persons who are experiencing the same kinds of problems meet regularly, without professionally trained leaders, to help one another cope with their problems. Unfortunately, little scientific evidence currently exists concerning the effectiveness of such groups.

**Deinstitutionalization:** A shifting of patients from public hospitals to the community, largely as a result of the development of effective drugs for treating mental disorders.

**Psychosocial Rehabilitation:** Efforts to help patients with serious mental disorders (e.g., schizophrenia, major mood disorders) to cope more effectively with their disorders and to prevent or lessen the crises that reduce these patients' ability to function in society.

groups are a fact of life; indeed, it has been estimated that more than 5 percent of all adults in the United States are or have been involved in such groups. What kinds of problems do these groups address? Almost everything you can imagine; in fact, several different types of groups, focusing on contrasting kinds of problems, exist. *Habit disturbance* self-help groups focus on specific behaviors (e.g., Alcoholics Anonymous, Gamblers Anonymous). *General-purpose* self-help groups address a wide range of difficulties (e.g., the death of a child or spouse, childhood sexual abuse, being a single parent, divorce, stuttering, breast cancer). *Lifestyle* organizations support individuals such as single parents or the elderly who feel that they are being treated unfairly by society (e.g., Parents Without Partners, Gray Panthers). *Physical handicap* organizations offer support to people with heart disease and other medical conditions (e.g., Mended Hearts). *Significant-other* organizations provide support and advocacy for relatives of disturbed persons (Gam-Anon for relatives of compulsive gamblers, Al-Anon for relatives of alcoholics). Finally, reflecting the tragic effects of AIDS, a growing number of self-help groups now focus on assisting persons who have been diagnosed with this illness as well as their friends, relatives, and significant others.

Do self-help groups succeed? Few scientific studies have been conducted on this question, partly because the groups themselves often strictly guard their privacy; but there is some indication that they can be beneficial (Christensen & Jacobson, 1994). In any case, these groups do provide members with emotional support and help them make new friends. These outcomes alone may justify their existence.

## Psychosocial Rehabilitation

As we'll soon see in more detail, the development of effective drugs for treating serious mental disorders during the 1950s and 1960s resulted in the release of large numbers of persons from public mental hospitals. Many applauded the **deinstitutionalization** trend—the shifting of patients from public hospitals to the community. But positive reactions to this change were soon muted by the fact that many of these persons failed to receive regular treatment of any kind after their release. The result? Many were unable to deal with the problems of everyday life and drifted into unemployment and homelessness (see Figure 15.14). As recognition of these sad facts has grown, efforts by psychologists and other mental health professionals to reach such persons and to help them deal with their disorders increased. Such efforts, known as **psychosocial rehabilitation,** center on teaching patients with serious mental disorders (schizophrenia, major mood disorders) to cope more effectively with their disorders and, especially, to avoid or lessen the crises that often stem from these disorders and make it virtually impossible for these patients to function in society. Psychosocial rehabilitation, in short, does not attempt to cure serious mental disorders; rather, it seeks to help persons with such disorders live as close to a normal life in the community as possible (Hunter, 1995).

**Figure 15.14**
**The Downside of Deinstitutionalization**

During the 1960s large numbers of persons were released from public mental hospitals, largely because of the development of effective drugs for treating mental disorders. Unfortunately, many of these persons received little or no treatment after their release and drifted into unemployment, crime, or homelessness.

Efforts to assist patients through psychosocial rehabilitation focus on achieving several goals. First, a key goal is to help such persons understand their disorders so that they can cope with them more effectively. For instance, patients may be taught to recognize early warning signs of deterioration and to avoid high-risk situations. Those with schizophrenia can be taught to recognize the hallucinations that often precede psychotic breaks and lead to arrest or hospitalization. Such steps can help individuals with serious mental disorders avoid serious trouble. Second, psychosocial rehabilitation focuses on teaching patients the practical skills they need to live in the community—how to use public transportation, shop for groceries, prepare meals, and interact with other persons. Third, efforts are made to have a single professional coordinate efforts to help the patient—efforts with respect to employment, housing, nutrition, transportation, medical care, and finances. Such *case management* helps to ensure that patients get all the help available to them and do not "slip between the cracks."

Growing evidence suggests that psychosocial rehabilitation works: It helps keep persons with serious mental disorders from having relapses or from experiencing serious problems with the law (Bond et al., 1990). However, such programs are most beneficial if they continue on a regular basis (Wallace, 1993). I'll have more to say about such programs in a later discussion of prevention.

**Biological Therapies:** Forms of therapy that attempt to reduce mental disorders through biological means.

**Drug Therapy:** Therapy based on the administration of psychoactive drugs.

**REVIEW QUESTIONS**

- What is marital or couples therapy?
- What is family therapy?
- What are self-help groups?
- What is psychosocial rehabilitation?

## Biological Therapies

Earlier, I noted that the development of effective drugs for treating serious mental disorders led to a sharp drop in the number of patients in public mental hospitals. What are these drugs, how do they work, and just how effective are they? We'll examine these questions in the course of our discussion of **biological therapies**—forms of therapy that attempt to alleviate mental disorders through biological means. Efforts along these lines have continued for hundreds, perhaps thousands of years. Indeed, skulls from early civilizations often show neatly drilled holes, suggesting that some persons, at least, may have received surgery on their brains as a means of eliminating mental disorders; presumably, the holes were intended to provide an escape route for the causes of such disorders (e.g., evil spirits). Even in the nineteenth century, many physicians used devices like the one in Figure 15.15, which delivered electric shocks, to treat a wide range of "nervous disorders."

Both brain surgery and the use of electric shock continue today. But by far the most popular form of biologically based therapy involves the use of various *psychoactive drugs*—drugs that alter feelings, thoughts, and behavior.

**Figure 15.15**
**Shocking Patients into Mental Health?**

Devices such as this one were widely used by physicians in the nineteenth and early twentieth centuries to treat "nervous disorders." They delivered jolts of electricity to patients and were, as far as I can tell, completely ineffective.

### Drug Therapy: The Pharmacological Revolution

In 1955, almost 600,000 persons were full-time resident patients in psychiatric hospitals in the United States. Twenty years later, this number had dropped below 175,000. Was the U.S. population achieving mental health at a dizzying pace? Absolutely not. What happened in those years was the advent of **drug therapy:** A wide

**Figure 15.16**
**Use of Drugs in Treating Mental Disorders**

As shown here, the percentage of patients receiving drugs as a treatment for mental disorders has increased sharply in recent decades.
(*Source:* Based on data reported by Nietzel et al., 1998.)

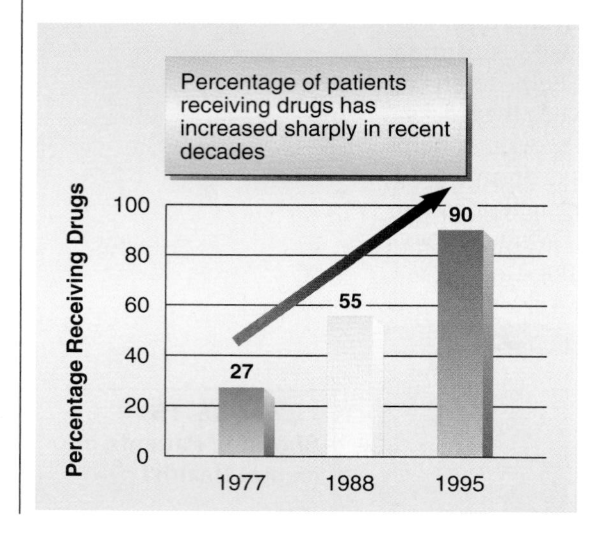


range of drugs effective in treating mental disorders were developed and put to use. And, as shown in Figure 15.16, such use has continued to increase, rising from 27 percent of patients in 1977 to more than 90 percent at present. This trend isn't due solely to the effectiveness of the drugs; it also reflects the fact that treating mental disorders with drugs is often less expensive than other forms of therapy—and changes in health care (e.g., the growth of managed care and HMOs) have made cost a primary consideration. Let's now take a closer look at these drugs and their effects.

**ANTIPSYCHOTIC DRUGS** If you had visited the wards of a psychiatric hospital for seriously disturbed persons before 1955, you would have witnessed some pretty wild scenes—screaming, bizarre actions, nudity. If you had returned a few years later, however, you would have seen a dramatic change: peace, relative tranquillity, and many patients now capable of direct, sensible communication. These startling changes were largely the result of the development of *antipsychotic drugs,* sometimes known as the *major tranquilizers* or *neuroleptics.* These drugs were highly effective in reducing the *positive* symptoms shown by schizophrenics (e.g., hallucinations, delusions), although they were less effective in reducing negative symptoms (e.g., withdrawal, lack of affect).

The most important group of antipsychotic drugs, *phenothiazines,* was discovered by accident. In the early 1950s a French surgeon, Henri Laborit, used a drug in this chemical family, *Thorazine* (chlorpromazine) to try to reduce blood pressure in patients before surgery. He found that their blood pressure didn't drop, but that they became much less anxious. French psychiatrists tried the drug with their patients, and found that it worked: It reduced anxiety—and, even more important, it also reduced hallucinations and delusions among schizophrenic patients. Chemists quickly analyzed chlorpromazine and developed many other drugs that are related to it but are even more effective in reducing psychotic symptoms (e.g., clozapine, haloperidol). (Throughout this discussion I'll present brand names of drugs; their chemical or generic names will appear in parentheses.)

CourseCompass
Web Link: *Tardive Dyskinesia*

CourseCompass
Audio Link 15.3: *Schizophrenia and Deficits in Selective Attention*

How do the antipsychotics produce such effects? Some block the action of the neurotransmitter *dopamine* on certain receptors in the brain ($D_2$ receptors). As noted in Chapter 14, the presence of an excess of this neurotransmitter, or increased sensitivity to it, may play a role in schizophrenia. Other antipsychotics—especially the newest, such as Novartis and Zeneca—influence many different chemicals in the brain: neurotransmitters and other compounds as well. In sum, many different antipsychotic drugs exist, and they do not all operate in the same way. Whatever the precise mechanism involved, however, it is clear that antipsychotic drugs are very helpful in reducing the bizarre symptoms of schizophrenia.

The use of these drugs, however, is not without drawbacks. They often produce side effects such as blurred vision and dry mouth. In addition, they produce more serious side effects known as *extrapyramidal symptoms*—for instance, fine tremor of the hands, muscular weakness, and rigidity. Additional and even more serious effects can involve uncontrollable contractions of muscles in the neck, head, tongue, and back, or uncontrollable restlessness and agitation. The most serious side effect of all, however, is **tardive dyskinesia.** After receiving antipsychotic drugs for prolonged periods of time, many patients develop this side effect, which involves loss of motor control, especially in the face. As a result, they show involuntary muscle movements of the tongue, lips, and jaw. Unfortunately, these effects don't occur until after patients have taken neuroleptics for several years, and at this

**Tardive Dyskinesia:** A common side effect produced by antipsychotic drugs, in which individuals experience loss of motor control, especially in the face.

point the disorder is irreversible. Schizophrenics often take antipsychotic drugs throughout life (Mueser & Glynn, 1995), and as a result they stand a very good chance of developing this side effect. One relatively new antipsychotic drug, Clozaril (clozapine), appears to be effective without producing tardive dyskinesia. However, clozapine has its own side effects, the most serious of which is *agranulocytosis*—a fatal blood disease. Additional antipsychotic drugs are under development (e.g., olanzapine), and it is hoped that they will cause even fewer side effects.

Although the antipsychotic drugs are clearly of great value and do reduce the most bizarre symptoms of schizophrenia, it should be emphasized that they do *not* cure this disorder. In the past, such drugs were more effective in reducing the positive symptoms of schizophrenia than in treating the negative symptoms. Thus, persons receiving them tended to remain somewhat withdrawn and to show the low levels of affect that are often part of schizophrenia. Newer drugs, however, do seem more successful in treating these negative symptoms. Such drugs are sometimes termed *atypicals,* because they influence many different chemicals in the brain rather than only one. In any case, although drugs for treating schizophrenia are improving, the likelihood that individuals with schizophrenia will regain normal functioning and be able to live on their own is increased when they receive psychotherapy too.

**ANTIDEPRESSANT DRUGS** Shortly after the development of chlorpromazine, drugs effective in reducing depression made their appearance. There are three basic types of such compounds, *tricyclics, selective serotonin reuptake inhibitors (SSRIs),* and *MAO inhibitors.* Again, as is true with virtually all drugs used to treat mental disorders, antidepressants seem to exert their effects by influencing neurotransmitters, especially serotonin and norepinephrine (Julien, 1995).

Among the SSRIs, *Prozac* (fluoxetine) is by far the most famous—and also the most commonly prescribed: More than 1.5 million prescriptions for it are written every month in the United States alone. Depressed persons taking this drug often report that they feel better than they have in their entire lives. However, Prozac, like other antidepressant drugs, appears to have serious side effects. About 30 percent of patients taking it report nervousness, insomnia, joint pain, weight loss, and sexual dysfunction (Hellerstein et al., 1993). A small number report suicidal thoughts (Teicher, Glod, & Cole, 1990). In contrast, MAO inhibitors can produce more dangerous side effects. They seem to virtually eliminate REM sleep; and if consumed with food containing tyramine (e.g., aged cheeses, beer, red wine), MAO inhibitors can cause a sudden extreme rise in blood pressure, thus putting patients at risk for strokes (Julien, 1995). For these reasons, these drugs are used less often than the other two types of antidepressants. Tricyclics also produce side effects, such as disturbances in sleep and appetite, but these tend to decrease within a few weeks. Widely prescribed tricyclics include Elavil (amitriptyline) and Tofranil (imipramine).

One final point: while these drugs *are* often effective in treating depression, research evidence suggests that they are not necessarily more effective than several forms of psychotherapy, especially cognitive and behavioral therapies (e.g., Bruder et al., 1997; Hollon, Shelton, & Loosen, 1991; Robinson, Berman, & Neimeyer, 1990). Indeed, as we saw in our discussion of cognitive therapies, growing evidence suggests that these may produce longer-lasting benefits than drugs (Segal, Gemar, & Williams, 1999). Also, antidepressants are most effective for treating major depression, but somewhat less so for milder conditions.

**LITHIUM** An entirely different kind of antidepressant drug is *lithium* (usually administered as *lithium chloride*). This drug has been found to be quite effective in treating people with bipolar (manic–depressive) disorders, and is successful with 60 to 70 percent of these persons (Julien, 1995). Because such persons are often quite agitated and even psychotic, lithium is generally administered along with antipsychotic or antidepressant medications. Unfortunately, lithium has serious side effects—excessive doses can cause delirium and even death. Thus, it has a very small "therapeutic window" or dose level that is effective without being dangerous. Exactly how lithium exerts its effects is not known; one possibility is that it influences the effects of *secondary messengers,* changes that occur in neurons after they have initially been stimulated by a neurotransmitter. Another possibility is that lithium affects electrolyte balances in the neurons. Whatever its mechanism, it is one of the few drugs effective in treating manic–depressive disorders, so its continued use seems likely.

**ANTIANXIETY DRUGS** Alcohol, a substance used by many people to combat anxiety, has been available for thousands of years. Needless to say, however, it has important negative side effects. Synthetic drugs with antianxiety effects—sometimes known as *minor tranquilizers*—have been manufactured for several decades. The most widely prescribed of these at present are the *benzodiazepines.* This group includes drugs whose names you may already know: Valium, Ativan, Xanax, and Librium.

The most common use for antianxiety drugs, at least ostensibly, is as an aid to sleep. They are safer for this purpose than *barbiturates* (see Chapter 4), being less addicting. However, substances derived from the benzodiazepines remain in the body for longer periods of time than those from barbiturates and can cumulate until they reach toxic levels. Thus, long-term use of these drugs can be quite dangerous. In addition, when they are taken with alcohol, their effects may be magnified; this is definitely a combination to avoid. Finally, the benzodiazepines tend to produce dependency; individuals experience withdrawal symptoms when they are abruptly stopped. These drugs seem to produce their effects by facilitating the postsynaptic binding of central nervous system neurotransmitters such as GABA, the brain's major inhibitor. Thus, the drugs seem to serve as a kind of braking system, reducing activity in the nervous system that would otherwise result in anxiety and tension. While benzodiazepines are effective—persons who take them report being calmer and less worried—they have potentially serious side effects: drowsiness, dizziness, fatigue, and reduced motor coordination. These can prove fatal to motorists or people operating dangerous machinery.

**Figure 15.17**
**Effects of Antianxiety Drugs on Motor Coordination**

Most antianxiety drugs produce drowsiness and seriously impair motor coordination. However, one drug useful in treating anxiety disorders, buspirone, does not seem to produce such effects. The figures in this drawing show the amount of body sway produced by this drug as compared to sway produced by alcohol, a placebo, and lorazepam, a benzodiazepine.

(*Source:* Based on data in Schuckit, 1982.)

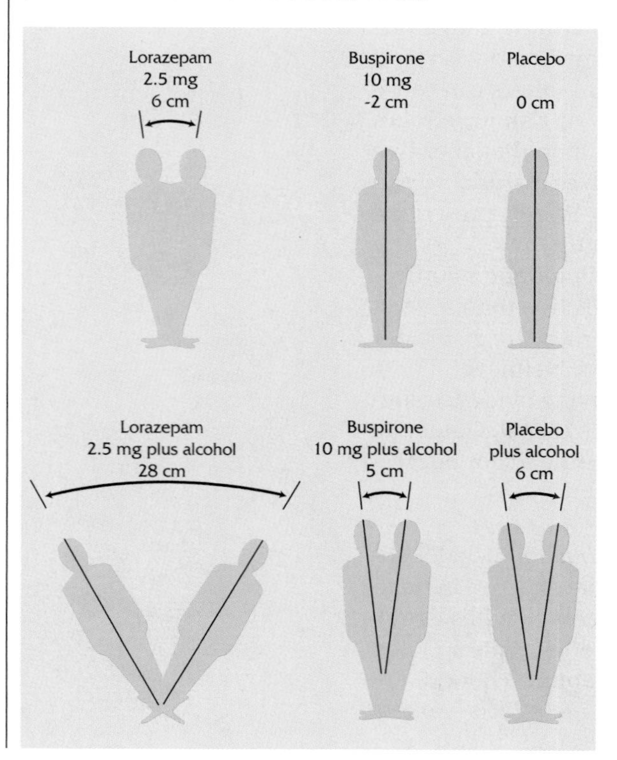


Fortunately, such effects are much smaller for an additional antianxiety drug that is not related to the benzodiazepines: BuSpar (buspirone). In fact, BuSpar produces little or no drowsiness and no more body sway than an inactive placebo (see Figure 15.17) (Long & Rybacki, 1994). There is a lag of one to three weeks before BuSpar produces its antianxiety effects. However, it does seem to be a useful alternative to the benzodiazepines.

In sum, many drugs are effective in treating serious mental disorders, and these drugs are being prescribed in ever increasing quantities. Some of these drugs are fairly new, however, so their long-term effects remain unknown. Moreover, as with all drugs, the benefits of these medications are offset, to a degree, by potentially serious side effects. Should society be more cautious in using drug therapy? This is a complex issue, but many psychologists feel that greater caution may be justified.

**ETHNIC DIFFERENCES IN REACTIONS TO PSYCHOACTIVE DRUGS** A basic question that arises with respect to all drugs is: How much is enough? In other words, what is the proper dose? Drugs used to treat mental disorders are no exception to this basic rule. Until recently, however, most studies concerning the effects and proper dosages of such drugs were conducted with males of European descent (e.g., Lin, Poland, & Nakasaki, 1993). The findings of such research could potentially be quite misleading, because it is well known that the effects of drugs can be strongly influenced by such factors as the age, body weight, and internal chemistry of the persons receiving them. And what about gender and ethnic differences—could these, too, influence the effects of psychoactive drugs? A growing body of evidence suggests that they can.

**Electroconvulsive Therapy:** A form of therapy in which strong electric shocks are delivered to the brain; often called ECT.

With respect to gender, females are usually smaller and lighter in weight than males. Further, gender differences exist in how much of a drug is absorbed through the gastrointestinal tract and how much accumulates in fat tissue. It is not surprising, then, that females require smaller doses of benzodiazepines and neuroleptics than do males—and that if females receive the full "standard" doses of such drugs (doses established primarily with males), they may experience stronger side effects. Further, the impact of drugs may vary in females as a function of where they are in their menstrual cycles and whether they are taking birth-control pills (e.g., Yonkers et al., 1992). Clearly, then, drug doses should be carefully adjusted to take account of patients' gender.

Ethnic differences in reactions to psychoactive drugs also exist. Asians seem to require only half the doses of some antidepressant drugs than persons of European descent (Silver, Poland, & Lin, 1993). Similarly, persons of African descent seem to require smaller doses than Europeans: They accumulate these drugs more quickly in their system and experience faster and stronger responses to them.

The effects of neuroleptics, too, vary with patients' ethnic background. Asians show higher blood concentrations of drugs such as haloperidol than do persons of European descent after receiving a standard dose (Jann, Lam, & Chang, 1993). This finding implies that Asians require lower doses of such drugs than Europeans. In view of these and related findings, it is clear that important ethnic and gender differences exist with respect to reactions to drugs used to treat many mental disorders. Failure to pay careful attention to such differences can reduce the effectiveness of such drugs or even put patients at serious risk.

## Electroconvulsive Therapy

Remember my grandmother's experience with depression? At the time when she had this disorder, the early 1950s, effective drugs for treating her depression did not exist. That's one of the main reasons why she received another kind of biological therapy: **electroconvulsive therapy (ECT).** In the modern form of ECT (somewhat different from what my grandmother received), physicians place electrodes on the patient's temples and deliver shocks of 70 to 130 volts for brief intervals (approximately one second). These shocks are continued until the patient has a seizure, a muscle contraction of the entire body, lasting at least twenty to twenty-five seconds. In order to prevent broken bones and other injuries, a muscle relaxant and a mild anesthetic are usually administered before the start of the shocks. Patients typically receive three treatments a week for several weeks (see Figure 15.18).

Surprisingly, ECT seems to work, at least for some disorders. It reduces severe depression, especially with persons who have failed to respond to other forms of

**Figure 15.18**
**Electroconvulsive Therapy Today**

In electroconvulsive therapy an electric current passes through the brain for about one second, causing a brief seizure. This treatment seems to be effective in reducing severe depression, although *how* it produces such benefits is still uncertain.

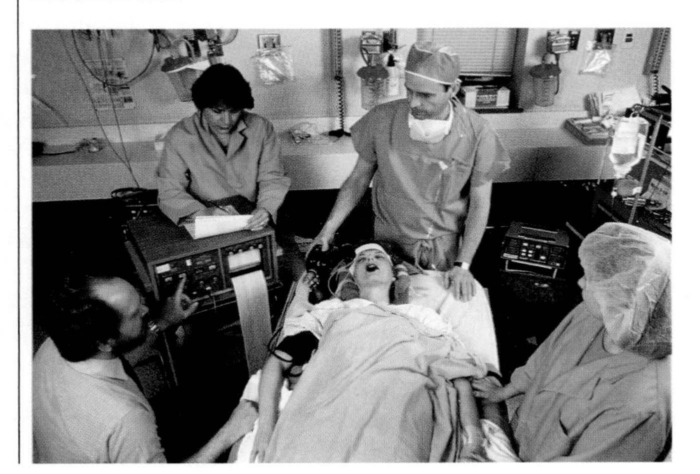

**Psychosurgery:** Brain operations designed to change abnormal behavior.

therapy (Effective Treatment, 1994; Fink, 1993). The American Psychiatric Association recommends ECT for use with patients who are severely suicidal or psychotically depressed (e.g., refusing to eat, in a stupor).

Unfortunately, there are important risks connected with ECT. It is designed to alter the brain—and it does, producing loss of *episodic memory* in many patients; that is, they forget events they have personally experienced. In some cases ECT does irreversible damage to portions of the brain. Further, although the shocks themselves are painless, many patients find the procedures frightening, to say the least; some, like my grandmother, are terrified of them. I remember her saying to me, "I only pray that *you* never have to experience it!" These facts have led some researchers to criticize the use of ECT and to call for its elimination as a form of therapy. However, the fact that ECT works for some severely depressed persons who have not responded to other forms of therapy has encouraged its continued use (e.g., Fink, 1994).

## Psychosurgery

In 1935 a Portuguese psychiatrist, Egas Moniz, attempted to reduce aggressive behavior in psychotic patients by severing neural connections between the prefrontal lobes and the remainder of the brain. The operation, known as *prefrontal lobotomy*, seemed to work: Aggressive behavior was reduced. Moniz received the 1949 Nobel Prize in Medicine for his work—but, in one of those strange twists of fate, he was later shot and killed by one of his lobotomized patients!

Encouraged by Moniz's work, psychiatrists all over the world rushed to treat mental disorders through various forms of **psychosurgery**—brain operations designed to change abnormal behavior. Tens of thousands of patients were given prefrontal lobotomies and related operations. Unfortunately, it soon became apparent that the results were not always positive. While some forms of objectionable or dangerous behavior did decrease, serious side effects sometimes occurred: Some patients became highly excitable and impulsive; others slipped into profound apathy and a total absence of emotion.

In view of these outcomes, most physicians stopped performing prefrontal lobotomies, and few are done today. However, other, more limited operations on the brain continue. For instance, in one modern procedure, *cingulotomy*, connections between a very small area of the brain and the limbic system are severed. Results indicate that this limited kind of psychosurgery may be effective with individuals suffering from depression, anxiety disorders, and especially obsessive–compulsive disorder who have not responded to any other type of treatment (e.g., Jenike et al., 1991). Still newer procedures involve inserting tiny video cameras into the brain or using computer-guided imagery (e.g., MRI scans) to help surgeons make very precise lesions in the brain. It is too early to tell whether such psychosurgery will yield long-term gains.

One final point: Even if such operations are successful, they raise important ethical questions. Is it right to destroy healthy tissue in a person's brain in the hopes that this will relieve symptoms of mental disorders? And given that the benefits are still uncertain, should such irreversible procedures be permitted? These and related issues have led most psychologists to conclude that psychosurgery should be viewed as a very drastic form of treatment, an approach to be tried only when everything else has failed.

### REVIEW QUESTIONS

- What drugs are used in the treatment of mental disorders?
- What is electroconvulsive therapy?
- What is psychosurgery?

## Psychotherapy: Is It Effective?

**Efficacy Studies:** Studies that apply basic methods of experimentation to find out whether a specific form of therapy really works—that is, whether the therapy produces beneficial outcomes for the persons who undergo it.

In the 1950s only 1 percent of the population of the United States had ever had contact with a trained therapist; currently this figure is about 10 percent. What accounts for this change? Part of the answer involves shifting attitudes toward the idea of participating in psychotherapy. Once, there was a stigma attached to this process. People spoke about it in hushed tones and often did their best to conceal the fact that someone in their family—or they themselves—had received therapy. This was certainly true in my own family; as you may recall, my parents refused to discuss my grandmother's problems with me.

While negative attitudes about psychotherapy have not entirely vanished, they have certainly weakened. As a result, growing numbers of people are now willing to seek assistance in dealing with problems that threaten their happiness and well-being. Another factor is the growing sophistication and effectiveness of various forms of psychotherapy. In recent decades many new forms of therapy have been introduced, and these are applicable to a wider range of disorders and a broader range of people than was true in the past. These trends, too, have contributed to the boom in psychotherapy.

But just how effective is psychotherapy? And is one kind of therapy best? These are the questions we'll now consider. Before summarizing what research findings indicate, however, we'll first examine the **Research Methods** described below that are used by psychologists to evaluate the effectiveness of all forms of psychotherapy.

## Research Methods: How Psychologists Study the Effectiveness of Psychotherapy

Does psychotherapy really work? That's a key question from the point of view of psychology. Clearly, this is a complex question that can be answered only through careful research. But what kind of research, specifically, can shed scientific light on this issue? Many procedures exist, but two appear to be most useful and revealing: *efficacy studies* (e.g., Seligman, 1995) and *effectiveness research.*

**Efficacy studies** must meet the following basic requirements, which, as you'll see, are very similar to the ones I outlined in Chapter 1 with respect to valid experimentation on virtually *any* topic in psychology:

- The study must include at least one *experimental* group (persons with a given psychological disorder who are exposed to the therapy) and at least one *control* group (persons with the same disorder who are *not* exposed to the therapy).
- Participants must be randomly assigned to these two conditions.
- Experimental treatments must be carefully standardized. Persons delivering the therapy must be thoroughly trained in it so that they know precisely what to do; and sessions should be videotaped to ensure that therapists are doing what the treatment requires but *nothing else* that might influence participants' behavior.
- A fixed number of sessions must be used, and participants in the control and experimental conditions must receive the same number of sessions.
- The dependent measures must be clearly specified: How will any changes in behavior be measured? This must be specified in advance.
- Participants must have only one psychological disorder—the one for which the therapy is designed. If they have several disorders, changes in one may influence changes in others, thus making it impossible to clearly assess effectiveness of the therapy.
- If the dependent variables involve ratings of participants' behavior, raters must be thoroughly trained and must *not* know whether participants were assigned to the experimental or the control condition.

Efficacy research using such methods, psychologists believe, provides a very rigorous test of the potential effects of any form of therapy. If, in such research, participants who receive therapy *do* show greater improvement than those who do not, we can have high confidence in the conclusion that "this form of therapy works—it is significantly better than no treatment."

Although there is no doubt that efficacy studies are very valuable in this respect, it is also clear that they are not totally conclusive. As noted by Martin Seligman (1995), a former president of the American Psychological Association, such studies have certain drawbacks, the most important of which is this: In efficacy studies psychotherapy is not practiced as it is in the real world. Thus, it is impossible to tell whether forms of therapy found to be effective in such studies would also succeed under natural conditions. For instance, in efficacy studies psychotherapy continues for a fixed number of sessions; but in actual practice this is rarely the case—therapy continues until people improve. Similarly, in efficacy studies only one type of therapy is used; under natural conditions therapists switch between techniques until they find one that works. Participants in efficacy studies are assigned to a type of therapy they have not necessarily sought; in actual practice individuals actively shop for and choose therapists. Finally, in efficacy studies participants have a single psychological disorder; in field settings patients often have several disorders.

Because of these differences, Seligman (1995) concludes, efficacy studies do not necessarily tell us whether a given form of therapy succeeds under natural conditions. To answer that question, he suggests, we need **effectiveness research**—research that examines how individuals respond to therapy as it is normally delivered in real-life settings. Such research must, of necessity, lack some of the rigor of efficacy studies—after all, it is purposely conducted under naturalistic conditions. To be useful, therefore, effectiveness research should be large-scale in scope, involving participation by thousands of persons.

One major study of this type has been conducted by an organization with no ax to grind in the field of mental health: *Consumer Reports,* a magazine that tests and compares a wide range of products for its subscribers. This study, which I'll describe in detail in the next section, involved responses to a questionnaire sent to more than 180,000 subscribers. The survey asked readers whether they had sought help with an emotional problem during the past three years, and if so, who had helped them—friends, clergy, family doctors, self-help groups, or a wide range of mental health professionals (psychiatrists, psychologists, social workers, marriage counselors, and so on). In addition, the survey asked questions about the duration and frequency of therapy respondents had received and—perhaps most important of all—about how helpful the therapy had been. I'll describe the results below; the main point here is to illustrate how an effectiveness study works. In essence, it is designed to obtain information on the experiences of large numbers of persons who actually received various kinds of therapy—or received no help at all. No, such studies don't have the scientific rigor of efficacy studies; but as compensation for this, they do reflect the impact of various kinds of therapy as people "out there" actually experience them.

By combining the rigor of efficacy studies with the large samples and real-life experiences of effectiveness research, psychologists believe that they can accurately determine whether and to what extent various kinds of psychotherapy succeed. This combination of approaches appears to be an especially powerful one, so now let's see what the findings of research using these methods have revealed.

Web Link: *The Efficacy of Psychotherapy*

## The Effectiveness of Psychotherapy: An Overview of Key Findings

In 1952 Hans Eysenck, a prominent psychologist, shocked many of his colleagues: He published a paper indicating that psychotherapy is ineffective. In his article Eysenck reported that about 67 percent of patients with a wide range of mental disorders improve after therapy, but that *about the same proportion of persons receiving no treatment also improve.* This was a disturbing conclusion for psychologists and quickly led to a great deal of research on this issue. After all, if the same proportion of people recover from mental disorders with and without therapy, why bother?

As you can probably guess, the findings of later studies—including results of efficacy studies and effectiveness research—pointed to a very different conclusion: Contrary to what Eysenck suggested, psychotherapy *is* helpful (Bergin & Lambert, 1978; Clum & Bowers, 1990). Apparently, Eysenck overestimated the proportion of persons who recover without any therapy, and also *under*estimated the proportion who improve after receiving therapy. In fact, many reviews of existing evidence—more than five hundred separate studies on the effects of therapy—suggest that therapy *does* work: More people who receive psychotherapy show improvements with respect to their mental disorders than persons who do not receive therapy (e.g., Elkin et al., 1989). Further, the more treatment people receive, the more they improve, the fewer symptoms they show, and the less distress they report (Howard et al., 1986; Orlinsky & Howard, 1987). Interestingly, however, the amount of professional experience therapists have—how long they have been doing therapy—does not seem to matter. Some studies suggest that experienced therapists obtain better outcomes than inexperienced ones (e.g., Stein & Lambert, 1995), but in general there is no significant difference between these groups (e.g., Berman & Norton,

**Effectiveness Research:** Research that examines individuals' responses to psychotherapy as it is normally delivered in real-life settings.

1985). Why? Perhaps because novice therapists make up for their lack of experience through greater enthusiasm.

In sum, available evidence (and there is a lot of it) points to the following overall conclusion: Psychotherapy is not perfect—it doesn't produce improvements for everyone. But yes, it *does* work—it helps many people suffering from mental disorders to recover from these problems.

## Are Some Forms of Therapy More Successful Than Others?

Web Link: *The Effectiveness of Psychotherapy: The Consumer Reports Study*

Now for another, and closely related, question: Are some forms of therapy better than others? The answer, surprisingly, is no. Although various forms of therapy differ greatly in methods and goals, there do not appear to be major differences among therapies in terms of the benefits they provide. In this context, the results of the effectiveness study conducted by *Consumer Reports* (mentioned earlier) are informative.

Once a year, *Consumer Reports* sends out a questionnaire to its 180,000 subscribers, asking for information about their experience with various products. In 1994 the annual survey focused on subscribers' experiences with mental health professionals. Results, which were based on replies from more than 7,000 persons, pointed to clear conclusions. First, as I've already noted, therapy did help: Most respondents indicated that it did make them feel much better and helped eliminate their problems and symptoms, especially if the therapy continued for six months or more. Second, such improvements were greatest when respondents received therapy from psychologists, psychiatrists, and social workers; improvements were somewhat less when they received therapy from physicians and marriage counselors (see Figure 15.19). Third, the longer therapy continued, the greater the respondents' improvement. Improvements began to occur for most people after the first six to eight sessions, and fully 75 percent of the clients showed improvement by the twenty-sixth session. Finally, and most relevant to the present discussion, it made little difference what kind of therapy respondents received: No particular approach was rated more highly than the others.

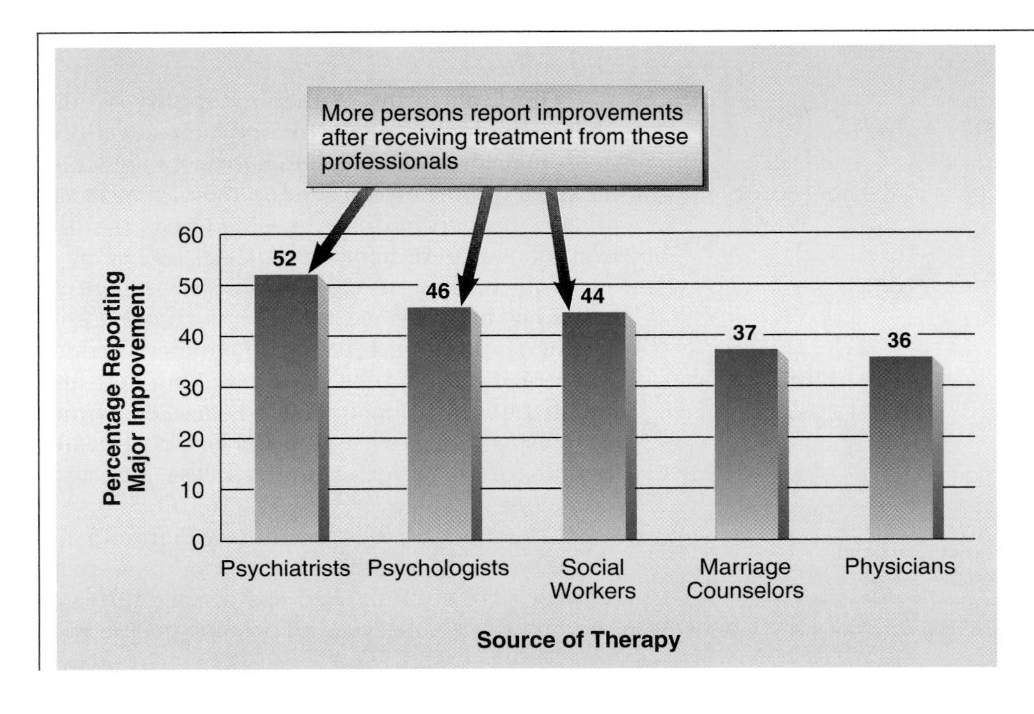


**Figure 15.19**
**Evidence for the Effectiveness of Psychotherapy**

The results of an effectiveness study involving thousands of participants indicate that therapy does indeed work: Large proportions of persons who received psychotherapy from trained therapists (psychiatrists, psychologists, social workers) reported feeling much better as a result of such treatment. Smaller proportions reported improvements after visiting marriage counselors or physicians.
(*Source:* Based on data reported by Seligman, 1995.)

Needless to add, this study was far from perfect from a research methods perspective. Results were based entirely on self-report—what participants *said* happened as a result of therapy. Further, the measures of change were somewhat informal, relying on questions such as "How much did therapy help you with the specific problems that led you to therapy?" Psychologists prefer more specific and more readily quantified questions. Third, there was no control group: All participants were people who had received therapy. What happened to people with similar problems who didn't receive therapy? We can't tell.

Balanced against these important flaws, however, is the fact that this effectiveness study was based on responses from thousands of persons who described their experiences with therapy as it actually occurs. Thus, it provides evidence that complements the findings of efficacy studies. In any case, putting these fine points of scientific design aside, it seems clear that available evidence indicates that although therapy is indeed beneficial, there are no major differences in effectiveness among the various types, and no one clear winner in the effectiveness stakes (Hollon, DeRubeis, & Evans, 1987; Hollon, Shelton, & Loosen, 1991).

How, you may be wondering, can this be so? How can therapies that use sharply different procedures yield similar results? The answer that has emerged in recent years goes something like this. Various forms of therapy do differ in their rationale and in their procedures, but under the surface all share common crucial features. It is this shared core that accounts for their effectiveness. What is this common core? It may include the following features.

First, all major forms of psychotherapy provide troubled individuals with a special type of setting—one in which they interact closely, usually one-on-one, with a highly trained and empathetic professional. For many clients this opportunity to interact with another person who seems to understand their problems and genuinely to care about them may be a unique and reassuring experience, and may play an important role in the benefits of many diverse forms of therapy.

Second, every form of therapy provides individuals with an explanation for their problems. No longer do these seem to be mysterious. Rather, as therapists explain, psychological disturbances stem from understandable causes, many of which lie outside the individual. This is something of a revelation to many persons who have sought in vain for a clue as to the causes of their difficulties.

Third, all forms of therapy specify actions that individuals can take to cope more effectively with their problems. No longer must they suffer in silence and despair. Rather, they are now actively involved in doing specific things that the confident, expert therapist indicates will help.

Fourth, all forms of therapy involve clients in what has been termed the *therapeutic alliance*—a partnership in which powerful emotional bonds are forged between the person seeking help and the therapist. This relationship is marked by mutual respect and trust, and it can be a big plus for people who previously felt helpless, hopeless, and alone.

Combining all these points (see Figure 15.20), the themes of *hope* and *personal control* seem to emerge very strongly. Perhaps diverse forms of therapy succeed because all provide people with

**Figure 15.20**
**Factors Common to Many Forms of Therapy**

The factors shown here are common to many forms of psychotherapy and seem to explain why, despite many differences in procedures, all therapies produce beneficial effects.

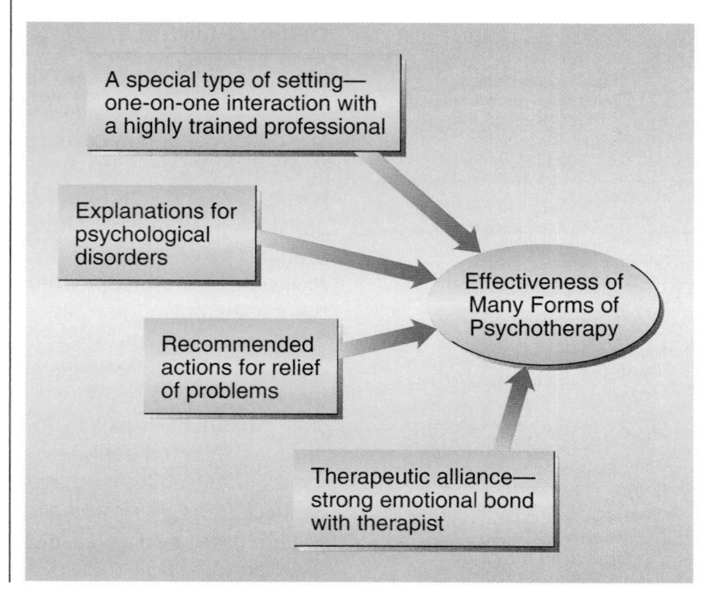

increased hope about the future plus a sense of heightened personal control. To the extent that this is the case, it is readily apparent why therapies that seem so different on the surface can all be effective. In a sense, all may provide the proverbial light at the end of the tunnel for people who have been struggling through the darkness of their emotional despair.

## Culturally Sensitive Psychotherapy

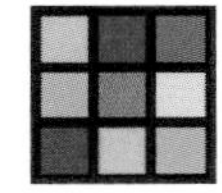

Despite improvements in the DSM–IV designed to make it more sensitive to cultural differences, existing evidence indicates that race, gender, ethnic background, and social class may all affect the process of diagnosis (e.g., Lopez, 1989). For instance, African Americans are more likely to be diagnosed as schizophrenic and less likely to be diagnosed as showing affective (mood) disorders than are persons of European descent (Snowden & Cheung, 1990).

If racial and ethnic factors can influence the diagnosis of mental disorders, it is not surprising to learn that they can also play a role in psychotherapy. For example, therapists and clients may find it difficult to communicate with one another across substantial culture gaps, with the result that the effectiveness of therapy is reduced. Even worse, most forms of psychotherapy were originally developed for, and tested with, persons of European descent. As a result, they may not be entirely suitable for use with individuals from very different backgrounds. Concern over these issues has led many psychologists to call for efforts to make various forms of therapy more *culturally sensitive.* This suggestion implies that all forms of therapy should take careful account of the values and traditions of minority cultures. To mention just one example, therapists working with people of Hispanic or Asian descent should be sensitive to the fact that views concerning the roles of males and females can be quite different in these cultural groups than they are in other groups living in the United States (Rogler, 1999; Rogler et al., 1987).

As I noted earlier, cultural factors may also play a role in individuals' willingness to enter therapy in the first place. In many Asian cultures, for instance, it is not considered appropriate to talk about one's personal feelings or even to focus on oneself individually; rather, emphasis is placed on being part of the social group. Such views may sometimes restrain persons in need of assistance from seeking it. Fortunately, growing evidence suggests that therapists can sometimes overcome such culturally derived reluctance to enter psychotherapy. For instance, Szapocznik and his colleagues (1990) have found that culturally sensitive procedures can help overcome the reluctance of persons of Hispanic descent in the United States to enter family therapy. When psychologists used culturally sensitive techniques to approach troubled families, fully 93 percent began therapy; this was much higher than the 42 percent who agreed when standard techniques that largely ignored culture were employed. Through careful attention to cultural factors and differences, psychologists can help ensure that psychotherapy is sensitive to the varied needs of persons from different cultures, and so increase the chances that it will accomplish its major goal: helping to alleviate mental disorders (e.g., Hammond & Yung, 1993).

**REVIEW QUESTIONS**

- What are efficacy studies and effectiveness research?
- Is psychotherapy effective?
- Are some types of psychotherapy more effective than others?
- What is culturally sensitive psychotherapy?

# The Prevention of Mental Disorders: Community Psychology and Its Legacy

The 1960s were a time of social turmoil in the United States and many other countries. Traditional ways of doing things were questioned and rejected in many spheres of life, ranging from education to styles of dress. I myself will never forget those years, because I was in college and graduate school then and began my career in 1968—the year in which these upheavals reached a peak. The field of mental health was no exception to the currents of change that swept through U.S. society, and one of the key shifts to emerge was the development of what came to be known as the *community mental health movement*—a new approach that focused on treating people with mental disorders in their local communities rather than in distant, huge, and often impersonal public mental hospitals. This movement was fueled, in part, by the passage of legislation that provided funds for the construction of *community mental health centers* throughout the United States.

While the community mental health movement produced many beneficial effects, it did not achieve all of the challenging goals it established for itself; and in some respects it was not fully in keeping with the scientific approach to mental disorders preferred by psychologists. But the movement did lead, gradually, to the emergence of a new subfield of psychology known as **community psychology**—an approach that focuses on promoting mental health through positive change in the community. The field of community psychology is identified by several additional principles as well. First, it adopts an *ecological perspective*—the view that the causes of mental disorders stem, at least in part, from the social, economic, and physical environments in which people live: factors such as poverty, disintegrating communities, and poor schools, to name just a few. This perspective contrasted sharply with the traditional view that mental disorders stem entirely—or at least primarily—from factors within individuals. Because ecological factors often play a role, community psychologists argued, effective treatment of mental disorders should involve efforts to change the social systems in which people live, not just the people themselves. Second, and perhaps most important of all, community psychology emphasizes *prevention*—interventions designed to prevent mental disorders from developing in the first place. Three distinct types of prevention became the focus of attention: primary prevention, secondary prevention, and tertiary prevention.

The term **primary prevention** refers to efforts to prevent new psychological problems from occurring. These efforts include programs aimed at both counteracting risk factors and strengthening protective factors—factors that prevent mental disorders. Most programs of primary prevention emphasize the following goals: *encouraging secure attachments and reducing family violence*—as we've seen repeatedly, secure attachments to parents or other caregivers appear to play a crucial role in children's healthy development; *teaching effective problem-solving skills*—skills that help people get along with others and regulate their own behavior; *changing environments*—making environments more supportive in many different ways; *enhancing stress-coping skills*—skills that help people deal with the major stressors they encounter in their lives; and *promoting empowerment*—helping people who, because of old age, poverty, homelessness, minority status, or physical disability, feel that they have little or no control over their own lives. As you can readily see, programs directed toward such goals must often involve an ecological approach that addresses the social and physical environments in which people live. For example, do we want to reduce the incidence of child abuse and the harmful effects it produces? Then we must, according to the ecological view, do more than simply provide counseling to parents; we must also try to counter the adverse effects of poverty so that parents have the resources to form warm, supportive bonds with their children and so that they experience less stress (e.g., stress generated by their inability to find decent affordable housing) (see Figure 15.21).

**Community Psychology:** A subfield of psychology that focuses on promoting mental health by making positive changes in the communities in which people live.

**Primary Prevention:** Efforts to prevent new psychological problems from occurring.

**Figure 15.21**
**Preventing Mental Disorders: An Ecological Perspective**

The ecological perspective adopted by *community psychology* suggests that mental disorders stem, at least in part, from the social, economic, and physical environments in which people live. Thus, countering factors such as poverty and disintegrating communities, and providing people with decent affordable housing, can be useful steps in preventing mental disorders.

In contrast, **secondary prevention** focuses on groups of people who are at risk for developing a disorder and involves efforts to detect psychological problems early, before they have escalated in intensity. *Diversion programs* aimed at helping juvenile offenders in the criminal justice system, provide an example of secondary prevention. It is a well-established fact that once young offenders are placed in prisons, they become more likely to continue their dangerous antisocial behaviors; such institutions are often more like training schools for criminal activities than anything else. In diversion programs, young offenders are steered away (diverted) from such institutions and given another chance to learn social skills and patterns of behavior that may help them lead happier and more productive lives (e.g., Davidson et al., 1987).

A third type of prevention, **tertiary prevention,** involves efforts to minimize the long-term harm stemming from mental disorders. Such programs are especially helpful for persons who are released from state facilities after years of confinement. One such program, *Training in Community Living,* attempts to repair the damage done by long years of what may amount to custodial care by teaching former mental-hospital patients the skills they need to live out in the community. The former patients are provided with living quarters and are visited every week by program staff. In other words, they are out in the community but are living in a protected environment, where they can learn the skills they need for an independent life (Levine, Toro, & Perkins, 1993). I have a relative (my wife's uncle) who went through such a program, and his reactions to it were extremely positive. In fact, he soon made a full adjustment to living on his own.

In sum, efforts at preventing or minimizing the harm of mental disorders do often seem to be quite effective. Their goal—like that of all forms of therapy—is reducing human suffering; but by operating *before* serious disorders occur, such programs take full advantage of the wisdom in the old saying "An ounce of prevention is worth a pound of cure."

**Secondary Prevention:** Efforts to detect psychological problems early, before they have escalated in intensity.

**Tertiary Prevention:** Efforts to minimize the long-term harm stemming from psychological disorders.

**REVIEW QUESTIONS**

- What is community psychology?
- What are primary, secondary, and tertiary prevention of mental disorders?

# Legal and Ethical Issues Relating to Mental Disorders

In 1981, President Ronald Reagan and three other people were shot by John Hinckley. There was no doubt that Hinckley had committed these crimes, but after a lengthy trial he was found *not guilty by reason of insanity.* Many people in the United States were outraged. They were far from convinced that Hinckley could not "substantially appreciate" the wrongfulness of his actions, or that he was unable to control his behavior—criteria that, at the time, were required for an insanity defense. In fact, the public outrage over this verdict soon led to changes in the law (the Insanity Defense Reform Act of 1984), which made it much harder for defendants to plead insanity as a defense for their actions.

Why do I begin with this distressing episode? Because it illustrates some of the complex legal and ethical issues relating to mental disorders. Are people with serious mental disorders responsible for their actions? Should they be forced to accept treatment if they do not wish to receive it? Is everything they tell a therapist during treatment *confidential*—or do therapists have an obligation to reveal such information to police if, in their judgment, a patient might pose real danger to himself or herself or to others? These are just a few of the issues that arise in connection with mental disorders. Although we can't examine all of them here, let's take a closer look at two: *patients' rights* and *ethical issues relating to psychotherapy.*

## The Rights of Individuals and the Rights of Society

Many old films featured the following plot: An individual wishes to get rid of his or her spouse, and to do so, this person tries to persuade a psychiatrist to have the spouse committed to a mental institution. This kind of plot is related to two important real-life questions: Under what conditions should individuals be hospitalized against their will? And should persons with mental disorders be allowed to refuse treatment?

With respect to the first issue, the legal pendulum in the United States and other countries has swung back and forth over the decades. Up until the 1960s people could indeed be committed to mental institutions against their will—and kept there—if physicians believed that that hospitalization was required; this was known as *civil commitment.* By the late 1960s, however, opinion had changed, and courts ruled that people could be committed against their will only if several conditions were met: only if they were mentally ill, they posed an imminent risk to themselves or others, treatment for their illness was available, and hospitalization was the *least restrictive alternative* available. Unfortunately, this trend in legal rulings coincided with the release from state mental hospitals of growing numbers of persons who, after their release, did *not* receive adequate follow-up treatment. Many of these persons became homeless wanderers who suffered much harm, and in some cases posed a danger to others as well. It gradually became apparent, then, that although these former patients' "rights" had been protected—they were no longer hospitalized against their will—they had been consigned to lives of poverty, danger, and despair. The result was a shift in legal opinion back toward allowing the state to hospitalize some mentally ill persons, provided that they are gravely disabled by their disorder, pose a danger to themselves or others, and are in danger of deteriorating further if not hospitalized. At present, then, involuntary commitment can occur by court order—or even without such an order in emergency situations. In addition, people can be committed involuntarily to *outpatient care,* in which the patient is ordered to appear for treatment at a community mental health center or other facility on a daily basis.

What about treatment—do individuals with mental disorders have a right to refuse it? Again, legal opinion has varied over the years. In general, though, the recent trend has been to protect individuals' rights to refuse treatment, unless it can be clearly shown such treatment is necessary to protect the patient's safety or that of others (e.g., *Riggins v. Nevada,* 1992, a Supreme Court ruling). Such rulings have led to much alarm among psychologists and mental health professionals, who feared that because persons with mental disorders often deny that they have any problems, many who could be helped would not receive appropriate assistance. Fortunately, such fears appear to be unfounded; very few patients refuse treatment—about 10 percent at most (Applebaum, 1994). Typically, patients object to a particular *kind* of treatment, not to treatment in general, so the result of strengthened patient rights has been mainly to give individuals a larger say in the type of treatment they receive.

In sum, legal issues relating to mental disorders involve efforts to strike a reasonable and useful balance between the rights of individuals and the rights of society. There are not—and perhaps can never be—any final, definite answers. Rather, the process is a continuous one, and the specific point of balance shifts over time in response to other changes in society.

## Ethical Issues in the Practice of Psychotherapy

Web Link: *Ethical Principles of Psychologists and Code of Conduct*

Suppose that you were a psychologist and that during psychotherapy with a patient, this individual told you that he was planning to kill a woman who had refused his advances. What should you do? Clearly, you face an ethical dilemma. On the one hand, you know that the information a patient supplies during therapy should be *confidential*—it is strictly between you and the patient and should not be revealed to anyone else. Yet you also know this person well enough to worry that he might actually murder the woman in question. Actually, a real-life case involving these circumstances occurred some years ago in California. In this famous case, known as the Tarasoff case, Prosenjit Poddar told his therapist that he would soon murder Tatania Tarasoff because she had spurned his romantic overtures (see Figure 15.22). The therapist broke confidentiality and told his supervisor, and Mr. Poddar was arrested. After promising to stay away from Ms. Tarasoff, however, he was released. Two months later he stabbed her to death. Her parents then sued the therapist and the university where he worked for failing to protect their daughter. Juries twice found in favor of the parents. As the court put it, "The protective privilege ends where the public peril begins" (*Tarasoff v. Regents of the University of California,* 1976). But just how dangerous does a client have to be before a therapist should notify police or other authorities? Clearly, this is a complex issue, and this complexity illustrates the kinds of ethical issues often faced by therapists—issues in which the welfare of their clients must be weighed against the welfare of others or of society.

**Figure 15.22**
**The Downside of Client Confidentiality**

Psychologists feel an ethical responsibility to hold everything their clients tell them in strict confidence. However, recent court rulings indicate that therapists have a legal obligation to inform police or other authorities in cases where clients pose a danger to themselves or others. In one famous case, juries awarded damages to the parents of Tatiana Tarasoff *(left),* who was murdered by Prosenjit Poddar *(right).* The reason? Mr. Poddar had told his therapist that he planned to kill her, and the therapist and the university where he worked did not take adequate steps to protect Ms. Tarasoff.

Issues relating to confidentiality are far from the only ones psychologists and other mental health professionals face, however. Another—and in some ways even more disturbing—set of issues is raised by a phenomenon first brought sharply into focus by Freud: sexual attraction on the part of clients toward their therapists. As you probably recall, Freud termed this attraction *transference* and felt that it often played a valuable role in psychoanalysis. In contrast, psychologists see such attraction in a much less positive light. In fact, ethical standards established by the American Psychological Association explicitly forbid any kind of sexual contact between clients and therapists—not just during therapy, but for at least two years after therapy ends. Indeed, an ethical psychologist who either feels sexual attraction toward a client or notices that the client is expressing such attraction toward him or her should end all contact with the client and transfer treatment to another therapist. Why is sexual contact between therapists and clients unethical? For many reasons, including these: If the therapist surrenders to such attraction, he or she is putting his or her own needs ahead of those of the client; a therapist who has a relationship with a client can no longer be objective in making judgments about proper treatment for that client; and clients, who are often in the midst of psychological crises, are not in any state to make sound decisions about forming intimate relationships. For all these reasons, ethical guidelines require that therapists avoid romances with their clients. In fact, any psychologist who engages in such behavior is subject to harsh punishment, including total exclusion from the field.

Again, this is just a small sample of the ethical issues associated with the treatment of mental disorders. These issues are indeed complex, and there is no choice and to deal with them in as careful and rational a manner as possible: Only in this way can both the rights of individuals and the rights of society be protected.

For guidelines on how to choose a therapist—one who is both competent *and* ethical—please see the **Making Psychology Part of Your Life** section that follows.

**REVIEW QUESTIONS**

- Under what conditions can individuals be committed to mental institutions against their will?
- When are psychologists required to break confidentiality and report information provided by clients during therapy to police or other authorities?

## Making Psychology Part of Your Life

### How to Choose a Therapist: A Consumer's Guide

The odds are high that at some time in your life, you or someone close to you will experience a mental disorder. Depression, phobias, anxiety—these are very common problems. If there's one point I hope this chapter has made clear, it is this: Effective help is available, and you should not hesitate to seek it. But how should you choose a therapist? Here are some basic guidelines.

**Getting Started** The first step is usually the hardest in any task, and searching for a therapist is no exception. While you are a student, this task is fairly simple. Virtually every college or university has a department of psychology and a student health center. Both are good places to start. Visit them and ask for help. Don't be shy; the people there *want* to help, but they can't approach you—you have to take the first step.

If you are no longer a student and don't have any contact with a college or university, you can still call your nearest psychology department and ask for help; the chances are that someone there will refer you to one or more excellent therapists. But if for some reason this is not practical, you can ask your physician or some member of the clergy to direct you to the help you need. Both will almost certainly know someone you can contact. If you have no local physician and don't know any clergy, contact your local Mental Health Association; it is probably listed in your phone book and is another good place to start.

**Choosing a Therapist** Let's assume that by following one of the routes above, you have obtained the names of several therapists. How can you choose among them? Several guidelines are useful.

First, always check for *credentials.* Therapists should be trained professionals. Before you consult one, be sure that this person has a Ph.D. in psychology, an M.D. degree plus a residency in psychiatry, or other equivalent training. While such credentials don't guarantee that the therapist can help you, they *are* important. Remember the results of the large-scale *Consumer Reports* study? Mental health professionals were more successful in helping than other persons.

Second, try to find out something about the kinds of disorders in which each therapist specializes. Most will readily give you this information, and what you are looking for is a good match between your needs and the therapist's expertise.

**Signs of Progress: How long should therapy last?** If therapy is going well, both you and the therapist will know it. You'll be able to see beneficial changes in your behavior, your thoughts, and your feelings. But what if it is not going well? When and how should you decide to go elsewhere? This is a difficult decision, but a rough rule of thumb is this: If you have been visiting a therapist regularly (once a week or more) for three months and see no change, it may be time to ask the therapist whether she or he is satisfied with your progress. Most forms of therapy practiced by psychologists are relatively short-term in nature. If several months have passed and your distress has not decreased, it is time to raise this issue with your therapist.

**Danger: When to Quit** Therapy is designed to help; unfortunately, though, there are instances in which it can hurt. How can you tell that you are in danger of such outcomes? There are several basic signals to watch for.

First, if you or the people around you notice that you are actually becoming more distressed—more depressed, more anxious, more nervous—you should ask yourself whether you are satisfied with what is happening. At the very least, discuss these feelings with your therapist.

Second, never under any circumstances should you agree to do anything during therapy that is against your own moral or ethical principles. A great majority of therapists would never dream of making such requests; but, sad to relate, there are a few who will take advantage of the therapeutic relationship to exploit their patients. The most common forms of such exploitation are sexual in nature. Unprincipled therapists may suggest that their clients engage in sexual relations with them as part of their "treatment." *This is never appropriate!* So if your therapist makes such suggestions, *get out of there fast!*

Third, beware of exaggerated claims. If a therapist tells you that she or he can guarantee to remake your life, turn you into a powerhouse of human energy, or assure you of total happiness, be cautious. Unrealistic promises are a good sign that you are dealing with an unprincipled—and probably poorly trained—individual.

All these suggestions are merely general guidelines to help you be a sophisticated consumer of psychological services. There may be particular situations, for instance, in which therapy requires much longer than the time period noted above, or in which a therapist has valid reasons for being reluctant to discuss procedures with you. These guidelines, however, should help you to avoid some of the pitfalls that exist in the search for a competent, caring therapist. Most important of all, always remember this: *Effective help is definitely out there if you take the trouble to look for it.*

## Summary and Review

### Psychotherapies: Psychological Approaches to Mental Disorders

- **What is psychoanalysis, and what are its major assumptions?** Psychoanalysis is the form of therapy developed by Freud. It assumes that mental disorders stem from hidden internal conflicts and that bringing these conflicts into consciousness will lead to improved adjustment.
- **What is the role of free association in psychoanalysis?** Free association supposedly brings hidden urges and conflicts into consciousness.
- **How are psychodynamic therapies practiced today?** At present psychodynamic therapies are shorter in length and focus more on the patients' current life than on events in her or his distant past.
- **According to phenomenological/experiential therapies, what is the cause of mental disorders?** Phenomenological/experiential or humanistic therapies assume that mental disorders stem from factors in the environment that block or interfere with personal growth.
- **What is the major goal of Rogers's client-centered therapy?** Rogers's client-centered therapy focuses on eliminating unrealistic conditions of worth in a therapeutic environment of unconditional positive regard.

- **What is the major goal of Gestalt therapy?** Gestalt therapy focuses on helping individuals acknowledge parts of their own feelings or thoughts that are not currently conscious so as to attain psychological "wholeness."
- **According to behavior therapies, what is the primary cause of mental disorders?** Behavior therapies are based on the view that mental disorders stem from faulty learning.
- **On what basic principles of learning are behavior therapies based?** Behavior therapies are based on principles of classical conditioning, operant conditioning, and observational learning.
- **What is modeling, and how can it be used in treating mental disorders?** Modeling is a process through which individuals acquire new information or learn new behaviors by observing the actions of others. Modeling is effective in treating several disorders, including phobias.
- **According to cognitive therapies, what is the primary cause of mental disorders?** Cognitive therapies assume that the major cause of mental disorders is distorted patterns of thought.
- **What is the major goal of rational–emotive therapy?** The major goal of rational–emotive therapy is to persuade individuals to recognize and reject irrational assumptions in their thinking.
- **What is the major goal of Beck's cognitive therapy for depression?** The major goal of Beck's cognitive therapy is to help individuals recognize and change irrational patterns of thought that induce negative affect and so contribute to their depression.

### Key Terms

psychotherapies, p. 578 • psychodynamic therapies, p. 580 • free association, p. 580 • resistance, p. 580 • transference, p. 581 • basic mistakes, p. 581 • phenomenological/experiential therapies (humanistic therapies), p. 582 • conditions of worth, p. 582 • client-centered therapy, p. 582 • Gestalt therapy, p. 582 • behavior therapies, p. 584 • systematic desensitization, p. 585 • token economies, p. 585 • cognitive therapies, p. 587 • rational–emotive therapy (RET), p. 587 • cognitive behavior therapy, p. 587

## Alternatives to Individual Psychotherapy: Group Therapy, Marital Therapy, Family Therapy, and Psychosocial Rehabilitation

- **Why are alternatives to individual psychotherapy needed?** Alternative approaches are needed because individual psychotherapy is too costly for many persons, and because cultural factors reduce the likelihood that persons in many groups will seek individual therapy.
- **What are group therapies?** Group therapies are procedures in which several people discuss their problems with one another under the guidance or leadership of a trained therapist.
- **What is marital or couples therapy?** Marital or couples therapy focuses on improving the relationship between members of a couple, often by enhancing their communication skills.
- **What is family therapy?** Family therapy is designed to change the relationships among family members in constructive ways.
- **What are self-help groups?** In self-help groups, persons who are experiencing the same kinds of problems meet regularly, without professionally trained leaders, to help one another cope with these difficulties.
- **What is psychosocial rehabilitation?** Psychosocial rehabilitation consists of efforts to teach patients with serious mental disorders (schizophrenia, major mood disorders) to cope more effectively with their disorders and, especially, to avoid or lessen the crises that often make it virtually impossible for these patients to function in society.

### Key Terms

group therapies, p. 590 • marital therapy, p. 592 • family therapy, p. 595 • family systems therapy, p. 595 • self-help groups, p. 595 • deinstitutionalization, p. 596 • psychosocial rehabilitation, p. 596

## Biological Therapies

- **What drugs are used in the treatment of mental disorders?** Many different psychoactive drugs are used to treat mental disorders. Antipsychotic or neuroleptic drugs reduce symptoms such as hallucinations and delusions. Antidepressant drugs counter depression. Antianxiety drugs reduce anxiety.
- **What is electroconvulsive therapy?** Electroconvulsive therapy involves delivery of strong shocks to the brain. It is used to treat depression.
- **What is psychosurgery?** Psychosurgery is surgery performed on the brain in an effort to reduce or eliminate mental disorders.

### Key Terms

biological therapies, p. 597 • drug therapy, p. 597 • Tardive dyskinesia, p. 598 • electroconvulsive therapy, p. 601 • psychosurgery, p. 602

## Psychotherapy: Is It Effective?

- **What are efficacy studies and effectiveness research?** Efficacy studies are studies designed to assess the effectiveness of specific forms of therapy through the use of rigorous experimental controls. Effectiveness research assesses the success of various forms of therapy in naturalistic settings.
- **Is psychotherapy effective?** Existing evidence suggests that psychotherapy is indeed effective relative to no treatment.
- **Are some types of psychotherapy more effective than others?** Research findings indicate that many types of therapy are roughly equal in their effectiveness.
- **What is culturally sensitive psychotherapy?** Culturally sensitive psychotherapy takes careful account of the values and traditions of persons from minority groups and attempts to match forms of therapy to the ethnic, cultural, educational, and economic backgrounds of clients.

#### Key Terms

efficacy studies, p. 603 • effectiveness research, p. 604

### The Prevention of Mental Disorders: Community Psychology and Its Legacy

- **What is community psychology?** Community psychology focuses on promoting mental health by making positive changes in the communities in which people live.
- **What are primary, secondary, and tertiary prevention of mental disorders?** Primary prevention involves efforts to prevent the occurrence of mental disorders. Secondary prevention emphasizes early detection of psychological problems, before they have escalated in intensity. Tertiary prevention consists of efforts to reduce the long-term harm stemming from mental disorders, especially the after-effects of institutionalizaton.

#### Key Terms

community psychology, p. 608 • primary prevention, p. 608 • secondary prevention, p. 609 • tertiary prevention, p. 609

### Legal and Ethical Issues Relating to Mental Disorders

- **Under what conditions can individuals be committed to mental institutions against their will?** Involuntary commitment can occur when patients are gravely disabled by their disorder, pose a danger to themselves or others, and are in danger of deteriorating further if not hospitalized.
- **When are psychologists required to break confidentiality and report information provided by clients during therapy to police or other authorities?** Psychologists must break confidentiality when, in their judgment, clients pose a danger to themselves or others.

## Critical Thinking Questions

### Appraisal

Despite evidence suggesting that Freudian psychoanalysis is relatively ineffective, many people continue to believe that it is *the* most important and successful kind of psychotherapy. Why do you think this is so?

### Controversy

Do you think it is ethical for courts to be able to commit individuals to mental institutions or to require that they receive outpatient treatment against their will? If so, why? If not, why?

### Making Psychology Part of Your Life

Now that you know how psychologists evaluate the success of various kinds of therapy, do you think you will be likely to refer to such information in choosing a therapist if *you* ever experience the symptoms of a mental disorder?

Chapter 16

# Social Thought and Social Behavior

## CHAPTER OUTLINE

**SOCIAL THOUGHT: THINKING ABOUT OTHER PEOPLE 619**

Attribution: Understanding the Causes of Others' Behavior

■ FROM SCIENCE TO PRACTICE *Attributional Augmenting and Perceptions of Female Entrepreneurs*

Social Cognition: How We Process Social Information

Attitudes: Evaluating the Social World

■ RESEARCH METHODS *How Psychologists Measure Attitudes—from Attitude Scales to the "Bogus Pipeline"*

**SOCIAL BEHAVIOR: INTERACTING WITH OTHERS 636**

Prejudice: Distorted Views of the Social World . . . and Their Effects

Social Influence: Changing Others' Behavior

■ BEYOND THE HEADLINES—As Psychologists See It: *What Happens When Social Norms Encourage a "Lifestyle to Die For"?*

Attraction and Love

Leadership: One Important Group Process

■ MAKING PSYCHOLOGY PART OF YOUR LIFE *Some Guidelines for Having a Happy Romantic Relationship*

Everyone has a favorite party story, so here's mine. For several years, my wife and I both did volunteer work for our local symphony. During that time we were invited to a lot of parties with people from outside the university, and my story involves one of these parties. The food and wine were especially good that evening, so I had a very nice time. But on the way home, my wife suddenly began to laugh out loud. Curious, I asked, "What's so funny?" Here's what she told me. At the party she had a long conversation with a local businesswoman—someone I had met several times before. This woman asked where we were from, and in answering, my wife told her about the positions I had held at various universities and all the different states in which we had lived as a result of these jobs. As my wife described these experiences, the woman seemed to become more and more concerned. Finally, shaking her head, she remarked: "I'm really surprised; I've met your husband and he seemed very nice; I didn't realize that he couldn't hold a job." Wow—talk about jumping to false conclusions! She didn't realize that all these moves were either steps *up* in my career or visiting professorships, and that I had actually received tenure many years earlier.

Why do I start with this story? Because for me, it provides a good illustration of the complexities of social life. Other people, it goes without saying, are a crucial part of our existence and play a key role in our happiness—can you imagine life without them? So not only do we interact with others many times each day, we also think about them when they are not present, try to figure them out, speculate about how they feel about us, wonder what they will do or say the next time we meet, and so on (see Figure 16.1).

Recognizing this basic fact, **social psychologists** have long specialized in the task of studying all aspects of social thought and social behavior (e.g., Baron & Byrne, 2000). In this chapter we'll examine a sample of the many fascinating findings they have uncovered. Specifically, we'll begin by considering several aspects of *social thought*—how, and what, we think about other persons. Included here will be discussions of three important topics: *attribution*—our efforts to understand the causes behind others' behavior, or *why* people act as they do; *social cognition*—how we process social information, remember it, and use it in making judgments or decisions about others; and *attitudes*—our evaluations of various features of the social world.

**Figure 16.1**
**Thinking about Other People: An Important Part of Daily Life**

As suggested by this cartoon, we think about other people many times each day—even if we haven't yet met them!
(*Source:* © 1995 Washington Post Writers Group.)

After considering these topics, we'll turn to important aspects of *social behavior*—how we interact with other people. Among the topics we'll examine are *prejudice*—negative attitudes and the harmful actions toward the members of various social groups they often produce; *social influence*—the many ways in which we attempt to change others' behavior and they attempt to change ours; *attraction and love*—why we like or dislike other people and why we fall in (and out) of love; and *leadership*—an important aspect of what social psychologists term *group processes*. Additional aspects of social behavior are covered elsewhere in this book—in our discussions of *social development* (Chapters 8 and 9) and *aggression* (Chapter 10).

## Social Thought: Thinking about Other People

Web Link: *The Social Psychology Network*

How many times each day do you think about other people? Your answer may well be "Who can count?"—because such thoughts are frequent indeed. Anytime you try to figure out why other people have acted in various ways, or attempt to make judgments about them (for example, will someone make a good roommate?), you are engaging in social thought. Let's take a closer look at several important aspects of this process.

### Attribution: Understanding the Causes of Others' Behavior

Imagine the following situation. You're standing at a counter in a store, waiting your turn, when suddenly another customer walks up and hands the clerk an item she wishes to purchase. How do you react? While your first response may be "With anger!" a more accurate answer is "It depends." And what it depends upon is your perceptions of *why* this other person has cut in front of you. Did she do it on purpose? In that case, you probably *would* get angry. But perhaps she just didn't see you. In that case, you might clear your throat or otherwise indicate your presence to see what would happen next. So it's not just what the person did that matters; your perception of *why* she did it matters too.

This question of *why* others act as they do is one we face every day in many different contexts. The process through which we attempt to answer this question—to determine the causes behind others' behavior—is known as **attribution.** In general, attribution is a fairly orderly process. We examine others' behavior for clues as to the causes behind what they say and do, then reach our decision. What kind of information do we consider? This depends on the specific question we want to answer. For instance, one basic issue is: Did another person's actions stem from *internal* causes (e.g., their own traits, intentions, or motives) or from *external* causes (e.g., luck or factors beyond their control in a given situation). To answer this question, we often focus on information about (1) **consensus**—whether other people behave in the same way as the person we're considering; (2) **consistency**—whether this person behaves in the same manner over time; and (3) **distinctiveness**—whether this person behaves in the same way in different situations. If very few people act like this person (consensus is low), this person behaves in the same way over time (consistency is high), and this person behaves in much the same manner in many situations (distinctiveness is low), we conclude that the behavior stems from *internal* causes: This is the kind of person the individual is and will probably remain. For instance, we'd probably draw this conclusion about a student who got up and criticized a professor harshly in class if no other students did this, if this student criticized the professor on other occasions, and if this student also criticized other professors, waitpersons in restaurants, and so on. In contrast, if all three factors

**Social Psychologists:** Psychologists who study all aspects of social behavior and social thought.

**Attribution:** The processes through which we seek to determine the causes behind others' behavior.

**Consensus:** Information regarding the extent to which behavior by one person is shown by others as well.

**Consistency:** Information regarding the extent to which a specific person shows similar behavior to a given stimulus across time.

**Distinctiveness:** Information regarding the extent to which a given person reacts in the same manner to different stimuli or situations.

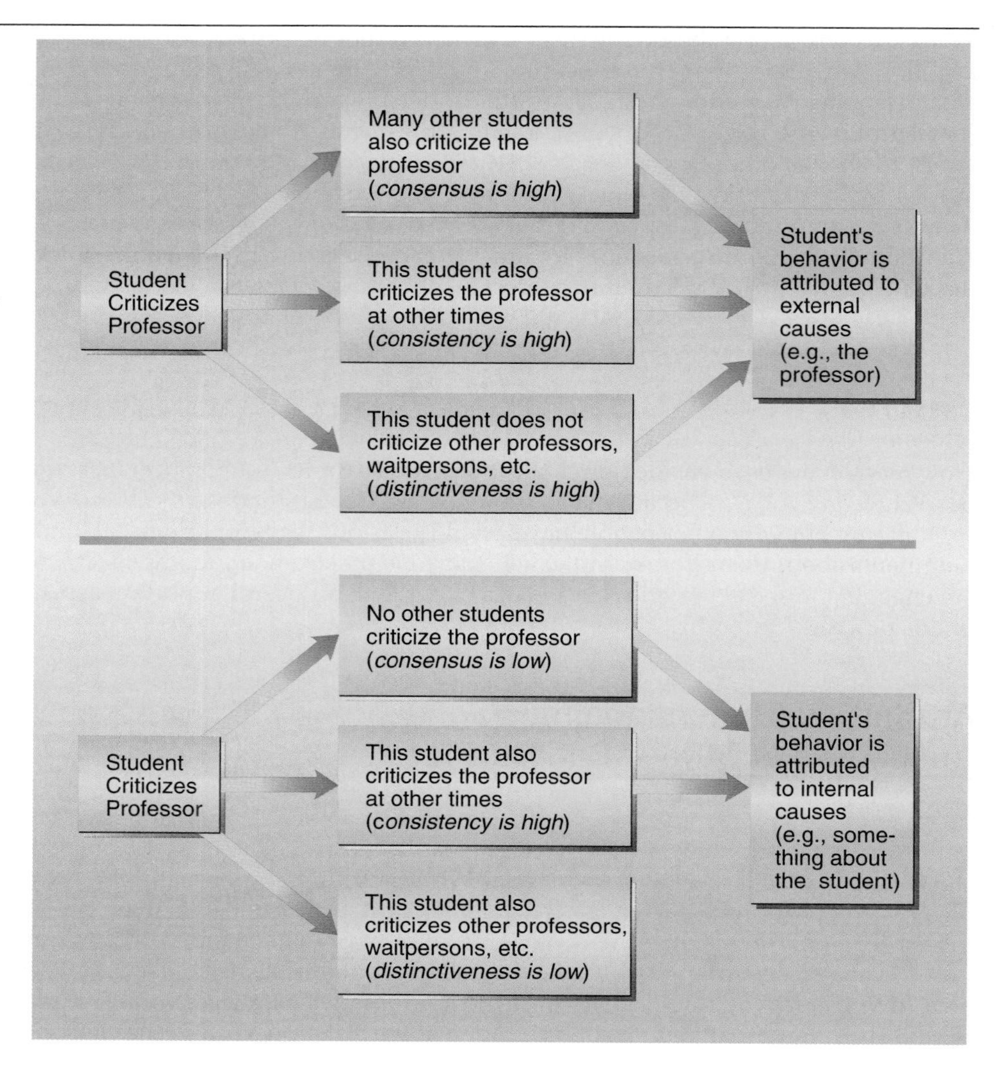


**Figure 16.2**
**Causal Attribution**

When consensus and distinctiveness are low but consistency is high, we tend to attribute others' behavior to internal causes *(upper diagram)*. When consensus, consistency, and distinctiveness are all high, in contrast, we attribute behavior to external causes *(lower diagram)*.

(consensus, consistency, and distinctiveness) are high, we are more likely to conclude that people behave as they do because of external causes—for instance, that they may have no choice (Kelley, 1972) (see Figure 16.2). We'd reach *this* conclusion if many other students also criticized the professor, if this student criticized the same professor on other occasions, and if this student did *not* criticize other professors.

**ATTRIBUTION: SOME BASIC SOURCES OF BIAS** Although attribution often involves the logical kind of reasoning I have just described, this is not always the case. In fact, the attribution process is subject to several kinds of errors, ones that can lead us to false conclusion about other persons. Let's consider some of these here.

***The Correspondence Bias: Overestimating the Role of Dispositional Causes.*** Suppose that you witness the following scene. A man arrives at a meeting thirty minutes late. On entering the room he drops his notes on the floor. While trying to pick them up, he falls over and breaks his glasses. How would you explain these events? Probably by concluding that he is disorganized and clumsy. In other words, you would emphasize *internal* causes in your explanation. Would you be correct? Perhaps. But it is also possible that you would be jumping to a false conclusion. It might be that this individual was late because of circumstances beyond his control (for instance, a major traffic jam), that he dropped his notes because they were printed on very slick paper, and that he fell down because the floor had just been waxed. The fact that you would be less likely to think of such *external* potential causes reflects one important source of error in attribution, the **correspondence bias** (also known as the *fundamental attribution error*)—our strong tendency to explain others' actions as corresponding to, or stemming from, dispositional (internal) causes even in the presence of clear situational (external) causes (e.g., Gilbert & Malone, 1995).

Why do we show this tendency? Many social psychologists accept the following explanation: When we focus on others' behavior, we tend to begin by assuming that their actions reflect their underlying characteristics. Then we attempt to correct for any possible effects of the external world—the current situation—by taking these into account. This correction, however, is often insufficient. We don't make enough allowance for the impact of external factors—we don't give enough weight to the possibility of a traffic jam or a slippery floor when reaching our conclusions (Leyens, Yzerbyt, & Corneille, 1996).

Is this tendency to emphasize dispositional causes truly universal, or is it influenced, like many other aspects of social behavior and thought, by cultural factors? Research findings indicate that in fact culture does play a role. Specifically, the fundamental attribution error appears to be more common or stronger in cultures that emphasize individual freedom—individualistic cultures such as those in western Europe or North America—than in collectivistic cultures that emphasize group membership, conformity, and interdependence (e.g., Morris & Pang, 1994; Triandis, 1990). For instance, consider a recent study by Choi and Nisbett (1998).

These researchers asked students in the United States and Korea to read essays supposedly written by another person; the essays were either in favor of or against capital punishment, and participants were led to believe either that the person who wrote each essay did so of his or her own free choice, or that in each case the person was told to write an essay favoring one point of view or the other. When asked questions about the writer's actual attitude toward capital punishment, U.S. students showed the correspondence bias quite strongly: They responded as if the essay reflected this person's true attitudes *even if the writer had been told to write the essay they read.* In contrast, Korean students showed this bias to a much weaker degree; indeed, in one condition, when it was made clear that the essay writer had simply repeated arguments given to him by the researchers, the Korean students showed no correspondence bias at all. Clearly, then, cultural factors play a role even in this very basic aspect of attribution.

***The Self-serving Bias: "I Can Do No Wrong; You Can Do No Right."*** Suppose that you write a term paper for one of your classes. After reading it, your professor gives you an A. To what will you attribute your success? If you are like most people, you will probably explain it in terms of internal causes—your own talent or hard work.

Now, in contrast, imagine that your professor gives you a D. How will you explain this outcome? The chances are good that you will focus mainly on external causes—the fact that you didn't have enough time for the project, your professor's unrealistically high standards, and so on. In situations like this one, you are showing another attributional error known as the **self-serving bias** (Brown & Rogers, 1991; Miller & Ross, 1975). This is our tendency to take credit for positive behaviors or outcomes by attributing them to internal causes, but to blame negative ones on external causes, especially on factors beyond our control.

**Correspondence Bias:** The tendency to attribute behavior to internal causes to a greater extent than is actually justified; also known as the *fundamental attribution error.*

**Self-Serving Bias:** Our tendency to attribute positive outcomes to our own traits or characteristics (internal causes) but negative outcomes to factors beyond our control (external causes).

Why does this tilt in our attributions occur? One possibility emphasizes cognitive factors, suggesting that the self-serving bias stems mainly from certain tendencies in the way we process social information. Specifically, this view suggests that we attribute positive outcomes to internal causes but negative ones to external causes because we expect to succeed and have a tendency to attribute expected outcomes to internal causes more than to external causes (see Chapter 7) (Ross, 1977). In contrast, another explanation emphasizes the role of motivation. This explanation suggests that the self-serving bias stems from our need to protect and enhance our self-esteem or the related desire to look good to others (Greenberg, Pyszczynski, & Solomon, 1983). While both cognitive and motivational factors may well play a role in this kind of attributional error, research evidence seems to offer more support for the motivational view (e.g., Brown & Rogers, 1991).

Whatever the origins of the self-serving bias, it can be the cause of much interpersonal friction. It often leads persons who work with others on a joint task to perceive that they, not their partners, have made the major contributions. I see this effect in my own classes every semester when students rate their own contributions and those of the other members of their team to the results of a required term project. Most students take lots of credit for themselves if the project has gone well, but tend to blame (and down-rate) their partners if it has not.

Is the self-serving bias a universal human tendency, occurring in all cultures? While it has been observed all over the world (e.g., Al-Zahrani & Kaplowitz, 1993), growing evidence suggests, once again, that this bias is more common in individualistic societies (e.g., many Western countries), which emphasize individual accomplishments, than in collectivistic societies (e.g., many Asian or African countries), which emphasize group outcomes and harmony (e.g., Oettingen, 1995; Oettingen & Seligman, 1990). In one study, for example, Lee and Seligman (1997) asked three groups of participants—U.S. citizens of European descent, U.S. citizens of Chinese descent, and Chinese citizens of the People's Republic of China—to complete a questionnaire relating to their attributions about positive and negative events. For each item (e.g., looking for a job unsuccessfully; going out on a date that turns out well) participants in the study indicated the extent to which these events stemmed from internal or external causes. In addition, they rated the extent to which the causes of these events were stable or unstable, and the extent to which they were specific or global (general) in nature.

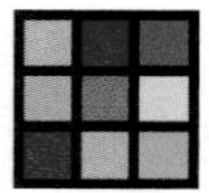

Lee and Seligman (1997) predicted that U.S. citizens of European descent would show a larger self-serving bias than either Chinese Americans or Chinese citizens. In other words, they would show a stronger tendency than the other two groups to attribute successes to themselves and failures to others and/or external events. As shown in Figure 16.3, this is precisely what happened. Interestingly,

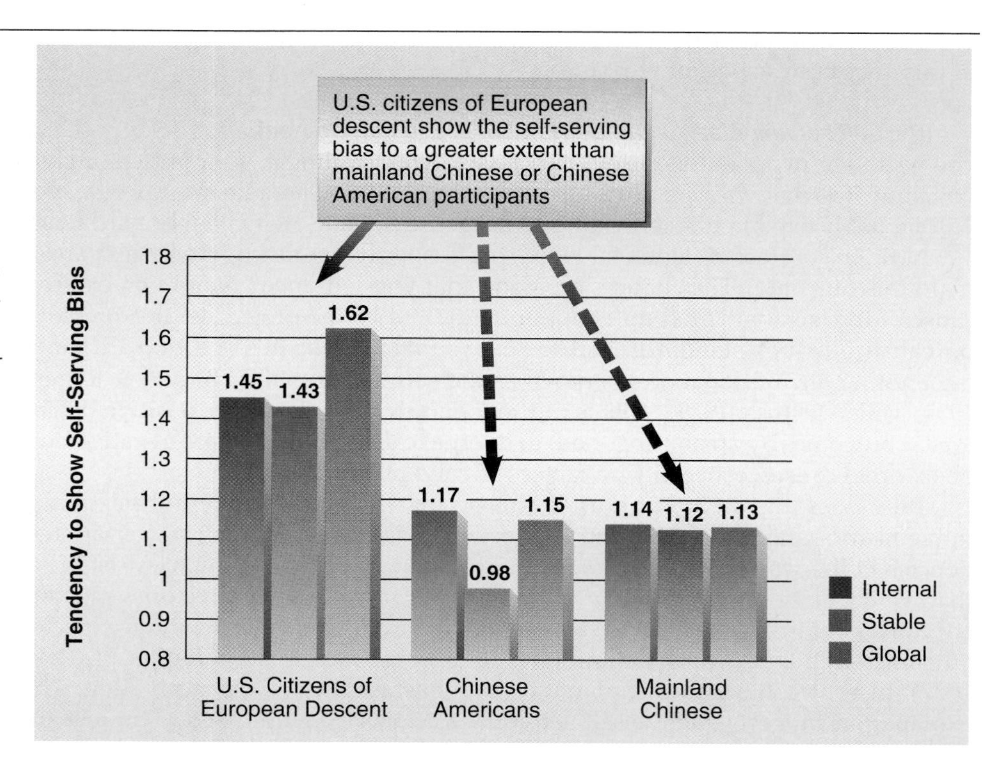


**Figure 16.3**
**Cultural Differences in the Self-Serving Bias**

As shown here, U.S. citizens of European descent showed a stronger tendency to attribute good events to stable, global, and internal causes than did either Chinese American or mainland Chinese participants. These findings indicate that cultural factors can strongly influence the nature of attributions individuals make concerning the causes of various events.
(*Source:* Based on data from Lee & Seligman, 1997.)

Chinese American and mainland Chinese participants did not differ in this respect: Both groups showed smaller susceptibility to the self-serving bias than did U.S. participants of European descent. Apparently, certain values central to Chinese culture—modesty, group orientation—combine to temper the tendency to pat ourselves on the back for good outcomes but to blame bad ones on factors outside our control. (See the **From Science to Practice** section below for a discussion of how attribution theory can be applied to important practical issues.)

**REVIEW QUESTIONS**

- What is the correspondence bias?
- What is the self-serving bias?
- Do cultural factors play a role in these forms of attributional error?

from SCIENCE to PRACTICE

## Attributional Augmenting and Perceptions of Female Entrepreneurs

Consider two possible situations: (1) an athlete competing in the Olympics sets a new record and wins a gold medal; (2) this athlete competes in the same event and sets a new record, but you know that this person is suffering from a painful injury. In which case would you be more impressed with the athlete's performance? Almost certainly, you would give the athlete "extra credit" in the second case. After all, this person has performed well despite the presence of a factor that might have reduced performance (a painful injury). Situations like this one illustrate the operation of *attributional augmenting*. This refers to the fact that if a factor that would be expected to facilitate some behavior or outcome *and* a factor that would be expected to inhibit some behavior or outcome are both present, yet the behavior or outcome actually occurs, we assign more weight or importance to the facilitating factor. In this case, we would attach greater weight to the athlete's ability or motivation, which allowed this person to win a gold medal despite a painful injury.

Recently, attributional augmenting has been employed to a very different context—entrepreneurship. It is widely agreed among economists that entrepreneurs—people who start new businesses—make major contributions to the prosperity of their countries, so studying the factors that help them succeed can yield important benefits. What does attributional augmenting have to do with entrepreneurship? Consider the following fact: A large majority of entrepreneurs (especially in high-tech industries) are males; further, in recent years, women have received less than two percent of the funds available from investors for starting new companies (Thomas, 1999). This suggests that women face important barriers as entrepreneurs, just as they do in many other business contexts (e.g., Lyness & Thomas, 1997). Indeed, a large body of evidence suggests that women often receive lower ratings as job applicants and ratings of their performance than males, especially when they seek or hold managerial-level jobs (e.g., Heilman, Martell, & Simon, 1988).

But here is where attributional augmenting might help. Once a woman actually becomes an entrepreneur, many people she meets may reason as follows: "Gee, she's an entrepreneur. This is unusual and means that she overcame a lot of barriers, so *she must be really good.*" In other words, attributional augmenting might lead people to perceive female entrepreneurs in a very favorable manner and this, in turn, could help them succeed.

I and my colleagues (Gideon Markman and Azita Hirsa) have recently obtained evidence for this reasoning (Baron, Hirsa, & Markman, 2000). We showed employed persons photos of females they did not know and asked them to rate these women on a number of different dimensions. We told half the raters that the women in the photos were entrepreneurs and the other half that they were managers. Results were clear: the women received higher ratings when they were described as being entrepreneurs. For instance, they were rated as more decisive and more serious about their careers, and their success was attributed more to their own abilities and less to luck. In addition, the women in the photos were also rated as being less stereotypically feminine when described as entrepreneurs. This suggests that not only did attributional augmenting enhance ratings of the women when they were described as being entrepreneurs, it also served to reduce the potential impact of negative gender stereotypes about women.

From a practical point of view, these findings suggest that principles of attribution can be used both to counter the effects of bias against females and to enhance the success of entrepreneurs. In fact, management schools that offer training to would-be entrepreneurs have recently begun to add information about basic principles of psychology (including attribution and social cognition) to their courses. I believe that such training will be invaluable to new entrepreneurs, and will help them to start companies that create millions of new jobs in the decades ahead.

Web Link: *Social Cognition Paper Archive and Information Center*

## Social Cognition: How We Process Social Information

Identifying the causes behind others' behavior is an important aspect of social thought, but it is far from the entire picture. Thinking about other persons involves many other tasks as well. In **social cognition** we must decide what information is most important, and so worthy of our attention. We must enter such information into long-term memory and be able to retrieve it at later times. And we must be able to combine this previously stored information about others in various ways in order to make judgments about people and predict their future actions (Wyer & Srull, 1999). It is only by accomplishing these tasks that we can make sense out of the social world in which we live—a world that, we soon learn, is anything but simple.

How do we accomplish these tasks? I have already explored parts of the answer in discussing memory and schemas (Chapter 6) and the use of *heuristics*—cognitive rules of thumb for making quick judgments or decisions (Chapter 7). Here, I'll focus on additional aspects of social thought, especially ones related to the following basic theme: As human beings we are definitely *not* perfect information-processing devices. On the contrary, in our efforts to understand others and make sense out of the social world, we are subject to a wide range of tendencies that together can lead us into serious error. In this section we'll consider several of these "tilts" in social cognition. Before turning to these sources of potential error, however, I should emphasize one point: Although these aspects of social thought do sometimes result in errors, they are also quite adaptive. They often help us to focus on the kinds of information that are usually most useful, and they reduce the effort required for understanding the social world.

**DEALING WITH INCONSISTENT INFORMATION: PAYING ATTENTION TO WHAT DOESN'T FIT** Imagine the following situation. You are watching a talk show on television, and one of the guests is Madonna. You only half listen as she makes several fairly extreme but, for her, not surprising comments about life, music, and sex. Then, in a quiet voice, Madonna says something totally unexpected: Since becoming a parent, she has lost interest in money and material things and has decided to retire to grow flowers and spend time with her husband and child. You sit up straight in disbelief: Can you believe your ears? Did she really say that?

This strange (and imaginary!) media event illustrates an important fact about social cognition: In general, we tend to pay much more attention to information that is unexpected or somehow inconsistent with our expectations than to information that is expected or consistent. Thus, a statement by the original "Material Girl" that she has lost interest in money would literally leap out at you, demanding close and careful attention.

This tendency to pay greater attention to information inconsistent with our expectations than to information consistent with them is an important and basic aspect of social cognition. It is apparent in a wide range of contexts (e.g., Belmore & Hubbard, 1987; Hilton, Klein, & von Hippel, 1991), and it seems to stem from the fact that we work harder to understand inconsistent information because it is unexpected and surprising. And because the greater the amount of attention we pay to information, the better its chance of entering memory and influencing our later

**Social Cognition:** The process through which we notice, store, remember, and later use social information.

judgments (Fiske & Neuberg, 1990), this tendency to notice what's inconsistent has important implications.

One final point: Although it is usually the case that information to which we pay particular attention exerts stronger effects on our social thought and judgments than other information, this is not always so. Sometimes, even though we readily notice information that is inconsistent with our expectations, we tend to discount it or downplay it: It's simply too unexpected to accept. For example, you probably can't help noticing the weird headlines on the tabloid newspapers displayed near the checkout lines in supermarkets (see Figure 16.4); but the likelihood that these headlines will influence you is slight, because they are so bizarre that you discount them. So the fact that we often pay careful attention to information inconsistent with our current views or thinking does not mean that such information is necessarily more influential with respect to social thought.

**Figure 16.4**
**When Information Is Too Extreme, We Discount It**

Although we readily notice unusual or extreme information such as tabloid headlines, we tend to discount such information and so are not strongly influenced by it.

**THE OPTIMISTIC BIAS FOR TASK COMPLETION: WE THINK WE CAN DO MORE, SOONER, THAN WE REALLY CAN** Several years ago one of my neighbors decided to build an addition to his house. The builder he chose estimated that the job would take about nine months. It is now more than two years since the work began, and it is still not done! In fact, I can hear the hammering today, as I write these words. This is not a rare event: Many projects seem to take longer, and cost more, than initially predicted.

Audio 16.1: *Planning Fallacy/Optimistic Bias*

Why is this the case? One possibility is as follows. In predicting how long a given task will take, people tend to be overly optimistic: They predict that they can get the job done much sooner than actually turns out to be the case. Or, turning this around somewhat, they expect to get more done in a given period of time than they really can. You probably recognize this tendency, often referred to as the *planning fallacy,* in your own thinking. Try to remember the last time you worked on a major project (for instance, a term paper). Did it take more time or less time to complete than you originally estimated? Probably your answer is "More time . . . of course!"

What features of social thought account for this common error? According to Buehler, Griffin, and Ross (1994), social psychologists who have studied the planning fallacy in detail, several factors play a role. One is that when individuals make predictions about how long it will take them to complete a given task, they enter a planning mode of thought in which they focus primarily on the future: how they will perform the task. This, in turn, prevents them from looking backward in time and remembering how long similar tasks took them in the past. The result: They tend to overlook important potential obstacles when predicting how long the task will take, and fall prey to the planning fallacy. These predictions have been confirmed in several studies (e.g., Buehler et al., 1994), so they do seem to provide important insights into the origins of the tendency to make optimistic predictions about task completion.

Additional research suggests that another factor, too, may play an important role in the planning fallacy: motivation to complete a task. When predicting what will happen in the future, individuals often guess that what *will* happen is what they *want* to happen (e.g., Johnson & Sherman, 1990). In cases where they are strongly motivated to complete a task, therefore, they make overoptimistic predictions concerning when this desired completion will occur.

**Counterfactual Thinking:** The tendency to evaluate events by thinking about alternatives to them—"what might have been."

To test the role of motivation in the planning fallacy, Buehler, Griffin, and MacDonald (1997) phoned people chosen at random from the telephone directory of a large Canadian city and asked these individuals whether they expected to receive an income tax refund. Then they asked them when, relative to the deadline, they expected to mail in their tax forms. Later, one week after the actual deadline for submitting the forms, the researchers phoned the same persons again and asked them when they had actually mailed their tax forms.

The researchers reasoned that persons expecting a refund would have stronger motivation to complete the task of filing their forms and so would make more optimistic predictions about when they would file them. This is precisely what happened. Although persons in both groups showed the planning fallacy, those expecting a refund were much more optimistic in their predictions: They estimated that they would submit their forms twenty-eight days before the deadline. In contrast, those not expecting a refund estimated that they would submit the forms about seventeen days before the deadline. Both groups actually submitted their forms later than they predicted—about fifteen days in advance for those expecting a refund and thirteen days in advance for those not expecting a refund.

These results, and those of a follow-up laboratory study (Buehler et al., 1997), indicate that the planning fallacy stems, at least in part, from motivation to complete a task. In other words, individuals' estimates of when they will complete a project are influenced by their hopes and desires: They want to finish early, so they predict that they will do so. Sad to relate, however, this appears to be one of the many situations in life where wishing does not necessarily make it so!

**COUNTERFACTUAL THINKING: THE EFFECTS OF CONSIDERING "WHAT MIGHT HAVE BEEN"** Suppose that you take an important exam, but when you receive your score, it is a C–, much lower than you hoped. What thoughts will enter your mind as you consider your grade? If you are like most people, you may imagine "what might have been"—receiving a higher grade—and reflect on how you could have obtained that better outcome. "If only I had studied more, or come to class more often," you may think to yourself. And then perhaps you may begin to formulate plans for actually doing better on the next test.

**Figure 16.5**
**Counterfactual Thinking in Action**

Athletes who win bronze medals at the Olympics report that they often imagine not winning any medal at all. The result of such *downward counterfactuals* is that the athletes experience positive feelings: They are glad they won *some* prize!

Such thoughts about what might have been are known in social psychology as **counterfactual thinking** and occur in a wide range of situations, not just in ones in which we experience disappointments. For instance, suppose you read an article in the newspaper about a woman who was injured by bricks falling off the front of a large office building. Certainly, you will feel some sympathy for this person. But now imagine that the article goes on to indicate either (1) that she is a stranger in town who had never been on that street before, or (2) that she works in the building next door and passes this way several times a day. Will you feel more sympathy for the injured person under condition (1) or condition (2)? Many studies indicate that you may actually experience more sympathy for the injured woman if she is a stranger in town than if she passes that building every day on the way to work or to lunch. Why? Because it is somewhat harder to imagine the woman *not* being injured when she walks past the building every day. And when it is harder to imagine an alternative outcome (such as the woman's not being injured), we feel less sympathy.

Here's another example: Will you feel more sympathy for a driver who never picks up hitchhikers but one day breaks his rule and is robbed by the person, or for a driver who frequently picks up hitchhikers and one day is robbed? Probably you'll have less sympathy for the driver who routinely picks up hitchhikers; after all, this person is asking for trouble. Moreover, because this driver takes many risks, it is harder for us to imagine another outcome (his not being robbed) (e.g.,

Macrae, 1992; Miller & McFarland, 1987). In general terms, research findings indicate that we feel more sympathy for people who experience harm as a result of *unusual* actions on their part than as a result of more typical behavior.

Engaging in counterfactual thinking can produce many other effects, too. For instance, such thinking can, depending on its focus, either boost or depress current moods. If individuals imagine better outcomes than actually occurred (upward counterfactuals), they may experience strong feelings of regret, dissatisfaction, or envy, especially if they do not feel capable of obtaining better outcomes in the future (Sanna, 1997). Alternatively, if individuals imagine worse outcomes than actually occurred, they may experience positive feelings of satisfaction or hopefulness. Such reactions, for example, have been found among Olympic athletes who win bronze medals and who comfort themselves by imagining what it would be like to have won no medal whatsoever (e.g., Gleicher et al., 1995) (see Figure 16.5). In sum, engaging in counterfactual thought can strongly influence affective states (Medvec & Savitsky, 1997).

In addition to these effects, counterfactual thinking can also help individuals understand *why* negative or disappointing outcomes occurred. This, in turn, can often help people plan changes in behavior or new strategies that can improve their future performance (e.g., McMullen, Markman, & Gavanski, 1995; Roese, 1997). Recent findings indicate that the magnitude of such changes in behavior is closely linked to the magnitude of improvements individuals desire. In other words, the greater the improvement desired, the larger the changes in behavior such persons imagine. If I receive a C in a course but would be happy with a B, I think about studying a little more for each exam. If, instead, I desire an A (a larger improvement in obtained outcome), I think about studying *much* more (Sim & Morris, 1998). Regardless of the specific thoughts involved, engaging in counterfactual thinking may be one technique that helps individuals learn from past experience and profit from their mistakes.

In sum, imagining what might have been in a given situation can yield many effects, ranging from despair and intense regret through hopefulness and increased determination to do better in the future. Our tendency to think not only about what is but also about what might be, therefore, can have far-reaching effects on many aspects of our social thought and social behavior (Baron, 2000). Figure 16.6 summarizes these potential effects.

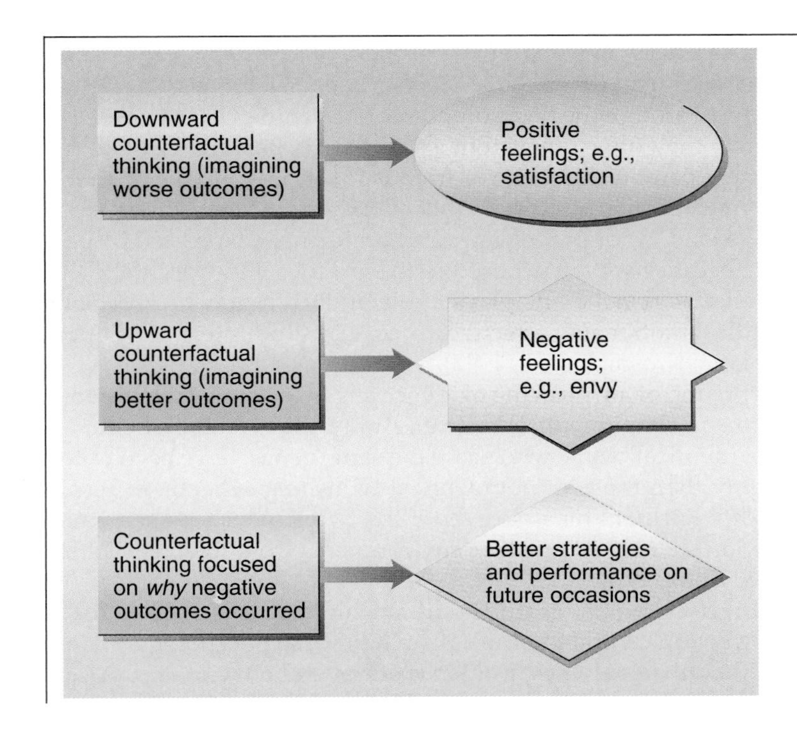


**Figure 16.6**
**Effects of Counterfactual Thinking**

As shown here, imagining "what might have been" can influence our affective states (moods) and our understanding of *why* we experienced negative outcomes, and so can improve our future performance.

REVIEW QUESTIONS

- How do we deal with social information that is inconsistent with our expectations?
- What is the optimistic bias for task completion?
- What is counterfactual thinking? How can it affect our affective states and performance?

Food for Thought

Some people seem to be more susceptible to the optimistic bias than others. Why do you think this is so?

**Attitudes:** Lasting evaluations of various aspects of the social world that are stored in memory.

**Persuasion:** The process through which one or more persons attempt to alter the attitudes of one or more others.

## Attitudes: Evaluating the Social World

Consider the following list:

Leonardo DiCaprio

Hillary Clinton

AIDS

Cheerios

Whoopi Goldberg

sport utility vehicles

Do you have any reactions to each item? Unless you have been living a life of total isolation, you probably do. You may like or dislike Leonardo DiCaprio, believe that Hillary Clinton would or would not make a good senator, be worried or unconcerned about AIDS, like or dislike Cheerios, find Whoopi Goldberg funny or not funny, and like or dislike sport utility vehicles. Such reactions, which social psychologists call *attitudes,* generally involve an emotional or affective component (for instance, liking or disliking), a cognitive component (beliefs), and a behavioral component (tendencies to act toward these items in various ways). More simply, **attitudes** can be defined as lasting evaluations of virtually any and every aspect of the social world—issues, ideas, persons, social groups, objects (Fazio & Roskos-Ewoldsen, 1994; Tesser & Martin, 1996).

Web Link: *Psychological Research on the Net*

Attitudes are formed through the basic processes of learning we considered in Chapter 5. For example, they often stem from *operant conditioning,* as we are frequently rewarded by our parents, teachers, or friends for expressing the "correct" views—the ones *they* hold. Similarly, attitudes also derive from *observational learning.* Throughout life we tend to adopt the views and preferences expressed by people we like or respect, because we are exposed to those views and want to be like those persons. Even *classical conditioning* plays a role; in fact, it may be especially influential in shaping the emotional or affective aspect of attitudes (e.g., Cacioppo, Priester, & Bernston, 1993; Krosnick et al., 1992).

Perhaps most surprising of all, growing evidence suggests that genetic factors, too, may play some role in shaping attitudes (e.g., Arvey et al., 1989; Keller et al., 1992). The attitudes of identical twins, who share the same genes, have been found to correlate more highly than those of nonidentical twins (e.g., Crealia & Tesser, 1996; Waller et al., 1990). Further, this is so even if the twins have been separated early in life and raised in sharply contrasting environments from then on (Hershberger, Lichtenstein, & Knox, 1994).

Whatever their precise origins, attitudes are an important aspect of social thought and have long been a central topic of research in social psychology, mainly because they often (although not always) influence our overt behavior (e.g., Ajzen,

1991; Gibbons et al., 1998). For instance, if you have a negative attitude toward Hillary Clinton, you probably won't vote for her if given the opportunity; if you like Cheerios, you may well eat them for breakfast. So an individual's attitudes are often good predictors of his or her behavior (although, again, this is *not* always the case, for reasons I'll discuss later). We'll now examine two key aspects of attitudes: *persuasion*—how attitudes can sometimes be changed; and *cognitive dissonance*—a process through which we sometimes change our own attitudes.

**Figure 16.7**
**Efforts at Persuasion: Will They Ever Go This Far?**

Efforts to change our attitudes haven't yet reached this stage, but no one can guarantee that technological advances won't someday make such tactics possible.
(*Source:* © The New Yorker Collection. 1995. Gahan Wilson from cartoonbank.com. All rights reserved)

*"Sometimes I wish they'd never perfected setless television."*

## PERSUASION: USING MESSAGES TO CHANGE ATTITUDES

In the early twenty-first century, the business of changing attitudes—or at least trying to change them—seems to grow ever bigger and more intense: television commercials, magazine ads, billboards, warning labels on products, and—who knows?—perhaps someday even the technique shown in Figure 16.7! The messages vary and are delivered in different ways, but the goal remains the same: to change people's attitudes and so, ultimately, their behavior. To what extent are such efforts at **persuasion**—efforts to change attitudes—really effective? Let's see what psychologists have learned about these issues.

1. Experts are more persuasive than nonexperts (Hovland & Weiss, 1951). The same arguments carry more weight when delivered by people who seem to know what they are talking about than when they are made by people lacking expertise.
2. Messages that do not appear to be designed to change our attitudes are often more successful in this respect than ones that seem intended to reach this goal (Walster & Festinger, 1962). In other words, we generally don't trust—and generally refuse to be influenced by—persons who deliberately set out to persuade us. This is one reason why the soft sell is so popular in advertising—and in politics.
3. Attractive sources are more effective in changing attitudes than unattractive ones (Kiesler & Kiesler, 1969). This is one reason why the models featured in many ads are highly attractive (see Figure 16.8) and why advertisers engage in a perpetual search for appealing new faces.

Video 16.1: *Pervasive Persuasion*

Web Link: *Persuasive Art from World War II*

4. People are sometimes more susceptible to persuasion when they are distracted by some extraneous event than when they are paying full attention to what is being said (Allyn & Festinger, 1961).
5. When an audience holds attitudes contrary to those of a would-be persuader, it is often more effective for the communicator to adopt a *two-sided approach,* in which both sides of the argument are presented, than a *one-sided approach.* Apparently, strongly supporting one side of an issue while acknowledging that the other side has a few good points in its favor serves to disarm the audience and makes it harder for them to resist the source's major conclusions.
6. People who speak rapidly are often more persuasive than persons who speak more slowly (Miller et al., 1976). So, contrary to popular belief, we do not always distrust fast-talking politicians and salespersons.
7. Persuasion can be enhanced by messages that arouse strong emotions (especially fear) in the audience,

**Figure 16.8**
**Beauty Sells!**

Research findings indicate that attractive persons are often more successful at persuasion than less attractive ones. Advertising executives are well aware of this fact and use it to promote many different products.

particularly when the message provides specific recommendations about how a change in attitudes or behavior will prevent the negative consequences described in the fear-provoking message (Leventhal, Singer, & Jones, 1965).

I'm confident that you find all these points to be reasonable ones that probably fit with your own experience, so early research on persuasion certainly provided important insights into the factors that influence persuasion. What such work *didn't* do, however, was offer a comprehensive account of *how* persuasion occurs. Fortunately, this question has been the focus of more recent research, and it is to this highly sophisticated work that we turn next.

**THE COGNITIVE APPROACH TO PERSUASION: SYSTEMATIC VERSUS HEURISTIC PROCESSING** What happens when you are exposed to a persuasive message—for instance, when you watch a television commercial or listen to a political speech? Your first answer may be something like "I think about what's happening or what's being said," and in a sense that's correct. But how much thinking of this type do we actually do, and how do we process (absorb, interpret, evaluate) the information contained in such messages? The answer that has emerged from many studies is that basically we process persuasive messages in two distinct ways.

The first of these is known as **systematic processing,** or the **central route** to persuasion; it involves careful consideration of message content, the ideas it contains, and so on. Such processing is quite effortful and absorbs much of our information-processing capacity. The second approach, known as **heuristic processing** or the **peripheral route** to persuasion, involves the use of simple rules of thumb or mental shortcuts, such as the belief that "experts' statements can be trusted" or the idea that "if it makes me feel good, I'm in favor of it." This kind of processing is much less effortful and allows us to react to persuasive messages in an automatic manner. It occurs in response to cues in the message or situation that evoke various mental shortcuts (e.g., "If someone so beautiful or famous or charismatic says it, then this message is worthy of careful attention").

When do we engage in each of these two distinct modes of thought? Modern theories of persuasion, such as the **elaboration-likelihood model (ELM)** (e.g., Petty & Cacioppo, 1986; Petty et al., 1994) and the **heuristic–systematic model** (e.g., Chaiken, Liberman & Eagly, 1989; Eagly & Chaiken, 1998), provide the following answer. We engage in the effortful type of processing (systematic processing) when our capacity to process information relating to the persuasive message is high (e.g., we have lots of knowledge about the subject or lots of time to engage in such thought) or when we are *motivated* to do so—when the issue is important to us, we believe it is important to form an accurate view, and so on (e.g., Maheswaran & Chaiken, 1991; Petty & Cacioppo, 1990). In contrast, we engage in the less effortful type of processing (heuristic processing) when we lack the ability or capacity to process more carefully (we must make up our minds very quickly or have little knowledge about the issue) or when our motivation to perform such cognitive work is low (the issue is unimportant to us, has little potential effect on us, and so on). Advertisers, politicians, salespersons, and others wishing to change our attitudes prefer to push us into the heuristic mode of processing; because, for reasons I'll soon describe, it is often easier for persuaders to change our attitudes when we think in this mode than when we engage in more careful and systematic processing.

Discovery of these two contrasting modes of processing provided an important key to understanding the process of persuasion. For instance, it has been found that when persuasive messages are not interesting or relevant to individuals, the amount of persuasion these messages produce is *not* strongly influenced by the strength of the arguments they contain. When such messages are highly relevant to individuals, however, they are much more successful in inducing persuasion when the arguments they contain are strong and convincing. The ELM and the heuristic–systematic model provide a clear explanation for why this is so. When relevance is low, individuals tend to process messages through the heuristic mode, by means of cognitive shortcuts. Thus, argument strength has little impact on them.

**Systematic Processing:** Careful consideration of the content of persuasive messages; also called the *central route* to persuasion. Such processing is quite effortful and absorbs much of our information-processing capacity.

**Central Route** (to persuasion): Careful consideration of the content of persuasive messages; also called *systematic processing.*

**Heuristic Processing:** The use of simple rules of thumb or mental shortcuts in the evaluation of persuasive messages; also called the *peripheral route* to persuasion.

**Peripheral Route** (to persuasion): The use of simple rules of thumb or mental shortcuts in the evaluation of persuasive messages; also called *heuristic processing.*

**Elaboration-Likelihood Model (ELM):** A cognitive model of persuasion suggesting that persuasion can occur through distinct routes.

**Heuristic–Systematic Model:** A cognitive model of persuasion suggesting that persuasion can occur through distinctly different routes.

In contrast, when relevance is high, people process persuasive messages through the systematic (central) route, and in this mode argument strength is important (e.g., Petty & Cacioppo, 1990).

Similarly, the systematic versus heuristic distinction helps explain why people are more easily persuaded when they are somehow distracted than when they are not. Our capacity to process the information in a persuasive message is limited, so when distracted we tend to adopt the heuristic mode of thought to conserve or stretch our cognitive resources. If the message contains the "right" cues (e.g., communicators who are attractive or seemingly expert), persuasion may occur because people respond to these cues and not to the arguments being presented. In sum, the modern cognitive approach has provided important new insights into the process of persuasion—into when and *how* persuasive messages succeed in changing attitudes.

In order to study changes in people's attitudes, psychologists must be able to measure these evaluations of the social world. How do they do this? Please see the **Research Methods** section below for information on this important question.

**Likert Scales:** Scales for measuring attitudes containing statements highly favorable or unfavorable toward the attitude object. Respondents indicate the extent to which they agree or disagree with each of these statements.

## Research methods: How Psychologists Measure Attitudes—from Attitude Scales to the "Bogus Pipeline"

If you've ever asked a friend for her or his views on some issue, you are already familiar with the most straightforward technique for measuring attitudes: simply asking people to state their opinions or preferences. Unfortunately, informal procedures like this suffer from several serious drawbacks. When asked to state their views, many persons begin to ramble and soon get far away from the issue at hand. Similarly, people are always concerned with "looking good" to others, so their statements may reflect what they think will put them in a favorable light rather than their actual views. To avoid these and related problems, social psychologists measure attitudes by more formal means, generally involving the use of *scales* or *questionnaires.* The items on these measuring instruments are carefully constructed to be related to a particular issue, object, or group of interests, and individuals' attitudes are revealed by their responses to these items. Many techniques for selecting the items to be included in an attitude questionnaire exist, but in essence, they all relate to the criteria of *reliability* and *validity* we discussed in Chapter 11: Researchers want to choose items that yield stable (i.e., reliable) scores and that actually measure the attitudes of interest (validity).

The items on attitude scales can be presented to respondents in many different formats, but one important approach involves what are known as **Likert scales.** On such scales, the items are statements either highly favorable or unfavorable toward the attitude object, and respondents indicate the extent to which they agree or disagree with each of these statements. To the extent that respondents agree with statements favorable to the attitude object or reject statements unfavorable to it, they are assumed to hold a positive attitude. To the extent that they endorse statements unfavorable to the attitude object or reject statements favorable to it, they are assumed to hold a negative attitude. (See Table 16.1 for examples of Likert scales.)

**TABLE 16.1**

### Measuring Attitudes with Likert Scales

Respondents completing Likert scales indicate the extent to which they agree or disagree with strong positive and negative statements about the attitude being studied.

Indicate the extent to which you agree or disagree with each statement below. Circle one number for each item.

1. President Clinton is one of the finest presidents the United States has ever had.

| Strongly Disagree | Disagree | Neutral | Agree | Strongly Agree |
|---|---|---|---|---|
| 1 | 2 | 3 | 4 | 5 |

2. President Clinton is the most corrupt president the United States has ever had.

| Strongly Disagree | Disagree | Neutral | Agree | Strongly Agree |
|---|---|---|---|---|
| 1 | 2 | 3 | 4 | 5 |

While attitude scales are often useful, they are not immune to one problem I mentioned above: Sometimes individuals want to conceal their true views so that they can shine in the eyes of others, or to avoid stating views they know to be unpopular (e.g., a racial bigot may claim to be unbiased to avoid strong disapproval from others). How can such problems be avoided? One ingenious technique is known as the **bogus pipeline.** In this procedure respondents are told that they will be attached to a special apparatus that, by measuring tiny changes in their muscles (or in brain waves or other physiological reactions) can assess their true opinions no matter what they say (see Figure 16.9). To convince respondents that this is actually the case, the researcher asks for their views on several issues—ones on which their real views are known (e.g., because they expressed these several weeks earlier). The researcher then "reads" the machine and reports these views to participants—who are often quite impressed! Once they believe that the machine can, in a sense, "see inside them," there is no reason to conceal their true attitudes. Presumably, then, their responses to questions or to an attitude scale will be quite truthful and provide an accurate picture of their attitudes. The bogus pipeline has been used in many different studies (e.g., De Vries et al., 1995) and does seem to be effective. However, because it involves temporary deception, it raises ethical issues, as described in Chapter 1; it should be used only with extreme caution.

These are only a few of the ways in which social psychologists measure attitudes—others exist as well. None of these methods is perfect. Together, however, they help researchers acquire useful information about important topics—information that might otherwise remain hidden from view.

**Figure 16.9**
**The Bogus Pipeline: An Ingenious Technique for Studying Attitudes**
In the bogus pipeline, individuals are told that the equipment shown here can, by measuring physiological reactions, reveal their true opinions. If the persons whose attitudes are being measured accept this description as accurate, there is no reason for them to fake their answers. (*Source:* Baron & Byrne, 1987.)

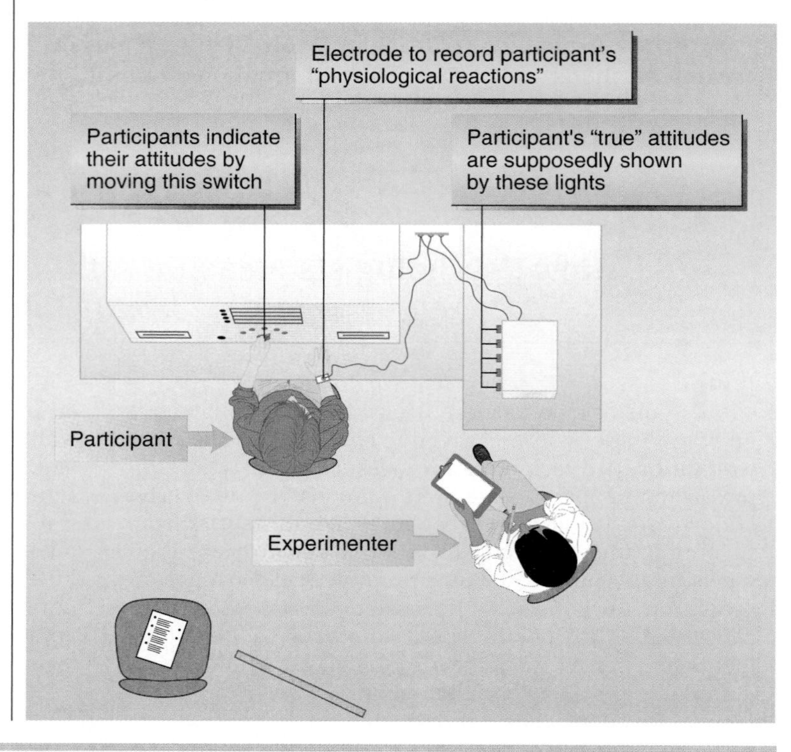


**Bogus Pipeline:** A procedure for measuring attitudes in which respondents are told that they will be attached to a special apparatus that, by measuring tiny changes in their muscles (or in brain waves or other physiological reactions) can assess their true opinions no matter what they say.

**Induced Compliance:** A technique for changing attitudes in which individuals are somehow induced to state positions different from their actual views.

**COGNITIVE DISSONANCE: HOW WE SOMETIMES CHANGE OUR OWN ATTITUDES** There are many occasions in everyday life when we feel compelled to say or do things inconsistent with our true attitudes. A couple of examples: Your friend shows you her new sweater and asks how you like it. You really hate the color, but you don't say that. Instead you say "Nice . . . really nice." Your boss describes his new idea for increasing sales. You think that it is totally idiotic, but you don't tell him that. Instead you respond, "Sounds really interesting."

The reasons for behaving in these polite—but slightly dishonest—ways are so obvious that social psychologists describe such situations as involving **induced compliance**—situations in which we feel compelled to say or do things inconsistent with our true attitudes. Now, here's the most interesting part: When we behave in this way—when we engage in *attitude-discrepant behavior*—this may sometimes produce changes in the attitudes we hold. In fact, our attitudes may shift toward what we felt compelled to do or say, thus reducing the size of the gap between our true attitudes and our overt actions.

Such effects were first predicted by a very famous theory known as the theory of *cognitive dissonance* (Festinger, 1957). The term **cognitive dissonance** (or *disso-*

*nance* for short) refers to the feelings we experience when we notice a gap between two attitudes we hold, or between our attitudes and our behavior. Dissonance, it appears, is quite unpleasant (e.g., Elliot & Devine, 1994); so when we experience it, we attempt to reduce it. We can accomplish this in several different ways. First, we can change our attitudes or our behavior so that these are more consistent with each other. For example, we can convince ourselves that the color of our friend's sweater is not really so bad. Second, we can acquire new information that supports our attitude or our behavior. For instance, we can seek out information indicating that our boss's plan does make some sense. Third, we can engage in *trivialization*—conclude that the attitudes or behaviors in question are not important (e.g., Simon, Greenberg, & Brehm, 1995).

All of these approaches can be viewed as *direct* ones to dissonance reduction: They focus on the attitude–behavior discrepancies that are causing the dissonance. Research by Steele and his colleagues (e.g., Steele, 1988; Steele & Lui, 1983), however, indicates that dissonance can also be reduced through *indirect* tactics—ones that leave the basic discrepancy between attitudes and behavior intact but reduce the negative feelings generated by dissonance. According to Steele (1988), adoption of such indirect routes to dissonance reduction is most likely to occur when attitude–behavior discrepancies involve important attitudes or self-beliefs. Under these conditions, Steele suggests (e.g., Steele, Spencer, & Lynch, 1993), individuals experiencing dissonance may focus not so much on reducing the gap between their attitudes and their behavior as on *self-affirmation*—efforts to restore positive self-evaluations that are threatened by the dissonance (e.g., Elliot & Devine, 1994; Tesser, Martin, & Cornell, 1996). How can they achieve self-affirmation? By focusing on their positive self-attributes—good things about themselves (e.g., Steele, 1988). For instance, if an individual experienced dissonance as a result of telling his boss that the boss's plan was good when in fact he thought it was silly, he could remind himself that he had recently served as a volunteer for a local charity, helped a friend move, and so on. Contemplating these positive self-attributes would help reduce the discomfort produced by dissonance.

Which of these tactics do we choose? As you might guess, whichever requires the least effort. In situations involving induced compliance, however, it is often the case that changing our attitudes is the easiest step to take, so it is not surprising that in such situations our attitudes often shift to match more closely what we have actually said or done. In other words, we change our attitudes because doing so helps us reduce cognitive dissonance.

***Dissonance and the Less-Leads-to-More Effect.*** The prediction that people sometimes change their own attitudes is surprising enough. But now get ready for an even bigger surprise: Dissonance theory also predicts that the weaker the reasons we have for engaging in attitude-discrepant behavior—for saying or doing things inconsistent with our initial attitudes—the greater the pressure to change these attitudes. Why is this so? Because when we have strong reasons for engaging in attitude-discrepant behavior, we realize that these reasons are responsible for our saying or doing things inconsistent with our true attitudes. As a result, we experience very little dissonance. When we have only weak reasons for engaging in attitude-discrepant behavior, however, dissonance is stronger, and so is the pressure to change our attitudes (see Figure 16.10 on page 634).

Social psychologists sometimes refer to this unexpected state of affairs as the **less-leads-to-more effect:** the fact that the stronger one's reasons for engaging in attitude-discrepant behavior, the weaker the pressures toward changing one's underlying attitudes. Surprising as it may seem, this effect has been confirmed in many different studies (e.g., Riess & Schlenker, 1977). In all these studies, people provided with a small reward for stating views contrary to their own attitudes changed these attitudes so that they became closer to the views they had expressed.

**Cognitive Dissonance:** The state experienced by individuals when they discover inconsistency between two attitudes they hold or between their attitudes and their behavior.

**Less-Leads-to-More Effect:** The fact that rewards just barely sufficient to induce individuals to state positions contrary to their own views often generate more attitude change than larger rewards.

**Figure 16.10**
**Why, Where Attitude Change Is Concerned, "Less" Sometimes Leads to "More"**

When individuals have strong reasons for engaging in behavior discrepant with their attitudes (e.g., when they receive large rewards for doing so), they experience little or no dissonance and show little attitude change. When they have weak reasons for engaging in such behavior (e.g., when they receive small rewards for doing so), dissonance is much greater—and attitude change, too, is increased. In such cases, "less" does indeed lead to "more."

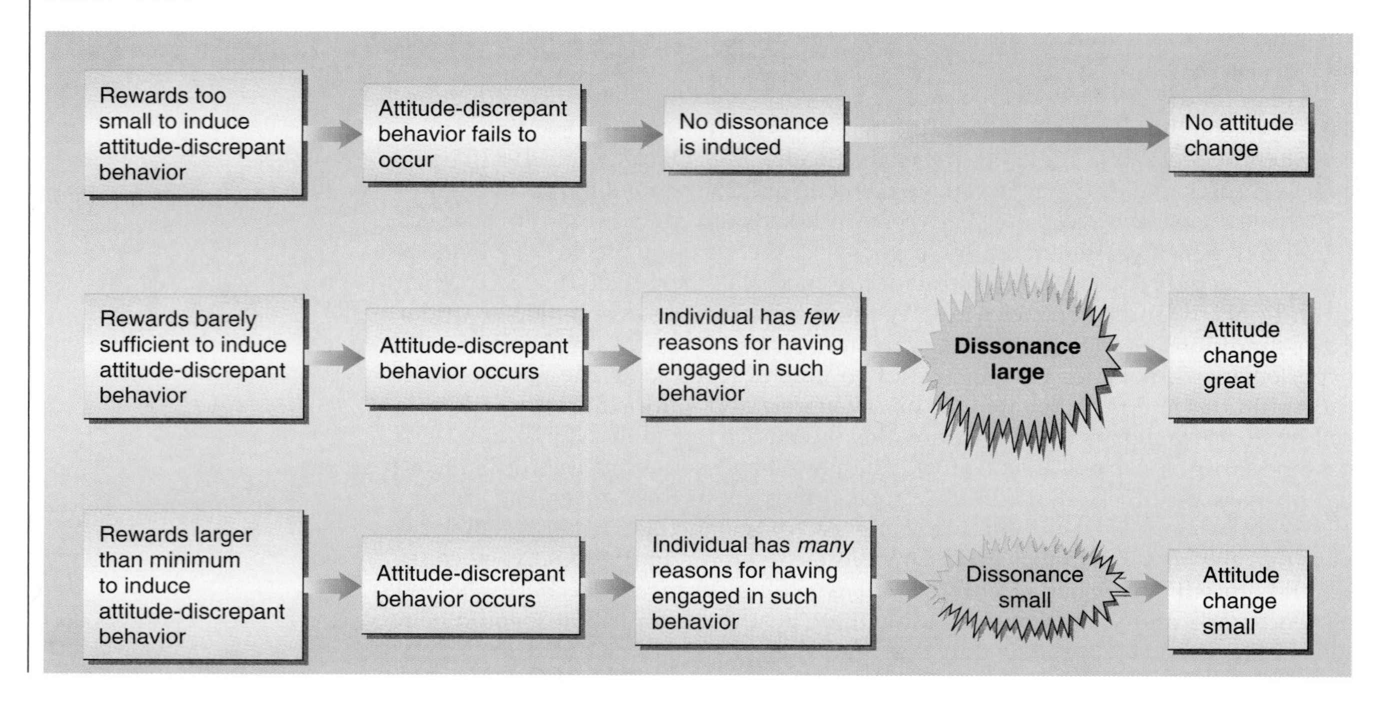


While the less-leads-to-more effect has been found in many studies, it does not occur under all conditions. Rather, it seems to happen only when several conditions exist (Cooper & Scher, 1994). First, the less-leads-to-more effect occurs only in situations in which people believe that they have a choice as to whether or not to perform the attitude-discrepant behavior. Second, small rewards lead to greater attitude change only when people believe that they were personally responsible for both the chosen course of action and any negative effects it produced. And third, the less-leads-to-more effect does not occur when people view the payment they receive as a bribe rather than as a well-deserved reward for services rendered. Because the necessary conditions do often exist, however, the strategy of offering others just barely enough to induce them to say or do things contrary to their true attitudes can often be an effective technique for inducing attitude change.

### *Putting Dissonance to Work: Hypocrisy and Safe Sex*

People who don't wear safety belts are much more likely to die in accidents than those who do.

People who smoke heavily are much more likely to develop lung cancer and heart disease than those who don't.

People who engage in unprotected sex are much more likely than those who engage in safe sex to contract dangerous diseases, including AIDS.

Most people know these statements are true (e.g., Carey, Morrison-Beedy, & Johnson, 1997), so their attitudes are generally favorable toward using seat belts, quitting smoking, and engaging in safe sex. Yet, as you well know, these attitudes

**Figure 16.11**
**Doing What We Know We Shouldn't Do**

Almost everyone knows that the behaviors shown here are dangerous. Yet many people continue to perform them. If people who engage in such actions can be induced to recommend avoiding them, they may experience feelings of hypocrisy and intense cognitive dissonance. The result? They may change their own behavior.

are often *not* translated into overt actions: People continue to drive without seat belts, to smoke, and so on (see Figure 16.11). What's needed, in other words, is not so much changes in attitudes as shifts in overt behavior. Can dissonance be useful in promoting such beneficial changes? A growing body of evidence suggests that it can (e.g., Gibbons, Eggleston, & Benthin, 1997; Stone et al., 1994), especially when it is generated by feelings of *hypocrisy*—awareness of publicly advocating some attitude or behavior but acting in a way inconsistent with that attitude or behavior. When people feel that they are being hypocritical, several researchers have reasoned (e.g., Aronson, Fried & Stone, 1991), they should experience strong dissonance. Moreover, such feelings would be so intense that adopting indirect modes of dissonance reduction (e.g., distracting oneself or bolstering one's ego by thinking about or engaging in other positively evaluated behaviors) would not do the trick; only actions that reduced dissonance directly, removing the discrepancy between words and deeds, would be effective.

These predictions have been tested in several studies. In one, for instance (Stone et al., 1994), students in a *hypocrisy* condition prepared a videotape urging others to engage in safe sex. Then they recalled situations in which they had failed to behave this way themselves. In contrast, other participants in the study engaged in only one of these two activities—they prepared the tape *or* remembered situations in which they had failed to engage in safe sex. Later, all groups were given an opportunity to buy condoms at a discounted price. It was expected that those in the hypocrisy condition would experience the strongest dissonance: After all, they had urged others to do something they themselves did not always do. Thus, they would be most likely to purchase condoms. Results indicated that this was the case: Fully 83 percent of those in the hypocrisy condition purchased condoms, compared with an average of only 38 percent in the other two conditions. Thus, exposing individuals to the strong dissonance induced by consciousness of their own hypocrisy seemed to be a highly effective means of changing their behavior.

A follow-up study on the same topic (Stone et al., 1997) indicated that when individuals are made to focus on the personal reasons why they have failed to engage in safe sex in the past, their sense of hypocrisy is intensified. As a result, they are more likely to change their overt behavior—purchase condoms offered to them at a reduced price—than to choose another, less direct route to dissonance reduction, such as making a donation to a charity. These findings suggest that using dissonance to generate hypocrisy can indeed be a powerful tool for changing people's behavior in desirable ways—ones that protect their health and safety.

**REVIEW QUESTIONS**

- What are attitudes?
- What factors were found to influence persuasion in early research?
- What are systematic and heuristic processing, and what role do they play in attitude change?
- What is cognitive dissonance, and how can it be reduced?
- What is induced compliance? The less-leads-to-more effect?
- How can hypocrisy be used to change behavior?

**Food for Thought**

Given the powerful effects of cognitive dissonance, how can people continue to do things like smoking or engaging in unsafe sex–actions they know are bad for them (and so are contrary to their attitudes)?

# Social Behavior: Interacting with Others

Thinking about other people is an important aspect of our social existence; but, as you know from your own life, we also *interact* with others in many ways. We work with others on various tasks; we attempt to influence them and are on the receiving end of *their* efforts at influence; we fall in and out of love; we join and leave various groups—the list goes on and on. In this section we'll consider several important aspects of *social interaction.*

## Prejudice: Distorted Views of the Social World . . . and Their Effects

**CourseCompass**

Web Link: *Understanding the Psychology of Prejudice and Racism*

"Ethnic cleansing" in Kosovo; mass murder of one ethnic group by another in Africa; seemingly perpetual suspicion and enmity between Moslem Pakistan and Hindu India . . . the list of atrocities based on racial, ethnic, or religious hatred seems endless. Such actions often stem from **prejudice**—powerful negative attitudes toward the members of specific social groups based solely on their membership in that group (Dovidio & Gaertner, 1986; Zanna & Olson, 1994). Where do such attitudes come from? And what can be done to reduce their impact? These are the issues we'll now examine.

**Prejudice:** Negative attitudes toward the members of some social group based on their membership in this group.

**Realistic Conflict Theory:** A theory proposing that prejudice stems, at least in part, from competition between social groups over valued commodities or opportunities.

**THE ORIGINS OF PREJUDICE: CONTRASTING PERSPECTIVES** Many different explanations for the origins of prejudice have been proposed. Here are four that have been especially influential.

***Direct Intergroup Conflict: Competition as a Source of Bias.*** It is sad but true that many of the things we value most—a good job, a nice home, high status—are in short supply; there's never enough to go around. This fact serves as the basis for one view of prejudice—**realistic conflict theory** (Bobo, 1983). According to this view, prejudice stems from competition between social groups over valued commodities or opportunities. The theory further suggests that as such competition persists, the members of each group involved come to view the other group in increasingly negative ways (White, 1977). They label members of the other group as enemies, view their own group as superior, and draw the boundaries between themselves and their opponents ever more firmly. As a result, what starts out as economic competition gradually turns into full-scale prejudice, with the hatred and anger this usually implies. Of course, competition between groups does not always produce such effects; but it *does* produce them in enough cases that this factor can be viewed as one important cause of prejudice.

**Social Categorization:** The tendency to divide the social world into two distinct categories: "us" and "them."

***Social Categorization: The Us-versus-Them Effect and the Ultimate Attribution Error.*** A second perspective on the origins of prejudice begins with a basic fact: We all tend to divide the social world into two distinct categories—*us* and *them* (Turner et al., 1987). We view other persons as belonging either to our own social group, usually termed the *in-group,* or to another group, an *out-group.* We make such distinctions on the basis of many dimensions, including race, religion, gender, age, ethnic background, occupation, and even the town or neighborhood where people live.

Web Link: *Little Rock Central High School—1957*

If this process of **social categorization**—the dividing of the world into distinct social categories—stopped there, it would have little connection to prejudice. Unfortunately, it does not. Sharply contrasting feelings and beliefs are usually attached to members of one's in-group and to members of various out-groups. Persons in the "us" category are viewed in favorable terms, whereas those in the "them" category are perceived negatively. Out-group members are assumed to possess more undesirable traits, are seen as being more alike (homogeneous) than members of the in-group, and are often disliked (e.g., Lambert, 1995; Linville & Fischer, 1993). This is often a very basic distinction; around the world, the word used by many different cultures to refer to themselves translates, roughly, as "human beings," whereas the word used for other groups translates as "nonhuman." In the U.S. Southwest, for instance, the Navaho refer to the long-vanished group that left impressive cliff dwellings and other ruins as the *Anasazi*—a word meaning "people who are not us." The in-group–out-group distinction also affects *attribution*—explanations for others' behaviors. We tend to attribute desirable behaviors by members of our in-group to stable, internal causes such as their admirable traits, but to attribute desirable behaviors by members of out-groups to temporary factors or to external ones such as luck (e.g., Hewstone, Bond, & Wan, 1983). This tendency to make more favorable attributions about members of one's own group than about members of other groups is sometimes referred to as the *ultimate attribution error,* for it carries the self-serving bias I described earlier into the area of intergroup relations—with potentially devastating effects.

**Figure 16.12**
**Social Learning as a Basis for Prejudice**

Parents and other adults often reward children for expressing the "right" attitudes–the attitudes they (the adults) hold. Prejudice is often transmitted to youngsters in this manner.

***The Role of Social Learning.*** A third perspective on the origins of prejudice begins with the obvious fact that such attitudes are *learned:* We acquire them from the people around us through the process of *social learning.* Prejudice emerges out of countless experiences in which children hear or observe their parents, friends, teachers, and others expressing prejudiced views. Because children want to be like these persons, and are often rewarded for expressing the "right" views (those held by adults), they quickly adopt such attitudes themselves (see Figure 16.12).

While persons with whom children interact play a key role in this process, the mass media, too, are important. If television, films, and other media present members of various social groups in an unflattering light, this may contribute to the development of prejudice on the part of children. And in fact African Americans, Asians, persons of Hispanic descent, and many other minority groups were indeed presented unflatteringly in films and on television in the United States in past decades. Fortunately, this situation has changed greatly in recent years (e.g., Weigel, Kim, & Frost, 1995); members of these groups are now being shown in a much more favorable manner. So at least one important source of prejudiced attitudes seems to be decreasing.

***Cognitive Sources of Prejudice: The Role of Stereotypes.*** The final source of prejudice we'll consider is in some ways the most disturbing. It involves the possibility that prejudice stems at least in part from basic aspects of social cognition—the ways in which we think about others and process social information (e.g., Kunda & Oleson, 1995). Several processes seem to play a role in this regard, but perhaps the most important of these involves **stereotypes.** These are cognitive frameworks consisting of knowledge and beliefs about specific social groups—frameworks suggesting that by and large, all members of these groups possess certain traits, at least to a degree (Judd, Ryan, & Park, 1991). Like other cognitive frameworks (schemas), stereotypes exert strong effects on the ways in which we process social information. For instance, information relevant to a particular stereotype is processed more quickly than information unrelated to it (e.g., Dovidio, Evans, & Tyler, 1986). Similarly, stereotypes lead us to pay attention to specific types of information—usually information consistent with the stereotypes. And when information inconsistent with stereotypes does manage to enter consciousness, it may be actively refuted or simply denied (O'Sullivan & Durso, 1984). In fact, research findings indicate that when individuals encounter persons who behave in ways contrary to stereotypes, they often perceive these persons as a new "subtype" rather than as an exception to their existing stereotype (Kunda & Oleson, 1995).

What is the relevance of such effects to prejudice? Together, they tend to make stereotypes somewhat self-confirming. Once an individual has acquired a stereotype about some social group, she or he tends to notice information that fits into this cognitive framework and to remember "facts" that are consistent with it more readily than "facts" inconsistent with it. As a result, the stereotype strengthens with time and may ultimately become invulnerable—new information or experiences simply can't change it. Indeed, given the strength of such effects, some researchers have described stereotypes as *inferential prisons*—mental frameworks from which it is difficult if not impossible to escape (Dunning & Sherman, 1997).

Given that stereotypes often lead us into serious errors and misjudgments in our social thought, why do they persist? One answer is that they are a kind of labor-saving device where social cognition is concerned (Macrae, Milne, & Bodenhausen, 1994). In other words, they allow us to make quick-and-dirty judgments about others without engaging in complex, effortful thought (e.g., Forgas & Fiedler, 1996). Another possibility is that stereotypes allow individuals to protect and bolster their social identity (e.g., Brewer, 1993). By perceiving all members of out-groups as alike, and as possessing more negative traits than members of our own in-group, we can boost our own group and our identification with it. Presumably, the greater the threat to our in-group, the stronger such tendencies, and therefore the stronger the relevant stereotypes.

**CHALLENGING PREJUDICE: TECHNIQUES THAT CAN HELP** Whatever the precise roots of prejudice, there can be no doubt that it is a negative, brutalizing force in human affairs. Reducing prejudice and countering its effects, therefore, are important tasks. What steps can be taken to reach these goals? Here is what the findings of careful research indicate.

**Stereotypes:** Cognitive frameworks suggesting that all members of specific social groups share certain characteristics.

***Breaking the Cycle of Prejudice: Learning Not to Hate.*** Bigots are clearly made, not born: They acquire their prejudices as a result of experience. Given this fact, one useful way to reduce prejudice involves discouraging the transmission of bigoted views while encouraging more positive attitudes toward others. But how can we induce parents, teachers, and other adults to encourage unbiased views among children in their care? One possibility involves calling the attention of such persons to their own prejudiced views. Few people actually see themselves as prejudiced. Instead, they view *their* negative attitudes toward others as justified. A key initial step, therefore, is convincing caregivers that the problem exists. Once they realize that it does, many are willing to modify their words and actions. True, some die-hard bigots *want* to turn children into hate-filled fanatics. Most people, though, realize that we live in a world of increasing diversity and that attitudes of tolerance are, in the long run, much more adaptive. Thus, campaigns designed to enhance awareness of prejudice and its harmful effects can sometimes be effective (Aronson, 1990).

Another argument that can be used to shift parents and other caregivers in the direction of teaching children tolerance lies in the fact that prejudice harms not only those who are its victims but those who hold such views (Dovidio & Gaertner, 1993). Growing evidence suggests that persons who are prejudiced live in a world filled with needless fears, anxieties, and anger. As result, they experience needless emotional turmoil that can adversely affect their health (Jussim, 1991). Most parents and teachers want to do everything possible to further children's well-being, so calling these potential costs to their attention may help persuade them to transmit tolerance rather than prejudice.

***Direct Intergroup Contact: The Potential Benefits of Acquaintance.*** At the present time many cities in the United States resemble a social donut: a disintegrating and crime-ridden core inhabited primarily by minority groups is surrounded by a ring of relatively affluent suburbs inhabited mainly by whites and a sprinkling of wealthy minority-group members. Needless to say, contact between the people living in these areas is minimal.

This state of affairs raises an intriguing question: Can prejudice be reduced if the degree of contact between different groups is somehow increased? The idea that it can is known as the **contact hypothesis,** and there are several good reasons for predicting that such a strategy might prove effective (Pettigrew, 1981, 1997). First, increased contact between persons from different groups can lead to a growing recognition of similarities between them. As we will see in a later section, perceived similarity can generate enhanced mutual attraction. Second, although stereotypes are resistant to change, they *can* be altered when people encounter sufficient information inconsistent with them or a sufficient number of "exceptions" to the stereotypes (Kunda & Oleson, 1995). Third, increased contact may help counter the illusion that all members of the stereotyped group are alike. For these and other reasons, it seems possible that direct intergroup contact may be one effective means of combating prejudice.

Is it? Existing evidence suggests that it is, but only when certain conditions are met: The groups interacting must be roughly equal in social status, the contact between them must involve cooperation and interdependence, the contact must permit them to get to know one another as individuals, norms favoring group equality must exist, and the persons involved must view one another as typical of their respective groups (see Figure 16.13 on page 640). When contact between initially hostile groups occurs under these conditions, prejudice between them does seem to decrease (e.g., Aronson, Bridgeman, & Geffner, 1978; Schwarzwald, Amir, & Crain, 1992). But unfortunately, such conditions are rare. Moreover, contact with persons from out-groups, especially when these groups are the target of strong prejudice, can generate negative emotions such as anxiety, discomfort, and fear of appearing to be prejudiced (Bodenhausen, 1993; Wilder, 1993). These reactions can work against

**Contact Hypothesis:** The suggestion that increased contact between members of different groups will reduce prejudice between them.

**Figure 16.13**
**Personal Contact as a Means of Reducing Prejudice**

When individuals from different groups meet under favorable circumstances (e.g., norms favoring equality exist, they get to know one another as individuals), any prejudice they formerly held may be sharply reduced. Recent findings suggest that such beneficial effects can occur even if people simply learn that other members of their own group have formed friendships with members from an out-group.

the potential benefits of contact. In view of such considerations, many social psychologists have voiced pessimism concerning the effectiveness of intergroup contact as a means of reducing prejudice.

Recently, however, a modified version of the contact hypothesis, known as the **extended contact hypothesis,** has helped to reverse these gloomy conclusions. This hypothesis suggests that direct contact between persons from different groups is not essential for reducing prejudice between them. In fact, such beneficial effects can be produced if the persons in question merely *know* that persons in their own group have formed close friendship with persons from the other group (e.g., Pettigrew, 1997; Wright et al., 1997). Knowledge of such cross-group friendship can help to reduce prejudice in several different ways. For instance, the existence of such friendship can indicate that contact with out-group members is acceptable—that the norms of the group are not so "anti-out-group" as individuals might initially have believed. Similarly, knowing that members of one's own group enjoy close friendships with members of an out-group can help to reduce anxiety about interacting with them: If someone we know enjoys such contact, why shouldn't we? Third, the existence of such cross-group friendships suggests that members of an out-group don't necessarily dislike members of our own in-group. Finally, awareness of such friendships can generate increased empathy and understanding between groups; in other words, we don't necessarily have to experience close contact with persons from an out-group to feel more positively toward them—learning that members of our own in-group have had such experiences can be sufficient.

A growing body of research evidence provides support for the accuracy of this reasoning and for the extended contact hypothesis (Pettigrew, 1997; Wright et al., 1997); so it appears that contact between persons belonging to different groups can be a highly effective means for reducing prejudice between them, especially if these contacts develop into close friendships. In sum, the English essayist Joseph Addison appears to have been correct when he wrote in 1794 that "The greatest sweetener of human life is friendship."

Audio 16.2: *Experiences with Recategorization*

**Extended Contact Hypothesis:** Suggestion that merely informing persons that members of their own group have formed close friendships with persons from an out-group can reduce prejudice.

**Recategorization:** A technique for reducing prejudice that involves inducing individuals to shift the boundary between "us" and "them" so that it now includes groups they previously viewed as "them."

***Recategorization: Resetting the Boundary Between "Us" and "Them."*** Suppose that a team from your college played against a team from a rival college: Which would be "us" and which would be "them"? The answer is obvious: Your own school's team would constitute your in-group; the other school's team would be the out-group. But now imagine that the team from the other school won many games and was chosen to represent your state in a national tournament. When it played against a team from another state, would you now perceive that team as "us" or "them"? Probably you would shift your view; now you would see this former "enemy" team as part of your own in-group. Situations like this suggest that the boundary between "us" and "them" is not fixed. On the contrary, it can be shifted so as to include—or exclude—various groups of people. This fact suggests another technique for reducing prejudice—**recategorization** (e.g., Gaertner et al., 1989, 1990). This involves somehow inducing individuals to shift the boundary between "us" and "them" so that it now includes groups they previously viewed as "them." The result: Their prejudice toward these persons is reduced.

Evidence for recategorization effects has been obtained in several studies (e.g., Dovidio et al., 1995). In one, for example, Gaertner and his colleagues (1993) investigated the attitudes of students at a multicultural high school in the United States. Students came from many different backgrounds—African American, Chinese, Hispanic, Japanese, Korean, Vietnamese, and Caucasian. More than 1,300 students completed a survey designed to measure their perceptions of the extent to which the student body at the school was a single group, consisted of distinct groups, or was composed of separate individuals. Results indicated that the greater the extent to which the students felt that they belonged to a single group, the more positive were their feelings toward persons from backgrounds other than their own. These findings, and those of several related studies (e.g., Gaertner et al., 1990), suggest that recategorization may be a very useful technique for reducing many forms of prejudice.

**REVIEW QUESTIONS**

- What are some of the major causes of prejudice?
- What techniques are effective in reducing prejudice?

## Social Influence: Changing Others' Behavior

Web Link: *Social Influence at Work*

How many times each day do others try to change your behavior? And how often do *you* try to do this to other persons? If you stop and count, you'll probably come up with a surprisingly large number; for efforts at **social influence**—attempts by one or more persons to change the attitudes or behavior of one or more others—are very common and take many different forms. We've already considered one important type of social influence—*persuasion*—in our discussion of attitudes. Here, we'll briefly examine three other important forms of influence: *conformity, compliance,* and *obedience.*

**CONFORMITY: TO GET ALONG, OFTEN, WE MUST GO ALONG** Have you ever been in a situation where you felt that you stuck out like a sore thumb? If so, you know how unpleasant the experience can be. In these circumstances we encounter powerful pressures to act or think like those around us. Such pressures toward **conformity**—toward thinking or acting like most other persons—stem from the fact that in many contexts there are spoken or unspoken rules indicating how we *should* behave. These rules are known as **social norms,** and they seem to take two basic forms (Cialdini, Kallgren, & Reno, 1991; Reno, Cialdini, & Kallgren, 1993). *Descriptive norms* tell us what most people do in a given situation; they inform us about what is generally seen as appropriate or adaptive behavior in that situation. In contrast, *injunctive norms* specify what *should* (or should not) be done, not merely what most people do. For instance, suppose you find yourself in a park where there are many people picnicking, but not one shred of paper blowing around; instead, all the trash cans are filled. The descriptive norm is clear: Most people don't litter in that park. But now suppose that you encounter a sign saying "$100 Fine for Littering." Clearly, this presents an injunctive norm: It tells you that littering is forbidden and that if you do it, you may be punished. Some injunctive norms can be detailed and precise—for example, written constitutions, athletic rule books, traffic signs. Others, in contrast, such as "Don't stare at strangers on the street," are implicit; yet they exert powerful effects on us. Whatever form they take, most social norms are obeyed by most persons most of the time (Cialdini, 1994).

Why is this the case? Apparently, for two important reasons. First, each of us has a strong desire to be liked by others. Experience teaches us that one way of

**Social Influence:** Efforts by one or more persons to change the attitudes or behavior of one or more others.

**Conformity:** A type of social influence in which individuals change their attitudes or behavior in order to adhere to existing social norms.

**Social Norms:** Rules indicating how individuals ought to behave in specific situations.

reaching this goal is to appear to be as similar to others as possible. (We'll return to this fact below, in our discussion of interpersonal attraction.) So one reason we often conform is that doing so can help us win the approval and acceptance of others. Social psychologists refer to this pattern as *normative social influence*—we conform in order to meet others' expectations and so to gain their approval. A second reason we conform is our strong desire to be right—to hold the "right" views, dress in the "right" style, and so on. Because we want to be correct about these matters, we turn to other persons for guidance as to what's appropriate, and this leads us to conform to existing social norms. This tendency is known as *informational social influence*—we conform because we depend on others for information about many aspects of the social world.

A clear illustration of such effects is provided by a study conducted by Robert S. Baron, Vandello, and Brunsman (1996) (this is another Robert Baron—not the author of this book!). These researchers showed participants a drawing of a person and then asked them to identify this person from among several other drawings in a kind of simulated eyewitness lineup. In one condition, the drawing was shown for only 0.5 seconds; this made the task quite difficult. In another condition, it was shown for 5.0 seconds, and the task was much easier. Another key aspect of the study involved the importance of making an accurate decision. Half the participants were told that the study was only preliminary, so the results were not very important. The others were told that the results were very important to the researchers.

To measure conformity, the researchers exposed participants to the answers of two assistants, who identified the *wrong* person first, before the participants made their own choice. It was predicted that when the study was described as being very important, participants would be more likely to conform to the assistants' false judgments when the task was difficult (they saw the drawing for only 0.5 seconds) than when it was easy (the drawing was shown for 5.0 seconds). When the study was described as being unimportant, however, task difficulty wouldn't matter: Conformity would be the same in both the easy and the difficult condition. As shown in Figure 16.14, this is what happened. These findings indicate that our desire to be correct can be a strong basis for conformity, especially when we feel that being accurate is quite important.

For information on how social norms can affect the lifestyles—and the personal health—of large numbers of people, please see the following **Beyond the Headlines** section.

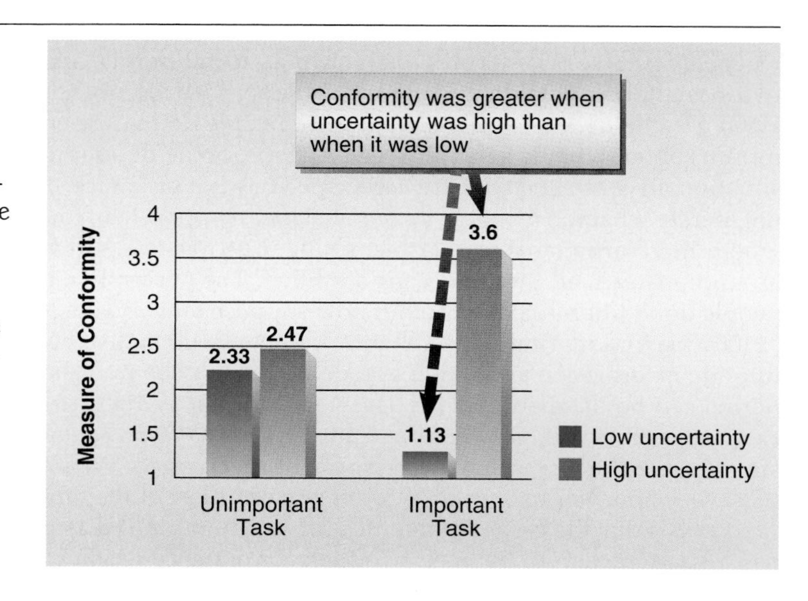


**Figure 16.14**
**Evidence for the Operation of Informational Social Influence**

When the motivation to be accurate was high (the task was described as important), research participants showed a greater tendency to conform to the judgments of others when the task was difficult than when the task was easy. When motivation to be accurate was low (the task was described as unimportant), no such differences occurred. These findings suggest that our susceptibility to informational social influence varies with several factors.
(*Source:* Based on data from Baron, Vandello, & Brunsman, 1996.)

## BEYOND the HEADLINES: As Psychologists See It

# What Happens When Social Norms Encourage a "Lifestyle to Die For"?

### Beer-Belly Blues: In New Orleans, Fat Is Where It's At, and It Shows in Grim Reports

*WALL STREET JOURNAL* (FEBRUARY 23, 1998)—Just before the start of the Mardi Gras Marathon, a runner takes a long last drag on his cigarette. . . . Midway through the race, contestants reach the "Red Dress Hydration Center" where men in drag bestow candy, beer, and X-rated cheers. At the finish there's still more free food and booze. . . . "In New Orleans, almost no one runs because they actually like running," says Coleen McEvoy, a 41-year-old banker. . . . "We run so we can eat and drink and party that much more."

Gluttony and excess are to New Orleans what pilgrims and prayer are to Mecca. . . . The city's catchphrase, "Let the Good Times Roll," has become a cliché. . . . But living the good life may also mean living the short life. Recent studies . . . have named New Orleanians the fattest people in America, the most likely to contract lung cancer, and among the shortest-lived. . . . Robert Post, a family physician, says about 75% of his female patients are obese . . . yet, few regard this as a problem. In fact, women whose weight is ideal often come to him for advice about how to gain pounds. Dr. Post says: "People here just have a very different body image than anywhere else." And fatalistic notions about health are common. Even Dr. Minyeard, the city's coroner, who often deals with premature deaths, believes that humans have little control over their life span. "When the good Lord wants you, he takes you," he says. . . . Others opt for good-humored denial. "We have complete disdain for the whole yuppie, Puritan ethos of exercise and denial," says the poet Mr. Codrescu, drinking in the French Quarter a few hours before start of a recent marathon. . . ." Most of the people I know think you shouldn't ever run—unless it's from someone."

New Orleans is famous for good food, wonderful jazz, and a relaxed lifestyle (see Figure 16.15)—but now, it seems, the city should also be famous for obesity, heart disease, and cancer. The statistics are grim: Rates for these serious ailments are much higher in New Orleans than in other large cities. Why? Psychologists would point to

**Figure 16.15**
**"Letting the Good Times Roll" Has a Downside**

Health statistics indicate that living the good life in New Orleans definitely has its costs. Rates of obesity, heart disease, and cancer are among the highest in the United States.

*social norms* as one important factor. In New Orleans, being overweight is viewed as being fully acceptable, not as something to be vigorously resisted. Similarly, other norms seem to favor a rich, high-calorie diet loaded with butter, cream, fat, and other ingredients that make people elsewhere shudder. Finally, living it up today with little worry about tomorrow seems to be a philosophy endorsed by most of the population. Given the choice of living cleanly and long or living hard and dying young, many people say they would opt for the latter.

Given such norms—and widespread acceptance of them—it 's no mystery why health statistics paint a grim picture of New Orleans. But psychologists see a silver lining in this situation: Because the population's health problems are related to lifestyle, they *can* be changed. Whether and to what extent change will occur in the years ahead, however, is anyone's guess. As one physician puts it, "For a lot of people here, every meal's a banquet and every day's a holiday, even the day you're buried." Until such attitudes change, the good times will probably continue to roll in New Orleans—and to take their toll on personal health.

## CRITICAL THINKING QUESTIONS

1. How do you think norms favoring the freewheeling lifestyle of New Orleans originated?
2. What steps could public health officials take to change these norms?
3. *Should* efforts be made to change these norms? Or is this the concern only of the people of New Orleans? Why do you hold the opinion on this issue that you do?

Audio 16.3: *Pique Technique for Generating Compliance*

**COMPLIANCE: TO ASK—SOMETIMES—IS TO RECEIVE** Suppose that you wanted someone to do something for you; how would you go about getting them to do it? If you think about this question for a moment, you'll soon realize that, like the character in Figure 16.16, you probably have quite a few tricks up your sleeve for getting the other person to say yes—for gaining what social psychologists term **compliance.** Careful study of these tactics by social psychologists, however, suggests that most of these rest on a small number of basic principles. These principles, and some of the strategies for gaining compliance related to them, are described below.

***Tactics Based on Liking: Ingratiation.*** Several tactics we use for gaining compliance from others involve causing them to have positive feelings about us. Among these, **ingratiation**—causing others to like us—is perhaps the most common (e.g., Liden & Mitchell, 1988). How do we accomplish this task? In general, in two basic ways. First, we may engage in various *self-enhancing tactics,* ones designed to enhance our personal appeal. These tactics include making ourselves as physically attractive as possible, showing friendliness toward the target person, and associating ourselves with positive events or people the target person already likes. Second, we often engage in *other-enhancing tactics,* such as flattering target persons, agreeing with them, or showing interest in them. All these tactics seem to work—they induce increased liking for us and therefore greater compliance (e.g., Wayne & Liden, 1995). However, if they are obvious or overdone, they may fail or even backfire, causing others to *dislike* us rather than to like us.

***Tactics Based on Commitment or Consistency: The Foot in the Door.*** Other tactics for getting others to say yes to our requests are based on obtaining an initial

**Figure 16.16**
**Getting Others to Say Yes: One Unusual Technique**
How do *you* get other persons to say yes to your requests—to show compliance? Your favorite tactics are probably different from the one shown here but also may be highly effective!
(*Source:* DILBERT reprinted by permission of United Feature Syndicate, Inc.)

small commitment from target persons. After making this small commitment, such persons often find it harder to refuse later requests. For instance, fund-raisers, people in sales, and other experts in gaining compliance often start with a trivial request and then, when this is granted, move on to a larger request—the one they really wanted all along. This is known as the **foot-in-the-door technique,** and the chances are good that you have encountered it or even used it yourself. Research findings indicate that it works (e.g., Beaman et al., 1983), and that one reason it does is that people want to be consistent. Once they have said yes to the first request, they feel it would be inconsistent to say no to the second.

***Tactics Based on Reciprocity: The Door in the Face.*** Reciprocity is a basic rule of social life: We tend to treat other people as they have treated us. Several tactics for gaining compliance are based on this fact. One of these, which is known as the **door-in-the-face technique,** is the opposite of the foot-in-the-door technique I just described. Instead of beginning with a small request and then escalating to a larger one, a person employing this tactic starts with a very large request. After that request is refused, a much smaller one is made—the one the requester wanted all along. The target person then feels a subtle pressure to reciprocate by saying yes. After all, the requester made a concession by scaling down the first request. This tactic is often successful, and its success seems to rest largely on the principle of reciprocity (Cialdini, 1994).

***Tactics Based on Scarcity: Playing Hard to Get.*** In general, the rarer or the harder to obtain something is, the more valuable it is perceived to be. This basic fact serves as the underlying principle for several tactics for gaining compliance. Perhaps the most popular of these is **playing hard to get**—a tactic in which individuals try to create the impression that they are very popular or very much in demand. This puts pressure on hoped-for romantic partners and employers, for example, to say yes to requests from the person using this tactic. The requests can range from "Let's get engaged" to "Pay me a high salary," but the underlying principle is the same: The persons on the receiving end feel that if they don't agree, they may lose a valuable partner or employee—so they often say yes (e.g., Williams et al., 1993).

I could go on to discuss other means for gaining compliance, but by now the main point should be clear: Many of these procedures seem to rest on basic principles well understood by psychologists. The success of top salespersons, fund-raisers, and others in getting people to say yes to their requests is, therefore, no mystery: These people are simply good applied psychologists, whether they realize it or not!

**OBEDIENCE: SOCIAL INFLUENCE BY DEMAND** Perhaps the most direct way in which one person can attempt to change the behavior of another is through *direct orders*—simply telling the target person what to do. This approach is less common than either conformity pressure or compliance tactics, but it is far from rare; it occurs in many situations in which one person has clear authority over another—in the military, in sports, and in business, to name a few. **Obedience** to the commands of sources of authority is far from surprising; military officers, coaches, and bosses have powerful means for enforcing their commands. More surprising, though, is the fact that even persons lacking in such authority can sometimes induce high levels of obedience in others. Unsettling evidence for such effects was first reported by Stanley Milgram in a series of famous—and controversial—experiments (Milgram, 1963, 1974).

In order to find out whether individuals would obey commands from a relatively powerless stranger, Milgram designed ingenious procedures very similar to those used by Arnold Buss to study human aggression (see Chapter 10). As in Buss's research, participants were told that they could deliver electric shocks to another person each time he made errors on a learning task, by means of the device shown in

**Compliance:** A form of social influence in which one or more persons acquiesce to direct requests from one or more others.

**Ingratiation:** A technique for gaining compliance by causing others to have positive feelings about us, or liking for us, before we attempt to influence them.

**Foot-in-the-Door Technique:** A technique for gaining compliance in which a small request is followed by a much larger one.

**Door-in-the-Face Technique:** A technique for gaining compliance in which a large request is followed by a smaller one.

**Playing Hard to Get:** A tactic for gaining compliance in which individuals try to create the image that they are very popular or very much in demand.

**Obedience:** A form of social influence in which one or more individuals behave in specific ways in response to direct orders from someone.

**Figure 16.17**
**Milgram's Research on Obedience**

The photo on the left shows the equipment used by Milgram in his famous studies. The photo on the right shows the experimenter and a participant (rear) attaching electrodes to the learner's (accomplice's) wrists. Results, as shown in the graph, indicated that fully 65 percent of all participants were fully obedient to the experimenter's commands—they advanced to the highest shock level, supposedly 450 volts.

(*Source:* Photos from the film *Obedience,* Copyright 1965 by Stanley Milgram: data based on Milgram, 1963.)

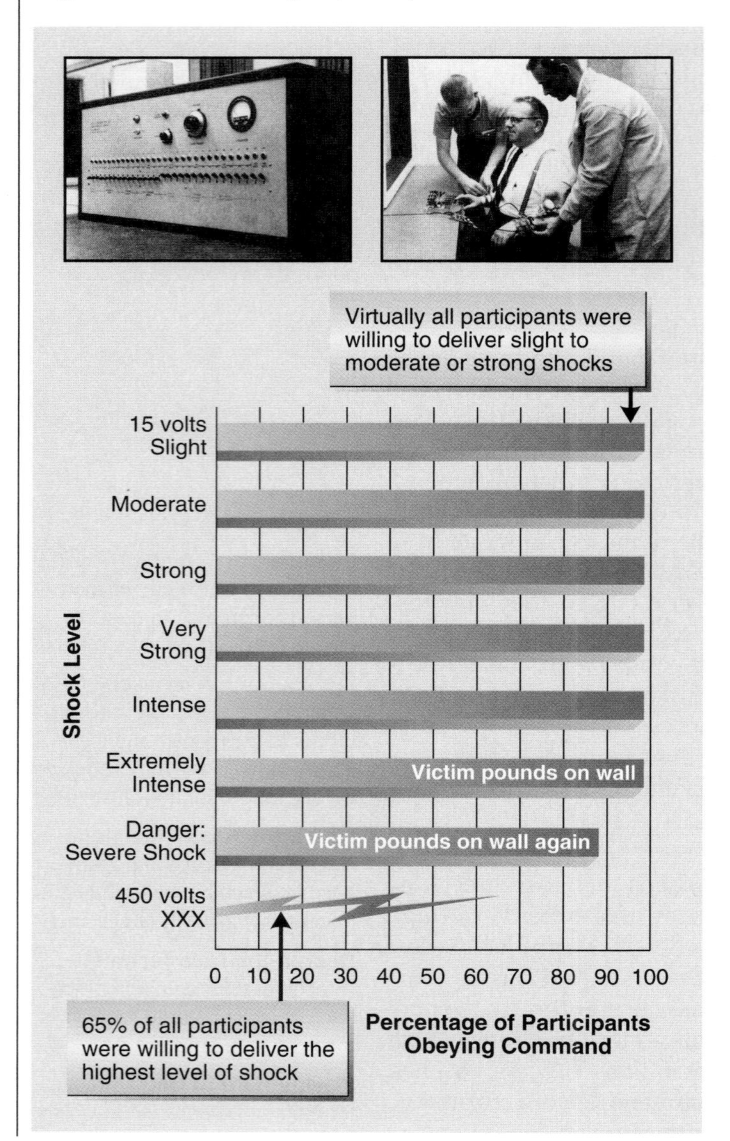


Figure 16.17. In contrast to participants in Buss's procedures, however, participants in Milgram's studies were told that they had to raise the shock level each time the learner made an error. If they refused, they were ordered to raise the level by the experimenter, in increasingly severe terms. Would they do as they were told—and thus show obedience? Given that the participants were volunteers and were paid in advance, you might predict that most would quickly refuse such "orders." In fact, though, *fully 65 percent were fully obedient,* continuing through the entire series to the final 450-volt shock (refer to Figure 16.17).

Of course, many persons protested and expressed concern over the learner's welfare. When ordered to proceed, however, most yielded to the experimenter's social influence and continued to obey. In fact, they did so even when the victim pounded on the wall and even when, later, he stopped responding altogether, as if he had passed out! Similar findings have been obtained in studies conducted around the world (Jordan, Germany, Australia) and with children as well as adults; so the tendency to obey commands from even a powerless source of authority seems to be frighteningly general in scope (e.g., Kilham & Mann, 1974; Shanab & Yahya, 1977).

Why do people show high levels of obedience in these laboratory studies—and in many tragic real-life situations too? Several factors seem to play a role. First, the experimenter began by explaining that he, not the participants, would be responsible for the learner's well-being. So, just as in many real-life situations in which soldiers or police commit atrocities, participants could say "I was only following orders" (e.g., Hans, 1992; Kelman & Hamilton, 1989). Second, the experimenter possessed clear signs of authority; and in most societies, individuals learn that persons holding authority are to be obeyed (Bushman, 1984, 1988). Third, the experimenter's commands were gradual in nature. He didn't request that participants jump to the 450-volt shock immediately; rather, he moved toward this request one step at a time. This is similar to many real-life situations in which police or military personnel are initially ordered merely to arrest or question future victims. Only later are they ordered to beat, torture, or even to kill them.

In sum, several factors probably contributed to the high levels of obedience observed in Milgram's research and related studies. Together, these factors produced a powerful force—one that most persons found difficult to resist. This does not imply that the commands of authority figures cannot be defied, however. In fact, history is filled with cases in which brave persons resisted the commands—and the power—of entrenched dictators and governments and, in the end, triumphed over them. The United States, of course, began with an act of rebellion against the British government (see Figure 16.18); and the events of

**Figure 16.18**
**Authority *Can* Be Resisted**

The United States was founded when large numbers of persons rebelled against British authority. At the start of the war, no one expected the colonists to win against the most powerful empire on earth—but they did!

the last decade in the former Soviet Union and throughout Eastern Europe provide clear illustrations of the fact that even powerful regimes can be resisted. What factors contributed to such dramatic events? Careful research on the nature of obedience indicates that important factors include clear evidence that the persons in authority are pursuing purely selfish goals (Saks, 1992); feelings of increased personal responsibility for the outcomes produced on the part of those who disobey (Hamilton, 1978); and exposure to *disobedient models*—persons who lead others by taking the first, dangerous steps (e.g., Rochat & Modigliani, 1995). When such conditions exist, persons in authority may lose their capacity to command, and may quickly find themselves on the outside looking in.

**REVIEW QUESTIONS**

- What is conformity, and what role do social norms play in it?
- What are some of the basic principles on which tactics of compliance are based?
- What is obedience, and how can it be reduced?

## Attraction and Love

Video 16.2: *Studying Flirtation*

Why do people like or dislike each other? And why, among the countless people we meet during our lives, do we have especially intense positive feelings toward only a few—the persons with whom we fall in love? Social psychologists have studied these and related questions for decades, and their findings have proved to be both revealing and—in many cases—surprising.

**INTERPERSONAL ATTRACTION: WHY WE LIKE OR DISLIKE OTHERS** Think of someone you like very much, someone you strongly dislike, and someone you'd place in the middle of this dimension. Now ask yourself this question: *Why* do you have these reactions? Revealing answers are provided by research on the nature and causes of liking and disliking, or **interpersonal attraction.**

**Interpersonal Attraction:** The extent to which we like or dislike other persons.

**Frequency-of-Exposure Effect:** The fact that the more frequently we are exposed to a given stimulus, the more—in general—we tend to like it.

***Propinquity: Nearness Makes the Heart Grow Fonder.*** Many friendships and romances start when individuals are brought into contact with one another, often by chance. We tend to form relationships with people who sit nearby in class, live in our dorm or in our neighborhood, or work in the same office. So *propinquity*—proximity or physical closeness to others—is an important factor in interpersonal attraction. In one sense, this *has* to be true, because we simply can't form relationships with people we never meet! But there seems to be more to the effects of propinquity than this. Many studies indicate that the more frequently we are exposed to a given stimulus, the more—in general—we tend to like it. This is known as the **frequency-of-exposure effect,** and it seems to extend to people as well as to objects (e.g., Moreland & Beach, 1992; Zajonc, 1968). The more often we encounter other people, the more we tend to like them, all other things being equal. Why is this so? Apparently because the more frequently we encounter a stimulus, the more familiar it becomes, and therefore the more comfortable or pleasant we feel in its presence. For this reason, propinquity is one important basis for interpersonal attraction.

***Similarity: Liking Others Who Are Like Ourselves.*** You've probably heard both of the following proverbs: "Birds of a feather flock together" and "Opposites attract." Which is true? Existing evidence leaves little room for doubt: Similarity wins hands down (see Figure 16.19) (e.g., Alicke & Largo, 1995; Byrne, 1971, 1992). Moreover, this is so whether such similarity relates to attitudes and beliefs, to personality traits, to personal habits such as drinking and smoking, to sexual preferences, to whether people accept traditional or less traditional gender roles, or even to whether people are morning or night persons (see Chapter 4) (Joiner, 1994).

Why do we like others who are similar to ourselves? The most plausible explanation is that such persons provide validation for our views or our personal characteristics (Goethals, 1986). That is, if another person agrees with us, or is similar to us in behavior, this indicates that our views, preferences, and actions are correct—or at least that they are shared by someone else. This makes us feel good, and our liking for the other person increases. Whatever the precise mechanisms involved, similarity is certainly one powerful determinant of attraction.

***Affective States: Positive Feelings as a Basis for Attraction.*** Suppose that you meet a stranger just after receiving some really good news: You got an A on an exam when you expected only a C. Will you like this person more than if you met him or her for the first time after receiving bad news that put you in a negative mood? Common sense suggests that this may be so, and research findings confirm this suggestion (e.g., Byrne & Smeaton, 1998). Positive feelings or moods—whatever their source—cause us to like others we meet while experiencing them; negative moods—again, whatever their source—cause us to dislike others we meet when we are feeling low. What do I mean by "whatever their source"? Simply this: If our positive feelings are produced by something another person says or (as we'll soon see) by the way the person looks, we will tend to like that individual. But even

**Figure 16.19**
**Similarity: One Basis for Attraction**

As this cartoon suggests, we often like persons who are similar to us in some respect.

(*Source:* DILBERT reprinted by permission of United Feature Syndicate, Inc.)

if our positive feelings have nothing to do with the person—as in the unexpectedly high grade incident, or if we meet someone in a pleasant setting (soft lights, pleasant music playing) (e.g., Baron, Rea, & Daniels, 1992)—we may still experience a boost in our liking for the person. In short, as noted in our Chapter 10 discussion of how feelings influence thought, anything that induces positive affect may lead us to like another person more than would otherwise be the case. As you might guess, such effects are most likely to occur when we are neutral to the person to start with and when we know little about him or her (e.g., Ottati & Isbell, 1996). Even so, these effects are both strong and general enough to be viewed as one important factor in interpersonal attraction.

Audio 16.4: *Evolutionary Psychology and Attractiveness*

***Physical Attractiveness: Beauty May Be Only Skin Deep, But We Pay Lots of Attention to Skin.*** Perhaps the most obvious factor affecting interpersonal attraction is *physical beauty.* Research findings indicate that, alas, we are indeed suckers for a pretty or handsome face (e.g., Collins & Zebrowitz, 1995; Sprecher & Duck, 1994). Moreover, this is true for both women and men, although the effects seem to be somewhat stronger for males (Feingold, 1990; Pierce, 1992). Why is this the case? One reason is that physically attractive people make us feel good—and, as we just saw, this can be one important ingredient in liking (Kenrick et al., 1993). Another reason, suggested by evolutionary psychology (e.g., Buss, 1999), is that physical attractiveness is associated with good health and good reproductive capacity; choosing attractive mates, therefore, is one strategy for increasing our chances of contributing our genes to the next generation.

Whatever the causes, we do tend to like physically attractive persons more than physically unattractive ones. Moreover, such effects occur across the entire life span (Singh, 1993). Indeed, even one-year-old infants show a preference for attractive rather than unattractive strangers (Langlois, Roggman, & Rieser-Danner, 1990). But what, precisely, makes other persons physically attractive? Clearly, this varies from culture to culture—but, surprisingly, less than you might guess. People tend to agree on what is or is not attractive even when judging other persons who differ from themselves in terms of race or ethnic background (Cunningham et al., 1995). So, to repeat, what makes another person physically attractive? One approach to this question has been to identify people viewed as attractive by a large majority of raters and then to see what those people have in common. Research using this approach suggests that among women, two distinct patterns of facial features are viewed as attractive: a "cute" pattern involving childlike features with large, widely spaced eyes and a small nose and chin (e.g., Meg Ryan), and a "mature" pattern involving prominent cheekbones, high eyebrows, large pupils, and a big smile; Julia Roberts fits this category well (Johnson & Oliver-Rodriguez, 1997) (see Figure 16.20).

Findings are less clear for males; but some results suggest that for men, too, there appear to be at least two clusters of facial features viewed as attractive: a youthful appearance such as that of Leonardo DiCaprio or Tom Hanks, and a mature, masculine appearance such as that of Harrison Ford or Jude Law.

**Figure 16.20**
**What Makes People Physically Attractive?**

Research findings indicate that two patterns of facial features—a "cute" pattern involving childlike features with large, widely spaced eyes and a small nose and chin and a "mature" pattern involving prominent cheekbones, high eyebrows, large pupils, and a big smile—are both considered attractive for females. Similar patterns may exist (with some differences) for males as well, although evidence on male attractiveness is less consistent.

Other, and perhaps more surprising, findings suggest that faces are perceived as attractive when they don't depart in any pronounced way from the "typical" face in their culture. To test this assertion, Langlois and Roggman (1990) constructed composite faces from photos of different individuals. They found that the more faces they used in constructing the composites, the more attractive the composites were rated as being. Why are "average" faces often judged to be attractive? Perhaps because they are more familiar than any specific face; and, as we have already seen, familiarity does often generate positive reactions.

Judgments of attractiveness do not depend solely on facial features, however. They are also influenced by other aspects of people's appearance. For example, there is currently a strong bias against being overweight in many Western cultures; in view of this fact, it's not surprising that *physique* is another important determinant of attraction, at least among young people. Persons whose physique matches the popular model—currently, slim but muscular—tend to receive higher evaluations than persons who depart from this model (e.g., Ryckman et al., 1995). However, the preferred physique may vary with social roles people play in their lives. For instance, although a rounded body build is usually down-rated, persons who show this build are rated favorably when they are described as being mothers, clowns, or (no surprise here!) Santa Claus. Similarly, reactions to males with a very thin body build who are described as being scholars are fairly positive, whereas reactions to super thin female fashion models are mixed (Ryckman et al., 1997). Such effects appear to be independent of other aspects of appearance. For example, in one ingenious study, Gardner and Tockerman (1994) used a computer to vary the apparent physique of several men and women. Results indicated that when these persons were made to appear overweight, they were rated as less attractive than when they were shown to be of normal weight or as very slim.

In sum, physical attractiveness plays an important role in our liking or disliking for others, and several features—facial and otherwise—enter into our judgments of what is and what is not attractive.

**LOVE: THE MOST INTENSE FORM OF ATTRACTION** If asked, nearly everyone living in Western cultures will report that they have been in love at some point in their lives. What do they mean by this statement? In other words, what is love, and how do we know that we are experiencing it? These questions have been pondered by countless poets, philosophers, and ordinary human beings for thousands of years—but only relatively recently has love become the subject of systematic research by psychologists (e.g., Hendrick & Hendrick, 1993). Let's take a look at the answers that have emerged from this work.

***Romantic Love: Its Nature.*** I should begin by noting that in this discussion I'll focus primarily on **romantic love**—a form of love involving feelings of strong attraction and sexual desire toward another person. However, there are several other kinds of love too, such as the love of parents for their children, or the kind of love one can observe in couples who reach their fiftieth wedding anniversary (known as *companionate love*). While these kinds of love are not the focus of as many television programs or films as passionate love, they too are recognized by psychologists as being very important (e.g., Meyers & Berscheid, 1997; Sternberg, 1988).

So what, precisely, does romantic love involve? Most experts agree that three components are central. First, before we can say that we are "in love," the idea of romantic love must be present in our culture. Not all cultures have this concept, and when it is lacking, it is difficult if not impossible for people to say, "I'm in love." Second, we must experience intense emotional arousal when in the presence of an appropriate person—someone defined by our culture as a suitable object for such feelings. And third, these feelings must be mixed with the desire to be loved by the object of our affection, coupled with fears that the relationship might end. Only if all of these conditions are present can we state with certainty, "I'm in love."

**Romantic Love:** A form of love in which feelings of strong attraction and sexual desire toward another person are dominant.

***Love: How and Why It Occurs.*** Although it is a powerful reaction—one of the strongest we ever experience—romantic love often develops quite suddenly. Many people report that falling in love feels like being struck by emotional lightning (Murray & Holmes, 1994). How can such powerful reactions develop so quickly? One explanation is that we are prepared to fall in love by our earlier relationships. As we saw in Chapter 8, infants form a powerful *attachment* to their parents or other caregivers; and such attachment is, in a sense, the forerunner of love. It prepares us for forming powerful bonds with other people when we are adults (e.g., Hatfield & Rapson, 1993).

Another, and very different, explanation for the sudden emergence of love relates to evolutionary theory (Buss, 1999; Buss & Schmitt, 1993). According to this view, through the ages the reproductive success of our species depended on two factors: (1) a desire on the part of both men and women to engage in sexual intercourse, and (2) an interest in investing the time and effort required to feed and protect offspring. According to this reasoning, love enhances both tendencies, because it leads to a lasting bond between males and females—a bond that is necessary for prolonged child care. Pure lust, which would ensure only sexual behavior, was not sufficient; so over time, human beings with a propensity to form long-term relationships—to fall in love—were more successful in passing on their genes to the next generation. The result: We are genetically programmed to fall in love.

Which of these views is more accurate? At present there is evidence for both; so the best conclusion is that both early experiences and our genetic heritage play a role in our tendency to fall in love, and so to form social relationships that sometimes last an entire lifetime.

***Love: Why It Sometimes Dies.*** ". . . And they lived happily ever after." This is the way many fairy tales—and movies from the 1940s and 1950s—end, with the characters riding off into a glowing, love-filled future. If only life could match these high hopes! Some romantic relationships do blossom into lifelong commitment; my own parents, for example, are approaching their fifty-eighth anniversary. But for many couples, the glow of love fades and leaves behind empty relationships from which one or both partners soon seek escape. In fact, for couples marrying today, the chances are less than one in three that they will remain together permanently. What causes such outcomes? Research on love and on other close relationships suggests that many factors are at work.

We have already considered one of these in our discussion of the importance of similarity in attraction. When partners discover that they are *dissimilar* in important ways, love can be weakened or even die. Such differences are often overlooked when the flames of passion run high but become increasingly obvious when these begin to subside. Also, as time passes, dissimilarities that weren't present initially may begin to emerge: The partners change and perhaps diverge. This, too, can weaken their love.

Another, and potentially serious, problem is simple *boredom.* Over time, the unchanging routines of living together may lead people to feel that they are in a rut and are missing out on the excitement of life—including, perhaps, new romantic partners (Fincham & Bradbury, 1993). Such reactions can have important consequences for the relationship.

Third, *jealousy* can undermine loving relationships. Interestingly, although both sexes experience jealousy, they differ in the pattern of such reactions. For women, the most intense jealousy is aroused by signs that a partner is transferring his emotional commitment to another woman. For men, the most intense jealousy is triggered by evidence (or suspicions) that a partner has been sexually unfaithful (Buunk, 1995).

Fourth, *changing patterns of affect*—positive and negative feelings—also play a role. Conflicts and disagreements generate negative affect, which may gradually become stronger than the positive feelings generated by love. Negative affect can be "imported" to the relationship from the outside, too: Negative emotions aroused at work are often brought home at the end of the day. Similarly, distress stemming from illness or aging parents, can also produce such effects. If enough sources of negative affect are present, partners may come to associate each other with unhappy feelings; this can ultimately destroy their love—and their relationship (e.g., Chan & Margolin, 1994).

Fifth, partly as function of early childhood experiences, people differ in their *attachment style.* As we saw in Chapter 8, some people—those who were securely attached to their caregivers—show a secure style. They feel positive about themselves and trust others. As a result, they seek interpersonal closeness and feel comfortable in relationships. Others, in contrast, were insecurely attached to their caregivers and, as adults, show a fearful–avoidant attachment style: They are negative about themselves, don't trust others, and so avoid rejection by minimizing interpersonal closeness. Other attachment patterns exist as well, but these two are sufficient for making the main point: People with a secure attachment style tend to experience happier and longer-lasting love relationships than those with a fearful–avoidant pattern (Carnelley, Pietromonaco, & Jaffe, 1996).

Finally, as relationships continue, interactions that can only be described as *self-defeating patterns of behavior* sometimes emerge. Dating couples and newlyweds frequently express positive evaluations and feelings to each other. As time passes, however, these supportive statements are sometimes replaced by negative ones: "You're so inconsiderate!" "I should never have married you!" These kinds of sentiments, either stated overtly or merely implied, become increasingly frequent. The result is that couples who began by seeing each other as perfect or nearly perfect (Murray & Holmes, 1994) and who frequently praised each other may shift to criticizing each other in the harshest terms imaginable (Miller, 1991). Further, their attributions about their partner's behavior may change. Instead of giving the partner the benefit of the doubt, they begin to attribute every action of which they disapprove or which causes them irritation as one that is done on purpose: "It's all your fault!" "You are so selfish!" When these patterns develop, love doesn't simply die; it is murdered by caustic, hurtful remarks. Figure 16.21 summarizes all of these factors.

Despite such factors, many relationships *do* succeed. Couples who stay together actively *work* at maintaining and strengthening their relationships: They practice the art of compromise, express positive feelings and sentiments toward their partners, and take each other's wishes and preferences into account on a daily basis. True, this is a lot of effort; but given the rewards of maintaining a long-term intimate relationship with someone we love and who loves us, it would appear to

**Figure 16.21**
**Why Love Fades**

The factors shown here have been found to be among the ones that contribute to the decline of love and the ending of relationships.

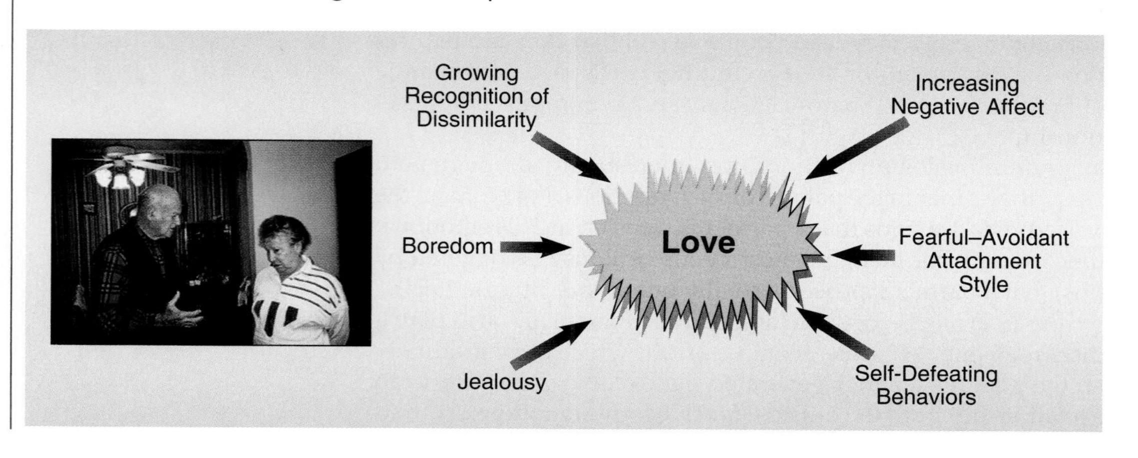

be well worthwhile. For some guidelines on how *you* can have the kind of happy, loving relationship nearly everyone desires, please see the **Making Psychology Part of Your Life** section at the end of this chapter.

**REVIEW QUESTIONS**

- What factors influence interpersonal attraction?
- Under what conditions do people conclude that they are in love?
- What factors cause love to fade and perhaps disappear?

## Leadership: One Important Group Process

Think of all the groups you have joined in your life—clubs, student associations, religious groups, teams. Do they have anything in common? Social psychologists would suggest that they do, because they probably all meet the requirements of the following definition: They consist of two or more persons who interact with one another, have shared goals, are somehow interdependent (what happens to one affects what happens to the other), and view themselves as members of the group. In other words, the groups you brought to mind are what psychologists describe as true social **groups.** In contrast, mere gatherings of people who are not interdependent, don't have common goals, and don't perceive themselves as members of a group (e.g., people standing at a bus stop or waiting outside a theater) are *not* true social groups—and probably weren't included in your list.

Why do I make this distinction? Because true social groups, in contrast to mere gatherings of people, often exert powerful effects on their members (e.g., Moreland, 1987). Such groups affect their members' task performance, the extent to which members coordinate their efforts (i.e., cooperate), the decisions members make (e.g., Henry et al., 2000), and many other processes (e.g., Witte & Davis, 1996). Obviously, we can't consider all of these effects here. As an example of how groups influence their members, therefore, I'll focus on one such effect—*leadership* (e.g., Vecchio, 1997).

For starters, try this simple demonstration with your friends. Ask them to rate themselves, on a seven-point scale ranging from 1 (very low) to 7 (very high), on leadership potential. Unless your friends are a very unusual group, here's what you'll find: Most will rate themselves as average or above on this dimension. This suggests that they view leadership very favorably. But what exactly is leadership? Definitions vary, but most psychologists view **leadership** as the process through which one member of a group (its leader) influences other group members toward attainment of shared group goals (Vecchio, 1997; Yukl, 1994). In other words, being a leader involves influence—a leader is the group member who exerts most influence within the group.

Research on leadership has long been part of social psychology, but it is also studied by other fields too (e.g., Bass, 1998). In this discussion we'll focus on two issues that have received a great deal of attention: (1) why some individuals, but not others, become leaders, and (2) the nature of charismatic leadership.

**WHO BECOMES A LEADER? THE ROLE OF TRAITS AND SITUATIONS** Are some people born to lead? Common sense suggests that this is so. Famous leaders such as Alexander the Great, Queen Elizabeth I, and Abraham Lincoln seem to differ from ordinary people in several respects. Such observations led early researchers to formulate the **great person theory of leadership:** the view that great leaders possess certain traits that set them apart from most human beings—traits that are possessed by all such leaders, no matter when or where they live (see Figure 16.22 on page 654).

**Groups:** Two or more persons who interact with one another, have shared goals, are somehow interdependent, and view themselves as members of the group.

**Leadership:** The process through which one member of a group (its leader) influences other group members toward attainment of shared goals.

**Great Person Theory of Leadership:** The view that great leaders possess certain traits that set them apart from most human beings—traits that are possessed by all such leaders, no matter when or where they live.

**Figure 16.22**
**The Great Person Theory of Leadership**

According to the great person theory, all great leaders—whenever and wherever they live—share similar characteristics. Research findings offer little support for this view, but growing evidence suggests that leaders do differ from other persons in some respects. (*Left:* Abraham Lincoln; *Right:* Queen Elizabeth I).

These are intriguing ideas, but until about 1980 research offered little support for them. Try as they might, researchers could not come up with a short list of key traits shared by all great leaders (Vecchio, 1997; Yukl, 1994). In recent years, however, this situation has changed. More sophisticated research methods, coupled with a better understanding of the basic dimensions of human personality, have led many researchers to conclude that leaders *do* differ from other persons in several important ways (Kirkpatrick & Locke, 1991). What special characteristics do leaders possess? Research findings point to the conclusion that leaders rate higher than most people on the following traits: *drive*—the desire for achievement coupled with high energy and resolution; *self-confidence; creativity;* and *leadership motivation*—the desire to be in charge and exercise authority over others. In addition, and perhaps most important of all, leaders—or at least successful ones—are high in *flexibility*—the ability to recognize what actions or approaches are required in a given situation and then to act accordingly (Zaccaro, Foti, & Kenny, 1991).

While certain traits do seem to be related to leadership, however, it is also clear that leaders do not operate in a social vacuum. On the contrary, different groups, facing different tasks and problems, seem to require different types of leaders—or at least leaders who demonstrate different styles (House & Podsakoff, 1994; Locke, 1991). So yes, traits do matter where leadership is concerned; but traits are definitely only part of the total picture, and it is misleading to conclude that all leaders, everywhere and at all times, share precisely the same traits.

**CHARISMATIC LEADERS: LEADERS WHO CHANGE THE WORLD** Have you ever seen films of John F. Kennedy? Franklin D. Roosevelt? Martin Luther King Jr.? If so, you may have noticed that there seemed to be something special about these leaders. As you listened to their speeches, you may have found yourself being moved by their words and stirred by the vigor of their presentations. You are definitely not alone in such reactions: These leaders exerted powerful effects on many millions of persons and by doing so, changed their societies. Leaders who accomplish such feats are described as being **charismatic** (or, sometimes, as *transformational*) (House & Howell, 1992; Kohl, Steers, & Terborg, 1995). How are charismatic leaders able to produce their profound effects? Apparently, through a combination of behaviors and characteristics that allow these leaders to establish a special type of relationship with followers—one in which followers have high levels of loyalty

**Charismatic** (transformational): Leaders who exert profound effects on their followers.

to the leader and a high level of enthusiasm for the leader's vision or goals. As one expert on this topic puts it, charismatic leaders somehow "make ordinary people do extraordinary things" (Conger, 1991).

But what, precisely, do charismatic leaders do to produce such effects? Research findings emphasize the importance of the following factors. First, such leaders usually propose a vision (Howell & Frost, 1989). They describe, in vivid, emotion-provoking terms, an image of what their society or group can and should become. To the extent followers accept this vision, their level of commitment to the leader and the leader's goals can be intense.

Second, charismatic leaders go beyond stating a dream or vision: They also offer a route for reaching it. They tell their followers, in straightforward terms, how to get from here to there. This too seems to be crucial, for a vision that seems out of reach is unlikely to motivate people to work to attain it.

Third, charismatic leaders engage in *framing* (Conger, 1991): They define the goals for their group in a way that gives extra meaning and purpose to the goals and to the actions needed to attain them. A clear illustration of such framing is provided by the story of two stonecutters working on a cathedral in the Middle Ages. When asked what they were doing, one replied, "Cutting this stone, of course." The other answered, "Building the world's most beautiful temple to the glory of God." Which person would be likely to work harder and, perhaps, to do "extraordinary things"? The answer is obvious—and it is also clear that any leader who can induce such thinking in her or his followers can also have profound effects upon them.

Other behaviors shown by charismatic leaders include high levels of self-confidence, a high degree of concern for followers' needs, an excellent communication style, and a stirring personal style (House, Spangler, & Woycke, 1991). Finally, research findings emphasize the importance of acts of *self-sacrifice* by charismatic leaders—such leaders give up important personal benefits (wealth, status, convenience) for the good of the group and for the sake of their vision (e.g., Shamir, House, & Arthur, 1993). Faced with such self-sacrifice, followers conclude that the leader is sincere and is acting on the basis of principle, and come to view this person as charismatic. These perceptions, in turn, enhance the leader's influence (e.g., Yorges, Wiss, & Strickland, 1999). In sum, charisma is not as mysterious as many people assume. Rather, it rests firmly on principles and processes well understood by social psychologists. (See Figure 16.23 for a summary of the factors that play a role in leaders' charisma.)

**Figure 16.23**
**The Bases of Charisma**

The powerful impact *charismatic leaders* exert on their followers seems to stem, at least in part, from the factors summarized here.

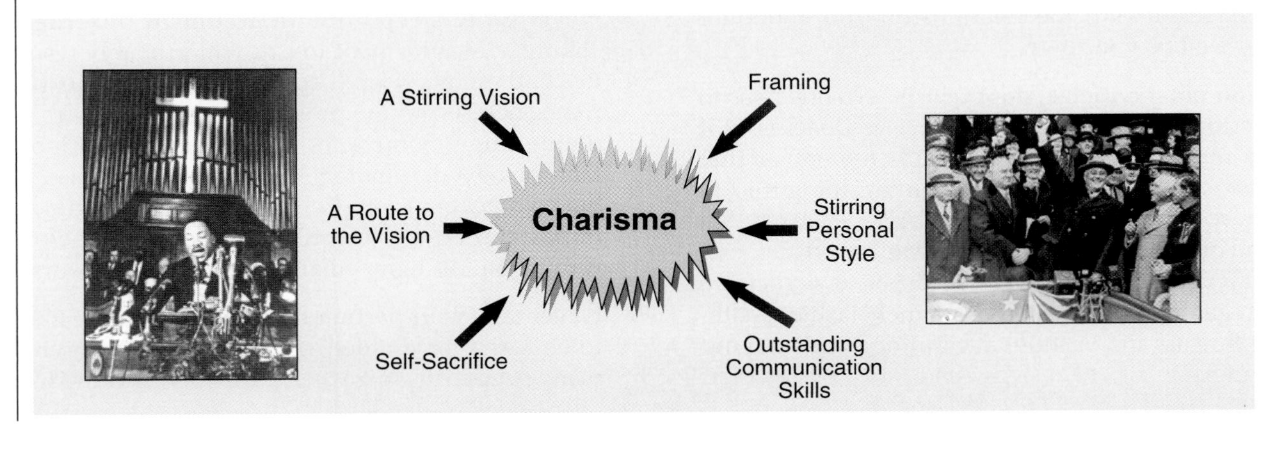

**REVIEW QUESTIONS**

- What are social groups?
- What is leadership?
- What factors play a role in leaders' charisma?

*Food for Thought*

Can you name any great leaders in the world today? If not, why do you think there are so few outstanding leaders at the present time?

# Making Psychology Part of Your Life

## Some Guidelines for Having a Happy Romantic Relationship

Nearly everyone lists "having a happy romantic relationship" as one of their life goals. Most of us recognize that playing the field is fun when we are young, but that settling down with someone we love, and who loves us, is one of the true foundations of long-term happiness. Yet, as we have already seen, a large proportion of marriages and romances fail. How can you increase the odds that your own relationship will be a happy one? Research suggests that the following steps are very helpful ones:

1. **Never both be angry at the same time.** One basic finding concerning the interface between emotions and cognition is this: When emotions are strong, the ability to reason or think clearly is greatly reduced. So avoid situations in which both you and your partner are angry; the result will be a shouting match (or worse!) that can undermine your relationship.
2. **If one of you has to win an argument, let it be your mate.** Conflicts are often intensified when one side wins and then rubs this in to the other. When one side adopts a conciliatory approach, the other usually reciprocates. So don't focus on winning every argument; the relationship you endanger may well be your own.
3. **If you must criticize, do it gently.** No one likes to be criticized—to receive negative feedback. But if you must deliver such feedback, remember that there is only one rational reason for doing this: to help the other person improve. Also, research that I and other psychologists have conducted suggests that if you decide to deliver criticism, it's crucial to do it gently, considerately, in a timely fashion, without threats, and without attributing blame to your partner.
4. **Never bring up mistakes of the past.** This guideline goes along with point 3: If you must criticize your partner, focus on the present. Talking about events in the past that can no longer be changed, and which your partner may deeply regret, can generate strong negative affect and will accomplish little—except, perhaps, to make your partner resentful.
5. **At least once a day, say something kind or complimentary to your partner.** Expressions of love and approval are frequent when relationships begin, but tend to decrease over time. Yet the need of both partners for such affirmation and praise remains strong. So by all means compliment your partner at least once a day, and more often if you can.
6. **When you have done something wrong, admit it and ask for forgiveness.** The ability to admit that you are wrong is a tremendously valuable skill. And asking for forgiveness gives your partner the chance to be generous and kind. So do learn to say "I'm sorry!" and mean it; doing so can strengthen your relationship greatly.
7. **Never go to sleep with an argument unsettled.** Taking a disagreement to bed will probably result in a bad night's sleep (I speak from personal experience here!), and the problem will still be there in the morning. Sometimes it will seem less important the next day, merely because time has passed, but on other occasions the issue will seem even *more* important. So try to settle disagreements before turning out the light—that's usually the best course.
8. **Never take your partner for granted.** No one likes to be taken for granted, yet this is precisely what many people do where their partner is concerned. In

a sense, this is really weird: After all, your partner is the most important person in your life. So always put her or him first and demonstrate, both in your words and in your actions, that you really do care.

Needless to say, these guidelines do not guarantee a happy relationship. But they do relate to some of the most important pitfalls relationships face—traps that can weaken or even demolish love over time. So paying careful attention to them can be a big step in the right direction. I wish you good luck, and much happiness!

# Summary and Review

## Social Thought: Thinking about Other People

- **What is the correspondence bias?** The correspondence bias, or fundamental attribution error, is our tendency to overestimate the importance of internal causes of others' behavior.
- **What is the self-serving bias?** The self-serving bias is our tendency to attribute our own positive outcomes to internal causes but our negative outcomes to external factors—including other people.
- **Do cultural factors play a role in these forms of attributional error?** Both forms of error are stronger in individualistic than in collectivistic societies.
- **How do we deal with social information that is inconsistent with our expectations?** In general, we tend to pay greater attention to information that is inconsistent with our expectations; but we also tend to reject information that is excessively bizarre.
- **What is the optimistic bias for task completion?** The optimistic bias for task completion, or planning fallacy, is the tendency to predict that we can do more in a given amount of time than we actually can.
- **What is counterfactual thinking? How can it affect our affective states and performance?** Counterfactual thinking involves imagining "what might have been." If we imagine better outcomes than occurred, this can lead to negative affect; if we imagine worse outcomes, this can lead to positive affect. Counterfactual thinking can provide insights as to why negative outcomes occurred and so can help us enhance our future performance.
- **What are attitudes?** Attitudes are lasting evaluations of various aspects of the social world—evaluations that are stored in memory.
- **What factors were found to influence persuasion in early research?** Early research on persuasion found that the success of persuasion was strongly affected by characteristics of the sources (e.g., their expertise), characteristics of the persuasive messages (e.g., whether they were one-sided or two-sided), and characteristics of the audience.
- **What are systematic and heuristic processing, and what role do they play in attitude change?** Systematic processing involves careful consideration of message content and is quite effortful. Heuristic processing involves the use of mental shortcuts (e.g., heuristics) to process message content and requires less effort. The differences between these two modes of processing provide important insights into the processes that occur during exposure to persuasive messages.
- **What is cognitive dissonance, and how can it be reduced?** Cognitive dissonance is an unpleasant state we experience when we notice that two attitudes we hold, or our attitudes and our behavior, are somehow inconsistent. The easiest way to reduce cognitive dissonance is often to change our attitudes.
- **What is induced compliance? The less-leads-to-more effect?** Induced compliance occurs in situations where we feel compelled to say or do something inconsistent with our true attitudes. The less-leads-to-more effect refers to the fact that the weaker the reasons we have for engaging in attitude-discrepant behavior, the more likely we are to change these attitudes.
- **How can hypocrisy be used to change behavior?** Inducing individuals to focus on gaps between their behavior and their attitudes can lead them to recognize their hypocrisy and so to experience intense levels of dissonance. Such dissonance, in turn, can cause people to change their overt behavior.

### Key Terms

social psychologists, p. 619 • attribution, p. 619 • consensus, p. 619 • consistency, p. 619 • distinctiveness, p. 619 • correspondence bias, p. 621 • self-serving bias, p. 621 • social cognition, p. 624 • counterfactual thinking, p. 626 • attitudes, p. 628 • persuasion, p. 628 • systematic processing, p. 630 • central route, p. 630 • heuristic processing, p. 630 • peripheral route, p. 630 • elaboration-likelihood model (ELM), p. 630 • heuristic–systematic model, p. 630 • Likert scales, p. 631 • bogus pipeline, p. 632 • induced compliance, p. 632 • cognitive dissonance, p. 633 • less-leads-to-more effect, p. 633

### Social Behavior: Interacting with Others

- **What are some of the major causes of prejudice?** Prejudice stems from direction competition between social groups, social categorization, social learning, and cognitive factors such as stereotypes.
- **What techniques are effective in reducing prejudice?** Societies can reduce prejudice by socializing children to be tolerant of others, through increased intergroup contact, and through recategorization—shifting the boundary between "us" and "them" so as to include previously excluded groups.
- **What is conformity, and what role do social norms play in it?** Conformity is the tendency to behave like others—to act in accordance with existing social norms.
- **What are some of the basic principles on which tactics of compliance are based?** Tactics of compliance are based on the principles of liking or friendship (e.g., ingratiation), commitment or consistency (e.g., the foot-in-the-door technique), reciprocity (e.g., the door-in-the-face technique), and scarcity (e.g., playing hard to get).
- **What is obedience, and how can it be reduced?** In obedience individuals follow the commands of persons in authority. Obedience can be reduced if the persons involved realize that authorities are pursuing selfish goals, if they are exposed to disobedient models, if they take increased personal responsibility for outcomes produced.
- **What factors influence interpersonal attraction?** Among the factors that influence interpersonal attraction are propinquity, similarity, positive and negative affect, and physical attractiveness.
- **Under what conditions do people conclude that they are in love?** Individuals conclude that they are in love when their culture has the concept of romantic love, when they experience strong emotional arousal in the presence of a person defined as appropriate for love by their culture, and when they also desire to be loved by that person.
- **What factors cause love to fade and perhaps disappear?** Love can be weakened by such factors as jealousy, increasing dissimilarity, boredom, increasing levels of negative affect, and a pattern in which negative statements and attributions replace positive ones.
- **What are social groups?** Social groups consist of two or more persons who interact, have shared goals, are interdependent, and perceive themselves as part of a group.
- **What is leadership?** Leadership is the process through which one member of a group (its leader) influences other group members toward attainment of shared group goals.
- **What factors play a role in leaders' charisma?** Factors that contribute to charisma include a stirring vision, a plan for realizing that vision, effective framing, high interpersonal and communication skills, and visible self-sacrifice.

#### Key Terms

prejudice, p. 636 • realistic conflict theory, p. 636 • social categorization, p. 637 • stereotypes, p. 638 • contact hypothesis, p. 639 • extended contact hypothesis, p. 640 • recategorization, p. 640 • social influence, p. 641 • conformity, p. 641 • social norms, p. 641 • compliance, p. 645 • ingratiation, p. 645 • foot-in-the-door technique, p. 645 • door-in-the-face technique, p. 645 • playing hard to get, p. 645 • obedience, p. 645 • interpersonal attraction, p. 647 • frequency-of-exposure effect, p. 648 • romantic love, p. 650 • groups, p. 653 • leadership, p. 653 • great person theory of leadership, p. 653 • charismatic, p. 654

## Critical Thinking Questions

### Appraisal

Social thought and social interaction occur together in everyday life. Do you think that studying them separately makes sense? Or should they be studied together, as they occur in most situations?

### Controversy

Do you think that racial, ethnic, and religious prejudices can ever be completely eliminated? Or do our human tendencies to divide the social world into "us" and "them" and to rely on stereotypes mean that such attitudes will always exist?

### Making Psychology Part of Your Life

Now that you know what psychologists have discovered about the factors that cause us to like or dislike other persons, can you think of any ways in which you might be able to put this knowledge to use? In what kinds of situations would you be most likely to do this—to engage in efforts to increase others' liking for you? How would you benefit from such efforts if they succeeded?

*Appendix*

# Statistics: Uses—and Potential Abuses

At many points in this text, I've noted that one benefit you should gain from your first course in psychology is the ability to think about human behavior in a new way. This appendix will expand on that theme by offering a basic introduction to one essential aspect of psychological thinking: statistics.

What does this special form of mathematics have to do with psychology or thinking like a psychologist? The answer involves the fact that all fields of science require two major types of tools. First, scientists need various kinds of equipment to gather the data they seek. Obviously, this equipment differs from field to field.

Second, all scientists need some means for interpreting the findings of their research—for determining the *meaning* of the information they have acquired and its relationship to important theories in their field. Again, this varies from one science to another. In most cases, though, some type of mathematics is involved. To understand the findings of their research, psychologists make use of *statistics*—or, more accurately, *statistical analysis* of the data they collect.

As you'll soon see, statistics are a flexible tool and can be used for many different purposes. In psychology, however, they are usually employed to accomplish one or more of the following tasks: (1) *summarizing* or *describing* large amounts of data; (2) *comparing* individuals or groups of individuals in various ways; (3) determining whether certain aspects of behavior are *related* (whether they vary together in a systematic manner); and (4) *predicting* future behavior from current information.

## Descriptive Statistics: Summarizing Data

Suppose that a psychologist conducts an experiment concerned with the effects of staring at others in public places. The procedures of the study are simple. He stares at people in stores, airports, and a variety of other locations, and he records the number of seconds until they look away—or until they approach to make him stop! After carrying out these procedures twenty times, he obtains the data shown in Table A.1 on page 660. Presented in this form, the scores seem meaningless. If they are grouped together in the manner shown in Figure A.1 on page 660, however, a much clearer picture emerges. Now we can see at a glance that the most frequent score is about 4 seconds; that fewer people look away after 3 or 5 seconds; and that even fewer look away very quickly (after 2 seconds) or after a longer delay (6 seconds). This graph presents a **frequency distribution:** It indicates the number of times each score occurs within an entire set of scores.

**Frequency Distribution:** The frequency with which each score occurs within an entire distribution of scores.

**Central Tendency:** The middle (center) of a distribution of scores.

**Dispersion:** The extent to which scores in a distribution spread out or vary around the center.

**Descriptive Statistics:** Statistics that summarize the major characteristics of an array of scores.

**Mean:** A measure of central tendency derived by adding all scores and dividing by the number of scores.

TABLE A.1

## Raw Data from a Simple Experiment

When a psychologist stares at strangers in a public place, these persons either look away or approach him in the number of seconds shown. Note that more people look away or approach after 4 seconds than any other value.

| | Seconds | | Seconds |
|---|---|---|---|
| Person 1 | 4 | Person 11 | 4 |
| Person 2 | 4 | Person 12 | 4 |
| Person 3 | 1 | Person 13 | 3 |
| Person 4 | 4 | Person 14 | 3 |
| Person 5 | 3 | Person 15 | 5 |
| Person 6 | 2 | Person 16 | 4 |
| Person 7 | 5 | Person 17 | 4 |
| Person 8 | 3 | Person 18 | 2 |
| Person 9 | 6 | Person 19 | 6 |
| Person 10 | 5 | Person 20 | 5 |

A graph such as the one in Figure A.1 provides a rough idea of the way a set of scores is distributed. In science, however, a rough idea is not sufficient: More precision is required. In particular, it would be useful to have an index of (1) the middle score of the distribution of scores (their **central tendency**) and (2) the extent to

**Figure A.1**
**A Frequency Distribution**

In a frequency distribution, scores are grouped together according to the number of times each occurs. This one suggests that most persons react to being stared at within about 4 seconds.

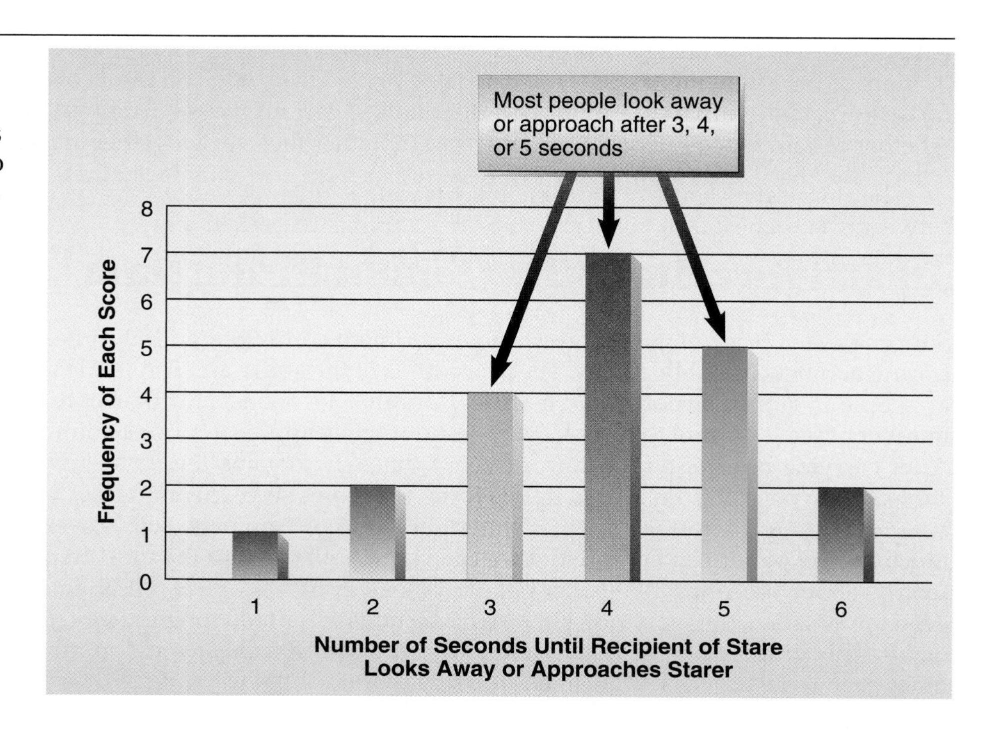

which the scores spread out around this point (their **dispersion**). Such measures are provided by **descriptive statistics.**

**Mode:** A measure of central tendency indicating the most frequent score in an array of scores.

**Median:** A measure of central tendency indicating the midpoint of an array of scores.

**Range:** The difference between the highest and lowest scores in a distribution of scores.

**Variance:** A measure of dispersion reflecting the average squared distance between each score and the mean.

**Standard Deviation:** A measure of dispersion reflecting the average distance between each score and the mean.

## Measures of Central Tendency: Finding the Center

You are already familiar with one important measure of central tendency: the **mean,** or average. We calculate a mean by adding all scores and then dividing by the total number of scores. The mean represents the typical score in a distribution and in this respect is often quite useful. Sometimes, though, it can be misleading. This is because the mean can be strongly affected by one or a few extreme scores. To see why this is so, consider the following example. Ten families live on a block. The number of children in each family is shown in Table A.2. Adding these numbers together and dividing by ten yields a mean of four. Yet, as you can see, *not one family actually has four children.* Most have none or two, but one has eight and another has nineteen.

In cases such as this, it is better to refer to other measures of central tendency. One of these is the **mode**—the most frequently occurring score. As you can see, the mode of the data in Table A.2 is 2: More families have two children than have any other number. Another useful measure of central tendency is the **median**—the midpoint of the distribution. Fifty percent of the scores fall at or above the median, while 50 percent fall at or below this value. Returning to the data in Table A.2, the median also happens to be 2: Half the scores fall at or below this value, while half fall at or above it.

As you can readily see, both the mode and the median provide more accurate descriptions of the data than does the mean in this particular example. However, this is true only in instances where extreme scores distort the mean. In fact, there is no single rule for choosing among these measures. The decision to employ one over the others should be made only after careful study of frequency distributions such as the one shown in Figure A.1.

**TABLE A.2**

**How the Mean Can Sometimes Be Misleading**

Ten families have a total of 40 children among them. The mean is 4.0; but, as you can see, not one family has this number of children. This illustrates the fact that the mean, while a useful measure of central tendency, can be distorted by a few extreme scores.

| | Number of Children |
|---|---|
| Family 1 | 0 |
| Family 2 | 0 |
| Family 3 | 2 |
| Family 4 | 2 |
| Family 5 | 2 |
| Family 6 | 2 |
| Family 7 | 2 |
| Family 8 | 3 |
| Family 9 | 19 |
| Family 10 | 8 |

Total = 40 children
Mean = 40/10 = 4.0

## Measures of Dispersion: Assessing the Spread

The mean, median, and mode each tell us something about the center of a distribution, but they provide no indication of its shape. Are the scores bunched together? Do they spread out over a wide range? This issue is addressed by measures of *dispersion.*

The simplest measure of dispersion is the **range**—the difference between the highest and lowest scores. For example, the range for the data in Table A.2 is 19 (19 – 0 = 19). Although the range provides some idea of the extent to which scores vary, it does not indicate how much the scores spread out around the center. Information on this important issue is provided by the *variance* and *standard deviation.*

The **variance** provides a measure of the average distance between scores in a distribution and the mean. It indicates the extent to which, on average, the scores depart from (vary around) the mean. Actually, the variance refers to the average *squared* distance of the scores from the mean; squaring eliminates negative numbers. The **standard deviation** then takes account of this operation of squaring by calculating the square root of the variance. So the standard deviation represents the average distance between scores and the mean in any distribution. The larger the standard deviation, the more the scores are spread out around the center of the distribution.

**Normal Curve:** A symmetrical, bell-shaped frequency distribution. Most scores are found near the middle, and fewer and fewer occur toward the extremes. Many psychological characteristics are distributed in this manner.

## The Normal Curve: Putting Descriptive Statistics to Work

Despite the inclusion of several examples, this discussion so far has been somewhat abstract. As a result, it may have left you wondering about the following question: Just what do descriptive statistics have to do with understanding human behavior or thinking like a psychologist? One important answer involves their relationship to a special type of frequency distribution known as the **normal curve.**

While you may never have seen this term before, you are probably quite familiar with the concept it describes. Consider the following characteristics: height, size of vocabulary, strength of motivation to attain success. Suppose you obtained measurements of each among thousands of persons. What would be the shape of each of these distributions? If you guessed that they would all take the form shown in Figure A.2, you are correct. In fact, on each dimension most scores would pile up in the middle, and fewer and fewer scores would occur farther away from this value.

What does the normal curve have to do with the use of descriptive statistics? A great deal. One key property of the normal curve is as follows: Specific proportions of the scores within it are contained in certain areas of the curve; moreover, these portions can be defined in terms of the standard deviation of all of the scores. Therefore, once we know the mean of a normal distribution and its standard deviation, we can determine the relative standing of any specific score within it. Perhaps a concrete example will help clarify both the nature and the value of this relationship.

Figure A.3 presents a normal distribution with a mean of 5.0 and a standard deviation of 1.0. Let's assume that the scores shown are those on a test of mathematical aptitude. Suppose that we now encounter an individual with a score of 7.0. We know that she is high on this characteristic, but *how* high? On the basis of descriptive statistics—the mean and standard deviation—plus the properties of the normal curve, we can tell. Statisticians have found that 68 percent of the scores in a normal distribution fall within one standard deviation of the mean, either above or below it. Similarly, fully 96 percent of the scores fall within two standard deviations of the mean. Given this information, we can conclude that a score of 7 on this test is very high indeed: Only 2 percent of persons taking the test attain a score equal to or higher than this one (refer to Figure A.3).

In a similar manner, descriptive statistics can be used to interpret scores in any other distribution, providing it approaches the normal curve in form. Because a

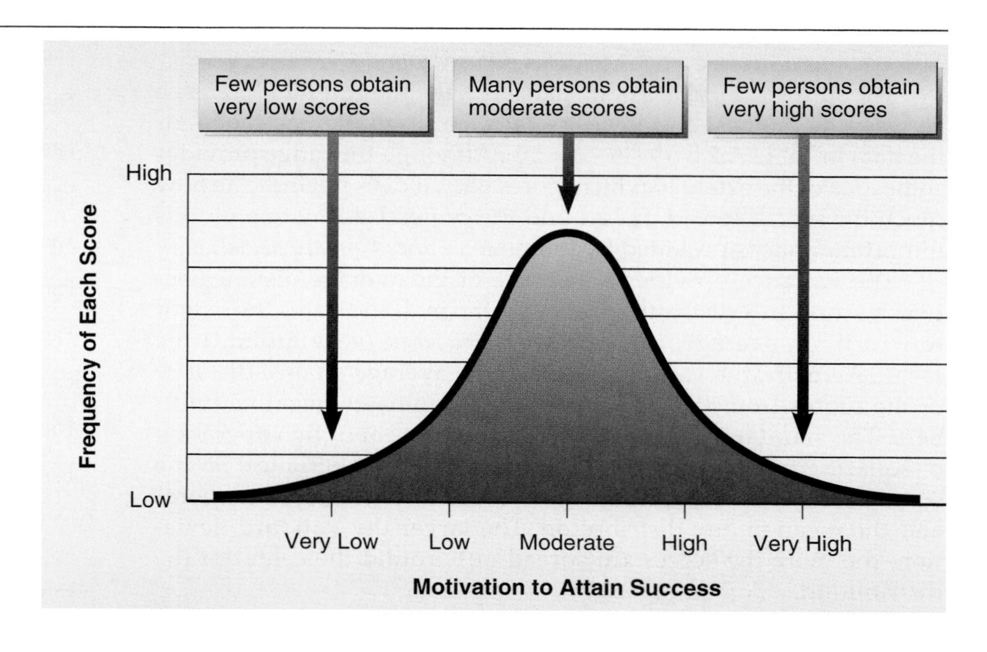


**Figure A.2**
**The Normal Curve**

On many dimensions relating to behavior, scores show the kind of frequency distribution illustrated here: the *normal curve.* Most scores pile up in the middle, and fewer and fewer occur toward the extremes. Thus, most people are found to be average height, to have average vocabularies, and to show average desire for success.

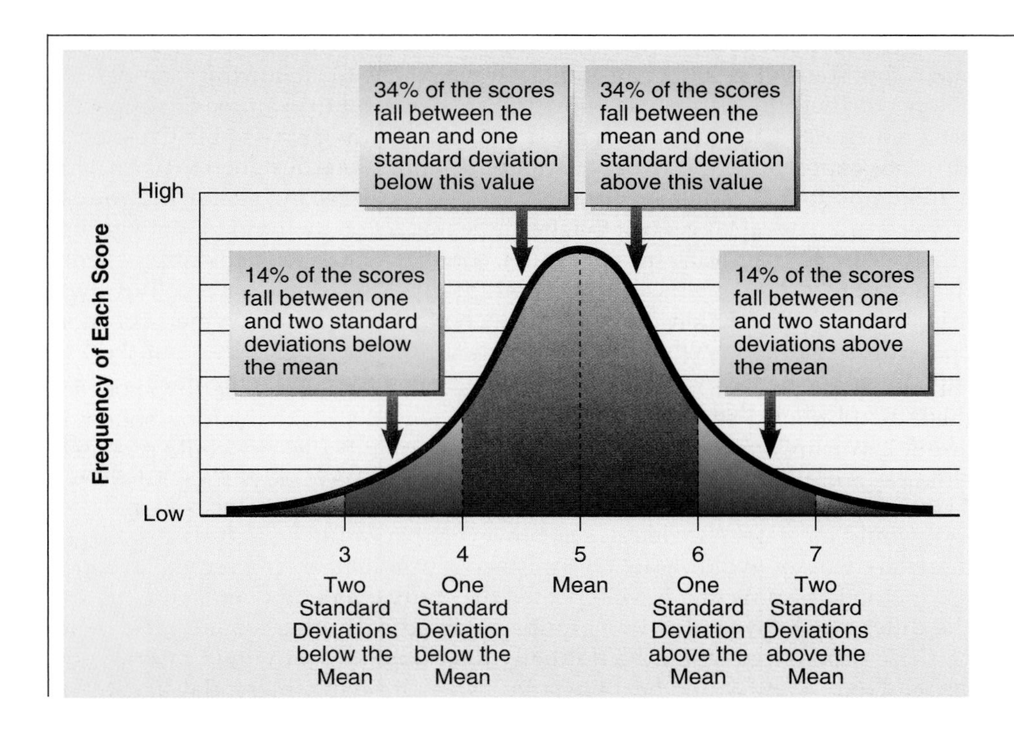


**Figure A.3**
**Interpreting Scores by Means of the Normal Distribution**

Sixty-eight percent of the scores in a normal distribution fall within one standard deviation of the mean (above or below it). Similarly, fully 96 percent of the scores fall within two standard deviations of the mean. Thus, on a test with a mean of 5.0 and a standard deviation of 1.0, only 2 percent of persons attain a score of 7.0 or higher.

vast array of psychological characteristics and behaviors do seem to be distributed in this manner, we can readily determine an individual's relative standing on any of these dimensions from just two pieces of information: the mean of all scores in the distribution and the standard deviation.

For one final example, imagine that your first psychology test contains fifty multiple-choice items. You obtain a score of 40. Did you do well or poorly? If your instructor provides two additional pieces of information—the mean of all the scores in the class and the standard deviation—you can tell. Suppose the mean is 35, and the standard deviation is 2.50. The mean indicates that most people got a lower score than you did. The relatively small standard deviation indicates that most scores were quite close to the mean—only about twice this distance *above* the mean. Further—and here is a key point—this conclusion would be accurate whether there were 30, 100, or 500 students in the class, assuming the mean and standard deviation remained unchanged. It is precisely this type of efficiency that makes descriptive statistics so useful for summarizing even large amounts of information.

## Inferential Statistics: Determining Whether Differences Are or Are Not Real

Throughout this book, the results of many experiments have been described. When these studies were discussed, differences between various conditions or groups were often mentioned. For example, we saw that participants exposed to one set of conditions or one level of an independent variable behaved differently from participants exposed to another set of conditions or another level of an independent variable. How did we know that such differences were real ones rather than differences that might have occurred by chance alone? The answer involves the use of **inferential statistics.** These methods allow us to reach conclusions about just this issue: whether a difference we have actually observed is large enough for us to conclude (to

**Inferential Statistics:** Statistical procedures that permit us to determine whether differences between individuals or groups are ones that are likely or unlikely to have occurred by chance.

*infer*) that it is indeed a real or *significant* one. The logic behind inferential statistics is complex, but some of its key points can be illustrated by the following example.

Suppose that a psychologist conducts an experiment to examine the impact of mood on memory. (As you may recall, such research was discussed in Chapter 6.) To do so, he exposes one group of participants to conditions designed to place them in a good mood: They watch a very funny videotape. A second group, in contrast, is exposed to a neutral tape—one that has little impact on their mood. Both groups are then asked to memorize lists of words, some of which refer to happy events, such as "party" and "success." Later, both groups are tested for recall of these words. Results indicate that those who watched the funny tape remember more happy words than those who watched the neutral tape; in fact, those in the first group remember 12 happy words, whereas those in the second remember only 8—a difference of 4.0. Is this difference a real one?

One way of answering this question would be to repeat the study over and over again. If a difference in favor of the happy group were obtained consistently, our confidence that it is indeed real (and perhaps due to differences in subjects' mood) would increase. As you can see, however, this would be a costly procedure. Is there any way of avoiding it? One answer is provided by inferential statistics. These methods assume that if we repeated the study over and over again, the size of the difference between the two groups obtained each time would vary; moreover, these differences would be normally distributed. Most would fall near the mean, and only a few would be quite large. When applying inferential statistics to the interpretation of psychological research, we make a very conservative assumption: We begin by assuming that there is no difference between the groups—that the mean of this distribution is zero. Through methods that are beyond the scope of this discussion, we then estimate the size of the standard deviation. Once we do, we can readily evaluate the difference obtained in an actual study. If an observed difference is large enough that it would occur by chance only 5 percent (or less) of the time, we can view it as significant. For example, assume that in the study we have been discussing, this standard deviation (a standard deviation of mean differences) is 2.0. This indicates that the difference we observed (4.0) is two standard deviations above the expected mean of zero (see Figure A.4). As you'll re-

**Figure A.4**
**Using Inferential Statistics to Determine Whether an Observed Difference Is a Real One**

Two groups in a study concerned with the effects of mood on memory attain mean scores of 12.0 and 8.0, respectively. Is this difference significant (real)? Through inferential statistics, we can tell. If the study were repeated over and over, and the two groups did not really differ, the mean difference in their scores would be zero. Assuming that the standard deviation is 2.0, we know that the probability of a difference this large is very small—less than 2 percent. In view of this fact, we conclude that this finding is indeed significant.

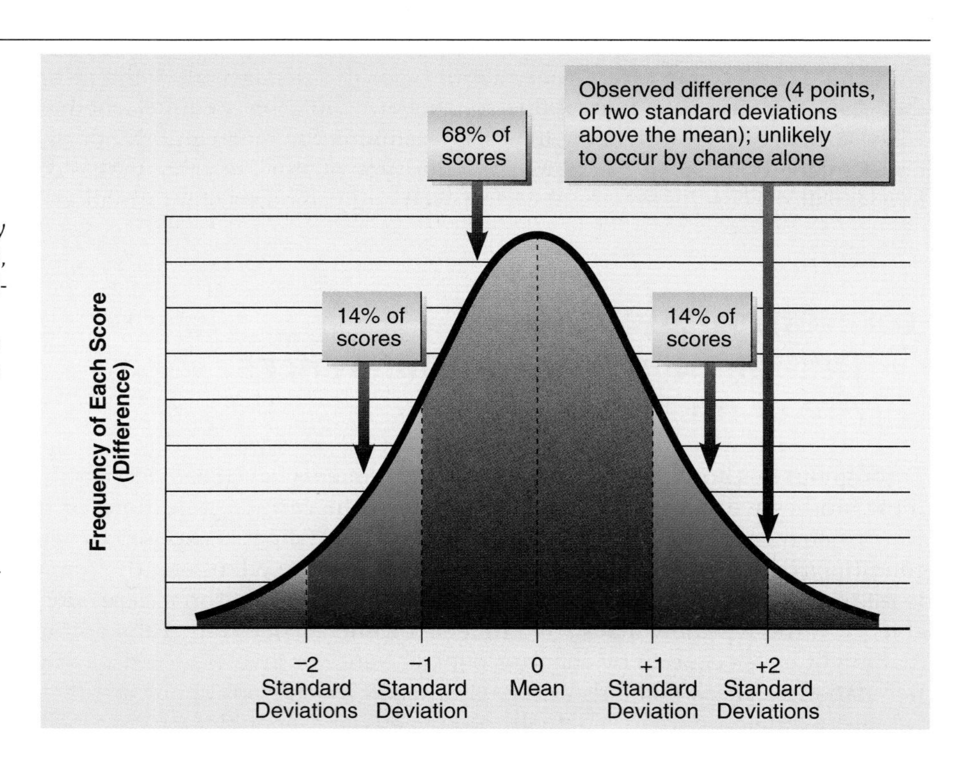

call from our discussion of the normal curve, this means that the difference is quite large and would occur by chance less than 2 percent of the time. Our conclusion: The difference between the two groups in our study is *probably* real. Thus, mood does indeed seem to affect memory.

Please note the word *probably* above. Since the tails of the normal curve never entirely level off, there is always some chance—no matter how slight—that even a huge observed difference is due to chance. If we accept a difference that really occurred by chance as being real, we make what statisticians describe as a Type I error. If, in contrast, we interpret a real difference as being one that occurred by chance, we make a Type II error. Clearly, both kinds can lead us to false conclusions about the findings of a research project.

## Correlation and Prediction

Does crime increase as temperatures rise? Does a candidate's chance of winning elections increase with his or her height? Does our ability to solve certain kinds of problems change with age? Psychologists are often interested in whether two or more variables are *related,* so that changes in one are associated with changes in the other. Remember: This is quite different from the issue of whether changes in one variable *cause* changes in another.

In order to answer such questions, we must gather information on each variable. For example, assume that we wanted to find out if political fortunes are indeed related to height. To do so, we might obtain information on (1) the heights of hundreds of candidates and (2) the percentage of votes they obtained in recent elections. Then we'd plot these two variables, heights against votes, by entering a single point for each candidate on a graph such as those in Figure A.5. As you can see, the first graph in this figure indicates that tallness is positively associated with political success; the second points to the opposite conclusion; and the third suggests that there is no relationship at all between height and political popularity.

**Figure A.5**
**Illustrating Relationships through Scatterplots**

Is height related to success in politics? To find out, we measure the heights of many candidates and obtain records of the percentage of votes they obtained. We then plot heights against votes in a scatterplot. Plot A indicates a positive relationship between height and political success. Plot B indicates a negative relationship between these variables. Plot C suggests that there is no relationship between these variables.

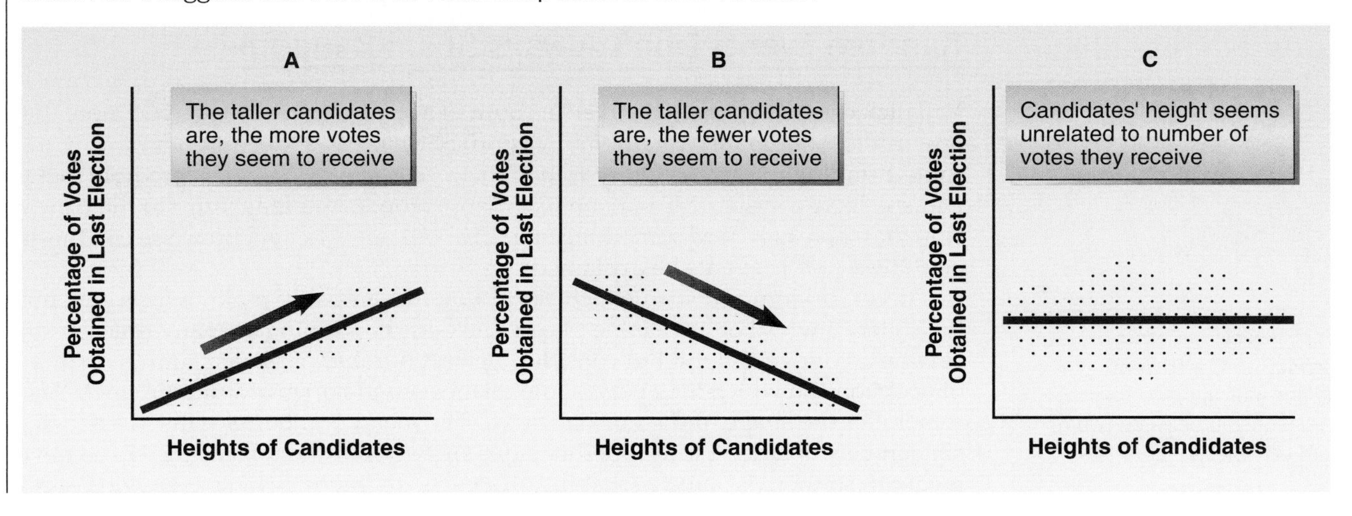

While such graphs, known as *scatterplots,* are useful, they don't by themselves provide a precise index of the strength of the relationship between two or more variables. To obtain such an index, we often calculate a statistic known as a **correlation coefficient.** Such coefficients can range from –1.00 to +1.00. Positive numbers indicate that as one variable increases, so does the other. Negative numbers indicate that as one factor increases, the other decreases. The greater the departure from 0.00 in either direction, the stronger the relationship between the two variables. Thus, a correlation of +0.80 is stronger than one of +0.39. Similarly, a correlation of –0.76 is stronger than one of –0.51.

Once we've computed a correlation coefficient, we can test its significance; we can determine whether it is large enough to be viewed as unlikely to occur by chance alone. Further, we can also compare correlations to determine if, in fact, one is significantly larger or smaller than another.

In addition to determining the extent to which two or more variables are related, statistical procedures also exist for determining the degree to which a specific variable can be *predicted* from one or more others. These methods of *regression analysis* are complex, but they are of great practical value. Knowing the extent to which individuals' performance can be predicted from currently available information—such as grades, past performance, or scores on psychological tests—can aid companies, schools, and many other organizations in selecting the best persons for employment or educational opportunities.

## The Misuse of Statistics: Numbers Don't Lie . . . or Do They?

A public figure once remarked that there are three kinds of lies: "lies, damned lies, and statistics"! By this he meant that statistics are often used for purposes quite different from the ones we've discussed here. Instead of helping us understand scientific data, interpret test scores, or make predictions about behavior, statistics are sometimes employed to confuse, deceive, or mislead their intended victims. To make matters worse, in the wrong hands statistics can be quite effective in this role. The reason for such success lies in the fact that most of us firmly accept another popular saying: "Numbers don't lie." Thus, when confronted with what appear to be mathematical data and facts, we surrender our usual skepticism and readily accept what we are told. Because the costs of doing so can be quite high, let's conclude this brief discussion of statistics by examining some of the more common—and blatant—*mis*uses of statistics.

### Random Events Don't Always Seem Random

You pick up the paper and read an account of a young woman who won more than one million dollars at a gambling casino. She placed sixteen bets in a row at a roulette table and won on every spin of the wheel. Why? Was she incredibly lucky? Did she have a system? If you are like many people, you may jump to the conclusion that there is indeed something special about her. After all, how else can this incredible series of events be explained?

If you do jump to such conclusions, you are probably making a serious mistake. Here's why. For any single player, the odds of winning so many times in succession are indeed slight. But consider the vast number of players and the number of occasions on which they play; some casinos remain open around the clock. Also, remember the shape of the normal curve. The mean number of wins in a series of sixteen bets is indeed low—-perhaps one or two. But the tails of the curve never level off, so there is some probability, however slight, of even sixteen wins occur-

**Correlation Coefficient:** A statistic indicating the degree of relationship between two or more variables.

ring in a row. In short, even events that would be expected to occur very rarely by chance *do* occur. The moral is clear: Don't overinterpret events that seem, at first glance, to border on impossible. They may actually be rare chance occurrences with no special significance of their own.

## Large Samples Provide a Better Basis for Reaching Conclusions Than Small Ones

Many television commercials take the following form. A single consumer is asked to compare three unlabeled brands of facial tissue or to compare the whiteness of three loads of wash. She then makes the "right" choice, selecting the sponsor's product as softest, brightest, or whitest. The commercial ends with a statement of the following type: "Here's proof. Our brand is the one most shoppers prefer." Should you take such evidence seriously? I doubt it. In most cases, it is not possible to reach firm statistical conclusions on the basis of the reactions of a single individual, or even of several individuals. Rather, a much larger number of participants is necessary. After watching such a commercial, then, you should ask what would happen if the same procedures were repeated with 20, 50, or 500 shoppers. Would the sponsor's brand actually be chosen significantly more often than the others? The commercials leave the impression that it would; but, as I'm sure you now realize, jumping to such conclusions is risky. So be skeptical of claims based on very small samples. They are on shaky grounds at best, and they may be purposely designed to be misleading.

## Unbiased Samples Provide a Better Basis for Reaching Conclusions Than Biased Ones

Here's another popular type of commercial, and another common misuse of statistics. An announcer, usually dressed in a white coat, states: "Three out of four dentists surveyed recommend *Jawbreak* sugarless gum." At first glance, the meaning of this message seems clear: Most dentists prefer that their patients chew a specific brand of gum. But look more closely; there's an important catch. Notice that the announcer says, "Three out of four dentists *surveyed. . . .*" Who were these people? A fair and representative sample of all dentists? Major stockholders in the Jawbreak company? Close relatives of the person holding the patent on this product? From the information given, it's impossible to tell. To the extent these or many other possibilities are true, the dentists surveyed represent a *biased* sample; they are *not* representative of the population to which the sponsor wishes us to generalize: all dentists.

So whenever you encounter claims about the results of a survey, ask two questions: (1) Who were the persons surveyed? (2) How were they chosen? If these questions can't be answered to your satisfaction, be on guard: Someone may be trying to mislead you.

## Unexpressed Comparisons Are Often Meaningless

Another all-too-common misuse of statistics involves what might be described as "errors of omission." Persons using this tactic mention a comparison but then fail to specify all of the groups or items involved. For example, consider the following statement: "In recent laboratory tests, *Plasti-spred* was found to contain fully 82 percent less cholesterol! So, if you care about your family's health, buy Plasti-spred, the margarine for modern life." Impressive, right? After all, Plasti-spred seems to contain much less of a dangerous substance than—what? There, in fact, is the rub: We have no idea as to the identity of the other substances in the comparison. Were they other brands of margarine? Butter? A jar of bacon drippings? A beaker full of cholesterol?

The lesson offered by such claims is clear. Whenever you are told that a product, candidate, or anything else is better or superior in some way, always ask the following question: Better than *what?*

## Some Differences Aren't Really There

Here's yet another type of commercial you've probably seen before. An announcer points to lines on a graph that diverge before your eyes and states, "Here's proof! *Gasaway* neutralizes stomach acid twice as fast as the other leading brand." And in fact, the line labeled Gasaway does seem to rise more quickly, leaving its poor competitor in the dust. Should you take such claims seriously? Again, the answer is no. First, such graphs are usually unlabeled. As a result, we have no idea as to what measure of neutralizing acids or how much time is involved. It is quite possible that the curves illustrate only the first few seconds after the medicine is taken and that beyond that period the advantage for the sponsor's product disappears.

# Summary and Review

### Descriptive Statistics: Summarizing Data

- All scientists require two types of tools in their research: equipment for collecting data and some means of interpreting their findings. In psychology statistics are often used for the latter purpose.
- Large quantities of data can be grouped into frequency distributions indicating the number of times each score occurs. Two important facts about any frequency distribution are its central tendency—its center—and its dispersion, or the extent to which scores spread out around this value.
- Common measures of central tendency include the mean, mode, and median. Dispersion is often measured in terms of variance and the standard deviation. This latter term refers to the average distance of each score from the mean.
- The frequency distributions for many behavioral characteristics show a bell-shaped form known as the normal distribution or normal curve. Most scores fall near the middle, and fewer occur at increasing distances from this value. Specific proportions of the scores are found under certain parts of the curve.

**Key Terms**

frequency distribution, p. 659 • central tendency, p. 660 • dispersion, p. 660 • descriptive statistics, p. 660 • mean, p. 660 • mode, p. 661 • median, p. 661 • range, p. 661 • variance, p. 661 • standard deviation, p. 661 • normal curve, p. 662

### Inferential Statistics: Determining Whether Differences Are or Are Not Real

- Psychologists use inferential statistics to determine whether differences between individuals or groups are significant, or real. Inferential statistics assume that the mean difference in question is zero and that observed differences are distributed normally around this value.
- If an observed difference is large enough that it would occur by chance only 5 percent of the time, it is viewed as significant.

**Key Term**

inferential statistics, p. 663

### Correlation and Prediction

- To determine whether two or more variables are related, psychologists compute correlation coefficients. These range from –1.00 to +1.00. The larger the departure from 0.00, the stronger the correlation between the variables in question.
- Correlations, and statistics derived from them, can be used to predict future behavior from current information. Such predictions are of great practical benefit to schools, companies, and others wishing to predict future performance from individuals' current behavior.

**Key Term**

correlation coefficient, p. 666

### The Misuse of Statistics: Numbers Don't Lie . . . or Do They?

- Although statistics have many beneficial uses, they are often employed to deceive or mislead.
- Misuse of statistics can involve the use of extremely small or biased samples, unexpressed comparisons, and misleading graphs and presentations.

# Glossary

**Absolute Threshold:** The smallest amount of a stimulus that we can detect 50 percent of the time.
**Accommodation:** In Piaget's theory, the modification of existing knowledge structures (schemas) as a result of exposure to new information or experiences.
**Achievement Motivation:** The desire to accomplish difficult tasks and to meet standards of excellence.
**Achievement Tests:** Tests designed to measure current knowledge—the results of previous learning.
**Acquisition:** The process by which a conditioned stimulus acquires the ability to elicit a conditioned response through repeated pairings of an unconditioned stimulus with the conditioned stimulus.
**Action Potential:** A rapidly moving wave of depolarization (shift in electrical potential) that travels along the cell membrane of a neuron. This disturbance along the membrane communicates information within the neuron.
**Acuity:** The visual ability to see fine details.
**Adolescence:** A period beginning with the onset of puberty and ending when individuals assume adult roles and responsibilities.
**Adrenal Glands:** Glands that release hormones to help the body handle emergencies by, for example, increasing heart rate, blood pressure, and blood sugar levels.
**Affect:** Relatively mild feelings and moods.
**Afferent Nerve Fibers:** Nerve fibers in the spinal cord that carry information from receptors throughout the body toward the brain.
**Aggression:** Behavior directed toward the goal of harming another living being that wishes to avoid such treatment.
**Aggression Machine:** A device used in the laboratory study of human aggression.
**Aggressive Motivation:** The desire to harm or injure others in some manner.
**Agonist:** A chemical substance that mimics the action of a neurotransmitter at a receptor site.
**Agoraphobia:** Intense fear of specific situations in which individuals suspect that help will not be available should they experience an incapacitating or embarrassing event.
**Agreeableness:** One of the "big five" dimensions of personality; ranges from good-natured, cooperative, trusting at one end to irritable, suspicious, uncooperative at the other.
**AIDS (Acquired Immune Deficiency Syndrome):** A viral infection that reduces the immune system's ability to defend the body against the introduction of foreign substances (antigens).
**Algorithm:** A rule that guarantees a solution to a specific type of problem.
**Alpha Waves:** Brain waves that occur when individuals are awake but relaxed.
**Alzheimer's Disease:** An illness primarily afflicting individuals over the age of sixty-five and involving severe mental deterioration, including severe amnesia.
**Amnesia:** Loss of memory stemming from illness, injury, drug abuse, or other causes.
**Amphetamines:** Drugs that act as stimulants, increasing feelings of energy and activation.
**Amygdala:** A limbic system structure involved in aspects of emotional control and formation of emotional memories.
**Anal Stage:** In Freud's theory, the psychosexual stage of development in which pleasure is focused primarily on he anal zone.
**Analogy:** A strategy for solving problems based on applying solutions that were previously successful with other problems similar in underlying structure.
**Anchoring-and-Adjustment Heuristic:** A cognitive rule of thumb for making decisions in which existing information is accepted as a reference point but then adjusted (usually insufficiently) in light of various factors.
**Anima:** According to Jung, the archetype representing the feminine side of males.
**Animus:** According to Jung, the archetype representing the masculine side of females.
**Anorexia Nervosa:** An eating disorder involving intense fears of gaining weight coupled with refusal to maintain normal body weight.
**Antagonist:** A chemical substance that inhibits the effect normally produced by a neurotransmitter at a receptor site.
**Anterograde Amnesia:** The inability to store in long-term memory information that occurs after an amnesia- inducing event.
**Antisocial Personality Disorder:** A personality disorder involving deceitfulness, impulsivity, callous disregard for the safety or welfare of others, and a total lack of remorse for actions that harm others.
**Anxiety Disorders:** Psychological disorders that take several different forms, but which are all related to a generalized feeling of anxiety.
**Anxiety:** In Freudian theory, unpleasant feelings of tension or worry experienced by individuals in reaction to unacceptable wishes or impulses.
**Apnea:** A sleep disorder in which sleepers stop breathing, and thus wake up, many times each night.
**Applied Behavior Analysis:** A field of psychology that specializes in the application of operant conditioning principles to solve problems of everyday life.
**Aptitude Tests:** Tests designed to measure the ability to acquire new information; used primarily to predict future performance.
**Archetypes:** According to Jung, inherited images in the collective unconscious that shape our perceptions of the external world.
**Arousal Theory:** A theory of motivation suggesting that human beings seek an optimal level of arousal, not minimal levels of arousal.
**Artificial Intelligence:** The capacity of computers to demonstrate performance that, if it were produced by human beings, would be described as showing intelligence.
**Assessment Interviews:** Interviews conducted by psychologists in which they seek information about individuals' past and present behaviors, current problems, interpersonal relations, and personality.
**Assimilation:** In Piaget's theory of cognitive development, incorporation of new information into existing mental frameworks (schemas).
**Attachment:** A strong affectional bond between infants and their caregivers.
**Attention-Deficit/Hyperactivity Disorder (ADHD):** A childhood mental disorder in which children simply can't pay attention, show hyperactivity or impulsivity, or show both of these symptoms.

**Attitudes:** Lasting evaluations of various aspects of the social world that are stored in memory.
**Attribution:** The processes through which we seek to determine the causes behind others' behavior.
**Autobiographical Memory:** Memory for information about events in our own lives.
**Automatic Processing:** Processing of information with minimal conscious awareness.
**Autonomic Nervous System:** The part of the peripheral nervous system that connects internal organs, glands, and involuntary muscles to the central nervous system.
**Availability Heuristic:** A cognitive rule of thumb in which the importance or probability of various events is judged on the basis of how readily they come to mind.
**Axon:** The part of the neuron that conducts the action potential away from the cell body.
**Axon Terminals:** Structures at the end of axons that contain transmitter substances.

**Babbling:** An early stage of speech development in which infants emit virtually all known sounds of human speech.
**Backward Conditioning:** A type of conditioning in which the presentation of the unconditioned stimulus (UCS) precedes the presentation of the conditioned stimulus (CS).
**Barbiturates:** Drugs that act as depressants, reducing activity in the nervous system and behavior output.
**Basic Anxiety:** According to Karen Horney, children's fear of being left alone, helpless, and insecure.
**Basic Mistakes:** False beliefs held by individuals that interfere with their mental health; a concept in psychotherapy devised by Adler.
**Behavior Therapies:** Therapies based on the belief that many mental disorders stem from faulty learning.
**Behaviorism:** The view that only observable, overt activities that can be measured scientifically should be studied by psychology.
**Bereavement:** The process of grieving for the persons we love who die.
**Binocular Cues:** Cues to depth or distance resulting from the fact that we have two eyes.
**Biofeedback:** A technique that enables people to monitor and self-regulate certain bodily functions through the use of specialized equipment.
**Biological Constraints on Learning:** Tendencies of some species to acquire some forms of conditioning less readily than other species do.
**Biological Rhythms:** Cyclic changes in bodily processes.
**Biological Therapies:** Forms of therapy that attempt to reduce mental disorders through biological means.
**Bipolar Disorder:** A mood disorder in which individuals experience very wide swings in mood, from deep depression to wild elation.
**Bisexual:** Motivated to engage in sexual relations with members of both sexes.
**Blind Spot:** The point in the back of the retina through which the optic nerve exits the eye. This exit point contains no rods or cones and is therefore insensitive to light.
**Blindsight:** A rare condition resulting from damage to the primary visual cortex in which individuals report being blind, yet respond to certain aspects of visual stimuli as if they could see.
**Body Language:** Nonverbal cues involving body posture or movement of body parts.
**Bogus Pipeline:** A procedure for measuring attitudes in which respondents are told that they will be attached to a special apparatus that, by measuring tiny changes in their muscles (or in brain waves or other physiological reactions) can assess their true opinions no matter what they say.
**Brightness:** The physical intensity of light.
**Brightness Constancy:** The tendency to perceive objects as having a constant brightness when they are viewed under different conditions of illumination.
**Broca's Area:** A region in the prefrontal cortex that plays a role in the production of speech.
**Bulimia Nervosa:** An eating disorder in which individuals engage in recurrent episodes of binge eating followed by some form of purging.

**Cancer:** A group of illnesses in which abnormal cells proliferate, invade, overwhelm normal tissues, and spread to distant sites in the body.
**Cannon–Bard Theory:** A theory of emotion suggesting that various emotion-provoking events simultaneously produce physiological arousal and subjective reactions labeled as emotions.
**Carcinogens:** Cancer-producing agents in our environment.
**Cardinal Trait:** According to Allport, a single trait that dominates an individual's entire personality.
**Cardiovascular Disease:** All diseases of the heart and bloodvessels.
**Case Method:** A research method in which detailed information about individuals is used to develop general principles about behavior.
**Cataplexy:** A symptom of the sleep disorder narcolepsy; in cataplexy individuals fall down suddenly, like a sack of flour.
**Catatonic Type** (of schizophrenia): A dramatic type of schizophrenia in which individuals show marked disturbances in motor behavior; many alternate between total immobility and wild, excited behavior in which they rush madly about.
**Central Nervous System:** The brain and the spinal cord.
**Central Route** (to persuasion): Careful consideration of the content of persuasive messages; also called *systematic processing*.
**Central Tendency:** The middle (center) of a distribution of scores.
**Central Traits:** According to Allport, the five or ten traits that best describe an individual's personality.
**Cerebellum:** A part of the brain concerned with the regulation of basic motor activities.
**Cerebral Cortex:** The outer covering of the cerebral hemispheres.
**Chaining:** A procedure that establishes a sequence of responses, which lead to a reward following the final response in the chain.
**Charismatic** (transformational): Leaders who exert profound effects on their followers.
**Childhood:** The years between birth and adolescence.
**Choking under Pressure:** Reduced performance that occurs under conditions in which pressures to perform well are very high.
**Chromosomes:** Threadlike structures containing genetic material, found in nearly every cell of the body.
**Chunk:** Items containing several separate bits of information.
**Circadian Rhythms:** Cyclic changes in bodily processes occurring within a single day.
**Classical Conditioning:** A basic form of learning in which one stimulus comes to serve as a signal for the occurrence of a second stimulus. During classical conditioning, organisms acquire information about the relations between various stimuli, not simple associations between them.
**Client-Centered Therapy:** Carl Rogers's approach to psychotherapy, which seeks to eliminate irrational "conditions of worth" in the client's mind by providing unconditional positive regard in a caring, empathetic environment.
**Climacteric:** A period during which the functioning of the reproductive system and various aspects of sexual activity change greatly.

**Cocaine:** A powerful stimulant that produces pleasurable sensations of increased energy and self-confidence.
**Cochlea:** A portion of the inner ear containing the sensory receptors for sound.
**Cognition:** The mental activities associated with thought, decision making, language, and other higher mental processes.
**Cognitive Behavior Therapy:** A form of cognitive therapy that focuses on changing illogical patterns of thought that underlie depression.
**Cognitive Dissonance:** The state experienced by individuals when they discover inconsistency between two attitudes they hold or between their attitudes and their behavior.
**Cognitive Restructuring:** A method of reducing stress by adjusting cognitive appraisals of stressors; clients learn to monitor and modify their self-talk and coping strategies.
**Cognitive Therapies:** Forms of therapy focused on changing distorted and maladaptive patterns of thought.
**Cohort Effects:** Differences between persons of different ages stemming from the fact that they have experienced contrasting social or cultural conditions.
**Collective Unconscious:** In Jung's theory, a portion of the unconscious shared by all human beings.
**Community Psychology:** A subfield of psychology that focuses on promoting mental health by making positive changes in the communities in which people live.
**Competency Assessment:** A technique for predicting future performance; involves identifying key differences between persons who are currently showing outstanding performance and those showing average performance.
**Complex Cells:** Neurons in the visual cortex that respond to stimuli moving in a particular direction and having a particular orientation.
**Compliance:** A form of social influence in which one or more persons acquiesce to direct requests from one or more others.
**Computerized Tomography (CT):** A method of brain scanning in which a series of X-ray images are synthesized and analyzed by computer.
**Concept:** A mental category for objects or events that are similar to one another in certain ways.
**Concrete Operations:** In Piaget's theory, a stage of cognitive development occurring roughly between the ages of seven and eleven. It is at this stage that children become aware of the permanence of objects.
**Concurrent Schedule of Reinforcement:** A situation in which two or more behaviors, each having its own reinforcement schedule, are simultaneously available.
**Conditioned Response (CR):** In classical conditioning, the response to the conditioned stimulus.
**Conditioned Stimulus (CS):** In classical conditioning, the stimulus that is repeatedly paired with an unconditioned stimulus.
**Conditioned Taste Aversion:** A type of conditioning in which the UCS (usually internal cues associated with nausea or vomiting) occurs several hours after the CS (often a novel food) and leads to a strong CS–UCS association in a single trial.
**Conditions of Worth:** In Rogers's client-centered therapy, individuals' beliefs that they must be something other than what they really are in order to be loved and accepted by others.
**Cones:** Sensory receptors in the eye that play a crucial role in sensations of color.
**Confirmation Bias:** The tendency to pay attention primarily to information that confirms existing views or beliefs.
**Confluence Approach:** An approach suggesting that for creativity to occur, multiple components must converge.
**Conformity:** A type of social influence in which individuals change their attitudes or behavior in order to adhere to existing social norms.
**Confounding (of variables):** Confusion that occurs when factors other than the independent variable are permitted to vary across experimental conditions; can invalidate the apparent results of an experiment.
**Conscientiousness:** One of the "big five" dimensions of personality; ranges from well-organized, careful, and responsible at one end to disorganized, careless, and unscrupulous at the other.
**Consensus:** Information regarding the extent to which behavior by one person is shown by others as well.
**Conservation:** The fact that certain physical attributes of an object remain unchanged even though its outward appearance changes.
**Consistency:** Information regarding the extent to which a specific person shows similar behavior to a given stimulus across time.
**Constancies:** Our tendency to perceive physical objects as unchanging despite shifts in the pattern of sensations these objects induce.
**Contact Hypothesis:** The suggestion that increased contact between members of different groups will reduce prejudice between them.
**Content Validity:** The extent to which items on a test are related in a straightforward way to the characteristic the test aims to measure.
**Context-Dependent Memory:** Refers to the fact that information entered into memory in one context or setting is easier to recall in that context than in others.
**Continuous Reinforcement Schedule:** A schedule of reinforcement in which every occurrence of a particular behavior is reinforced.
**Controlled Processing:** Processing of information with relatively high levels of conscious awareness.
**Conventional Level (of morality):** According to Kohlberg, a stage of moral development during which individuals judge morality largely in terms of existing social norms or rules.
**Conversion Disorder:** A somatoform disorder in which individuals experience actual physical impairment such as blindness, deafness, or paralysis for which there is no underlying medical cause.
**Convoy Model:** A model of social networks suggesting that from midlife on, we tend to maintain close relationships with a small number of people.
**Cornea:** The curved transparent layer through which light rays enter the eye.
**Corpus Callosum:** A band of nerve fibers connecting the two hemispheres of the brain.
**Correlation Coefficient:** A statistic indicating the degree of relationship between two or more variables. Correlational Method: A research method in which researchers attempt to determine whether, and to what extent, different variables are related to each other.
**Correspondence Bias:** The tendency to attribute behavior to internal causes to a greater extent than is actually justified; also known as the *fundamental attribution error.*
**Counterfactual Thinking:** The tendency to evaluate events by thinking about alternatives to them—"what might have been."
**Crack:** A derivative of cocaine that can be smoked. It acts as a powerful stimulant.
**Creativity:** The ability to produce work that is both novel (original, unexpected) and appropriate (it works—it is useful or meets task constraints).
**Criterion-Related Validity:** The extent to which scores on a test are related to behaviors (criteria) that are relevant to the characteristics the test purports to measure.
**Critical Thinking:** Thinking that avoids blind acceptance of conclusions

or arguments but instead closely examines all assumptions, evidence, and conclusions.
**Cross-Sectional Research:** Research comparing groups of persons of different ages in order to determine how certain aspects of behavior or cognition change with age.
**Cross-Tolerance:** Increased tolerance for one drug that develops as a result of taking another drug.
**Crystallized Intelligence:** Aspects of intelligence that draw on previously learned information—our accumulated knowledge.
**Cultural Bias:** The tendency of items on a test of intelligence to require specific cultural experience or knowledge.

**Dark Adaptation:** The process through which our visual system increases its sensitivity to light under low levels of illumination.
**Debriefing:** Providing research participants with full information about all aspects of a study after they have participated in it.
**Deception:** The temporary withholding of information about a study from participants.
**Decision Making:** The process of choosing among various courses of action or alternatives.
**Defense Mechanisms:** Techniques used by the ego to keep threatening and unacceptable material out of consciousness, and so to reduce anxiety.
**Deinstitutionalization:** A shifting of patients from public hospitals to the community, largely as a result of the development of effective drugs for treating mental disorders.
**Delay Conditioning:** A form of forward conditioning in which the onset of the unconditioned stimulus (UCS) begins while the conditioned stimulus (CS) is still present.
**Delta Activity:** Slow (3.5 Hz or less), high-amplitude brain waves that occur during several stages of sleep, but especially during Stage 4.
**Delusions:** Firmly held beliefs that have no basis in reality.
**Dendrites:** The parts of neurons that conduct action potentials toward the cell body.
**Dependence:** Strong need for a particular drug and inability to function without it.
**Dependent Variable:** The variable that is measured in an experiment.
**Depressants:** Drugs that reduce activity in the nervous system and therefore slow many bodily and cognitive processes. Depressants include alcohol and barbiturates.
**Depression:** A mood disorder in which individuals experience extreme unhappiness, lack of energy, and several related symptoms.
**Descriptive Statistics:** Statistics that summarize the major characteristics of an array of scores.
**Developmental Psychology:** The branch of psychology that focuses on the many ways we change throughout life.
**Developmental Psychopathology Perspective:** A view emphasizing the fact that problems that first appear during childhood or adolescence are often precursors for disorders that occur later in life.
**Diagnostic and Statistical Manual of Mental Disorders–IV (DSM–IV):** A manual designed to help all mental health practitioners to recognize and correctly diagnose specific disorders; known as DSM–IV.
**Diathesis–Stress Model:** A model suggesting that genetic or other factors may predispose an individual to develop a mental disorder but that the disorder will develop only if the person is exposed to certain kinds of stressful environmental conditions.
**Difference Threshold:** The amount by which two stimuli must differ in order to be just noticeably different.
**Discriminative Stimulus:** Stimulus that signals the availability of reinforcement if a specific response is made.
**Disorganized or Disoriented Attachment:** A pattern of attachment in which infants show contradictory reactions to their caregiver after being reunited with her in the strange situation test.
**Dispersion:** The extent to which scores in a distribution spread out or vary around the center.
**Disruptive Behaviors:** Childhood mental disorders involving poor control of impulses, conflict with other children and adults, and, in some cases, more serious forms of antisocial behavior.
**Dissociative Amnesia:** Profound amnesia stemming from the active motivation to forget specific events or information.
**Dissociative Disorders:** Disorders involving disruptions in a person's memory, consciousness, or identity.
**Dissociative Fugue:** A sudden and extreme disturbance of memory in which individuals wander off, adopt a new identity, and are unable to recall their own past.
**Dissociative Identity Disorder:** A condition previously called *multiple personality disorder,* in which a single person seems to possess two or more distinct identities or personality states and these take control of the person's behavior at different times.
**Distinctiveness:** Information regarding the extent to which a given person reacts in the same manner to different stimuli or situations.
**Door-in-the-Face Technique:** A technique for gaining compliance in which a large request is followed by a smaller one.
**Double-Blind Procedure:** Procedure in which the researchers who have contact with participants do not know the hypothesis under investigation.
**Down Syndrome:** A genetically caused condition that results in mental retardation.
**Dream:** (1) In Levinson's theory of adult development, a vision of future accomplishments—what a person hopes to achieve in the years ahead. (2) Cognitive event, often vivid but disconnected, that occurs during sleep. Most dreams take place during REM sleep.
**Dreams of Absent-Minded Transgression:** Dreams in which persons attempting to change their behavior, as in quitting smoking, see themselves slipping into the unwanted behavior in an absent-minded or careless manner.
**Drive Theory:** A theory of motivation suggesting that behavior is "pushed" from within by drives stemming from basic biological needs.
**Drug Abuse:** Instances in which individuals take drugs purely to change their moods and experience impaired behavior or social functioning as a result.
**Drug Therapy:** Therapy based on the administration of psychoactive drugs.
**Drugs:** Chemical compounds that change the functioning of biological systems.
**Dysfunctional Families:** Families that do not meet the needs of children and in fact do them serious harm.

**Ecological Systems Theory:** Bronfenbrenner's theory suggesting that in order to fully understand human development, we must focus on relationships between individuals and their environments—ecology.
**Effectiveness Research:** Research that examines individuals' responses to psychotherapy as it is normally delivered in real-life settings.
**Efferent Nerve Fibers:** Nerve fibers in the spinal cord that carry information from the brain to muscles and glands throughout the body.

**Efficacy Studies:** Studies that apply basic methods of experimentation to find out whether a specific form of therapy really works—that is, whether the therapy produces beneficial outcomes for the persons who undergo it.
**Ego:** In Freud's theory, the part of personality that takes account of external reality in the expression of instinctive sexual and aggressive urges.
**Egocentrism:** The inability of young children to distinguish their own perspective from that of others.
**Elaboration-Likelihood Model (ELM):** A cognitive model of persuasion suggesting that persuasion can occur through distinct routes.
**Electroconvulsive Therapy:** A form of therapy in which strong electric shocks are delivered to the brain; often called ECT.
**Electroencephalogram (EEG):** A record of electrical activity within the brain. EEGs play an important role in the scientific study of sleep.
**Electroencephalography (EEG):** A technique for measuring the electrical activity of the brain via electrodes placed at specified locations on the skull.
**Electromyogram (EOM):** A record of electrical activity in various muscles.
**Electrooculogram (EOG):** A record of changes in electrical potentials in the eyes.
**Embryo:** The developing child during the second through the eighth week of prenatal development.
**Emotional Intelligence (EQ):** A cluster of traits or abilities relating to the emotional side of life—abilities such as recognizing and managing one's own emotions, being able to motivate oneself and restrain one's impulses, recognizing and managing others' emotions, and handling interpersonal relationships in an effective manner.
**Emotional Stability:** One of the "big five" dimensions of personality; ranges from poised, calm, and composed at one end to nervous, anxious, and excitable at the other; also called *neuroticism.*
**Emotions:** Reactions consisting of subjective cognitive states, physiological reactions, and expressive behaviors.
**Empathy:** Our ability to recognize the emotions of others, to understand these feelings, and to experience them ourselves, at least to a degree.
**Encoding:** The process through which information is converted into a form that can be entered into memory.
**Encoding Specificity Principle:** Principle stating that retrieval of information is successful to the extent that the retrieval cues match the cues the learner used during the study phase.
**Endocrine System:** A system for communication within our bodies; it consists of several glands that secrete hormones directly into the bloodstream.
**Epidemiological Studies:** Large-scale research conducted to identify risk factors that lead to the development of certain diseases.
**Episodic Memory:** Memory for factual information that we acquired at a specific time.
**Escalation of Commitment:** The tendency to become increasingly committed to bad decisions even as losses associated with them increase.
**Evolutionary Psychology:** A branch of psychology suggesting that as a result of evolution, human beings possess many evolved psychological mechanisms that help (or once helped) us to deal with important problems relating to survival.
**Exemplar:** An example of a category of things that is readily brought to mind.
**Expectancy Theory:** A theory of motivation suggesting that behavior is "pulled" by expectations of desirable outcomes.
**Experimentation (the Experimental Method):** A research method in which researchers systematically alter one or more variables in order to determine whether such changes influence some aspect of behavior.
**Experimenter Effects:** Unintended effects, caused by researchers, on participants' behavior.
**Extended Contact Hypothesis:** Suggestion that merely informing persons that members of their own group have formed close friendships with persons from an out-group can reduce prejudice.
**Externals:** In Rotter's term, individuals who believe that they have little control over the outcomes they experience.
**Extinction:** The process through which a conditioned stimulus gradually loses the ability to evoke conditioned responses when it is no longer followed by the unconditioned stimulus.
**Extrasensory Perception:** Perception without a basis in sensory input.
**Extraversion:** One of the "big five" dimensions of personality; ranges from sociable, talkative, and enthusiastic at one end to sober, reserved, and cautious at the other.
**Extroverts:** In Jung's theory, individuals who are open and and confident and make friends readily.
**Eyewitness Testimony:** Information provided by witnesses to crimes or accidents.

**Facial Feedback Hypothesis:** A hypothesis indicating that facial expressions can produce changes in emotional states.
**Family Systems Therapy:** A form of family therapy in which therapists treat families as dynamic systems in which each member has an important major role.
**Family Therapy:** Therapy designed to change the relationships among family members in constructive ways.
**Farsightedness:** A condition in which the visual image entering our eye is focused behind rather than directly on the retina. Therefore, close objects appear out of focus, whereas distant objects are in clear focus.
**Fatal Familial Insomnia:** A genetic disorder in which individuals experience increasing disturbances in sleep; the disorder is, as its name suggests, fatal.
**Feature Detectors:** Neurons at various levels within the visual cortex that respond primarily to stimuli possessing certain features.
**Feeding and Eating Disorders:** Disturbances in eating behavior that involve maladaptive and unhealthy efforts to control body weight.
**Fetus:** The developing child during the last seven months of pregnancy.
**Figure–Ground Relationship:** Our tendency to divide the perceptual world into two distinct parts—discrete figures and the background against which they stand out.
**Fixation:** Excessive investment of psychic energy in a particular stage of psychosexual development; this results in various types of psychological disorders.
**Fixed-Interval Schedule:** A schedule of reinforcement in which a specific interval of time must elapse before a response will yield reinforcement.
**Fixed-Ratio Schedule:** A schedule of reinforcement in which reinforcement occurs only after a fixed number of responses have been emitted.
**Flashbulb Memories:** Vivid memories of what we were doing at the time of an emotion-provoking event.
**Fluid Intelligence:** Our abilities (largely inherited) to think and reason.
**Foot-in-the-Door Technique:** A technique for gaining compliance in which a small request is followed by a much larger one.
**Formal Operations:** In Piaget's theory, the final stage of cognitive development,

during which individuals may acquire the capacity for deductive or propositional reasoning.
**Fovea:** The area in the center of the retina in which cones are highly concentrated.
**Framing:** Presentation of information concerning potential outcomes in terms of gains or in terms of losses.
**Free Association:** A verbal reporting by persons undergoing psychoanalysis of everything that passes through their minds, no matter how trivial it may appear to be.
**Frequency Distribution:** The frequency with which each score occurs within an entire distribution of scores.
**Frequency Theory:** A theory suggesting that sounds of different frequencies (heard as differences in pitch) induce different rates of neural activity in the hair cells of the inner ear.
**Frequency-of-Exposure Effect:** The fact that the more frequently we are exposed to a given stimulus, the more—in general—we tend to like it.
**Freudian Slips:** Errors in speech that in fact betray unconscious thoughts or impulses.
**Friendships:** Relationships involving strong affective (emotional) ties between two persons.
**Frontal Lobe:** The portion of the cerebral cortex that lies in front of the central fissure.
**Frustration:** The blocking of ongoing, goal-directed behavior.
**Fully Functioning Persons:** In Rogers's theory, psychologically healthy persons who live life to the fullest.
**Functional Autonomy:** In Allport's theory, maintenance of patterns of behavior by motives other than the ones originally responsible for the behavior's occurrence.
**Functional Fixedness:** The tendency to think of using objects only as they have been used in the past.
**Functionalism:** An early view of psychology suggesting that it should focus on the functions of consciousness.

**Gate-Control Theory:** A theory of pain suggesting that the spinal cord contains a mechanism that can block transmission of pain to the brain.
**Gateway Hypothesis:** The view that use of marijuana is uniquely linked to the use of other drugs. This hypothesis is not supported by existing evidence.
**Gender:** A society's beliefs about the traits and behavior of males and females.
**Gender Consistency:** Children's understanding that their gender will not change even if they adopted the behavior, dress, or hairstyles of the other gender.
**Gender Differences:** Differences in the behavior of females and males. Often, these are exaggerated by *gender stereotypes.*
**Gender Identity Disorder:** A disorder in which individuals believe that they were born with the wrong sexual identity.
**Gender Identity:** Understanding of the fact that one is male or female.
**Gender Roles:** Expected behaviors of males and females in many situations.
**Gender Schema Theory:** Theory that children develop a cognitive framework reflecting the beliefs of their society about the characteristics and roles of males and females; this gender schema then strongly affects the processing of new social information.
**Gender Stability:** Children's understanding that gender is stable over time.
**Gender Stereotypes:** Cultural beliefs about differences between women and men.
**General Adaptation Syndrome (GAS):** A three-step profile of response to stress: (1) alarm, a nonspecific mobilization phase that promotes sympathetic nervous system activity; (2) resistance, during which the organism makes efforts to cope; and (3) exhaustion, which occurs if the organism fails to overcome the threat and depletes its coping resources.
**Genes:** Segments of DNA that serve as biological blueprints, shaping development and all basic bodily processes.
**Genetic Hypothesis:** The view that group differences in intelligence are due, at least in part, to genetic factors.
**Genital Stage:** In Freud's theory, the final stage of psychosexual development—one in which individuals acquire the adult capacity to combine lust with affection.
**Gestalt Psychologists:** German psychologists intrigued by our tendency to perceive sensory patterns as well-organized wholes rather than as separate, isolated parts.
**Gestalt Therapy:** A humanistic therapy that focuses on helping individuals to acknowledge hidden aspects of their thoughts and feelings.
**Gestures:** Movements of various body parts that convey specific meanings in a given culture.
**Glial Cells:** Cells in the nervous system that surround, support, and protect neurons.
**Goal-Setting Theory:** The view that motivation can be strongly influenced by goals.
**Gonads:** The primary sex glands.
**Graded Potential:** A basic type of signal within neurons that results from external physical stimulation of the dendrite or cell body. In contrast to the all-or-nothing nature of action potentials, graded potentials vary in proportion to the size of the stimulus that produced them.
**Grammar:** Rules within a given language indicating how words can be combined into meaningful sentences.
**Great Person Theory of Leadership:** The view that great leaders possess certain traits that set them apart from most human beings—traits that are possessed by all such leaders, no matter when or where they live.
**Group:** Two or more persons who interact with one another, have shared goals, are somehow interdependent, and view themselves as members of the group.
**Group Therapies:** Procedures in which several people discuss their problems with one another under the guidance or leadership of a trained therapist.

**Hallucinations:** Vivid sensory experiences that have no basis in physical reality.
**Hallucinogens:** Drugs that generate sensory perceptions for which there are no external stimuli (e.g., LSD).
**Halstead–Reitan Neuropsychological Battery:** A battery of tests of auditory, visual, and psychomotor functioning (e.g., eye–hand coordination). The pattern of scores obtained by a given individual can point to the existence of specific forms of brain damage.
**Hassles:** Annoying minor events of everyday life that cumulatively can affect psychological well-being.
**Health Belief Model:** A theory of health behaviors; the model predicts that whether or not a person practices a particular health behavior may depend on the degree to which the person perceives a personal health threat and believes that practicing the behavior will reduce that threat.
**Health Psychology:** The study of the relation between psychological variables and health, which reflects the view that both mind and body are important determinants of health and illness.
**Heredity:** Biologically determined characteristics passed from parents to their offspring.
**Heritability:** The proportion of the variance in any trait within a given population that is attributable to genetic factors.
**Heterosexual (sexual orientation):** A sexual orientation in which individuals

prefer sexual relations with members of the other sex.

**Heuristic Processing:** The use of simple rules of thumb or mental shortcuts in the evaluation of persuasive messages; also called the *peripheral route* to persuasion.

**Heuristic–Systematic Model:** A cognitive model of persuasion suggesting that persuasion can occur through distinctly different routes.

**Heuristics:** Mental rules of thumb that permit us to make decisions and judgments in a rapid and efficient manner.

**Hierarchy of Needs:** In Maslow's theory of motivation, an arrangement of needs from the most basic to those at the highest levels.

**Hindsight Effect:** The tendency to assume that we would have been better at predicting actual events than is really true.

**Hippocampus:** A structure of the limbic system that plays a role in the formation of certain types of memories.

**Homeostasis:** A state of physiological balance within the body.

**Homosexual (sexual orientation):** A sexual orientation in which individuals prefer sexual relations with members of their own sex.

**Hormones:** Substances secreted by endocrine glands that regulate a wide range of bodily processes.

**Hue:** The color that we experience due to the dominant wavelength of a light.

**Humanistic Theories:** Theories of personality emphasizing personal responsibility and innate tendencies toward personal growth.

**Hunger Motivation:** The motivation to obtain and consume food.

**Huntington's Disease:** A genetically based fatal neuromuscular disorder characterized by the gradual onset of jerky, uncontrollable movements.

**Hypercomplex Cells:** Neurons in the visual cortex that respond to complex aspects of visual stimuli, such as width, length, and shape.

**Hypertension:** High blood pressure, a condition in which the pressure within the blood vessels is abnormally high.

**Hypnosis:** An interaction between two persons in which one (the hypnotist) induces changes in the behavior, feelings, or cognitions of the other (the subject) through suggestions. Hypnosis involves expectations on the part of subjects and their attempts to conform to social roles (e.g., the role of the hypnotized person).

**Hypochondriasis:** A disorder involving preoccupation with fears of disease or illness.

**Hypohedonia:** A genetically inherited impairment in the ability to experience pleasure.

**Hypothalamus:** A small structure deep within the brain that plays a key role in the regulation of the autonomic nervous system and of several forms of motivated behavior such as eating and aggression.

**Hypotheses:** Testable predictions derived from theories.

**Hypothetico–Deductive Reasoning:** In Piaget's theory, a type of reasoning first shown by individuals during the stage of formal operations. It involves formulating a general theory and deducing specific hypotheses from it.

**Id:** In Freud's theory, the portion of personality concerned with immediate gratification of primitive needs.

**Identity Fusion:** A pattern in which bicultural or multicultural children combine their different cultural identities into one.

**Illusions:** Instances in which perception yields false interpretations of physical reality.

**Incentives:** Rewards individuals seek to attain.

**Independent Variable:** The variable that is systematically changed in an experiment.

**Induced Compliance:** A technique for changing attitudes in which individuals are somehow induced to state positions different from their actual views.

**Industrial/Organizational Psychologists:** Psychologists who study all aspects of behavior in work settings.

**Infantile Amnesia:** Our supposed inability to remember experiences during the first two or three years of life.

**Inferential Statistics:** Statistical procedures that permit us to determine whether differences between individuals or groups are ones that are likely or unlikely to have occurred by chance.

**Information-Processing Perspective:** An approach to human memory that emphasizes the encoding, storage, and later retrieval of information.

**Informed Consent:** A principle requiring that research participants be provided with information about all events and procedures a study will involve before they agree to participate in it.

**Ingratiation:** A technique for gaining compliance by causing others to have positive feelings about us, or liking for us, before we attempt to influence them.

**Insecure/Ambivalent Attachment:** A pattern of attachment in which infants seek contact with their caregiver children before separation but then, after she leaves and then returns, first seek her but then resist or reject her offers of comfort.

**Insecure/Avoidant Attachment:** A pattern of attachment in which children don't cry when their caregiver leaves in the strange situation test, and are slow to greet their caregiver when this person returns.

**Insomnia:** Disorder involving the inability to fall asleep or to maintain sleep once it is attained.

**Inspection Time:** The minimum amount of time a particular stimulus must be exposed for individuals to make a judgment about it that meets some preestablished criterion of accuracy.

**Intelligence:** Individuals' abilities to understand complex ideas, to adapt effectively to the environment, to learn from experience, to engage in various forms of reasoning, to overcome obstacles by careful thought.

**Interactionist Perspective:** The view that behavior in any situation is a function of both personality and external factors.

**Internals:** In Rotter's theory, individuals who believe that they exert considerable control over the outcomes they experience.

**Interpersonal Attraction:** The extent to which we like or dislike other persons.

**Interpropositional Thinking:** In Piaget's theory, thinking in which a child seeks to test the validity of several propositions.

**Intrinsic Motivation:** Motivation to perform activities because they are rewarding in and of themselves.

**Introverts:** In Jung's theory, individuals who are hesitant and cautious and do not make friends easily.

**IQ:** Originally, "intelligent quotient," a number that examiners derived by dividing an individual's mental age by his or her chronological age. Now IQ simply indicates an individual's performance on an intelligence test relative to those of other persons.

**Iris:** The colored part of the eye; adjusts the amount of light that enters by constricting or dilating the pupil.

**James–Lange Theory:** A theory of emotion suggesting that emotion-provoking events produce various physiological reactions and that recognition of these is responsible for subjective emotional experiences.

**Just Noticeable Difference (jnd):** The smallest amount of change in a physical stimulus necessary for an individual to notice a difference in the intensity of the stimulus.

**Kinesthesia:** The sense that gives us information about the location of our body parts with respect to one another and allows us to perform movement.
**Korsakoff's Syndrome:** An illness caused by long-term abuse of alcohol; often involves profound retrograde amnesia.

**Language:** A system of symbols, plus rules for combining them, used to communicate information.
**Late-Adult Transition:** In Levinson's theory of adult development, a transition in which individuals must come to terms with their impending retirement.
**Latency Stage:** In Freud's theory, the psychosexual stage of development that follows resolution of the Oedipus complex. During this stage, sexual desires are relatively weak.
**Lateralization of Function:** Specialization of the two hemispheres of the brain for the performance of different functions.
**Laws of Grouping:** Simple principles describing how we tend to group discrete stimuli together in the perceptual world.
**Leadership:** The process through which one member of a group (its leader) influences other group members toward attainment of shared goals.
**Learned Helplessness:** Feelings of helplessness that develop after exposure to situations in which no effort succeeds in affecting outcomes.
**Learning:** Any relatively permanent change in behavior (or behavior potential) resulting from experience.
**Lens:** A curved structure behind the pupil that bends light rays, focusing them on the retina.
**Less-Leads-to-More Effect:** The fact that rewards just barely sufficient to induce individuals to state positions contrary to their own views often generate more attitude change than larger rewards.
**Levels of Processing View:** A view of memory suggesting that the greater the effort expended in processing information, the more readily the information will be recalled later.
**Libido:** According to Freud, the psychic energy that powers all mental activity.
**Life Structure:** In Levinson's theory of adult development, then underlying patterns or design of a person's life.
**Lifestyle:** In the context of health psychology, the overall pattern of decisions and behaviors that determine health and quality of life.
**Likert Scales:** Scales for measuring attitudes containing statements highly favorable or unfavorable toward the attitude object. Respondents indicate the extent to which they agree or disagree with each of these statements.
**Limbic System:** Several structures deep within the brain that play a role in emotional reactions and behavior.
**Linguistic Relativity Hypothesis:** The view that language shapes thought.
**Localization:** The ability of our auditory system to determine the direction of a sound source.
**Logical Concepts:** Concepts that can be clearly defined by a set of rules or properties.
**Long-Term Memory:** A memory system for the retention of large amounts of information over long periods of time.
**Longitudinal Research:** Research in which the same individuals are studied across relatively long periods of time.
**Longitudinal–Sequential Design:** A research method in which several groups of individuals of different ages are studied across time.
**LSD:** A powerful hallucinogen that produces profound shifts in perception; many of these are frightening in nature.

**Magnetic Resonance Imaging (MRI):** A method for studying the intact brain in which technicians obtain images by exposing the brain to a strong magnetic field.
**Marital Therapy:** Therapy designed to help couples improve the quality of their relationship.
**Maturation:** Changes determined largely by our genes.
**Mean:** A measure of central tendency derived by adding all scores and dividing by the number of scores.
**Median:** A measure of central tendency indicating the midpoint of an array of scores.
**Medulla:** A structure in the brain concerned with the regulation of vital bodily functions such as breathing and heartbeat.
**Memory:** Our cognitive system(s) for storing and retrieving information.
**Menopause:** Cessation of the menstrual cycle.
**Mental Contamination:** A process in which our judgments, emotions, or behavior are influenced by mental processing that is not readily under our control.
**Mental Disorders:** Disturbances of an individual's behavioral or psychological functioning that are not culturally expected and that lead to psychological distress, behavioral disability, and/or impaired overall functioning.
**Mental Models:** Knowledge structures that guide our interactions with objects and events in the world around us.
**Mental Retardation:** Considerably below-average intellectual functioning combined with varying degrees of difficulty in meeting the demands of everyday life.
**Mental Set:** The impact of past experience on present problem solving; specifically, the tendency to retain methods that were successful in the past even if better alternatives now exist.
**Mentor:** Older and more experienced individual who helps guide a young adult.
**Metacognitive Processing:** An expanded level of awareness that allows us, in a sense, to observe ourselves in the problem-solving process.
**Midbrain:** A part of the brain containing primitive centers for vision and hearing. It also plays a role in the regulation of visual reflexes.
**Midlife Transition:** In Levinson's theory of adult development, a turbulent transitional period occurring between the ages of forty and forty-five.
**Millon Clinical Multiaxial Inventory (MCMI):** An objective test of personality specifically designed to assist psychologists in diagnosing various psychological disorders.
**Mitosis:** Cell division in which chromosome pairs split and then replicate themselves so that the full number is restored in each of the cells produced by division.
**MMPI:** A widely used objective test of based on empirical keying.
**Mode:** A measure of central tendency indicating the most frequent score in an array of scores.
**Models of Abnormality:** Frameworks that provide comprehensive accounts of how and why mental disorders develop and how they can best be treated.
**Monocular Cues:** Cues to depth or distance provided by one eye.
**Mood Congruence Effects:** Our tendency to notice or remember information congruent with our current mood.
**Mood-Dependent Memory:** Our enhanced ability, when we are in a given mood, to remember what we learned when previously in that same mood.
**Mood Disorders:** Psychological disorders in which individuals experience swings in their emotional states that are much more extreme and prolonged than is true of most people.
**Moral Development:** Changes in the capacity to reason about the rightness or wrongness of various actions that occur with age.
**Motivation:** Internal processes that activate, guide, and maintain behavior over time.

**Multicultural Perspective:** In psychology, an approach that pays careful attention to the effects of ethnic and cultural forces on behavior.
**Munchausen's Syndrome:** A syndrome in which individuals pretend to have various medical problems in order to get attention from health practitioners.

**Narcolepsy:** A sleep disorder in which individuals are overcome by sleep attacks—the uncontrollable urge to sleep during waking hours.
**Natural Concepts:** Concepts that are not based on a precise set of attributes or properties, do not have clear-cut boundaries, and are often defined by prototypes.
**Naturalistic Decision Making:** Decision making as it occurs in real-world settings.
**Naturalistic Observation:** A research method in which behavior is studied in the settings were it usually occurs.
**Nearsightedness:** A condition in which the visual image entering our eye is focused slightly in front of our retina rather than directly on it. Therefore, near objects can be seen clearly, whereas distant objects appear fuzzy or blurred.
**Negative Afterimages:** Sensations of complementary color that we experience after staring at a stimulus of a given hue.
**Negative Reinforcers:** Stimuli that strengthen responses that permit the organism to avoid or escape from their presence.
**NEO Personality Inventory (NEO–PI):** An objective measure of personality designed to assess individuals' relative standing on each of the "big five" dimensions of personality.
**Neodissociation Theory:** A theory of hypnosis suggesting that hypnotized individuals enter an altered state of consciousness in which consciousness is divided.
**Neo-Freudians:** Personality theorists who accepted basic portions of Freud's theory but rejected or modified other portions.
**Nervous System:** The complex network of neurons that regulates bodily processes and is ultimately responsible for all aspects of conscious experience.
**Neural Network Models:** Models of memory that describe parallel (simultaneous) processing of information by numerous neural modules in the brain; each of these processing units is dedicated to a specific task, and all are interconnected.
**Neural Networks:** Computer systems modeled after the brain and made up of highly interconnected elementary computational units that work together in parallel.
**Neurons:** Cells specialized for communicating information, the basic building blocks of the nervous system.
**Neurotransmitters:** Chemicals, released by neurons, that carry information across synapses.
**Nicotine:** The addictive substance in tobacco.
**Night Terrors:** Extremely frightening dreamlike experiences that occur during non-REM sleep.
**Nodes of Ranvier:** Small gaps in the myelin sheath surrounding the axons of many neurons.
**Nonverbal Cues:** Outward signs of others' emotional states, such as facial expressions, eye contact, and body language.
**Normal Curve:** A symmetrical, bell-shaped frequency distribution. Most scores are found near the middle, and fewer and fewer occur toward the extremes. Many psychological characteristics are distributed in this manner.
**Nucleus Accumbens:** A structure in the forebrain that plays an important role in the reinforcing effects of many addictive drugs.

**Obedience:** A form of social influence in which one or more individuals behave in specific ways in response to direct orders from someone.
**Object Permanence:** The fact that objects continue to exist when they pass from view.
**Observational Learning:** The acquisition of new forms of behavior, information, or concepts through exposure to others and the consequences they experience.
**Obsessive–Compulsive Disorder:** An anxiety disorder in which individuals have recurrent, disturbing thoughts (obsessions) they can't prevent unless they engage in specific behaviors (compulsions).
**Occipital Lobe:** The portion of the cerebral cortex involved in vision.
**Oedipus Complex:** In Freud's theory, a crisis of psychosexual development in which children must give up their sexual attraction to their opposite-sex parent.
**Openness to Experience:** One of the "big five" dimensions of personality; ranges from imaginative, witty, and intellectual at one end to down-to-earth, simple, and narrow in interests at the other.
**Operant Conditioning:** A process through which organisms learn to repeat behaviors that yield positive outcomes or permit them to avoid or escape from negative outcomes.
**Opiates:** Drugs that induce a dreamy, relaxed state and, in some persons, intense feelings of pleasure. Opiates exert their effects by stimulating special receptor sites within the brain.
**Opponent-Process Theory:** Theory that describes the processing of sensory information related to color at levels above the retina. The theory suggests that we possess six different types of neurons, each of which is either stimulated or inhibited by red, green, blue, yellow, black, or white.
**Opponent-Process Theory of Emotion:** A theory suggesting that an emotional reaction is followed automatically by an opposite reaction.
**Optic Nerve:** A bundle of nerve fibers that exit the back of the eye and carry visual information to the brain.
**Oral Stage:** In Freud's theory, the stage of psychosexual development during which pleasure is centered in the region of the mouth.

**Panic Disorder:** Condition characterized by periodic, unexpected attacks of intense, terrifying anxiety known as panic attacks.
**Paraphilias:** Disorders in which sexual arousal cannot occur without the presence of unusual imagery or acts.
**Parapsychologists:** Individuals who study ESP and other paranormal events.
**Parasympathetic Nervous System:** The portion of the autonomic nervous system that readies the body for restoration of energy.
**Parental Demandingness:** The extent to which parents are strict or controlling and confront their children (often angrily) when they do not meet the parents' expectations.
**Parental Responsiveness:** The extent to which parents are involved in and supportive of their children's activities.
**Parietal Lobe:** A portion of the cerebral cortex, lying behind the central fissure, that plays a major role in the skin senses: touch, temperature, pressure.
**Peak Experiences:** According to Maslow, intense emotional experiences during which individuals feel at one with the universe.
**Perception:** The process through which we select, organize, and interpret input from our sensory receptors.
**Peripheral Nervous System:** The portion of the nervous system that connects internal organs, glands, and voluntary and involuntary muscles to the central nervous system.
**Peripheral Route** (to persuasion): The use of simple rules of thumb or mental

shortcuts in the evaluation of persuasive messages; also called *heuristic processing.*
**Person–Environment (P–E) Fit:** The appropriateness of the fit, or match, between a person and his or her work environment; a poor P–E fit may produce stress.
**Personality:** Individuals' unique and relatively stable patterns of behavior, thoughts, and feelings.
**Personality Disorders:** Disorders involving extreme and inflexible personality traits that are distressing to the persons who have them or cause them problems in school, at work, or in interpersonal relations.
**Personality Traits:** Specific dimensions along which individuals differ in consistent, stable ways.
**Persuasion:** The process through which one or more persons attempt to alter the attitudes of one or more others.
**Pervasive Developmental Disorders:** Disorders involve lifelong impairment in mental or physical functioning.
**Phallic Stage:** In Freud's theory, an early stage of psychosexual development during which pleasure is centered in the genital region. It is during this stage that the Oedipus complex develops.
**Phenomenological/Experiential Therapies (Humanistic Therapies):** Therapies based on the view that understanding people requires trying to see the world through their eyes (a phenomenological approach) and on the belief that the therapist's therapeutic relationship with the client is central to the benefits of therapy.
**Phenylketonuria (PKU):** A genetically based disorder in which persons lack the enzyme to break down phenylalanine, a substance present in many foods. The gradual buildup of body phenylalanine levels contributes to subsequent outcomes that include retardation.
**Phobias:** Intense, irrational fears of objects or events.
**Phonological Development:** Development of the ability to produce recognizable speech.
**Physical Reasoning:** The ways in which people perceive physical objects and the cognitive processes that allow people to make predictions about events involving these objects.
**Physiological Dependence:** Strong urges to continue using a drug based on organic factors such as changes in metabolism.
**Pineal Gland:** A portion of the brain that secretes the hormone melatonin, and plays a role in biological rhythms.
**Pinna:** The external portion of the ear.
**Pitch:** The characteristic of a sound that is described as high or low. Pitch is mediated by the frequency of a sound.
**Pituitary Gland:** An endocrine gland that releases hormones to regulate other glands and several basic biological processes.
**Place Theory:** A theory of pitch perception suggesting that sounds of different frequencies stimulate different areas of the basilar membrane, the portion of the cochlea containing sensory receptors for sound.
**Placenta:** A structure that surrounds, protects, and nourishes the developing fetus.
**Playing Hard to Get:** A tactic for gaining compliance in which individuals try to create the image that they are very popular or very much in demand.
**Pleasure Principle:** The principle on which the id operates, according to which immediate pleasure is the sole motivation for behavior.
**Pons:** A portion of the brain through which sensory and motor information passes and which contains structures relating to sleep, arousal, and the regulation of muscle tone and cardiac reflexes.
**Positive Reinforcers:** Stimuli that strengthen responses that precede them.
**Positron Emission Tomography (PET):** An imaging technique that detects the activity of the brain by measuring glucose utilization or blood flow.
**Postconventional Level (of morality):** According to Kohlberg, the final stage of moral development, in which individuals judge morality in terms of abstract principles.
**Posttraumatic Stress Disorder:** A disorder in which people persistently reexperience a traumatic event in their thoughts or dreams, feel as if they are reliving this event from time to time, persistently avoid stimuli associated with the traumatic event, and may experience several other symptoms.
**Practical Intelligence:** Intelligence useful in solving everyday problems.
**Preconventional Level (of morality):** According to Kohlberg, the earliest stage of moral development, in which individuals judge morality in terms of the effects produced by various actions.
**Prejudice:** Negative attitudes toward the members of some social group based on their membership in this group.
**Premack Principle:** Principle stating that a more preferred activity can be used to reinforce a less preferred activity.
**Preoperational Stage:** In Piaget's theory, a stage of cognitive development during which children become capable of mental representations of the external world.
**Prevention Strategies:** Techniques designed to reduce the occurrence of disease and other physical and psychological problems.
**Primary Aging:** Changes in our bodies caused by the passage of time and, perhaps, by genetic factors.
**Primary Prevention:** Efforts to prevent new psychological problems from occurring.
**Proactive Interference:** Interference with the learning or storage of current information by information previously entered into memory.
**Problem Solving:** Efforts to develop or choose among various responses in order to attain desired goals.
**Procedural Memory:** Memory system that retains information we cannot readily express verbally—for example, information necessary to perform skilled motor activities such as riding a bicycle. Also called *implicit memory.*
**Programmed Theories of Aging:** Theories that attribute physical aging primarily to genetic programming.
**Progressive Relaxation:** A stress-reduction technique in which people learn to relax by alternately flexing and relaxing, one by one, muscle groups throughout the body.
**Propositions:** Sentences that relate one concept to another and can stand as separate assertions.
**Prosopagnosia:** A rare condition in which brain damage impairs a person's ability to recognize faces.
**Prototype:** Abstract, idealized representation that captures an average or typical member of a category of things.
**Psi:** Unusual processes of information or energy transfer that are currently unexplained in terms of known physical or biological mechanisms. Included under the heading of psi are such supposed abilities as telepathy (reading others' thoughts) and clairvoyance (perceiving distant objects).
**Psychedelics:** Drugs that alter sensory perception and so may be considered mind-expanding (e.g., marijuana).
**Psychoanalysis:** A method of therapy based on Freud's theory of personality, in which the therapist attempts to bring repressed unconscious material into consciousness.
**Psychodynamic Therapies:** Therapies based on the idea that mental disorders stem primarily from the kind of hidden inner conflicts first described by Freud.
**Psychological Dependence:** Strong desires to coninue using a drug even

though it is not physiologically addicting.
**Psychology:** The science of behavior and cognitive processes.
**Psychophysical Methods:** A set of procedures psychologists have developed to investigate sensory thresholds.
**Psychosexual Stages of Development:** According to Freud, an innate sequence of stages through which all human beings pass. At each stage, pleasure is focused on a different region of the body.
**Psychosocial Rehabilitation:** Efforts to help patients with serious mental disorders (e.g., schizophrenia, major mood disorders) to cope more effectively with their disorders and to prevent or lessen the crises that reduce these patients' ability to function in society.
**Psychosurgery:** Brain operations designed to change abnormal behavior.
**Psychotherapies:** Procedures in which persons with mental disorders interact with a trained psychotherapist who helps them change certain behaviors, thoughts, or emotions so that they feel and function better.
**Puberty:** The period of rapid growth and change during which individuals reach sexual maturity.
**Punishment:** A procedure by which the application or removal of a stimulus decreases the strength of a behavior.
**Pupil:** An opening in the eye, just behind the cornea, through which light rays enter the eye.

**Random Assignments of Participants to Experimental Conditions:** Ensuring that all research participants have an equal chance of being exposed to each level of the independent variable (that is, of being assigned to each experimental condition).
**Range:** The difference between the highest and lowest scores in a distribution of scores.
**Rational–Emotive Therapy (RET):** A form of therapy that focuses on persuading individuals to recognize and change irrational assumptions that underlie their thinking.
**Raven Progressive Matrices:** A popular test of intelligence that was designed to be relatively free of cultural bias.
**Reaction Time:** Time that elapses between the presentation of a stimulus and a person's reaction to it.
**Realistic Conflict Theory:** A theory proposing that prejudice stems, at least in part, from competition between social groups over valued commodities or opportunities.
**Reality Monitoring:** The process of deciding whether specific memories are based on external (real) sources or on internal sources (e.g., imagination, thoughts).
**Reality Principle:** The principle according to which the ego operates, in which the external consequences of behavior are considered in the expression of impulses from the id.
**Reasoning:** Cognitive activity in which we transform information in order to reach specific conclusions.
**Recategorization:** A technique for reducing prejudice that involves inducing individuals to shift the boundary between "us" and "them" so that it now includes groups they previously viewed as "them."
**Reconditioning:** The rapid recovery of a conditioned response (CR) to a CS–UCS pairing following extinction.
**Reflexes:** Inherited responses to stimulation in certain areas of the body.
**Reinforcement:** The application or removal of a stimulus to increase the strength of a specific behavior.
**Relative Size:** A visual cue based on comparison of the size of an unknown object to objects of known size.
**Reliability:** The extent to which any measuring device (including psychological tests) yields the same result each time it is applied to the same quantity.
**REM Sleep:** A state of sleep in which brain activity resembling waking restfulness is accompanied by deep muscle relaxation and movements of the eyes. Most dreams occur during periods of REM sleep.
**Representativeness Heuristic:** A mental rule of thumb suggesting that the more closely an event or object resembles typical examples of some concept or category, the more likely it is to belong to that concept or category.
**Repression:** The active elimination from consciousness of memories of experiences we find threatening.
**Resilience in Development:** The capacity of some adolescents raised in harmful environments to somehow rise above these disadvantages and achieve healthy development.
**Resistance:** In psychoanalysis, a patient's stubborn refusal to report certain thoughts, motives, and experiences or overt rejection of the analyst's interpretations.
**Reticular Activating System:** A structure within the brain concerned with sleep, arousal, and the regulation of muscle tone and cardiac reflexes.
**Retina:** The surface at the back of the eye containing the rods and cones.
**Retrieval:** The process through which information stored in memory is located.
**Retrieval Cues:** Stimuli associated with information stored in memory that can aid in its retrieval.
**Retrieval Inhibition:** The inhibition of information in memory we don't try to remember produced by our retrieval of other, related information.
**Retroactive Interference:** Interference with retention of information already present in memory by new information being entered into memory.
**Retrograde Amnesia:** Loss of memory of events that occurred prior to an amnesia-inducing event.
**Risk Factors:** Aspects of our environment or behavior that influence our chances of developing or contracting a particular disease, within the limits established through our genetic structure.
**Rods:** One of the two types of sensory receptors for vision found in the eye.
**Romantic Love:** A form of love in which feelings of strong attraction and sexual desire toward another person are dominant.
**Rorschach Test:** A widely used projective test of personality in which individuals are asked to describe what they see in a series of inkblots.

**Saccadic Movements:** Quick movements of the eyes from one point of fixation to another.
**Sampling:** In the survey method, the methods used to select persons who respond to the survey.
**Saturation:** The degree of concentration of the hue of light. We experience saturation as the purity of a color.
**Schachter–Singer Theory:** A theory of emotion suggesting that our subjective emotional states are determined, at least in part, by the cognitive labels we attach to feelings of arousal; also known as *two-factor theory.*
**Schedules of Reinforcement:** Rules determining when and how reinforcements will be delivered.
**Schemas:** Cognitive frameworks representing our knowledge and assumptions about specific aspects of the world.
**Schizophrenia:** A complex disorder characterized by hallucinations (e.g., hearing voices), delusions (beliefs with no basis in reality), disturbances in speech, and several other symptoms.
**Secondary Aging:** Changes in our bodies due to disease, disuse, or abuse.
**Secondary Prevention:** Efforts to detect psychological problems early, before they have escalated in intensity.
**Secondary Traits:** According to Allport, traits that exert relatively specific and weak effects on behavior.
**Secure Attachment:** A pattern of attachment in which infants actively seek contact with their caregiver and take

comfort from her presence when she returns in the strange situation test.
**Selective Attention:** Our ability to pay attention to only some aspects of the world around us while largely ignoring others.
**Self-Actualization:** In Maslow's theory, the stage of personal development in which individuals reach their maximum potential.
**Self-Awareness:** A state of consciousness in which we focus our attention inward, upon ourselves.
**Self-Concept:** All the information and beliefs individuals have about their own characteristics and themselves.
**Self-Determination Theory:** In relation to health and lifestyle, theory suggesting that motivation for health-promoting behaviors is highest when it is autonomous and lowest when these behaviors are prompted by others.
**Self-Efficacy:** Individuals' expectations concerning their ability to perform various tasks.
**Self-Help Groups:** Groups of persons who are experiencing the same kinds of problems and who meet regularly, without professionally trained leaders, to help one another in their efforts to cope with these difficulties.
**Self-Reinforcement:** A process in which individuals reward themselves for reaching their own goals.
**Self-Serving Bias:** Our tendency to attribute positive outcomes to our own traits or characteristics (internal causes) but negative outcomes to factors beyond our control (external causes).
**Self-System:** In Bandura's social cognitive theory, the set of cognitive processes by which a person perceives, evaluates, and regulates his or her own behavior.
**Semantic Development:** Development of understanding of the meaning of spoken or written language.
**Semantic Memory:** A memory system that stores general, abstract knowledge about the world—information we cannot remember acquiring at a specific time and place.
**Sensation:** Input about the physical world provided by our sensory receptors.
**Sensation Seeking:** The desire to seek out novel, intense, experiences.
**Sensorimotor Stage:** In Piaget's theory, the earliest stage of cognitive development.
**Sensory Adaptation:** Reduced sensitivity to unchanging stimuli over time.
**Sensory Memory:** A memory system that retains representations of sensory input for brief periods of time.
**Sensory Receptors:** Cells of the body specialized for the task of transduction—converting physical energy (light, sound) into neural impulses.
**Serial Position Curve:** The greater accuracy of recall of words or other information early and late in a list of information than of words or information in the middle of the list.
**Serum Cholesterol:** The cholesterol in our blood.
**Sex-Category Constancy:** Complete understanding of one's sexual identity, centering around a biologically based categorical distinction between males and females.
**Sexual Abuse:** Sexual contact or activities forced on children or adolescents by other persons, usually adults.
**Sexual Arousal Disorders:** The inability to attain or maintain an erection (males) or the absence of vaginal swelling and lubrication (females).
**Sexual Desire Disorders:** Disorders involving a lack of interest in sex or active aversion to sexual activity.
**Sexual Motivation:** Motivation to engage in various forms of sexual activity.
**Shape Constancy:** The tendency to perceive a physical object as having a constant shape even when the image it casts on the retina changes.
**Shaping:** A technique in which closer and closer approximations to desired behavior are required for the delivery of positive reinforcement.
**Signal Detection Theory:** A theory suggesting that there are no absolute thresholds for sensations. Rather, detection of stimuli depends on their physical energy and on internal factors such as the relative costs and benefits associated with detecting their presence.
**Simple Cells:** Cells within the visual system that respond to specific shapes presented in certain orientations (e.g., horizontal, vertical, etc.).
**Simultaneous Conditioning:** A form of conditioning in which the conditioned stimulus (CS) and the unconditioned stimulus (UCS) begin and end at the same time.
**Size Constancy:** The tendency to perceive a physical object as having a constant size even when the size of the image it casts on the retina changes.
**Sleep:** A process in which important physiological changes (e.g., shifts in brain activity, slowing of basic bodily functions) are accompanied by major shifts in consciousness.
**Social Age Clocks:** Internalized calendars telling us when certain events should occur in our lives and what we should be doing at certain ages.
**Social Categorization:** The tendency to divide the social world into two distinct categories: "us" and "them."
**Social Cognition:** The process through which we notice, store, remember, and later use social information.
**Social Cognitive Theory:** A theory of behavior suggesting that human behavior is influenced by many cognitive factors as well as by reinforcement contingencies, and that human beings have an impressive capacity to regulate their own actions.
**Social–Cognitive or Role-Playing View:** A view suggesting that effects produced by hypnosis are the result of hypnotized persons' expectations about hypnosis and their social role as "hypnotized subject."
**Social Influence:** Efforts by one or more persons to change the attitudes or behavior of one or more others.
**Social Network:** A group of people with whom one interacts regularly.
**Social Norms:** Rules indicating how individuals ought to behave in specific situations.
**Social Psychologists:** Psychologists who study all aspects of social behavior and social thought.
**Sociocultural Theory:** Vygotsky's theory of cognitive development, which emphasizes the role of social factors and language.
**Somatic Nervous System:** The portion of the peripheral nervous system that connects the brain and spinal cord to voluntary muscles.
**Somatization Disorder:** A condition in which an individual has a history of many physical complaints, beginning before age thirty, that occur over a period of years and result in treatment being sought for significant impairments in social, occupational, or other important areas of life.
**Somatoform Disorders:** Disorders in which individuals experience physical symptoms for which there is no apparent physical cause.
**Somnambulism:** A sleep disorder in which individuals actually get up and move about while still asleep.
**Source Monitoring:** The process of identifying the origins of specific memories.
**Source Traits:** According to Cattell, key dimensions of personality that underlie many other traits.
**Split-Half Reliability:** The correlation between scores on two parts of a test.
**Spontaneous Recovery:** Reappearance of a weakened conditioned response to a conditioned stimulus after an interval of time following extinction.
**SQUID (Superconducting Quantum Interference Device):** An imaging technique that captures images of the brain through its ability to detect tiny changes in magnetic fields in the brain.

**Stage Theory:** Any theory proposing that all human beings move through an orderly and predictable series of changes.
**Standard Deviation:** A measure of dispersion reflecting the average distance between each score and the mean.
**Stanford–Binet Test:** A widely used individual test of intelligence.
**State-Dependent Retrieval:** Occurs when aspects of our physical states serve as retrieval cues for information stored in long-term memory.
**States of Consciousness:** Varying degress of awareness of ourselves and the external world.
**Stereotypes:** Cognitive frameworks suggesting that all members of specific social groups share certain characteristics.
**Stimulants:** Drugs that increase activity in the nervous system (e.g., amphetamines, caffeine, nicotine).
**Stimulus:** A physical event capable of affecting behavior.
**Stimulus Control:** Consistent occurrence of a behavior in the presence of a discriminative stimulus.
**Stimulus Discrimination:** The process by which organisms learn to respond to certain stimuli but not to others.
**Stimulus Generalization:** The tendency of stimuli similar to a conditioned stimulus to evoke conditioned responses.
**Stochastic Theories of Aging:** Theories suggesting that we grow old because of cumulative damage to our bodies from both external and internal sources; also known as *wear-and-tear theories of aging*.
**Storage:** The process through which information is retained in memory.
**Strange Situation Test:** A procedure for studying attachment in which a caregiver leaves a child alone with a stranger for several minutes and then returns.
**Stress:** Our response to events that disrupt, or threaten to disrupt, our physical or psychological functioning.
**Stressors:** Events or situations in our environment that cause stress.
**Striving for Superiority:** Attempting to overcome feelings of inferiority. According to Adler, this is the primary motive for human behavior.
**Structuralism:** An early view of psychology suggesting that the field should focus on identifying the basic structures of the human mind.
**Subjective Well-Being:** Individuals' global judgments of their own life satisfaction.
**Sublimation:** A defense mechanism in which threatening unconscious impulses are channeled into socially acceptable forms of behavior.
**Subliminal Perception:** The presumed ability to perceive a stimulus that is below the threshold for conscious experience.
**Substance Abuse:** A maladaptive pattern of substance use that results in repeated, significant adverse effects and maladaptive behaviors: failure to meet obligations at work, in school, or at home; repeated use of a psychoactive substance in hazardous ways; recurrent legal problems related to the substance; and continued use of the substance despite its negative effects on social relationships.
**Substance-Related Disorders:** Disorders related to the use of psychoactive substances.
**Successful Aging:** Aging with minimal physiological losses in many bodily functions relative to younger persons; results from a healthy lifestyle.
**Suicide:** The voluntary taking of one's own life.
**Superego:** According to Freud, the portion of human personality representing the conscience.
**Suprachiasmatic Nucleus (SCN):** A portion of the hypothalamus that seems to play an important role in the regulation of circadian rhythms.
**Survey Method:** A research method in which large numbers of people answer questions about aspects of their views or their behavior.
**Symbolic Play:** Play in which children pretend that one object is another object.
**Sympathetic Nervous System:** The portion of the autonomic nervous system that readies the body for expenditure of energy.
**Synapse:** A region where the axon of one neuron closely approaches other neurons or the cell membrane of other types of cells such as muscle cells.
**Synaptic Vesicles:** Structures in the axon terminals that contain various neurotransmitters.
**Syntax:** Rules about how units of speech can be combined into sentences in a given language.
**Systematic Desensitization:** A form of behavior therapy for phobias in which individuals first learn how to induce a relaxed state in their own bodies. Then, while in a relaxed state, they are exposed to stimuli that elicit fear.
**Systematic Observation:** A basic method of science in which the natural world, or various events or processes in it, are observed and measured in a very careful manner.
**Systematic Processing:** Careful consideration of the content of persuasive messages; also called the *central route* to persuasion. Such processing is quite effortful and absorbs much of our information-processing capacity.

**Tardive Dyskinesia:** A common side effect produced by antipsychotic drugs, in which individuals experience loss of motor control, especially in the face.
**Teleomeres:** Caps consisting of DNA that cover the ends of chromosomes and seem to regulate the number of times a cell can divide.
**Telepresence:** A process in which a person's perceptual, cognitive, and psychomotor capabilities are projected virtually into simulated environments.
**Temperament:** Stable individual differences in the quality and intensity of emotional reactions.
**Temporal Lobe:** The lobe of the cerebral cortex that is involved in hearing.
**Teratogens:** Factors in the environment that can harm the developing fetus.
**Tertiary Prevention:** Efforts to minimize the long-term harm stemming from psychological disorders.
**Test–Retest Reliability:** A measure of the extent to which scores on a test remain stable over time.
**Thalamus:** A structure deep within the brain that receives sensory input from other portions of the nervous system and then transmits this information to the cerebral hemispheres and other parts of the brain.
**Thematic Apperception Test (TAT):** A psychological test used to assess individual differences in several different motives (e.g., achievement motivation, power motivation).
**Theories:** In science, frameworks for explaining various events or processes.
**Theory of Dissociated Control:** A theory of hypnosis suggesting that hypnotism weakens control by the central function over other cognitive and behavioral subsystems, thus permitting these subsystems to be invoked directly by the hypnotist's suggestions.
**Theory of Mind:** Refers to children's growing understanding of their own mental states and those of others.
**Timbre:** The quality of a sound, resulting from the complexity of a sound wave; timbre helps us to distinguish the sound of a trumpet from a saxophone.
**Token Economies:** A form of behavior therapy in which patients in hospital settings earn tokens they can exchange for various rewards by engaging in desirable forms of behavior.
**Tolerance:** Habituation to a drug, causing larger and larger doses to be required to produce effects of the same magnitude.

**Trace Conditioning:** A form of forward conditioning in which the onset of the conditioned stimulus (CS) precedes the onset of the unconditioned stimulus (UCS) and the presentation of the CS and UCS does not overlap.
**Trait Theories:** Theories of personality that focus on identifying the key dimensions along which people differ.
**Transduction:** The translation of a physical energy into electrical signals by specialized receptor cells.
**Transference:** Intense emotional feelings of love or hate toward the analyst on the part of a patient undergoing psychoanalysis.
**Trial and Error:** A method of solving problems in which possible solutions are tried until one succeeds.
**Triarchic Theory:** A theory suggesting that there are three basic forms of intelligence: componential, experiential, and contextual.
**Trichromatic Theory:** A theory of color perception suggesting that we have three types of cones, each primarily receptive to different wavelengths of light.
**Type A Behavior Pattern:** A cluster of traits that includes competitiveness, impatience, and hostility; related to important aspects of health, social behavior, and task performance.
**Type D:** A personality type characterized by a general tendency to cope with stress by keeping negative emotions to oneself. People who exhibit this behavior pattern are more likely to experience suppressed immune systems and health-related problems.

**Unconditional Positive Regard:** In Rogers's theory, a therapeutic atmosphere that communicates that a person will be respected or loved regardless of what he or she says or does.
**Unconditioned Response (UCR):** In classical conditioning, the response evoked by an unconditioned stimulus.
**Unconditioned Stimulus (UCS):** In classical conditioning, a stimulus that can evoke an unconditioned response the first time it is presented.

**Validity:** The extent to which a test actually measures what it claims to measure.
**Variable-Interval Schedule:** A schedule of reinforcement in which a variable amount of time must elapse before a response will yield reinforcement.
**Variable-Ratio Schedule:** A schedule of reinforcement in which reinforcement is delivered after a variable number of responses have been performed.
**Variance:** A measure of dispersion reflecting the average squared distance between each score and the mean.
**Vestibular Sense:** Our sense of balance.
**Visual Images:** Mental pictures or representations of objects or events.
**Wavelength:** The peak-to-peak distance in a sound or light wave.

**Wear-and-Tear Theories of Aging:** Theories suggesting that aging results from the continuous use of cells and organs in our bodies.
**Wernicke's Area:** An area in the temporal lobe that, through its connection with other brain areas, plays a role in the comprehension of speech.
**Working Memory:** A memory system that holds information we are processing at the moment; formerly called *short-term memory.* Recent findings suggest that working memory involves more complex levels and forms of processing than was previously believed.
**Workplace Violence:** Violent outbursts in which employees attack and even kill other persons with whom they work.

**Yerkes–Dodson Law:** The suggestion that the level of arousal beyond which performance begins to decline is a function of task difficulty.

# References


Abram, S. E. (1993). Advances in chronic pain management since gate control. *Regional Anesthesia, 18,* 66–81.

Achenbach, T. M. (1997). *Empirically based assessment of child and adolescent psychopathology.* Thousand Oaks, CA: Sage.

Acocella, J. (1998, April 6). The politics of hysteria. *The New Yorker,* 64–79.

Adams, R. J. (1987). An evaluation of color preference in early infancy. *Infant Behavior and Development, 10,* 143–150.

Ader, R., & Cohen, N. (1984). Behavior and the immune system. In W. D. Gentry (Ed.), *Handbook of behavioral medicine.* New York: Guilford.

Ader, R., Kelly, K., Moynihan, J. A., Grota, L. J., & Cohen, N. (1993). Conditioned enhancement of antibody production using antigen as the unconditioned stimulus. *Brain, Behavior, and Immunity, 7,* 334–343.

Adler, N. J., & Bartholomew, S. (1992). Managing globally competent people. *Academy of Management Executive, 6,* 52–65.

Adolphs, R. (in press). The human amygdala and emotion. *The Neuroscientist.*

Adolphs, R., Russell, J. A., & Tranel, D. (1999). A role for the human amygdala in recognizing emotional arousal from unpleasant stimuli. *Psychological Science, 10,* 167–171.

Aiken, L. R. (1991). *Psychological testing and assessment* (7th ed.). Boston: Allyn and Bacon.

Aiken, L. S., West, S. G., Woodward, C. K., Reno, R. R., & Reynolds, K. D. (1994). Increasing screening mammography in asymptomatic women: Evaluation of a second-generation, theory-based program. *Health Psychology, 13,* 526–538.

Ainsworth, M. D. S. (1973). The development of infant-mother attachment. In B. Caldwell & H. Riciutti (Eds.), *Review of child development research* (Vol. 3, pp. 1–94). Chicago: University of Chicago Press.

Ajzen, J. (1991). The theory of planned behavior: special issue: Theories of cognitive self-regulation. *Organizational Behavior and Human Decision Processes, 509,* 179–211.

Akerstedt, T., & Froberg, J. E. (1976). Interindividual differences in circadian pattern of catecholamine excretion, body temperature, performance, and subjective arousal. *Biological Psychology, 4,* 277–292.

Alicke, M. D., & Largo, E. (1995). The role of the self in the false consensus effect. *Journal of Experimental Social Psychology, 31,* 28–47.

Al-Issa, I. (1977). Social and cultural aspects of hallucinations. *Psychological Bulletin, 84,* 570–587.

Allen, J. P., & Litten, R. Z. (1993). Psychometric and laboratory measures to assist in the treatment of alcoholism. *Clinical Psychology Review, 13,* 223–240.

Allen, L. S., & Gorski, R. A. (1992). Biology, brain architecture, and human sexuality. *Journal of National Institute of Health Research, 4,* 53–59.

Allport, G. W. (1965). *Letters from Jenny.* New York: Harcourt, Brace & World.

Allred, J. B. (1993). Lowering serum cholesterol: Who benefits? *Journal of Nutrition, 123,* 1453–1459.

Allyn, J., & Festinger, L. (1961). The effectiveness of unanticipated persuasive communications. *Journal of Abnormal and Social Psychology, 62,* 35–40.

Aloise-Young, P. A., Graham, J. W., & Hansen, W. B. (1994). Peer influence on smoking initiation during early adolescence: A comparison of group members and group outsiders. *Journal of Applied Psychology, 79,* 281–287.

Alvarez-Borda, B., Ramirez-Amaya, V., Perez-Montfort, R., & Bermudez-Rattoni, F. (1995). Enhancement of antibody production by a learning paradigm. *Neurobiology of Learning and Memory, 64,* 103–105.

Al-Zahrani, S. S., & Kaplowitz, S. A. (1993). Attributional biases in individualistic and collective cultures: A comparison of Americans with Saudis. *Social Psychology Quarterly, 56,* 223–233.

Amabile, T. M. (1983). *The social psychology of creativity.* New York: Springer-Verlag.

Amaro, H. (1995). Love, sex, and power: Considering women's realities in HIV prevention. *American Psychologist, 50,* 437–447.

Amato, P. R. (1990). Parental divorce and attitudes toward marriage and family life. *Journal of Marriage and the Family, 50,* 453–461.

Amato, P. R., & Keith, B. (1991). Parental divorce and the well-being of children: A meta-analysis. *Psychological Bulletin, 110,* 26–46.

Ambuel, B. (1995). Adolescents, unintended pregnancy, and abortion: The struggle for a compassionate social policy. *Current Directions in Psychological Science, 4,* 1–5.

American Cancer Society. (1989). *Cancer facts and figures—1989.* Atlanta, GA: Author.

American Psychiatric Association (1994). *Diagnostic and statistical manual of mental disorders* (4th ed.). Washington, DC: American Psychiatric Association.

American Psychological Association. (1993b). Guidelines for providers of psychological services to ethnic, linguistic, and culturally diverse populations. *American Psychologist, 48,* 45–48.

American Psychological Association. (1995). Training in and dissemination of empirically-validated psychological procedures. Report and recommendations. *The Clinical Psychologist, 48,* 22–23.

American Psychological Association. (1999). The scope of psychology. Washington, DC: Author.

Amoore, J. (1970). *Molecular basis of odor.* Springfield, IL: Thomas.

Amoore, J. (1982). Odor theory and odor classification. In E. Theimer (Ed.), *Fragrance chemistry-the science of the sense of smell.* New York: Academic Press.

Anderson, C. A., & Bushman, B. J. (1997). External validity of "trivial" experiments: The case of laboratory aggression. *Review of General Psychology, 1,* 19–41.

Anderson, C. A., Anderson, K. B., & Deuser, W. E. (1996). Examining an affective aggression framework: Weapon and temperature effects on aggressive thoughts, affect, and attitudes. *Personality and Social Psychology Bulletin, 22,* 366–376.

Anderson, C. A., Deuser, W. E., & DeNeve, K. M. (1995). Hot temperatures, hostile affect, hostile cognition, and arousal: Tests of a general theory of affective aggression. *Personality and Social Psychology Bulletin, 21,* 434–448.

Anderson, C. A., Lindsay, J. J., & Bushman, B. J. (1999). Research in the psychological laboratory: Truth or triviality? *Current Directions in Psychological Science, 8,* 1–9.

Anderson, J. R. (1993). *Rules of the mind.* Hillsdale, NJ: Erlbaum.

Anderson, J. R., & Spellman, B. A. (1995). On the status of inhibitory mechanisms in cognition: Memory retrieval as a model case. *Psychological Review, 102,* 68–100.

Anderson, J. R., Bjork, R. A., & Bjork, E. L. (1994). Mechanisms of inhibition in long-term memory: A new taxonomy. *Journal of Experimental Psychology: Learning, Memory, and Cognition, 20,* 1063–1087.

Anderson, J. R., Reder, L. M., & Lebiere, C. (1996). Working memory: Activation, limitations on retrieval. *Cognitive Psychology, 30,* 221–256.

Andreason, N. C., & Black, D. (1995). *Introductory textbook of psychiatry* (2nd ed.) Washington, DC: American Psychiatric Press.

Andreasen, N. C., Flaum, M., Swayze, V., II, O'Leary, D. S., Alliger, R., Cohen, G., Ehrhardt, J., & Yuhn, W. T. C. (1993). Intelligence and brain structure in normal individuals. *American Journal of Psychiatry, 150,* 130–134.

Andrews, E. A., Gosse, V. F., Gaulton, R. S., & Maddigan, R. I. (1999). Teaching introductory psychology at a distance by two-way interactive video. *Teaching of Psychology, 2,* 115–118.

Andrews, J. D. W. (1967). The achievement motive and advancement in two types of organization. *Journal of Personality and Social Psychology, 6,* 163–168.

Antrobus, J. (1991). Dreaming: Cognitive processes during cortical activation and high afferent thresholds. *Psychological Review, 98,* 96–212.

Applebaum, P. S. (1994). *Almost a revolution: Mental health law and the limits of change.* New York: Oxford University Press.

Archer, J. (1994). Testosterone and aggression. *Journal of Offender Rehabilitation, 5,* 3–25.

Arena, J. G., Bruno, G. M., Hannah, S. L., & Meador, J. K. (1995). A comparison of frontal electromyographic biofeedback training, trapezius electromyographic biofeedback training, and progressive muscle relaxation therapy in the treatment of tension headache. *Headache, 35,* 411–419.

Arking, R. (1991). *Biology of aging: Observations and principles.* Englewood Cliffs, NJ: Prentice-Hall.

Arndt, J., Greenberg, J., Pyszcynski, T., Solomon, S. (1997). Subliminal exposure to death-related stimuli increases defense of the cultural worldview. *Psychological Science, 8,* 379–385.

Aronoff, J., Woike, B. A., & Hyman, L. M. (1992). Which are the stimuli in facial displays of anger and happiness? Configurational bases of emotional recognition. *Journal of Personality and Social Psychology, 62,* 1050–1066.

Aronoff, S. R., & Spilka, B. (1984–1985). Patterning of facial expressions among terminal cancer patients. *Omega, 15,* 101–108.

Aronson, E. (1990). Applying social psychology to desegregation and energy conservation. *Personality and Social Psychology Bulletin, 16,* 118–132.

Aronson, E., Bridgeman, D. L., & Geffner, R. (1978). Interdependent interactions and prosocial behavior. *Journal of Research and Development in Education, 12,* 16–27.

Aronson, E., Fried, C., & Stone, J. (1991). Overcoming denial: Increasing the intention to use condoms through induction of hypocrisy. *American Journal of Public Health, 18,* 1636–1640.

Arvey, R. D., Bouchard, T. J., Jr., Segal, N. L., & Abraham, L. M. (1989). Job satisfaction: Genetic and environmental components. *Journal of Applied Psychology, 74,* 187–192.

Ashcraft, M. H. (1998). *Fundamentals of Cognition.* New York: Addison-Wesley.

Astington, J. W. (1995). Talking it over with my brain. In J. Flavell, F. Green, & E. Flavell, (Eds.),

*Monographs of the Society for Research in Child Development, 60,* 104–113.

Atkinson, R. C., & Shiffrin, R. M. (1968). Human memory: A proposed system and its control processes. In K. W. Spence & J. T. Spence (Eds.), *The psychology of learning and motivation: Advances in research and theory* (pp. 89–195). New York: Academic Press.

Awh, D., Jonides, J., Smith, E. E., Buxton, R. B., Frank, L. R., Love, T., Wong, E. C., & Gmeindl, L. (1999). Rehearsal in spatial working memory: Evidence from neuroimaging. *Psychological Science, 10,* 433–437.

Awh, D., Jonides, J., Smith, E. E., Schumacher, E. H., Koeppe, R. A., & Katz, S. (1996). Dissociation of storage and rehearsal in verbal working memory: Evidence from positron emission tomography. *Psychological Science, 7,* 25–31.

Azar, B. (1996, August). Why men lose keys—and women find them. *American Psychological Association Monitor,* p. 32.

Azar, B. (1999, June). Tailored interventions prove more effective. *APA Monitor, 30*(6), 38–39.

Azmitia, M. (1988). Peer interaction and problem-solving: When two heads are better than one? *Child Development, 59,* 87–96.

Békésy, G. von. (1960). *Experiments in hearing.* New York: McGraw-Hill.

Bachman, J. G. (1987, February). An eye on the future. *Psychology Today,* pp. 6–7.

Baddeley, A. (1990). *Human memory: Theory and practice.* Boston: Allyn and Bacon.

Baddeley, A. D. (1992). Working memory. *Science, 255,* 556–559.

Baddeley, A. D. (1996). Exploring the central executive. *Quarterly Journal of Experimental Psychology, 49A,* 5–28.

Baddeley, A. D., & Hitsch, G. (1994). Developments in the concept of working memory. *Neuropsychology, 8,* 485–493.

Bader, S. A., & Braude, R. M. (1998). Patient informatics: Creating new partnerships in medical decision making. *Academic Medicine, 73,* 408–411.

Baghurst, P. A., McMichael, A. J., Wigg, N. R., Vimpahni, G. V., Robertson, E. F., Roberts, R. J., & Tongs, S. L. (1992). Environmental exposure to lead and children's intelligence at the age of seven years: The Port Pirie cohort study. *New England Journal of Medicine, 327,* 1279–1284.

Bailey, J. H., & Witmer, B. G. (1994). Learning and transfer of spatial knowledge in virtual environments. In *Proceedings of the Human Factors and Ergonomics Society 38th Annual Meeting* (pp. 1158–1162). Santa Monica, CA: Human Factors and Ergonomics Society.

Bailey, J. M., & Pillard, R. C. (1991). A genetic study of male sexual orientation. *Archives of General Psychiatry, 48,* 1089–1096.

Baillargeon, R. (1987). Object permanence in 3.5– and 4.5–month-old infants. *Developmental Psychology, 23,* 655–664.

Baillargeon, R. (1994). Physical reasoning in young infants: Seeking explanations for possible events. *British Journal of Developmental Psychology, 12,* 9–33.

Baillargeon, R., Needham, A., & DeVos, J. (1992). The development of young infants' intuitions about support. *Early Development and Parenting, 1,* 69–78.

Baker, A. G., & Mackintosh, N. J. (1977). Excitatory and inhibitory conditioning following uncorrelated presentations of CS and US. *Animal Learning and Behavior, 5*(3), 315–319.

Baker, R. R., & Bellis, M. A. (1995). *Human sperm competition.* London: Chapman & Hall.

Balogh, R. D., & Porter, R. H. (1986). Olfactory preferences resulting from mere exposure in human neonates. *Infant Behavior and Development, 9,* 395–401.

Baltes, P. B. (1987). Theoretical propositions of life-span developmental psychology: On the dynamics between growth and decline. *Developmental Psychology, 23,* 611–626.

Bandura, A. (1977). *Social learning theory.* Englewood Cliffs, NJ: Prentice-Hall.

Bandura, A. (1977). Self-efficacy: toward a unifying theory of behavioral change. *Psychological Review, 84,* 191–215.

Bandura, A. (1986). *Social foundations of thought and action: A social cognitive theory.* Englewood Cliffs, NJ: Prentice Hall.

Bandura, A. (1992). Exercise of personal agency through the self-efficacy mechanism. In R. Schwarzer (Ed.), *Self-efficacy: Thought control of action* (pp. 3–38). Washington, DC: Hemisphere.

Bandura, A. (1997). *Self-efficacy: The exercise of control.* New York: Freeman.

Bandura, A. (1999). A social cognitive theory of personality. In L. Pervin & D. John (Eds.), *Handbook of personality* (2nd ed.). New York: Guilford.

Bandura, A., Ross, D., & Ross, S. (1963). Imitation of film-mediated aggressive models. *Journal of Abnormal and Social Psychology, 66,* 3–11.

Banks, S. M., Salovey, P., Greener, S., Rothman, A. J., Moyer, A., Beauvais, J. & Epel, E. (1995). The effects of message framing on mammography utilization. *Health Psychology, 14,* 178–184.

Bar, M., & Biederman, I. (1998). Subliminal visual priming. *Psychological Science, 9,* 464–469.

Barber, T. X., Chauncey, H. H., & Winer, R. A. (1964). Effects of hypnotic and nonhypnotic suggestions on parotid gland response to gustatory stimuli. *Psychosomatic Medicine, 26,* 374–380.

Barbur, J. L., Watson, J. D. G., Frackowiak, R. S. J., & Zeki, S. (1993). Conscious visual perception without V1. *Brain, 116,* 1293.

Barch, D. M., & Berenbaum, H. (1996). Language production and thought disorder in schizophrenia. *Journal of Abnormal Psychology, 105,* 81–88.

Barfield, W., & Weghorst, S. (1993). The sense of presence within virtual environments: A conceptual framework. In G. Salvendy & M. Smith (Eds.), *Human–computer interaction: Software and hardware interfaces* (pp. 699–704). Amsterdam: Elsevier.

Bargh, J. A., Raymond, P., Pryor, J. B., & Strack, F. (1995). Attractiveness of the underling: An automatic power—sex association and its consequences for sexual harassment and aggression. *Journal of Personality and Social Psychology, 68,* 768–781.

Bargones, J. Y., & Werner, L. A. (1994). Adults listen selectively; infants do not. *Psychological Science, 5,* 170–174.

Barkley, R. A., DuPaul, G. J., & McMurray, M. B. (1990). Comprehensive evaluation of attention deficit disorder with and without hyperactivity as defined by research criteria. *Journal of Consulting and Clinical Psychology, 58,* 775–789.

Barlow, D. H. (1988). *Anxiety and its disorders.* New York: Guilford Press.

Barlow, D. H. (1993). Disorders and emotion. *Psychological Inquiry, 2,* 58–71.

Barnier, A. (1997). *Experiments on posthypnotic suggestion.* Unpublished doctoral dissertation, University of New South Wales, Australia.

Baron, J. (1988). *Thinking and deciding.* Cambridge, England: Cambridge University Press.

Baron, R. A. (1970). Attraction toward the model and model's competence as determinants of adult imitative behavior. *Journal of Personality and Social Psychology, 14,* 335–344.

Baron, R. A. (1983). The control of human aggression: A strategy based on incompatible responses. In R. G. Geen & E. I. Donnerstein (Eds.), *Aggression: Theoretical and empirical reviews.* New York: Academic Press.

Baron, R. A. (1987). Mood of interviewer and the evaluation of job candidates. *Journal of Applied Social Psychology, 17,* 911–926.

Baron, R. A. (1993a). Criticism (informal negative feedback) as a source of perceived unfairness in organizations: Effects, mechanisms, and countermeasures. In R. Cropanzano (Ed.), *Justice in the workplace: Approaching fairness in human resource management* (pp. 155–170). Hillsdale, NJ: Erlbaum.

Baron, R. A. (1993b). Interviewers' moods and evaluations of job applicants: The role of applicant qualifications. *Journal of Applied Social Psychology, 23,* 253–271.

Baron, R. A. (1993c). Reducing aggression and conflict: The incompatible response approach. Or: Why people who feel good usually won't be bad. In G. G. Brannigan & M. R. Merrens (Eds.), *The undaunted psychologist* (pp. 203–218). Philadelphia: McGraw-Hill.

Baron, R. A. (1994). The physical environment of work settings: Effects on task performance, interpersonal relations, and job satisfaction. In M. Staw & L. L. Cummings (Eds.), *Research in organizational behavior* (Vol. 16, pp. 1–46). Greenwich, CT: JAI Press.

Baron, R. A. (1997). The sweet smell of . . . helping: Effects of pleasant ambient odors on helping in shopping malls. *Personality and Social Psychology Bulletin, 2,* 498–503.

Baron, R. A. (1998). Cognitive mechanisms in entrepreneurship: Why, and when, entrepreneurs think differently than other persons. *Journal of Business Venturing, 13,* 275–294.

Baron, R. A. (2000). Psychological perspectives on entrepreneurship: Social and cognitive factors in entrepreneurs' success. *Current Directions in Psychological Science, 9,* 15–18.

Baron, R. A., & Bronfen, M. I. (1994). A whiff of reality: Empirical evidence concerning the effects of pleasant fragrances on work-related behavior. *Journal of Applied Social Psychology, 13,* 1179–1203.

Baron, R. A., & Byrne, D. (2000). *Social psychology* (9th ed.). Boston: Allyn & Bacon.

Baron, R. A., Hirsa, A., & Markman, G. D. (2000). Perceptions of female entrepreneurs: Evidence for the beneficial effects of attributional augmenting. Manuscript submitted for publication.

Baron, R. A., & Kalsher, M. J. (1998). The sweet smell of . . . safety? *Proceedings of the Human Factors and Ergonomics Society, 40,* 1282.

Baron, R. A., & Kalsher, M. J. (1998). Effects of a pleasant ambient fragrance on simulated driving performance: The sweet smell of . . . safety? *Environment and Behavior, 30,* 535–552.

Baron, R. A., & Markman, G. D. (2000). Beyond social capital: The role of social skills in entrepreneurs' success. *Academy of Management Executive.*

Baron, R. A., & Neuman, J. H. (1996). Workplace violence and workplace aggression: Evidence on their relative frequency and potential causes. *Aggressive Behavior, 22,* 161–173.

Baron, R. A., & Neuman, J. H. (1998). Workplace aggression—the iceberg beneath the tip of workplace violence: Evidence on its forms, frequency, and potential causes. *Public Administration Quarterly, 21,* 446–464.

Baron, R. A., Neuman, J. H., & Geddes, D. (1999). Social and personal determinants of workplace aggression: Evidence for the impact of perceived injustice and the Type A behavior pattern. *Aggressive Behavior, 25,* 281–296.

Baron, R. A., Rea, M. S., & Daniels, S. G. (1992). Lighting as a source of environmentally-generated positive affect in work settings: Impact on cognitive tasks and interpersonal behavior. *Motivation and Emotion, 14,* 1–34.

Baron, R. A., & Richardson, D. (1994). *Human aggression* (2nd ed.). New York: Plenum.

Baron, R. A., & Thomley, J. (1994). A whiff of reality: Positive affect as a potential mediator of the effects of pleasant fragrances on task performance and helping. *Environment and Behavior, 26,* 766–784.

Baron, R. S., Vandello, U.S., & Brunsman, B. (1996). The forgotten variable in conformity research: Impact of task importance on social influence. *Journal of Personality and Social Psychology, 71,* 915–927.

Baron-Cohen, S., Campbell, R., Kamiloff-Smith, A., Grant, J., & Walker, J. (1995). Are children with autism blind to the mentalistic significance of the eyes? *British Journal of Developmental Psychology, 13,* 379–398.

Barrett, L. F., & Russell, J. A. (1999). The structure of current affect: Controversies and emerging consensus. *Current Directions in Psychological Science, 9,* 10–14.

Barrick, M. R., & Mount, M. K. (1993). Autonomy as a moderator of the relationships between the big five personality dimensions and job performance. *Journal of Applied Psychology, 78,* 111–118.

Barrick, M. R., Stewart, G. L., Neubert, M. J., & Mount, M. K. (1998). Relating member ability and personality to work-team processes and team effectiveness. *Journal of Applied Psychology, 83,* 377–391.

Bartlett, J. G., & Moore, R. D. (1998, July). Improving HIV therapy. *Scientific American,* 84–87, 89, 91–93.

Bashore, T. R., Ridderinkhof, K. R., & van der Molen, M. W. (1997). The decline of cognitive processing in old age. *Current Directions in Psychological Science, 6,* 163–169.

Basoglu, M., Paker, M., Ozmen, E., Tasdemir, O., Sahin, D., Ceyhanli, A., & Incesu, C. (1996). Appraisal of self, social environment, and state authority as a possible mediator of posttraumatic stress disorder in tortured political activists. *Journal of Abnormal Psychology, 105,* 232–236.

Bass, B. I. (1998). *Leadership* (2nd ed.). New York: Free Press.

Bauer, P. (1996). What do infants recall of their lives? *American Psychologist 51,* 29–41.

Baum, A., & Posluszny, D. M. (1999). Health psychology: Mapping biobehavioral contributions to health and illness. *Annual Review of Psychology, 50,* 137–163.

Baum, D. R., & Jonides, J. J. (1979). Cognitive maps: Analysis of comparative judgments of distance. *Memory and Cognition, 7,* 462–468.

Baumeister, R. F. (1984). Choking under pressure: Self-consciousness and paradoxical effects of incentives on skillful performance. *Journal of Personality and Social Psychology, 46,* 610–620.

Baumeister, R. F. (1990). Suicide as an escape from self. *Psychological Review, 97,* 90–113.

Baumeister, R. F. (1998). The self. In D. T. Gilbert, S. T. Fiske, & G. Lindzey (Eds.), *Handbook of social psychology* (4th ed.), (Vol 1, pp. 689–740). New York: McGraw-Hill.

Baumeister, R. F., & Leary, M. R. (1995). The need to belong: Desire for interpersonal attachments as a fundamental human motivation. *Psychological Bulletin, 117,* 497–529.

Baumeister, R. F., & Steinhilber, A. (1984). Paradoxical effects of supportive audiences on performance under pressure: The home field disadvantage in sports championships. *Journal of Personality and Social Psychology, 47,* 85–93.

Baumrind, D. (1991). The influence of parenting style on adolescent competence and substance abuse. *Journal of Early Adolescence, 11,* 56–95.

Beaman, A. L., Cole, N., Preston, M., Glentz, B., & Steblay, N. M. (1983). Fifteen years of the foot-in-the-door research: A meta-analysis. *Personality and Social Psychology Bulletin, 9,* 181–186.

Bechara, A., Tranel, D., Damasio, H., Adolphs, R., Fockland, C., & Damasio, A. F. (1997). Double dissociation of conditioning and declarative knowledge relative to the amygdala and hippocampus in humans. *Science, 269,* 1115–1118.

Beck, A. T. (1976). *Cognitive therapy and the emotional disorders.* New York: International Universities Press.

Beck, A. T. (1985). *Anxiety disorders and phobias: A cognitive perspective.* New York: Basic Books.

Beck, A. T., Rush, A. J., Shaw, B. F., & Emery, G. (1979). *Cognitive theory of depression.* New York: Guilford Press.

Becker, H. C., Randall, C. L., Salo, A. L., Saulnier, J. L., & Weathersby, R. T. (1994). Animal research: Charting the course for FAS. *Alcohol Health and Research World, 18,* 10–16.

Beckstead, J. W. (1991). Psychological factors influencing judgments and attitude regarding animal research: An application of functional measurement and structural equation modeling. Unpublished doctoral dissertation, State University of New York, Albany.

Bednar, R. L., & Kaul, T. (1994). Experiential group research. In A. E. Bergin & S. L. Garfield (Eds.), *Handbook of psychotherapy and behavior change.* New York: John Wiley & Sons (pp. 631–663).

Belli, R. F., & Loftus, E. F. (1996). The pliability of autobiographical memory: Misinformation and the false memory problem. In D.C. Rubin (Ed.), *Remembering our past* (pp. 157–179). New York: Cambridge University Press.

Belmore, S. M., & Hubbard, M. L. (1987). The role of advance expectancies in person memory. *Journal of Personality and Social Psychology, 53,* 61–70.

Belsky, J., & Cassidy, J. (1995). Attachment: Theory and evidence. In M. Rutter & D. Hay (Eds.), *Development through life: A handbook for clinicians* (pp. 373–402). Oxford, England: Blackwell.

Bem, D. J. (1996). Exotic becomes erotic: A developmental theory of sexual orientiaton. *Psychological Review, 103,* 320–335.

Bem, D. J., & Honorton, C. (1994). Does psi exist? Replicable evidence for an anomalous process of information transfer. *Psychological Bulletin, 115,* 4–18.

Bem, S. L. (1984). Adrogyny and gender schema theory: A conceptual and empirical integration. In R. A. Dientsbier & T. B. Sondregger (Eds.), *Nebraska Symposium on Motivation* (Vol. 34, pp. 179–226). Lincoln: University of Nebraska Press.

Bem, S. L. (1989). Genital knowledge and gender constancy in preschool children. *Child Development, 60,* 649–662.

Benjamin, L. T., Jr., & Dixon, D. N. (1996). Dream analysis by mail: An American woman seeks Freud's advice. *American Psychologist, 51,* 461–468.

Berardi-Coletta, B., Buyer, L. S., Dominowski, R. L., & Rellinger, E. R. (1995). Metacognition and problem solving: A process-oriented approach. *Journal of Experimental Psychology: Learning, Memory, and Cognition, 21,* 205–223.

Berenbaum, H., & Oltmanns, T. F. (1992). Emotional experience and expression in schizophrenia and depression. *Journal of Abnormal Psychology, 101,* 37–44.

Bergin, A. E., & Lambert, M. J. (1978). The evaluation of therapeutic outcomes. In S. L. Garfield & A. E. Bergin (Eds.), *Handbook of psychotherapy and behavior change: An empirical analysis* (2nd ed., pp. 139–190). New York: Wiley.

Berglas, S., & Jones, E. E. (1978). Drug choice as a self-handicapping strategy in response to noncontingent success. *Journal of Personality and Social Psychology, 36,* 405–417.

Berkowitz, L. (1984). Some effects of thoughts on anti- and pro-social influences of media events: A cognitive-neoassociation analysis, *Psychological Bulletin, 95,* 410–427.

Berkowitz, L. (1989). Frustration-aggression hypothesis: Examination and reformulation. *Psychological Bulletin, 106,* 59–73.

Berkowitz, L. (1993). *Aggression: Its causes, consequences, and control.* New York: McGraw-Hill.

Berlyne, D. E. (1967). Arousal and reinforcement. In D. Levine (Ed.), *Nebraska Symposium on Motivation* (Vol. 15, pp. 279–286). Lincoln: University of Nebraska Press.

Berman, J. S., & Norton, N. C. (1985). Does professional training make a therapist more effective? *Psychological Bulletin, 98,* 401–406.

Berry, D. S. (1991). Attractive faces are not all created equal: Joint effects of facial babyishness and attractiveness on social perception. *Personality and Social Psychology Bulletin, 17,* 523–531.

Berry, D. S., & McArthur, L. Z. (1986). Perceiving character in faces: The impact of age-related craniofacial changes on social perception. *Psychological Bulletin, 100,* 3–18.

Besson, J., & Chaouch, A. (1987). Peripheral spinal mechanisms of nociception. *Psychological Review, 67,* 67–186.

Besson, M., Faita, F., Peretz, I., Bonnel, A.-M., & Requin, J. (1998). Singing in the brain: Independence of lyrics and tunes. *Psychological Science, 9,* 494–498.

Betz, E. L. (1982). Need fulfillment in the career development of women. *Journal of Vocational Behavior, 20,* 53–66.

Biederman, J., Rosenbaum, J. F., Hirshfield, D. R., Faraone, S. V., Bolduc, E. A., Gersten, M., Menninger, S. R., Kagan, J., Snidman, N., & Reznick, J. S. (1990). Psychiatric correlations of behavioral inhibition in young children of parents with and without psychiatric disorders. *Archives of General Psychiatry, 47,* 21–26.

Bixler, E. O., Kales, A., Soldatos, C. R., Kales, J. D., & Healey, S. (1979). Prevalence of sleep disorders in the Los Angeles metropolitan area. *American Journal of Psychiatry, 136,* 1257–1262.

Black, J. S., & Mendenhall, M. (1990). Cross-cultural training effectiveness: A review and a theoretical framework for future research. *Academy of Management Review, 15,* 113–136.

Blackmore, S. (1986). A critical guide to parapsychology. *Skeptical Inquirer, 11*(1), 97–102.

Blakemore, C., & Cooper, G. F. (1970). Development of the brain depends on the visual environment. *Nature, 228,* 477–478.

Blaney, P. H. (1986). Affect and memory: A review. *Psychological Bulletin, 99,* 229–246.

Blatt, S. J., Zuroff, D. C., Quinlan, D. M., & Pilkonis, P. (1996). Interpersonal factors in brief treatment of depression: Further analysis of the NIMH Treatment of Depression Collaborative Research Program. *Journal of Consulting and Clinical Psychology, 64,* 162–171.

Block, J. H. (1995). A contrarian view of the five-factor approach to personality description. *Psychological Bulletin, 117,* 187–215.

Block, V., Hennevin, E., & Leconte, P. (1977). Interaction between post-trial reticular stimulation and subsequent paradoxical sleep in memory consolidation processes. In R. R. Drucker-Colin & J. L. McGaugh (Eds.), *Neurology of sleep and memory.* New York: Academic Press.

Blyth, D. A., Bulcroft, R., & Simmons, R. G. (1981, August). *The impact of puberty on adolescents: A longitudinal study.* Paper presented at the annual meetings of the American Psychological Association, Los Angeles.

Bobo, L. (1983). Whites' opposition to busing: Symbolic racism or realistic group conflict? *Journal of Personality and Social Psychology, 45,* 1196–1210.

Bobocel, D. R., & Meyer, J. P. (1994). Escalating commitment to a failing course of action: Separating the roles of choice and justification. *Journal of Applied Psychology, 79,* 360–363.

Bodenhausen, G. F. (1993). Emotion, arousal, and stereotypic judgment: A heuristic model of affect and stereotyping. In D. Mackie & D. Hamilton (Eds.), *Affect, cognition, and stereotyping: Intergroup processes in intergroup perception* (pp. 13–37). San Diego, CA: Academic Press.

Boivin, M., & Hymel, S. (1997). Peer expectations and social self-perceptions: A sequential model. *Developmental Psychology, 33,* 135–145.

Boling, N. C., & Robinson, D. H. (1999). Individual study, interactive multimedia, or cooperative learning: Which activity best supplements lecture-based distance education? *Journal of Educational Psychology, 91,* 169–174.

Bonardi, C., Honey, R. C., & Hall, G. (1990). Context specificity of conditioning in flavor-aversion learning: Extinction and blocking tests. *Animal Learning & Behavior, 18,* 229–237.

Bond, G. R., Witheridge, T. C., Dincin, J., Wasner, D., Webb, J. U., & Graff-Kaser, R. (1990). Assertive community treatment for frequent users of psychiatric hospitals in a large city: A controlled study. *American Journal of Community Psychology, 18,* 865–891.

Bongar, B. (1991). *The suicidal patient: Clinical and legal standards of care.* Washington, DC: American Psychological Association.

Bookstein, F. L., Sampson, P. D., Streissgarth, A. P., & Barr, H. M. (1996). Exploiting redundant measurement of dose and developmental outcome: New methods from the behavioral teratology of alcohol. *Developmental Psychology, 32,* 404–415.

Bootzin, R. R., Acocella, J. R., & Alloy, L. B. (1993). *Abnormal psychology* (6th ed.). New York: McGraw-Hill.

Borges, G., & Rosovsky, H. (1996). Suicide attempts and alcohol consumption in an emergency room sample. *Journal of Studies on Alcohol, 57,* 543–548.

Borke, H. (1975). Piaget's mountains revisited: Changes in the egocentric landscape. *Developmental Psychology, 11,* 240–243.

Bornstein, R. F. (1992). Subliminal mere exposure effects. In R. Bornstein & T. S. Pittman (Eds.), *Perception without awareness: Cognitive, clinical, and social perspectives* (pp. 191–210). New York: Guilford Press.

Borod, J. C. (1993). Cerebral mechanisms underlying facial, prosodic, and lexical emotional expressions: A review of neuropsychological studies and methodological issues. *Neuropsychology, 7,* 445–463.

Bouchard, T. J., Jr., Lykken, D. T., McGue, M., Segal, N. L. & Tellegen, A. (1990). Sources of human psychological differences: The Minnesota Study of Twins Reared Apart. *Science, 250,* 223–228.

Bounds, W. (1996, May 6). Sounds and scents to jolt drowsy drivers. *Wall Street Journal,* pp. B1, B5.

Bowers, K. S. (1992). Imagination and dissociation in hypnotic responding. *International Journal of Clinical and Experimental Hypnosis, 40,* 253–275.

Bowers, K. S., & Farvolden, P. (1996). Revisiting a century-old Freudian slip: From suggestion disavowed to the truth repressed. *Psychological Bulletin,* 119, 355–380.

Bowlby, J. (1969). *Attachment and loss: Vol. 1. Attachment.* New York: Basic Books.

Bowles, N., & Hynds, F. (1978). *Psy search: The comprehensive guide to psychic phenomena.* New York: Harper & Row.

Bowman, E. S., & Nurnberger, J. K. (1993). Genetics of psychiatry diagnosis and treatment. In D. L. Dunner (Ed.), *Current psychiatric therapy* (p. 46–56). Philadelphia: Saunders.

Boyle, P. (1993). The hazards of passive-and active-smoking. *New England Journal of Medicine, 328,* 1708–1709.

Brainerd, C. J. (1996). Piaget: A centennial celebration. *Psychological Science, 7,* 191–195.

Brainerd, C. J., & Reyna, V. F. (1998). When things that were never experienced are easier to "remember" than things that were. *Psychological Science, 9,* 484–489.

Braungart, M. M., & Braungart, R. G. (1990). The life course development of left- and right-wing youth activist leaders from the 1960s. *Political Psychology, 11,* 242–282.

Braverman, N. S., & Bronstein, P. (Eds.). (1985). Experimental assessments and clinical applications of conditioned food aversions. *Annals of the New York Academy of Sciences, 443,* 1–41.

Brean, H. (1958, March 31). What hidden sell is all about. *Life,* pp.104–114.

Breazeal (Ferrell), C., & Scassellati, B. (in press). Infant-like social interactions between a robot and a human caretaker. *Adaptive Behavior* [Special issue on Simulation Models of Social Agents, guest ed. K. Dautenhahn].

Breland, K., & Breland, M. (1961). The misbehavior of organisms. *American Psychologist, 16,* 681–684.

Brewer, M. B. (1993). Social identity, distinctiveness, and in-group homogeneity. *Social Cognition, 11,* 150–154.

Brockner, J., & Rubin, J. Z. (1985). *Entrapment in escalating conflicts.* New York: Springer-Verlag.

Bronfenbrenner, U. (1989). Ecological systems theory. In R. Vasta (Ed.), *Annals of child development: Vol. 6. Six theories of child development: Revised formulations and current issues* (pp. 187–249). Greenwich, CT: JAI Press.

Broussaud, D., di Pellegrino, G., & Wise, S. P. (1996). Frontal lobe mechanisms subserving vision-for-action versus vision-for-perception. *Behavioural Brain Research, 72,* 1–15.

Brown, J. (1968). Reciprocal facilitation and impairment in free recall. *Psychonomic Science, 10,* 41–42.

Brown, J. D., & McGill, K. L. (1989). The cost of good fortune: When positive life events produce negative health consequences. *Journal of Personality and Social Psychology, 57,* 1103–1110.

Brown, J. D., & Rogers, R. J. (1991). Self-serving attributions: The role of physiological arousal. *Personality and Social Psychology Bulletin, 17,* 501–506.

Brown, R. W., & Kulik, J. (1977). Flashbulb memories. *Cognition, 5,* 73–99.

Brownell, K. D., & Cohen, L. R. (1995). Adherence to dietary regimens 1: An overview of research. *Behavioral Medicine, 20,* 149–154.

Bruder, G. E., Stewart, M. W., Mercier, M. A., Agosti, V., Leite, P., Donovan, S., & Quitkin, F. M. (1997). Outcome of cognitive-behavioral therapy for depression: Relation to hemispheric dominance for verbal processing. *Journal of Abnormal Psychology, 106,* 138–144.

Bruhn, J. G., & Phillips, B. U. (1987). A developmental basis for social support. *Journal of Behavioral Medicine, 10,* 213–229.

Bryant, D., & Maxwell, K. (1997). The effectiveness of early intervention for disadvantaged children. In M. Guralnick (Ed.), *The effectiveness of early intervention* (pp. 23–46). Baltimore: Brookes.

Buehler, R., Griffin, D., & MacDonald, H. (1997). The role of motivated reasoning in optimistic time predictions. *Personality and Social Psychology Bulletin, 23,* 238–247.

Buehler, R., Griffin, D., & Ross, M. (1994). Exploring the "planning fallacy": Why people underestimate their task completion times. *Journal of Personality and Social Psychology, 67,* 355–381.

Bullock, M. (1985). Animism in childhood thinking: A new look at an old question. *Developmental Psychology, 21,* 217–225.

Burish, T. G., & Carey, M. P. (1986). Conditioned aversive response in cancer chemotherapy patients: Theoretical and developmental analysis. *Journal of Consulting and Clinical Psychology, 54,* 593–600.

Burns, B. D. (1996). Meta-analogical transfer: Transfer between episodes of analogical reasoning. *Journal of Experimental Psychology: Learning, Memory, and Cognition, 22,* 1032–1048.

Burrell, C. (1996, March 23). Number of fatherless children in U.S. quadruples in 45 years. Associated Press, *Albany Times Union,* p. B1.

Bushman, B. J. (1984). Perceived symbols of authority and their influence on compliance. *Journal of Applied Social Psychology, 14,* 501– 508.

Bushman, B. J. (1988). The effects of apparel on compliance: A field experiment with a female authority figure. *Personality and Social Psychology Bulletin, 14,* 459–467.

Bushman, B. J. (1995). Moderating role of trait aggressiveness in the effects of violent media on aggression. *Journal of Personality and Social Psychology, 69,* 950–960.

Bushman, B. J. (1998). Effects of television violence on memory for commercial messages. *Journal of Experimental Psychology: Applied, 4,* 291–307.

Bushman, B. J., Baumeister, R. F., & Stack, A. D. (1999). Catharsis, aggression, and persuasive influence: Self-fulfilling or self-defeating prophecies? *Journal of Personality and Social Psychology, 76,* 367–376.

Buss, A. H. (1961). *The psychology of aggression.* New York: Wiley.

Buss, D. H. (1999). *Evolutionary psychology.* Boston: Allyn and Bacon.

Buss, D. M. (1999). *Evolutionary psychology.* Boston: Allyn & Bacon.

Buss, D. M. (1999). *Evolutionary psychology.* Boston: Allyn & Bacon.

Buss, D. M. (1999). *Evolutionary psychology: The new science of the mind.* Boston: Allyn & Bacon.

Buss, D. M., & Schmitt, D. P. (1993). Sexual strategies theory: An evolutionary perspective on human mating. *Psychological Review, 100,* 204–232.

Buss, D. M., & Shackelford, T. K. (1997). Human aggression in evolutionary psychological perspective. *Clinical Psychology Review, 17,* 605–691.

Butcher, J. N. (1990). *MMPI–2 in psychological treatment.* New York: Oxford University Press.

Buunk, B. P. (1995). Sex, self-esteem, dependency, and extradyadic sexual experience as related to jealousy responses. *Journal of Social and Personal Relationships, 12,* 147–153.

Byrne, D. (1971). *The attraction paradigm.* New York: Academic Press.

Byrne, D. (1982). Predicting human sexual behavior. In A. G. Kraut (Ed.), *The G. Stanley Hall Lecture Series* (Vol. 2, pp. 363–364, 368). Washington, DC: American Psychological Association.

Byrne, D. (1992). The transition from controlled laboratory experimentation to less controlled settings: Surprise! Additional variables are operative. *Communication Monographs, 59,* 190–198.

Byrne, D., & Smeaton, G. (1998). The Feeling Scale: Positive and negative affective responses. In C. M. Davis, W. L. Yarger, R. Bauserman, G. Scheer, & S. L. Davis (Eds.), *Handbook of sexuality-related measures* (pp. 50–52). Thousand Oaks, CA: Sage.

Cacioppo, J. T., Petty, R. E., & Quintanar, L. R. (1982). Individual differences in relative hemisphere alpha abundance and cognitive responses persuasive communications. *Journal of Personality and Social Psychology, 43,* 623–626.

Cacioppo, J. T., Priester, J. R., & Berntson, G. G. (1993). Rudimentary determinants of attitude: II. Arm flexion and extension have differential effects on attitudes. *Journal of Personality and Social Psychology, 65,* 5–17.

Cadoret, R. J., Troughton, E., & O'Gorman, T. W. (1987). Genetic and environmental factors in alcohol abuse and antisocial personality. *Journal of Studies on Alcohol, 48,* 1–8.

Campbell, J. N., & LaMotte, R. H. (1983). Latency to detection of first pain. *Brain Research, 266,* 203–208.

Campbell, S. C., Ewing, L. J., Breaux, A. M., & Szumowski, E. K. (1986). Problem three-year-olds: Follow-up at school entry. *Journal of Child Psychology and Psychiatry, 27,* 473–488.

Campos, J. J., Langer, A., & Krowitz, A. (1970). Cardiac responses on the visual cliff in prelocomotor human infants. *Science, 170,* 196–197.

Cannon-Bowers, J. A., Salas, E., & Pruitt, J. S. (1996). Establishing the boundaries of a paradigm for decision-making research. *Human Factors, 38,* 193–205.

Cantor, N., & Sanderson, C. A. (in press). Life task participation and well-being: The importance of taking part in daily life. In D. Kahneman, E. Diener, & N. Schwarz (Eds.), *Well-being: The foundations of hedonid psychology.* New York: Russell Sage.

Capaldi, E. J. (1978). Effects of schedule and delay of reinforcement on acquisition speed. *Animal Learning and Behavior, 6,* 330–334.

Capaldi, E. J., Alptekin, S., & Birmingham, K. (1997). Discriminating between reward-produced memories: Effects of differences in reward magnitude. *Animal Learning & Behavior, 25,* 171–176.

Capaldi, E. J., & Birmingham, K. M. (1998). Reward produced memories regulate memory-discrimination learning, extinction, and other forms of discrimination learning. *Journal of Experimental Psychology: Animal Behavior Processes, 24,* 254–264.

Capaldi, E. J., Birmingham, K. M., & Alptekin, S. (1995). Memories of reward events and expectancies of reward events may work in tandem. *Animal Learning & Behavior, 23,* 40–48.

Carey, M. P., Morrison-Beedy, D., & Johnson B. T. (1997). The HIV-Knowledge Questionnaire: Development and evaluation of a reliable, valid, and practical self-administered questionnaire. *AIDS and Behavior, 1* , 61–74.

Carlo, G., Koller, S. H., Eisenberg, N., Da Silva, M. S., & Frohlich, C. B. (1996). A cross-national study on the relations among prosocial moral reasoning, gender role orientations, and prosocial behavior. *Developmental Psychology, 32,* 231–240.

Carlson, N. R. (1998). *Physiology of behavior* (6th ed.). Needham Heights, MA: Allyn & Bacon.

Carlson, N. R. (1999). *Foundations of physiological psychology* (4th ed.). Boston: Allyn & Bacon.

Carnelley, K. B., Pietromonaco, P. R., & Jaffe, K. (1996). Attachment, caregiving, and relationship functioning in couples: Effects of self and partner. *Personal Relationships, 3,* 257–278.

Carpendale, J. L. M., & Krebs, D. L. (1995). Variations in moral judgment as a function of type of dilemma and moral choice. *Journal of Personality, 63,* 289–313.

Carroll, J. M., & Russell, J. A. (1996). Do facial expressions signal specific emotions? Judging emotion from the face in context. *Journal of Personality and Social Psychology, 70,* 205–218.

Carstensen, L. I., Isaacowitz, D. M., & Charles, S. T. (1999). Taking time seriously: A life-span theory of social selectivity. *American Psychologist, 54,* 165–181.

Carstensen, L. I., Pasupathi, M., & Mary, U. (1998). *Emotion experiences in the daily lives of older and younger adults.* Manuscript submitted for publication.

Carstensen, L. L., & Charles, S. T. (1998). Emotion in the second half of life. *Current Directions in Psychological Science, 7,* 144–149.

Carver, C. S., Pozo, C., Harris, S. D., Noriega, V., Scheier, M. F., Robinson, D. S., Ketcham, A. S., Moffat, F. L., & Clark, K. C. (1993). How coping mediates the effect of optimism on distress: A study of women with early stage breast cancer. *Journal of Personality and Social Psychology, 65,* 375–390.

Carver, C. S., & Scheier, M. F. (1981). *Attention and self-regulation: A control-theory approach to human behavior.* New York: Springer-Verlag.

Catania, A. C. (1992). *Learning* (3rd ed.). Englewood Cliffs, NJ: Prentice-Hall.

Cattell, R. B. (1963). Theory of fluid and crystallized intelligence: A critical experiment. *Journal of Educational Psychology, 54,* 1–22.

Cattell, R. B., & Dreger, R. M. (Eds.). (1977). *Handbook of modern personality theory.* Washington, DC: Hemisphere.

Ceci, S. J. (1995). False beliefs: Some developmental and clinical considerations. In D. L. Schachter (Ed.), *Memory distortions* (pp. 91–125). Cambridge, MA: Harvard University Press.

Centers for Disease Control. (1993). Smoking Cessation During Previous Year Among Adults—United States, 1990 and 1991. *Mortality and Morbidity Weekly Report, 42*(26), 504–507.

Centers for Disease Control. (1996a). Cigarette smoking among adults: United States, 1994. *Morbidity and Mortality Weekly Report, 45,* 588–590.

Centers for Disease Control. (1996b). *HIV/AIDS Surveillance Report, 8,* 1–33.

Centers for Disease Control. (1997). Average annual number of deaths: 1990–1994. *Mortality and Morbidity Weekly Report, 46,* 448–451.

Centers for Disease Control. (1999). Achievements in Public Health, 1900–1999: Tobacco Use—United States, 1900–1999. *Mortality and Morbidity Weekly Report, 48*(43), 986–993.

Centers for Disease Control. (1999). At-a-Glance 1999: *Targeting Tobacco Use: The Nation's Leading Cause of Death.* Atlanta, GA: Author. Retrieved December 26, 1999 from the World Wide Web: http://www.cdc.gov/tobacco/oshaag.htm.

Centerwall, B. S. (1989). Exposure to television as a cause of violence. In G. Comstock (Ed.), *Public communication and behavior* (Vol. 2). San Diego: Academic Press.

Cerella, J., Poon, L. W., & Williams, D. M. (1980). Age and the complexity hypothesis. In L. Poon (Ed.), *Aging in the 1980s: Psychological issues* (pp. 332–340). Washington, DC: American Psychological Association.

Cerelli, E. (1989). *Older drivers, the age factor in traffic safety* (DOT HS-807–402). Washington, DC: National Highway Traffic and Safety Administration.

Chaiken, S., Liberman, A., & Eagly, A. H. (1989). Heuristic and systematic processing within and beyond persuasion context. In J. S. Uleman & J. A. Bargh (Eds.), *Unintended thought* (pp. 212–252). New York: Guilford Press.

Chan, C. J., & Margolin, G. (1994). The relationship between dual-earner couples' daily work mood and home affect. *Journal of Social and Personal Relationships, 11,* 573–586.

Chang, E. C. (1996). Cultural differences in optimism, pessimism, and coping: Predictors of subsequent adjustment in Asian American and Caucasian American college students. *Journal of Counseling Psychology, 43,* 113–123.

Cherek, D. R., Schnapp, W., Gerard Moeller, F., & Dougherty, D. M. (1996). Laboratory measures of aggressive responding in male parolees with violent and nonviolent histories. *Aggressive Behavior, 22,* 27–36.

Cherry, E. C. (1953). Some experiments on the recogniton of speech with one and with two ears. *Journal of Acoustical Society of America, 25,* 975–979.

Chess, S., & Thomas, A. (1984). *Origins and evolution of behavior disorders.* New York: Brunner/Mazel.

Choi, L., & Nisbett, R. E. (1998). Situational salience and cultural differences in the correspondence bias and actor–observer bias. *Personality and Social Psychology Bulletin, 24,* 949–960.

Chokar, J. S., & Wallin, J. A. (1984). A field study of the effect of feedback frequency on performance. *Journal of Applied Psychology, 68,* 524–530.

Chomsky, N. (1968). *Language and mind.* New York: Harcourt Brace.

Chorney, M. J., Chorney, K., Seese, N., Owen, M. J., Daniels, J., McGuffin, P., Thompson, L. A., Detterman, D. K., Benbow, C., Lubinski, D., Eley, T., & Plomin, R. (1998). A quantitative trait locus associated with cognitive ability in children. *Psychological Science, 9,* 159–166.

Christenfeld, N. (1995). Choices from identical options. *Psychological Science, 6,* 50–55.

Christensen, A., & Jacobson, N. S. (1994). Who (or what) can do psychotherapy: The status and challenge of nonprofessional therapies. *Psychological Science, 5,* 8–14.

Christensen-Szalanski, J. J. J., & Willham, C. F. (1991). The hindsight bias: A meta-analysis. *Organizational Behavior and Human Decision Processes, 48,* 147–168.

Christiansen, C., Alreu, B. C., & Huffman, R. K. (1996). Creating a virtual environment for brain injury rehabilitation and research: A preliminary report. *Journal of Medicine and Virtual Reality, 1,* 6–9.

Cialdini, R. B. (1994). Interpersonal influence. In S. Shavitt & T. C. Brock (Eds.), *Persuasion* (pp. 195–218). Boston: Allyn & Bacon.

Cialdini, R. B., Kallgren, C. A., & Reno, R. R. (1991). A focus theory of normative conduct. *Advances in Experimental Social Psychology, 24,* 201–234.

Clark, A. E., & Oswald, A. J. (1994). Unhappiness and unemployment. *Economic Journal, 104,* 648–659.

Clark, H., & Clark, E. (1977). *Psychology and language: An introduction to psycholinguistics.* New York: Harcourt Brace Jovanovich.

Clark, R. E., & Squire, L. R. (1999). Human eyeblink classical conditioning: Effects of manipulating awareness of the stimulus contingencies. *Psychological Science, 10,* 14–18.

Clarke-Stewart, A., Friedman, S., & Koch, J. (1985). *Child development: A topical approach.* New York: John Wiley & Sons.

Clum, G. A., & Bowers, T. G. (1990). Behavior therapy better than placebo treatments: Fact or artifact? *Psychological Bulletin, 107,* 110–113.

Coates, T. J., & Collins, C. (1998, July). Preventing HIV infection. *Scientific American,* 96–97.

Cohen, S., Frank, E., Doyle, W. J., Skoner, D. P., Rabin, B. S., & Gwaltney, J. M. (1998). Types of stressors that increase susceptibility to the common cold in healthy adults. *Health Psychology, 3,* 214–223.

Cohen, S., Kaplan, J. R., Cunnick, J. E., Manuck, S. B., & Rabin, B. S. (1992). Chronic social stress, affiliation, and cellular immune response in nonhuman primates. *Psychological Science, 3,* 301–304.

Cohn, E. G., & Rotton, J. (1997). Assault as a function of time and temperature: A moderator-variable time-series analysis. *Journal of Personality and Social Psychology, 72,* 1322–1334.

Colborn, T., Dumanoski, D., & Myers, J. P. (1996). *Our stolen future: How we are threatening our fertility, intelligence, and survival—a scientific detective story.* New York: Penguin Books.

Collins, M. A., & Zebrowitz, L. A. (1995). The contributions of appearance to occupational outcomes in civilian and military settings. *Journal of Applied Social Psychology, 25,* 129–163.

Colwill, R. M. (1993). An associative analysis of instrumental learning. *Current Directions in Psychological Science, 2,* 111–116.

Colwill, R. M., & Rescorla, R. A. (1985). Postconditioning devaluation of a reinforcer affects instrumental responding. *Journal of Experimental Psychology, 11,* 120–132.

Colwill, R. M., & Rescorla, R. A. (1988). Associations between the discriminative stimulus and the reinforcer in instrumental learning. *Journal of Experimental Psychology, 14,* 155–164.

Compas, B. E., Haaga, D. A. F., Keefe, F. J., Leitenberg, H., & Williams, D. A. (1998). *Journal of Consulting & Clinical Psychology, 66,* 89–112.

Conger, J. A. (1991). Inspiring others: The language of leadership. *Academy of Management Executive, 5,* 31–45.

Conway, M. A. (1995). *Flashbulb memories.* Hillsdale, NJ: Erlbaum.

Cooper, J., & Scher, S. J. (1990). Actions and attitude: The role of responsibility and aversive consequences in persuasion. In T. Brock & S. Shavitt (Eds.), *The psychology of persuasion.* San Francisco: Freeman.

Cooper, M. L., Frone, M. R., Russell, M., & Mudar, P. (1995). Drinking to regulate positive and negative emotions: A motivational model of alcohol use. *Journal of Personality and Social Psychology, 69,* 990–1005.

Coren, S., & Girgus, J. S. (1978). *Seeing is deceiving: The psychology of visual illusion.* Hillsdale, NJ: Lawrence Erlbaum.

Coren, S., Girgus, J. S., Erlichman, H., & Hakstean, A. R. (1976). An empirical taxonomy of visual illusions. *Perception & Psychophysics, 20,* 129–137.

Coren, S., Ward, L. M., & Enns, J. T. (1999). *Sensation and perception* (5th ed.). Fort Worth, TX: Harcourt Brace College.

Corso, J. F. (1977). Auditory perception and communication. In J. E. Birren & K. W. Schaie (Eds.), *Handbook of the psychology of aging* (pp. 535–553). New York: Van Nostrand Reinhold.

Costa, P. T., Jr., & McCrae, R. R. (1989). *The NEO-PI/NEO-FFI manual supplement.* Odessa, FL: Psychological Assessment Resources.

Costa, P. T., Jr., & McCrae, R. R. (1994). The Revised NEO Personality Inventory (NEO-PI-R). In R. Briggs & J. M. Cheek (Eds.), *Personality measures: Development and evaluation* (Vol. 1.). Greenwich, CT: JAI Press.

Coyle, J. T. (1987). Alzheimer's disease. In G. Adelman (Ed.), *Encyclopedia of neuroscience* (pp. 29–31). Boston: Birkhauser.

Coyle, J. T., Price, D. L., & DeLong, M. R. (1983). Alzheimer's disease: A disorder of cortical cholinergic innervation. *Science, 219,* 1184–1190.

Craik, F. I. M., & Lockhart, R. S. (1972). Levels of processing: A framework for memory research. *Journal of Verbal Learning and Verbal Behavior, 11,* 671–684.

Craik, F. I. M., & Tulving, E. (1975). Depth of processing and the retention of words in episodic memory. *Journal of Experimental Psychology: General, 104,* 268–294.

Crawford, H. J., Knebel, T., Vendemia, J. M. (1998). The nature of hypnotic analgesia: Neurophysiological foundation and evidence. *Contemporary Hypnosis, 15,* 22–33.

Crealia, R., & Tesser, A. (1996). Attitude heritability and attitude reinforcement: A replication. *Personality and Individual Differences, 21,* 803–808.

Crespi, L. P. (1942). Quantitative variation of incentive and performance in the white rat. *American Journal of Psychology, 55,* 467–517.

Crick, F., & Mitchison, G. (1995). REM sleep and neural nets. *Behavioral Brain Research, 69,* 147–155.

Croyle, R. T. (1992). Appraisal of health threats: Cognition, motivation, and social comparison. *Cognitive Therapy and Research, 16,* 165–182.

Csikszentmihalyi, M., & Larson, R. (1984). *Being adolescent: Conflict and growth in the teenage years.* New York: Basic Books.

Culbertson, F. M. (1997). Depression and gender: An international review. *American Psychologist, 52,* 25–31.

Cunningham, J., Dockery, D. W., & Speizer, F. E. (1994). Maternal smoking during pregnancy as a predictor of lung functions in children. *American Journal of Epidemiology, 139,* 1139–1152.

Cunningham, M. R., Roberts, A. R., Wu, C. H., Barbee, A. P., & Druen, P. B. (1995). "Their ideas of beauty are, on the whole, the same as ours": Consistency and variability in the cross-cultural perception of female physical attractiveness. *Journal of Personality and Social Psychology, 68,* 261–279.

Curfman, G. O. (1993). Is exercise beneficial—or hazardous—to your heart? *The New England Journal of Medicine, 329,* 173.

Czeisler, C. A., Moore-Ede, M. C., & Coleman, R. M. (1982). Rotating shift work schedules that disrupt sleep are improved by applying Circadian principles. *Science, 217,* 460–462.

Dabbs, J. M., Jr. (1992). Testosterone measurements in social and clinical psychology. *Journal of Social and Clinical Psychology, 11,* 302–321.

Dabbs, J. M., Jr., Carr, T. S., Frady, R. L., & Riad, J. K. (1995). Testosterone, crime, and misbehavior among 692 male prison inmates. *Personality and Individual Differences, 18,* 627–633.

Dadds, M. R., Bovbjerg, D. H., Redd, W. H., & Cutmore, T. R. (1997). Imagery in human classical conditioning. *Psychological Bulletin, 122,* 89–103.

Daniel, J., & Potasova, A. (1989). Oral temperature and performance in 8 hour and 12 hour shifts. *Ergonomics, 32,* 689–696.

Datan, N., Antonovsky, A., & Moaz, B. (1984). Love, war, and the life cycle of the family. In K. A. McCluskey & H. W. Reese (Eds.), *Life-span developmental psychology: Historical and generational effects* (pp. 143–159). New York: Academic Press.

Daum, I., Ackermann, H., Schugens, M. M., Reimold, C., Dichgans, J., & Birbaumer, N. (1993). The cerebellum and cognitive functions in humans. *Behavioral Neuroscience, 104,* 411–419.

Daum, I., & Schugens, M. M. (1996). On the cerebellum and classical conditioning. *Current Directions in Psychological Science, 5,* 58–61.

Davidson, K., & Hopson, J. L. (1988). Gorilla business. *Image* (San Francisco Chronicle), 14–18.

Davidson, W. S., II, Redne, R., Blakely, C. H., Mitchell, C. M., & Emshoff, J. G. (1987). Diversion of juvenile offenders: An experimental comparison. *Journal of Consulting and Clinical Psychology, 55,* 68–75.

Davies, M., Stankov, L., & Roberts, R. D. (1998). Emotional intelligence: In search of an elusive construct. *Journal of Personality and Social Psychology, 75,* 989–1015.

Dawson, N. V., Arkes, H. R., Siciliano, C., Blinkhorn, R., Lakshmanan, M., & Petrelli, M. (1988). Hindsight bias: An impediment to accurate probability estimation in clinicopathologic conferences. *Medical Decision Making, 8,* 259–264.

Day, D. V., Bedeian, G. F., & Conte, J. M. (1998). Personality as predictor of work-related outcomes: Test of a mediated latent structural model. *Journal of Applied Social Psychology, 28,* 2068–2088.

De Villiers, J. G., & De Villiers, P. A. (1978). *Language acquisition.* Cambridge, MA: Harvard University Press.

De Vries, H., Backbier, E., Kok, G., & Dijkstra, M. (1995). The impact of social influences in the context of attitude, self-efficacy, intention, and previous behavior as predictors of smoking onset. *Journal of Applied Social Psychology, 25,* 237–257.

Deacon, S., & Arendt, J. (1996). Adapting to phase shifts I: An experimental model for jet lag and shift work. *Physiology and Behavior, 59,* 665–673.

Deary, I. J. (1995). Auditory inspection time and intelligence: What is the direction of causation? *Developmental Psychology, 31,* 237–250.

Deary, I. J., & Stough, C. (1996). Intelligence and inspection time. *American Psychologist, 51,* 599–608.

Deaux, K. (1993). Commentary: Sorry, wrong number—a reply to Gentile's call. *Psychological Science, 4,* 125–126.

Deci, E. L. (1975). *Intrinsic motivation.* New York: Plenum.

Deci, E. L., & Ryan, R. M. (1985). *Intrinsic motivation and self-determination in human behavior.* New York: Plenum Press.

Delgado, P. L., Charney, D. S., Price, L. H., Aghajanian, G. K., Landis, H., & Heninger, G. R. (1990). Serotonin function and mechanism of antidepressant action: Reversal of antidepressant-induced remission by rapid depletion of plasma atryptophan. *Archives of General Psychiatry, 47,* 411–418.

Delis, D.C., Squire, L. R., Bihrle, A., & Massman, P. S. (1992). Componential analysis of problem-solving ability: Performance of patients with frontal lobe damage and amnesic patients on a new sorting test. *Neuropsychologia, 30,* 680–697.

DeLongis, A., Folkman, S., & Lazarus, R. S. (1988). The impact of daily stress on health and mood: Psychological and social resources as mediators. *Journal of Personality and Social Psychology, 54,* 486–495.

Dement, W. C. (1975). *Some must watch while some must sleep.* San Francisco: W. H. Freeman.

Dement, W. C., & Kleitman, N. (1957). The relation of eye movement during sleep to dream activity: An objective method for the study of dreaming. *Journal of Experimental Psychology, 53,* 339–353.

Dement, W. C., & Wolpert, E. A. (1958). The relation of eye movements, body mobility and external stimuli to dream content. *Journal of Experimental Psychology, 55,* 543–553.

DeNeve, K. (1999). Happy as an extraverted clam? The role of personality for subjective well-being. *Current Directions in Psychological Science, 8,* 141–144.

DeNeve, K. M., & Cooper, H. (1998). The happy personality: A meta-analysis of 137 personality traits and subjective well-being. *Psychological Bulletin, 124,* 197–229.

Denning, P. J. (1992). Neural networks. *American Scientist, 80,* 426–429.

Denollet, J. (1998). Personality and coronary heart disease: The Type-D Scale-16 (DS16). *Annals of Behavioral Medicine, 20,* 209–215.

Deppe, R. K., & Harackiewicz, J. M. (1996). Self-handicapping and intrinsic motivation: Buffering intrinsic motivation from the threat of failure. *Journal of Personality and Social Psychology, 70,* 868–876.

Desimone, R. (1991). Face-selective cells in the temporal cortex of monkeys. *Journal of Cognitive Neuroscience, 3,* 1–8.

Desimone, R., Albright, T. D., Gross, C. G., & Bruce, D. (1984). Stimulus-selective properties of inferior temporal neurons in the macaque. *Journal of Neuroscience, 8,* 2051–2062.

Desimone, R., & Ungerleider, L. G. (1989). Neural mechanisms of visual processing in monkeys. In F. Boller & J. Garfman (Eds.), *Handbook of neuropsychology* (pp. 267–299). New York: Elsevier.

Detweiler, J. B., Bedell, B. T., Salovey, P., Pronin, E., & Rothman, A. J. (1999). Message framing and sunscreen use: Gain-framed messages motivate beach-goers. *Health Psychology, 18,* 189–196.

DeValois, R. L., Abramov, I., & Jacobs, G. H. (1996). Analysis of response patterns of LGN cells. *Journal of the Optical Society of America, 56,* 96–97.

DeValois, R. L., & DeValois, K. K. (1975). Neural coding of color. In E. C. Carterette & M. P. Friedman (Eds.), *Handbook of perception* (pp. 117–166). New York: Academic Press.

Di Chiara, G. (1995). The role of dopamine in drug abuse viewed from the perspective of its role in motivation. *Drug and Alcohol Dependency, 38,* 95–137.

Diego, M. A., Jones, N. A., Field, T., Hernandez-Reif, M., Schanberg, S., Kuhn, C., McAdam, V., Galamaga, R., & Galamaga, M. (1998). Aromatherapy positively affects mood, EEG patterns of alertness and math computations. *International Journal of Neuroscience, 96,* 217–224.

Diekmann, K. A., Tenbrunsel, A. E., Shah, P. P., Schroth, H. A., & Bazerman, M. H. (1996). The descriptive and prescriptive use of previous purchase price in negotiations. *Organizational Behavior and Human Decision Processes, 66,* 179–191.

Diener, E., & Diener, C. (1996). Most people are happy. *Psychological Science, 7,* 181–185.

Diener, E., Eunkook, Suh, M., Lucas, R. E., & Smith, H. L. (1999). Subjective well-being: Three decades of progress. *Psychological Bulletin, 125,* 276–302.

Diener, E., Gohm, C., Suh, E., & Oishi, S. (1998). *Do the effects of marital status on subjective well-being vary across cultures?* Manuscript submitted for publication.

Diener, E., & Lucas, R. (in press). Personality and subjective well-being. In D. Kahneman, E. Diener, & N. Schwarz (Eds.), *Well-being: The foundations of hedonic psychology.* New York: Russell Sage.

Diener, E., & Suh, M. E. (1997). Subjective well-being and age: An international analysis. In K. W. Schaie & M. P. Lawton (Eds.), *Annual review of gerontology and geriatrics: Vol. 17. Focus on emotion and adult development* (pp. 304–324). New York: Springer-Verlag.

Diener, E., & Suh, E. (Eds.) (1998). *Subjective well-being across cultures.* Cambridge, MA: MIT Press.

Diener, E., Suh, E. M., Lucas, R. E., & Smith, H. L. (1999). Subjective well-being: Three decades of progress. *Psychological Bulletin, 125,* 276–302.

Diener, E., Wolsic, B., & Fujita, F. (1995). Physical attractiveness and subjective well-being. *Journal of Personality and Social Psychology, 69,* 120–129.

DiMatteo, M. R., & Di Nicola, D. D. (1982). *Achieving patient compliance: The psychology of the medical practitioner's role.* New York: Pergamon Press.

Dingle, G. A., & Oei, T. P. S. (1997). Is alcohol a cofactor of HIV and AIDS? Evidence from immunological and behavioral studies. *Psychological Bulletin, 122,* 56–71.

Dishman, R. K. (1988). *Exercise adherence: Its impact on public health.* Champaign, IL: Human Kinetic Books.

Dollard, J., Doob, L., Miller, N., Mowrer, O. H., & Sears, R. R. (1939). *Frustration and aggression.* New Haven, CT: Yale University Press.

Dondi, M., Simion, F., & Caltran, G. (1999). Can newborns discriminate between their own cry and the cry of another newborn infant? *Developmental Psychology, 35,* 418–426.

Donovan, J. J., & Radosevich, D. J. (1998). The moderating role of goal commitment on the goal difficulty–performance relationship: A meta-analytic review and critical reanalysis. *Journal of Applied Psychology, 83,* 308–315.

Dorfman, J., & Kihlstrom, J. F. (1994). *Semantic priming in posthypnotic amnesia.* Paper presented at the annual meeting of the Psychonomic Society, St. Louis, MO.

Douek, E. (1988). Olfaction and medicine. In S. Van Toller & G. Doll (Eds.), *Perfumery: The psychology and biology of fragrance.* London: Chapman Hall.

Dougherty, M. R. P., Gettys, C. F., & Ogden, E. E. (1999). MINERVA–DM: A memory processes model for judgments of likelihood. *Psychological Review, 106,* 180–209.

Dovidio, J. F., Evans, N., & Tyler, R. B. (1986). Racial stereotypes: The contents of their cognitive representations. *Journal of Experimental Social Psychology, 22,* 22–37.

Dovidio, J. F., & Gaertner, S. L. (1993). Stereotype and evaluative intergroup bias. In D. M. Mackie & D. L. Hamilton (Eds.), *Affect, cognition, and stereotyping: Interactive processes in group perception.* Orlando, FL: Academic Press.

Dovidio, J. F., & Gaertner, S. L. (Eds.). (1986). *Prejudice, discrimination, and racism.* Orlando, FL: Academic Press.

Dovidio, J. F., Gaertner, S. L., Isen A. M., & Lawrance, R. E. (1995). Group representations and intergroup bias: Positive affect, similarity, and group size. *Personality and Social Psychology Bulletin, 21,* 856–865.

Dragoi, V., & Staddon, J. E. R. (1999). The dynamics of operant conditioning. *Psychological Bulletin, 1,* 20–61.

Draper, J. V., Kaber, D. B., & Usher, J. M. (1998). Telepresence. *Human Factors, 40,* 354–375.

Dreher, N. (1995). Women and smoking. *Current Health, 21,* 16–19.

Dubbert, P. M. (1992). Exercise in behavioral medicine. *Journal of Consulting and Clinical Psychology, 60,* 613–618.

Dubbert, P. M. (1995). Behavioral (lifestyle) modification in the prevention and treatment of hypertension. *Clinical Psychology Review, 15*(3), 187–216.

Duffy, D. L., Hamerman, D., & Cohen, M. A. (1980). Communication skills of house officers: A study in a medical clinic. *Annals of Internal Medicine, 93,* 354–357.

Dufour, M. C. (1996). Risks and benefits of alcohol use over the life span. *Alcohol Health & Research World, 20,* 145–151.

Duncan, L. E., & Agronick, G. S. (1995). The intersection of life stage and social events: Personality and life outcomes. *Journal of Personality and Social Psychology, 69,* 558–658.

Duncker, K. (1945). On problem solving. *Psychological Monographs* (whole No. 270).

Dunning, D., Leuenberger, A., & Sherman, D. A. (1995). A new look at motivated inference: Are self-serving theories of success a product of motivational forces? *Journal of Personality and Social Psychology, 69,* 58–68.

Dunning, D., & Sherman, D. A. (1997). Stereotypes and tacit inference. *Journal of Personality and Social Psychology, 73,* 459–471.

Dutton, D. G., & Aron, A. P. (1974). Some evidence for heightened sexual attraction under conditions of high anxiety. *Journal of Personality and Social Psychology, 30,* 510–517.

Dweck, C. S., & Licht, B. G. (1980). Learned helplessness and intellectual achievement. In M. E. P. Seligman & J. Garber (Eds.), *Human helplessness: Theory and application.* New York: Academic Press.

Dyer, F. C. (1991). Bees acquire route-based memories but not cognitive maps in a familiar landscape. *Animal Behaviour, 41,* 239–246.

Eagly, A. H., & Chaiken, S. (1998). Attitude structure and function. In G. Lindsey, S. T. Fiske, & D. T. Gilbert (Eds.), *Handbook of social psychology* (4th ed.). New York: Oxford University Press and McGraw-Hill.

Eagly, A. H., & Wood, W. (1999). The origins of sex differences in human behavior. *American Psychologist, 54,* 408–423.

Ebbinghaus, H. (1885). *Uber das Gedachtnis.* Leipzig: Dunker. (Translation by H. Ruiyer & C. E. Bussenius [1915]. *Memory.* New York: Teachers College Press Columbia University.)

Eccleston, C., & Crombez, G. (1999). Pain demands attention: A cognitive-affective model of the interruptive function of pain. *Pychological Bulletin, 125,* 356–366.

Eden, D., & Aviram, A. (1993). Self-efficacy training to speed reemployment: Helping people to help themselves. *Journal of Applied Psychology, 78,* 352–360.

Edwards, J. R., & Harrison, R. V. (1993). Job demands and worker health: Three-dimensional reexamination of the relationship between person-environment fit and strain. *Journal of Applied Psychology, 78,* 628–648.

Edwards, K., & Bryan, T. S. (1997). Judgmental biases produced by instructions to disregard: The (paradoxical) case of emotional information. *Personality and Social Psychology Bulletin, 23,* 849–864.

Edwards, K., Heindel, W., & Louis-Dreyfus, E. (1996). *Directed forgetting of emotional and nonemotional words: Implications for implicit and explicit memory processes.* Manuscript submitted for publication.

Effective treatment for treating depression (1994, April). *Johns Hopkins Medical Letter, 6*(2), 6–7.

Egan, S. K., & Perry, D. G. (1998). Does low self-regard invite victimization? *Developmental Psychology, 34,* 299–309.

Egeland, J. A., Gerhard, D. S., Pauls, D. L., Sussex, J. N., Kidd, K. K., Allen, C. R., Hostetter, A. M., & Housman, D. E. (1987). Bipolar affective disorders linked to DNA markers on chromosome 11. *Nature, 325,* 783–787.

Ehrman, R. N., Robbins, S. J., Childress, A. R., & O'Brien, C. P. (1992). Conditioned responses to cocaine-related stimuli in cocaine abuse patients. *Psychopharmacology, 107,* 523–529.

Eich, E. (1995). Searching for mood dependent memory. *Psychological Science, 6,* 67–75.

Eich, J. E. (1985). Levels of processing, encoding specificity, elaboration, and CHARM. *Psychological Review, 92,* 1–38.

Eichenbaum, H., & Bunsey, M. (1995). On the binding of associations in memory: Clues from studies on the role of the hippocampal region in paired-associate learning. *Current Directions in Psychological Science, 4,* 19–23.

Eimas, P. D., & Tarter, V. C. (1979). The development of speech perception. In H. W. Reese & L. P. Lipsitt (Eds.), *Advances in child development and behavior* (Vol. 13, pp. 155–193). New York: Academic Press.

Ekman, P. (1992). Facial expressions of emotion: New findings, new questions. *Psychological Science, 3,* 34–38.

Ekman, P., Davidson, R. J., & Friesen, W. V. (1990). The Duchenne smile: Emotional expression and brain physiology II. *Journal of Personality and Social Psychology, 58,* 342–353.

Ekman, P., & Friesen, W. V. (1975). *Unmasking the face.* Englewood Cliffs, NJ: Prentice Hall.

Elisberg, M., Caldera, T., Herrera, A., Winkvist, A., & Kullgren, G. (1999). Domestic violence and emotional distress among Nicaraguan women. *American Psychologist, 54,* 30–36.

Elkin, J., Shea, T., Watkins, J. T., Imber, S. D., Stotsky, S. M., Collins, J. F., Glass, D. R., Pilkonis, P. A., Leber, W. R., Docherty, J. P., Fiester, S. J., & Parloff, M. B. (1989). National Institutes of Mental Health treatment of depression and collaborative research program. *Archives of General Psychiatry, 46,* 971–982.

Elliot, A. J. (1981) *Child language.* Cambridge, England: Cambridge University Press.

Elliot, A. J., & Devine, P. G. (1994). On the motivational nature of cognitive dissonance: Dissonance as psychological discomfort. *Journal of Personality and Social Psychology, 67,* 382–394.

Ellis, A. (1987). The impossibility of achieving consistently good mental health. *American Psychologist, 42,* 364–375.

Ellis, L. (1995). Dominance and reproductive success among nonhuman animals: A cross-species comparison. *Ethology and Sociobiology, 16* , 257–333.

Elsmore, T. F., & McBride, S. A. (1994). An eight-alternative concurrent schedule: Foraging in a radial maze. *Journal of Applied Behavior Analysis, 28,* 236.

Emmelkamp, P. (1982). *Phobics and obsessive–compulsive disorders: Theory, research, and practice.* New York: Plenum.

Empson, J. A. C. (1984). Sleep and its disorders. In R. Stevens (Ed.), *Aspects of consciousness.* New York: Academic Press.

Engel, S., Zhang, X., & Wandell, B. (1997). Colour tuning in human visual cortex measured with functional magnetic resonance imaging. *Nature, 388,* 68–71.

Engen, T. (1982). *The perception of odors.* New York: Academic Press.

Engen, T. (1986). *Remembering odors and their names.* Paper presented at the First International Conference on the Psychology of Perfumery, University of Warwick, England.

Engen, T. (1987). Remembering odors and their names. *American Scientist, 75,* 497–503.

Engen, T., & Ross, B. M. (1973). Long-term memory of odors with and without verbal descriptions. *Journal of Experimental Psychology, 100,* 221–227.

Epley, N., & Huff, C. (1998). Suspicion, affective response, and educational benefit as a result of deception in psychology research. *Personality and Social Psychology Bulletin, 24,* 759–768.

Epstein, L. H. (1992). Role of behavior theory in behavioral medicine. Special Issue: Behavioral medicine: An update for the 1990s. *Journal of Consulting and Clinical Psychology, 60,* 493–498.

Epstein, S. (1994). An integration of the cognitive and psychodynamic unconscious. *American Psychologist, 49,* 709–724.

Erdelyi, M. H., & Kleinbard, J. (1978). Has Ebbinghaus decayed with time? The growth of recall (hypermnesia) over days. *Journal of*

*Experimental Psychology: Human Learning and Memory, 4,* 275–289.
Erdley, C. A., & D'Agostino, P. R. (1989). Cognitive and affective components of automatic priming effects. *Journal of Personality and Social Psychology, 54,* 741–746.
Erev, I. (1998). Signal detection by human observers: A cutoff reinforcement learning model of categorization decisions under uncertainty. *Psychological Review, 105,* 280–298.
Ericsson, K. A., & Polson, P. G. (1988). A cognitive analysis of exceptional memory for restaurant orders. In M. T. H. Chi, R. Glaser, & J. J. Farr (Eds.), *The nature of expertise* (pp. 23–70). Hillsdale, NJ: Erlbaum.
Erikson, E. H. (1950). *Childhood and society.* New York: Norton.
Erikson, E. H. (1987). *A way of looking at things: Selected papers from 1930 to 1980* (S. Schlein, Ed.). New York: Norton.
Eron, L. D. (1987). The development of aggressive behavior from the perspective of a developing behaviorist. *American Psychologist, 42,* 435–442.
Eron, L. D., Huesmann, L. R., Lefkowitz, M. M., & Walder, L. O. (1996). Does television violence cause aggression? In D. F. Greenberg (Ed.), Criminal careers: Vol 2. *The international library of criminology, criminal justice and penology* (pp. 311–321). Aldershot, England: Dartmouth Publishing Company.
Estrada, C. A., Isen, A. M., & Young, M. J. (1995). Positive affect improves creative problem solving and influences reported source of practice satisfaction in physicians. *Motivation and Emotion, 388,* 300–385.
Evans, L. (1991). Traffic safety and the driver. New York: Van Nostrand Reinhold.
Evert, D. L., & Oscar-Berman, M. (1995). Alcohol-related cognitive impairments: An overview of how alcoholism may affect the workings of the brain. *Alcohol Health & Research World, 19,* 89–96.
Exner, J. E. (1993). *The Rorschach: A comprehensive system: Vol. 1. Basic Foundations* (3rd ed.). New York: Wiley.
Eysenck, H. J. (1994). The big five or giant three: Criteria for a paradigm. In C. F. Halverson, Jr., G. A. Honhnstamm, & R. P. Martin ( Eds.), *The developing structure of temperament and personality from infancy to adulthood* (pp. 37–51). Hillsdale, NJ: Erlbaum.
Fagot, B. I., & Kavanagh, K. (1990). The prediction of anti-social behavior from avoidant attachment classification. *Child Development, 61,* 864–873.
Fantz, R. L. (1961). The origin of form perception. *Scientific American, 204,* 66–72.
Farah, M. J. (1988). Is visual imagery really visual? Overlooked evidence from neuropsychology. *Psychological Review, 95,* 307–317.
Farah, M. J., Wilson, K. D., Drain, M., & Tanaka, J. N. (1998). What is "special" about face perception? *Psychological Review, 3,* 482–498.
Fazio, R. H., & Roskos-Ewoldsen, D. R. (1994). Acting as we feel: When and how attitudes guide behavior. In S. Shavitt & T. C. Brock (Eds.), *Persuasion* (pp. 71–93). Boston: Allyn & Bacon.
Feingold, A. (1992). Cognitive gender differences: A developmental perspective. *Sex Roles, 29,* 91–112.
Feingold, A. J. (1990). Gender differences in the effects of physical attractiveness on romantic attraction: A comparison across five research paradigms. *Journal of Personality and Social Psychology, 59,* 981–993.
Feingtstein, A. (1987). On the nature of public and private self-consciousness. *Journal of Personality, 55,* 543–553.
Feldman, D. C., & Tompson, H. B. (1993). Entry shock, culture shock: Socializing the new breed of global managers. *Human Resource Management, 31,* 345–362.
Felleman, D. J., & Van Essen, D. C. (1991). Distributed hierarchical processing in the primate cerebral cortex. *Cerebral Cortex, 1,* 1–47.
Ferrari, J. R., Johnson, J. L., & McCown, W. G. (Eds.). (1995). *Procrastination and task avoidance: Theory, research, and treatment.* New York: Plenum.
Ferster, C. B., & Skinner, B. F. (1957). *Schedules of reinforcement.* New York: Appleton-Century-Crofts.
Festinger, L. (1957). *A theory of cognitive dissonance.* Evanston, IL: Row, Peterson.
Fibiger, H. C., Murray, C. L., & Phillips, A. G. (1983). Lesions of the nucleus basalis magnocellularis impair long-term memory in rats. *Society for Neuroscience Abstracts, 9,* 332.
Field, T. T. M, Cohen, D., Garcia, R., & Greenberg, R. (1984). Mother-stranger face discrimination by the newborn. *Infant Behavior and Development, 7,* 19–25.
Fields, H. L., & Basbaum, A. (1984). Endogenous pain control mechanisms. In P. D. Wall & R. Melzack (Eds.), *Textbook of pain* (pp. 142–152). Edinburgh: Churchill Livingstone.
Fierman, J. (1995, August 21). It's 2:00 A.M., let's go to work. *Fortune,* pp. 82–86.
Fincham, F. D., & Bradbury, T. N. (1993). Marital satisfaction, depression and attributions: A longitudinal analysis. *Journal of Personality and Social Psychology, 64,* 442–452.
Fink, M. (1993). Who should get ECT? In C. E. Coffey (Ed.), *The clinical science of electroconvulsive therapy* (pp. 3–16). Washington, DC: American Psychiatric Association Press.
Fink, M. (1994). Can ECT be an effective treatment for adolescents? *Harvard Mental Health Letter, 10,* 8.
Finkel, D., Pederson, J. L., Plomin, R., & McClearn, G. E. (1998). Longitudinal and cross-sectional twin data on cognitive abilities in adulthood: The Swedish adoption/twin study of aging. *Developmental Psychology, 34,* 1400–1413.
Finney, J. W., Weist, M. D., & Friman, P. C. (1995). Evaluation of two health education strategies for testicular self-examination. *Journal of Applied Behavior Analysis 28,* 39–46.
Fischhoff, B. (1996). The real world: What good is it? *Organizational Behavior and Human Decision Processes, 65,* 232–248.
Fisher, J. D., Fisher, W. A., Misovich, S. J., Kimble, D. L, & Malloy, T. E. (1996). Changing AIDS risk behavior: Effects of an intervention emphasizing AIDS risk reduction information, motivation, and behavioral skills in a college population. *Health Psychology, 15,* 114–123.
Fisher, J. D., Fisher, W. A., Williams, S. S., & Malloy, T. E. (1994). Empirical tests of an information-motivation-behavioral skills model of AIDS preventive behavior with gay men and heterosexual university students. *Health Psychology 13,* 238–250.
Fisher, L., Harris, V. G., & VanGuren, J. (1980). Assessment of a pilot child playground injury prevention project in New York State. *American Journal of Public Health, 70,* 1000–1007.
Fiske, S. T., & Neuberg, S. L. (1990). A continuum model of impression formation, from category based to individuating processes: Influences of information and motivation in attention and interpretation. In M. P. Zanna (Ed.), *Advances in experimental social psychology* (Vol. 23). New York: Academic Press.
Fivush, R., Kuebli, J., & Clubb, P. A. (1992). The structure of events and event representations: A developmental analysis. *Child Development, 63,* 188–201.
Flack, W. F., Laird, J. D., & Cavallero, R. (1999). Additive effects of facial expressions and postures on emotional feelings. *European Journal of Social Psychology, 29,* 203–217.
Flaherty, C. F., & Largen, J. (1975). Within-subjects positive and negative contrast effects in rats. *Journal of Comparative and Physiological Psychology, 88,* 653–664.
Flanagan, P., McAnally, K., Martin, R. L., Meehan, J. W., & Oldfield, S. R. (1998). Aurally and visually guided visual search in a virtual environment. *Human Factors, 40,* 461–468.
Flavell, J. H. (1985). *Cognitive development* (2nd ed.). Englewood Cliffs, NJ: Prentice-Hall.
Flavell, J. H., Green, F. L., & Flavell, E. R. (1995). Young children's knowledge about the appearance–reality distinction. *Monographs of the Society for Research in Child Development,* 51 (1, Serial 212).
Flin, R., Slaven, G., & Stewart, K. (1996). Emergency decision making in the offshore oil and gas industry. *Human Factors, 38,* 262–277.
Flynn, J. R. (1980). *Race, IQ, and Jensen.* London: Routledge.
Flynn, J. R. (1987). Massive IQ gains in 14 nations: What IQ tests really measure. *Psychological Bulletin, 101,* 171–191.
Flynn, J. R. (1993). Skodak and Skeels: The inflated mother–child IQ gap. *Intelligence, 17,* 557–661.
Flynn, J. R. (1996). Group differences: Is the good society impossible? *Journal of Biosocial Science, 28,* 573–585.
Flynn, J. R. (1999). Searching for justice: The discovery of IQ gains over time. *American Psychologist, 54,* 5–20.
Folger, R., & Baron, R. A. (1996). Violence and hostility at work: A model of reactions to perceived injustice. In C. VandenBos & E. Q. Bulato (Eds.), pp. 51–86. *Workplace violence.* Washington, DC: American Psychological Association.
Folk, C. L., & Remington, R. W. (1996). When knowledge does not help: Limitations on the flexibility of attentional control. In A. F. Kramer, M. G. H. Coles, & G. D. Logan (Eds.), *Converging operations in the study of selective attention* (pp. 271–295). Washington, DC: American Psychological Association.
Ford, S., Fallowfield, L., & Lewis, S. (1996). Doctor-patient interactions in oncology. *Social Science Medicine, 12,* 1511–1519.
Forgas, J. P. (1995a). Mood and judgment: The affect infusion model (AIM). *Psychological Bulletin, 117,* 39–66.
Forgas, J. P. (1995b). The role of emotion in social judgments: An introductory review and an affect infusion model (AIM). *European Journal of Social Psychology.*
Forgas, J. P. (1998a). On being happy and mistaken: Mood effects on the fundamental attribution error. *Journal of Personality and Social Psychology, 75,* 318–331.
Forgas, J. P. (1998b). On feeling good and getting your way: Mood effects on negotiator cognition and bargaining strategies. *Journal of Personality and Social Psychology, 74,* 565–577.
Forgas, J. P., & Fiedler, K. (1996). Us and them: Mood effects on intergroup discrimination. *Journal of Personality and Social Psychology, 70,* 28–40.
Foulkes, D. (1985). *Dreaming: A cognitive-psychological analysis.* Hillsdale, NJ: Erlbaum.
Fowles, D. C. (1994). A motivational theory of psychopathology. In W. Spaulding (Ed.), *Nebraska symposium on motivation: Integrated views of motivation and emotion* (Vol. 41, pp. 181–238). Lincoln: University of Nebraska Press.
Frederiksen, N. (1994). The integration of testing with teaching: Applications of cognitive psychology in instruction. *American Journal of Education, 102,* 527–564.
Freedman, J. L. (1986). Television violence and aggression: A rejoinder. *Psychological Bulletin, 100,* 372–378.
French, D.C., Conrad, J., & Turner, T. M. (1995). Adjustment of antisocial and nonantisocial adolescents. *Development and Psychopathology, 7,* 857–874.

Frese, M. (1985). Stress at work and psychosomatic complaints: A causal interpretation. *Journal of Applied Psychology, 70,* 314–328.
Frese, M. (1999). Social support as a moderator of the relationship between work stressors and psychological dysfunctioning. *Journal of Occupational Health Psychology, 4,* 179–192.
Friedman, H. S., Hawley, P. H., & Tucker, J. S. (1994). Personality, health, and longevity. *Current Directions in Psychological Science, 3,* 37–41.
Friedman, H. W., & Schustack, M. W. (1999). *Personality: Classic theories and modern research.* Boston: Allyn & Bacon.
Friedman, H. W., Tucker, J. S., Schwartz, J. E., Tomlinson-Keasey, C., Martin, L. R., Wingart, D. L., & Criqui, M. H. (1995). Psychosocial and behavioral predictors of longevity: The aging and death of the "termites." *American Psychologist, 50,* 69–78.
Friedman, M., & Rosenman, R. H. (1974). *Type A behavior and your heart.* New York: Knopf.
Fry, A. F., & Hale, S. (1996). Processing speed, working memory, and fluid intelligence. *Psychological Science, 7,* 237–241.
Fry, W. A., Menck, H. R., & Winchester, D. P. (1996). The national cancer data base report on lung cancer. *Cancer, 77,* 1947–1955.
Fuligni, A. J. (1998). The adjustment of children from immigrant families. *Current Directions in Psychological Science, 7,* 99–104.
Funder, D. C., & Colvin, C. R. (1991). Explorations in behavioral consistency: Properties of persons, situations, and behavior. *Journal of Personality and Social Psychology, 60,* 773–794.
Funder, D. C., & Sneed, C. D. (1993). Behavioral manifestations of personality: An ecological approach to judgmental accuracy. *Journal of Personality and Social Psychology, 64,* 479–490.
Fung, H., Carstensen, L. I., & Lutz, A. (1999). The influence of time on social preferences: Implications for life-span development. *Psychology and Aging, 14,* 595–604.
Furnham, A., Kirkcaldy, B. D., & Lynn, R. (1994). National attitudes to competitiveness, money, and work among young people: First, second, and third world differences. *Human Relations, 47,* 119–132.
Furnham, A., & Salpe, J. (1993). Personality correlates of convicted drivers. *Personality and Individual Differences, 14,* 329–336.
Gaertner, S. L., Mann, J. A., Dovidio, J. F., & Murrell, J. A. (1990). How does cooperation reduce intergroup bias? *Journal of Personality and Social Psychology, 57,* 239–249.
Gaertner, S. L., Mann, J., Murrell, A., & Dovidio, J. F. (1989). Reducing intergroup bias: The benefits of recategorization. *Journal of Personality and Social Psychology, 57,* 239–249.
Gaertner, S. L., Rust, M. C., Dovidio, J. F., Bachman, B. A., & Anastasio, P. A. (1993). The contact hypothesis: The role of common ingroup identity on reducing intergroup bias. *Small Groups Research, 25,* 224–249.
Gaffney, G. R., Kuperman, S., Tsai, L. Y., & Minchin, S. (1989). Forebrain structure in infantile autism. *Journal of the American Academy of Child and Adolescent Psychiatry, 28,* 534–537.
Galanter, E. (1962). Contemporary psychophysics. In R. Brown, E. Galanter, E. G. Hess, & G. Mandler (Eds.), *New Directions in Psychology.* New York: Holt, Rinehart, & Winston.
Gallassi, R., Morreale, A., Montagna, P., Cortelli, P., Avoni, P., Castelanni, R., Gambetti, P., & Lugaresi, E. (1996). Fatal familial insomnia: Behavioral and cognitive features. *Newsday, 46,* 935–939.
Galotti, K. (1989). Approaches to studying formal and everyday reasoning. *Psychological Bulletin, 105,* 331–351.
Garcia, J., Hankins, W. G., & Rusiniak, K. W. (1974). Behavioral regulation of the milieu interne in man and rat. *Science, 185,* 824–831.
Garcia, J., & Koelling, R. A. (1966). Relation of cue to consequence in avoidance learning. *Psychonomic Science, 4,* 123.
Garcia, J., Rusiniak, K. W., & Brett, L. P. (1977). Conditioning food-illness aversions in wild animals: Caveat Canonici. In H. Davis & H. M. B. Hurwitz (Eds.), *Operant-Pavlovian interactions.* Hillsdale, NJ: Erlbaum.
Gardner, B. T., & Gardner, R. A. (1975). Evidence for sentence constituents in the early utterances of child and chimpanzee. *Journal of Experimental Psychology: General, 4,* 244–267.
Gardner, H. (1983). *Frames of mind: The theory of multiple intelligences.* New York: Basic Books.
Gardner, R. M., & Tockerman, Y. R. (1994). A computer–TV methodology for investigating the influence of somatotype on perceived personality traits. *Journal of Social Behavior and Personality, 9,* 555–563.
Garland, A. F., & Zigler, E. (1993). Adolescent suicide prevention: Current research and social policy implications. *American Psychologist, 48,* 169–182.
Garland, H., & Newport, S. (1991). Effects of absolute and relative sunk costs on the decision to persist with a course of action. *Organizational Behavior and Human Decision Processes, 48,* 55–69.
Garner, D. M., & Wooley, S. C. (1991). Confronting the failure of behavioral and dietary treatments for obesity. *Clinical Psychology Review, 11,* 729–780.
Gati, I., Houminer, D., & Aviram, T. (1998). Career compromises: Framings and their implications. *Journal of Counseling Psychology, 45,* 505–514.
Gawande, A. (1999, February 1). When doctors make mistakes. *New Yorker,* 40–55.
Gazzaniga, M. S. (1984). Right hemisphere language: Remaining problems. *American Psychologist, 39,* 1494–1495.
Gazzaniga, M. S. (1985, November). The social brain. *Psychology Today,* pp. 29–38.
Gazzaniga, M. S., Fendrich, R., & Wessinger, C. M. (1994). Blindsight reconsidered. *Current Directions in Psychological Science, 3,* 93–96.
Ge, X., Conger, R. D., Lorenz, F. O., Shanahan, M., & Elder, G. H., Jr. (1995). Mutual influences in parent and adolescent psychological distress. *Developmental Psychology, 2,* 406–419.
Geen, R., & Donnerstein, E. (Eds.) (1998). *Human aggression: Theories, research and implications for policy.* Pacific Grove, CA: Brooks/Cole.
Geen, R. G., Beatty, W. W., & Arkin, R. M. (1984). *Human motivation.* Boston: Allyn and Bacon.
Gehring, R. E., & Toglia, M. P. (1989). Recall of pictorial enactments and verbal descriptions with verbal and imagery study strategies. *Journal of Mental Imagery, 13,* 83–98.
Geiselman, R. E., & Fisher, R. P. (1997). Ten years of cognitive interviewing. In D. G. Payne & F. G. Conrad (Eds.), *Intersections in basic and applied memory research* (pp. 291–310). Mahwah, NJ: Erlbaum.
Geller, E. S. (1995). Integrating behaviorism and humanism for environmental protection. *Journal of Social Issues, 4,* 179–195.
Geller, E. S. (1996). Managing the human element of occupational health and safety. In R. W. Lack (Ed.), *Essentials of safety and health management.* Boca Raton, FL: Lewis Publishers.
Geller, E. S. (1996a). *The psychology of safety: How to improve behaviors and attitudes on the job.* Radnor, PA: Chilton.
Geller, E. S. (1996b). *The psychology of safety.* Radnor, PA: Chilton.
Gentner, D. (1982). Why nouns are learned before verbs: Linguistic relativity versus natural partitioning. In S. A. Kuczaj (Ed.), *Language development, Vol. 2. Language, thought, and culture* (pp. 301–334). Hillsdale, NJ: Erlbaum.
Gentner, D., & Holyoak, K. J. (1997). Reasoning and learning by analogy introduction. *American Psychologist, 52,* 32–34.
Gibbons, B. (1986). The intimate sense of smell. *National Geographic, 170,* 324–361.
Gibbons, F. X. (1990). Self-attention and behavior: a review and theoretical update. In M. P. Zanna (Ed.), *Advances in experimental social psychology* (Vol. 23, pp. 249–303). New York: Academic Press.
Gibbons, F. X., Eggleston, T. J., & Benthin, A. C. (1997). Cognitive reactions to smoking relapse: The reciprocal relation between dissonance and self-esteem. *Journal of Personality and Social Psychology, 72*(1), 184–195.
Gibbons, F. X., Gerrard, M., Blanton, H., & Russell, D. W. (1998). Reasoned action and social reaction: Willingness and intention as independent predictors of health risk. *Journal of Personality and Social Psychology, 74,* 1164–1180.
Gibson, E. J., & Walk, R. D. (1960). The "visual cliff." *Scientific American, 202,* 64–71.
Gidron, Y., & Davidson, K. (1996). Development and preliminary testing of a brief intervention for modifying CHD-predictive hostility components. *Journal of Behavioral Medicine, 19*(3), 203–220.
Gilbert, A. N., & Wysocki, C. J. (1987). The smell survey results. *National Geographic, 172,* 514–525.
Gilbert, D. T., & Malone, P. S. (1995). The correspondence bias. *Psychological Bulletin, 117,* 21–38.
Gill, J. (1985, August, 22). Czechpoints. *Time Out,* p. 15.
Gilligan, C. F. (1982). *In a different voice.* Cambridge, MA: Harvard University Press.
Giordani, B., Berent, S., Boivin, M. J., & Penney, J. B. (1995). Longitudinal neuropsychological and genetic linkage analysis of persons at risk for Huntington's disease. *Archives of Neurology, 52,* 59–64.
Gladwell, M. (1996, September 30). The new age of man. *The New Yorker,* pp. 56–67.
Gladwell, M. (1998, February 2). The Pima paradox. *The New Yorker,* 42–57.
Gleicher, F., Boninger, D., Strathman, A., Armor, D., Hetts, J., & Ahn, M. (1995). With an eye toward the future: Impact of counterfactual thinking on affect, attitudes, and behavior. In N. J. Roese & J. M. Olson (Eds.), *What might have been: The social psychology of counterfactual thinking* (pp. 283–304). Mahwah, NJ: Erlbaum.
Gluck, M. A., & Myers, C. E. (1995). Representation and association in memory: A neurocomputational view of hippocampal function. *Current Directions in Psychological Science, 4,* 23–29.
Godden, D., & Baddeley, A. D. (1975). Context-dependent memory in two natural environments: On land and under water. *British Journal of Psychology, 66,* 325–331.
Goethals, G. R., (1986). Fabricating and ignoring social reality: Self-serving estimates of consensus. In J. Olson, C. P. Herman, & N. P. Zanna (Eds.), *Relative deprivation and social comparison: The Ontario symposium on social cognition IV.* Hillsdale, NJ: Erlbaum.
Goldberg, L. R., & Saucier, G. (1995). So what do you propose we use instead? A reply to Block. *Psychological Bulletin, 117,* 221–225.
Goleman, D. (1995). *Emotional intelligence.* New York: Bantam.
Goleman, D. R. (1998). *Working with emotional intelligence.* New York: Bantam.
Goodale, M. A., Meeman, H. P., Bulthoff, H. H., Nicolle, D. A., Murphy, K. H., & Racicot, C. L. (1994). Separate neural pathways for the visual analysis of object shape and perception and prehension. *Current Biology, 4,* 604–610.
Goodman, G. S., Quas, J. A., Batterman-Faunce, J. M., Riddlesberger, M. M., & Kuhn, J. (1996). Predictors of accurate and inaccurate memories of traumatic events experienced in childhood. In K. Pedzek & W. P. Banks (Eds.), *The*

*recovered/false memory debate* (pp. 3–28). San Diego, CA: Academic Press.
Gopnik, A. (1996). The post-Piaget era. *Psychological Science, 7,* 221–225.
Gordon, P. (1990). Learnability and feedback: A commentary on Bohannon and Stanowicz. *Developmental Psychology, 26,* 215–218.
Gordon, W. C. (1989). *Learning and memory.* Belmont, CA: Brooks/Cole Publishing Company.
Gorman, J., Leibowitz, M., Fryer, A., & Stein, J. (1989). A neuroanatomical hypothesis for panic disorder. *American Journal of Psychiatry, 146,* 148–161.
Gotlieb, I. H., & McCabe, S. B. (1990). Marriage and psychopathology. In F. F. Fincham & T. N. Brabury (Eds.), *The psychology of marriage* (pp. 226–257). New York: Guilford Press.
Gottesman, I. I. (1993). Origins of schizophrenia: Past as a prologue. In R. Plomin & G. E. McClearn (Eds.), *Nature, nurture, and psychology* (pp. 2231–2344). Washington, DC: American Psychological Association.
Gottfredson, L. S. (1987). The practical significance of black–white differences in intelligence. *Behavioral and Brain Science, 10,* 510–512.
Gottfried, A. W. (Ed.). (1984). *Home environment and early cognitive development.* San Francisco: Academic.
Graham, C. H., & Hsia, Y. (1958). Color defect and color theory. *Science, 127,* 675–682.
Graham, K. S., & Hodges, J. R. (1997). Differentiating the roles of the hippocampal complex and the neocortex in long-term memory storage: Evidence from the study of semantic dementia and Alzheimer's disease. *Neuropsychology, 11,* 77–89.
Granchrow, J. R., Steiner, J. E., & Daher, M. (1983). Neonatal facial expressions in response to different qualities and intensities of gustatory stimuli. *Infant Behavior and Development, 6,* 189–200.
Grant, B. F., Harford, T. C., Dawson, D. A., Chou, P., Dufour, M., & Pickering, R. (1994). Prevalence of DSM–IV alcohol abuse and dependence in United States, 1992. *NIAAA's Epidemiological Bulletin No. 35, 13,* 243–248.
Grant, S. C., Magee, L. E. (1998). Contributions of proprioception to navigation in virtual environments. *Human Factors, 40,* 489–497.
Green, J. D., & Sedikides, C. (1999). Affect and self-focused attention revisited: The role of affect orientation. *Personality and Social Psychology Bulletin, 25,* 104–119.
Green, J. P., & Lynn, S. J. (1995). Hypnosis, dissociation, and simultaneous task performance. *Journal of Personality and Social Psychology, 69,* 728–735.
Green, L., Fry, A. F., & Myerson, J. (1994). Discounting of delayed rewards: A life-span comparison. *Psychological Science, 5,* 33–36.
Green, R. (1987). *The "sissy boy syndrome" and the development of homosexuality.* New Haven, CT: Yale University Press.
Green, R., & Blanchard, K. (1995). Gender identity disorders. In H. J. Kaplan & B. J. Sadock (Eds.), *Comprehensive textbook of psychiatry/VI* (pp. 1345–1360). Baltimore: Williams & Wilkins.
Greenberg, J., & Alge, B. J. (in press). Aggressive reactions to workplace injustice. In R. W. Griffin, A. O'Leary-Kelly, & J. Collins (Eds.), *Dysfunctional behavior in organizations: Vol 1. Violent behaviors in organizations.* Greenwich, CT: JAI Press.
Greenberg, J., Pyszcynski, T., & Solomon, S. (1982). The self-serving attributional bias: Beyond self-presentation. *Journal of Experimental Social Psychology, 18,* 56–67.
Greenberg, L. S., Elliott, R. K., & Lietaer, G. (1994). Research on experiential psychotherapies. In A. E. Bergin & S. L. Garfield (Eds.), *Handbook of psychotherapy and behavior change* (pp. 509–539). New York: John Wiley & Sons.
Greene, B. F., Winett, R. A., Van Houten, R., Geller, E. S., & Iwata, B. A. (1987). (Eds.). *Behavior analysis in the community: Readings from the Journal of Applied Behavior Analysis.* Lawrence, KS: University of Kansas Press.
Greenwald, A. G. (1992). New look 3: Unconscious cognition reclaimed. *American Psychologist, 47,* 766–779.
Greenwald, A. G., Draine, S. C., & Abrams, R. L. (1996). Three cognitive markers of unconscious semantic activation. *Science, 273,* 1699–1702.
Greenwald, A. G., Spangenberg, E. R., Pratkanis, A. R., & Eskenazi, J. (1991). Double-blind tests of subliminal self-help audiotapes. *Psychological Science, 2,* 119–122.
Greist-Bousquet, S., Watson, M., & Schiffman, H. R. (1990). *An examination of illusion decrement with inspection of wings-in and wings-out Müller-Lyer figures: The role of corrective and contextual information perception.* New York: Wiley.
Grilly, D. M. (1989). *Drugs and human behavior.* Boston: Allyn and Bacon.
Grilo, C. M., & Pogue-Geile, M. F. (1991). The nature of environmental influences on weight and obesity: A behavior genetic analysis. *Psychological Bulletin, 110,* 520–537.
Groopman, J. (1999). Congation: A sometimes lethal sexual epidemic that condoms can't stop. *The New Yorker,* September 13, pp. 34–37.
Gruneberg, M. M., Morris, P., & Sykes, R. N. (1988). *Practical aspects of memory: Current research and issues* (Vols. 1 & 2). Chichester, England: John Wiley & Sons.
Guerin, D. W., & Gottfried, A. W. (1994). Developmental stability and change in parent reports of temperament: A ten-year longitudinal investigation from infancy through preadolescence. *Merrill-Palmer Quarterly,* 40, 334–355.
Guilford, J. P. (1950). Creativity. *American Psychologist, 5,* 444–454.
Gully, K. J., & Dengerink, H. A. (1983). The dyadic interaction of persons with violent and nonviolent histories. *Aggressive Behavior, 9,* 13–20.
Gur, R. E., & Pearlson, G. D. (1993). Neuroimaging in schizophrenia research. In *Schizophrenia 1993: Special report* (pp. 163–179). Washington, DC: National Institute of Mental Health, Schizophrenia Research Board.
Gur, R., Mozley, P., Resnick, S., Gottlieb, G., Kohn, M., Zimmerman, R., Herman, G., Atlas, S., Grossman, R., Beretta, D., Erwin, R., & Gur, R. E. (1991). Gender differences in age effect on brain atrophy measured by magnetic resonance imaging. *Proceedings of the National Academy of Sciences, 88,* 2845–2849.
Guralnick, M. J. (Ed.). (1997). *The effectiveness of early intervention.* Baltimore: Brookes.
Gurman, A. S., Kniskern, D. P., & Pinsof, W. M. (1986). Research on marital and family therapies. In S. L. Garfield & A. E. Bergin (Eds.), *Handbook of psychotherapy and behavior change* (pp. 565–626). New York: Wiley.
Gustavson, C. R., Garcia, J., Hawkins, W. G., & Rusiniak, K. W. (1974). Coyote predation control by aversive conditioning. *Science, 184,* 581–583.
Guthrie, J. P., Ash, R. A., & Bendapudi, V. (1995). Additional validity evidence for a measure of Morningness. *Journal of Applied Psychology, 80,* 186–190.
Haas, E. C. (1998). Can 3-D auditory warnings enhance helicopter cockpit safety? *Proceedings of the Human Factors and Ergonomics Society,* 42nd Annual Meeting, 1117–1121.
Haas, E. C, & Edworthy, J. (1996). Measuring perceived urgency to create safe auditory warnings. *Proceedings of the Human Factors and Ergonomics Society,* 40th Annual Meeting, 845–849.
Haas, E. C., & Schmidt, J. (1995). Auditory icons as warning and advisory signals in the U.S. army battlefield combat identification system ( BCIS). *Proceedings of the Human Factors and Ergonomics Society,* 39th Annual Meeting, 999–1003.
Haberlandt, K. (1999). *Human memory: Exploration and application.* Boston: Allyn & Bacon.
Haggerty, R. J., Garmezy, N., Rutter, M., & Sherrod, L. (1994). *Stress, risk, and resilience in children and adolescents: Processes, mechanisms, and interventions.* New York: Cambridge University Press.
Hahn, G., Charlin, V. L., Sussman, S., Dent, C. W., Manzi, J., Stacy, A. W., Flay, B., Hansen, W. B., & Burton, D. (1990). Adolescents' first and most recent use situations of smokeless tobacco and cigarettes: Similarities and differences. *Addictive Behaviors, 15,* 439–448.
Haier, R. J. (1993). Cerebral glucose metabolism and intelligence. In P. A. Vernon (Ed.), *Biological approaches to the study of human intelligence* (pp. 317–332). Norwood, NJ: Ablex.
Hajek, P., & Belcher, M. (1991). Dreams of absent-minded transgression: An empirical study of a cognitive withdrawal symptom. *Journal of Abnormal Psychology, 100,* 487–491.
Hall, J. A., Roter, D. L., & Milburn, M. A. (1999). Illness and satisfaction with medical care. *Current Directions in Psychological Science, 8,* 96–99.
Hall, J. A., & Veccia, E. M. (1991). More "touching" observations: New insights on men, women, and interpersonal touch. *Journal of Personality and Social Psychology, 59,* 1155–1162.
Hall, S. (1998, February 15). Our memories, our selves. *The New York Times Magazine, 26.*
Hamburg, S. (1998). Inherited hypohedonia leads to learned helplessness: A conjecture updated. *Review of General Psychology, 2,* 384–403.
Hamilton, G. V. (1978). Obedience and responsibility: A jury simulation. *Journal of Personality and Social Psychology, 36,* 126–146.
Hammond, W. R., & Yung, B. (1993). Psychology's role in the public health response to assaultive violence among young African-American men. *American Psychologist, 48,* 142–154.
Hanisch, K. A. (1995). Behavioral families and multiple causes: Matching the complexity of responses to the complexity of antecedents. *Current Directions in Psychological Science, 4,* 156–161.
Hans, V. P. (1992). Obedience, justice, and the law: PS reviews recent contributions to a field ripe for new research efforts by psychological scientists. *Psychological Science, 3,* 218–221.
Harlow, H. F., & Harlow, M. H. (1966). Learning to love. *American Scientist, 54,* 244–272.
Harrigan, J. A., Luci, K. S., Kay, D., McLaney, A., & Rosenthal, R. (1991). Effects of expresser role and type of self-touching on observers' perceptions. *Journal of Applied Social Psychology, 21,* 585–609.
Harrington, A. (1995). Unfinished business: Models of laterality in the nineteenth century. In R. J. Davidson & K. Hugdahl (Eds.), *Brain asymmetry* (pp. 24–37). Cambridge, MA: MIT Press.
Harris, J. A., Rushton, J. P., Hampson, E., & Jackson, D. N. (1996). Salivary testosterone and self-report aggressive and pro-social personality characteristics in men and women. *Aggressive Behavior, 22,* 321–331.
Harris, J. R., (1998). *The nurture assumption: Why children turn out the way they do.* New York: Simon & Schuster.
Harris, K. M. (1999). The health status and risk behavior of adolescents in immigrant families. In D. J. Hernandez (Ed.), *Children of immigrants: Health, adjustment, and public assistance.* Washington, DC: National Academy Press.
Harrison, J. K. (1992). Individual and combined effects of behavior modeling and the cultural assimilator in cross-cultural management training. *Journal of Applied Psychology, 77,* 952–962.
Harrison, R. V. (1985). The person-environment fit model and the study of job stress. In T. A. Beehr & R. S. Bhagat (Eds.), *Human stress and cognition in organizations* (pp. 23–55). New York: Wiley.

Hart, D., Stinson, C., Field, N., Ewert, M., & Horowitz, M. (1995). A semantic space approach to representations of self and other in pathological grief: A case study. *Psychological Science, 6,* 96–100.
Hartmann, E. L. (1973). *The functions of sleep.* New Haven: Yale University Press.
Harvard Center for Cancer Prevention. (1996). Harvard Report on Cancer Prevention Volume 1: Causes of Human Cancer. *Can Causes Control, 7,* 7–15.
Harvey, E. (1999). Short-term and long-term effects of early parental employment on children of the national longitudinal survey of youth. *Developmental Psychology, 35,* 445–459.
Hatch, T. (1990). Social intelligence in young children. Paper presented at the meeting of the American Psychological Association.
Hatfield, E., & Rapson, R. L. (1993). *Love, sex, and intimacy: Their psychology, biology, and history.* New York: HarperCollins.
Haugaard, J. J., Repucci, N. D., Laurd, J., & Nauful, T. (1991). Children's definitions of the truth and their competency as witnesses in legal proceedings. *Law and Human Behavior, 15,* 253–273.
Hauser, M. D. (1993). Right hemisphere dominance for the production of facial expression in monkeys. *Science, 264,* 475–477.
Hawkins, J. D., Catalano, R. F., & Miller, J. Y. (1992). Risk and protective factors for alcohol and other drug problems in adolescence and early adulthood: Implications for substance abuse prevention. *Psychological Bulletin, 112,* 64–105.
Hawkins, S. A., & Hastie, R. (1990). Hindsight: Biased judgments of past events after the outcomes are known. *Psychological Bulletin, 107,* 311–327.
Haworth, N. L., Triggs, T. J., & Grey, E. M. (1988, June). Diver fatigue research: Development of methodology. Melbourne, Australia: Monash University, Accident Research Centre.
Haxby, J. V., Horwitz, B., Ungerleider, L. G., Maisog, J. M., Pietrini, P., & Grady, C. O. (1994). The functional organization of human extrastriatecortex: APET-$_r$CBF study of selective attention to faces and locations. *Journal of Neuroscience, 14,* 6336–6353.
Hazan, C., & Shaver, P. R. (1990). Love and work: An attachment-theoretical perspective. *Journal of Personality and Social Psychology, 59,* 270–280.
Hazelrigg, M. D., Cooper, H. M., & Borduin, C. M. (1987). Evaluating the effectiveness of family therapies: An integrative review and analysis. *Psychological Bulletin, 101,* 428–442.
Heatherton, T. F., Mahamedi, F., Striepe, M., & Field, A. E. (1997). A 10–year longitudinal study of body weight, dieting, and eating disorder symptoms. *Journal of Abnormal Psychology, 106,* 117–125.
Heatherton, T., & Weinberger, J. L. (1994). *Can personality change?* Washington, DC: American Psychological Association.
Heilman, M. E., Martell, R. F., & Simon, M. C. (1988). The vagaries of sex bias: Conditions regulating the undervaluation, equivaluation, and overvaluation of female job applicants. *Organizational Behavior and Human Decision Processes, 41,* 98–110.
Heller, W. (1997). Emotion. In M. T. Banich (Ed.), *Neuropsychology: The neural bases of mental function* (pp. 398–429). Boston: Houghton Mifflin.
Heller, W., Etienne, M. A., & Miller, G. A. (1995). Patterns of perceptual asymmetry in depression and anxiety: Implications for neuropsychological models of emotion and psychopathology. *Journal of Abnormal Psychology, 104,* 327–333.
Heller, W., Nitschke, J. B., & Miller, G. A. (1998) Lateralization in emotion and emotional disorders. *Current Directions in Psychological Science, 7,* 26–32.
Hellerstein, D., Yanowitch, P., Rosenthal, J., Samstag, L. W., Maurer, M., Kasch, K., Burrow, L., Porter, M., Cantillon, M., & Winston, R. (1993). A randomized double-blind study of fluoxetine versus placebo in the treatment of dysthymia. *American Journal of Psychiatry, 150,* 1169–1175.
Helweg-Larsen, M., & Collins, B. E. (1997). A social psychological perspective on the role of knowledge about AIDS in AIDS prevention. *Current Directions in Psychological Science, 6,* 23–26.
Hendrick, C., & Hendrick S. S. (1993). Lovers as friends. *Journal of Social and Personal Relationships, 10,* 459–466.
Henggler, S. W., Melton, G. B., & Smith, L. A. (1992). Family preservation using multisystematic therapy: An effective alternative to incarcerating juvenile offenders. *Journal of Consulting and Clinical Psychology, 60,* 953–961.
Hennekens, C. H. (1996). Alcohol and Risk of Coronary Events. In *Alcohol and the cardiovascular system* (NIAAA Research Monograph). Washington, DC: U.S. Department of Health and Human Services.
Hennig, P., & Knowles, A. (1990). Factors influencing women over 40 years to take precautions against cervical cancer. *Journal of Applied Social Psychology, 20,* 1612–1621.
Henry, R. A., Kmet, J., Desrosiers, E., & Landa, A. (in press). Examining the impact of interpersonal cohesiveness on group accuracy interventions: The importance of matching versus buffering. *Organizational Behavior and Human Processes.*
Herman, L. M., Richards, D. G., & Wolz, J. P. (1984). Comprehension of sentences by bottlenosed dolphins. *Cognition, 16,* 129–219.
Hermann, C., Blanchard, E. B., & Flor, H. (1997). *Journal of Consulting & Clinical Psychology, 65,* 611–616.
Herrnstein, R. J. (1961). Relative and absolute strength of response as a function of frequency of reinforcement. *Journal of Experimental Analysis of the Behavior 4,* 267–272.
Herrnstein, R. J. (1970). On the law of effect. *Journal of the Experimental Analysis of Behavior, 13,* 243–266.
Herrnstein, R. J., & Murray, C. (1994). *The bell curve.* New York: The Free Press.
Hershberger, S. L., Lichtenstein, P., & Knox, S. S. (1994). Genetic and environmental influences on perceptions of organizational climate. *Journal of Applied Psychology, 79,* 24–33.
Hetzel, B., & McMichael, T. (1987). *The LS factor: Lifestyle and health.* Ringwood, Victoria: Penguin.
Hewstone, M., Bond, M. H., & Wan, K. C. (1983). Social factors and social attributions: The explanation of intergroup differences in Hong Kong. *Social Cognition, 2,* 142–157.
Hilgard, E. R. (1979). Divided consciousness in hypnosis: Implications of the hidden observer. In E. Fromm & R. E. Shor (Eds.), *Hypnosis: Developments in research and new perspectives* (2nd ed). Chicago: Aldine.
Hilgard, E. R. (1986). *Divided consciouseness: Multiple controls in human thought and action* (2nd ed.). New York: Wiley.
Hilgard, E. R. (1993). Dissociation and theories of hypnosis. In E. Fromm & M. R. Nash (Eds.), *Contemporary hypnosis research* (pp. 69–101). New York: Guilford Press.
Hilton, D. J. (1995). The social context of reasoning: Conversational inference and rational judgment. *Psychological Bulletin, 118,* 248–271.
Hilton, J. L., Klein, J. G., & von Hippel, W. (1991). Attention allocation and impression formation. *Personality and Social Psychology Bulletin, 17,* 548–559.
Hilts, P. J. (1996, July 2). In research scans, telltale signs sort false memories from true. *New York Times,* p. C3.
Hingson, R., Strunin, L., Berlin, B., & Heeren, T. (1990). Beliefs about AIDS, use of alcohol and drugs, and unprotected sex among Massachusetts adolescents. *American Journal of Public Health, 80,* 295–299.
Hobfoll, S. E., Jackson, A. P., Lavin, J., Britton, P. J., & Shepherd, J. B. (1994). Reducing inner-city women's AIDS risk activities: A study of single, pregnant women. *Health Psychology, 13,* 397–403.
Hobson, J. A. (1988). *The dreaming brain.* New York: Basic Books.
Hodges, E. V. E., Boivin, M., Vitaro, F., & Bukowski, W. M. (1999). The power of friendship: Protection against an escalating cycle of peer victimization. *Developmental Psychology, 35,* 94–101.
Hofmann, D. A., & Morgeson, F. P. (1999). Safety-related behavior as a social exchange: The role of organizational support and leader–member exchange. *Journal of Applied Psychology, 84,* 286–296.
Hogan, R., Hogan, J., & Roberts, B. W. (1996). Personality measurement and employment decisions: Questions and answers. *American Psychologist, 51,* 469–477.
Holland, D., Witty, T., Lawler, J., & Lanzisera, D. (1999). Biofeedback-assisted relaxation training with brain injured patients in acute stages of recovery. *Brain Injury, 13,* 53–57.
Hollon, S. D., DeRubeis, R. J., & Evans, M. D. (1987). Causal mediation of change in treatment for depression: Discriminating between nonspecificity and noncausality. *Psychological Bulletin, 102,* 139–149.
Hollon, S. D., Shelton, R. C., & Loosen, P. T. (1991). Cognitive therapy and pharmacotherapy for depression. *Journal of Consulting and Clinical Psychology, 59,* 88–99.
Holmes, D. S., McGilley, B. M., & Houston, B. K. (1984). Take-related arousal of Type A and Type B persons: Level of challenge and response specificity. *Journal of Personality and Social Psychology, 46,* 1322–1327.
Holmes, T. H., & Masuda, M. (1974). Life change and illness susceptibility. In B. S. Dohrenwend and B. P. Dohrenwend (Eds.), *Stressful life events: Their nature and effects.* New York: Wiley.
Holmes, T. H., & Rahe, R. H. (1967). The social readjustment rating scale. *Journal of Psychosomatic Research, 11,* 213–218.
Holtzman, A. D., & Levis, D. J. (1991). Differential aversive conditioning of an external (visual) and internal (imaginal) CS: Effects of transfer between and within CS modalities. *Journal of Mental Imagery, 15,* 77–90.
Holyoak, K. J., & Thagard, P. (1997). The analogical mind. *American Psychologist, 52,* 35–44.
Honig, W. K., & Staddon, J. E. R. (Eds.). (1977). *Handbook of operant behavior.* Englewood Cliffs, NJ: Prentice-Hall.
Honig, W. K., & Urcuioli, P. J. (1981). The legacy of Guttman and Kalish: Twenty-five years of research on stimulus generalization. *Journal of the Experimental Analysis of Behavior, 36,* 405–445.
Hoppe, R. B. (1988). In search of a phenomenon: Research in parapsychology. *Contemporary Psychology, 33,* 129–130.
Hoptman, M. J., & Davidson, R. J. (1994). How and why do the two cerebral hemispheres interact? *Psychological Bulletin, 116,* 195–219.
Horne, J. A. (1998). *Why we sleep: The function of sleep in humans and other mammals.* Oxford, England: Oxford University Press.
Horne, S. (1999). Domestic violence in Russia. *American Psychologist, 54,* 55–61.
Hornstein, G. A. (1992). The return of the repressed: Psychology's problematic relations with psychoanalysis, 1909–1960. *American Psychologist, 47,* 254–263.
Houfman, L. G., House, M., & Ryan, J. B. (1981). Dynamic visual acuity: A review. *Journal of the American Optometric Association, 52,* 883–887.
Houpt, T. A., & Berlin, R. (1999). Rapid, labile, and protein synthesis–independent short-term

memory in conditioned taste aversion. *Learning & Memory, 6,* 37–46.

Houpt, T. A., Boulos, Z., & Moore-Ede, M. C. (1996). Midnight Sun: Software for determining light exposure and phase-shifting schedules during global travel. *Physiology and Behavior, 59,* 561–568.

House, R. J., & Howell, J. M. (1992). Personality and charismatic leadership. *Leadership Quarterly, 3,* 81–108.

House, R. J., & Podsakoff, P. M. (1994). Leadership effectiveness: Past perspectives and future directions for research. In J. Greenberg (Ed.), *Organizational behavior: The state of the sceince* (pp. 45–82). Hillsdale, NJ: Erlbaum.

House, R. J., Spangler, W. D., & Woycke, J. (1991). Personality and charisma in the U.S. presidency: A psychological theory of leader effectiveness. *Administrative Science Quarterly, 36,* 263–296.

Hovland, C. I., & Weiss, W. (1951). The influence of source credibility on communication effectiveness. *Public Opinion Quarterly, 1,* 635–650.

Howard, K. I., Kopta, S. M., Krause, M. S., & Orlinsky, D. E. (1986). The dose-effect relationship in psychotherapy. *American Psychologist, 41,* 159–164.

Howe, M. L., & Courage, M. L. (1993). On resolving the enigma of infantile amnesia. *Psychological Bulletin, 113,* 305–326.

Howell, J. M., & Frost, P. J. (1989). A laboratory study of charismatic leadership. *Organizational Behavior and Human Decision Processes, 43,* 243–269.

Hubel, D. H., & Wiesel, T. N. (1979). Brain mechanisms of vision. *Scientific American, 241,* 150–162.

Huesmann, L. R. (Ed.). (1994). *Aggressive behavior: Current perspectives.* New York: Plenum.

Hughes, J. R., Smith, T. W., Kosterlitz, H. W., Fothergill, L. A., Morgan, B. A., & Morris, H. R. (1975). Identification of two related pentapeptides from the brain with potent opiate agonist activity. *Nature, 258,* 577–581.

Hultsch, D. F., & Dixon, R. A. (1990). Learning and memory in aging. In J. E. Birren & K. W. Schaie (Eds.), *Handbook of the psychology of aging* (3rd ed., pp. 359–374). San Diego: Academic Press.

Humbaugh, K., & Garrett, J. (1974). Sensation seeking among skydivers. *Perceptual and Motor Skills, 38,* 103–111.

Hummell, J. E. (1994). Reference frames and relations in computational models of object recognition. *Current Directions in Psychological Science, 3,* 111–116.

Hunt, E. (1993). What do we need to know about aging? In J. Cerella, J. Rybash, W. Hoyer, & M. L. Commons (Eds.), *Adult information processing: Limits on loss* (pp. 587–598). San Diego, CA: Academic Press.

Hunt, E., & Agnoli, F. (1991). The Whorfian hypothesis: A cognitive psychology perspective. *Psychological Review, 98,* 377–389.

Hunter, R. H. (1995). Benefits of competency-based treatment programs. *American Psychologist,* 50, 509–513.

Hurvich, L. M. (1981). *Color vision.* Sunderland, MA: Sinauer Associates.

Husband, A. J., Lin, W., Madsen, G., & King, M. G. (1993). A conditioning model for immunostimulation: Enhancement of the antibody response to ovalbumin by behavioral conditioning in rats. In A. J. Husband (Ed.), *Psychoimmunology: CNS-Immune Interactions* (pp. 139–147). Boca Raton, FL: CRC Press.

Hymowitz, C. (1995, December 21). High anxiety: In the name of Freud, why are psychiatrists complaining so much? *Wall Street Journal,* pp. A1, A6.

Ingram, R. (1990). Self-focused attention in clinical disorders: Review and a conceptual model. *Psychological Bulletin, 107,* 156–176.

Institute of Medicine. (1989). *Prevention and treatment of alcohol problems: Research opportunities.* Washington, DC: National Academy of Sciences.

Isabella, R. (1993). Origins of attachment: Maternal interactive behavior across the first year. *Child Development, 64,* 605–621.

Isen, A. M. (1993). Positive affect and decision making. In M. Lewis & J. M. Haviland (Eds.), *Handbook of emotion* (pp. 216–277). New York: Guilford Press.

Isen, A. M., & Baron, R. A. (1991). Positive affect and organizational behavior. In B. M. Staw & L. L. Cummings (Eds.), *Research in organizational behavior* (Vol. 14, pp. 1–48). Greenwich, CT: JAI Press.

Ittelson, W. H. (1996). Visual perception of markings. *Psychonomic Bulletin & Review, 3,* 171–187.

Ivkovich, D., Collins, K. L., Eckerman, C. O., Krasnegor, N. A., & Stanton, M. E. (1999). Classical delay eyeblink conditioning in 4- and 5-month-old human infants. *Psychological Science, 10,* 4–7.

Iwahashi, M. (1992). Scents and science. *Vogue,* pp. 212–214.

Izard, C. E. (1991). *The psychology of emotions.* New York: Plenum.

Izard, C. E., Hembree, E. A., & Huebner, R. R. (1987). Infants' emotion expressions to acute pain. *Developmental Psychology, 23,* 105–113.

Jacobson, S., Fein, G., Jacobson, J., Schwartz, P., & Dowler, J. (1984). Neonatal correlates of prenatal exposure to smoking, caffeine, and alcohol. *Infant Behavior and Development, 7,* 253–265.

Jahnke, J. C., & Nowaczyk, R. H. (1998). *Cognition.* Upper Saddle River, NJ: Prentice-Hall.

James, W. J. (1890). *Principles of psychology.* New York: Holt.

Jameson, D., & Hurvich, L. M. (1989). Essay concerning color constancy. *Annual Review of Psychology, 40,* 1–22.

Janicak, P., Sharma, R., Israni, T., Dowd, S., Altman, E., & Davis, J. (1991). Effects of unilateral-non-dominant vs. bilateral ECT on memory and depression: A preliminary report. *Psychopharmacology Bulletin, 27,* 353–57.

Jann, M., Lam, T. W., & Chang, W. H. (1993). Haloperidol and reduced haloperidol plasma concentrations in different ethnic populations and interindividual variabilities in haloperidol metabolism. In K. M. Lin, R. Poland, & G. Nakasaki (Eds.), *Psychopharmacology and psychobiology of ethnicity.* Washington, DC: American Psychiatric Association Press.

Jefferson, D. J. (1993, August 12). Dr. Brown treats what ails the rides at amusement parks. *The Wall Street Journal,* p. 1.

Jencks, D. (1972). *Inequality: A reassessment of the effect of family and school in America.* New York: Basic Books.

Jenike, M. A., Baer, L., Ballantine, H. T., Martuza, R. L., Tynes, S., Giriunas, I., Buttolph, M. L., & Cassem, N. H. (1991). Cingulotomy for refractory obsessive compulsive disorder: A long-term follow-up of 33 cases. *Archives of General Psychiatry, 48,* 548–557.

Jenkins, J. G., & Dallenbach, K. M. (1924). Obliviscence during sleep and waking. *American Journal of Psychology, 35,* 605–612.

Jessor, R. (1993). Successful adolescent development among youth in high-risk settings. *American Psychologist, 48,* 117–126.

Johnson, B. T., & Eagly, A. H. (1989). Effects of involvement on persuasion: A meta-analysis. *Psychological Bulletin, 106,* 290–314.

Johnson, E. J. (1985). Expertise and decision under uncertainty: Performance and process. In M. Chi, R. Glasse, & M. Farr (Eds.), *The nature of expertise.* Columbus, OH: National Center for Research in Vocational Education.

Johnson, M. K., Hashtroudi, S., & Lindsay, D. S. (1993). Source monitoring. *Psychological Bulletin, 114,* 3–28.

Johnson, M. K., & Sherman, S. J. (1990). Constructing and reconstructing the past and the future in the present. In E. T. Higgins & R. M. Sorrentino (Eds.), *Handbook of motivation and social cognition: Foundations of social behavior* (pp. 482–526). New York: Guilford.

Johnson, V. S., & Oliver-Rodriguez, J. C. (1997). Facial beauty and the late positive component of event-related potentials. *Journal of Sex Research, 34,* 188–198.

Johnson-Laird, P. N., Byrne, R. M. J., & Shaeken, W. (1992). Propositional reasoning by model. *Psychological Review, 99,* 418–439.

Johnson-Laird, P. N., Byrne, R. M. J., Tabossi, P. (1989). Reasoning by model: The case of multiple quantification. *Psychological Review, 96,* 658–673.

Johnston, J. C., McCann, R. S., & Remington, R. W. (1995). Chronometric evidence for two types of attention. *Psychological Science, 6,* 365–369.

Johnston, L. D., O'Malley, P. M., & Bachman, J. G. (1997). *National survey results on drug use from the Monitoring the Future study, 1975–1996,* (Vol. 1). Rockville, MD: National Institute on Drug Abuse.

Johnston, W., & Dark, V. (1986). Selective attention. *Annual Review of Psychology, 37,* 43–75.

Johnstone, B. (1999, May/June). Japan's friendly robots. *MITs Magazine of Innovation Technology Review.* www.techreview.com/articles/may99/johnstone.htm

Joiner, T. E., Jr. (1994). The interplay of similarity and self-verification in relationship formation. *Social Behavior and Personality, 22,* 195–200.

Joiner, T. E., Jr., Alfano, M. S., & Metalsky, G. I. (1993). When depression breeds contempt: Reassurance seeking, self-esteem, and rejection of depressed college students by their roommates. *Journal of Abnormal Psychology, 101* 165–173.

Joiner, T. E., Jr., Heatheton, T. F., Rudd, M. D., & Schmidt, N. B. (1997). Perfectionism, perceived with status, and bulimic symptoms: Two studies testing a diathesis-stress model. *Journal of Abnormal Psychology, 106,* 145–153.

Jones, D. M., & Broadbent, D. E. (1987). Noise. In G. Salvendy (Ed.), *Handbook of human factors.* New York: John Wiley & Sons.

Jonides, J. (1995). Working memory and thinking. In E. E. Smith & F. N. Osherson (Eds.), *An invitation to cognitive science: Thinking* (Vol. 3, pp. 215–265). Cambridge, MA: MIT Press.

Jou, J., Shanteau, J., & Harris, R. J. (1996). An information processing view of framing effects: The role of causal schemes in decision making. *Memory & Cognition, 24,* 1–15.

Judd, C. M., Ryan, C. N., & Park, B. (1991). Accuracy in the judgment of in-group and out-group variability. *Journal of Personality and Social Psychology, 61,* 366–379.

Judge, T. A., Martocchio, J. J., & Thorsen, C. J. (1998). Five-factor model of personality and employee absence. *Journal of Applied Psychology, 82,* 745–755.

Julien, R. M. (1995). *A primer of drug action* (7th ed.). New York: Freeman.

Jussim, L. (1991). Interpersonal expectations and social reality: A reflection-construction model and reinterpretation of evidence. *Psychological Review, 98,* 54–73.

Just, M. A., & Carpenter, P. A. (1987). *The psychology of reading and language comprehension.* Newton, MA: Allyn and Bacon.

Kaempf, G. L., Klein, G. A., Thordsen, M. L., & Wolf, S. (1996). Decision making in complex naval command-and-control environments. *Human Factors, 38,* 220–231.

Kagan, J., & Snidman, N. (1991). Temperamental factors in human development. *American Psychologist, 46,* 856–862.

Kahneman, D., & Tversky, A. (1982). Judgment under uncertainty: Heuristics and biases. In D. Kahneman, P. Slovic, & A. Tversky (Eds.), *Judgment under uncertainty: Heuristics and biases*

(pp. 3–22). Cambridge, England: Cambridge University Press.
Kalivas, P. W., & Samson, H. H. (Eds.). (1992). *The neurobiology of drug and alcohol addiction.* Annals of the New York Academy of Sciences, Vol. 654. New York: Academy of Sciences.
Kamin, L. J. (1965). Temporal and intensity characteristics of the conditioned stimulus. In W. F. Prokasy (Ed.), *Classical conditioning: A symposium.* New York: Appleton-Century-Crofts.
Kanner, A. D., Coyne, J. C., Schaefer, C., & Lazarus, R. S. (1981). Comparison of two modes of stress measurement: Daily hassles and uplifts versus major life events. *Journal of Behavioral Medicine, 4,* 1–39.
Kaplan, H. I., & Sadock, B. J. (1991). *Synopsis of psychiatry: Behavioral sciences and clinical psychiatry* (6th ed.). Baltimore, MD: Williams & Wilkins.
Karasek, R., & Theorell, T. (1990). *Healthy work: Job stress, productivity, and the reconstruction of working life.* New York: Basic Books.
Kattler, H., Djik, D. J., & Borbely, A. A. (1994). Effects of unilateral somatosensory stimulation prior to sleep on the sleep EEG in humans. *Journal of Sleep Research, 4,* 159–164.
Kaufman, A. S., & Kaufman, N. L. (1993). Kaufman adolescent and adult intelligence test. Circle Pines, MN: American Guidance.
Kavanagh, D. J. (1992). Recent developments in expressed emotion in schizophrenia. *British Journal of Psychiatry, 148,* 601–620.
Kazdin, A. E. (1982). The token economy: A decade later. *Journal of Applied Behavior Analysis, 15,* 431–446.
Keary, K., & Fitzpatrick, C. (1994). Children's disclosure of sexual abuse during formal investigation. *Child Abuse and Neglect, 18,* 543–548.
Keller, I. M., Bouchard, T. J., Jr., Arvey, R. D., Segaln, N. L., & Dawis, R. V. (1992). Work values: Genetic and environmental influences. *Journal of Applied Psychology, 77,* 79–88.
Keller, P. A. (1999). Converting the unconverted: The effect of inclination and opportunity to discount health-related fear appeals. *Journal of Applied Psychology, 84,* 403–415.
Kelley, H. H. (1972). Attribution in social interaction. In E. E. Jones et al. (Eds.), *Attribution: Perceiving the causes of behavior.* Morristown, NJ: General Learning Press.
Kelly, D. D. (1981). Disorders of sleep and consciousness. In E. Kandel & J. Schwartz (Eds.), *Principles of neural science.* New York: Elsevier-North Holland.
Kelly, J. A., & Kalichman, S. C. (1998). Reinforcement value of unsafe sex as a predictor of condom use and continued HIV/AIDS risk behavior among gay and bisexual men. *Health Psychology, 17,* 328–335.
Kelman, H. C., & Hamilton, V. L. (1989). *Crimes of obedience.* New Haven, CT: Yale University Press.
Kelsey, F. O. (1969). Drugs and pregnancy. *Mental Retardation, 7,* 7–10.
Kendall-Tackett, K. A. (1991). Characteristics of abuse that influence when adults molested as children seek treatment. *Journal of Interpersonal Violence, 6,* 486–493.
Kendall-Tackett, K. A., Williams, L. M., & Finkelhor, D. (1993). Impact of sexual abuse on children: A review and synthesis of recent empirical studies. *Psychological Bulletin, 113,* 164–180.
Kendler, K. S., Prescott, C. A., Neale, M. C., & Pedersen, N. L. (1997). Temperance Board registration for alcohol abuse in a national sample of Swedish male twins, born 1902 to 1949. *Archives of General Psychiatry, 54,* 178–184.
Kendzierski, D., & Whitaker, D. J. (1997). The role of self-schema in linking intentions with behavior. *Personality and Social Psychology Bulletin, 23,* 139–147.
Kenrick, D. T., Groth, G. E., Trost, M. R., & Sadalla, E. K. (1993). Integrating evolutionary and social exchange perspectives on relationships: Effects of gender, self-appraisal, and involvement level on mate selection criteria. *Journal of Personality and Social Psychology, 64,* 951–969.
Kessler, R. C., McGonagle, K. A., Zhao, S., Nelson, C. B., Hughes, M., Eshleman, S., Witchen, H-U., & Kendler, K. S. (1994). Lifetime and 12–month prevalence of DSM-III-R psychiatric disorders in the United States. *Archives of General Psychiatry, 5,* 8–19.
Kiecolt-Glaser, J. K., & Glaser, R. (1992). Psychoneuroimmunology: Can psychological interventions modulate immunity? *Journal of Consulting and Clinical Psychology, 60,* 569–575.
Kiecolt-Glaser, J. K., Fisher, L., Ogrocki, P., Stout, J. C., Speicher, C. E., & Glaser, R. (1987). Marital quality, marital disruption, and immune function. *Psychosomatic Medicine, 49,* 13–34.
Kiecolt-Glaser, J. K., Kennedy, S., Malkoff, S., Fisher, L., Speicher, C. E., & Glaser, R. (1988). Marital discord and immunity in males. *Psychosomatic Medicine, 50,* 213–229.
Kiesler, C. A., & Kiesler, S. B. (1969). *Conformity.* Reading, MA: Addison-Wesley.
Kihlstrom, J. F. (1998). Dissociation and dissociation theory in hypnosis: Comment on Kirsch & Lynn (1998). *Psychological Bulletin, 123,* 186–191.
Kilham, W., & Mann, L. (1974). Level of destructive obedience as function of transmitter and executant roles in the Milgram obedience paradigm. *Journal of Personality and Social Psychology, 29,* 696–702.
Kim, J. E., Nesselroade, J. R., & Feaherman, D. L. (1996). The state component in self-reported world views and religious beliefs of older persons: The MacArthur successful aging studies. *Psychology and Aging, 11,* 396–407.
Kinnunen, T., Zamansky, T., & Block, M. (1994). Is the hypnotized subject lying? *Journal of Abnormal Psychology, 103,* 184–191.
Kinsey, A. C., Pomeroy, W., & Martin, C. (1984). *Sexual behavior in the human male.* Philadelphia: W. B. Saunders.
Kinsey, A. C., Pomeroy, W., Martin, C., & Gebhard, P. (1953). *Sexual behavior in the human female.* Philadelphia: W. B. Saunders.
Kintsch, W. (1997). *Memory and cognition.* New York: Wiley.
Kirby, S. L., & Davis, M. A. (1998). A study of escalating commitment in principal–agent relationships: Effects of monitoring and personal responsibility. *Journal of Applied Psychology, 83,* 206–217.
Kirkpatrick, S. A., & Locke, E. A. (1991). Leadership: Do traits matter? *Academy of Management Executive, 5*(2), 48–60.
Kirmeyer, S. L., & Biggers, K. (1988) Environmental demand and demand engendering behavior: An observational analysis of the Type A pattern. *Journal of Personality and Social Psychology, 54,* 997–1005.
Kirsch, I., & Lynn, S. J. (1998). Dissociation theories of hypnosis. *Psychological Bulletin, 123,* 100–115.
Klaczynski, P. A. (1997). Bias in adolescents' everyday reasoning and its relationships with intellectual ability, personal theories, and self-serving motivation. *Developmental Psychology, 33,* 273–383.
Klag, M. J., Ford, D. E., Mead, L. A., He, J., Whelton, P. K., Liang, K., & Levine, D. M. (1993). Serum cholesterol in young men and subsequent cardiovascular disease. *New England Journal of Medicine, 328,* 313–318.
Klausner, J., Sweeney, J., Deck, M., Hass, G., & Kelly, A. B. (1992). Clinical correlates of cerebral ventricular enlargement on schizophrenia. Further evidence for frontal lobe disease. *Journal of Nervous and Mental Disease, 180,* 407–412.
Kluft, R. P. (1995). Current controversies surrounding dissociative identity disorder. In L. M. Cohen, J. N. Berzoff, & M. R. Elin (Eds.), *Dissociative identity disorder: Theoretical and treatment controversies* (pp. 347–348). Northvale, NJ: Jason Aronson.
Knapp, D. N. (1988). Behavioral management techniques and exercise promotion. In R. K. Dishman (Ed.), *Exercise adherence: Its impact on public health.* Champaign, IL: Human Kinetics Books.
Knapp, R. (1987, July). When a child dies. *Psychology Today,* 60–67.
Knipling, R. R., & Wang, J. S. (1994, November). Crashes and fatalities related to driver drowsiness/fatigue. NHTSA Research Note.
Koehler, J. J. (1996). The base rate fallacy reconsidered: Descriptive, normative, and methodological challenges. *Behavioral and Brain Sciences, 19,* 1–53.
Kohl, W. L., Steers, R., & Terborg, J., Jr. (1995). The effects of transformational leadership on teacher attitudes and student performance in Singapore. *Journal of Organizational Behavior, 73,* 695–702.
Kohlberg, L. (1984). *Essays on moral development: Vol. 2. The Psychology of moral development.* San Francisco: Harper & Row.
Kohler, I. (1962, May). Experiments with goggles. *Scientific American,* pp. 62–72.
Koocher, G. P., Goodman, G. S., White, C. S., Friedrich, W. N., Sivan, A. B., & Reynolds, C. R. (1995). Psychological science and the use of anatomically detailed dolls in child sexual-abuse assessments. *Psychological Bulletin, 118,* 119–222.
Kosslyn, S. (1994). *Image and brain.* Cambridge, MA: MIT Press.
Kosslyn, S. M. (1994). *Image and brain: The resolution of the imagery debate.* Cambridge, MA: MIT Press.
Kosslyn, S. M., Segar, C., Pani, J., & Hilger, L. A. (1991). When is imagery used? A diary study. *Journal of Mental Imagery.*
Kotre, J. (1984). *Outliving the self: Generativity and the interpretation of lives.* Baltimore: Johns Hopkins University Press.
Kounious, J. (1996). On the continuity of thought and the representation of knowledge: Electrophysiological and behavioral time-course measures reveal levels of structure in semantic memory. *Psychonomic Bulletin and Review, 3,* 265–286.
Kozu, J. (1999). Domestic violence in Japan. *American Psychologist, 54,* 50–54.
Krakauer, J. (1997). *Into thin air: A personal account of the Mount Everest disaster.* New York: Random House.
Krakoff, L. R., Dziedzic, S., Mann, S. J., Felton, K., & Yeager, K. (1985). Plasma epinephrine concentrations in healthy men: Correlation with systolic blood pressure and rate-pressure product. *Journal of American College of Cardiology, 5,* 352.
Kramer, A. F., Hahn, S., Cohen, N. J., Banich, M. T., McAuley, E., Harrison, C. R., Chason, J., Vakil, E., Bardell, L., Boileau, R. A., & Colcombe, A. (1999). Ageing, fitness and neurocognitive function. *Nature, 400,* 418–419.
Kranzler, J., & Jensen, A. R. (1989). Inspection time and intelligence: A meta-analysis. *Intelligence, 13,* 329–247.
Kring, A. M., Smith, D. A., & Neale, J. M. (1994). Individual differences in dispositional expressiveness: Development and validation of the emotional expressivity scale. *Journal of Personality and Social Psychology, 66,* 934–949.
Krosnick, J. A., Beta, A. L., Jussim, L. J., & Lynn, A. R. (1992). Subliminal conditioning of attitudes. *Personality and Social Psychology Bulletin, 18,* 152–162.
Kubany, E. S., Bauer, G. B., Muraoka, M. Y., Richard, D. C., & Read, P. (1995). Impact of labeled anger and blame in intimate relationships. *Journal of Social and Clinical Psychology, 14,* 53–60.

Kübler-Ross, E. (1974). *Questions and answers on death and dying.* New York: Macmillan.

Kuhn, L., Stein, Z. A., Thomas, P. A., Singh, T., & Tasai, W. (1994). Maternal–infant HIV transmission and circumstances of delivery. *American Journal of Public Health, 84,* 1110–1115.

Kulman, L. (1999, April 26). What'd you say? A high-volume world takes a toll on ever younger ears. *U.S. News & World Report,* 66–68, 71–74.

Kunda, Z., & Oleson, K. C. (1995). Maintaining stereotypes in the face of disconfirmation: Construction grounds for subtyping deviants. *Journal of Personality and Social Psychology, 68,* 565–579.

Kutchinsky, B. (1992). The child sexual abuse panic. *Nordisk Sexologist, 10,* 30–42.

Ladavas, E., Umilta, C., & Ricci-Bitti, P. E. (1980). Evidence for sex differences in right-hemisphere dominance for emotions. *Neuropsychologia, 18,* 361–366.

Lahey, B. B., Hart, E. L., Pilszka, S., & Applegate, B. (1993). Neurophysiological correlates of conduct disorder: A rationale and a review of research. *Journal of Clinical Child Psychology, 22,* 141–153.

Laird, J. D. (1984). The real role of facial responses in the experience of emotion: A reply to Tourangeua and Ellsworth, and others. *Journal of Personality and Social Psychology, 47,* 909–917.

Lamb, M. E. (1977). Father-infant and mother-infant interactions in the first year of life. *Child Development, 48,* 167–181.

Lamb, M. R., London, B., Pond, H. M., & Whitt, K. A. (1998). Automatic and controlled processes in the analysis of hierarchical structure. *Psychological Science, 9,* 14–19.

Lambert, A. J. (1995). Stereotypes and social judgment: The consequences of group variability. *Journal of Personality and Social Psychology, 68,* 388–403.

Landis, S. H., Murray, T., Bolden, S., & Wingo, P. A. (1998). Cancer statistics, 1998. *CA Cancer J Clin, 48,* 6–29.

Landro, L. (1998, October 19). Alone together: Cancer patients and survivors find treatment, and support, online. *Wall Street Journal,* p. R12.

Lange, J. D., Brown, W. A., Wincze, J. P., & Zwick W. (1980). Serum testosterone concentration and penile tumescence changes in men. *Hormones and Behavior, 14,* 267–270.

Langlois, J. H., & Roggman, L. A. (1990). Attractive faces are only average. *Psychological Science, 1,* 115–121.

Langlois, J. H., Roggman, L. A., & Riesser-Danner, L. A. (1990). Infants' differential social responses to attractive and unattractive faces. *Developmental Psychology, 26,* 153–159.

Laumann, E. O., Gagnon, J. H., Michael, R. T., & Michaels, S. (1994). *The social organization of sexuality: Sexual practices in the United States.* Chicago: University of Chicago Press.

Law, D. J., Pellegrino, J. W., & Hunt, E. B. (1993). Comparing the tortoise and the hare: Gender differences and experience in dynamic spatial reasoning tasks. *Psychological Science, 4,* 35–40.

Lawless, H., & Engen, T. (1977). Associations to odors: Interference, mnemonics, and verbal labeling. *Journal of Experimental Psychology: Human Learning and Memory, 3,* 52–59.

Layman, J., Gidycz, C. A., & Lynn, S. J. (1996). Unacknowledged versus acknowledged rape victims: Situational factors and posttraumatic stress. *Journal of Abnormal Psychology, 105,* 124–131.

Lazarus, R. S., & Folkman, S. (1984). *Stress, appraisal, and coping.* New York: Springer.

Lazarus, R. S., Opton, E. M., Nomikos, M. S., & Rankin, N. O. (1985). The principle of short-circuiting of threat: Further evidence. *Journal of Personality, 33,* 622–635.

Lee, K., Eskritt, M., Symons, L. A., & Muir, D. (1998). Children's use of triadic eye gaze information for "mind reading." *Developmental Psychology, 34,* 525–539.

Lee, Y. T., & Seligman, M. E. P. (1997). Are Americans more optimistic than the Chinese? *Personality and Social Psychology Bulletin, 23,* 32–40.

Leitenberg, H., & Henning, K. (1995). Sexual fantasy. *Psychological Bulletin, 117,* 469–496.

Lemery, K. S., Goldsmith, H. H., Klinnert, M. D., & Mrazek, D. A. (1999). Developmental models of infant and childhood temperament. *Developmental Psychology, 35,* 189–204.

Lemme, B. H. (1999). *Development in adulthood* (2nd ed.). Boston: Allyn & Bacon.

Leonard, J. R., & Sloboda, B. A. (1996, April). *Workplace violence: A review of current literature.* Paper presented at the Annual Meeting of the Society for Industrial and Organizational Psychology, San Diego, CA.

Lepper, M., & Green, D. (Eds.). (1978). *The hidden costs of reward.*

Lepper, M. R., & Cordova, D. I. (1992). A desire to be taught: Instructional consequences of intrinsic motivation. *Motivation and Emotion, 16,* 187–208.

Lerman, C., Caporaso, N. E., Audrain, J., Main, D., Bowman, E. D., Lockshin, B., Boyd, N. R., & Shields, P. G. (1999). Evidence suggesting the role of specific genetic factors in cigarette smoking. *Health Psychology, 18,* 14–20.

Lerner, M. J. (1980). *The belief in a just world: A fundamental delusion.* New York: Plenum.

Lerner, R. M. (1990). Plasticity, person-context relations, and cognitive training in the aged years: A developmental contextual perspective. *Developmental Psychology, 26,* 911–915.

Lerner, R. M. (1993). The demise of the nature-nurture dichotomy. *Human Development, 36,* 119–124.

Lester, N., Smart, L., & Baum, A. (1994). Measuring coping flexibility. *Psychology and Health, 9,* 409–424.

LeVay, S. (1991). A difference in hypothalamic structure between heterosexual and homosexual men. *Science, 253,* 1–36.

Levenson, R. W. (1992). Autonomic nervous system differences among emotions. *Psychological Science, 3,* 23–27.

Levenson, R. W., Carstensen, L. L., Friesen, W. V., & Ekman, P. (1991). Emotion, physiology, and expression in old age. *Psychology and Aging, 6,* 28–35.

Leventhal, H., Singer, R., & Jones, S. (1965). The effects of fear and specifying of recommendation upon attitudes and behavior. *Journal of Personality and Social Psychology, 2,* 20–29.

Levine, D. S. (1991). *Introduction to neural and cognitive modeling.* Hillsdale, NJ: Erlbaum.

Levine, M., Toro, P. A., & Perkins, D. V. (1993). Social and community interventions. *Annual Review of Psychology, 44,* 525–558.

Levinson, D. (1996). *The seasons of a woman's life.* New York: Knopf.

Levinson, D. J. (1986). A conception of adult development. *American Psychologist, 41,* 3–13.

Levinthal, C. F. (1999). *Drugs, behavior, and modern society.* Boston: Allyn & Bacon.

Levis, D. J. (1985). Implosive theory: A comprehensive extension of conditioning theory of fear/anxiety to psychology. In S. Reiss & R. R. Bootzin (Eds.), *Theoretical issues in behavior therapy.* New York: Academic Press.

Levy, S. M. (1990). Psychosocial risk factors and cancer progression: Mediating pathways linking behavior and disease. In K. D. Craig & S. M. Weiss (Eds.), *Health enhancement, disease prevention, and early intervention: Biobehavioral perspectives.* New York: Springer.

Levy, S. M., Herberman, R., Maluish, A., Achlien, B., & Lippman, M. (1985). Prognostic risk assessment in primary breast cancer by behavioral and immunological parameters. *Health Psychology, 4,* 99–113.

Levy, S. M., Herberman, R. B., Simons, A., Whiteside, T., Lee, J., McDonald, R., & Beadle, M. (1989). Persistently low natural killer cell activity in normal adults: Immunological, hormonal and mood correlates. *Natural Immune Cell Growth Regulation, 8,* 173–186.

Levy, S. M., Lee, J., Bagley, C., & Lippman, M. (1988). Survival hazards analysis in first recurrent breast cancer patients: Seven-year follow-up. *Psychosomatic Medicine, 50,* 520–528.

Lewkowicz, D. J. (1996). Infants' response to the audible and visible properties of the human face 1. Role of lexical-syntactic content, temporal synchrony, gender, and manner of speech. *Developmental Psychology, 32,* 347–366.

Lewy, A. J., Sack, R. I., & Singer, C. M. (1992). Bright light, melatonin, and biological rhythms in humans. In J. Montplaisir & R. Godbout (Eds.), *Sleep and biological rhythms: Basic mechanisms and applications to psychiatry.* New York: Oxford University Press.

Leyens, J. P., Yzerbyt, V., & Corneille, O. (1996). The role of applicability in the emergence of the overattribution bias. *Journal of Personality and Social Psychology, 70,* 291–229.

Liddell, F. D. K. (1982). Motor vehicle accidents (1973–6) in a cohort of Montreal drivers. *Journal of Epidemiological Community Health, 36,* 140–145.

Liden, R. C., & Mitchell, T. R. (1988). Ingratiatory behaviors in organizational settings. *Academy of Management Review, 13,* 572–587.

Lieberman, D. A. (1990). *Learning: Behavior and cognition.* Belmont, CA: Wadsworth Publishing Company.

Lieberman, J. A., & Koreen, A. R. (1993). Neurochemistry and neuroendocrinology of schizophrenia. *Schizophrenia Bulletin, 19,* 197–256.

Lin, K. M., Poland, R., & Nakasaki, G. (Eds.), (1993). *Psychopharmacology and psychobiology of ethnicity.* Washington, DC: American Psychiatric Association Press.

Linden, E. (1992). Chimpanzees with a difference: Bonobos. *National Geographic, 181*(3), 46–53.

Lindsay, D. S., & Read, J. D. (1995). Memory, remembering, and misremembering. *PTSD Research Quarterly, 6,* 1–7.

Linville, P. W., & Fischer, G. W. (1993). Exemplar and abstraction models of perceived group variability and stereotypicality. *Social Cognition, 11,* 92–125.

Lipshitz, R., & Bar-Ilan, O. (1996). How problems are solved: Reconsidering the phase theorem. *Organizational Behavior and Human Decision Processes, 65,* 48–60.

Locke, B. Z., & Slaby, A. E. (1982). Preface. In D. Mechanic (Ed.), *Symptoms, illness behavior, and help-seeking* (pp. xi-xv). New York: Prodist.

Locke, E. A. (1991). *The essence of leadership.* New York: Lexingon Books.

Locke, E. A., & Latham, G. P. (1990). *A theory of goal setting and task performance.* Englewood Cliffs, NJ: Prentice-Hall.

Loehlin, J. C., Lindzey, G., & Spuhle, J. N. (1975). Race differences in intelligence. New York: Freeman.

Loftus, E. F. (1991). The glitter of everyday memory . . . and the gold. *American Psychologist, 46,* 16–18.

Loftus, E. F. (1992). When a lie becomes memory's truth: Memory distortion after exposure to misinformation. *Current Directions in Psychological Science, 1,* 121–123.

Loftus, E. F. (1993). The reality of repressed memories. *American Psychologist, 48,* 518–537.

Loftus, E. F., & Coan, D. (1995). The construction of childhood memories. In D. Peters (Ed.), *The child in context: Cognitive, social and legal perspectives.* New York: Kluwer.

Loftus, E. F., & Herzog, C. (1991). Unpublished data, University of Washington. Cited in Loftus, E. F. (1993). The reality of repressed memories. *American Psychologist, 48,* 518–537.

Loftus, E. F., & Ketcham, K. (1994). *The myth of repressed memory.* New York: St. Martin's.

Logan, G. D. (1985). Skill and automaticity: Relations, implications, and future directions. *Canadian Journal of Psychology, 39,* 367–386.

Logan, G. D. (1988). Toward an instance theory of automotization. *Psychological Review, 95,* 492–527.

Logie, R. H., Gilhooly, K. J., & Wynn, V. (1994). Counting on working memory in mental arithmetic. *Memory and Cognition, 22,* 395–410.

Logotheris, N. K., Pauls, J., & Poggio, T. (1995). Shape representations in the inferior temporal cortex of monkeys. *Current Biology, 5,* 552–563.

Logue, A. W. (1988). Research on self-control: An integrating framework. *Behavioral and Brain Sciences, 11,* 665–679.

Logue, A. W., Logue, K. R., & Strauss, K. E. (1983). The acquisition of taste aversion in humans with eating and drinking disorders. *Behavioral Research and Therapy, 21,* 275–289.

Logue, A. W., Ophir, I., & Strauss, K. E. (1981). The acquisition of taste aversion in humans. *Behavior Research and Therapy, 19,* 319–333.

Long, G. M., & Crambert, R. F. (1990). The nature and basis of age-related change in dynamic visual acuity. *Psychology and Aging, 5,* 138–143.

Long, J. W., & Rybacki, J. J. (1994). *The essential guide to prescription drugs.* New York: HarperCollins.

Lopez, S. R. (1989). Patient variable biases in clinical judgment: Conceptual overview and methodological considerations. *Psychological Bulletin, 106,* 184–203.

Louie, T. A. (1999). Decision makers' hindsight bias after receiving favorable and unfavorable feedback. *Journal of Applied Psychology, 84,* 29–41.

Lubart, T. I. (1994). Creativity. In R. J. Sternberg (Ed.), *Thinking problem solving* (pp. 289–332). San Diego, CA: Academic Press.

Lubart, T. T., & Sternberg, R. J. (1995). An investment approach to creativity: Theory and data. In S. M. Smith, T. B. Ward, & R. A. Finke (Eds.), *The creative cognition approach* (pp. 269–302). Cambridge, MA: MIT Press.

Luchins, A. S. (1942). Mechanization in problem solving. *Psychological Monographs, 54* (whole No. 248).

Lucy, J. A. (1992). *Language diversity and thought: A reformulation of the Whorfian hypothesis.* Cambridge, England: Cambridge University Press.

Lykken, D. T., McGue, M., Tellegen, A., & Bouchard, T. J. (1992). Emergenesis: Genetic traits that may not run in families. *American Psychologist, 47,* 1565–1577.

Lykken, D., & Tellegen, A. (1996). Happiness is a stochastic phenomenon. *Psychological Science, 7,* 186–189.

Lyman, B. J., & McDaniel, M. A. (1986). Effects of encoding strategy on long-term memory for odours. *Quarterly Journal of Experimental Psychology, 38A,* 753–765.

Lyman, B. J., & McDaniel, M. A. (1987, April). *Effects of experimenter and subject provided verbal and visual elaborations on long-term memory for odors.* Paper presented at the annual meeting of the Eastern Psychological Association, Arlington, VA.

Lyness, K. S., & Thompson, D. E. (1997). Above the glass ceiling? A comparison of matched samples of female and male executives. *Journal of Applied Psychology, 82,* 359–375.

Lynn, R. (1994). Sex differences in intelligence and brain size: A paradox resolved. *Personality and Individual Differences, 17,* 257–271.

Lynn, R. (1996). Racial and ethnic differences in intelligence in the United States on the Difference Ability Scale. *Personality and Individual Differences, 20,* 271–273.

Lynn, S. J., Rhue, J. W., & Weekes, J. R. (1990). Hypnotic involuntariness: A social cognitive analysis. *Psychological Review, 974,* 169–184.

Lytton, H. (1990). Child and parent effects in boys' conduct disorders. *Developmental Psychology, 26,* 683–697.

Macnichol, E. F. (1964). Retinal mechanisms of color vision. *Vision Research, 4,* 119–133.

Macrae, C. N. (1992). A tale of two curries: Counterfactual thinking and accident-related judgments. *Personality and Social Psychology Bulletin, 18,* 84–87.

Macrae, C. N., Milne, A. B., & Bodenhausen, G. V. (1994). Stereotypes as energy-saving devices: A peek inside the cognitive toolbox. *Journal of Personality and Social Psychology, 66,* 37–47.

Magai, C., & McFadden, S. H. (1995). The role of emotions in social and personality development. *History, theory, and research.* New York: Plenum Press.

Magee, L. M. (1997). Virtual reality simulator (VRS) for training ship handling skills. In R. J. Seidel & P. R. Chatelier (Eds.), Virtual reality training's future? Perspectives on virtual reality and related emerging technologies. *Proceedings of NATO Defense Research Group* (pp. 12–29). New York: Plenum.

Maheswaran, D., & Chaiken, S. (1991). Promoting systematic processing in low-motivation settings: Effect of incongruent information on processing and judgment. *Journal of Personality and Social Psychology, 61,* 13–25.

Maier, S. F., & Jackson, R. L. (1979). Learned helplessness: All of us were right (and wrong): Inescapable shock has multiple effects. In G. H. Bower (Ed.), *The psychology of learning and motivation* (Vol. 13). New York: Academic Press.

Malandro, L. A., Barker, L., & Barker, D. A. (1994). *Nonverbal communication* (3rd ed.). New York: Random House.

Mandel, D. R., Jusczyk, P. W., & Pisoni, D. B. (1995). Infants' recognition of the sound patterns of their own names. *Psychological Science, 6,* 314–317.

Mandler, J. M., Bauer, P. J., & McDonough, L. (1991). Separating the sheep from the goats: Differentiating global categories. *Cognitive Psychology, 23,* 263–298.

Mann, J. M., & Tarantola, D. J. M. (1998, July). HIV 1998: The global picture. *Scientific American,* 82–83.

Mann, T. (1994). Informed consent for psychological research: Do subjects comprehend consent forms and understand their legal rights? *Psychological Science, 5,* 140–143.

Mannheim, K. (1972). The problem of generations. In P. G. Altbach & R. S. Laufer (Eds.), *The new pilgrims: Youth protest in transition* (pp. 101–138). New York: David McKay.

Marcia, J. E. (1988). Ego identity, cognitive/moral development, and individuation. In D. K. Lapsley & F. C. Power (Eds.), *Self, ego, and identity: Integrative approaches* (pp. 211–225). New York: Springer-Verlag.

Marcia, J. E. (1991). Identity and self-development. In R. M. Lerner, A. C. Petersen, & E. J. Brooks, *Encyclopedia of Adolescence* (Vol. 1) (pp. 527–531). New York: Garland.

Mark, M. M., & Mellor, S. (1991). Effect of self-relevance of an event on hindsight bias: The foreseeability of a layoff. *Journal of Applied Psychology, 76,* 569–577.

Markus, H. M. & Nurius, P. (1986). Possible selves. *American Psychologist, 41,* 954–969.

Marlatt, G. A., Baer, J. S., Donovan, D. M., & Kivlahan, D. R. (1988). Addictive behaviors: Etiology and treatment. *Annual Review of Psychology, 58,* 265–272.

Marr, D. (1982). *Vision: A computational investigation into the human representation and processing of visual information.* San Francisco: W. H. Freeman.

Marsolek, C. J. (1999). Dissociable neural subsystems underlie abstract and specific object recognition. *Psychological Science, 10,* 111–118.

Marsolek, C. J., & Burgund, E. D. (1997). Computational analyses and hemispheric asymmetries in visual-form recognition. In S. Christman (Ed.), *Cerebral asymmetries in sensory and perceptual processing* (pp. 125–158). Amsterdam: Elsevier.

Martin, C. L., & Little, J. K. (1990). The relation of gender understanding to children's sex-typed preferences and gender stereotypes. *Child Development, 61,* 1427–1439.

Maslow, A. H. (1970). *Motivation and personality* (2nd ed.). New York: Harper & Row.

Masters, W. H., & Johnson, V. E. (1966). *Human sexual response.* Boston: Little, Brown.

Matarazzo, J. D. (1992). Psychological testing and assessment in the 21st century. *American Psychologist, 47,* 1007–1018.

Mathews, T. J. (1998, November 19). Smoking during pregnancy, 1990–1996. *National Vital Statistics Reports, 47*(10), 1–12. Retrieved December 26, 1999 from the World Wide Web: http://www.cdc.gov/nchs/data/nvs47-10.pdf.

Matlin, M. W., & Foley, H. J. (1997). *Sensation and perception.* Needham Heights, MA: Allyn & Bacon.

Mattheson, P. B., Shooenbaum, E., Greenberg, B., & Pliner, V. (1997). Association of maternal drug use during pregnancy with mother-to-child HIV transmission. *AIDS, 11,* 941–942.

Mattila, M., Aranko, K., & Seppala, T. (1982). Acute effects of buspirone and alcohol on psychomotor skills. *Journal of Clinical Psychiatry, 43,* 56–61.

Maturi, R. (1992, July 20). Stress can be beaten. *Industry Week,* pp. 23–26.

Maurer, D., & Barrera, M. (1981). Infants' perception of natural and distorted arrangements of a schematic face. *Child Development, 52,* 196–202.

Maurer, T. J., & Pierce, H. R. (1998). A comparison of Likert scale and traditional measures of self-efficacy. *Journal of Applied Psychology, 83,* 324–329.

May, C. P., Hasher, L., & Stoltzfus, E. R. (1993). Optimal time of day and the magnitude of age differences in memory. *Psychological Science, 4,* 326–330.

Mayer, J. D., Caruso, D. R., & Salovey, P. (1998). *Emotional intelligence meets traditional standards for intelligence.* Manuscript submitted for publication.

Mayer, J. D., & Salovey, P. (in press). What is emotional intelligence? In P. Salovey & D. Suyter (Eds.), *Emotional development, emotional literacy, and emotional intelligence.* New York: Basic Books.

Mayes, A. R. (1996). The functional deficits that underlie amnesia: Evidence from amnesic forgetting rate and item-specific implicit memory. In D. J. Herman, C. McEvoy, C. Hertzog, P. Hertel, & M. K. Johnson (Eds.), *Basic and applied memory research: Practical applications* (Vol. 2, pp. 391–405). Mahwah, NJ: Erlbaum.

Mazur, A., Helpern, C., & Udry, J. R. (1994). Dominant-looking male teenagers copulate earlier. *Ethology and Sociobiology, 15,* 87–94.

Mazur, J. E. (1996). Procrastination by pigeons: Preference for larger, more delayed work requirements. *Journal of the Experimental Analysis of behavior, 65,* 159–171.

Mazzoni, G. A. L., Lombardo, E., Malvagia, C., & Loftus, E. F. (1999). Dream interpretation and false belief. *Professional Psychology: Research and Practice, 30,* 45–50.

McCall, R. B. (1994). Academic underachievers. *Current Directions in Psychological Science, 3,* 15–19.

McClearn, G. E., Plomin, R., Gora-Maslak, G., & Crabbe, J. C. (1991). The gene chase in behavioral science. *Psychological Science, 2,* 222–229.

McClelland, D. C. (1985). *Human motivation.* New York: Cambridge University Press.

McClelland, D. C. (1995). Achievement motivation in relation to achievement-related recall, performance, and urine flow, a marker associated with release of vasopressin. *Motivation and Emotion, 19,* 59–76.

McClelland, D. C. (1998). Identifying competencies with behavioral-event interview. *Psychological Science, 9,* 331–340.

McClelland, J. L., & Rumelhart, D. E. (1981). An interactive activation model of context effects in letter perception: Part I. An account of basic findings. *Psychological Review, 102,* 375–407.

McConkey, K. M. (1991). The construction and resolution of experience and behavior in hypnosis. In S. J. Lynn & J. W. Rhue (Eds.), *Theories of hypnosis: Current models and perspectives* (pp. 542–563). New York: Guilford Press.

McConkie, G. W., & Zola, D. (1984). Eye movement control during reading. The effect of word units. In W. Prinz & A. F. Sanders (Eds.), *Cognition and motor processes* (pp. 63–74). Berlin: Springer-Verlag.

McDonald, H. E., & Hirt, E. R. (1997). When expectancy meets desire: Motivational effects in reconstructive memory. *Journal of Personality and Social Psychology, 72,* 5–23.

McFadden, D. (1982). *Tinnitus: Facts, theories, and treatments.* Washington, DC: National Academy Press.

McGinnis, J. M., & Meyers, L. D. (1995). Dietary change and health: Policy implications. *Behavioral Medicine, 20,* 165–169.

McGowin, D. F. (1993). *Living in the labyrinth: A personal journey through the maze of Alzheimer's.* San Francisco: Elder Books.

McGue, M. (1999). The behavioral genetics of alcoholism. *Current Directions in Psychological Science, 8,* 109–115.

McGue, M., Bouchard, T. J., Jr., Iaconon, W. G., & Lykken, D. T. (1993). Behavioral genetics of cognitive ability: A life-span perspective. In R. Plomin & G. E. McClearn (Eds.), *Nature, nurture, and psychology* (pp. 59–76). Washington, DC: American Psychological Association.

McGue, M., Sharma, A., & Benson, P. (1996). Parent and sibling influences on adolescent alcohol use and misuse: Evidence from a U.S. adoption cohort. *Journal of Studies on Alcohol, 57,* 8–18.

McGuire, P. A. (1999, June). Psychology and medicine connecting in war on cancer. *APA Monitor,* 8–9.

McKenry, P. C., Kotch, J. B., & Browne, D. H. (1991). Correlates of dysfunctional parenting attitudes among low-income adolescent mothers. *Journal of Adolescent Research, 6,* 212–234.

McMullen, M. N., Markman, K. D., & Gavanski, I. (1995). Living in neither the best nor the worst of all possible worlds: Antecedents and consequences of upward and downward counterfactual thinking. In N.J. Roese & J. M. Olson (Eds.), *What might have been: The social psychology of counterfactual thinking* (pp. 133–167). Mahwah, NJ: Erlbaum.

McNeil, B. J., Pauker, S. G., & Tversky, A. (1988). On the framing of medical decisions. In D. E. Bell (Ed.), *Decision making: Descriptive, normative, and prescriptive interactions* (pp. 562–568). New York: Cambridge University Press.

McWhirter, P. T. (1999). La violencia privada: Domestic violence in Chile. *American Psychologist, 54,* 37–40.

Medvec, V. H., & Savitsky, K. (1997). When doing better means feeling worse: The effects of categorical cutoff points on counterfactual thinking and satisfaction. *Journal of Personality and Social Psychology, 72,* 1284–1296.

Meehl, P. E. (1975). Hedonic capacity: Some conjectures. *Bulletin of the Menninger Clinic, 39,* 295–307.

Meichenbaum, D. H. (1977). *Cognitive-behavior modification.* New York: Plenum.

Meijmann, T., van der Meer, O., & van Dormolen, M. (1993). The after-effects of night work on short-term memory performance. *Ergonomics, 36,* 37–42.

Mellers, B. A., Schwartz, A., Ho, K., & Ritov, I. (1997). Decision affect theory: Emotional reactions to the outcomes of risky options. *Psychological Science, 8,* 423–429.

Mellors, J. W. (1998, July). Viral-load tests provide valuable answers. *Scientific American,* 90.

Melzack, R. (1976). Pain: Past, present, and future. In M. Weisenberg & B. Tursky (Eds.), *Pain: New perspectives in therapy and research.* New York: Plenum.

Melzack, R. (1993). Pain: Past, present, and future. *Canadian Journal of Experimental Psychology, 47,* 615–629.

Melzack, R. (1994). Folk medicine and the sensory modulation of pain. In P. D. Wall & R. Melzack (Eds.), *Textbook of pain* (pp. 1209–1217). Edinburgh: Churchill Livingstone.

Mento, A. J., Locke, E. A., & Klein, H. J. (1992). Relationship of goal level to valence and instrumentality. *Journal of Applied Psychology, 77,* 395–405.

Merikle, P. M. (1992). Perception without awareness. *American Psychologist, 47,* 792–795.

Merikle, P. M., & Daneman, M. (1998). Psychological investigations of unconscious perception. *Journal of Consciousness Studies, 5,* 5–18.

Merkelbach, H., deJong, P. J., Muris, P., & van den Hout, M. A. (1996). The etiology of specific phobias: A review. *Clinical Psychology Review, 16,* 337–361.

Metcalfe, J., & Mischel, W. (1999). A hot/cool-system analysis of delay of gratification: Dynamics of willpower. *Psychological Bulletin, 1,* 3–19.

Metzger, A. M. (1980). A methodological study of the Kübler-Ross stage theory. *Omega, 10,* 291–301.

Meyer, A. J., Maccoby, N., & Farquhar, J. W. (1980). Skills training in a cardiovascular health education campaign. *Journal of Consulting and Clinical Psychology, 48,* 129–142.

Meyers, S. A., & Berscheid, E. (1997). The language of love: The difference a reposition makes. *Personality and Social Psychology Bulletin, 23,* 347–362.

Milgram, S. (1963). Behavioral study of obedience. *Journal of Abnormal and Social Psychology, 67,* 371–378.

Milgram, S. (1974). *Obedience to authority.* New York: Harper.

Millenson, J. R., & Leslie, J. C. (1979). *Principles of behavioral analysis* (2nd ed.). New York: Macmillan.

Miller, C. L., Miceli, P. J., Whitman, T. L., & Borkowski, J. G. (1996). Cognitive readiness to parent and intellectual-emotional development in children of adolescent mothers. *Developmental Psychology, 32,* 533–541.

Miller, C. L., Miceli, P. J., Whitman, T. L., & Borkowski, J. G. (1996). Cognitive readiness to parent and intellectual-emotional development in children of adolescent mothers. *Developmental Psychology, 33,* 533–541.

Miller, D. T., & McFarland, C. (1987). Counterfactual thinking and victim compensation: A test of norm theory. *Personality and Social Psychology Bulletin, 12,* 513–519.

Miller, D. T., & Ross, M. (1975). Self-serving biases in attribution of causality: Fact or fiction? *Psychological Bulletin, 82,* 313–325.

Miller, G. A. (1956). The magic number seven plus or minus two: Some limits on our capacity for processing information. *Psychological Review, 63,* 81–97.

Miller, G. E., Dopp, J. M., Myers, H. F., Stevens, S. Y., & Fahey, J. L. (1999). Psychosocial predictors of natural killer cell mobilization during marital conflict. *Health Psychology, 18,* 262–271.

Miller, M. E., & Bowers, K. S. (1993). Hypnotic analgesia: Dissociated experience or dissociated control? *Journal of Abnormal Psychology, 102,* 29–38.

Miller, N. E. (1985). The value of behavioral research on animals. *American Psychologist, 40,* 423–440.

Miller, N., Maruyama, G., Beaber, R. J., & Valone, K. (1976). Speed of speech and persuasion. 615–624.

Miller, R. S. (1991). On decorum in close relationships: Why aren't we polite to those we love? *Contemporary Social Psychology, 15,* 63–65.

Miller, S. M., Shoda, Y., & Hurley, K. (1996). Applying cognitive-social theory to health-protective behavior: Breast self-examination in cancer screening. *Psychological Bulletin, 119,* 70–94.

Miller, T. Q., Smith, T. W., Turner, C. W., Guijarro, M. L., & Hallet, A. J. (1996). A meta-analytic review of research on hostility and physical health. *Psychological Bulletin. 119,* 322–348.

Miller, T. Q., Turner, C. W., Tindale, R. S., Posavac, E. J., & Dugoni, B. I. (1991). Reasons for the trend toward null findings in research on Type A behavior. *Psychological Bulletin, 110,* 469–485.

Millon, T. (1987). *Millon clinical multiaxial inventory-II: Manual for MCMI-II* (2nd ed.). Minneapolis, MN: National Computer System.

Millon, T. (1991). Classification psychopathology: Rationale, alternatives, and standards. *Journal of Abnormal Psychology, 100,* 245–261.

Millon, T. A. (Ed.) (1997). *The Millon inventories: Clinical and personality assessment.* New York: Guilford Press.

Minami, H., & Dallenbach, K. M. (1946). The effect of activity upon learning and retention in the cockroach. *American Journal of Psychology, 59,* 1–58.

Minuchin, S., & Fishman, H. C. (1981). *Family therapy techniques.* Cambridge, MA: Harvard University Press.

Mischel, W. (1985). *Personality: Lost or found? Identifying when individual differences make a difference.* Paper presented at the meetings of the American Psychological Association, Los Angeles.

Mischel, W., & Shoda, Y. (1995). A cognitive–affective system theory of personality: Reconceptualizing situations, dispositions, dynamics, and invariance in personality structure. *Psychological Review, 102,* 246–268.

Mitchell, H. (1988, February). Why are women still dying of cervical cancer? *Australian Society,* pp. 34–35.

Montepare, J., & Lachman, M. (1989). "You're only as old as you feel": Self-perceptions of age, fears of aging, and life satisfaction from essence to old age. *Psychology and Aging, 4,* 73–78.

Montgomery, G., & Kirsch, I. (1996). Mechanisms of placebo pain reduction: An empirical investigation. *Psychological Science, 7,* 174–176.

Moore, B. C. J. (1982). *An introduction to the psychology of hearing* (2nd ed.). New York: Academic.

Moore, B. C. J., & Oxenham, A. J. (1998). Psychoacoustic consequences of compression in the peripheral auditory system. *Psychological Review, 105,* 108–124.

Moore, R. Y., & Card, J. P. (1985). Visual pathways and the entrainment of circadian rhythms: The medical and biological effects of light. In R. J. Wurtman, M. J. Baum, J. T. Potts, Jr. (Eds.), *Annals of the New York Academy of Science, 453,* 123–133.

Moore-Ede, M. C., Sulzman, F. M., & Fuller, C. A. (1982). *The clocks that time us.* Cambridge, MA: Harvard University Press.

Moray, N. (1959). Attention in dichotic listening: Affective cues and the influence of instruction. *Quarterly Journal of Experimental Psychology, 11,* 59–60.

Moreland, R. L. (1987). The formation of small groups. In C. Hendrick (Ed.), *Review of Personality and Social Psychology* (Vol. 8, pp. 80–110). Newbury Park, CA: Sage.

Moreland, R. L., & Beach, S. R. (1992). Exposure effects in the classroom: The development of affinity among students. *Journal of Experimental Social Psychology, 28,* 255–276.

Morris, M. W., & Pang, K. (1994). Culture and cause: American and Chinese attributions for social and physical events. *Journal of Personality and Social Psychology, 67,* 949–971.

Morrongiello, B. A., & Clifton, R. K. (1984). Effects of sound frequency on behavioral and cardiac orienting in newborn and five-month-old infants. *Journal of Experimental Child Psychology, 38,* 429–446.

Morrow, K. B., & Sorell G. T. (1989). Factors affecting self-esteem, depression, and negative behaviors in sexually abused female adolescents. *Journal of Marriage and the Family, 51,* 677–686.

Morse, J. M., & Morse, R. M. (1988). Cultural variation in the inference of pain. *Journal of Cross Cultural Psychology, 19,* 232–242.

Mosak, H. H. (1995). Adlerian psychotherapy. In R. J. Corsini & D. Wedding (Eds.), *Current psychotherapies* (5th ed., pp. 51–94). Itasca, IL: F. E. Peacock.

Moscovitch, M. (1985). Memory from infancy to old age: Implications for theories of normal and pathological memory. *Annals of the New York Academy of Sciences, 444,* 79–96.

Motowidlo, S. J., Packard, J. S., & Manning, M. R. (1986). Occupational stress: Its causes and consequences for job performance. *Journal of Applied Psychology, 71,* 618–629.

Mowrer, O. H., & Jones, H. M. (1945). Habit strength as a function of the pattern of reinforcement. *Journal of Experimental Psychology, 35,* 293–311.

Mueller, U. & Mazur, A. (1996). Facial dominance of West Point cadets as predictors of later military rank. *Social Forces, 74,* 823–850.

Mueser, K. T., & Glynn, S. M. (1995). *Behavioral family therapy for psychiatric disorders.* Boston: Allyn & Bacon.

Mulkens, S. A. N., deJong, P. J., & Merckelbach, H. (1996). Disgust and spider phobia. *Journal of Abnormal Psychology, 105,* 464–468.

Munsinger, H. A. (1978). The adopted child's IQ: A crucial review. *Psychological Bulletin, 82,* 623–659.

Murphy, S. T., & Zajonc, R. B. (1993). Affect, cognition, and awareness: Affective priming with suboptimal and optimal stimulus. *Journal of Personality and Social Psychology, 64,* 723–739.

Murray, B. (1999, April). Technology invigorates teaching, but is the pazzazz worth the price? *APA Monitor Online, 30.*

Murray, B. (1999, June). Customized appeals may increase cancer screening. *APA Monitor,* 35.

Murray, S. L., & Holmes, J. G. (1994). Storytelling in close relationships: The construction of confidence. *Personality and Social Psychology Bulletin, 20,* 650–663.

Murrey, G. J., Cross, H. J., & Whipple, J. (1992). Hypnotically created pseudomemories: Further investigation into the "memory distortion or response bias" question. *Journal of Abnormal Psychology, 101,* 75–77.

Myers, D. G., & Diener, E. (1995). Who is happy? *Psychological Science, 6,* 10–19.

Myers, N. A., Clifton, R. K., & Clarkson, M. C. (1987). When they were young: Almost-threes remember two years ago. *Infant Behavior and Development, 10,* 123–132.

Naglieri, J. A. (1997). IQ: Knowns and unknowns, hits and misses. *American Psychologist, 52,* 75–76.

Naito, M., Komatsu, S., & Fuke, T. (1994). Normal and autistic children's understanding of their own and others' false beliefs: A study from Japan. *British Journal of Developmental Psychology, 12,* 403–416.

Nakajima, S., Kobayashi, Y., & Imada, H. (1995). Contextual control of taste aversion in rats: The effects of context extinction. *The Psychological Record, 45,* 309–318.

Nakano, K. (1990). Effects of two self-control procedures on modifying the Type A behavior pattern. *Journal of Clinical Psychology, 46,* 652–656.

Nathans, J. (1989). The genes for color vision. *Scientific American, 260,* 42–49.

Nathans, J., Thomas, D., & Hogness, D. S. (1986). Molecular genetics of human color vision: The genes encoding blue, green, and red pigments. *Science, 232,* 193–202.

National Center for Health Statistics. (1999). *Healthy People 2000 Review: 1998–99.* Hyattsville, MD: Public Health Service.

National Institute for Occupational Safety and Health, Centers for Disease Control and Prevention. (1993, December 5). *Homicide in the workplace.* Document #705003.

National Television Violence Study. (1996). *National television violence study* (Vol. 1). Thousand Oaks, CA: Sage.

National Television Violence Study. (1997). *National television violence study* (Vol. 2). Studio City, CA: Mediascope.

Neher, A. (1991). Maslow's theory of motivation: A critique. *Journal of Humanistic Psychology, 31,* 89–112.

Neher, A. (1996). Jung's theory of archetypes: A critique. *Journal of Humanistic Psychology, 36,* 61–91.

Neisser, U. (1991). A case of misplaced nostalgia. *American Psychologist, 46,* 34–36.

Neisser, U. (1997). Never a dull moment. *American Psychologist, 52,* 79–81.

Neisser, U., Boodoo, G., Bouchard, T. J., Jr., Bykin, A. W., Brody, N., Ceci, S. J., Halpern, D. F., Loehlin, J. C., Perloff, R., Sternberg, R. J., & Urbina, S. (1996). Intelligence: Knowns and unknowns. *American Psychologist, 51,* 77–101.

Nelson, L. J., & Miller, D. T. (1995). The distinctiveness effect in social categorization: You are what makes you unusual. *Psychological Science, 6,* 246–249.

Nelson, M. J., Lamke, T. A., & French, J. L. (1973). *The Henmon-Nelson Tests of Mental Ability.* Riverside, CA: Riverside Publishing.

Nelson, W. T., Hettinger, L. J., Cunningham, J. A., Brickman, B. J., Haas, M. W., & McKinley, R. L. (1998). Effects of localized auditory information on visual target detection performance using a helmet-mounted display. *Human Factors, 40,* 452–460.

Neugarten, B. L. (1987). The changing meaning of age. *Psychology Today, 21,* 29–33.

Neuman, J. H., & Baron, R. A. (1998). Workplace violence and workplace aggression: Evidence concerning specific forms, potential causes, and preferred targets. *Journal of Management, 24,* 391–420.

Newcomb, A. F., & Bagwell, C. L. (1995). Children's friendship relations: A meta-analytic review. *Psychological Bulletin, 117,* 306–347.

Newcombe, N., & Huttenlocher, J. (1992). Children's early ability to solve perspective-taking problems. *Developmental Psychology, 28,* 635–643.

Newton, J., Toby, O., Spence, S. H., & Schotte, D. (1995). Cognitive-behavioral therapy versus EMG biofeedback in the treatment of chronic low back pain. *Behaviour Research and Therapy, 33,* 691–697.

NICHD Early Child Care Research Network (1999). Child care and mother-child interaction in the first 3 years of life. *Developmental Psychology, 35,* 1399–1413.

Nickerson, R. S. (1998). Confirmation Bias: A ubiquitous phenomenon in many guises. *Review of General Psychology, 2,* 175–220.

Nicoladis, E., Mayberry, R. I., & Genesee, F. (1999). Gesture and early bilingual development. *Developmental Psychology, 35,* 514–526.

Nietzel, M. T., Speltz, M. L., McCauley, E. A., & Bernstein, D. A. (1998). *Abnormal psychology.* Boston: Allyn & Bacon.

Nisan, M., & Kohlberg, L. (1982). Universality and variation in moral judgment: A longitudinal and cross-sectional study in Turkey. *Child Development, 53,* 865–876.

Nixon, S. J. (1999). Neurocognitive performance in alcoholics: Is polysubstance abuse important? *Psychological Science, 10,* 181–185.

Nixon, S. J., Paul, R., & Phillips, M. (1998). Cognitive efficiency in alcoholics and polysubstance abusers. *Alcoholism: Clinical and Experimental Research, 22,* 1414–1420.

Noble, J., & McConkey, K. M. (1995). Hypnotic sex change: Creating and challenging a delusion in the laboratory. *Journal of Abnormal Psychology, 104,* 69–74.

Nolen-Hoeksema, S., & Rusting, C. L. (in press). Gender differences in well-being. In D. Kahneman, E. Diener, & N. Schwarz (Eds.), *Well-being: The foundations of hedonic psychology.* New York: Russell Sage.

Noller, P. (1994). Relationships with parents in adolescence: Process and outcome. In R. Montemayor, G. R. Adams, & T. P. Gullota (Eds.), *Personal relationships during adolescence.* Thousand Oaks, CA: Sage.

Noonan, E. (1999, April 29). Hospital misread biopsies. *Albany Times Union.*

Norman, D. A., & Shallice, T. (1985). Attention to action: Willed and automatic control of behavior. In R. J. Davidson, G. E. Schwartz, & D. Shapiro (Eds.), *Consciousness and self-regulation: Vol. 4. Advances in research and theory* (pp. 2–18). New York: Plenum Press.

Norris, F. H., & Murrell, S. A. (1990). Social support, life events, and stress as modifiers of adjustment to bereavement by older adults. *Psychology and Aging, 5,* 429–436.

Northcraft, G. B., & Neale, M. A. (1987). Experts, amateurs, and real estate: An anchoring-and-adjustment perspective on property pricing in decision. *Organizational Behavior and Human Decision Processes, 39,* 94–97.

Norton, A., & Moorman, J. E. (1987). Current trends in marriage and divorce among American women. *Journal of Marriage and the Family, 49,* 3–14.

Novy, D. M., Nelson, D. V., Francis, D., & Turk, D. C. (1995). Perspectives of chronic pain: An evaluative comparison of restrictive and comprehensive models. *Psychological Bulletin, 118,* 238–247.

Nygren, D. J., & Ukeritis, M. D. (1993). *The future of religious orders in the United States: Transformation and commitment.* Westport, CT: Praeger.

Nyhan, W. L. (1987). Phenylalanine and mental retardation (PKU). In G. Adelman (Ed.), *Encyclopedia of neuroscience* (Vol. 2, pp. 940–942). Boston: Birkhauser.

O'Connor, K., Gareau, D., & Borgeat, F. (1995). *Biofeedback and Self-Regulation, 20,* 111–122.

O'Leary, K. D., Vivian, D., & Malone, J. (1992). Assessment of physical aggression in marriage: The need for multimodal assessment. Behavior *Research and Therapy, 14,* 1–10.

O'Sullivan, C. S., & Durso, F. T. (1984). Effects of schema-incongruent information on memory for stereotypical attributes. *Journal of Personality and Social Psychology, 47,* 55–70.

Oaksford, M., Morris, F., Grainger, B., & Williams, J. M. G. (1996). Mood, reasoning, and central executive processes. *Journal of Experimental Psychology: Learning, Memory and Cognition, 22,* 476–492.

Oettingen, G. (1995). Explanatory style in the context of culture. In G. M. Buchanan & M. E. P. Seligman (Eds.), *Explanatory style.* Hillsdale, NJ: Erlbaum.

Oettingen, G., & Seligman, M. E. P. (1990). Pessimism and behavioral signs of depression in East versus West Berlin. *European Journal of Social Psychology, 20,* 207–220.

Ogloff, J. R., & Wong, S. (1990). Electrodermal and cardiovascular evidence of a coping response in psychopaths. *Criminal Justice and Behavior, 17,* 231–245.

Ohbuchi, K. I., Kameda, M., & Agarie, N. (1989). Apology as aggression control: Its role in mediating appraisal of and response to harm. *Journal of Personality and Social Psychology, 56,* 219–227.

Ohbuchi, K. I., & Ogura, S. (1984). The experience of anger (1): The survey for adults and university students with Averill's questionnaire (Japanese). *Japanese Journal of Criminal Psychology, 22*, 1–35.

Olsson, P. A. (1989). Psychodrama and group therapy approaches to alexithymia. In D. A. Halperin (Ed.), *Group Psychodynamics: New paradigms and new perspectives.* Chicago: Year Book Medical.

Olweus, D. (1995). Bullying or peer abuse at school: Facts and intervention. *Current Directions in Psychological Science, 4*, 196–200.

Orasanu, J., & Connolly, T. (1993). The reinvention of decision making. In G. A. Klein, J. Orasanu, R. Calderwood, & C. E. Zsambok (Eds.), *Decision making in action: Models and methods* (pp. 3–20). Norwood, NJ: Ablex.

Orlinsky, D. E., & Howard, K. E. (1987). The relation of process to outcome in psychotherapy. In S. L. Garfield & A. E. Bergin (Eds.), *Handbook of psychotherapy and behavior change* (3rd ed.). New York: Wiley.

Oscar-Berman, M., Shagrin, B., Evert, D. L., & Epstein, C. (1997). Impairments of brain and behavior: The neurological effects of alcohol. *Alcohol Health & Research World, 21*, 63–75.

Osterling, J., & Dawson, G. (1994). Early recognition of children with autism: A study of first birthday home videotapes. *Journal of Autism and Development Disorders, 24*, 247–257.

Osterman, K., Björkqvist, K., Lagerspetz, K., Kaukianainen, A., Hauesmann, L. W., & Fraczek, A. (1994). Peer and self-estimated aggression and victimization in 8–year-old children from five ethnic groups. *Aggressive Behavior, 20*, 411–428.

Otis, A. S., & Lennon, R. T. (1967). *The Otis-Lennon mental ability tests.* Los Angeles: Psychological Corp.

Ottati, V. C., & Isbell, L. M. (1996). Effects of mood during exposure to target information on subsequently reported judgments: An online model of misattribution and correction. *Journal of Personality and Social Psychology, 71*, 39–53.

Oulette-Kobasa, S. C., & Puccetti, M. C. (1983). Personality and social resources in stress resistance. *Journal of Personality and Social Psychology, 45*, 836–850.

Padian, N. S., Shiboski, S., & Jewell, N. (1990). The effect of the number of exposures on the risk of heterosexual HIV transmission. *Journal of Infectious Diseases. 161*, 883–887.

Page, J. B., Fletcher, J., & True, W. R. (1988). Psychosociocultural perspectives on chronic cannabis use: The Costa Rica follow-up. *Journal of Psychoactive Drugs, 20*, 57–65.

Palace, E. M. (1995). Modification of dysfunctional patterns of sexual response through autonomic arousal and false physiological feedback. *Journal of Consulting and Clinical Psychology, 63*(4), 604–615.

Paller, K. A., Kutas, M., & McIsaac, H. K. (1995). Monitoring conscious recollection via the electrical activity of the brain. *Psychological Science, 6*, 107–111.

Pani, J. R. (1993). Limits on the comprehension of rotational motion: Mental imagery of rotations with oblique components. *Perception, 22*, 785–808.

Pani, J. R. (1997). Descriptions of orientation in physical reasoning. *Current Directions in Psychological Science, 6*, 121–126.

Pani, J. R., Zhou, H., & Friend, S. M. (1997). Perceiving and imagining Plato's solids: The generalized cylinder in spatial organization of 3D structures. *Visual Cognition, 4*, 225–264.

Papp, L., Klein, D., Martinez, J., Schneier, F., Cole, R., Liebowitz, M., Hollander, E., Fryer, A., Jordan, F., & Gorman, J. (1993). Diagnostic and substance specificity of carbon-dioxide-induced panic. *American Journal of Psychiatry, 150*, 250–257.

Park, D.C., Smith, A. D., Lautenschlager, G., Earles, J. L., Frieske, D., Zwahr, M., & Gaines, C. L. (1996). Mediators of long-term memory-performance across the lifespan. *Psychology and Aging, 11*, 621–637.

Parkin, A. J., & Walter, B. M. (1992). Recollective experience, normal aging, and frontal dysfunction. *Psychology and Aging, 7*, 290–298.

Passman, R. H., & Weisberg, P. (1975). Mothers and blankets as agents for promoting play and exploration by young children in a novel environment: The effects of social and nonsocial attachment objects. *Developmental Psychology, 11*, 170–177.

Pastor, D. L. (1981). The quality of mother-infant attachment and its relationship to toddlers' initial sociability with peers. *Developmental Psychology, 17*, 326–335.

Patel, A., Gibson, E., Ratner, J., Besson, M., & Holcomb, P. (in press). Processing grammatical relations in language and music: An event-related potential study. *Journal of Cognitive Neuroscience.*

Patrick, C. J., Bradley, M. M., & Lang, P. J. (1993). Emotion in the criminal psychopath: Startle reflex modulation. *Journal of Abnormal Psychology, 102*, 83–92.

Patterson, F. (1978). Conversations with a gorilla. *National Geographic, 154*, 438–465.

Paul, G. L. (1982). *The development of a "transportable" system of behavioral assessment for chronic patients.* Invited address, University of Minnesota, Minneapolis.

Paul, G. L., & Lentz, R. J. (1977). *Psychosocial treatment of chronic mental patients: Milieu versus social-learning programs.* Cambridge, MA: Harvard University Press.

Paxton, S. J., Schutz, H. K., Wertheim, E. H., & Muir, S. L. (1999). Friendship clique and peer influences on body image concerns, dietary restraint, extreme weight-loss behaviors, and binge eating in adolescent girls. *Journal of Abnormal Psychology, 108*, 255–266.

Pearce, J. M. (1986). A model for stimulus generalization in Pavlovian conditioning. *Psychological Review, 94*, 61–73.

Pelletier, K. R. (1986). Longevity: What can centenarians teach us? In K. Dychtwald (Ed.), *Wellness and health promotion for the elderly.* Rockville, MD: Aspen Publishers.

Pennington, N., & Hastie, R. (1993). A theory of explanation-based decision making. In G. A. Klein, J. Orasanu, R. Calderwood, & C. E. Zsambok (Eds.), *Decision making in action: Models and methods* (pp. 188–201). Norwood, NJ: Ablex.

Perkins, D. N. (1997). Creativity's camel: The role of analogy in invention. In T. S. Ward, S. M. Smith, & J. Vaid (Eds.), *Creative thought.* Washington, DC: American Psychological Association.

Peters, R. D., Kloeppel, E., Alciandri, E., Fox, J. E., Thomas, M. L., Thorne, D. R., Sing, H. C., & Baliwinski, S. M. (1995). Effects of partial and total sleep deprivation on driving performance. *Proceedings of the Human Factors and Ergonomics Society*, 39th Annual Meeting.

Peterson, A. C. (1987, September). Those gangly years. *Psychology Today*, pp. 28–34.

Peterson, C., & Siegal, M. (1999). Representing inner worlds: Theory of mind in autistic, deaf, and normal hearing children. *Psychological Science, 10*, 126–129.

Pettigrew, T. E. (1997). Generalized intergroup contact effects on prejudice. *Personality and Social Psychology Bulletin, 23*, 175–185.

Pettigrew, T. F. (1981). Extending the stereotype concept. In D. L. Hamilton (Ed.), *Cognitive processes in stereotyping and intergroup behavior* (pp. 303–331). Hillsdale, NJ: Erlbaum.

Petty, R. E., & Cacioppo, J. T. (1986). The elaboration likelihood model of persuasion. In L. Berkowitz (Ed.), *Advances in experimental social psychology* (Vol. 19, pp. 123–205). New York: Academic Press.

Petty, R. E., & Cacioppo, J. T. (1990). Involvement and persuasion: Tradition versus integration. *Psychological Bulletin, 107*, 367–374.

Petty, R. E., Cacioppo, J. T., Strathman, A. J., & Priester, J. R. (1994). To think or not to think; Exploring two routes to persuasion. In S. Shavitt & T. C. Brock (Eds.), *Persuasion* (pp. 113–147). Boston: Allyn and Bacon.

Pfaffman, C. (1978). The vertebrate phylogeny, neural code, and integrative processes of taste. In E. C. Carterrette & M. P. Friedman (Eds.), *Handbook of perception* (vol. 6A). New York: Academic.

Pham, L. B., & Taylor, S. E. (1999). From thought to action: Effects of process- versus outcome-based mental simulations on performance. *Personality and Social Psychology Bulletin, 25*, 250–260.

Phillips, A. G., & Fibiger, H. C. (1989). Neuroanatomical bases of intracranial self-stimulation: Untangling the Gordian knot. In J. M. Leibman & S. J. Cooper (Eds.), *The neuropharmacological bases of reward* (pp. 66–105). Oxford, England: Clarendon Press.

Phillips, D. P., & Brugge, J. F. (1985). Progress in neurophysiology of sound localization. *Annual Review of Psychology, 36*, 245–274.

Phillips, J. M., & Gully, S. M. (1997). Role of goal orientation, ability, and need for achievement, and locus of control in the self-efficacy and goal-setting process. *Journal of Applied Psychology, 82*, 792–802.

Piaget, J. (1965). *The moral judgment of the child.* New York: Free Press. (Original work published 1932.)

Piaget, J. (1975). *The child's conception of the world.* Totowa, NJ: Littlefield, Adams. (Originally published in 1929.)

Pierce, C. A. (1992). *The effects of physical attractiveness and height on dating choice: Meta-analysis.* Unpublished masters thesis, University at Albany, State University of New York, Albany.

Pierce, P. F. (1996). When the patient chooses: Describing unaided decisions in health care. *Human Factors, 38*, 278–287.

Pierce, W. D., & Epling, W. F. (1994). The applied importance of research on the matching law. *Journal of Applied Behavior Analysis, 28*, 237–241.

Pihl, R. O., Lau, M. L., & Assaad, J. M. (1997). Aggressive disposition, alcohol, and aggression. *Aggressive Behavior, 23*, 11–18.

Pinel, J. P. J. (1993). *Biopsychology* (2nd ed.). Boston: Allyn and Bacon.

Pinker, S. (1989). *Learnability and cognition.* Cambridge, MA: MIT Press.

Pinker, S. (1997). *How the mind works.* New York: Norton.

Plante, T. G., & Rodin, J. (1990). Physical fitness and enhanced psychological health. *Current Psychology: Research & Reviews, 9*, 3–24.

Plomin, R. (1997). Genetics and intelligence: What's new? *Intelligence, 24*, 45–65.

Plomin, R., Emde, R. N., Braungart, J. M., Campos, J., Corley, R., Fulker, D. W., Kagan, J., Reznick, J. S., Robinson, J., Zahn-Waxler, C., & DeFries, J. C. (1993). Genetic change and continuity from fourteen to twenty months: The MacArthur Longitudinal Twin Study. *Child Development, 64*, 1354–1376.

Plomin, R., Fulker, D. W., Corley, R., & DeFries, J. C. (1997). Nature, nurture, and cognitive development from 1 to 16 years: A parent–offspring adoption study. *Psychological Science, 8*, 442–447.

Pomerleau, O. F. (1995). Individual differences in sensitivity to nicotine: Implications for genetic research on nicotine dependence. *Behavior Genetics, 25*, 161–177.

Pomerleau, O. F., & Kardia, S. L. R. (1999). Introduction to the featured section Genetic Research on Smoking. *Health Psychology, 18*, 3–6.

Poon, L. W., & Fozard, J. L. (1980). Age and word frequency effects in continuous recognition memory. *Journal of Gerontology, 35*, 77–86.

Pope, A. W., & Bierman, K. L. (1999). Predicting adolescent peer problems and antisocial activities: The relative roles of aggression and dysregulation. *Developmental Psychology, 35,* 335–346.

Popenoe, D., & Whitehead, B. D. (1999). *The state of our unions.* New Brunswick, NJ: Rutgers University Press.

Porter, L. S., & Stone, A. A. (1995). Are there really gender differences in coping? A reconsideration of previous data and results from a daily study. *Journal of Social and Clinical Psychology. 14,* 184–202.

Posner, M. I., & Peterson, S. E. (1990). The attention system of the human brain. *Annual Review of Neuroscience,* 13, 25–42.

Posner, M. I., & Rossman, E. (1965). Effects of size and location of informational transforms upon short-term retention. *Journal of Experimental Psychology, 70,* 496–505.

Pratto, F. (1996). Sexual politics: The gender gap in the bedroom, the cupboard, and the cabinet. In D. M. Buss & N. M. Malamuth (Eds.), *Sex, power, conflict: Evolutionary and feminist perspectives* (pp. 179–230). New York: Oxford University Press.

Prochaska, J. O. (1996). A stage paradigm for integrating clinical and public health approaches to smoking cessation. *Addictive Behaviors, 21,* 721–732.

Psotka, J. (1995). Immersive training systems: Virtual reality and education and training. *Instructional Science, 23,* 405–431.

Ptacek, J. T., Smith, R. E, & Dodge, K. L. (1994). Gender differences in coping with stress: When stressor and appraisals do not differ. *Personality and Social Psychology Bulletin, 20,* 421–430.

Raajimakers, J. G., & Shiffrin, R. M. (1981). SAM: Search of associative memory. *Psychological Review, 88,* 93–134.

Rabin, M. D., & Cain, W. S. (1984). Determinants of measured olfactory sensitivity. *Perception & Psychophysics, 39,* 281–286.

Rachlin, H. (1995). The value of temporal patterns in behavior. *Current Directions in Psychological Science, 4,* 188–192.

Raine, A., Bihrle, S., Venebles, P. H., Mednick, S. A., & Pollock V. (1999). Skin-conductance orienting deficits and increased alcoholism in schizotypal criminals. *Journal of Abnormal Psychology, 108,* 299–306.

Raine, A., Venebles, P. H., & Williams, M. (1990). Relationships between central and autonomic measure of arousal at age 15 years and criminality at age 24 years. *Archives of General Psychiatry, 47,* 1003–1007.

Rajaram, S. (1993). Remembering and knowing: Two means of access to the personal past. *Memory and Cognition, 21,* 89–102.

Ramey, C. T., & Ramey, S. L. (1998). Early intervention and early experience. *American Psychologist, 53,* 109–120.

Raphael, B., Cubis, J., Dunne, M., Lewin, T., & Kelly, B. (1990). The impact of parental loss on adolescents' psychosocial characteristics. *Adolescence, 25,* 689–700.

Rauschecker, J. P. (1995). Compensatory plasticity and sensory substitution in the cerebral cortex. *Trends in Neuroscience, 18,* 36–43.

Raven, J. C. (1977). *Raven Progressive Matrices.* Los Angeles: Psychological Corp.

Raynor, J. O. (1970). Relationships between achievement-related motives, future orientation, and academic performance. *Journal of Personality and Social Psychology, 15,* 28–33.

Rechtschaffen, A., & Bergmann, B. M. (1995). Sleep deprivation in the rat by the disk-over-water method. *Behavioural Brain Research, 69,* 55–63.

Rechtschaffen, A,. Gilliland, M. A., Bergmann, B. M, & Winter, J. B. Physiological correlates of prolonged sleep deprivation in rats. *Science, 221,* 182–184

Redd, W. H., Dadds, M. R., Futterman, A. D., Taylor, K., & Bovbjerg, D. (1993). Nausea induced by mental images of chemotherapy. *Cancer, 72,* 629–636.

Reder, I. M., & Gordon, J. S. (1997). Subliminal perception: Nothing special cognitively speaking. In J. D. Cohen & J. W. Schooler (Eds.), *Scientific approaches to consciousness* (pp. 125–234). Mahwah, NJ: Erlbaum.

Reed, S. B., Kirsch, I., Wickless, C., Moffitt, K. H., & Taren, P. (1996). Reporting biases in hypnosis: Suggestion or compliance? *Journal of Abnormal Psychology, 105,* 142–145.

Reed, T. E., & Jensen, A. R. (1993). Choice reaction time and visual pathway conduction velocity both correlate with intelligence but appear not to correlate with each other: Implications for information processing. *Intelligence, 17,* 191–203.

Reichle, E. D., Pollatsek, A., Fisher, D. L., & Rayner, K. (1998). Toward a model of eye movement control in reading. *Psychological Review, 105,* 125–157.

Reid, L. D. (1990). Rates of cocaine addiction among newborns. Personal communication, Rensselaer Polytechnic Institute.

Reiman, E. M., Fusselman, M. J., Fox, P. T., & Raichle, M. E. (1989). Neuroanatomical correlates of anticipatory anxiety. *Science, 243,* 1071–1074.

Reinecke, J., Schmidt, P., & Ajzen, I. (1996). Application of the theory of planned behavior to adolescents' condom use: A panel study. *Journal of Applied Social Psychology, 26,* 749–772.

Reisenzein, R. (1983). The Schachter theory of emotion: Two decades later. *Psychological Bulletin, 94,* 239–264.

Remschmidt, H., Schulz, E., Mart, W., Warnke, A., & Trott, G. E. (1994). Childhood onset schizophrenia: History of the concept and recent studies. *Schizophrenia Bulletin, 20,* 727–745.

Reno, R. R., Cialdini, R. B., & Kallgren, C. A. (1993). The transsituational influence of social norms. *Journal of Personality and Social Psychology, 64,* 104–112.

Rensberger, B. (1993, May 3). The quest for machines that not only listen, but also understand. *Washington Post,* p.3.

Rensink, R. A., O'Regan, J. K., & Clark, J. J. (1997). To see or not to see: The need for attention to perceive changes in scenes. *Psychological Science, 8,* 368–373.

Rentsch, J. R., & Heffner, T. S. (1994). Assessing self-concept: Analysis of Gordon's coding scheme using "Who am I?" responses. *Journal of Social Behavior and Personality, 9,* 283–300.

Rescorla, R. A., & Wagner, A. R. (1972). A theory of Pavlovian conditioning: Variations in the effectiveness of reinforcement and nonreinforcement. In A. Black & W. F. Prokasy (Eds.), *Classical conditioning: II. Current research and theory.* New York: Appleton.

Reyna, V. F., & Titcomb, A. (1996). Constraints on the suggestibility of eyewitness testimony: A fuzzy-trace theory analysis. In D. Payne & F. Conrad (Eds.), *Intersections in basic and applied memory research.* Hillsdale, NJ: Erlbaum.

Rhodewalt, F., & Fairfield, M. (1991). Claimed self-handicaps and the self-handicapper: The relations of reduction in intended effort to performance. *Journal of Research in Personality, 245,* 402–417.

Rice, F. P. (1992). *Intimate relationships, marriages, and families.* Mountain View, CA: Mayfield.

Richardson, G., Day, N., & Goldschmidt, L. (1995). *A longitudinal study of prenatal cocaine exposure: Infant development at 12 months.* Paper presented at Biennial Meetings of the Society for Research in Child Development, Indianapolis, IN.

Richardson, J. T. E., & Zucco, G. M. (1989). Cognition and olfaction: A review. *Psychological Bulletin, 105,* 352–360.

Richman, D. D. (1998, July). How drug resistance arises. *Scientific American,* 88.

Riess, M., & Schlenker, B. R. (1977). Attitude changes and responsibility avoidance as modes of dilemma resolution in forced-compliance situations. *Journal of Personality and Social Psychology, 35,* 21–30.

Rigby, C. S., Deci, E. L., Patrick, B. C., & Ryan, R. M. (1992). Beyond the intrinsic-extrinsic dichotomy: Self-determination in motivation and learning. *Motivation and Emotion, 16,* 165–185.

Riggins v. Nevada, 112 S. Ct. 1810 (1992).

Rissman, E. F. (1995). An alternative animal model for the study of female sexual behavior. *Current Directions in Psychological Science, 4,* 6–10.

Robbin, A. L., & Foster, L. (1988). *Negotiating adolescence: A behavioral family systems approach to parent/teen conflict.* New York: Guilford Press.

Roberts, M. (1997). *The man who listens to horses.* New York: Random House.

Robin, N., & Holyoak, K. J. (1995). Relational complexity and the function of prefrontal cortex. In M. S. Gazzaniga (Ed.), *The cognitive neurosciences* (pp. 987–997). Cambridge, MA: MIT Press.

Robins, L. N., & Rutter, M. (1990). Childhood prediction of psychiatric status in the young adulthood of hyperactive boys: A study controlling for chance association. In L. Robins & M. Rutter (Eds.), *Straight and deviant pathways from childhood to adulthood* (pp. 279–299). Cambridge, MA: Cambridge University Press.

Robinson, L. A., Berman, J. S., & Neimeyer, R. A. (1990). Psychotherapy for the treatment of depression: A comprehensive review of controlled outcome research. *Psychological Bulletin, 108,* 30–49.

Rochat, F., & Modigliani, A. (1995). The ordinary quality of resistance: From Milgram's laboratory to the village of Le Chambon. *Journal of Social Issues, 5,* 195–210.

Rodin, J. (1984, April). A sense of control. *Psychology Today,* 38–45.

Rodin, J., & Plante, T. (1989). The psychological effects of exercise. In R. S. Williams & A. Wellece (Eds.), *Biological effects of physical activity.* Champaign, IL: Human Kinetics.

Rodin, J., & Salovey, P. (1989). Health psychology. *Annual Review of Psychology, 40,* 533–580.

Rodin, J., & Slochower, J. (1976). Externality in the nonobese: Effects of environmental responsiveness on weight. *Journal of Personality and Social Psychology, 33,* 338–344.

Roediger, H. L., III., & McDermott, K. B. (1996). False perceptions of false memories. *Journal of Experimental Psychology: Learning, Memory, and Cognition, 22,* 814–816.

Roese, N.J. (1997). Counterfactual thinking. *Psychological Bulletin, 121,* 133–148.

Rogers, C. R. (1970). *Carl Rogers on encounter groups.* New York: Harper & Row.

Rogers, C. R. (1977). *Carl Rogers on personal power: Inner strength and its revolutionary impact.* New York: Delacorte.

Rogers, C. R. (1980). *A way of being.* Boston: Houghton Mifflin.

Rogers, C. R. (1982, August). Nuclear war: A personal response. *American Psychological Association,* pp. 6–7.

Rogler, L. H. (1999). Methodological sources of cultural insensitivity in mental health research. *American Psychologist, 54,* 424–433.

Rogler, L. H., Malgady, R. G., Constantino, G., & Blumenthal, R. (1987). What do culturally sensitive mental health services mean? The case of Hispanics. *American Psychologist, 42,* 565–570.

Rogoff, B., & Chavajay, P. (1995). What's become of research on the cultural basis of cognitive development? *American Psychologist, 50,* 859–877.

Romani, C., & Martin, R. (1999). A deficit in the short-term retention of lexical–semantic information: Forgetting words but remembering a story. *Journal of Experimental Psychology: General, 128,* 57–77.

Rosch, E. H. (1975). The nature of mental codes for color categories. *Journal of Experimental Psychology: Human Perception and Performance, 1,* 303–322.

Rosen, K. S., & Rothbaum, F. (1993). Quality of parental caregiving and security of attachment. *Developmental Psychology, 29,* 358–367.

Rosenberg, E. L., & Ekman, P. (1995). Conceptual and methodological issues in the judgment of facial expressions of emotion. *Motivation and Emotion, 19,* 111–138.

Rosenblith, J. F. (1992). *In the beginning: Development from conception to age two.* Newbury Park, CA: Sage.

Rosenfeld, I. (1999, May 16). Is laser eye surgery for you? *Parade,* p. 4–6.

Rosenfield, D., Folger, R., & Adelman, H. F. (1980). When rewards reflect competence: A qualification of the overjustification effect. *Journal of Personality and Social Psychology, 39,* 368–376.

Rosenman, R. H. (1988). The impact of certain emotions in cardiovascular disorders. In M. P. Janisse (Ed.), *Individual differences, stress, and health psychology* (pp. 1–23). New York: Springer-Verlag.

Rosenstock, I. M. (1974). The health belief model and preventive health behavior. *Health Education Monographs, 2,* 354–386.

Ross, E. D., Homan, R. W., & Buck, R. (1994). Differential hemispheric lateralization of primary and social emotions. *Neuropsychiatry, Neuropsychology, and Behavioral Neurology, 7,* 1–19.

Ross, L. (1977). The intuitive scientist and his shortcoming. In L. Berkowitz (Ed.), *Advances in experimental social psychology,* Vol. 10 (pp. 174–221). New York: Academic Press.

Ross, L. L., & McBean, D. (1995). A comparison of pacing contingencies in classes using a personalized system of instruction. *Journal of Applied Behavior Analysis, 28,* 87–88.

Rothenberg, R. B., & Koplan, J. P. (1990). Chronic disease in the 1990s. *Annual Review of Public Health, 11,* 267–296.

Rothenberg, R., Nasca, P., Mikl, J., Burnett, W., & Reynolds, B. (1987). In R. W. Amler & H. B. Dull (Eds.), *Closing the gap: The burden of unnecessary Illness.* New York: Oxford University Press.

Rothgerber, H. (1997). External intergroup threat as an antecedent to perceptions of in-group and out-group homogeneity. *Journal of Personality and Social Psychology, 73,* 1206–1212.

Rothland, J. C., Brandt, J., Zee, D., & Codori, A. M. (1993). Unimpaired verbal memory with oculomotor control in asymptomatic adults with the genetic marker for Huntington's disease. *Archives of Neurology, 50,* 799–802.

Rothman, A. J., & Hardin, C. D. (1997). Differential use of the availability heuristic in social judgment. *Personality and Social Psychology Bulletin, 23,* 123–138.

Rothman, A. J., & Salovey, P. (1997) Shaping perceptions to motivate healthy behavior. The role of message framing. *Psychological Bulletin, 121*(1), 3–19.

Rotter, J. B. (1954). *Social learning and clinical psychology.* Englewood Cliffs, NJ: Prentice-Hall.

Rotter, J. B. (1982). *The development and applications of social learning theory: Selected papers.* New York: Praeger.

Rowe, D.C., Vazsonyi, A. T., & Flannery, D. J. (1994). No more than skin deep: Ethnic and racial similarity in developmental process. *Psychological Review, 101,* 396–413.

Rowe, D. C., Vazsonyi, A. T., & Flannery, D. J. (1995). Ethnic and racial similarity in developmental process: A study of academic achievement. *Psychological Science, 6,* 33–38.

Rowland, D. L., Cooper, S. E., & Slob, A. K. (1996). Genital and psychoaffective response to erotic stimulation in sexually functional and dysfunctional men. *Journal of Abnormal Psychology, 105,* 194–203.

Rozin, P. (1996). Toward a psychology of food and eating: From motivation to module to model to marker, morality, meaning, and metaphor. *Current Directions in Psychological Science, 6,* 18–20.

Rozin, P., Dow, S., Moscovitch, M., & Rajaram, S. (1998). What causes humans to begin and end a meal? A role for memory for what has been eaten, as evidenced by a study of multiple meal eating in amnesic patients. *Psychological Science, 9,* 392–396.

Rubin, D.C. (1982). On the retention function for autobiographical memory. *Journal of Verbal Learning and Verbal Behavior, 21,* 21–38.

Rubin, D.C., & Schulkind, M. D. (1997). The distribution of autobiographical memories across the lifespan. *Memory & Cognition, 25,* 859–866.

Rubin, D.C., Wetzler, S. E., & Nebes, R. D. (1986). Autobiographical memory across the adult lifespan. In D. C. Rubin (Ed.), *Autobiographical memory* (pp. 202–221). New York: Cambridge University Press.

Ruble, D. N., & Martin, C. (1998). Gender development. In W. Damon (Series Ed.) & N. Eisenberg (Vol. Ed.), *Handbook of child psychology: Vol 3. Social, emotional, and personality development* (5th ed., pp. 933–1016). New York: Wiley.

Rushton, J. P. (1989a). Genetic similarity, human altruism, and group selection. *Behavioral and Brain Sciences, 12,* 503–559.

Rushton, J. P. (1989b). Genetic similarity in male friendships. *Ethology and Sociobiology, 10,* 361–373.

Rushton, J. P. (1997). Race, intelligence, and the brain: The errors and omissions of the "revised" edition of S. J. Gould's *The Mismeasure of Man. Personality and Individual Differences, 23,* 169–180.

Rushton, W. A. H. (1975). Visual pigments and color blindness. *Scientific American, 232,* 64–74.

Russell, J. A. (1994). Is there universal recognition of emotion from facial expression? A review of the cross-cultural studies. *Psychological Bulletin, 115,* 102–141.

Rutter, M., Macdonald, H., LeCouteur, A., Harrington, R., Bolton, P., & Bailey, A. (1990). Genetic factors in child psychiatric disorders, II: Empirical findings. *Journal of Child Psychology and Psychiatry, 31,* 39–83.

Rutter, M., & Plomin, R. (1997). Opportunities for psychiatry from genetic findings. *British Journal of Psychiatry, 171,* 209–219.

Ryan, R. M. (1982). Control and information in the intrapersonal sphere: An extension of cognitive evaluation theory. *Journal of Personality and Social Psychology, 43,* 450–561.

Ryckman, R. M., Butler, J. C., Thornton, B., & Lindner, M. A. (1995, April). Identification and assessment of physique subtype stereotypes. Paper presented at the meeting of the Eastern Psychological Association, Boston.

Ryckmann, R. M., Butler, J. C., Thornton, B., & Lindner, M. A. (1997). Assessment of physique subtype stereotypes. *Genetic, Social, and General Psychology Monographs, 123,* 101–128.

Saarni, C. (1993). Socialization of emotion. In M. Lewis & J. Haviland (Eds.), *Handbook of emotions* (pp. 435–446).

Sabol, S. Z., Nelson, M. L., Fisher, C., Gunzerath, L., Brody, C. L., Hu, S., Sirota, L. A., Marcus, S. E., Greenberg, B. D., Lucas, F. R., Benjamin, J., Murphy, D. L., & Hamer, D. H. (1999). A genetic association for cigarette smoking behavior. *Health Psychology, 18,* 7–13.

Sachs, J. J., Holt, K. W., Holmgreen, P., Colwell, L. S., & Brown, J. M. (1990). Playground hazards in Atlanta child-care centers. *American Journal of Public Health, 80,* 986–988.

Sackheim, H. A., & Gur, R. C. (1978). Lateral asymmetry in intensity of emotional expression. *Neuropsychologia, 16,* 473–482.

Sacks, O. (1993, May 10). To see and not see: A neurologist's notebook. *The New Yorker,* pp. 59–73.

Saffran, E. M., Schwartz, M. F., & Marin, O. S. M. (1980). Evidence from aphasia: Isolating the components of a production model. In B. Butterworth (Ed.), *Language production.* London: Academic Press.

Saks, M. J. (1992). Obedience versus disobedience to legitimate versus illegitimate authorities issuing good versus evil directions. *Psychological Science, 3,* 221–223.

Salgado, J. F. (1997). The five factor model of personality and job performance in the European community. *Journal of Applied Psychology, 82,* 30–43.

Salovey, P. (1992). Mood-induced self-focused attention. *Journal of Personality and Social Psychology, 62,* 699–707.

Salovey, P., & Mayer, J. D. (1994). Some final thoughts about personality and intelligence. In R. J. Sternberg (Ed.), *Personality and intelligence* (pp. 303–318). New York: Cambridge University Press.

Samson, L. F. (1988). Perinatal viral infections and neonates. *Journal of Perinatal and Neonatal Nursing, 1,* 56–65.

Sanna, L. J. (1997). Self-efficacy and counterfactual thinking: Up a creek with and without a paddle. *Personality and Social Psychology Bulletin, 23,* 654–666.

Sansavini, A., Bertonicini, J., & Giovanelli, G. (1997). Newborns discriminate the rhythm of multisyllabic stressed words. *Developmental Psychology, 33,* 3–11.

Sargent, C. (1984). Between death and shame: Dimensions in pain in Bariba culture. *Social Science Medicine, 19,* 1299–1304.

Savage-Rumbaugh, S., Romski, M. A., Hopkins, W. D., & Sevcik, R. A. (1989). Symbol acquisition and use by *Pan troglodytes, Pan paniscus, Homo sapiens.* In P. G. Heltne, & L. A. Marquardt (Eds.), *Understanding chimpanzees* (pp. 266–295). Cambridge, MA: Harvard University Press.

Saxby, E., & Peniston, E. G., (1995) Alpha-theta brainwave neurofeedback training: An effective treatment for male and female alcoholics with depressive symptoms. *Journal of Clinical Psychology, 51*(5), 685–693.

Schab, F. R. (1991). Odor memory: Taking stock. *Psychological Bulletin, 109,* 242–251.

Schachter, D. L. (1996). *Searching for memory.* New York: Basic Books.

Schachter, D. L., & Kihlstrom, J. F. (1989). Functional amnesia. In F. Boller & J. Grafman (Eds.), *Handbook of neuropsychology* (Vol. 3, pp. 209–230). New York: Elsevier.

Schachter, S., & Singer, J. E. (1962). Cognitive, social, and physiological determinants of emotional states. *Psychological Review, 69,* 379–399.

Schaie, K. W. (1974). Translations in gerontology-from lab to life: Intellectual functioning. *American Psychologist, 29,* 802–807.

Schaie, K. W. (1986). *Adult development and aging* (2nd ed.). Boston: Little, Brown.

Schaie, K. W. (1990). Intellectual development in adulthood. In J. E. Birren & K. W. Schaie (Eds.), *Handbook of the psychology of aging* (3rd ed., pp. 291–309). San Diego: Academic Press.

Schaie, K. W. (1993). The Seattle longitudinal studies of adult intelligence. *Current Directions in Psychological Science, 2,* 171–175.

Schaie, K. W. (1994). The course of adult intellectual development. *American Psychologist, 49,* 304–313.

Schaubroeck, J., Ganster, D.C., & Kemmerer, B. E. (1994). Job complexity, "Type A" behavior, and cardiovascular disorder: A prospective study. *Academy of Management Journal, 37,* 426–439.

Scheier, M. F., & Carver, C. S. (1988). *Perspectives on personality.* Boston: Allyn and Bacon.

Scheier, M. F., & Carver, C. S. (1992). Effects of optimism on psychological and physical wellbeing: Theoretical overview and empirical update. *Cognitive Therapy and Research, 16,* 201–228.

Scheier, M. F., Weintraub, J. K., & Carver, C. S. (1986). Coping with stress: Divergent strategies of optimists and pessimists. *Journal of Personality and Social Psychology, 51,* 1257–1264.

Schickedanz, J. A., Schickedanz, D. I., Forsyth, P. D., & Forsyth, G. A. (1998). Understanding children and adolescents (3rd ed.). Boston: Allyn & Bacon.

Schiffman, H. R. (1990). *Sensation and perception: An integrated approach* (3rd ed). New York: John Wiley & Sons.

Schiffman, S. E., Graham, B. G., Sattely-Miller, E. A., & Warwick, Z. S. (1998). Orosensory perception of sensory fat. *Current Directions in Psychological Science, 7,* 137–143.

Schiller, P. H. (1994). Area V4 of the primate visual cortex. *Current Directions in Psychological Science, 3,* 89–92.

Schnider, A., Regard, M., & Landis, T. (1994). Anterograde and retrograde amnesia following bitemporal infarction. *Behavioral Neurology, 7,* 87–92.

Schnurr, P., Friedman, M. J., & Rosenberg, S. D. (1993). Preliminary MMPI scores as predictors of combat-related PTSD symptoms. *American Journal of Psychiatry, 150,* 479–483.

Schreiber, F. R. (1973). *Sybil.* Chicago: Henry Regnery.

Schroots, J. J. F., & Birren, J. (1990). Concepts of time and aging in science. In J. E. Birren & K. W. Schaie (Eds.), *Handbook of the psychology of aging* (3rd ed., pp. 45–64). San Diego, CA: Academic Press.

Schuckit, R. (1982). Symposium on buspirone. *American Journal of Medicine, 82(suppl 5A),* 29.

Schul, Y., & Ganzach, Y. (1995). The effects of accessibility of standards and decision framing on product evaluations. *Journal of Consumer Psychology, 4,* 61–84.

Schulze, C., Karie, T., & Dickens, W. (1996). *Does the bell curve ring true?* Washington, DC: Brookings Institution.

Schunn, C. D., & Dunbar, K. (1996). Priming, analogy, and awareness in complex reasoning. *Memory & Cognition, 24,* 271–284.

Schwarzwald, J., Amir, Y., & Crain, R. L. (1992). Long-term effects of school desegregation experiences on interpersonal relations in the Israeli defense forces. *Personality and Social Psychology Bulletin, 18,* 357–368.

Schweinberger, S. R., Klos, T., & Sommer, W. (1995). Covert face recognition in prosopagnosia: A dissociable function? *Cortex, 31,* 517–529.

Scott, J. P. (1992). Aggression: Functions and control in social systems. *Aggressive Behavior, 18,* 1–20.

Seabrook, J. (1995). *In the cities of the south: Scenes from a developing world.* New York: Verso.

Searle, J. (1980). Minds, brains, and programs. *Behavioral and Brain Science, 3,* 417–457.

Sedikides, C. (1992). Mood as a determinant of attentional focus. *Cognition and Emotion, 6,* 129–148.

Sedikides, C., & Skowronski, J. J. (1997). The symbolic self in evolutionary context. *Personality and Social Psychology Review, 1,* 80–102.

Segal, N. L., & Bouchard, T. J. (1993). Grief intensity following the loss of a twin and other relatives: Test of kinship-genetic hypotheses. *Human Biology, 65,* 87–105.

Segal, Z. V., Gemar, M., & Williams, S. (1999). Differential cognitive response to a mood challenge following successful cognitive therapy or pharmacotherapy for unipolar depression. *Journal of Abnormal Psychology, 108,* 5–10.

Segerstrom, S. C., Taylor, S. E., Kemeny, M. E., & Fahey, J. L. (1998). Optimism is associated with mood, coping, and immune change in response to stress. *Journal of Personality and Social Psychology, 74,* 1646–1655.

Seifer, R., Sameroff, A. J., Barrett, L. C., & Krafchuk, E. (1994). Infant temperament measured by multiple observations and mother report. *Child Development, 65,* 1478–1490.

Seifer, R., Schiller, M., Sameroff, A. J., Resnick, S., & Riordan, K. (1996). Attachment, maternal sensitivity, and infant temperament during the first year of life. *Developmental Psychology, 32,* 12–25.

Sekuler, R., & Blake, R. (1990). *Perception.* New York: Alfred A. Knopf.

Seligman, M. E. P. (1975). *Helplessness: On depression, development, and death.* San Francisco: W. H. Freeman.

Seligman, M. E. P. (1995). The effectiveness of psychotherapy: The Consumer Reports study. *American Psychologist, 50,* 965–974.

Seligman, M. E. P., Castellon, C., Cacciola, J., Schulman, P., Luborsky, L., Ollove, M., & Downing, R. (1988). Explanatory style change during cognitive therapy for unipolar depression. *Journal of Abnormal Psychology, 97,* 13–18.

Seligman, M. E. P., & Hager, J. L. (1972). *Biological boundaries of learning.* New York: Appleton-Century-Crofts.

Selye, H. (1976). *The stress of life* (2nd ed.). New York: McGraw-Hill.

Shaffer, D. (1990). *Adolescent suicide.* Presentation at the ADAMHOL Clinical training meetings, Reston, VA.

Shafir, E. (1993). Choosing versus rejecting: Why some options are both better and worse than others. *Memory and Cognition, 21,* 546–556.

Shamir, B., House, R. J., & Arthur, M. B. (1993). The motivational effects of charismatic leadership: A self-concept based concept. *Organizational Science, 4,* 577–594.

Shanab, M. E., & Spencer, R. E. (1978). Positive and negative contrast effects obtained following shifts in delayed water reward. *Bulletin of the Psychonomic Society, 12,* 199–202.

Shanab, N. E., & Yahya, K. A. (1977). A behavioral study of obedience in children. *Journal of Personality and Social Psychology, 35,* 530–536.

Shane, S., & Venkataraman, S. (in press). The promise of entrepreneurship as a field of research. *Academy of Management Review.*

Sharp, M. J., & Getz, J. G. (1996). Substance use as impression management. *Personality and Social Psychology Bulletin, 22,* 60–67.

Sharpe, D., Adair, J. G., & Roese, N. J. (1992). Twenty years of deception research: A decline in subjects' trust? *Personality and Social Psychology Bulletin, 18,* 585–590.

Shaver, P. R., & Brennan, K. A. (1992). Attachment styles and the "big five" personality traits: Their connections with each other and with romantic relationship outcomes. *Personality and Social Psychology Bulletin, 18,* 536–545.

Shaver, P. R., & Hazan, C. (1994). Attachment. In A. L. Weber & J. H. Harvey (Eds.), *Perspectives on close relationships* (pp. 110–130). Boston: Allyn & Bacon.

Shepherd, G. M. (1994). Discrimination of molecular signals by the olfactory receptor neuron. *Neuron, 13,* 771–790.

Shepard, R. N. (1964). Circularity in judgments of relative pitch. *Journal of the Acoustical Society of America, 36,* 2346–2353.

Sher, K. J., & Trull, T. J. (1994). Personality and disinhibitory psychopathology: Alcoholism and antisocial personality disorder. *Journal of Abnormal Psychology, 103,* 92–102.

Sherman, S. L., Defries, J. C., Gottesman, L. I., Loehlin, J. C., Meyer, J. M., Pelias, M. Z., Rice, J., & Waldman, I. (1997). Behavioral genetics '97: ASHG Statement. Recent developments in human behavioral genetics: Past accomplishments and future directions. *American Journal of Human Genetics, 60,* 1265–1275.

Sherrick, C. E., & Cholewiak, R. W. (1986). Cutaneous sensitivity. In K. R. Boff, L. Kaufamn, & J. P. Thomas (Eds.), *Handbook of perception and human performance* (pp. 12.1–12.58). New York: Wiley.

Shettleworth, S. J. (1993). Where is the comparison in comparative cognition? *Psychological Science, 4,* 179–183.

Shiffrin, R. M. (1993). Short-term memory: A brief commentary. *Memory & Cognition, 21,* 193–197.

Shiffrin, R. M., & Dumais, S. T. (1981). The development of automatism. In J. R. Anderson (Ed.), *Cognitive skills and their acquisition.* Hillsdale, NJ: Erlbaum.

Shiffrin, R. M., & Schneider, W. (1977). Controlled and automatic human information processing. II: Perceptual learning, automatic attending, and a general theory. *Psychological Review, 84,* 127–190.

Shimamura, A. P., Berry, J. M., Mangela, J. A., Rusting, C. L., & Jurica, P. J. (1995). Memory and cognitive abilities in university professors: Evidence for successful aging. *Psychological Science, 6,* 271–277.

Shimamura, A. P., & Jurica, P. J. (1994). Memory interference effects and aging: Findings from a test of frontal lobe function. *Neuropsychology, 8,* 408–412.

Shoda, Y., Mischel, W., & Peake, P. K. (1990). Predicting adolescent cognitive and self-regulatory competencies from preschool delay of gratification. *Developmental Psychology, 26,* 978–986.

Shulman, C., Yirmiya, N., & Greenbaum, C. W. (1995). From categorization to classification: A comparison among individuals with autism, mental retardation, and normal development. *Journal of Abnormal Psychology, 104,* 601–609.

Shum, M. S. (1998). The role of temporal landmarks in autobiographical memory processes. *Psychological Bulletin, 1214,* 423–442.

Sicard, G., & Holley, A. (1984). Receptor cell responses to odorants: Similarities and differences among odorants. *Brain Research, 292,* 282–296.

Siegal, M., & Peterson, C. C. (1996). Breaking the mold: A fresh look at children's understanding of questions about lies and mistakes. *Developmental Psychology, 32,* 322–334.

Siegel, S. (1975). Evidence from rats that morphine tolerance is a learned response. *Journal of Comparative and Physiological Psychology, 89,* 598–606.

Siegel, S. (1983). Classical conditioning, drug tolerance, and drug dependence. In R. G. Smart, F. B. Glaser, Y. Israel, H. Kalant, R. E. Popham, & W. Schmidt (Eds.), *Research advances in alcohol and drug problems* (Vol. 7). New York: Plenum.

Siegel, S. (1984). Pavlovian conditioning and heroin overdose: Reports by overdose victims. *Bulletin of the Psychonomic Society, 22,* 428–430.

Siegel, S., Hinson, R. E., Krank, M. D., & McCully, J. (1982). Heroin "overdose" death: The contribution of drug-associated environmental cues. *Science, 216,* 436–437.

Siegler, R. S., & Ellis, S. (1996). Piaget on childhood. *Psychological Science, 7,* 211–215.

Siegman, A. W., & Boyle, S. (1993). Voices of fear and anxiety and sadness and depression: The effects of speech rate and loudness on fear and anxiety and sadness and depression. *Journal of Abnormal Psychology, 102,* 430–437.

Sigman, M. (1995). Nutrition and child development: More food for thought. *Current Directions in Psychological Science, 4,* 52–55.

Sigvardsson, S., Bohman, M., & Cloninger, R. C. (1996). Replication of the Stockholm adoption study of alcoholism. *Archives of General Psychiatry, 53,* 681–687.

Silagy, C., Mant, D., Fowler, G., & Lodge, M. (1994). Metaanalysis of efficacy of nicotine replacement therapies in smoking cessation. *Lancet, 343,* 139–142.

Silva, C. E., & Kirsch, I. (1992). Interpretive sets, expectancy, fantasy proneness, and dissociation as predictors of hypnotic response. *Journal of Personality and Social Psychology, 63,* 847–856.

Silver, B., Poland, R., & Lin, K. M. (1993). Ethnicity and pharmacology of tricyclic antidepressants. In K. M. Lin, R. Poland, & G. Nakasaki (Eds.), *Psychopharmacology and psychobiology of ethnicity.* Washington, DC: American Psychiatric Association Press.

Silverman, I., & Eals, M. (1992). Sex differences in spatial abilities. Evolutionary theory and data. In J. H. Barkow, L. Cosmides, & J. Tooby (Eds.), *The adapted mind.* (pp. 533–549). New York: Oxford University Press.
Silverman, I., & Phillips, K. (1998). The evolutionary psychology of spatial sex differences In C. Crawford & D. L. Krebs (Eds.)., *Handbook of evolutionary psychology* (pp. 595–612). Mahwah, NJ: Erlbaum.
Sim, D. L. H., & Morris, M. W. (1998). Representativeness and counterfactual thinking: The principle that antecedent and outcome are correspondent in magnitude. *Personality and Social Psychology Bulletin, 24,* 595–609.
Simon, L., Greenberg, J., & Brehm, J. (1995). Trivialization: The forgotten mode of dissonance reduction. *Journal of Personality and Social Psychology, 68,* 247–260.
Simonson, I., & Staw, B. M. (1992). De-escalation strategies: A comparison of techniques for reducing commitment to losing courses of action. *Journal of Applied Psychology, 77,* 419–426.
Simonton, D. K. (1990). Creativity and wisdom in aging. In J. E. Birren & K. W. Schaie (Eds.), *Handbook of the psychology of aging* (3rd ed., pp. 320–329). San Diego: Academic Press.
Simonton, D. K. (1994). Individual differences, developmental changes, and social context. *Behavioral and Brain Sciences, 17,* 552–563.
Simonton, D. K. (1988). Age and outstanding achievement: What do we know after a century of research? *Psychological Bulletin, 104,* 251–267.
Simpson, E. (1974). Moral development research: A case study of scientific cultural bias. *Human Development, 17,* 81–105.
Sinclair, R. C., Hoffman, C., Mark, M. M., Martin, L. L., & Pickering, T. L. (1994). Construct accessibility and the misattribution of arousal: Schachter and Singer revisited. *Psychological Science, 5,* 15–19.
Singh, D. (1993). Adaptive significance of female's physical attractiveness: Role of waist-to-hip ratio. *Journal of Personality and Social Psychology, 65,* 293–307.
Siquelande, E. R., & Lipsitt, L. P. (1996). Conditioned head-turning in human newborns. *Journal of Experimental Child Psychology, 3,* 356–376.
Skarlicki, D. P., Folger, R., & Tesluk, P. (1999). Personality as a moderator in the relationship between fairness and retaliation. *Academy of Management Journal, 42,* 100–110.
Skeels, H. M. (1938). Mental development of children in foster homes. *Journal of Consulting Psychology, 2,* 33–43.
Skeels, H. M. (1966). Ability status of children with contrasting early life experience. *Society for Research in Child Development Monographs, 31*(3), 1–65.
Skinner, B. F. (1938). *The behavior of organisms.* New York: Appleton-Century-Crofts.
Skinner, B. F. (1971). *Beyond freedom and dignity.* New York: Alfred A. Knopf.
Skinner, B. F. (1974). *About behaviorism.* New York: Vintage Books.
Slobin, D. I. (1979). *Psycholinguistics* (2nd ed.). Glenview, IL: Scott, Foresman.
Smith, C. P. (Ed.). (1992). *Motivation and personality: Handbook of thematic content analysis.* New York: Cambridge University Press.
Smith, E. E., & Jonides, J. (1997). Working memory: A view from neuroimaging. *Cognitive Psychology, 33,* 5–42.
Smith, G. T., Goldman, M., Greenbaum, P. E., & Christiansen, B. A. (1995). Expectancy for social facilitation from drinking: The divergent paths of high-expectancy and low-expectancy adolescents. *Journal of Abnormal Psychology, 104,* 32–40.
Smith, J. F., & Kida, T. (1991). Heuristics and biases: Expertise and task realism in auditing. *Psychological Bulletin, 109,* 472–489.
Smith, S. M. (1979). Remembering in and out of context. *Journal of Experimental Psychology: Human Learning and Memory, 5,* 460–471.
Snowden, L. R., & Cheung, F. K. (1990). Use of inpatient mental health services by members of ethnic minority groups. *American Psychologist, 45,* 347–355.
Snyder, D. K., Wills, R. M., & Grady-Fletcher, A. (1991). Long-term effectiveness of behavioral versus insight-oriented marital therapy: A 4-year follow-up study. *Journal of Consulting and Clinical Psychology, 59,* 138–141.
Snyder, S. (1991). Movies and juvenile delinquency: An overview. *Adolescence, 26,* 121–132.
Solomon, R. L. (1982). The opponent-process in acquired motivation. In D. W. Pfaff (Ed.), *The physiological mechanisms of motivation.* New York: Springer-Verlag.
Sommers, K., Whitman, T. L., Borkowski, J. G., Schellenbach, C., Maxwell, S., & Keogh, D. (1993). Cognitive readiness and adolescent parenting. *Developmental Psychology, 29,* 389–398.
Spanos, N. P. (1991). A sociocognitive approach to hypnosis. In S. J. Lynn & J. R. Rhue (Eds.), *Hypnosis theories: Current models and perspectives* (pp. 324–361). New York: Guilford Press.
Spanos, N. P., Burgess, C. A., & Perlini, A. H. (1992). Compliance and suggested deafness in hypnotic and nonhypnotic subjects. *Imagination, Cognition, and Personality, 11,* 211–223.
Spanos, N. P., Perlini, A. H., Patrick, L., Bell, S., & Gwynne, M. I. (1990). The role of compliance in hypnotic and nonhypnotic analgesia. *Journal of Research in Personality, 24,* 433–453.
Spearman, C. E. (1927). *The abilities of man.* London: Macmillan.
Specter, M. (1999, January 18). Decoding Iceland. *New Yorker,* 39–51.
Spence, A. P. (1989). *Biology of human aging.* Englewood Cliffs, NJ: Prentice-Hall.
Spencer, L. M., Jr., & Spencer, S. M. (1993). *Competence at work: Models for superior performance.* New York: Wiley.
Sperry, R. W. (1968). Hemisphere deconnection and unity of conscious experience. *American Psychologist, 29,* 723–733.
Spirduso, W. W., & MacRae, P. G. (1990). Motor performance and aging. In J. E. Birren & K. W. Schaie (Eds.), *Handbook of the psychology of aging* (3rd ed., pp. 184–200). San Diego: Academic Press.
Sprecher, S., & Duck, S. (1994). Sweet talk: The importance of perceived communication for romantic and friendship attraction experienced during a get-acquainted date. Personality and *Social Psychology Bulletin, 20,* 391–400.
Springer, S. P., & Deutsch, G. (1985). *Left brain, right brain.* San Francisco: Freeman.
Squire, L. R. (1991). Closing remarks. In L. R. Squire & E. Lindenlaub (Eds.), *The biology of memory* (pp. 643–644). Stuttgart, Germany: F. K. Schattauer Verlag.
Squire, L. R. (1995). Biological foundations of accuracy and inaccuracy of memory. In D. L. Schachter (Ed.), *Memory distortions* (pp. 197–225). Cambridge, MA: Harvard University Press.
Squire, L. R., & Spanis, C. W. (1984). Long gradient of retrograde amnesia in mice: Continuity with the findings in humans. *Behavioral Neuroscience, 98,* 345–348.
Sroufe, L. A., & Waters, E. (1976). The ontogenesis of smiling and laughter on the organization of development in infancy. *Psychological Review, 83,* 173–189.
Stangor, C., & Ruble, D. N. (1989). Strength of expectancies and memory for social information: What we remember depends on how much we know. *Journal of Experimental Social Psychology, 39,* 1408–1423.
Stanley, J. (1993). Boys and girls who reason well mathematically. In G. R. Bock & K. Ackrill (Eds.), *The origins and development of high ability.* Chichester, England: Wiley.
Stanovich, K. E. (Ed.), (1993). The development of rationality and critical thinking. [Special issue]. *Merrill-Palmer Quarterly, 39,* 47–103.
Staw, B. M., & Ross, J. (1987). Behavior in escalation situations: Antecedents, prototypes, and solutions. In L. L. Cummings & B. M. Staw (Eds.), *Research in organizational behavior* (Vol. 9, pp. 29–78). Greenwich, CT: JAI Press.
Staw, B. M., & Ross, J. (1989). Understanding behavior in escalation situations. *Science, 246,* 216–220.
Steel, R. P., & Rentsch, J. R. (1997). The dispositional model of job attitudes revisited: Findings of a 10-year study. *Journal of Applied Psychology, 82,* 873–879.
Steele, C. M. (1988). The psychology of self-affirmation: Sustaining the integrity of the self. In L. Berkowitz (Ed.), *Advances in experimental social psychology* (pp. 261–302). Hillsdale, NJ: Erlbaum.
Steele, C. M., & Aronson, E. (1996). Stereotype threat and the intellectual test performance of African Americans. *Journal of Personality and Social Psychology, 69,* 797–811.
Steele, C. M., & Josephs, R. A. (1990). Alcohol myopia: Its prized and dangerous effects. *American Psychologist, 45,* 921–933.
Steele, C. M., & Lui, T. J. (1983). Dissonance processes as self-affirmation. *Journal of Personality and Social Psychology, 45,* 5–19.
Steele, C. M., Spencer, S. J., & Lynch, M. (1993). Self-image resilience and dissonance: The role of affirmational resources. *Journal of Personality and Social Psychology, 64,* 885–896.
Steers, R. M. (1984). *Organizational behavior* (2nd ed.). Glenview, IL: Scott Foresman.
Steffen, V. J. (1990). Men's motivation to perform the testicular self-exam: Effect of prior knowledge and an educational brochure. *Journal of Applied Social Psychology, 20,* 681–702.
Stein, D. M., & Lambert, M. J. (1995). Graduate training in psychotherapy: Are therapy outcomes enhanced? *Journal of Consulting and Clinical Psychology, 63,* 182–196.
Steinmetz, J. E. (1996). The brain substrates of classical eyeblink conditioning in rabbits. In J. R. Bloedel, T. J. Ebner, & S. P. Wide (Eds.), *The acquisition of motor behavior in vertebrates* (pp. 89–114). Cambridge, MA: MIT Press.
Steinmetz, J. E. (1999). A renewed interest in human classical conditioning. *Psychological Science, 10,* 24–25.
Stellar, E. (1985, April). *Hunger in animals and humans.* Lecture to the Eastern Psychological Association, Boston.
Sternberg, R. J. (1985). *Beyond IQ.* Cambridge: Cambridge University Press.
Sternberg, R. J. (1988). Triangulating love. In R. J. Sternberg & H. J. Barnes (Eds.), *The psychology of love* (pp. 119–138). New Haven, CT: Yale University Press.
Sternberg, R. J. (1995). For whom the bell curve tolls: A review of The Bell Curve. *Psychological Science, 6,* 257–261.
Sternberg, R. J., & Lubart, T. I. (1996). Investing in creativity. American Psychologist, 51, 677–688.
Sternberg, R. J., Wagner, R. K., Williams, W. M., & Horvath, J. A. (1995). Testing common sense. *American Psychologist, 50,* 912–927.
Stewart, A. J., Copeland, A. P., Chester, N. L., Malley, J. E., & Barenbaum, N. B. (1997). *Separating together: How divorce transforms families.* New York: Guilford Press.
Stewart, A. J., & Vandewater, E. A. (1999). "If I had it to do over again . . . ": Midlife review, midcourse corrections, and women's well-being in midlife. *Journal of Personality and Social Psychology, 76,* 270–283.
Stice, E., & Barrera, M., Jr. (1995). A longitudinal examination of the reciprocal relations between perceived parenting and adolescents' sub-

stance use and externalizing behaviors. *Developmental Psychology, 31,* 332–334.
Stipp, D. (1990, May 17). Einstein bird has scientists atwitter over mental feats. *Wall Street Journal,* pp. 1, 7.
Stone, A. A., Kessler, R. C., & Haythornthwaite, J. A. (1991). Measuring daily events and experiences: Decisions for the researchers. *Journal of Personality, 59,* 575–607.
Stone, J., Aronson, E., Crain, A. L., Winslow, M. P., & Fried, C. B. (1994). Inducing hypocrisy as a means of encouraging young adults to use condoms. *Personality and Social Psychology Bulletin, 20,* 116–128.
Stone, J., Wiegand, A. W., Cooper, J., & Aronson, E. (1997). When exemplification fails: Hypocrisy and the motives for self-integrity. *Journal of Personality and Social Psychology, 72,* 54–65.
Storms, M. D. (1983). *Development of sexual orientation.* Washington, DC: Office of Social and Ethical Responsibility, American Psychological Association.
Story, M., & Faulkner, P. (1990). The prime time diet: A content analysis of eating behavior and food messages in television program content and commercials. *American Journal of Public Health, 80,* 738–740.
Strean, H. S. (1985). *Resolving resistances in psychotherapy.* New York: Wiley Interscience.
Streissguth, A. P. (1994). A long-term perspective of FAS. *Alcohol Health and Research World, 18,* 74–81.
Streissguth, A. P., Bookstein, F. L., Sampson, P. D., Olson, H. C., & Barr, H. M. (1995, March). *Measurement and analysis of main effects, covariates, and moderators in the behavioral teratology of alcohol.* Paper presented at the Biennial Meetings of the Society for Research in Child Development, Indianapolis, IN.
Strickland, B. R. (1992). Women and depression. *Current Directions in Psychological Science, 1,* 132–134.
Stroessner, S. J., & Mackie, D. M. (1992). The impact of induced affect on the perception of variability in social groups. *Personality and Social Psychology Bulletin, 18,* 546–554.
Struckman-Johnson, C. J., Gilliland, R. C., Struckman-Johnson, D. L., & North, T. C. (1990). The effects of fear of AIDS and gender on responses to fear-arousing condom advertisements. *Journal of Applied Social Psychology, 20,* 1396–1410.
Sullivan, M. J. L., Bishop, S. R., & Pivik, J. (1995). The pain catastrophizing scale: Development and validation. *Psychological Assessment, 7,* 524–532.
Super, C. M. (1981). Behavioral development in infancy. In R. H. Monroe, R. I. Monroe, & B. B. Whiting (Eds.), *Handbook of cross-cultural human development* (pp. 181–270). New York: Garland.
Sutton, J., & Smith, P. K. (1999). Bullying as a group process: An adaptation of the participant role approach. *Aggressive Behavior, 25,* 97–111.
Swets, J. A. (1992). The science of choosing the right decision threshold in high-stakes diagnostics. *American Psychologist, 47,* 522–532.
Syvalahti, E. K. G. (1994). Biological factors in schizophrenia: Structural and functional aspects. *British Journal of Psychiatry, 146* (Suppl. 23), 9–14.
Szapocznik, J., Kurtines, W., Santisteban, D. A., & Rio, A. T. (1990). Interplay of advances between theory, research, and application in treatment interventions aimed at behavior problem children and adolescents. *Journal of Consulting and Clinical Psychology, 58,* 69–70.
Szkrybalo, J., & Ruble, D. N. (1999). "God made me a girl": Sex-category constancy judgments and explanations revisited. *Developmental Psychology, 35,* 392–402.
Takahashi, T. (1989). Social phobia syndrome in Japan. *Comprehensive Psychiatry, 30,* 45–52.
Tang, J. L., Law, M., & Wald, N. (1994). How effective is nicotine replacement therapy in helping people to stop smoking? *British Medical Journal, 308,* 21–26.
Tangney, J. P., Miller, R. S., Flicker, L., & Barlow, D. H. (1996). Are shame, guilt, and embarrassment distinct emotions? *Journal of Personality and Social Psychology, 70,* 1256–1269.
Tanouye, E. (1999a, August 25). Clues to a sudden attack on the mind. *Wall Street Journal,* pp. B1, B8.
Tanouye, E. (1999b, August 25). For drug makers, high-stakes race inside the brain. *Wall Street Journal,* pp. B1, B8.
Tarasoff v. Regents of the University of California, 17 Cal. 3d 425, 551 P.2d 334, 131 Cal. Reptr. 14 (1976).
Tardif, T. (1996). Nouns are not always learned before verbs: Evidence from Mandarin speakers' early vocabularies. *Developmental Psychology, 32,* 492–504.
Taylor, R. L. (1991). Poverty and adolescent black males: The subculture of disengagement. In P. B. Edelman & J. Ladner (Eds.), *Adolescence and poverty: Challenge for the 1990s* (pp. 139–162). Washington, DC: Center for National Policy Press.
Taylor, S. E. (1999). *Health psychology* (4th ed.). New York: McGraw-Hill.
Taylor, S. E., & Brown, J. (1988). Illusion and well-being: A social psychological perspective on mental health. *Psychological Bulletin, 103,* 193–210.
Taylor, S. E., Pham, L. B., Rivkin, I. D., & Armor, D. A. (1998). Harnessing the imagination: Mental stimulation, self-regulation, and coping. *American Psychologist, 55,* 429–439.
Taylor, S. P. (1967). Aggressive behavior and physiological arousal as a function of provocation and the tendency to inhibit aggression. *Journal of Personality, 35,* 297–310.
Teicher, M. H., Glod, C., & Cole, O. J. (1990). Emergence of intense suicidal preoccupation during fluoxetine treatment. *American Journal of Psychiatry, 147,* 207–210.
Teichman, M., Barnea, Z., & Rahav, G. (1989). Sensation seeking, state and trait anxiety, and depressive mood in adolescent substance abusers. *International Journal of the Addictions, 24,* 87–99.
Tennen, H., & Eller, S. J. (1977). Attributional components of learned helplessness. *Journal of Personality and Social Psychology, 35,* 265–271.
Terman, L. M. (1954). The discovery and encouragement of exceptional talent. *American Psychologist, 9,* 221–230.
Terrace, H. S. (1985). In the beginning was the "name." *American Psychologist, 40,* 1011–1028.
Tesser, A., & Martin, L. (1996). The psychology of evaluation. In E. T. Higgins & A. W. Kruglanski (Eds.), *Social psychology: Handbook of basic principles* (pp. 400–432). New York: Guilford Press.
Tesser, A., Martin, L. L., & Cornell, D. P. (1996). On the substitutability of the self-protecting mechanism. In Pl. Gollwitzerr & J. Bargh (Eds.), *The psychology of action* (pp. 48–68). New York: Guilford.
Teyler, T. J., & DiScenna, P. (1984). Long-term potentiation as a candidate mnemonic device. *Brain Research Reviews, 7,* 15–28.
*The World Health Report 1999: Making a difference.* (1999). Geneva: The World Health Organization. Retrieved December 26, 1999 from the World Wide Web: http://www.who.org/whr/1999/en/report.htm.
Thiele, T. E., Marsh, D. J., Marie, L. S., Bernstein, I. L., & Palmiter, R. D. (November 26, 1998). Ethanol consumption and resistance are inversely related to neuropeptide Y levels. *Nature,* 396, 366–369.
Thigpen, C. H., & Cleckley, H. (1957). *The three faces of Eve.* New York: McGraw-Hill.
Thoma, S. J. (1986). Estimating gender differences in the comprehension and preference of moral issues. *Developmental Review, 6,* 165–180.
Thomas, A., & Chess, S. (1989). Temperament and development. In G. A. Kohnstamm, J. E. Bates, & M. K. Rothbart (Eds.), *Temperament in childhood.* New York: Wiley.
Thomas, J. L. (1992). *Adulthood and aging.* Boston: Allyn and Bacon.
Thomas, M. H. (1982). Physiological arousal, exposure to a relatively lengthy aggressive film, and aggressive behavior. *Journal of Research in Personality, 16,* 72–181.
Thomas, P. (1999). When Venus talks to Mars. *Wall Street Journal,* February 25: B1, B8.
Thompson, J. K. (1992). Body image: Extent of disturbance, associated features, theoretical models, assessment methodologies, intervention strategies, and a proposal for a new DSM-IV diagnostic category-Body Image Disorder. In M. Hesen, R. M. Eisler, & P. M. Miller (Eds.), *Progress in behavior modification* (pp. 3–54). Sycamore, IL: Sycamore Publishing.
Thompson, R. F. (1989). A model system approach to memory. In P. R. Solomon, G. R. Goethals, C. M. Kelley, & B. R. Stephens (Eds.), *Memory: Interdisciplinary approaches.* New York: Springer-Verlag.
Thompson, R. F., Bao, S., Chen, L., Cipriano, B. D., Grethe, J. S., Kim, J. J., Thompson, J. K., Tracy, J. A., Weninger, M. S., & Krupa, D. J. (1997). Associative learning. In R. J. Bradley, R. A. Harris, & P. Jenner (Series Eds.) & J. D. Schmahmann (Vol. Ed.), *International review of neurobiology: Vol. 41. The cerebellum and cognition* (pp. 152–189). San Diego: Academic Press.
Thompson, R. F., & Krupa, D. J. (1994). Organization of memory traces in the mammalian brain. *Annual Review of Neuroscience, 17,* 519–549.
Thorndike, R. L., & Hagen, E. (1982). *Ten thousand careers.* New York: Wiley.
Thurstone, E. L. (1938). *Primary mental abilities.* Chicago: University of Chicago Press.
Tice, D. M., & Baumeister, R. F. (1997). Longitudinal study of procrastination, performance, stress, and health: The costs and benefits of dawdling. *Psychological Science, 8,* 454–458.
Tiernari, P. (1991). Interaction between genetic vulnerability and family environment: The Finnish adoptive family study of schizophrenia. *Acta Psychiatrica Scandanavica, 84,* 460–465.
Tiffany, S. T. (1990). A cognitive model of drug urges and drug-use behavior: Role of automatic and nonautomatic processes. *Psychological Review, 97,* 147–168.
Tisserand, R. B. (1977). *The art of aromatherapy.* Rochester, VT: Healing Arts Press.
Tolman, E. C., & Honzik, C. H. (1930). Introduction and removal of reward, and maze performance in rats. *University of California Publications in Psychology, 4,* 257–275.
Tomaka, J., Blascovich, J., Kelsey, R. M., & Leitten, C. L. (1993). Subjective, physiological, and behavioral effects of threat and challenge appraisal. *Journal of Personality and Social Psychology, 65,* 248–260.
Topf, M. D. (1999, June). Chicken/egg/chegg!: The merits of a holistic, integrated approach vs. a behavior-based approach, to create lasting changes in unsafe attitudes and behaviors. *Occupational Health & Safety,* 60–66.
Topka, H., Valls-Sole, J., Massaquoi, S. G., & Hallett, M. (1993). Deficit in classical conditioning in patients with cerebellar degeneration. *Brain, 116,* 961–969.
Torrance, E. P. (1974). *Torrance tests of creative thinking.* Lexington, MA: Personnel Press.
Tracy, J., Ghose, S. S., Stecher, T., McFall, R. M., & Steinmetz, J. E. (1999). *Psychological Science, 10,* 9–13.
Trapnell, P. D., & Campbell, J. D. (1999). Private self-consciousness and the five-factor model of personality: Distinguishing rumination from reflection. *Journal of Personality and Social Psychology, 76,* 284–304.

Treffinger, D. J. (1995). Creative problem solving: Overview and educational implications. *Educational Psychology Review, 7,* 301–312.

Tremblay, R. E., Pagani-Kurtzi, L., Masse, L. C., Vitario, F., & Pihl, R. O. (1995). A bimodal preventive intervention for disruptive kindergarten boys: Its impact through mid-adolescence. *Journal of Consulting and Clinical Psychology, 63,* 560–568.

Triandis, H. C. (1990). Cross-cultural studies of individualism and collectivism. In J. J. Berman (Ed.), *Nebraska symposium on motivation, 1989* (pp. 41–133). Lincoln: University of Nebraska Press.

Trillin, C. (1999, February 8). The chicken vanishes. *The New Yorker,* 38–41.

Tronick, E. Z. (1989). Emotions and emotional communication in infants. *American Psychologist, 44,* 112–119.

Tulving, E. (1989). Remembering and knowing the past. *American Scientist, 77,* 361–367.

Tulving, E. (1993). What is episodic memory? *Current Directions in Psychological Science, 2,* 67–70.

Tulving, E., & Psotka, L. (1971). Retroactive inhibition in free recall: Inaccessibility of information available in the memory store. *Journal of Experimental Psychology, 87,* 1–8.

Tulving, E., & Watkins, M. J. (1973). Continuity between recall and recognition. *American Journal of Psychology, 86,* 739–748.

Turban, D. B., & Keon, T. O. (1993). Organizational attractiveness: An interactionist perspective. *Journal of Applied Psychology, 78,* 184–193.

Turk, D. C. (1994). Perspectives on chronic pain: The role of psychological factors. *Current Directions in Psychological Science, 3,* 45–48.

Turk, D. C., & Rudy, T. E. (1992). Cognitive factors and persistent pain: A glimpse into Pandora's box. *Cognitive Therapy and Research, 16,* 99–122.

Turkheimer, E. (1998). Heritability and biological explanation. *Psychological Review , 105,* 782–791.

Turner, J. C., Hogg, M. A., Oakes, P. J., Richer, S. D., & Wetherell, M. S. (1987). *Rediscovering the social group: A self-categorization theory.* Oxford, England: Blackwell.

Tversky, A., & Kahneman, D. (1974). Judgment under uncertainty: Heuristics and biases. *Science, 185,* 1124–1131.

Tversky, A., & Kahneman, D. (1981). The framing of decisions and the psychology of choice. *Science, 211,* 453–458.

Tyler, T. R., & Cook, F. L. (1984). The mass media and judgment of risk: Distinguishing impact on personal and societal level judgments. *Journal of Personality and Social Psychology, 47,* 693–708.

Uchino, B. N., Cacioppo, J. T., & Kiecolt-Glaser, J. K. (1996). The relationship between social support and physiological processes: A review with emphasis on underlying mechanisms and implications for health. *Psychological Bulletin, 119,* 488–531.

UNAIDS. (December, 1998). *AIDS Epidemic Update: December 1998.* UNAIDS Joint United Nations Programme on HIV/AIDS. Retrieved December 27, 1999 from the World Wide Web: http://www.unaids.org/publications/documents/epidemiology/surveillance/wad1998/wadr98e.pdf.

Unger, R. K., & Crawford, M. (1992). *Women and gender: A feminist psychology.* Philadelphia: Temple University Press.

Ungerleider, L. G., & Mishkin, M. (1982). Two cortical visual systems. In D. J. Ingle, M. A. Goodale, & R. J. W. Mansfield (Eds.), *Analysis of visual behavior.* Cambridge, MA: MIT Press.

United States Department of Health and Human Services. (1989). *Aging in the eighties: The prevalence of comorbidity and its associations with disability* (DHHS Publication No. PHS 89–1250). Washington, DC: U.S. Government Printing Office.

U.S. Department of Health and Human Services. (1994). *Preventing Tobacco Use Among Young People: A Report of the Surgeon General.* Atlanta, Georgia: U.S. Department of Health and Human Services, Public Health Service, Centers for Disease Control and Prevention, National Center for Chronic Disease Prevention and Health Promotion, Office on Smoking and Health.

United States Senate Special Committee on Aging. American Association of Retired Persons, Federal Council on Aging, and U.S. Administration on Aging. *Aging America: Trends and projections.* (DHHS Publication No. FoA 91-28001). Washington, DC: U.S. Department of Health and Human Services.

Urban, M. J. (1992) Auditory subliminal stimulation: A reexamination. *Perceptual and Motor Skills, 74,* 515–541.

Urberg, K. A., Degirmencioglu, S. M., Tolson, J. M., & Halliday-Scher, K. (1995). The structure of adolescent peer networks. *Developmental Psychology, 31,* 540–547.

Usher, J. A, & Neisser, U. (1995). Childhood amnesia and the beginnings of memory for four early life events. *Journal of Experimental Psychology: General.*

Valenza, E., Simion, F., Cassia, V. M., & Umilta, C. (1996). Face preference at birth. *Journal of Experimental Psychology, 22,* 892–903.

Vanman, E. J., Paul, B. Y., Ito, T. A., & Miller, N. (1997). The modern face of prejudice and structure features that moderate the effect of cooperation on affect. *Journal of Personality and Social Psychology, 73,* 941–959.

Vansteelandt, K., & Van Mechelan, I. (1999). Individual differences in situation-behavior profiles: A triple typology model. *Journal of Personality and Social Psychology, 75,* 751–765.

Vecchio, R. P. (Ed.). (1997). *Leadership.* Notre Dame, IN: University of Notre Dame Press.

Vecra, S., & Johnson, M. H. (1995). Gaze detection and the cortical processing of faces: Evidence from infants and adults. *Visual Perception, 2,* 101–129.

Velicer, W. F., & Prochaska, J. O. (1999). An expert system intervention for smoking cessation. *Patient Education & Counseling, 36,* 119–129.

Vernberg, E. M., LaGreca, A. M., Silverman, W. K., & Prinstein, M. J. (1996). Prediction of posttraumatic stress symptoms in children after hurricane Andrew. *Journal of Abnormal Psychology, 105,* 237–248.

Vernon, P. A. (1987). *Speed of information processing and intelligence.* Norwood, NJ: Ablex.

Vernon, P. A. (1993). *Biological approaches to the study of human intelligence.* Norwood, NJ: Ablex.

Volpe, J. J. (1992). The effect of cocaine use on the fetus. *New England Journal of Medicine, 327,* 399–407.

Von Senden, M. (1960). *Space and sign.* Trans. by P. Heath. New York: Free Press.

Vredenburgh, A. G., & Cohen, H. H. (1995). Does culture affect risk perception?: Comparisons among Mexicans, African-Americans, Asians, and Caucasians. *Proceedings of the Human Factors and Ergonomics Society, 39,* 1015–1019.

Vredenburgh, A. G., McLeod, J. S., & Nebeker, D. M. (1999). Under what circumstances do extrinsic rewards decrease intrinsic motivation? *Proceedings of the Human Factors and Ergonomics Society, 43,* 830–834.

Vredenburgh, A. G., Weinger, M. B., Williams, K. J., Kalsher, M. J., Macario, A., & Smith, B. (in press). Developing a technique to measure anesthesiologists' real-time workload. Proceedings of the IEA 2000/HFES Congress.

Vygotsky, L. S. (1987). Thinking and speech. In R. W. Rieber, A. S. Carton (Eds.), & N. Minick (Trans.), *The collected works of L. S. Vygotsky: Vol 1. Problems of general psychology* (pp. 37–285). New York: Plenum. (Original work published in 1934.)

Wagenaar, W. A., (1986). My memory: A study of autobiographical memory over six years. *Cognitive Psychology, 18,* 225–252.

Wagner, A., Desmond, J., Demb, J., Glover, G., & Gabrielli, J. (1997). Semantic repetition priming for verbal and pictorial knowledge: A functional MRI study of left inferior prefrontal cortex. *Journal of Cognitive Neuroscience, 9,* 714–726.

Walden, T. A., & Ogan, T. A. (1988). The development of social referencing. *Child Development, 29,* 1230–1240.

Walker, L. J. (1989). A longitudinal study of moral reasoning. *Child Development, 60,* 157–166.

Walker, L. J. (1991). Sex differences in moral reasoning. In W. M. Kurtines & J. L. Gewirtz (Eds.), *Handbook of moral behavior and development,* Vol. 2 (pp. 164–193). Hillsdale, NJ: Erlbaum.

Walker, L. W. (1999). Psychology and domestic violence around the world. *American Psychologist, 54,* 21–29.

Wallace, B. (1993). Day persons, night persons, and variability in hypnotic susceptability. *Journal of Personality and Social Psychology, 64,* 827–833

Wallace, C. J. (1993). Psychiatric rehabilitation. *Psychopharmacology Bulletin, 29,* 537–548.

Wallace, R. K., & Fisher, L. E. (1987). *Consciousness and behavior* (2nd ed.). Boston: Allyn and Bacon.

Wallace-Broscious, A., Serafica, F. C., & Osipow, S. H. (1994). Adolescent career development: Relationships to self-concept and identity status. *Journal of Research on Adolescence, 4,* 122–149.

Waller, N. G., Kojetin, B. A., Bouchard, T. J., Jr., Lykken, D. T., & Tellgen, A. (1990). Genetic and environmental influences on religious interests, attitudes, and values: A study of twins reared apart and together. *Psychological Science, 1,* 138–142.

Walsh, S. (1993). Cited in Toufexis, A. (1993, February 15), *Time,* pp. 49–51.

Walster, E., & Festinger, L. (1962). The effectiveness of "overheard" persuasive communication. *Journal of Abnormal and Social Psychology, 65,* 395–402.

Walton, G. E., Bower, N.J. A., & Bower, T. G. R. (1992). Recognition of familiar faces by newborns. *Infant Behavior and Development, 15,* 265–269.

Waltz, J. A., Knowlton, B. J., Holyoak, K. J., Boone, K. B., Mishkin, F. S., de Menezes, M., Thomas, C. R., & Miller, B. L. (1999). A system for relational reasoning in human prefrontal cortex. *Psychological Science, 10,* 119–125.

Wanberg, C. R., Kanfer, R., & Rotundo, M. (1999). Unemployed individuals: Motives, job-search constraints as predictors of job seeking and reemployment. *Journal of Applied Psychology, 54,* 897–910.

Wang, G., Tanaka, K., & Tanifuji, M. (1996). Optical imaging of functional organization in the monkey inferotemporal cortex. *Science, 272,* 665–1668.

Wang, X. T. (1996). Framing effects: Dynamics and task domains. *Organizational Behavior & Human Decision Processes, 68*(2), 145–157.

Wannamethee, S. G., & Shaper, A. G. (1998). Alcohol, coronary heart disease and stroke: An examination of the J-shaped curve. *Neuroepidemiology, 17,* 288–295.

Ward, T. S., Smith, S. M., & Vaid, J. (Eds.), *Creative thought.* Washington, DC: American Psychological Association.

Wark, G. R., & Krebs, D. L. (1996). Gender and dilemma differences in real-life moral judgment. *Developmental Psychology, 32,* 220–230.

Warren, S. (1999 March 16). Toy makers say bye-bye to "plasticizers." *Wall Street Journal,* pp. B1, B8.

Warwick, Z. S., & Schiffman, S. S. (1992). Role of dietary fat in calorie intake and weight gain. *Neuroscience & Biobehavioral Reviews, 16,* 585–596.

Watson, A. C., Nixon, C. L., Wilson, A., & Capage, L. (1999). Social interaction skills and theory of mind in young children. *Developmental Psychology, 35,* 386–391.

Watson, D. (1989). Strangers' ratings of the five robust personality factors: Evidence of a surprising convergence with self-report. *Journal of Personality and Social Psychology, 57,* 120–128.

Watson, J. B. (1924). *Behaviorism.* New York: Norton.

Watson, T. S. (1996). A prompt plus delayed contingency procedure for reducing bathroom graffiti. *Journal of Applied Behavior Analysis, 29,* 121–124.

Wayne, S. J., & Liden, R. C. (1995). Effects of impression management on performance ratings: A longitudinal study. *Academy of Management Journal, 38,* 232–260.

Webb, W. (1975). *Sleep: The gentle tyrant.* Englewood Cliffs, NJ: Prentice-Hall.

Wechsler, H., Levine, S., Idelson, R. K., Schor, E. L., & Coakley, E. (1996). The physicians' role in health promotion revisited: A survey of primary care practitioners. *The New England Journal of Medicine, 334,* 996–998.

Wegner, D. M. (1994). Ironic processes of mental control. *Psychological Review, 101,* 34–52.

Wegner, D. M. (1997). When the antidote is the poison: Ironic mental control processes. *Psychological Science, 8,* 148–150.

Wegner, D. M., Ansfield, M., & Pilloff, D. (1998). The putt and the pendulum: Ironic effects of the mental control of action. *Psychological Science, 9,* 196–199.

Wegner, D. M., Broome, A., & Blumberg, S. (1997). Ironic effects of trying to relax under stress. *Behaviour Research and Therapy, 35,* 11–21.

Wegner, D. M., & Gold, D. B. (1995). Fanning old flames: Emotional and cognitive effects of suppressing thoughts of a past relationship. *Journal of Personality and Social Psychology, 68,* 782–792.

Wehner, R., & Menzel, R. (1990). Do insects have cognitive maps? *Annual Review of Neuroscience, 13,* 403–414.

Weigel, R. H., Kim, E. L., & Frost, J. L. (1995). Race relations on prime time television reconsidered: Patterns of continuity and change. *Journal of Applied Social Psychology, 25,* 223–236.

Weinberger, D. R. (1994). Biological basis of schizophrenia: Structural/functional considerations relevant to potential for antipsychotic drug reasons. *Journal of Clinical Psychiatry, Monograph Series, 12,* 4–7.

Weiner, B. (1989). *Human motivation.* Hillsdale, NJ: Erlbaum.

Weinstein, N. D. (1998). Accuracy of smokers' risk perceptions. *Annals of Behavioral Medicine, 20,* 135–140.

Weisberg, R., & Suls, J. M. (1973). An information-processing model of Duncker's candle problem. *Cognitive Psychology, 4,* 255–276.

Weisenberg, M. (1982). Cultural and ethnic factors in reaction to pain. In I. Al-Issa (Ed.), *Culture and psychopathology.* Baltimore: University Park Press.

Weisenberg, M., Raz, T., & Hener, T. (1998). The influence of film-induced mood on pain perception. *Pain, 76,* 365–375.

Weiskrantz, L. (1995). Blindsight—not an island unto itself. *Current Directions in Psychological Science, 4,* 146–150.

Weiss, H. M., & Cropanzano, R. (1996). Affective events theory: A theoretical discussion of the structure, causes, and consequences of affective experiences at work. In B. M. Staw & L. L. Cummings (Eds.), *Research in organizational behavior* (Vol. 19, pp. 1–745). Greenwich, CT: JAI Press.

Wells, G. L. (1993). What do we know about eyewitness identification? *American Psychologist, 48,* 553–571.

Welsh, D. K., Logothetis, D. E., Meister, M., & Reppert, S. M. (1995). Individual neurons dissociated from rat suprachiasmatic nucleus express independently phased circadian firing rhythms. *Neuron, 14,* 697–706.

Wen, S. W., Goldenberg, R. L., Cutter, G. R., Hoffman, H. J., Cliver, S. P., Davis, R. O., & DuBard, M. B. (1990). Smoking, maternal age, fetal growth, and gestational age at delivery. *American Journal of Obstetries and Gynecology, 162,* 53–58.

Werker, J. F., & Desjardins, R. N. (1995). Listening to speech in the 1st year of life: Experiential influences on phoneme perception. *Current Directions in Psychological Science, 4,* 76–80.

Werkhoven, P. J., & Groen, J. (1998). Manipulation performance in interactive virtual environments. *Human Factors, 40,* 432–442.

Werner, E. E. (1995). Resilience in development. *Current Directions in Psychological Science, 44,* 81–84.

Werts, M. G., Caldwell, N. K., & Wolery, M. (1996). Peer modeling of response chains: Observational learning by students with disabilities. *Journal of Applied Behavior Analysis, 29,* 53–66.

Wetter, D. W., Fiore, M. C., Gritz, E. R., Lando, H. A., Stitzer, M. L., Hasselblad, V., Baker, T. B. (1998). The Agency for Health Care Policy and Research Smoking Cessation Clinical Practice Guideline: Findings and implications for psychologists. *American Psychologist, 53,* 657–669.

White, J. M. (1992). Marital status and well-being in Canada. *Journal of Family Issues, 13,* 390–409.

White, R. K. (1977). Misperception in the Arab-Israeli conflict. *Journal of Social Issues, 25,* 41–78.

Whitla, D. A. (1975). *Value added: Measuring the impact of undergraduate education.* Cambridge, MA: Harvard University Office of Instructional Research and Evaluation.

WHO (World Health Organization). (1992). *International Statistical Classification of Diseases* (ICD-10). Geneva, Switzerland: Author.

Whorf, B. L. (1956). Science and linguistics. In J. B. Carroll (Ed.), *Language, thought, and reality: Selected writings of Benjamin Whorf.* Cambridge, MA: MIT Press.

Whyte, G. (1991). Diffusion of responsibility: Effects on the escalation tendency. *Journal of Applied Psychology, 76,* 408–415.

Widiger, T., & Spitzer, R. (1991). Sex bias in the diagnosis of personality disorders. *Clinical Psychology Review, 11,* 1–22.

Widom, C. S. (1989). Does violence beget violence? A critical examination of the literature. *Psychological Bulletin, 106,* 3–28.

Wielkiewicz, R. M., & Calvert, C. R. X. (1989). *Training and habilitating developmentally disabled people: An introduction.* Newbury Park, CA: Sage.

Wierwille, W. W., Wreggit, S. S., Kirn, C. L., Ellsworth, L. E., & Fairbanks, R. J. (1994, December). *Research on vehicle-based driver status/performance monitoring: Three year report.* Vehicle Analysis and Simulation Laboratory, Virginia Polytechnic Institute and State University, VPISU Report No. ISE 94–04, NHTSA Report No. DOT HS 808 247.

Wilcoxon, H. C., Dragoin, W. B., & Kral, P. A. (1971). Illness-induced aversions in rats and quail: Relative salience of visual and gustatory cues. *Science, 171,* 826–828.

Wilder, D. A. (1993). Freezing intergroup evaluations: Anxiety fosters resistance to counterstereotypic information. In M. A. Hogg & D. Abrams (Eds.), *Group motivation: Social psychological perspectives* (pp. 68–86). London: Harvester Wheatsheaf.

Wiley, J. A., & Camacho, T. C. (1980). Life-style and future health: Evidence from the Alameda County study. *Preventive Medicine, 9,* 1–21.

Wilhelm, K., & Parker, G. (1994). Sex differences in lifetime depression rates: Fact or artifact? Psychological Medicine, 24, 97–111.

Williams, B. F., Howard, V. F., & McLaughlin, T. F. (1994). Fetal alcohol syndrome: Developmental characteristics and directions for further research. *Education and Treatment of Children, 17,* 86–97.

Williams, D. E., & Page, M. M. (1989). A multi-dimensional measure of Maslow's hierarchy of needs. *Journal of Research in Personality, 23,* 192–213.

Williams, D. P., Going, S. B., Lohman, T. G., Harsha, D. W., Srinivasan, S. R., Weber, L. S., & Berenson, G. S. (1992). Body fatness and risk for elevated blood pressure, total cholesterol, and serum lipoprotein ratios in children and adolescents. *American Journal of Public Health, 82,* 363–368.

Williams, G. C., Grow, V. M., Freedman, Z. R., Ryan, R. M., & Deci, E. I. (1996). Motivational predictors of weight loss and weight-loss maintenance. *Journal of Personality and Social Psychology, 70,* 115–126.

Williams, I. M. (1994). Recall of childhood trauma: A prospective study of women's memories of childhood abuse. *Journal of Consulting and Clinical Psychology, 62,* 1167–1176.

Williams, K. B., Radefeld, P. A. Binning J. F., & Suadk, J. R. (1993). When job candidates are "hard" versus "easy-to-get": Effects of candidate availability on employment decisions. *Journal of Applied Social Psychology, 23,* 169–198.

Williams, W. (1998). Are we raising smarter kids today? School and home-related influences on IQ. In U. Neisser (Ed.), *The rising curve: Long-term gains in IQ and related measures* (pp. 125–154). Washington, DC: American Psychological Association.

Williamson, D. A., Cubic, B. A., & Gleaves, D. H. (1993). Equivalence of body image disturbances in anorexia and bulimia nervosa. *Journal of Abnormal Psychology, 102,* 177–180.

Willis, S. L., & Nesselroade, C. S. (1990). Long-term effects of fluid ability training in old-old age. *Developmental Psychology, 26,* 905–910.

Willis, W. D. (1985). *The pain system. The neural basis of nociceptive transmission in the mammalian nervous system.* Basel: Karger.

Wills, T. A., McNamara, G., Vaccaro, D., & Hirky, A. E. (1996). Escalated substance use: A longitudinal grouping analysis from early to middle adolescence. *Journal of Abnormal Psychology, 105,* 166–180.

Wilson, B. A., & Wearing, D. (1995). Prisoner of consciousness: A state of just awakening following herpes simplex encaphalitis. In R. Campbell & M. A. Conway (Eds.), *Broken memories: Case studies in memory impairment* (pp. 14–30). Cambridge, MA: Blackwell.

Wilson, G. T., Nathan, P. E., O'Leary, K. D., & Clark, L. A. (1996). *Abnormal psychology: Integrating perspectives.* Boston: Allyn & Bacon.

Wilson, J. M. (1999). Just-in-time training: Distance learning on the desktop. *Syllabus, 11,* 52–54.

Wilson, T. D., & Brekke, N. (1994). Mental contamination and mental correction: Unwanted influences on judgments and evaluations. *Psychological Bulletin, 116,* 117–142.

Wilson, T. D., Houston, C. E., Etling, K. M., & Brekke, N. (1996). A new look at anchoring effects: Basic anchoring and its antecedents. *Journal of Experimental Psychology: General, 125*(4), 387–402.

Winett, R. A. (1995). A framework for health promotion and disease prevention programs. *American Psychologist, 50,* 341–350.

Winett, R. A. (1998). Developing more effective health-behavior programs: Analyzing the epidemiological and biological bases for activity and exercise programs. *Applied & Preventive Psychology, 7,* 209–224.

Winn, P. (1995). The lateral hypothalamus and motivated behavior: An old syndrome reassessed and a new perspective gained. *Current Directions in Psychological Science*, 4, 182–187.

Winokur, G. (1986). Unipolar depression. In G. Winokur & P. Clayton (Eds.), *The medical basis of psychiatry* (pp. 60–79). Philadelphia: Saunders.

Winter, D. G. (1983). *Development of an integrated system for scoring motives in verbal running text.* Unpublished manuscript, Wesleyan University.

Wise, R. A., & Bozarth, M. A. (1987). A psychomotor stimulant theory of addiction. *Psychological Review, 94,* 469–492.

Wisniewski, H. M., & Terry, R. D. (1976). Neuropathology of the aging brain. In R. D. Terry & S. Gershod (Eds.), *Neurobiology of aging* (pp. 65–78). New York: Raven.

Witelson, S. (1991). Sex differences in neuroanatomical changes with aging. *New England Journal of Medicine, 325,* 211–212.

Witte, E., & Davis, J. H. (Eds.), (1996). *Understanding group behavior: Consensual action by small groups.* Hillsdale, NJ: Erlbaum.

Wolfe, B. M., & Baron, R. A. (1971). Laboratory aggression related to aggression in naturalistic social situations: Effects of an aggressive model on the behavior of college student and prisoner observers. *Psychonomic Science, 24,* 193–194.

Wood, J. M., Nezworski, M. T., & Stejskal, W. J. (1996). The comprehensive system for the Rorschach: A critical examination. *Psychological Science, 7,* 3–10.

Wood, J. V., Saltzberg, J. A., & Goldsamt, L. A. (1990). Does affect induce self-focused attention? *Journal of Personality and Social Psychology, 8,* 890–908.

Wood, R. A., & Locke, E. A. (1990). Goal setting and strategy effects on complex tasks. In B. M. Staw & L. L. Cummings (Eds.), *Research in organizational behavior* (Vol. 12, pp. 73–110). Greenwich, CT: JAI Press.

Wood, W., Wong, F. Y., & Chachere, J. G. (1991). Effects of media violence on viewers' aggression in unconstrained social interaction. *Psychological Bulletin, 109,* 373–383.

Woodcock, R. W., & Johnson, M. B. (1989). Woodcock-Johnson Tests of Cognitive Ability: Standard and Supplemental Batteries.

Woodruff-Pak, D. S. (1999). New directions for a classical paradigm: Human eyeblink conditioning. *Psychological Science, 10,* 1–3.

Woody, E. Z., & Bowers, K. S. (1994). A frontal assault on dissociated control. In S. J. Lynn & J. W. Rhue (Eds.), *Dissociation: Theoretical and clinical perspectives* (pp. 52–79). New York: Guilford Press.

World Cancer Research Fund. (1997). *Food, Nutrition and the Prevention of Cancer: A Global Perspective.* Washington DC: American Institute for Cancer Research.

Wright, P. M., O'Leary-Kelly, A. M., Cortinak, J. M., Klein, H. J., & Hollenbeck, J. R. (1994). On the meaning and measurement of goal commitment. *Journal of Applied Psychology, 79,* 795–803.

Wright, R. W. (1982). *The sense of smell.* Boca Raton, FL: CRC Press.

Wright, S. C., Aron, A., McLaughlin-Volpe, T., & Ropp, S. A. (1997). The extended contact effect: Knowledge of cross-group friendships and prejudice. *Journal of Personality and Social Psychology, 73,* 73–90.

Wrightsman, L. S. (1988). *Personality development in adulthood.* Newbury Park, CA: Sage.

Wyer, R. S. Jr., & Srull, T. K. (Eds.). (1994). *Handbook of social cognition* (2nd ed., Vol. 1). Hillsdale, NJ: Erlbaum.

Wyer, R. S., Jr., & Srull, T. K. (Eds.). (1999). *Handbook of social cognition* (3rd ed.). Mahwah, NJ: Erlbaum.

Yankner, J., Johnson, S. T., Menerdo, T., Cordell, B., & Firth, C. L. (1990). Relations of neural APP-751/APP-695 in RNA ratio and neuritic plaque density in Alzheimer's disease. *Science, 248,* 854–856.

Yik, M. S. M., Bond, M. H., & Paulhus, D. L. (1998). Do Chinese self-enhance or self-efface? It's a matter of domain. *Personality and Social Psychology Bulletin, 24,* 399–406.

Yonas, A., Arterberry, M. E., & Granrud, C. E. (1987). Four-month-old infants' sensitivity to binocular and kinetic information for three-dimensional object shape. *Child Development, 58,* 910–927.

Yonkers, K., Kando, J., Cole, J., & Blumenthal, S. (1992). Gender differences in pharmacokinetics and pharmacodynamics of psychotropic medication. *The American Journal of Psychiatry, 149,* 587–595.

Yorges, S. L., Weiss, H. M., & Strickland, O. J. (1999). The effect of leader outcomes on influence, attributions, and perceptions of charisma. *Journal of Applied Psychology, 84,* 428–436.

Young, A. M., & Herling, S. (1986). Drugs as reinforcers: Studies in laboratory animals. In S. R. Goldberg & I. P. Stolerman (Eds.), *Behavioral analysis of drug dependence* (pp. 9–67). New York: Academic Press.

Yukl, G. (1994). *Leadership in organizations* (3rd ed.). Englewood Cliffs, NJ: Prentice-Hall.

Zaccaro, S. J., Foti, R. J., & Kenny, D. A. (1991). Self-monitoring and trait-based variance in leadership: An investigation of leader-flexibility across multiple group situations. *Journal of Applied Psychology, 76,* 308–315.

Zahn-Waxler, C., Radke-Yarrow, M., Wagner, E., & Chapman, M. (1992). Development of concern for others. *Developmental Psychology, 28,* 126–136.

Zajonc, R. B. (1968). Attitudinal effects of mere exposure. *Journal of Personality and Social Psychology Monograph Supplement, 9,* 1–27.

Zajonc, R. B., & McIntosh, D. N. (1992). Emotions research: Some promising questions and some questionable promises. *Psychological Science, 3,* 70–74.

Zajonc, R. B., Murphy, S. T., & Inglehart, M. (1989). Feeling and facial efference: Implications of the vascular theory of emotion. *Psychological Review, 96,* 395–416.

Zanna, M. P., & Olson, J. M. (1994). The psychology of prejudice. *The Ontario Symposium* (Vol. 7). Hillsdale, NJ: Erlbaum.

Zatzick, D. F., & Dimsdale, J. E. (1990). *Psychosomatic Medicine,* 52, 544–557.

Zebrowitz, L. A., & Collins, M. A. (1997). Accurate social perception at zero acquaintance: The affordances of a Gibsonian approach. *Personality and Social Psychology Review, 1,* 204–223.

Zebrowitz, L. A., Collins, M. A., Lee, S. Y., & Blumenthal, J. (1998). Bright, bad, babyfaced boys: Appearance stereotypes do not always yield self-fulfilling prophecy effects. *Journal of Personality and Social Psychology, 75,* 1300–1320.

Zeki, S. (1992, September). The visual image in mind and brain. *Scientific American,* pp. 69–76.

Zeman, J., & Shipman, K. (1996). Children's expression of negative affect: Reasons and method. *Developmental Psychology, 32,* 842–849.

Zhang, S., & Schmitt, B. (1998). Language-dependent classification: The mental representation of classifiers in cognition, memory, and ad evaluations. *Journal of Experimental Psychology: Applied, 4,* 375–385.

Zill, N., Morrison, D. R., & Coiro, M. J. (1993). Long-term effects of parental divorce on parent–child relationships, adjustment, and achievement in young adulthood. *Journal of Family Psychology, 7,* 91–103.

Zillmann, D. (1993). Mental control of angry aggression. In D. M. Wegner & J. W. Pennebaker (Eds.), *Handbook of mental control.* Englewood Cliffs, NJ: Prentice-Hall.

Zillmann, D. (1996). Anger. In *Encyclopedia of Mental Health.* New York: Harcourt Brace.

Zillmann, D., Schweitzer, K. J., & Mundorf, N. (1994). Menstrual cycle variation in women's interest in erotica. *Archives of Sexual Behavior, 23,* 579–597.

Zinberg, R. E., & Barlow, D. H. (1996). Structure of anxiety and the anxiety disorders: A hierarchical model. *Journal of Abnormal Psychology, 105,* 181–193.

Zuckerman, M. (1990). The psychophysiology of sensation seeking. *Journal of Personality, 58,* 313–345.

Zuckerman, M. (1994). *Behavioral expressions and biosocial bases of sensation seeking.* New York: Cambridge University Press.

Zuckerman, M. (1995). Good and bad humors: Biochemical bases of personality and its disorders. *Psychological Science, 6,* 325–332.Zuroff, D.C., Blatt, S. J., Sanislow III, C. A., Bondi, C. M., & Pilkonis, P. A. (1999). Vulnerability to depression: Reexamining state dependence and relative stability. *Journal of Abnormal Psychology, 108,* 76–89.

# Name Index


Abraham, L.M., 628
Abram, S.E., 105
Abrams, R.L., 89, 90
Achenbach, T.M., 542
Achlien, B., 517
Ackerman, H., 56
Acocella, J., 228, 559
Acocella, J.R., 584
Adair, J.G., 33
Adams, R.J., 295
Adelman, H.F., 395
Ader, R., 180, 500
Adler, N.J., 203
Adolphs, R., 71, 399
Agarie, N., 404
Aghajanian, G.K., 550
Agnoli, F., 279
Agosti, V., 588, 599
Agronick, G.S., 330, 346
Ahn, M., 627
Aiken, L.R., 418, 419
Aiken, L.S., 525
Ainsworth, M.D.S., 313
Ajzen, I., 519
Ajzen, J., 628-629
Akerstedt, T., 132
Al-Issa, I., 568
Al-Zahrani, S.S., 622
Albright, T.D., 68
Alfano, M.S., 551
Alge, B.J., 484
Alicke, M.D., 648
Allen, C.R., 550
Allen, J.P., 541
Allens, L.S., 385
Alliger, R., 426
Alloy, L.B., 584
Allport, G.W., 469
Allred, J.B., 514
Allyn, J., 629
Aloise-Young, P.A., 203, 511
Alptekin, S., 197
Alreu, B.C., 111
Altman, E., 578
Alvarez-Borda, B., 180
Amabile, T.M., 443
Amaro, H., 520
Amato, P.R., 341, 493
Ambuel, B., 562
American Cancer Society, 509, 525
American Psychiatric Association, 419, 538
American Psychological Association, 12, 14, 540
Amir, Y., 639
Amoore, J., 107
Anastasio, P.A., 640
Anderson, C.A., 387, 388, 390
Anderson, J.R., 211, 224, 226
Anderson, K.B., 387, 388, 390
Andreason, N.C., 426, 551
Andrews, E.A., 199
Andrews, J.D.W., 391
Ansfield, M., 138
Antonovsky, A., 349
Antrobus, J., 149
Applebaum, P.S., 611
Applegate, B., 564
Archer, J., 43
Arena, J.G., 199
Arendt, J., 134
Arkes, H.R., 256
Arkin, R.M., 373, 387
Arking, R., 349
Armor, D., 627
Armor, D.A., 252
Arnoff, J., 402
Arnoff, S.R., 362
Aron, A., 640
Aron, A.P., 397
Aronson, E., 434, 635, 639
Arterberry, M.E., 296
Arthur, M.B., 655
Arvey, R.D., 628
Ash, R.A., 132
Ashcraft, M.H., 253
Assaad, J.M., 157
Astington, J.W., 304
Atkinson, R.C., 211
Atlas, S., 352
Audrain, J., 511
Aviram, A., 474
Aviram, T., 261
Avoni, P., 145
Awh, E., 216, 217
Azar, B., 438, 522
Azmitia, M., 304

Bachman, B.A., 640
Bachman, J.G., 155, 333
Backbier, E., 632
Baddeley, A., 216, 217, 235
Baddeley, A.D., 220, 232, 240
Bader, S.A., 507
Baer, J.S., 398
Baer, L., 602
Baghurst, P.A., 433
Bagley, C., 517
Bagwell, C.L., 317
Bailey, A., 548
Bailey, J.H., 111
Bailey, J.M., 386
Baillargeon, R., 302, 303
Baker, A.G., 173
Baker, R.R., 385
Baker, T.B., 511, 512
Ballantine, H.T., 602
Balogh, R.D., 295
Baltes, P.B., 416
Bandura, A., 169, 200, 323, 472, 473, 475, 586
Banich, M.T., 523
Banks, S.M., 522
Bar, M., 90
Bar-Ilan, O., 267
Barbee, A.P., 331, 649
Barber, T.X., 179
Barbur, J.L., 98
Barch, D.M., 568
Bardell, L., 523
Barenbaum, N.B., 195
Bargh, J.A., 89
Bargones, J.Y., 295
Barker, D.A., 440
Barker, L., 440
Barkley, R.A., 544
Barlow, D.H., 396, 553, 554, 555
Barnea, Z., 394
Barnier, A., 152
Baron, J., 255
Baron, R.A., 25, 58, 109, 135, 170, 201, 323, 338, 386, 387, 388, 390, 403, 405, 420, 441, 442, 445, 482, 483, 484, 570, 592, 618, 627, 641, 649
Baron-Cohen, S., 306
Barr, H.M., 288, 289
Barrera, M., 296
Barrera, M., Jr., 341
Barrett, L.C., 312
Barrett, L.F., 403
Barrick, M.R., 482, 483
Bartholomew, S., 203
Bartlett, J.G., 519
Basbaum, A., 49
Bashore, T.R., 254
Basoglu, M., 557
Bass, B.I., 653
Batterman-Faunce, J.M., 231
Bauer, G.B., 592
Bauer, P., 233
Bauer, P.J., 303
Baum, A., 491, 502
Baum, D.R., 252
Baumeister, R.F., 139, 141, 189, 190, 373, 376, 445, 466
Baumrind, D., 334
Bazerman, M.H., 260
Beaber, R.J., 629
Beach, S.R., 648
Beaman, A.L., 645
Beatty, W.W., 373, 387
Beauvais, J., 522
Bechara, A., 71
Beck, A.T., 551, 587
Becker, H.C., 289
Beckstead, J.W., 33
Bedeian, G.F., 482
Bedell, B.T., 522
Bednar, R.L., 591
Békésy, G.von., 101
Belcher, M., 150
Bell, S., 153
Belli, R.F., 227
Bellis, M.A., 385
Belmore, S.M., 624
Belsky, J., 315
Bem, D.J., 123, 323, 386
Bem, S.L., 323
Benbow, C., 430
Bendapudi, V., 132
Benjamin, J., 511
Benson, P., 517
Benthin, A.C., 635
Berardi-Coletta, B., 270
Berenbaum, H., 568
Berenson, G.S., 325
Berent, S., 73
Beretta, D., 352
Bergin, A.E., 604
Berglas, S., 395
Bergmann, B.M., 145
Berkowitz, L., 202, 387, 388
Berlin, B., 496
Berlin, R., 178
Berlyne, D.E., 501
Berman, J.S., 599, 604-605
Bermudez-Rattoni, F., 180
Bernstein, D.A., 533, 541, 545, 560, 567, 579, 598, 600
Bernstein, I.L., 516
Berntson, G.G., 628
Berrry, J.M., 351, 352, 353
Berry, D.S., 331
Berscheid, E., 650
Bertonicini, J., 294, 295
Besson, J., 104
Besson, M., 43, 71, 72
Beta, A.L., 628
Betz, E.L., 377
Biederman, I., 90
Biederman, J., 543
Bierman, K.L., 341, 342
Biggers, K., 480
Bihrle, A., 70
Bihrle, S., 564
Binning, J.F., 645
Birbaumer, N., 56
Birmingham, K.M., 197
Birren, J., 346
Bishop, S.R., 106
Bixler, E.O., 146
Bjork, E. L., 226
Bjork, R.A., 226
Bjorkqvist, K., 387
Black, D., 551
Black, J.S., 203
Blackmore, S., 123

Blake, R., 116, 118
Blakely, C.H., 609
Blakemore, C., 122
Blanchard, E.B., 199
Blanchard, K., 563
Blaney, P.H., 235
Blanton, H., 629
Blasccovich, J., 495
Blatt, S.J., 551, 588
Blay, N.M., 645
Blinkhorn, R., 256
Block, J.H., 471, 472
Block, M., 152
Block, V., 144
Blumberg, S., 138
Blumenthal, J., 331
Blumenthal, R., 607
Blumenthal, S., 601
Blyth, D.A., 332
Bobo, L., 636
Bobocel, D.R., 262
Bodenhausen, G.F., 639
Bodenhausen, G.V., 638
Bohman, M., 157
Boileau, R.A., 523
Boivin, M., 296, 318
Boivin, M.J., 73
Bolden, S., 513
Bolduc, E.A., 543
Boling, N.C., 199
Bolton, P., 548
Bonardi, C., 178
Bond, G.R., 597
Bond, M.H., 466, 637
Bondi, C.M., 551
Bongar, B., 552
Boninger, D., 627
Bonnel, A.-M., 43, 72
Boodoo, G., 413, 425, 428, 431, 433
Bookstein, F.L., 288, 289
Boone, K.B., 43, 71
Bootzin, R.R., 584
Borbely, A.A., 144
Borduin, C.M., 594, 595
Borgeat, F., 199
Borges, G., 516
Borke, H., 303
Borkowski, J.G., 339, 340, 480
Bornstein, R.F., 458
Borod, J.C., 399
Bouchard, T.J., 73, 75
Bouchard, T.J., Jr., 413, 425, 428, 430, 431, 433, 628
Boulos, Z., 134
Bounds, W., 136
Bovbjerg, D.H., 178, 181
Bower, N.J.A., 296
Bower, T.G.R., 296
Bowers, K.S., 152, 153, 231
Bowers, T.G., 604
Bowlby, J., 314
Bowles, N., 123
Bowman, E.D., 511
Bowman, E.S., 550
Boyd, N.R., 511
Boyle, P., 513
Boyle, S., 397
Bozarth, M.A., 156
Bradbury, T.N., 651
Bradley, M.M., 43, 565
Brainerd, C.J., 228, 231, 304
Brando, M., 383
Brandt, J., 73
Braude, R.M., 507
Braungart, J.M., 312
Braungart, M.M., 346
Braungart, R.G., 346
Braverman, N.S., 176
Brean, H., 89
Breaux, A.M., 543
Breazeal (Ferrell), C., 272
Brehm, J., 633
Breland, K., 187
Breland, M., 187
Brennan, K.A., 313
Brett, L.P., 177
Brewer, M.B., 638
Brickman, B.J., 111
Bridgeman, D.L., 639
Britton, P.J., 520
Brockner, J., 262, 281
Brody, C.L., 511
Brody, N., 413, 425, 428, 431, 433
Bronfen, M.I., 109
Bronfenbrenner, U., 345
Bronstein, P., 176
Broome, A., 138
Broussaud, D., 65
Brown, J., 226, 505
Brown, J.D., 621, 622, 949
Brown, J.M., 319
Brown, R.W., 234
Brown, W.A., 382
Browne, D.H., 341
Brownell, K.D., 514
Bruce, D., 68
Bruder, G.E., 588, 599
Brugge, J.F., 101
Bruhn, J.G., 527
Bruno, G.M., 199
Brunsman, B., 641
Bryan, T.S., 236, 403
Bryant, D., 432
Buck, R., 63
Buehler, R., 625, 626
Bukowski, W.M., 296, 318
Bulcroft, R., 332
Bullock, M., 303
Bulthoff, H.H., 65, 68
Bunsey, M., 57
Burgess, C.A., 153
Burgund, E.D., 119
Burish, T.G., 177
Burnett, W., 524
Burns, B.D., 269
Burrell, C., 339
Burrow, L., 599
Burton, D., 203
Bushman, B.J., 202, 388, 390, 445, 646
Buss, A.H., 389
Buss, D.H., 76, 383, 384, 649, 651
Buss, D.M., 15, 383, 384, 651
Butcher, J.N., 477
Butler, J.C., 650
Buttolph, M.L., 602
Buunk, B.P., 651
Buxton, R.B., 216, 217
Buyer, L.S., 270
Bykin, A.W., 413, 425, 428, 431, 433
Byrne, D., 170, 382, 385, 618, 648
Byrne, R.M.J., 249, 251

Cacciola, J., 551, 578
Cacioppo, J.T., 63, 500, 628, 630, 631
Cadoret, R.J., 517
Cain, W.S., 108
Caldera, T., 14
Caldwell, N.K., 204
Caltran, G., 295, 313
Calvert, C.R.X., 419
Camacho, T.C., 493
Campbell, J.D., 139
Campbell, J.N., 104
Campbell, R., 306
Campbell, S.C., 543
Campos, J.J., 296
Cannon-Bowers, J.A., 266
Cantillon, M., 599
Cantor, N., 405
Capage, L., 304, 317
Capaldi, E.J., 188, 197
Caporaso, N.E., 511
Card, J.P., 131
Carey, M.P., 177, 634
Carlo, G., 308
Carlson, N.R., 104, 107, 143, 144, 149, 159
Carnelley, K.B., 652
Carpendale, J.L.M., 308
Carpenter, P.A., 95
Carroll, J.M., 401
Carroll, T.K., 396, 403
Carstensen, L.I., 334, 356
Carstensen, L.L., 355, 356
Cartland, B., 383
Caruso, D.R., 441
Carver, C.S., 139, 502
Cassem, N.H., 602
Cassia, V.M., 121
Cassidy, J., 315
Castelanni, R., 145
Castellon, C., 551, 578
Catalano, R.F., 203
Catania, A.C., 184, 192
Cattell, R.B., 416, 470
Cavallero, R., 397
Ceci, S.J., 231, 413, 425, 428, 431, 433
Centers for Disease Control, 510, 511, 518, 519
Cerella, J., 253
Cerelli, E., 351
Ceyhanli, A., 557
Chachere, J.G., 201
Chaiken, S., 630
Chan, C.J., 652
Chang, E.C., 503
Chang, W.H., 601
Chaouch, A., 104
Chapman, M., 313
Charles, S.T., 355, 356
Charlin, V.L., 203
Charney, D.S., 550
Chason, J., 523
Chauncey, H.H., 179
Chavajay, P., 332
Cherek, D.R., 390
Cherry, E.C., 112
Chess, S., 312
Chester, N.L., 195
Cheung, F.K., 607
Childress, A.R., 180
Choi, L., 621
Chokar, J.S., 375, 376
Cholewiak, R.W., 104
Chomsky, N., 275
Chorney, K., 430
Chorney, M.J., 430
Chou, P., 571
Christenfeld, N., 258
Christensen, A., 595, 596
Christensen-Szalanski, J.J.J., 256
Christiansen, B.A., 572
Christiansen, C., 111
Cialdini, R.B., 641, 645
Clark, A.E., 405
Clark, E., 278
Clark, H., 278
Clark, J.J., 112
Clark, K.C., 502
Clark, L.A., 569, 586
Clark, R.E., 175
Clarkson, M.C., 233
Clark-Stewart, A., 294
Cleckley, H., 558
Clifton, R.K., 233, 295
Cliver, S.P., 289
Cloninger, R.C., 157
Clubb, P.A., 307
Clum, G.A., 604
Coakley, E., 506
Coan, D., 231
Coates, T.J., 519
Codori, A.M., 73
Cohen, D., 296
Cohen, G., 426
Cohen, H.H., 511
Cohen, L.R., 514
Cohen, M.A., 505
Cohen, N., 180, 500
Cohen, N.J., 523
Cohen, S., 497, 500, 501
Cohn, E.G., 388
Coiro, M.J., 493
Colborn, T., 290
Colcombe, A., 523
Cole, J., 601
Cole, N., 645
Cole, O.J., 599

Cole, R., 555
Coleman, R.M., 134
Collins, B.E., 519
Collins, C., 519
Collins, J.F., 604
Collins, K.L., 175
Collins, M.A., 331, 471, 649
Colvin, C.R., 470-471
Colwell, L.S., 319
Colwill, R.M., 194, 197
Compas, B.E., 491
Conger, J.A., 655
Conger, R.D., 341
Connolly, T., 266
Conrad, J., 341
Constantino, G., 607
Conte, J.M., 482
Conway, M.A., 234
Cook, F.L., 259
Cooper, G.F., 122
Cooper, H., 405
Cooper, H.M., 594, 595
Cooper, J., 634, 635
Cooper, M.L., 157
Cooper, S.E., 561
Copeland, A.P., 195
Cordell, B., 239
Cordova, D.I., 395
Coren, S., 86, 93, 96, 97, 116, 117
Corley, R., 430, 431
Corneille, O., 621
Cornell, D.P., 633
Corso, J.F., 350
Cortelli, P., 145
Cortinak, J.M., 375
Costa, P.T., Jr., 470, 478
Courage, M.L., 233
Coyle, J.T., 49, 239
Coyne, J.C., 498
Crabbe, J.C., 74
Craik, F.I.M., 220
Crain, A.L., 635
Crain, R.L., 639
Crambert, R.F., 350
Crawford, H.J., 106
Crawford, M., 322
Crealia, R., 628
Crespi, L.P., 195
Crick, F., 144
Criqui, M.H., 330, 361, 419, 481, 493
Crombez, G., 105
Cropanzano, R., 405
Cross, H.J., 154
Croyle, R.T., 495
Csikszentmihalyi, M., 333
Cubic, B.A., 545, 546, 547
Cubis, J., 339
Culbertson, F.M., 549
Cunnick, J.E., 497, 500
Cunningham, J., 289
Cunningham, J.A., 111
Cunningham, M.R., 331, 649
Curfman, G.O., 524
Cutmore, T.R., 178, 181
Cutter, G.R., 289
Czeisler, C.A., 134

D'Agostino, P.R., 223
Da Silva, M.S., 308
Dabbs, J.M., Jr., 389
Dadds, M.R., 178, 181
Daher, M., 295
Dallenbach, K.M., 225
Damasio, A.F., 71
Damasio, H., 71
Daneman, M., 89
Daniel, J., 131
Daniels, J., 430
Daniels, S.G., 649
Dark, V., 112
Datan, N., 349
Daum, I., 56, 175
Davidson, K., 280, 517
Davidson, R.J., 61, 397
Davidson, W.S., II, 609
Davies, M., 441
Davis, J., 578
Davis, J.H., 658
Davis, M.A., 262
Davis, R.O., 289
Dawis, R.V., 628
Dawson, D.A., 571
Dawson, G., 548
Dawson, N.V., 256
Day, D.V., 482
Day, N., 289
De Menezes, M., 43, 71
De Villiers, J.G., 276
De Villiers, P.A., 276
De Vries, H., 632
Deacon, S., 134
Deary, I.J., 425
Deaux, K., 322
Deci, E.I., 514, 515
Deci, E.L., 395, 514
Deck, M., 570
DeFries, J.C., 312, 430, 431
Defries, J.C., 430
DeJong, P.J., 74, 554
Delgado, P.L., 550
Delis, D.C., 70
DeLong, M.R., 49
DeLongis, A., 498
Demb, J., 89
Dement, W.C., 142, 143, 148
DeNeve, K., 405
DeNeve, K.M., 388
Dengerink, H.A., 390
Denning, P.J., 273
Denollet, J., 517
Dent, C.W., 203
Deppe, R.K., 395
Desimone, R., 122, 240
Desimore, R., 68
Desjardins, R.N., 277
Desmond, J., 89
Detterman, D.K., 430
Detweiler, J.B., 522
Deuser, W.E., 387, 388, 390
Deutsch, G., 63
DeValois, K.K., 96
DeValois, R.L., 96
Devine, P.G., 633
DeVos, J., 302
Di Chiara, G., 156
Di Nicola, D.D., 506
Di Pellegrino, G., 65
Dichgans, J., 56
Dickens, W., 436
Diego, M.A., 109
Diekmann, K.A., 260
Diener, C., 333, 404
Diener, E., 333, 337, 404, 405, 406
Dijkstra, M., 632
DiMatteo, M.R., 506
Dimsdale, J.E., 105
Dincin, J., 597
Dingle, G.A., 516
DiScenna, P., 240
Dishman, R.K., 523
Dixon, D.N., 457
Djik, D.J., 144
Docherty, J.P., 604
Dockery, D.W., 289
Dodge, K.L., 502
Dollard, J., 387
Dominowski, R.L., 270
Dondi, M., 295, 313
Donovan, D.M., 398
Donovan, J.J., 375
Donovan, S., 588, 599
Doob, L., 387
Dopp, J.M., 500
Dorfman, J., 152
Douek, E., 109
Dougherty, D.M., 390
Dougherty, M.R.P., 258
Dovidio, J.F., 636, 638, 639, 640, 641
Dow, S., 378, 379
Dowd, S., 578
Dowler, J., 288
Downing, R., 551, 578
Doyle, W.J., 501
Dragoi, V., 193
Dragoin, W.B., 177
Drain, M., 121, 122
Draine, S.C., 89, 90
Draper, J.V., 111
Dreger, R.M., 470
Dreher, N., 289
Druen, P.B., 331, 649
DuBard, M.B., 289
Dubbert, P.M., 199, 523
Duck, S., 649
Duffy, D.L., 505
Dufour, M., 571
Dufour, M.C., 515
Dumais, S.T., 137
Dumanoski, D., 290
Dunbar, K., 269
Duncan, L.E., 330, 346
Duncker, K., 271
Dunne, M., 339
Dunning, D., 256, 638
DuPaul, G.J., 544
Durso, F.T., 638
Dutton, D.G., 397
Dweck, C.S., 194
Dyer, F.C., 197
Dziedzic, S., 517

Eagly, A.H., 22, 322, 630
Eals, M., 17, 437
Earles, J.L., 351
Eccleston, C., 105
Eckerman, C.O., 175
Eden, D., 474
Edwards, J.R., 500
Edwards, K., 236, 403
Edworthy, J., 135
Egan, S.K., 318
Egeland, J.A., 550
Eggleston, T.J., 635
Ehram, R.N., 180
Ehrhardt, J., 426
Eich, E., 235
Eich, J.E., 221
Eichenbaum, H., 57
Eimas, P.D., 295
Eisenberg, N., 308
Ekman, P., 356, 397, 401
Elder, G.H., Jr., 341
Eley, T., 430
Elisberg, M., 14
Elkin, J., 604
Eller, S.J., 194
Elliott, A.J., 276, 633
Elliott, R.K., 583
Ellis, A., 587
Ellis, L., 76
Ellis, S., 299
Ellsworth, L.E., 135
Elsmore, T.F., 192
Emde, R.N., 312
Emery, G., 551
Emmelkamp, P., 556
Empson, J.A.C., 146, 147
Emshoff, J.G., 609
Engen, T., 107, 108, 109
Enns, J.T., 86, 93, 96, 97, 116
Epel, E., 522
Epley, N., 33
Epling, W.F., 191, 192
Epstein, L.H., 491
Epstein, S., 22
Erdelyi, M.H., 225
Erdley, C.A., 223
Erev, I., 88
Ericsson, K.A., 224
Eriskson, E.H., 335, 344
Erlichman, H., 116
Eron, L.D., 202
Erwin, R., 352
Eshleman, S., 549, 554
Eskenazi, J., 90
Eskritt, M., 306
Estrada, C.A., 403
Etienne, M.A., 399
Evans, L., 135
Evans, N., 638
Evert, D.L., 515
Ewert, M., 364
Ewing, L.J., 543

Exner, J.E., 478
Eysenck, H.J., 471

Fagot, B.I., 315
Fahey, J.L., 500, 502
Fairbanks, R.J., 135
Fairfield, M., 395
Faita, F., 43, 72
Fallowfield, L., 505
Fantz, R.L., 295
Farah, M.J., 121, 122, 179
Faraone, S.V., 543
Farquhar, J.W., 522
Farvolden, P., 231
Faulkner, P., 522
Fazio, R.H., 628
Fein, G., 288
Feingold, A., 437
Feingold, A.J., 649
Feldman, D.C., 203
Felleman, D.J., 97
Felton, K., 517
Fendrich, R., 98
Fengtstein, A., 140
Ferrari, J.R., 189
Ferster, C.B., 190
Festinger, L., 629, 632
Fibiger, H.C., 159, 239
Fiedler, K., 403, 638
Field, A.E., 646
Field, N., 364
Field, T., 109
Field, T.T.M., 296
Fields, H.L., 49
Fiester, S.J., 604
Finchman, F.D., 651
Fink, M., 602
Finkel, D., 353
Finkelhor, D., 341
Finney, J.W., 525
Fiore, M.C., 511, 512
Firth, C.L., 239
Fischer, G.W., 637
Fischhoff, B., 266
Fisher, C., 511
Fisher, D.L., 95
Fisher, J.D., 519, 520
Fisher, L., 319, 501
Fisher, L.E., 151, 155
Fisher, R.P., 229
Fisher, W.A., 519, 520
Fishman, H.C., 595
Fiske, S.T., 625
Fitzpatrick, C., 232
Fivush, R., 307
Flack, W.F., 397
Flaherty, C.F., 195
Flanagan, P., 111
Flannery, D.J., 391, 434
Flaum, M., 426
Flavell, E.R., 299, 307
Flavell, J.H., 299, 307
Flay, B., 203
Fletcher, J., 160
Flicker, L., 396
Flin, R., 266
Flor, H., 199
Flynn, J.R., 431, 432, 434, 435
Fockland, C., 71
Foley, H.J., 95, 97, 104, 105, 110, 112, 116
Folger, R., 387, 395, 484
Folk, C.L., 136
Folkman, S., 494, 498
Ford, D.E., 514
Ford, S., 505
Forgas, J.P., 255, 371, 403, 638
Forsyth, G.A., 288, 303, 305, 320
Forsyth, P.D., 288, 303, 305, 320
Foster, L., 595
Fothergill, L.A., 49
Foti, R.J., 654
Foulkes, D., 149
Fowler, G., 511
Fowles, D.C., 569
Fox, P.T., 555
Fozard, J.L., 351
Frackowiak, R.S.J., 98
Fraczek, A., 387
Frady, R.L., 389
Francis, D., 106
Frank, E., 501
Frank, L.R., 216, 217
Frederiksen, N., 307
Freedman, J.L., 202
Freedman, Z.R., 514, 515
French, D.C., 341
French, J.L., 422
Frese, M., 500
Fried, C., 635
Fried, C.B., 635
Friedman, H.S., 502
Friedman, H.W., 330, 361, 419, 450, 451, 470, 474, 481, 493
Friedman, M., 480
Friedman, M.J., 557
Friedman, S., 294
Friedrich, W.N., 232
Friend, S.M., 257
Friesen, W.V., 356, 397, 401
Frieske, D., 351
Friman, P.C., 525
Froberg, J.E., 132
Frohlich, C.B., 308
Frone, M.R., 157
Frost, J.L., 638
Frost, P.J., 655
Fry, A.F., 188, 425
Fry, W.A., 510
Fryer, A., 555
Fujita, F., 404
Fuke, T., 306
Fuligni, A.J., 320
Fulker, D.W., 430, 431
Fuller, C.A., 131, 132
Funder, D.C., 470-471
Fung, H., 334, 356
Furnham, A., 392
Fusselman, M.J., 555

Gabrielli, J., 89
Gaertner, S.L., 636, 639, 640, 641
Gaffney, G.R., 548
Gagnon, J.H., 385
Gaines, C.L., 351
Galamaga, M., 109
Galamaga, R., 109
Galanter, E., 86
Gallassi, R., 145
Galotti, K., 254
Gambetti, P., 145
Ganster, D.C., 480
Ganzach, Y., 261
Garcia, J., 176, 177
Garcia, R., 296
Gardner, B.T., 279
Gardner, H., 414
Gardner, R.A., 279
Gardner, R.M., 650
Gareau, D., 199
Garland, A.F., 552
Garland, H., 262, 263
Garmezy, N., 195
Garner, D.M., 514
Garrett, J., 394
Gati, I., 261
Gaulton, R.S., 199
Gavanski, I., 627
Gazzaniga, M.S., 62, 98
Ge, X., 341
Gebhard, P., 383
Geddes, D., 25, 387, 484
Geen, R.G., 373, 387
Geffner, R., 639
Gehring, R.E., 243
Geiselman, R.E., 229
Geller, E.S., 197, 199
Gemar, M., 588, 589, 599
Genesee, F., 277
Gentner, D., 269, 277
Gerard, 390
Gerhard, D.S., 550
Gerrard, M., 629
Gersten, M., 543
Gettys, C.F., 258
Getz, J.G., 156
Gibbons, B., 107
Gibbons, F.X., 139, 629, 635
Gibson, E., 71
Gibson, E.J., 296
Gidron, Y., 517
Gidycz, C.A., 557
Gilbert, A.N., 107
Gilbert, D.T., 621
Gilhooly, K.J., 217
Gill, J., 149
Gilligan, C.F., 310
Gilliland, M.A., 145
Gilliland, R.C., 522
Giordani, B., 73
Giovanelli, G., 294, 295
Girgus, J.S., 116, 117
Giriunas, I., 602
Gladwell, M., 380, 381, 390
Glaser, R., 500, 501, 509
Glass, D.R., 604
Gleaves, D.H., 545, 546, 547
Gleicher, F., 627
Glentz, B., 645
Glod, C., 599
Glover, G., 89
Gluck, M.A., 51
Glynn, S.M., 599
Gmeindl, L., 216, 217
Godden, D., 220
Goethals, G.R., 648
Gohm, C., 405
Going, S.B., 325
Gold, D.B., 236
Goldberg, L.R., 472
Goldenberg, R.L., 289
Goldman, M., 572
Goldmsith, H.H., 312
Goldsamt, L.A., 139
Goldschmidt, L., 289
Goleman, D., 413, 439, 441
Goodale, M.A., 65, 68
Goodman, G.S., 231, 232
Gopnik, A., 304
Gora-Maslak, G., 74
Gordon, J.S., 461
Gordon, P., 276
Gordon, W.C., 276
Gorman, J., 555
Gorski, R.A., 385
Gosse, V.F., 199
Gotlieb, I.H., 592
Gottesman, I.I., 569
Gottesman, L.I., 430
Gottfredon, L.S., 424
Gottfried, A.W., 312, 432
Gottlieb, G., 352
Grady, C.O., 68
Graff-Kaser, R., 597
Graham, B.G., 514
Graham, C.H., 93
Graham, J.W., 203, 511
Graham, K.S., 71
Grainger, B., 255
Granchrow, J.R., 295
Granrud, C.E., 296
Grant, B.F., 571
Grant, J., 306
Green, D., 395
Green, F.L., 299, 307
Green, J.D., 139, 140
Green, J.P., 152, 154
Green, L., 188
Green, R., 385, 563
Greenbaum, C.W., 548
Greenbaum, P.E., 572
Greenberg, B., 288
Greenberg, B.D., 511
Greenberg, J., 484, 622, 633
Greenberg, L.S., 583
Greenberg, R., 296
Greene, B.F., 199
Greener, S., 522
Greenwald, A.G., 89, 90
Greist-Bousquet, S., 117
Grey, E.M., 135
Griffin, D., 625, 626
Grilly, D.M., 155
Grilo, C.M., 514
Gritz, E.R., 511, 512
Groen, J., 111
Groopman, J., 339
Gross, C.G., 68

Grossman, R., 352
Grota, L.J., 180
Groth, G.E., 649
Grow, V.M., 514, 515
Gruneberg, M.M., 225
Guerin, D.W., 312
Guilford, J.P., 442
Gully, K.J., 390
Gully, S.M., 375
Gunzerath, L., 511
Gur, R., 352
Gur, R.C., 63
Gur, R.E., 352, 570
Guralnick, M.J., 432
Gurman, A.S., 591–592
Gustavson, C.R., 177
Guthrie, J.P., 132
Gwaltney, J.M., 501
Gwynne, M.I., 153

Haaga, D.A.F., 491
Haas, E.C., 135, 136
Haas, M.W., 111
Haberlandt, K., 215, 226, 239
Hagan, E., 422
Hager, J.L., 177
Haggerty, R.J., 195
Hahn, G., 203
Hahn, S., 523
Haier, R.J., 426
Hajek, P., 150
Hakstean, A.R., 116
Hale, S., 425
Hall, G., 178
Hall, J.A., 24, 506
Hall, S., 241
Hallett, M., 175
Halpern, D.F., 413, 425, 428, 431, 433
Hamburg, S., 195
Hamerman, D., 505
Hamilton, G.V., 647
Hamilton, V.L., 646
Hammer, D.H., 511
Hammond, W.R., 607
Hampson, E., 389, 479
Hanisch, K.A., 191
Hankins, W.G., 176
Hannah, S.L., 199
Hans, V.P., 646
Hansen, W.B., 203, 511
Harackiewicz, J.M., 395
Hardin, C.D., 22
Harford, T.C., 571
Harlow, H.F., 316
Harlow, M.H., 316
Harrigan, J.A., 399, 402
Harrington, R., 548
Harris, J.A., 389, 479
Harris, J.R., 334
Harris, K.M., 320
Harris, R.J., 261
Harris, S.D., 502
Harris, V.G., 319
Harrison, C.R., 523
Harrison, J.K., 203
Harrison, R.V., 500
Harsha, D.W., 325
Hart, D., 364
Hart, E.L., 564
Hartmann, E.L., 143
Harvard Center for Cancer Prevention, 514
Harvey, E., 320
Hasher, L., 352
Hashtroudi, S., 228, 231
Hass, G., 570
Hasselblad, V., 511, 512
Hastie, R., 249, 256, 266
Hatch, T., 441
Hatfield, E., 651
Haugaard, J.J., 231
Hauser, M.D., 63
Hauesmann, L.W., 387
Hawkins, J.D., 203
Hawkins, S.A., 249, 256
Hawkins, W.G., 177
Hawley, P.H., 502
Haworth, N.L., 135
Haxby, J.V., 68
Haythornthwaite, J.A., 479
Hazan, C., 315
Hazelrigg, M.D., 594, 595
Hazen, C., 313, 315
He, J., 514
Healey, S., 146
Heatherton, T., 450
Heatherton, T.F., 546, 646
Heeren, T., 496
Heffner, T.S., 466
Heilman, M.E., 623
Heindel, W., 236
Heller, W., 399
Hellerstein, D., 599
Helpern C., 77
Helweg-Larsen, M., 519
Hembree, E.A., 311
Hendrick, C., 650
Hendrick, S.S., 650
Hener, T., 106
Henggler, S.W., 595
Heninger, G.R., 550
Hennekens, C.H., 515
Hennevin, E., 144
Hennig, P., 525
Henning, K., 385
Herberman, R., 517
Herling, S., 156
Herman, G., 352
Herman, L.M., 280
Hermann, C., 199
Hernandez-Reif, M., 109
Herrera, A., 14
Herrnstein, R.J., 192, 436
Hershberger, S.L., 75, 628
Herzog, C., 230
Hettinger, L.J., 111
Hetts, J., 627
Hetzel, B., 504
Hewstone, M., 637
Hilgard, E.R., 152
Hilger, L.A., 252
Hilton, D.J., 254
Hilton, J.L., 624
Hilts, P.J., 232
Hingston, R., 496
Hinson, R.E., 179
Hirky, A.E., 572
Hirsa, A., 627
Hirshfield, D.R., 543
Hirt, E.R., 227
Ho, K., 263
Hobfoll, S.E., 520
Hobson, J.A., 149
Hodges, E.V.E., 296, 318
Hodges, J.R., 71
Hoffman, C., 397
Hoffman, H.J., 289
Hofmann, D.A., 375
Hogan, J., 471
Hogan, R., 471
Hogg, M.A., 637
Hogness, D.S., 96
Holcomb, P., 71
Holland, D., 199
Hollander, E., 555
Hollenbeck, J.R., 375
Holley, A., 107
Hollon, S.D., 599, 606
Holmes, D.S., 480
Holmes, J.G., 651, 652
Holmes, T.H., 497, 498, 499
Holmgreen, P., 319
Holt, K.W., 319
Holyoak, K.J., 43, 70, 71, 269
Holzman, A.D., 179
Homan, R.W., 63
Honey, R.C., 178
Honig, W.K., 174, 190
Honorton, C., 123
Honzik, C.H., 196
Hopkins, W.D., 280
Hoppe, R.B., 123
Hopson, J.L., 280
Hoptman, M.J., 61
Horne, J.A., 144
Horne, S., 14
Hornstein, G.A., 581
Horowitz, M., 364
Horvath, J.A., 354, 416
Horwitz, B., 68
Hostetter, A.M., 550
Houfman, L.G., 94
Houminer, D., 261
Houpt, T.A., 134, 178
House, M., 94
House, R.J., 654, 655
Housman, D.E., 550
Houston, B.K., 480
Hovland, C.I., 629
Howard, K.E., 604
Howard, K.I., 604
Howard, V.F., 289
Howe, M.L., 233
Howell, J.M., 654, 655
Hsia, Y., 93
Hu, S., 511
Hubbard, M.L., 624
Hubel, D.H., 97
Huebner, R.R., 311
Huesmann, L.R., 202, 388
Huff, C., 33
Huffman, R.K., 111
Hughes, J.R., 49
Hughes, M., 549, 554
Humbaugh, K., 394
Hummell, J.E., 118
Hunt, E., 279, 351
Hunt, E.B., 437
Hunter, R.H., 596
Hurley, K., 525
Hurvich, L.M., 97
Husband, A.J., 180
Huttenlocher, J., 303
Hyman, L.M., 402
Hymel, S., 318
Hymowitz, C., 579
Hynds, F., 123

Idelson, R.K., 506
Imada, H., 178
Imber, S.D., 604
Incesu, C., 557
Ingram, R., 139, 141
Institute of Medicine, 571
Isaacowitz, D.M., 355
Isabella, R., 314
Isbell, L.M., 649
Isen, A.M., 403, 640
Israni, T., 578
Ito, T.A., 459, 460
Ittelson, W.H., 118
Ivkovich, D., 175
Iwahashi, M., 108
Iwata, B.A., 199
Izard, C.E., 311, 397

Jackson, A.P., 520
Jackson, D.N., 389, 479
Jackson, R.L., 194
Jacobson, J., 288
Jacobson, N.S., 595, 596
Jacobson, S., 288
Jaconon, W.G., 428, 431
Jaffe, K., 652
Jahnke, J.C., 250
James, W.J., 396
Jameson, D., 97
Janicak, P., 578
Jann, M., 601
Jefferson, D.J., 110
Jencks, D., 429
Jenike, M.A., 602
Jenkins, J.G., 225
Jensen, A.R., 425, 426
Jessor, R., 342
Jewell, N., 520
Johnson, B.T., 22, 634
Johnson, E.J., 270
Johnson, J.L., 189
Johnson, M.B., 425
Johnson, M.H., 306
Johnson, M.K., 228, 231, 625
Johnson, S.T., 239
Johnson, V.E., 383
Johnson, V.S., 649
Johnson-Laird, P.N., 249, 251
Johnston, J.C., 212

Johnston, L.D., 155
Johnston, W., 112
Johnstone, B., 273
Joindes, J., 216
Joiner, T.E., Jr., 546, 551
Jones, E.E., 395
Jones, H.M., 191
Jones, N.A., 109
Jones, S., 630
Jonides, J., 216, 217
Jonides, J.J., 252
Jordan, F., 555
Josephs, R.A., 188, 450
Jou, J., 261
Judd, C.M., 638
Judge, T.A., 473, 483
Julien, R.M., 289, 570, 599
Jurcia, P.J., 351
Jurica, P.J., 351, 352, 353
Jusczyk, P.W., 295
Jussim, L., 639
Jussim, L.J., 628
Just, M.A., 95

Kaber, D.B., 111
Kaempf, G.L., 266
Kagan, J., 312, 320, 543
Kahneman, D., 259, 260, 281
Kales, A., 146
Kales, J.D., 146
Kalichman, S.C., 505
Kalivas, P.W., 49
Kallgren, C.A., 641
Kalsher, M.J., 109, 135, 249
Kameda, M., 404
Kamiloff-Smith. A., 306
Kamin, L.J., 173
Kando, J., 601
Kanfer, R., 475
Kanner, A.D., 498
Kaplan, H.I., 552, 559
Kaplan, J.R., 497, 500
Kaplowitz, S.A., 622
Karasek, R., 495
Kardia, S.L.R., 511
Karie, T., 436
Kasch, K., 599
Kattler, H., 144
Katz, S., 216
Kaufman, A.S., 425
Kaufman, N.L., 425
Kaukianainen, A., 387
Kaul, T., 591
Kavanagh, D.J., 570
Kavanagh, K., 315
Kay, D., 399, 402
Kazdin, A.E., 585
Keary, K., 232
Keefe, F.J., 491
Keith, B., 493
Keller, I.M., 628
Keller, P.A., 513
Kelley, H.H., 620
Kelly, A.B., 570
Kelly, B., 339
Kelly, D.D., 143
Kelly, J.A., 505
Kelsey, F.O., 288
Kelsey, R.M., 495
Kemeny, M.E., 502
Kemmerer, B.E., 480
Kendall-Tackett, K.A., 341
Kendler, K.S., 516, 549, 554
Kendrick, D.T., 649
Kendzierski, D., 466
Kenny, D.A., 654
Keogh, D., 339
Keon, T.O., 392
Kessler, R.C., 479, 549, 554
Ketcham, A.S., 502
Ketcham, K., 220
Kida, T., 249
Kidd, K.K., 550
Kiecolt-Glaser, J.K., 500, 501, 509
Kiesler, C.A., 629
Kiesler, S.B., 629
Kihlstrom, J.F., 152, 235
Kilham, W., 646
Kim, E.L., 638
Kimble, D.L., 519
King, M.G., 180
Kinnunen, T., 152
Kinsey, A.C., 383
Kirby, S.L., 262
Kirkcaldy, B.D., 392
Kirkpatrick, S.A., 654
Kirmeyer, S.L., 480
Kirn, C.L., 135
Kirsch, I., 106, 151, 152, 154, 177
Kivlahan, D.R., 398
Klaczynski, P.A., 333
Klag, M.J., 514
Klausner, J., 570
Klein, D., 555
Klein, G.A., 266
Klein, H.J., 375
Klein, J.G., 624
Kleinbard, J., 225
Kleitman, N., 148
Klinnert, M.D., 312
Klos, T., 98
Kluft, R.P., 559
Knapp, D.N., 364, 524
Knebel, T., 106
Knipling, R.R., 135
Kniskern, D.P., 591-592
Knowles, A., 525
Knowlton, B.J., 43, 71
Knox, S.S., 75, 628
Kobayashi, Y., 178
Koch, J., 294
Koehler, J.J., 266
Koelling, R.A., 176
Kohl, W.L., 654
Kohlberg, L., 308, 310
Kohler, I., 122
Kohn, M., 352
Kojetin, B.A., 628
Kok, G., 632
Koller, S.H., 308
Komatsu, S., 306
Koocher, G.P., 232
Koplan, J.P., 510
Kopta, S.M., 604
Koreen, A.R., 570
Kosslyn, S., 179
Kosslyn, S.M., 252
Kosterlitz, H.W., 49
Kotch, J.B., 341
Kotre, J., 345
Kounious, J., 223
Kozu, J., 14
Krafchuk, E., 312
Krakauer, J., 257
Krakoff, L.R., 517
Kral, P.A., 177
Kramer, A.F., 523
Krank, M.D., 179
Kranzler, J., 425
Krasnegor, N.A., 175
Krause, M.S., 604
Krebs, D.L., 308, 310
Kring, A.M., 471
Krosnick, J.A., 628
Krowitz, A., 296
Krupa, D.J., 175
Kubany, E.S., 592
Kübler-Ross, E., 362
Kuebli, J., 307
Kuhn, C., 109
Kuhn, J., 231
Kuhn, L., 288
Kulik, J., 234
Kullgren, G., 14
Kunda, Z., 638, 639
Kuperman, S., 548
Kurtines, W., 607
Kutas, M., 237
Kutchinsky, B., 387

Lachman, M., 346, 347
Ladavas, E., 399
Lagerspetz, K., 387
LaGreca, A.M., 557
Lahey, B.B., 564
Laird, J.D., 397
Lakshmanan, M., 256
Lam, T.W., 601
Lamb, M.E., 137
Lambert, A.J., 637
Lambert, M.J., 604
Lamke, T.A., 422
LaMotte, R.H., 104
Landis T., 237
Landis, H., 550
Landis, S.H., 513
Lando, H.A., 511, 512
Landro, L., 509
Lang, P.J., 43, 565
Lange, J.D., 382
Langer, A., 296
Langlois, J.H., 649, 650
Lanzisera, D., 199
Largen, J., 195
Largo, E., 648
Larson, R., 333
Latham, G.P., 374
Lau, M.L., 157
Laumann, E.O., 385
Laurd, J., 231
Lautenschlager, G., 351
Lavin, J., 520
Law, D.J., 437
Law, M., 511
Lawler, J., 199
Lawless, H., 109
Lawrence, R.E., 640
Layman, J., 557
Lazarus, R.S., 494, 498, 499
Leary, M.R., 373, 376, 466
Leber, W.R., 604
Lebiere, C., 216
Leconte, P., 144
LeCouteur, A., 548
Lee, J., 517
Lee, K., 306
Lee, S.Y., 331
Lee, Y.T., 622
Lefkowitz, M.M., 202
Leibowitz, M., 555
Leite, P., 588, 599
Leitenberg, H., 385, 491
Leitten, C.L., 495
Lemery, K.S., 312
Lemme, B.H., 339, 345, 346
Lennon, R.T., 422
Lentz, R.J., 585
Leonard, J.R., 483
Lepper, M., 395
Lepper, M.R., 395
Lerman, C., 511
Lerner, R.M., 74, 354
Leslie, J.C., 184
Lester, N., 502
Leuenberger, A., 256
LeVay, S., 385
Levenson, R.W., 356, 397
Leventhal, H., 630
Levine, D.M., 514
Levine, D.S., 273
Levine, M., 609
Levine, S., 506
Levinson, D., 356, 357, 359
Levinson, D.J., 345
Levinthal, C.F., 155, 159, 161
Levis, D.J., 179, 585
Levy, S.M., 517
Lewin, T., 339
Lewis, S., 505
Lewy, A.J., 131
Leyens, J.P., 621
Liang, K., 514
Liberman, A., 630
Licht, B.G., 194
Lichtenstein, P., 75, 628
Liddell, F.D.K., 134
Liden, R.C., 644
Lieberman, D.A., 173
Lieberman, J.A., 570
Liebowitz, M., 555
Lietaer, G., 583
Lin, K.M., 601
Lin, W., 180
Linden, E., 24
Lindner, M.A., 650
Lindsey, D.S., 214, 228, 231

Lindsay, J.J., 390
Lindzay, J.C., 435
Linville, P.W., 637
Lippman, M., 517
Lipshitz, R., 267
Lipsitt, L.P., 294
Litten. R.Z., 541
Little, J.K., 325
Locke, B.Z., 504
Locke, E.A., 374, 375, 654
Lockhart, R.D., 220
Locksin, B., 511
Lodge, M., 511
Loehlin, J.C., 413, 425, 428, 430, 431, 433, 435
Loftus, E.F., 220, 227, 230, 231, 232, 272
Logan, G.D., 136, 137
Logie, R.H., 217
Logothetis, D.E., 131
Logothetis, N.K., 68
Logue, A.W., 177, 188
Logue, K.R., 177
Lohman, T.G., 325
Lombardo, E., 231
Long, G.M., 350
Long, J.W., 600
Loosen, P.T., 599, 606
Lopez, S.R., 607
Lorenz, F.O., 341
Louie, T.A., 256
Louis-Dreyfus, E., 236
Love, T., 216, 217
Lubart, T.I., 413, 442, 443, 444
Lubart, T.T., 444
Lubinski, D., 430
Luborsky, L., 551, 578
Lucas, F.R., 511
Lucas, R., 404
Lucas, R.E., 404, 405
Luchins, A.S., 271
Luci, K.S., 399, 402
Lugaresi, E., 145
Lui, T.J., 633
Lutz, A., 334, 356
Lykken, D., 405
Lykken, D.T., 75, 428, 430, 431, 628
Lyman, B.J., 109
Lynch, M., 633
Lyness, K.S., 623
Lynn, A.R., 628
Lynn, R., 392, 435, 437
Lynn, S.J., 152, 154, 557
Lytton, H., 312

McAdam, V., 109
McAnally, K., 111
McArthur, L.Z., 331
McAuley, E., 523
McBean, D., 199
McBride, S.A., 192
McCabe, S.B., 592
McCall, R.B., 339
McCann, R.S., 212
McCauley, E.A., 533, 541, 545, 560, 567, 579, 598, 600
McClearn, G.E., 74, 353
McClelland, D.C., 391, 392, 424, 427
McClelland, J.L., 213
McConkey, K.M., 152, 154
McConkie, G.W., 95
McCown, W.G., 189
McCrae, R.R., 470, 478
McCully, J., 179
McDaniel, M.A., 109
McDonald, H.E., 227
McDonough, L., 303
McFadden, S.H., 312
McGill, K.L., 949
McGilley, B.M., 480
McGinnis, J.M., 514
McGonagle, K.A., 549, 554
McGowin, D.F., 239
McGue, M., 75, 428, 430, 431, 517
McGuffin, P., 430
McGuire, P.A., 509
McIntosh, D.N., 396, 397
McIsaac, H.K., 237
McKenry, P.C., 341
McKinley, R.L., 111
McLaney, A., 399, 402
McLaughlin, T.F., 289
McLaughlin-Volpe, T., 640
McLeod, J.S., 499
McMichael, A.J., 433
McMichael, T., 504
McMullen, M.N., 627
McMurray, M.B., 544
McNamara, G., 572
McNeil, B.J., 261
McWhirter, P.T., 14
Macario, A., 249
Maccoby, N., 522
MacDonald, H., 548, 626
Mackie, D.M., 403
Mackintosh, N.J., 173
Macrae, C.N., 626, 638
MacRae, P.G., 350
Maddigan, R.I., 199
Madsen, G., 180
Magai, C., 312
Mahamedi, F., 646
Maheswaran, D., 630
Maier, S.F., 194
Main, D., 511
Maisog, J.M., 68
Malandro, L.A., 440
Malgady, R.G., 607
Malley, J.E., 195
Malloy, T.E., 519, 520
Malone, J., 593
Malone, P.S., 621
Maluish, A., 517
Malvagia, C., 231
Mandel, D.R., 295
Mandler, J.M., 303
Mangela, J.A., 351, 352, 353
Mann, J.A., 640, 641
Mann, J.M., 518
Mann, L., 646
Mann, S.J., 517
Mann, T., 33
Mannheim, K., 346
Manning, M.R., 501
Mant, D., 511
Manuck, S.B., 497, 500
Manzi, J., 203
Marcia, J.E., 337
Marcus, S.E., 511
Margolin, G., 652
Marie, L.S., 516
Marin, O.S.M., 69
Mark, M.M., 256, 397
Markman, G.D., 442, 627
Markman, K.D., 627
Markus, H.M., 337
Marlatt, G.A., 398
Marr, D., 118
Marsh, D.J., 516
Marsolek, C.J., 119
Mart, W., 568
Martell, R.F., 623
Martin, C., 321, 383
Martin, C.L., 325
Martin, L., 628
Martin, L.L., 397, 633
Martin, L.R., 330, 361, 419, 481, 493
Martin, R., 217
Martin, R.L., 111
Martinez, J., 555
Martocchio, J.J., 473, 483
Martuza, R.L., 602
Maruyama, G., 629
Mary, U., 356
Maslow, A.H., 376, 463, 465
Massaquoi, S.G., 175
Masse, L.C., 543
Massman, P.S., 70
Masters, W.H., 383
Masuda, M., 498
Matarazzo, J.D., 426
Matlin, M.W., 95, 97, 104, 105, 110, 112, 116
Mattheson, P.B., 288
Maturi, R., 500
Maurer, D., 296
Maurer, M., 599
Maurer, T.J., 473
Maxwell, K., 432
Maxwell, S., 339
May, C.P., 352
Mayberry, R.I., 277
Mayer, J.D., 413, 441
Mayes, A.R., 240
Mazur, A., 74, 77
Mazur, J.E., 189
Mazzoni, G.A.L., 231
McFarland, C., 626
Mead, L.A., 514
Meador, J.K., 199
Mednick, S.A., 564
Medvec, V.H., 627
Meehan, J.W., 111
Meehl, P.E., 195
Meeman, H.P., 65, 68
Meichenbaum, D.H., 527
Meijmann, T., 134
Meister, M., 131
Mellers, B.A., 263
Mellor, S., 256
Mellors, J.W., 519
Melton, G.B., 595
Melzack, R., 104, 105, 124
Melzak, R., 124
Menck, H.R., 510
Mendenhall, M., 203
Menerdo, T., 239
Menninger, S.R., 543
Mento, A.J., 375
Menzel, R., 197
Mercier, M.A., 588, 599
Merckelbach, H., 554
Merikle, P.M., 89
Merkelbach, H., 74, 554
Metalsky, G.I., 551
Metcalfe, J., 188
Meyer, A.J., 522
Meyer, J.M., 430
Meyer, J.P., 262
Meyers, L.D., 514
Meyers, S.A., 650
Miceli, P.J., 339, 340, 480
Michael, R.T., 385
Michaels, S., 385
Mikl, J., 524
Milburn, M.A., 506
Milgram, S., 645
Millenson, J.R., 184
Miller, B.L., 43, 71
Miller, C.L., 339, 340, 480
Miller, D.T., 450, 621, 626
Miller, G.A., 216, 399
Miller, G.E., 500
Miller, J.Y., 203
Miller, M.E., 153
Miller, N., 387, 459, 460, 629
Miller, N.E., 34
Miller, R.S., 396, 652
Miller, S.M., 525
Millon, T., 538
Millon, T.A., 478
Milne, A.B., 638
Minami, H., 225
Minchin, S., 548
Minuchin, S., 595
Mischel, W., 188, 440, 450, 451, 452
Mishkin, F.S., 43, 71
Mishkin, M., 68
Misovich, S.J., 519
Mitchell, C.M., 609
Mitchell, H., 524
Mitchell, T.R., 644
Mitchison, G., 144
Moaz, B., 349
Modigliani, A., 647
Moeller, F., 390
Moffat, F.L., 502
Moffitt, K.H., 152, 154, 177
Montagna, P., 145
Montepare, J., 346, 347
Montgomery, G., 106
Moore, B.C.J., 101
Moore, R.D., 519

Moore, R.Y., 131
Moore-Ede, M.C., 131, 132, 134
Moorman, J.E., 339
Moray, N., 113
Moreland, R.L., 648, 653
Morgan, B.A., 49
Morgeson, F.P., 375
Morreale, A., 145
Morris, F., 255
Morris, H.R., 49
Morris, M.W., 621, 627
Morris, P., 225
Morrison, D.R., 493
Morrison-Beedy, D., 634
Morrongiello, B.A., 295
Morrow, K.B., 341
Morse, J.M., 105
Morse, R.M., 105
Mosak, H.H., 591
Moscovitch, M., 233, 378, 379
Motowidlo, S.J., 501
Mount, M.K., 482, 483
Mowrer, O.H., 191, 387
Moyer, A., 522
Moynihan, J.A., 180
Mozley, P., 352
Mrazek, D.A., 312
Mudar, P., 157
Mueller, U., 74
Mueser, K.T., 599
Muir, D., 306
Muir, S.L., 545
Mulkens, S.A.N., 554
Mundorf, N., 382
Munsinger, H.A., 429
Muraoka, M.Y., 592
Muris, P., 74, 554
Murphy, D.L., 511
Murphy, K.H., 65, 68
Murphy, S.T., 89
Murray, B., 199, 524
Murray, C., 436
Murray, C.L., 239
Murray, S.L., 651, 652
Murray, T., 513
Murrell, J.A., 640
Murrell, S.A., 363
Murrey, G.J., 154
Myers, C.E., 51
Myers, D.G., 404
Myers, H.F., 500
Myers, J.P., 290
Myers, N.A., 233
Myerson, J., 188

Naglieri, J.A., 425
Naito, M., 306
Nakajima, S., 178
Nakano, K., 480
Nakasaki, G., 601
Nasca, P., 524
Nathan, P.E., 569, 586
Nathans, J., 96
National Center for Health Statistics, 492, 510
National Institute for Occupational Safety and Health, Center for Disease Control and Prevention, 483
National Television Violence Study, 201
Nauful, T., 231
Neale, J.M., 471
Neale, M.A., 260, 281
Neale, M.C., 516
Nebeker, D.M., 499
Nebes, R.D., 233
Needham, A., 302
Neher, A., 462, 465
Neimeyer, R.A., 599
Neisser, U., 233, 234, 413, 425, 428, 431, 433
Nelson, C.B., 549, 554
Nelson, D.V., 106
Nelson, L.J., 450
Nelson, M.J., 422
Nelson, M.L., 511
Nelson, W.T., 111
Nesselroade, C.S., 354
Neuberg, S.L., 625
Neubert, M.J., 483
Neugarten, B.L., 345
Neuman, J.H., 25, 387, 482, 483, 484
Newcomb, A.F., 317
Newcombe, N., 303
Newport, S., 262, 263
Newton, J., 199
Nezworski, M.T., 478
NICHD Early Child Care Research Network, 320
Nickerson, R.S., 255
Nicoladis, E., 277
Nicolle, D.A., 65, 68
Nietzel, M.T., 533, 541, 545, 560, 567, 579, 598, 600
Nisan, M., 310
Nisbett, R.E., 621
Nitschke, J.B., 399
Nixon, C.L., 304, 317
Nixon, S.J., 515
Noble, J., 152, 154
Nolen-Hoeksema, S., 405
Noller, P., 337
Nomikos, M.S., 498, 499
Noonan, E., 88
Noriega, V., 502
Norman, D.A., 137
Norris, F.H., 363
North, T.C., 522
Northcraft, G.B., 260, 281
Norton, A., 339
Norton, N.C., 604-605
Novy, D.M., 106
Nowaczyk, R.H., 250
Nurius, P., 337
Nurnberger, J.K., 550
Nygren, D.J., 427
Nyhan, W.L., 74

O'Brien, C.P., 180
O'Connor, K., 199
O'Gorman, T.W., 517
O'Leary, D.S., 426
O'Leary, K.D., 569, 586, 593
O'Leary-Kelly, A.M., 375
O'Malley, P.M., 155
O'Regan, J.K., 112
O'Sullivan, C.S., 638
Oakes, P.J., 637
Oaksford, M., 255
Oei, T.P.S., 516
Oettingen, G., 622
Ogan, T.A., 311
Ogden, E.E., 258
Ogloff, J.R., 565
Ogrocki, P., 501
Ogura, S., 388
Ohbuchi, K.I., 388, 404
Oishi, S., 405
Oldfield, S.R., 111
Oleson, K.C., 638, 639
Oliver-Rodriguez, J.C., 649
Ollove, M., 551, 578
Olson, H.C., 289
Olson, J.M., 636
Olsson, P.A., 590
Oltmanns, T.F., 568
Olweus, D., 296
Ophir, I., 177
Opton, E.M., 498, 499
Orasanu, J., 266
Orlinsky, D.E., 604
Oscar-Berman, M., 515
Osipow, S.H., 337
Osterman, K., 387
Osterling, J., 548
Oswald, A.J., 405
Otis, A.S., 422
Ottati, V.C., 649
Oulette-Kobasa, S.C., 497
Owen, M.J., 430
Ozmen, E., 557

Packard, J.S., 501
Padian, N.S., 520
Pagani-Kurtzi, L., 543
Page, J.B., 160
Page, M.M., 376
Paker, M., 557
Palace, E.M., 199
Paller, K.A., 237
Palmiter, R.D., 516
Pang, K., 621
Pani, J., 252
Pani, J.R., 257
Papp, L., 555
Park, B., 638
Park, D.C., 351
Parker, G., 550
Parkin, A.J., 352
Parloff, M.B., 604
Passman, R.H., 317
Pastor, D.L., 315
Pasupathi, M., 356
Patel, A., 71
Patrick, C.J., 43, 565
Patrick, L., 153
Patterson, F., 279
Pauker, S.G., 261
Paul, B.Y., 459, 460
Paul, G.L., 585
Paul, R., 515
Paulhus, D.L., 466
Pauls, D.L., 550
Pauls, J., 68
Paxton, S.J., 545
Peake, P.K., 440
Pearce, J.M., 174
Pearlson, G.D., 570
Pedersen, N.L., 516
Pederson, J.L., 353
Pelias, M.Z., 430
Pellegrino, J.W., 437
Pelletier, K.R., 521
Peniston, E.G., 199
Penney, J.B., 73
Pennington, N., 266
Peretz, I., 43, 72
Perez-fort, R., 180
Perkins, D.N., 443
Perkins, D.V., 609
Perlini, A.H., 153
Perloff, R., 413, 425, 428, 431, 433
Perry, D.G., 318
Peterson, A.C., 332
Peterson, C., 548
Peterson, C.C., 302
Peterson, S.E., 212
Petrelli, M., 256
Pettigrew, T.E., 639, 640
Petty, R.E., 63, 630, 631
Pfaffman, C., 107
Pham, L.B., 252
Phillips, A.G., 159, 239
Phillips, B.U., 527
Phillips, D.P., 101
Phillips, J.M., 375
Phillips, K., 15
Phillips, M., 515
Piaget, J., 299
Pickering, R., 571
Pickering, T.L., 397
Pierce, C.A., 649
Pierce, H.R., 473
Pierce, P.F., 266
Pierce, W.D., 191, 192
Pietrini, P., 68
Pietromonaco, P.R., 652
Pihl, R.O., 157, 543
Pilkonis, P., 588
Pilkonis, P.A., 551, 604
Pillard, R.C., 386
Pilloff, D., 138
Pilszka, S., 564
Pinel, J.P.J., 55, 73
Pinker, S., 15, 276
Pinsof, W.M., 591-592
Pisoni, D.B., 295
Pittman, T.S., 458
Pivik, J., 106
Plante, T., 523
Plante, T.G., 523
Pliner, V., 288

Plomin, R., 74, 312, 353, 428, 429, 430, 431, 433
Podsakoff, P.M., 654
Poggio, T., 68
Pogue-Geile, M.F., 514
Poland, R., 601
Pollatsek, A., 95
Pollock, V., 564
Polson, P.G., 224
Pomerleau, O.F., 511, 513
Pomeroy, W., 383
Poon, L.W., 253, 351
Pope, A.W., 341, 342
Popenoe, D., 592
Porter, L.S., 502
Porter, M., 599
Porter, R.H., 295
Posluszny, D.M., 491
Posner, M.I., 212, 216
Potasova, A., 131
Pozo, C., 502
Pratkanis, A.R., 90
Pratto, F., 76
Prescott, C.A., 516
Preston, M., 645
Price, D.L., 49
Price, L.H., 550
Priester, J.R., 628, 630
Prinstein, M.J., 557
Prochaska, J.O., 522
Pronin, E., 522
Pruitt, J.S., 266
Pryor, J.B., 89
Psotka, L., 225
Ptacek, J.T., 502
Puccetti, M.C., 497
Pyszcynski, T., 622

Quas, J.A., 231
Quinlan, D.M., 588
Quintanar, L.R., 63
Quitkin, F.M., 588, 599

Raajimakers, J.G., 211
Rabin, B.S., 497, 500, 501
Rabin, M.D., 108
Rachlin, H., 188
Racicot, C.L., 65, 68
Radefeld, P.A., 645
Radke-Yarrow, M., 313
Radosevich, D.J., 375
Rahav, G., 394
Rahe, R.H., 497, 499
Raichle, M.E., 555
Raine, A., 543, 564
Rajaram, S., 223, 378, 379
Ramey, C.T., 421, 432
Ramey, S.L., 421, 432
Ramirez-Amaya, V., 180
Randall, C.L., 289
Rankin, N.O., 498, 499
Raphael, B., 339
Rapson, R.L., 651
Ratner, J., 71
Rauschecker, J.P., 122
Raven, J.C., 434
Raymond, P., 89
Rayner, K., 95
Raynor, J.O., 391
Raz, T., 106
Rea, M.S., 649
Read, J.D., 214
Read, P., 592
Rechtschaffen, A., 145
Redd, W.H., 178, 181
Reder, I.M., 461
Reder, L.M., 216
Redne, R., 609
Reed, S.B., 152, 154, 177
Reed, T.E., 426
Regard, M., 237
Reichle, E.D., 95
Reid, L.D., 159
Reiman, E.M., 555
Reimold, C., 56
Reinecke, J., 519
Reisenzein, R., 397
Rellinger, E.R., 270
Remington, R.W., 136, 212
Remschmidt, H., 568
Reno, R.R., 525, 641
Rensberger, B., 273
Rensink, R.A., 112
Rentsch, J.R., 466
Reppert, S.M., 131
Repucci, N.D., 231
Requin, J., 43, 72
Rescorla, R.A., 178, 197
Resnick, S., 312, 315, 352
Reyna, V.F., 228, 231
Reynolds, B., 524
Reynolds, C.R., 232
Reynolds, K.D., 525
Reznick, J.S., 543
Rhodewalt, F., 395
Rhue, J.W., 152
Riad, J.K., 389
Ricci-Bitti, P.E., 399
Rice, F.P., 330
Rice, J., 430
Richard, D.C., 592
Richards, D.G., 280
Richardson, D., 201, 338, 386, 390
Richardson, G., 289
Richardson, J.T.E., 108
Richer, S.D., 637
Richman, D.D., 519
Ridderinkhof, K.R., 254
Riddlesberger, M.M., 231
Riess, M., 633
Riesser-Danner, L.A., 649
Riggins v. Nevada, 611
Rio, A.T., 607
Riordan, K., 312, 315
Rissman, E.F., 382
Ritov, I., 263
Rivkin, I.D., 252
Robbin, A.L., 595
Robbins, S.J., 180
Roberts, A.R., 331, 649
Roberts, B.W., 471
Roberts, M., 185
Roberts, R.D., 441
Roberts, R.J., 433
Robertson, E.F., 433
Robin, N., 70
Robins, L.N., 552
Robinson, D.H., 199
Robinson, D.S., 502
Robinson, L.A., 599
Rochart, F., 647
Rodin, J., 380, 381, 495, 523
Roese, N.J., 33, 627
Rogers, C.R., 463, 582
Rogers, R.J., 621, 622
Roggman, L.A., 649, 650
Rogler, L.H., 590, 607
Rogoff, B., 332
Romani, C., 217
Romski, M.A., 280
Ropp, S.A., 640
Rosch, E.H., 250
Rosen, K.S., 315
Rosenbaum, J.F., 543
Rosenberg, E.L., 401
Rosenberg, S.D., 557
Rosenblith, J.F., 288
Rosenfeld, J., 95
Rosenfield, D., 395
Rosenman, R.H., 480, 517
Rosenstock, I.M., 504
Rosenthal, J., 599
Rosenthal, R., 399, 402
Roskos-Ewoldsen, D.R., 628
Rosovsky, H., 516
Ross, B.M., 108
Ross, D., 200
Ross, E.D., 63
Ross, J., 262, 263
Ross, L., 621
Ross, L.L., 199
Ross, M., 621, 625
Ross, S., 200
Rossman, E., 216
Roter, D.L., 506
Rothbaum, F., 315
Rothenberg, R., 524
Rothenberg, R.B., 510
Rothland, J.C., 73
Rothman, A.J., 22, 262, 522
Rotter, J.B., 472, 473
Rotton, J., 388
Rotundo, M., 475
Rowe, D.C., 391, 434
Rowland, D.L., 561
Rozin, P., 378, 379, 581
Rubin, D.C., 233
Rubin, J.Z., 262, 281
Ruble, D.N., 227, 321, 322
Rudd, M.D., 546
Rudy T.E., 106, 124
Rumelhart, D.E., 213
Rush, A.J., 551
Rushton, J.P., 72, 96, 389, 436, 479
Rusiniak, K., 177
Rusiniak, K.W., 176, 177
Russell, D.W., 629
Russell, J.A., 396, 399, 401, 403
Russell, M., 157
Rust, M.C., 640
Rusting, C.L., 351, 352, 353, 405
Rutter, M., 195, 430, 548, 552
Ryan, C.N., 638
Ryan, J.B., 94
Ryan, R.M., 395, 514, 515
Rybacki, J.J., 600
Ryckman, R.M., 650

Saarni, C., 312
Sabol, S.Z., 511
Sachs, J.J., 319
Sack, R.I., 131
Sackhein, H.A., 63
Sadalla, E.K., 649
Sadock, B.J., 552, 559
Saffran, E.M., 69
Sahin, D., 557
Saks, M.J., 122, 647
Salas, E., 266
Salgado, J.F., 482
Salo, A.L., 289
Salovey, P., 139, 262, 413, 441, 495, 522
Saltzberg, J.A., 139
Sameroff, A.J., 312, 315
Sampson, H.H., 49
Sampson, L.F., 288
Sampson, P.D., 288, 289
Samstag, L.W., 599
Sanderson, C.A., 405
Sanislow, C.A. III, 551
Sanna, L.J., 627
Sansavini, A., 294, 295
Santisteban, D.A., 607
Sargent, C., 105
Sattely-Miller, E.A., 514
Saucier, G., 472
Saulnier, J.L., 289
Savage-Rumbaugh, S., 280
Savitsky, K., 627
Saxby, E., 199
Scassellati, B., 272
Schab, F.R., 108
Schachter, D.L., 235
Schachter, S., 397, 403
Schaefer, C., 498
Schaie, K.W., 352, 353
Schanberg, S., 109
Schauabroeck, J., 480
Scheier, M.F., 139, 502
Schellenbach, C., 339
Scher, S.J., 634
Schickedanz, D.I., 288, 303, 305, 320
Schickedanz, J.A., 288, 303, 305, 320
Schiffman, H.R., 95, 110, 117, 121
Schiffman, S.E., 514
Schiffman, S.S., 514
Schiller, M., 312, 315
Schiller, P.H., 98
Schlenker, B.R., 633
Schmidt, J., 136
Schmidt, N.B., 546

Schmitt, B., 279
Schmitt, D.P., 383, 384, 651
Schmmidt, P., 519
Schnapp, W., 390
Schneider, F., 555
Schneider, W., 137
Schnider, A., 237
Schnurr, P., 557
Schor, E.L., 506
Schotte, D., 199
Schreiber, F.R., 558
Schroots, J.J.F., 346
Schroth, H.A., 260
Schugens, M.M., 56, 175
Schul, Y., 261
Schulkind, M.D., 233
Schulman, P., 551, 578
Schulz, E., 568
Schulze, C., 436
Schunn, C.D., 269
Schustack, M.W., 450, 451, 470, 474
Schutz, H.K., 545
Schwartz, A., 263
Schwartz, J.E., 330, 361, 419, 481, 493
Schwartz, M.F., 69
Schwartz, P., 288
Schwarzwald, J., 639
Schweinberger, S.R., 98
Schweitzer, K.J., 382
Scott, J.P., 387
Seabrook, J., 195
Searle, J., 273
Sears, R.R., 387
Sedikides, C., 139, 140, 466
Seese, N., 430
Segal, N.L., 73, 430, 628
Segal, Z.V., 588, 589, 599
Segaln, N.L., 628
Segar, C., 252
Segerstrom, S.C., 502
Seifer, R., 312, 315
Sekuler, R., 116, 118
Seligman, M.E.P., 177, 194, 550, 551, 578, 603, 604, 605, 622
Selye, H., 495
Serafica, F.C., 337
Sevcik, R.A., 280
Shackelford, T.K., 387
Shafir, E., 261
Shah, P.P., 260
Shallice, T., 137
Shamir, B., 655
Shanab, M.E., 195
Shanab, N.E., 646
Shanahan, M., 341
Shane, S., 442
Shanteau, J., 261
Shaper, A.G., 515
Sharma, A., 517
Sharma, R., 578
Sharp, M.J., 156
Sharpe, D., 33
Shaver, P.R., 313, 315
Shaw, B.F., 551
Shea, T., 604
Shelton, R.C., 599, 606
Shepherd, J.B., 520
Sher, K.J., 564
Sherman, D.A., 256, 638
Sherman, S.J., 625
Sherman, S.L., 430
Sherrick, C.E., 104
Sherrod, L., 195
Shettleworth, S.J., 177
Shiboski, S., 520
Shields, P.G., 511
Shiffin, R.M., 211
Shiffrin, R.M., 137, 211, 217
Shimamura, A.P., 351, 352, 353
Shipman, K., 312
Shoda, Y., 440, 451, 452, 525
Shooenbaum, E., 288
Shulman, C., 548
Shum, M.S., 234
Sicard, G., 107
Siciliano, C., 256
Siegal, M., 302, 548
Siegel, S., 179, 180
Siegler, R.S., 299
Siegman, A.W., 397
Sigman, M., 433
Sigvardsson, S., 157
Silagy, C., 511
Silva, C.E., 151
Silver, B., 601
Silverman, I., 15, 17, 437
Silverman, W.K., 557
Sim, D.L.H., 627
Simion, F., 121, 295, 313
Simmons, R.G., 332
Simon, L., 633
Simon, M.C., 623
Simonson, I., 263
Simonton, D.K., 354, 443
Simpson, E., 310
Sinclair, R.C., 397
Singer, C.M., 131
Singer, J.E., 397, 403
Singer, R., 630
Singh, D., 649
Singh, T., 288
Siquelande, E.R., 294
Sirota, L.A., 511
Sivan, A.B., 232
Skarlicki, D.P., 484
Skeels, H.M., 432
Skinner, B.F., 190, 193, 197, 472
Skoner, D.P., 501
Skowronski, J.J., 466
Slaby, A.E., 504
Slaven, G., 266
Slob, A.K., 561
Slobin, D.I., 278
Sloboda, B.A., 483
Slohower, J., 380
Smart, L., 502
Smeaton, G., 648
Smith, A.D., 351
Smith, B., 249
Smith, C.P., 391
Smith, D.A., 471
Smith, E.E., 216, 217
Smith, G.T., 572
Smith, H.L., 404, 405
Smith, J.F., 249
Smith, L.A., 595
Smith, P.K., 463
Smith, R.E., 502
Smith, S.M., 220, 443
Smith, T.W., 49
Sneed, C.D., 471
Snidman, N., 312, 320, 543
Snowden, L.R., 607
Snyder, S., 201
Soldatos, C.R., 146
Solomon, R.L., 398
Solomon, S., 622
Sommer, W., 98
Sommers, K., 339
Sorell, G.T., 341
Spangenberg, E.R., 90
Spangler, W.D., 655
Spanis, C.W., 240
Spanos, N.P., 152, 153
Spearman, C.E., 414
Specter, M., 75
Speicher, C.E., 501
Speizer, F.E., 289
Spellman, B.A., 226
Speltz, M.L., 533, 541, 545, 560, 567, 579, 598, 600
Spence, A.P., 350
Spence, S.H., 199
Spencer, L.M., Jr., 426
Spencer, R.E., 195
Spencer, S.J., 633
Spencer, S.M., 426
Sperry, R.W., 62
Spilka, B., 362
Spirduso, W.W., 350
Sprecher, S., 649
Springer, S.P., 63
Spuhle, J.N., 435
Squire, L.R., 25, 70, 175, 240
Srinivasan, S.R., 325
Sroufe, L.A., 311
Srull, T.K., 227, 624
Stack, A.D., 445
Stacy, A.W., 203
Staddon, J.E.R., 190, 193
Stangor, C., 227
Stankov, L., 441
Stanley, J., 437
Stanovich, K.E., 332
Staw, B.M., 262, 263
Steele, C.M., 188, 434, 450, 633
Steers, R., 654
Steers, R.M., 501
Steffen, V.J., 525
Stein, D.M., 604
Stein, J., 555
Stein, Z.A., 288
Steiner, J.E., 295
Steinhilber, A., 141
Steinmetz, J.E., 175
Stejskal, W.J., 478
Stellar, E., 378
Sternberg, R.J., 354, 413, 415, 416, 425, 428, 431, 433, 436, 443, 444, 650
Stevens, S.Y., 500
Stewart, A.J., 195, 358
Stewart, G.L., 483
Stewart, K., 266
Stewart, M.W., 588, 599
Stice, E., 341
Stinson, C., 364
Stipp, D., 279
Stitzer, M.L., 511, 512
Stoltzfus, E.R., 352
Stone, A.A., 479, 502
Stone, J., 635
Storms, M.D., 385
Story, M., 522
Stotsky, S.M., 604
Stough, C., 425
Stout, J.C., 501
Strack, F., 89
Strathman, A., 627
Strathman, A.J., 630
Strauss, K.E., 177
Strean, H.S., 581
Streissgarth, A.P., 288, 289
Streissguth, A.P., 289
Strickland, B.R., 549-550
Strickland, O.J., 655
Striepe, M., 646
Stroessner, S.J., 403
Struckman-Johnson, C.J., 522
Struckman-Johnson, D.L., 522
Strunin, L., 496
Suadk, J.R., 645
Suh, E., 404, 405, 406
Suh, E.M., 404, 405
Suh, M.E., 337
Sullivan, M.J.L., 106
Suls, J.M., 271
Sulzman, F.M., 131, 132
Super, C.M., 294
Sussex, J.N., 550
Sussman, S., 203
Sutton, J., 463
Swayze, V., II, 426
Sweeney, J., 570
Swets, J.A., 88
Sykes, R.N., 225
Symons, L.A., 306
Syvalahti, E.K.G., 570
Szapocznik, J., 607
Szkrybalo, J., 321, 322
Szumowski, E.K., 543

Tabossi, P., 249, 251
Takahashi, T., 554
Tanaka, J.N., 121, 122
Tanaka, K., 68
Tang, J.L., 511
Tangney, J.P., 396
Tanifuji, M., 68
Tanouye, E., 570
Tarantola, D.J.M., 518
Tarasoff v. Regents of the University of California, 611
Tardif, T., 277

Taren, P., 152, 154, 177
Tarter, V.C., 295
Tasai, W., 288
Tasdemir, O., 557
Taylor, R.L., 342
Taylor, S.E., 252, 419, 494, 501, 502, 505
Taylor, S.P., 390
Teicher, M.H., 599
Teichman, M., 394
Tellegen, A., 75, 405, 430
Tellgen, A., 628
Tenbrunsel, A.E., 260
Tennen, H., 194
Terborg, J., Jr., 654
Terman, L.M., 419
Terrace, H.S., 280
Terry, R.D., 352
Tesluk, P., 484
Tesser, A., 628, 633
Teyler, T.J., 240
Thagard, P., 269
Theorell, T., 495
Thiele, T.E., 516
Thigpen, C.H., 558
Thoma, S.J., 310
Thomas, A., 312
Thomas, C.R., 43, 71
Thomas, D., 96
Thomas, J.L., 350, 352, 362, 546
Thomas, M.H., 202
Thomas, P., 623
Thomas, P.A., 288
Thomley, J., 109
Thompson, D.E., 623
Thompson, H.B., 203
Thompson, L.A., 430
Thompson, R.F., 175, 240
Thordsen, M.L., 266
Thorndike, R.L., 422
Thornton, B., 650
Thorsen, C.J., 473, 483
Thurstone, E.L., 414
Tice, D.M., 189, 190
Tiernari, P., 569
Tiffany, S.T., 157
Tisserand, R.B., 108
Titcomb, A., 228
Toby, O., 199
Tockerman, Y.R., 650
Toglia, M.P., 243
Tolman, E.C., 196
Tomaka, J., 495
Tomlinson-Keasey, C., 330, 361, 419, 481, 493
Tongs, S.L., 433
Topf, M.D., 199
Topka, H., 175
Toro, P.A., 609
Torrance, E.P., 443
Trandel, D., 399
Tranel, D., 71
Trapnell, P.D., 139
Treffinger, D.J., 267
Tremblay, R.E., 543
Triandis, H.C., 621
Triggs, T.J., 135
Trillin, C., 187
Tronick, E.Z., 311
Trost, M.R., 649
Trott, G.E., 568
Troughton, E., 517
True, W.R., 160
Trull, T.J., 564
Tsai, L.Y., 548
Tucker, J.S., 330, 361, 419, 481, 493, 502
Tulving, E., 220, 223, 225
Turban, D.B., 392
Turk, D.C., 106, 124
Turkheimer, E., 121, 122
Turner, J.C., 637
Turner, T.M., 341
Tversky, A., 259, 260, 261, 281
Tyler, R.B., 638
Tyler, T.R., 259
Tynes, S., 602

Uchino, B.N., 500
Udry, J.R., 77
Ukeritis, M.D., 427
Umilta, C., 121, 399
UNAIDS, 518, 519, 520
Unger, R.K., 322
Ungerleider, L.G., 68, 240
United States Department of Health and Human Services, 350, 511
United States Senate Special Committee on Aging, 350
Urban, M.J., 90
Urberg, K.A., 334
Urbina, S., 413, 425, 428, 431, 433
Urcuioli, P.J., 174
Usher, J.A., 233
Usher, J.M., 111

Vaccaro, D., 572
Vaid, J., 443
Vakil, E., 523
Valenz, E., 121
Valls-Sole, J., 175
Valone, K., 629
Van den Hout, M.A., 74, 554
Van der Meer, O., 134
Van der Molen, M.W., 254
Van Dormolen, M., 134
Van Essen, D.C., 97
Van Houten, R., 199
Van Mechelan, I., 451
Vandello, U.S., 641
Vandewater, E.A., 358
VanGuren, J., 319
Vanman, E.J., 459, 460
VanSteelandt, K., 451
Vazsonyi, A.T., 391, 434
Vecchio, R.P., 653, 654
Veccia, E.M., 24
Vecra, S., 306
Velicer, W.F., 522
Vendemia, J.M., 106
Venebles, P.H., 543, 564
Venkataraman, S., 442
Vernberg, E.M., 557
Vernon, P.A., 425, 426
Vimpahni, G.V., 433
Vitaro, F., 296, 318, 543
Vivian, D., 593
Volpe, J.J., 289
von Hippel, W., 624
Von Senden, M., 121
Vredenburgh, A.G., 249, 499, 511
Vygotsky, L.S., 304

Wagenaar, W.A., 232
Wagner, A., 89
Wagner, A.R., 178
Wagner, E., 313
Wagner, R.K., 354, 416
Wald, N., 511
Walden, T.A., 311
Walder, L.O., 202
Waldman, I., 430
Walk, R.D., 296
Walker, J., 306
Walker, L.J., 310
Walker, L.W., 14
Wallace, B., 132
Wallace, C.J., 597
Wallace, R.K., 151, 155
Wallace-Broscious, A., 337
Waller, N.G., 628
Wallin, J.A., 375, 376
Walsh, S., 382
Walster, E., 629
Walter, B.M., 352
Walton, G.E., 296
Waltz, J.A., 43, 71
Wan, K.C., 637
Wanberg, C.R., 475
Wang, G., 68
Wang, J.S., 135
Wang, X.T., 261
Wannamethee, S.G., 515
Ward, L.M., 86, 93, 96, 97, 116
Ward, T.S., 443
Wark, G.R., 310
Warnke, A., 568
Warren, S., 290
Warwick, Z.S., 514
Wasner, D., 597
Waters, E., 311
Watkins, J.T., 604
Watkins, M.J., 220
Watson, A.C., 304, 317
Watson, J.D.G., 98
Watson, M., 117
Watson, T.S., 197, 198
Wayne, S.J., 644
Wearing, D., 238
Weathersby, R.T., 289
Webb, J.U., 597
Webb, W., 142, 144
Weber, L.S., 325
Wechsler, H., 506
Weekes, J.R., 152
Wegner, D.M., 137, 138, 236
Wehner, R., 197
Weigel, R.H., 638
Weinberger, J.L., 450
Weiner, B., 374
Weinger, M.B., 249
Weinstein, N.D., 511
Weintraub, J.K., 502
Weisberg, P., 317
Weisberg, R., 271
Weisenberg, M., 105, 106, 569
Weiskrantz, L., 98
Weiss, H.M., 405, 655
Weiss, W., 629
Weist, M.D., 525
Wells, G.L., 229
Welsh, D.K., 131
Wen, S.W., 289
Werker, J.F., 277
Werkhoven, P.J., 111
Werner, E.E., 342, 343
Werner, L.A., 295
Wertheim, E.H., 545
Werts, M.G., 204
Wessinger, C.M., 98
West, S.G., 525
Wetherell, M.S., 637
Wetter, D.W., 511, 512
Wetzler, S.E., 233
Whelton, P.K., 514
Whipple, J., 154
Whitaker, D.J., 466
White, C.S., 232
White, J.M., 405
White, R.K., 156, 637
Whitehead, B.D., 592
Whitla, D.A., 426
Whitman, T.L., 339, 340, 480
WHO (World Health Organization), 538
Whorf, B.L., 278
Whyte, G., 262
Wickless, C., 152, 154, 177
Widom, C.S., 202
Wiegand, A.W., 635
Wielkiewicz, R.M., 419
Wierwille, W.W., 135
Wiesel, T.N., 97
Wigg, N.R., 433
Wilcoxon, H.C., 177
Wilder , D.A., 639
Wiley, J.A., 493
Wilhelm, K., 550
Willham, C.F., 256
Williams, B.F., 289
Williams, D.A., 491
Williams, D.E., 376
Williams, D.M., 253
Williams, D.P., 325
Williams, G.C., 514, 515
Williams, I.M., 232
Williams, J.M.G., 255
Williams, K.B., 645
Williams, K.J., 249
Williams, L.M., 341
Williams, M., 543
Williams, S., 588, 589, 599
Williams, S.S., 519, 520
Williams, W., 432
Williams, W.M., 354, 416

Williamson, D.A., 545, 546, 547
Willis, S.L., 354
Willis, W.D., 104
Wills, T.A., 572
Wilson, A., 304, 317
Wilson, B.A., 238
Wilson, G.T., 569, 586
Wilson, K.D., 121, 122
Winchester, D.P., 510
Wincze, J.P., 382
Winer, R.A., 179
Winett, R.A., 199, 493, 522, 523
Wingart, D.L., 330, 361, 419, 481, 493
Wingo, P.A., 513
Winkvist, A., 14
Winn, P., 57, 373, 378
Winokur, G., 550
Winslow, M.P., 635
Winston, R., 599
Winter, D.G., 391
Winter, J.B., 145
Wise, R.A., 156
Wise, S.P., 65
Wisniewski, H.M., 352
Witchen, H-U., 549, 554
Witelson, S., 386
Witheridge, T.C., 597
Witmer, B.G., 111
Witte, E., 658
Witty, T., 199
Woike, B.A., 402
Wolery, M., 204
Wolf, S., 266
Wolfe, B.M., 390
Wolpert, E.A., 148
Wolsic, B., 404
Wolz, J.P., 280
Wong, E.C., 216, 217
Wong, F.Y., 201
Wong, S., 565
Wood, J.M., 478
Wood, J.V., 139
Wood, R.A., 375
Wood, W., 201, 322
Woodcock, R.W., 425
Woodruff-Pak, D.S., 175
Woodward, C.K., 525
Woody, E.Z., 152
Wooley, S.C., 514
World Cancer Research Fund, 514
Woycke, J., 655
Wreggit, S.S., 135
Wright, P.M., 375
Wright, R.W., 107
Wright, S.C., 640
Wrightsman, L.S., 358
Wu, C.H., 331, 649
Wyer, R.S., Jr., 227, 624
Wynn, V., 217
Wysocki, C.J., 107

Yahya, K.A., 646
Yankner, J., 239
Yanowitch, P., 599
Yeager, K., 517
Yik, M.S.M., 466
Yirmiya, N., 548
Yonas, A., 296
Yonkers, K., 601
Yorges, S.L., 655
Young, A.M., 156
Young, M.J., 403
Yuhn, W.T.C., 426
Yung, B., 607
Yzerbyt, V., 621

Zaccaro, S.J., 654
Zahn-Waxler, C., 313
Zajonc, R.B., 89, 396, 397, 648
Zamansky, T., 152
Zanna, M.P., 636
Zatzick, D.F., 105
Zebrowitz, L.A., 331, 649
Zebrowski, L.A., 471
Zee, D., 73
Zeki, S., 97, 98
Zeman, J., 312
Zhang, S., 279
Zhao, S., 549, 554
Zhou, H., 257
Zigler, E., 552
Zill, N., 493
Zillman, D., 382, 404, 440
Zimmerman, R., 352
Zinberg, R.E., 553
Zola, D., 95
Zucco, G.M., 108
Zuckerman, M., 374, 394, 450, 453, 470, 480, 481
Zuroff, D.C., 551, 588
Zwahr, M., 351
Zwick, W., 382

# Subject Index


Ablation, experimental, 65, 65*f*
Abreaction, 580
Absolute threshold, 87
Absorption, hypnotizability and, 151
Abstract-category subsystem, 119
Acceptance, of terminal illness, 362
Accommodation, 299, 299*f*
Accuracy, scientific method and, 20
Acetylcholine
effects of, 48–49, 48*f*
location of, 48*f*
memory and, 239
Achievement motivation
definition of, 390–392
individual differences in, 391–392
measuring, 391, 391*f*
societal effects of, 392–393, 393*f*
Achievement tests, 418, 419
Acoustic trauma, 102–103
Acquaintance, in reducing prejudice, 639
Acquired immune deficiency syndrome (AIDS)
distribution of, 518–519, 518*f*
drug therapy for, 519
health beliefs and, 504–505
health-promotion messages, 522, 523*f*
prevention of, 519–520, 519*f*
transmission of, 288, 519, 520
in women, 520
Acquisition
biological constraints/characteristics, 175–178, 176*f*
in classical conditioning, 172–172
Action potential, 46, 46*f*
Activating events, 587
Activation effects, 381
Active control processes, of memory systems, 212
Active touch, 104
Acuity, 94
Acupuncture, 124
ADHD (attention-deficit/hyperactivity disorder), 544
Adler, Alfred, 462–463, 581
Adolescence. *See also* Adolescents
cognitive development during, 332–333
definition of, 330
effects of parenting styles on, 333–334, 334*f*
emotional development during, 333–334
growth spurt during, 292
physical development during, 330–332, 331*f*, 332*f*
social development during, 334–337, 335*f*, 336*t*, 337*f*
Adolescents
alcohol abuse/dependence, 571–572
drug usage of, 156*f*
friendships and, 334–335, 335*f*
personality of, 341, 342*f*
pregnancy and, 339–340
resilient, 342–343, 343*f*
at risk, 338–343, 338*f*
suicide and, 552–553
Adoption studies
of intelligence, 429–430, 429*f*
purpose of, 74–75
Adrenal glands, 54
Adrenaline (epinephrine), 53, 132
Adulthood
cognitive change during, 351–365, 353*f*, 354*f*
emotional development during, 356–359, 357*f*, 358*f*
physical change during, 347–351, 348*f*
social development during, 355–359, 355*f*, 357*f*, 358*f*
stages of, 356–357, 357*f*
Advertising
antismoking, 512–513, 513*f*
health-promotion messages, 521–522, 523*f*
persuasion and, 629
Aerial perspective, 120
Affect
cognition influence on, 403–404
influence on cognition, 403
Affective states
counterfactual thinking and, 626–627, 627*f*
influence on cognition, 403
interpersonal attraction and, 648–649
self-awareness and, 139
Afferent nerve fibers, 50
Affiliation, 405
Affiliation motivation, 391
Ageism, 345
Age-related changes
event-related brain potentials, 253–254, 253*f*
physical, 347–351, 348*f*
in reaction time, 253
Aggreeableness, 470
Aggression
"Bobo doll" experiments, 200
brain dysfunction and, 57–58
environmental factors, 388
frustration and, 387, 387*f*
hormonal factors, 388–389
innate *vs.* learned, 386–387
observational learning and, 201–202, 202*f*
origins of, 564
social factors and, 387–388
study of, methods for, 389–390, 389*f*
testosterone levels and, 43
workplace
personality and, 483–484, 483*f*
survey on, 25–26, 26*f*
Aggression machine, 389–390, 389*f*
Aggressive coping style, 463
Aggressive motivation, 386–390, 386*f*, 387*f*, 389*f*
Aging
creativity and, 354–355, 354*f*
emotions and, 356
intelligence and, 352–354, 353*f*
memory and, 351–352
primary, 350
secondary, 350
successful, 349, 360–361
theories of, 359–360
Agonists, 49, 50*t*
Agoraphobia, 554–555
Agranulocytosis, 599
Agreeableness, 470
AIDS. *See* Acquired immune deficiency syndrome
Alarm stage, of general adaptation syndrome, 495
Alcohol abuse/dependence
binge drinking, 158
concordance rates, 516–517, 516*t*
genetic factors in, 157–158, 158*f*
longevity and, 361
parental, 341
risks of, 571–572, 572*f*
Alcohol consumption
binge-type, 158
genetic factors in, 516–517, 516*f*
health benefits of, 515
maternal, prenatal influences of, 289, 289*f*
negative effects of, 515–516
Alcoholism. *See* Alcohol abuse/dependence
Alertness, fragrances for, 109
Algorithm, 269
"All-nighter" study method, 36*f*
"All-or-nothing" response, 46
Alogia, 568
Alpha waves, 142, 143
Alternative personalities (alters), 558
Alzheimer's disease, 49, 239, 239*f*
American Sign Language (ASL), 279
Amitriptyline (Elavil), 599
Amnesia, 237, 238*f*, 239, 239*f*
Amotivational syndrome, 161
Amphetamines, 158, 382
Amplitude, of sound waves, 99
Amygdala, 57, 175, 399
Amyloid beta protein, 239
Analogy, 269
Anal stage, 457
Anasazi, 637
Anchoring-and-adjustment heuristic, 260
Anchors, decision-making, 281
Androstenedione, 161–162
Anger
blood pressure and, 517
expressions, of infants, 311
management, 445
at terminal illness, 362
Angular velocity, 94
Anima, 462
Animals
cognitive processes in learning and, 196–197, 196*f*
language and, 279–281, 280*f*
research on, ethical issues of, 33–34, 34*f*
training
chaining for, 187–188, 187*f*
reinforcement for, 185–186, 186*f*
shaping for, 187–188, 187*f*
Animus, 462
Anorexia nervosa, 545
Anosmia, 108
Antagonists, 49, 50*t*
Anterior commissure, 385
Anterograde amnesia, 237, 238*f*
Antianxiety drugs, 600, 600*f*
Anticipation, errors of, 87
Antidepressant drugs, 599
Antigens, 500
Antioxidants, phenolic, 515
Antipsychotic drugs, 598–599
Antismoking campaigns, 512–513, 513*f*
Antisocial behavior, 341
Antisocial personality disorder, 564, 564*f*, 565*t*, 566
Anxiety
basic, 463
biological basis for, 399, 553
definition of, 553
reactions to, 456, 456*t*

Anxiety disorders
agoraphobia, 554–555
definition of, 553
panic disorder, 554, 555*f*
phobias. *See* Phobias
Apnea, 146, 147
Applied behavior analysis, 197–198, 198*f*
Aptitude tests, 418, 419
Archetypes, 462
Area, illusions of, 117–118, 117*f*
Army Alpha, 421
Army Beta, 421–422
Aromatherapy, 108–109
Arousal, 399, 400
Arousal theory, 373–374, 377*t*
Arteriosclerosis, 514
Artificial intelligence, 272–274, 272*f*, 274*f*
Ascending trials, 87
ASL (American Sign Language), 279
Assertiveness training, 586, 590
Assessment interviews, 540, 541*f*
Assimilation, 299, 299*f*
Association cortex, 61
Asylums, 534
Atmospheric perspective, 120
Attachment
contact comfort and, 315–317, 316*f*
definition of, 313
love and, 651, 652
measurement of, 313–315
origins of, 313–315
patterns, 314
secure, promotion of, 608
style, long-term effects of, 315, 315*f*
Attention
in observational learning, 200–201, 201*f*
selective, perception and, 112–113
Attention-deficit/hyperactivity disorder (ADHD), 544
Attitude
change, cognitive dissonance and, 632–636, 634*f*, 635*f*
definition of, 618, 628
measurement of, 631–632, 631*t*, 632*f*
persuasion and, 629–630
Attitude-discrepant behavior, 632
Attraction
definition of, 619
social influence and, 647–650, 648*f*, 649*f*
Attribution
bias and, 620–623, 622*f*
causal, 619–620, 620*f*
definition of, 618, 619
Attributional augmenting, 623
Atypical antipsychotics, 599
Auditory nerve, 99, 99*f*
Authoritarian parents, 334
Authoritative parents, 334
Autism, 546–549, 548*f*
Autobiographical memory
definition of, 210
infantile autism and, 232–234
organization of, 233–234, 233*f*
self-concept and, 233
Automatic priming, 224
Automatic processing, 130, 137, 137*f*, 138–139
Autonomic nervous system, 51–52, 53*f*, 396
Autonomous motivation, 514
Autonomy versus shame and doubt, 335, 336*t*
Availability heuristic, 22, 259, 259*f*
Avoidant personality disorder, 565*t*
Avolition, 568
Axis I, 538, 539*t*
Axis II, 538, 539*t*
Axons, 44–45
Axon terminals, 45

Babbling, 277
Babinski reflex, 292*t*
Backward conditioning, 172, 172*f*, 173
Backward masking, 89
Bain, Alexander, 6
Balance, sense of, 110, 110*f*
Barbiturates, 158, 600
Bargaining, terminal illness and, 362
Base-rate problem, 266–267
Basic anxiety, 463
Basic mistakes, 581
Basilar membrane, 100–101
Beauty, physical, interpersonal attraction and, 649–650, 649*f*
Behavior
attitude-discrepant, 632
autonomic vs. controlled, drug abuse and, 156–157
brain and, 43, 43*f*
consistency of, 450–451, 472
definition of, 5
disruptive, 542–543, 542*f*
external causes, 619
functionally equivalent, 451
genetic factors and, 15, 15*f*
genetic factors in, 44, 78–79
internal causes, 619
motivation for. *See* Motivation
new perspective on, 4–5
observations, for mental disorder assessment, 541
of others, changing. *See* Social influence
perspectives of, 11–12, 12*t*
stimulus control of, 193, 193*f*
strengthening. *See* Reinforcement
suppression. *See* Punishment
uniqueness of, 472
violent. *See* Violence
Behavioral approaches, for family members, 595
Behavioral coping techniques, 526, 526*t*
Behavioral-event interviews, 426
Behavioral group therapies, 590
Behavioral management programs, for ADHD, 544
Behavioral marital therapy, 592
Behavioral medicine, 491
Behavioral modeling, 203–204, 204*f*
Behavioral perspective, 11, 12*t*
Behavioral signature, 451
Behaviorism, 7–9, 7*f*
Behavior therapies
classical conditioning in, 584–585, 585*f*
operant conditioning in, 585–586, 586*f*
Beliefs, reasoning and, 255
The Bell Curve, 435–436
Benzodiazepines, 600
Bereavement, 363–365, 364*f*
Beta waves, 143
Bias
attribution and, 620–623, 622*f*
correspondence, 620–621
hindsight, 256–257, 265
optimistic, 405, 625–626
self-serving, 621–623, 622*f*
source, competition as, 636–637
Bicultural adolescents, identity formation of, 337, 337*f*
Bidis, 513
Bigots, 639
Binge drinking, 158
Binge-purge cycle, 546
Binocular cues, for distance perception, 120
Binocular parallax, 120
Biochemical factors, in schizophrenia, 570
Biofeedback, 199
Biological clock, 131
Biological constraints on learning, 176–177, 176*f*
Biological factors
of aggression, 387
of emotion, 399–400, 400*f*
of homosexuality, 385–386
in psychology, 42–43, 43*f*
Biological markers, 541
Biological measures
in mental disorder assessment, 541
of personality, 479
Biological model, 535
Biological perspective, 11, 12*t*
Biological rhythms
circadian, 131–132
definition of, 130, 131
longer-term, 131, 131*f*, 132
Biological sex, 322
Biological therapies
drug-based, 597–601, 598*f*, 600*f*
electroconvulsive, 578, 601–602, 601*f*
historical aspects, 597, 597*f*
psychosurgery, 602
Biology, mental disorders and, 43
Bipolar affective reactions, 403
Bipolar cells, 93
Bipolar disorder, 550
Biracial adolescents, identity formation of, 337, 337*f*
Birth order, importance of, 463
Bisexual sexual orientation, 385–386
Blanks, Billy, 205*f*
Blended families, 339
Blindness, temporary, 95
Blindsight, 98
Blind spot, 93
Blinking reflex, 292*t*
Blocking, 178
Blood-brain barrier, 45
Blood pressure, emotion and, 517
Blood sugar, 378
"Bobo doll" experiments, 200
Bodily-kinesthetic intelligence, 414, 414*f*
Body image distortion, 546, 547*f*
Body language, 402
Body weight. *See* Weight
Bogus pipeline, 632, 632*f*
Bonding, resilience in development and, 342
Bonobo chimpanzees, language usage, 280, 280*f*
Borderline personality disorder, 564, 565*t*
Boredom, love and, 651
Bottom-up approach, 118
Brain. *See also* specific brain components
behavior and, 43, 43*f*
damage
amnesia from, 240
naturally occurring, effects of, 64–65, 65*f*
dysfunction
in schizophrenia, 569–570
violent behavior and, 57–58
emotions and, 399–400, 400*f*
function
music and, 71–72
relational reasoning, 70–71, 71*t*
speech and, 69–70, 70*f*
vs. computers, 67
hemispheres
connected, 63–64
emotional expression and, 62–63, 63*f*, 399, 400*f*
unconnected, 61–63, 62*f*, 63*f*
higher mental processes and, 44, 70–72, 71*f*
lateralization of function, 61–63, 63*f*, 64*f*
of panic-disordered patients, 555
pattern recognition and, 119
potentials. *See* Event-related potentials
rest, sleep and, 144
structure, 55–56, 56*f*
structure, intelligence and, 426
study methods for, 64–65, 65*f*, 66*f*
temperature, sleep and, 144
vision and, 97–98
visual perception and, 67–68, 67*f*, 68*f*
vs. computer, 55*f*

Brain death, 362
Brain Gum, 241, 242*f*
Brain stem, 55–56, 175
Brightness, 94
Brightness constancy, 115–116
Broca's aphasia, 69
Broca's area, 69
Bulimia, 546
Bully, 317–318
BuSpar (buspirone), 600

Caffeine, 159
CAI (computer-assisted instruction), 199, 199*f*
Cancer, 509, 513–514
Cannon-Bard theory, 396, 396*f*, 398*t*
Carcinogens, 509
Cardiac output, 348
Cardinal traits, 469
Cardiovascular disease, 510, 514
Care-based principles, 310
Career age, 354
Career success, predicting, 426–427
Carlson, Elizabeth, 559, 559*f*
Case management, 597
Case method, 24–25, 32*t*
Castration anxiety, 457
CAT (Cognitive Abilities Test), 422
Cataplexy, 146, 147
Catatonia, 568, 568*f*
Catatonic type of schizophrenia, 569, 569*t*
Catecholamines, 517
Catecholamine system, 481
Causation, vs. correlation, 28*f*
Cause and effect concept, in sensorimotor stage, 299–300
Cell body, of neuron, 44
Central executive, in working memory, 216, 217
Central fissure, 59
Central nervous system, 50–51
Central route, to persuasion, 630
Central tendency, 660, 661, 661*t*
Central traits, 469
Cerebellum, 56, 175
Cerebral cortex, 58–60, 59*f*, 60*f*
Cerebral death, 362
Cerebral hemispheres, 59
Chaining, 187–188, 187*f*
Change
  human development and, 287*f*
  vs. stability, 10, 286
Charismatic leaders, 654–655, 655*f*
Chemicals, hormone-disrupting, 290–291, 290*f*
Chemical senses
  smell, 106–109, 107*f*
  taste, 107–109, 108*f*
Chemotherapy, conditioned taste aversions and, 177
Child, death of, 364
Childhood, 286
  emotional development in, 311–313, 312*f*, 313*f*
  obesity, 324–325, 324*f*
  personality, health-related outcomes and, 493
  physical development in, 291–292, 292*t*, 293*f*, 294
  sexual abuse, repression of, 230–231
Children
  difficult, 312
  easy, 312
  slow-to-warm-up, 312
  understanding of others' wishes, 306–307, 306*f*
Chinese, self-serving bias and, 622–623, 622*f*
Chinese-Americans, self-serving bias and, 622–623, 622*f*
Chlorpromazine (thorazine), 598
Choking under pressure, 141–142, 141*f*
Cholesterol, serum, 514
Chromosomes, 72, 73, 73*f*, 287
Chronic illnesses, 350
Chunk, 216
Cigarettes. *See also* Smoking
  candy-flavored, 513
Cingulotomy, 602
Circadian rhythm
  definition of, 131–132
  disturbances in, 133–135, 134*f*
  individual differences in, 132, 133*t*
  melatonin and, 132
Circular causality, 595
Civil commitment, 610
Clairvoyance, 123
Classical conditioning
  attitudes and, 628
  cognitive perspective, 178–179
  counteracting violence and, 181
  definition of, 169–170, 170*f*
  drug overdose and, 179–180
  early work on, 171, 171*f*
  example of, 169–170, 170*f*
  exceptions to, 175–178, 176*f*
  neural basis of, 175
  of newborns, 294
  phobias and, 554
  principles of, 171–174, 172*f*, 174*f*
  stimulus for, 170
  therapies based on, 584–585, 585*f*
Classifiers, in language, 279
Client-centered therapy, 582–583, 583*f*
Climacteric, 348–349
Clinical psychologists, 17
Clinical psychology, 13*t*, 543
Clinical scales, MMPI-2, 477–478, 477*t*
Closure, laws of, 115*f*
Cocaine
  prenatal influences on development, 288–289
  stimulant effects, 158–159, 159*f*
Cochlea, 99, 99*f*
Cocktail party phenomenon, 113
Cognition
  affect influence on, 403
  changes, during adulthood, 351–355, 353*f*, 354*f*
  definition of, 249
  eating and, 378–379
  emotion and, 402–404
  influence on affect, 403–404
  personality and, 472–474
  reasoning in. *See* Reasoning
  smoking and, 511
Cognitive Abilities Test (CAT), 422
Cognitive appraisal, of stressors, 495–496, 496*f*
Cognitive approach, to persuasion, 630–631
Cognitive behavior therapy
  for depression, 587–588, 588*f*
  for pain management, 106, 124
Cognitive coping techniques, 526–527
Cognitive development
  during adolescence, 332–333
  discrete stages in, 304
  emotional development and, 311–313, 312*f*, 313*f*
  information-processing perspective, 307
  Piaget's theory of, 298–301, 302*t*
  social context of, 304
Cognitive development theory, 323
Cognitive dissonance
  attitude change and, 629, 632–636, 634*f*, 635*f*
  hypocrisy and, 634–635, 635*f*
Cognitive frameworks (schemas), 638
Cognitive interviews, of eyewitnesses, 229
Cognitive map, 196–197, 196*f*
Cognitive mechanisms, in depression, 551, 552*f*
Cognitive perspective
  of drug abuse, 156–157
  in psychology, 11, 12*t*
Cognitive processes
  definition of, 5
  in learning, 196–197, 196*f*
  in pain perception, 105–106
  study methods for, 253–254, 253*f*
Cognitive psychology, 13*t*
Cognitive restructuring, 526–527
Cognitive revolution, 8
Cognitive scaffold, 299
Cognitive sources, of prejudice, 638
Cognitive theory, of language development, 275
Cognitive therapies, 587–589, 588*f*, 589*f*
Cog project, 272–273, 272*f*
Cohort effects
  definition of, 296, 346
  in developmental studies, 297–298
  in intelligence, age-related, 353, 353*f*
Collective unconscious, 462
Collectivistic culture, 466
Color blindness, 96
Colorectal cancer, 513–514
Color perception, development of, 295
Color vision, 96–97, 96*f*
Common region, laws of, 115*f*
Common sense, behavioral conclusions and, 21–22
Communication problems, marital therapy for, 592–593
Community factors, resilience in development and, 342–343
Community mental health centers, 608
Community mental health movement, 608
Community psychology, 608, 609*f*
Comparisons, unexpressed, 667–668
Compassionate love, 650
Compensatory tracking task, 135
Competencies, 426
Competency assessment, 426–427, 427*f*
Competition, as bias source, 636–637
Complex cells, 97
Compliance, social influence and, 644–645, 644*f*
Componential (analytic) intelligence, 415, 424
Comprehension, speech, 70, 70*f*
Compulsions, 556
Compulsive personality, 457, 458*f*
Computer-assisted instruction (CAI), 199, 199*f*
Computerized tomography (CT), 64, 65, 541
Computers
  artificial intelligence and, 272–273, 272*f*
  wearable, 273–274, 274*f*
Concepts, 221–222, 250–251
Concordance, 535
Concordance rates, for alcoholism, 516–517, 516*t*
Concrete operations, 301, 302*t*
Concurrent schedules of reinforcement, 191–193
Concurrent task paradigm, 217
Concurrent validity, 424
Conditional positive regard, 465
Conditioned fear, in combating teen violence, 181
Conditioned reinforcers, 183, 183*f*
Conditioned response (CR), 171
Conditioned stimulus (CS)
  biological constraints/characteristics, 175–178, 176*f*
  definition of, 171
  familiarity of, 173
  intensity of, 173
  temporal arrangement of, 172–173, 172*f*

Conditioned taste aversion, 177–178
Conditions of worth, 582
Condolence behaviors, 365
Condoms, for HIV/AIDS prevention, 520
Conduct disorder
  disruptive behavior and, 542
  preventing, 543–544, 543*f*
Cones, 92*f*, 93, 96, 96*f*
Confidentiality, 611–612, 611*f*
Confirmation bias, 22, 255, 256*f*
Confluence approach, 443–444, 444*f*
Conformity, social influence and, 641–642, 642*f*
Confounding, of variables, 30–31, 30*f*
Conscientiousness
  job performance and, 482
  longevity and, 361, 481
  personality and, 470
Conscious level, of consciousness, 453, 454*f*
Consciousness
  levels of, 453–455, 454*f*
  state of, hypnotic alteration of, 152–153
Consciousness-altering drugs
  depressants, 157–158, 158*f*
  hallucinogens, 159–161
  opiates, 159
  psychedelics, 159–161
  reward properties of, 156
  stimulants, 158–159, 159*f*
Consensus, 619
Conservation, 301, 303
Consistency, 619
Constancies, 114–116, 116*f*
Constant stimuli, method of, 87–88
Construction, of memory, 227, 228–229, 228*f*
Constructivism, 299
Consumer Reports, 604, 605
Contact comfort, attachment and, 315–317, 316*f*
Contact hypothesis, 639–640, 640*f*
Content validity, 424
Context-dependent memory, 220
Continuous reinforcement schedule (CRF), 190
Contraception, Depo-Provera injections, 340
Contracting programs, for childhood obesity, 325
Contrast effect, 195–196
Control, 29
Control delusions, 567
Controlled motivation, 514
Controlled processing, 130, 137, 139
Control theory, 139
Conventional level of morality, 308, 309*t*
Convergence, 120
Conversion disorder, 560
Convoy model, 354, 355–356, 355*f*
Coping
  behavioral techniques, 526, 526*t*
  optimistic vs. pessimistic, 502–503, 503*t*
  problem-focused, 502
  psychological techniques, 526
Coping techniques, cognitive, 526–527
Coprophilia, 562*t*
Cornea, 92, 92*f*
Corpus callosum, 61–64, 62*f*, 63*f*
Correlation, 665–666, 665*f*
Correlational method (correlation), 26–28
  advantages vs. disadvantages of, 32*t*
  causation and, 28*f*
  example of, 27
Correlation coefficient, 666
Correspondence bias, 620–621
Counseling psychology, 13*t*
Counterfactual thinking, 263, 626–627, 626*f*
Counterirritants, for pain relief, 124
Couples therapy (marital therapy), 591–593, 592*f*, 593*f*
CR (conditioned response), 171
Crack, 159, 159*f*
Creativity
  aging and, 354–355, 354*f*
  contrasting views of, 443–444, 444*f*
  definition of, 442–443, 442*f*
  exceptional, 443
  mundane, 443
  research, 444
Creativity leadership and, 654
CRF (continuous reinforcement schedule), 190
Criterion-related validity, 424
Critical period, for language development, 276
Critical thinking, 23
Cross-dressing, 563
Cross-sectional research, 296, 297, 297*t*
Cross-tolerance, 155
Crystallized intelligence, 353–354, 416
CS (conditioned stimulus), 171
CT (computerized tomography), 64, 65, 541
Cue-word method, 233–234
Cultural bias, 434
Culturally related features, 538
Culturally sensitive psychotherapy, 607
Culture
  achievement motivation and, 392–393, 393*f*
  aggression and, 387
  differences
    in self-serving bias, 622–623, 622*f*
    in suicide rates, 552
  diversity, 12, 13–14
  domestic violence and, 14, 14*f*
  eating and, 378
  interpersonal attraction and, 649–650, 649*f*
  moral development and, 310–311
  observational learning and, 202–203, 203*f*
  pain perception and, 105
  in psychology, 11, 12*t*
  in sexual behavior, 383
Culture-fair tests, 434, 435*f*
Curare, 49
Cyborg (bionic man), 273–274, 274*f*
Cynical hostility, type A behavior pattern and, 479

Daily life, hassles of, 498–499
DAMIT (dreams of absent-minded transgression), 149–150
Dark adaptation, 95, 350
Darwin, Charles, 15
Death
  causes of, 491, 491*t*
  of child, 364
  dignity in, 362, 363*f*
  high-grief, 364
  legal issues of, 363
  low-grief, 364
  patient rights and, 362, 362*f*
  suicide, 551–553
  types of, 361–362
Debriefing, 33, 33*f*
Decentration, 300
Deception, 31–33
Decision making
  better, steps for, 281
  definition of, 258
  emotions and, 263–264
  framing and, 260–262, 261*f*
  naturalistic, 266–267, 266*f*
  process of, 249, 249*f*
Declarative memory, 218, 219
Decontextualization, 300
Defended realism approach, 332
Defense mechanisms
  psychoanalysis of, 580, 580*f*
  self-concept and, 464
  types of, 456, 456*t*
Deficiency needs, 376, 376*f*
Deinstitutionalization, 596, 596*f*
Delay conditioning, 172–173, 172*f*
Delta activity, 142, 143
Delusions, 567
Dendrites, 44
Denial, 362, 464
Deoxyribonucleic acid (DNA)
  aging and, 359–360
  genetics and, 73, 73*f*, 75–76
Dependence, 155
Dependent personality disorder, 565*t*
Dependent variables, 29
Depersonalization disorder, 558
Depo-Provera injections, 340
Depressants, 157–158, 158*f*
Depression
  antidepressant drugs for, 599
  brain in, 399
  causes of, 550–551, 552*f*
  cognitive therapy for, 588–589
  description of, 549–550, 550*f*
  terminal illness and, 362
  theories, 535
Depth
  binocular cues, 120
  monocular cues, 119–120
  perception, 296, 296*f*
DES (diethylstilbestrol), 290–291
Descartes, René, 6
Descending trials, 87
Descriptive norms, 641
Descriptive statistics, 659–661, 660*f*, 660*t*
Desensitization, 388
Despair, bereavement and, 363–364
Detachment, bereavement and, 364
Determinism, 468
Development
  adult, 343–344
    childhood events and, 346–347
    contextual approaches, 345–345, 345*f*
    stage theory of, 344–345
  cognitive, 298–301, 302*t*
  as continuous process, 330, 330*f*
  emotional, 311–313, 312*f*, 313*f*
  gender, 322–324, 323*f*
  locomotor, 292, 293*t*, 294
  moral, 307–311, 308*f*, 309*t*
  perceptual, 293–296, 295*f*, 296*f*
  physical
    during adolescence, 330–332, 331*f*, 332*f*
    early childhood, 291–292, 292*t*, 293*f*, 294
  potential, level of, 304
  prenatal influences on, 288–291, 288*f*-290*f*
  prenatal period, 287–288
  proximal, zone of, 304
  study methods for, 296–298, 297*f*
  theory of mind, 305–307, 305*f*, 306*f*
Developmental perspective, 11, 12*t*
Developmental psychology, 13*t*, 286
Developmental psychopathology perspective, 537
Diagnostic and Statistical Manual of Mental Disorders-IV (DSM-IV), 538–540, 539*t*, 563
Diagnostic features, 538
Diary studies, 232
Diathesis-stress model, 536–537, 537*f*, 555
Diet
  cardiovascular disease and, 514
  childhood obesity and, 325
  colorectal cancer and, 513–514
  longevity and, 361
  weight control and, 407

Dietary supplements, 161–162
Diethylstilbestrol (DES), 290–291
Difference thresholds, 88*f*, 89
Dignity, end-of-life, 362, 363*f*
Dimensional approach, 540
Direct evidence, for environmental factors, in group differences in intelligence test scores, 435
Direct intergroup contact, in reducing prejudice, 639–640, 640*f*
Direct orders, social influence from, 645–646, 646*f*
Discontinuous development stages, 304
Discriminative stimulus, 193
Disobedient models, 647, 647*f*
Disorganized/disoriented attachment, 314
Disorganized type of schizophrenia, 569*t*
Dispersion, 660–661, 661
Displacement, 456*t*
Dispositional causes, overestimating role of, 620–621
Disruptive behavior, 542–543, 542*f*
Dissociable subsystems, 119, 119*f*
Dissociated control, theory of, 152
Dissociative amnesia, 558
Dissociative disorders, 558–559
Dissociative fugue, 558
Dissociative identity disorder, 558–559, 559*f*
Dissonance. *See* Cognitive dissonance
Distance perception, 119–120, 120*f*
Distinctiveness, 619
Distortion
  as defense mechanism, 464
  of memory, 227–228
Distractions, studying and, 36
Distress, mental disorders and, 533
Distribution, normal, 662–663, 662*f*, 663*f*
Diversity, psychology and, 12, 13–14
Divorced families, 339
DNA. *See* Deoxyribonucleic acid
Doctor-patient interactions, 505–507
Dogmatism-skepticism, 332
DO IT process, 197–198, 198*f*
Dolphins, language usage, 280–281
Domain specific, 304
Domestic violence, cultural values and, 14, 14*f*
Dominance motivation, 76–77, 77*f*
Door-in-the face technique, 645
Dopamine
  blockage, by antipsychotic drugs, 598
  in depression, 550
  drug abuse and, 156
  effects of, 48*t*
  location of, 48*t*
  Ritalin and, 544
  in schizophrenia, 570
  stimulants and, 158
Double-blind procedure, 31
Double depression, 550
Downsizing, 474
Down syndrome, 418, 419
Downward counterfactuals, 626*f*, 627
Dream, life structure and, 356
Dreams
  brain activity in, 143
  cognitive view of, 149–150, 149*f*
  interpretation of, 148–149, 455
  nightmares, 147
  physiological view of, 149
  psychodynamic view of, 148–149
Dreams of absent-minded transgression (DAMIT), 149–150
Drive, leadership and, 654
Drive theory, 372–373, 373*f*, 377*t*
"Drowsy driver" syndrome, counteracting, 135–136, 135*f*
Drug abuse, 155
  cognitive perspective of, 156–157
  longevity and, 361
  parental, 341
  psychological mechanisms, 156–157
  social perspective of, 156
Drug addiction, 155
Drug-dependency insomnia, 147
Drugs. *See also* specific drugs
  adolescent usage of, 156*f*
  consciousness-altering. *See* Consciousness-altering drugs
  consciousness and, 154–155
  dependence on, 155
  for memory improvement, 241, 242*f*
  nervous system effects, 49, 50*t*
  overdose of, classical conditioning and, 179–180
  over-the-counter drugs, prenatal influences of, 288
  physiological dependence on, 155
  psychoactive, reaction differences in, 600–601
  psychological dependence on, 155
  tolerance, 155
  vs. dietary supplements, 161–162
Drug therapy, 597–601, 598*f*, 600*f*
Drug withdrawal, 156
DSM-IV (Diagnostic and Statistical Manual of Mental Disorders-IV), 538–540, 539*t*, 563
Dualism, 6
Durable power of attorney for health care, 363
Dynamic visual acuity (DVA), 94
Dysexecutive syndrome, 217
Dysfunctional families, 340–341
Dysthymic disorder, 550

Ear, 98–99, 99*f*
Eardrum, 99, 99*f*
Eating
  habits, childhood obesity and, 325
  hunger and, 406
  regulation of, 378–379
Ecocentrism, 300–301
Ecological perspective, 608
Ecological systems theory, 345–346, 345*f*
Ecology, 595
ECT (electroconvulsive therapy), 578, 601–602, 601*f*
Ectopic pregnancy, 287
Educational psychology, 13*t*
EEG (electroencephalography), 64, 65, 142–143
Efferent nerve fibers, 50
Efficacy research, 603–604
Efficacy studies, 603
Ego, 455, 456, 456*t*, 580
Egocentrism, 303
Elaboration, 307
Elaboration-likelihood model (ELM), 630
Elaborative rehearsal, 212
Elavil (amitriptyline), 599
Electroconvulsive therapy (ECT), 578, 601–602, 601*f*
Electroencephalography (EEG), 64, 65, 142–143
Electromyogram (EOM), 142
Electrooculogram (EOG), 142, 143
Elicitation research, 519–520
ELM (elaboration-likelihood model), 630
Embryo, 287
Emotion
  aging and, 356
  biological basis of, 399–400, 400*f*
  cognition and, 402–404
  decision making and, 263–264
  definition of, 370–371, 395
  development
    in adolescence, 333–334
    in adulthood, 356–359, 357*f*, 358*f*
    in childhood, 311–313, 312*f*, 313*f*
  expression, 395–396, 395*f*
    external, 401–402, 401*f*
    facial, 311, 401, 401*f*
  health and, 517–518
  management of, 440
  nonverbal cues of, 401–402, 401*f*
  of others, recognizing/influencing, 440, 440*f*
  perception, 442
  personal, recognition/knowledge of, 439–440
  theories of, 398*t*
    Cannon-Bard, 396, 396*f*, 398*t*
    James-Lange, 396–397, 396*f*, 398*t*
    opponent-process, 397–398, 398*t*
    Schacter-Singer or two-factor, 397, 398*t*
  thoughts and, 23
Emotional intelligence (EQ)
  anger management and, 445
  components of, 439–441
  effects of, 441–442
  evidence of, 441–442
Emotional stability, 470, 471, 482
Empathy, 295, 313, 313*f*
Empirical keying, 477
Empowerment, promotion, 608
Empty chair technique, 583, 583*f*
Encoding, 210, 211
Encoding specificity principle, 221
Encounter groups, 590–591
Endocrine system, 52, 54, 54*f*
End-of-life stages, 362
Endorphins, 49, 159
Entrepreneurs, 420
Entrepreneurship, attributional augmenting and, 623–624
Environment
  aggression and, 388
  alcohol abuse and, 158
  deprivation, 432
  enrichment, 432
  group differences in IQ scores and, 434–435, 435*f*
  intelligence and, 431–433, 431*f*
  for mental disorder prevention, 608
  temperament and, 312–313
  vs. genetics. *See* Nature-versus-nurture controversy
  in weight regulation, 380
Environmental cues, drug overdose and, 179–180
EOG (electrooculogram), 142, 143
EOM (electromyogram), 142
Epidemiological studies, 492, 493
Epinephrine (adrenaline), 54, 132
Episodic memory
  autobiographical memory, 232–234, 233*f*
  definition of, 219
  electroconvulsive therapy and, 602
  influencing factors, 219–221
  study methods for, 218
  vs. semantic memory, 222–223

EQ. *See* Emotional intelligence
Erikson, Erik, stages of life, 335–337, 336*t*
ERPs. *See* Event-related potentials
Errors of anticipation, 87
Errors of habituation, 87
Errors of omission, 667
Escalation of commitment, 20–21, 262–263, 263*f*, 265
ESP (extrasensory perception), 123–124
Esteem needs, 376, 376*f*
Estrogen, 382
Ethical issues
  in psychological research, 31–34
  in psychotherapy, 611–612, 611*f*
  for wearable computers, 274
Ethnic cleansing, 636
Ethnicity
  cognitive differences in, genetic factors in, 436
  culturally sensitive psychotherapy and, 607
  differences in psychoactive drug reactions and, 600–601
  diversity and, 12, 13–14
  smoking and, 511
Ethologist, 387
Evaluation, in problem solving, 268
Event-related potentials (ERPs)
  of cognitive processes, 253–254, 253*f*
  definition of, 65
  music and, 71–72
Everyday reasoning, 254
Evolution, 12, 15–16, 16*f*
Evolutionary perspective
  in psychology, 11, 12*t*
  on sexual behavior, 383–385, 384*f*
Evolutionary psychology
  definition of, 10, 13*f*, 15
  genetics and, 76–77, 77*f*
  overview of, 15–17, 16*f*
  psychologists in, 13*t*
Evolutionary theory, love and, 651
Excitement phase, of sexual behavior, 383
Exemplar, 222
Exercise
  for childhood obesity, 325
  colorectal cancer and, 513–514
  longevity and, 361
  motivation for, 523–524, 523f
  slow-wave sleep and, 144
  weight control and, 406–407
Exhaustion, in general adaptation syndrome, 495
Exhibitionism, 562*t*
Exorcisms, 534
Exosystem, 345
Expectancy theory, 374, 377*t*
Experience sampling method, 479
Experiential (creative) intelligence, 415
Experimental psychology, 6, 6*f*, 13*t*
Experimentation (experimental method)
  advantages vs. disadvantages of, 32*t*
  basic nature of, 29
  definition of, 28–29
  requirements for, 29–31
Experimenter effects, 30–31
Explicit memory, 218, 219
Expressiveness, 440, 440*f*
Extended contact hypothesis, 640
External causes, of behavior, 619, 621
Externalizing behaviors, 341
Externalizing problems, 542
External rewards, 395
Externals, 474
Extinction, 173–174
Extrapyramidal symptoms, 598–599
Extrasensory perception (ESP), 123–124
Extrastriate cortex, 68*f*
Extraversion, 470
Extroverts, 462
Eye, 91–93, 92*f*
Eye-blink classical conditioning, 175
Eye movements, visual acuity and, 95
Eyewitness testimony, 228–229, 229*f*
Eysenck, Hans, 604

Face validity, 477
Facial dominance, 77, 77*f*
Facial expressions, emotions and, 311, 401, 401*f*
Facial features, during puberty, 331
Facial feedback hypothesis, 397
Facial recognition, 296
Factor, 416
Factor analysis, 416, 470
Fainting game, 393–394
False memories, 228, 231–232, 231*f*
Family relationship, intelligence and, 428–431, 428*f*-430*f*
Family systems therapy, 595
Family therapy, 579, 594–595
Family violence, reduction, 608
Farsightedness, 94–95
FAS (fetal alcohol syndrome), 289, 289*f*, 516
Fatal familial insomnia, 145
Father-absent families, 339
Fats, 378
FDA (Food and Drug Administration), 162
Fear. *See also* Phobias
  conditioned, in combating teen violence, 181
  messages, for health promotion, 522, 523*f*
  self-awareness and, 141
Feature detectors, 97
Fechner, Gustav, 6
Feeding and eating disorders, 544–546, 545*f*, 547*f*
Feeding schedule, infant, 291
Female entrepreneurs, attributional augmenting and, 623–624
Females, feeding and eating disorders and, 545–546, 545*f*
Fertilization, 287
Fetal alcohol syndrome (FAS), 289, 289*f*, 516
Fetishism, 562, 562*t*
Fetus, 287–288
Fight-or-flight syndrome, 495
Figure-ground relationship, 113–114, 114*f*
Fitness, learning principles in, 204–205, 205*f*
Fixation, in psychosexual development, 457
Fixations, visual, 95
Fixed-interval schedule, 190
Fixed-ratio schedule, 191
Flashbulb memories, 234
Flat affect, 568
Flexibility
  in decision making, 281
  leadership and, 654
  optimism and, 502
Flooding, 584–585
Fluid intelligence, 354, 416, 434
Fluoxetine (Prozac), 599
Flynn effect, 431–432
Food
  eating regulation and, 378
  external cues, obese persons and, 380–381
  flavors, taste and, 107–108, 108*f*
  high-fat, taste preference for, 514
  snack, 406
Food and Drug Administration (FDA), 162
Foot-in-the-door technique, 644–645
Forensic psychologists, 236
Forgetting
  definition of, 210
  interference and, 225–226, 225*f*
  retrieval inhibition and, 226
  time and, 225
Form, recognition of, 295
Formal operations, 301, 302*t*
Formal reasoning, 254
Form discrimination task, for vision assessment, 68
Four-card problem, 255
Fovea, 93
Framing, 260–262, 261*f*, 655
Fraternal twins, 73
Free association, 580
Free nerve endings, 104
Free radicals, 359
Free recall, 218, 218*f*
Free will, 468
Frequency, of sound waves, 99–100
Frequency distribution, 659–660, 660*f*, 660*t*
Frequency-of-exposure effect, 648
Frequency theory, 101
Freud, Sigmund
  case method and, 25
  dreams and, 148–149
  psychoanalysis and, 452–453, 453*f*, 580–581
  unconscious and, 8
Freudian slips, 455
Friendships
  during adolescence, 334–335, 335*f*
  during adulthood, 355–356, 355*f*
  social development and, 317, 334–335
Frontal lobe
  aging and, 352
  anatomy, 59
  in memory, 239–240
Frotteurism, 562, 562*t*
Frustration, 387
Frustration-aggression hypothesis, 387, 387*f*
Fully functioning persons, 464
Functional autonomy, 469
Functional fixedness, 270–271, 271*f*
Functionalism, 7, 17–18
Fundamental attribution error, 621
Funerals, 364, 364*f*

Gamma-amino-butyric acid (GABA), 48*t*, 600
Ganglion cells, 93
GAS (general adaptation syndrome), 495
Gate-control theory, 104–105
Gateway hypothesis, 161
Gender
  development, 322–324, 323*f*
  division of labor and, 17
Gender bias, in DSM-IV, 540
Gender consistency, 321, 322
Gender differences
  in dominance motivation, 76–77
  in intelligence, 437–438, 438*f*
  in mating strategies, 383–385, 384*f*
  in moral development, 310
  in obsessive-compulsive disorder, 556
  in personal happiness, 405
Gender identity, 321, 322
Gender identity disorders, 563
Gender roles, 322
Gender schema theory, 323–324
Gender stability, 321, 322
Gender stereotypes, 322
General adaptation syndrome (GAS), 495
General factor (g), 414
Generalized expectancies, 474

Generativity, 280
Generativity versus self-absorption, 336*t*, 344
Genes, 73
Genetic disorders, 75–76
Genetic hypothesis, 436
Genetics
aggression and, 387
alcohol abuse and, 157–158, 158*f*, 516–517, 516*t*
attitudes and, 628
DNA and, 73, 73*f*, 75–76
evolutionary psychology and, 76–77, 77*f*
homosexuality and, 385–386
human behavior and, 15, 15*f*, 78–79
human disorders and, 75–76
intelligence and, 428–431, 428*f*-430*f*
IQ score group differences and, 435–436, 437*f*
learned helplessness and, 195
longevity and, 521
mental disorders and, 75–76
principles of, 73–74, 73*f*
schizophrenia and, 569
smoking behavior and, 511
subjective well-being and, 405
temperament and, 312–313
vs. environment. *See* Nature-versus-nurture controversy
in weight regulation, 379–380
Genital herpes, 288
Genital stage, 458
German measles, 288
Gestalt psychologists, 113
Gestalt therapy, 582, 583, 583*f*
Gestures
animal language and, 280–281
emotions and, 401–402, 402*f*
Giddings State School approach, for teen violence, 181
Glial cells, 44–45, 292
Glucose, 378
Goals
attainability of, 375
challenge of, 375
self-set, 473
setting, to increase occupational safety, 375–376
specificity of, 375
Goal-setting theory, 374–376, 375*f*, 376*f*, 377*t*
Gonads, 331, 381–382
Good continuation, laws of, 115*f*
Graded potential, 45–46
Grammar, 277, 278
Grandeur, delusions of, 567
Graphs, unlabeled, 668
Grasping reflex, 290–291, 292*t*
Gratification, delay in, 188–189
Great person theory of leadership, 653–654, 654*f*
Grief, 364
Grouping, laws of, 114, 115*f*
Groups, 653
Group therapy, 579, 590–591, 591*f*
Growth
in early childhood, 291
needs, 376, 376*f*
physical, prenatal period, 287–288
Growth spurt, adolescent, 292, 330–331
Guided imagery, 559

Habit disturbances, self-help groups for, 596
Habituation, errors of, 87
Hair cells
inner, 102–103
outer, 102–103
structure, 99, 99*f*, 101
Hall, G. Stanley, 6–7
Hallucinations, 567
Hallucinogens, 159–161, 161
Halstead-Reitan Neuropsychological Battery, 541
Hardy individuals, 498
Hassles, of daily life, 498–499
HDL cholesterol, 514, 515
Health
alcohol consumption and, 515–517, 516*f*
diet and, 513–515
emotions and, 517–518
problems, behavior responsible for, 504
risks, from smoking, 510–511
stress and, 500–501
thoughts/actions and, 509–510
Health behavior, study methods for, 493–494
Health belief model, 504–505, 505*f*
Health-promotion messages, 521–522, 523*f*
Health psychology, 490–492
Health status, seeking information on, 524–525
Healthy People 2000 Initiative, 491–492, 492*t*
Hearing
development of, 295
ear anatomy and, 98–99, 99*f*
premature loss of, 102–103, 103*f*
sound and, 99–100, 100*f*
Heart attacks, type A behavior pattern and, 479, 479*f*
Height cues, 120
Helper T cells, optimism and, 502
Henmon-Nelson Tests, 422
Hereditary factors, in alcohol abuse, 157–158, 158*f*
Heredity. *See also* Genetics
definition of, 72
influence on intelligence, 428–431, 428*f*-430*f*
Heritability
definition of, 75
of intelligence, 431
Heroin, 159
Heterosexual intercourse, AIDS transmission and, 519
Heterosexual sexual orientation, 385–386
Heuristic processing, 630
Heuristics, 258–260, 269, 624
Heuristic-systematic model, 630
Hibernation, 132
Hidden observer, 152
Hierarchy of needs, 376–377, 376*f*
Higher mental processes, brain function and, 70–72, 71*f*
Hinckley, John, 610
Hindsight effect, 256–257, 265
Hippocampus
aging and, 352
damage, 238
definition of, 57
eye-blink conditioning and, 175
lateral, 57
in memory, 239
Histrionic personality disorder, 564, 565*t*
HIV (human immunodeficiency virus), 518, 520. *See also* Acquired immune deficiency syndrome
Holophrases, 277
Homemakers, regrets of, 358, 358*f*
Homeostasis, 56, 87, 373
Homicide, adolescent, 338
Homosexual intercourse, AIDS transmission and, 519
Homosexual sexual orientation, 385–386
Hope, in psychotherapy, 606–607
Hormone-disrupting chemicals, 290–291, 290*f*
Hormone replacement therapy (HRT), 349
Hormones. *See also* specific hormones
aggression and, 388–389
definition of, 52
sexual behavior and, 381–382
Horney, Karen, 462–463
Horse whisperer, 185–186, 186*f*
Hostility, blood pressure and, 517
Host personality, 558
Hot flashes, 349
HRT (hormone replacement therapy), 349
Hue, 93–94
Human behavior. *See* Behavior
Human factors, 18–19
Human immunodeficiency virus (HIV), 518, 520. *See also* Acquired immune deficiency syndrome
Humanism, 8
Humanistic theories, of personality, 463–468, 465*f*, 466*f*
Humanistic therapies, 582–584, 583*f*
Human nature, evolutionary psychology view of, 15–16
Humors, 534
Hunger cues, infant, 291
Hunger motivation, 378–381, 379*f*, 380*f*, 406
Huntington's disease, 73
Hypercomplex cells, 97
Hypertension, 517
Hypnosis
to improve eyewitness testimony, 229
neodissociation theory of, 152, 154
pain perception and, 105–106
performance of, 150–151
social-cognitive or role-playing view of, 151–154, 151*f*, 153*f*
suggestions for, 150–151
theory of dissociated control, 152
Hypnotic amnesia, 152
Hypnotizability, individual differences in, 151
Hypochondriasis, 560
Hypocrisy, cognitive dissonance and, 634–635, 635*f*
Hypohedonia, 195
Hypothalamus
hunger and, 378
sexual orientation and, 385
suprachiasmatic nucleus, 131
ventromedial damage, 56–57
Hypothesis, 20–21
Hypothetico-deductive reasoning, 301
Hysteria, 453

ICD-10 (International Statistical Classification of Diseases, Injuries, and Causes of Death), 538
Id, 455, 580
Identity achievement, 337
Identity diffusion, 337
Identity foreclosure, 337
Identity formation, among bicultural adolescents, 337, 337*f*
Identity fusion, 337
Identity moratorium, 337
Identity versus role confusion, 336, 336*t*
Illness, stress and, 497
Illusion of outgroup homogeneity, 229
Illusions, 116–118, 116*f*, 117*f*
Images, 252–253, 252*f*
IMB (information-motivation-behavioral) skills model, 519–520, 519*f*
Imipramine (Tofranil), 599
Immune system
classical conditioning and, 180, 180*f*
emotions and, 517
stress and, 500–501

Implicit memory. *See* Procedural memory
Impossible event condition, 302–303, 303*f*
Impotence, smoking and, 512–513, 513*f*
Impulsiveness, 188
Impulsivity, 564
Incentives, 374
Independent variables, 29, 30
Individualistic culture, 466
Induced compliance, 632
Industrial/organizational psychologists, 17, 482
Industrial/organizational psychology, 13*t*, 374
Industry versus inferiority, 335, 336*t*
Infantile amnesia, 232–233
Infants
  learning abilities of, 293
  pattern recognition, 295–296
  visual perception of, 121–122, 121*f*
Infectious agents, prenatal influences on development, 288
Inferential prisons, 638
Inferential statistics, 663–665, 664
Inflection, 501
Information
  factual, in memory, study methods for, 218
  inconsistent, dealing with, 624–625, 625*f*
Informational social influence, 642, 642*f*
Information-motivation-behavioral (IMB) skills model, 519–520, 519*f*
Information-processing capacity, 136
Information-processing perspective, 212, 307
Informed consent, 33
Ingratiation, 644
Inheritance, in evolution, 16, 16*f*
Initiative versus guilt, 335, 336*t*
Injunctive norms, 641
Insanity defense, 610
Insanity Defense Reform Act of 1984, 610
Insecure/ambivalent attachment, 314
Insecure/avoidant attachment, 314
Insomnia, 146–147
Inspection time, 425, 425*f*
Instinctive drift, 188
Instrumentality, 374
Integration, 300
Integrity versus despair, 336*t*, 344
Intellectual abilities, creativity and, 443, 444*f*
Intellectually gifted persons, 419–420
Intelligence
  aging and, 352–354, 353*f*
  cognitive basis of, 424–425
  crystallized, 353–354
  definition of, 413
  environmental factors of, 433
  in evaluating others, 413, 413*f*
  fluid, 354
  gender differences in, 437–438, 438*f*
  group tests, 421–422
  hereditary factors of, 433
  hereditary influences on, 428–431, 428*f*-430*f*
  interpersonal, 440
  measurement of, 416–420, 418*t*, 419*f*-420*f*
  multifaceted view of, 414
  nature of, 413–416
  neural basis of, 425–426
  practical, 354
  tests, 414
    group differences in scores, 434–438, 435*f*, 437*f*, 438*f*
    individual, 419–420, 419*t*, 420*t*
  theories of, 414–416
  unitary view of, 413–414
Intelligence quotient (IQ)
  definition of, 417
  entrepreneurs and, 420, 420*f*
  environmental factors and, 431–433, 431*f*
  group differences in, 435–436, 437*f*
  Williams syndrome and, 421, 421*f*
Intentional operating process, 137
Interactionism, 6
Interactionist perspective, 451, 451*f*
Interference, memory and, 243
Intermittent reinforcement, 190
Internal causes, of behavior, 619, 620, 621
Internal consistency, 423
Internalizing behaviors, 318
Internalizing problems, 542
Internal rewards, 395
Internals, 474
International Statistical Classification of Diseases, Injuries, and Causes of Death (ICD-10), 538
Internet, medical advise searches on, 507, 508*f*, 509
Interpersonal attraction
  love, 650–653, 652*f*
  social influence and, 647–650, 648*f*, 649*f*
Interpersonal intelligence, 440
Interpersonal relationships
  handling, 440–441
Interpersonal relationships, mental disorders and, 581–582, 591–592
Interposition, 120
Interpropositional thinking, 301
Interviews, for personality measurement, 479
Intimacy versus isolation, 336*t*, 344
Intrinsic motivation, 394–395
Introspection, 7, 249–250
Introverts, 462
Intuitive thought, vs. rational thought, 22–23, 23*f*
Involuntary eye movements, 95
Involuntary response, 186–187
IQ. *See* Intelligence quotient
Iris, 93
Ironic monitoring process, 137–138, 138*f*
Irrational beliefs, overcoming, cognitive therapies for, 587–589, 588*f*, 589*f*
Irrationality, vs. rationality, 10, 11*f*
Irritable-inattentive behavior, 341

James-Lange theory, 396–397, 396*f*, 398*t*
Jealousy, love and, 651
Jet lag, 133–134, 134*f*
Jnd (just noticeable difference), 88–89
Job performance, personality and, 482–483, 483*f*
Job search, self-efficacy and, 474–475, 475*f*
"Join up" method, for horse training, 185–186, 186*f*
Jung, Carl, 462
Jury trials, mental contamination and, 236, 236*f*
Just noticeable difference (jnd), 88–89

Kaufman Adult Intelligence Test, 425
Kaufman Assessment Battery for Children, 425
K complexes, 143
Kennedy, John F. Jr., 264–265, 265*f*
Kevorkian, Dr. Jack, 362, 362*f*
Kinesics, 402
Kinesthesia, 109–110
Kismet, 272–273, 272*f*
Klismaphilia, 562*t*
Klondike spaces, 443
"Knockout" mice, 516
Knowing, vs. remembering, 223
Knowledge, creativity and, 443, 444*f*
Kohlberg, Lawrence, moral development theory, 308–311, 309*t*
Koro, 538
Korsakoff's syndrome, 239

Labels, DSM-IV, 540
Language, 249, 275
  basic nature of, 275
  development of, 275–278, 276*t*
    components of, 277–278
    critical period for, 276
    milestones for, 276*t*
    theories of, 275–276, 276*t*
  nonhuman, 279–281, 280*f*
  thought and, 278–279
Language acquisition device, 275
Language area, posterior, 69
LASIK surgery, 95, 95*f*
Late-adult transition, 357–358, 357*f*
Latency stage, 458
Lateralization of function, 61–63, 63*f*, 64*f*
Laws of grouping, 114, 115*f*
LDL cholesterol, 514, 515
Leadership, 619, 653–655
Leading questions, memory distortion and, 227
Learned helplessness
  depression and, 550–551
  operant conditioning and, 194–195, 194*f*
Learning
  approach, evaluation of, 475–476
  based on consequences. *See* Operant conditioning
  biological constraints on, 176–177, 176*f*
  classical conditioning, 169
  cognitive processes in, 196–197, 196*f*
  disabilities, 418
  mental disorders and, 535
  neural basis of, 175
  observational. *See* Observational learning
  operant conditioning, 169
  in perception, 122
  REM sleep and, 144
Learning theories of personality, 471–476, 473*f*, 475*f*
Least restrictive alternative, 610
Left hemisphere, emotions and, 399, 400*f*
Legal issues
  mental disorders, 610–611
  related to death, 363
Lens, 93
Leptin, 381
Less-lead-to-more effect, 633–634, 634*f*
Libido, 457
Life events, stressful, 497–498, 498*t*
Life experiences, health-related outcomes and, 493
Life records, 540
Life structure, 356
Lifestyle
  definition of, 491
  healthy, marketing of, 521–522, 523*f*
  longevity and, 521
  organizations, 596
Light
  intensity, 94
  vision and, 93–94, 93*f*, 94*f*

wavelength of, 93, 94*f*
as zeitgeber, 133–134, 134*f*
Likert scales, 631, 631*t*
Limbic system, 57
Limits, method of, 87
Linear perspective, 119
Linguistic relativity hypothesis, 278
Lipids, 378
Lithium, 599–600
Living will, 363
Localization, of sound, 101–102
Location task, for vision assessment, 68
Loci, method of, 243
Locomotor development, 292, 293*t*, 294
Locus ceruleus, in panic disorder, 555
Logical concepts, 250
Logical thought, 301
Longevity
guidelines for, 360–361
healthy lifestyle and, 521
personality and, 481
Longitudinal research, 296–297, 297*f*
Longitudinal-sequential design, 298
Long-term memory
aging and, 352
definition of, 212
neuron structural changes and, 240
Loudness, 99, 100*f*
Love
in adult development, 344
decline of, 651–653, 652*f*
physical attraction and, 619, 650
romantic, 650
LSD (lysergic acid diethylamide), 161
Lymphocytes, 500
Lysergic acid diethylamide (LSD), 161

Macroelectrodes, 65
Macrosystem, 345
Magnetic resonance imaging (MRI), 64, 65, 541
Magnitude, of sound waves, 99
Maintenance rehearsal, 212
Major depressive episode, 549
Major tranquilizers, 598–599
Maladaptive habits/reactions, 584
Maladaptive nature, of mental disorders, 533
Mania, 550
MAO inhibitors, 599
Marijuana, 160–161, 160*f*
Marital relationship
subjective well-being and, 405
Viagra and, 593–594, 594*f*
Marital therapy, 579, 591–593, 592*f*, 593*f*
Maslow, Abraham, 465
Masochism, 562, 562*t*
Matching law, 192–193
Maternal sensitivity, attachment and, 314–315
Maturation, 286
MCMI (Millon Clinical Multiaxial Inventory), 478
Mean, 660–661
Meaning, language and, 275
Media, health-promotion messages, 521–522, 523*f*
Median, 661
Media violence, 201–202, 202*f*, 388
Medical information, on Internet, 507, 508*f*, 509
Medulla, of brain, 55
Melatonin, 132, 134
Memory/memories
aging and, 351–352
biological bases, neuroimaging studies of, 219
brain and, 237–241
construction, 227, 228–229, 228*f*
decision making and, 281
definition of, 210
distortion, 227–228
distributed vs. massed practice, 210
dreams and, 149, 149*f*
for emotionally laden events, 234–235, 235*f*
encoding, 210, 211
for factual information. *See* Episodic memory; Semantic memory
false, 228, 231–232, 231*f*
implicit. *See* Procedural memory
improvement
drugs for, 241, 242*f*
steps for, 242–243
information sources, confusion about, 228
kinds of information stored in, 214–215, 214*f*
lapses, 241
levels of processing view, 220
long-term, 212
loss. *See* Amnesia
modal model of, 211–212, 211*f*
mood effects on, 235
neural network models, 212–214, 213*f*
for odors, 108
processes, models of, 210–211
recovered, 559
repression, 230–232, 231*f*
retrieval, 210, 211
semantic, 221–223
sensory, 212
short-term, 212
for skills. *See* Procedural memory
storage, 210, 211
study methods for, 218–219, 218*f*
working, 212
Memory trace, 240
Menopause, 349, 382
Menstrual cycle, 382
Menstruation, 331
Mental contamination, 236, 236*f*, 237
Mental disorders. *See also* specific mental disorders
assessment
methods for, 537–538
by psychologists, 540–541
biological causes of, 43
classification, 538
definition of, 532–533, 533
developmental perspective, 542
diagnosis, 538
drug therapy for, 597–601, 598*f*, 600*f*
faulty learning and, 584–586, 585*f*, 586*f*
genetic factors in, 75–76
historical aspects, 533–534, 535*f*
legal issues, 610–611
medical view of, 534
modern perspectives, 535
poor social skills in, 586, 586*f*
prevention, 608–609, 609*f*
psychotherapies for, 578–579
sociocultural factors in, 536, 536*f*
vulnerability to, 536
Mental health, exercise and, 523
Mental hospitals, commitment to, 610
Mental hygiene movement, 534
Mental imagery
benefits of, 252–253, 252*f*
in conditioning process, 178–179
Mental models, 251
Mental retardation, 418, 419, 419*f*, 538
Mental set, 271–272, 271*t*
Mentor, 344, 356
Merit-based pay systems, 392
Mesosystem, 345
Metacognitive processing, 270
Method of constant stimuli, 87–88
Method of limits, 87
Method of loci, 243
Microelectrodes, 65
Microsystem, 345
Midbrain, 56
Midlife transition, 357, 357*f*
Millon Clinical Multiaxial Inventory (MCMI), 478
Mind, theory of. *See* Theory of mind
Mind-body connection, 6
Minnesota Multiphasic Personality Inventory (MMPI-2), 477–478, 477*t*
Minor tranquilizers, 600
Mirages, 116
Mirroring, 590
Misapplied constancy, theory of, 117
Mitosis, 73
MMPI-2 (Minnesota Multiphasic Personality Inventory), 477–478, 477*t*
Mneumonics, for memory improvement, 243
Modal model of memory, 211–212, 211*f*
Mode, 661
Modeling, 586
Models of abnormality, 533
Modules, 67, 67*f*
Monocular cues, for distance perception, 119–120
Monozygotic twins, 73, 75*f*
Mood, 255, 403. *See also* Affective states
Mood congruence effects, 235, 235*f*
Mood-dependent memory, 235, 235*f*
Mood disorders, 549
Moon illusion, 117
Moral development
cultural differences in, 310–311
gender differences in, 310
stages in, 307–311, 308*f*, 309*t*
Moral judgments, consistency of, 310
Moral treatment, 534, 535*f*
Morning person, 132, 133*t*
Moro reflex, 291, 292*t*
Morphine, 159
Mothers, schizophrenic, 569
Motion parallax, 120
Motivation
achievement, 390–394, 391*f*, 393*f*
action and, 371–372, 372*f*
affiliation, 391
aggressive, 386–390, 386*f*, 387*f*, 389*f*
arousal theory, 377*t*
arousal theory of, 373–374
autonomous, 514
controlled, 514
definition of, 370, 371*f*
drive theory, 377*t*
drive theory of, 372–373, 373*f*
exercise, 523–524, 523f
expectancy theory, 374, 377*t*
goal-setting theory, 374–375, 375*f*, 377*t*
hierarchy of needs and, 376–377, 376*f*
hunger, 378–381, 379*f*, 380*f*
intrinsic, 394–395
leadership, 654
in observational learning, 201, 201*f*
personal, 440
in planning fallacy, 625–626
power, 391
sexual, 381–386, 382*f*, 384*f*
theories of, 377*t*
Motivational factors, 88
Motives, in memory distortion, 227
Motor cortex, 59

Motor deficits, 560
Movements, emotions and, 401–402, 401*f*
Mr. Yuk stickers, 193
MRI (magnetic resonance imaging), 64, 65
Müller, Johannes, 6
Müller-Lyer illusion, 117, 117*f*
Multicultural perspective, 14
Multiple-baseline design, 198
Multiple intelligences, theory of, 414–415
Multiple personality disorder, 558–559, 559*f*
Multiple sclerosis, 44
Munchausen's syndrome, 560
Music, brain function and, 71–72
Musical intelligence, 414
Myelin, 44
Myelin sheath, 44, 46

Names, occupational choice and, 467
Narcissistic personality disorder, 564, 565*t*
Narcolepsy, 146, 147
Natural concepts, 250
Naturalistic decision making, 266–267, 266*f*
Naturalistic observation, 24, 24*f*
Natural killer cells
  cancer rates and, 509
  optimism and, 502
Natural opiates, 514
Natural selection, in evolution, 16–17, 16*f*
Nature-versus-nurture controversy, 10, 286
  balanced view of, 78–79
  parenting and, 319–321, 320*f*
  research strategies for, 74–75
  resolution of, 122–123
Nearsightedness, 94
Necrophilia, 562*t*
Need for achievement. *See* Achievement motivation
Needs, hierarchy of, 465
Need to belong, adolescent friendships and, 334–335, 335*f*
Negative affect, love and, 651–652
Negative afterimages, 96
Negative cognitive triad, 551
Negative contrast effect, 196
Negative punishment, 184, 185*t*
Negative reinforcement, 185–186, 185*t*, 186*f*, 205
Negative reinforcers, 184
Neodissociation theory of hypnosis, 152, 154
Neo-Freudians, 462–463
NEO-PI (NEO Personality Inventory), 478
Nerve conduction velocity, 426
Nerve fibers, 50
Nervous system
  anatomy, 50–51, 51*f*, 51*t*
  autonomic, 51–52, 53*f*
  study methods for, 64–66, 65*f*, 66*f*
Neural network models of memory, 212–214, 213*f*
Neural networks, 240, 273
Neurohormones, 52
Neuroimaging
  for studying biological bases of memory, 219
  during working memory tasks, 216–217
Neuroleptics, 598–599
Neurons
  communication between, 46–48, 47*t*
  communication within, 45–46, 46*f*
  definition of, 85
  function of, 45–48, 46*f*, 47*f*
  structure of, 44–45, 45*f*
Neuropeptide Y, 516
Neuropsychological tests, 541
Neuroticism, 405
Neurotransmitters, 48–49, 48*t*. *See also* specific neurotransmitters
  barbiturates and, 158
  in depression, 550
  drug effects and, 49, 50*f*
  endorphins, 49
  excitatory effects, 48
  inhibitory effects, 48
  in memory, 239
  in schizophrenia, 570
  stimulants and, 158
Newborns
  learning abilities of, 293
  visual perception of, 121–122, 121*f*
NICHD Study of Early Child Care, 320
Nicotine, 159, 511
Nightmares, 147
Night person, 132, 133*t*
Night terrors, 146, 147
Nodes of Ranvier, 46
Noise
  hearing loss and, 102–103, 103*f*
  longevity and, 361
Nonconscious thoughts, 458–459, 460*f*
Nonverbal cues, of emotions, 401–402, 401*f*
Norepinephrine (noradrenaline)
  in depression, 550
  effects of, 48*t*
  function of, 54
  localization of, 48*t*
  Ritalin and, 544
  stimulants and, 158
Normal curve
  interpretation of, 662–663, 662*f*, 663*f*
  test standardization and, 422, 423*f*
Normative social influence, 642
Nouns, acquisition of, 277
Nuclei, medullary, 55
Nucleus accumbens, 156
Number, as primary mental ability, 414

Obedience, social influence and, 645–647, 646*f*, 647*f*
Obesity
  childhood, 324–325, 324*f*
  Pima Indians, 380, 380*f*
Objective tests of personality, 476–478, 477*t*
Objectivity, scientific method and, 20
Object permanence, 300, 302–303
Observation
  naturalistic, 24, 24*f*
  of naturally occurring brain damage, 64–65, 65*f*
  survey method and, 25–26, 26*f*
  systematic, 24
    advantages vs. disadvantages of, 32*t*
    case method and, 24–25
Observational learning
  from actions of others and, 167–168, 169*f*
  aggression and, 201–202, 202*f*
  applications, practical, 203–204, 204*f*
  attitudes and, 628
  culture and, 202–203, 203*f*
  definition of, 169, 200, 200*f*
  physical fitness and, 205
  principles, 200–201, 201*f*
  social cognitive theory and, 473
Obsessions, 556
Obsessive-compulsive disorder
  description of, 555–556, 556*f*, 565*t*
  eye-blink classical conditioning in, 175
Occipital lobe, 60
Occupational choices, last names and, 467
Occupational safety, goal-setting for, 375–376, 376*f*
Odors
  effects of, 108–109
  memory for, 108
  primary, 107
Oedipus complex, 457
Olfactory epithelium, 107, 107*f*
Omission, errors of, 87
One-trial learning, 177
Open-mindedness
  critical thinking and, 23
  scientific method and, 20
Openness to experience, 470, 470*f*, 471
Operant conditioning
  applications
    for daily life, 199
    for horses, 185–186, 186*f*
    study of, 197–198, 198*f*
  attitudes and, 628
  in behavior therapies, 585–586, 586*f*
  cognitive perspective, 194–198, 194*f*, 196*f*
  consequential operations and, 183–186, 183*f*, 185*t*, 186*f*
  definition of, 169, 182, 182*f*
  principles, 186, 193*f*
    chaining, 187–188, 187*f*
    reward delay, 188–189, 190*f*
    schedules of reinforcement, 189–193, 192*f*
    shaping, 187–188, 187*f*
    stimulus control, 193, 193*f*
Operating principles, of language development, 275–276
Opiates, 159, 514
Opium, 159
Opponent-process theory
  color-vision and, 96–97
  of emotion, 397–398, 398*t*
Oppositional defiant disorder, 542, 542*f*
Optic nerve, 93
Optimism, 502–503, 503*t*
Optimistic bias, 405, 625–626
Options, decision making, 281
Oral stage, 457
Orgasm disorders, 561
Orgasmic phase, of sexual behavior, 383
Orientation, 257–258, 257*f*
Osteoporosis, 349
Other-enhancing tactics, 644
Otis-Lennon School Ability Test, 422
Outcomes, negative/disappointing, 626–627, 627*f*
Outpatient care, for mental disorders, 610
Oval window, 99, 99*f*
Overextensions, 278
Overlap, 120
Overload, 400
Over-the-counter drugs, prenatal influences of, 288
Ovum, 287

Pain
  expressions, of infants, 311
  gate-control theory, 104–105
  management, 105, 106, 124
  perception, 104–106
    cognitive processes in, 105–106
    culture and, 105
  perception, placebo effect, 106
  purpose of, 124
  role of, 104
  threshold, 105
  types of, 104
Palmar grasping reflex, 291–292, 292*t*
Panic disorder, 554, 555*f*
Papillae, tongue, 107, 108*f*
Papilloma infections, 339
Paracelsus, 534
Parallel processing

neural networks and, 212–213
vs. serial, 67, 67*f*
Paranoid personality disorder, 563, 565*t*
Paranoid type of schizophrenia, 569*t*
Paranormal events, 123
Paraphilias, 561–562, 561*f*, 562*t*
Parapsychologists, 123
Parasympathetic nervous system, 52, 53*f*
Parent-absent families, 339
Parental demandingness, 334
Parental responsiveness, 334
Parenting styles, 333–334, 334*f*
Parietal lobe, 60, 68*f*
Partial reinforcement, 190
Partial reinforcement effect, 191
Passive coping style, 463
Passive smoking, prenatal development and, 289
Passive touch, 104
Patients, interaction with physicians, 505–507
Pattern recognition
of infants, 295–296
perception and, 118–119, 119*f*
Pavlov, Ivan, 170, 171, 171*f*
P-E (person-environment fit), 500
PEA (phenylethylamine), 382
Peak experiences, 465
Pedophilia, 562, 562*t*
Penis envy, 457
Perception
active role of, 84, 85*f*
attention and, 112–113
constancies, 114–116, 116*f*
definition of, 85
development of, 293–296, 295*f*, 296*f*
distance, 119–120, 120*f*
extrasensory, 123–124
figure-ground relationship and, 113–114, 114*f*
illusions of, 116–118, 116*f*, 117*f*
innate, 121–122, 121*f*
laws of grouping, 114, 115*f*
learning in, 122
organizational principles, 113–114, 113*f*, 114*f*
pain, 104–106
cognitive processes in, 105–106
culture and, 105
pattern recognition and, 118–119, 119*f*
of pitch, 100–101
selective attention and, 112–113
species differences in, 118
subliminal, 85, 89–90, 90*f*
Performance appraisals, 400
Peripheral feedback effect, 397
Peripheral nervous system, 50
Peripheral route, to persuasion, 630
Perls, Fritz, 583
Permanent threshold shift (PTS), 102
Permissive parents, 334
Persecution, delusions of, 567
Personal control, in psychotherapy, 606–607
Personal growth, 464
Personal happiness, subjective well-being, 404–405, 406*f*
Personal identity, 335
Personality
adolescent, 341, 342*f*
behavioral observations, 479
biological measures, 479
definition of, 450
dimensions of, 470–471, 470*f*
dominant aspects of, 469, 469*f*
health-related outcomes and, 493
interviews, 479
job performance and, 482–483, 483*f*
learning theories of, 471–476, 473*f*, 475*f*
longevity and, 361, 481
measurement of, 476–479, 477*t*, 478*f*
projective measures of, 478, 478*f*
reality of, 450–452, 451*f*
research, 479–484, 480*f*, 481*f*
self-report tests of, 476–478, 477*t*
structure of, 455
theories
Freudian, 453–461
humanistic, 463–468, 465*f*, 466*f*
trait, 468–472, 469*f*, 470*f*
workplace aggression and, 483–484, 483*f*
Personality attributes, creativity and, 444, 444*f*
Personality disorders. *See also* specific personality disorders
description of, 538, 563–566, 564*f*, 565*t*
DSM-IV classification, 563
Personality traits
basic, 469–472, 469*f*, 470*f*
definition of, 468
secondary, 469
Personal responsibility, 464, 468
Personal styles (strategies), 451
Person-environment fit (P-E), 500
Person-job fit, 482
Persuasion
central route, 630
cognitive approach, 630–631
effects of, 629–630, 629*f*
one-sided approach, 629
peripheral route, 630
subliminal messages and, 90
theories of, 630
two-sided approach, 629
Pervasive developmental disorders, 546
Pessimism, 502–503, 503*t*
PET (positron emission tomography), 65–66, 66*f*, 541
Phallic stage, 457
Phenolic antioxidants, 515
Phenomenological/experiential therapies, 582–584, 583*f*
Phenothiazines, 598
Phenylalanine, 73–74
Phenylethylamine (PEA), 382
Phenylketonuria (PKU), 73–74
Philosophy, psychology and, 6
Phobias
anxiety disorders, 553–554, 554*f*
behavior therapies for, 584
learning and, 535
systematic desensitization for, 585, 585*f*
Phonological development, 277
Phonological loop, in working memory, 216
Phosphatidylserine, 241
Phthalate esters, risks to infants, 290–291, 290*f*
Physical appearance, persuasive advertising and, 629, 629*f*
Physical attractiveness, interpersonal attraction and, 649–650, 649*f*
Physical change
during early adulthood, 348, 348*f*
in later life, 349–351, 350*f*
during midlife, 348–349
Physical contact, attachment and, 315–317, 316*f*
Physical handicap organizations, 596
Physical reasoning, 257–258, 258*f*
Physical violence, HIV/AIDS and, 520
Physicians
changing role of, 506*f*
interaction with patients, 505–507
Physiological death, 361–362
Physiological dependence, 155
Physiological needs, 376, 376*f*
Physiology, 6
Physique, interpersonal attraction and, 650
Piaget, Jean, 298–299
Pima Indians, obesity and, 380, 380*f*
Pineal gland, 6, 132
Pinel, Philippe, 534
Pinna, 98–99
Pitch, 99–101, 100*f*
Pituitary gland, 52, 54, 57
PKU (phenylketonuria), 73–74
Placebo effect, pain perception and, 106
Placenta, 288
Place theory, 100–101
Planning fallacy, 252–253, 625–626
Plasticity, 59
Plasticizers, risks to infants, 290–291, 290*f*
Plateau phase, of sexual behavior, 383
Playground safety, 318–319, 318*f*
Playing hard to get, 645
Pleasure principle, 455
Poggendorf illusion, 117–118, 117*f*
Pons, 55
Positive contrast effect, 195–196
Positive emotionality, 312
Positive mood state, reasoning and, 255
Positive punishment, 184, 185*t*
Positive reinforcement
effects of, 185*t*
for exercise motivation, 205
for horse training, 185–186, 186*f*
Positive reinforcers, 183, 183*f*
Positron emission tomography (PET), 65–66, 66*f*, 541
Possible event condition, 302–303
Postconventional level of morality, 309, 309*t*
Posterior language area, 69
Postskeptical rationalism, 333
Posttraumatic stress disorder (PTSD), 536–537, 556–557, 557*f*
Posture, emotions and, 401–402, 401*f*
Power motivation, 391
Practical intelligence, 354, 420*t*
Practical (contextual) intelligence, 415, 415*f*
Practice
episodic memory and, 219
memory and, 243
Practice effects, 297
Preadult era, 356
Precognition, 123
Preconscious level, of consciousness, 453, 454*f*
Preconventional level of morality, 308, 309*t*
Prediction, 665–666, 665*f*
Predictions, 26–27
Predictive validity, 424
Prefrontal cortex, in relational reasoning, 70–71, 71*f*
Prefrontal lobotomy, 602
Pregnancy
adolescent, 339–340
alcohol consumption during, 289, 289*f*
smoking during, 289
Prejudice
nonconscious thought and, 460, 460*f*
origins of, 636–638, 637*f*
reducing, 638–641, 640*f*
Premack principle, 183
Premature ejaculation, 561
Prenatal period, 287–288
Preoperational stage, 300, 302*t*
Preschooler, competent, stage theory and, 302–303

Prescription drugs, prenatal influences on development, 288
Preservation, 217
Prevention
  behaviors, 522
  primary, 608
  secondary, 609
  strategies, 521
  tertiary, 609
Primary aging, 350
Primary appraisal, of stressors, 495
Primary prevention, 521–524, 523*f*, 608
Primary reinforcers, 183
Primates, sign language and, 279
Priming, 218–219
Priming effect, 223–224
Primitive thinking, 551
Private self-consciousness, 560
Proactive interference, 225–226, 225*f*, 351
Problem identification, 267
Problem solving
  effective
    facilitation of, 269–270
    interference with, 270–272, 270*f*, 271*f*, 271*t*
  methods, 268–269
  mood and, 255
  stages of, 267–268, 268*f*
Problem-solving skills, teaching, 608
Problem-solving therapy, 595
Procedural memory, 218, 223–224, 224*f*, 458–459, 460*f*
Procrastination, 189, 190*f*
Prodromal pruning theory of schizophrenia, 569–570
Production, speech, 70, 70*f*
Production processes, in observational learning, 201, 201*f*
Programmed theories of aging, 360
Progressive relaxation, 526
Progress rewards, for studying, 37
Projection, 456*t*
Projective tests of personality, 478, 478*f*
Propinquity, 648
Propositions, 251
Prosocial behavior, 313
Prosopagnosia, 98
Prostate gland, 349
Protease inhibitors, 519
Protective factors, 342
Protest, bereavement and, 363
Prototypes, 222, 250, 251*t*
Proximity, laws of, 115*f*
Prozac (fluoxetine), 599
Psi, 123–124
Psychedelics, 159–161, 160*f*
Psychiatrist, 534
Psychoactive drugs, reactions to
  ethnic differences in, 600–601
  gender differences in, 601
Psychoanalysis, 454–455, 580–581, 580*f*
Psychoanalytically oriented psychotherapy, 581
Psychobiology, 13*t*
Psychodrama, 590
Psychodynamic perspective, 11, 12*t*
Psychodynamic theory, 385
Psychodynamic therapies, 580–582, 581*f*
Psychodynamic view, of dreams, 148–149
Psychokinesis, 123
Psychological coping techniques, 526
Psychological dependence, 155
Psychological factors
  in autism, 548
  in escalation of commitment, 262
  in mental disorders, 535
  in schizophrenia, 570–571
Psychological tests, 422–424, 541
Psychology
  applications, 17–19
  behavior and, 4–5
  biological factors in, 42–43, 43*f*
  definition of, 5
  diversity and, 12, 13–14
  evolutionary, 15–17, 16*f*
  grand issues of, 10
  historical aspects of, 6–8, 6*f*, 9*f*
  human factors, 18–19
  humanistic, 8
  modern, 8–9
    perspectives in, 11–12, 12*t*
    trends in, 12
  research in. *See* Research, psychological
  scientific field of, 6
  scientific nature of, 5
  study methods for, 36–37, 36*f*
  subfields, 13*t*
Psychophysical methods, 87–88
Psychosexual stages of development, 457–458, 459*f*
Psychosocial factors, in smoking, 511
Psychosocial rehabilitation, 579, 596–597, 596*f*
Psychosurgery, 602
Psychotherapist, selection of, 612–613
Psychotherapy, 578–579
  culturally sensitive, 607
  effectiveness, 603–607, 605*f*, 606*f*
  ethical issues in, 611–612, 611*f*
  forms of, common factors in, 606, 606*f*
  individual
    alternatives to, group therapies, 590–591, 591*f*
    limitations of, 589–590
  phenomenological/experiential, 582–584, 583*f*
  popular view of, 579–580, 579*f*
  psychodynamic, 580–582, 581*f*
  termination, 613
PTS (permanent threshold shift), 102
PTSD (posttraumatic stress disorder), 536–537, 556–557, 557*f*
Puberty, 330, 331–332, 331*f*, 332*f*
Punishment, 183, 184, 185*t*
Pupil, 92–93, 92*f*
Pure word deafness, 69
Pursuit movements, 96

Quantitative trait loci (QTLs), 430
Questionnaires, 631

Race, culturally sensitive psychotherapy and, 607
Random access memory, 211
Random assignment of participants to experimental conditions, 30
Randomization, 666–667
Range, 661
Rapid eye-movement sleep. *See* REM sleep
Rational-emotive therapy (RET), 587
Rational factors, in escalation of commitment, 262
Rationalism, 6
Rationality, vs. irrationality, 10, 11*f*
Rationalization, 456*t*
Rational thought, vs. intuitive thought, 22–23, 23*f*
Raven Progressive Matrices, 434
Reaction time, 253, 350, 425
Realist approach, 332
Realistic conflict theory, 636–637
Reality monitoring, 228
Reality principle, 455
Reasoning
  definition of, 254
  error, sources of, 255–257, 256*f*
  faulty, 264–265, 265*f*
Recategorization, in reducing prejudice, 640–641
Recency effect, 215–216
Receptors, sensory. *See* Sensory receptors
Reciprocal teaching, 304
Recognition, 218
Reconditioning, 173–174
Recovered memories, 559
Recovery, bereavement and, 364
Reflection, 141, 163
Reflexes, 50–51, 291–292, 292*t*
Regression, 456*t*
Regression analysis, 666
Rehearsal, 307
Reinforcement
  concurrent schedules of, 191–193
  definition of, 183
  effects of, 185*t*
  negative, 184
  partial or intermittent, 190
  physical fitness and, 205
  positive, 183
  schedules of, 189–193, 192*f*, 472
Reinforcement value, 474
Rejecting/neglecting parents, 334
Relational reasoning, prefrontal cortex in, 70–71, 71*f*
Relationships
  adult, attachment and, 315, 315*f*
  interpersonal
    handling, 440–441
    mental disorders and, 581–582
  marital
    subjective well-being and, 405
    Viagra and, 593–594, 594*f*
  romantic
    attachment and, 315, 315*f*
    guidelines for, 656–657
Relative size, 115
Relativist approach, 332
Reliability, 422–423, 631
Religious faith, longevity and, 361
Remembering, 223. *See also* Memory
REM sleep
  disorders of, 147
  dreams and, 148
  functions of, 144
  slow-wave, functions of, 144
  studying, 142, 143, 143*f*
  without atonia, 147
Representativeness heuristic, 259–260
Repression
  Freudian view of, 454, 456*t*
  psychoanalysis of, 580
  purpose of, 230–232, 231*f*
Research, psychological
  with animals, 33–34, 34*f*
  ethical issues in, 31–34
  methods
    advantages vs. disadvantages of, 32*t*
    case studies, 32*t*
    correlation, 26–28, 32*t*
    experimentation, 28–31, 32*t*
    observation, 24–26, 24*f*, 26*f*
    surveys, 32*t*
    systematic observation, 32*t*
Residual type of schizophrenia, 569*t*
Resilience in development, 342–343, 343*f*
Resistance
  in general adaptation syndrome, 495
  in psychoanalysis, 580–581

Resolution phase, of sexual behavior, 383
Responsibility, diffusion, escalation of commitment and, 262
RET (rational-emotive therapy), 587
Retention, in observational learning, 201, 201*f*
Reticular activating system, 55
Retina, 93
Retinal disparity, 120, 120*f*
Retrieval
  memory, 210, 211
  state-dependent, 220–221
Retrieval cues, 220, 221*f*, 243
Retrieval inhibition, 226
Retroactive interference, 225–226, 225*f*
Retrograde amnesia, 237, 237*f*
Reversibility, 301
Reward delay, 188–189
Riggins vs. Nevada, 611
Right hemisphere, emotional expression and, 62–63, 63*f*, 399, 400*f*
Rights of individuals vs. societal rights, 610–611
Right to die, 362, 362*f*
Risk averse, 261
Risk factors, 493, 509
Risk prone, 261
Ritalin, for ADHD, 544
Rods, 92*f*, 93
Rogers, Carl, 464–465, 583
Role conflict, 400
Role-playing view of hypnosis, 151–154, 151*f*, 153*f*
Role reversal, 590
Romantic love, 650
Romantic relationships
  attachment and, 315, 315*f*
  guidelines for, 656–657
Rooting reflex, 292, 292*t*
Rotational acceleration, semicircular canals and, 110*f*
Rubella, 288
Rumination, 141, 163

Saccadic eye movements, 95
Sadism, 562, 562*t*
Safe sex, hypocrisy and, 634–636
Safety needs, 376, 376*f*
Sample
  size, statistics and, 667
  unbiased vs. biased, 667
Sampling, 25–26
Saturation, 94
Scaffolding, 304
Scales, 631
Scatter plots, 665*f*, 666
SCC (sex-category constancy), 321
Schacter-Singer theory (two-factor), 397, 398*t*, 403–404
Schedules of reinforcement, 189–193, 192*f*, 472
Schemas
  concepts and, 251
  definition of, 299
  distortion and, 227
  emotions and, 404
  framing and, 261
  gender, 323–324
Schizoid personality disorder, 563, 565*t*
Schizophrenia
  causes, 569–571
  course, 568–569
  definition of, 567
  nature of, 567–568
  negative symptoms, 567, 568
  onset, 568
  positive symptoms, 567–568, 568*f*
  relapses, 570
  types, 569, 569*t*
  vampires and, 566
Schizotypal personality disorder, 563–564, 565*t*
Scientific method
  advantages of, 21–23
  components of, 20
  definition of, 6, 19–20
  theory in, 20–21
SCN (suprachiasmatic nucleus), 131
Screening, disease, 524–525
Secondary aging, 350
Secondary appraisal, of stressors, 495–496
Secondary messengers, 600
Secondary prevention, 521, 524–525, 525*f*, 609
Secondary traits, 469
Secure attachment, 314
Security blankets, 316
Sedentary individuals, exercise motivation for, 523–524, 523f
Selection, in evolution, 16–17, 16*f*
Selective attention, 112–113, 212, 568
Selective-serotonin reuptake inhibitors (SSRIs), 599
Self-actualization, 465
Self-actualization needs, 376, 376*f*
Self-affirmation, 633
Self-awareness
  choking under pressure and, 141–142
  definition of, 130, 139
  depression and, 551
  effects of, 140–141
  increased, effects of, 139–140, 140*f*
  test for, 162–163
Self-concept
  autobiographical memory and, 233
  culture and, 466, 466*f*
  definition of, 464
  empathy and, 313
  gaps with experience, 464–465, 465*f*
  research on, 466–467
Self-confidence, leadership and, 654
Self-consciousness
  private, 140, 560
  public, 140
  test for, 162–163
Self-control, teaching, 590
Self-defeating patterns of behavior, 652
Self-determination theory, 514–515
Self-efficacy
  boosting, benefits of, 474–475, 475*f*
  definition of, 473
  mood and, 523
Self-enhancing tactics, 644
Self-examination, 525, 525*f*
Self-handicapping, 395
Self-healers, 502
Self-help groups, 579, 595–596
Self-identity, 336–337
Self-justification, in escalation of commitment, 262
Self-monitoring, 325, 541
Self-reinforcement, 473
Self-report tests, of personality, 476–478, 477*t*
Self-sacrifice, by charismatic leaders, 655
Self-schema, 251, 337, 551
Self-serving bias, 621–623, 622*f*
Self-system, 473
Semantic development, 277–278
Semantic memory
  aging and, 352
  concepts and, 221–223
  definition of, 219
  study methods for, 218
  temporal lobes and, 238–239
  vs. episodic memory, 222–223
Semicircular canals, 110, 110*f*
Sensation, 84–85
Sensation seeking, 393–394, 479–480, 480*f*
Sensitivity-training, 590–591
Sensorimotor stage, 299–300, 302*t*
Sensory abilities, age-related decline in, 350
Sensory adaptation, 90–91, 91*f*
Sensory cortex, 61
Sensory deficits, 560
Sensory deprivation, 86
Sensory memory, 212
Sensory processes
  role of, 86*f*
  virtual environment technologies and, 111, 111*f*
Sensory receptors
  definition of, 85, 86
  olfactory, 107, 107*f*
  for taste, 107, 108*f*
  touch, 104
  visual, 92*f*, 93, 96, 96*f*
Sensory thresholds, 86–87
  measurement of, 87–88
  signal detection theory and, 88
Sentence verification task, 218
Serial position curve, 215–216, 215*f*
Serial processing, 67, 67*f*, 213
Serotonin, 48*t*, 550
Serum cholesterol, 514
Set point, 381
Sex-category constancy (SCC), 321
Sex-change operation, 563
Sexual abuse, 341
Sexual arousal, 385
Sexual arousal orders, 561
Sexual attraction, between therapist and client, 611
Sexual behavior, 382–385, 384*f*
Sexual contact, between therapist and client, 611–612
Sexual desire orders, 561
Sexually transmitted diseases, adolescent, 339
Sexual masochism, 562, 562*t*
Sexual maturation, early, 331–332, 332*f*
Sexual motivation, 381–386, 382*f*, 384*f*
Sexual orientation, 385–386
Sexual sadism, 562, 562*t*
Shadow grief, 364
Shape, illusions of, 117–118, 117*f*
Shape constancy, 115, 116*f*
Shaping, 187–188, 187*f*, 205
Shift work, 134, 134*f*
Shock, bereavement and, 363
Shorthand codes, for memory improvement, 224, 243
Short-term memory, 215
Shyness, 313, 320
Signal detection theory, 88, 89
Significant-other organizations, 596
Similarity
  interpersonal attraction and, 648, 648*f*
  laws of, 115*f*
Simple cells, 97
Simplicity, laws of, 115*f*
Simultaneous conditioning, 172, 172*f*, 173
Single-parent families, 339
Situational (external) factors, of behavior, 451
Size, illusions of, 116–117, 116*f*, 117*f*
Size constancy, 114–115
Size cues, 119
Size-distance invariance, 115
Skepticism
  critical thinking and, 23
  scientific method and, 20
Skin, touch receptors, 104
Skinner, B.F., 7*f*, 8, 197
SLC6A3–9 gene, 511
Sleep
  deprivation, 145, 146*f*
  promotion, 146
  rapid-eye movement or REM, 142, 143, 143*f*
  slow-wave, disorders of, 147

Sleep, *continued*
stages of, 143, 143*f*
study of, 142–143
Sleep attacks, 147
Sleep disorders
insomnia, 146–147
with REM sleep, 147
with slow-wave sleep, 147
Sleeping pills, 147, 158
Sleep laboratory, 142–143
Sleep spindles, 143
Sleep walking, 147, 147*f*
Slips of the tongue, 580
Slow-wave sleep, functions of, 144
Smell, sense of, 106–109, 107*f*, 295
Smoking
cessation, 511–513, 512*t*
health risks of, 510–511
longevity and, 361
observational learning and, 203–204
prenatal influences on development, 289
Snorting, cocaine, 159
Social age clocks, 345–346, 347*f*
Social behavior
definition of, 619, 636
prejudice, 636–641, 637*f*, 640*f*
Social categorization, 637
Social cognition, 618, 624–627, 625*f*
Social cognitive theory, 473–474, 473*f*
Social-cognitive view of hypnosis, 151–152, 152*f*, 153*f*, 153–154
Social death, 362
Social development
during adolescence, 334–337, 335*f*, 336*t*, 337*f*
in adulthood, 355–359, 355*f*, 357*f*, 358*f*
Social factors
aggression and, 387–388
in psychology, 11, 12*t*
Social influence
compliance and, 644–645, 644*f*
conformity and, 641–642, 642*f*
informational, 642
interpersonal attraction and, 647–650, 648*f*, 649*f*
normative, 642, 643–644
obedience and, 645–647, 646*f*, 647*f*
Social interaction, 636
Social learning
language and, 275
prejudice and, 637–638, 637*f*
Social learning theory, 322–323, 323*f*, 473–474
Social needs, 376, 376*f*
Social networks, 334, 354, 355
Social norms, 641, 643–644, 643*f*
Social phobias, 554, 554*f*
Social pressure
anorexia nervosa and, 545
drug abuse and, 156
Social psychologists, 618, 619
Social psychology, 13*t*
Social referencing, 311–312, 312*f*
Social skills
poor, in mental disorders, 586, 586*f*
teaching, 590
Social smiling, 311
Social thought
attribution and, 619–623, 620*f*, 622*f*
importance of, 618, 618*f*
Societal effects, of achievement motivation, 392–393, 393*f*
Societal rights, vs. rights of individuals, 610–611
Sociocultural factors, in mental disorders, 536, 536*f*
Sociocultural theory, 304
Solutions, problem, potential, formulation of, 267–268
Somatic nervous system, 51
Somatization disorder, 158, 560
Somatoform disorders, 560
Somatosensory cortex, 60
Somnambulism, 146, 147, 147*f*
Sound
intensities, 103*f*
localization of, 101–102
physical characteristics, 99–100, 100*f*
Sound shadow, 101
Source monitoring, 228, 229
Source traits, 470
Space, as primary mental ability, 414
Species differences, in cerebral cortex, 59*f*
Specific-exemplar subsystem, 119
Speech, brain function and, 69–70, 70*f*
Spirituality, longevity and, 361
Split-brain persons, research on, 61–63, 63*f*, 64*f*
Split-half reliability, 423
Spontaneous recovery, 174
SQUID (superconducting quantum interference device), 65, 66
SSRIs (selective-serotonin reuptake inhibitors), 599
Stability versus change, 10, 286
Stages of life, 335–337, 336*t*
Stage theory
of adult development, 344–345
description of, 298–299
modern assessment of, 302–304, 303*f*
Staircase method, 87
Standard deviation, 661, 662–663, 663*f*
Standardization, test, 422, 423*f*
Stanford-Binet test, 416–417, 424
State-dependent retrieval, 220–221
States of consciousness, 130, 130*f*, 136–139
Static visual acuity (SVA), 94
Statistical analysis, 659
Statistical conclusions, sample size and, 667
Statistics, 659
descriptive, 659–661, 660*f*, 660*t*
inferential, 663–665, 664
misuse of, 666–668
Stepping reflex, 292*t*
Stereochemical theory, 107
Stereogram, 120, 120*f*
Stereotaxis apparatus, 65, 65*f*
Stereotypes, 638
Stimulants, 158–159, 159*f*
Stimulus
for classical conditioning, 170
conditioned. *See* Conditioned stimulus
control, 193, 193*f*, 205
discrimination, 174, 174*f*
generalization, 174
subliminal or below threshold, 89–90
unconditioned. *See* Unconditioned stimulus
Stochastic theories of aging, 359–360
Storage
definition of, 210, 211
information in, 214–215, 214*f*
memory disturbances and, 226–227
Strange situation test, 314
Stress
activators of, 494–495
causes of, 497–500, 498*t*, 499*f*
definition of, 494
health and, 500–501
management, 525–527, 526*t*
resistance to, individual differences in, 502–503, 503*t*
task performance and, 501–502, 502*f*
type A behavior pattern and, 479, 479*f*
work-related, 499–500, 499*f*
Stress-coping skills, 608
Stressors
cognitive appraisal of, 495–496, 496*f*
definition of, 494–495
physiological responses to, 495, 495*f*
Stress reduction, longevity and, 361
Stress-resistant individuals, 498
Striving for superiority, 463
Structuralism, 7
Studying
active vs. passive, 37
goals for, 36–37
methods, 36–37, 36*f*
for aggression, 389–390, 389*f*
for brain/nervous system, 64–65, 65*f*, 66*f*
for cognitive processes, 253–254, 253*f*
for development, 296–298, 297*f*
Subject attrition, 297
Subjective well-being, 404–405, 406*f*
Subjectivity, 595
Sublimation, 456
Subliminal perception, 85, 89–90, 90*f*, 460–461
Substance abuse, 571
Substance-induced disorders, 571
Substance-related disorders, 571–572, 572*f*
Substance-use disorders, 571
Successful aging, 349
Successive approximations, 187
Sucking reflex, 292, 292*t*
Suggestibility, 228
Suicide
factors in, 551–553
prevention, 553, 572–573
Sullivan, Henry Stack, 581
Sun exposure, longevity and, 361
Superconducting quantum interference device (SQUID), 65, 66
Superego, 455, 580
Superiority complex, 463
Supermemory, 224, 224*f*
Suprachiasmatic nucleus (SCN), 131
Surface traits, 470
Survey method, 25–26, 26*f*, 32*t*
SVA (static visual acuity), 94
Swan-song phenomenon, 354
Sybil, 558
Syllables, nonsense, 210, 218
Symbolic play, 300
Sympathetic nervous system, 52, 53*f*
Sympathy, counterfactual thinking and, 626
Synapse, 45
Synaptic transmission, 46–48, 47*t*
Synaptic vesicles, 47, 47*f*
Syntax, 280
Systematic desensitization, 585, 585*f*
Systematic observation
advantages vs. disadvantages of, 32*t*
definition of, 24
methods
case studies, 24–25
surveys, 25–26
Systematic processing, 630
Systems theory, 595

Tae-Bo, 205*f*
Tarasoff v. Regents of the University of California, 611, 611*f*
Tardive dyskinesia, 598

Task completion, optimistic bias for, 625–626
Task performance, stress and, 501–502, 502*f*
Taste
  food flavors and, 107–108, 108*f*
  sense of, 107–109, 108*f*
  sensory receptors for, 107, 108*f*
Taste buds, 107, 108*f*
TAT (Thematic Apperception Test), 391, 391*f*
Teenagers. *See* Adolescents
Telegraphic speech, 278
Telomeres, 360
Telepathy, 123
Telepresence, 110, 111
Television violence, 201–202, 202*f*
Temperament, 312–313, 342
Temperature regulation, by infants, 291
Temporal lobe
  anatomy, 60–61
  in memory, 240
  semantic memory and, 238–239
Temporary threshold shift (TTS), 102
Temptation, food as, 406
TENS (transcutaneous electrical nerve stimulation ), 124
Teratogens, 288
Terminal illness, right to die and, 362, 362*f*
Termites, 493–494
Tertiary prevention, 609
Testicular cancer, 525, 525*f*
Testosterone
  aggression and, 43, 388–389
  sexual behavior and, 382
Test-test reliability, 423
Textural gradient, 119
Thalamus, 57
Thematic Apperception Test (TAT), 391, 391*f*
Theories, 20–21
Theory of dissociated control, 152
Theory of mind
  adolescent development and, 332
  in autism, 548, 548*f*
  childhood development and, 305–307, 305*f*
Theory of misapplied constancy, 117
Therapeutic alliance, 606
Therapeutic window, 599–600
Therapist, selection of, 612–613
Theta activity, 143
Thinking, 249–250. *See also* Cognition
  concepts and, 250–251
  images and, 252–253
  nature of, 249
  propositions and, 251
  style, creativity and, 444, 444*f*
Thorazine (chlorpromazine), 598
Thought
  language and, 278–279
  logical, emergence of, 301
  rational vs. intuitive, 22–23, 23*f*
Threatening posture, 402
The Three Faces of Eve, 558
Timbre, 100, 100*f*
Time management, 526, 526*t*
Time-out, 184
"Tip-of-the-nose" phenomenon, 108
Tobacco. *See also* Smoking
  candy-flavored cigarettes, 513
Tofranil (imipramine), 599
Token economies, 585
Tolerance, 155, 639
Tongue, papillae, 107, 108*f*
Tonic neck reflex, 292*t*
Top-down approach, 119
Touch
  passive vs. active, 104
  temperature illusion, 118
Trace conditioning, 172, 172*f*
Traits, leadership, 653–654
Trait theories, 462, 468–472, 469*f*, 470*f*
Tranquilizers
  major, 598–599
  minor, 600
Transcriptase inhibitors, 519
Transcutaneous electrical nerve stimulation (TENS), 124
Transduction, 85
Transference, 581, 611
Transformational leaders, 654–655, 655*f*
Transition periods, 356–357, 357*f*
Tranvestic fetishism, 562*t*
Traumatic experiences, psychological disorders caused by, 557, 557*f*
Traveling wave theory, 100–101
Treatment refusal, 611
Trial and error, 268–269
Trials
  eyewitness testimony, 228–229, 228*f*
  leading questions in, 227
Triarchic theory, 415
Trichromatic theory, 96
Tricyclic antidepressants, 599
Trivialization, 633
Trust versus mistrust, 335, 336*t*
TTS (temporary threshold shift), 102
Twins
  fraternal, 73
  identical or monozygotic, 75*f*
  monozygotic, 73
Twin studies
  alcoholism, 516, 516*t*
  autism, 548
  intelligence, 430–431, 430*f*
  purpose of, 74–75
Two-factor theory (Schacter-Singer), 397, 398*t*, 403–404
Tympanic membrane, 99, 99*f*
Type A behavior pattern, 479, 484–485, 517
Type D personality, 517

UCR (unconditioned response), 171
UCS. *See* Unconditioned stimulus
Ultimate attribution error, 637
Unconditional positive regard, 465
Unconditioned response (UCR), 171
Unconditioned stimulus (UCS)
  biological constraints/characteristics, 175–178, 176*f*
  definition of, 171
  familiarity of, 173
  intensity of, 173
  temporal arrangement of, 172–172, 172*f*
Unconscious level, of consciousness, 453, 454*f*
Underextensions, 278
Underload, 400
Undifferentiated type of schizophrenia, 569*t*
Unusual Uses Test, 442
Upward counterfactuals, 627
Us-versus-them effect, 637
Uterus, 287

Valence, 374, 399, 400
Validity, 423–424, 631
Validity scales, MMPI-2, 477
Variability, in sexual behavior, 383
Variable-interval schedule, 191
Variable-ratio schedule, 191
Variables
  confounding of, 30–31, 30*f*
  correlational method and, 26
  dependent, 29
  experimental method and, 29–30
  independent, 29, 30
Variance, 661
Variation, in evolution, 15, 16*f*
Verbal meaning, as primary mental ability, 414
Verbal salad, 568
Verbs, acquisition of, 277
Vergence eye movements, 95
Version eye movements, 95
Vestibular sacs, 110, 110*f*
Vestibular sense, 110, 110*f*
VE technologies, sensory processes and, 111, 111*f*
Viagra, marital relationships and, 593–594, 594*f*
Violence
  adolescent, treatment method for, 181
  brain dysfunction and, 57–58
  in media, 388
  television/media, 201–202, 202*f*
Virtual environment technologies, sensory processes and, 111, 111*f*
Vision. *See also* Visual perception
  brain and, 97–98
  color, 96–97, 96*f*
  eye structure and, 91–93, 92*f*
  farsighted, 94–95
  light and, 93–94, 93*f*, 94*f*
  nearsighted, 94
  retinal imaging and, 93, 93*f*
  selective, 98
Visual acuity, 94–95
Visual cliff, 296, 296*f*
Visual cortex, 97, 98
Visual imagery, for memory improvement, 243
Visual images, 250
Visual perception
  brain function and, 67–68, 67*f*, 68*f*
  development of, 294–295
  innate, 121–122, 121*f*
  in newborns, 121–122, 121*f*
Visual priming, 89, 90*f*
Visuo-spatial abilities, gender differences in, 437–438, 438*f*
Visuospatial sketch pad, in working memory, 216
Vocabulary, development of, 277–278
Volley principle, 101
Von Helmholtz, Hermann, 6
Voyeurism, 562*t*

WAIS-3 (Weschsler Adult Intelligence-Revised), 418, 418*t*
Waking states of consciousness, 130, 136–139, 137*f*
Water consumption, weight control and, 407
Watson, John B., 7, 7*f*
Wavelength, of light, 93, 94*f*
Wear-and-tear theories of aging, 359–360
WearComp, 273–274, 274*f*
Wearing, Clive, 238
Wechsler scales, 417–419, 418*t*, 424
Weight
  control, tips for, 406–407
  gain, 379–381, 379*f*, 380*f*
  gain, factors in, 379–381, 379*f*, 380*f*
  loss, 514–515
Wellness promotion, 521–525
Wernicke's aphasia, 69
Wernicke's area, 69
Weschsler Adult Intelligence-Revised (WAIS-3), 418, 418*t*
Weschsler Intelligence Scale for Children (WISC), 418
Williams syndrome, 420–421, 421*f*
Windigo, 538

WISC (Weschsler Intelligence Scale for Children), 418
Withdrawal, drug, 156
Withdrawn coping style, 463
Women
HIV/AIDS in, 520
midlife change and, 358–359, 358f
regrets of, 358–359, 358f
Woodcock-Johnson Test of Cognitive Abilities, 425
Word deafness, pure, 69
Working memory
definition of, 215
dissociation with long-term memory, 237–238
early research on, 215–216
multiple components model of, 216–217, 217f
processing in, 216
Work-related stress, 499–500, 499f
Work settings
aggression in
personality and, 483–484, 483f
survey, 25–26, 26f
personal health/behavior in, 479–481, 480f
personality and behavior in, 482–484, 483f
violence in, 387
Wundt, Wilhelm, 6, 6f, 7
Yearning, bereavement and, 363
Yerkes-Dodson law, 374
Zeitgeber, 132, 133–134, 134f
Zone of proximal development, 304
Zoophilia, 562t

*Continued from copyright page*

Weintraub/Science Source/Photo Researchers, Inc.; p. 182: Vincent Laforet/AllSport; p. 183(l): John Coletti; p. 183(r) Courtesy of Michael J. Kalsher; p. 186: Eric Sander/Liaison Agency; p. 187: Stone/Tim Flach; p. 194: Courtesy of Michael J. Kalsher; p. 199: Courtesy of the Office of Professional and Distance Education, Rensselaer Polytechnic Institute; p. 200: Courtesy of Michael J. Kalsher; p. 202: The Everett Collection; p. 203: Stone/David Austen; p. 204: Christopher Brown/Stock, Boston; p. 205: Courtesy of Integrity Global Marketing; **Chapter 6:** p. 214(l): Syracuse Newspapers/The Image Works; p. 214(r): Stone/Frank Herholdt; p. 218: Courtesy of Robert A. Baron; p. 224: Bettmann/Corbis; p. 229: Mark Richards/PhotoEdit; p. 231: Courtesy of Robert A. Baron; p. 236: John Neubauer/PhotoEdit; p. 239: Reuters/Fred Prouser/Archive; **Chapter 7:** p. 251: Stone/Paul Chesley; p. 253: Hank Morgan; p. 265: S. Connolly/Liaison Agency; p. 266: Stone/James Schnepf; p. 272: Sam Ogden; p. 274: Courtesy of Steve Mann, University of Toronto, image available through http://wearcomp.org/steve5.htm; p. 276: John Eastcott & Eva Momatiuk/The Image Works; p. 280: AnimalsAnimals/©OSF/M. Colbeck; **Chapter 8:** p. 287(l): Jeff Greenberg/Rainbow; p. 287(middle): Will & Deni McIntyre/Photo Researchers, Inc.; p. 287(r): Jeff Greenberg/Photo Researchers, Inc.; p. 288: Jennie Woodcock/Reflections Photolibrary/Corbis; p. 289: Fetal Alcohol & Drug Unit/University of Washington/School of Medicine; p. 290: Bob Rowan/Progressive Image/Corbis; p. 296: Courtesy of J. Campos, B. Bertenthal & R. Kermoian; p. 300: Cassy Cohen/PhotoEdit; p. 312: Stone/Pauline Cutler; p. 313: Stone/Robert Van Der Hilst; p. 315: Courtesy of Robert A. Baron; p. 316(l): Martin Rogers/Woodfin Camp & Associates; p. 316(r): Stone/Martin Rogers; p. 318(l): Bonnie Kamin/PhotoEdit; p. 318(r): Jennie Woodcock/Reflections Photolibrary/Corbis; p. 323(l): Stone/Andy Sacks; p. 323(r): Caroline Wood/International Stock; p. 324(l): Donna Binder/Impact Visuals; p. 324(r): Bob Daemmrich/The Image Works; **Chapter 9:** p. 331(l): Stone/Cary Wolinsky; p. 331(r): John Annerino/Liaison Agency; p. 332: Brian Smith; p. 335: Catherine Smith/Impact Visuals; p. 337: Nancy Richmond/The Image Works; p. 338: Peter Turnley/Corbis; p. 348: Courtesy of Robert A. Baron; p. 354(l): AP/Wide World Photos; p. 354(r): Culver Pictures; p. 355: Stone/David Young-Wolff; p. 362: Reuters/Corbis-Bettmann; p. 364: AP/Wide World Photos; **Chapter 10:** p. 372(r,top): AP/Wide World Photos; p. 372(r,bottom): G. Heidorn/laif/Impact Visuals; p. 372(l): Reuters/Peter Morgan/Archive Photos; p. 379(l): Reuters/Jeff Christensen/Archive Photos; p. 379(r): Mike Brinson/Image Bank; p. 380: Dennis Stock/Magnum Photos; p. 382: Billy Barnes/Stock, Boston; p. 386: Anders Patterson/Black Star; p. 389: Courtesy of Robert A. Baron; p. 391: Lew Merrim/Monkmeyer; p. 393(l): Jack Kurtz/Impact Visuals; p. 393(r): Louise Gubb/The Image Works; p. 395: The Everett Collection; p. 401(l): Dan McCoy/Rainbow; p. 401(r): Terje Rakke/Image Bank; p. 402: Courtesy of Robert A. Baron; **Chapter 11:** p. 414: Steven E. Sutton/Duomo; p. 415: John Eastcott & Eva Momatiuk/The Image Works; p. 420: Paul A. Souders; p. 421: Courtesy of Professor Howard M. Lenhoff, Williams Syndrome Foundation; p. 424: Courtesy of Robert A. Baron; p. 428: Martha Bates/Stock, Boston; p. 430: Arnold Zann/Black Star; **Chapter 12:** p. 451: Dennis MacDonald/PhotoEdit; p. 453: National Library of Medicine; p. 460: Lisa Quinones/Black Star; p. 462: PhotoFest; p. 466(l): Duomo/Corbis; p. 466(r): A. Ramey/PhotoEdit; p. 469(l): Bettmann/Corbis; p. 469(r): Francis G. Mayer/Corbis; p. 473: Stone/Sylvain Grandadam; p. 475: Bob Daemmrich/The Image Works; p. 480: Courtesy of Robert A. Baron; p. 481: F. Ferreira/Agence Mission/Liaison Agency; p. 483: Courtesy of Robert A. Baron; **Chapter 13:** p. 495: Courtesy of Michael J. Kalsher; p. 502: Bob Daemmrich/The Image Works; p. 505: Courtesy of Michael J. Kalsher; p. 508: Courtesy of Traumatic Brain Injury Resource Guide; Indiana Prevention Resource Center; Doctor's Guide/PSL Group; Virtual Hospital Home Page; p. 513: Courtesy of California Department of Health Services/Tobacco Control Services; p. 519: Stephen Marks; p. 523: Tom Prettyman/PhotoEdit; p. 525: Tom Able-Green/AllSport; **Chapter 14:** p. 535(l): North Wind Picture Archives; p. 535(r): Jerry Cooke/Photo Researchers, Inc.; p. 536(l): J. Nordell/The Image Works; p. 536(r): Bronstein/Liaison Agency; p. 541: Courtesy of Robert A. Baron; p. 545(l): Corbis/Bettmann; p. 545(r): Christensen Big Pictures/Archive Photos; p. 550: Will Hart; p. 554: Bob Daemmrich/Stock, Boston; p. 557: AFP/Corbis; p. 559: Sally Savage; p. 561: Courtesy of Robert A. Baron; p. 564: The Kobal Collection; p. 568: Mary Ellen Mark;p. 572(l): Michael Newman/PhotoEdit; p. 572(r): Donald C. Wetter/The Stock Shop, Inc.; **Chapter 15:** p. 583: Courtesy of Robert A. Baron; p. 585: Courtesy of Robert A. Baron; p. 591: Courtesy of Pearson Education; p. 594: David Young-Wolff/PhotoEdit; p. 595: Hank Morgan/Rainbow; p. 596: ChromoSohm/Sohm/Photo Researchers, Inc.; p. 597: Courtesy of Robert A. Baron; p. 601: James Wilson/Woodfin Camp & Associates; p. 609(l): Spencer Grant/PhotoEdit; p. 609(r): Michael Newman/PhotoEdit; p. 611: AP/Wide World Photos; **Chapter 16:** p. 625: Courtesy of Robert A. Baron; p. 626: Gary M. Prior/AllSport; p. 629: Bill Aron/PhotoEdit; p. 635(l): Patrick Ward/Stock, Boston; p. 635(r): Bill Bachman/PhotoEdit; p. 637: Bettmann/Corbis; p. 640: Stone/ David Young-Wolff; p. 643: Lee Celano/SABA Press Photos, Inc.; p. 646: From the film *Obedience* ©1965 Stanley Milgram and distributed by Penn State Media Sales. Permission granted by Alexandra Milgram; p. 647: Archive Photos; p. 649(l,top): Liaison Agency; p. 649(r,top & l,bottom): The Everett Collection; p. 649(r,bottom): Kostas Alexander/Fotos International/Archive Photos; p. 652: Courtesy of Robert A. Baron; p. 654(l): Folio, Inc.; p. 654(r): Archive Photos; p. 655(l): Archive Photos/PictureQuest; p. 655(r): Hulton Getty/Liaison Agency.

**Figure Credits:** p. 53: From Carlson, *Foundations of Physiological Psychology*, 4/e, 1999, Allyn & Bacon. Reprinted by permission. p. 63: Reprinted from *Neuropsychologia*, Vol. 16, Sackheim et al., "Lateral asymmetry in intensity of emotional expression," p. 29, Copyright © 1978, with permission from Elsevier Science. p. 65: From Carlson, *Foundations of Physiological Psychology*, 4/e, 1999, Allyn & Bacon. Reprinted by permission. p. 66: Reprinted with permission from SUNY/Brookhaven National Laboratory. p. 68: From Carlson, *Foundations of Physiological Psychology*, 4/e, 1999, Allyn & Bacon. Reprinted by permission. p. 70: From Carlson, *Foundations of Physiological Psychology*, 4/e, 1999, Allyn & Bacon. Reprinted by permission. p. 96: Reprinted from *Vision Research*, Vol. 4, Macnichol, E. F., "Retinal mechanisms of color vision," pp. 119–133, Copyright 1964, with permission from Elsevier Science. p. 293: From Schickedanz, et al., *Understanding Children and Adolescents,* 3e, Allyn and Bacon, 1998, p. 157. Reprinted by permission. p. 303: Adapted from R. Baillargeon (1994). Physical reasoning in young infants: Seeking explanations for impossible events. *British Journal of Developmental Psychology*, 12, 9–33. p. 305: From Schickedanz, et al., *Understanding Children and Adolescents*, 3e, Allyn and Bacon, 1998, p. 335. Reprinted by permission. p. 345: From Lemme, *Development in Adulthood,* 2e, Allyn and Bacon, 1999, p. 43. Reprinted by permission. p. 600: Reprinted from *American Journal Of Medicine*, Vol. 82 (suppl 5A), Schuckit, "Symposium on Buspirone," p. 29, Copyright © 1987, with permission from Excerpta Medica. p. 632: From Baron & Byrne, *Social Psychology*, 4e, Allyn and Bacon. Reprinted by permission. p. 634: From Baron & Byrne, *Social Psychology*, 4e, Allyn and Bacon. Reprinted by permission. p. 646: Adapted from drawings in Schickedanz et al., 1998 and Baillargeon, 1994.